PHILIP'S

ATLAS
OF THE
WORLD

PAPERBACK EDITION

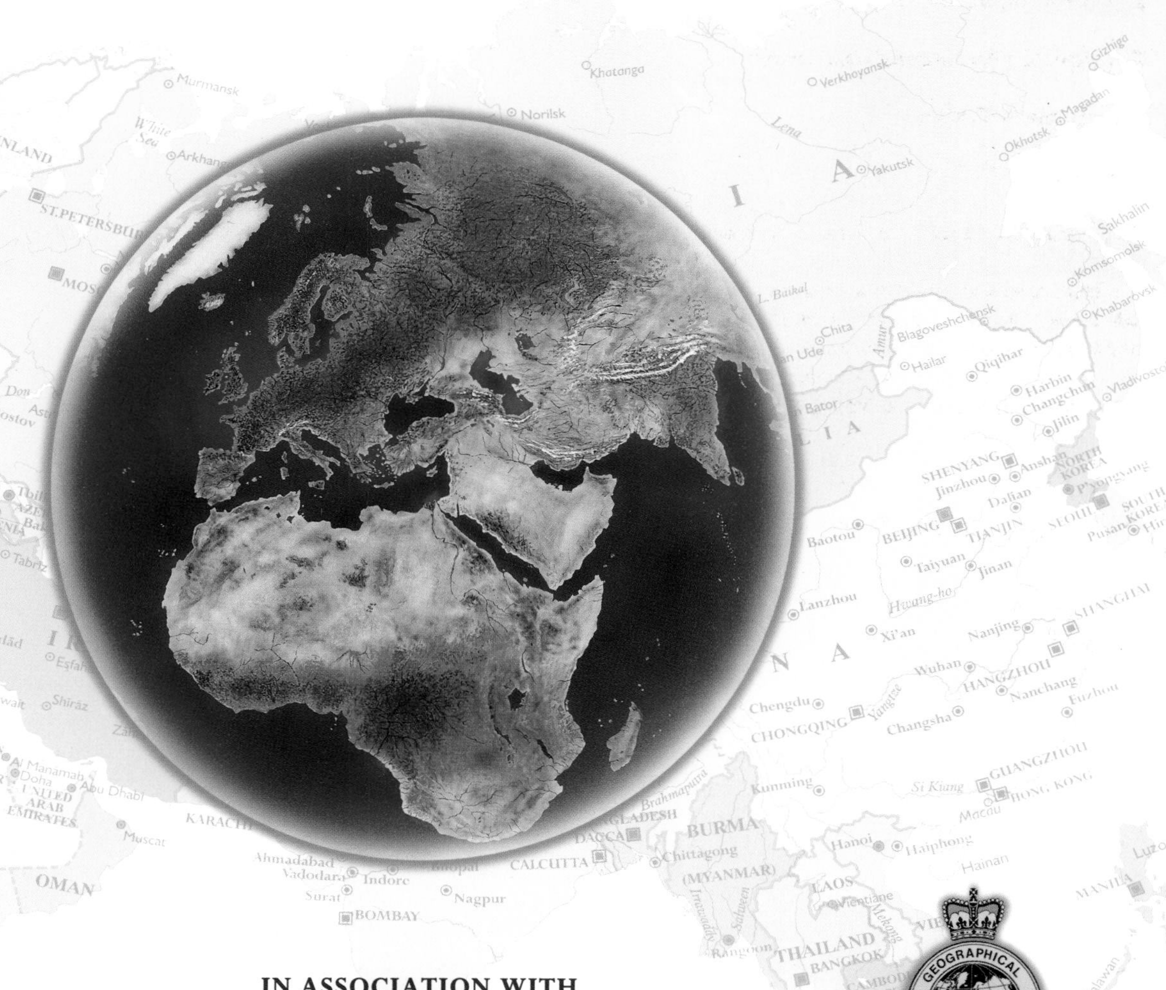

IN ASSOCIATION WITH
THE ROYAL GEOGRAPHICAL SOCIETY
WITH THE INSTITUTE OF BRITISH GEOGRAPHERS

Contents

PHILIP'S

ATLAS
OF THE
WORLD

PAPERBACK EDITION

The World in Focus
Cartography by Philip's

Picture Acknowledgements
Page 14
Science Photo Library/NOAA

Illustrations
Stefan Chabluk

CONSULTANTS
Philip's are grateful to the following people for acting as specialist
geography consultants on 'The World in Focus' front section:

Professor D. Brunsden, Kings College, University of London, UK
Dr C. Clarke, Oxford University, UK
Dr I. S. Evans, Durham University, UK
Professor P. Haggett, University of Bristol, UK
Professor K. McLachlan, University of London, UK
Professor M. Monmonier, Syracuse University, New York, USA
Professor M-L. Hsu, University of Minnesota, Minnesota, USA
Professor M. J. Tooley, University of St Andrews, UK
Dr T. Unwin, Royal Holloway, University of London, UK

Published in Great Britain in 1999
by George Philip Limited,
a division of Octopus Publishing Group Limited,
2–4 Heron Quays, London E14 4JP

Cartography by Philip's

ISBN 0–540–07707–0

A CIP catalogue record for this book is available from the British Library.

Printed in China

Details of other Philip's titles and services can be found on our website at: www.philips-maps.co.uk

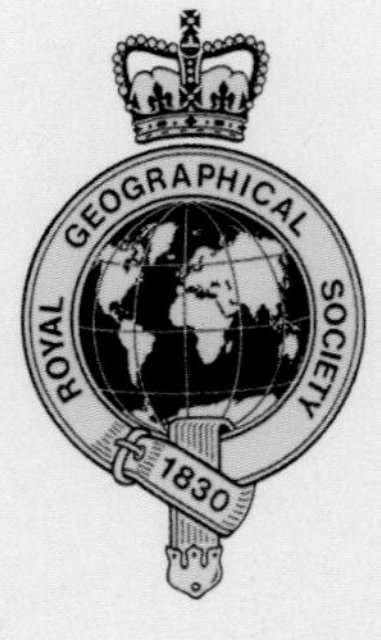

Philip's is proud to announce that its World Atlases
are now published in association with The Royal
Geographical Society (with The Institute of British
Geographers).

The Society was founded in 1830 and given a
Royal Charter in 1859 for 'the advancement of
geographical science'. It holds historical collections
of national and international importance, many of
which relate to the Society's association with and
support for scientific exploration and research
from the 19th century onwards. It was pivotal
in establishing geography as a teaching and research
discipline in British universities close to the turn of
the century, and has played a key role in geographical
and environmental education ever since.

Today the Society is a leading world centre for
geographical learning – supporting education, teaching,
research and expeditions, and promoting public
understanding of the subject.

The Society welcomes those interested in geography
as members. For further information, please visit the
website at: www.rgs.org

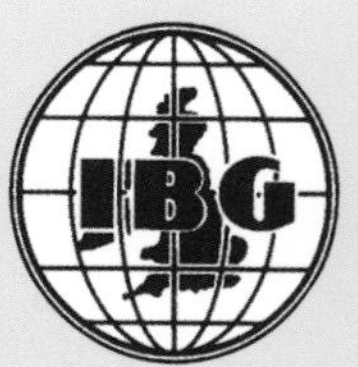

v

World Statistics: Countries

This alphabetical list includes all the countries and territories of the world. If a territory is not completely independent, then the country it is associated with is named. The area figures give the total area of land, inland water and ice. The population figures are 1998 estimates. The annual income is the Gross National Product per capita in US dollars. The figures are the latest available, usually 1997.

Country/Territory	Area km² Thousands	Area miles² Thousands	Population Thousands	Capital	Annual Income US $
Adélie Land (France)	432	167	0.03	–	–
Afghanistan	652	252	24,792	Kabul	600
Albania	28.8	11.1	3,331	Tirana	750
Algeria	2,382	920	30,481	Algiers	1,490
American Samoa (US)	0.20	0.08	62	Pago Pago	2,600
Andorra	0.45	0.17	75	Andorra La Vella	16,200
Angola	1,247	481	11,200	Luanda	340
Anguilla (UK)	0.1	0.04	11	The Valley	6,800
Antigua & Barbuda	0.44	0.17	64	St John's	7,330
Argentina	2,767	1,068	36,265	Buenos Aires	8,750
Armenia	29.8	11.5	3,422	Yerevan	530
Aruba (Netherlands)	0.19	0.07	69	Oranjestad	15,890
Ascension Is. (UK)	0.09	0.03	1.5	Georgetown	–
Australia	7,687	2,968	18,613	Canberra	20,540
Austria	83.9	32.4	8,134	Vienna	27,980
Azerbaijan	86.6	33.4	7,856	Baku	510
Azores (Portugal)	2.2	0.87	238	Ponta Delgada	–
Bahamas	13.9	5.4	280	Nassau	11,940
Bahrain	0.68	0.26	616	Manama	7,840
Bangladesh	144	56	125,000	Dhaka	270
Barbados	0.43	0.17	259	Bridgetown	6,560
Belarus	207.6	80.1	10,409	Minsk	2,150
Belgium	30.5	11.8	10,175	Brussels	26,420
Belize	23	8.9	230	Belmopan	2,700
Benin	113	43	6,101	Porto-Novo	380
Bermuda (UK)	0.05	0.02	62	Hamilton	31,870
Bhutan	47	18.1	1,908	Thimphu	390
Bolivia	1,099	424	7,826	La Paz/Sucre	950
Bosnia-Herzegovina	51	20	3,366	Sarajevo	300
Botswana	582	225	1,448	Gaborone	4,381
Brazil	8,512	3,286	170,000	Brasília	4,720
British Indian Ocean Terr. (UK)	0.08	0.03	0	–	–
Brunei	5.8	2.2	315	Bandar Seri Begawan	15,800
Bulgaria	111	43	8,240	Sofia	1,140
Burkina Faso	274	106	11,266	Ouagadougou	240
Burma (= Myanmar)	677	261	47,305	Rangoon	1,790
Burundi	27.8	10.7	5,531	Bujumbura	180
Cambodia	181	70	11,340	Phnom Penh	300
Cameroon	475	184	15,029	Yaoundé	650
Canada	9,976	3,852	30,675	Ottawa	19,290
Canary Is. (Spain)	7.3	2.8	1,494	Las Palmas/Santa Cruz	–
Cape Verde Is.	4	1.6	399	Praia	1,010
Cayman Is. (UK)	0.26	0.10	35	George Town	20,000
Central African Republic	623	241	3,376	Bangui	320
Chad	1,284	496	7,360	Ndjaména	240
Chatham Is. (NZ)	0.96	0.37	0.05	Waitangi	–
Chile	757	292	14,788	Santiago	5,020
China	9,597	3,705	1,236,915	Beijing	860
Christmas Is. (Australia)	0.14	0.05	2	The Settlement	–
Cocos (Keeling) Is. (Australia)	0.01	0.005	1	West Island	–
Colombia	1,139	440	38,581	Bogotá	2,280
Comoros	2.2	0.86	545	Moroni	450
Congo	342	132	2,658	Brazzaville	660
Congo (= Zaïre)	2,345	905	49,001	Kinshasa	110
Cook Is. (NZ)	0.24	0.09	20	Avarua	900
Costa Rica	51.1	19.7	3,605	San José	2,640
Croatia	56.5	21.8	4,672	Zagreb	4,610
Cuba	111	43	11,051	Havana	1,300
Cyprus	9.3	3.6	749	Nicosia	13,420
Czech Republic	78.9	30.4	10,286	Prague	5,200
Denmark	43.1	16.6	5,334	Copenhagen	32,500
Djibouti	23.2	9	650	Djibouti	850
Dominica	0.75	0.29	78	Roseau	3,090
Dominican Republic	48.7	18.8	7,999	Santo Domingo	1,670
Ecuador	284	109	12,337	Quito	1,590
Egypt	1,001	387	66,050	Cairo	1,180
El Salvador	21	8.1	5,752	San Salvador	1,810
Equatorial Guinea	28.1	10.8	454	Malabo	530
Eritrea	94	36	3,842	Asmara	570
Estonia	44.7	17.3	1,421	Tallinn	3,330
Ethiopia	1,128	436	58,390	Addis Ababa	110
Falkland Is. (UK)	12.2	4.7	2	Stanley	–
Faroe Is. (Denmark)	1.4	0.54	41	Tórshavn	23,660
Fiji	18.3	7.1	802	Suva	2,470
Finland	338	131	5,149	Helsinki	24,080
France	552	213	58,805	Paris	26,050
French Guiana (France)	90	34.7	162	Cayenne	10,580
French Polynesia (France)	4	1.5	237	Papeete	7,500
Gabon	268	103	1,208	Libreville	4,230
Gambia, The	11.3	4.4	1,292	Banjul	320
Georgia	69.7	26.9	5,109	Tbilisi	840
Germany	357	138	82,079	Berlin/Bonn	28,260
Ghana	239	92	18,497	Accra	370
Gibraltar (UK)	0.007	0.003	29	Gibraltar Town	5,000
Greece	132	51	10,662	Athens	12,010
Greenland (Denmark)	2,176	840	59	Nuuk (Godthåb)	15,500
Grenada	0.34	0.13	96	St George's	2,880
Guadeloupe (France)	1.7	0.66	416	Basse-Terre	9,200
Guam (US)	0.55	0.21	149	Agana	6,000
Guatemala	109	42	12,008	Guatemala City	1,500
Guinea	246	95	7,477	Conakry	570
Guinea-Bissau	36.1	13.9	1,206	Bissau	240
Guyana	215	83	820	Georgetown	690
Haiti	27.8	10.7	6,781	Port-au-Prince	330
Honduras	112	43	5,862	Tegucigalpa	700
Hong Kong (China)	1.1	0.40	6,707	–	22,990
Hungary	93	35.9	10,208	Budapest	4,430
Iceland	103	40	271	Reykjavik	26,580
India	3,288	1,269	984,000	New Delhi	390
Indonesia	1,905	735	212,942	Jakarta	1,110
Iran	1,648	636	64,411	Tehran	4,700
Iraq	438	169	21,722	Baghdad	2,000
Ireland	70.3	27.1	3,619	Dublin	18,280
Israel	27	10.3	5,644	Jerusalem	15,810
Italy	301	116	56,783	Rome	20,120
Ivory Coast (Côte d'Ivoire)	322	125	15,446	Yamoussoukro	690
Jamaica	11	4.2	2,635	Kingston	1,560
Jan Mayen Is. (Norway)	0.38	0.15	1	–	–
Japan	378	146	125,932	Tokyo	37,850
Johnston Is. (US)	0.002	0.0009	1	–	–
Jordan	89.2	34.4	4,435	Amman	1,570
Kazakstan	2,717	1,049	16,847	Astana	1,340
Kenya	580	224	28,337	Nairobi	330
Kerguelen Is. (France)	7.2	2.8	0.7	–	–
Kermadec Is. (NZ)	0.03	0.01	0.1	–	–
Kiribati	0.72	0.28	85	Tarawa	920
Korea, North	121	47	21,234	Pyŏngyang	1,000
Korea, South	99	38.2	46,417	Seoul	10,550
Kuwait	17.8	6.9	1,913	Kuwait City	17,390
Kyrgyzstan	198.5	76.6	4,522	Bishkek	440
Laos	237	91	5,261	Vientiane	400
Latvia	65	25	2,385	Riga	2,430
Lebanon	10.4	4	3,506	Beirut	3,350

Country/Territory	Area km² Thousands	Area miles² Thousands	Population Thousands	Capital	Annual Income US $
Lesotho	30.4	11.7	2,090	Maseru	670
Liberia	111	43	2,772	Monrovia	770
Libya	1,760	679	4,875	Tripoli	6,510
Liechtenstein	0.16	0.06	32	Vaduz	33,000
Lithuania	65.2	25.2	3,600	Vilnius	2,230
Luxembourg	2.6	1	425	Luxembourg	45,360
Macau (China)	0.02	0.006	429	Macau	7,500
Macedonia	25.7	9.9	2,009	Skopje	1,090
Madagascar	587	227	14,463	Antananarivo	250
Madeira (Portugal)	0.81	0.31	253	Funchal	–
Malawi	118	46	9,840	Lilongwe	220
Malaysia	330	127	20,993	Kuala Lumpur	4,680
Maldives	0.30	0.12	290	Malé	1,080
Mali	1,240	479	10,109	Bamako	260
Malta	0.32	0.12	379	Valletta	12,000
Marshall Is.	0.18	0.07	63	Dalap-Uliga-Darrit	1,890
Martinique (France)	1.1	0.42	407	Fort-de-France	10,000
Mauritania	1,030	412	2,511	Nouakchott	450
Mauritius	2.0	0.72	1,168	Port Louis	3,800
Mayotte (France)	0.37	0.14	141	Mamoundzou	1,430
Mexico	1,958	756	98,553	Mexico City	3,680
Micronesia, Fed. States of	0.70	0.27	127	Palikir	2,070
Midway Is. (US)	0.005	0.002	2	–	–
Moldova	33.7	13	4,458	Chişinău	540
Monaco	0.002	0.0001	32	Monaco	25,000
Mongolia	1,567	605	2,579	Ulan Bator	390
Montserrat (UK)	0.10	0.04	12	Plymouth	4,500
Morocco	447	172	29,114	Rabat	1,250
Mozambique	802	309	18,641	Maputo	90
Namibia	825	318	1,622	Windhoek	2,220
Nauru	0.02	0.008	12	Yaren District	10,000
Nepal	141	54	23,698	Katmandu	210
Netherlands	41.5	16	15,731	Amsterdam/The Hague	25,820
Netherlands Antilles (Neths)	0.99	0.38	210	Willemstad	10,400
New Caledonia (France)	18.6	7.2	192	Nouméa	8,000
New Zealand	269	104	3,625	Wellington	16,480
Nicaragua	130	50	4,583	Managua	410
Niger	1,267	489	9,672	Niamey	200
Nigeria	924	357	110,532	Abuja	260
Niue (NZ)	0.26	0.10	2	Alofi	–
Norfolk Is. (Australia)	0.03	0.01	2	Kingston	–
Northern Mariana Is. (US)	0.48	0.18	50	Saipan	11,500
Norway	324	125	4,420	Oslo	36,090
Oman	212	82	2,364	Muscat	4,950
Pakistan	796	307	135,135	Islamabad	490
Palau	0.46	0.18	18	Koror	5,000
Panama	77.1	29.8	2,736	Panama City	3,080
Papua New Guinea	463	179	4,600	Port Moresby	940
Paraguay	407	157	5,291	Asunción	2,010
Peru	1,285	496	26,111	Lima	2,460
Philippines	300	116	77,736	Manila	1,220
Pitcairn Is. (UK)	0.03	0.01	0.05	Adamstown	–
Poland	313	121	38,607	Warsaw	3,590
Portugal	92.4	35.7	9,928	Lisbon	10,450
Puerto Rico (US)	9	3.5	3,860	San Juan	7,800
Qatar	11	4.2	697	Doha	11,600
Queen Maud Land (Norway)	2,800	1,081	0	–	–
Réunion (France)	2.5	0.97	705	Saint-Denis	4,500
Romania	238	92	22,396	Bucharest	1,420
Russia	17,075	6,592	146,861	Moscow	2,740
Rwanda	26.3	10.2	7,956	Kigali	210
St Helena (UK)	0.12	0.05	7	Jamestown	–
St Kitts & Nevis	0.36	0.14	42	Basseterre	5,870
St Lucia	0.62	0.24	150	Castries	3,500
St Pierre & Miquelon (France)	0.24	0.09	7	Saint Pierre	–
St Vincent & Grenadines	0.39	0.15	120	Kingstown	2,370
San Marino	0.06	0.02	25	San Marino	20,000
São Tomé & Príncipe	0.96	0.37	150	São Tomé	330
Saudi Arabia	2,150	830	20,786	Riyadh	6,790
Senegal	197	76	9,723	Dakar	550
Seychelles	0.46	0.18	79	Victoria	6,850
Sierra Leone	71.7	27.7	5,080	Freetown	200
Singapore	0.62	0.24	3,490	Singapore	32,940
Slovak Republic	49	18.9	5,393	Bratislava	3,700
Slovenia	20.3	7.8	1,972	Ljubljana	9,680
Solomon Is.	28.9	11.2	441	Honiara	900
Somalia	638	246	6,842	Mogadishu	500
South Africa	1,220	471	42,835	C. Town/Pretoria/Bloem.	3,400
South Georgia (UK)	3.8	1.4	0.05	–	–
Spain	505	195	39,134	Madrid	14,510
Sri Lanka	65.6	25.3	18,934	Colombo	800
Sudan	2,506	967	33,551	Khartoum	800
Surinam	163	63	427	Paramaribo	1,000
Svalbard (Norway)	62.9	24.3	4	Longyearbyen	–
Swaziland	17.4	6.7	966	Mbabane	1,210
Sweden	450	174	8,887	Stockholm	26,220
Switzerland	41.3	15.9	7,260	Bern	44,220
Syria	185	71	16,673	Damascus	1,150
Taiwan	36	13.9	21,908	Taipei	12,400
Tajikistan	143.1	55.2	6,020	Dushanbe	330
Tanzania	945	365	30,609	Dodoma	210
Thailand	513	198	60,037	Bangkok	2,800
Togo	56.8	21.9	4,906	Lomé	330
Tokelau (NZ)	0.01	0.005	2	Nukunonu	–
Tonga	0.75	0.29	107	Nuku'alofa	1,790
Trinidad & Tobago	5.1	2	1,117	Port of Spain	4,230
Tristan da Cunha (UK)	0.11	0.04	0.33	Edinburgh	–
Tunisia	164	63	9,380	Tunis	2,090
Turkey	779	301	64,568	Ankara	3,130
Turkmenistan	488.1	188.5	4,298	Ashkhabad	630
Turks & Caicos Is. (UK)	0.43	0.17	16	Cockburn Town	5,000
Tuvalu	0.03	0.01	10	Fongafale	600
Uganda	236	91	22,167	Kampala	320
Ukraine	603.7	233.1	50,125	Kiev	1,040
United Arab Emirates	83.6	32.3	2,303	Abu Dhabi	17,360
United Kingdom	243.3	94	58,970	London	20,710
United States of America	9,373	3,619	270,290	Washington, DC	28,740
Uruguay	177	68	3,285	Montevideo	6,020
Uzbekistan	447.4	172.7	23,784	Tashkent	1,010
Vanuatu	12.2	4.7	185	Port-Vila	1,290
Vatican City	0.0004	0.0002	1	–	–
Venezuela	912	352	22,803	Caracas	3,450
Vietnam	332	127	76,236	Hanoi	320
Virgin Is. (UK)	0.15	0.06	13	Road Town	–
Virgin Is. (US)	0.34	0.13	118	Charlotte Amalie	12,000
Wake Is.	0.008	0.003	0.3	–	–
Wallis & Futuna Is. (France)	0.20	0.08	15	Mata-Utu	–
Western Sahara	266	103	280	El Aaiún	300
Western Samoa	2.8	1.1	224	Apia	1,170
Yemen	528	204	16,388	Sana	270
Yugoslavia	102.3	39.5	10,500	Belgrade	2,000
Zambia	753	291	9,461	Lusaka	380
Zimbabwe	391	151	11,044	Harare	750

World Statistics: Physical Dimensions

Each topic list is divided into continents and within a continent the items are listed in order of size. The bottom part of many of the lists is selective in order to give examples from as many different countries as possible. The order of the continents is the same as in the atlas, beginning with Europe and ending with South America. The figures are rounded as appropriate.

World, Continents, Oceans

	km²	miles²	%
The World	509,450,000	196,672,000	–
Land	149,450,000	57,688,000	29.3
Water	360,000,000	138,984,000	70.7
Asia	44,500,000	17,177,000	29.8
Africa	30,302,000	11,697,000	20.3
North America	24,241,000	9,357,000	16.2
South America	17,793,000	6,868,000	11.9
Antarctica	14,100,000	5,443,000	9.4
Europe	9,957,000	3,843,000	6.7
Australia & Oceania	8,557,000	3,303,000	5.7
Pacific Ocean	179,679,000	69,356,000	49.9
Atlantic Ocean	92,373,000	35,657,000	25.7
Indian Ocean	73,917,000	28,532,000	20.5
Arctic Ocean	14,090,000	5,439,000	3.9

Ocean Depths

Atlantic Ocean	m	ft
Puerto Rico (Milwaukee) Deep	9,220	30,249
Cayman Trench	7,680	25,197
Gulf of Mexico	5,203	17,070
Mediterranean Sea	5,121	16,801
Black Sea	2,211	7,254
North Sea	660	2,165

Indian Ocean	m	ft
Java Trench	7,450	24,442
Red Sea	2,635	8,454

Pacific Ocean	m	ft
Mariana Trench	11,022	36,161
Tonga Trench	10,882	35,702
Japan Trench	10,554	34,626
Kuril Trench	10,542	34,587

Arctic Ocean	m	ft
Molloy Deep	5,608	18,399

Mountains

Europe		m	ft
Elbrus	*Russia*	5,642	18,510
Mont Blanc	*France/Italy*	4,807	15,771
Monte Rosa	*Italy/Switzerland*	4,634	15,203
Dom	*Switzerland*	4,545	14,911
Liskamm	*Switzerland*	4,527	14,852
Weisshorn	*Switzerland*	4,505	14,780
Taschorn	*Switzerland*	4,490	14,730
Matterhorn/Cervino	*Italy/Switzerland*	4,478	14,691
Mont Maudit	*France/Italy*	4,465	14,649
Dent Blanche	*Switzerland*	4,356	14,291
Nadelhorn	*Switzerland*	4,327	14,196
Grandes Jorasses	*France/Italy*	4,208	13,806
Jungfrau	*Switzerland*	4,158	13,642
Grossglockner	*Austria*	3,797	12,457
Mulhacén	*Spain*	3,478	11,411
Zugspitze	*Germany*	2,962	9,718
Olympus	*Greece*	2,917	9,570
Triglav	*Slovenia*	2,863	9,393
Gerlachovka	*Slovak Republic*	2,655	8,711
Galdhöpiggen	*Norway*	2,468	8,100
Kebnekaise	*Sweden*	2,117	6,946
Ben Nevis	*UK*	1,343	4,406

Asia		m	ft
Everest	*China/Nepal*	8,848	29,029
K2 (Godwin Austen)	*China/Kashmir*	8,611	28,251
Kanchenjunga	*India/Nepal*	8,598	28,208
Lhotse	*China/Nepal*	8,516	27,939
Makalu	*China/Nepal*	8,481	27,824
Cho Oyu	*China/Nepal*	8,201	26,906
Dhaulagiri	*Nepal*	8,172	26,811
Manaslu	*Nepal*	8,156	26,758
Nanga Parbat	*Kashmir*	8,126	26,660
Annapurna	*Nepal*	8,078	26,502
Gasherbrum	*China/Kashmir*	8,068	26,469
Broad Peak	*China/Kashmir*	8,051	26,414
Xixabangma	*China*	8,012	26,286
Kangbachen	*India/Nepal*	7,902	25,925
Trivor	*Pakistan*	7,720	25,328
Pik Kommunizma	*Tajikistan*	7,495	24,590
Demavend	*Iran*	5,604	18,386
Ararat	*Turkey*	5,165	16,945
Gunong Kinabalu	*Malaysia (Borneo)*	4,101	13,455
Fuji-San	*Japan*	3,776	12,388

Africa		m	ft
Kilimanjaro	*Tanzania*	5,895	19,340
Mt Kenya	*Kenya*	5,199	17,057
Ruwenzori (Margherita)	*Ug./Congo (Z.)*	5,109	16,762
Ras Dashan	*Ethiopia*	4,620	15,157
Meru	*Tanzania*	4,565	14,977
Karisimbi	*Rwanda/Congo (Zaïre)*	4,507	14,787
Mt Elgon	*Kenya/Uganda*	4,321	14,176
Batu	*Ethiopia*	4,307	14,130
Toubkal	*Morocco*	4,165	13,665
Mt Cameroon	*Cameroon*	4,070	13,353

Oceania		m	ft
Puncak Jaya	*Indonesia*	5,029	16,499
Puncak Trikora	*Indonesia*	4,750	15,584
Puncak Mandala	*Indonesia*	4,702	15,427
Mt Wilhelm	*Papua New Guinea*	4,508	14,790
Mauna Kea	*USA (Hawaii)*	4,205	13,796
Mauna Loa	*USA (Hawaii)*	4,170	13,681
Mt Cook (Aoraki)	*New Zealand*	3,753	12,313
Mt Kosciuszko	*Australia*	2,237	7,339

North America		m	ft
Mt McKinley (Denali)	*USA (Alaska)*	6,194	20,321
Mt Logan	*Canada*	5,959	19,551
Citlaltepetl	*Mexico*	5,700	18,701
Mt St Elias	*USA/Canada*	5,489	18,008
Popocatepetl	*Mexico*	5,452	17,887
Mt Foraker	*USA (Alaska)*	5,304	17,401
Ixtaccihuatl	*Mexico*	5,286	17,342
Lucania	*Canada*	5,227	17,149
Mt Steele	*Canada*	5,073	16,644
Mt Bona	*USA (Alaska)*	5,005	16,420
Mt Whitney	*USA*	4,418	14,495
Tajumulco	*Guatemala*	4,220	13,845
Chirripó Grande	*Costa Rica*	3,837	12,589
Pico Duarte	*Dominican Rep.*	3,175	10,417

South America		m	ft
Aconcagua	*Argentina*	6,960	22,834
Bonete	*Argentina*	6,872	22,546
Ojos del Salado	*Argentina/Chile*	6,863	22,516
Pissis	*Argentina*	6,779	22,241
Mercedario	*Argentina/Chile*	6,770	22,211
Huascaran	*Peru*	6,768	22,204
Llullaillaco	*Argentina/Chile*	6,723	22,057
Nudo de Cachi	*Argentina*	6,720	22,047
Yerupaja	*Peru*	6,632	21,758
Sajama	*Bolivia*	6,542	21,463
Chimborazo	*Ecuador*	6,267	20,561
Pico Colon	*Colombia*	5,800	19,029
Pico Bolivar	*Venezuela*	5,007	16,427

Antarctica		m	ft
Vinson Massif		4,897	16,066
Mt Kirkpatrick		4,528	14,855

Rivers

Europe		km	miles
Volga	*Caspian Sea*	3,700	2,300
Danube	*Black Sea*	2,850	1,770
Ural	*Caspian Sea*	2,535	1,575
Dnepr (Dnipro)	*Black Sea*	2,285	1,420
Kama	*Volga*	2,030	1,260
Don	*Black Sea*	1,990	1,240
Petchora	*Arctic Ocean*	1,790	1,110
Oka	*Volga*	1,480	920
Dnister (Dniester)	*Black Sea*	1,400	870
Vyatka	*Kama*	1,370	850
Rhine	*North Sea*	1,320	820
N. Dvina	*Arctic Ocean*	1,290	800
Elbe	*North Sea*	1,145	710

Asia		km	miles
Yangtze	*Pacific Ocean*	6,380	3,960
Yenisey–Angara	*Arctic Ocean*	5,550	3,445
Huang He	*Pacific Ocean*	5,464	3,395
Ob–Irtysh	*Arctic Ocean*	5,410	3,360
Mekong	*Pacific Ocean*	4,500	2,795
Amur	*Pacific Ocean*	4,400	2,730
Lena	*Arctic Ocean*	4,400	2,730
Irtysh	*Ob*	4,250	2,640
Yenisey	*Arctic Ocean*	4,090	2,540
Ob	*Arctic Ocean*	3,680	2,285
Indus	*Indian Ocean*	3,100	1,925
Brahmaputra	*Indian Ocean*	2,900	1,800
Syrdarya	*Aral Sea*	2,860	1,775
Salween	*Indian Ocean*	2,800	1,740
Euphrates	*Indian Ocean*	2,700	1,675
Amudarya	*Aral Sea*	2,540	1,575

Africa		km	miles
Nile	*Mediterranean*	6,670	4,140
Congo	*Atlantic Ocean*	4,670	2,900
Niger	*Atlantic Ocean*	4,180	2,595
Zambezi	*Indian Ocean*	3,540	2,200
Oubangi/Uele	*Congo (Zaïre)*	2,250	1,400
Kasai	*Congo (Zaïre)*	1,950	1,210
Shaballe	*Indian Ocean*	1,930	1,200
Orange	*Atlantic Ocean*	1,860	1,155
Cubango	*Okavango Swamps*	1,800	1,120
Limpopo	*Indian Ocean*	1,600	995
Senegal	*Atlantic Ocean*	1,600	995

Australia		km	miles
Murray–Darling	*Indian Ocean*	3,750	2,330
Darling	*Murray*	3,070	1,905
Murray	*Indian Ocean*	2,575	1,600
Murrumbidgee	*Murray*	1,690	1,050

North America		km	miles
Mississippi–Missouri	*Gulf of Mexico*	6,020	3,740
Mackenzie	*Arctic Ocean*	4,240	2,630
Mississippi	*Gulf of Mexico*	3,780	2,350
Missouri	*Mississippi*	3,780	2,350
Yukon	*Pacific Ocean*	3,185	1,980
Rio Grande	*Gulf of Mexico*	3,030	1,880
Arkansas	*Mississippi*	2,340	1,450
Colorado	*Pacific Ocean*	2,330	1,445
Red	*Mississippi*	2,040	1,270
Columbia	*Pacific Ocean*	1,950	1,210
Saskatchewan	*Lake Winnipeg*	1,940	1,205

South America		km	miles
Amazon	*Atlantic Ocean*	6,450	4,010
Paraná–Plate	*Atlantic Ocean*	4,500	2,800
Purus	*Amazon*	3,350	2,080
Madeira	*Amazon*	3,200	1,990
São Francisco	*Atlantic Ocean*	2,900	1,800
Paraná	*Plate*	2,800	1,740
Tocantins	*Atlantic Ocean*	2,750	1,710
Paraguay	*Paraná*	2,550	1,580
Orinoco	*Atlantic Ocean*	2,500	1,550
Pilcomayo	*Paraná*	2,500	1,550
Araguaia	*Tocantins*	2,250	1,400

Lakes

Europe		km²	miles²
Lake Ladoga	*Russia*	17,700	6,800
Lake Onega	*Russia*	9,700	3,700
Saimaa system	*Finland*	8,000	3,100
Vänern	*Sweden*	5,500	2,100

Asia		km²	miles²
Caspian Sea	*Asia*	371,800	143,550
Lake Baykal	*Russia*	30,500	11,780
Aral Sea	*Kazakstan/Uzbekistan*	28,687	11,086
Tonlé Sap	*Cambodia*	20,000	7,700
Lake Balqash	*Kazakstan*	18,500	7,100

Africa		km²	miles²
Lake Victoria	*East Africa*	68,000	26,000
Lake Tanganyika	*Central Africa*	33,000	13,000
Lake Malawi/Nyasa	*East Africa*	29,600	11,430
Lake Chad	*Central Africa*	25,000	9,700
Lake Turkana	*Ethiopia/Kenya*	8,500	3,300
Lake Volta	*Ghana*	8,500	3,300

Australia		km²	miles²
Lake Eyre	*Australia*	8,900	3,400
Lake Torrens	*Australia*	5,800	2,200
Lake Gairdner	*Australia*	4,800	1,900

North America		km²	miles²
Lake Superior	*Canada/USA*	82,350	31,800
Lake Huron	*Canada/USA*	59,600	23,010
Lake Michigan	*USA*	58,000	22,400
Great Bear Lake	*Canada*	31,800	12,280
Great Slave Lake	*Canada*	28,500	11,000
Lake Erie	*Canada/USA*	25,700	9,900
Lake Winnipeg	*Canada*	24,400	9,400
Lake Ontario	*Canada/USA*	19,500	7,500
Lake Nicaragua	*Nicaragua*	8,200	3,200

South America		km²	miles²
Lake Titicaca	*Bolivia/Peru*	8,300	3,200
Lake Poopo	*Peru*	2,800	1,100

Islands

Europe		km²	miles²
Great Britain	*UK*	229,880	88,700
Iceland	*Atlantic Ocean*	103,000	39,800
Ireland	*Ireland/UK*	84,400	32,600
Novaya Zemlya (N.)	*Russia*	48,200	18,600
Sicily	*Italy*	25,500	9,800
Corsica	*France*	8,700	3,400

Asia		km²	miles²
Borneo	*Southeast Asia*	744,360	287,400
Sumatra	*Indonesia*	473,600	182,860
Honshu	*Japan*	230,500	88,980
Sulawesi (Celebes)	*Indonesia*	189,000	73,000
Java	*Indonesia*	126,700	48,900
Luzon	*Philippines*	104,700	40,400
Hokkaido	*Japan*	78,400	30,300

Africa		km²	miles²
Madagascar	*Indian Ocean*	587,040	226,660
Socotra	*Indian Ocean*	3,600	1,400
Réunion	*Indian Ocean*	2,500	965

Oceania		km²	miles²
New Guinea	*Indonesia/Papua NG*	821,030	317,000
New Zealand (S.)	*Pacific Ocean*	150,500	58,100
New Zealand (N.)	*Pacific Ocean*	114,700	44,300
Tasmania	*Australia*	67,800	26,200
Hawaii	*Pacific Ocean*	10,450	4,000

North America		km²	miles²
Greenland	*Atlantic Ocean*	2,175,600	839,800
Baffin Is.	*Canada*	508,000	196,100
Victoria Is.	*Canada*	212,200	81,900
Ellesmere Is.	*Canada*	212,000	81,800
Cuba	*Caribbean Sea*	110,860	42,800
Hispaniola	*Dominican Rep./Haiti*	76,200	29,400
Jamaica	*Caribbean Sea*	11,400	4,400
Puerto Rico	*Atlantic Ocean*	8,900	3,400

South America		km²	miles²
Tierra del Fuego	*Argentina/Chile*	47,000	18,100
Falkland Is. (E.)	*Atlantic Ocean*	6,800	2,600

Philip's World Maps

The reference maps which form the main body of this atlas have been prepared in accordance with the highest standards of international cartography to provide an accurate and detailed representation of the Earth. The scales and projections used have been carefully chosen to give balanced coverage of the world, while emphasizing the most densely populated and economically significant regions. A hallmark of Philip's mapping is the use of hill shading and relief colouring to create a graphic impression of landforms: this makes the maps exceptionally easy to read. However, knowledge of the key features employed in the construction and presentation of the maps will enable the reader to derive the fullest benefit from the atlas.

Map sequence

The atlas covers the Earth continent by continent: first Europe; then its land neighbour Asia (mapped north before south, in a clockwise sequence), then Africa, Australia and Oceania, North America and South America. This is the classic arrangement adopted by most cartographers since the 16th century. For each continent, there are maps at a variety of scales. First, physical relief and political maps of the whole continent; then a series of larger-scale maps of the regions within the continent, each followed, where required, by still larger-scale maps of the most important or densely populated areas. The governing principle is that by turning the pages of the atlas, the reader moves steadily from north to south through each continent, with each map overlapping its neighbours. A key map showing this sequence, and the area covered by each map, can be found on the endpapers of the atlas.

Map presentation

With very few exceptions (e.g. for the Arctic and Antarctica), the maps are drawn with north at the top, regardless of whether they are presented upright or sideways on the page. In the borders will be found the map title; a locator diagram showing the area covered and the page numbers for maps of adjacent areas; the scale; the projection used; the degrees of latitude and longitude; and the letters and figures used in the index for locating place names and geographical features. Physical relief maps also have a height reference panel identifying the colours used for each layer of contouring.

Map symbols

Each map contains a vast amount of detail which can only be conveyed clearly and accurately by the use of symbols. Points and circles of varying sizes locate and identify the relative importance of towns and cities; different styles of type are employed for administrative, geographical and regional place names. A variety of pictorial symbols denote features such as glaciers and marshes, as well

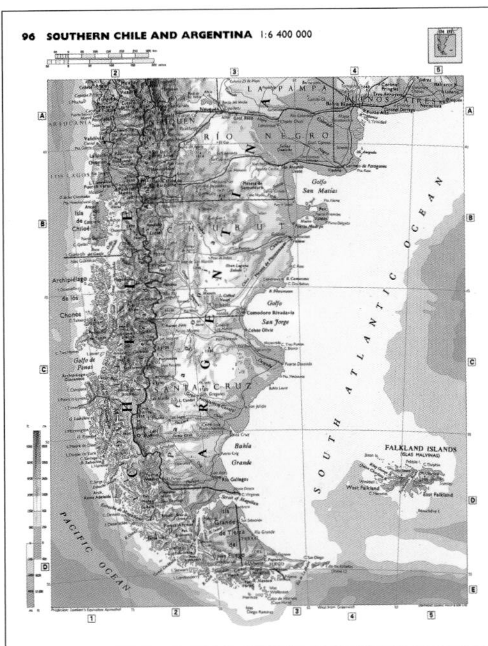

as man-made structures including roads, railways, airports and canals. International borders are shown by red lines. Where neighbouring countries are in dispute, for example in the Middle East, the maps show the *de facto* boundary between nations, regardless of the legal or historical situation. The symbols are explained on the first page of the World Maps section of the atlas.

Map scales

The scale of each map is given in the numerical form known as the 'representative fraction'. The first figure is always one, signifying one unit of distance on the map; the second figure, usually in millions, is the number by which the map unit must be multiplied to give the equivalent distance on the Earth's surface. Calculations can easily be made in centimetres and kilometres, by dividing the Earth units figure by 100 000 (i.e. deleting the last five 0s). Thus 1:1 000 000 means 1 cm = 10 km. The calculation for inches and miles is more laborious, but 1 000 000 divided by 63 360 (the number of inches in a mile) shows that the ratio 1:1 000 000 means approximately 1 inch = 16 miles. The table below provides distance equivalents for scales down to 1:50 000 000.

LARGE SCALE		
1:1 000 000	1 cm = 10 km	1 inch = 16 miles
1:2 500 000	1 cm = 25 km	1 inch = 39.5 miles
1:5 000 000	1 cm = 50 km	1 inch = 79 miles
1:6 000 000	1 cm = 60 km	1 inch = 95 miles
1:8 000 000	1 cm = 80 km	1 inch = 126 miles
1:10 000 000	1 cm = 100 km	1 inch = 158 miles
1:15 000 000	1 cm = 150 km	1 inch = 237 miles
1:20 000 000	1 cm = 200 km	1 inch = 316 miles
1:50 000 000	1 cm = 500 km	1 inch = 790 miles
SMALL SCALE		

Measuring distances

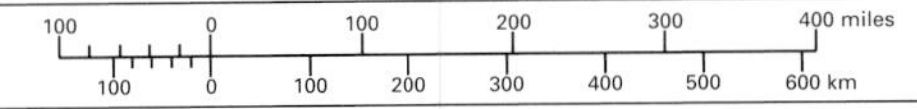

Although each map is accompanied by a scale bar, distances cannot always be measured with confidence because of the distortions involved in portraying the curved surface of the Earth on a flat page. As a general rule, the larger the map scale (i.e. the lower the number of Earth units in the representative fraction), the more accurate and reliable will be the distance measured. On small-scale maps such as those of the world and of entire continents, measurement may only be accurate along the 'standard parallels', or central axes, and should not be attempted without considering the map projection.

Latitude and longitude

Accurate positioning of individual points on the Earth's surface is made possible by reference to the geometrical system of latitude and longitude. Latitude *parallels* are drawn west-east around the Earth and numbered by degrees north and south of the Equator, which is designated 0° of latitude. Longitude *meridians* are drawn north–south and numbered by degrees east and west of the *prime meridian*, 0° of longitude, which passes through Greenwich in England. By referring to these co-ordinates and their subdivisions of minutes (^{1}/60th of a degree) and seconds (^{1}/60th of a minute), any place on Earth can be located to within a few hundred metres. Latitude and longitude are indicated by blue lines on the maps; they are straight or curved according to the projection employed. Reference to these lines is the easiest way of determining the relative positions of places on different maps, and for plotting compass directions.

Name forms

For ease of reference, both English and local name forms appear in the atlas. Oceans, seas and countries are shown in English throughout the atlas; country names may be abbreviated to their commonly accepted form (e.g. Germany, not The Federal Republic of Germany). Conventional English forms are also used for place names on the smaller-scale maps of the continents. However, local name forms are used on all large-scale and regional maps, with the English form given in brackets only for important cities – the large-scale map of Russia and Central Asia thus shows Moskva (Moscow). For countries which do not use a Roman script, place names have been transcribed according to the systems adopted by the British and US Geographic Names Authorities. For China, the Pin Yin system has been used, with some more widely known forms appearing in brackets, as with Beijing (Peking). Both English and local names appear in the index, the English form being cross-referenced to the local form.

The WORLD IN FOCUS

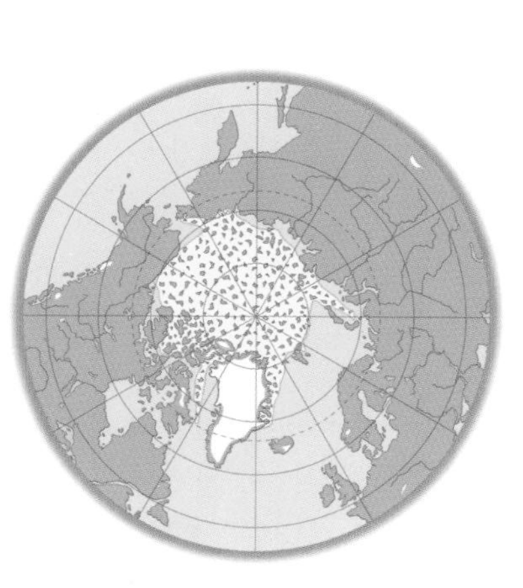

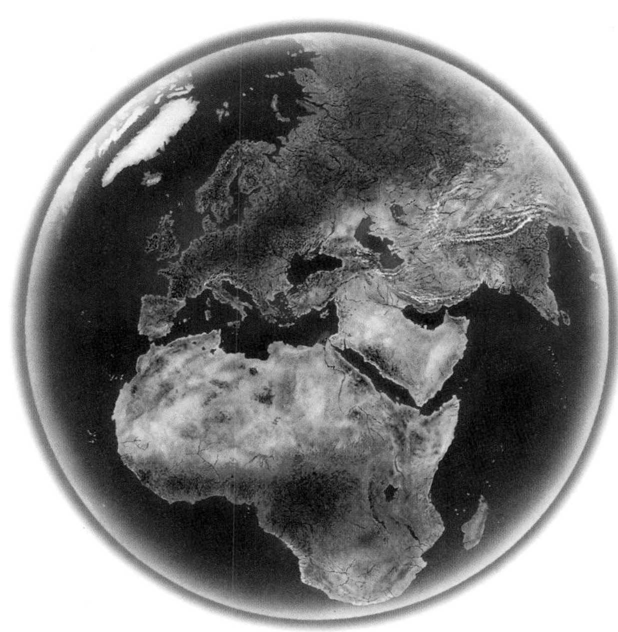

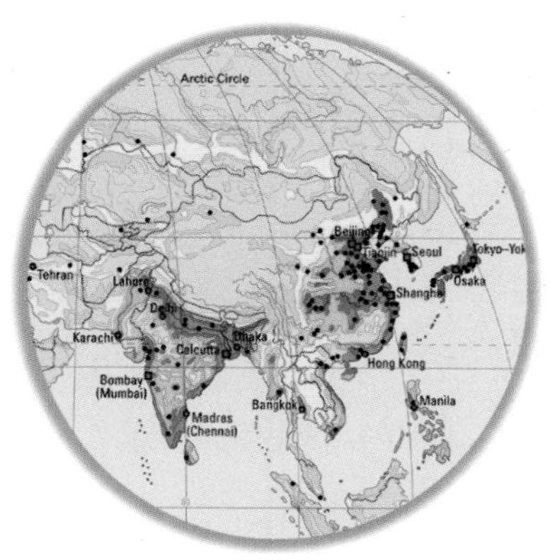

Planet Earth

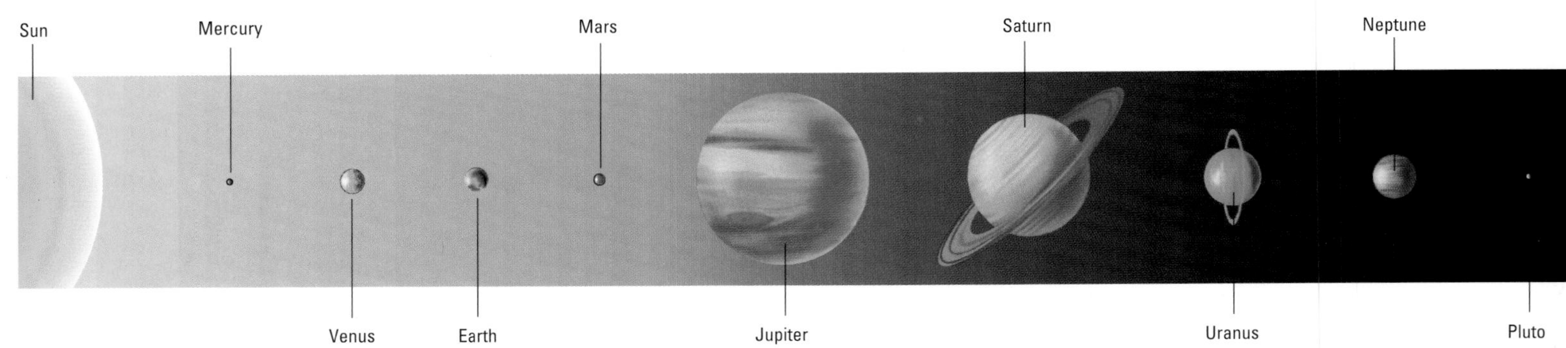

Sun · Mercury · Mars · Saturn · Neptune · Venus · Earth · Jupiter · Uranus · Pluto

The Solar System

A minute part of one of the billions of galaxies (collections of stars) that comprises the Universe, the Solar System lies some 27,000 light-years from the centre of our own galaxy, the 'Milky Way'. Thought to be over 4,700 million years old, it consists of a central sun with nine planets and their moons revolving around it, attracted by its gravitational pull. The planets orbit the Sun in the same direction – anti-clockwise when viewed from the Northern Heavens – and almost in the same plane. Their orbital paths, however, vary enormously.

The Sun's diameter is 109 times that of Earth, and the temperature at its core – caused by continuous thermonuclear fusions of hydrogen into helium – is estimated to be 15 million degrees Celsius. It is the Solar System's only source of light and heat.

Profile of the Planets

	Mean distance from Sun (million km)	Mass (Earth = 1)	Period of orbit (Earth years)	Period of rotation (Earth days)	Equatorial diameter (km)	Number of known satellites
Mercury	57.9	0.055	0.24 years	58.67	4,878	0
Venus	108.2	0.815	0.62 years	243.00	12,104	0
Earth	149.6	1.0	1.00 years	1.00	12,756	1
Mars	227.9	0.107	1.88 years	1.03	6,787	2
Jupiter	778.3	317.8	11.86 years	0.41	142,800	16
Saturn	1,427	95.2	29.46 years	0.43	120,000	20
Uranus	2,871	14.5	84.01 years	0.75	51,118	15
Neptune	4,497	17.1	164.80 years	0.80	49,528	8
Pluto	5,914	0.002	248.50 years	6.39	2,320	1

All planetary orbits are elliptical in form, but only Pluto and Mercury follow paths that deviate noticeably from a circular one. Near perihelion – its closest approach to the Sun – Pluto actually passes inside the orbit of Neptune, an event that last occurred in 1983. Pluto did not regain its station as outermost planet until February 1999.

The Seasons

Seasons occur because the Earth's axis is tilted at a constant angle of 23½°. When the northern hemisphere is tilted to a maximum extent towards the Sun, on 21 June, the Sun is overhead at the Tropic of Cancer (latitude 23½° North). This is midsummer, or the summer solstice, in the northern hemisphere.

On 22 or 23 September, the Sun is overhead at the Equator, and day and night are of equal length throughout the world. This is the autumn equinox in the northern hemisphere. On 21 or 22 December, the Sun is overhead at the Tropic of Capricorn (23½° South), the winter solstice in the northern hemisphere. The overhead Sun then tracks north until, on 21 March, it is overhead at the Equator. This is the spring (vernal) equinox in the northern hemisphere.

In the southern hemisphere, the seasons are the reverse of those in the north.

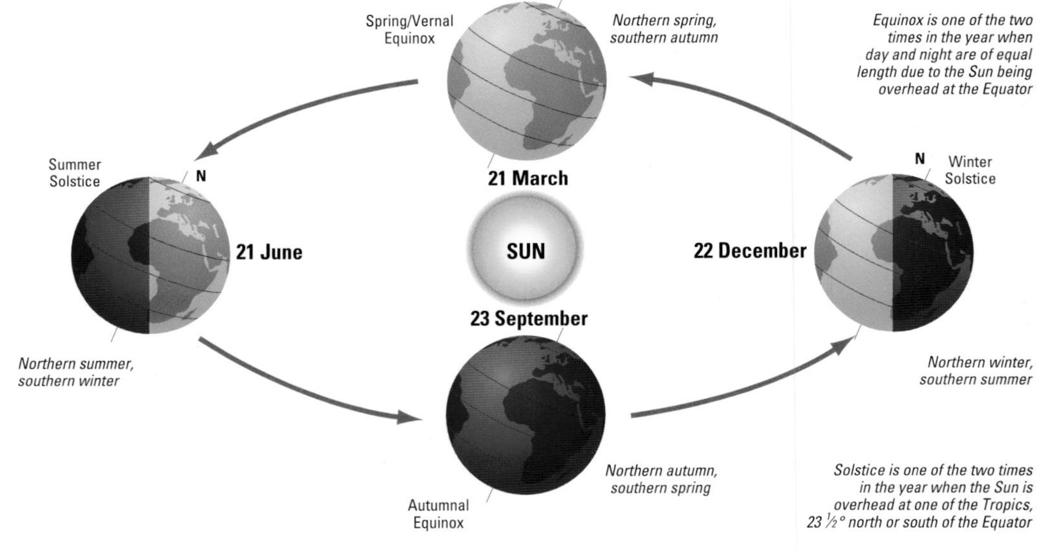

Spring/Vernal Equinox — Northern spring, southern autumn — Equinox is one of the two times in the year when day and night are of equal length due to the Sun being overhead at the Equator

Summer Solstice — N — 21 March — Winter Solstice — N

21 June — SUN — 22 December

23 September

Northern summer, southern winter — Northern winter, southern summer

Autumnal Equinox — Northern autumn, southern spring — Solstice is one of the two times in the year when the Sun is overhead at one of the Tropics, 23½° north or south of the Equator

Day and Night

The Sun appears to rise in the east, reach its highest point at noon, and then set in the west, to be followed by night. In reality, it is not the Sun that is moving but the Earth rotating from west to east. The moment when the Sun's upper limb first appears above the horizon is termed sunrise; the moment when the Sun's upper limb disappears below the horizon is sunset.

At the summer solstice in the northern hemisphere (21 June), the Arctic has total daylight and the Antarctic total darkness. The opposite occurs at the winter solstice (21 or 22 December). At the Equator, the length of day and night are almost equal all year.

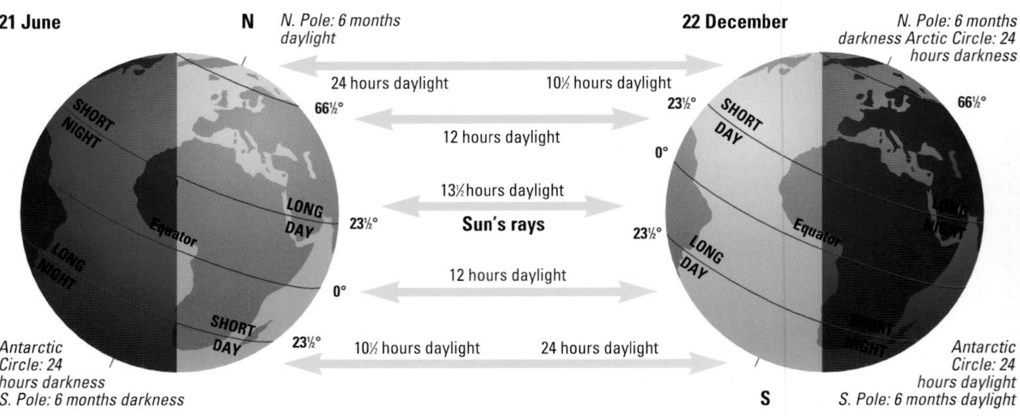

21 June — N — N. Pole: 6 months daylight
24 hours daylight — 10½ hours daylight — 66½°
12 hours daylight
13½ hours daylight
23½° — Sun's rays
12 hours daylight
0°
SHORT NIGHT — LONG DAY — LONG NIGHT — SHORT DAY — Equator
Antarctic Circle: 24 hours darkness — 23½° — 10½ hours daylight — S. Pole: 6 months darkness

22 December — N. Pole: 6 months darkness Arctic Circle: 24 hours darkness
23½° — 66½° — SHORT DAY
0°
23½° — LONG DAY — Equator
24 hours daylight
Antarctic Circle: 24 hours daylight — S. Pole: 6 months daylight — S

Time

Year: The time taken by the Earth to revolve around the Sun, or 365.24 days.

Leap Year: A calendar year of 366 days, 29 February being the additional day. It offsets the difference between the calendar and the solar year.

Month: The approximate time taken by the Moon to revolve around the Earth. The 12 months of the year in fact vary from 28 (29 in a Leap Year) to 31 days.

Week: An artificial period of 7 days, not based on astronomical time.

Day: The time taken by the Earth to complete one rotation on its axis.

Hour: 24 hours make one day. Usually the day is divided into hours AM (ante meridiem or before noon) and PM (post meridiem or after noon), although most timetables now use the 24-hour system, from midnight to midnight.

Sunrise

Sunset

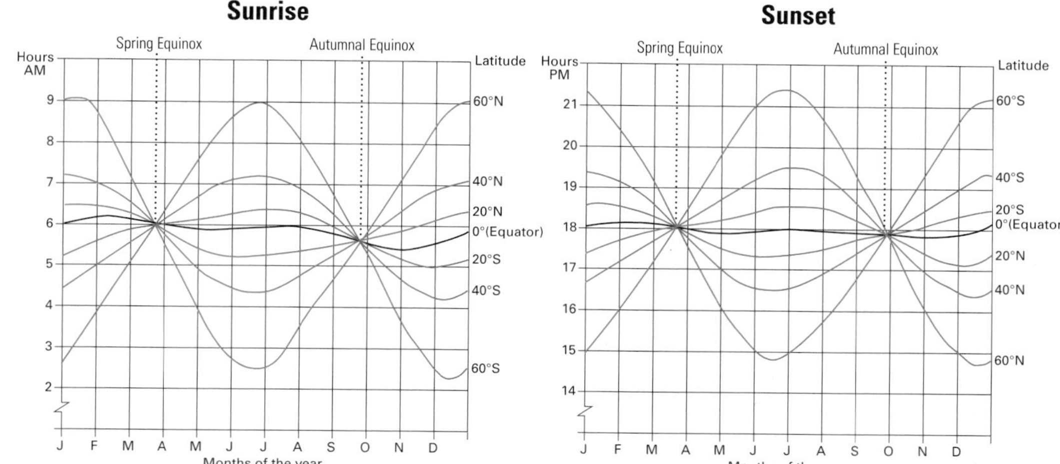

The Moon

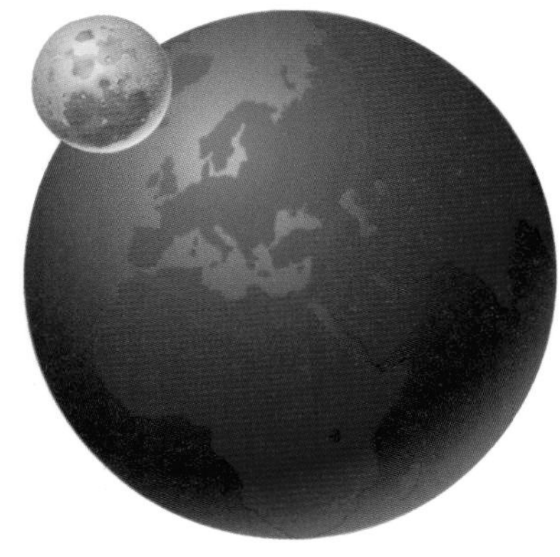

The Moon rotates more slowly than the Earth, making one complete turn on its axis in just over 27 days. Since this corresponds to its period of revolution around the Earth, the Moon always presents the same hemisphere or face to us, and we never see 'the dark side'. The interval between one full Moon and the next (and between new Moons) is about 29½ days – a lunar month. The apparent changes in the shape of the Moon are caused by its changing position in relation to the Earth; like the planets, it produces no light of its own and shines only by reflecting the rays of the Sun.

Phases of the Moon

Distance from Earth: 356,410 km – 406,685 km; Mean diameter: 3,475.1 km; Mass: approx. 1/81 that of Earth; Surface gravity: one-sixth of Earth's; Daily range of temperature at lunar equator: 200°C; Average orbital speed: 3,683 km/h

New Moon — Crescent — First quarter — Gibbous — Full Moon — Gibbous — Last quarter — Crescent — New Moon

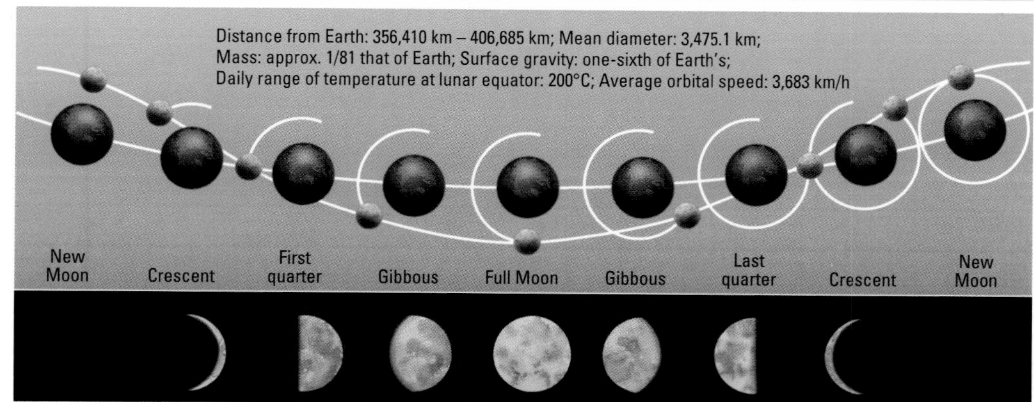

Eclipses

When the Moon passes between the Sun and the Earth it causes a partial eclipse of the Sun (1) if the Earth passes through the Moon's outer shadow (P), or a total eclipse (2) if the inner cone shadow crosses the Earth's surface. In a lunar eclipse, the Earth's shadow crosses the Moon and, again, provides either a partial or total eclipse.

Eclipses of the Sun and the Moon do not occur every month because of the 5° difference between the plane of the Moon's orbit and the plane in which the Earth moves. In the 1990s only 14 lunar eclipses are possible, for example, seven partial and seven total; each is visible only from certain, and variable, parts of the world. The same period witnesses 13 solar eclipses – six partial (or annular) and seven total.

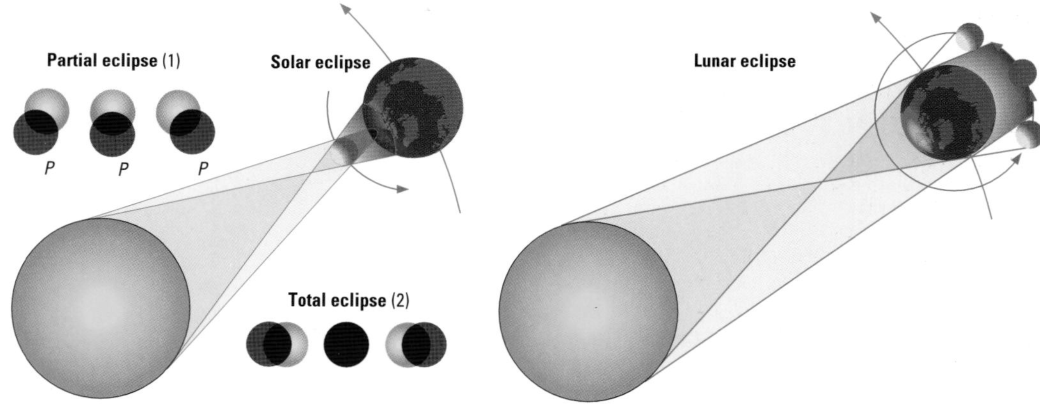

Tides

The daily rise and fall of the ocean's tides are the result of the gravitational pull of the Moon and that of the Sun, though the effect of the latter is only 46.6% as strong as that of the Moon. This effect is greatest on the hemisphere facing the Moon and causes a tidal 'bulge'. When the Sun, Earth and Moon are in line, tide-raising forces are at a maximum and Spring tides occur: high tide reaches the highest values, and low tide falls to low levels. When lunar and solar forces are least coincidental with the Sun and Moon at an angle (near the Moon's first and third quarters), Neap tides occur, which have a small tidal range.

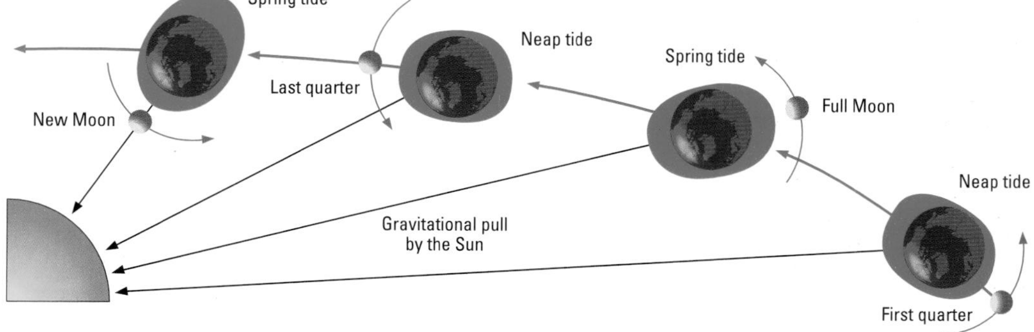

Restless Earth

The Earth's Structure

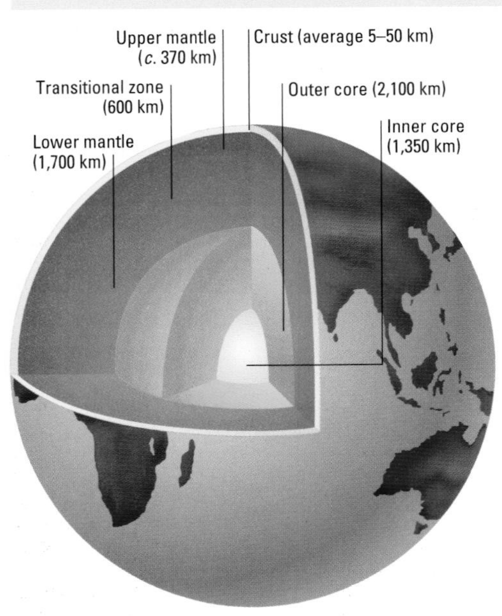

Upper mantle (c. 370 km)

Crust (average 5–50 km)

Transitional zone (600 km)

Outer core (2,100 km)

Lower mantle (1,700 km)

Inner core (1,350 km)

Continental Drift

About 200 million years ago the original Pangaea landmass began to split into two continental groups, which further separated over time to produce the present-day configuration.

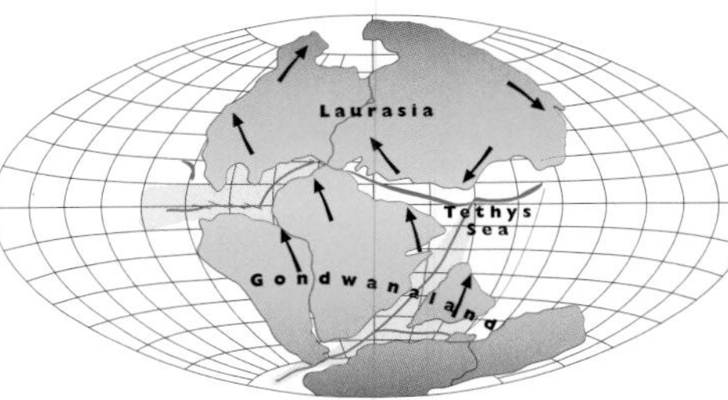

180 million years ago

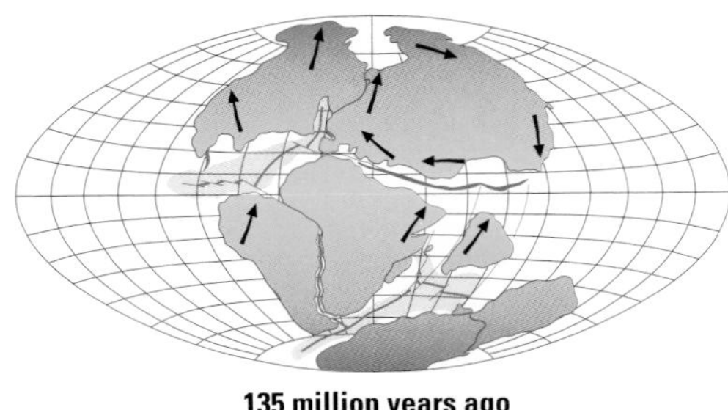

135 million years ago

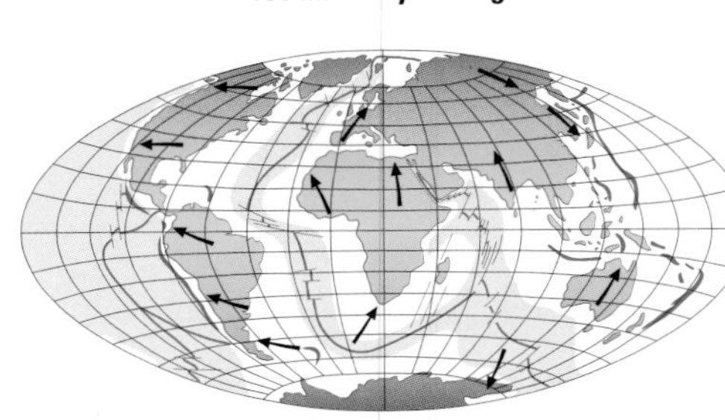

Present day

— Trench
— Rift
New ocean floor
— Zones of slippage

Notable Earthquakes Since 1900

Year	Location	Richter Scale	Deaths
1906	San Francisco, USA	8.3	503
1906	Valparaiso, Chile	8.6	22,000
1908	Messina, Italy	7.5	83,000
1915	Avezzano, Italy	7.5	30,000
1920	Gansu (Kansu), China	8.6	180,000
1923	Yokohama, Japan	8.3	143,000
1927	Nan Shan, China	8.3	200,000
1932	Gansu (Kansu), China	7.6	70,000
1933	Sanriku, Japan	8.9	2,990
1934	Bihar, India/Nepal	8.4	10,700
1935	Quetta, India (now Pakistan)	7.5	60,000
1939	Chillan, Chile	8.3	28,000
1939	Erzincan, Turkey	7.9	30,000
1960	Agadir, Morocco	5.8	12,000
1962	Khorasan, Iran	7.1	12,230
1968	N.E. Iran	7.4	12,000
1970	N. Peru	7.7	66,794
1972	Managua, Nicaragua	6.2	5,000
1974	N. Pakistan	6.3	5,200
1976	Guatemala	7.5	22,778
1976	Tangshan, China	8.2	255,000
1978	Tabas, Iran	7.7	25,000
1980	El Asnam, Algeria	7.3	20,000
1980	S. Italy	7.2	4,800
1985	Mexico City, Mexico	8.1	4,200
1988	N.W. Armenia	6.8	55,000
1990	N. Iran	7.7	36,000
1993	Maharashtra, India	6.4	30,000
1994	Los Angeles, USA	6.6	51
1995	Kobe, Japan	7.2	5,000
1995	Sakhalin Is., Russia	7.5	2,000
1997	N.E. Iran	7.1	2,500
1998	Takhar, Afghanistan	6.1	4,200
1998	Rostaq, Afghanistan	7.0	5,000

The highest magnitude recorded on the Richter scale is 8.9 in Japan on 2 March 1933 which killed 2,990 people.

Earthquakes

Earthquake magnitude is usually rated according to either the Richter or the Modified Mercalli scale, both devised by seismologists in the 1930s. The Richter scale measures absolute earthquake power with mathematical precision: each step upwards represents a tenfold increase in shockwave amplitude. Theoretically, there is no upper limit, but the largest earthquakes measured have been rated at between 8.8 and 8.9. The 12–point Mercalli scale, based on observed effects, is often more meaningful, ranging from I (earthquakes noticed only by seismographs) to XII (total destruction); intermediate points include V (people awakened at night; unstable objects overturned), VII (collapse of ordinary buildings; chimneys and monuments fall) and IX (conspicuous cracks in ground; serious damage to reservoirs).

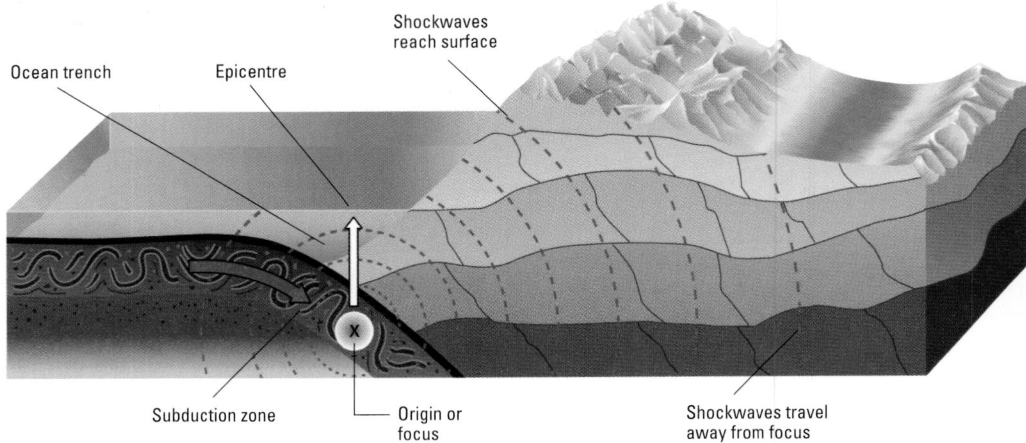

Ocean trench

Epicentre

Shockwaves reach surface

Subduction zone

Origin or focus

Shockwaves travel away from focus

Structure and Earthquakes

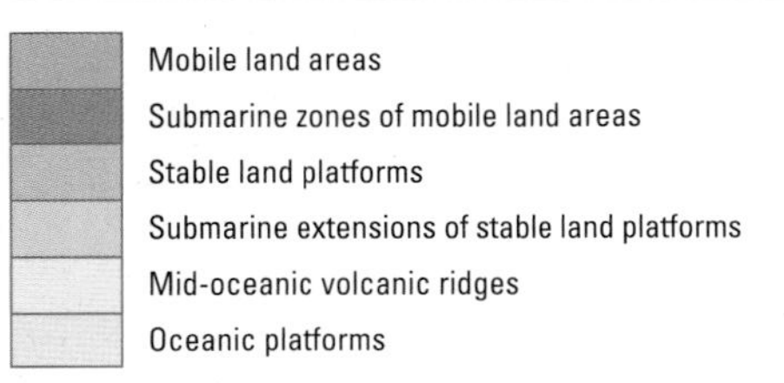

Mobile land areas

Submarine zones of mobile land areas

Stable land platforms

Submarine extensions of stable land platforms

Mid-oceanic volcanic ridges

Oceanic platforms

1976 ○ Principal earthquakes and dates

Earthquakes are a series of rapid vibrations originating from the slipping or faulting of parts of the Earth's crust when stresses within build up to breaking point. They usually happen at depths varying from 8 km to 30 km. Severe earthquakes cause extensive damage when they take place in populated areas, destroying structures and severing communications. Most initial loss of life occurs due to secondary causes such as falling masonry, fires and flooding.

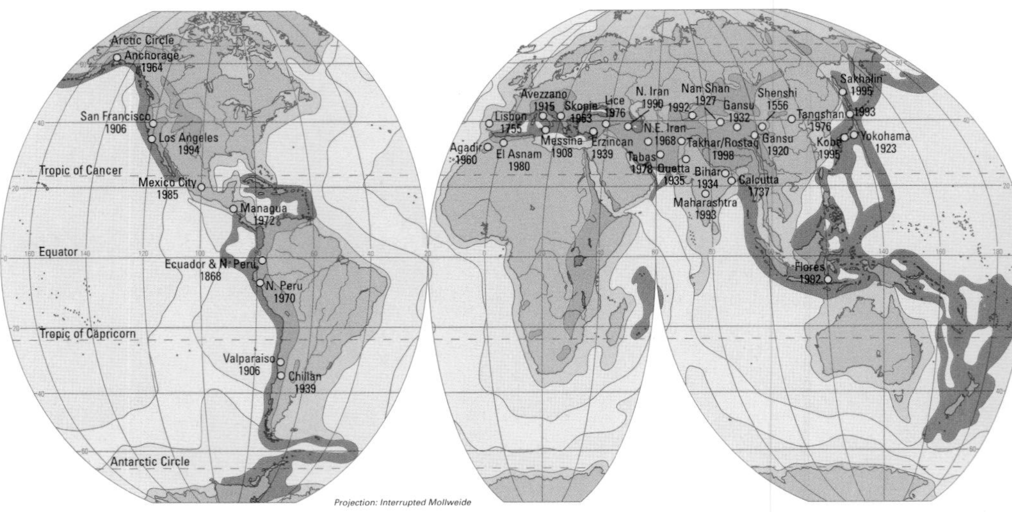

Projection: Interrupted Mollweide

Plate Tectonics

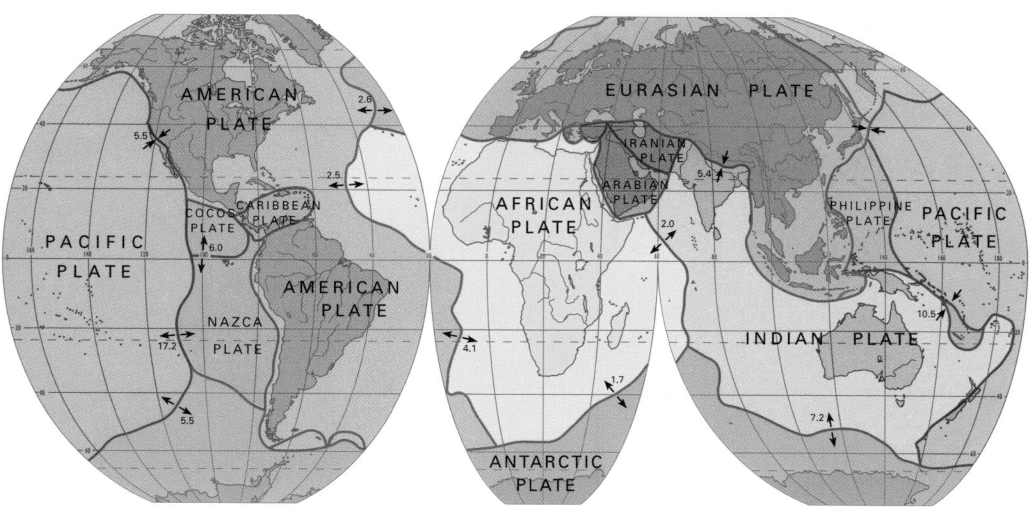

— Plate boundaries   PACIFIC Major plates

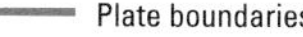

➤ Direction of plate movements and rate of movement (cm/year)

The drifting of the continents is a feature that is unique to Planet Earth. The complementary, almost jigsaw-puzzle fit of the coastlines on each side of the Atlantic Ocean inspired Alfred Wegener's theory of continental drift in 1915. The theory suggested that the ancient super-continent, which Wegener named Pangaea, incorporated all of the Earth's landmasses and gradually split up to form today's continents.

The original debate about continental drift was a prelude to a more radical idea: plate tectonics. The basic theory is that the Earth's crust is made up of a series of rigid plates which float on a soft layer of the mantle and are moved about by continental convection currents within the Earth's interior. These plates diverge and converge along margins marked by seismic activity. Plates diverge from mid-ocean ridges where molten lava pushes upwards and forces the plates apart at rates of up to 40 mm [1.6 in] a year.

The three diagrams, left, give some examples of plate boundaries from around the world. Diagram (a) shows sea-floor spreading at the Mid-Atlantic Ridge as the American and African plates slowly diverge. The same thing is happening in (b) where sea-floor spreading at the Mid-Indian Ocean Ridge is forcing the Indian plate to collide into the Eurasian plate. In (c) oceanic crust (sima) is being subducted beneath lighter continental crust (sial).

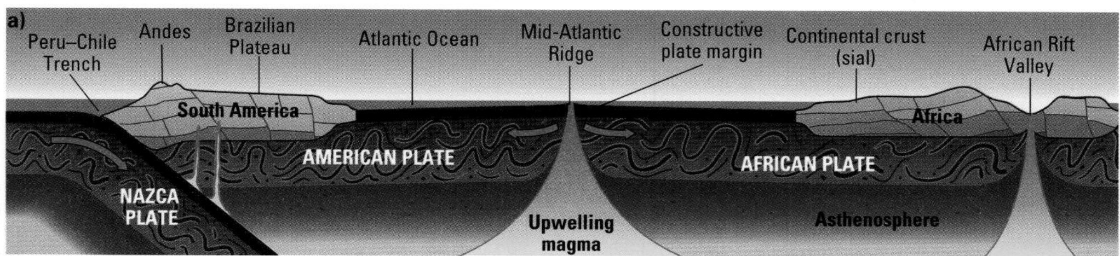

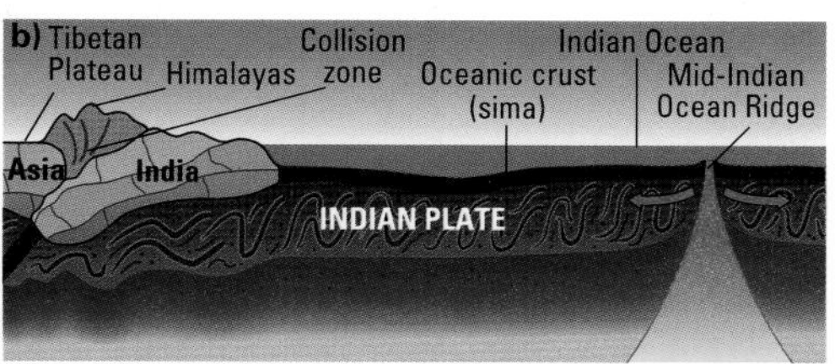

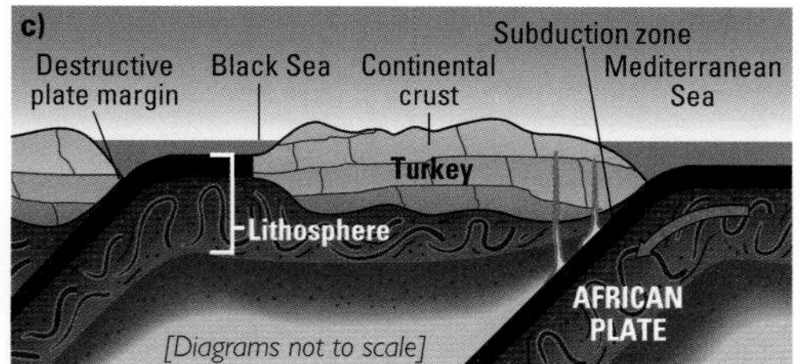

Volcanoes

Volcanoes occur when hot liquefied rock beneath the Earth's crust is pushed up by pressure to the surface as molten lava. Some volcanoes erupt in an explosive way, throwing out rocks and ash, whilst others are effusive and lava flows out of the vent. There are volcanoes which are both, such as Mount Fuji. An accumulation of lava and cinders creates cones of variable size and shape. As a result of many eruptions over centuries, Mount Etna in Sicily has a circumference of more than 120 km [75 miles].

Climatologists believe that volcanic ash, if ejected high into the atmosphere, can influence temperature and weather for several years afterwards. The 1991 eruption of Mount Pinatubo in the Philippines ejected more than 20 million tonnes of dust and ash 32 km [20 miles] into the atmosphere and is believed to have accelerated ozone depletion over a large part of the globe.

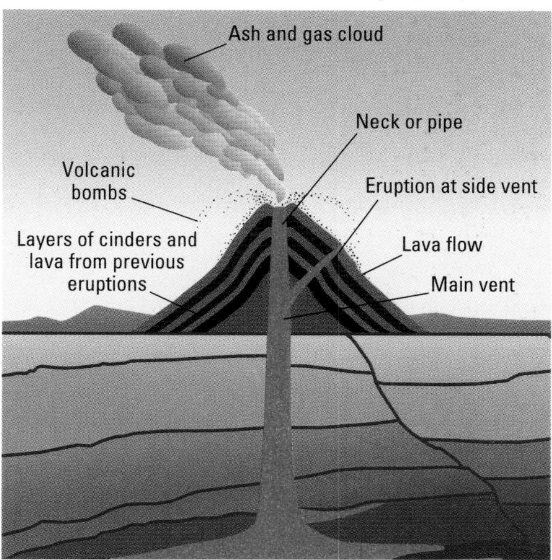

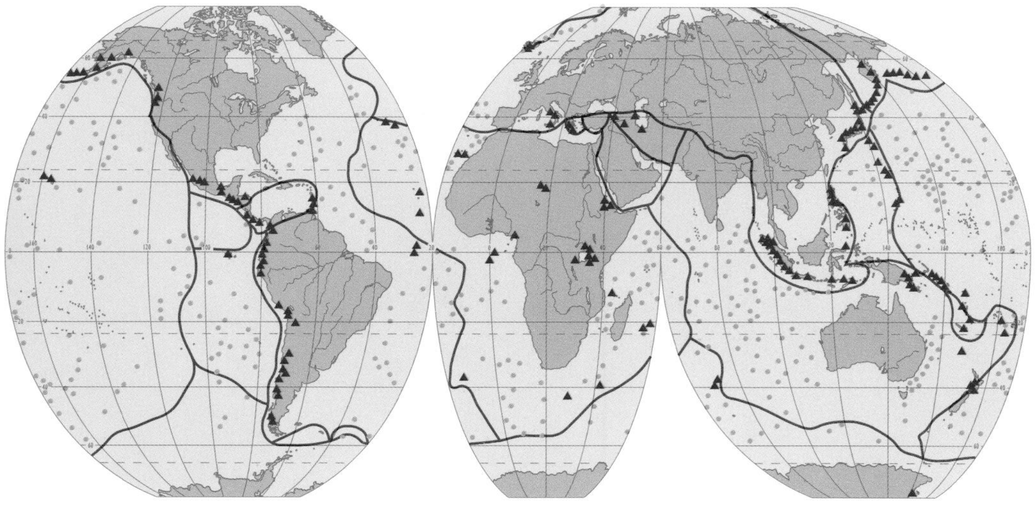

Distribution of Volcanoes

Volcanoes today may be the subject of considerable scientific study but they remain both dramatic and unpredictable: in 1991 Mount Pinatubo, 100 km [62 miles] north of the Philippines capital Manila, suddenly burst into life after lying dormant for more than six centuries. Most of the world's active volcanoes occur in a belt around the Pacific Ocean, on the edge of the Pacific plate, called the 'ring of fire'. Indonesia has the greatest concentration with 90 volcanoes, 12 of which are active. The most famous, Krakatoa, erupted in 1883 with such force that the resulting tidal wave killed 36,000 people and tremors were felt as far away as Australia.

• Submarine volcanoes

▲ Land volcanoes active since 1700

— Boundaries of tectonic plates

CARTOGRAPHY BY PHILIP'S. COPYRIGHT GEORGE PHILIP LTD

5

Landforms

The Rock Cycle

James Hutton first proposed the rock cycle in the late 1700s after he observed the slow but steady effects of erosion.

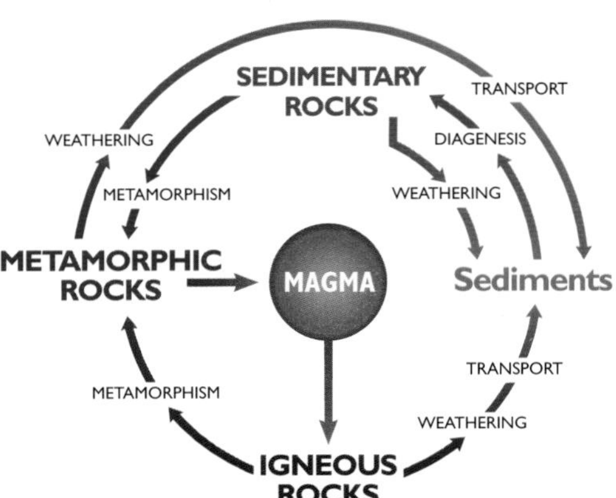

Above and below the surface of the oceans, the features of the Earth's crust are constantly changing. The phenomenal forces generated by convection currents in the molten core of our planet carry the vast segments or 'plates' of the crust across the globe in an endless cycle of creation and destruction. A continent may travel little more than 25 mm [1 in] per year, yet in the vast span of geological time this process throws up giant mountain ranges and creates new land.

Destruction of the landscape, however, begins as soon as it is formed. Wind, water, ice and sea, the main agents of erosion, mount a constant assault that even the most resistant rocks cannot withstand. Mountain peaks may dwindle by as little as a few millimetres each year, but if they are not uplifted by further movements of the crust they will eventually be reduced to rubble and transported away.

Water is the most powerful agent of erosion – it has been estimated that 100 billion tonnes of sediment are washed into the oceans every year. Three Asian rivers account for 20% of this total, the Huang He, in China, and the Brahmaputra and Ganges in Bangladesh.

Rivers and glaciers, like the sea itself, generate much of their effect through abrasion – pounding the land with the debris they carry with them. But as well as destroying they also create new landforms, many of them spectacular: vast deltas like those of the Mississippi and the Nile, or the deep fjords cut by glaciers in British Columbia, Norway and New Zealand.

Geologists once considered that landscapes evolved from 'young', newly uplifted mountainous areas, through a 'mature' hilly stage, to an 'old age' stage when the land was reduced to an almost flat plain, or peneplain. This theory, called the 'cycle of erosion', fell into disuse when it became evident that so many factors, including the effects of plate tectonics and climatic change, constantly interrupt the cycle, which takes no account of the highly complex interactions that shape the surface of our planet.

Mountain Building

Mountains are formed when pressures on the Earth's crust caused by continental drift become so intense that the surface buckles or cracks. This happens where oceanic crust is subducted by continental crust or, more dramatically, where two tectonic plates collide; the Rockies, Andes, Alps, Urals and Himalayas resulted from such impacts. These are all known as fold mountains because they were formed by the compression of the rocks, forcing the surface to bend and fold like a crumpled rug. The Himalayas are formed from the folded former sediments of the Tethys Sea which was trapped in the collision zone between the Indian and Eurasian plates.

The other main mountain-building process occurs when the crust fractures to create faults, allowing rock to be forced upwards in large blocks; or when the pressure of magma within the crust forces the surface to bulge into a dome, or erupts to form a volcano. Large mountain ranges may reveal a combination of those features; the Alps, for example, have been compressed so violently that the folds are fragmented by numerous faults and intrusions of molten igneous rock.

Over millions of years, even the greatest mountain ranges can be reduced by the agents of erosion (most notably rivers) to a low rugged landscape known as a peneplain.

Types of faults: Faults occur where the crust is being stretched or compressed so violently that the rock strata break in a horizontal or vertical movement. They are classified by the direction in which the blocks of rock have moved. A normal fault results when a vertical movement causes the surface to break apart; compression causes a reverse fault. Horizontal movement causes shearing, known as a strike-slip fault. When the rock breaks in two places, the central block may be pushed up in a horst fault, or sink (creating a rift valley) in a graben fault.

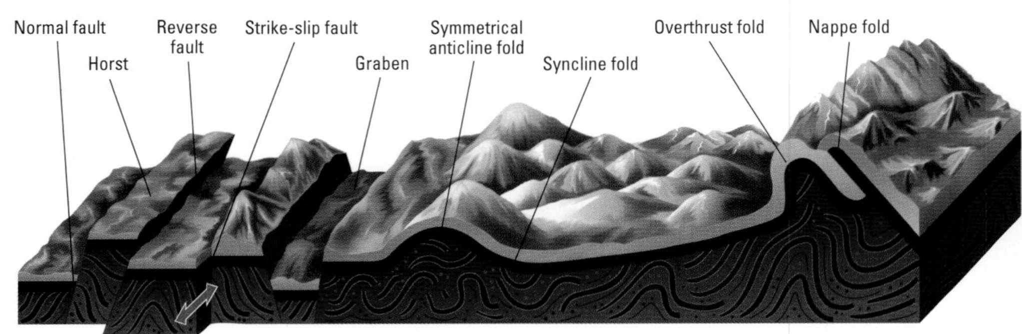

Normal fault | Reverse fault | Strike-slip fault | Symmetrical anticline fold | Overthrust fold | Nappe fold
Horst | Graben | Syncline fold

Types of fold: Folds occur when rock strata are squeezed and compressed. They are common therefore at destructive plate margins and where plates have collided, forcing the rocks to buckle into mountain ranges. Geographers give different names to the degrees of fold that result from continuing pressure on the rock. A simple fold may be symmetric, with even slopes on either side, but as the pressure builds up, one slope becomes steeper and the fold becomes asymmetric. Later, the ridge or 'anticline' at the top of the fold may slide over the lower ground or 'syncline' to form a recumbent fold. Eventually, the rock strata may break under the pressure to form an overthrust and finally a nappe fold.

Continental Glaciation

Ice sheets were at their greatest extent about 200,000 years ago. The maximum advance of the last Ice Age was about 18,000 years ago, when ice covered virtually all of Canada and reached as far south as the Bristol Channel in Britain.

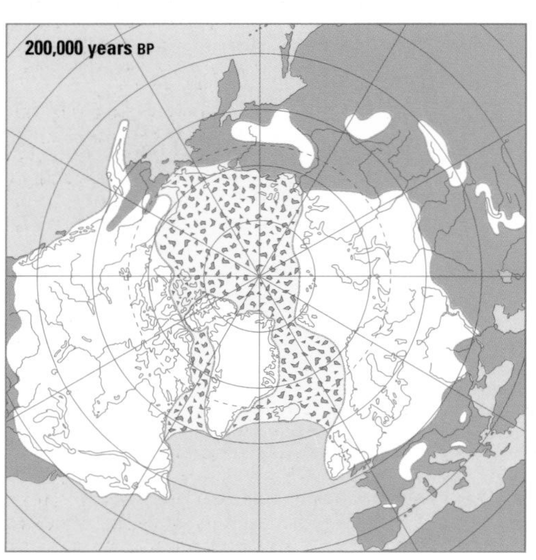

200,000 years BP

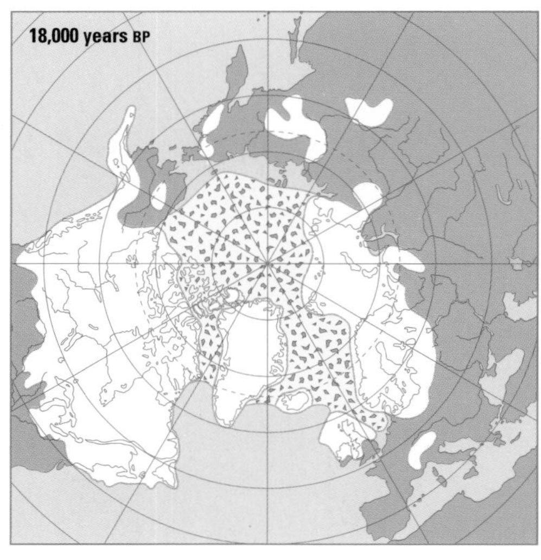

18,000 years BP

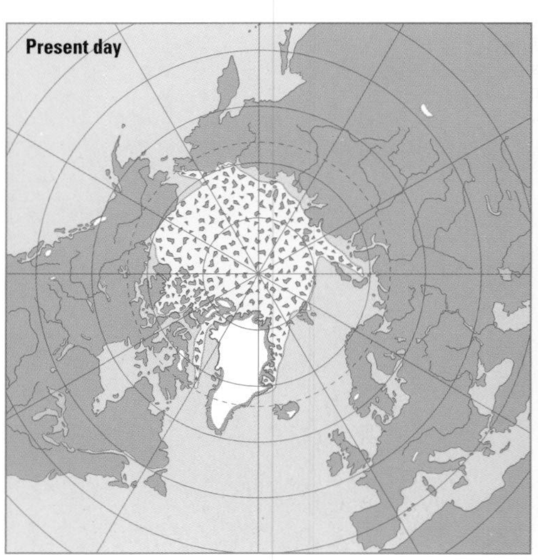

Present day

Natural Landforms

A stylized diagram to show a selection of landforms found in the mid-latitudes.

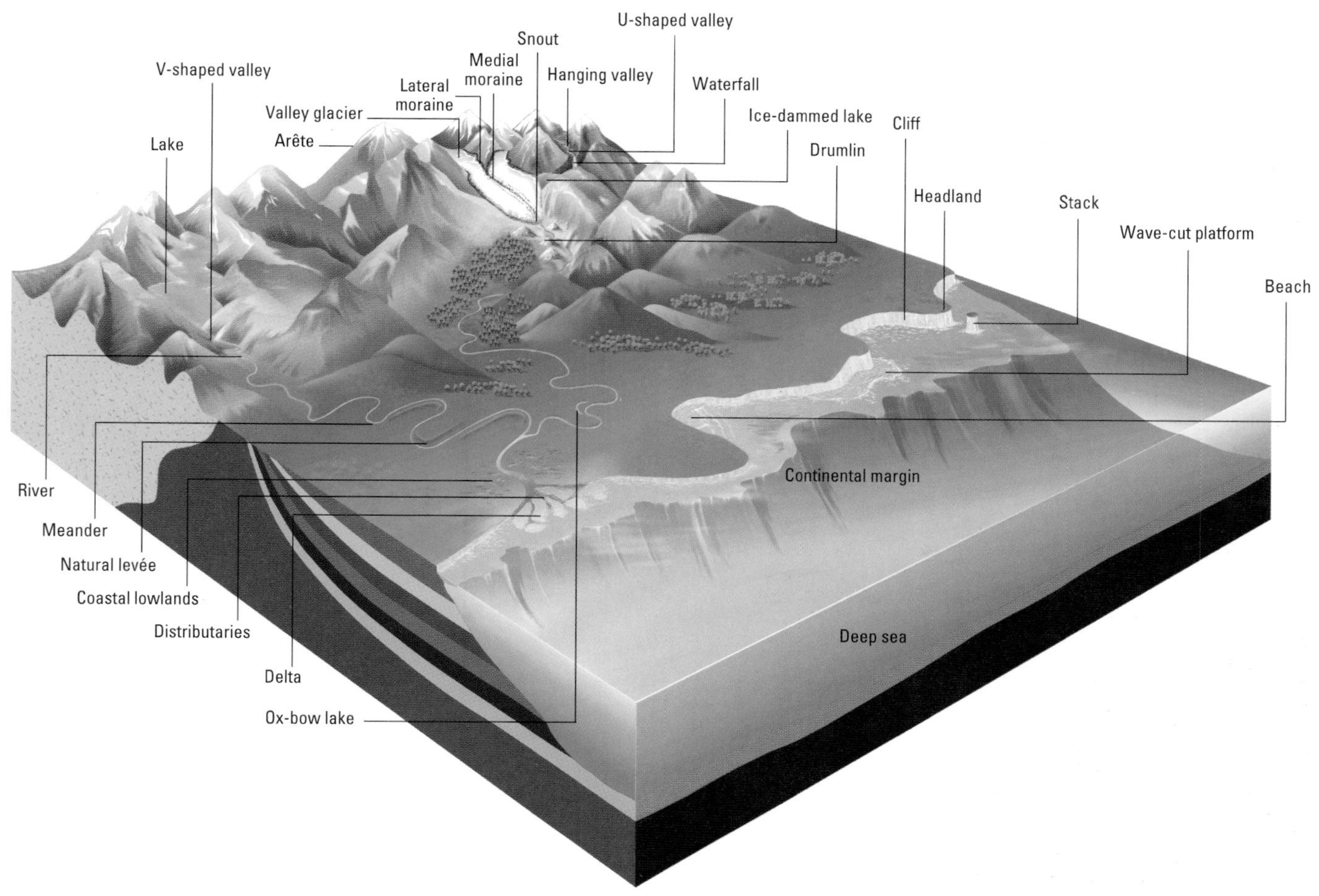

U-shaped valley

Snout

Medial moraine

Hanging valley

Waterfall

V-shaped valley

Lateral moraine

Ice-dammed lake

Cliff

Valley glacier

Arête

Drumlin

Headland

Stack

Lake

Wave-cut platform

Beach

River

Meander

Natural levée

Coastal lowlands

Distributaries

Delta

Ox-bow lake

Continental margin

Deep sea

Desert Landscapes

The popular image that deserts are all huge expanses of sand is wrong. Despite harsh conditions, deserts contain some of the most varied and interesting landscapes in the world. They are also one of the most extensive environments – the hot and cold deserts together cover almost 40% of the Earth's surface.

The three types of hot desert are known by their Arabic names: sand desert, called *erg*, covers only about one-fifth of the world's desert; the rest is divided between *hammada* (areas of bare rock) and *reg* (broad plains covered by loose gravel or pebbles).

In areas of *erg*, such as the Namib Desert, the shape of the dunes reflects the character of local winds. Where winds are constant in direction, crescent-shaped *barchan* dunes form. In areas of bare rock, wind-blown sand is a major agent of erosion. The erosion is mainly confined to within 2 m [6.5 ft] of the surface, producing characteristic, mushroom-shaped rocks.

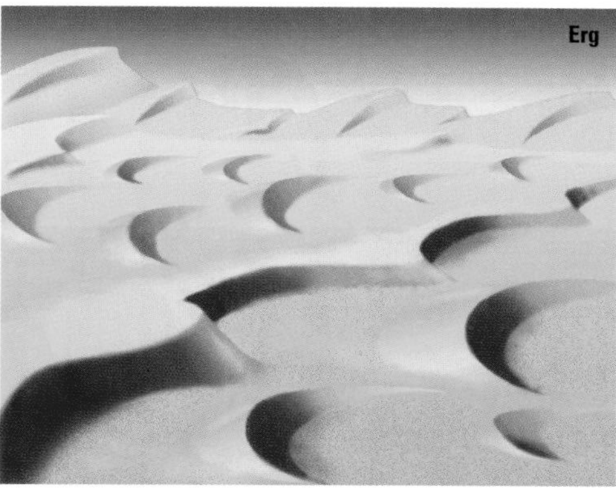

Erg

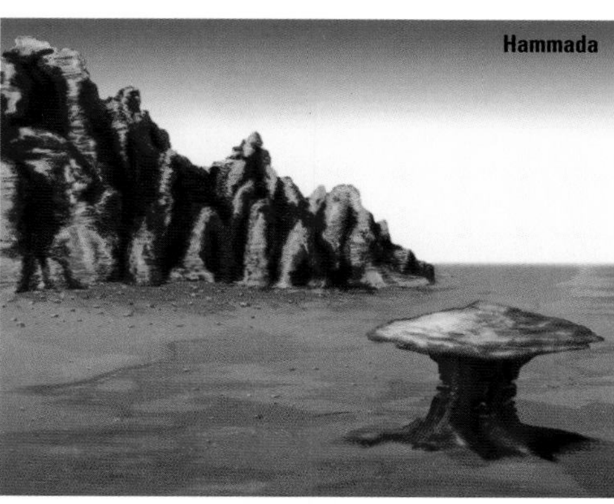

Hammada

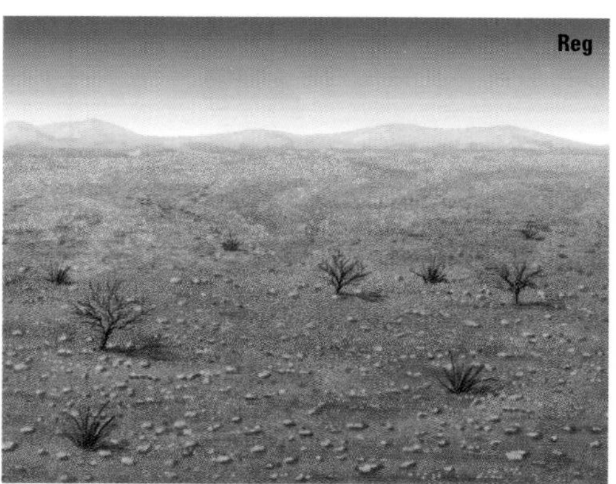

Reg

Surface Processes

Catastrophic changes to natural landforms are periodically caused by such phenomena as avalanches, landslides and volcanic eruptions, but most of the processes that shape the Earth's surface operate extremely slowly in human terms. One estimate, based on a study in the United States, suggested that 1 m [3 ft] of land was removed from the entire surface of the country, on average, every 29,500 years. However, the time-scale varies from 1,300 years to 154,200 years depending on the terrain and climate.

In hot, dry climates, mechanical weathering, a result of rapid temperature changes, causes the outer layers of rock to peel away, while in cold mountainous regions, boulders are prised apart when water freezes in cracks in rocks. Chemical weathering, at its greatest in warm, humid regions, is responsible for hollowing out limestone caves and decomposing granites.

The erosion of soil and rock is greatest on sloping land and the steeper the slope, the greater the tendency for mass wasting – the movement of soil and rock downhill under the influence of gravity. The mechanisms of mass wasting (ranging from very slow to very rapid) vary with the type of material, but the presence of water as a lubricant is usually an important factor.

Running water is the world's leading agent of erosion and transportation. The energy of a river depends on several factors, including its velocity and volume, and its erosive power is at its peak when it is in full flood. Sea waves also exert tremendous erosive power during storms when they hurl pebbles against the shore, undercutting cliffs and hollowing out caves.

Glacier ice forms in mountain hollows and spills out to form valley glaciers, which transport rocks shattered by frost action. As glaciers move, rocks embedded into the ice erode steep-sided, U-shaped valleys. Evidence of glaciation in mountain regions includes cirques, knife-edged ridges, or arêtes, and pyramidal peaks.

Oceans

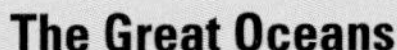

The Great Oceans

Relative sizes of the world's oceans

Pacific
Atlantic
Indian
Arctic

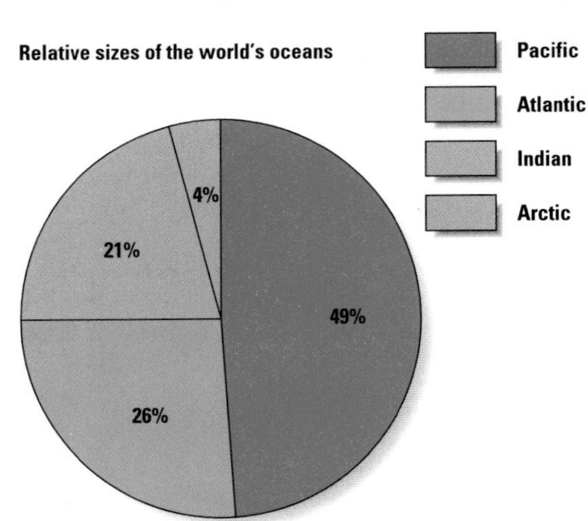

In a strict geographical sense there are only three true oceans – the Atlantic, Indian and Pacific. The legendary 'Seven Seas' would require these to be divided at the Equator and the addition of the Arctic Ocean – which accounts for less than 4% of the total sea area. The International Hydrographic Bureau does not recognize the Antarctic Ocean (even less the 'Southern Ocean') as a separate entity.

The Earth is a watery planet: more than 70% of its surface – over 360,000,000 sq km [140,000,000 sq miles] – is covered by the oceans and seas. The mighty Pacific alone accounts for nearly 36% of the total, and 49% of the sea area. Gravity holds in around 1,400 million cu. km [320 million cu. miles] of water, of which over 97% is saline.

The vast underwater world starts in the shallows of the seaside and plunges to depths of more than 11,000 m [36,000 ft]. The continental shelf, part of the landmass, drops gently to around 200 m [650 ft]; here the seabed falls away suddenly at an angle of 3° to 6° – the continental slope. The third stage, called the continental rise, is more gradual with gradients varying from 1 in 100 to 1 in 700. At an average depth of 5,000 m [16,500 ft] there begins the aptly-named abyssal plain – massive submarine depths where sunlight fails to penetrate and few creatures can survive.

From these plains rise volcanoes which, taken from base to top, rival and even surpass the tallest continental mountains in height. Mount Kea, on Hawaii, reaches a total of 10,203 m [33,400 ft], some 1,355 m [4,500 ft] more than Mount Everest, though scarcely 40% is visible above sea level.

In addition, there are underwater mountain chains up to 1,000 km [600 miles] across, whose peaks sometimes appear above sea level as islands such as Iceland and Tristan da Cunha.

The Ocean Depths

Average and maximum depths of the world's great oceans, in metres

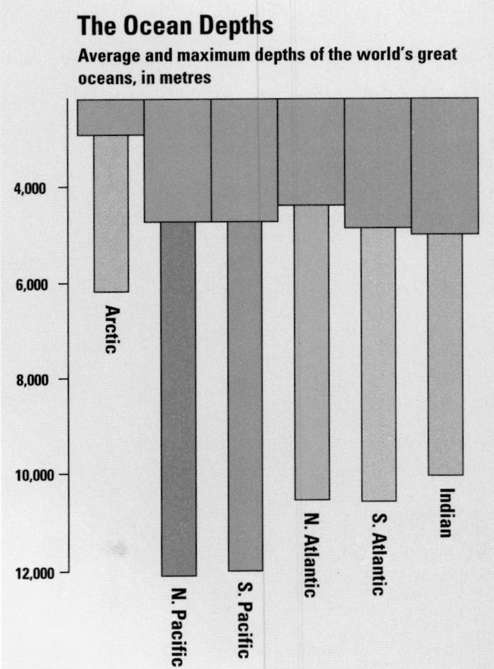

Ocean Currents

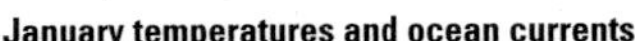

January temperatures and ocean currents

ACTUAL SURFACE TEMPERATURE
°C
30
20
10
0
– 10
– 20
– 30
– 40

OCEAN CURRENTS
Cold   Warm   Speed (knots)
              Less than 0.5
              0.5 – 1.0
              Over 1.0

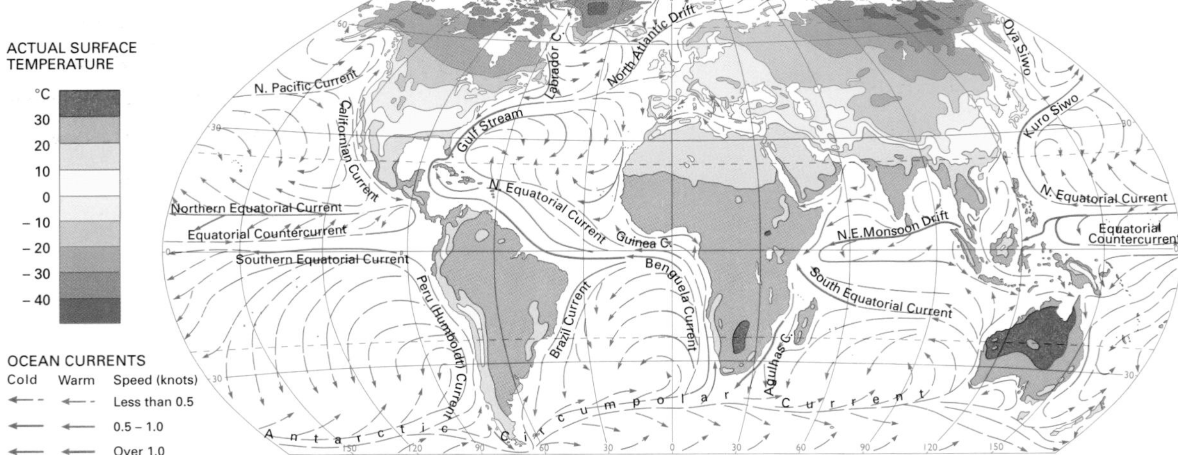

July temperatures and ocean currents

ACTUAL SURFACE TEMPERATURE
°C
30
20
10
0
–10

OCEAN CURRENTS
Cold   Warm   Speed (knots)
              Less than 0.5
              0.5 – 1.0
              Over 1.0

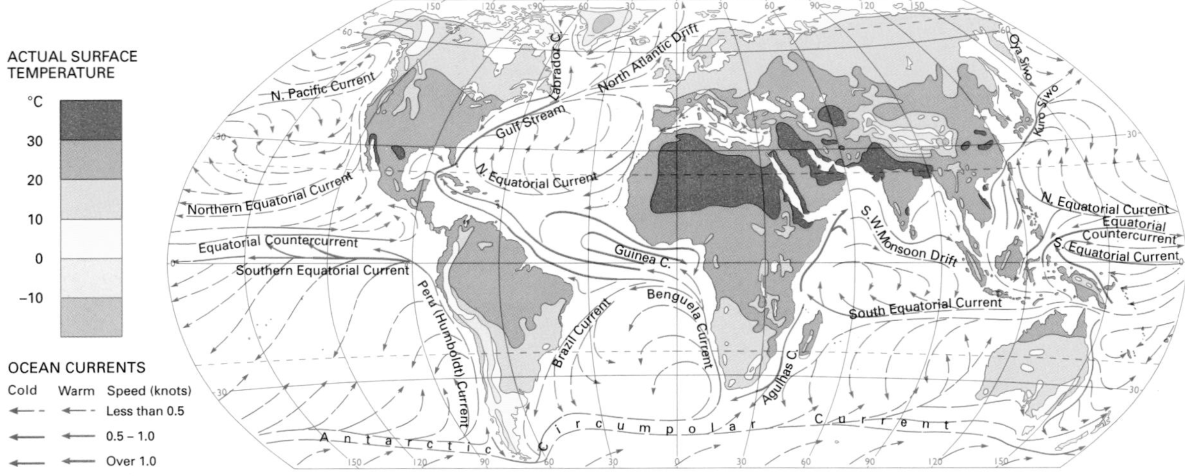

Moving immense quantities of energy as well as billions of tonnes of water every hour, the ocean currents are a vital part of the great heat engine that drives the Earth's climate. They themselves are produced by a twofold mechanism. At the surface, winds push huge masses of water before them; in the deep ocean, below an abrupt temperature gradient that separates the churning surface waters from the still depths, density variations cause slow vertical movements.

The pattern of circulation of the great surface currents is determined by the displacement known as the Coriolis effect. As the Earth turns beneath a moving object – whether it is a tennis ball or a vast mass of water – it appears to be deflected to one side. The deflection is most obvious near the Equator, where the Earth's surface is spinning eastwards at 1,700 km/h [1,050 mph]; currents moving polewards are curved clockwise in the northern hemisphere and anti-clockwise in the southern.

The result is a system of spinning circles known as gyres. The Coriolis effect piles up water on the left of each gyre, creating a narrow, fast-moving stream that is matched by a slower, broader returning current on the right. North and south of the Equator, the fastest currents are located in the west and in the east respectively. In each case, warm water moves from the Equator and cold water returns to it. Cold currents often bring an upwelling of nutrients with them, supporting the world's most economically important fisheries.

Depending on the prevailing winds, some currents on or near the Equator may reverse their direction in the course of the year – a seasonal variation on which Asian monsoon rains depend, and whose occasional failure can bring disaster to millions.

World Fishing Areas

Main commercial fishing areas (numbered FAO regions)

Catch by top marine fishing areas, thousand tonnes (1992)

1. Pacific, NW	[61]	24,199	29.3%
2. Pacific, SE	[87]	13,899	16.8%
3. Atlantic, NE	[27]	11,073	13.4%
4. Pacific, WC	[71]	7,710	9.3%
5. Indian, W	[51]	3,747	4.5%
6. Indian, E	[57]	3,262	4.0%
7. Atlantic, EC	[34]	3,259	3.9%
8. Pacific, NE	[67]	3,149	3.8%

Principal fishing areas

Leading fishing nations

China 17.3% Peru 8.3% Japan 8.0% Chile 5.9% U.S.A. 5.9% Russia 4.4% India 4.3% Indonesia 3.6%

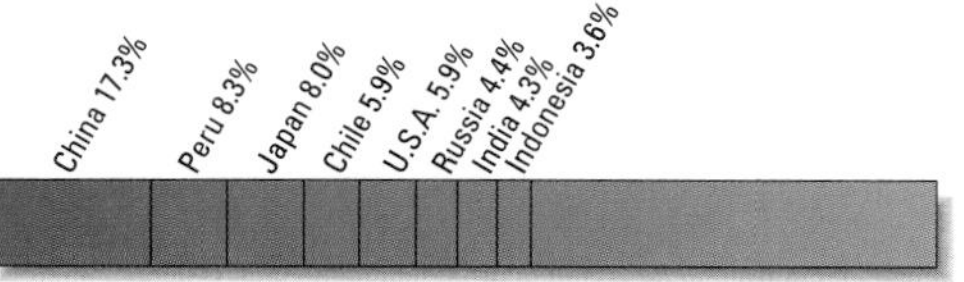

World total (1993): 101,417,500 tonnes
(Marine catch 83.1% Inland catch 16.9%)

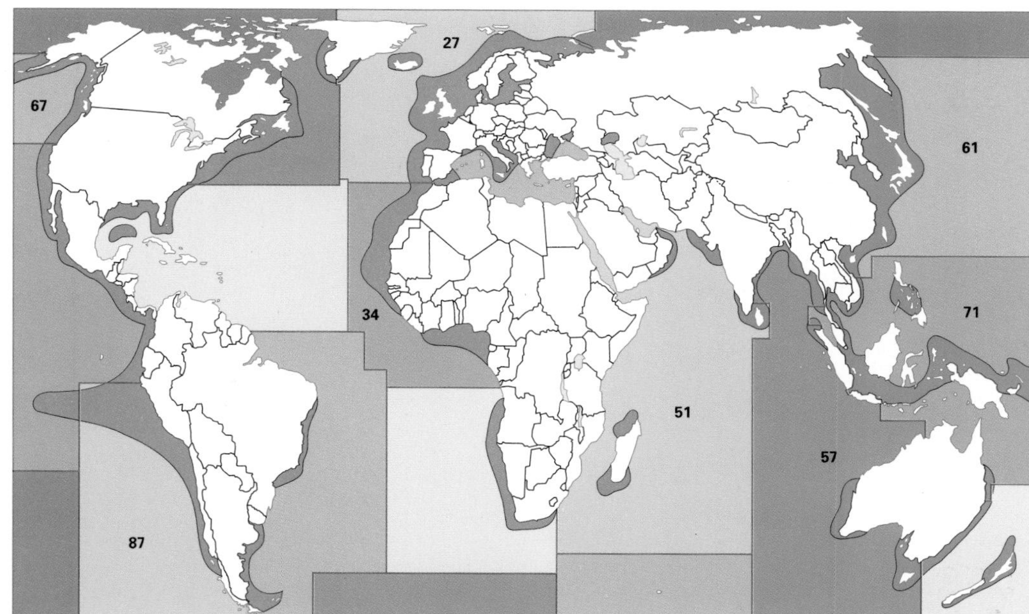

Marine Pollution

Sources of marine oil pollution (latest available year)

- Tanker operations
- Municipal wastes
- Tanker accidents
- Bilge and fuel oils
- Natural seeps
- Industrial waste
- Urban runoff
- Coastal oil refining
- Offshore oil rigs
- River runoffs
- Other

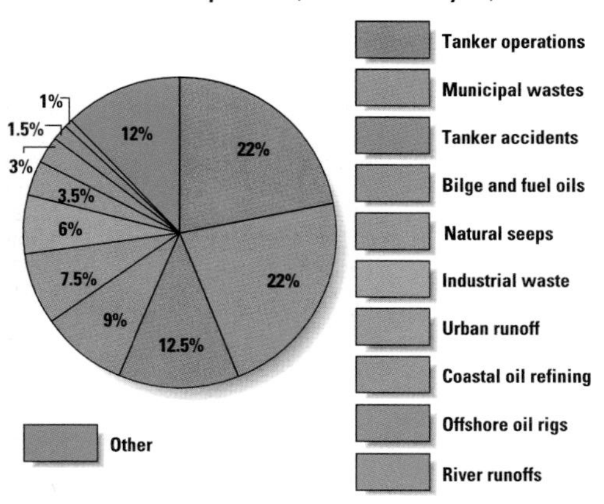

Oil Spills

Major oil spills from tankers and combined carriers

Year	Vessel	Location	Spill (barrels)**	Cause
1979	Atlantic Empress	West Indies	1,890,000	collision
1983	Castillo De Bellver	South Africa	1,760,000	fire
1978	Amoco Cadiz	France	1,628,000	grounding
1991	Haven	Italy	1,029,000	explosion
1988	Odyssey	Canada	1,000,000	fire
1967	Torrey Canyon	UK	909,000	grounding
1972	Sea Star	Gulf of Oman	902,250	collision
1977	Hawaiian Patriot	Hawaiian Is.	742,500	fire
1979	Independenta	Turkey	696,350	collision
1993	Braer	UK	625,000	grounding
1996	Sea Empress	UK	515,000	grounding

Other sources of major oil spills

1983	Nowruz oilfield	The Gulf	4,250,000†	war
1979	Ixtoc 1 oilwell	Gulf of Mexico	4,200,000	blow-out
1991	Kuwait	The Gulf	2,500,000†	war

** 1 barrel = 0.136 tonnes/159 lit./35 Imperial gal./42 US gal. † estimated

River Pollution

Sources of river pollution, USA (latest available year)

- Agriculture
- Mining
- Forestry
- Urban runoff
- Hydro-engineering
- Construction
- Land disposal
- Other

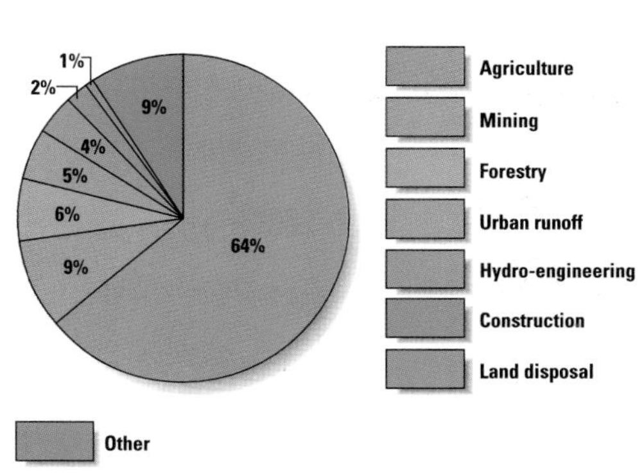

Water Pollution

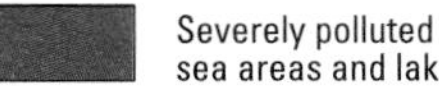

- Severely polluted sea areas and lakes
- Polluted sea areas and lakes
- Areas of frequent oil pollution by shipping
- ◣ Major oil tanker spills
- ▲ Major oil rig blow-outs
- ▼ Offshore dumpsites for industrial and municipal waste
- —— Severely polluted rivers and estuaries

The most notorious tanker spillage of the 1980s occurred when the *Exxon Valdez* ran aground in Prince William Sound, Alaska, in 1989, spilling 267,000 barrels of crude oil close to shore in a sensitive ecological area. This rates as the world's 28th worst spill in terms of volume.

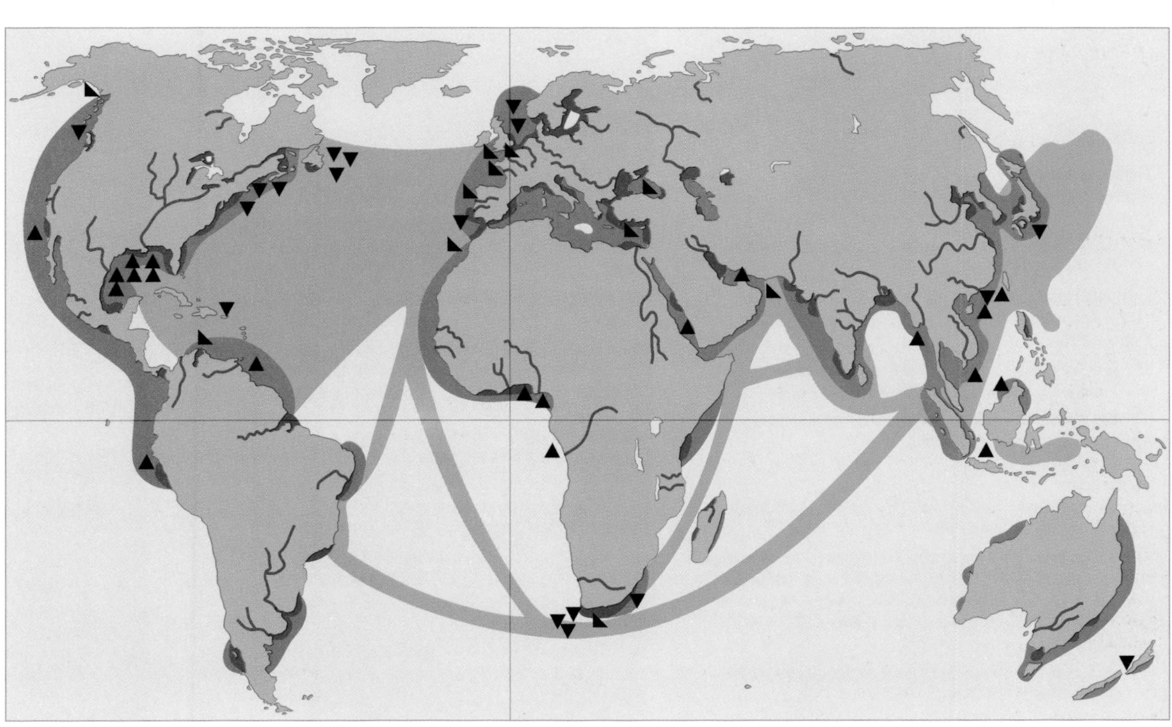

Climate

Climatic Regions

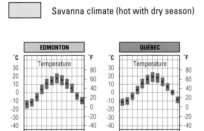

Colour of climate region on map — Name of place

SINGAPORE

Average monthly temperature

Average monthly daily maximum temperature
Average monthly daily minimum temperature

Temperature

Average annual precipitation — Precipitation 2413mm/95in

Average monthly precipitation

Months of the year — J F M A M J J A S O N D

(Map of the world showing climatic regions, with labelled places: Arctic Circle, Eismitte, Krasnoyarsk, Edmonton, Québec, Bahrain, Ouagadougou, Addis Ababa, Tropic of Cancer, Equator, Singapore, Tropic of Capricorn, Buenos Aires, Antarctic Circle)

Legend:
- Tropical climate (hot with rain all year)
- Desert climate (hot and very dry)
- Savanna climate (hot with dry season)
- Steppe climate (warm and dry)
- Mild climate (warm and wet)
- Continental climate (wet with cold winter)
- Subarctic climate (very cold winter)
- Polar climate (very cold and dry)
- Mountainous climate (altitude affects climate)

Climate graphs

EDMONTON Temperature — Precipitation 460mm/18in

QUÉBEC Temperature — Precipitation 1053mm/41in

BUENOS AIRES Temperature — Precipitation 950mm/37in

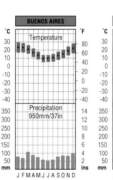

EISMITTE Temperature — Precipitation 109mm/4in

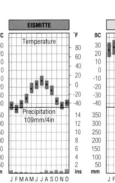

OUAGADOUGOU Temperature — Precipitation 889mm/35in

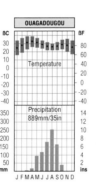

ADDIS ABABA Temperature — Precipitation 1072mm/42in

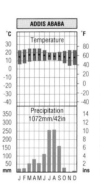

BAHRAIN Temperature — Precipitation 81mm/3in

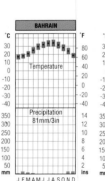

KRASNOYARSK Temperature — Precipitation 249mm/10in

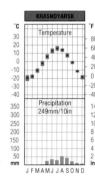

Climate Records

Temperature
Highest recorded shade temperature: Al Aziziyah, Libya, 58°C [136.4°F], 13 September 1922.

Highest mean annual temperature: Dallol, Ethiopia, 34.4°C [94°F], 1960–66.

Longest heatwave: Marble Bar, W. Australia, 162 days over 38°C [100°F], 23 October 1923 to 7 April 1924.

Lowest recorded temperature (outside poles): Verkhoyansk, Siberia, –68°C [–90°F], 6 February 1933.

Lowest mean annual temperature: Plateau Station, Antarctica, –56.6°C [–72.0°F]

Pressure
Longest drought: Calama, N. Chile, no recorded rainfall in 400 years to 1971.

Wettest place (12 months): Cherrapunji, Meghalaya, N. E. India, 26,470 mm [1,040 in], August 1860 to August 1861. Cherrapunji also holds the record for the most rainfall in one month: 2,930 mm [115 in], July 1861.

Wettest place (average): Mawsynram, India, mean annual rainfall 11,873 mm [467.4 in].

Wettest place (24 hours): Cilaos, Réunion, Indian Ocean, 1,870 mm [73.6 in], 15–16 March 1952.

Heaviest hailstones: Gopalganj, Bangladesh, up to 1.02 kg [2.25 lb], 14 April 1986 (killed 92 people).

Heaviest snowfall (continuous): Bessans, Savoie, France, 1,730 mm [68 in] in 19 hours, 5–6 April 1969.

Heaviest snowfall (season/year): Paradise Ranger Station, Mt Rainier, Washington, USA, 31,102 mm [1,224.5 in], 19 February 1971 to 18 February 1972.

Pressure and winds
Highest barometric pressure: Agata, Siberia (at 262 m [862 ft] altitude), 1,083.8 mb, 31 December 1968.

Lowest barometric pressure: Typhoon Tip, Guam, Pacific Ocean, 870 mb, 12 October 1979.

Highest recorded wind speed: Mt Washington, New Hampshire, USA, 371 km/h [231 mph], 12 April 1934. This is three times as strong as hurricane force on the Beaufort Scale.

Windiest place: Commonwealth Bay, Antarctica, where gales frequently reach over 320 km/h [200 mph].

Climate

Climate is weather in the long term: the seasonal pattern of hot and cold, wet and dry, averaged over time (usually 30 years). At the simplest level, it is caused by the uneven heating of the Earth. Surplus heat at the Equator passes towards the poles, levelling out the energy differential. Its passage is marked by a ceaseless churning of the atmosphere and the oceans, further agitated by the Earth's diurnal spin and the motion it imparts to moving air and water. The heat's means of transport – by winds and ocean currents, by the continual evaporation and recondensation of water molecules – is the weather itself. There are four basic types of climate, each of which can be further subdivided: tropical, desert (dry), temperate and polar.

Composition of Dry Air

Nitrogen	78.09%	Sulphur dioxide	trace
Oxygen	20.95%	Nitrogen oxide	trace
Argon	0.93%	Methane	trace
Water vapour	0.2–4.0%	Dust	trace
Carbon dioxide	0.03%	Helium	trace
Ozone	0.00006%	Neon	trace

El Niño

In a normal year, south-easterly trade winds drive surface waters westwards off the coast of South America, drawing cold, nutrient-rich water up from below. In an El Niño year (which occurs every 2–7 years), warm water from the west Pacific suppresses up-welling in the east, depriving the region of nutrients. The water is warmed by as much as 7°C [12°F], disturbing the tropical atmospheric circulation. During an intense El Niño, the south-east trade winds change direction and become equatorial westerlies, resulting in climatic extremes in many regions of the world, such as drought in parts of Australia and India, and heavy rainfall in south-eastern USA. An intense El Niño occurred in 1997–8, with resultant freak weather conditions across the entire Pacific region.

Normal year

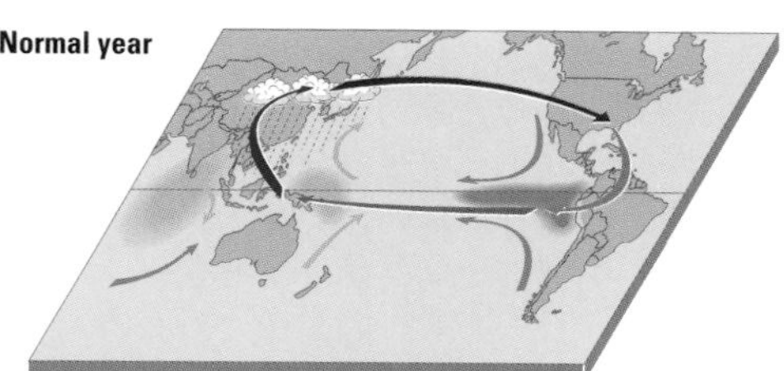

El Niño event

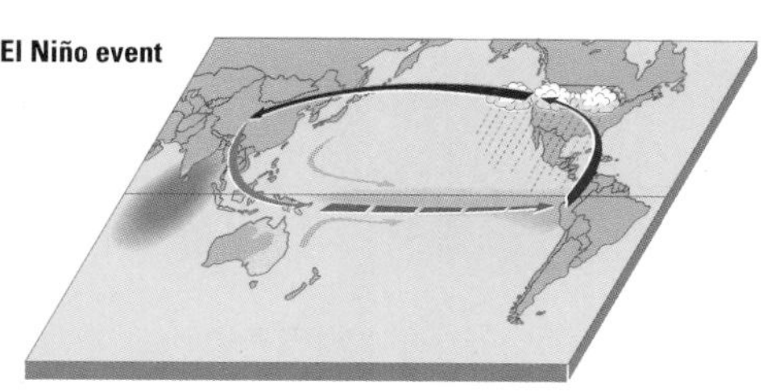

Beaufort Wind Scale

Named after the 19th-century British naval officer who devised it, the Beaufort Scale assesses wind speed according to its effects. It was originally designed as an aid for sailors, but has since been adapted for use on the land.

Scale	Wind speed		Effect
	km/h	mph	
0	0–1	0–1	**Calm**
			Smoke rises vertically
1	1–5	1–3	**Light air**
			Wind direction shown only by smoke drift
2	6–11	4–7	**Light breeze**
			Wind felt on face; leaves rustle; vanes moved by wind
3	12–19	8–12	**Gentle breeze**
			Leaves and small twigs in constant motion; wind extends small flag
4	20–28	13–18	**Moderate**
			Raises dust and loose paper; small branches move
5	29–38	19–24	**Fresh**
			Small trees in leaf sway; wavelets on inland waters
6	39–49	25–31	**Strong**
			Large branches move; difficult to use umbrellas
7	50–61	32–38	**Near gale**
			Whole trees in motion; difficult to walk against wind
8	62–74	39–46	**Gale**
			Twigs break from trees; walking very difficult
9	75–88	47–54	**Strong gale**
			Slight structural damage
10	89–102	55–63	**Storm**
			Trees uprooted; serious structural damage
11	103–117	64–72	**Violent storm**
			Widespread damage
12	118+	73+	**Hurricane**

Conversions

°C = (°F − 32) × 5/9; °F = (°C × 9/5) + 32; 0°C = 32°F
1 in = 25.4 mm; 1 mm = 0.0394 in; 100 mm = 3.94 in

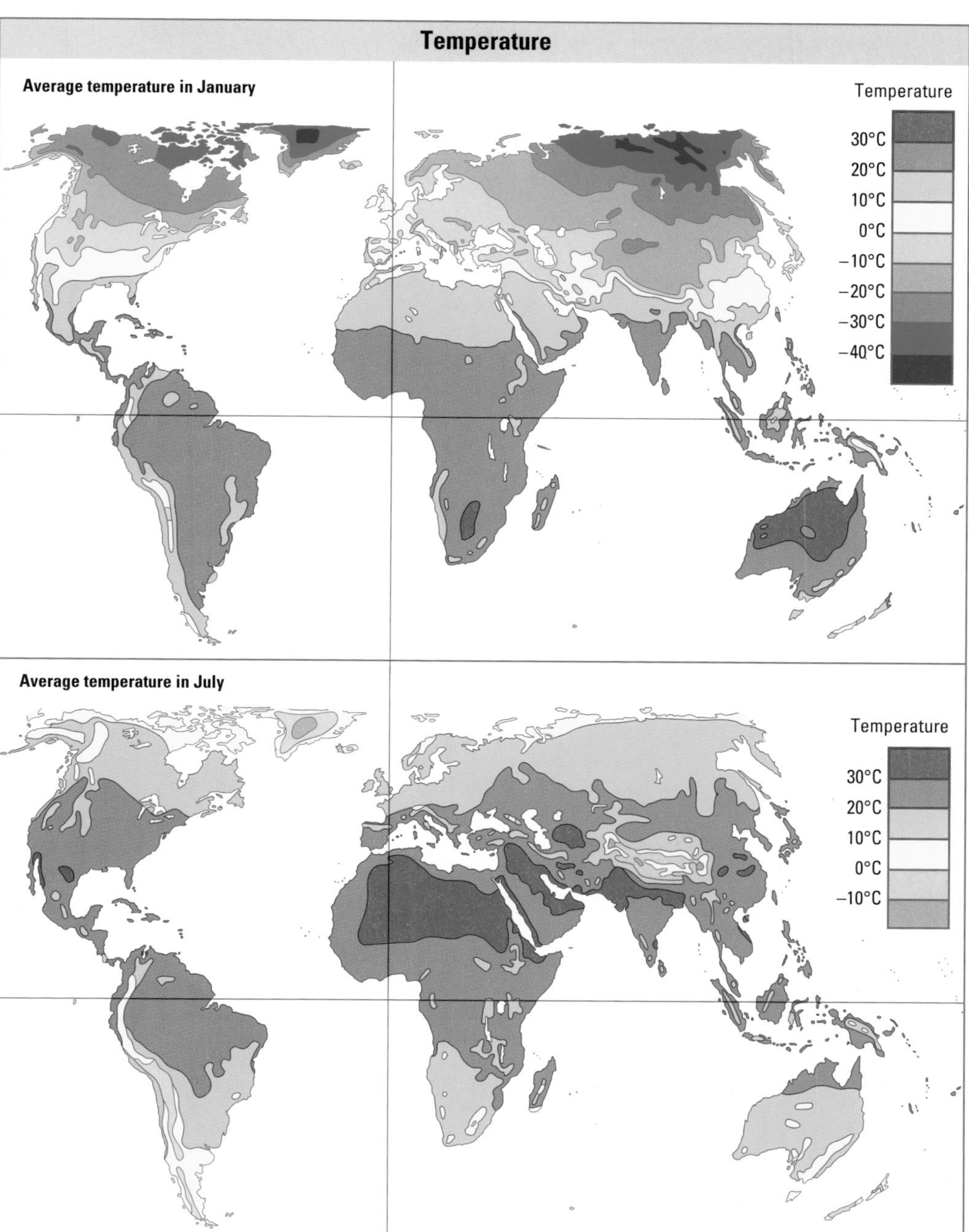

Temperature

Average temperature in January

Temperature

30°C
20°C
10°C
0°C
−10°C
−20°C
−30°C
−40°C

Average temperature in July

Temperature

30°C
20°C
10°C
0°C
−10°C

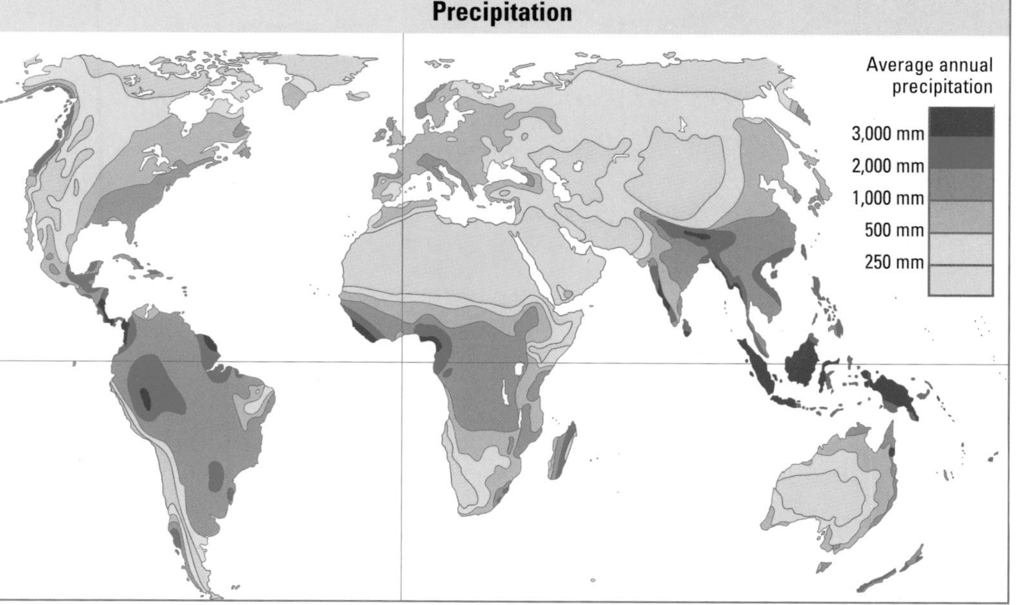

Precipitation

Average annual precipitation

3,000 mm
2,000 mm
1,000 mm
500 mm
250 mm

Water and Vegetation

The Hydrological Cycle

The world's water balance is regulated by the constant recycling of water between the oceans, atmosphere and land. The movement of water between these three reservoirs is known as the hydrological cycle. The oceans play a vital role in the hydrological cycle: 74% of the total precipitation falls over the oceans and 84% of the total evaporation comes from the oceans.

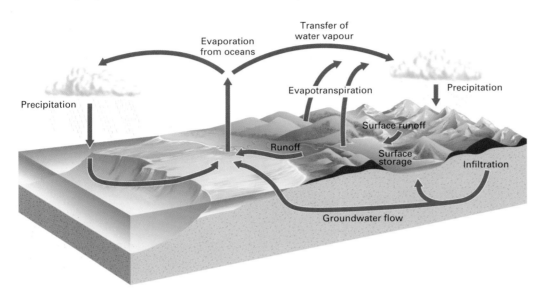

Water Distribution

The distribution of planetary water, by percentage. Oceans and ice-caps together account for more than 99% of the total; the breakdown of the remainder is estimated.

All water

97.4%
2.6%

Oceans
Fresh water

Fresh water

76.6%
0.5%
22.7%

Ice-caps and glaciers
Groundwater
Active water

Active water

52%
1.4%
7.1%
3.5%
36%

Lakes
Soil moisture
Atmosphere
Rivers
Living things

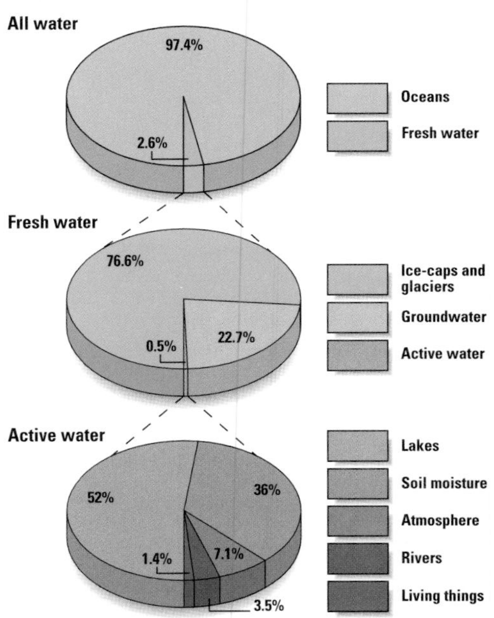

Water Utilization

Domestic   Industrial   Agriculture

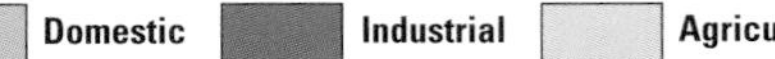

The percentage breakdown of water usage by sector, selected countries (1996)

Algeria
Australia
Russian Fed.
Egypt
France
Ghana
India
Mexico
Poland
Saudi Arabia
UK
USA

0   20   40   60   80   100

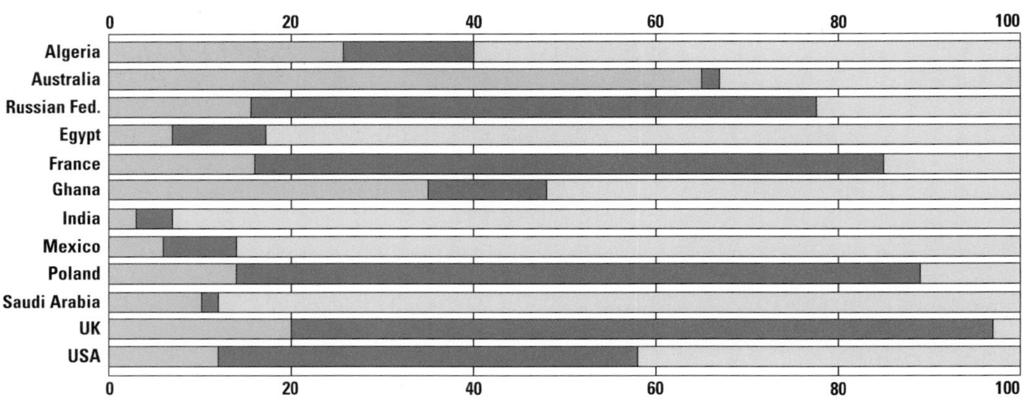

Water Usage

Almost all the world's water is 3,000 million years old, and all of it cycles endlessly through the hydrosphere, though at different rates. Water vapour circulates over days, even hours, deep ocean water circulates over millennia, and ice-cap water remains solid for millions of years.

Fresh water is essential to all terrestrial life. Humans cannot survive more than a few days without it, and even the hardiest desert plants and animals could not exist without some water. Agriculture requires huge quantities of fresh water: without large-scale irrigation most of the world's people would starve. In the USA, agriculture uses 42% and industry 45% of all water withdrawals.

The United States is one of the heaviest users of water in the world. According to the latest figures the average American uses 380 litres a day and the average household uses 415,000 litres a year. This is two to four times more than in Western Europe.

Water Supply

Percentage of total population with access to safe drinking water (1995)

Over 90% with safe water
75 – 90% with safe water
60 – 75% with safe water
45 – 60% with safe water
30 – 45% with safe water
Under 30% with safe water

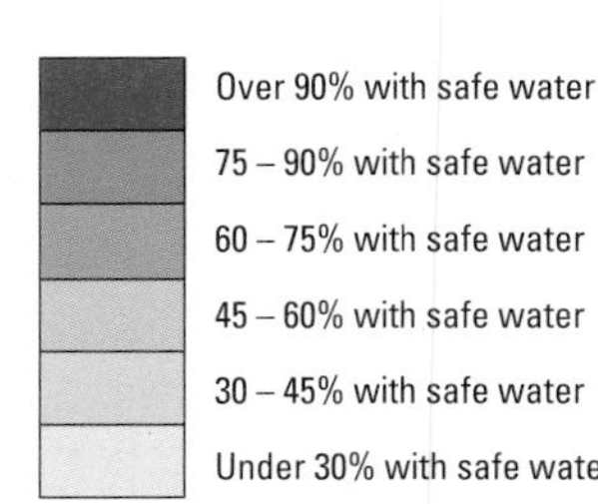

⬠ Under 80 litres per person per day domestic water consumption

⬢ Over 320 litres per person per day domestic water consumption

NB: 80 litres of water a day is considered necessary for a reasonable quality of life.

Least well-provided countries

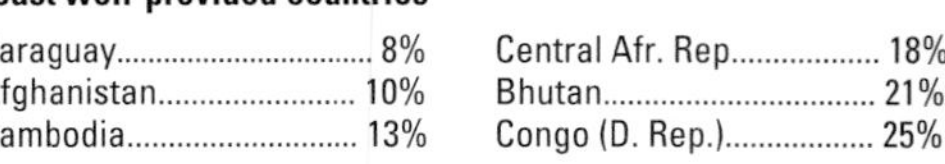

Paraguay	8%	Central Afr. Rep	18%
Afghanistan	10%	Bhutan	21%
Cambodia	13%	Congo (D. Rep.)	25%

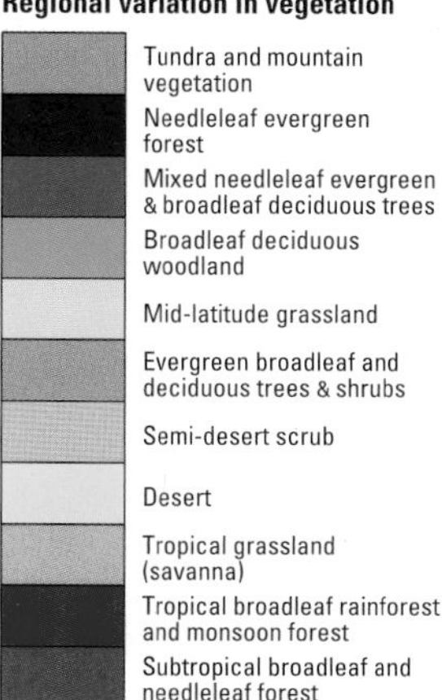

Natural Vegetation

Regional variation in vegetation

- Tundra and mountain vegetation
- Needleleaf evergreen forest
- Mixed needleleaf evergreen & broadleaf deciduous trees
- Broadleaf deciduous woodland
- Mid-latitude grassland
- Evergreen broadleaf and deciduous trees & shrubs
- Semi-desert scrub
- Desert
- Tropical grassland (savanna)
- Tropical broadleaf rainforest and monsoon forest
- Subtropical broadleaf and needleleaf forest

The map shows the natural 'climax vegetation' of regions, as dictated by climate and topography. In most cases, however, agricultural activity has drastically altered the vegetation pattern. Western Europe, for example, lost most of its broadleaf forest many centuries ago, while irrigation has turned some natural semi-desert into productive land.

Land Use by Continent

- Forest
- Permanent pasture and rough grazing
- Permanent crops and plantations
- Arable
- Non-productive

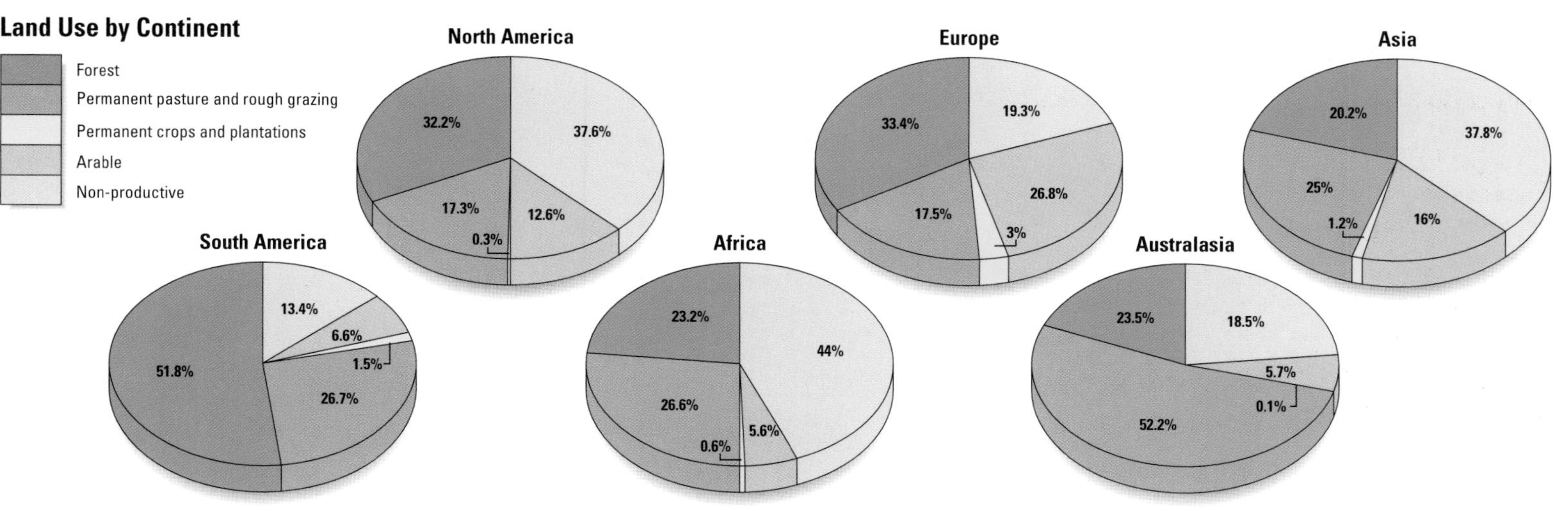

North America: 37.6%, 12.6%, 0.3%, 17.3%, 32.2%

Europe: 19.3%, 26.8%, 3%, 17.5%, 33.4%

Asia: 37.8%, 16%, 1.2%, 25%, 20.2%

South America: 13.4%, 6.6%, 1.5%, 26.7%, 51.8%

Africa: 44%, 5.6%, 0.6%, 26.6%, 23.2%

Australasia: 18.5%, 5.7%, 0.1%, 52.2%, 23.5%

Forestry: Production

Forest and woodland (million hectares)	Annual production (1996, million cubic metres)	
	Fuelwood and charcoal	Industrial roundwood*
World 3,987.9	*1,864.8*	*1,489.5*
S. America 829.3	193.0	129.9
N. & C. America 709.8	155.4	600.4
Africa 684.6	519.9	67.9
Asia 131.8	905.2	280.2
Europe 157.3	82.4	369.7
Australasia 157.2	8.7	41.5

Paper and Board

Top producers (1996)**		Top exporters (1996)**	
USA	85,173	Canada	13,393
China	30,253	USA	9,113
Japan	30,014	Finland	8,529
Canada	18,414	Sweden	7,483
Germany	14,733	Germany	6,319

* roundwood is timber as it is felled
** in thousand tonnes

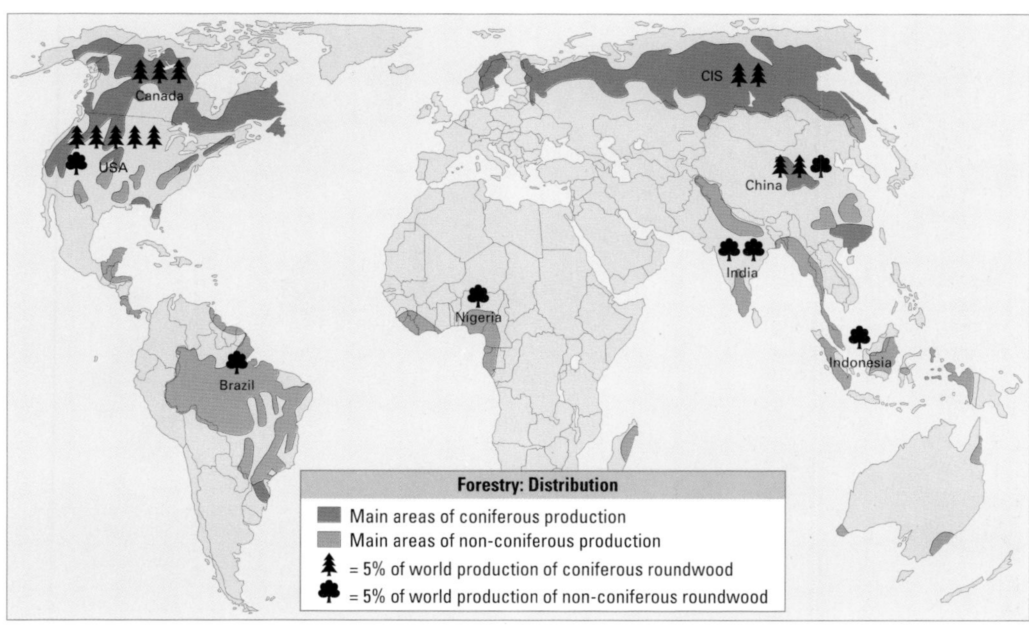

Forestry: Distribution

- Main areas of coniferous production
- Main areas of non-coniferous production
- = 5% of world production of coniferous roundwood
- = 5% of world production of non-coniferous roundwood

Environment

Humans have always had a dramatic effect on their environment, at least since the development of agriculture almost 10,000 years ago. Generally, the Earth has accepted human interference without obvious ill effects: the complex systems that regulate the global environment have been able to absorb substantial damage while maintaining a stable and comfortable home for the planet's trillions of lifeforms. But advancing human technology and the rapidly-expanding populations it supports are now threatening to overwhelm the Earth's ability to compensate.

Industrial wastes, acid rainfall, desertification and large-scale deforestation all combine to create environmental change at a rate far faster than the great slow cycles of planetary evolution can accommodate. As a result of overcultivation, overgrazing and overcutting of groundcover for firewood, desertification is affecting as much as 60% of the world's croplands. In addition, with fire and chain-saws, humans are destroying more forest in a day than their ancestors could have done in a century, upsetting the balance between plant and animal, carbon dioxide and oxygen, on which all life ultimately depends.

The fossil fuels that power industrial civilization have pumped enough carbon dioxide and other so-called greenhouse gases into the atmosphere to make climatic change a near-certainty. As a result of the combination of these factors, the Earth's average temperature has risen by approximately 0.5°C [1°F] since the beginning of the 20th century, and it is still rising.

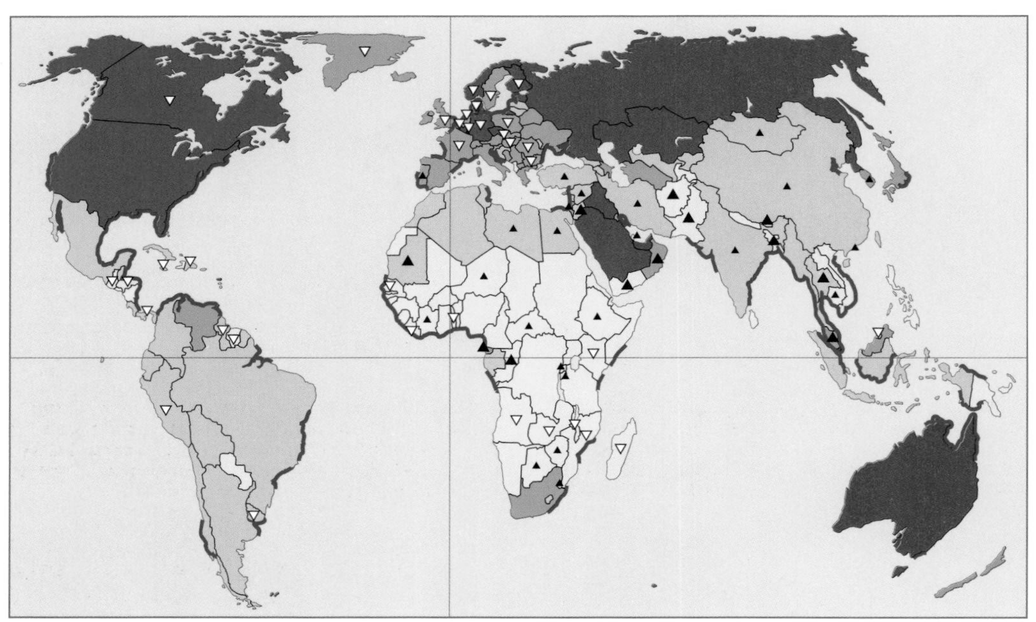

Global Warming

Carbon dioxide emissions in tonnes per person per year (1995)

Over 10 tonnes of CO_2

5 – 10 tonnes of CO_2

1 – 5 tonnes of CO_2

Under 1 tonne of CO_2

Changes in CO_2 emissions 1980–90

▲ Over 100% increase in emissions

▲ 50–100% increase in emissions

▽ Reduction in emissions

— Coastal areas in danger of flooding from rising sea levels caused by global warming

High atmospheric concentrations of heat-absorbing gases, especially carbon dioxide, appear to be causing a steady rise in average temperatures worldwide – up to 1.5°C [3°F] by the year 2020, according to some estimates. Global warming is likely to bring with it a rise in sea levels that may flood some of the Earth's most densely populated coastal areas.

Greenhouse Power

Relative contributions to the Greenhouse Effect by the major heat-absorbing gases in the atmosphere.

The chart combines greenhouse potency and volume. Carbon dioxide has a greenhouse potential of only 1, but its concentration of 350 parts per million makes it predominate. CFC 12, with 25,000 times the absorption capacity of CO_2, is present only as 0.00044 ppm.

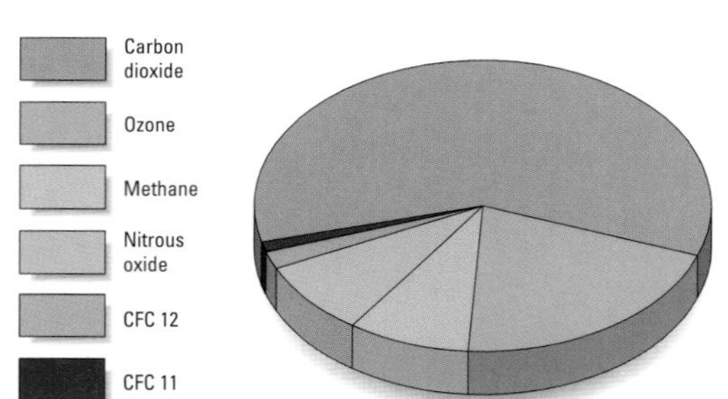

- Carbon dioxide
- Ozone
- Methane
- Nitrous oxide
- CFC 12
- CFC 11

Ozone Layer

The ozone 'hole' over the northern hemisphere on 12 March 1995.

The colours represent Dobson Units (DU). The ozone 'hole' is seen as the dark blue and purple patch in the centre, where ozone values are around 120 DU or lower. Normal levels are around 280 DU. The ozone 'hole' over Antarctica is much larger.

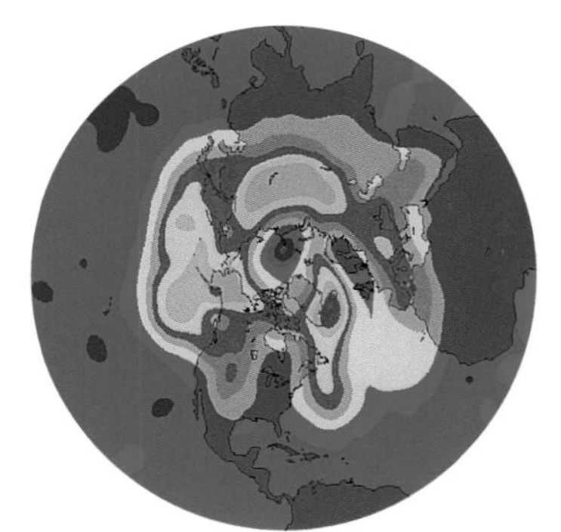

Carbon Dioxide

Carbon dioxide released in millions of tonnes (1992)

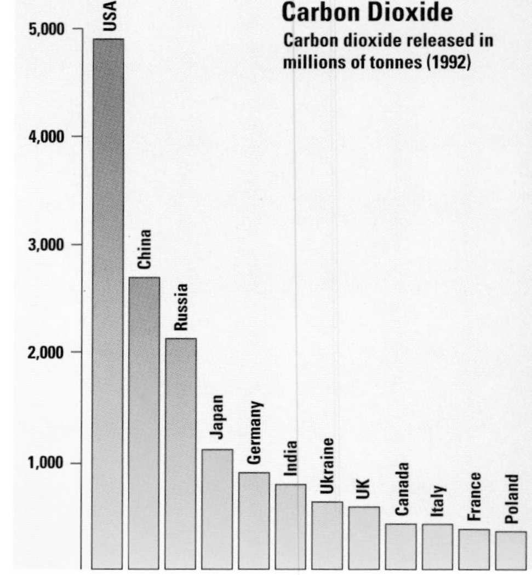

The Greenhouse Effect

Carbon dioxide is increased by burning fossil fuels and cutting forests

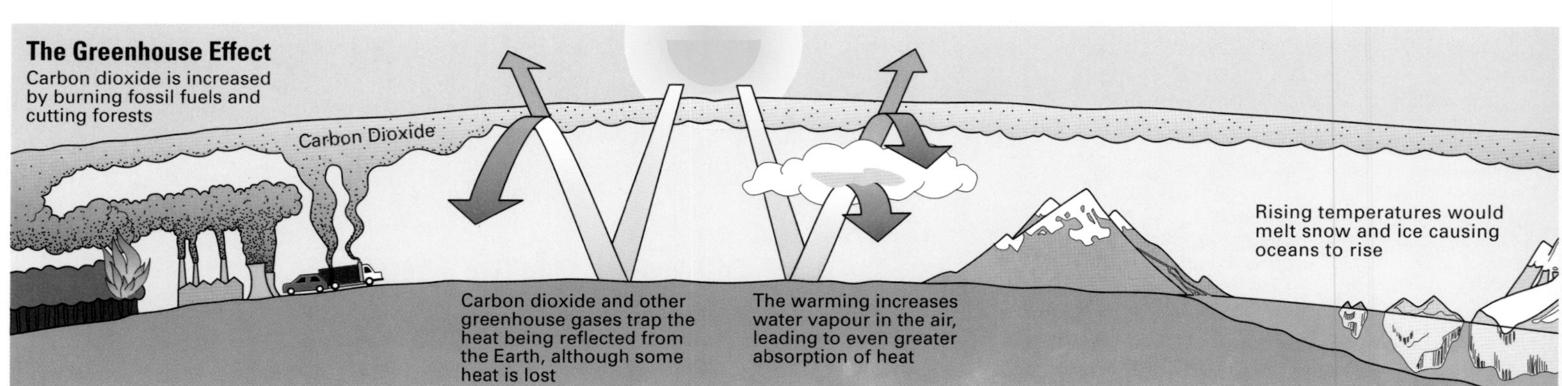

Carbon Dioxide

Carbon dioxide and other greenhouse gases trap the heat being reflected from the Earth, although some heat is lost

The warming increases water vapour in the air, leading to even greater absorption of heat

Rising temperatures would melt snow and ice causing oceans to rise

Desertification

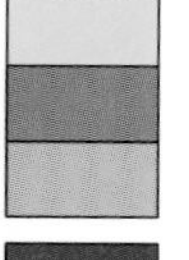

- Existing deserts
- Areas with a high risk of desertification
- Areas with a moderate risk of desertification
- Former areas of rainforest
- Existing rainforest

Forest Clearance

Thousands of hectares of forest cleared annually, tropical countries surveyed 1981–85 and 1987–90. Loss as a percentage of remaining stocks is shown in figures on each column.

	1987–90	1981–85
Brazil	1.5	0.4
India	4.1	0.3
Indonesia	0.8	0.5
Burma	2.1	0.3
Thailand	2.5	2.4
Vietnam	2.0	0.7
Philippines	1.5	1.0
Costa Rica	7.6	4.0
Cameroon	0.6	0.4

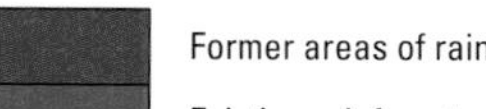

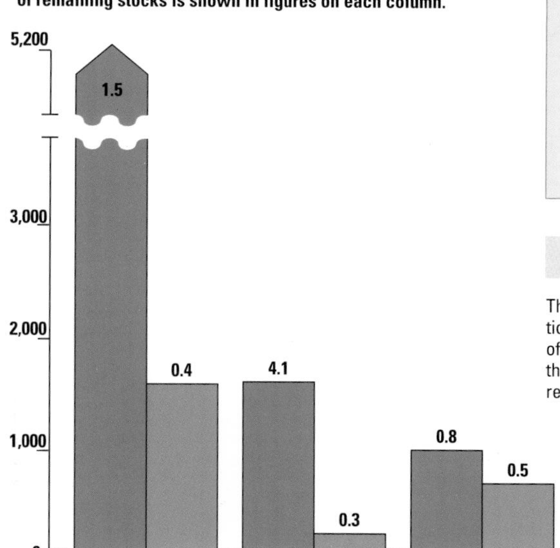

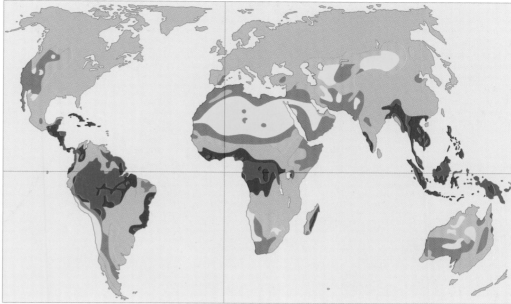

Deforestation

The Earth's remaining forests are under attack from three directions: expanding agriculture, logging, and growing consumption of fuelwood, often in combination. Sometimes deforestation is the direct result of government policy, as in the efforts made to resettle the urban poor in some parts of Brazil; just as often, it comes about despite state attempts at conservation. Loggers, licensed or unlicensed, blaze a trail into virgin forest, often destroying twice as many trees as they harvest. Landless farmers follow, burning away most of what remains to plant their crops, completing the destruction.

 1987–90   1981–85

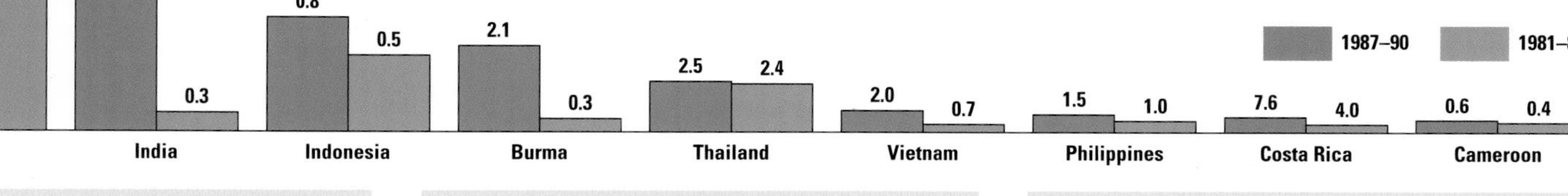

Ozone Depletion

The ozone layer, 25–30 km [15–18 miles] above sea level, acts as a barrier to most of the Sun's harmful ultra-violet radiation, protecting us from the ionizing radiation that can cause skin cancer and cataracts. In recent years, however, two holes in the ozone layer have been observed during winter: one over the Arctic and the other, the size of the USA, over Antarctica. By 1996, ozone had been reduced to around a half of its 1970 amount. The ozone (O_3) is broken down by chlorine released into the atmosphere as CFCs (chlorofluorocarbons) – chemicals used in refrigerators, packaging and aerosols.

Air Pollution

Sulphur dioxide is the main pollutant associated with industrial cities. According to the World Health Organization, at least 600 million people live in urban areas where sulphur dioxide concentrations regularly reach damaging levels. One of the world's most dangerously polluted urban areas is Mexico City, due to a combination of its enclosed valley location, 3 million cars and 60,000 factories. In May 1998, this lethal cocktail was added to by nearby forest fires and the resultant air pollution led to over 20% of the population (3 million people) complaining of respiratory problems.

Acid Rain

Killing trees, poisoning lakes and rivers and eating away buildings, acid rain is mostly produced by sulphur dioxide emissions from industry and volcanic eruptions. By the mid 1990s, acid rain had sterilized 4,000 or more of Sweden's lakes and left 45% of Switzerland's alpine conifers dead or dying, while the monuments of Greece were dissolving in Athens' smog. Prevailing wind patterns mean that the acids often fall many hundred kilometres from where the original pollutants were discharged. In parts of Europe acid deposition has slightly decreased, following reductions in emissions, but not by enough.

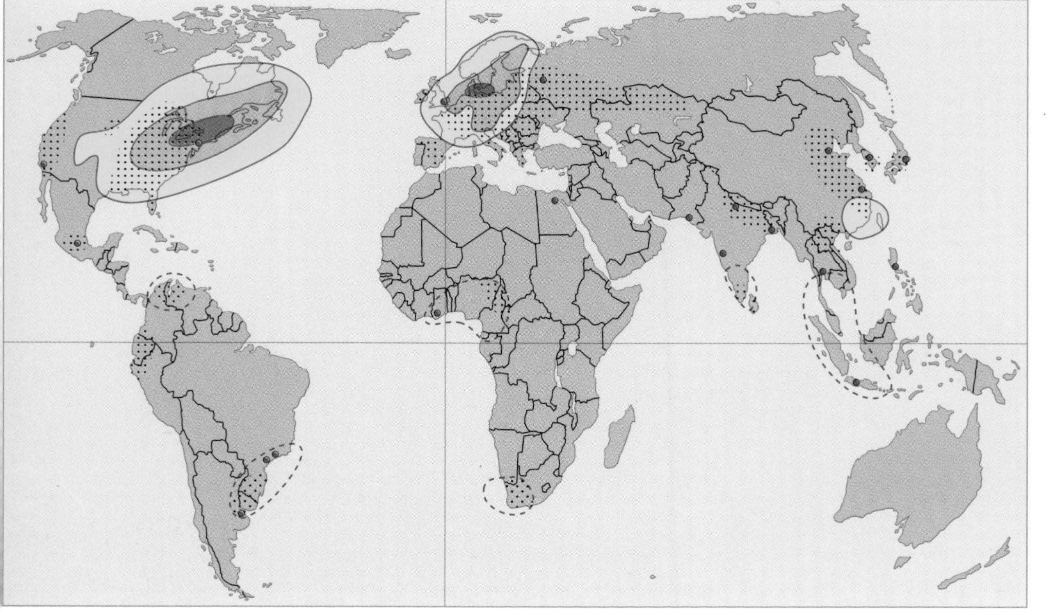

World Pollution

Acid rain and sources of acidic emissions (latest available year)

Acid rain is caused by high levels of sulphur and nitrogen in the atmosphere. They combine with water vapour and oxygen to form acids (H_2SO_4 and HNO_3) which fall as precipitation.

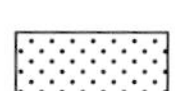

- Regions where sulphur and nitrogen oxides are released in high concentrations, mainly from fossil fuel combustion
- Major cities with high levels of air pollution (including nitrogen and sulphur emissions)

Areas of heavy acid deposition

pH numbers indicate acidity, decreasing from a neutral 7. Normal rain, slightly acid from dissolved carbon dioxide, never exceeds a pH of 5.6.

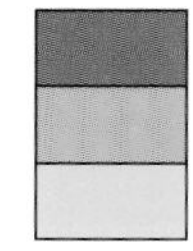

- pH less than 4.0 (most acidic)
- pH 4.0 to 4.5
- pH 4.5 to 5.0
- Areas where acid rain is a potential problem

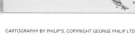

Population

Developed nations such as the UK have populations evenly spread across the age groups and, usually, a growing proportion of elderly people. The great majority of the people in developing nations, however, are in the younger age groups, about to enter their most fertile years. In time, these population profiles should resemble the world profile (even Kenya has made recent progress with reducing its birth rate), but the transition will come about only after a few more generations of rapid population growth.

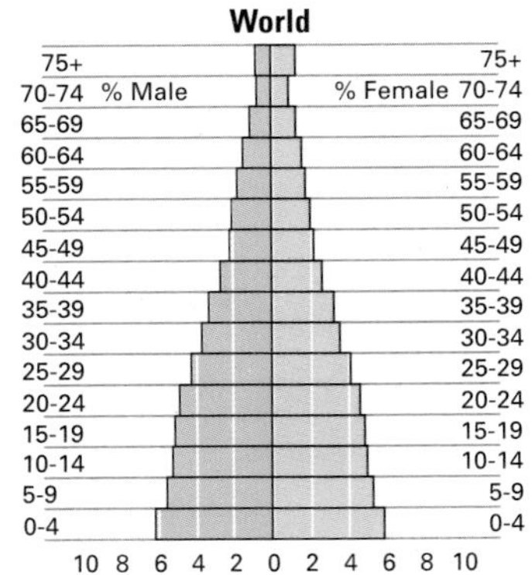

World

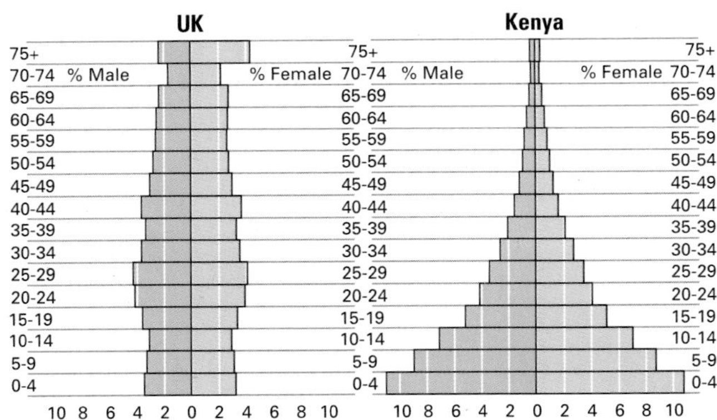

UK | Kenya

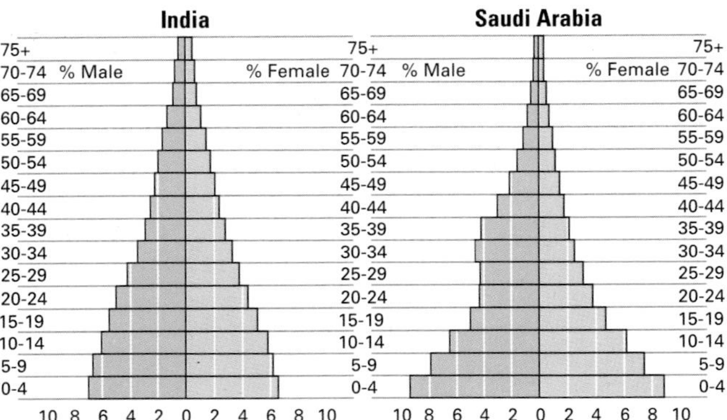

India | Saudi Arabia

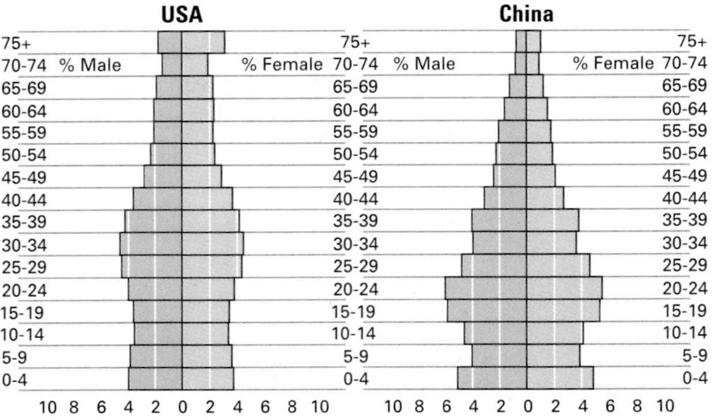

USA | China

Most Populous Nations [in millions (1998 estimates)]

1.	China	1,237	9.	Bangladesh	125	17.	Iran	64
2.	India	984	10.	Nigeria	111	18.	Thailand	60
3.	USA	270	11.	Mexico	99	19.	France	59
4.	Indonesia	213	12.	Germany	82	20.	UK	59
5.	Brazil	170	13.	Philippines	78	21.	Ethiopia	58
6.	Russia	147	14.	Vietnam	76	22.	Italy	57
7.	Pakistan	135	15.	Egypt	66	23.	Ukraine	50
8.	Japan	126	16.	Turkey	65	24.	Congo (=Zaïre)	49

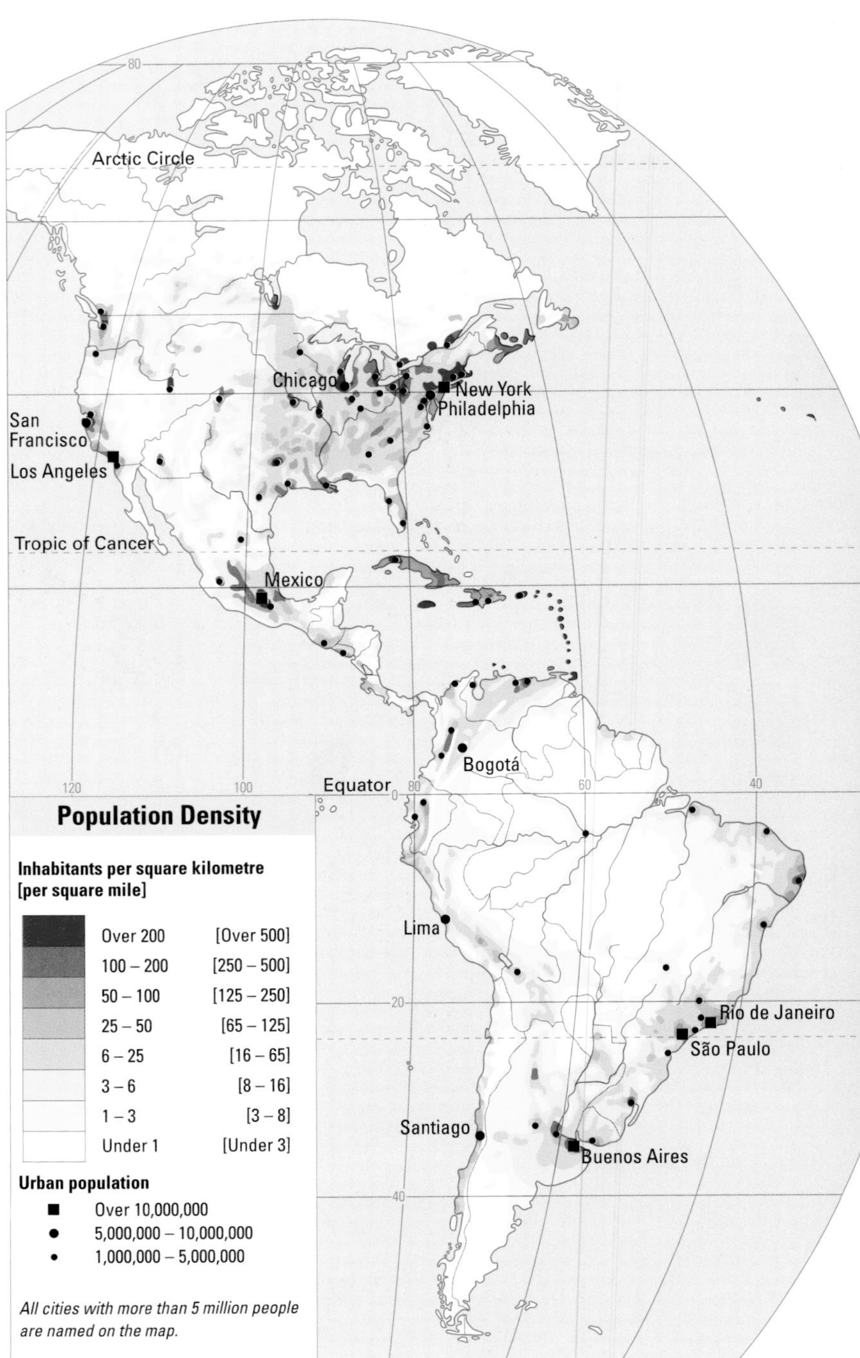

Population Density

Inhabitants per square kilometre [per square mile]

Over 200	[Over 500]
100 – 200	[250 – 500]
50 – 100	[125 – 250]
25 – 50	[65 – 125]
6 – 25	[16 – 65]
3 – 6	[8 – 16]
1 – 3	[3 – 8]
Under 1	[Under 3]

Urban population

■ Over 10,000,000
● 5,000,000 – 10,000,000
• 1,000,000 – 5,000,000

All cities with more than 5 million people are named on the map.

Continental Comparisons

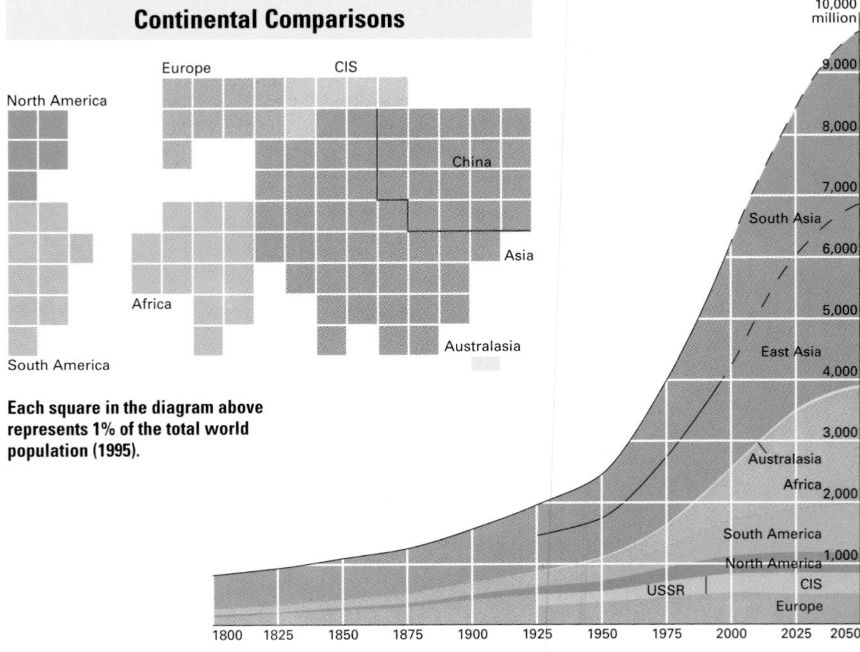

Each square in the diagram above represents 1% of the total world population (1995).

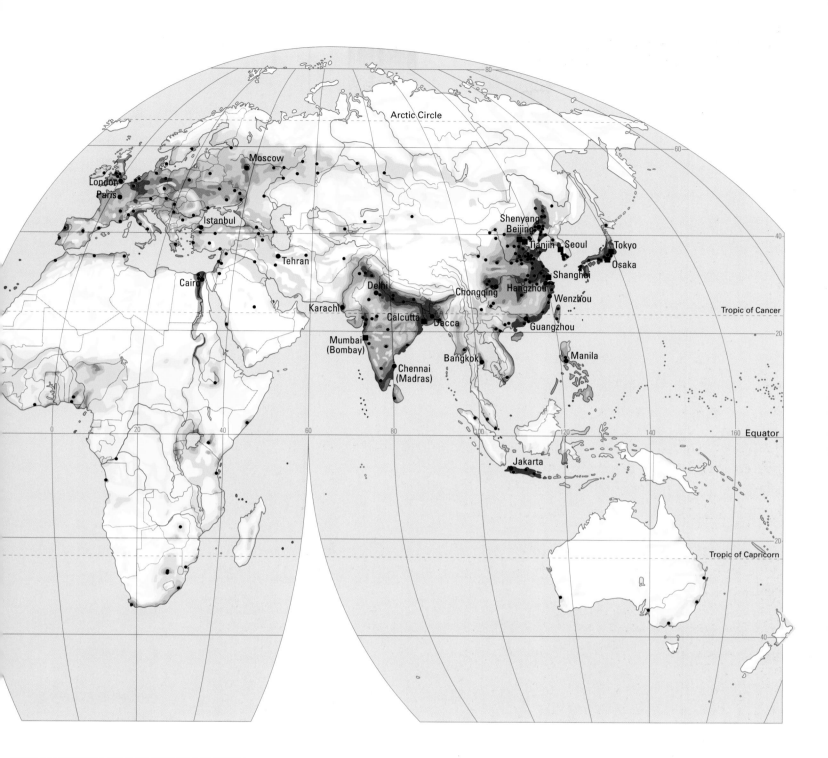

Arctic Circle

London
Paris

Moscow

Istanbul

Tehran

Cairo

Shenyang
Beijing
Tianjin   Seoul   Tokyo
Osaka
Shanghai
Delhi
Chongqing   Hangzhou
Wenzhou
Karachi
Calcutta   Dacca
Guangzhou
Mumbai
(Bombay)
Chennai
(Madras)   Bangkok   Manila

Tropic of Cancer

Equator

Jakarta

Tropic of Capricorn

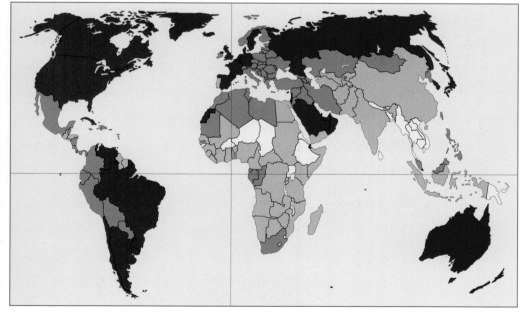

Urban Population

Percentage of total population living in towns and cities (1997)

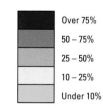

	Over 75%
	50 – 75%
	25 – 50%
	10 – 25%
	Under 10%

Most urbanized		Least urbanized	
Singapore	100%	Rwanda	6%
Belgium	97%	Bhutan	8%
Israel	91%	Burundi	8%
Uruguay	91%	Nepal	11%
Netherlands	89%	Swaziland	12%

[UK 89%]

The Human Family

Predominant Languages

Languages of the World

Language can be classified by ancestry and structure. For example, the Romance and Germanic groups are both derived from an Indo-European language believed to have been spoken 5,000 years ago.

Mother tongues (in millions)
Chinese 1,069 (Mandarin 864), English 443, Hindi 352, Spanish 341, Russian 293, Arabic 197, Bengali 184, Portuguese 173, Malay-Indonesian 142, Japanese 125, French 121, German 118, Urdu 92, Punjabi 84, Korean 71.

Official languages (% of total population)
English 27%, Chinese 19%, Hindi 13.5%, Spanish 5.4%, Russian 5.2%, French 4.2%, Arabic 3.3%, Portuguese 3%, Malay 3%, Bengali 2.9%, Japanese 2.3%.

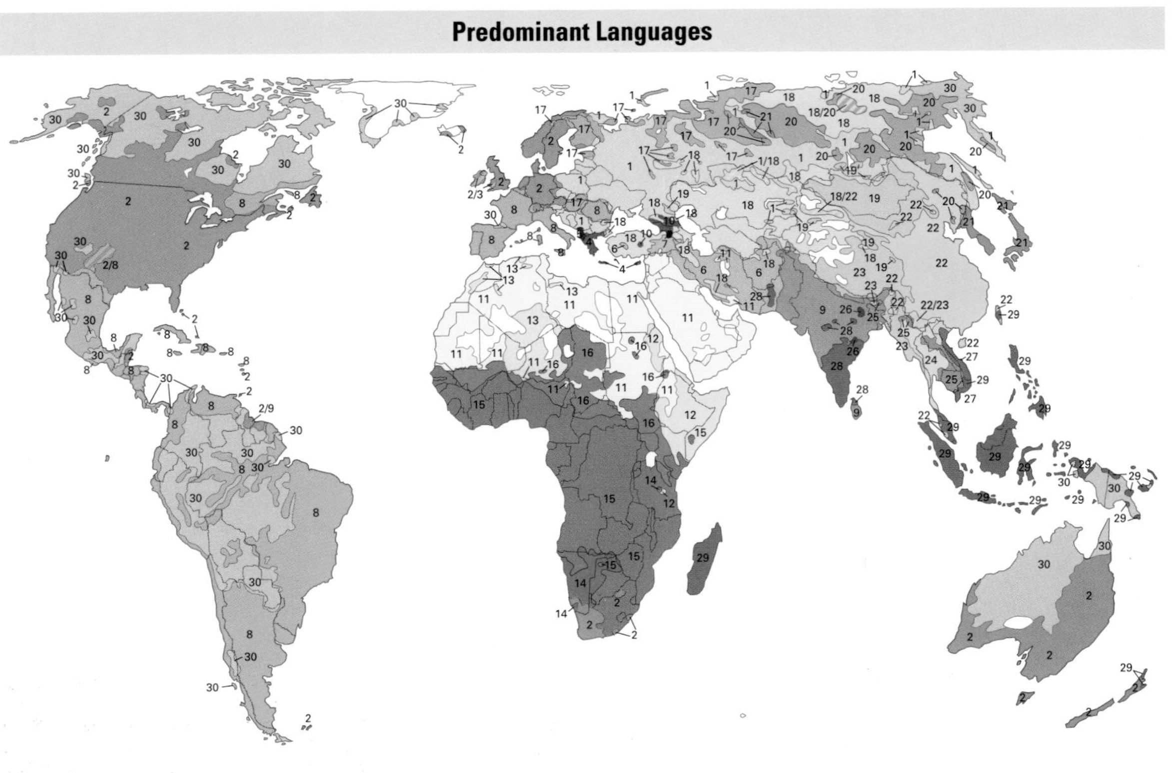

INDO-EUROPEAN FAMILY

1. Balto-Slavic group (incl. Russian, Ukrainian)
2. Germanic group (incl. English, German)
3. Celtic group
4. Greek
5. Albanian
6. Iranian group
7. Armenian
8. Romance group (incl. Spanish, Portuguese, French, Italian)
9. Indo-Aryan group (incl. Hindi, Bengali, Urdu, Punjabi, Marathi)
10. CAUCASIAN FAMILY

AFRO-ASIATIC FAMILY

11. Semitic group (incl. Arabic)
12. Kushitic group
13. Berber group

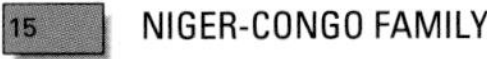

14. KHOISAN FAMILY

15. NIGER-CONGO FAMILY

16. NILO-SAHARAN FAMILY

17. URALIC FAMILY

ALTAIC FAMILY

18. Turkic group
19. Mongolian group
20. Tungus-Manchu group
21. Japanese and Korean

SINO-TIBETAN FAMILY

22. Sinitic (Chinese) languages
23. Tibetic-Burmic languages

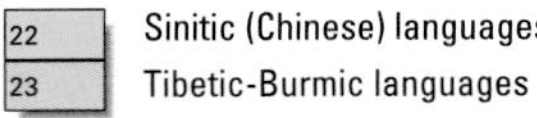

24. TAI FAMILY

AUSTRO-ASIATIC FAMILY

25. Mon-Khmer group
26. Munda group
27. Vietnamese

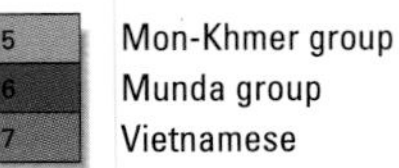

28. DRAVIDIAN FAMILY (incl. Telugu, Tamil)

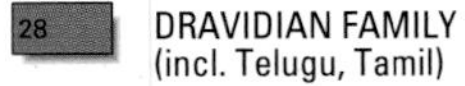

29. AUSTRONESIAN FAMILY (incl. Malay-Indonesian)

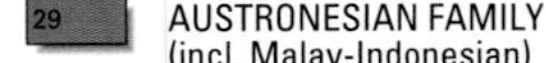

30. OTHER LANGUAGES

Predominant Religions

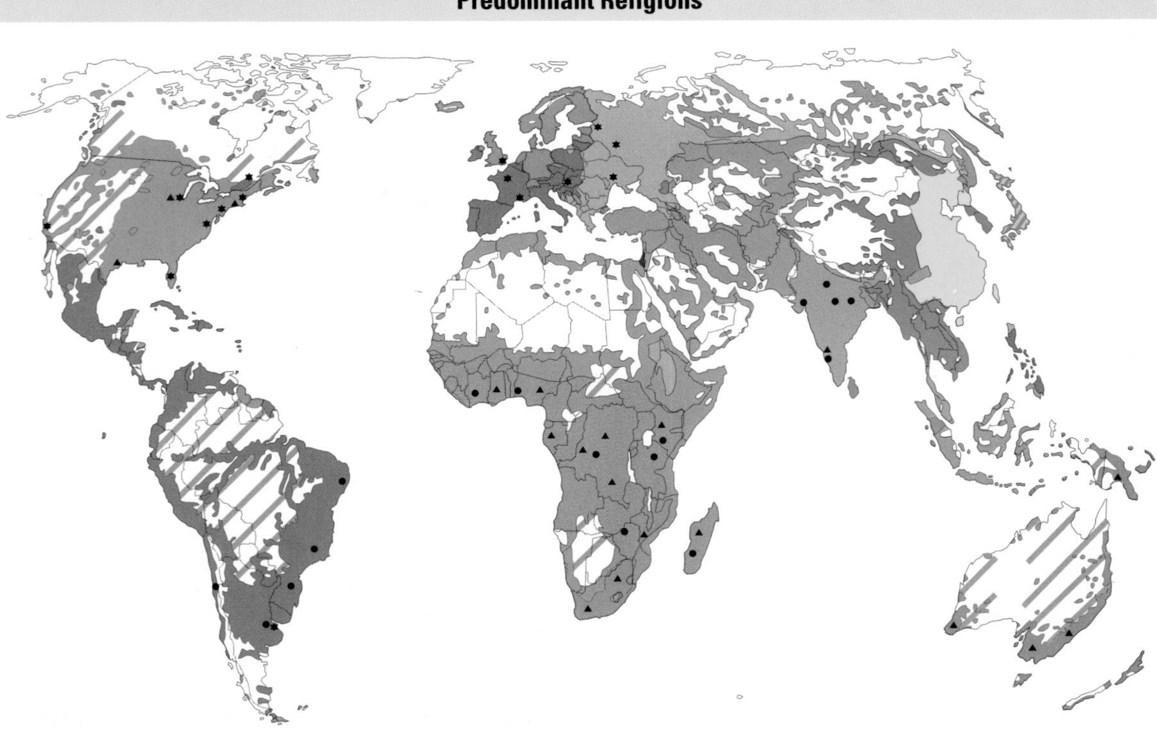

Religious Adherents

Religious adherents in millions:

Christian	1,669	Hindu	663
Roman Catholic	*952*	Buddhist	312
Protestant	*337*	Chinese Folk	172
Orthodox	*162*	Tribal	92
Anglican	*70*	Jewish	18
Other Christian	*148*	Sikhs	17
Muslim	966		
Sunni	*841*		
Shia	*125*		

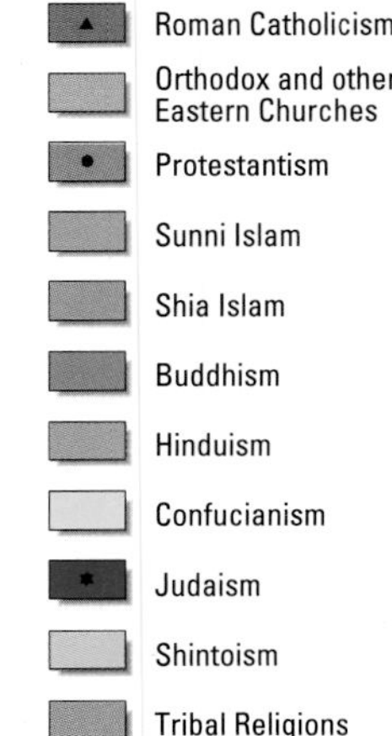

- Roman Catholicism
- Orthodox and other Eastern Churches
- Protestantism
- Sunni Islam
- Shia Islam
- Buddhism
- Hinduism
- Confucianism
- Judaism
- Shintoism
- Tribal Religions

United Nations

Created in 1945 to promote peace and co-operation and based in New York, the United Nations is the world's largest international organization, with 185 members and an annual budget of US $2.6 billion (1996–97). Each member of the General Assembly has one vote, while the permanent members of the 15-nation Security Council – USA, Russia, China, UK and France – hold a veto. The Secretariat is the UN's principal administrative arm. The 54 members of the Economic and Social Council are responsible for economic, social, cultural, educational, health and related matters. The UN has 16 specialized agencies – based in Canada, France, Switzerland and Italy, as well as the USA – which help members in fields such as education (UNESCO), agriculture (FAO), medicine (WHO) and finance (IFC). By the end of 1994, all the original 11 trust territories of the Trusteeship Council had become independent.

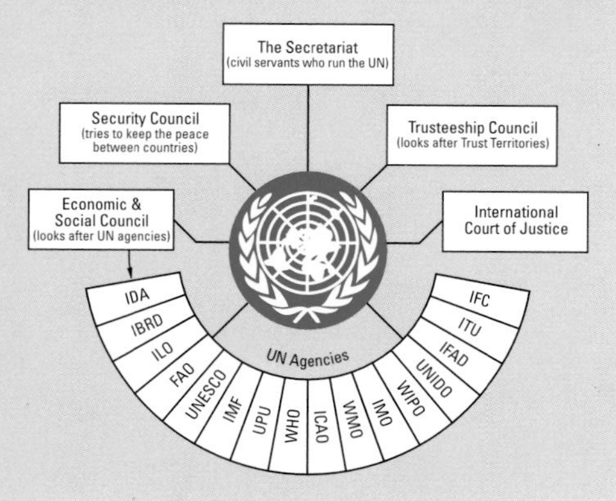

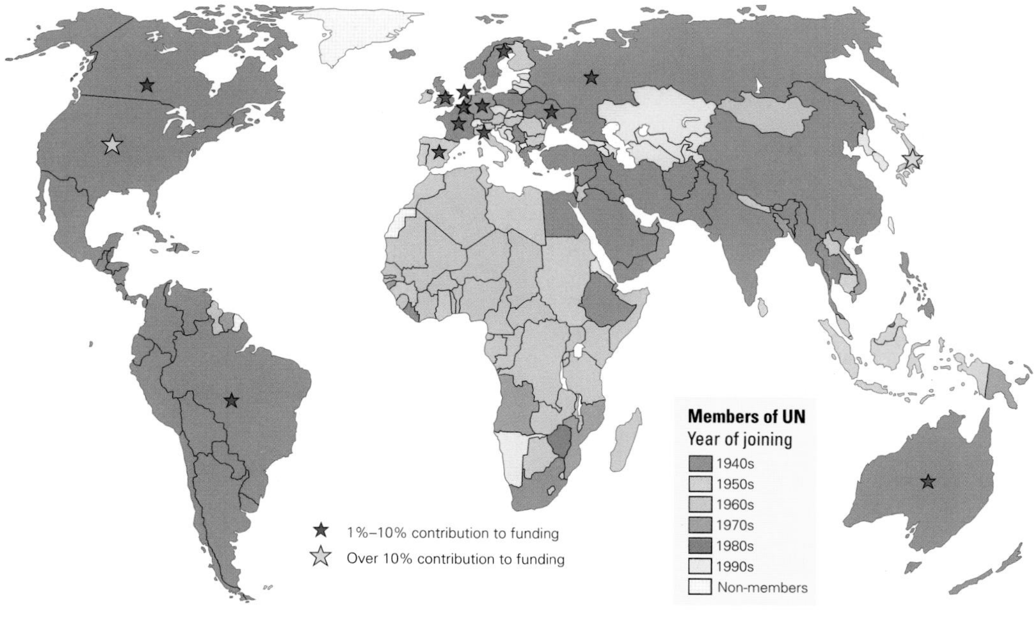

Members of UN
Year of joining
- 1940s
- 1950s
- 1960s
- 1970s
- 1980s
- 1990s
- Non-members

★ 1%–10% contribution to funding
☆ Over 10% contribution to funding

MEMBERSHIP OF THE UN In 1945 there were 51 members; by December 1994 membership had increased to 185 following the admission of Palau. There are 7 independent states which are not members of the UN – Kiribati, Nauru, Switzerland, Taiwan, Tonga, Tuvalu and the Vatican City. All the successor states of the former USSR had joined by the end of 1992. The official languages of the UN are Chinese, English, French, Russian, Spanish and Arabic.

FUNDING The UN budget for 1996–97 was US $2.6 billion. Contributions are assessed by the members' ability to pay, with the maximum 25% of the total, the minimum 0.01%. Contributions for 1996 were: USA 25.0%, Japan 15.4%, Germany 9.0%, France 6.4%, UK 5.3%, Italy 5.2%, Russia 4.5%, Canada 3.1%, Spain 2.4%, Brazil 1.6%, Netherlands 1.6%, Australia 1.5%, Sweden 1.2%, Ukraine 1.1%, Belgium 1.0%.

International Organizations

EU European Union (evolved from the European Community in 1993). The 15 members – Austria, Belgium, Denmark, Finland, France, Germany, Greece, Ireland, Italy, Luxembourg, Netherlands, Portugal, Spain, Sweden and the UK – aim to integrate economies, co-ordinate social developments and bring about political union. These members of what is now the world's biggest market share agricultural and industrial policies and tariffs on trade. The original body, the European Coal and Steel Community (ECSC), was created in 1951 following the signing of the Treaty of Paris.

EFTA European Free Trade Association (formed in 1960). Portugal left the original 'Seven' in 1989 to join what was then the EC, followed by Austria, Finland and Sweden in 1995. Only 4 members remain: Norway, Iceland, Switzerland and Liechtenstein.

ACP African-Caribbean-Pacific (formed in 1963). Members have economic ties with the EU.

NATO North Atlantic Treaty Organization (formed in 1949). It continues after 1991 despite the winding up of the Warsaw Pact. The Czech Republic, Hungary and Poland were the latest members to join in 1999.

OAS Organization of American States (formed in 1948). It aims to promote social and economic co-operation between developed countries of North America and developing nations of Latin America.

ASEAN Association of South-east Asian Nations (formed in 1967). Burma and Laos joined in 1997.

OAU Organization of African Unity (formed in 1963). Its 53 members represent over 94% of Africa's population. Arabic, French, Portuguese and English are recognized as working languages.

LAIA Latin American Integration Association (1980). Its aim is to promote freer regional trade.

OECD Organization for Economic Co-operation and Development (formed in 1961). It comprises the 29 major Western free-market economies. Poland, Hungary and South Korea joined in 1996. 'G8' is its 'inner group' comprising Canada, France, Germany, Italy, Japan, Russia, the UK and the USA.

COMMONWEALTH The Commonwealth of Nations evolved from the British Empire; it comprises 16 Queen's realms, 32 republics and 5 indigenous monarchies, giving a total of 53.

OPEC Organization of Petroleum Exporting Countries (formed in 1960). It controls about three-quarters of the world's oil supply. Gabon left the organization in 1996.

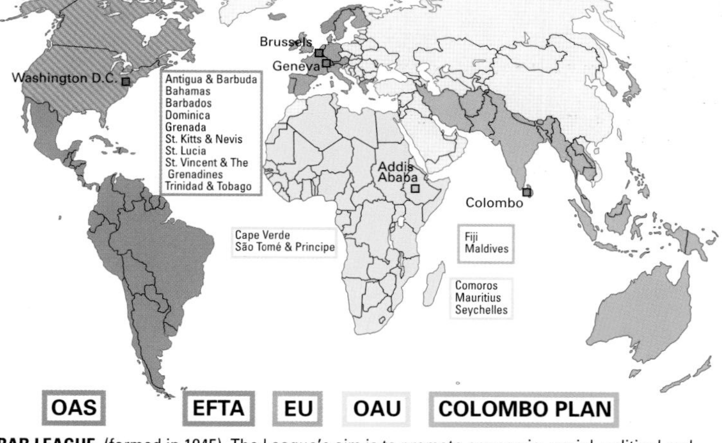

| OAS | EFTA | EU | OAU | COLOMBO PLAN |

ARAB LEAGUE (formed in 1945). The League's aim is to promote economic, social, political and military co-operation. There are 21 member nations.

COLOMBO PLAN (formed in 1951). Its 26 members aim to promote economic and social development in Asia and the Pacific.

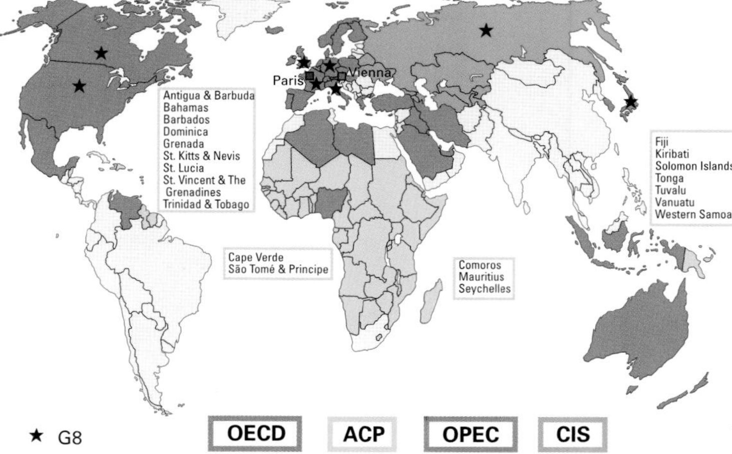

★ G8

| OECD | ACP | OPEC | CIS |

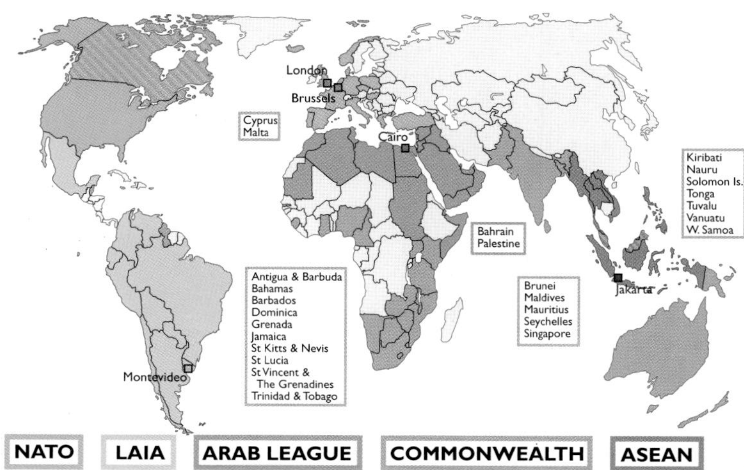

| NATO | LAIA | ARAB LEAGUE | COMMONWEALTH | ASEAN |

Wealth

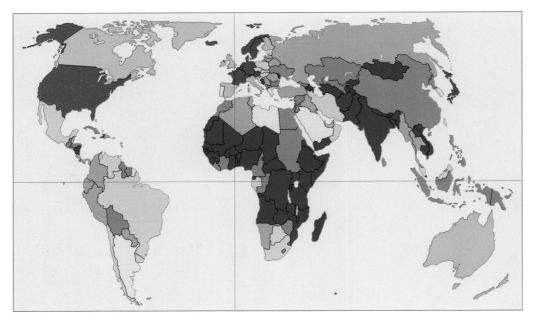

Gross National Product per capita: the value of total production divided by the population (1997)

- Over 400% of world average
- 200 – 400% of world average
- 100 – 200% of world average

[World average wealth per person US $6,316]

- 50 – 100% of world average
- 25 – 50% of world average
- 10 – 25% of world average
- Under 10% of world average

GNP per capita growth rate (%), selected countries, 1985–94

Thailand	8.2	Brazil	−0.4
Chile	6.9	Zimbabwe	−0.6
Japan	3.2	USA	−1.3
Germany	1.9	UK	−1.4
Australia	1.2	Armenia	−12.9

Wealth Creation

The Gross National Product (GNP) of the world's largest economies, US $ million (1997)

1.	USA	7,690,100	23.	Turkey	199,500
2.	Japan	4,772,300	24.	Denmark	171,400
3.	Germany	2,319,300	25.	Thailand	169,600
4.	France	1,526,400	26.	Hong Kong	164,400
5.	UK	1,220,200	27.	Norway	158,900
6.	Italy	1,155,400	28.	Poland	138,900
7.	China	1,055,400	29.	South Africa	130,200
8.	Brazil	773,400	30.	Saudi Arabia	128,900
9.	Canada	583,900	31.	Greece	126,200
10.	Spain	570,100	32.	Finland	123,800
11.	South Korea	485,200	33.	Portugal	103,900
12.	Russia	403,500	34.	Singapore	101,800
13.	Netherlands	402,700	35.	Malaysia	98,200
14.	Australia	380,000	36.	Philippines	89,300
15.	India	373,900	37.	Israel	87,600
16.	Mexico	348,600	38.	Colombia	86,800
17.	Switzerland	313,500	39.	Venezuela	78,700
18.	Argentina	305,700	40.	Chile	73,300
19.	Belgium	268,400	41.	Egypt	71,200
20.	Sweden	232,000	42.	Pakistan	67,200
21.	Austria	225,900	43.	Ireland	66,400
22.	Indonesia	221,900	44.	Peru	60,800

The Wealth Gap

The world's richest and poorest countries, by Gross National Product per capita in US $ (1997)

1.	Luxembourg	45,360	1.	Mozambique	90
2.	Switzerland	44,220	2.	Ethiopia	110
3.	Japan	37,850	3.	Congo (D. Rep.)	110
4.	Norway	36,090	4.	Burundi	180
5.	Liechtenstein	33,000	5.	Sierra Leone	200
6.	Singapore	32,940	6.	Niger	200
7.	Denmark	32,500	7.	Rwanda	210
8.	Bermuda	31,870	8.	Tanzania	210
9.	USA	28,740	9.	Nepal	210
10.	Germany	28,260	10.	Malawi	220
11.	Austria	27,980	11.	Chad	240
12.	Iceland	26,580	12.	Madagascar	250
13.	Belgium	26,420	13.	Mali	260
14.	Sweden	26,220	14.	Yemen	270
15.	France	26,050	15.	Cambodia	300
16.	Netherlands	25,820	16.	Bosnia-Herzegovina	300
17.	Monaco	25,000	17.	Gambia, The	320
18.	Hong Kong	22,990	18.	Haiti	330
19.	Finland	20,580	19.	Kenya	330
20.	UK	18,700	20.	Angola	340

GNP per capita is calculated by dividing a country's Gross National Product by its total population.

Continental Shares

Shares of population and of wealth (GNP) by continent

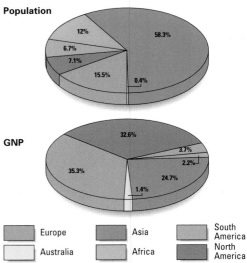

Population

GNP

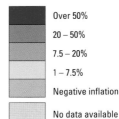

- Europe
- Asia
- South America
- Australia
- Africa
- North America

Inflation

Average annual rate of inflation (1990–96)

- Over 50%
- 20 – 50%
- 7.5 – 20%
- 1 – 7.5%
- Negative inflation
- No data available

Highest average inflation

Congo (D. Rep.)	2747%
Georgia	2279%
Angola	1103%
Turkmenistan	1074%
Armenia	897%

Lowest average inflation

Oman	−3.0%
Bahrain	−0.5%
Brunei	−0.0%
Saudi Araba	1.0%
Japan	1.0%

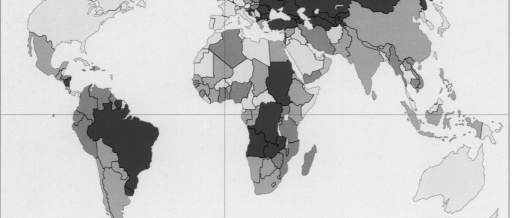

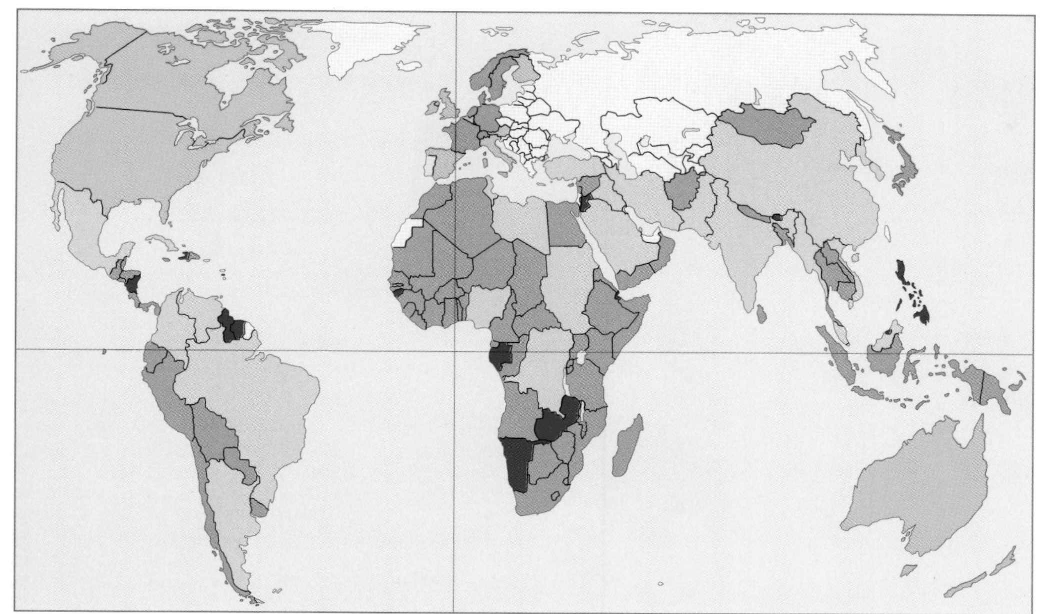

Aid provided or received, divided by the total population, in US $ (1995)

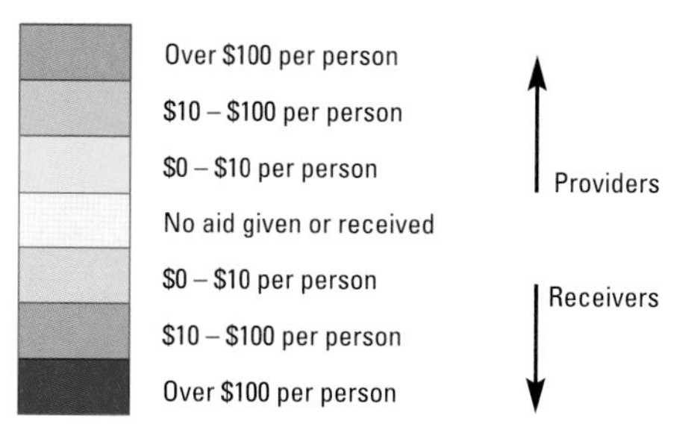

Over $100 per person
$10 – $100 per person
$0 – $10 per person
No aid given or received
$0 – $10 per person
$10 – $100 per person
Over $100 per person

Providers

Receivers

Top 5 providers per capita (1994)		Top 5 receivers per capita (1994)	
France	$279	São Tomé & P.	$378
Denmark	$260	Cape Verde	$314
Norway	$247	Djibouti	$235
Sweden	$201	Surinam	$198
Germany	$166	Mauritania	$153

Debt and Aid

International debtors and the aid they receive (1996)

Although aid grants make a vital contribution to many of the world's poorer countries, they are usually dwarfed by the burden of debt that the developing economies are expected to repay. In 1992, they had to pay US $160,000 million in debt service charges alone – more than two and a half times the amount of Official Development Assistance (ODA) the developing countries were receiving, and US $60,000 million more than total private flows of aid in the same year. In 1990, the debts of Mozambique, one of the world's poorest countries, were estimated to be 75 times its entire earnings from exports.

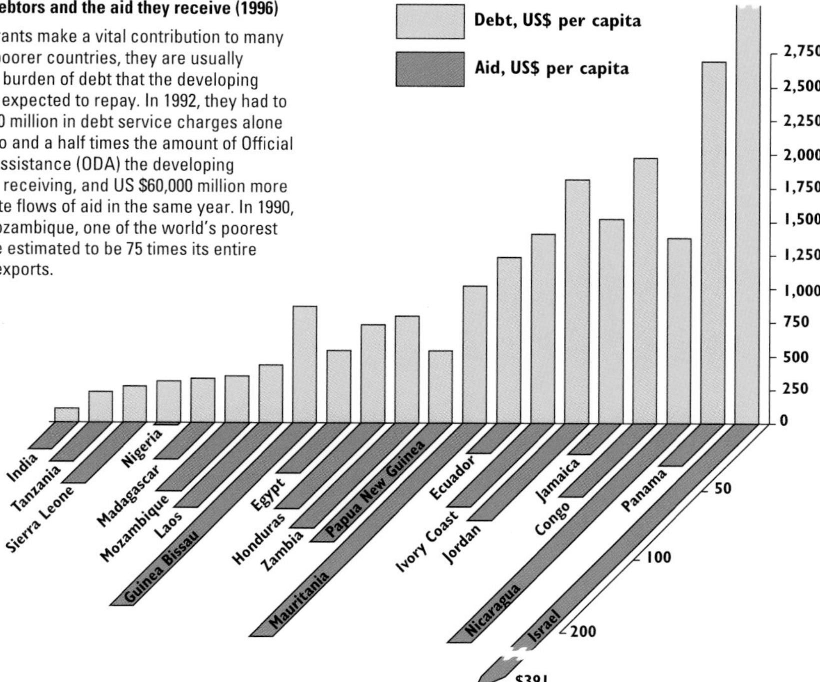

Debt, US$ per capita

Aid, US$ per capita

$5,014

$391

Distribution of Spending

Percentage share of household spending, selected countries

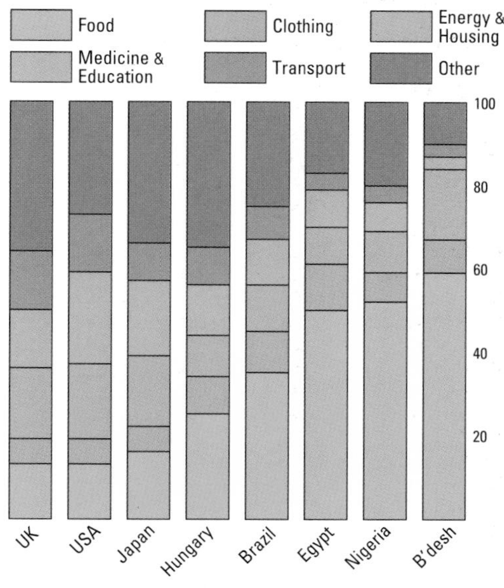

Food
Medicine & Education
Clothing
Transport
Energy & Housing
Other

UK USA Japan Hungary Brazil Egypt Nigeria B'desh

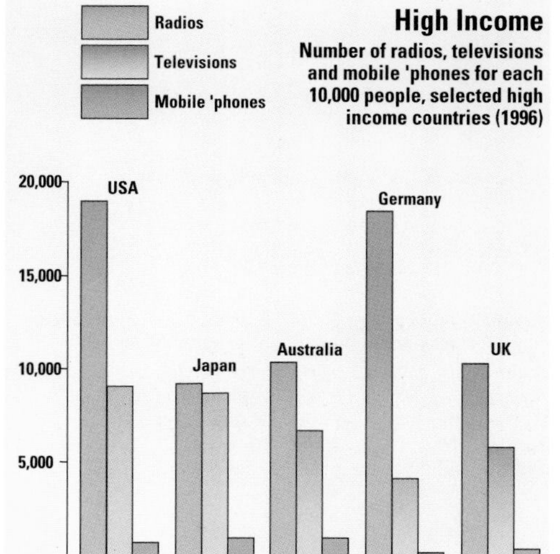

Radios
Televisions
Mobile 'phones

High Income

Number of radios, televisions and mobile 'phones for each 10,000 people, selected high income countries (1996)

USA Germany Japan Australia UK

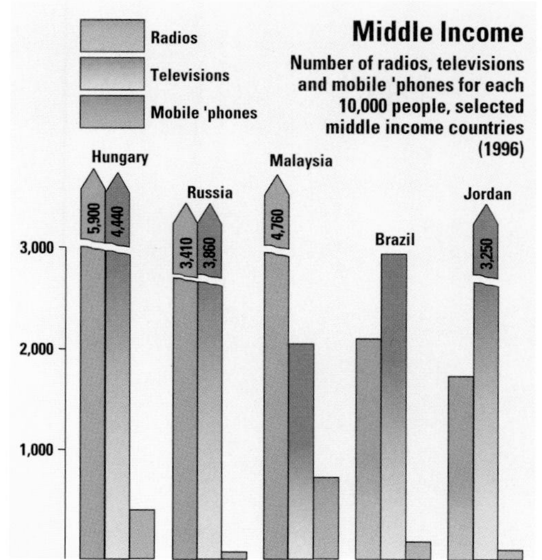

Radios
Televisions
Mobile 'phones

Middle Income

Number of radios, televisions and mobile 'phones for each 10,000 people, selected middle income countries (1996)

Hungary 5,900 4,440 Russia 3,410 3,860 Malaysia 4,760 Brazil Jordan 3,250

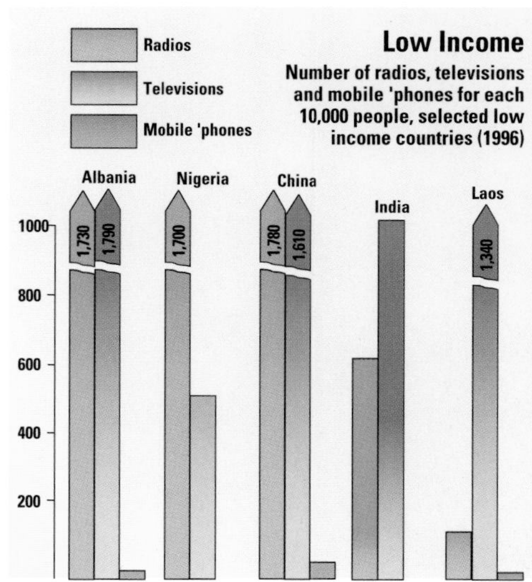

Radios
Televisions
Mobile 'phones

Low Income

Number of radios, televisions and mobile 'phones for each 10,000 people, selected low income countries (1996)

Albania 1,730 1,790 Nigeria 1,700 China 1,780 1,610 India Laos 1,340

Quality of Life

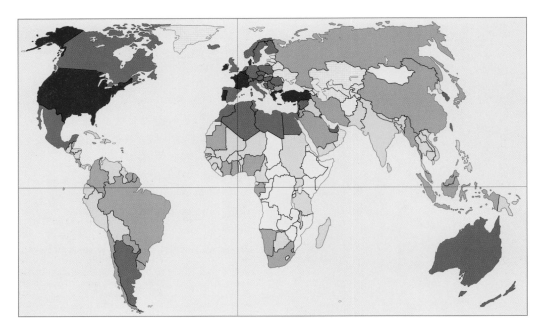

Daily Food Consumption

Average daily food intake in calories per person (1995)

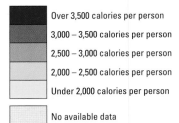

Over 3,500 calories per person

3,000 – 3,500 calories per person

2,500 – 3,000 calories per person

2,000 – 2,500 calories per person

Under 2,000 calories per person

No available data

Top 5 countries		Bottom 5 countries	
Cyprus	3,708 cal.	Congo (D.Rep.)	1,879 cal.
Denmark	3,704 cal.	Djibouti	1,831 cal.
Portugal	3,639 cal.	Togo	1,754 cal.
Ireland	3,638 cal.	Burundi	1,749 cal.
USA	3,603 cal.	Mozambique	1,678 cal.

[UK 3,149 calories]

Hospital Capacity

Hospital beds available for each 1,000 people (1996)

Highest capacity		Lowest capacity	
Switzerland	20.8	Benin	0.2
Japan	16.2	Nepal	0.2
Tajikistan	16.0	Afghanistan	0.3
Norway	13.5	Bangladesh	0.3
Belarus	12.4	Ethiopia	0.3
Kazakstan	12.2	Mali	0.4
Moldova	12.2	Burkina Faso	0.5
Ukraine	12.2	Niger	0.5
Latvia	11.9	Guinea	0.6
Russia	11.8	India	0.6

[UK 4.9] [USA 4.2]

Although the ratio of people to hospital beds gives a good approximation of a country's health provision, it is not an absolute indicator. Raw numbers may mask inefficiency and other weaknesses: the high availability of beds in Kazakstan, for example, has not prevented infant mortality rates over three times as high as in the United Kingdom and the United States.

Life Expectancy

Years of life expectancy at birth, selected countries (1997)

The chart shows combined data for both sexes. On average, women live longer than men worldwide, even in developing countries with high maternal mortality rates. Overall, life expectancy is steadily rising, though the difference between rich and poor nations remains dramatic.

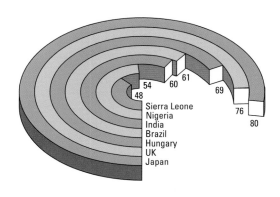

Sierra Leone 48
Nigeria 54
India 60
Brazil 61
Hungary 69
UK 76
Japan 80

Causes of Death

Causes of death for selected countries by % (1992–94)

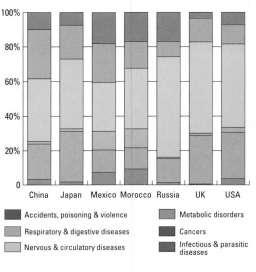

China Japan Mexico Morocco Russia UK USA

Accidents, poisoning & violence

Respiratory & digestive diseases

Nervous & circulatory diseases

Metabolic disorders

Cancers

Infectious & parasitic diseases

Child Mortality

Number of babies who will die under the age of one, per 1,000 births (average 1990–95)

Over 150 deaths per 1,000 births

100 – 150 deaths per 1,000 births

50 – 100 deaths per 1,000 births

20 – 50 deaths per 1,000 births

10 – 20 deaths per 1,000 births

Under 10 deaths per 1,000 births

Highest child mortality		Lowest child mortality	
Afghanistan	162	Hong Kong	6
Mali	159	Denmark	6
Sierra Leone	143	Japan	5
Guinea-Bissau	140	Iceland	5
Malawi	138	Finland	5

[UK 8 deaths]

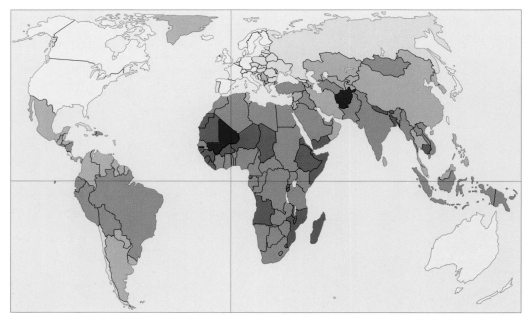

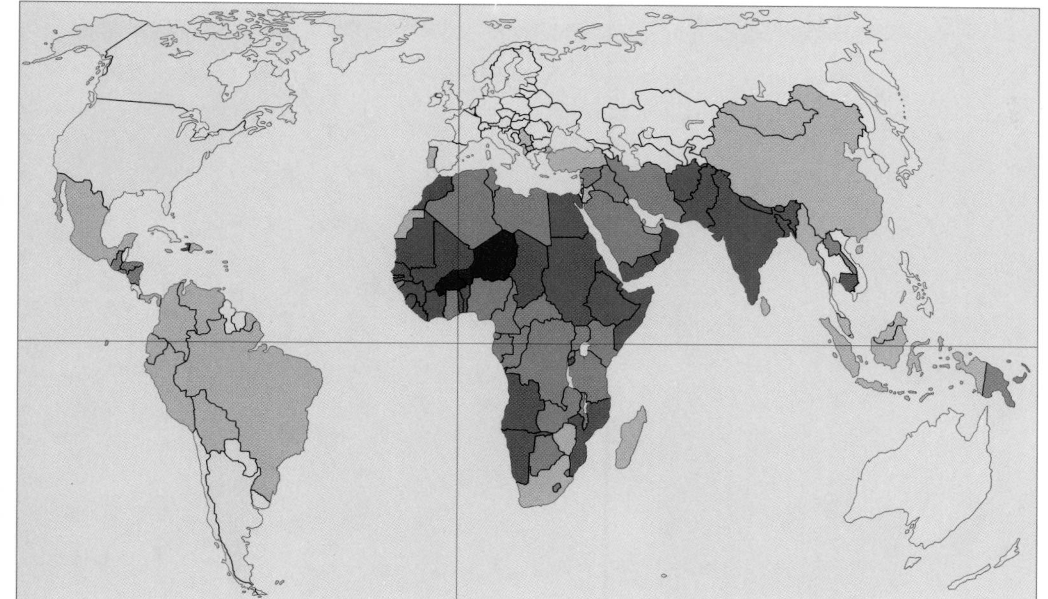

Illiteracy

Percentage of the total population unable to read or write (latest available year)

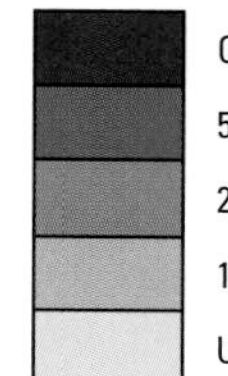

Over 75% of population illiterate

50 – 75% of population illiterate

25 – 50% of population illiterate

10 – 25% of population illiterate

Under 10% of population illiterate

Educational expenditure per person (latest available year)

Top 5 countries		Bottom 5 countries	
Sweden	$997	Chad	$2
Qatar	$989	Bangladesh	$3
Canada	$983	Ethiopia	$3
Norway	$971	Nepal	$4
Switzerland	$796	Somalia	$4

Fertility and Education

Fertility rates compared with female education, selected countries (1992–95)

Percentage of females aged 12–17 in secondary education

Fertility rate: average number of children borne per woman

Denmark, Austria, France, Canada, Belgium, Switzerland, UK, Poland, Australia, Sri Lanka, Malaysia, Turkey, Saudi Arabia, Thailand, Bolivia, Nigeria, Sierra Leone, Niger

Living Standards

At first sight, most international contrasts in living standards are swamped by differences in wealth. The rich not only have more money, they have more of everything, including years of life. Those with only a little money are obliged to spend most of it on food and clothing, the basic maintenance costs of their existence; air travel and tourism are unlikely to feature on their expenditure lists. However, poverty and wealth are both relative: slum dwellers living on social security payments in an affluent industrial country have far more resources at their disposal than an average African peasant, but feel their own poverty nonetheless. A middle-class Indian lawyer cannot command a fraction of the earnings of a counterpart living in New York, London or Rome; nevertheless, he rightly sees himself as prosperous.

The rich not only live longer, on average, than the poor, they also die from different causes. Infectious and parasitic diseases, all but eliminated in the developed world, remain a scourge in the developing nations. On the other hand, more than two-thirds of the populations of OECD nations eventually succumb to cancer or circulatory disease.

Women in the Workforce

Women in paid employment as a percentage of the total workforce (latest available year)

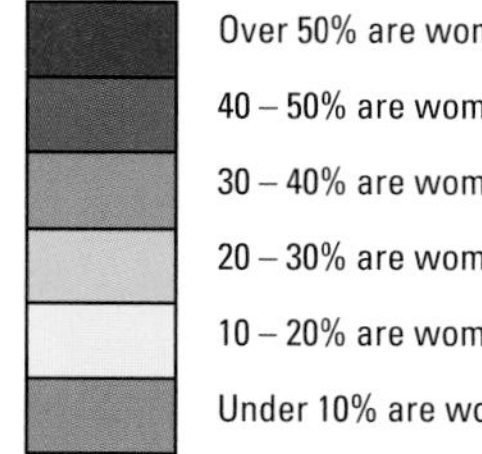

Over 50% are women

40 – 50% are women

30 – 40% are women

20 – 30% are women

10 – 20% are women

Under 10% are women

Most women in the workforce		Fewest women in the workforce	
Cambodia	56%	Saudi Arabia	4%
Kazakstan	54%	Oman	6%
Burundi	53%	Afghanistan	8%
Mozambique	53%	Algeria	9%
Turkmenistan	52%	Libya	9%

[USA 45] [UK 44]

Energy

Production

[Each square represents 1% of world energy production]

North America

Europe

CIS

Middle East

Japan

Africa

Asia

South America

Australasia

Consumption

[Each square represents 1% of world energy consumption]

North America

Europe

CIS

Middle East

Japan

Africa

Asia

South America

Australasia

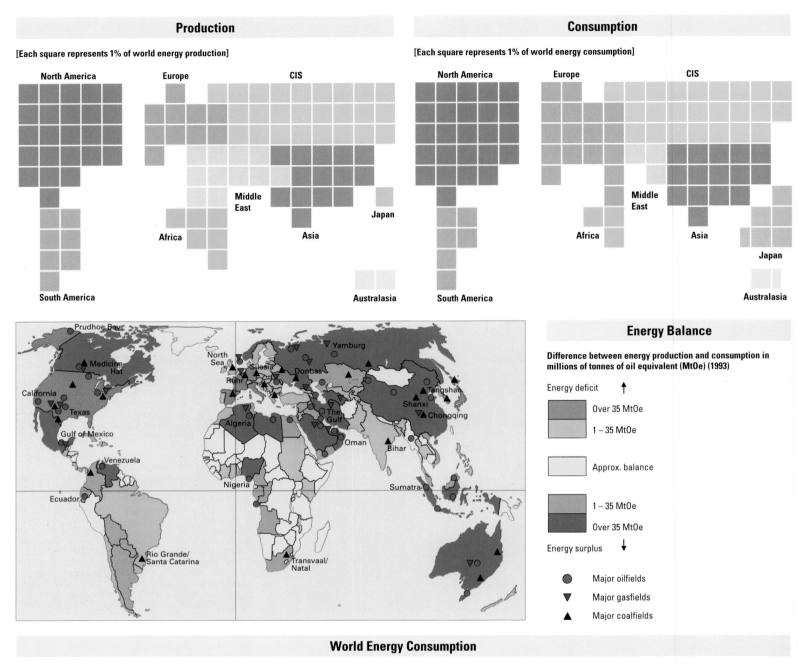

Energy Balance

Difference between energy production and consumption in millions of tonnes of oil equivalent (MtOe) (1993)

Energy deficit ↑

Over 35 MtOe

1 – 35 MtOe

Approx. balance

1 – 35 MtOe

Over 35 MtOe

Energy surplus ↓

● Major oilfields

▽ Major gasfields

▲ Major coalfields

Map labels: Prudhoe Bay, Medicine Hat, California, Texas, Gulf of Mexico, Venezuela, Ecuador, Rio Grande/Santa Catarina, North Sea, Silesia, Ruhr, Algeria, Nigeria, Transvaal/Natal, Yamburg, Donbas, The Gulf, Oman, Shanxi, Tangshan, Chongqing, Bihar, Sumatra

World Energy Consumption

Energy consumed by world regions, measured in million tonnes of oil equivalent in 1997. Total world consumption was 8,509 MtOe. Only energy from oil, gas, coal, nuclear and hydroelectric sources are included. Excluded are fuels such as wood, peat, animal waste, wind, solar and geothermal which, though important in some countries, are unreliably documented in terms of consumption statistics.

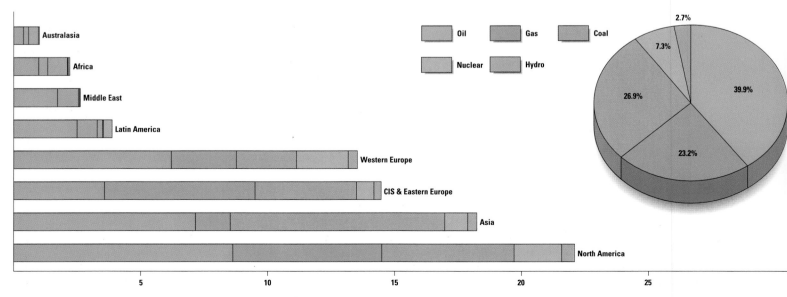

Legend: Oil, Gas, Coal, Nuclear, Hydro

Bar chart regions: Australasia, Africa, Middle East, Latin America, Western Europe, CIS & Eastern Europe, Asia, North America

Scale: 5, 10, 15, 20, 25

Pie chart: 39.9%, 23.2%, 26.9%, 7.3%, 2.7%

Energy

Energy is used to keep us warm or cool, fuel our industries and our transport systems, and even feed us; high-intensity agriculture, with its use of fertilizers, pesticides and machinery, is heavily energy-dependent. Although we live in a high-energy society, there are vast discrepancies between rich and poor; for example, a North American consumes 13 times as much energy as a Chinese person. But even developing nations have more power at their disposal than was imaginable a century ago.

The distribution of energy supplies, most importantly fossil fuels (coal, oil and natural gas), is very uneven. In addition, the diagrams and map opposite show that the largest producers of energy are not necessarily the largest consumers. The movement of energy supplies around the world is therefore an important component of international trade. In 1995, total world movements in oil amounted to 1,815 million tonnes.

As the finite reserves of fossil fuels are depleted, renewable energy sources, such as solar, hydro-thermal, wind, tidal and biomass, will become increasingly important around the world.

Nuclear Power

Percentage of electricity generated by nuclear power stations, leading nations (1995)

1. Lithuania..............85%	11. Spain....................33%
2. France.................77%	12. Finland................30%
3. Belgium..............56%	13. Germany..............29%
4. Slovak Rep. 49%	14. Japan..................29%
5. Sweden................48%	15. UK........................27%
6. Bulgaria.............41%	16. Ukraine...............27%
7. Hungary..............41%	17. Czech Rep. 22%
8. Switzerland.........39%	18. Canada................19%
9. Slovenia.............38%	19. USA.....................18%
10. South Korea........33%	20. Russia................12%

Although the 1980s were a bad time for the nuclear power industry (major projects ran over budget, and fears of long-term environmental damage were heavily reinforced by the 1986 disaster at Chernobyl), the industry picked up in the early 1990s. However, whilst the number of reactors is still increasing, orders for new plants have shrunk. This is partly due to the increasingly difficult task of disposing of nuclear waste.

Hydroelectricity

Percentage of electricity generated by hydroelectric power stations, leading nations (1995)

1. Paraguay...........99.9%	11. Rwanda.............97.6%
2. Congo (Zaïre)....99.7%	12. Malawi..............97.6%
3. Bhutan.............99.6%	13. Cameroon.........96.9%
4. Zambia.............99.5%	14. Nepal................96.7%
5. Norway.............99.4%	15. Laos.................95.3%
6. Ghana..............99.3%	16. Albania.............95.2%
7. Congo..............99.3%	17. Iceland.............94.0%
8. Uganda.............99.1%	17. Brazil 92.2%
9. Burundi............98.3%	19. Honduras.........87.6%
10. Uruguay............98.0%	20. Tanzania...........87.1%

Countries heavily reliant on hydroelectricity are usually small and non-industrial: a high proportion of hydroelectric power more often reflects a modest energy budget than vast hydroelectric resources. The USA, for instance, produces only 9% of power requirements from hydroelectricity; yet that 9% amounts to more than three times the hydropower generated by all of Africa.

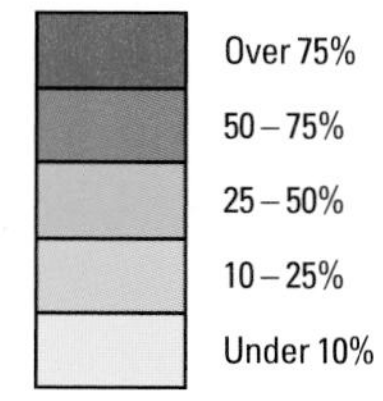

Fuel Exports

Fuels as a percentage of total value of exports (1990–94)

- Over 75%
- 50 – 75%
- 25 – 50%
- 10 – 25%
- Under 10%

Conversion Rates

1 barrel = 0.136 tonnes or 159 litres or 35 Imperial gallons or 42 US gallons

1 tonne = 7.33 barrels or 1,185 litres or 256 Imperial gallons or 261 US gallons

1 tonne oil = 1.5 tonnes hard coal or 3.0 tonnes lignite or 12,000 kWh

1 Imperial gallon = 1.201 US gallons or 4.546 litres or 277.4 cubic inches

Measurements
For historical reasons, oil is traded in 'barrels'. The weight and volume equivalents (shown right) are all based on average-density 'Arabian light' crude oil.

The energy equivalents given for a tonne of oil are also somewhat imprecise: oil and coal of different qualities will have varying energy contents, a fact usually reflected in their price on world markets.

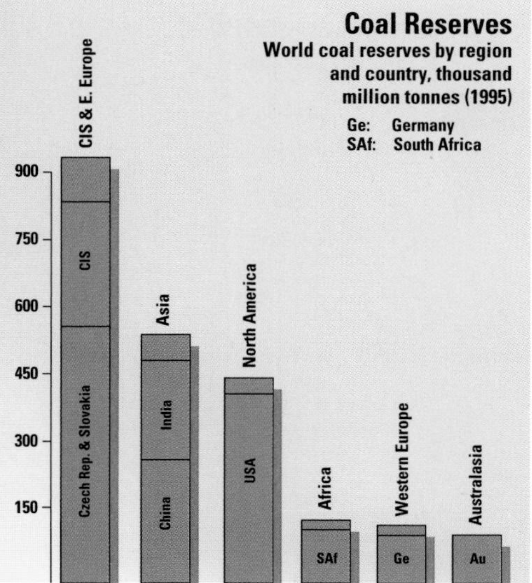

Coal Reserves

World coal reserves by region and country, thousand million tonnes (1995)

Ge: Germany
SAf: South Africa

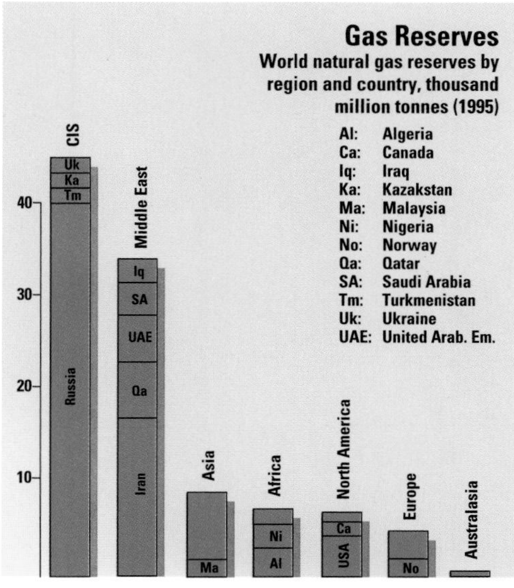

Gas Reserves

World natural gas reserves by region and country, thousand million tonnes (1995)

Al: Algeria
Ca: Canada
Iq: Iraq
Ka: Kazakhstan
Ma: Malaysia
Ni: Nigeria
No: Norway
Qa: Qatar
SA: Saudi Arabia
Tm: Turkmenistan
Uk: Ukraine
UAE: United Arab. Em.

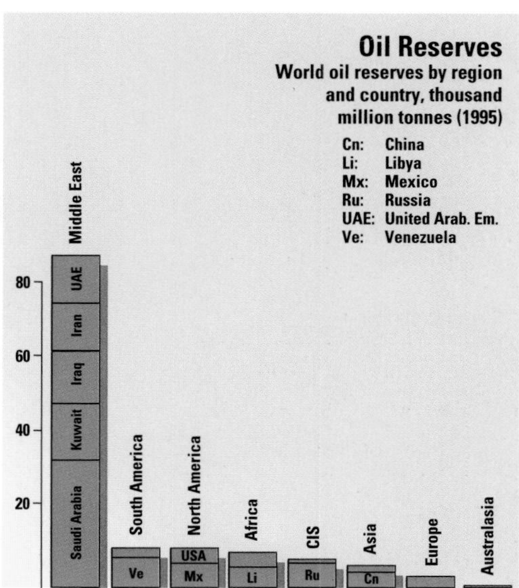

Oil Reserves

World oil reserves by region and country, thousand million tonnes (1995)

Cn: China
Li: Libya
Mx: Mexico
Ru: Russia
UAE: United Arab. Em.
Ve: Venezuela

Production

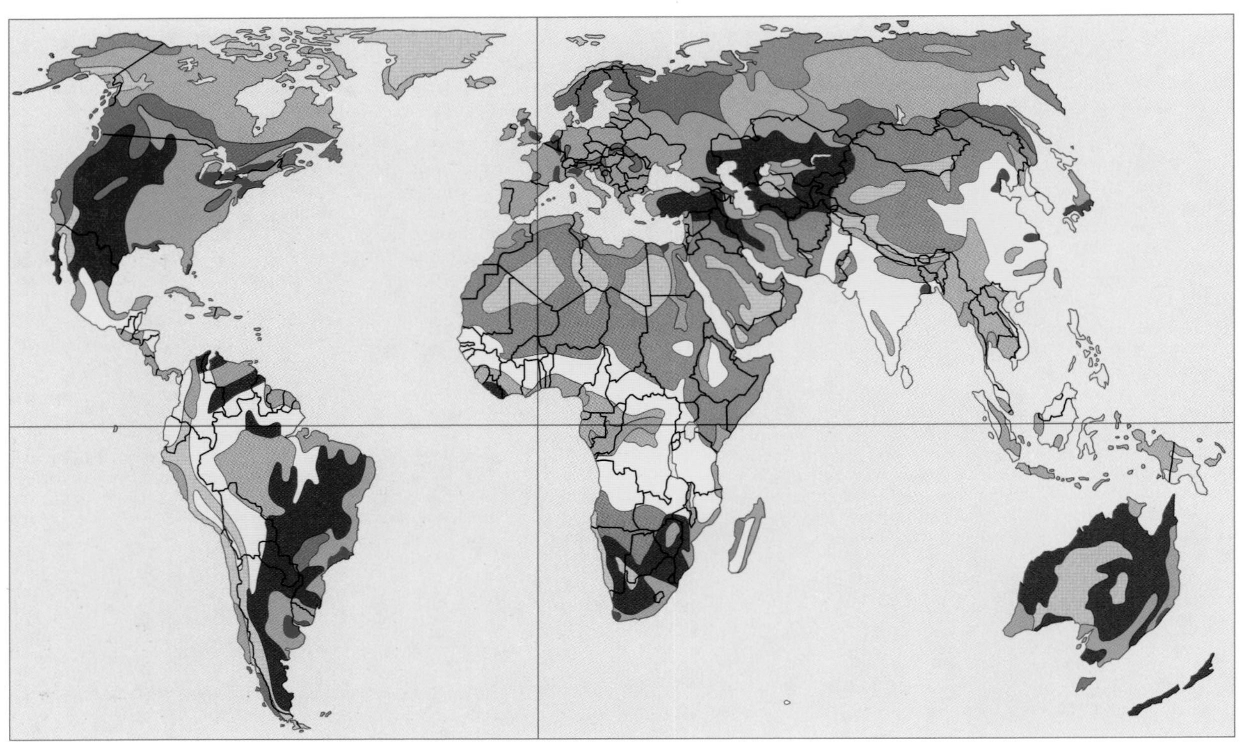

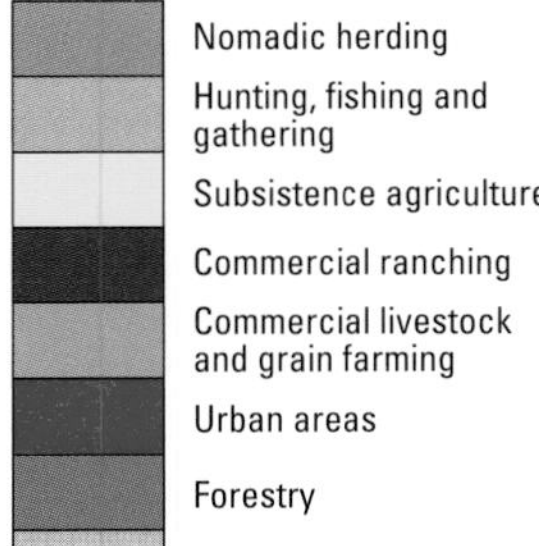

The development of agriculture has transformed human existence more than any other. The whole business of farming is constantly developing: due mainly to the new varieties of rice and wheat, world grain production has increased by over 70% since 1965. New machinery and modern agricultural techniques enable relatively few farmers to produce enough food for the world's 6 billion or so people.

Staple Crops

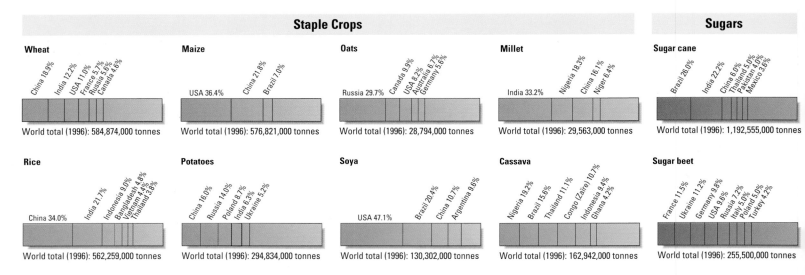

Wheat

China 18.9% | India 12.2% | USA 11.0% | France 5.7% | Russia 5.6% | Canada 4.6%

World total (1996): 584,874,000 tonnes

Maize

USA 36.4% | China 21.8% | Brazil 7.0%

World total (1996): 576,821,000 tonnes

Oats

Russia 29.7% | Canada 9.9% | USA 8.2% | Australia 6.7% | Germany 5.6%

World total (1996): 28,794,000 tonnes

Millet

India 33.2% | Nigeria 18.3% | China 16.1% | Niger 6.4%

World total (1996): 29,563,000 tonnes

Rice

China 34.0% | India 21.7% | Indonesia 9.0% | Bangladesh 4.8% | Vietnam 4.4% | Thailand 3.8%

World total (1996): 562,259,000 tonnes

Potatoes

China 16.0% | Russia 14.0% | Poland 8.7% | India 6.3% | Ukraine 5.2%

World total (1996): 294,834,000 tonnes

Soya

USA 47.1% | Brazil 20.4% | China 10.7% | Argentina 9.6%

World total (1996): 130,302,000 tonnes

Cassava

Nigeria 19.2% | Brazil 15.6% | Thailand 11.1% | Congo (Zaïre) 10.7% | Indonesia 9.4% | Ghana 4.2%

World total (1996): 162,942,000 tonnes

Sugars

Sugar cane

Brazil 26.0% | India 22.2% | China 6.0% | Thailand 5.0% | Pakistan 4.0% | Mexico 3.6%

World total (1996): 1,192,555,000 tonnes

Sugar beet

France 11.5% | Ukraine 11.2% | Germany 9.8% | USA 9.6% | Russia 7.2% | Italy 5.0% | Poland 5.0% | Turkey 4.2%

World total (1996): 255,500,000 tonnes

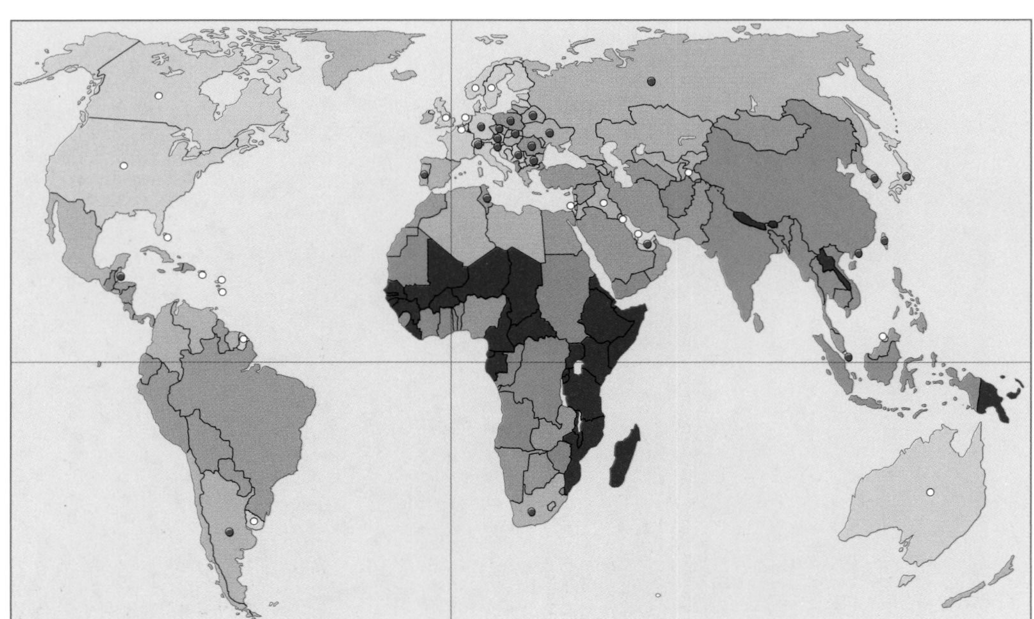

Balance of Employment

Percentage of total workforce employed in agriculture, including forestry and fishing (1990–92)

- Over 75% in agriculture
- 50 – 75% in agriculture
- 25 – 50% in agriculture
- 10 – 25% in agriculture
- Under 10% in agriculture

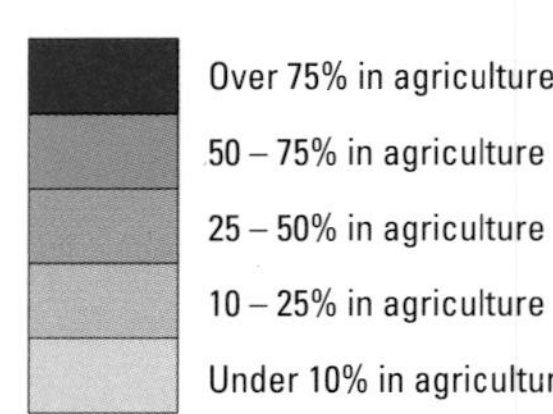

Employment in industry and services

- Over a third of total workforce employed in manufacturing
- Over two-thirds of total workforce employed in service industries (work in offices, shops, tourism, transport, construction and government)

Mineral Production

*Figures for aluminium are for refined metal; all other figures refer to ore production.

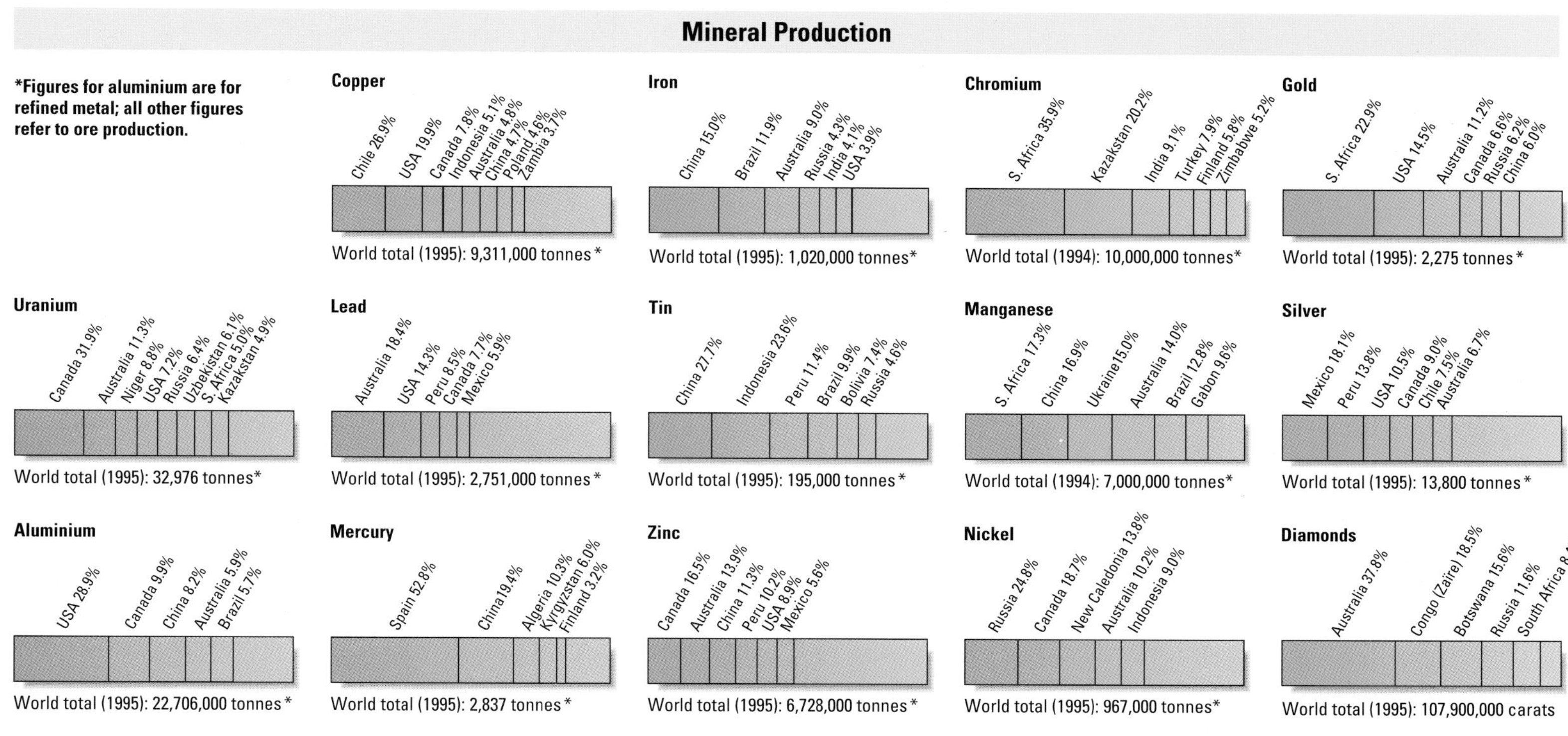

Copper
Chile 26.9% | USA 19.9% | Canada 7.8% | Indonesia 5.1% | Australia 4.8% | Poland 4.7% | Zambia 3.7%
World total (1995): 9,311,000 tonnes*

Iron
China 15.0% | Brazil 11.9% | Australia 9.0% | Russia 4.3% | India 4.1% | USA 3.9%
World total (1995): 1,020,000 tonnes*

Chromium
S. Africa 35.5% | Kazakstan 20.2% | India 9.1% | Turkey 7.9% | Finland 5.8% | Zimbabwe 5.2%
World total (1994): 10,000,000 tonnes*

Gold
S. Africa 22.9% | USA 14.5% | Australia 11.2% | Canada 6.6% | Russia 6.2% | China 6.0%
World total (1995): 2,275 tonnes*

Uranium
Canada 31.9% | Australia 11.3% | Niger 8.6% | USA 7.2% | Russia 6.4% | Uzbekistan 6.1% | S. Africa 5.0% | Kazakstan 4.9%
World total (1995): 32,976 tonnes*

Lead
Australia 18.4% | USA 14.3% | Peru 8.5% | Canada 7.7% | Mexico 5.9%
World total (1995): 2,751,000 tonnes*

Tin
China 27.7% | Indonesia 23.6% | Peru 11.4% | Brazil 9.9% | Bolivia 7.4% | Russia 4.6%
World total (1995): 195,000 tonnes*

Manganese
S. Africa 17.3% | China 16.9% | Ukraine 15.0% | Australia 14.0% | Brazil 12.6% | Gabon 9.6%
World total (1994): 7,000,000 tonnes*

Silver
Mexico 18.1% | Peru 13.8% | USA 10.5% | Canada 9.0% | Chile 7.5% | Australia 6.7%
World total (1995): 13,800 tonnes*

Aluminium
USA 28.9% | Canada 9.9% | China 8.2% | Australia 5.9% | Brazil 5.7%
World total (1995): 22,706,000 tonnes*

Mercury
Spain 52.8% | China 19.4% | Algeria 10.3% | Kyrgyzstan 6.0% | Finland 3.2%
World total (1995): 2,837 tonnes*

Zinc
Canada 16.5% | Australia 13.9% | China 11.3% | Peru 10.2% | USA 8.9% | Mexico 5.6%
World total (1995): 6,728,000 tonnes*

Nickel
Russia 24.8% | Canada 18.7% | New Caledonia 13.8% | Australia 10.2% | Indonesia 9.0%
World total (1995): 967,000 tonnes*

Diamonds
Australia 37.8% | Congo (Zaire) 18.5% | Botswana 15.6% | Russia 11.6% | South Africa 8.4%
World total (1995): 107,900,000 carats

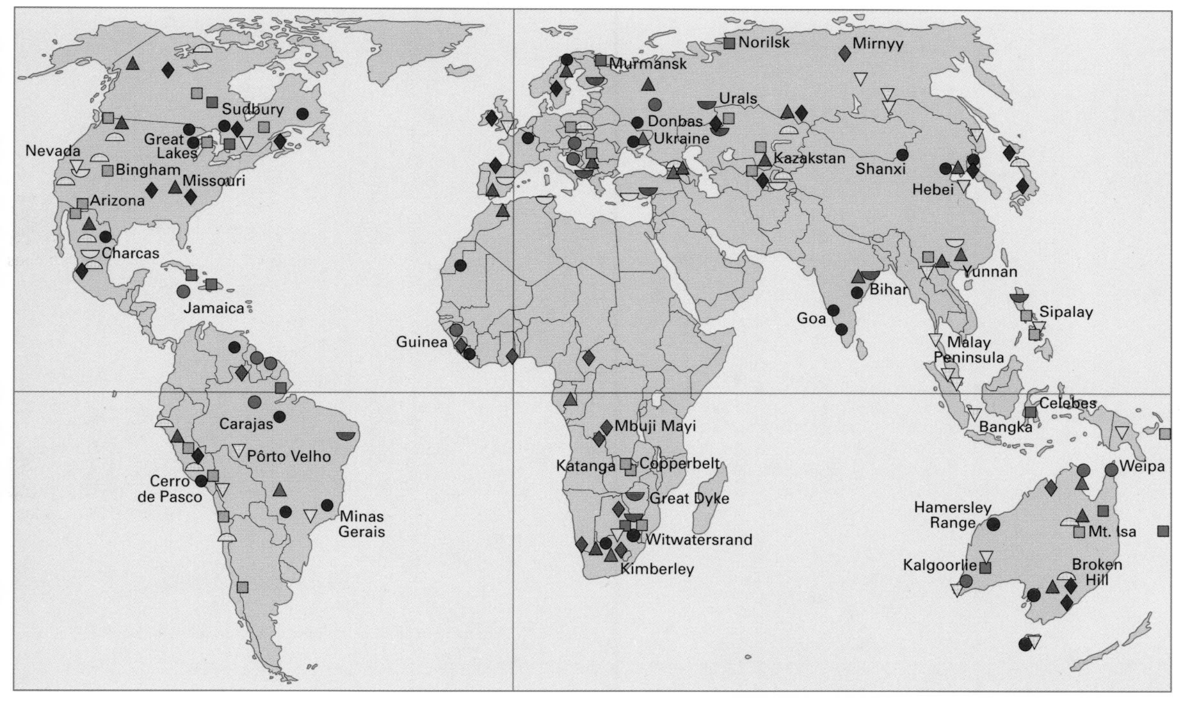

Mineral Distribution

The map shows the richest sources of the most important minerals. Major mineral locations are named.

Light metals
- Bauxite

Base metals
- Copper
- Lead
- Mercury
- Tin
- Zinc

Iron and ferro-alloys
- Iron
- Chrome
- Manganese
- Nickel

Precious metals
- Gold
- Silver

Precious stones
- Diamonds

The map does not show undersea deposits, most of which are considered inaccessible.

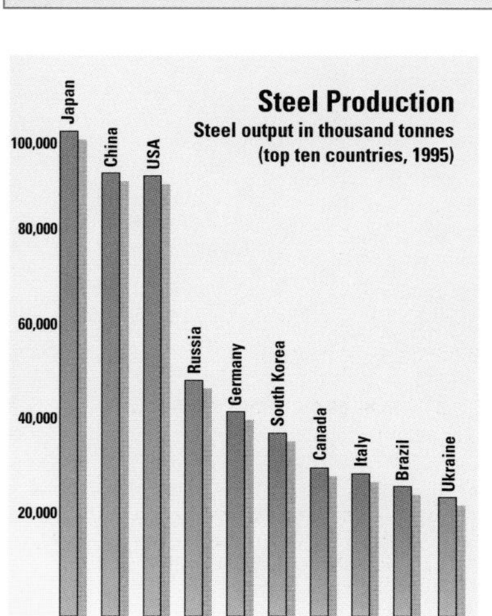

Steel Production
Steel output in thousand tonnes (top ten countries, 1995)
Japan, China, USA, Russia, Germany, South Korea, Canada, Italy, Brazil, Ukraine

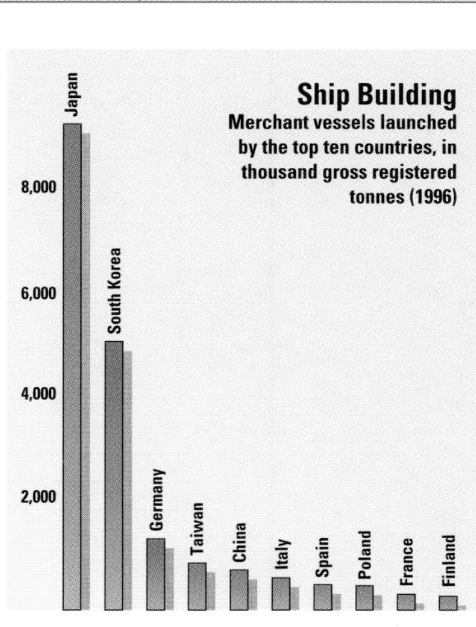

Ship Building
Merchant vessels launched by the top ten countries, in thousand gross registered tonnes (1996)
Japan, South Korea, Germany, Taiwan, China, Italy, Spain, Poland, France, Finland

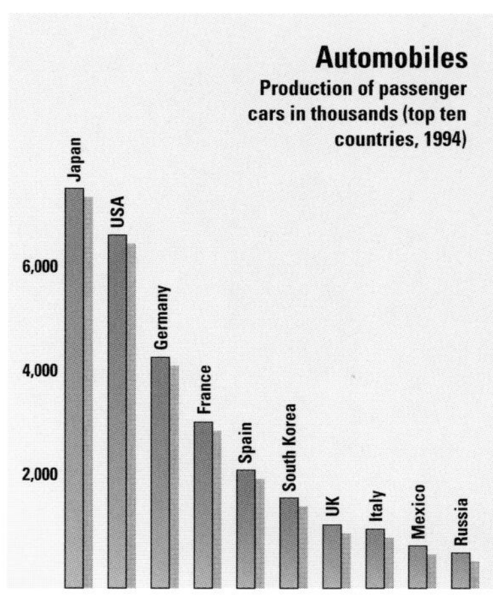

Automobiles
Production of passenger cars in thousands (top ten countries, 1994)
Japan, USA, Germany, France, Spain, South Korea, UK, Italy, Mexico, Russia

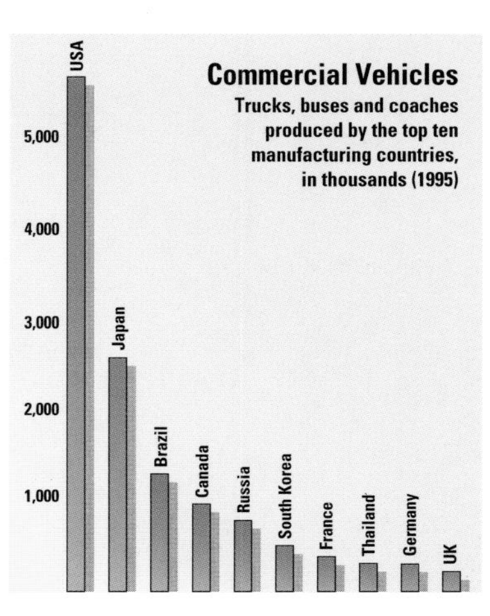

Commercial Vehicles
Trucks, buses and coaches produced by the top ten manufacturing countries, in thousands (1995)
USA, Japan, Brazil, Canada, Russia, South Korea, France, Thailand, Germany, UK

Trade

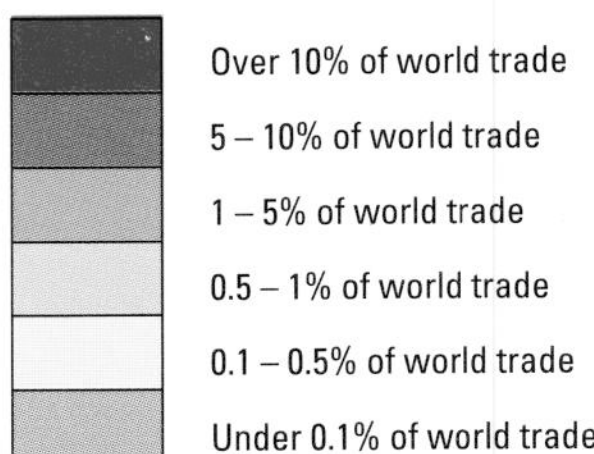

Share of World Trade

Percentage share of total world exports by value (1996)

- Over 10% of world trade
- 5 – 10% of world trade
- 1 – 5% of world trade
- 0.5 – 1% of world trade
- 0.1 – 0.5% of world trade
- Under 0.1% of world trade

International trade is dominated by a handful of powerful maritime nations. The members of 'G8', the inner circle of OECD (see page 19), and the top seven countries listed in the diagram below, account for more than half the total. The majority of nations – including all but four in Africa – contribute less than one quarter of 1% to the worldwide total of exports; the EU countries account for 40%, the Pacific Rim nations over 35%.

The Main Trading Nations

The imports and exports of the top ten trading nations as a percentage of world trade (1994). Each country's trade in manufactured goods is shown in dark blue.

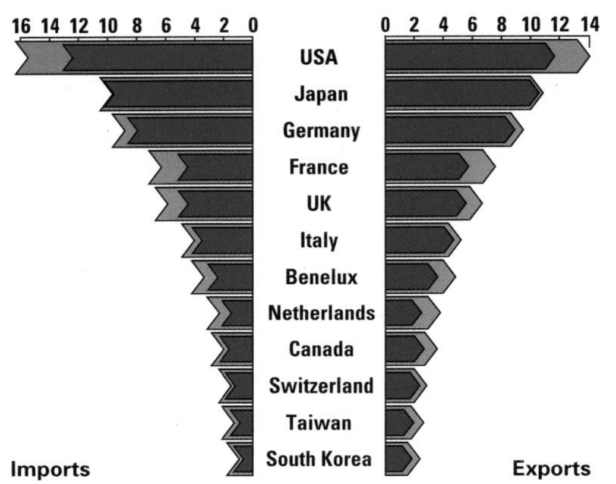

16 14 12 10 8 6 4 2 0   0 2 4 6 8 10 12 14

USA
Japan
Germany
France
UK
Italy
Benelux
Netherlands
Canada
Switzerland
Taiwan
South Korea

Imports   **Exports**

Patterns of Trade

Thriving international trade is the outward sign of a healthy world economy, the obvious indicator that some countries have goods to sell and others the means to buy them. Global exports expanded to an estimated US $3.92 trillion in 1994, an increase due partly to economic recovery in industrial nations but also to export-led growth strategies in many developing nations and lowered regional trade barriers. International trade remains dominated, however, by the rich, industrialized countries of the Organization for Economic Development: between them, OECD members account for almost 75% of world imports and exports in most years. However, continued rapid economic growth in some developing countries is altering global trade patterns. The 'tiger economies' of South-east Asia are particularly vibrant, averaging more than 8% growth between 1992 and 1994. The size of the largest trading economies means that imports and exports usually represent only a small percentage of their total wealth. In export-concious Japan, for example, trade in goods and services amounts to less than 18% of GDP. In poorer countries, trade – often in a single commodity – may amount to 50% of GDP.

Traded Products

Top ten manufactures traded, by value in billions of US $ (latest available year)

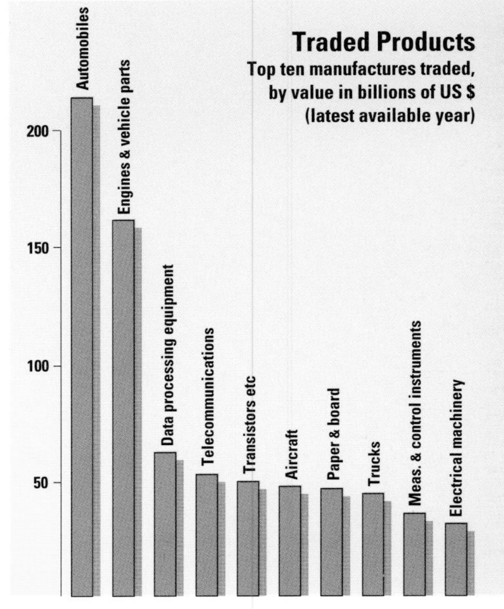

Automobiles · Engines & vehicle parts · Data processing equipment · Telecommunications · Transistors etc · Aircraft · Paper & board · Trucks · Meas. & control instruments · Electrical machinery

Balance of Trade

Value of exports in proportion to the value of imports (1995)

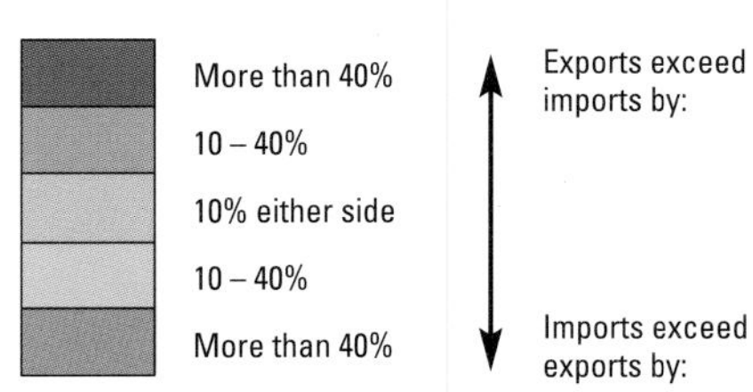

- More than 40%   Exports exceed imports by:
- 10 – 40%
- 10% either side
- 10 – 40%
- More than 40%   Imports exceed exports by:

The total world trade balance should amount to zero, since exports must equal imports on a global scale. In practice, at least $100 billion in exports go unrecorded, leaving the world with an apparent deficit and many countries in a better position than public accounting reveals. However, a favourable trade balance is not necessarily a sign of prosperity: many poorer countries must maintain a high surplus in order to service debts, and do so by restricting imports below the levels needed to sustain successful economies.

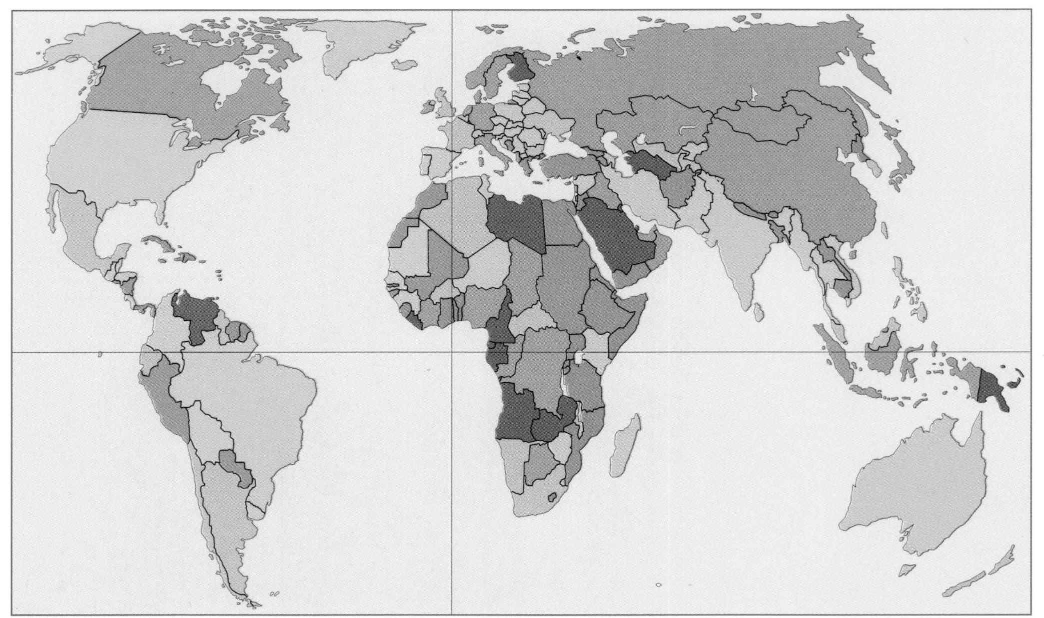

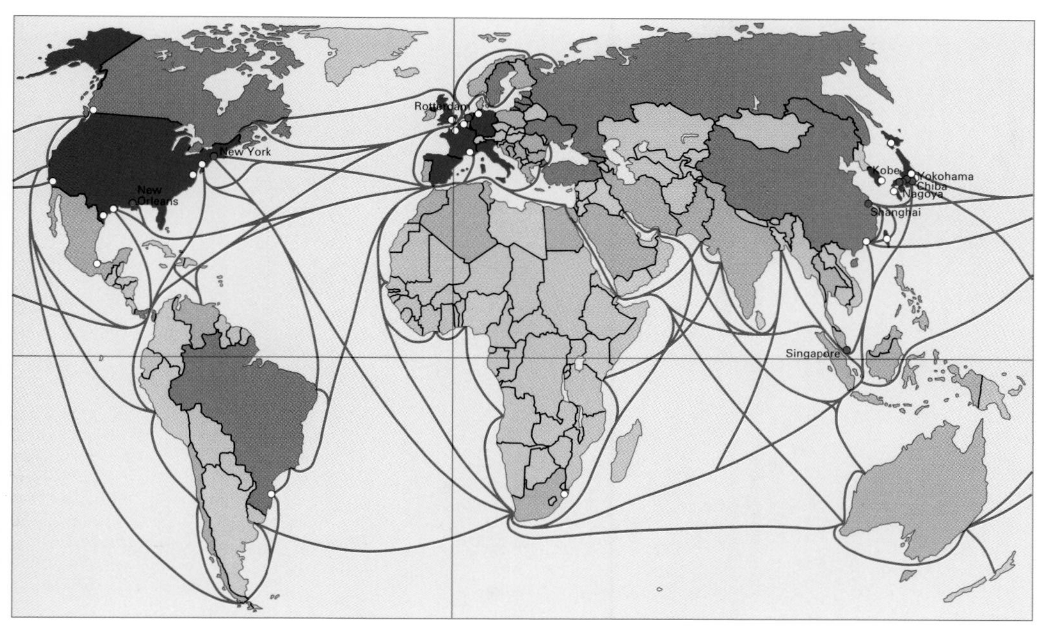

Seaborne Freight

Freight unloaded in millions of tonnes (latest available year)

- Over 100
- 50 – 100
- 10 – 50
- 5 – 10
- Under 5
- Landlocked countries

Major seaports

- ● Over 100 million tonnes per year
- ○ 50–100 million tonnes per year
- ▬ Major shipping routes

Cargoes

Type of seaborne freight

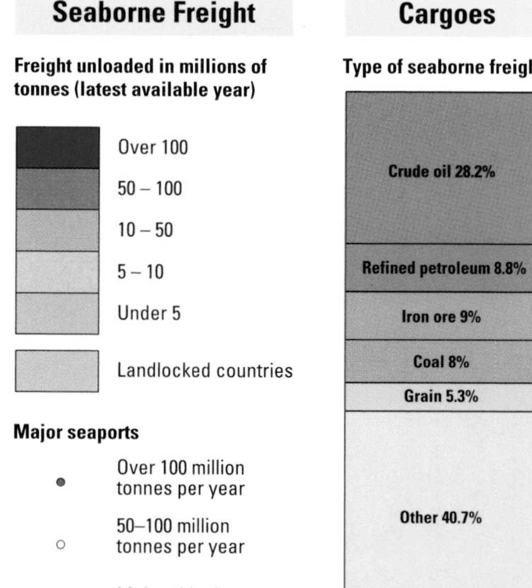

- Crude oil 28.2%
- Refined petroleum 8.8%
- Iron ore 9%
- Coal 8%
- Grain 5.3%
- Other 40.7%

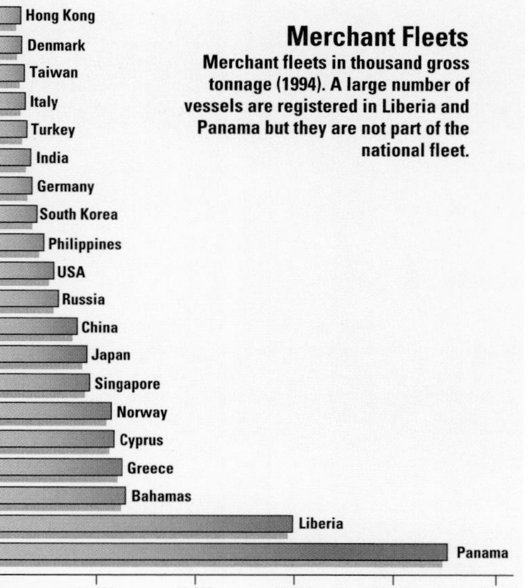

Merchant Fleets
Merchant fleets in thousand gross tonnage (1994). A large number of vessels are registered in Liberia and Panama but they are not part of the national fleet.

Hong Kong, Denmark, Taiwan, Italy, Turkey, India, Germany, South Korea, Philippines, USA, Russia, China, Japan, Singapore, Norway, Cyprus, Greece, Bahamas, Liberia, Panama

20,000 40,000 60,000 80,000 100,000

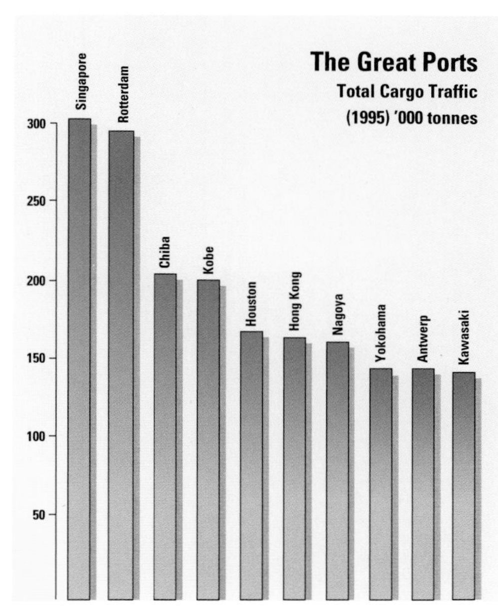

The Great Ports
Total Cargo Traffic (1995) '000 tonnes

Singapore, Rotterdam, Chiba, Kobe, Houston, Hong Kong, Nagoya, Yokohama, Antwerp, Kawasaki

50 100 150 200 250 300

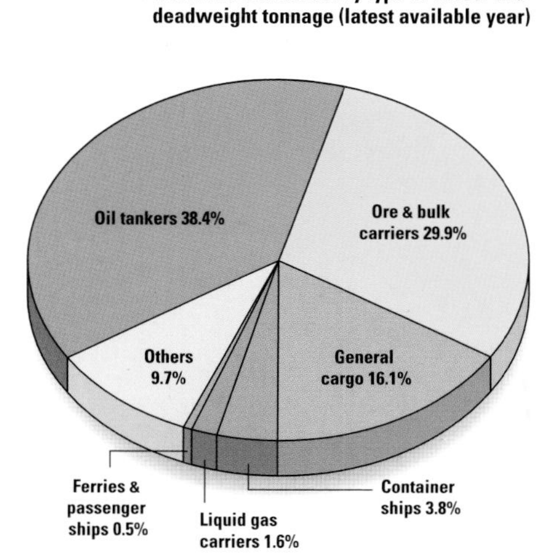

World Shipping
World merchant fleet by type of vessel and deadweight tonnage (latest available year)

- Oil tankers 38.4%
- Ore & bulk carriers 29.9%
- General cargo 16.1%
- Others 9.7%
- Ferries & passenger ships 0.5%
- Liquid gas carriers 1.6%
- Container ships 3.8%

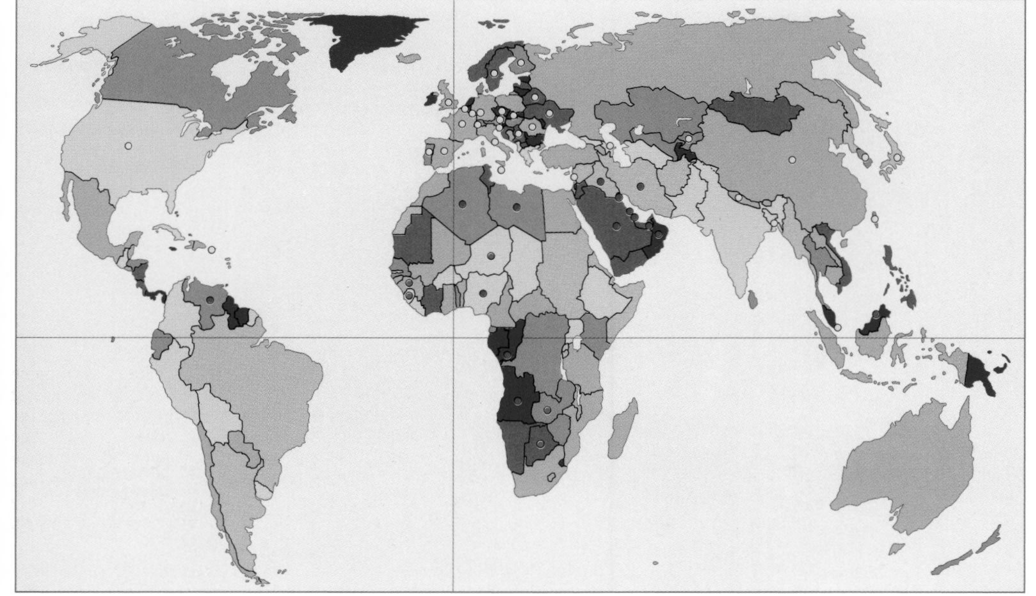

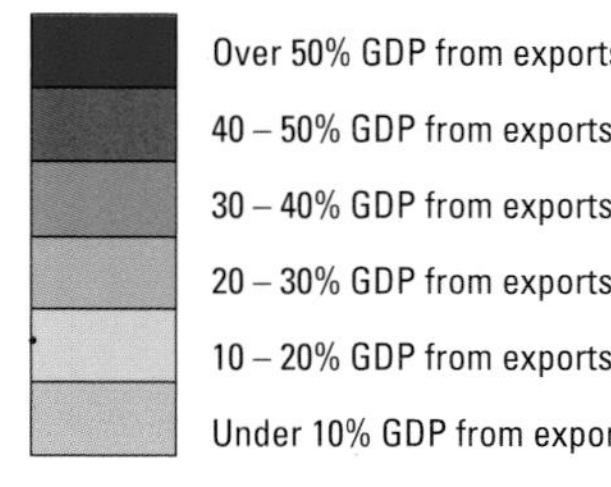

Dependence on Trade

Value of exports as a percentage of Gross Domestic Product (1997)

- Over 50% GDP from exports
- 40 – 50% GDP from exports
- 30 – 40% GDP from exports
- 20 – 30% GDP from exports
- 10 – 20% GDP from exports
- Under 10% GDP from exports

- ○ Most dependent on industrial exports (over 75% of total exports)
- ● Most dependent on fuel exports (over 75% of total exports)
- ● Most dependent on mineral and metal exports (over 75% of total exports)

Travel and Tourism

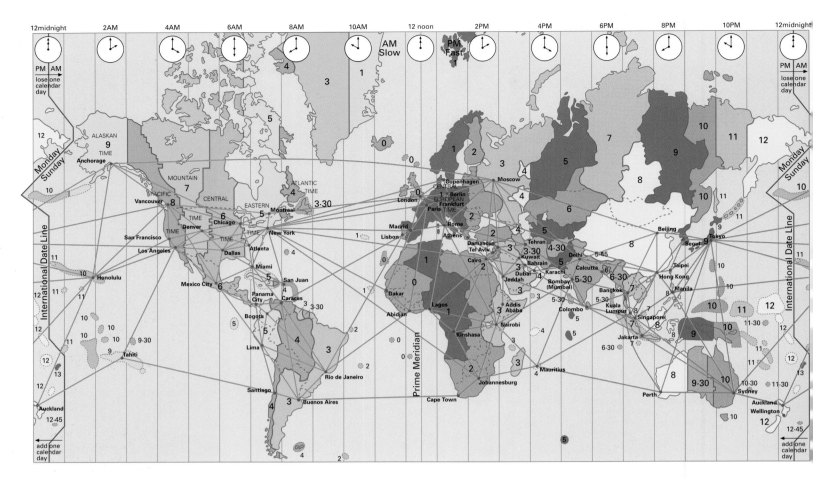

Time Zones

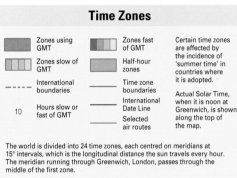

Zones using GMT	Zones fast of GMT
Zones slow of GMT	Half-hour zones
International boundaries (- - -)	Time zone boundaries
10 Hours slow or fast of GMT	International Date Line
	Selected air routes

Certain time zones are affected by the incidence of 'summer time' in countries where it is adopted.

Actual Solar Time, when it is noon at Greenwich, is shown along the top of the map.

The world is divided into 24 time zones, each centred on meridians at 15° intervals, which is the longitudinal distance the sun travels every hour. The meridian running through Greenwich, London, passes through the middle of the first zone.

Rail and Road: The Leading Nations

	Total rail network ('000 km) (1995)	Passenger km per head per year		Total road network ('000 km)		Vehicle km per head per year		Number of vehicles per km of roads	
1.	USA 235.7	Japan 2,017		USA 6,277.9		USA...................12,505		Hong Kong 284	
2.	Russia 87.4	Belarus 1,880		India 2,962.5		Luxembourg 7,989		Taiwan 211	
3.	India 62.7	Russia.................1,826		Brazil 1,824.4		Kuwait.................7,251		Singapore 152	
4.	China 54.6	Switzerland 1,769		Japan 1,130.9		France 7,142		Kuwait 140	
5.	Germany 41.7	Ukraine 1,456		China 1,041.1		Sweden 6,991		Brunei..................96	
6.	Australia 35.8	Austria 1,168		Russia 884.0		Germany 6,806		Italy.....................91	
7.	Argentina 34.2	France 1,011		Canada.................849.4		Denmark 6,764		Israel...................87	
8.	France 31.9	Netherlands 994		France 811.6		Austria 6,518		Thailand 73	
9.	Mexico................26.5	Latvia 918		Australia 810.3		Netherlands 5,984		Ukraine 73	
10.	South Africa.........26.3	Denmark 884		Germany 636.3		UK 5,738		UK 67	
11.	Poland 24.9	Slovak Rep. 862		Romania.................461.9		Canada 5,493		Netherlands 66	
12.	Ukraine 22.6	Romania 851		Turkey 388.1		Italy.....................4,852		Germany 62	

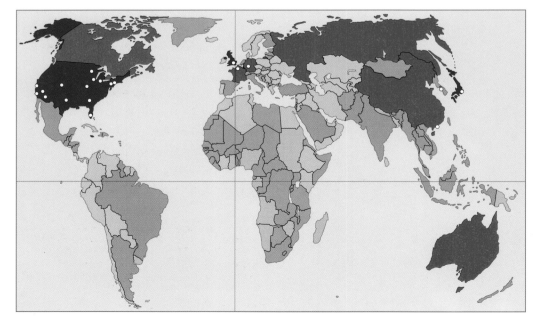

Air Travel

Passenger kilometres (the number of passengers – international and domestic – multiplied by the distance flown by each passenger from the airport of origin) (1996)

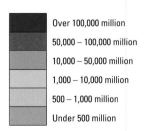

	Over 100,000 million
	50,000 – 100,000 million
	10,000 – 50,000 million
	1,000 – 10,000 million
	500 – 1,000 million
	Under 500 million

○ Major airports (handling over 25 million passengers in 1995)

World's busiest airports (total passengers)
1. Chicago   (O'Hare)
2. Atlanta   (Hatsfield)
3. Dallas   (Dallas/Ft Worth)
4. Los Angeles   (Intern'l)
5. London   (Heathrow)

World's busiest airports (international passengers)
1. London   (Heathrow)
2. London   (Gatwick)
3. Frankfurt   (International)
4. New York   (Kennedy)
5. Paris   (De Gaulle)

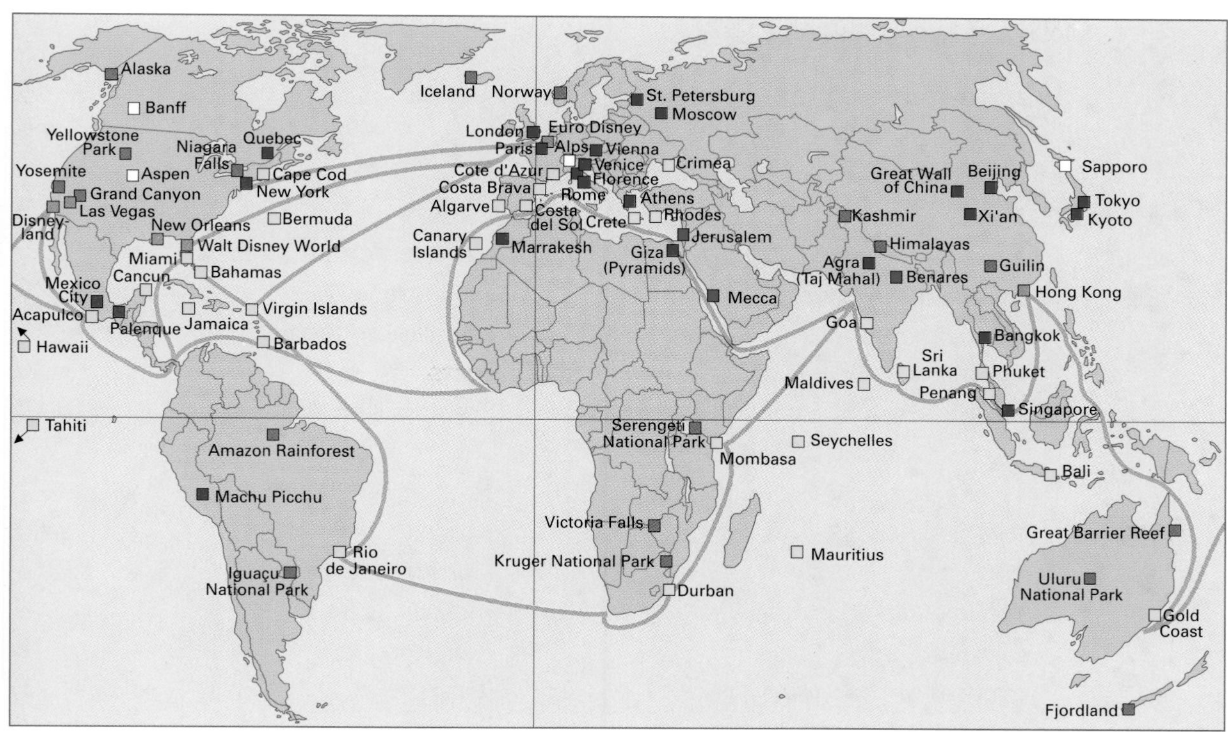

Destinations

- ◼ Cultural and historical centres
- ◻ Coastal resorts
- ◻ Ski resorts
- ◼ Centres of entertainment
- ◼ Places of pilgrimage
- ◼ Places of great natural beauty
- —— Popular holiday cruise routes

Visitors to the USA

Overseas travellers to the USA, thousands (1997 estimates)

1.	Canada	13,900
2.	Mexico	12,370
3.	Japan	4,640
4.	UK	3,350
5.	Germany	1,990
6.	France	1,030
7.	Taiwan	885
8.	Venezuela	860
9.	South Korea	800
10.	Brazil	785

In 1996, the USA earned the most from tourism, with receipts of more than US $75 billion.

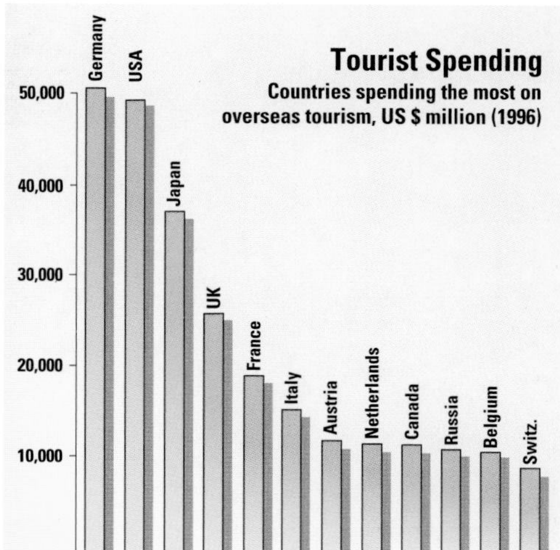

Tourist Spending
Countries spending the most on overseas tourism, US $ million (1996)

Importance of Tourism

		Arrivals from abroad (1996)	% of world total (1996)
1.	France	66,800,000	10.2%
2.	USA	49,038,000	7.5%
3.	Spain	43,403,000	6.6%
4.	Italy	34,087,000	5.2%
5.	UK	25,960,000	3.9%
6.	China	23,770,000	3.6%
7.	Poland	19,514,000	3.0%
8.	Mexico	18,667,000	2.9%
9.	Canada	17,610,000	2.7%
10.	Czech Republic	17,400,000	2.7%
11.	Hungary	17,248,000	2.6%
12.	Austria	16,642,000	2.5%

In 1996, there was a 4.6% rise, to 593 million, in the total number of people travelling abroad. Small economies in attractive areas are often completely dominated by tourism: in some West Indian islands, for example, tourist spending provides over 90% of total income.

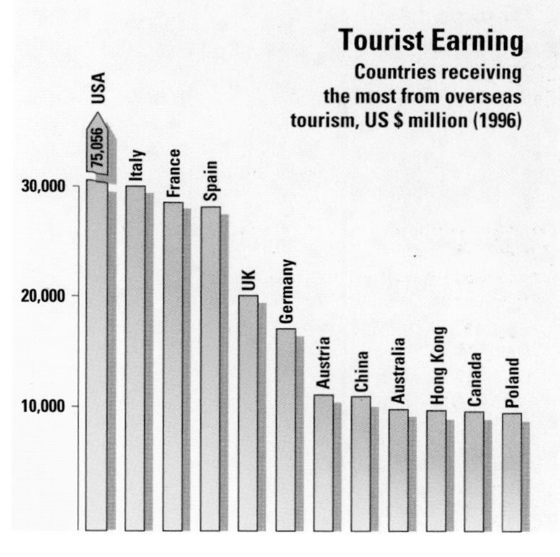

Tourist Earning
Countries receiving the most from overseas tourism, US $ million (1996)

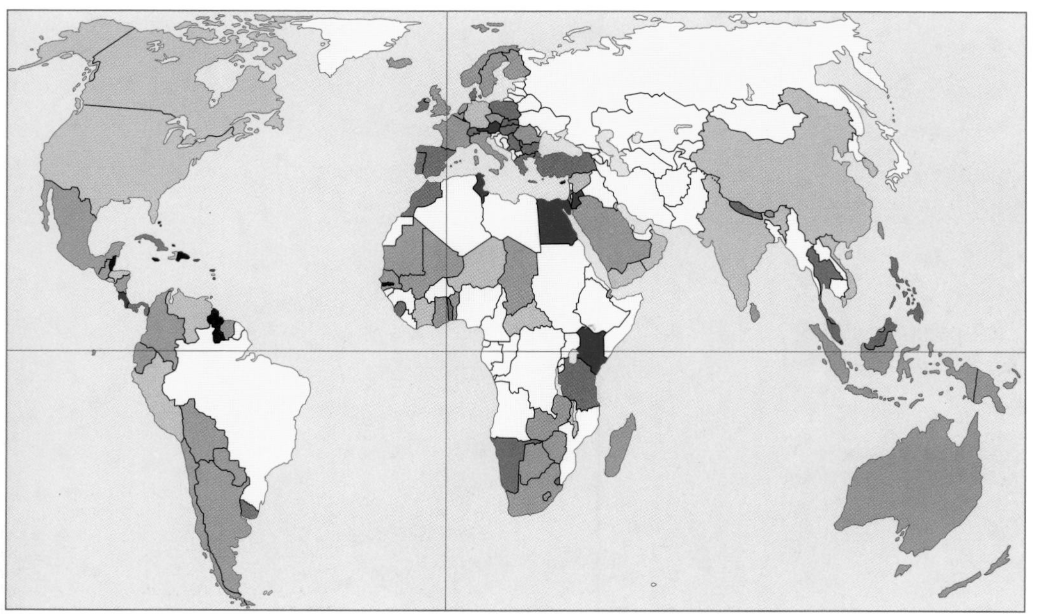

Tourism

Tourism receipts as a percentage of Gross National Product (1994)

- ◼ Over 10% of GNP from tourism
- ◼ 5 – 10% of GNP from tourism
- ◼ 2.5 – 5% of GNP from tourism
- ◼ 1 – 2.5% of GNP from tourism
- ◻ 0.5 – 1% of GNP from tourism
- ◻ Under 0.5% of GNP from tourism

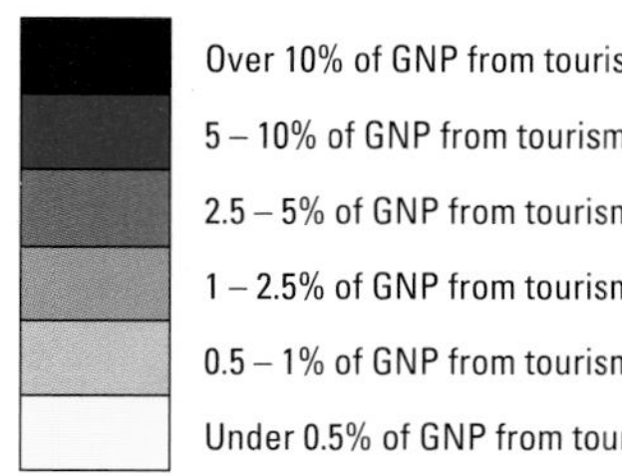

Countries spending the most on promoting tourism, millions of US $ (1996)		Fastest growing tourist destinations, % change in receipts (1994–5)	
Australia	88	South Korea	49%
Spain	79	Czech Republic	27%
UK	79	India	21%
France	73	Russia	19%
Singapore	54	Philippines	18%

CARTOGRAPHY BY PHILIP'S. COPYRIGHT GEORGE PHILIP LTD

31

The World In Focus: Index

WORLD MAPS

SETTLEMENTS

◼ PARIS   ◼ Berne   ◉ Livorno   ◎ Brugge   ◎ Algeciras   ○ *Frejus*   ○ Oberammergau   ○ Thira

Settlement symbols and type styles vary according to the scale of each map and indicate the importance
of towns on the map rather than specific population figures

∴ Ruins or Archæological Sites   Wells in Desert

ADMINISTRATION

―――― International Boundaries

----- International Boundaries
(Undefined or Disputed)

············ Internal Boundaries

National Parks

Country Names
NICARAGUA

Administrative
Area Names

KENT

CALABRIA

International boundaries show the *de facto* situation where there are rival claims to territory

COMMUNICATIONS

―――― Principal Roads

〰 Other Roads

⊣---⊢ Road Tunnels

⨝ Passes

⊕ Airfields

―――― Principal Railways

---- Railways
Under Construction

―― Other Railways

⊣---⊢ Railway Tunnels

········· Principal Canals

PHYSICAL FEATURES

〰 Perennial Streams

--- Intermittent Streams

⬭ Perennial Lakes

⬭ Intermittent Lakes

Swamps and Marshes

Permanent Ice
and Glaciers

▲ 8848 Elevations in metres

▼ 8500 Sea Depths in metres

1134 Height of Lake Surface
Above Sea Level in metres

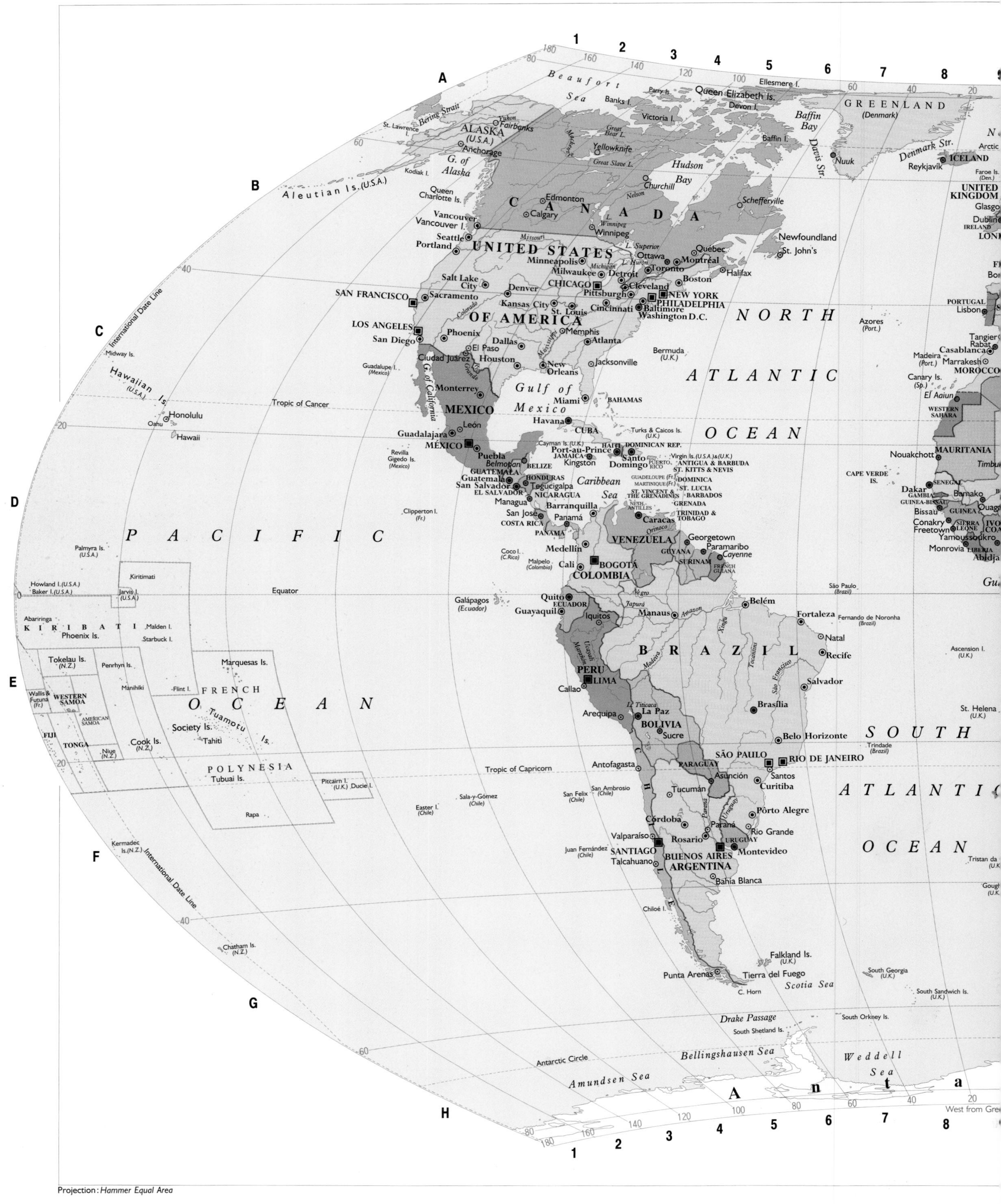

Projection: *Hammer Equal Area*

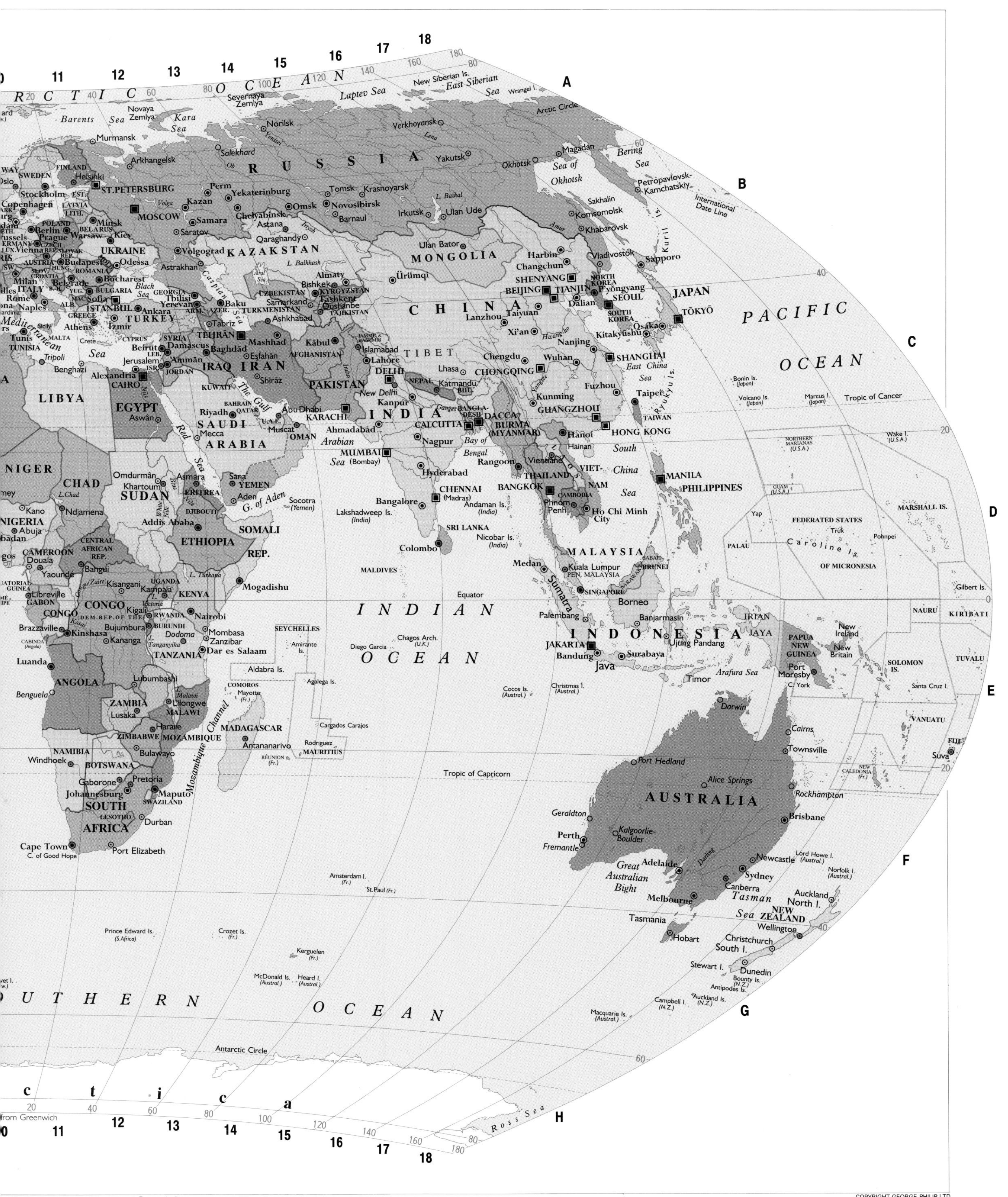

ARCTIC   OCEAN

A

Barents Sea   Novaya Zemlya   *Kara Sea*   Severnaya Zemlya   New Siberian Is.   *Laptev Sea*   *East Siberian Sea*   Wrangel I.   Arctic Circle

WAY   SWEDEN   FINLAND   Helsinki   Murmansk   Arkhangelsk   Salekhard   Norilsk   *Ob*   *Yenisey*   Verkhoyansk   *Lena*   Yakutsk   Magadan   Bering Sea   B

Oslo   Stockholm   EST.   ST.PETERSBURG   Perm   Yekaterinburg   Tomsk   Krasnoyarsk   L. Baikal   Irkutsk   Okhotsk   Sea of Okhotsk   Petropavlovsk-Kamchatskiy   International Date Line

Copenhagen   LATVIA   MOSCOW   Kazan   Chelyabinsk   Omsk   Novosibirsk   Ulan Ude   Sakhalin   Komsomolsk   60

ARK   Berlin   LITH.   Minsk   *Volga*   Samara   *Irtysh*   Barnaul   *Amur*   Khabarovsk   Kuril

am   POLAND   BELARUS   Saratov   Astana   Vladivostok   Sapporo

THE   GERMANY   Warsaw   UKRAINE   Volgograd   KAZAKSTAN   Ulan Bator   Harbin   Changchun   NORTH KOREA   40

LUX.   Vienna   Prague   Budapest   Odessa   Astrakhan   *L. Balkhash*   MONGOLIA   SHENYANG   Pyongyang   SEOUL   JAPAN

AUSTRIA   HUNG.   ROMANIA   *Caspian Sea*   Ürümqi   BEIJING   TIANJIN   SOUTH KOREA   Ōsaka   TŌKYŌ   PACIFIC

Milan   Belgrade   BULGARIA   *Black Sea*   GEORGIA   Baku   UZBEKISTAN   Bishkek   KYRGYZSTAN   Almaty   Dalian   Kitakyūshū

Rome   CROATIA   Sofia   Tbilisi   Yerevan   Samarkand   Tashkent   CHINA   Lanzhou   Taiyuan   OCEAN

na   ITALY   YUG.   Istanbul   ARM.   AZER.   TURKMENISTAN   Dushanbe   TAJIKISTAN   Xi'an   Nanjing   C

iles   ALB.   GREECE   Ankara   TURKEY   Izmir   Ashkhabad   *Huang He*   SHANGHAI   *East China Sea*   Bonin Is. (Japan)

Mediterranean   Athens   CYPRUS   SYRIA   TEHRĀN   Mashhad   Kābul   TIBET   Chengdu   Wuhan   CHONGQING   Taipei   Volcano Is. (Japan)   Marcus I. (Japan)   Tropic of Cancer

Tunis   MALTA   Crete   Beirut   Damascus   Baghdād   AFGHANISTAN   Islamabad   Lhasa   NEPAL   Kunming   GUANGZHOU   TAIWAN   Wake I. (U.S.A.)   20

TUNISIA   *Sea*   Jerusalem   LEB.   JORDAN   IRAQ   IRAN   Eşfahān   Lahore   DELHI   Katmandu   BHU.   Fuzhou   HONG KONG   Ryukyus

LIBYA   Alexandria   ISR.   Ammān   Shīrāz   PAKISTAN   New Delhi   BANGLA-DESH   DACCA   NORTHERN MARIANAS (U.S.A.)

CAIRO   KUWAIT   *The Gulf*   Karachi   INDIA   *Ganges*   CALCUTTA   BURMA (MYANMAR)   Hanoi   South China Sea

EGYPT   Aswân   BAHRAIN   QATAR   Abu Dhabi   Kanpur   Hainan   D

Riyadh   U.A.E.   Muscat   Ahmadabad   Nagpur   *Bay of Bengal*   Rangoon   VIET-   MANILA   PHILIPPINES   GUAM (U.S.A.)

NIGER   Mecca   SAUDI   OMAN   MUMBAI (Bombay)   *Arabian*   Hyderabad   THAILAND   NAM   *Sea*   FEDERATED STATES   MARSHALL IS.

CHAD   Omdurmân   ARABIA   *Sea*   BANGKOK   CAMBODIA   Yap   Truk   Pohnpei

Kano   Khartoum   Sana'   YEMEN   CHENNAI (Madras)   Andaman Is. (India)   Phnom   Ho Chi Minh   PALAU   *Caroline Is.*   OF MICRONESIA

NIGERIA   Ndjamena   SUDAN   Asmara   ERITREA   Aden   *G. of Aden*   Bangalore   Penh   City   Gilbert I.

Abuja   DJIBOUTI   Socotra (Yemen)   Lakshadweep Is. (India)   SRI LANKA   Nicobar Is. (India)   MALAYSIA   NAURU   KIRIBATI

adan   CAMEROON   Douala   CENTRAL AFRICAN REP.   ETHIOPIA   SOMALI REP.   Colombo   Medan   Kuala Lumpur   SABAH   BRUNEI

gos   Yaounde   Bangui   UGANDA   *L. Turkana*   MALDIVES   PEN. MALAYSIA   IRIAN   New Ireland

TORIAL   Libreville   GABON   Kisangani   Kampala   KENYA   Equator   SINGAPORE   Borneo   JAYA   PAPUA NEW GUINEA   New Britain   SOLOMON IS.   E

NEA   CONGO   DEM.REP.OF THE   Kigali   RWANDA   Nairobi   *INDIAN*   Palembang   Banjarmasin   Port Moresby   Santa Cruz I.

PF   Brazzaville   CONGO   Bujumbura   BURUNDI   Dodoma   Mombasa   SEYCHELLES   *Sumatra*   INDONESIA   C. York   TUVALU

CABINDA (Angola)   Kinshasa   Kananga   TANZANIA   Zanzibar   Dar es Salaam   Amirante Is.   Chagos Arch. (U.K.)   *OCEAN*   JAKARTA   Ujung Pandang   VANUATU

Luanda   Diego Garcia   Bandung   Surabaya   *Arafura Sea*   NEW CALEDONIA (Fr.)   FIJI

ANGOLA   Lubumbashi   COMOROS   Aldabra Is.   Agalega Is. (Fr.)   *Java*   Timor   Darwin   Suva

Benguela   ZAMBIA   Malawi   MALAWI   MADAGASCAR   Cargados Carajos   Cocos Is. (Austral.)   Christmas I. (Austral.)   Cairns   20

Lusaka   Lilongwe   Antananarivo   Rodriguez I.   MAURITIUS   Townsville

ZIMBABWE   MOZAMBIQUE   RÉUNION (Fr.)   Port Hedland   Tropic of Capricorn

NAMIBIA   Harare   Bulawayo   *Mozambique Channel*   Alice Springs   Rockhampton

Windhoek   BOTSWANA   Gaborone   Pretoria   *Tropic of Capricorn*   Geraldton   AUSTRALIA   Brisbane   F

Johannesburg   SWAZILAND   Maputo   Amsterdam I. (Fr.)   Prince Edward Is. (S.Africa)   Perth   Kalgoorlie-Boulder   *Great Australian Bight*   Adelaide   Sydney   Lord Howe I. (Austral.)

SOUTH   LESOTHO   Durban   St.Paul (Fr.)   Fremantle   Canberra   Newcastle   Norfolk I. (Austral.)

AFRICA   Cape Town   Port Elizabeth   Crozet Is. (Fr.)   Melbourne   *Tasman*   Auckland   North I.

C. of Good Hope   *Sea*   NEW ZEALAND

Kerguelen (Fr.)   McDonald Is. (Austral.)   Heard I. (Austral)   Tasmania   Hobart   Christchurch   South I.   Wellington   40

SOUTHERN   OCEAN   Stewart I.   Dunedin

vet I.   Bounty Is. (N.Z.)   Antipodes Is. (N.Z.)

N.Z.)   Campbell I. (N.Z.)   Auckland Is. (N.Z.)   G

Macquarie Is. (Austral.)

Antarctic Circle   Ross Sea   H

Hanoi ⊙ Capital Cities

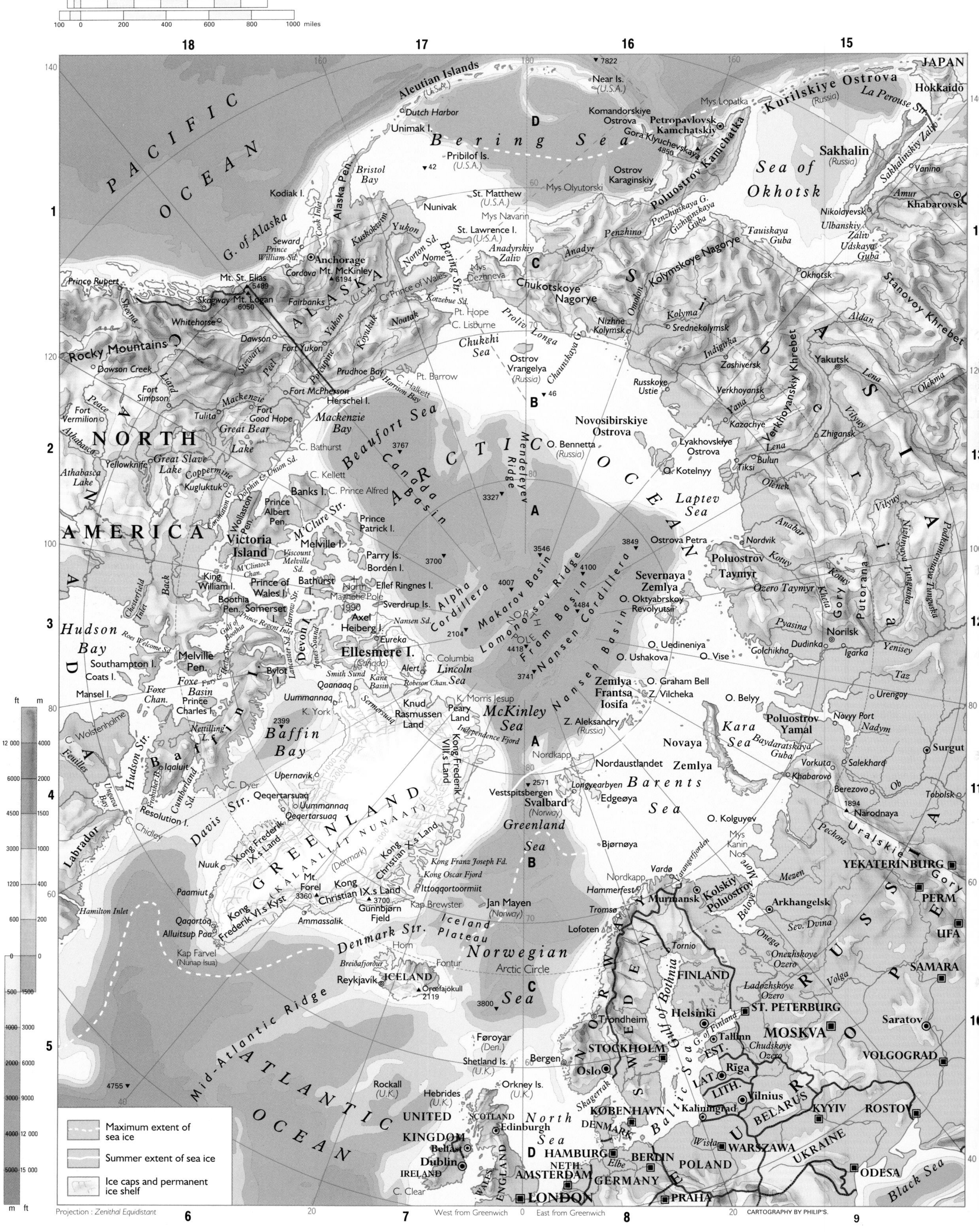

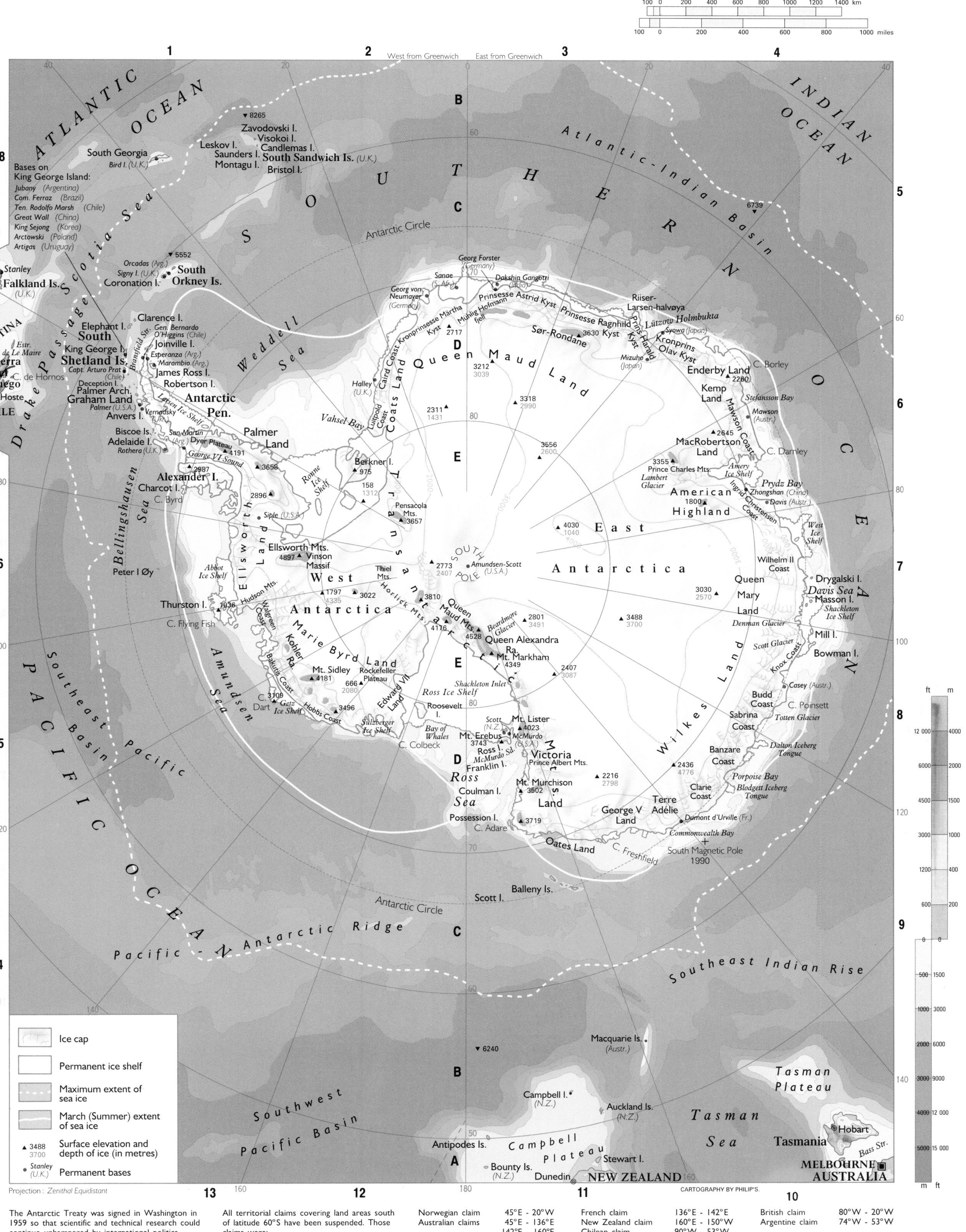

Projection : Zenithal Equidistant

▱	Ice cap
▱	Permanent ice shelf
▱	Maximum extent of sea ice
▱	March (Summer) extent of sea ice
▲ 3488 / 3700	Surface elevation and depth of ice (in metres)
● Stanley (U.K.)	Permanent bases

The Antarctic Treaty was signed in Washington in 1959 so that scientific and technical research could continue unhampered by international politics.

All territorial claims covering land areas south of latitude 60°S have been suspended. Those claims were:

Norwegian claim	45°E – 20°W
Australian claims	45°E – 136°E
	142°E – 160°E
French claim	136°E – 142°E
New Zealand claim	160°E – 150°W
Chilean claim	90°W – 53°W
British claim	80°W – 20°W
Argentine claim	74°W – 53°W

Bases on King George Island:
Jubany (Argentina)
Com. Ferraz (Brazil)
Ten. Rodolfo Marsh (Chile)
Great Wall (China)
King Sejong (Korea)
Arctowski (Poland)
Artigas (Uruguay)

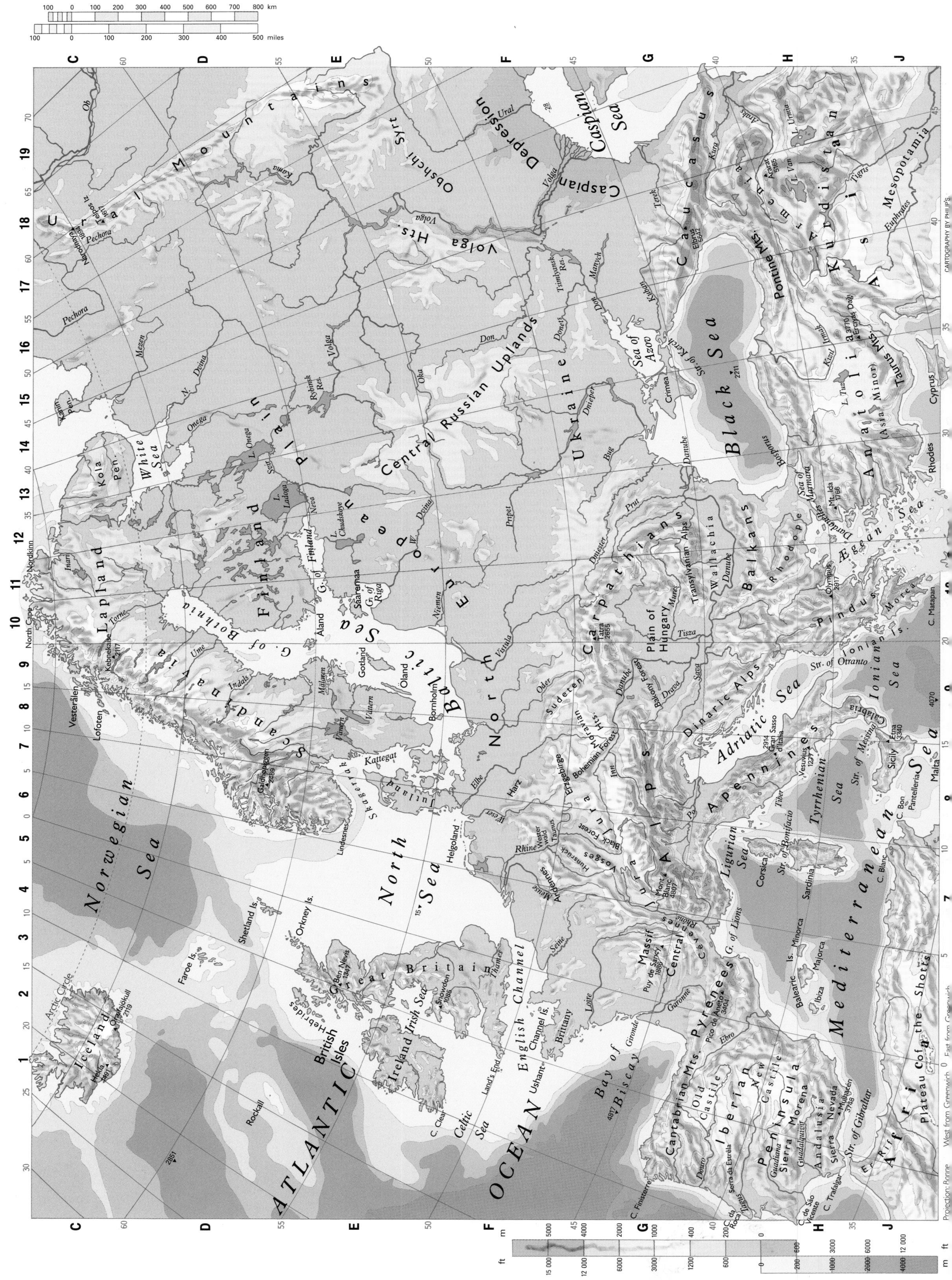

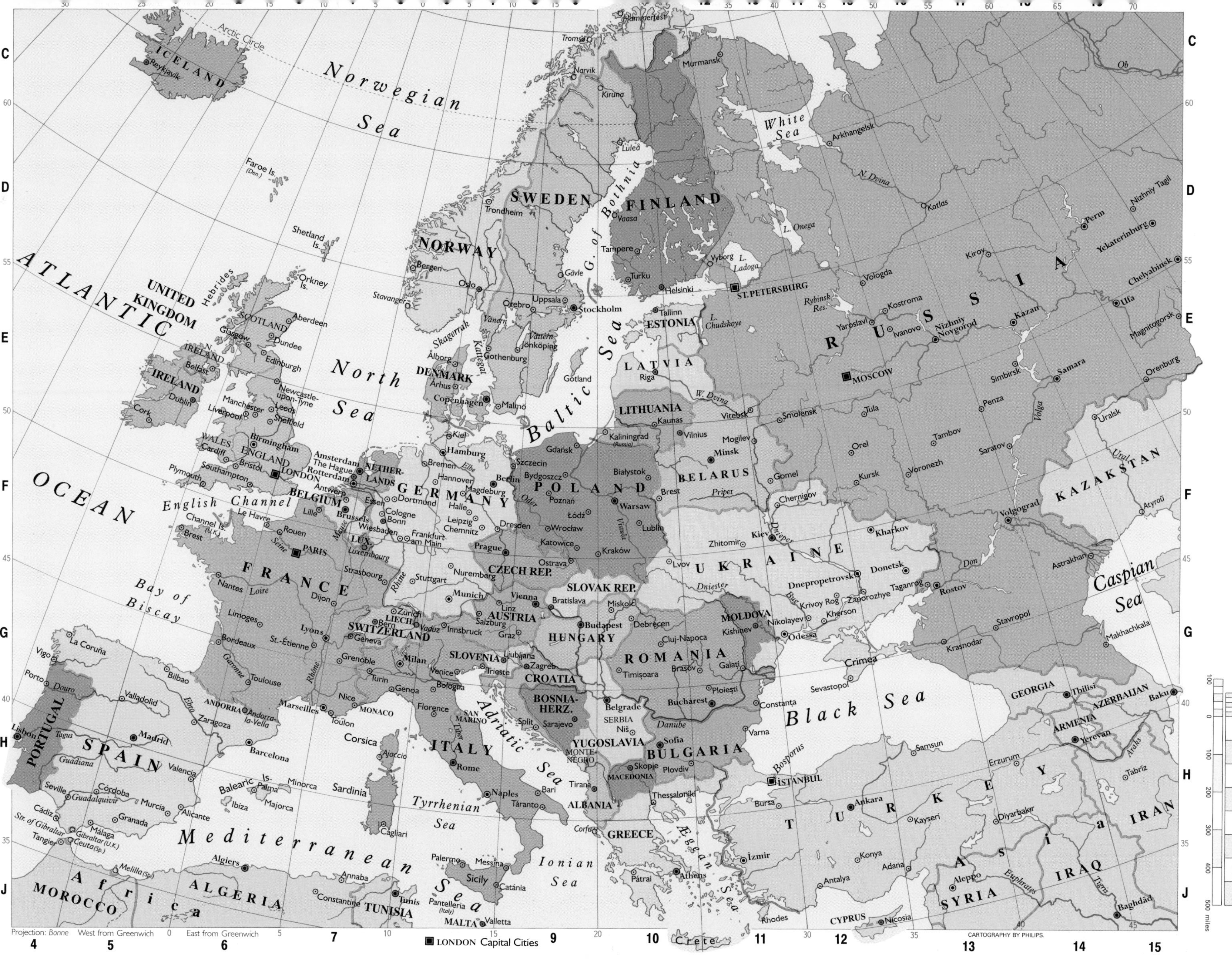
100 0 100 200 300 400 500 600 700 800 km
100 0 100 200 300 400 500 miles
ICELAND
Reykjavík
Arctic Circle
Norwegian Sea
Faroe Is. (Den.)
Shetland Is.
Orkney Is.
Hebrides
UNITED KINGDOM
SCOTLAND
ENGLAND
WALES
N. IRELAND
IRELAND
LONDON
ATLANTIC
OCEAN
North Sea
English Channel
Channel Is. (U.K.)
Bay of Biscay
NORWAY
SWEDEN
FINLAND
DENMARK
ESTONIA
LATVIA
LITHUANIA
BELARUS
RUSSIA
UKRAINE
MOLDOVA
POLAND
GERMANY
NETHER-LANDS
BELGIUM
LUX.
FRANCE
SWITZERLAND
LIECH.
AUSTRIA
CZECH REP.
SLOVAK REP.
HUNGARY
ROMANIA
SLOVENIA
CROATIA
BOSNIA-HERZ.
YUGOSLAVIA
SERBIA
MONTE-NEGRO
MACEDONIA
ALBANIA
BULGARIA
GREECE
TURKEY
CYPRUS
SYRIA
IRAQ
IRAN
GEORGIA
ARMENIA
AZERBAIJAN
KAZAKSTAN
ITALY
SAN MARINO
MALTA
MONACO
ANDORRA
SPAIN
PORTUGAL
MOROCCO
ALGERIA
TUNISIA
Africa
Asia
Baltic Sea
G. of Bothnia
White Sea
Kattegat
Skagerrak
Black Sea
Caspian Sea
Adriatic Sea
Tyrrhenian Sea
Ionian Sea
Ægean Sea
Mediterranean Sea
Bosporus
Crete
Corsica
Sardinia
Sicily
Balearic Is.
Str. of Gibraltar
MOSCOW
ST. PETERSBURG
PARIS
Volga
Danube
Dnieper
Vistula
Rhine
Rhône
Loire
Seine
Ebro
Tagus
Douro
Projection: Bonne
West from Greenwich
East from Greenwich
■ LONDON Capital Cities
CARTOGRAPHY BY PHILIPS

SCANDINAVIA 1:5 000 000

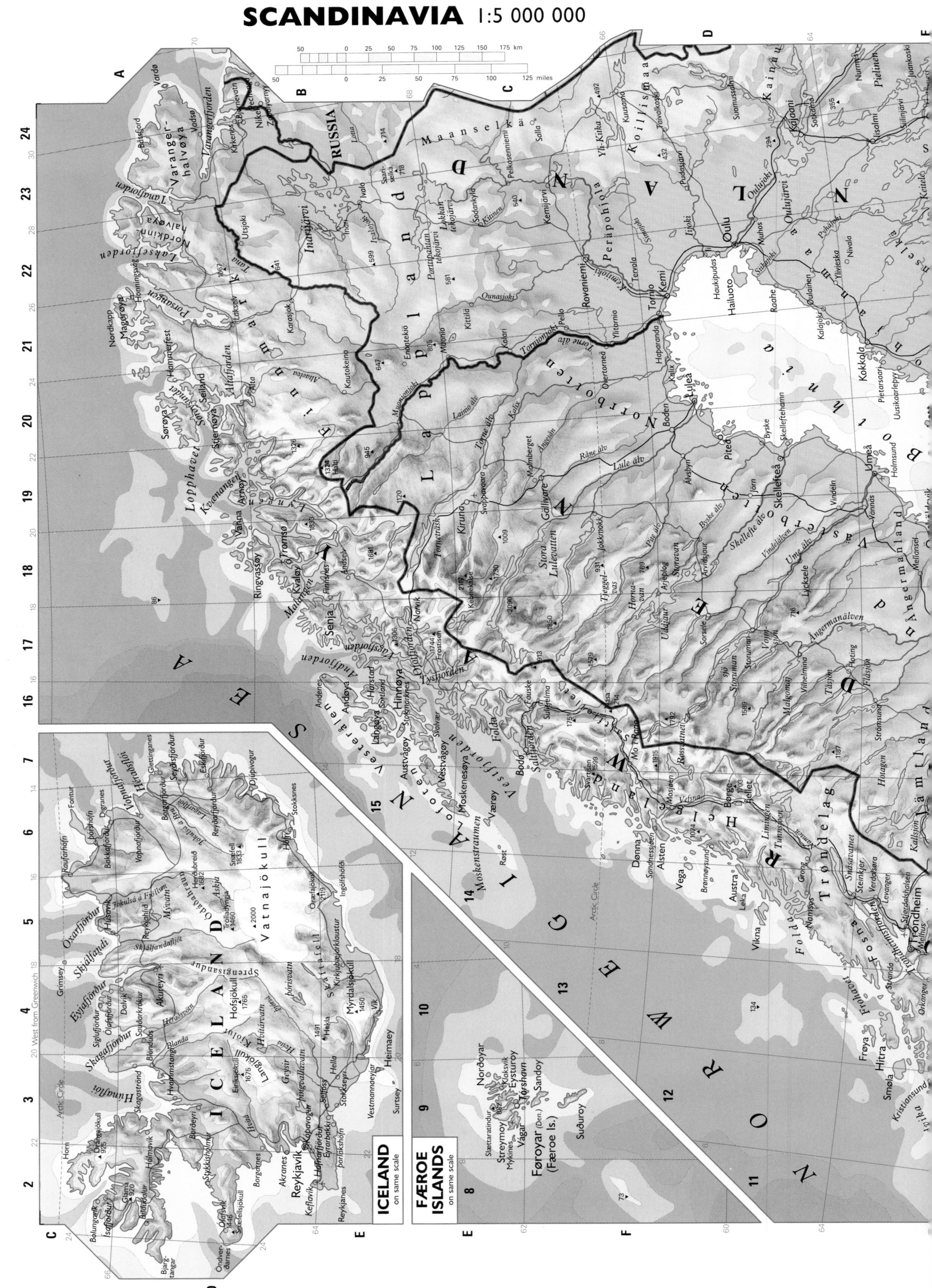

50 0 25 50 75 100 125 150 175 km
50 0 25 50 75 100 125 miles

ICELAND
on same scale

FÆROE ISLANDS
on same scale

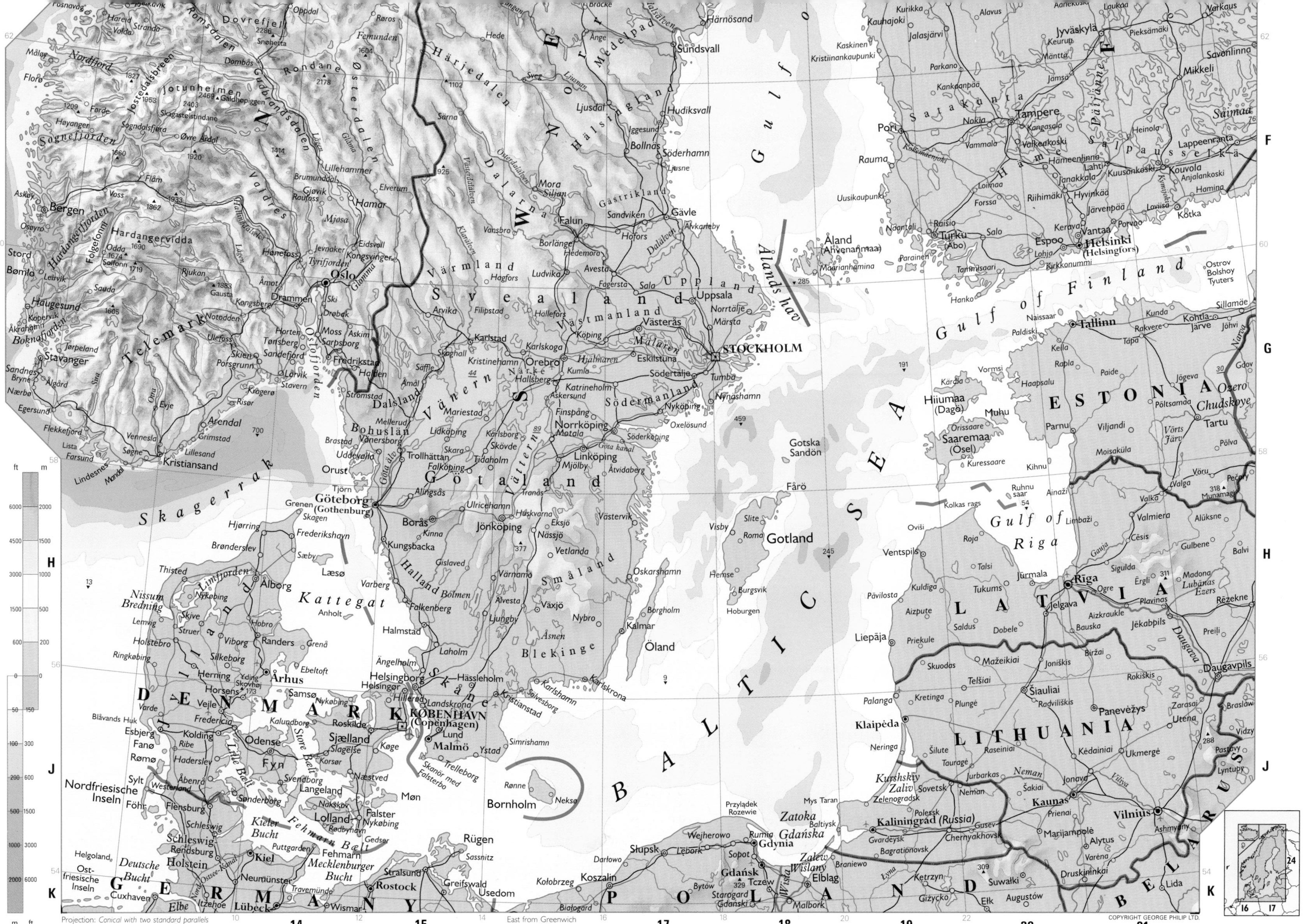

Suomi

Lappland

P a u s s e l k ä

F i n l a n d

Jyväskylä
Mikkeli
Savonlinna
Lappeenranta
Kouvola
Tampere
Nokia
Pori
Rauma
Uusikaupunki
Turku (Åbo)
Helsinki (Helsingfors)
Espoo
Vantaa
Porvoo
Kotka

Gulf of Finland

Åland (Ahvenanmaa)

Ålands hav

E S T O N I A
Tallinn
Tartu
Pärnu
Narva
Ozero Chudskoye

Hiiumaa (Dagö)
Saaremaa (Ösel)

Gulf of Riga

L A T V I A
Riga
Jelgava
Daugavpils
Liepāja
Ventspils
Daugava

L I T H U A N I A
Vilnius
Kaunas
Panevėžys
Šiauliai
Klaipėda
Kaliningrad (Russia)

B A L T I C   S E A

Gotland
Visby
Öland
Gotska Sandön
Fårö

S W E D E N
Stockholm
Uppsala
Västerås
Eskilstuna
Norrköping
Linköping
Örebro
Gävle
Sundsvall
Härnösand
Falun
Borlänge
Karlstad
Jönköping
Göteborg (Gothenburg)
Borås
Halmstad
Helsingborg
Malmö
Kalmar
Karlskrona
Kristianstad

Dalarna
Värmland
Svealand
Götaland
Småland
Blekinge
Skåne
Halland
Bohuslän
Dalsland
Västergötland
Östergötland
Södermanland
Västmanland
Uppland
Norrland

Vänern
Vättern

Kattegat
Skagerrak

N O R W A Y
Oslo
Bergen
Stavanger
Kristiansand
Drammen
Tønsberg
Sandefjord
Arendal
Hamar
Lillehammer
Oslofjorden

Dovrefjell
Jotunheimen
Hardangervidda
Gudbrandsdalen
Østerdalen

Bornholm
Rønne
Nexø

D E N M A R K
København (Copenhagen)
Århus
Ålborg
Odense
Esbjerg
Randers
Kolding
Vejle
Horsens
Fyn
Sjælland
Lolland
Falster
Langeland

Little Bælt
Store Bælt

G E R M A N Y
Kiel
Lübeck
Rostock
Flensburg
Schleswig
Holstein
Rügen
Usedom
Mecklenburger Bucht
Deutsche Bucht
Nordfriesische Inseln
Ostfriesische Inseln
Helgoland
Cuxhaven

P O L A N D
Gdańsk
Gdynia
Słupsk
Koszalin
Kołobrzeg
Elbląg
Malbork
Zatoka Gdańska

m ft
6000 2000
4500 1500
3000 1000
1500   500
 600   200
   0   0

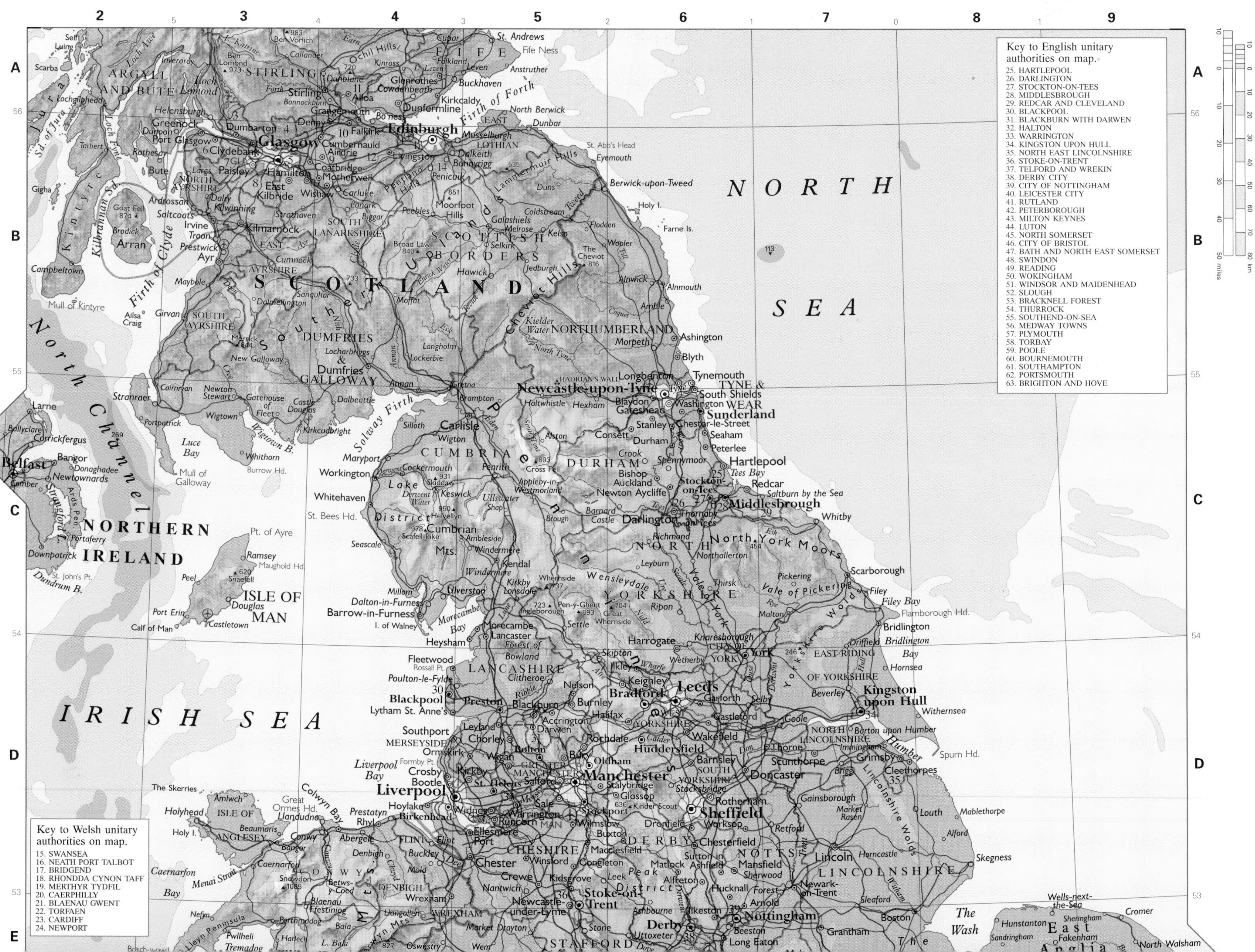

Key to English unitary
authorities on map.

25. HARTLEPOOL
26. DARLINGTON
27. STOCKTON-ON-TEES
28. MIDDLESBROUGH
29. REDCAR AND CLEVELAND
30. BLACKPOOL
31. BLACKBURN WITH DARWEN
32. HALTON
33. WARRINGTON
34. KINGSTON UPON HULL
35. NORTH EAST LINCOLNSHIRE
36. STOKE-ON-TRENT
37. TELFORD AND WREKIN
38. DERBY CITY
39. CITY OF NOTTINGHAM
40. LEICESTER CITY
41. RUTLAND
42. PETERBOROUGH
43. MILTON KEYNES
44. LUTON
45. NORTH SOMERSET
46. CITY OF BRISTOL
47. BATH AND NORTH EAST SOMERSET
48. SWINDON
49. READING
50. WOKINGHAM
51. WINDSOR AND MAIDENHEAD
52. SLOUGH
53. BRACKNELL FOREST
54. THURROCK
55. SOUTHEND-ON-SEA
56. MEDWAY TOWNS
57. PLYMOUTH
58. TORBAY
59. POOLE
60. BOURNEMOUTH
61. SOUTHAMPTON
62. PORTSMOUTH
63. BRIGHTON AND HOVE

Key to Welsh unitary
authorities on map.

15. SWANSEA
16. NEATH PORT TALBOT
17. BRIDGEND
18. RHONDDA CYNON TAFF
19. MERTHYR TYDFIL
20. CAERPHILLY
21. BLAENAU GWENT
22. TORFAEN
23. CARDIFF
24. NEWPORT

ENGLAND

WALES

FRANCE

NORMANDIE

HAUTE-

SEINE-MARITIME

CALVADOS

MANCHE

Cotentin

ENGLISH CHANNEL

Strait of Dover

Bristol Channel

Cardigan Bay

Lyme Bay

Baie de la Somme

Baie de la Seine

CHANNEL ISLANDS (U.K.)

ISLE OF WIGHT

CORNWALL

DEVON

DORSET

SOMERSET

WILTSHIRE

HAMPSHIRE

WEST SUSSEX

EAST SUSSEX

KENT

SURREY

BERKSHIRE

GLOUCS.

HEREFORD

WORCESTERSHIRE

WARWICK

WEST MIDLANDS

SHROPSHIRE

POWYS

CEREDIGION

PEMBROKESHIRE

CARMARTHENSHIRE

GLAMORGAN

VALE OF GLAMORGAN

MONMOUTHSHIRE

GWENT

SUFFOLK

ESSEX

HERTS

BUCKS

OXON

NORTHAMPTON

CAMBRIDGESHIRE

NORFOLK

BEDFORD

LONDON

GREATER LONDON

LONDON

Birmingham

Bristol

Bath

Cardiff

Swansea

Plymouth

Southampton

Portsmouth

Bournemouth

Brighton

Hove

Worthing

Exeter

Gloucester

Cheltenham

Oxford

Cambridge

Northampton

Coventry

Le Havre

Rouen

Cherbourg

Caen

Dieppe

Calais

Boulogne-sur-Mer

Le Touquet-Paris-Plage

Le Tréport

Fécamp

Évreux

Lisieux

St. Ives

Penzance

Newlyn

Land's End

Lizard Pt.

Lundy

Isles of Scilly
On same scale

St. Mary's

Tresco

Camborne

Hayle

Newquay

Redruth

Truro

Falmouth

Fowey

Bodmin

Launceston

Bude

Barnstaple or Bideford Bay

Ilfracombe

Minehead

Bridgwater

Taunton

Yeovil

Dorchester

Weymouth

Portland Bill

I. of Portland

Chesil Beach

Poole

Swanage

St. Alban's Head

Christchurch

New Forest

Salisbury

Winchester

Andover

Basingstoke

Newbury

Reading

Guildford

Crawley

Horsham

Chichester

Bognor Regis

Littlehampton

Selsey Bill

Hayling I.

Gosport

Fareham

Ryde

Newport

Cowes

Ventnor

St. Catherine's Pt.

The Needles

Lymington

Eastbourne

Beachy Head

Bexhill

Hastings

Rye Bay

Dungeness

Romney

Folkestone

Hythe

Ashford

Dover

Deal

Ramsgate

Margate

North Foreland

South Foreland

Canterbury

Whitstable

Herne Bay

Sheppey

Gillingham

Chatham

Rochester

Maidstone

Tonbridge

Tunbridge Wells

Royal Tunbridge Wells

Sevenoaks

Gravesend

Dartford

Croydon

Bromley

Epsom

Leatherhead

Reigate

Redhill

Dorking

Woking

Aldershot

Farnham

Alton

Petersfield

Haslemere

Midhurst

Lewes

East Grinstead

Haywards Heath

Uckfield

Cuckfield

Shoreham by Sea

Southend-on-Sea

Canvey Island

Basildon

Brentwood

Chelmsford

Braintree

Witham

Colchester

Clacton-on-Sea

Walton-on-the-Naze

The Naze

Harwich

Felixstowe

Ipswich

Woodbridge

Orford Ness

Aldeburgh

Southwold

Lowestoft

Beccles

Bungay

Diss

Stowmarket

Bury St. Edmunds

Sudbury

Halstead

Saffron Walden

Bishop's Stortford

Harlow

Cheshunt

Hertford

Welwyn Garden City

Hatfield

St. Albans

Hemel Hempstead

Watford

High Wycombe

Maidenhead

Windsor

Slough

Bracknell

Wokingham

Luton

Dunstable

Stevenage

Hitchin

Letchworth

Biggleswade

Bedford

Milton Keynes

Bletchley

Buckingham

Banbury

Bicester

Aylesbury

Thame

Witney

Woodstock

Abingdon

Wantage

Wallingford

Chipping Norton

Cirencester

Stroud

Chepstow

Newport

Cwmbran

Pontypool

Abergavenny

Ebbw Vale

Merthyr Tydfil

Aberdare

Rhondda

Pontypridd

Caerphilly

Bridgend

Port Talbot

Neath

Llanelli

Carmarthen

Pembroke

Milford Haven

Fishguard

St. David's

St. David's Hd.

Aberystwyth

Cardigan

New Quay

Aberaeron

Lampeter

Brecon

Brecon Beacons

Hereford

Leominster

Ludlow

Kidderminster

Stourbridge

Dudley

Halesowen

Solihull

Worcester

Droitwich

Redditch

Bromsgrove

Evesham

Stratford-upon-Avon

Royal Leamington Spa

Warwick

Tewkesbury

Ross-on-Wye

Monmouth

Hay-on-Wye

Builth Wells

Llandrindod Wells

Rhayader

Newtown

Welshpool

Machynlleth

Montgomery

St. Helier

Jersey

Guernsey

St. Peter Port

Alderney

Sark

Herm

Dinard

Coutances

Granville

Carteret

La Haye-du-Puits

Valognes

Ste-Mère-Église

Barfleur

Pte. de Barfleur

Montebourg

Carentan

Périers

St-Lô

Bayeux

Courseulles-sur-Mer

Arromanches-les-Bains

Port-en-Bessin

Ouistreham

Deauville

Trouville

Honfleur

Pont-l'Évêque

Pont-Audemer

Bernay

Elbeuf

Louviers

Gisors

Les Andelys

St-Valéry-en-Caux

Yvetot

Bolbec

Lillebonne

Étretat

Berck

Montreuil

Rue

St-Valéry-sur-Somme

Cayeux-sur-Mer

Ault

Eu

Gris-Nez

Wissant

Étaples

Wimereux

East from Greenwich

West from Greenwich

Projection: Lambert's Conformal Conic

ft m
3000 1000
1500 500
600 200
300 100
0 0
m ft

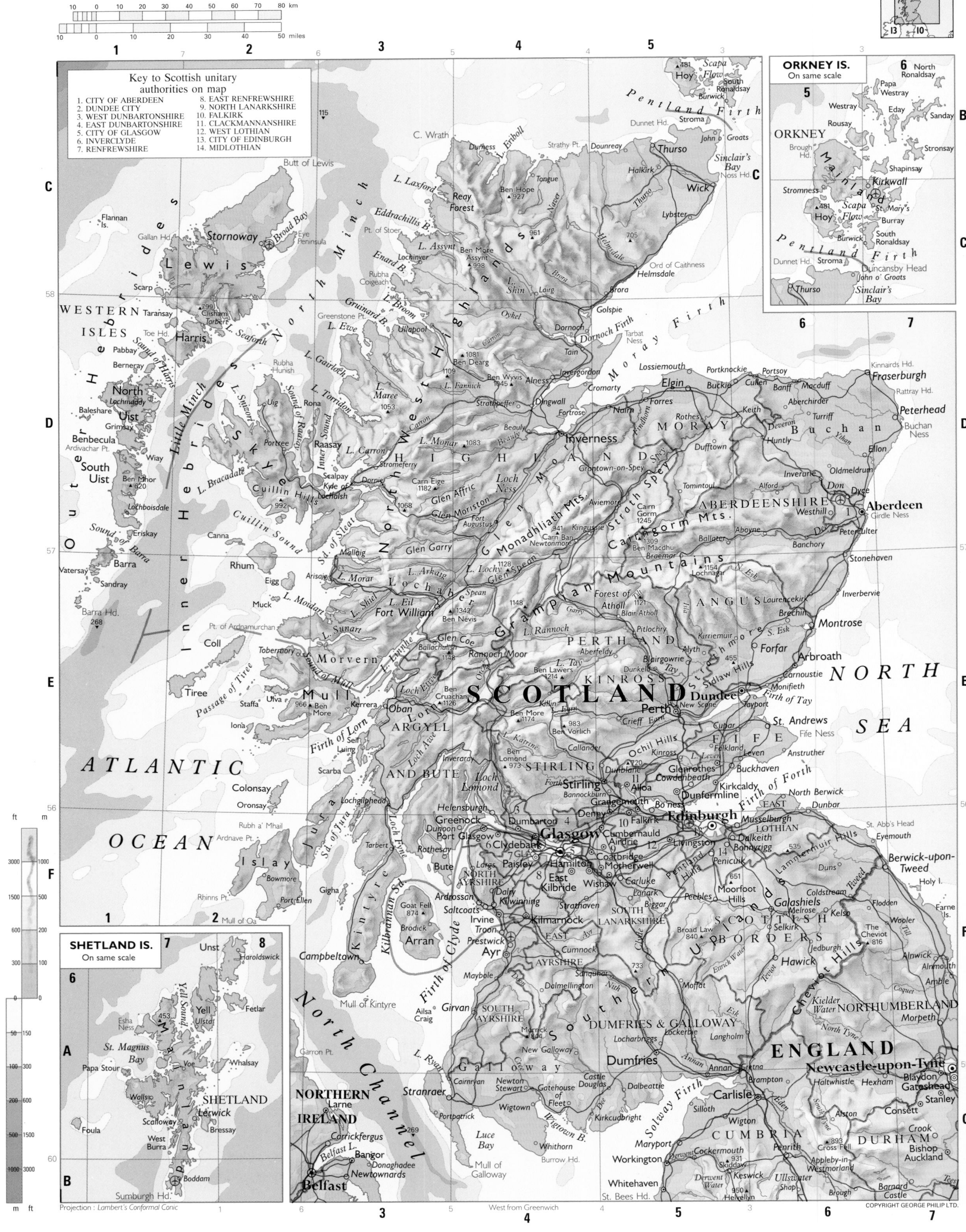

Key to Scottish unitary authorities on map

1. CITY OF ABERDEEN
2. DUNDEE CITY
3. WEST DUNBARTONSHIRE
4. EAST DUNBARTONSHIRE
5. CITY OF GLASGOW
6. INVERCLYDE
7. RENFREWSHIRE
8. EAST RENFREWSHIRE
9. NORTH LANARKSHIRE
10. FALKIRK
11. CLACKMANNANSHIRE
12. WEST LOTHIAN
13. CITY OF EDINBURGH
14. MIDLOTHIAN

ORKNEY IS. On same scale

ORKNEY

SHETLAND IS. On same scale

Projection : Lambert's Conformal Conic

West from Greenwich

COPYRIGHT GEORGE PHILIP LTD.

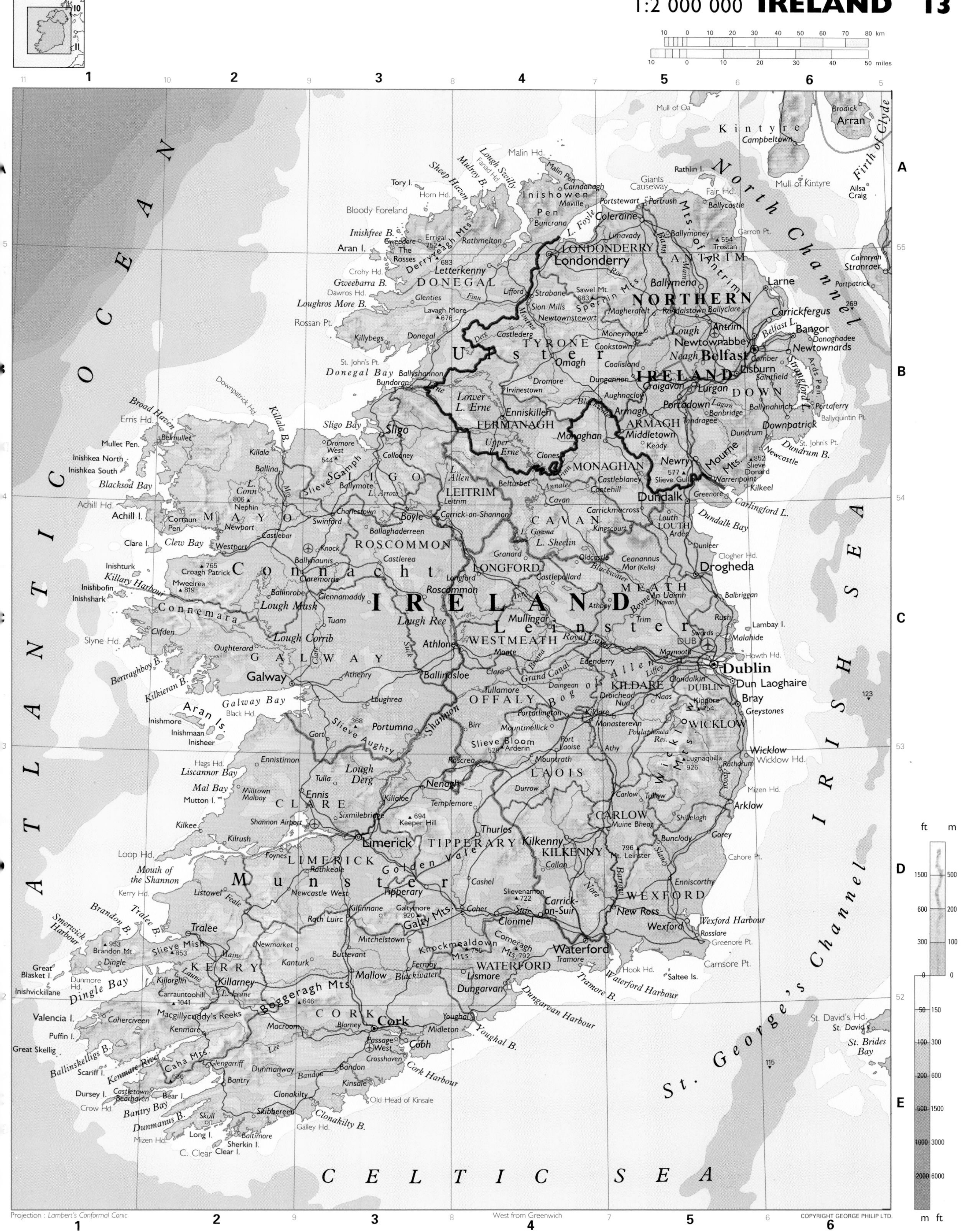

Projection : Lambert's Conformal Conic

West from Greenwich

COPYRIGHT GEORGE PHILIP LTD.

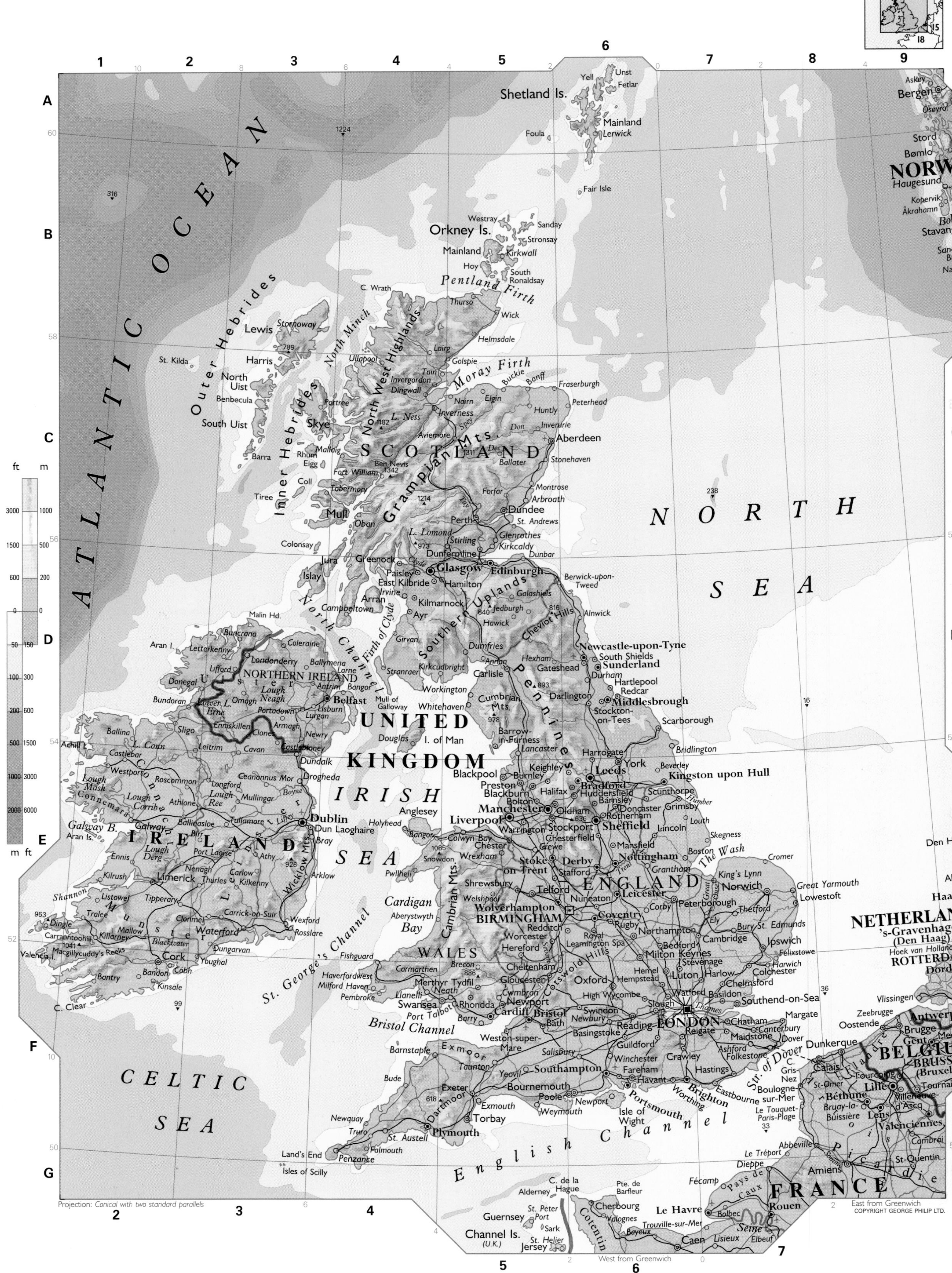
ATLANTIC OCEAN
NORTH SEA
CELTIC SEA
IRISH SEA
English Channel
Bristol Channel
St. George's Channel
North Channel
Shetland Is.
Orkney Is.
Outer Hebrides
Inner Hebrides
SCOTLAND
UNITED KINGDOM
NORTHERN IRELAND
IRELAND
ENGLAND
WALES
FRANCE
NETHERLANDS
BELGIUM
NORWAY
Grampian Mts.
Southern Uplands
Pennines
Cambrian Mts.
Cotswold Hills
Cheviot Hills
North West Highlands
Moray Firth
Pentland Firth
Firth of Clyde
The Wash
Str. of Dover
Cardigan Bay
Galway B.
Edinburgh
Glasgow
Aberdeen
Dundee
Inverness
Belfast
Londonderry
Dublin
Cork
Limerick
Galway
Waterford
LONDON
BIRMINGHAM
Manchester
Liverpool
Leeds
Sheffield
Bradford
Newcastle-upon-Tyne
Sunderland
Middlesbrough
Kingston upon Hull
Nottingham
Leicester
Coventry
Bristol
Cardiff
Swansea
Southampton
Portsmouth
Plymouth
Exeter
Norwich
Cambridge
Oxford
Brighton
Channel Is. (U.K.)
Guernsey
Jersey
I. of Man
Anglesey
Isles of Scilly
Land's End
Projection: Conical with two standard parallels
East from Greenwich
West from Greenwich
COPYRIGHT GEORGE PHILIP LTD.

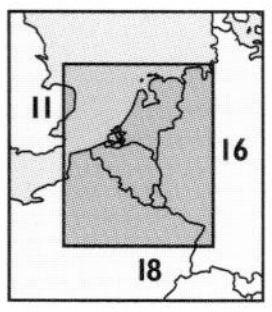

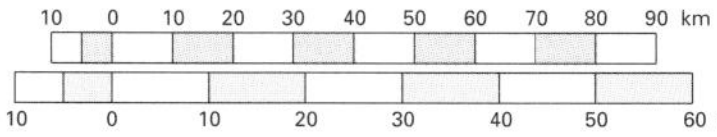

10 0 10 20 30 40 50 60 70 80 90 km
10 0 10 20 30 40 50 60 miles

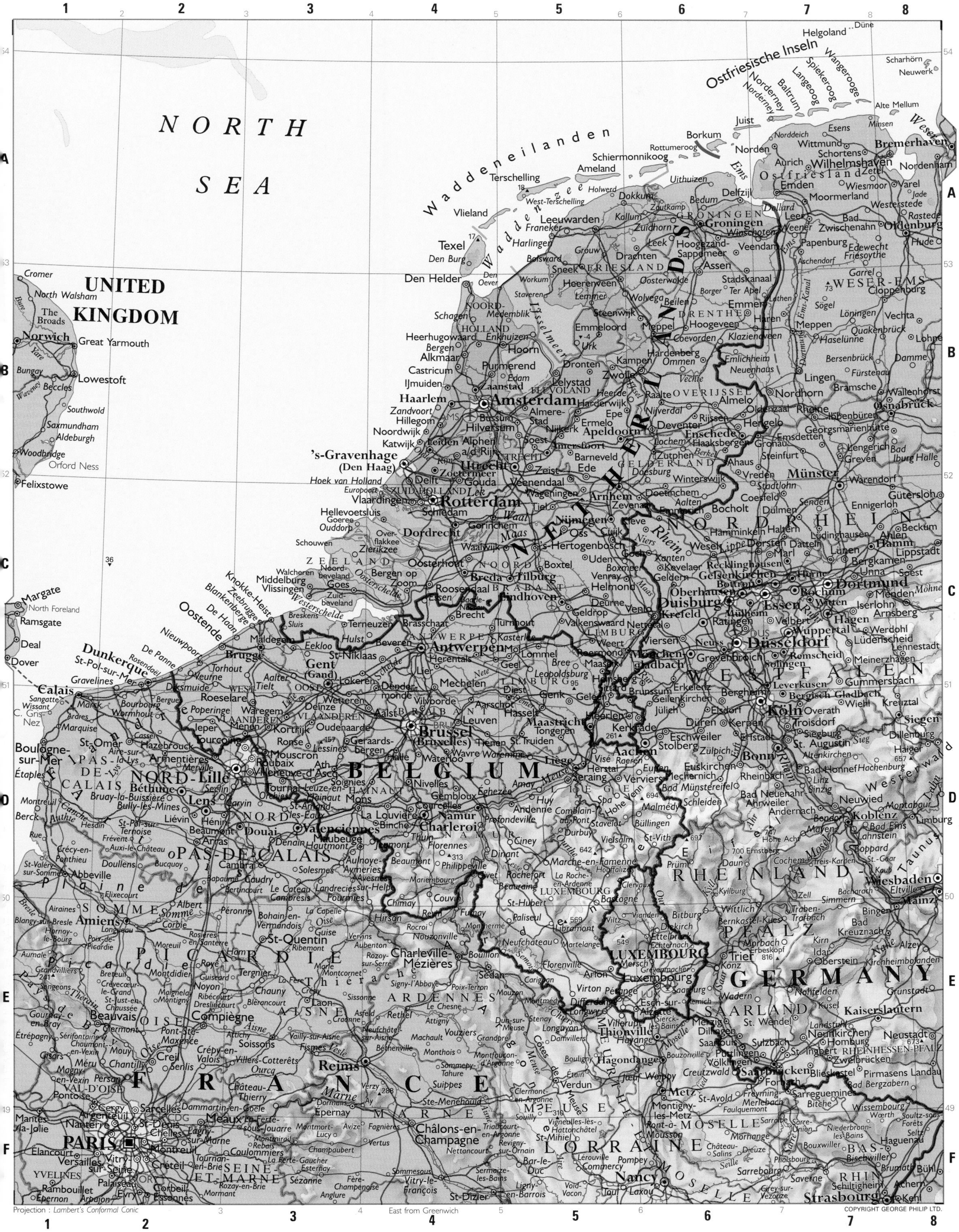

NORTH

SEA

UNITED
KINGDOM

Cromer
North Walsham
The Broads
Norwich Great Yarmouth
Bungay Lowestoft
Waveney Beccles
Southwold
Saxmundham Aldeburgh
Woodbridge
Orford Ness
Felixstowe

Margate
North Foreland
Ramsgate
Deal
Dover
Calais
C. Gris Nez
Boulogne-sur-Mer
Étaples
Berck
Montreuil

Waddeneilanden

Ostfriesische Inseln
Helgoland Düne
Scharhörn
Neuwerk
Wangerooge
Spiekeroog
Langeoog
Baltrum
Norderney
Juist
Borkum
Memmert

Texel
Den Burg
Den Helder
Vlieland
Terschelling
West-Terschelling
Ameland
Schiermonnikoog
Rottumeroog

Leeuwarden
Franeker
Harlingen
Bolsward
Sneek
Dokkum
Holwerd
Grouw
Drachten
FRIESLAND
Heerenveen
Oosterwolde

GRONINGEN
Groningen
Delfzijl
Winschoten
Veendam
Hoogezand-Sappemeer
Stadskanaal
Assen
DRENTHE
Hoogeveen
Emmen
Klazienaveen

Bremerhaven
Wilhelmshaven
Nordenham
Aurich
Emden
Leer
Oldenburg
WESER-EMS
Cloppenburg
Papenburg
Meppen
Lingen
Nordhorn
Osnabrück

Schagen
Heerhugowaard
Bergen
Alkmaar
Castricum
IJmuiden
Haarlem
Zandvoort
Hillegom
Noordwijk
Katwijk

Hoorn
Enkhuizen
Purmerend
Edam
Zaanstad
Amsterdam
HOLLAND
NOORD-HOLLAND

NETHERLANDS

Lelystad
Dronten
FLEVOLAND
Almere
Harderwijk
Ermelo
Nijkerk
Apeldoorn
GELDERLAND
Deventer
Zutphen
Zwolle
OVERIJSSEL
Almelo
Hengelo
Enschede

's-Gravenhage
(Den Haag)
Delft
Zoetermeer
Leiden
Gouda
Utrecht
UTRECHT
Amersfoort
Barneveld
Ede
Arnhem
Doetinchem
Winterswijk

Münster
NORDRHEIN

Vlaardingen
Rotterdam
Schiedam
ZUID-HOLLAND
Dordrecht
Hellevoetsluis
Goeree
Ouddorp
Schouwen
Zierikzee
Oosterhout
Breda
's-Hertogenbosch
Oss
Nijmegen
Cuijk
Kleve
Wesel
Xanten

ZEELAND
Middelburg
Vlissingen
Goes
Bergen op Zoom
Roosendaal
NOORD-BRABANT
Tilburg
Boxtel
Eindhoven
Helmond
Venlo
Oberhausen
Duisburg
Essen
Krefeld
Düsseldorf
Dortmund
Bochum

Knokke-Heist
Zeebrugge
Blankenberge
De Haan
Oostende
Nieuwpoort
Brugge
ANTWERPEN
Antwerpen
LIMBURG
Weert
Roermond
Mönchen-gladbach
Neuss
WESTFALEN
Köln
Bonn
Aachen

Dunkerque
St-Pol-sur-Mer
Gravelines
Veurne
Diksmuide
Roeselare
Ieper
Menen
Kortrijk
Gent
(Gand)
OOST-VLAANDEREN
Aalst
Dendermonde
Mechelen
Lier
Turnhout
Geel
Diest
Hasselt
Genk
Maastricht
Tongeren
Kerkrade
Sittard
Heerlen

Cassel
Hazebrouck
Armentières
NORD
Lille
Roubaix
Tourcoing
Oudenaarde
Ronse
BRABANT
Brussel
(Bruxelles)
Leuven
Tienen
St-Truiden

St-Omer
Béthune
Lens
Liévin
Hénin
Douai
Valenciennes
Maubeuge
PAS-DE-CALAIS
Arras
Cambrai
HAINAUT
Mons
Soignies
Nivelles
Charleroi
La Louvière
NAMUR
Namur
LIÈGE
Liège
Seraing
Verviers
Spa
Eupen
Malmédy
St-Vith
RHEINLAND-PFALZ
Euskirchen
Koblenz

BELGIUM

Bapaume
Albert
Péronne
Bohain-en-Vermandois
St-Quentin
Guise
La Capelle
Avesnes
Philippeville
Dinant
Marche-en-Famenne
Rochefort
La Roche-en-Ardenne
Bastogne
Prüm
Bitburg
Wittlich
Bernkastel-Kues
Bad Neuenahr

SOMME
Amiens
Corbie
Montdidier
Noyon
Chaulnes
Ham
Laon
AISNE
Vervins
ARDENNES
Charleville-Mézières
Sedan
Bouillon
LUXEMBOURG
Neufchâteau
Florenville
Virton
Arlon
Luxembourg
LUXEMBOURG
Mersch
Diekirch
Echternach
Trier
Konz
SAARLAND
GERMANY

PICARDIE
Beauvais
OISE
Compiègne
Clermont
Senlis
Creil
Soissons
Reims
MARNE
Épernay
Châlons-en-Champagne
Vouziers
Verdun
MEUSE
Metz
Thionville
MOSELLE
Saarbrücken
Saarlouis
St. Wendel
Neunkirchen
Homburg
Kaiserslautern
RHEINLAND-PFALZ
PFALZ

Paris
Versailles
YVELINES
SEINE-ET-MARNE
Meaux
VAL-D'OISE
Pontoise
Mantes-la-Jolie
St-Denis
Nanterre
Créteil
Melun
Provins
Sézanne
Vitry-le-François
St-Dizier
Bar-le-Duc
Commercy
Toul
Nancy
MOSELLE
LORRAINE
Sarreguemines
Bitche
Wissembourg
Haguenau
BAS-RHIN
Saverne
Strasbourg
Kehl

FRANCE

Projection : Lambert's Conformal Conic
East from Greenwich
COPYRIGHT GEORGE PHILIP LTD.

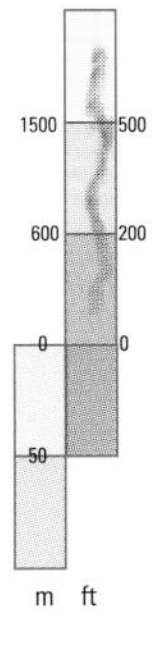

ft m
1500 500
600 200
0
50

Underlined towns give their name to the
administrative area in which they stand.

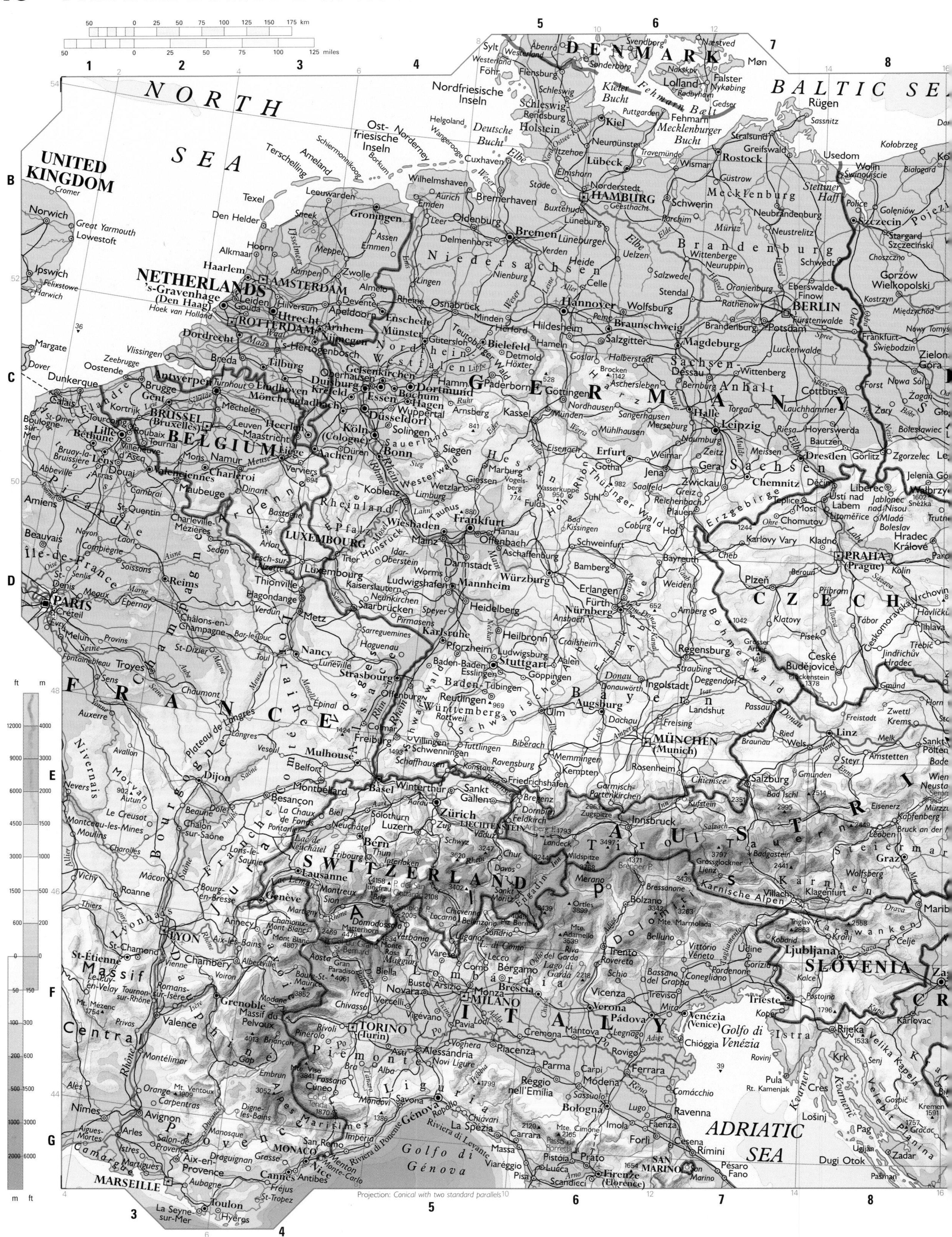

9 10 11 12 13 14 15 16

LITHUANIA

BELARUS

POLAND

UKRAINE

SLOVAK REP.

HUNGARY

ROMANIA

MOLDOVA

YUGOSLAVIA

BOSNIA-HERZEGOVINA

BULGARIA

Carpathians

Transilvania

Carpaţii Meridionali

Vojvodina

Podolska Vysochyna

Basarabia

Dobruja

Walachia

Pripet Marshes

Pojezierze Mazurskie

Zatoka Gdańska

Zalew Wiślany

Kaliningrad (Russia)

Vilnius

MINSK

WARSZAWA (Warsaw)

KYYIV (Kiev)

BUDAPEST

BUCUREŞTI (Bucharest)

BEOGRAD (Belgrade)

Chişinău

Gdańsk

Gdynia

Elbląg

Olsztyn

Bydgoszcz

Toruń

Włocławek

Płock

Łódź

Radom

Lublin

Kielce

Częstochowa

Kraków

Katowice

Wrocław

Opole

Rzeszów

Tarnów

Białystok

Hrodna

Brest

Pinsk

Baranavichy

Babruysk

Homyel

Mahilyow

Mazyr

Lviv (Lvov)

Lutsk

Rivne

Ternopil

Khmelnytskyy

Vinnytsya

Zhytomyr

Bila Tserkva

Chernivtsi

Ivano-Frankivsk

Uzhhorod

Košice

Prešov

Bratislava

Miskolc

Debrecen

Nyiregyháza

Szeged

Pécs

Győr

Székesfehérvár

Kecskemét

Cluj-Napoca

Oradea

Arad

Timişoara

Braşov

Sibiu

Iaşi

Bacău

Galaţi

Brăila

Constanţa

Ploieşti

Craiova

Piteşti

Novi Sad

Subotica

Osijek

Sarajevo

Tuzla

Ruse

Varna

Dobrich

Tiraspol

Bălţi

Wisła (Vistula)

Bug

San

Dnister

Prut

Siret

Mureş

Tisza

Dunaj

Duna

Dunav

Dunărea (Danube)

Sava

Drava

Dnyapro (Dnieper)

Pripyat'

East from Greenwich

9 10 11 12 13 14 15

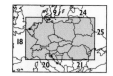

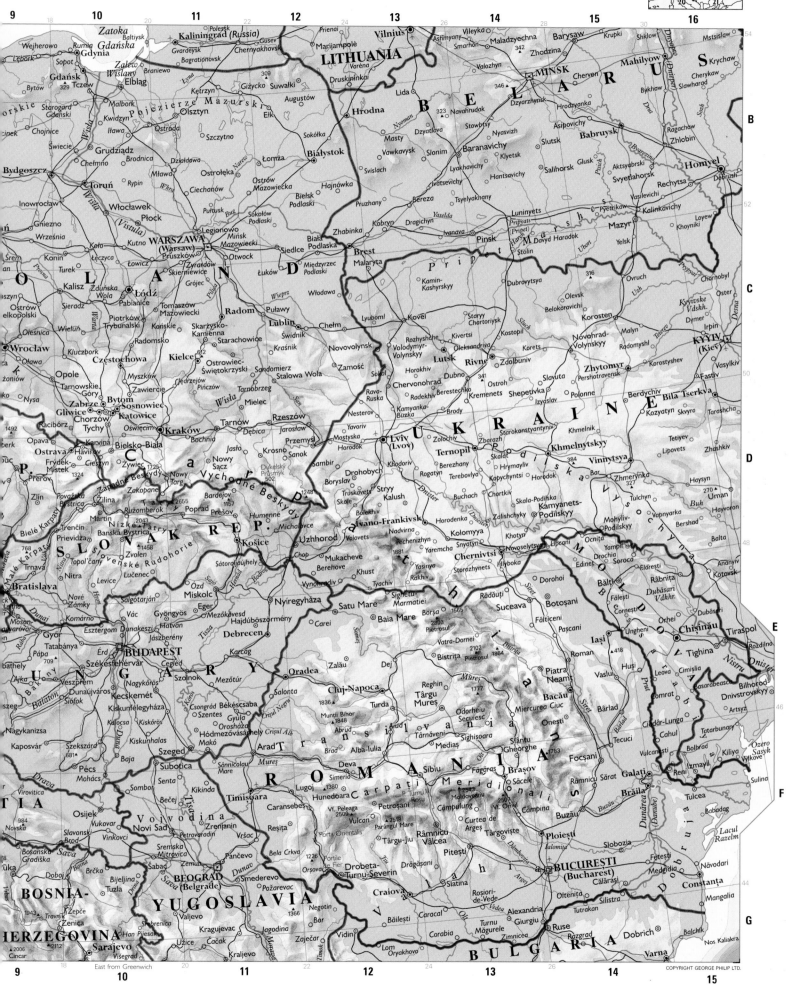

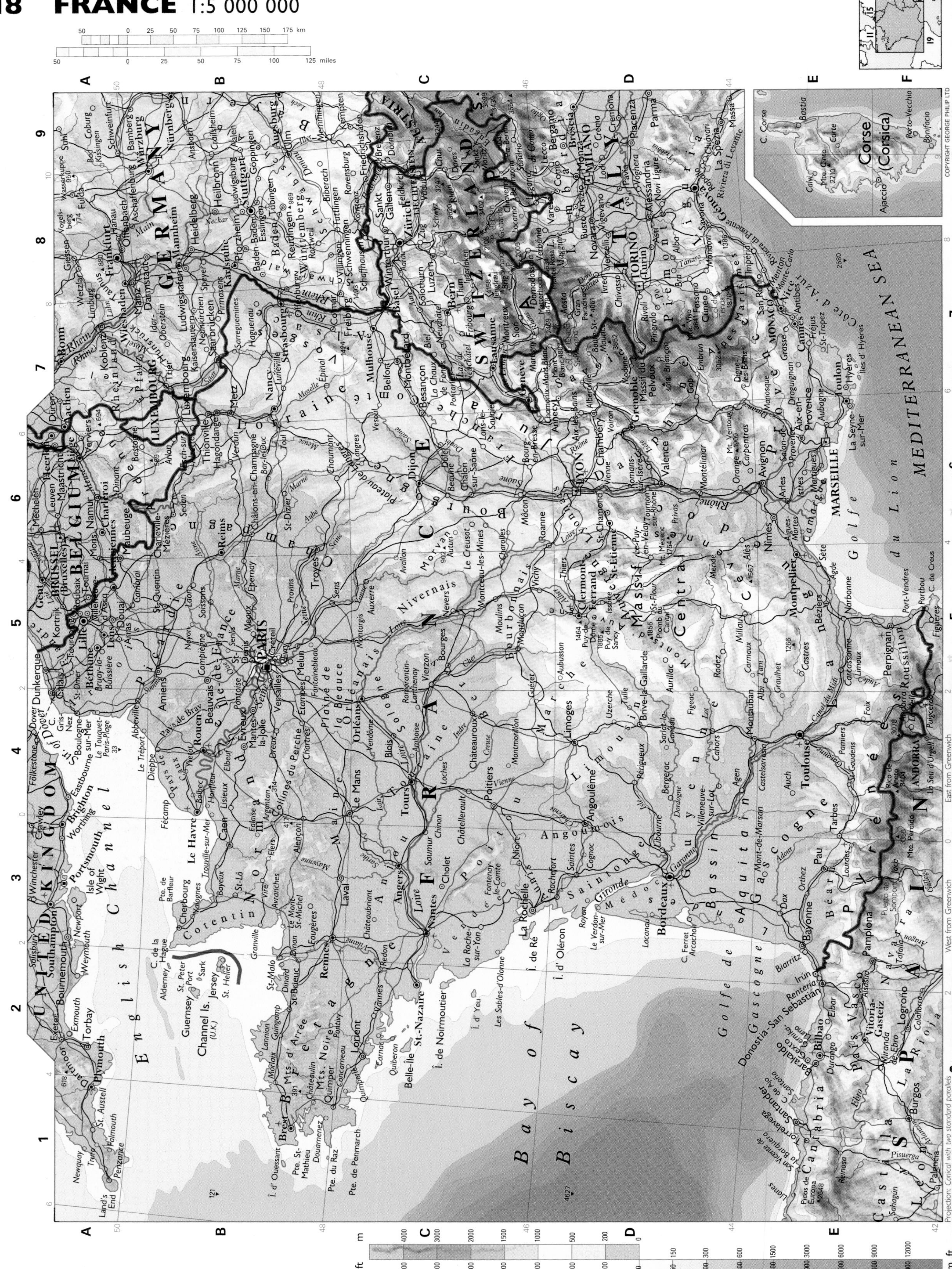

Corse (Corsica)

MEDITERRANEAN SEA

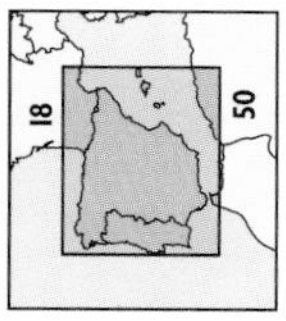

50 0 25 50 75 100 125 150 175 km

50 0 25 50 75 100 125 miles

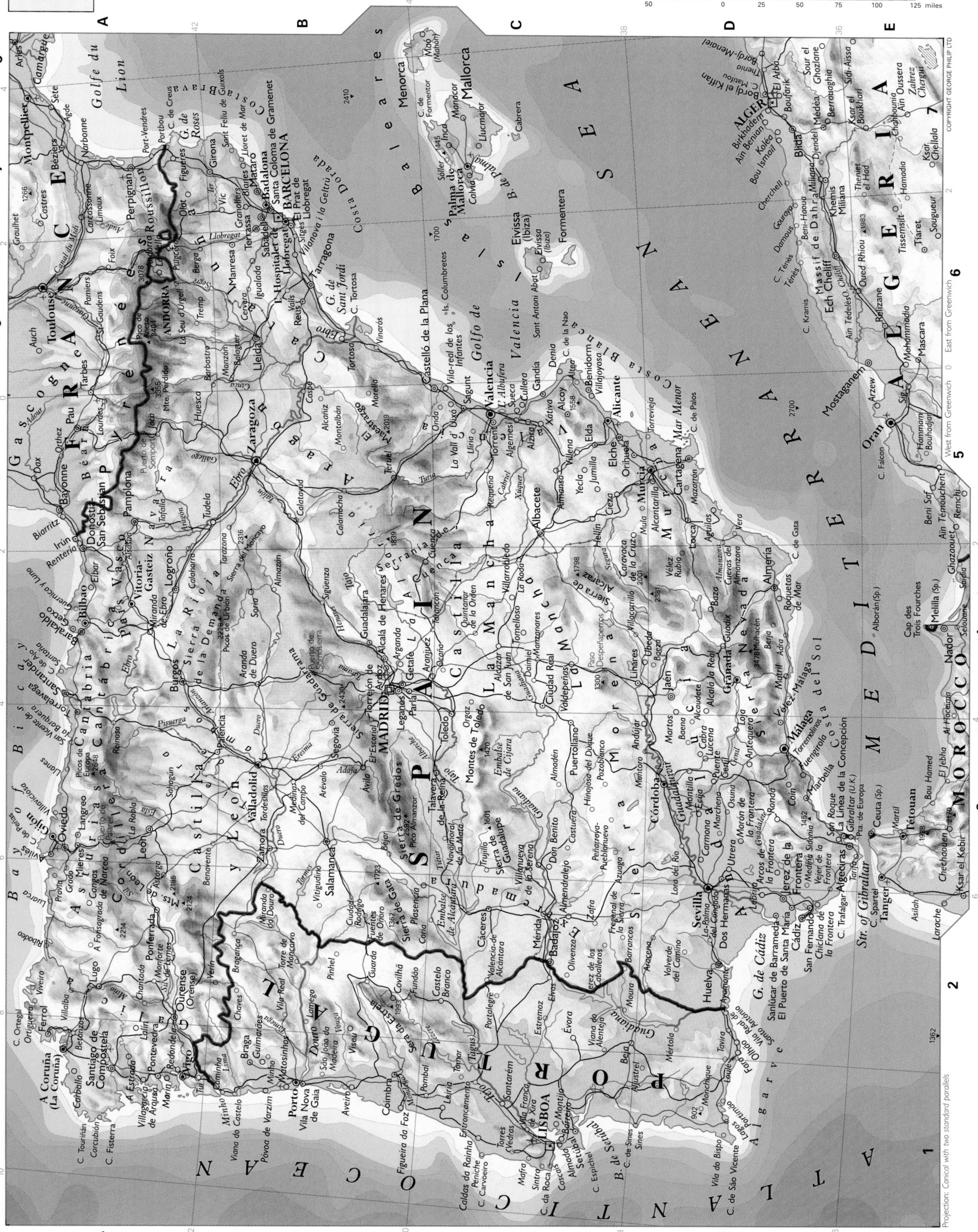

COPYRIGHT GEORGE PHILIP LTD

Projection: Conical with two standard parallels

West from Greenwich 0 East from Greenwich

FRANCE

SPAIN

PORTUGAL

ANDORRA

MOROCCO

ALGERIA

MADRID

BARCELONA

LISBOA

Valencia

Sevilla

Málaga

ALGER

Oran

P y r e n e e s

MEDITERRANEAN SEA

ATLANTIC OCEAN

Bay of Biscay

Golfe du Lion

Islas Baleares

Mallorca

Menorca

Eivissa (Ibiza)

m ft
6000
4500
3000
1500
600
200
0
50 – 150

50 0 25 50 75 100 125 150 175 km
50 0 25 50 75 100 125 miles

SWITZERLAND
AUSTRIA
Graz
Wolfsberg
Klagenfurt
Villach
Maribor
Nagykan
SLOVENIA
Ljubljana
Zagreb
CROATIA
Trieste
Venézia (Venice)
Golfo di Venézia

FRANCE
LYON
Grenoble
Chambéry
Aix-les-Bains
Valence
Montélimar
Orange
Avignon
MARSEILLE
Toulon
Hyères
MONACO
Nice
Cannes
Antibes

TORINO (Turin)
Pinerolo
Piemonte
MILANO
Monza
Brescia
Verona
Pádova
Vicenza
Lombardia
Novara
Vercelli
Pavia
Cremona
Mántova
Parma
Módena
Bologna
Ferrara
Ravenna
Rímini
Toscana
Firenze (Florence)
Pisa
Livorno
Siena
Arezzo
SAN MARINO
Ancona
Perúgia
Lázio
ROMA
VATICAN CITY
Tívoli
Latina
Frosinone

LIGURIAN SEA
Génova
La Spézia
Golfo di Génova
Côte d'Azur

Corse
Ajaccio
Bastia
Corte
Bonifacio
Bouches de Bonifacio

Sardegna
Sássari
Ólbia
Nuoro
Oristano
Cágliari
Iglésias
Carbónia
Sant' Antioco
G. di Oristano
G. di Cágliari
G. di Pálmas

TYRRHENIAN SEA

ADRIATIC SEA
Pula
Zadar
Split
Hvar
Brač
Korčula

Pescara
Chieti
L'Áquila
Campobasso
Foggia
Barletta
Trani
Bari
NÁPOLI
Salerno
Avellino
Potenza
Matera
Calábria
Cosenza
Catanzaro
Crotone
Messina
Réggio di Calábria
Str. di Messina

Sicília
Palermo
Trápani
Marsala
Mázara del Vallo
Agrigento
Caltanissetta
Enna
Catánia
Siracusa
Ragusa
Gela
Etna
Ísole Eólie
Strómboli
Lípari
Vulcano

ALGERIA
Annaba
Constantine
Guelma
Skikda

TUNISIA
Tunis
Bizerte
Golfe de Tunis
Golfe de Hammamet
Kairouan
Sousse
Monastir

Pantelleria (Italy)
Ísole Pelagie (Italy)
Lampedusa
MALTA
Valletta
Gozo
MEDITER

ft m
12000 4000
9000 3000
6000 2000
4500 1500
3000 1000
1500 500
600 200
0 0

Projection: Conical with two standard parallels

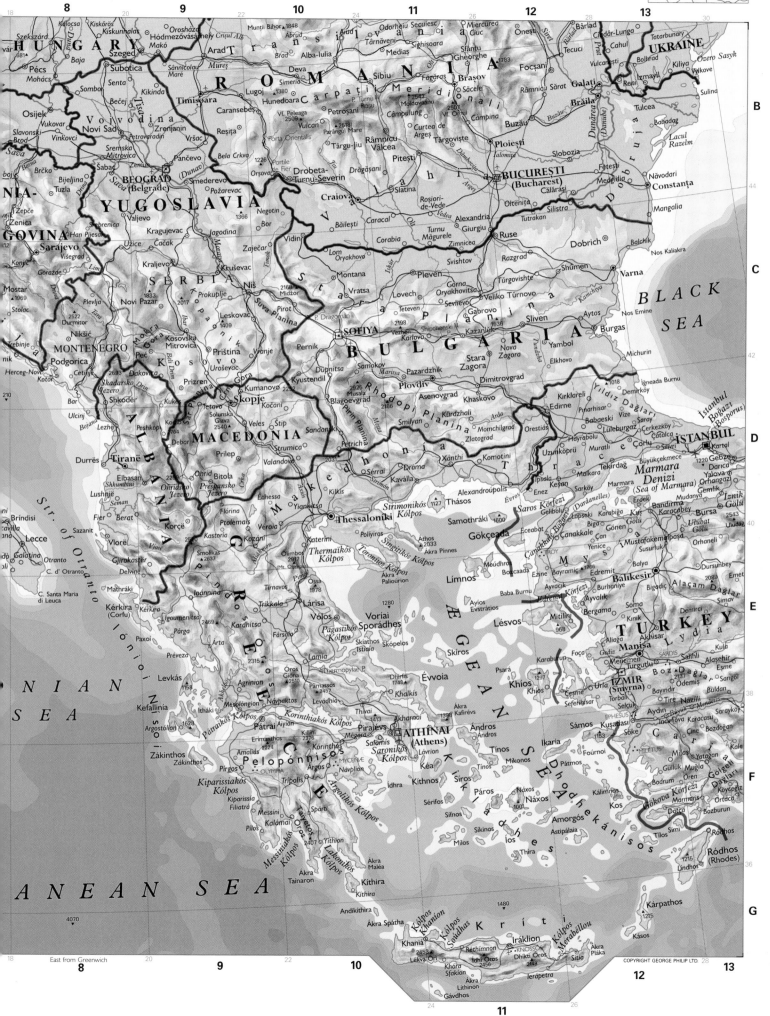

8 9 10 11 12 13

HUNGARY
ROMANIA
UKRAINE
YUGOSLAVIA
BULGARIA
MACEDONIA
ALBANIA
GREECE
TURKEY
BLACK SEA
ÆGEAN SEA
IONIAN SEA
MEDITERRANEAN SEA

East from Greenwich

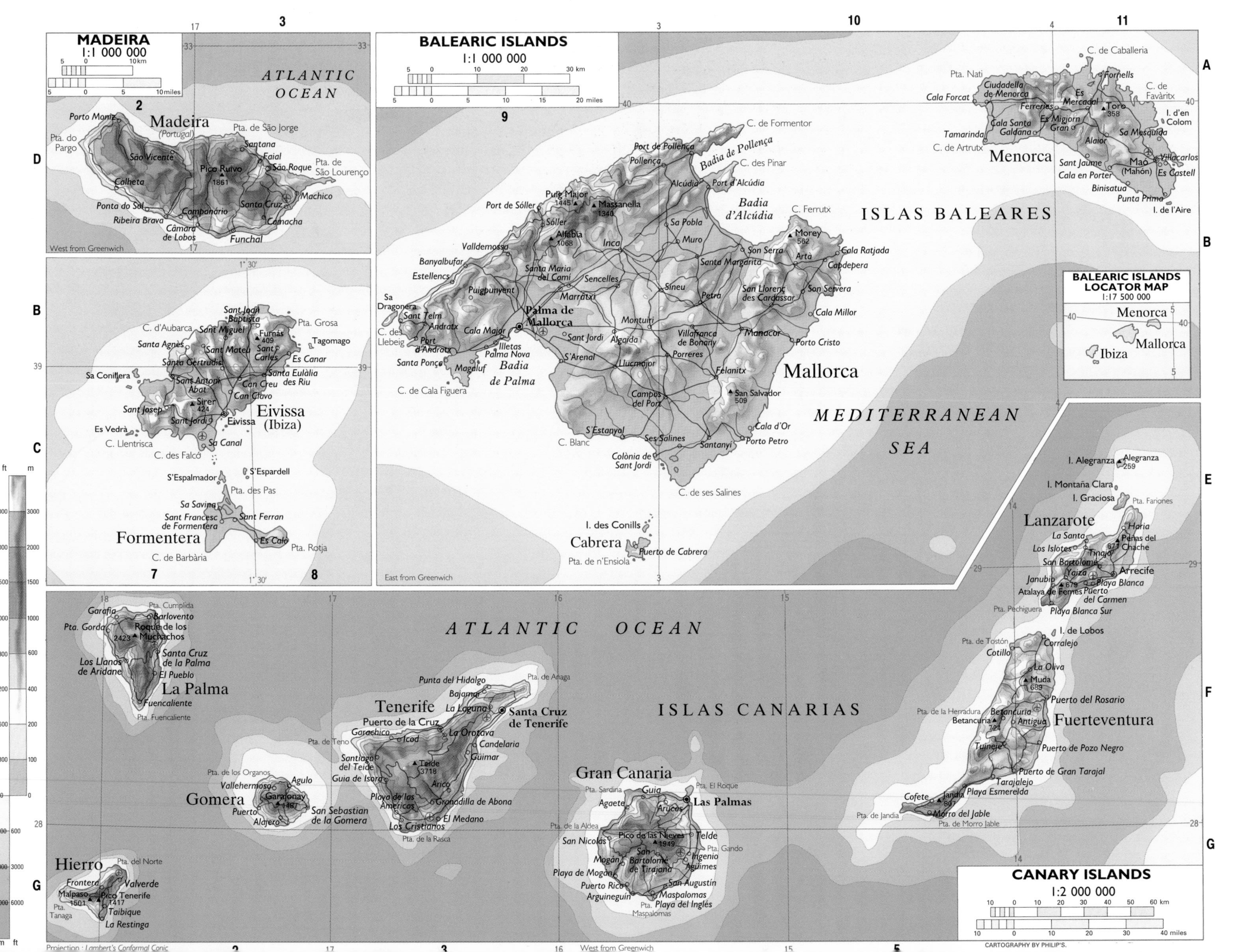

BALEARIC ISLANDS LOCATOR MAP
1:17 500 000

Menorca
Mallorca
Ibiza

BALEARIC ISLANDS
1:1 000 000

CANARY ISLANDS
1:2 000 000

CARTOGRAPHY BY PHILIP'S

MADEIRA
1:1 000 000

Menorca

ISLAS BALEARES

MEDITERRANEAN SEA

Mallorca

Palma de Mallorca

Cabrera

ATLANTIC OCEAN

Madeira
(Portugal)

Funchal

Eivissa (Ibiza)

Formentera

ISLAS CANARIAS

Lanzarote

Fuerteventura

Gran Canaria

Las Palmas

Tenerife

Santa Cruz de Tenerife

Teide 3718

Gomera

La Palma

Hierro

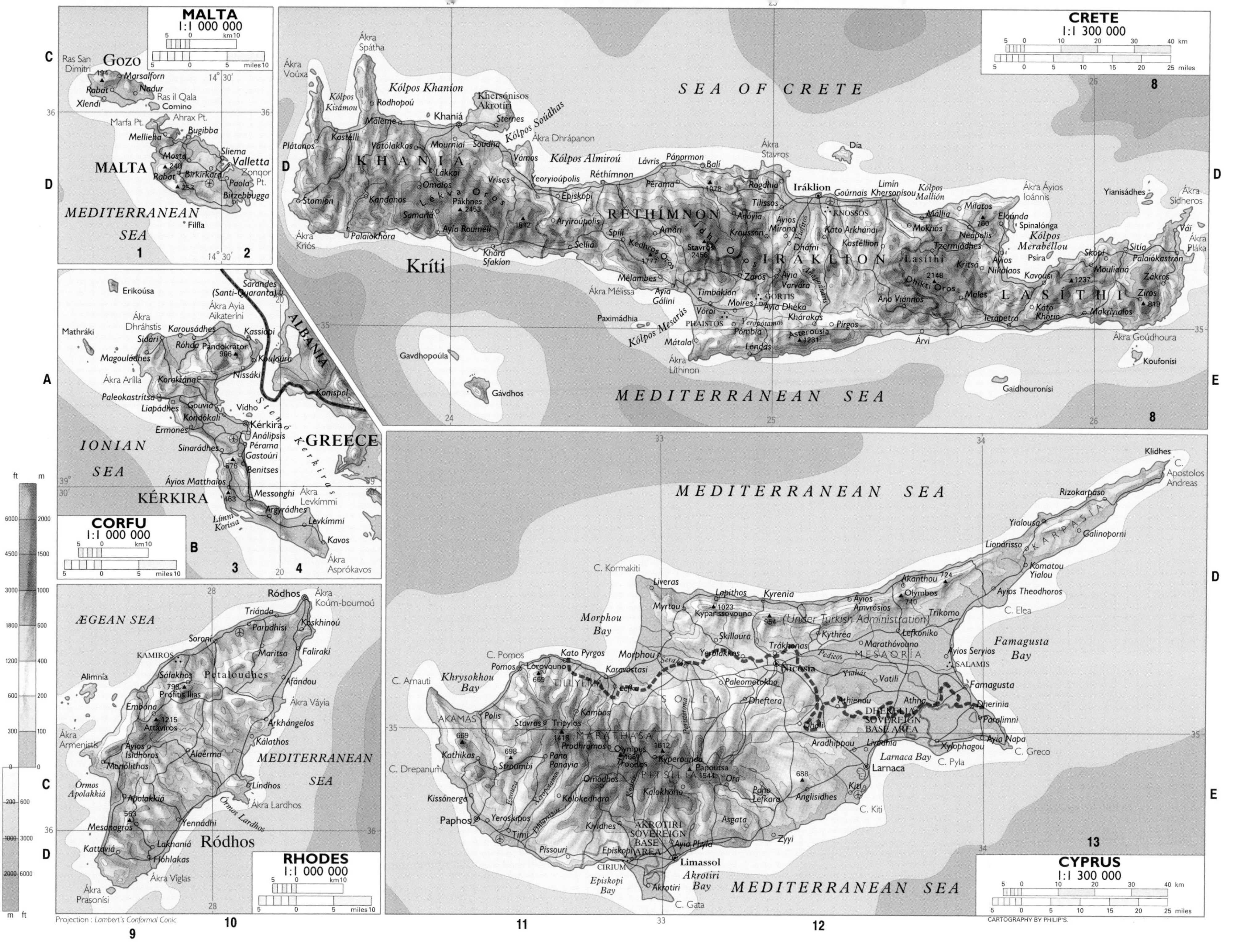

CRETE
1:1 300 000

CYPRUS
1:1 300 000

CARTOGRAPHY BY PHILIP'S.

MALTA
1:1 000 000

CORFU
1:1 000 000

RHODES
1:1 000 000

Projection: Lambert's Conformal Conic

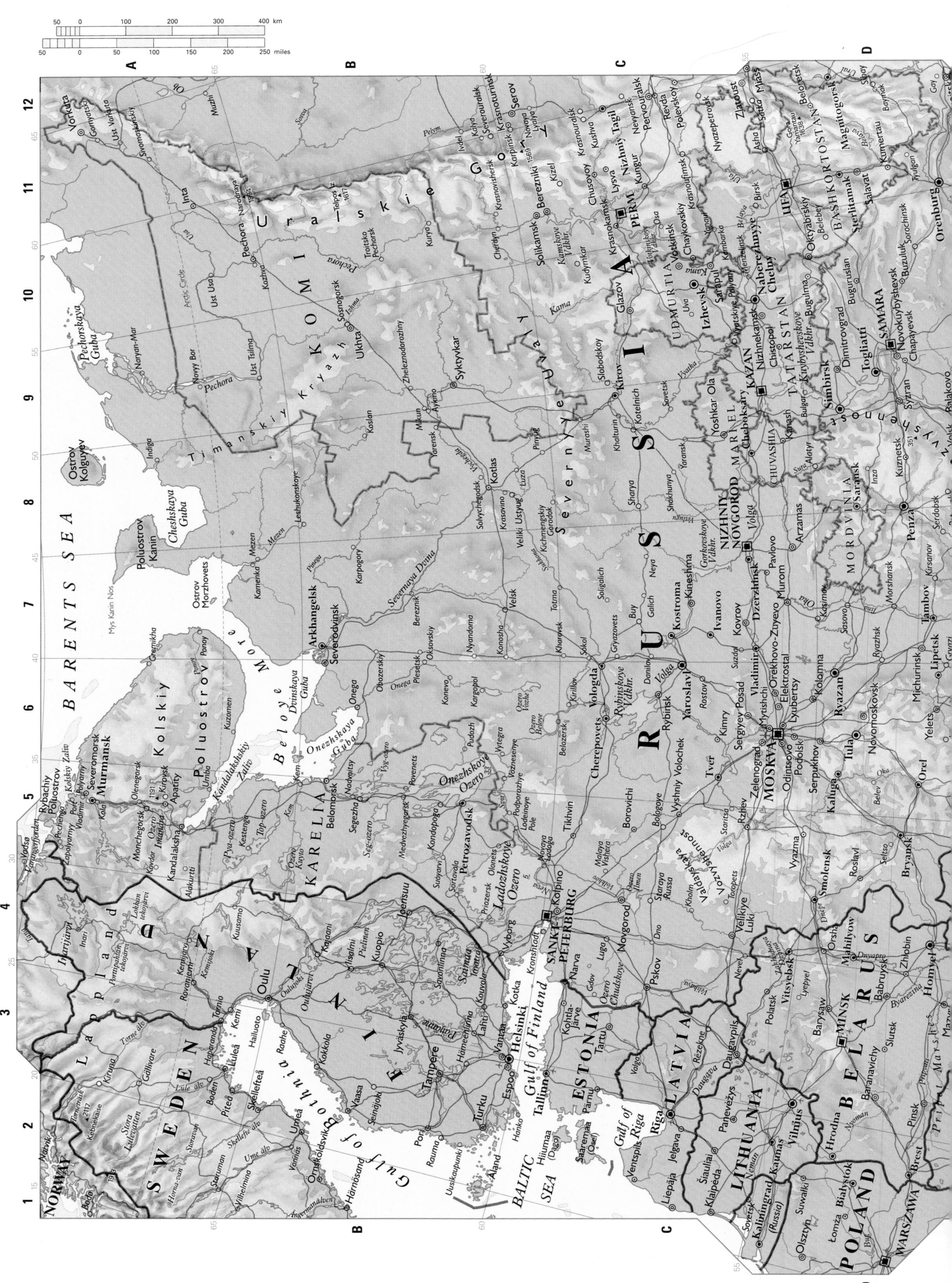

UKRAINE
MOLDOVA
ROMANIA
BULGARIA
KAZAKSTAN
GEORGIA
ARMENIA
AZERBAIJAN
TURKMENISTAN
TURKEY
SYRIA
IRAQ
IRAN
LEBANON
CYPRUS
KALMYKIA
CRIMEA

BLACK SEA
CASPIAN SEA
MEDITERRANEAN SEA
Sea of Azov
Caucasus Mountains
Carpathians
Kirgiziya Steppe
Caspian Depression
Anadolu
Kuzey Anadolu Dağları
Toros Dağları
Kurdistan
Reshteh-ye Kūhhā-ye Alborz
Zāgros
Bādiyat ash Shām
Dasht-e Kavīr
Garabogazköl Aylagy

KYYIV
KHARKIV
DNIPROPETROVSK
DONETSK
ODESA
VOLGOGRAD
ROSTOV
BUCUREŞTI
Chişinău
İSTANBUL
ANKARA
İZMIR (Smyrna)
BURSA
KONYA
ADANA
TBILISI
YEREVAN
BAKI
TABRĪZ
TEHRĀN
HALAB
DIMASHQ
BAYRŪT
Nicosia
Astrakhan
Atyraū
Krasnodar
Stavropol
Grozny
Makhachkala
Trabzon
Samsun
Erzurum
Diyarbakır
Al Mawşil

E
F
G
H

Projection: Conical with two standard parallels

East from Greenwich

4 5 6 7 8 9

ft m
12 000 4000
9000 3000
6000 2000
4500 1500
3000 1000
1500 500
600 200
0 0
200 600
500 1500
1000 3000
2000 6000
m ft

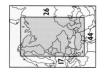

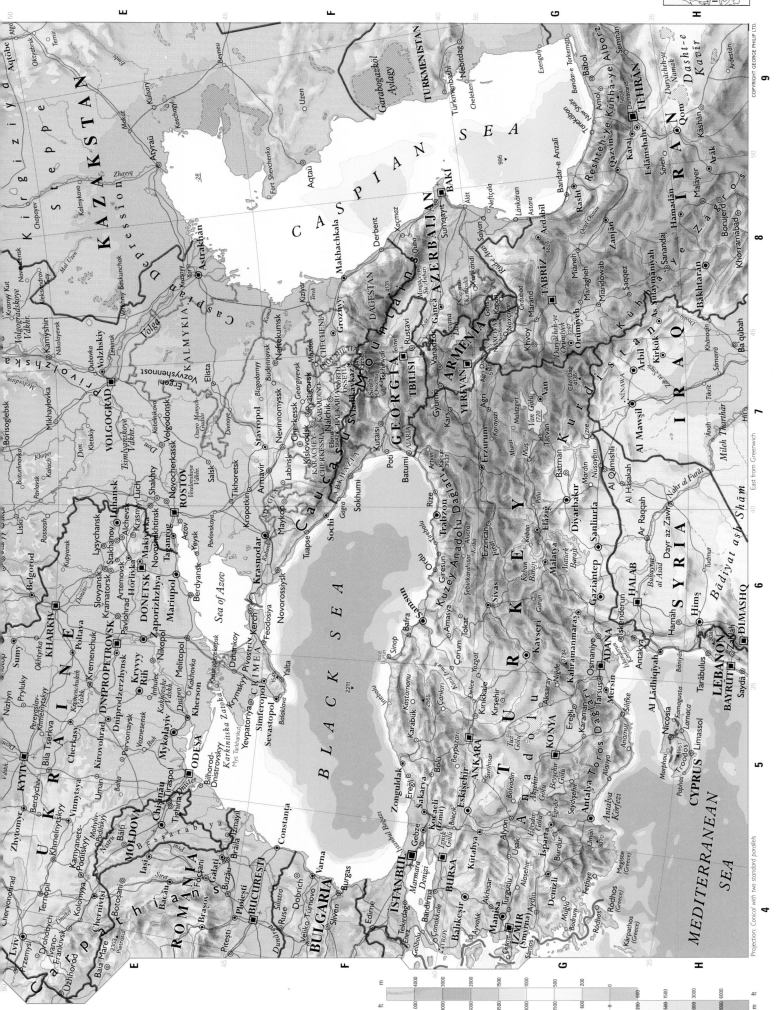

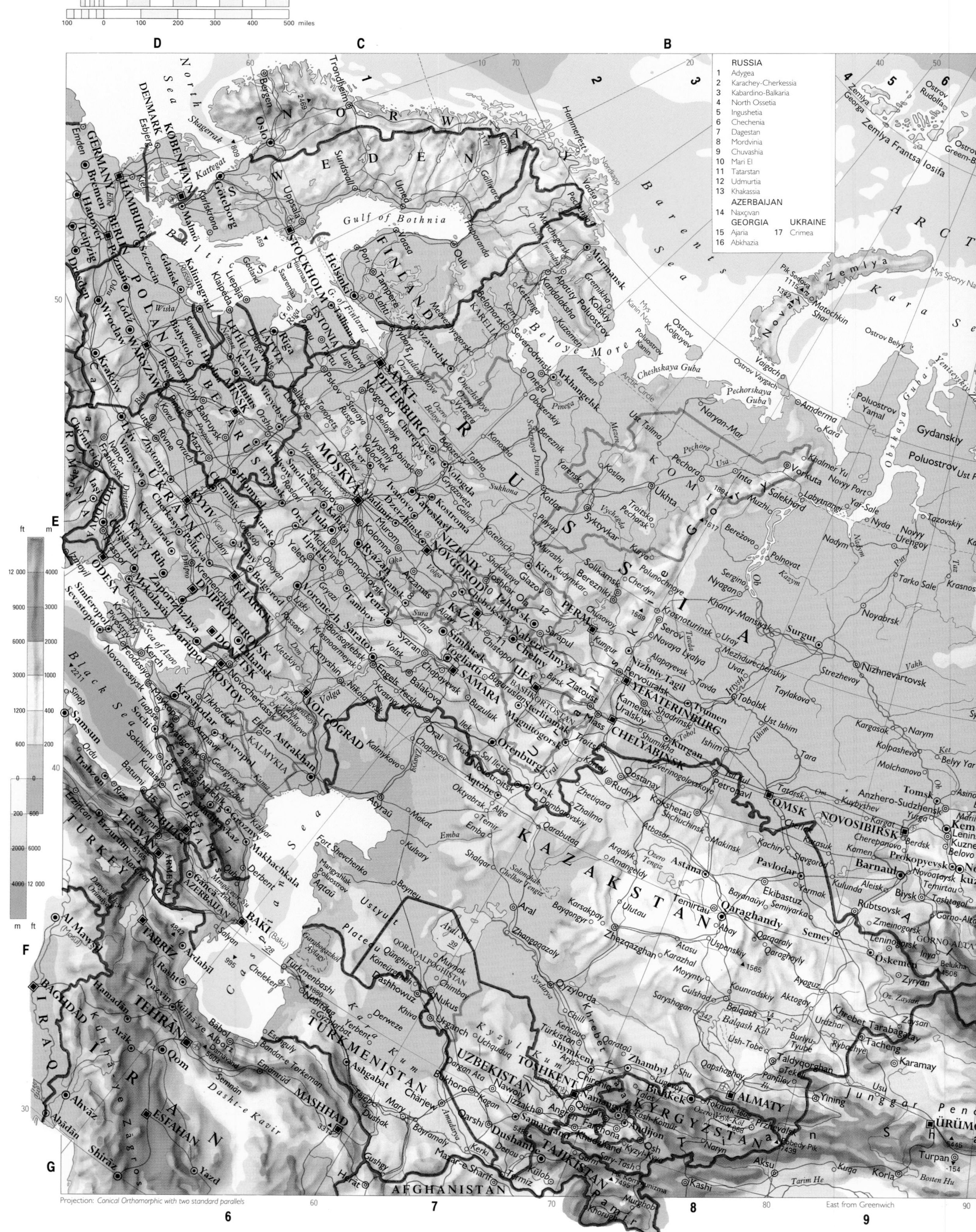

RUSSIA
1 Adygea
2 Karachey-Cherkessia
3 Kabardino-Balkaria
4 North Ossetia
5 Ingushetia
6 Chechenia
7 Dagestan
8 Mordvinia
9 Chuvashia
10 Mari El
11 Tatarstan
12 Udmurtia
13 Khakassia

AZERBAIJAN
14 Naxçıvan

GEORGIA   **UKRAINE**
15 Ajaria   17 Crimea
16 Abkhazia

Projection: Conical Orthomorphic with two standard parallels

East from Greenwich

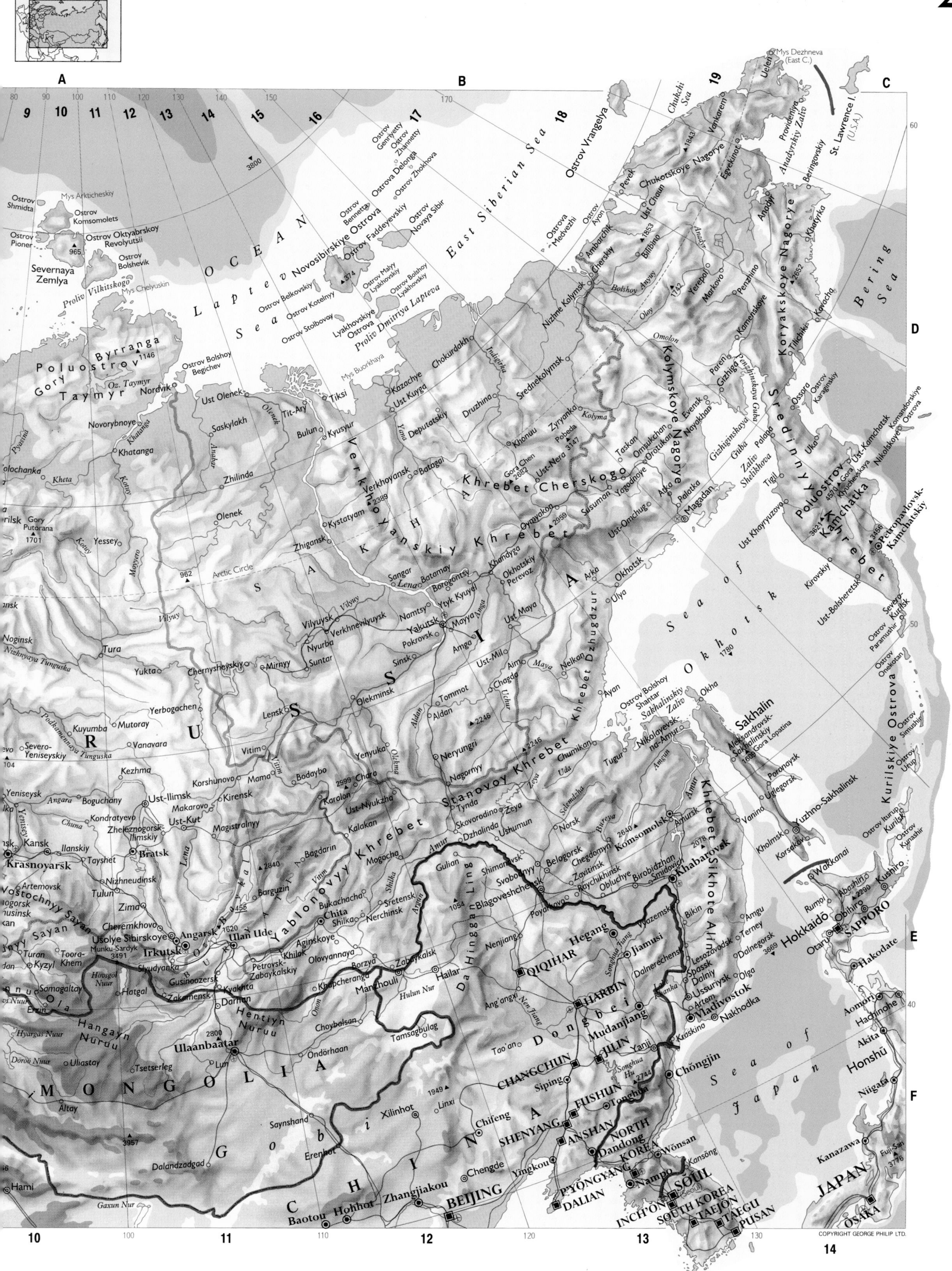

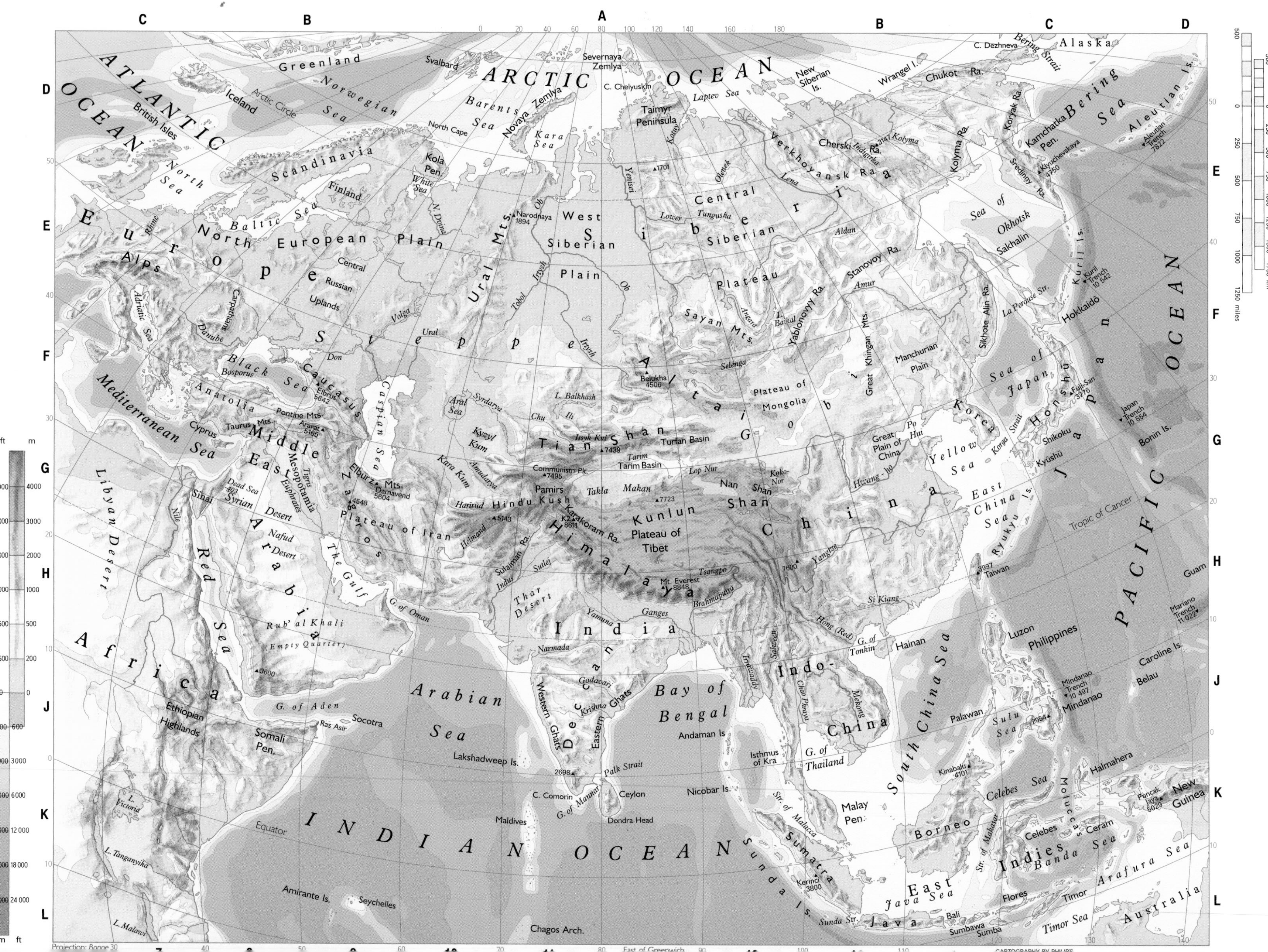

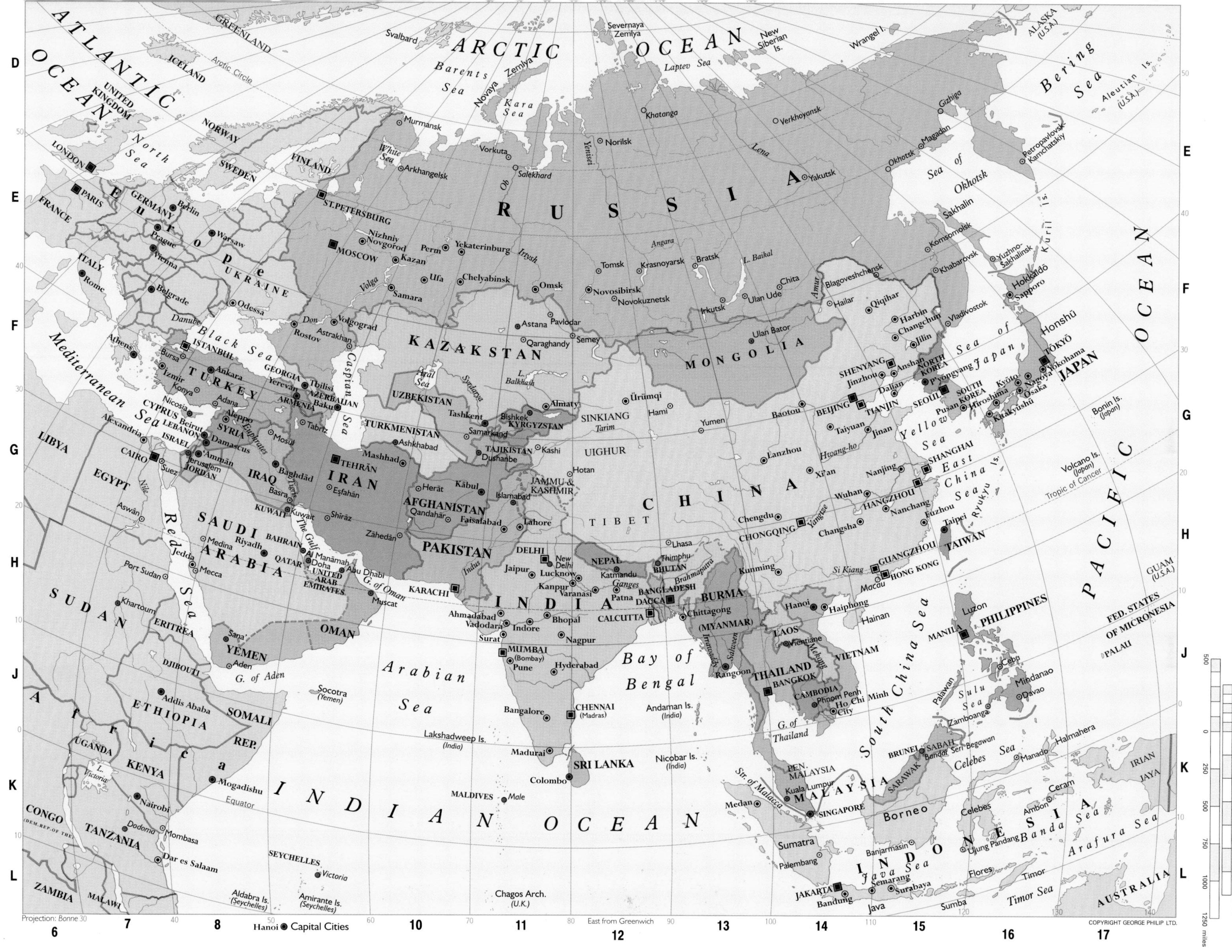
ARCTIC OCEAN
PACIFIC OCEAN
INDIAN OCEAN
ATLANTIC OCEAN
RUSSIA
CHINA
MONGOLIA
KAZAKSTAN
INDIA
PAKISTAN
AFGHANISTAN
IRAN
IRAQ
SAUDI ARABIA
TURKEY
SYRIA
JORDAN
ISRAEL
LEBANON
CYPRUS
GEORGIA
ARMENIA
AZERBAIJAN
TURKMENISTAN
UZBEKISTAN
TAJIKISTAN
KYRGYZSTAN
NEPAL
BHUTAN
BANGLADESH
BURMA (MYANMAR)
THAILAND
LAOS
VIETNAM
CAMBODIA
MALAYSIA
SINGAPORE
INDONESIA
PHILIPPINES
TAIWAN
JAPAN
NORTH KOREA
SOUTH KOREA
SRI LANKA
MALDIVES
OMAN
YEMEN
KUWAIT
BAHRAIN
QATAR
UNITED ARAB EMIRATES
EGYPT
SUDAN
ETHIOPIA
SOMALI REP.
KENYA
TANZANIA
ERITREA
DJIBOUTI
UGANDA
LIBYA
Caspian Sea
Black Sea
Mediterranean Sea
Red Sea
Arabian Sea
Bay of Bengal
South China Sea
East China Sea
Yellow Sea
Sea of Japan
Sea of Okhotsk
Bering Sea
Laptev Sea
Kara Sea
Barents Sea
Java Sea
Timor Sea
Hanoi ● Capital Cities
Projection: Bonne
East from Greenwich
COPYRIGHT GEORGE PHILIP LTD.
500 0 250 500 750 1000 1250 1500 1750 km
500 0 250 500 750 1000 1250 miles

JAPAN 1:5 000 000

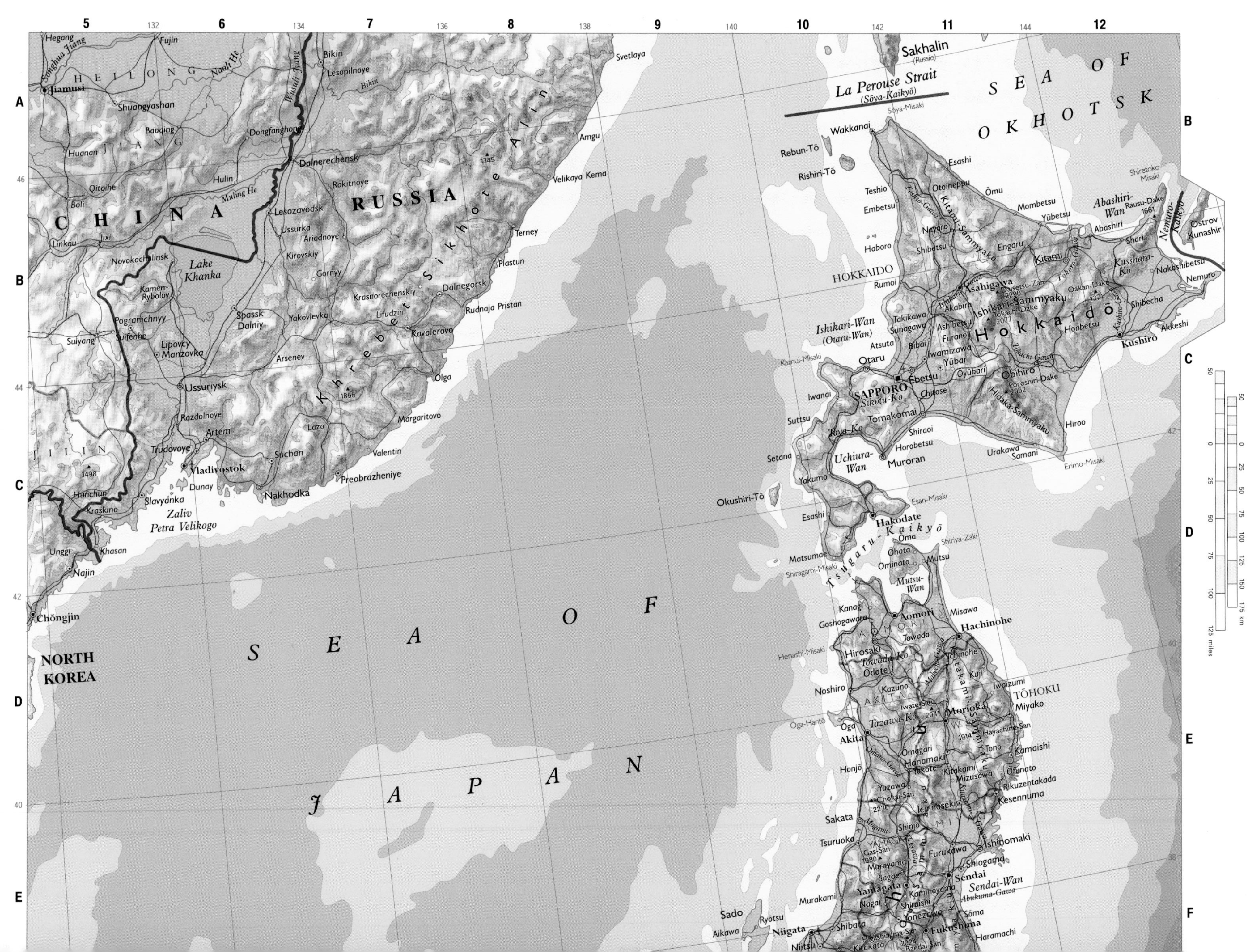

50   0   25   50   75   100 125 150 175 km

50   0   25   50   75   100 125 miles

SEA OF OKHOTSK

Sakhalin
(Karafuto)

La Perouse Strait
(Sōya-Kaikyō)

HOKKAIDO

SEA OF JAPAN

RUSSIA

S i k h o t e   A l i n

CHINA

HEILONG JIANG

JILIN

NORTH KOREA

Lake Khanka

Wusuli Jiang

TOHOKU

OU   SANMYAKU

HOKKAIDO

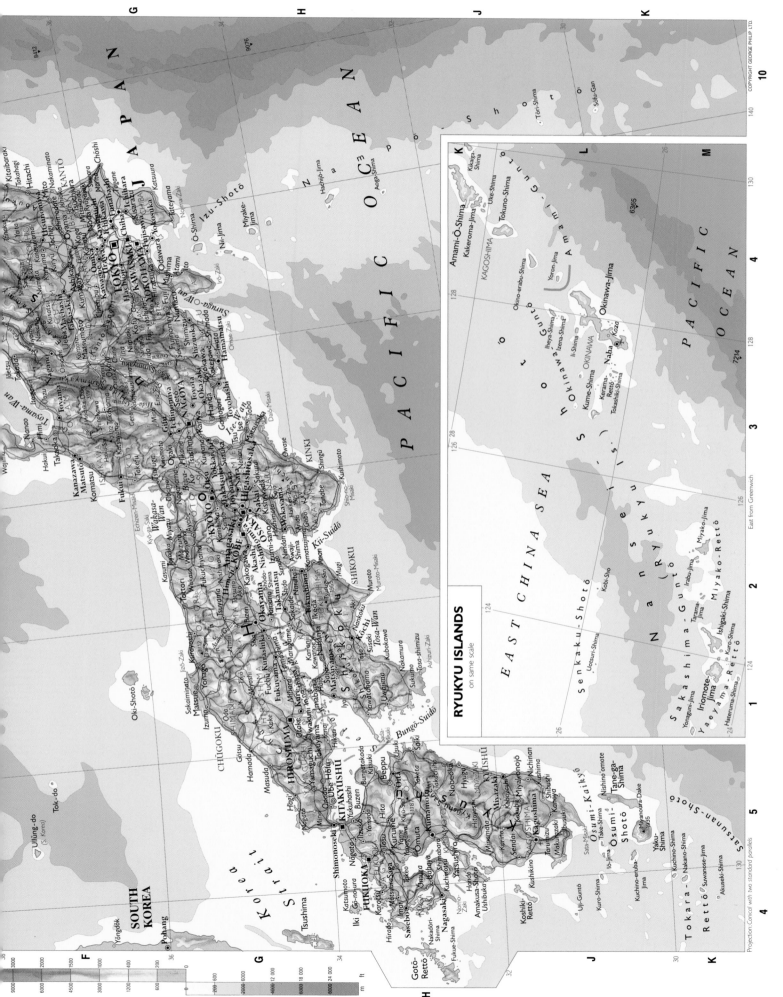

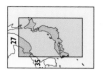

10

J A P A N

S O U T H K O R E A

P A C I F I C   O C E A N

RYUKYU ISLANDS
on same scale

E A S T   C H I N A   S E A

P A C I F I C   O C E A N

KAGOSHIMA

OKINAWA

Amami-Ō-Shima

Okinawa-Jima

Naha

Miyako-Rettō

Ishigaki-Shima

East from Greenwich

Projection: Conical with two standard parallels

m ft

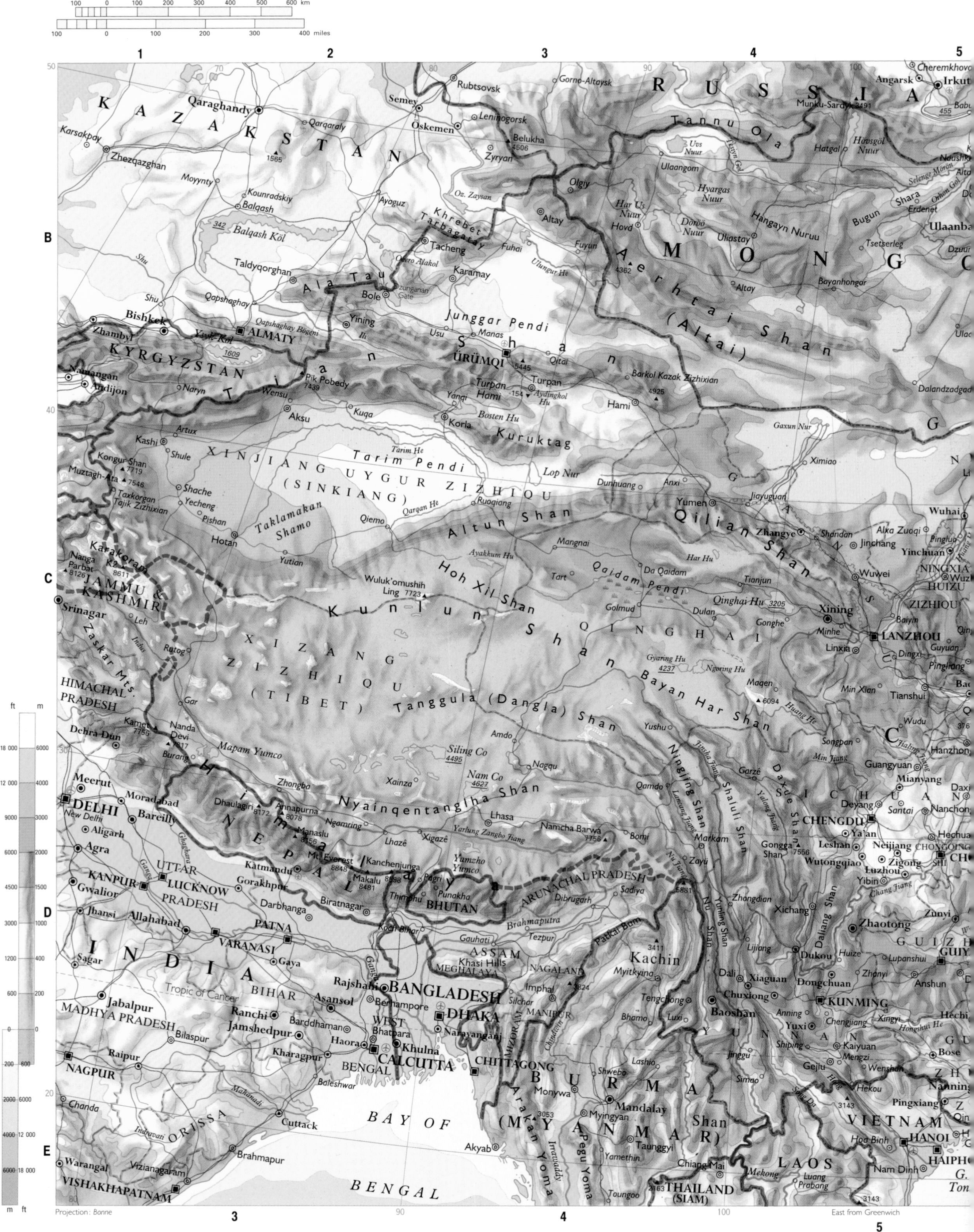

100 0 100 200 300 400 500 600 km
100 0 100 200 300 400 miles

1 2 3 4 5

KAZAKSTAN

Qaraghandy
Karsakpay
Zhezqazghan
Moyynty
Kounradskiy
Balqash
Balqash Köl
342

Semey
Qarqaraly
Öskemen
Leninogorsk
Rubtsovsk
Belukha
4506
Zyryan
Oz. Zaysan
Ayaguz
Osero Alakol
Zungarian
Gate
Tacheng

RUSSIA

Gorno-Altaysk
Angarsk
Irkut
Cheremkhova
Munku-Sardyk
4491
455

Tannu Ola
Uvs
Nuur
Ulaangom
Hovsgol
Ntur
Hatgal

Olgiy
Altay
Har Us
Nuur
Hova

MONGO
Aerhtai Shan
(Altai)

Hyargas
Nuur
Doroo
Nuur
Uliastay
Bayanhongor

Hangayn Nuruu
Bugun
Shara
Erdenet
Selenge Moron
Okhon Gol
Ulaanba

Dalandzadgad

B

Bishkek
Zhambyl
KYRGYZSTAN
Almaty
Qapshaghay
Qapshaghay Bogeni
Issyk-Kul
1609
Namangan
Andijon
Naryn
Pik Pobedy
7439
T i a n

Yining
Ili
Usu
Manas
URUMQI
5445
Turpan
Aydingkol
Hu
-154
Hami
Turpan
Yanqi
Korla
Kuruktag

Khrebet
Tarbagatay
Fuhai
Ulungur He
Karamay
Junggar Pendi

Altay
4362

Qitai
Barkol Kazak Zizhixian
Hami
4925

Gaxun Nur

G

Ximiao

G
Dalandzadgad

40

Nanga
Parbat
8126
Kongur Shan
7719
Muztagh-Ata
7546
Taxkorgan
Tajik Zizhixian
Kashi
Artux
Shule
Shache
Yecheng
Pishan
Yutian
Hotan

Aksu
Wensu
Kuqa
Tarim He
Taklamakan
Shamo
Qarqan He
Qiemo
Ruoqiang

XINJIANG
UYGUR ZIZHIQU
(SINKIANG)
Tarim Pendi
Lop Nur

Altun Shan
Dunhuang
Anxi
Yumen
Jiayuguan

Qilian Shan
Zhangye
Shandan
Alxa Zuoqi

Wuhai
NINGXIA
HUIZU
ZIZHIQU

C

JAMMU &
KASHMIR
K2
8611
Karakoram
Srinagar
Leh
Zaskar Mts.
Ratog

HIMACHAL
PRADESH
Dehra Dun

Ayakkum Hu
Hoh Xil Shan
Wuluk'omushih
Ling 7723
Kun l u n S h a n

Tart
Mangnai
Qaidam Pendi
Da Qaidam
Golmud

QINGHAI
Har Hu
Tianjun
Qinghai Hu
3205
Dulan
Gonghe
Linxia
Xining
Minhe
Baiyin
Guyuan
Dingxi
Pingliang

LANZHOU

D

DELHI
New Delhi
Meerut
Moradabad
Aligarh
Agra
KANPUR
Gwalior
Jhansi
LUCKNOW
Allahabad
UTTAR
PRADESH

Kamet
7756
Nanda
Devi
7817
Mapam Yumco
Burang
Dhaulagiri
8172
Annapurna
8078
Manaslu
8156
Zhongba
Ngamring
NEPAL
Katmandu
Gorakhpur
Darbhanga
Biratnagar

Xizang
Gar

XIZANG
ZIZHIQU
(TIBET)
Siling Co
4495
Xainza
Nam Co
4627
Zhongba
Nyainqentanglha Shan
Lhasa
Mt Everest
8848
Kanchenjunga
Xigaze
Lhaze
Makalu 8198
8481
Yarlung Zangbo Jiang
Thimphu
Bagri
Punakha
BHUTAN

Tanggula (Dangla) Shan
Amdo
Nagqu
Yushu
Songpan

Bayan Har Shan
6094
Magen

Qamdo
Ningjing Shan

Namcha Barwa
7756
Bomi

Zayu
ARUNACHAL PRADESH
Dibrugarh
Sadiya
6881
Zhongdian

Shaluli Shan
Daxue Shan
Garze
Gongga
Shan 7556
Yalan
Xichang
Daliang Shan

Yala
Deyang
CHENGDU
Neijiang
CHONGQING
Zigong
Yibin
Leshan
Wutongqiao
Luzhou

SICHUAN
Mianyang
Santai
Nanchon
Guangyuan
Min Jiang
Daxi

Wudu
Songpan
C

Hanzho
SHI

E

INDIA
Sagar
Jabalpur
MADHYA PRADESH
Raipur
NAGPUR
Chanda
ORISSA
Warangal
Vizianagaram
VISHAKHAPATNAM
Brahmapur
Indravati
Mahanadi
80

Jhansi
Allahabad
VARANASI
Gaya
PATNA
BIHAR
Tropic of Cancer
Ranchi
Barddhaman
Jamshedpur
Bilaspur
Kharagpur
Baleshwar
Cuttack
20

Gauhati
Kochi Bihar
ASSAM
MEGHALAYA
Khasi Hills
Rajshahi
Berhampore
BANGLADESH
Asansol
WEST
Bhatpara
Khulna
Narayanganj
DHAKA
Haora
CALCUTTA
BENGAL
Tezpur
NAGALAND
Imphal
MANIPUR
Silchar
3411
Kachin
Myitkyina
3824
MIZORAM
CHITTAGONG
Monywa
Arakan
Yoma
(MYANMAR)
3053
Akyab
Yamethin
Pegu Yoma
Toungoo

BAY OF
BENGAL

BURMA
Bhamo
Lashio
Mandalay
Myingyan
Taunggyi
Shwebo
Irrawaddy
Chindwin
Salween

THAILAND
(SIAM)
Chiang Mai
Mekong
Luang
Prabang
LAOS
3143

Tengchong
Baoshan
Luxi
Dali
Xiaguan
Chuxiong
KUNMING
Anning
Yuxi
Chengjiang
Shiping
Jinggu
Simao
Gejlu
Kaiyuan
Mengzi
Wenshan

YUNNAN
Dongchuan
Zhaotong
Dukou
Lijiang
Huize
Anshun
Lupanshui
Zhonyi
GUIZHOU
GUIY

VIETNAM
HANOI
Hoa Binh
Nam Dinh
HAIPHO
Pingxiang
Nanning
Bose
ZH
Hekou
3143

1500
18 000
12 000
9000
6000
4500
3000
1200
600
0
200
2000
4000
6000
ft m
6000
4000
3000
2000
1500
1000
400
200
0
600
6000
12 000
18 000
m ft

Projection: Bonne
East from Greenwich

3 90 4 100 5

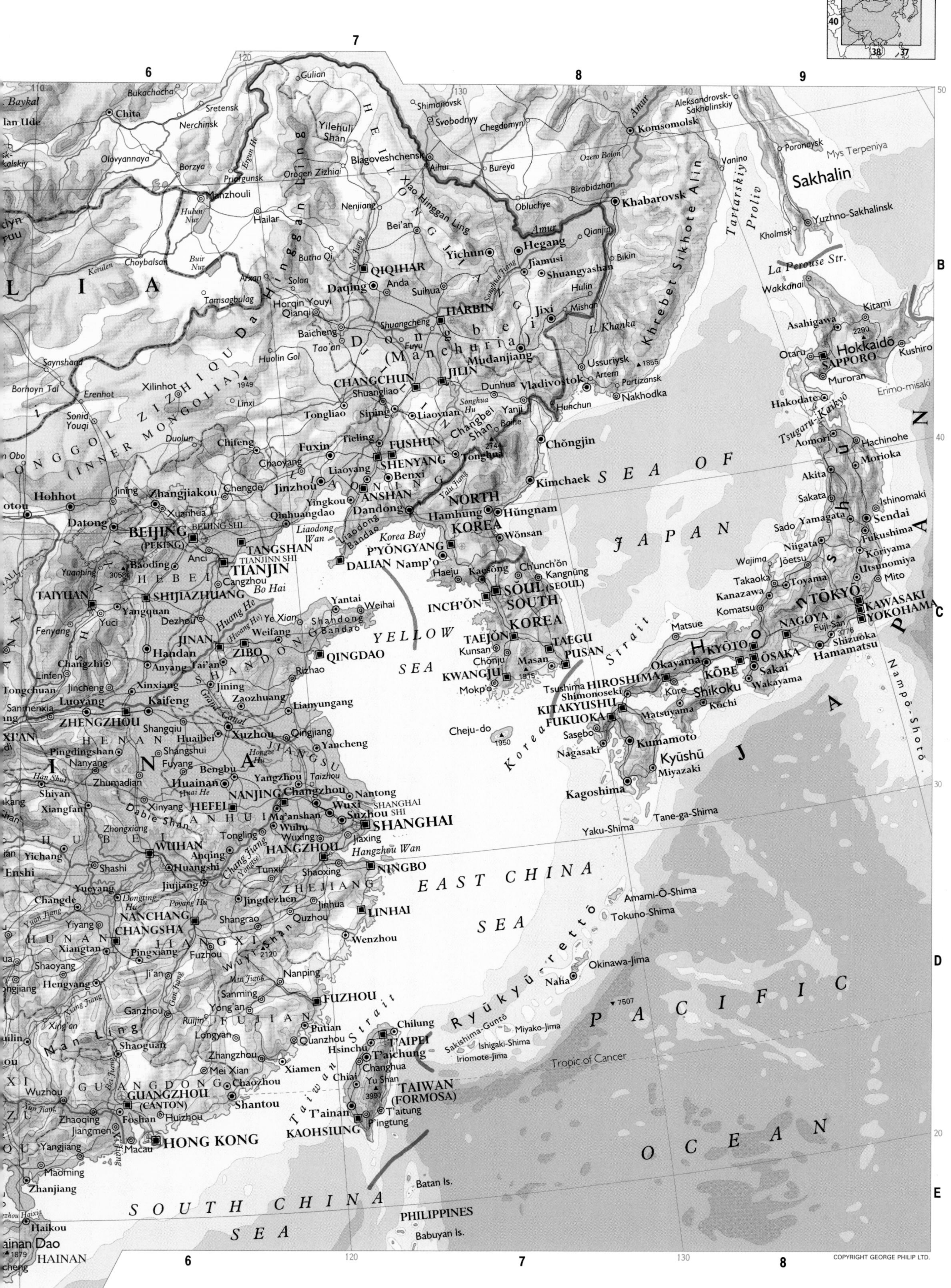
SEA OF JAPAN
YELLOW SEA
EAST CHINA SEA
SOUTH CHINA SEA
PACIFIC OCEAN
NORTH KOREA
SOUTH KOREA
BEIJING
TIANJIN
SHANGHAI
PUSAN
HONG KONG
TAIWAN (FORMOSA)
Hokkaidō
Sakhalin
Tropic of Cancer

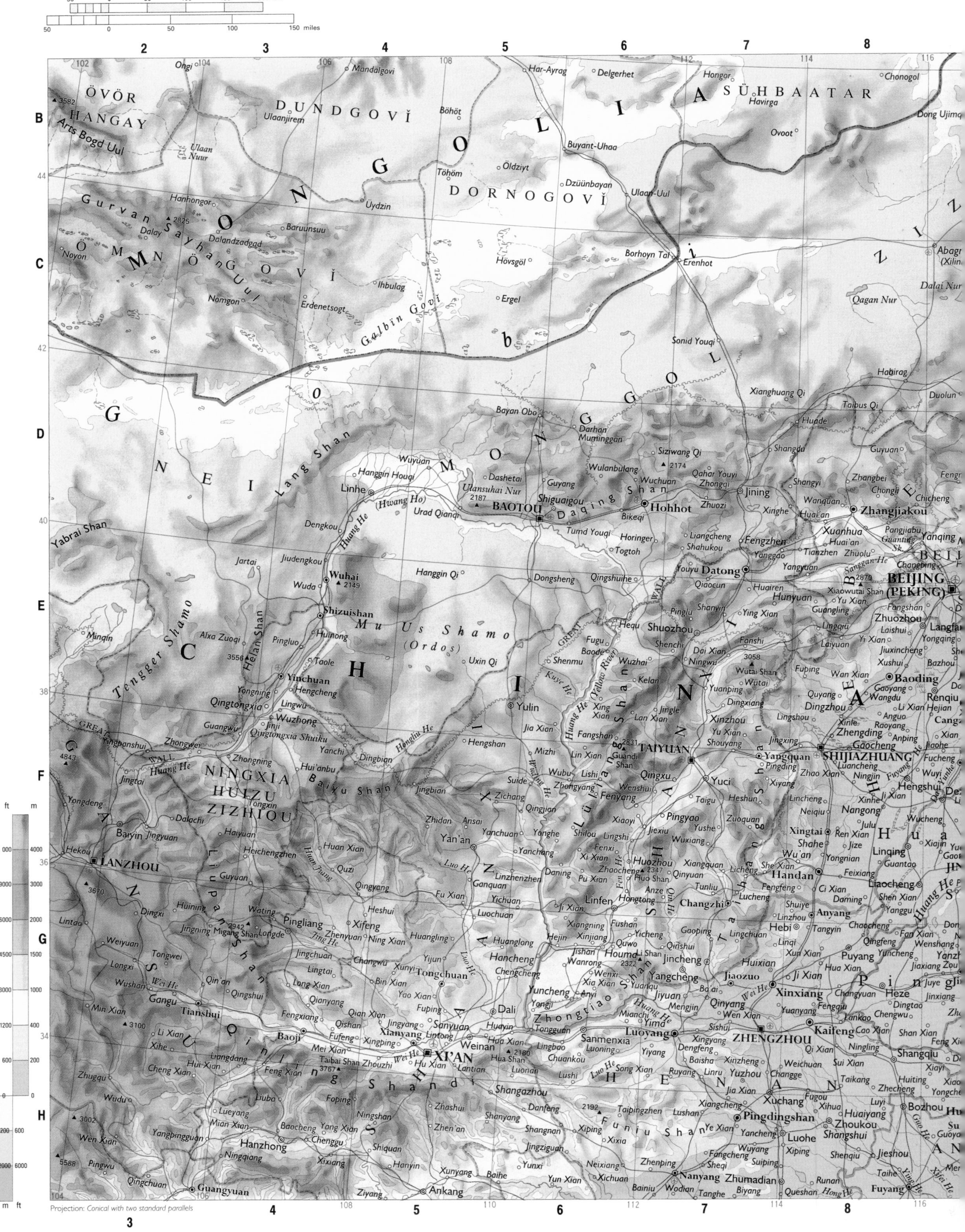

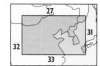

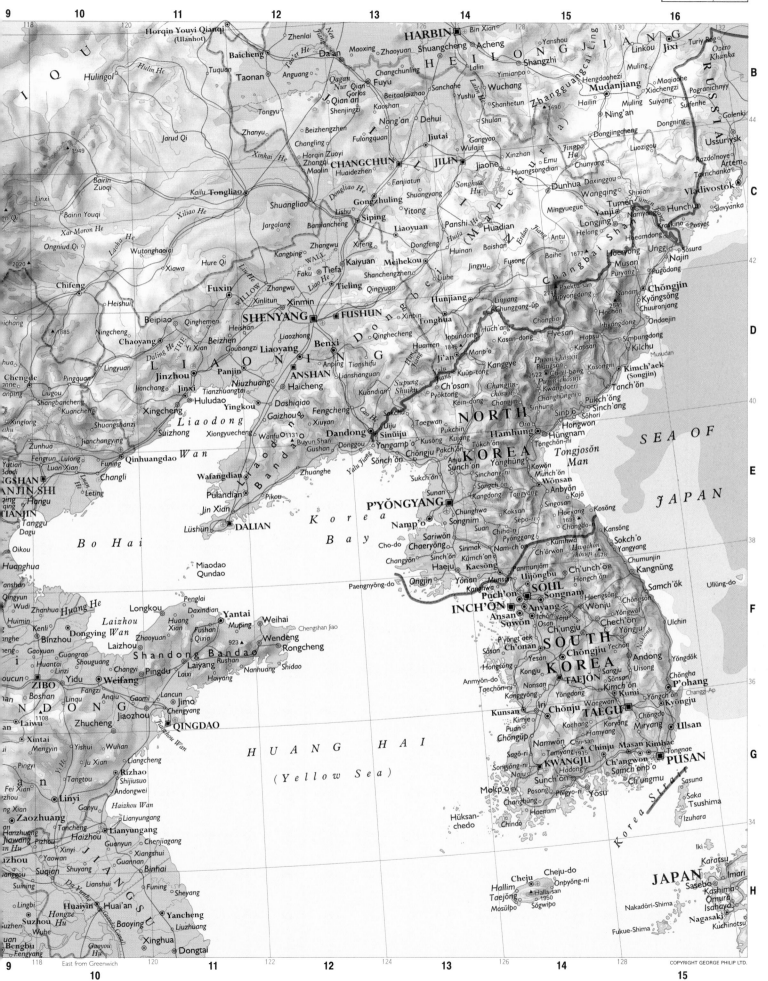

COPYRIGHT GEORGE PHILIP LTD.

9 10 11 12 13 14 15 16
Horqin Youyi Qianqi (Ulanhot) Zhenlai Nen Jiang HARBIN Bin Xian Yanshou Linkou Jixi Turiy Rog Ozero Khanka
Baicheng Tao'er He Da'an Maoxing Zhaoyuan Shuangcheng Acheng Shangzhi H E I L O N G J I A N G Muling
Hulingol Hulin He Tuquan Taonan Anguang Qagan Nur Qian Gorlos Changchunling Fuyu Lalin Yimianpo Hengdaohezi Mudanjiang Maqiaohe Xiachengzi Pogranichnyy Suifenhe R U S S I A
Tongyu Qian an Shenjingzi Beitaolaizhao Sanchahe Yushu Wuchang Shanhetun Zhangguangcai Ling 1690 Hailin Muling Suiyang Golenki
Kaoshan Nong'an Dehui Shulan Ning'an Dongning
Zhanyu Beizhengzhen Jarud Qi 1949 Changling Fulongquan Jiutai Gangyao Wulajie Dongjingcheng Luozigou Ussuriysk
Xinkai He Horqin Zuoyi Zhongqi Maolin Huaidezhen CHANGCHUN JILIN Jiaohe Xinzhan Emu Huangsongdian Jingpo Hu Chunyang Razdolnoye Artem Tavrichanka
Bairin Zuoqi Kailu Tongliao Fanjiatun Songhua Hu Dunhua Daxinggou Vladivostok
Linxi Shuangliao Dongliao He Gongzhuling Shuangyang Wangqing Shixian Tumen Hunchun Slavyanka
Bairin Youqi Xiliao He Lishu Siping Yitong Mingyuegue Yanji Namyang Tumen Jiang Kraskino Posyet
Xar Moron He Jargalang Bamiancheng Liaoyuan Panshi Huadian Longjing Helong
Ongniud Qi Laoha He Wutonghaolai Zhangwu Xifeng Dongfeng Huinan Huifa He Erdao Jiang Antu Hoeamdong Unggi Sosura
2020 Xiawa Kangping WALL Kaiyuan Meihekou Baishan Baihe 1677 Hoeryong Najin
Hure Qi Liuhe Faku Tiefa Shanchengzhen Jingyu Fusong Musan Puryong Pugodong
Chifeng Fuxin THE WILLOW Zhangwu Liao He Tieling Qingyuan Liuhe Changbai Shan Paektu-san 2744 Yupyongdong Nanam Chongjin Kyongsong
Heishui Xinlitun Xinmin Hunjiang Linjiang Chunggang-up 2541 Chuuronjang
Beipiao Qinghemen SHENYANG FUSHUN Xinbin Tonghua Changbai Haechon Ondaejin
Ningcheng 1885 Heishan Liaozhong Qingyuan Huch'ang Hyesan Irhyangdong
Chaoyang Daling He Yi Xian Beizhen Goubangzi Liaoyang Benxi Qinghecheng Huanren Inpundong Kosan-dong Hapsu Kapsan Simpungdong Kilchu
L I A O N I N G Jinzhou Panjin Anping Tianshifu 1845 Manp'o Pujon-chosuji Musudan
Lingyuan Chengde Pingquan ANSHAN Lianshanguan Ji'an Yalu Jiang Kanggye P'ungsan 2522 Ch'ail-bong Kosongni Kimch'aek (Songjin)
Liugou Jianchang Jinxi Niuzhuang Haicheng Kuandian Supung Shuiku Ch'osan Changjin-chosuji Pujon-chosuji Kwangdaeri Tanch'on
Shangbancheng Tianzhuangtai Huludao Yingkou Dashiqiao Pyoktong Koin-dong Changjin Changhungni Pukch'ong
Kuancheng Xingcheng Gaizhou Fengcheng Sakchu Sinhung Sinch'ang
Xinglong Shuangshanzi Liaodong Suizhong Xiuyan Cao He Uiju Sinp'o Sohori
Jianchangying Xiongyuecheng Wanfu 1131 Dandong Sinuiju Taegwan Pukchin N O R T H Oro Hongwon
Zunhua Buyun Shan Gushan Donggou Yongamp'o Kusong Kujang Hamhung Hungnam
Qinhuangdao Wan Tokch'on Tongchon-ni S E A O F
Fengrun Lulong Funing Yalu Jiang Chongju Pakch'on K O R E A Yonghung Tongjoson Man
Luan Xian Changli Wafangdian Sonch'on Anju Kowon
Luan He Leting Zhuanghe Sukch'on Sunch'on Sinchang-ni Munch'on Wonsan J A P A N
TIANJIN SHI Pulandian Songch'on Anbyon
Hangu Jin Xian Pikou Sunan Kangdong Tongyang Kojo
TIANJIN Tanggu Dagu Lushun DALIAN K o r e a B a y P'YONGYANG Chunghwa Koksan Singosan Kosong
Nampo Songnim Sepo-ri Hoeyang 1638 Changdo-ri Kansong
Oikou B o H a i Sariwon Suan Chiha-ri Pyonggang Sokch'o
Cho-do Chaeryong Sinmak Nam-ch'on Kumhwa Hwachon-chosuji Yangyang 1578
Huanghua Miaodao Qundao Changyon Sinch'on Kumch'on Ch'orwon Chumunjin
Haeju Kaesong Panmunjom Ch'unch'on Kangnung
Paengnyong-do Ongjin Yonan Uijongbu Hongch'on Samch'ok Ullung-do
Penglai Kanghwa Munsan SOUL
Longkou Daxindian Yantai Weihai Puch'on Songnam Hoengsong Chongson
Huang He Laizhou Wan Huang Xian Muping Chengshan Jiao INCH'ON Ansan Anyang Wonju Yongwol Ulchin
Huimin Kenli Dongying Fushan Qixia Wendeng Suwon Ich'on Osan Yoju Han'gang Chech'on
Binzhou Zhaoyuan 923 Rongcheng Ch'ungju Yongju
Laizhou S h a n d o n g B a n d a o Rushan P'yongt'aek Ch'onan S O U T H Yech'on
Gaoyuan Guangrao Shouguang Laiyang Nanhuang Shidao Sosan Yesan Chongju Andong Yongdok
Huantai Linzi Changyi Pingdu Laixi Haiyang Hongsong Kongju K O R E A Sangju Uisong
ZIBO Yidu Weifang Anmyon-do TAEJON Sonsan Chongha
Boshan Linqu Fangzi Anqiu Gaomi Lancun Jimo Taechon-ni Nonsan Kimch'on P'ohang
D O N G Jiaozhou Chengyang Kanggyong Yongdong Kumi Yongch'on Kyongju Changgi-Ap
Laiwu 1108 Zhucheng QINGDAO Kunsan Iri Chonju Waegwan TAEGU Chongdo
Xintai Jiaozhou Wan Kimje Kochang Koryong Miryang Ulsan
Mengyin Yishui Wulian Puan Hamyang Kimhae
Ju Xian Liangcheng H U A N G H A I Chongup Namwon Chii-san 1915 Chinju Masan Tongnae PUSAN
Pingyi Yi He Tangtou Rizhao Sago-ri Tamyang Ch'angwon
Fei Xian Shijiusuo (Y e l l o w S e a) Songjong-ni KWANGJU Hadong Samch'onp'o Sasuna
Andongwei Naju Sunch'on Ch'ungmu
Linyi Haizhou Wan Mokp'o Posong Polgyo-ri Yosu Saka Tsushima
Ganyu Lianyungang Hūksan-chedo Changhung Haenam Korea Strait Izuhara
Zaozhuang Tancheng Lianyungang Chindo
Pizhou Haizhou Guanyun Chenjiagang Iki
J I A N G S U Xinyi Xiangshui Karatsu
Yaowan Guannan Imari
Suqian Shuyang Binhai Cheju Cheju-do JAPAN Sasebo
Suining Da Yunhe Lianshui Funing Hallim Onpyong-ni Kashima
Lingbi Huaiyin Huai'an Sheyang Taejong Halla-san 1950 Omura
Hongze Hu Yancheng Mosulpo Sogwipo Nakadori-Shima Isahaya
Suzhou Wuhe Baoying Liuzhuang Nagasaki
Grand Canal Fukue-Shima Kuchinotsu
Bengbu Fengyang Gaoyou Hu Xinghua Dongtai
B C D E F G H
44 42 40 38 36 34
118 120 122 124 126 128 130 132
East from Greenwich
9 10 11 12 13 14 15

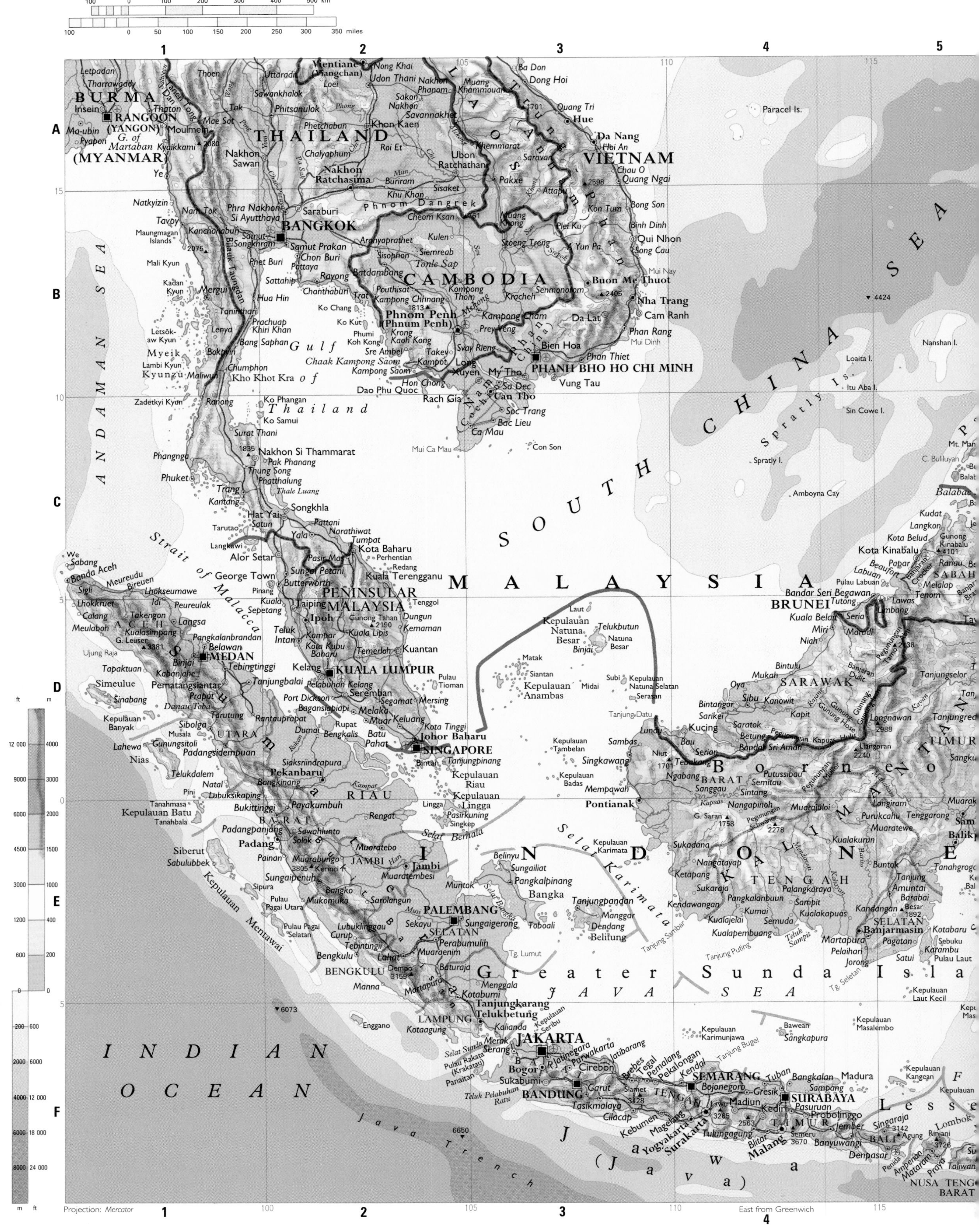

Projection: Mercator

East from Greenwich

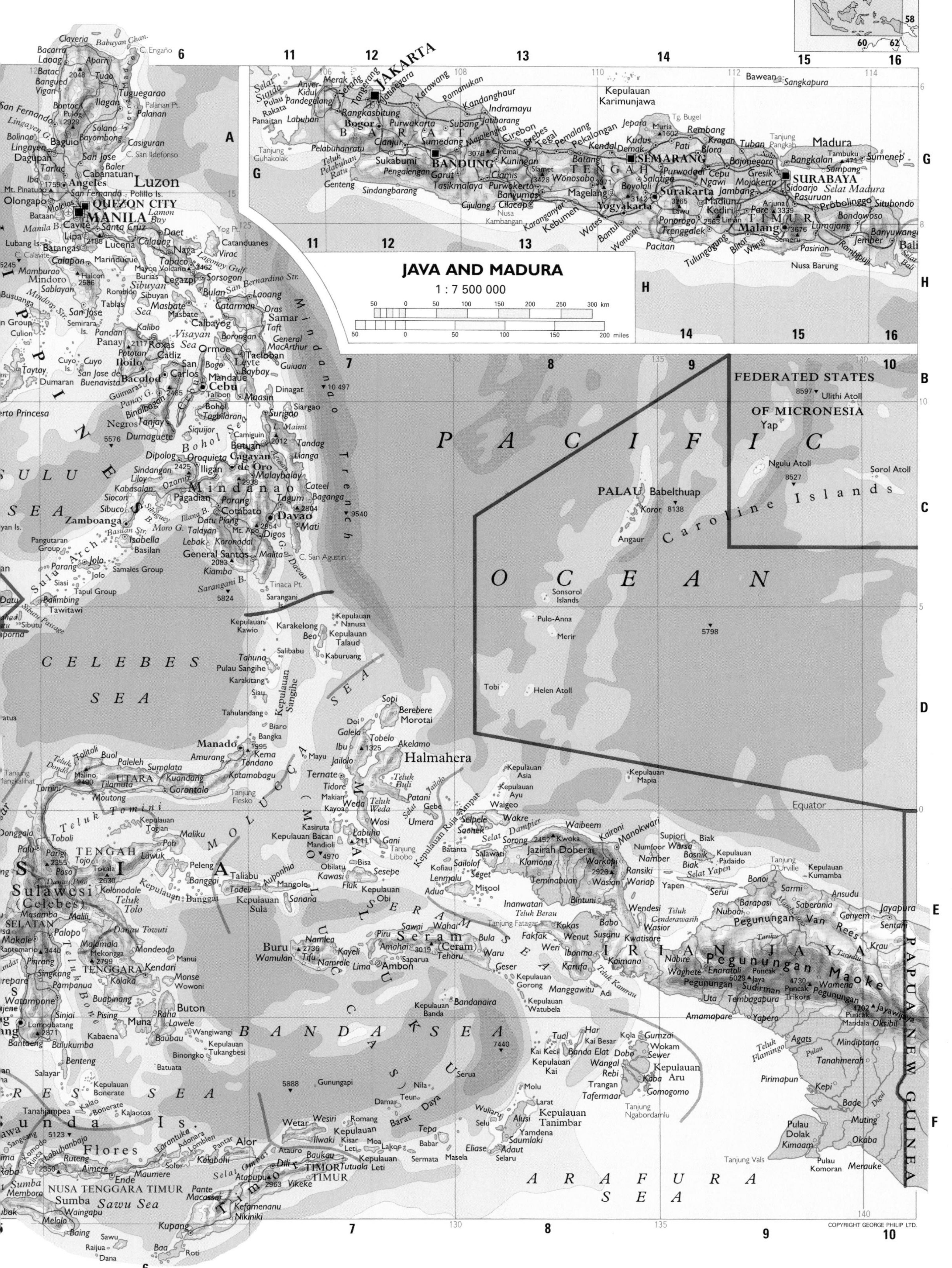

JAVA AND MADURA

1 : 7 500 000

50 0 50 100 150 200 250 300 km

50 0 50 100 150 200 miles

PACIFIC

OCEAN

FEDERATED STATES

OF MICRONESIA

Yap

Ngulu Atoll

8527

Sorol Atoll

PALAU Babelthuap

Koror 8138

Angaur

Caroline Islands

Sonsorol
Islands

Pulo-Anna

Merir

5798

Tobi

Helen Atoll

CELEBES

SEA

Ulithi Atoll

8597

Kepulauan
Kawio

Karakelong

Beo

Kepulauan
Nanusa

Kepulauan
Talaud

Salibabu

Kaburuang

Tahuna

Pulau Sangihe

Karakitang

Siau

Kepulauan
Sanghie

Tahulandang

Biaro

Bangka

Sopi

Berebere

Morotai

Doi

Galela

Ibu

Tobelo

Akelamo

Manado

1995

Amurang

Kema

Tondano

Kotamobagu

UTARA

Kuandang

Gorontalo

Tanjung
Flesko

Halmahera

Ternate

Tidore

Makian

Kayoa

Weda

Teluk
Buli

Patani

Teluk
Weda

Sagea

Kepulauan
Asia

Kepulauan
Ayu

Waigeo

Kepulauan
Mapia

Equator

ARAFURA

SEA

COPYRIGHT GEORGE PHILIP LTD.

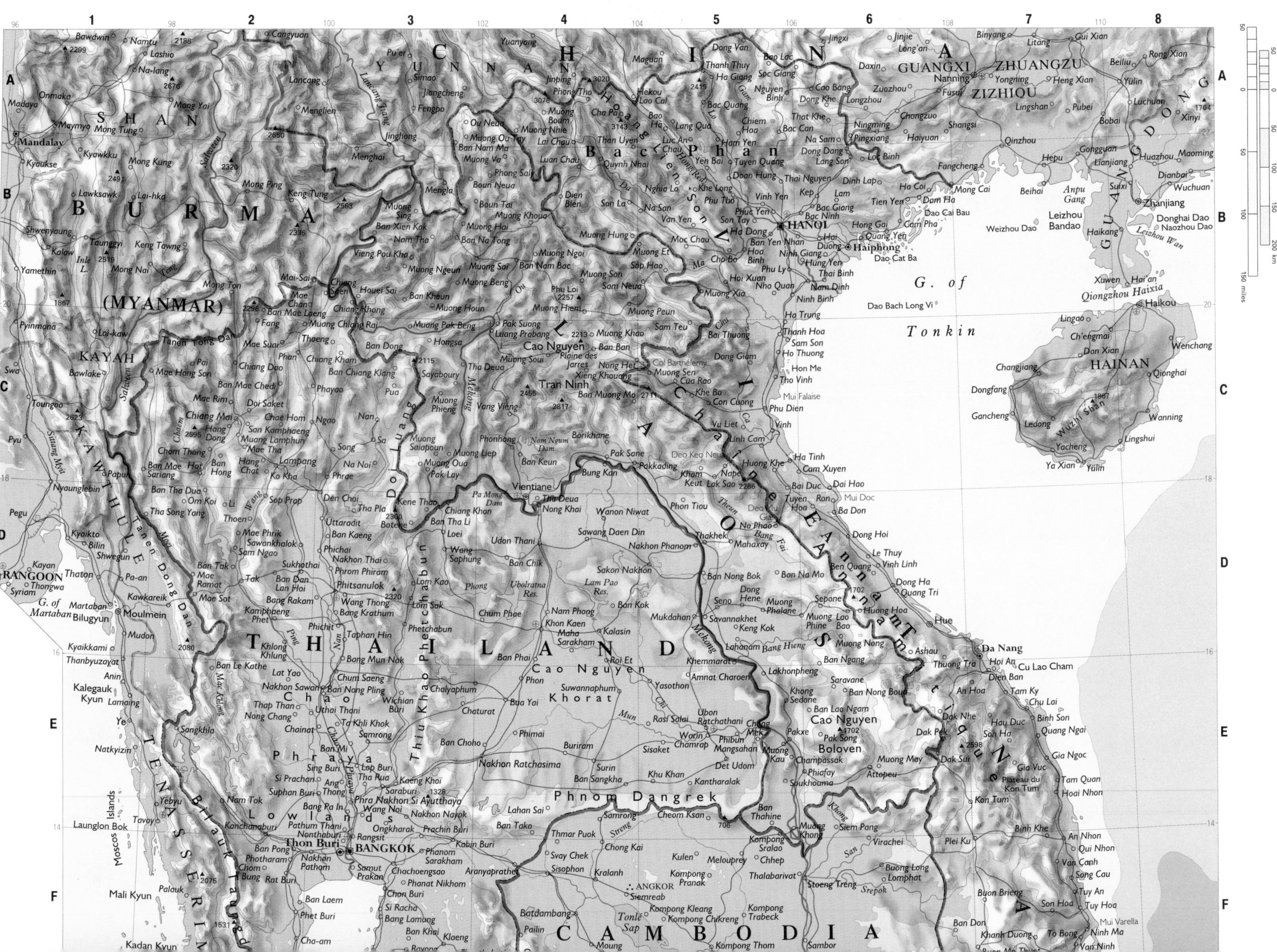

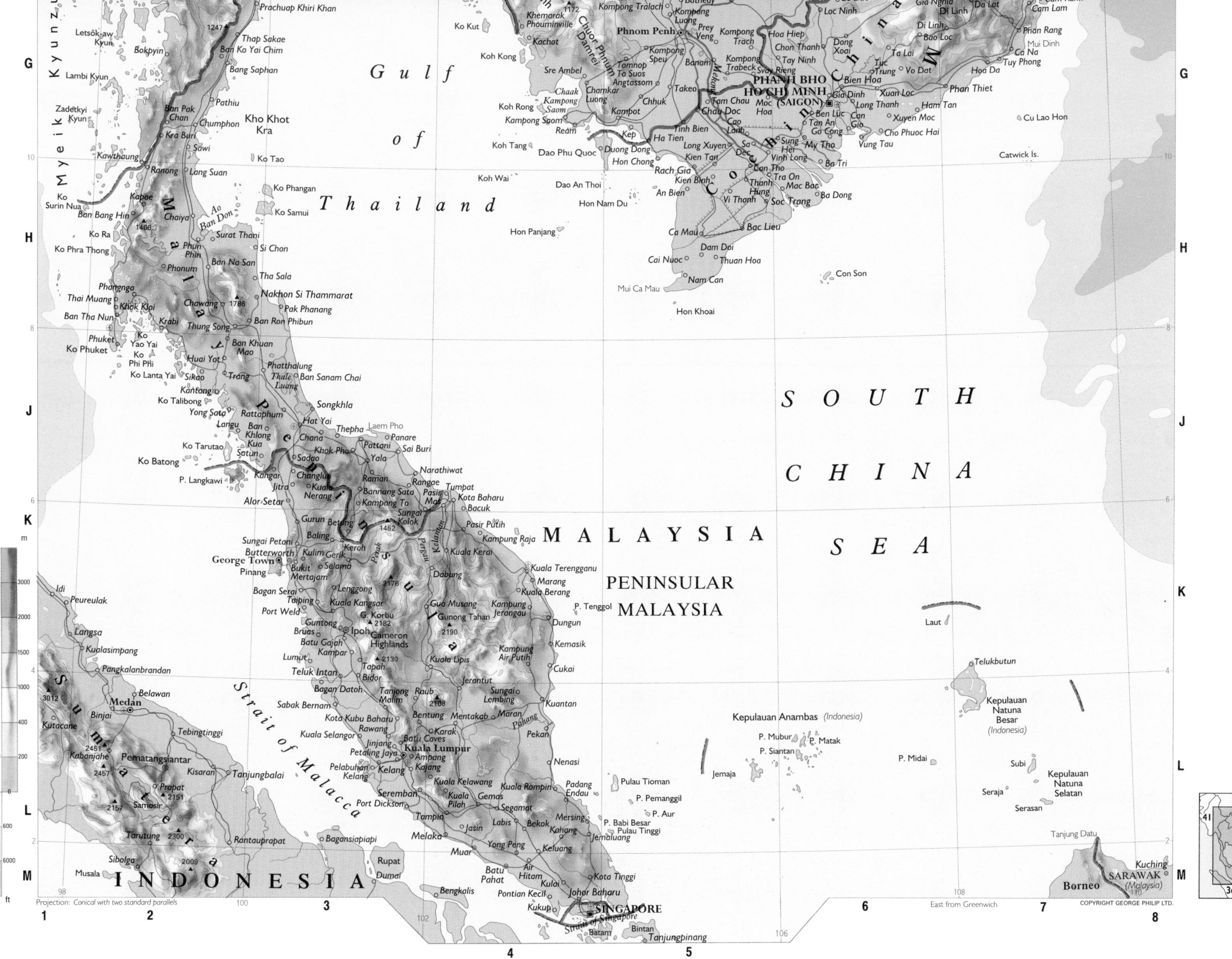

SOUTH

CHINA

SEA

MALAYSIA

PENINSULAR
MALAYSIA

Gulf

of

Thailand

INDONESIA

Strait of Malacca

Sumatera

Borneo
SARAWAK
(Malaysia)
Kuching

Kepulauan
Natuna
Selatan

Kepulauan Anambas (Indonesia)

East from Greenwich

Projection: Conical with two standard parallels

m   ft
9000
6000
4500
3000
1500
1200
600
400
200
0

ft   m
6000 2000
600
200
0

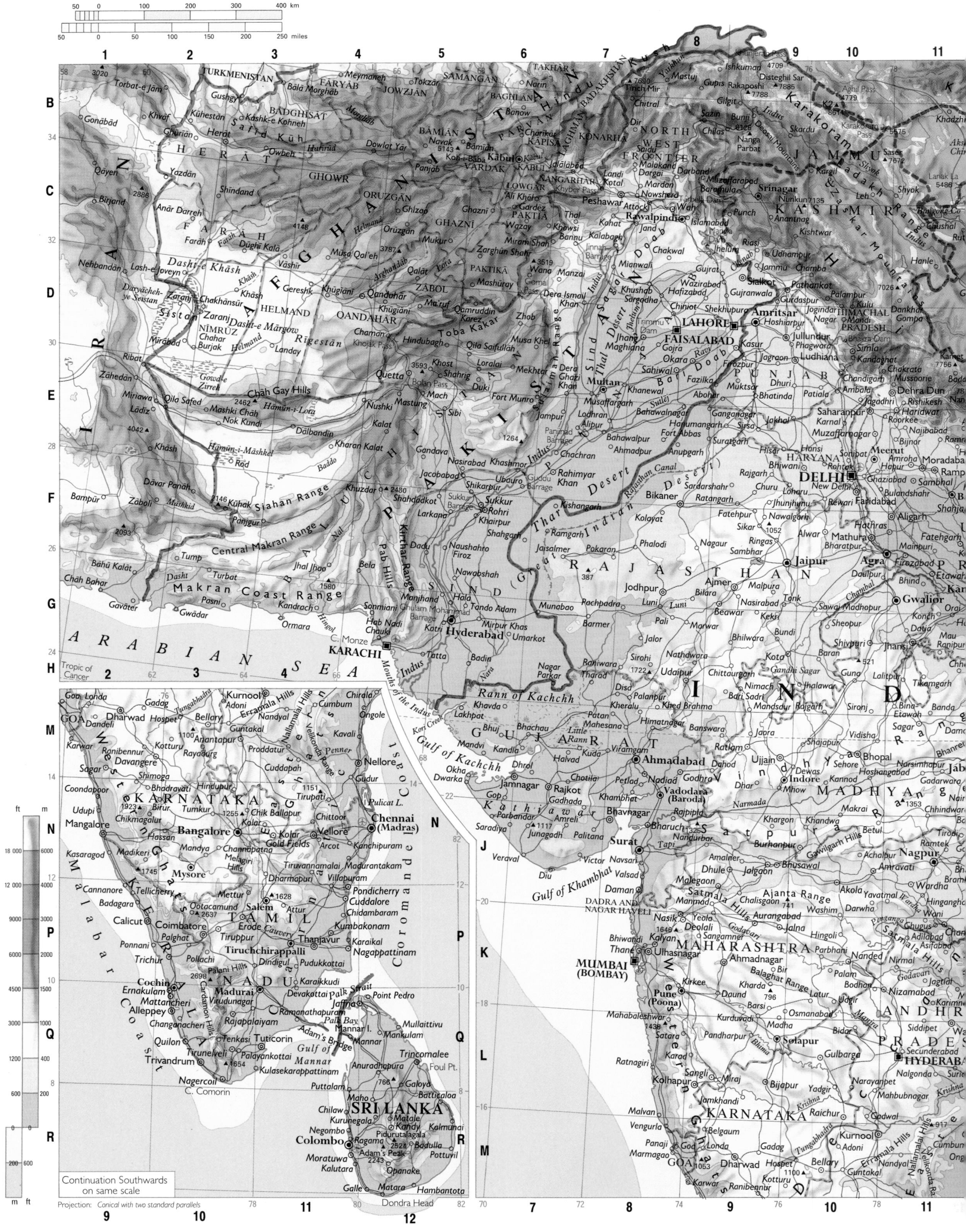

50 0   100   200   300   400 km
50   0   50   100   150   200   250 miles

Continuation Southwards
on the same scale

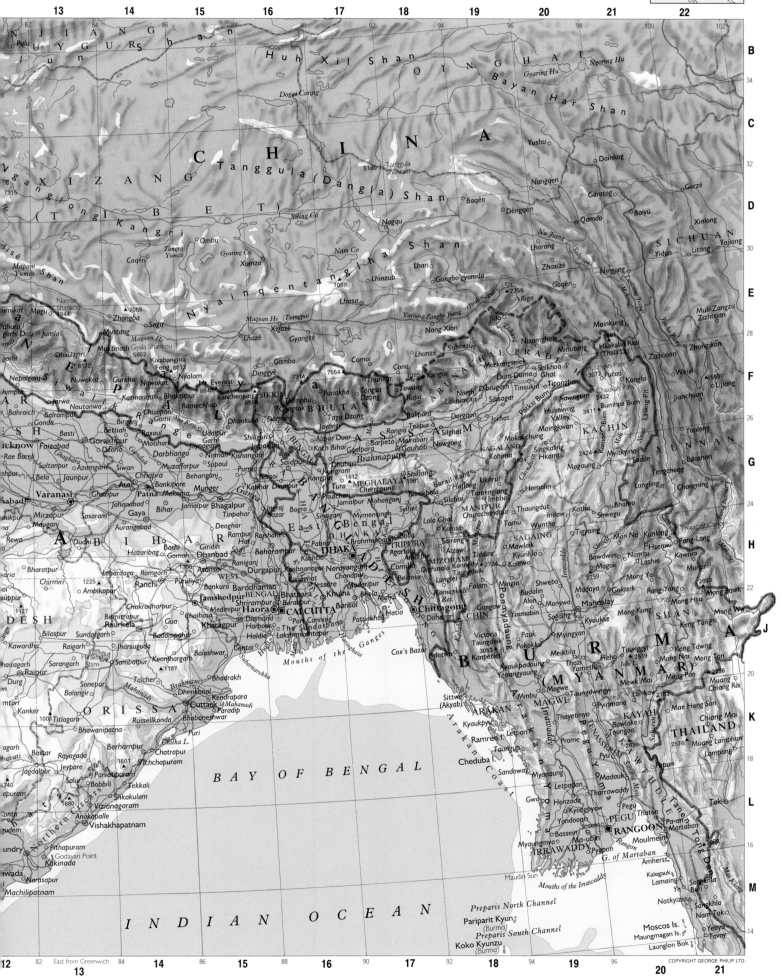

BAY OF BENGAL

INDIAN OCEAN

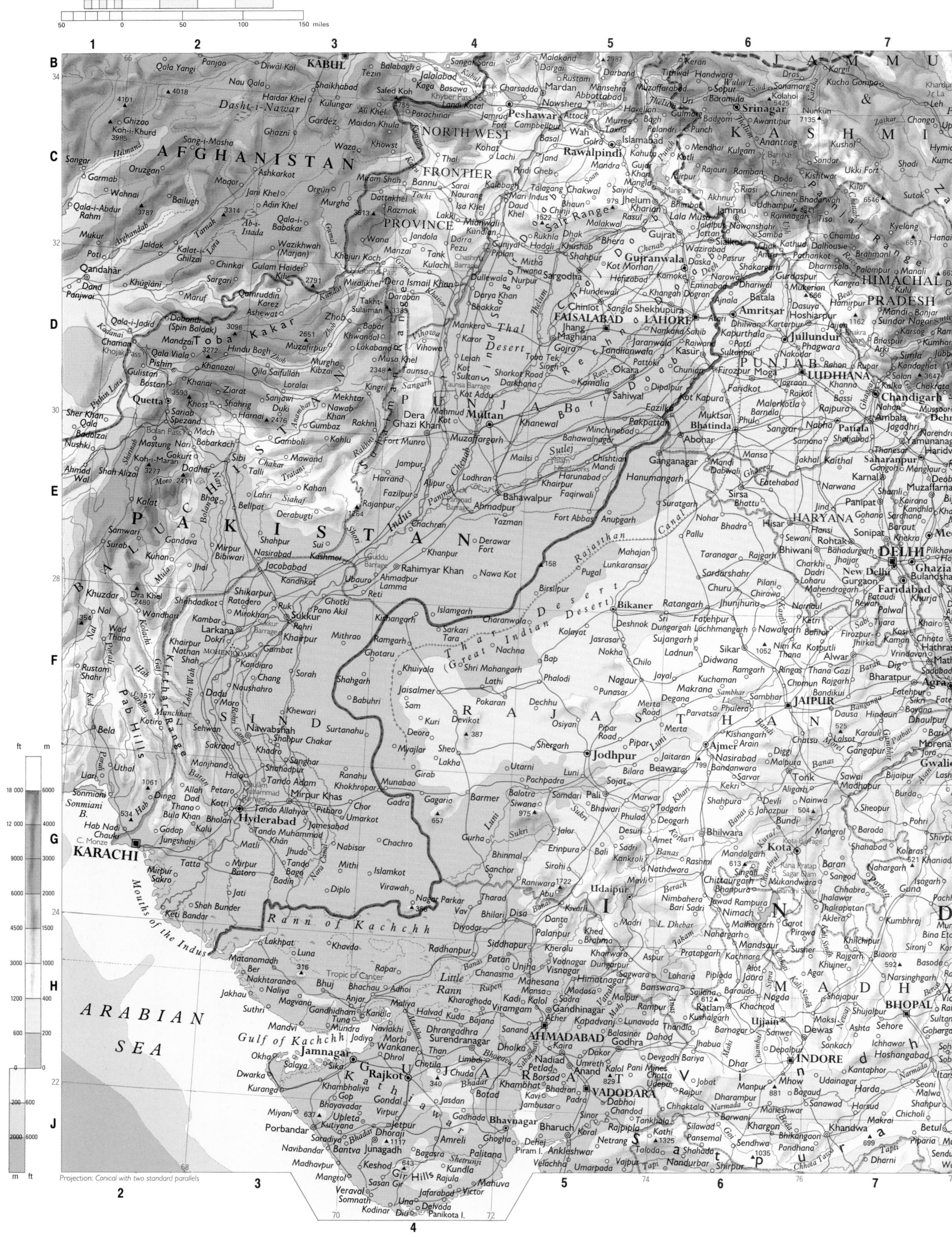
50 0 50 100 150 200 km
50 0 50 100 150 miles
AFGHANISTAN
PAKISTAN
NORTH WEST FRONTIER PROVINCE
BALUCHISTAN
PUNJAB
SIND
RAJASTHAN
HARYANA
HIMACHAL PRADESH
JAMMU & KASHMIR
KATHIAWAR
MADHYA PRADESH
ARABIAN SEA
Gulf of Kachchh
Rann of Kachchh
Mouths of the Indus
Thar Desert (Great Indian Desert)
Thal Desert
Salt Range
Dasht-i-Nawar
Kirthar Range
Pab Hills
Toba Kakar
Tropic of Cancer
KABUL
Qandahār
Quetta
Peshawar
Rawalpindi
Islamabad
Srinagar
FAISALABAD
LAHORE
Amritsar
Multan
Hyderabad
KARACHI
Sukkur
Bahawalpur
Jodhpur
Bikaner
JAIPUR
DELHI
New Delhi
Chandigarh
LUDHIANA
Jullundur
AHMADABAD
VADODARA
Rajkot
Jamnagar
Bhavnagar
Ujjain
INDORE
BHOPAL
Kota
Ajmer
Udaipur
Agra
Projection: Conical with two standard parallels

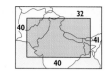

JAMMU AND KASHMIR
On same scale as Main Map

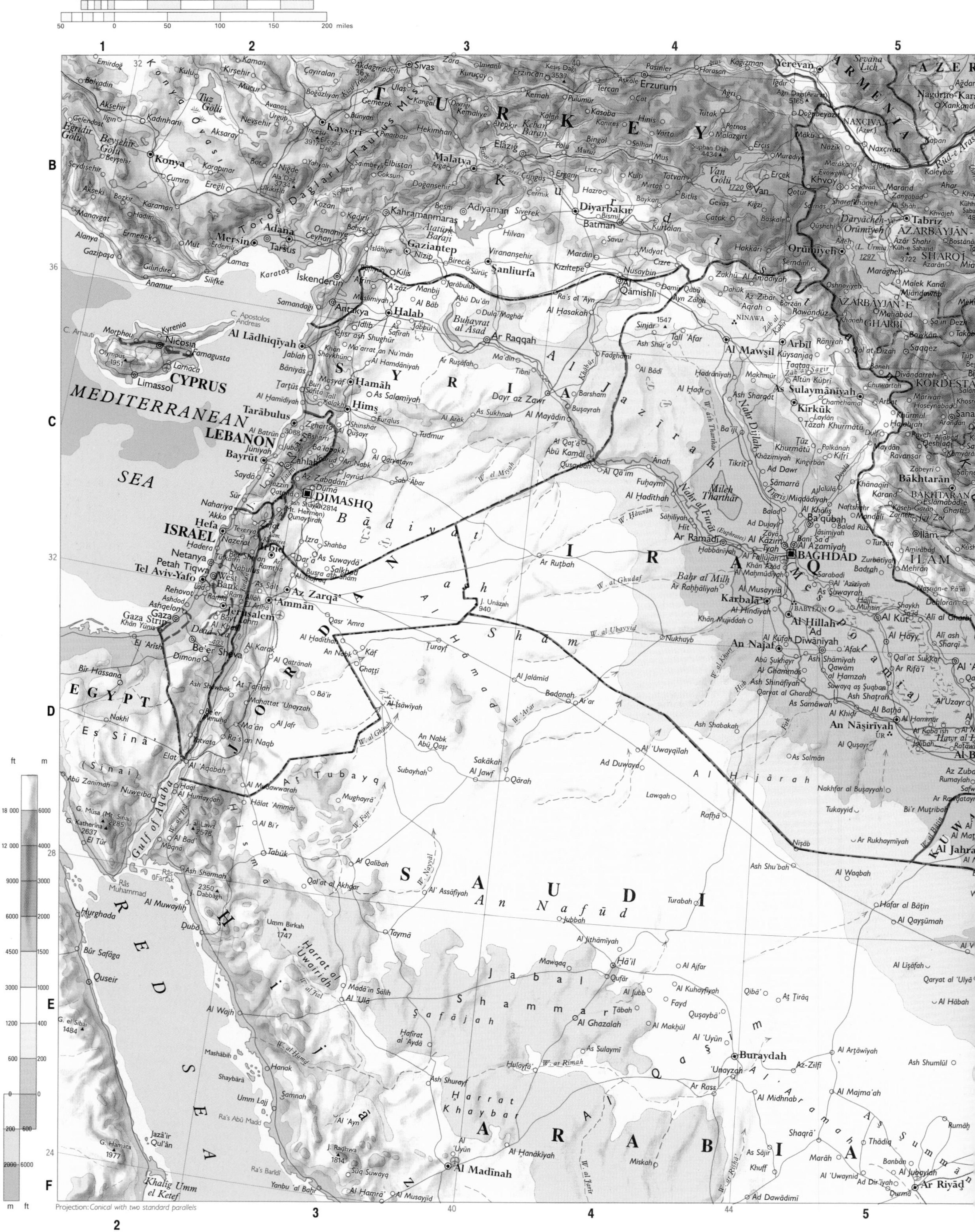

Projection: Conical with two standard parallels

6 7 8 9 10

TURKMENISTAN

Kara Kum

Kopet Dagh

CASPIAN SEA

-28

995

IRAN

Dasht-e Kavīr

Dasht-e Lūt

Reshteh-ye Kūhhā-ye Alborz

Kūhhā-ye Zāgros

AFGHANISTAN

PAKISTAN

THE GULF

Gulf of Oman

QATAR

BAHRAIN

UNITED ARAB EMIRATES

OMAN

MAZANDARAN

SEMNĀN

MARKAZĪ

KHORĀSĀN

EŞFAHĀN

YAZD

KERMĀN

FĀRS

HORMOZGĀN

SĪSTĀN VA BALŪCHESTĀN

KHUZESTĀN

BUSHEHR

KOHKILUYEH VA BUYER AHMADĪ

CHAHAR MAHALL VA BAKHTIARI

GĪLĀN

HERĀT

FARĀH

NĪMRŪZ

Safīd Kūh

Dasht-e Mārgow

Gowd-e Zirreh

Hamun-i Mashkel

Makran

Namakzār-e Shahdād

Daryācheh-ye Namak

Daryācheh-ye Sīstān

Daryācheh-ye Namakzar

Daryācheh-ye Tashk

Bīābān-e Kermān

Hāmūn-e Jaz Mūrīān

Al Jāfūrah

Str. of Hormuz

Amudarya

Shatt al Arab

Ashgabat

Mary

Chārjew

Tejen

Türkmenbashi

Nebitdag

Gazanjyk

Bakı

Rasht

Gorgān

Sārī

Qazvin

Karaj

TEHRĀN

Qom

Kāshān

Arāk

Eşfahān

Yazd

Mashhad

Sabzevār

Neyshābūr

Kermān

Zāhedān

Shīrāz

Bandar-e 'Abbās

Būshehr

Ahvāz

Dezfūl

Herāt

Farāh

Zābol

Ad Dammām

Al Manāmah

Ad Dawhah

Dubayy

Abū Zāby

Ash Shāriqah

Al 'Ayn

Al Hufūf

Ra's Masandam (Oman)

Kūh-e Bazmān 3489

Kūh-e Taftān 4042

Kūh-e Hazārān 4419

Kūh-e Dīnār 4431

Kūh-e Bīnālūd 3314

Damāvand 5604

Kūh-e Darband 2499

Kūh-e Hormoz 2804

J. al Hafit 1372

East from Greenwich

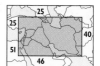

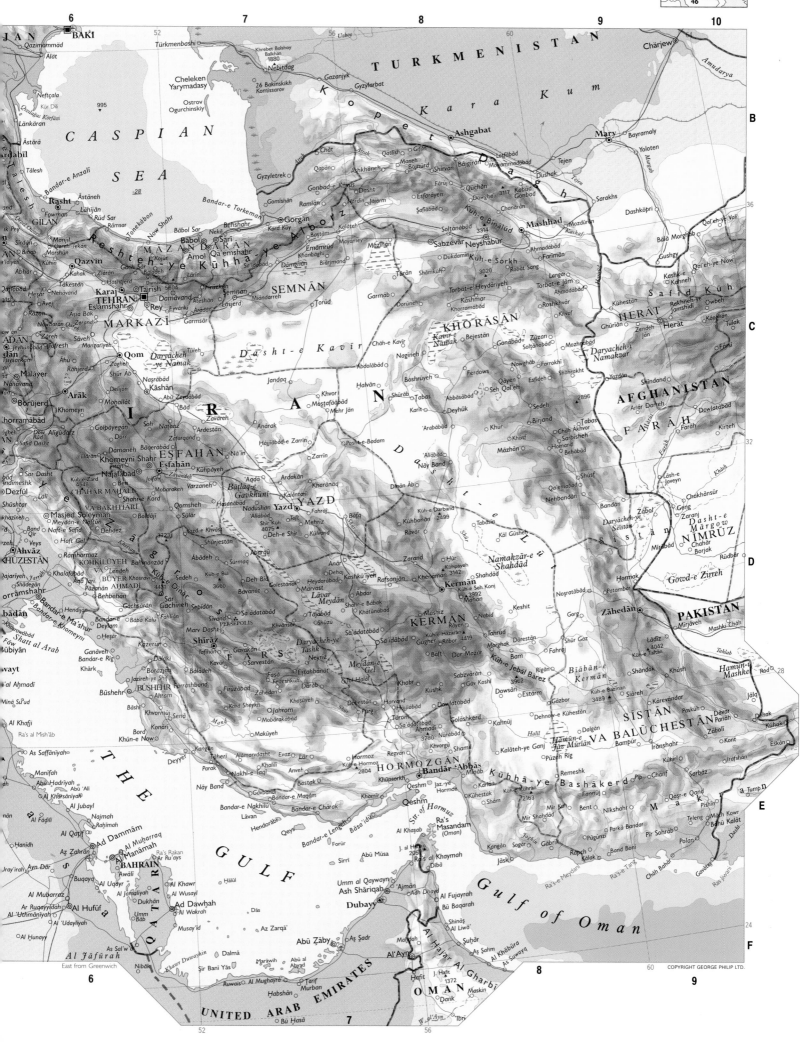

ARABIA AND THE HORN OF AFRICA 1:15 000 000

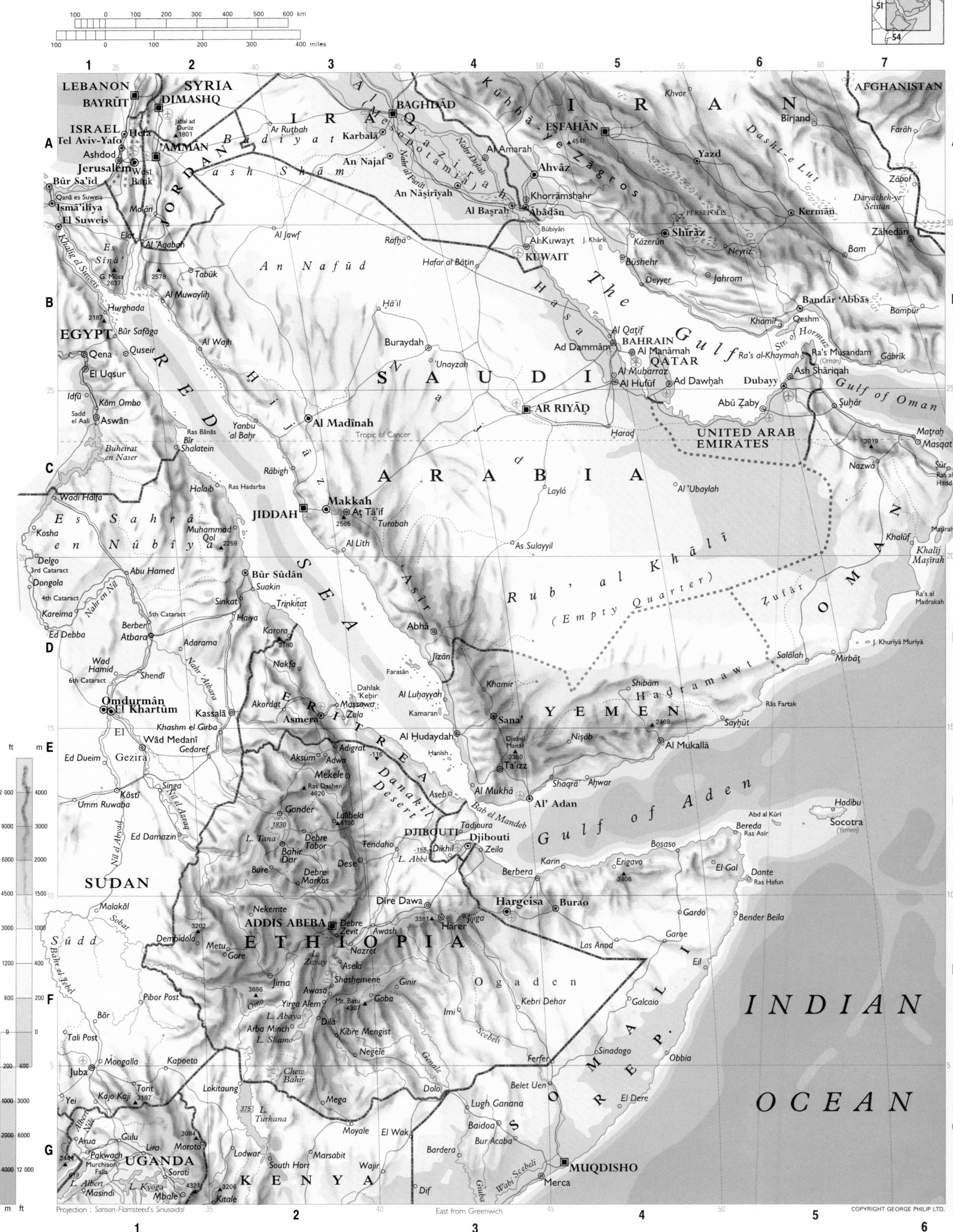

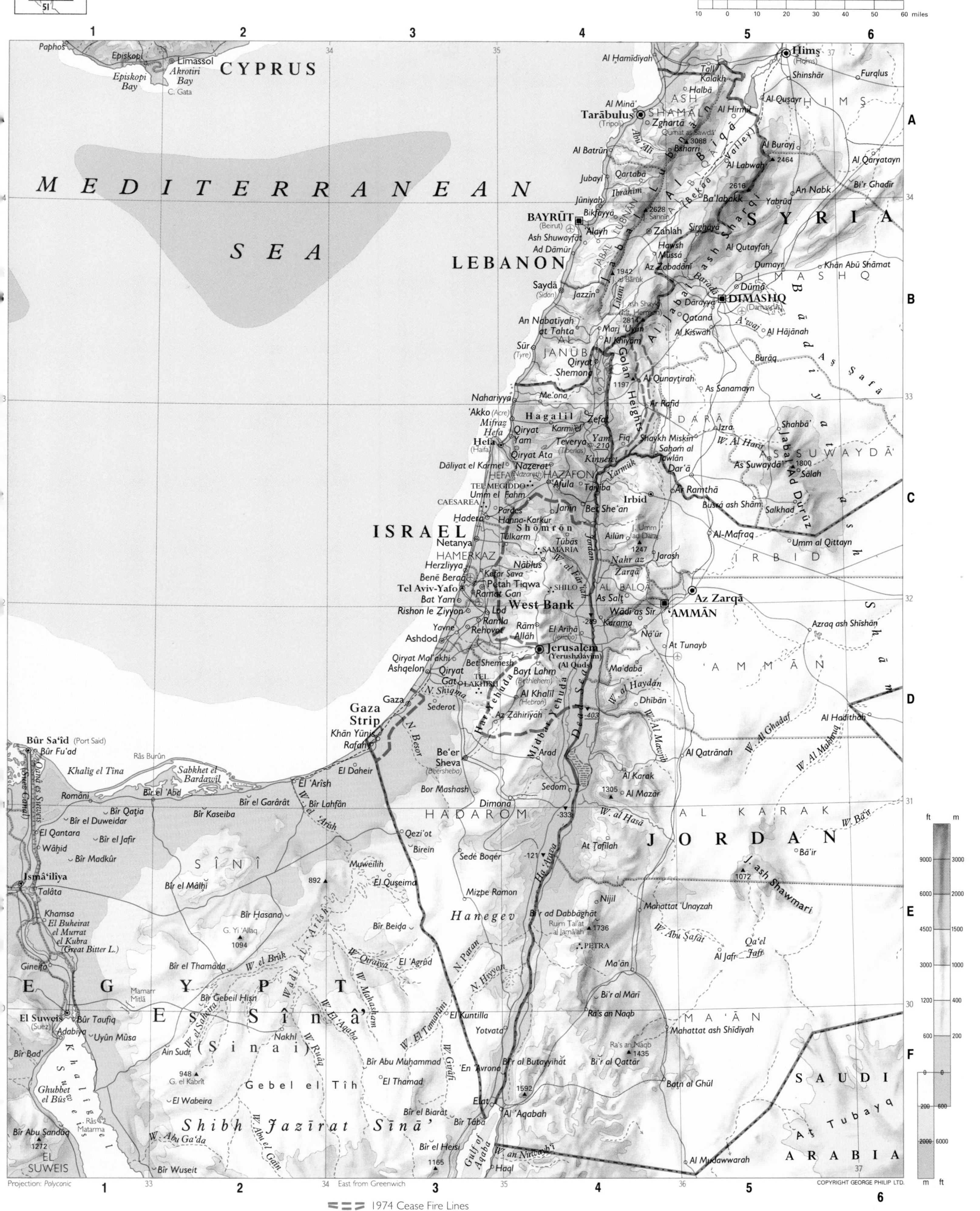
CYPRUS
MEDITERRANEAN
SEA
LEBANON
SYRIA
ISRAEL
West Bank
Gaza Strip
JORDAN
EGYPT
SAUDI ARABIA
Sînâ' (Sinai)
Hanegev
Tarābulus (Tripoli)
BAYRŪT (Beirut)
DIMASHQ (Damascus)
Ḥimş (Homs)
Tel Aviv-Yafo
Jerusalem (Yerushalayim) (Al Quds)
'AMMĀN
Az Zarqā
Gaza
Bûr Sa'îd (Port Said)
Ismâ'ilîya
El Suweis (Suez)
Gulf of Aqaba
Elat
Al 'Aqabah
Dead Sea
Jordan
Golan Heights
Projection: Polyconic
East from Greenwich
COPYRIGHT GEORGE PHILIP LTD.
1974 Cease Fire Lines

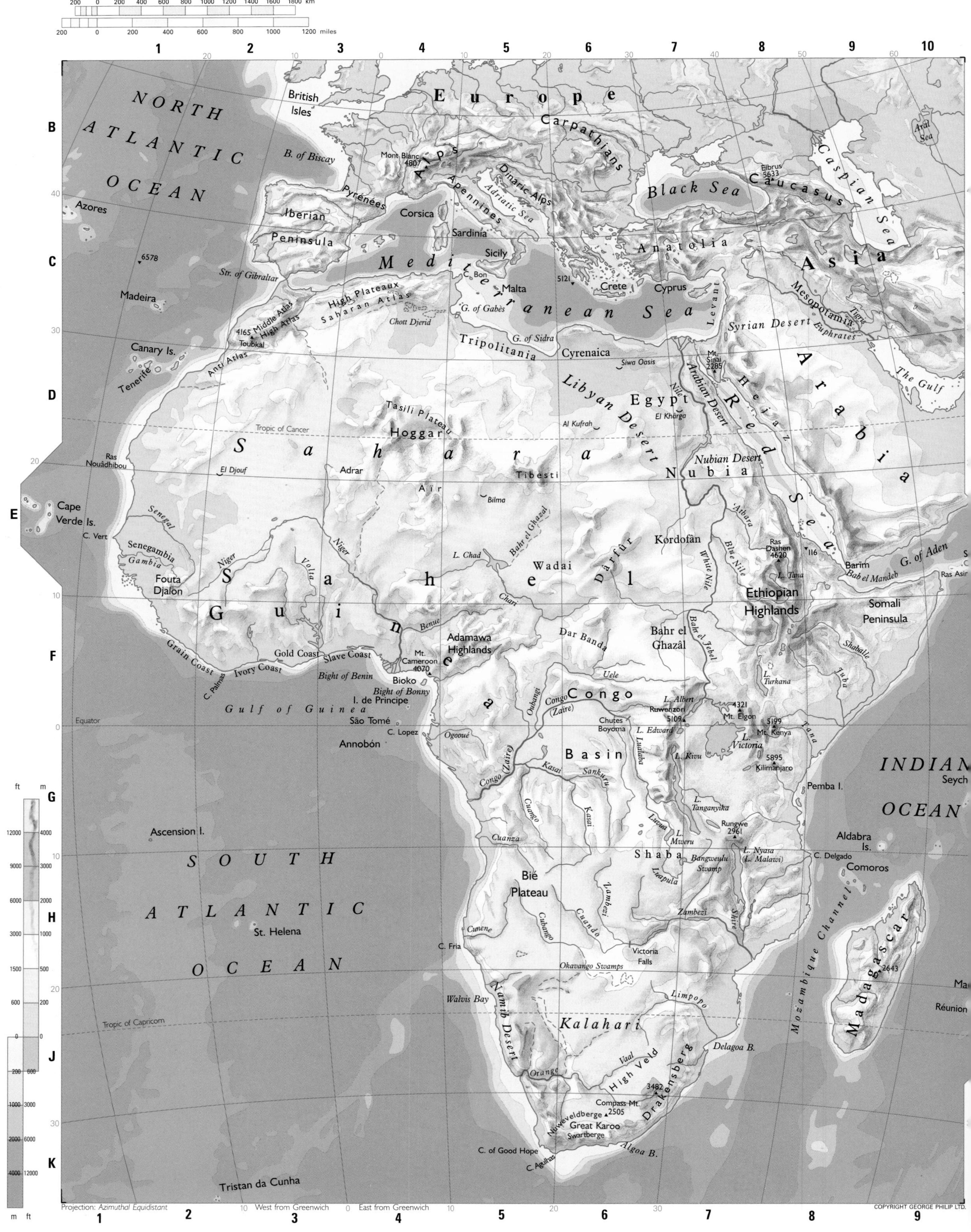

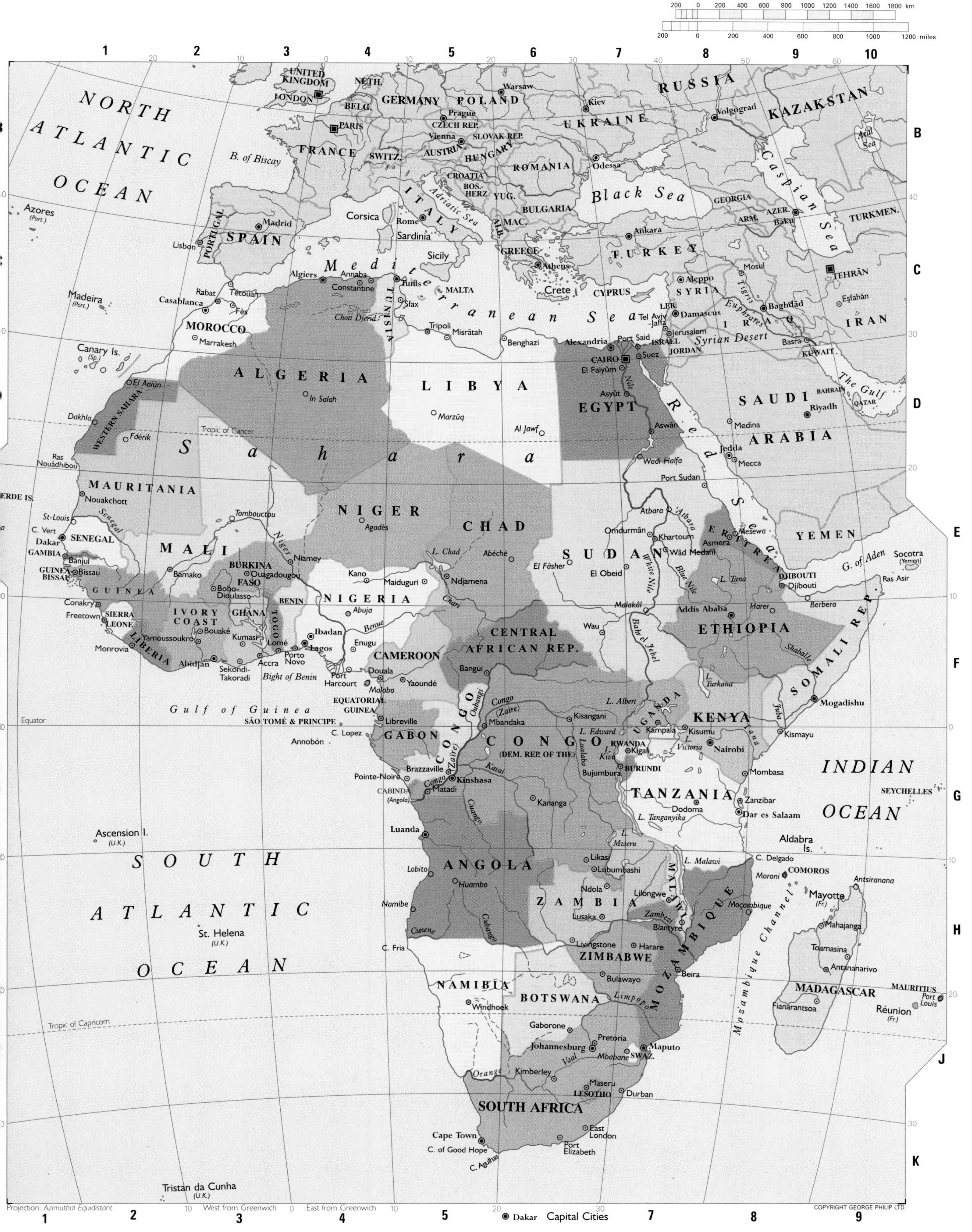

200   0   200   400   600   800   1000 1200 1400 1600 1800 km
200   0   200   400   600   800   1000 1200 miles

NORTH
ATLANTIC
OCEAN

B. of Biscay

Azores
(Port.)

Madeira
(Port.)

Canary Is.
(Sp.)

VERDE IS.

SOUTH
ATLANTIC
OCEAN

Ascension I.
(U.K.)

St. Helena
(U.K.)

Tristan da Cunha
(U.K.)

UNITED
KINGDOM
LONDON
PARIS
FRANCE
NETH.
BELG.
GERMANY POLAND
Warsaw
Prague
CZECH REP.
Vienna
SWITZ. AUSTRIA HUNGARY
SLOVAK REP.
CROATIA
BOS.-
HERZ.
YUG.
ITALY
Rome
Corsica
Sardinia
Madrid
SPAIN
PORTUGAL
Lisbon
ROMANIA
BULGARIA
ALB.
MAC.
GREECE
Athens
Crete
Sicily
MALTA
Kiev
UKRAINE
Odessa
Black Sea
GEORGIA
ARM. AZER.
Baku
TURKEY
Ankara
Volgograd
RUSSIA
KAZAKSTAN
Aral
Sea
Caspian Sea
TURKMEN.

Mediterranean Sea

Algiers
Annaba
Constantine
Tunis
TUNISIA
Sfax
Tripoli
Misrātah
Benghazi
Rabat
Tétouan
Fès
Casablanca
Marrakesh
MOROCCO
Chott Djerid

ALGERIA
In Salah

LIBYA
Marzūq
Al Jawf
Tropic of Cancer

El Aaiún
WESTERN SAHARA
Dakhla
Fdérik
Ras Nouâdhibou

Sahara

EGYPT
Alexandria
Port Said
CAIRO
El Faiyûm
Suez
Asyût
Aswân
Wadi Halfa
Port Sudan
Nile

SAUDI
ARABIA
Medina
Jedda
Mecca
Riyadh
BAHRAIN
QATAR
The Gulf
KUWAIT
Basra
Baghdād
IRAQ
Euphrates
Tigris
Mosul
Aleppo
SYRIA
Damascus
LEB.
Tel Aviv-
Jaffa
Jerusalem
ISRAEL
JORDAN
Syrian Desert
CYPRUS
Tehrān
Eşfahān
IRAN
AZER.

MAURITANIA
Nouakchott
St-Louis
C. Vert
Dakar
SENEGAL
GAMBIA
Banjul
GUINEA-
BISSAU
Bissau
Tombouctou
Senegal
MALI
Bámako
GUINEA
Conakry
SIERRA
LEONE
Freetown
IVORY
COAST
Yamoussoukro
Monrovia
LIBERIA
Abidjan
BURKINA
FASO
Ouagadougou
Bobo
Dioulasso
GHANA
Kumasi
Bouaké
Sekondi-
Takoradi
Accra
TOGO
BENIN
Lomé
Porto
Novo
Lagos
Ibadan
NIGERIA
Abuja
Enugu
Kano
Maiduguri
Niger
Namey
Agadès
NIGER
L. Chad
CHAD
Ndjamena
Abéché
El Fásher
Chari
Benue

CAMEROON
Yaoundé
Douala
Malabo
EQUATORIAL
GUINEA
Port
Harcourt
Bight of Benin
Gulf of Guinea
SÃO TOMÉ & PRINCIPE
C. Lopez
Annobón
Equator

GABON
Libreville

CONGO
Brazzaville
Pointe-Noire
CABINDA
(Angola)
Matadi
Kinshasa
CONGO
(ZAIRE)
CONGO
(DEM. REP. OF THE)
Mbandaka
Kisangani
Congo
(Zaire)
Ubangi
Kasai
Luanda
ANGOLA
Lobito
Huambo
Namibe
C. Fria
Cunene
Cuando
Cuango
Kananga
Likasi
Lubumbashi
Ndola
ZAMBIA
Lusaka
Livingstone
Kafue
Zambezi

SUDAN
Khartoum
Omdurmán
El Obeid
Wad Medani
Atbara
Atbara
White Nile
Blue Nile
Malakâl
Wau
Bahr el Jebel

CENTRAL
AFRICAN REP.
Bangui

ETHIOPIA
Addis Ababa
Harer
L. Tana
Asmera
ERITREA
Massawa
DJIBOUTI
Djibouti
G. of Aden
Berbera
Ras Asir
Socotra
(Yemen)
YEMEN
Red Sea

SOMALI REP.
Mogadishu
Kismayu
Juba
Shabelle

UGANDA
Kampala
L. Albert
L. Edward
L. Kivu
RWANDA
Kigali
BURUNDI
Bujumbura
L. Victoria
Kisumu
Nairobi
KENYA
Mombasa
Dodoma
Dar es Salaam
Zanzibar
TANZANIA
L. Tanganyika
L. Turkana
Tana

INDIAN
OCEAN
SEYCHELLES
Aldabra
Is.
COMOROS
Moroni
Mayotte
(Fr.)
Antsiranana
Mahajanga
Toamasina
MADAGASCAR
Antananarivo
MAURITIUS
Port
Louis
Réunion
(Fr.)
Fianarantsoa
Mozambique Channel

L. Mweru
L. Malawi
MALAWI
Lilongwe
Blantyre
Harare
ZIMBABWE
Bulawayo
MOZAMBIQUE
Moçambique
Beira
C. Delgado
Zambezi
Limpopo

NAMIBIA
Windhoek
BOTSWANA
Gaborone
Orange
Vaal
SOUTH AFRICA
Johannesburg
Pretoria
Kimberley
Maputo
Mbabane
SWAZ.
LESOTHO
Maseru
Durban
East
London
Port
Elizabeth
Cape Town
C. of Good Hope
C. Agulhas

Equator

Tropic of Capricorn

West from Greenwich
East from Greenwich

Dakar   Capital Cities

COPYRIGHT GEORGE PHILIP LTD.

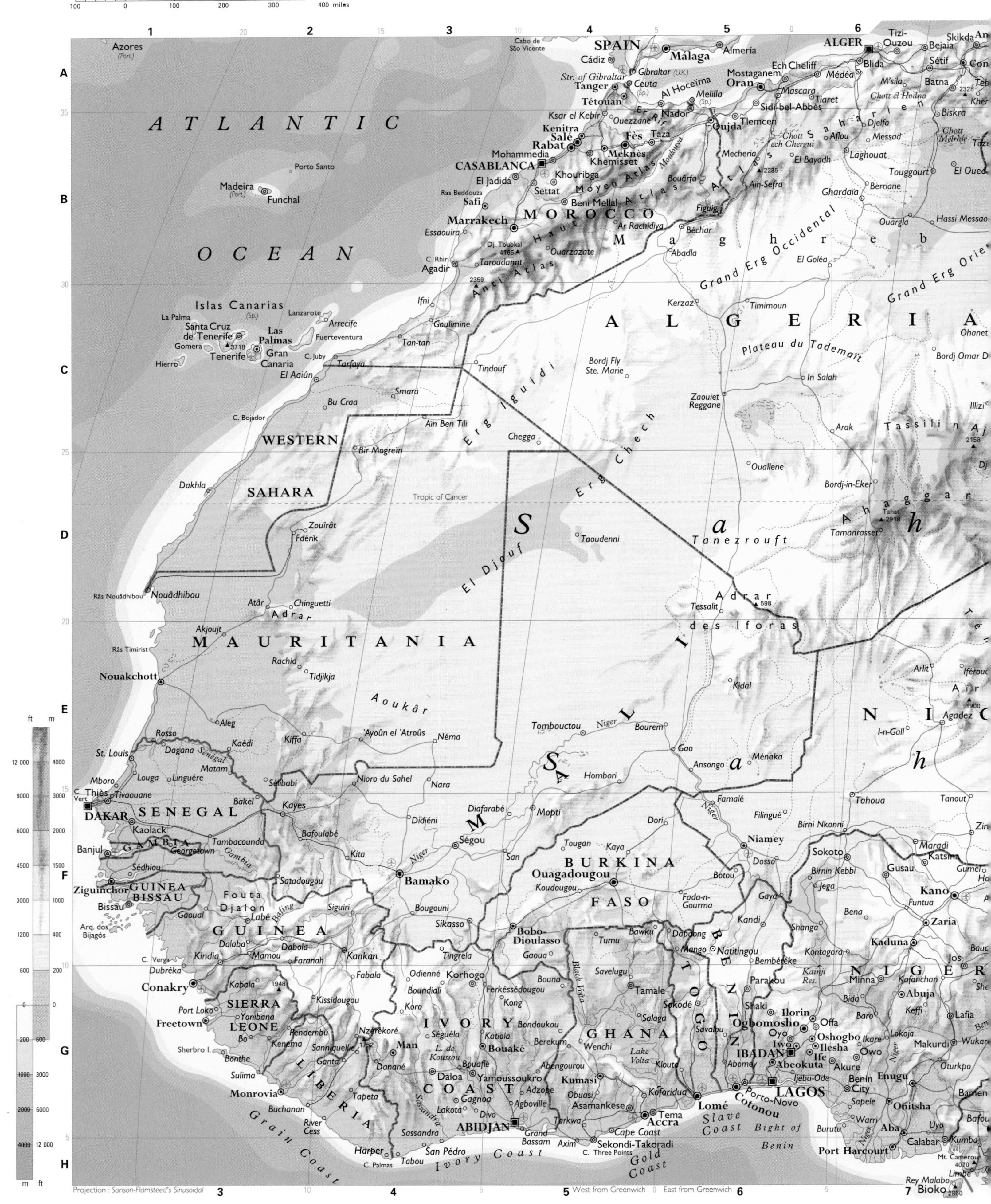

Projection : Sanson-Flamsteed's Sinusoidal

West from Greenwich   East from Greenwich

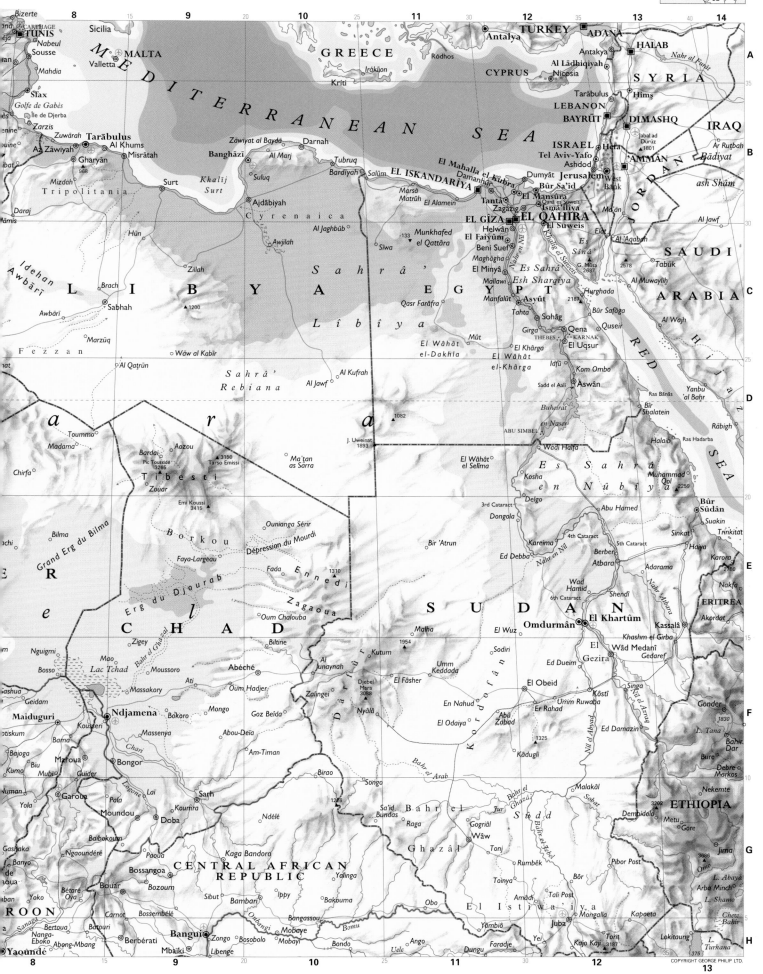

8 15 9 20 10 25 11 30 12 35 13 40 14

A B C D E F G H

MEDITERRANEAN SEA
GREECE
TURKEY
CYPRUS
SYRIA
LEBANON
IRAQ
ISRAEL
JORDAN
SAUDI ARABIA
LIBYA
EGYPT
SUDAN
CHAD
CENTRAL AFRICAN REPUBLIC
ETHIOPIA
ERITREA
RED SEA

Bizerte
CARTHAGE
TUNIS
Nabeul
Sousse
Mahdia
Sfax
Golfe de Gabès
Île de Djerba
Zarzis
Sicilia
MALTA
Valletta
Kríti
Iráklion
Ródhos
Antalya
ADANA
Antakya
HALAB
Nahr al Furat
Al Lādhiqīyah
Nicosia
Tarābulus
Hims
BAYRŪT
DIMASHQ
Jabal ad Durūz 1801
Tel Aviv-Yafo
Ashdod
Hefa
'AMMĀN
Jerusalem
West Bank
Ar Rutbah
Bādiyat ash Shām
Ma'ān
Al Jawf
Elat
Al 'Aqabah
Tabūk
Al Muwaylih
Al Wajh
Hijaz
Yanbu 'al Bahr
Rābigh
Ras Hadarba

Zuwārah
Tarābulus
Az Zāwiyah
Al Khums
Misrātah
Gharyān 968
Mizdah
Tripolitania
Surt
Khalīj Surt
Zāwiyat al Baydā
Darnah
Al Marj
Banghāzī
Suluq
Tubruq
Bardīyah
Salūm
Ajdābiyah
Cyrenaica
Al Jaghbūb
Awjilah
Hūn
Zillah
Idehan Awbārī
Brach
Sabhah
Awbārī
1200
Marzūq
Fezzan
Wāw al Kabīr
Al Qatrūn
Sahrâ' Rebiana
Al Jawf
Al Kufrah
Sahrâ' Lîbîya

EL ISKANDARÎYA
El Mahalla el Kubra
Damanhûr
Dumyât
Bûr Sa'îd
Marsâ Matrûh
El Alamein
Tanta
El Mansûra
Zagazig
Qanâ es Suweis
Isma'iliya
EL GÎZA
EL QAHIRA
El Suweis
Helwân
El Faiyûm
Beni Suef
Maghâgha
El Minyâ
Mallawi
Manfalût
Asyût
Tahta
Sohâg
Girga
Qena
THEBES
KARNAK
El Uqsur
Idfu
Kom Ombo
Sadd el Aali
Aswân
Buheirat en Naser
ABU SIMBEL
Siwa
Munkhafed el Qattâra -133
Qasr Farâfra
Mût
El Wâhât el-Dakhla
El Khârga
El Wâhât el-Khârga
Nahr en Nil
Khalîg el Suweis
Es Sînâ'
G. Mûsa 2637
2578
Es Sahrâ Esh Sharqîya
2187
Hurghada
Bûr Safâga
Quseir
Ras Bânâs
Bîr Shalatein
Halaib
1082
J. Uweinat 1893

Wadi Halfa
El Wâhât el Selîma
Es Sahrâ en Nûbîya
Kosha
Delgo
3rd Cataract
Dongola
Abu Hamed
Muhammad Qol
2259
Bûr Sûdân
Suakin
Trinkitat
Sinkat
Haiya
Karora
2180
Nakfa
Akordat
Kareima
4th Cataract
5th Cataract
Berber
Atbara
Ed Debba
Nahr en Nîl
Bir 'Atrun
Adarama
Nahr 'Atbara
Wad Hamid
6th Cataract
Shendî
Omdurmân
El Khartûm
Kassalâ
El Wuz
Khashm el Girba
Wâd Medanî
Gedaref
El Gezira
Sodiri
Ed Dueim
Umm Keddada
El Obeid
Umm Ruwaba
Kôstî
Singa
Nîl el Azraq
En Nahud
Er Rahad
Abû Zabad
El Odaiya
Kordofân
Ed Damazin
Nîl el Abyad
1325
Kâdugli
Gonder 1830
L. Tana
Bahir Dar
Bure
Debre Markos
Nekemte
Malakâl
Sobat
3202
Dembidolo
Metu
Gore
Bahr el Ghazâl
Sudd
Bahr el Jebel
Bahr el Arab
Jur
Gogriâl
Wâw
Tonj
Rumbêk
Pibor Post
Jima
3686
Omo
L. Abaya
Arba Minch
L. Shamo
Chew Bahir
Bôr
Toinya
Amadi
Tali Post
El Istiwa'iya
Mongalla
Kapoeta
Juba
Yambio
Torit
Kajo Kaji 3187
Yei
Faradje
Lokitaung
L. Turkana
375

Ma'tan as Sarra
Toummo
Madama
Aozou
Bardai
Pic Toussidé 3265
3150 Tarso Emissi
Tibesti
Zouar
Emi Koussi 3415
Chirfa
Bilma
Grand Erg du Bilma
Borkou
Ounianga Sérir
Dépression du Mourdi
Faya-Largeau
Fada
Ennedi
1310
Erg du Djourab
Zagaoua
Oum Chalouba
Sahara
Biltine
Malha
1954
Kutum
Al Junaynah
Dârfûr
Djebel Mara 3088
El Fâsher
Zalingei
Nyâlâ
Zigey
Bahr el Ghazal
Nguigmi
Mao
Lac Tchad
Moussoro
Bosso
Abéché
Ati
Oum Hadjer
Massakory
Geidam
Maiduguri
Ndjamena
Bokoro
Mongo
Goz Beïda
Kousseri
Massenya
Abou-Deïa
Am-Timan
Bama
Chari
Bajoga
Maroua
Bongor
Biu
Mubi
Guider
Birao
Songo
Garoua
Logone
Laï
Sarh
Pala
Moundou
Koumra
Doba
1236
Ndélé
Sa'id Bundas
Raga
Baïbokoum
Ngaoundéré
Paoua
Kaga Bandoro
Bossangoa
Yalinga
Bozoum
Bouar
Bétaré Oya
Yoko
Sibut
Bambari
Ippy
Bakouma
Obo
Carnot
Bossembélé
Batouri
Bertoua
Sanaga
Bangassou
Oubangi
Bomu
Mobaye
Mobayi
Bangui
Zongo
Bosobolo
Berbérati
Nanga-Eboko
Abong-Mbang
Bondo
Ango
Uele
Dungu
Mbaïki
Libenge
Yaoundé
CAMEROON

8 15 9 20 10 25 11 30 12 35 13

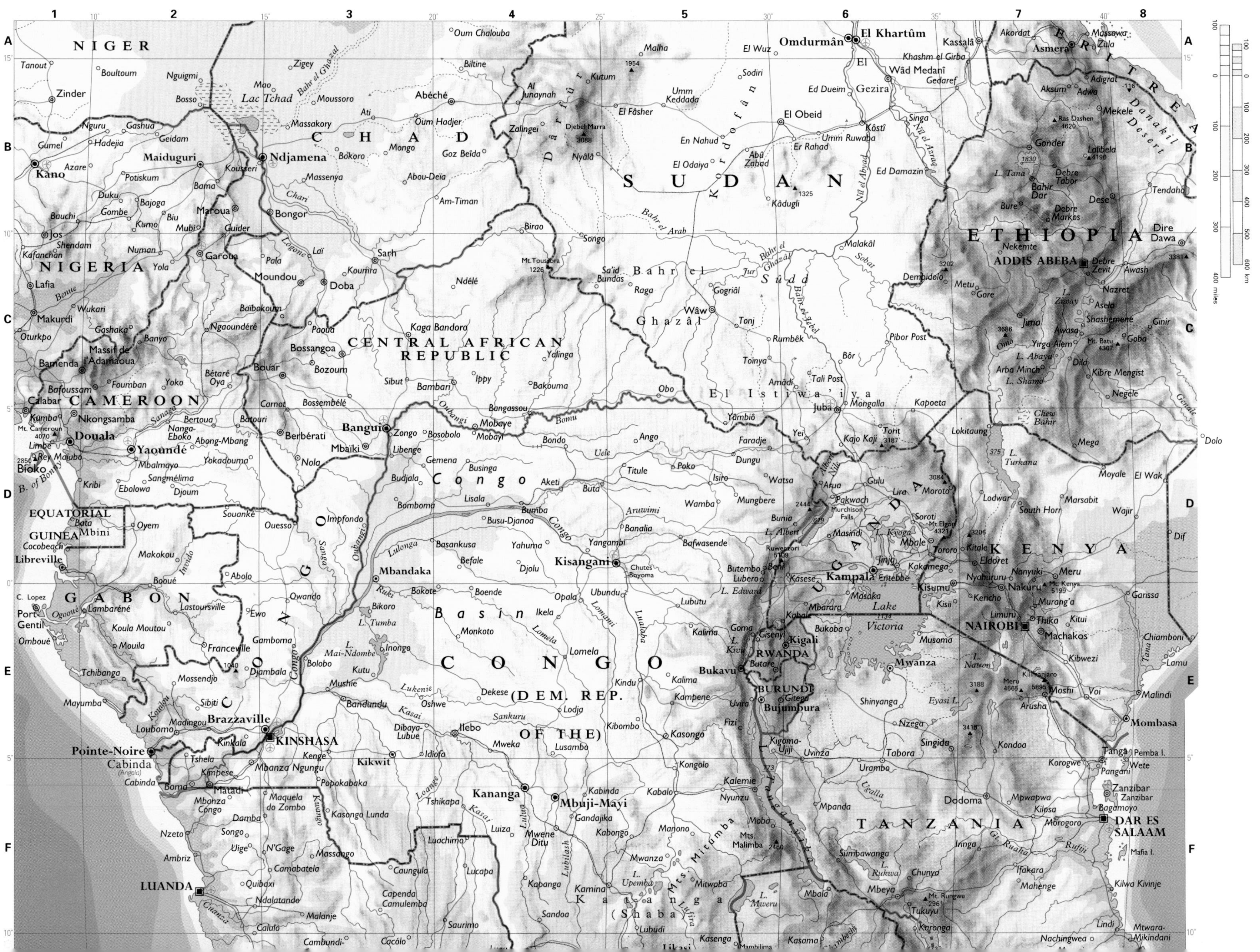

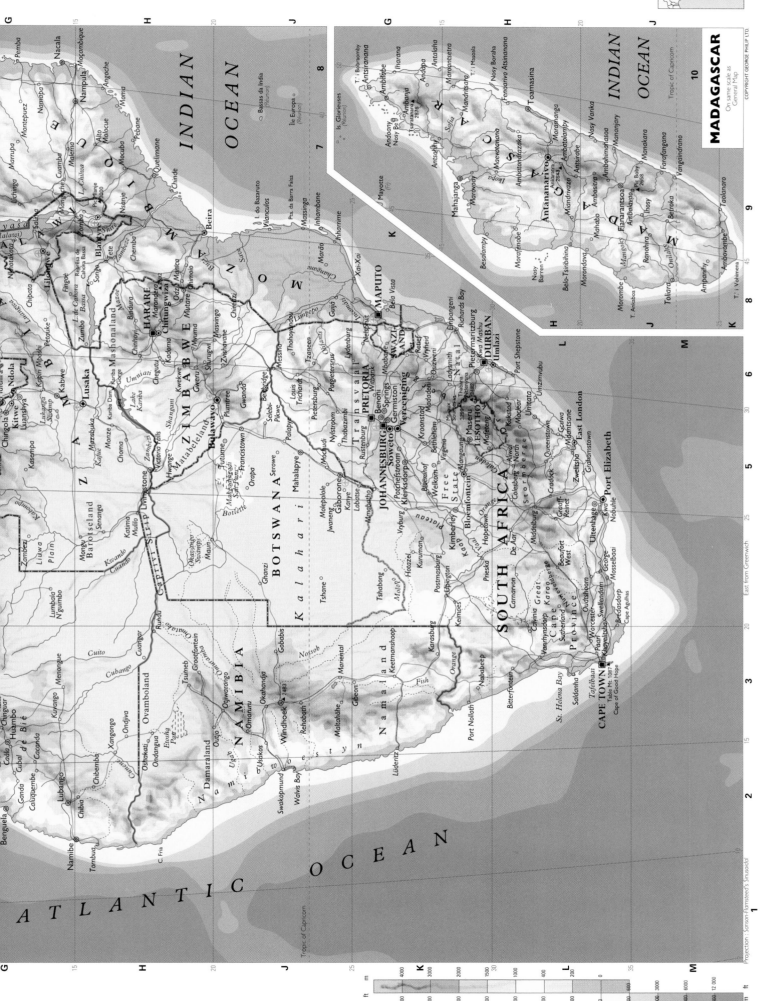

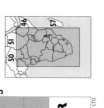

MADAGASCAR

On same scale as
General Map

COPYRIGHT GEORGE PHILIP LTD.

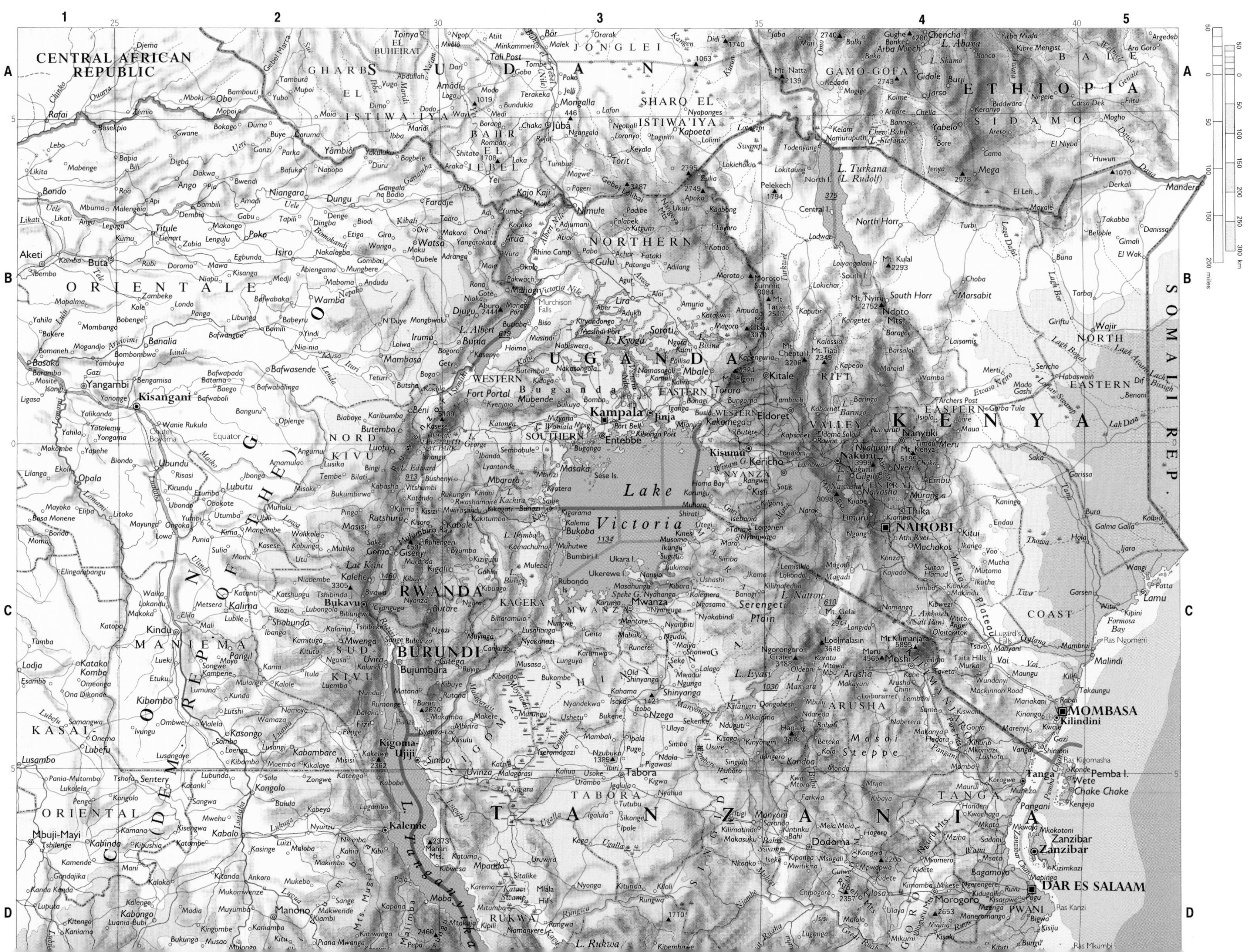

I N D I A N
O C E A N
L. Nyasa
Malawi
ANGOLA
NAMIBIA
BOTSWANA
SOUTH AFRICA
Z A M B I A
M A L A W I
Z I M B A B W E
M O Z A M B I Q U E
Lusaka
Harare
Lilongwe
Blantyre
Bulawayo
Lubumbashi
Ndola
Kitwe
Beira
Mocambique
Nampula
Quelimane
Tete
Livingstone
Victoria Falls
Lake Kariba
Cahora Bassa
Zambeze
Limpopo
Mtwara-Mikindani
Lindi
Chipata
Mutare
Masvingo
Gweru
Kwekwe
Kasama
Mpika
Kabwe
Mufulira
Chingola
Luanshya
Francistown
Serowe
Palapye
Messina
Caprivi Strip
Makgadikgadi Salt Pans
COPPERBELT
CABO DELGADO
NAMPULA
NIASSA
ZAMBEZIA
MANICA
SOFALA
GAZA
INHAMBANE
MATABELELAND
MASHONALAND
MASVINGO
LUAPULA
NORTHERN
EASTERN
CENTRAL
SOUTHERN
WESTERN
NORTH WESTERN
Projection: Lambert's Equivalent Azimuthal
East from Greenwich

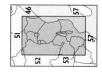

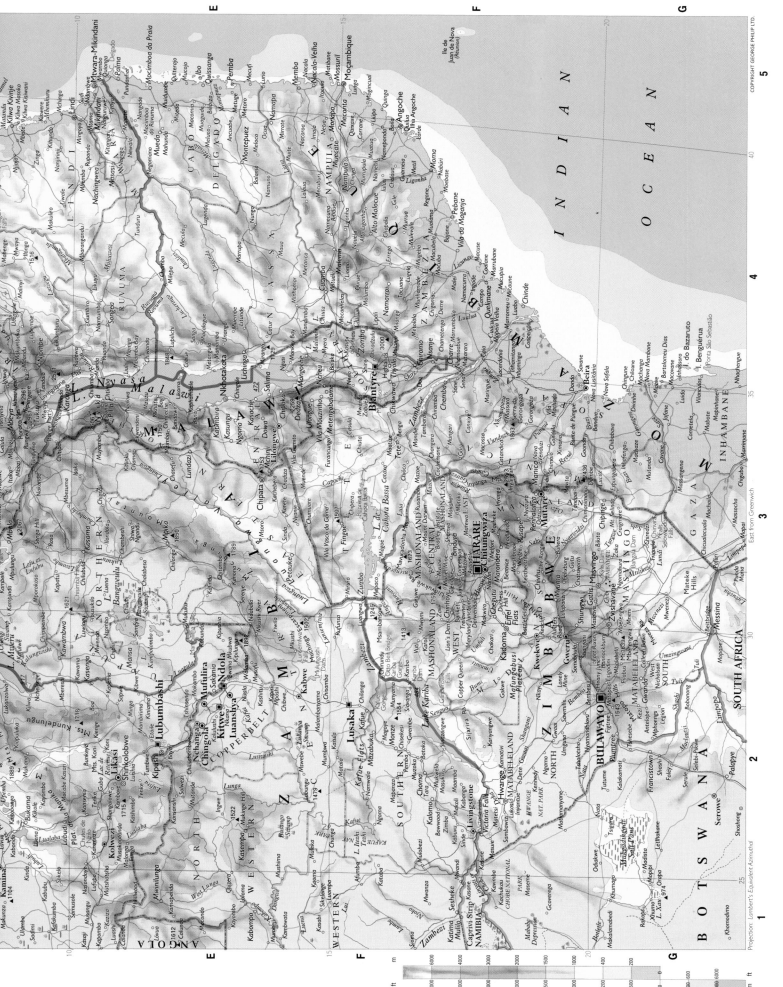

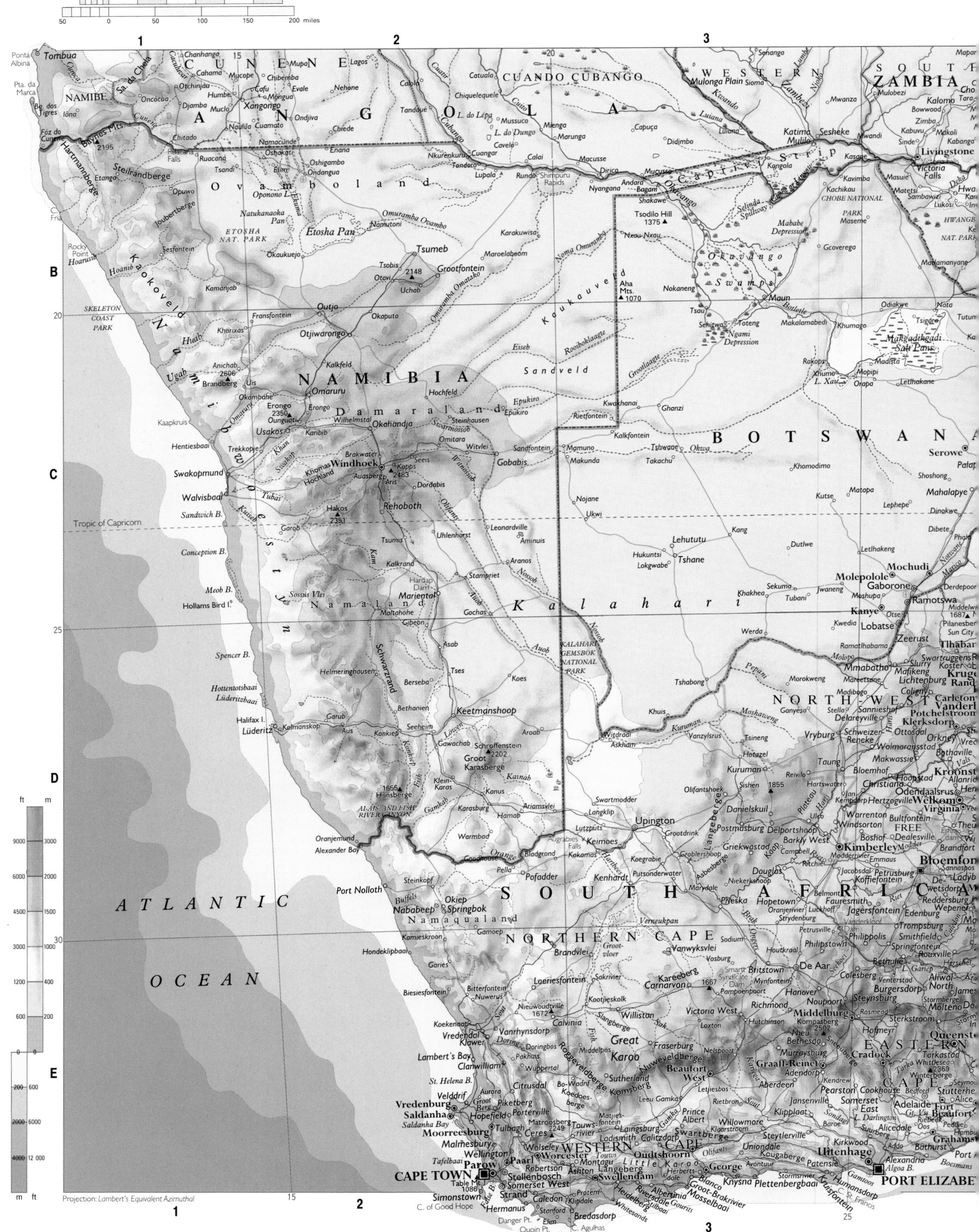

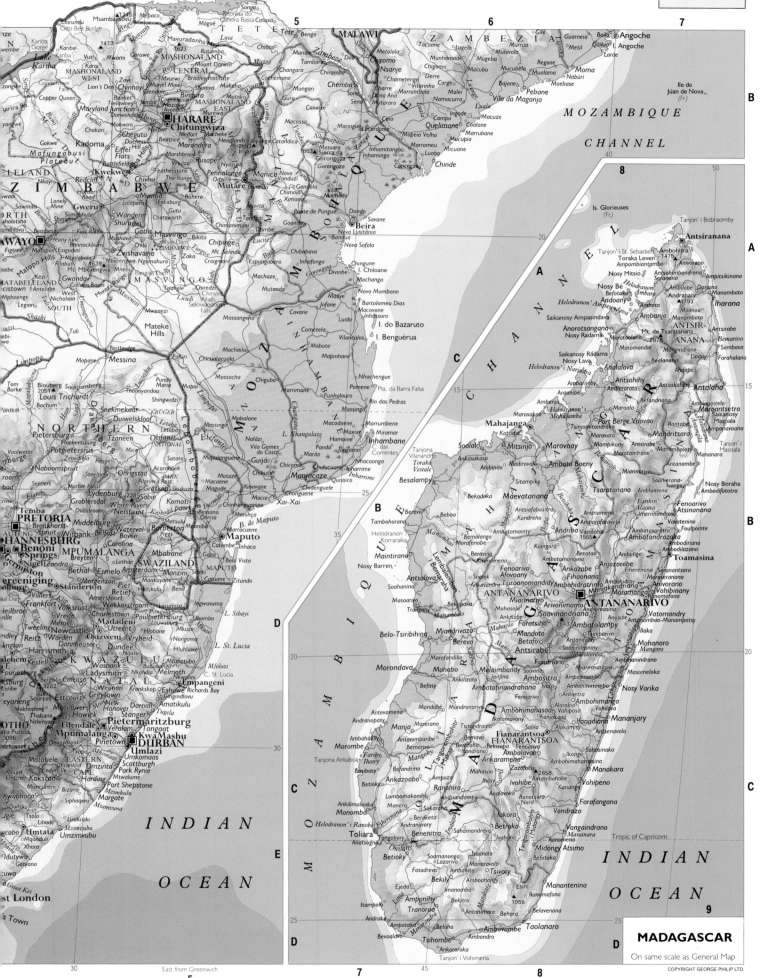

MADAGASCAR

On same scale as General Map

COPYRIGHT GEORGE PHILIP LTD.

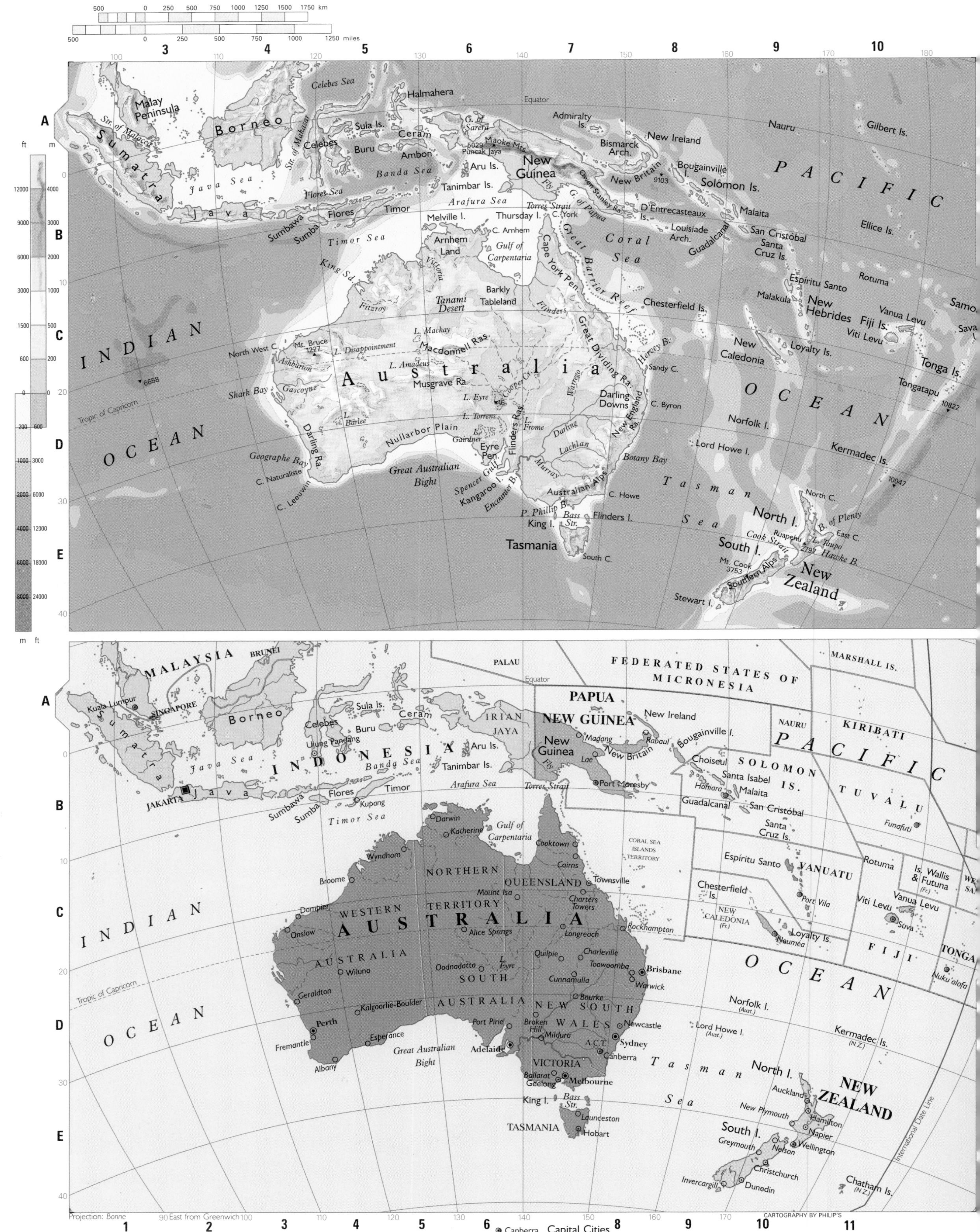

64
64 64
64

50 0 50 100 150 200 km
50 0 50 100 150 miles

North Island

South Island

TASMAN

SEA

PACIFIC

OCEAN

C. Reinga
C. Maria van Diemen
North C.
Houhora Heads
Rangaunu B.
Mangonui
Whangaroa Harb.
Ahipara B.
Kaitaia
Tauroa Pt.
Okaihau
Doubtless B.
C. Brett
B. of Islands
Rawene
Kaikohe
Hikurangi
Hokianga Harbour
Whangarei
Whangarei Harb.
Donnelly's Crossing
Bream Hd.
Bream B.
Dargaville
Waipu
Little Barrier I.
Great Barrier I.
Kaipara Harbour
Warkworth
C. Rodney
C. Colville
Cuvier I.
Helensville
Hauraki Gulf
Coromandel
Takapuna
Devonport
Whitianga
AUCKLAND
Manukau
Papakura
Thames
Waiuku
Pukekohe
Mercer
Waihi
Mayor I.
Waikato
Paeroa
Tauranga Harb.
Huntly
Te Aroha
Mount Maunganui
Bay of Plenty
White I.
C. Runaway
Morrinsville
Tauranga
Te Puke
Hamilton
Cambridge
Whakatane
Raglan
Te Awamutu
Kawerau
Opotiki
Rotorua
Raukumara Ra.
Mt. Hikurangi 1753
Kawhia Harbour
Otorohanga
Putaruru
Rotorua
Tarawera
L. Tarawera
Tauranga
Matu
Te Kuiti
Tokoroa
Kinleith
Kaingaroa
Murupara
Waipiro
Mokau
Mokai
Wairakei
Forest
Waikaremoana
Ormond
Tolaga Bay
North Taranaki Bight
Ongarue
Taupo
L. Taupo
Rotongaio
L. Waikaremoana
Gisborne
Waitara
New Plymouth
Turangi
Kaimanawa Mts.
Tangiwera
Nuhaka
Poverty Bay
Inglewood
Mt. Egmont 2518
Taumarunui
Ruapehu 2797
Wairoa
Waikokopu
Opunake
Kapuni
Stratford
Eltham
Ohakune
Waiouru
Bay View
Hawke Bay
Mahia Pen.
Napier
Hawera
South Taranaki Bight
Patea
Raetihi
Waverley
Taihape
Rangitikei
Hastings
Waipawa
Wanganui
Mangaweka
Hunterville
Waipukurau
Marton
Halcombe
Feilding
Dannevirke
Bulls
Palmerston North
Woodville
C. Farewell
Foxton
Pahiatua
Golden B.
D'Urville I.
Shannon
Levin
Collingwood
Tasman B.
Otaki
C. Turnagain
Takaka
Paraparaumu
Tasman Mts.
Motueka
Kapiti I.
Masterton
Karamea Bight
Nelson
Pelorus Sd.
Upper Hutt
Carterton
Greytown
Havelock
Feather ston
Martinborough
Seddonville
Matiri Ra.
Richmond
Picton
Petone
Wairarapa
Granity
Wakefield
WELLINGTON
Lower Hutt
Westport
Lyell
Blenheim
Eastbourne
Murchison
Seddon
Cook Strait
Inangahua Junction
Rotoroa
Ward
Mt. Tapuaenuku 2885
Reefton
Spenser Mts.
Blackball
Runanga
Stillwater
Mt. Travers 2338
Hanmer Springs
Kaikoura
Greymouth
Kumara
Hanmer
Waiau
Kumara
L. Brunner
Pass
Culverden
Hokitika
Jacksons
Hurunui
Waiau
Ross
Arthur's Pass
Waikari
Waipara
Amberley
Oxford
Rangiora
Pegasus Bay
Waimakariri
Kaiapoi
Coleridge
Springfield
New Brighton
South Island
Whitecliffs
Riccarton
Christchurch
Mt. Cook 3753
Methven
Lincoln
Lyttelton
Westland Bight
Staveley
Banks Pen.
Abut Hd.
Okuru
Southbridge
Akaroa
Rakaia
Little River
Southern Alps
L. Tekapo
Rakaia
Ashburton Bight
Jackson B.
Mt. Aspiring 3027
Rangitata
Fairlie
Timaru
Pukaki
Timaru
Milford Sd.
Mt. Earnslaw 2818
Wanaka L.
Ohau
St. Andrews
Bligh Sound
George Sound
Wanaka
Tekapo
Kurow
Waimate
Arrowtown
Cromwell
Tokarahi
Ngapara
Queenstown
Clyde
Naseby
Oamaru
Wakatipu L.
Alexandra
Maheno
Secretary I.
Roxburgh
Hampden
Doubtful Sd.
Dunback
Palmerston
Te Anau
Kingston
Umbrella Mts.
Waikouaiti
Garvie Mts.
Otago
Port Chalmers
Resolution I.
Manapouri
Mossburn
Otago Harbour
Saunders C.
Breaksea Sd.
Eyre Mts.
Lumsden
Waipori
Dusky Sd.
Ohai
Nightcaps
Lawrence
Mosgiel
Dunedin
Southland
Edievale
Milton
Preservation Inlet
Clifden
Tapanui
Kelso
Balclutha
Te Waewae B.
Orepuki
Winton
Clinton
Kaitangata
Riverton
Mataura
Wyndham
Nugget Pt.
Invercargill
Gore
Tokanui
Tahakopa
Bluff
Ruapuke I.
Halfmoon Bay
Foveaux Str.
Stewart I.
Southwest C.
Port Pegasus

SAMOA ISLANDS
1:12 000 000
WESTERN SAMOA
AMERICAN SAMOA
Savai'i
Apia
Upolu
Pago Pago
Tutuila
West from Greenwich

FIJI AND TONGA ISLANDS
1:12 000 000
Wallis & Futuna (Fr.)
Futuna
Niuafo'ou (Tonga)
Thikombia
Lambasa
Vanua Levu
FIJI
Yasawa Group
Taveuni
Koro
Vanua Mbalavu
Lautoka 1323
Levuka
Ovalau
TONGA (Friendly Is.)
Nandi
Viti Levu
Gau
Lau Group
Suva
Koro Sea
Lakemba
Vava'u
Moala
Kandavu
Tofua
Vatoa
Tongatapu
Nuku'alofa

ft m
9000 3000
6000 2000
3000 1000
1200 400
600 200
0
200 600
2000 6000
4000 12 000
6000 18 000
m ft

50 0 50 100 150 200 km
50 0 50 100 150 miles

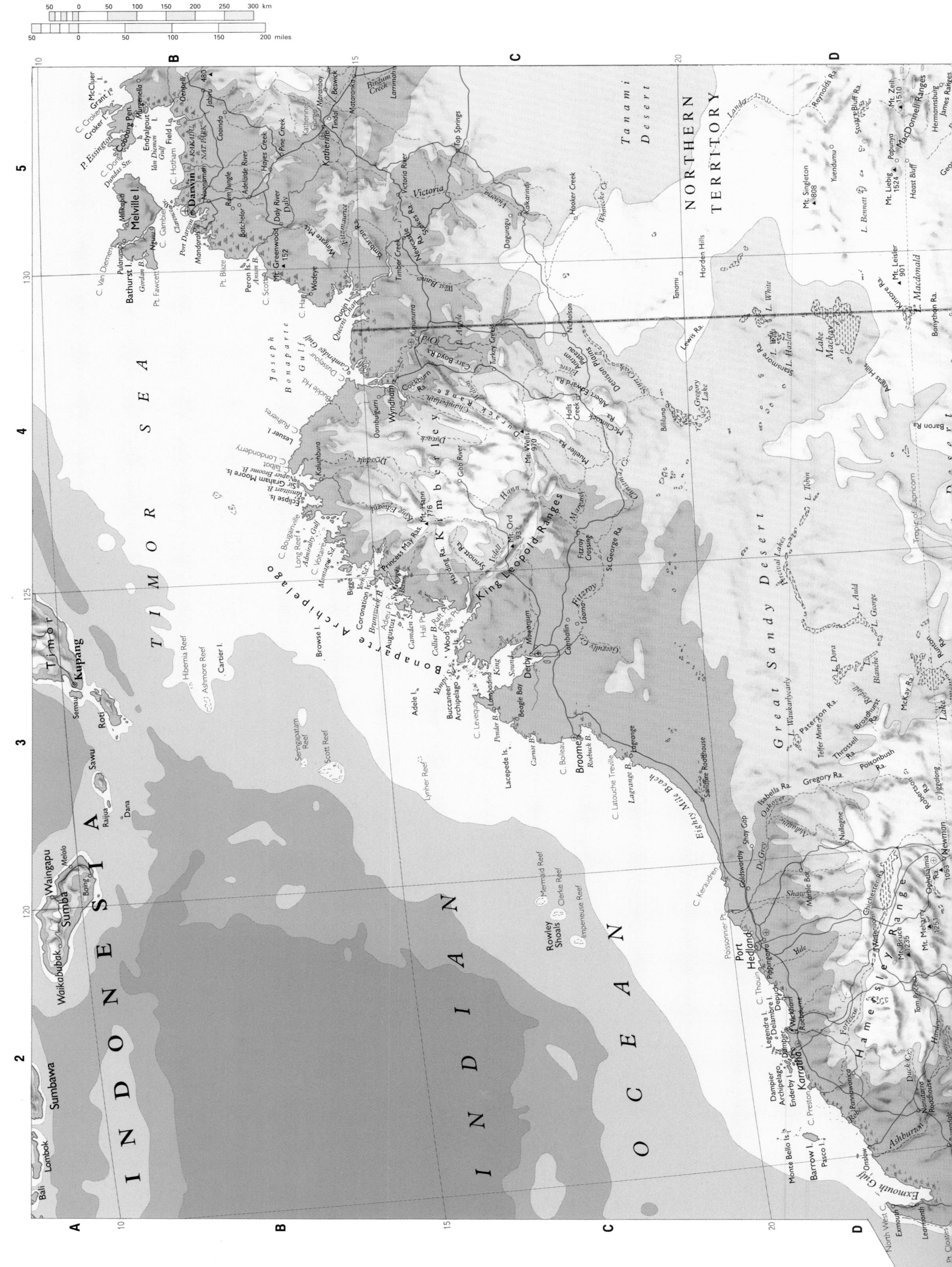

37
62
63

WESTERN AUSTRALIA
SOUTH AUSTRALIA
Great Victoria Desert
Nullarbor Plain
Hampton Tableland
Great Australian Bight
INDIAN OCEAN
SOUTHERN OCEAN
PERTH
Fremantle
Kwinana
Rockingham
Mandurah
Bunbury
Busselton
Albany
Esperance
Kalgoorlie-Boulder
Geraldton
Carnarvon
Norseman
Merredin
Northam
Katanning
Shark Bay
Dirk Hartog I.
Houtman Abrolhos
Archipelago of the Recherche
Eastern Group
Petermann Ranges
Musgrave Ranges
Everard Ranges
Ayers Rock 868
Mt. Olga 1069
L. Carnegie
L. Wells
L. Carey
L. Barlee
L. Moore
L. Austin
L. Cowan
L. Dundas
L. Lefroy
L. Ballard
L. Yindarlgooda
Eucla
Nullarbor
Cook
Ooldea
Head of Bight
Wilson Bluff
▼ 5632
E
F
G
1
2
3
4
5
115
120
125
130
30
35
East from Greenwich
Projection: Bonne
m
ft
3000
1000
1200
400
600
200
0
200
600
2000
6000
4000
12 000

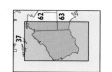

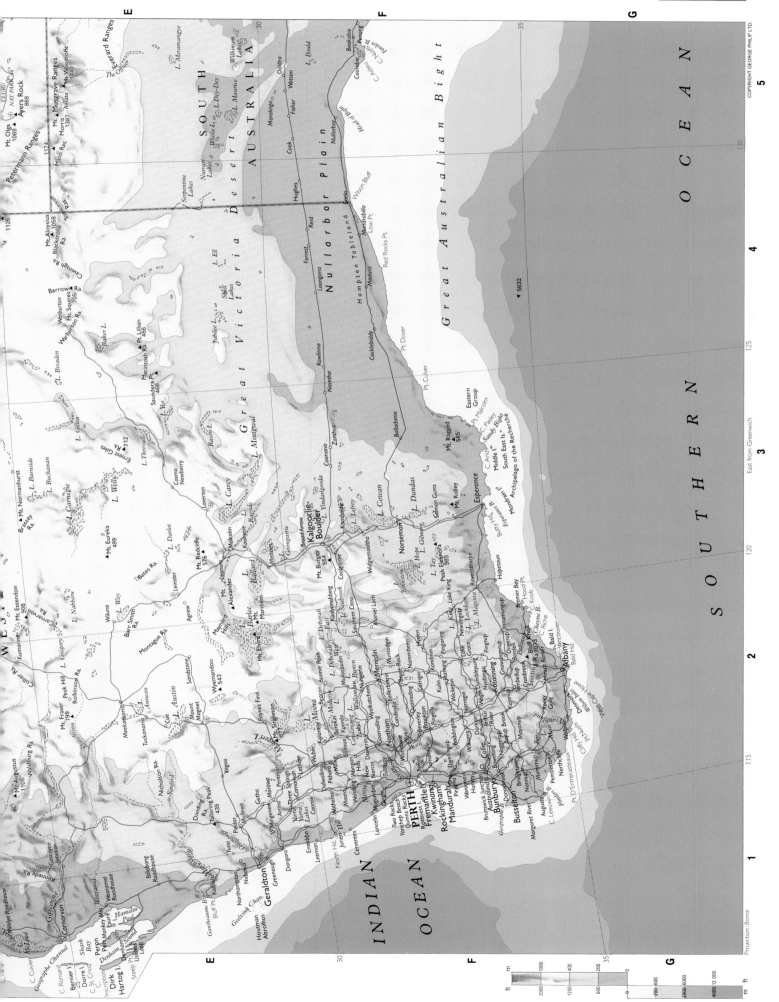

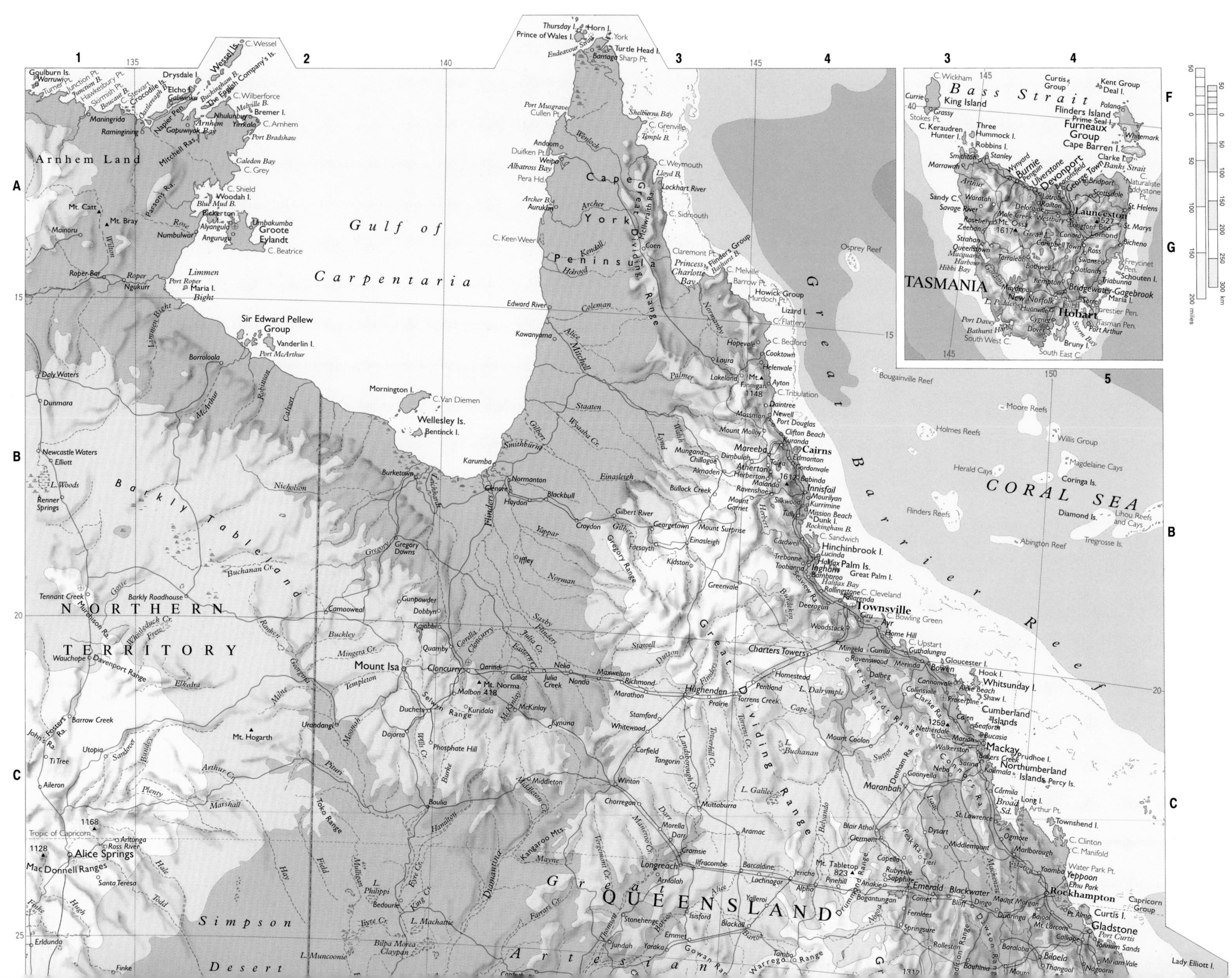

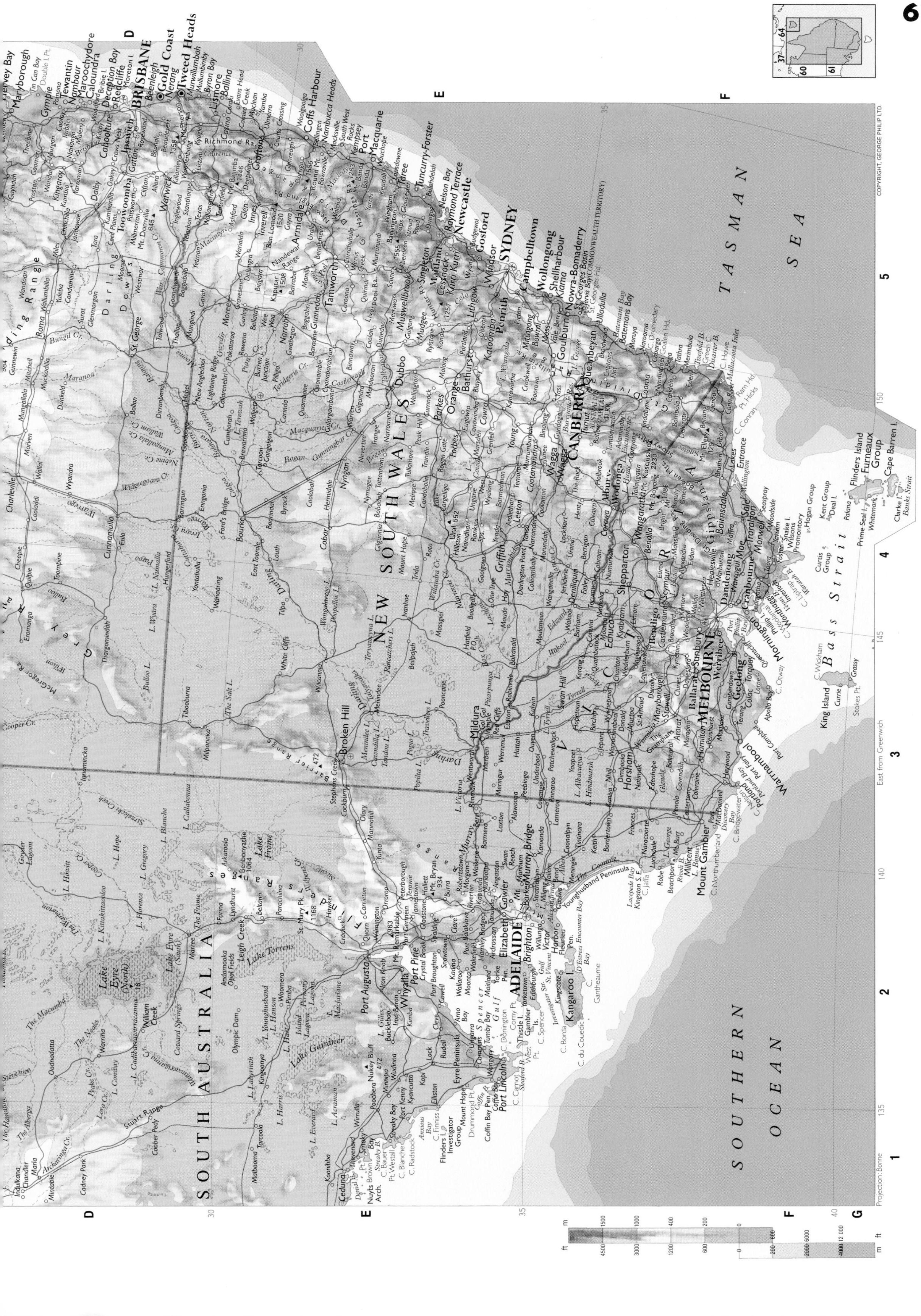

Map — Southeastern Australia

BRISBANE

NEW SOUTH WALES

SOUTH AUSTRALIA

VICTORIA

SYDNEY

CANBERRA

ADELAIDE

MELBOURNE

TASMAN SEA

SOUTHERN OCEAN

Bass Strait

East from Greenwich

Projection Bonne

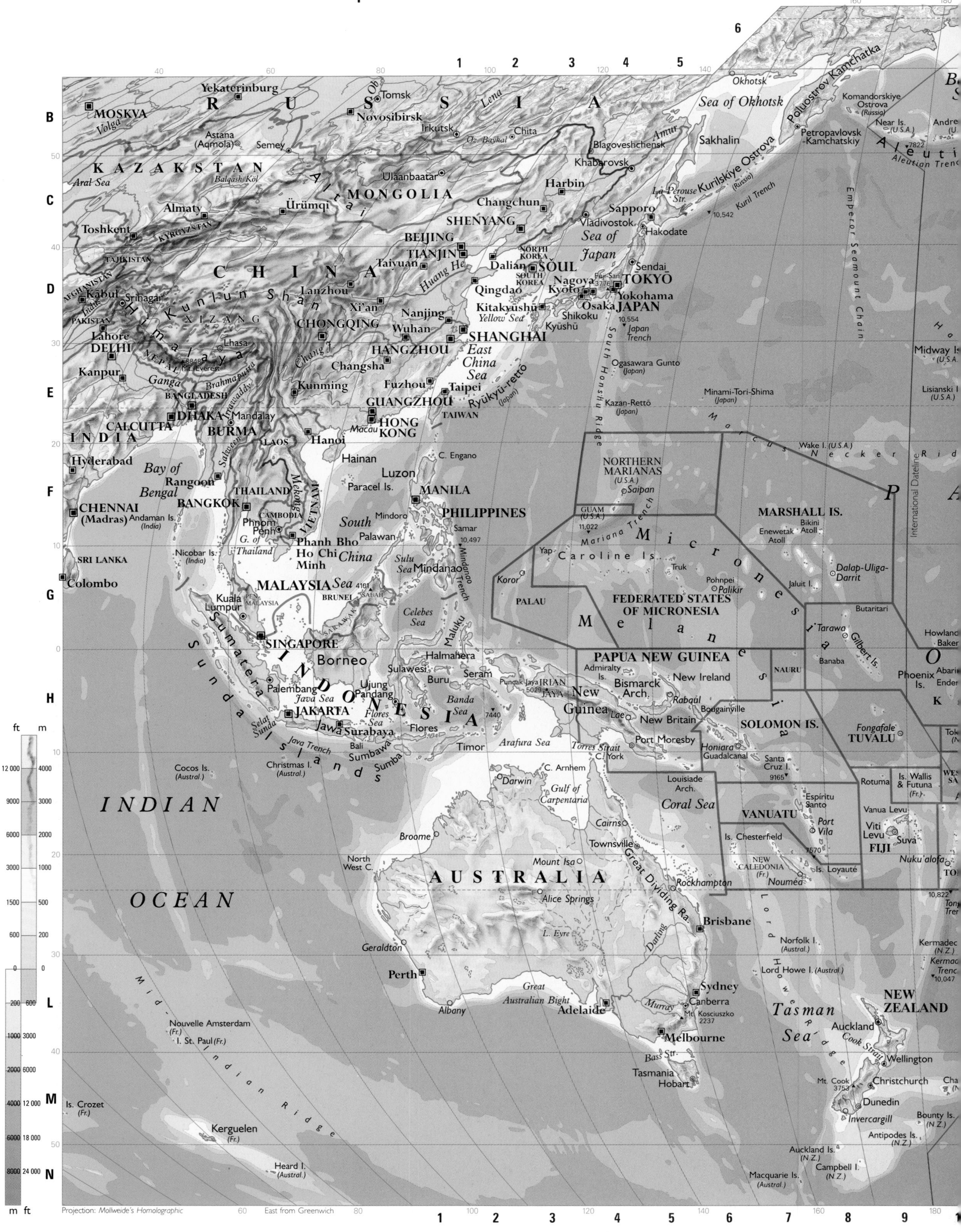

RUSSIA

Yekaterinburg
MOSKVA
Volga
Tomsk
Novosibirsk
Astana (Aqmola)
Semey
Irkutsk
Oz. Baykal
Chita
Lena
Ob'
Blagoveshchensk
Amur
Sea of Okhotsk
Okhotsk
Poluostrov Kamchatka
Komandorskiye Ostrova (Russia)
Petropavlovsk-Kamchatskiy
Near Is. (U.S.A.)
Andre
Be
S
Aleutian
Aleutian Trench

KAZAKSTAN
Aral Sea
Balqash Köl
Ulaanbaatar
MONGOLIA
Khabarovsk
Sakhalin
Kurilskiye Ostrova (Russia)
La Pérouse Str.
Kuril Trench
10,542
7822
Aleu

Almaty
Ürümqi
Changchun
Harbin
Sapporo
Vladivostok
Hakodate
Sea of Japan
Emperor Seamount Chain

Toshkent
KYRGYZSTAN
SHENYANG
NORTH KOREA
Sendai
TAJIKISTAN
BEIJING
TIANJIN
Taiyuan
Dalian
SOUL
SOUTH KOREA
Nagoya
TOKYO
JAPAN
Yokohama
Osaka
3776
Fuji-San

AFGHANISTAN
Kabul
Srinagar
CHINA
Lanzhou
Xi'an
Qingdao
Kyoto
Kitakyushu
Shikoku
Ho
Midway Is. (U.S.A.)

PAKISTAN
Lahore
DELHI
Himalaya
8848
Mt. Everest
Lhasa
XIZANG
Kunlun Shan
Chongqing
CHONGQING
Nanjing
Wuhan
SHANGHAI
Huang He
Yellow Sea
Kyūshū
10,554
Japan Trench
Ogasawara Gunto (Japan)
Lisianski I. (U.S.A.)

Kanpur
Ganga
NEPAL
Brahmaputra
Changsha
HANGZHOU
East China Sea
Ryūkyū-rettō (Japan)
Minami-Tori-Shima (Japan)

INDIA
Hyderabad
CALCUTTA
DHAKA
BANGLADESH
Mandalay
BURMA
Kunming
Fuzhou
GUANGZHOU
HONG KONG
Macau
Taipei
TAIWAN
Kazan-Rettō (Japan)
Wake I. (U.S.A.)
Necker
Ri

Bay of Bengal
Rangoon
Irrawaddy
Salween
LAOS
Hanoi
Hainan
C. Engaño
Luzon
NORTHERN MARIANAS (U.S.A.)
Saipan
MARSHALL IS.

CHENNAI (Madras)
Andaman Is. (India)
BANGKOK
THAILAND
Mekong
VIETNAM
Paracel Is.
MANILA
PHILIPPINES
GUAM (U.S.A.)
11,022
Mariana Trench
Enewetak Atoll
Bikini Atoll
Micronesia

SRI LANKA
Colombo
Nicobar Is. (India)
G. of Thailand
South China Sea
Phnom Penh
CAMBODIA
Phanh Bho Ho Chi Minh
Mindoro
Palawan
Samar
10,497
Yap
Caroline Is.
Truk
Jaluit I.
Dalap-Uliga-Darrit

Kuala Lumpur
MALAYSIA
Sulu Sea
Mindanao
Mindanao Trench
Koror
PALAU
FEDERATED STATES OF MICRONESIA
Pohnpei
Palikir
Butaritari
Tarawa
Gilbert Is.
Howland Baker

SINGAPORE
Sumatera
Borneo
Celebes Sea
BRUNEI
SABAH
SARAWAK
4101
Banaba
Phoenix Is.
O
Ender

INDONESIA
Palembang
Sulawesi
Halmahera
Seram
Buru
Maluku
PAPUA NEW GUINEA
Admiralty Is.
New Ireland
Bismarck Arch.
Rabaul
NAURU
Melanesia
Fongafale
TUVALU

JAKARTA
Jawa
Java Sea
Ujung Pandang
Flores Sea
Banda Sea
7440
Puncak Jaya
5029
IRIAN JAYA
New Guinea
New Britain
Lae
Bougainville
SOLOMON IS.
Is. Wallis & Futuna (Fr.)
Rotuma
WES SA

Surabaya
Bali
Flores
Sumbawa
Sumba
Timor
Arafura Sea
Torres Strait
C. York
Port Moresby
Honiara
Guadalcanal
Santa Cruz I.
9165
VANUATU
Viti Levu
FIJI
Suva
Nuku'alofa
TO

Selat Sunda
Java Trench
C. Arnhem
Gulf of Carpentaria
Darwin
Louisiade Arch.
Coral Sea
Espiritu Santo
Vanua Levu
Is. Chesterfield
Port Vila

Cocos Is. (Austral.)
Christmas I. (Austral.)
Broome
Cairns
Townsville
NEW CALEDONIA (Fr.)
Nouméa
Is. Loyauté
7570

INDIAN
North West C.
Mount Isa
AUSTRALIA
Rockhampton
Great Dividing Ra.
Norfolk I. (Austral.)
10,822
Ton
Trer

OCEAN
Alice Springs
Brisbane
L. Eyre
Darling
Kermadec (N.Z.)
Lord Howe I. (Austral.)

Geraldton
Murray
Sydney
Canberra
Mt. Kosciuszko
2237
Kermadec Trench
10,047

Perth
Albany
Great Australian Bight
Adelaide
Melbourne
Bass Str.
Tasman Sea
Auckland
NEW ZEALAND
Cook Strait
Wellington

Nouvelle Amsterdam (Fr.)
I. St. Paul (Fr.)
Tasmania
Hobart
Mt. Cook
3753
Christchurch
Cha

Mid Indian Ridge
Is. Crozet (Fr.)
Dunedin
Invercargill
Bounty Is. (N.Z.)

Kerguelen (Fr.)
Auckland Is. (N.Z.)
Antipodes Is. (N.Z.)

Heard I. (Austral.)
Macquarie Is. (Austral.)
Campbell I. (N.Z.)

Elevation scale (ft / m):
12 000 / 4000
9000 / 3000
6000 / 2000
3000 / 1000
1500 / 500
600 / 200
0 / 0
200 / 600
1000 / 3000
2000 / 6000
4000 / 12 000
6000 / 18 000
8000 / 24 000
m ft

1 12 13 14 15 16 17 18 19 20

B C D E F G H J K L M N

Arctic Circle

ALASKA (U.S.A.)
Anchorage
5959
Bristol Bay
Juneau
Gulf of Alaska

ROCKY
C A N A D A

Prince of Wales I. (U.S.A.)
Prince Rupert (U.S.A.)
Queen Charlotte Is. (Canada)

Vancouver
Vancouver I.
Victoria
Seattle
Portland

Edmonton
Calgary
Regina
Winnipeg
L. Winnipeg

Boise
Salt Lake City
Sacramento
C. Mendocino
SAN FRANCISCO
6741
4418

Snake
Colorado
MTS

Minneapolis
Missouri

L. Superior
L. Michigan
L. Huron
Toronto
Detroit
CHICAGO
Denver
Kansas City
St. Louis
Cincinnati

Québec
Montréal
Ottawa
L. Ontario
L. Erie
Buffalo
Pittsburgh

St. Lawrence
Newfoundland
St. John's

NORTH

N E W Y O R K C I T Y
PHILADELPHIA
Baltimore
Washington D.C.
Boston

ATLANTIC

UNITED STATES
LOS ANGELES
San Diego
Phoenix
Oklahoma City
Memphis
Dallas
Atlanta
Appalachian Mts.
C. Hatteras

Bermuda (U.K.)

OCEAN

Ciudad Juárez
Guadalupe (Mex.)
Houston
San Antonio
New Orleans
Mississippi

Tropic of Cancer

C. San Lucas
Gulfo de California
Baja California

Monterrey
Gulf of Mexico
Miami
Florida Str.
BAHAMAS

Sargasso Sea

OCEAN

Honolulu
Oahu 4205
HAWAIIAN IS. (U.S.A.)
Hawaii

Guadalajara
MEXICO
5700
Puebla
Acapulco
Mérida

La Habana
CUBA
Canal de Yucatán
JAMAICA
Kingston
HAITI
7680
DOMINICAN REP.
9200
PUERTO RICO (U.S.A.)
Leeward Is.

West Indies

Is. Revilla Gigedo (Mex.)

BELIZE
GUATEMALA
Guatemala
San Salvador
EL SALVADOR
HONDURAS
NICARAGUA
Managua
San José
Caribbean Sea

BARBADOS
Windward Is.

C I F I C

I. Clipperton (Fr.)

COSTA RICA
Colón
PANAMA
Panamá

Barranquilla
Maracaibo
Caracas
Orinoco

VENEZUELA

Palmyra Is. (U.S.A.)
Teraina
Tabuaeran
Kiritimati

Jarvis I. (U.S.A.)

E A N

Equator

I. del Coco (Costa Rica)
I. de Malpelo (Colombia)
Medellín
Cali
Bogotá
COLOMBIA

Galápagos (Ecuador)
Quito
ECUADOR

Amazonas

nix Is.
B A T I
Malden I.
Starbuck I.

Tongareva
Pukapuka
Manihiki
Caroline I.
Vostok I.
Flint I.

Suwarrow Is.
Cook Is. (N.Z.)
Is. de la Société
Tahiti
Papeete
Is. Marquises

Is. Tuamotu

Guayaquil
Iquitos
C. Paliñas

BRAZIL

Trujillo

PERU
6369
LIMA
Cuzco

Rarotonga
Austral Seamount Chain
Is. Tubuai
Mururoa
FRENCH POLYNESIA
Tuamotu Ridge

L. Titicaca
Nevada Ancohuma 6550
Arequipa
6866
Peru-
Arica
La Paz
BOLIVIA

Tropic of Capricorn
Ducie I.
Pitcairn I. (U.K.)
Rapa

Iquique
Chile
Antofagasta
8050
Trench

PARAGUAY
Asunción

San Miguel de Tucumán

Sala-y-Gómez (Chile)
I. de Pascua (Chile)
San Félix (Chile)
San Ambrosio (Chile)

Córdoba
Aconcagua 6960
Rosario
Pôrto Alegre

Arch. de Juan Fernández (Chile)
Valparaíso
SANTIAGO
BUENOS AIRES
Concepción
URUGUAY
Montevideo
Río de la Plata
ARGENTINA

SOUTH

East Pacific Ridge
Chile Rise

ATLANTIC

Pacific-Antarctic Ridge

OCEAN
6212

Punta Arenas
Est. de Magallanes
Tierra del Fuego
C. de Hornos
Falkland Is. (U.K.)
South Georgia (U.K.)

160 140 120 100 80 60 West from Greenwich 40 20
11 12 13 14 15 16 17 18 19 20

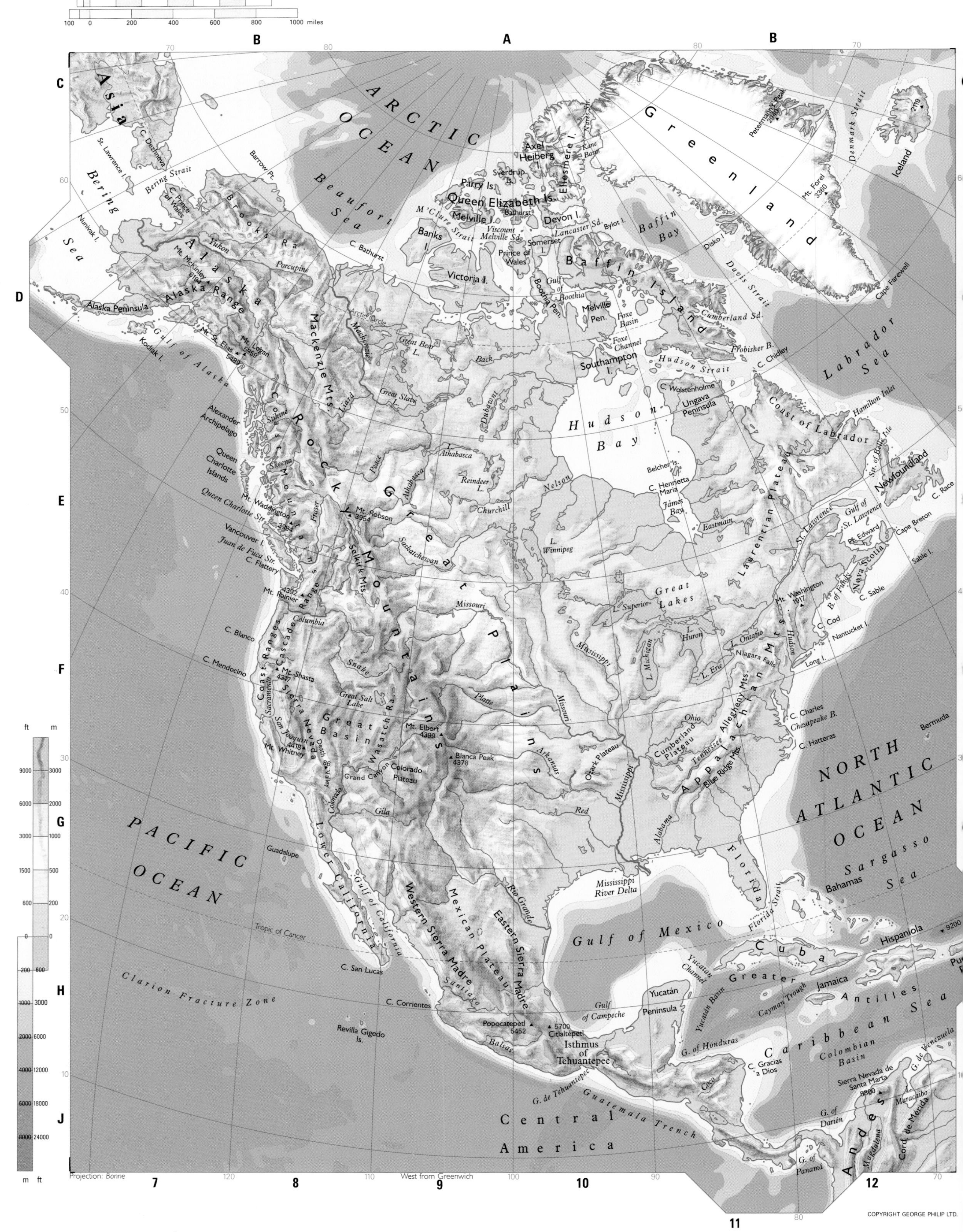

Projection: Bonne

West from Greenwich

COPYRIGHT GEORGE PHILIP LTD.

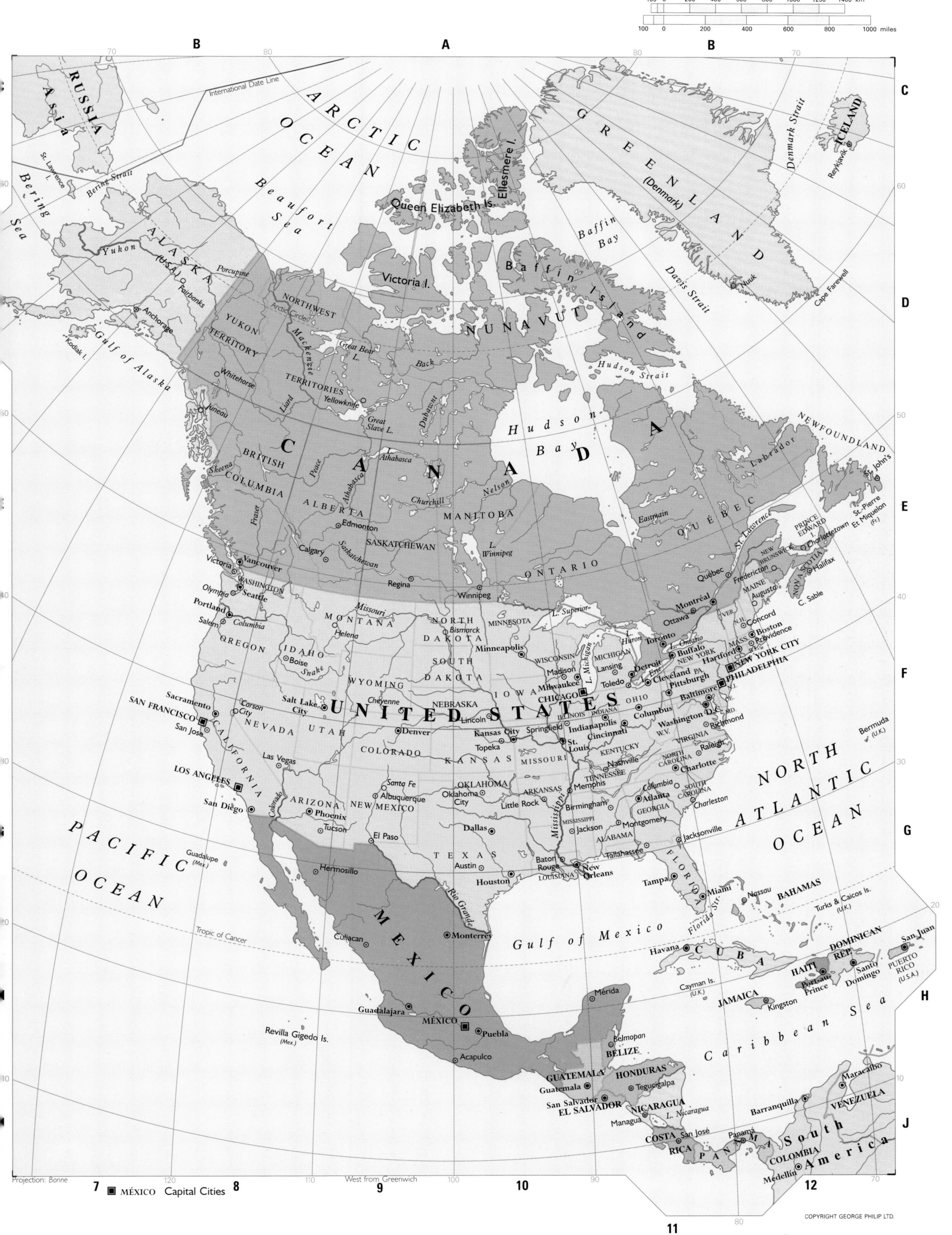
ARCTIC OCEAN
Beaufort Sea
GREENLAND (Denmark)
Baffin Bay
Baffin Island
Queen Elizabeth Is.
Ellesmere I.
Victoria I.
NUNAVUT
NORTHWEST TERRITORIES
YUKON TERRITORY
ALASKA (U.S.A.)
RUSSIA
Asia
Bering Sea
Bering Strait
International Date Line
Gulf of Alaska
Hudson Bay
Hudson Strait
Davis Strait
Denmark Strait
ICELAND
Reykjavik
Nuuk
Cape Farewell
CANADA
BRITISH COLUMBIA
ALBERTA
SASKATCHEWAN
MANITOBA
ONTARIO
QUÉBEC
NEWFOUNDLAND
Labrador
PRINCE EDWARD I.
NEW BRUNSWICK
NOVA SCOTIA
St.-Pierre Et Miquelon (Fr.)
UNITED STATES
NORTH ATLANTIC OCEAN
PACIFIC OCEAN
Gulf of Mexico
MEXICO
MÉXICO
Caribbean Sea
CUBA
BAHAMAS
JAMAICA
HAITI
DOMINICAN REP.
PUERTO RICO (U.S.A.)
BELIZE
GUATEMALA
HONDURAS
EL SALVADOR
NICARAGUA
COSTA RICA
PANAMA
COLOMBIA
VENEZUELA
South America
Tropic of Cancer
Projection: Bonne
West from Greenwich
MÉXICO Capital Cities
COPYRIGHT GEORGE PHILIP LTD.

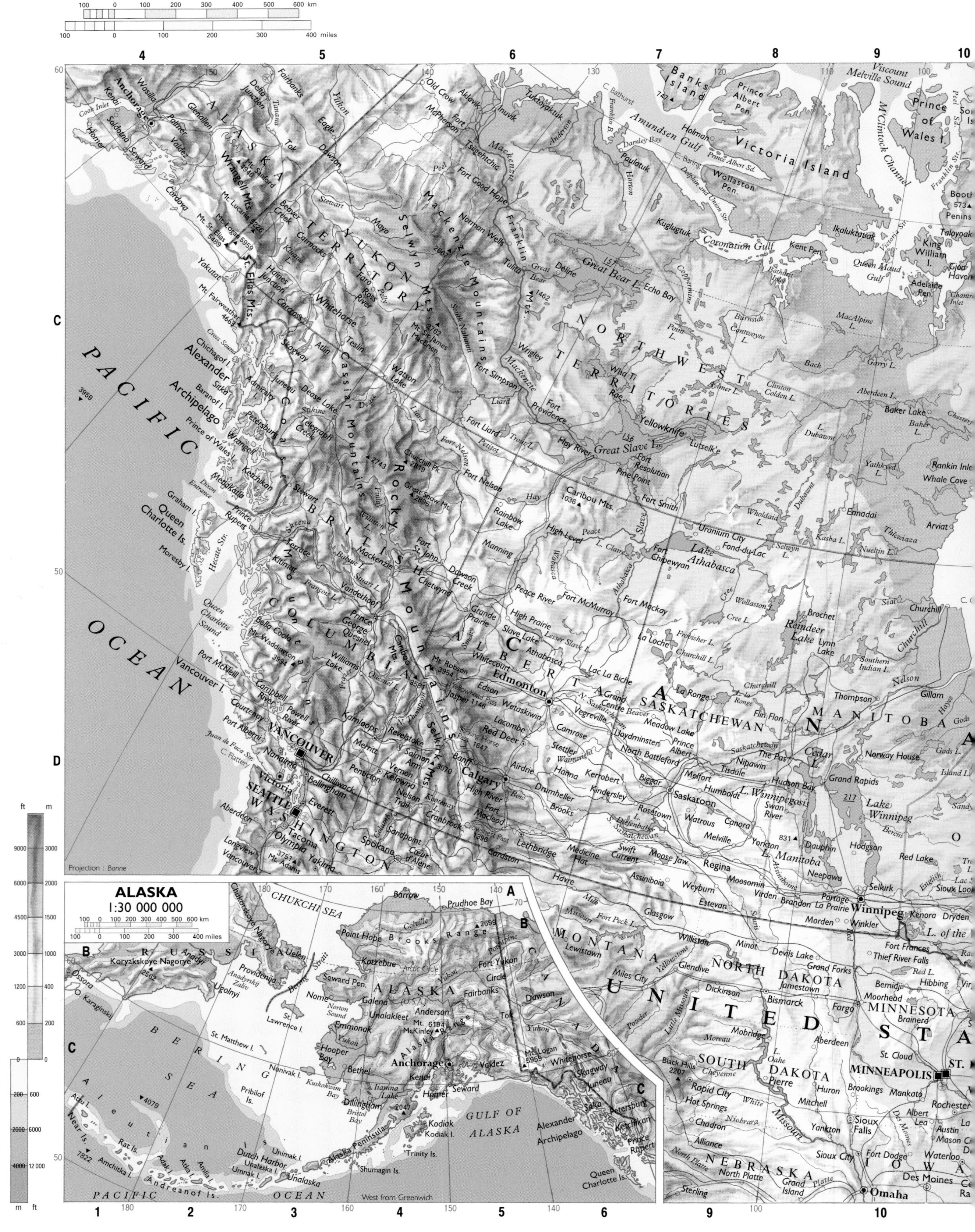

PACIFIC OCEAN

ALASKA TERRITORY

YUKON TERRITORY

BRITISH COLUMBIA

ROCKY MOUNTAINS

Coast Mountains

Cassiar Mountains

Selwyn Mts

Mackenzie Mountains

NORTHWEST TERRITORIES

Victoria Island

Banks Island

Prince Albert Pen.

Prince of Wales I.

ALBERTA

SASKATCHEWAN

MANITOBA

Great Bear L.

Great Slave L.

Lake Athabasca

Reindeer Lake

Lake Winnipeg

Lake Winnipegosis

L. Manitoba

Anchorage
Fairbanks
Whitehorse
Yellowknife
Edmonton
Calgary
VANCOUVER
Victoria
Seattle
Saskatoon
Regina
Winnipeg

WASHINGTON
MONTANA
NORTH DAKOTA
SOUTH DAKOTA
NEBRASKA
MINNESOTA
IOWA

UNITED STATES

Queen Charlotte Is.
Vancouver I.
Alexander Archipelago

GULF OF ALASKA

Minneapolis
Omaha

Projection : Bonne

ALASKA
1:30 000 000

RUSSIA

CHUKCHI SEA

BERING SEA

PACIFIC OCEAN

Brooks Range

ALASKA (U.S.A.)

Aleutian Is.

Anchorage

GULF OF ALASKA

Arctic Circle

West from Greenwich

11 12 13 14 15 16

B
C
D
E

Devon I.
Lancaster Sound
Bylot I.
1890
Arctic Bay
Borden Pen.
Pond Inlet
Baffin Bay
2136
Nunavik
Uummannaq
Qeqertarsuaq
Qeqertarsuaq
Ilulissat
Qasigiannguit
C. Adair
Clyde River
C. Raper
Home B.
Baffin Island
Fury and Hecla Str.
Igloolik
Sanirajak
Melville Peninsula
Committee B.
Foxe Basin
Prince Charles I.
Air Force I.
2591
Cumberland Peninsula
Qikiqtarjuaq
C. Dyer
Pangnirtung
Hoare B.
Cumberland Sd.
Mercy C.
Nettilling L.
Rae Isthmus
Repulse Bay
NUNAVUT
C. Dorchester
Amadjuak L.
Foxe Pen.
Cape Dorset
Foxe Channel
Roes Welcome Sd.
Southampton I.
Salliq
Bell Pen.
Nottingham I.
Salisbury I.
Meta Incognita Peninsula
Kimmirut
Iqaluit
Hall Peninsula
Frobisher Bay
Resolution I.
Hudson Strait
Coats I.
Mansel I.
Ivujivik
Salluit
Kangiqsujuaq
Quaqtaq
Akpatok I.
C. Chidley
Péninsule d'Ungava
Puvirnituq
L. Payne
Arnaud
Kangirsuk
Ungava Bay
1652
Kangiqsualujjuaq
Hebron
Hudson Bay
Ottawa Is.
257
Inukjuak
Feuilles
Koksoak
Kuujjuaq
George
Baleine
Nain
Caniapiscau
Mélèzes
L. Minto
Sleeper Is.
King George Is.
Baker's Dozen Is.
Belcher Is.
L. à l'Eau Claire
Kuujjuarapik
Grande Baleine
L. Bienville
Schefferville
Petitsikapau
Esker
Smallwood Res.
Labrador
Churchill Falls
Churchill
North West River
Happy Valley-Goose Bay
Hopedale
C. Harrison
Rigolet
Cartwright
NEWFOUNDLAND
Port Hope Simpson
Belle Isle
C. Bauld
St. Anthony
Str. of Belle Isle
Notre Dame B.
C. Henrietta Maria
Pte. Louis XIV
Peawanuck
Winisk
Kanaaupscow
La Grande
Rés. de Caniapiscau
Labrador City
Fermont
Ashuanipi
Natashquan
Romaine
St-Augustin
Moisie
Chisasibi
James Bay
Akimiski I.
Wemindji
1135
Gagnon
QUÉBEC
Rés. Manicouagan
Manicouagan
Havre-St-Pierre
Natashquan
Î. d'Anticosti
Sept-Îles
Port-Cartier
Big Trout L.
Attawapiskat
Attawapiskat
Charlton I.
Eastmain
Eastmain
Waskaganish
Rupert
L. Albanel
L. Mistassini
Fort Albany
Albany
ONTARIO
Moosonee
Nottaway
Harricana
Missinaibi
Kenogami
Nakina
Joseph
Chibougamau
Peribonca
Baie Comeau
St. Lawrence
Matane
Gaspé
Pén. de Gaspé
Rimouski
Gulf of St. Lawrence
Cabot Str.
Îs. de la Madeleine
Deer Lake
Baie Verte
Grand Falls
Lewisporte
Gander
Bonavista
Trinity B.
Carbonear
St. John's
Corner Brook
Newfoundland
814
Stephenville
Channel-Port aux Basques
Marystown
Placentia B.
Placentia
C. Race
C. Ray
ST.-PIERRE et MIQUELON (Fr.)
North C.
Cape Breton I.
Sydney
Glace Bay
Port Hawkesbury
Antigonish
Dolbeau
L. St-Jean
Chicoutimi
Roberval
Jonquière
Matagami
L. Matagami
Hearst
Mattagami
Cochrane
Abitibi L.
Amos
Rés. Gouin
Rivière-du-Loup
Campbellton
Bathurst
Edmundston
Miramichi
PR. EDWARD I.
Summerside
Charlottetown
Northumberland Str.
NEW BRUNSWICK
Moncton
NOVA SCOTIA
New Glasgow
Truro
Geraldton
Kapuskasing
Timmins
Oba
Marathon
Nipigon
Kirkland Lake
Rouyn-Noranda
Val-d'Or
La Tuque
1190
Québec
Grand Falls
Woodstock
Fredericton
Saint John
Amherst
Kentville
Dartmouth
Halifax
Sable I. (Nova Scotia)
Thunder Bay
Lake Superior
Wawa
Chapleau
New Liskeard
Rés. Cabonga
Mont-Laurier
Shawinigan
Trois-Rivières
Joliette
Lévis
Thetford Mines
St-Hyacinthe
MAINE
B. of Fundy
Digby
Bridgewater
Liverpool
Yarmouth
C. Sable
Houghton
183
Sault Ste. Marie
Elliot Lake
Sudbury
North Bay
Ottawa
L. Nipissing
MONTRÉAL
Hull
Sherbrooke
Bangor
Augusta
Lewiston
Portland
Marquette
Sault Ste. Marie
Manitoulin I.
Parry Sound
Pembroke
Ottawa
Granby
L. Champlain
Montpelier
Manistique
MICHIGAN
Georgian Bay
Huntsville
Cornwall
Burlington
VERMONT
NEW HAMPSHIRE
Concord
Manchester
Escanaba
Menominee
Petoskey
Lake Huron
Barrie
Peterborough
Kingston
Traverse City
Owen Sound
Oshawa
Belleville
Green Bay
Cadillac
TORONTO
L. Ontario
Syracuse
MASS.
BOSTON
C. Cod
Kitchener
Hamilton
Rochester
Albany
Springfield
Providence
L. Michigan
Grand Rapids
Saginaw
Flint
London
Niagara Falls
BUFFALO
NEW YORK
HARTFORD
CONN.
R.I.
New Haven
MILWAUKEE
Lansing
Sarnia
174
L. Erie
Elmira
Binghamton
Bridgeport
Racine
Kenosha
DETROIT
Windsor
Erie
Jamestown
Scranton
Newark
NEW YORK
CHICAGO
Gary
South Bend
Toledo
CLEVELAND
PENNSYLVANIA
Allentown
N.J.
Trenton
INDIANA
OHIO
GREENLAND (KALAALLIT NUNAAT) (Denmark)
Kangerlussuaq
Sisimiut
Maniitsoq
Nuuk
2850
Kong Frederik VI's Kyst
Ammassalik
Davis Strait
Qeqertarsuatsiaat
Paamiut
Arsuk
Qaqortoq
Narsaq
Nanortalik
Alluitsup Paa
Uummannarsuaq
Labrador Sea
3809
ATLANTIC OCEAN
6309

80 70 60 50 40 30
60 50 40
80 70 60

West from Greenwich

11 12 13 14

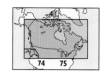

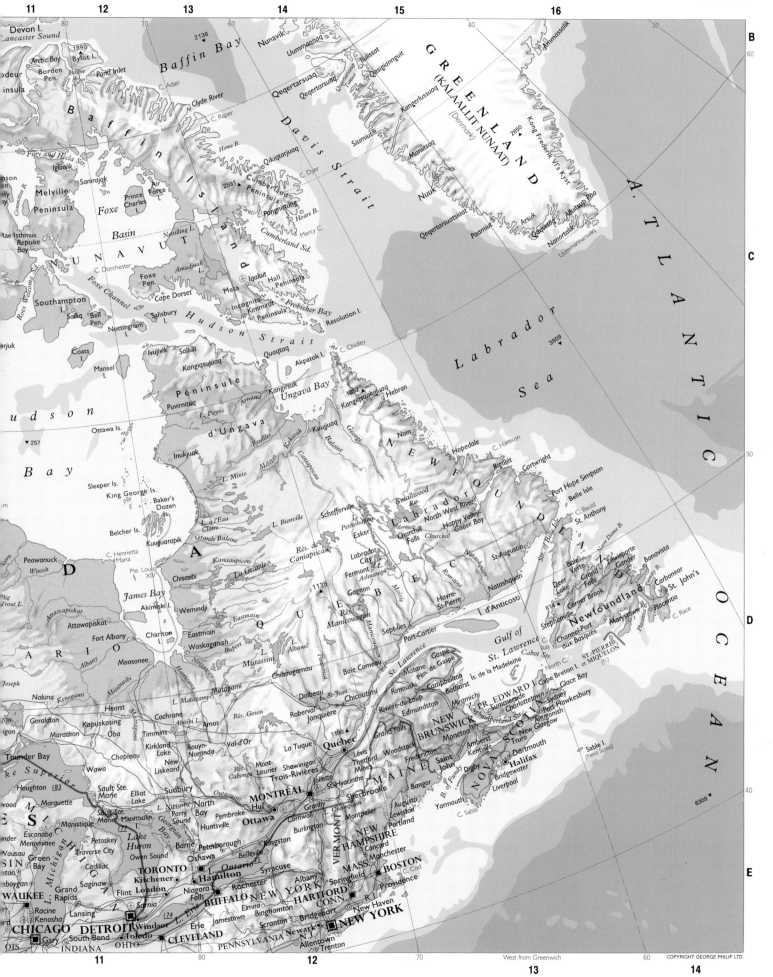

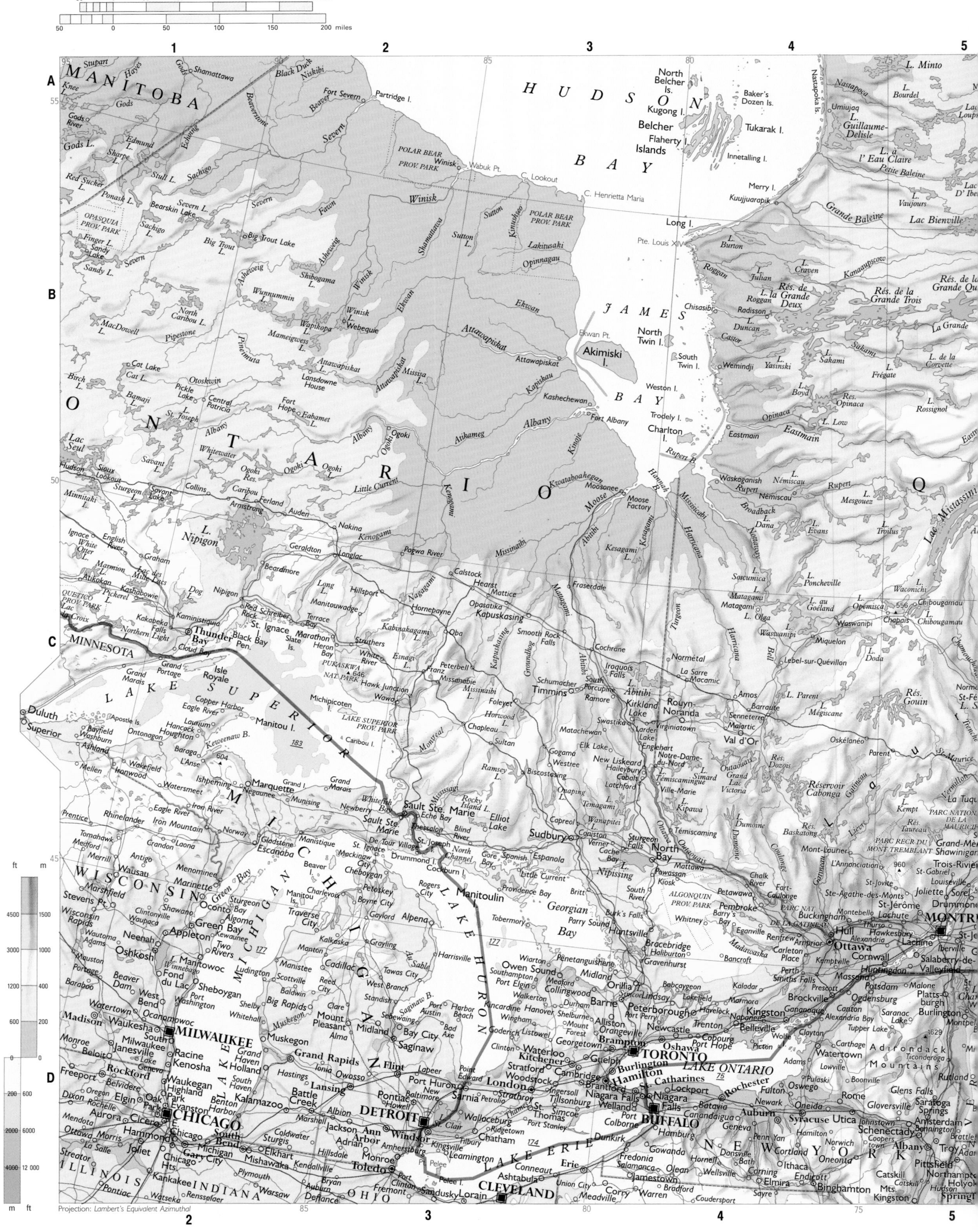

6 7 8 9

A B C D

LABRADOR SEA

NEWFOUNDLAND

Labrador

Newfoundland

QUÉBEC

Smallwood Reservoir

Churchill Falls

Happy Valley-Goose Bay

North West River

Mealy Mts.

Nain

Hopedale

Makkovik

Postville

Rigolet

Cartwright

Schefferville

Labrador City

Wabush

Fermont

Rés. de Caniapiscau

Rés. Manicouagan

Sept-Îles

Port-Cartier

Baie Comeau

Havre-St-Pierre

Natashquan

Blanc-Sablon

L'Anse aux Meadows

St. Anthony

Str. of Belle Isle

Long Range Mts.

Corner Brook

Stephenville

Deer Lake

Grand Falls

Windsor

Gander

Botwood

Lewisporte

Channel-Port aux Basques

Cabot Strait

St. John's

Mt. Pearl

Conception B.

Avalon Peninsula

C. Race

Trinity B.

Bonavista

Placentia

Marystown

Burin

ST.-PIERRE ET MIQUELON (France)

Î. d'Anticosti

GULF OF ST. LAWRENCE

Gaspé

Pén. de Gaspé

Chic-Chocs

Rimouski

Matane

Chicoutimi

Jonquière

St. Lawrence

Rivière-du-Loup

Îs. de la Madeleine

Cape Breton Island

Sydney

Glace Bay

Louisbourg

Bras d'Or L.

PRINCE EDWARD ISLAND

Charlottetown

Summerside

NEW BRUNSWICK

Moncton

Fredericton

Saint John

Bathurst

Miramichi

Edmundston

NOVA SCOTIA

Halifax

Dartmouth

Truro

Yarmouth

Sable I. (Nova Scotia)

Bay of Fundy

MAINE

Bangor

Augusta

Portland

Lewiston

UNITED STATES

BOSTON

Manchester

Concord

ATLANTIC OCEAN

70 65 60 55 50 45

West from Greenwich

6 7 8

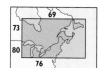

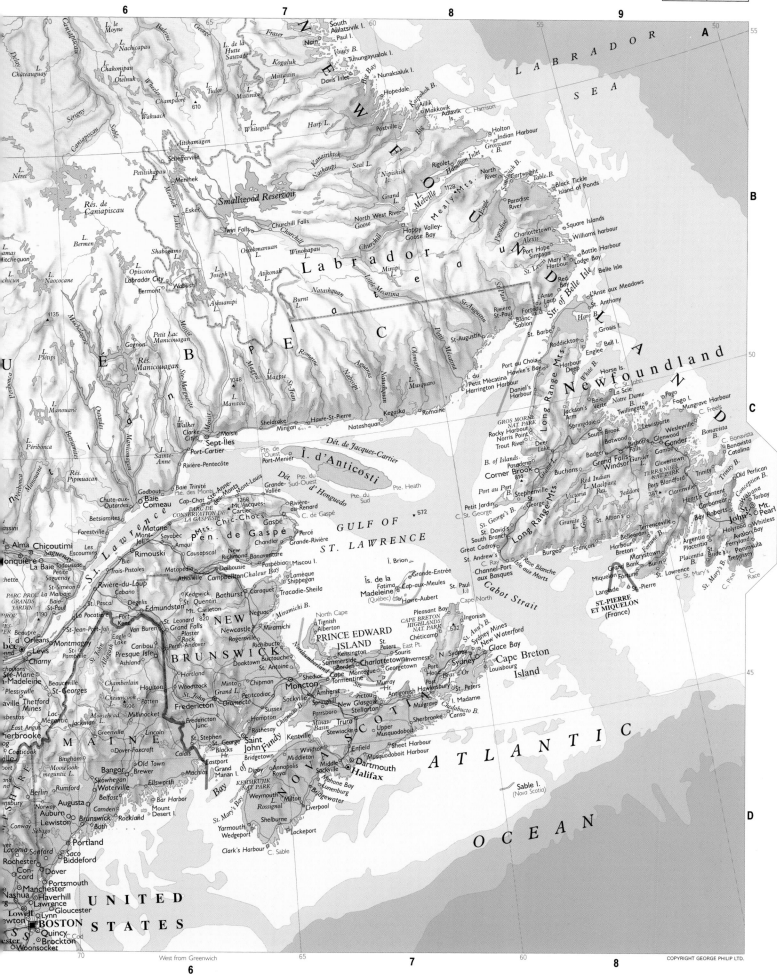

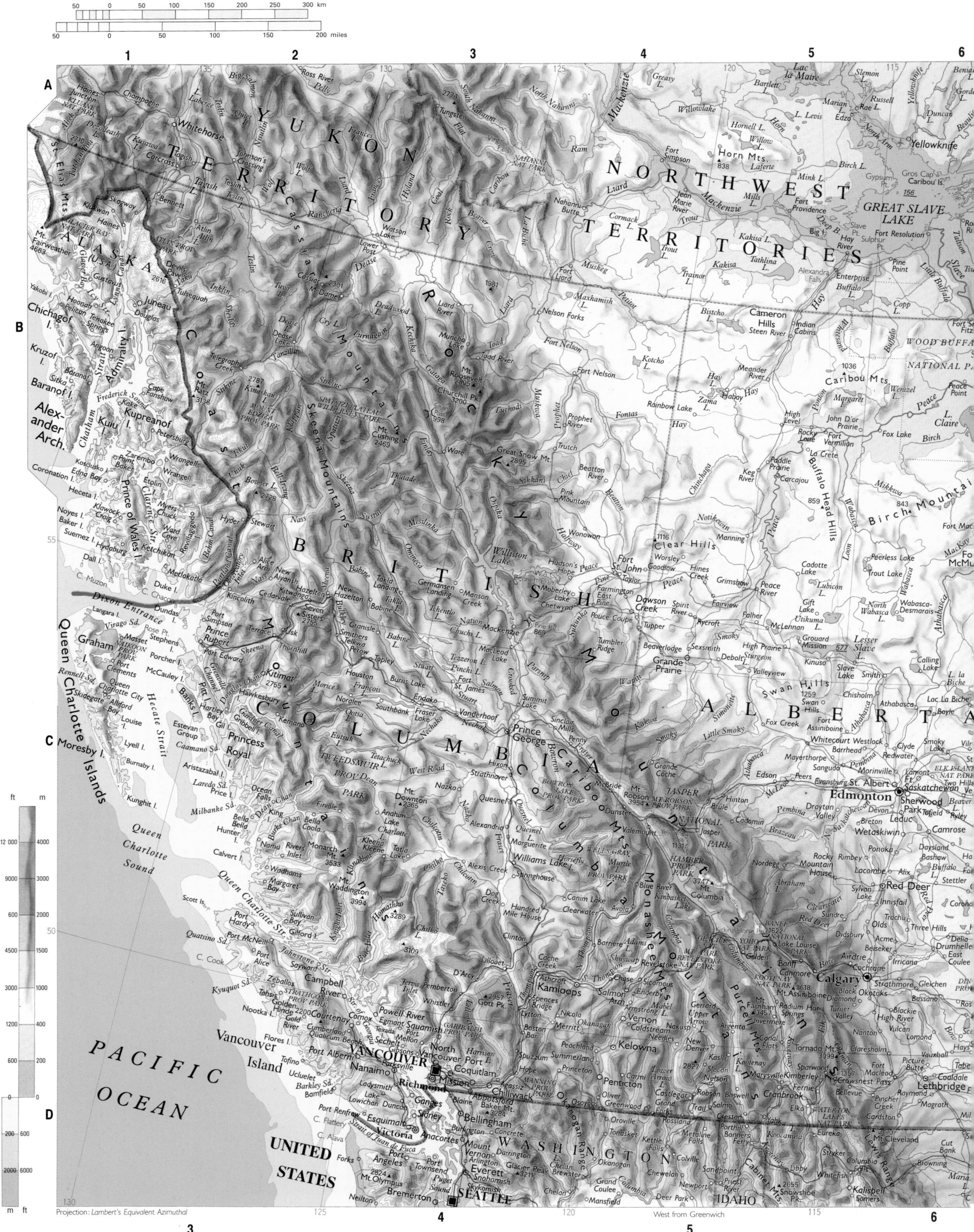
YUKON TERRITORY
NORTHWEST TERRITORIES
BRITISH COLUMBIA
ALBERTA
ALASKA (U.S.A.)
PACIFIC OCEAN
UNITED STATES
WASHINGTON
IDAHO
GREAT SLAVE LAKE
Whitehorse
Yellowknife
Prince George
Edmonton
Calgary
Kamloops
Kelowna
VANCOUVER
Victoria
SEATTLE
Vancouver Island
Queen Charlotte Islands
Coast Mountains
Rocky Mountains
Skeena Mountains
Cassiar Mountains
Cariboo Mts
Columbia Mountains
Monashee Mts
Purcell Mts
Projection: Lambert's Equivalent Azimuthal
West from Greenwich

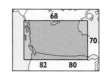

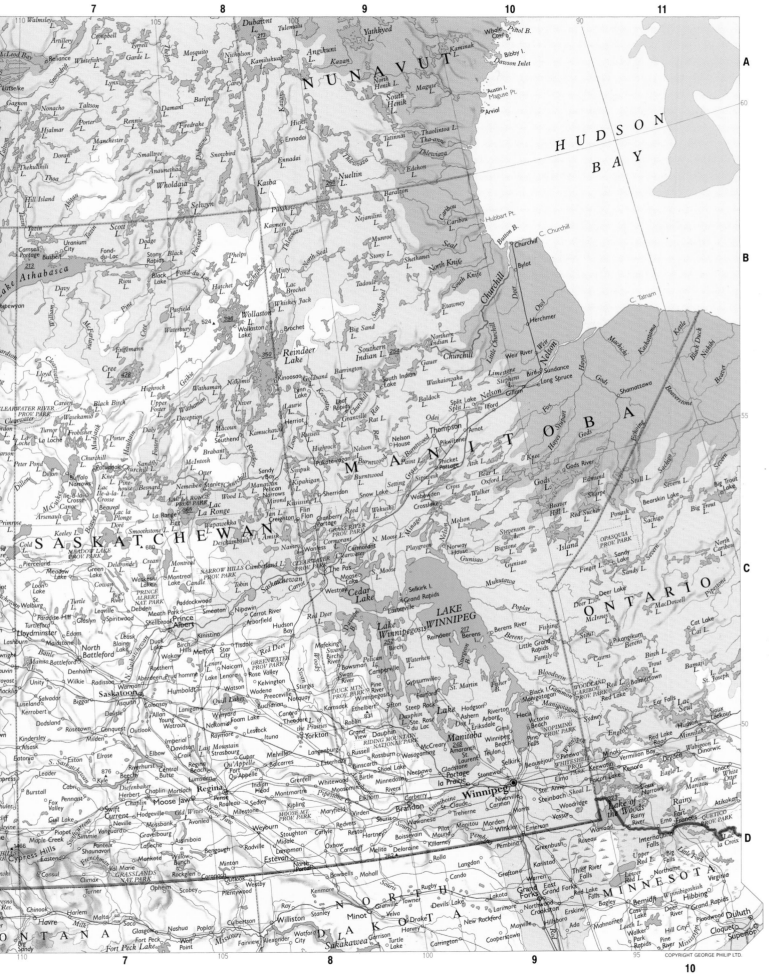

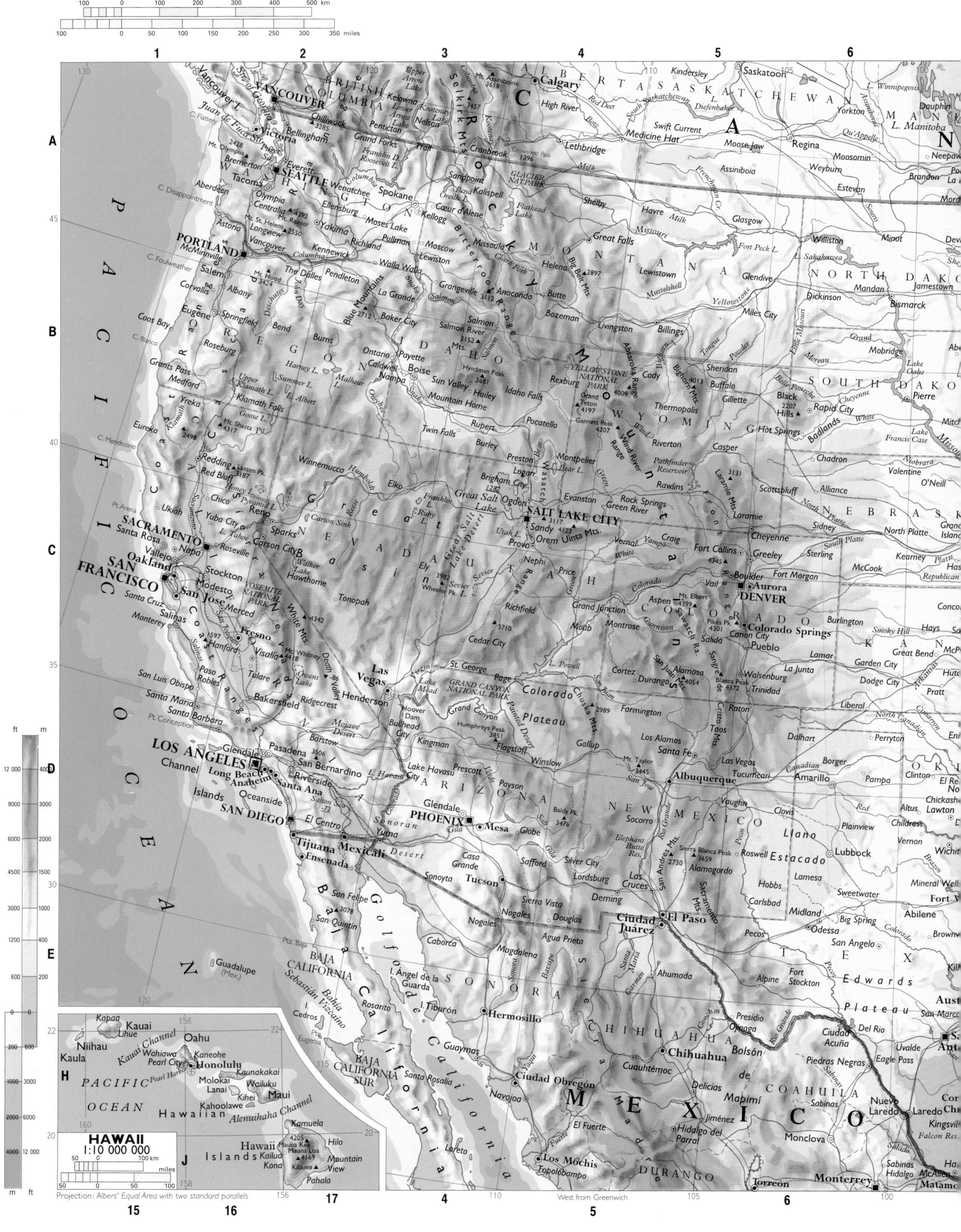

Scale: 100 0 100 200 300 400 500 km / 100 0 50 100 150 200 250 300 350 miles

Elevation scale (ft / m): 12 000, 9000, 6000, 3000, 1200, 600, 0

HAWAII 1:10 000 000
50 0 100 km
Hawaiian Islands

Projection: Albers' Equal Area with two standard parallels

West from Greenwich

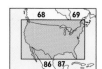

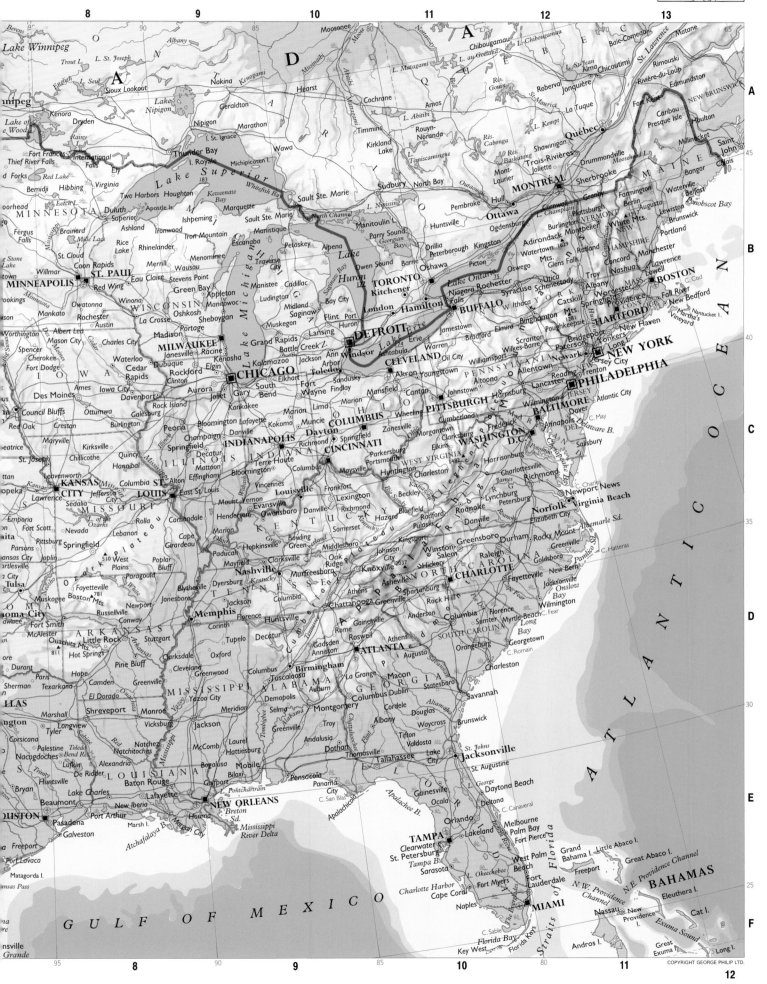

COPYRIGHT GEORGE PHILIP LTD.

8 9 10 11 12 13
A B C D E F
CANADA
ONTARIO
QUEBEC
NEW BRUNSWICK
ATLANTIC OCEAN
GULF OF MEXICO
BAHAMAS
MINNESOTA
WISCONSIN
IOWA
ILLINOIS
INDIANA
OHIO
MICHIGAN
MISSOURI
KENTUCKY
TENNESSEE
ARKANSAS
MISSISSIPPI
ALABAMA
GEORGIA
LOUISIANA
FLORIDA
SOUTH CAROLINA
NORTH CAROLINA
VIRGINIA
WEST VIRGINIA
PENNSYLVANIA
NEW YORK
NEW JERSEY
MAINE
VERMONT
NEW HAMPSHIRE
MASS.
CONN.
Lake Winnipeg
Lake Superior
Lake Michigan
Lake Huron
Lake Erie
Lake Ontario
Appalachian Mts.
Cumberland Plateau
Ozark Plateau
MONTREAL
Ottawa
TORONTO
Québec
CHICAGO
DETROIT
CLEVELAND
PITTSBURGH
BUFFALO
NEW YORK
PHILADELPHIA
BALTIMORE
WASHINGTON D.C.
BOSTON
HARTFORD
MINNEAPOLIS
ST. PAUL
MILWAUKEE
INDIANAPOLIS
COLUMBUS
CINCINNATI
KANSAS CITY
ST. LOUIS
Memphis
Nashville
CHARLOTTE
ATLANTA
NEW ORLEANS
Jacksonville
TAMPA
MIAMI
Straits of Florida
Florida Keys
Mississippi River Delta

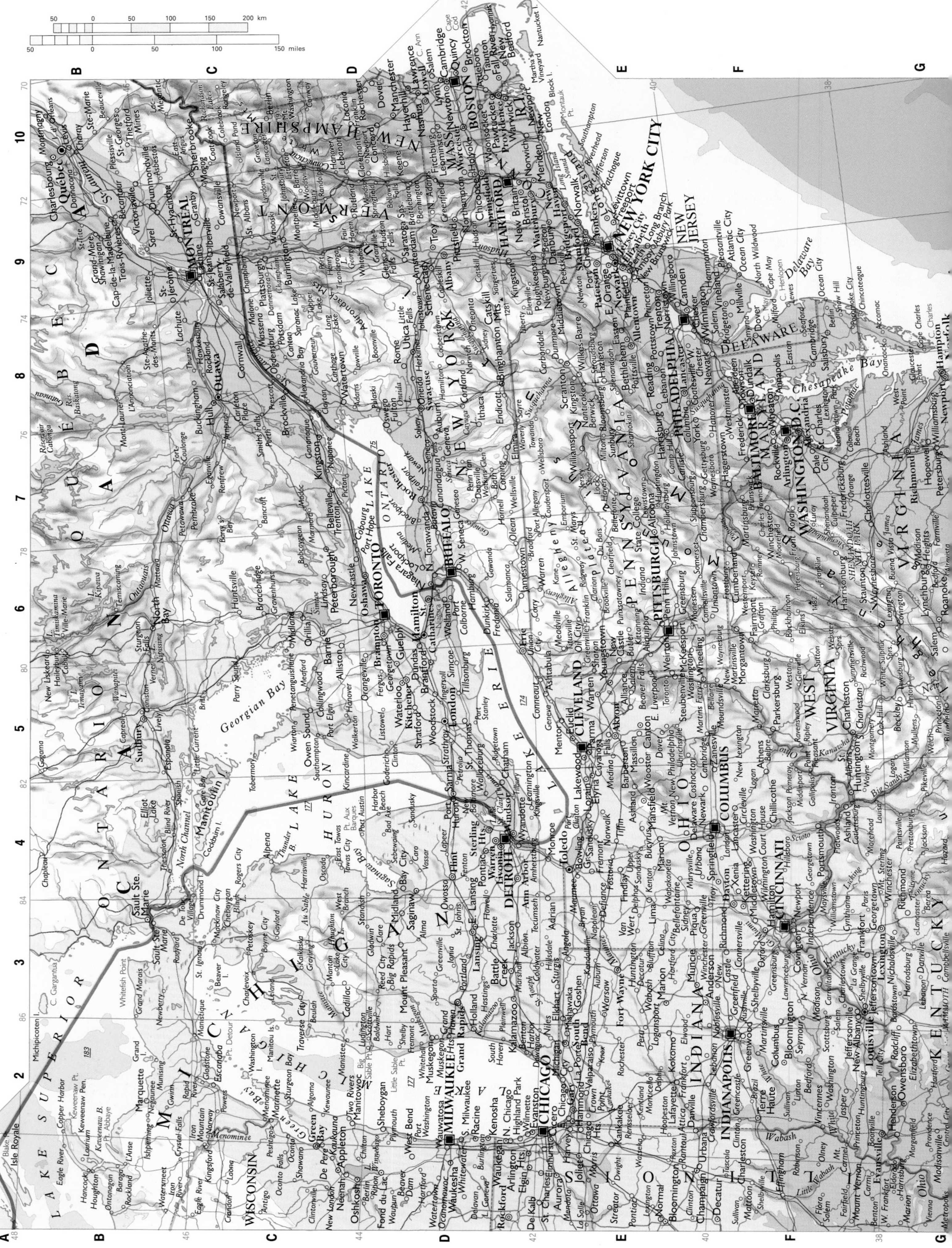

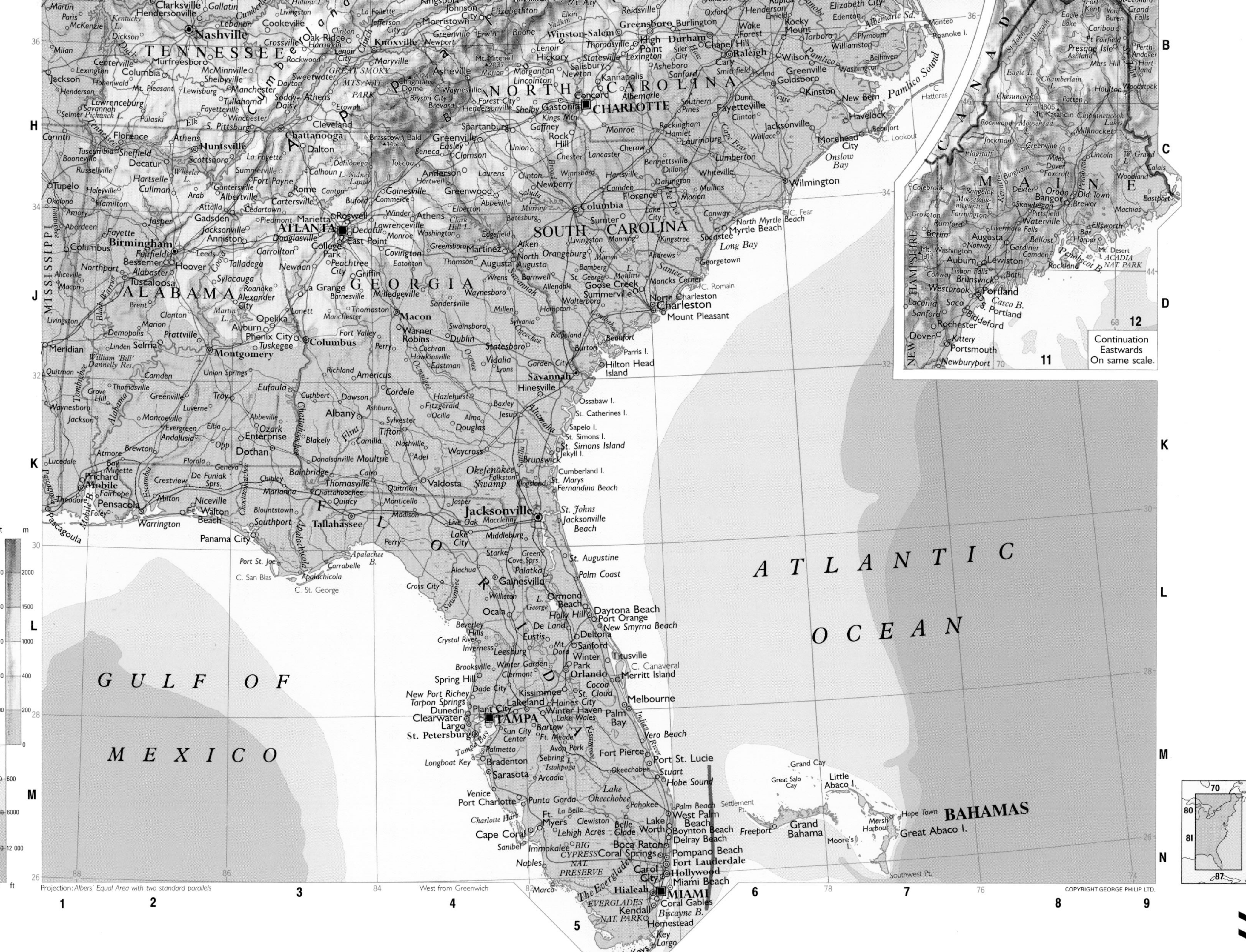
ATLANTIC OCEAN
GULF OF MEXICO
BAHAMAS
TENNESSEE
NORTH CAROLINA
SOUTH CAROLINA
GEORGIA
ALABAMA
FLORIDA
MISSISSIPPI
MAINE
NEW HAMPSHIRE
Nashville
Knoxville
Chattanooga
Huntsville
CHARLOTTE
Raleigh
Durham
Greensboro
Winston-Salem
Wilmington
Columbia
Charleston
Savannah
ATLANTA
Augusta
Macon
Columbus
Birmingham
Montgomery
Mobile
Pensacola
Tallahassee
Jacksonville
Gainesville
Daytona Beach
Orlando
TAMPA
St. Petersburg
Clearwater
Sarasota
Cape Coral
Fort Lauderdale
West Palm Beach
MIAMI
Florida Keys
Freeport
Grand Bahama
Great Abaco I.
Portland
Bangor
Lewiston
Augusta
Continuation Eastwards On same scale.
Projection: Albers' Equal Area with two standard parallels
West from Greenwich
COPYRIGHT GEORGE PHILIP LTD.

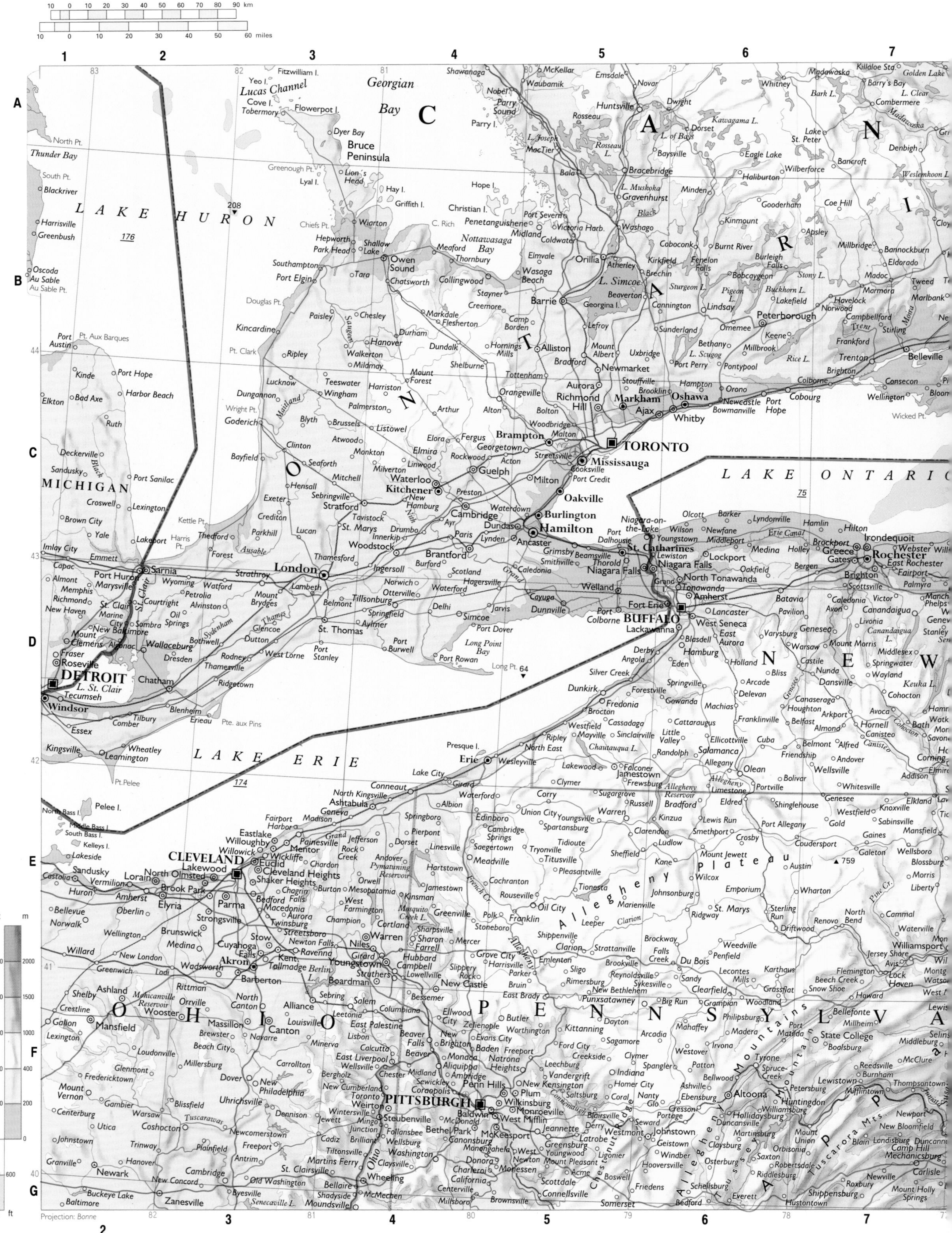
LAKE HURON
Georgian Bay
Bruce Peninsula
LAKE ONTARIO
LAKE ERIE
MICHIGAN
OHIO
PENNSYLVANIA
ONTARIO
TORONTO
DETROIT
CLEVELAND
BUFFALO
PITTSBURGH
Hamilton
Mississauga
London
Kitchener
Rochester
Windsor
Akron
Erie
Allegheny Plateau
Projection: Bonne

8 9 10 11 12 13 14

A B C D E F G

QUÉBEC

ADIRONDACK MOUNTAINS

NEW YORK

VERMONT

GREEN MOUNTAINS

WHITE MOUNTAINS

NEW HAMPSHIRE

MAINE

MASSACHUSETTS

CONNECTICUT

RHODE ISLAND

NEW JERSEY

Catskill Mts.

Long Island

ATLANTIC OCEAN

MONTREAL · Ottawa · BOSTON · HARTFORD · NEW YORK · PHILADELPHIA

from Greenwich

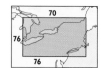

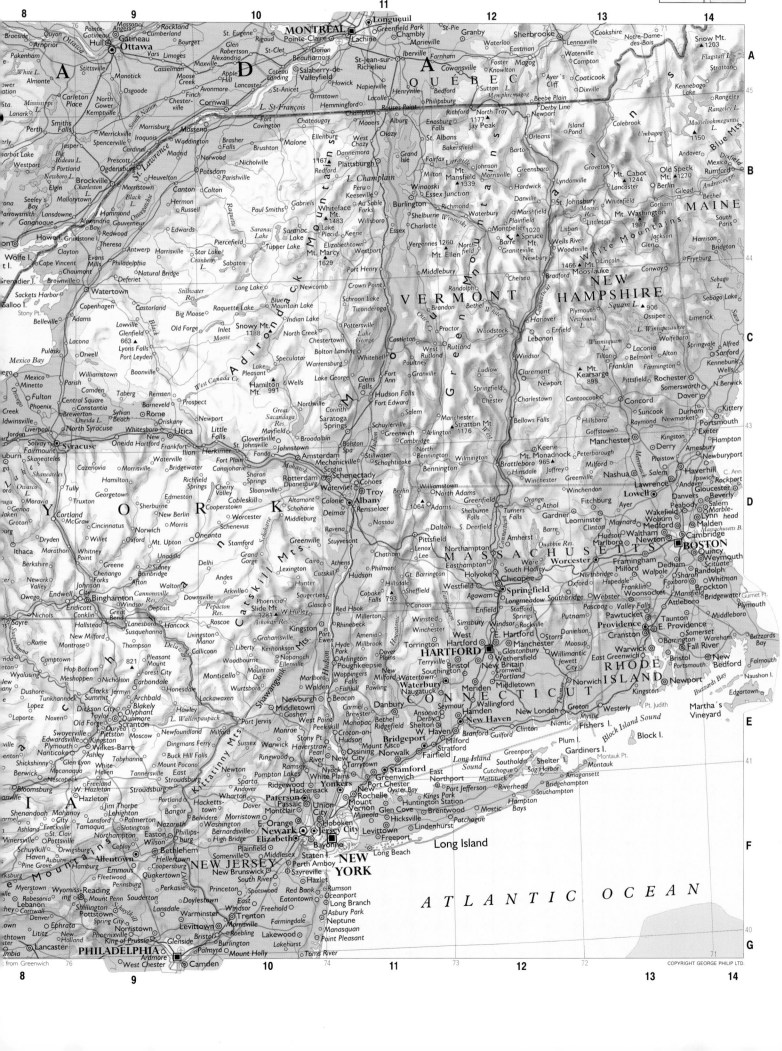

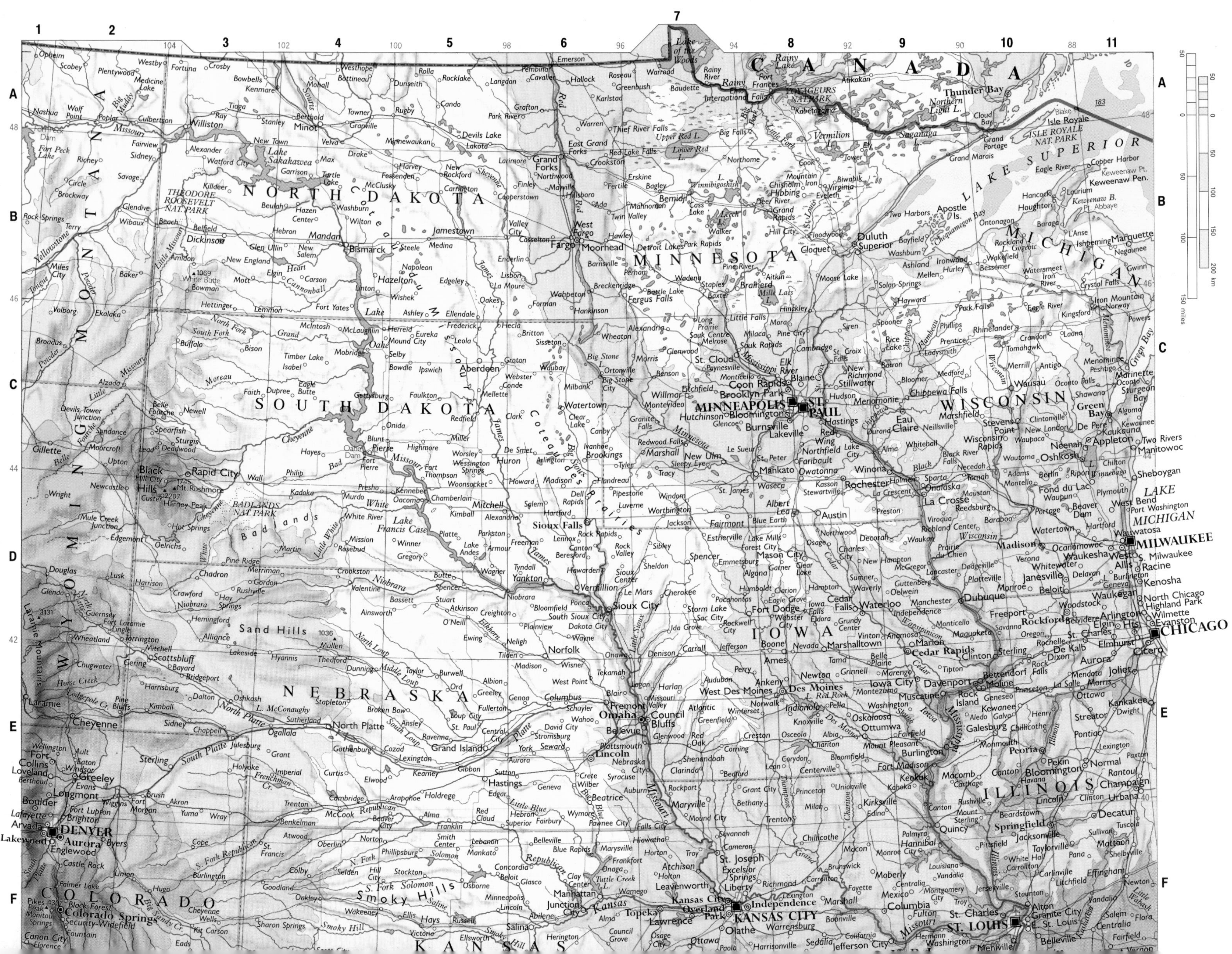

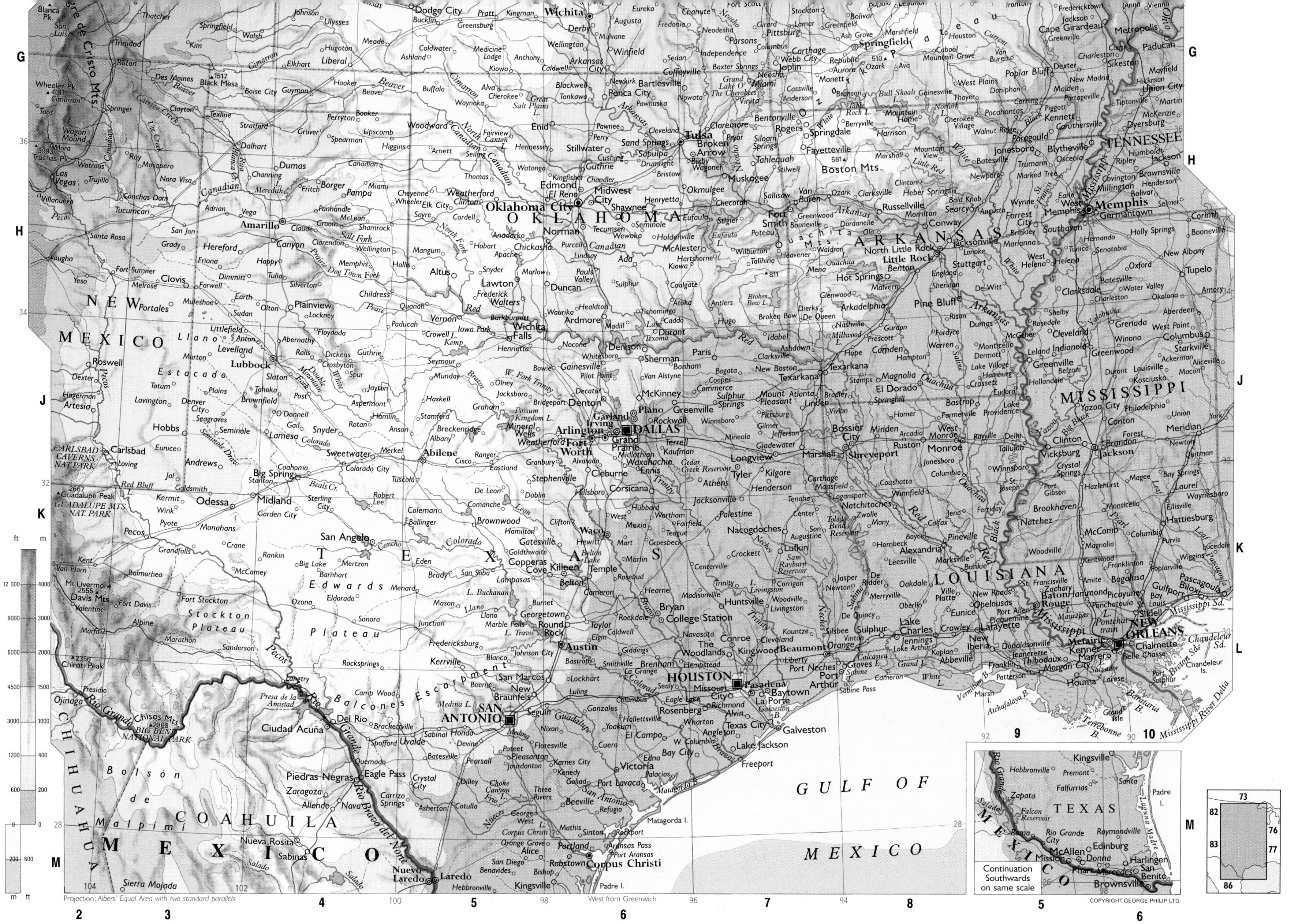

TENNESSEE

MISSISSIPPI

ARKANSAS

LOUISIANA

OKLAHOMA

NEW MEXICO

TEXAS

MEXICO

COAHUILA

CHIHUAHUA

GULF OF MEXICO

New Orleans

Houston

San Antonio

Dallas

Fort Worth

Oklahoma City

Tulsa

Wichita

Memphis

Corpus Christi

Laguna Madre

Rio Grande

Rio Bravo del Norte

Edwards Plateau

Llano Estacado

Sierra de Cristo Mts.

Projection: Albers Equal Area with two standard parallels

COPYRIGHT GEORGE PHILIP LTD.

West from Greenwich

Continuation Southwards on same scale

ft / m scale bar: 12 000, 9000, 6000, 4500, 3000, 1500, 1200, 600, 400, 200, 0

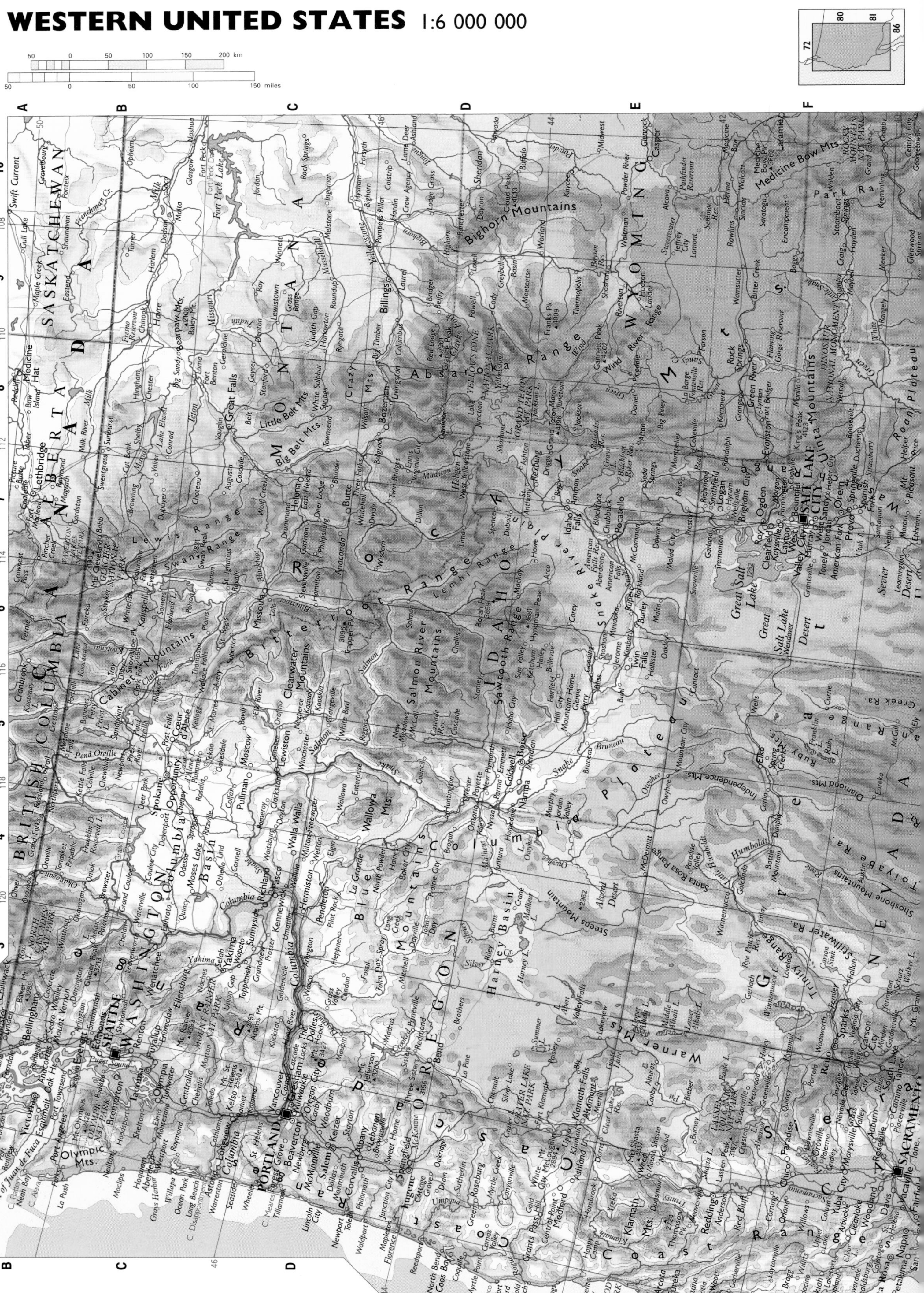

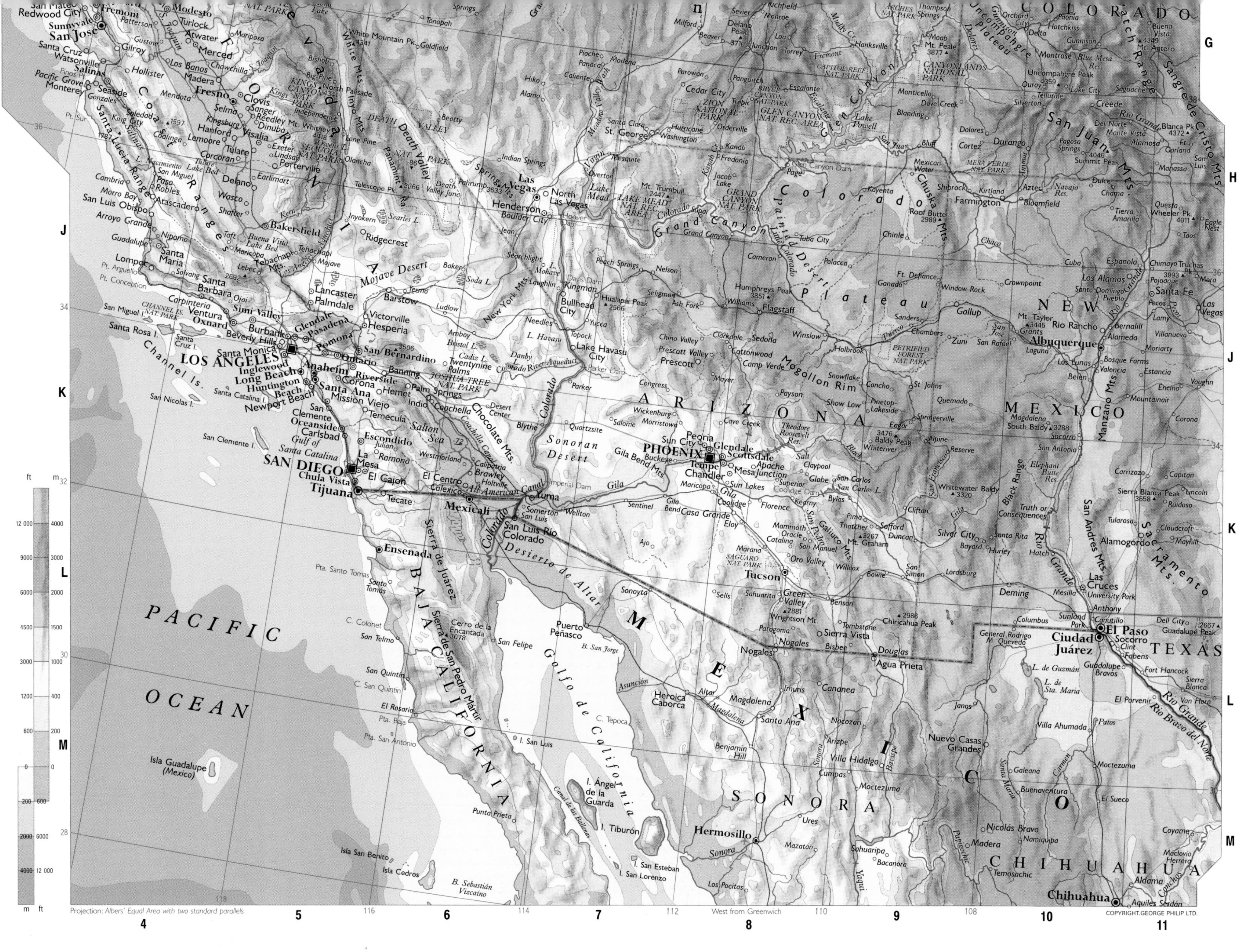
PACIFIC OCEAN
BAJA CALIFORNIA
SONORA
CHIHUAHUA
ARIZONA
NEW MEXICO
TEXAS
COLORADO
Golfo de California
Colorado Plateau
Sonoran Desert
Mojave Desert
Painted Desert
Desierto de Altar
Death Valley
Grand Canyon
Sierra de Juárez
Sierra de San Pedro Mártir
Sacramento Mts.
San Juan Mts.
Sangre de Cristo Mts.
Chuska Mts.
Mogollon Rim
Channel Is.
LOS ANGELES
SAN DIEGO
PHOENIX
Tijuana
Mexicali
Tucson
Albuquerque
El Paso
Ciudad Juárez
Chihuahua
Hermosillo
Las Vegas
Santa Fe
Fresno
Bakersfield
Flagstaff
Yuma
Ensenada
Nogales
Isla Guadalupe (Mexico)
Isla Cedros
I. Tiburón
Projection: Albers' Equal Area with two standard parallels
West from Greenwich
COPYRIGHT.GEORGE PHILIP LTD.
ft m
12 000 4000
9000 3000
6000 2000
4500 1500
3000 1000
1200 400
600 200
0 0
200 600
2000 6000
4000 12 000
m ft

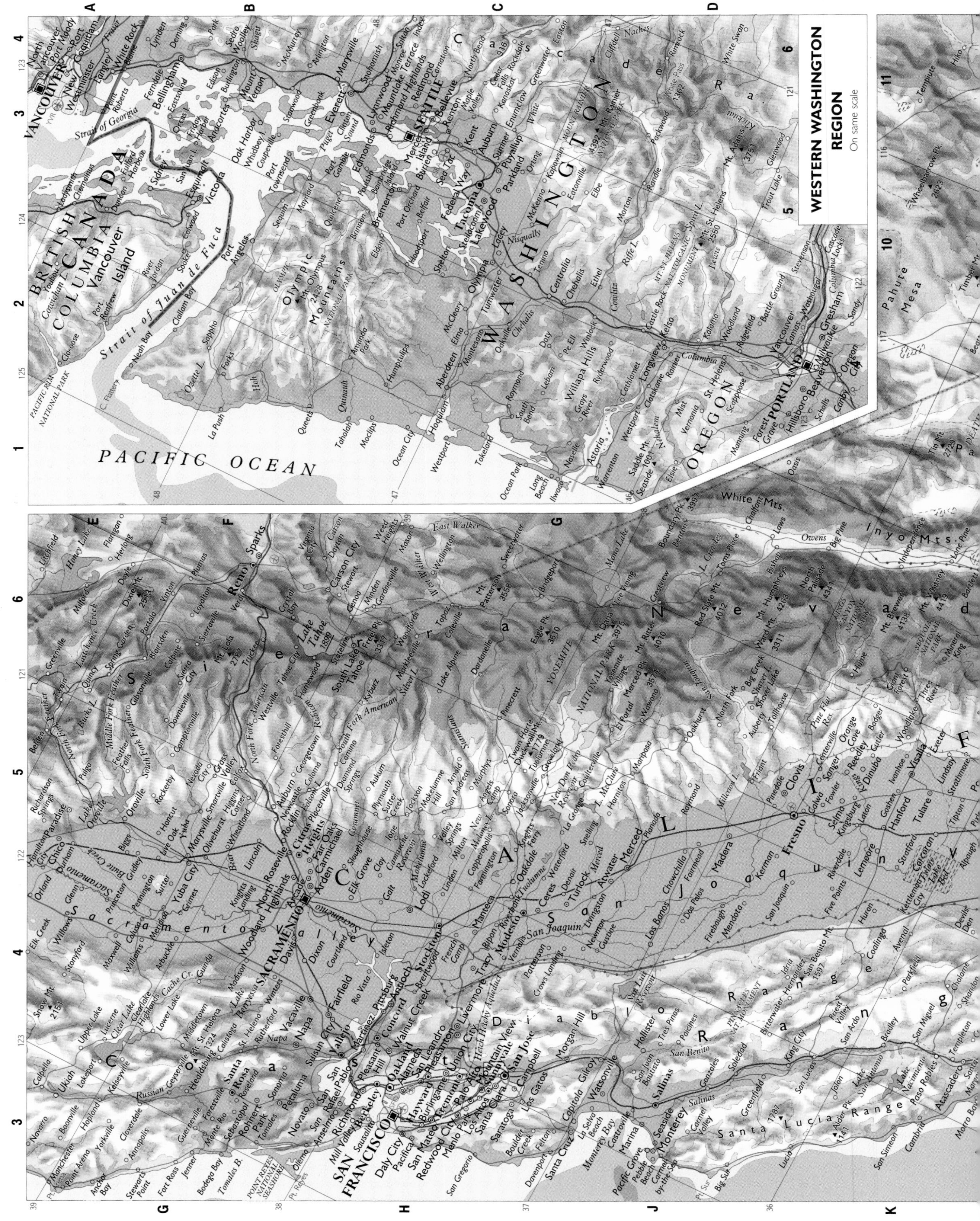

WESTERN WASHINGTON REGION
On same scale

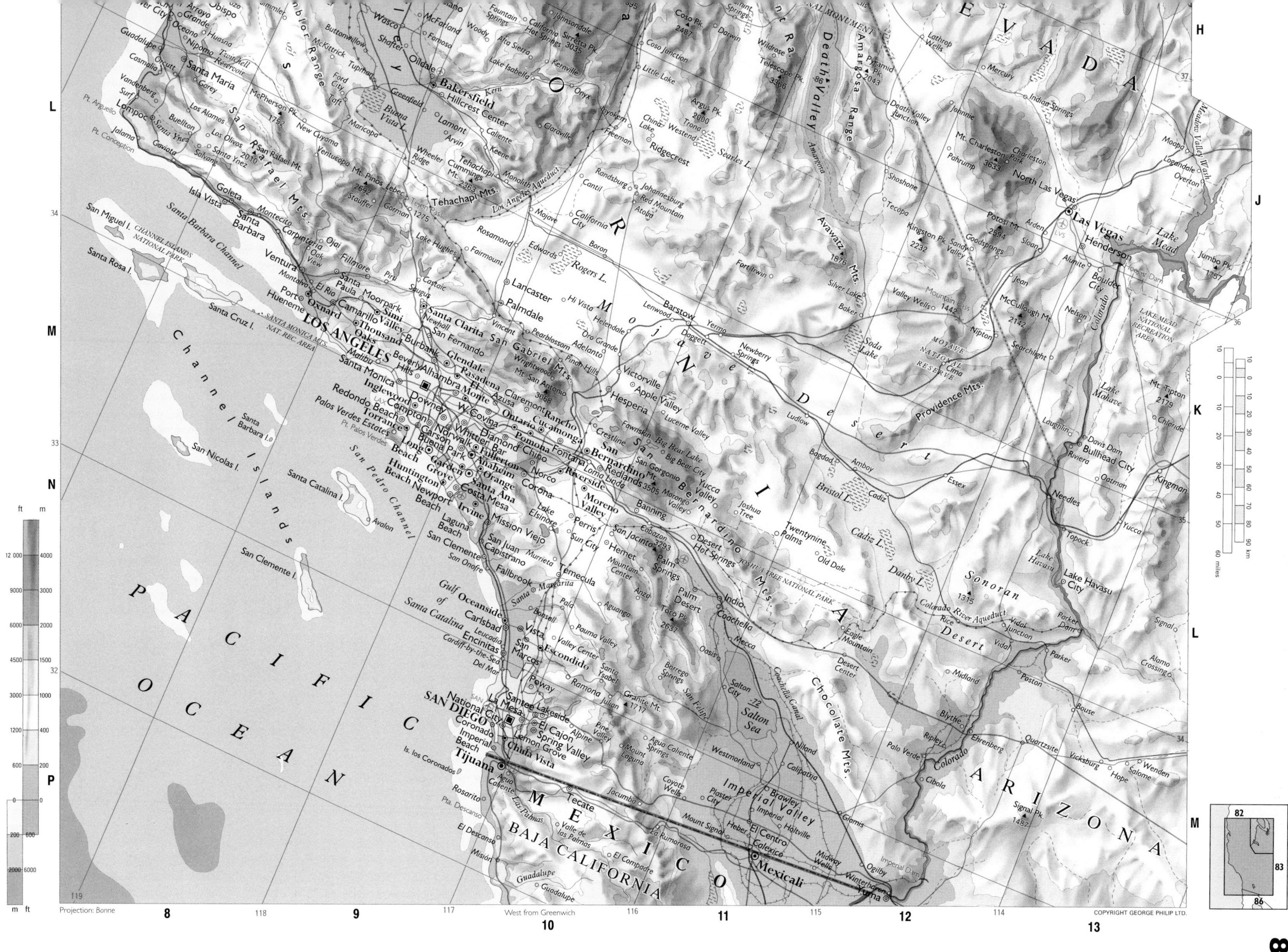
N E V A D A
A R I Z O N A
C A L I F O R N I A
M E X I C O
BAJA CALIFORNIA
P A C I F I C O C E A N
Mojave Desert
Sonoran Desert
Death Valley
Amargosa Range
Chocolate Mts.
San Bernardino Mts.
San Gabriel Mts.
Tehachapi Mts.
San Rafael Mts.
Providence Mts.
Channel Islands
Santa Barbara Channel
San Pedro Channel
Gulf of Santa Catalina
Salton Sea
Imperial Valley
Lake Mead
Las Vegas
Henderson
North Las Vegas
Boulder City
Bullhead City
Kingman
Needles
Lake Havasu City
Parker
Blythe
Yuma
Mexicali
Calexico
El Centro
Brawley
Indio
Palm Springs
Palm Desert
Barstow
Victorville
Hesperia
Lancaster
Palmdale
Bakersfield
Ridgecrest
San Bernardino
Riverside
Ontario
Pomona
LOS ANGELES
Long Beach
Santa Ana
Anaheim
Oxnard
Ventura
Santa Barbara
Santa Maria
Lompoc
Oceanside
Escondido
SAN DIEGO
Chula Vista
Tijuana
Tecate
Santa Catalina I.
San Clemente I.
San Nicolas I.
Santa Cruz I.
Santa Rosa I.
San Miguel I.
Projection: Bonne
West from Greenwich

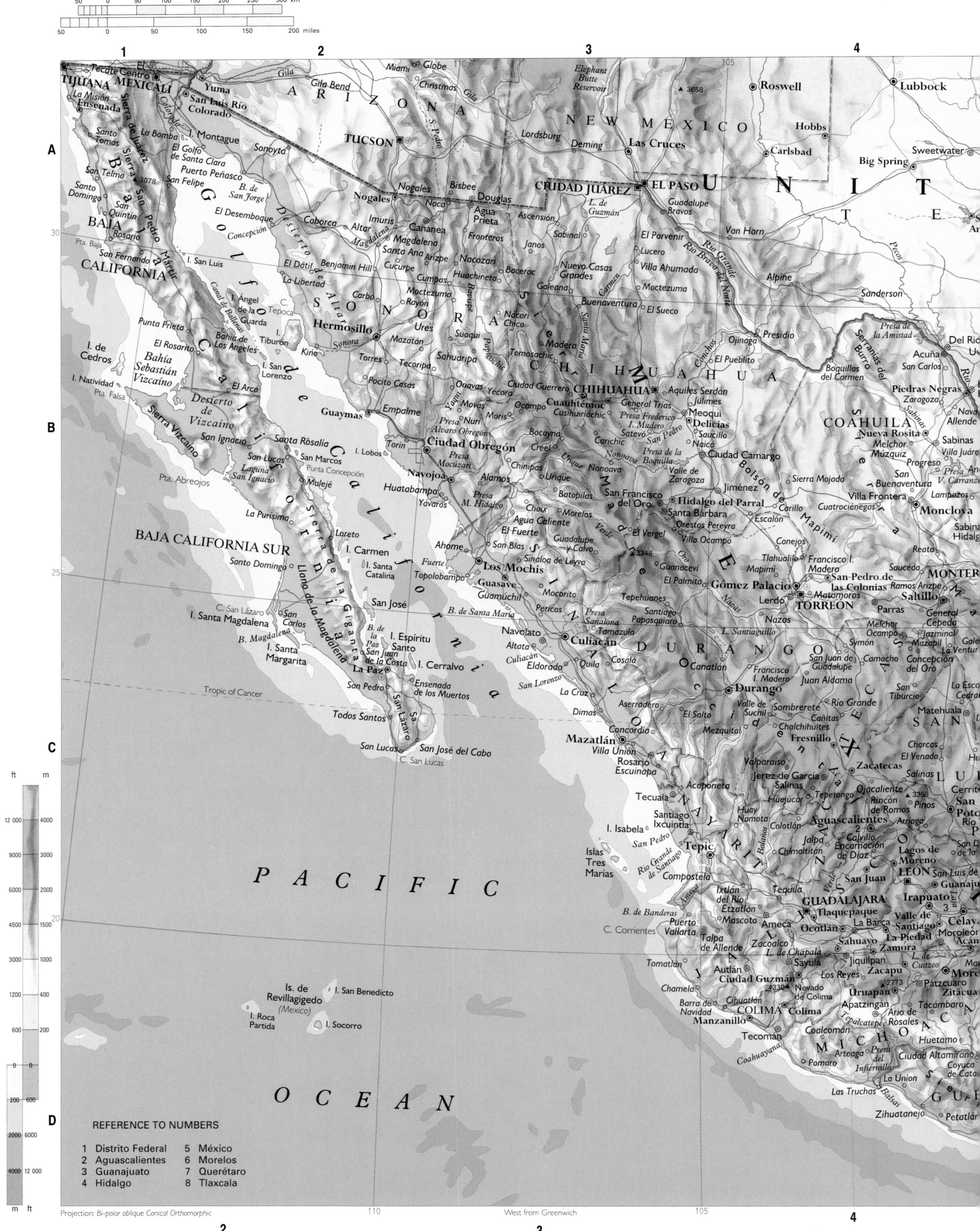

REFERENCE TO NUMBERS

1 Distrito Federal 5 México
2 Aguascalientes 6 Morelos
3 Guanajuato 7 Querétaro
4 Hidalgo 8 Tlaxcala

Projection: Bi-polar oblique Conical Orthomorphic

West from Greenwich

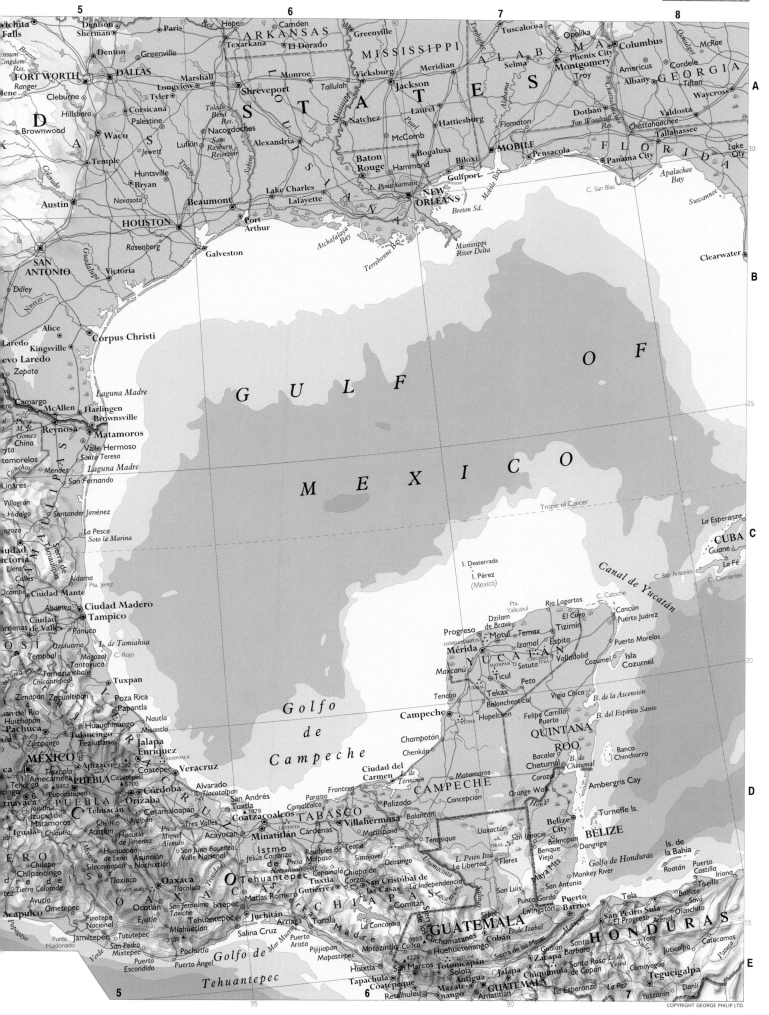

Wichita
Falls
Denison
Sherman
Paris
Hope
Camden
A R K A N S A S
Greenville
Tuscaloosa
Opelika
McRae
Omulgee
Possum
Kingdom
Res.
Ranger
Denton
Greenville
Texarkana
El Dorado
M I S S I S S I P P I
Selma
Montgomery
Americus
Cordele
Tifton
Tombigbee

FORT WORTH
DALLAS
Marshall
Longview
Monroe
Vicksburg
Meridian
Selma
A L A B A M A
Phenix City
Columbus
Americus
G E O R G I A

Cleburne
Hillsboro
Corsicana
Tyler
Shreveport
Jackson
Laurel
Troy
Albany
Waycross
Valdosta
A

D
Brownwood
Waco
Palestine
Nacogdoches
Alexandria
Natchez
Hattiesburg
Flomaton
Dothan
Chattahoochee
Chattahoochee
Tallahassee

Temple
Huntsville
Bryan
Lufkin
Jewett
Toledo
Bend
Res.
Sam
Rayburn
Reservoir
McComb
Bogalusa
Biloxi
MOBILE
Pensacola
Panama City
F L O R I D A
Lake
City

Austin
Colorado
Navasota
Trinity
Sabine
Baton
Rouge
Hammond
L. Pontchartrain
Gulfport
Mobile Bay
C. San Blas
Apalachee
Bay
Suwannee

HOUSTON
Beaumont
Lake Charles
Lafayette
NEW
ORLEANS
Breton Sd.
B

SAN
ANTONIO
Rosenberg
Port
Arthur
Atchafalaya
Bay
Terrebonne Bay
Mississippi
River Delta
Clearwater

Dilley
Victoria
Galveston

Nueces
Guadalupe

Alice
Laredo
Kingsville
Corpus Christi
G U L F
O F

evo Laredo
Zapata
Laguna Madre

Camargo
McAllen
Harlingen
Brownsville
M E X I C O

ero
China
Reynosa
Matamoros
Presa
M. R.
Gómez
Valle Hermoso
Santa Teresa
C

temorelos
Conchos
Mendez
Laguna Madre
San Fernando
Tropic of Cancer
La Esperanza

Villagrán
Hidalgo
agoza
Santander Jiménez
I. Desterrada
I. Pérez
(Mexico)
CUBA
Guane

Linares
La Pesca
Soto la Marina
Canal de Yucatán
C. San Antonio
La Fé
C. Corrientes

iudad
ictoria
Llera
Calles
Aldama
Pta.
Yalkubul
Rio Lagartos
C. Catoche

campo
Ciudad Mante
Dzilam
de Bravo
El Cuyo
Tizimin
Cancún
Puerto Juárez

Altamira
Ciudad Madero
Tampico
Progreso
DZIBILCHALTUN
Motul
Temax
Izamal
Espita
Puerto Morelos

ardenas de Valles
Ciudad
Valles
Pánuco
Ozuluama
L. de Tamiahua
Mérida
MAYAPAN
Sotuta
Y U C A T Á N
CHICHEN
ITZA
Valladolid
Cozumel
Isla
Cozumel

OSÍ
Tem60al
Magozal
C. Rojo
Maxcanú
Ticul
Peto
Sotuta

Tempoal
Tamazunchale
Tantoyuca
UXMAL
Tekax
Tenabo
Vigia Chico
B. de la Ascensión

Chicontepec
Zimapán
Zacualtipan
Tuxpan
Poza Rica
Papantla
Campeche
Balonchenticul
Hopelchén
Felipe Carrillo
Puerto
B. del Espíritu Santo

Jan del Rio
Huichapan
Pachuca
Huauchinango
Misantla
Nautla
Golfo
de
Champotón
Chenkán
QUINTANA
ROO
Banco
Chinchorro

ula
Zumpango
Tulancingo
Teziutlán
Jalapa
Enriquez
ZEMPOALA
Campeche
Bacalar
Chetumal
B. de
Chetumal

MÉXICO
Tlaxcala
Apizaco
4282
Coatepec
Veracruz
Ciudad del
Carmen
Matamoros
Corozal
Ambergris Cay

ca
Tenango
Amecameca
PUEBLA
Citlaltépetl
5700
Alvarado
Tlacotalpan
San Andrés
Frontera
L. de
Términos
CAMPECHE
Concepción
Orange Walk
Turneffe Is.
D

rnavaca
6
Popocatépetl
PUEBLA
Orizaba
Córdoba
Paraíso
Palizada
Belize
City

Jojutla
Izúcar de
Matamos
5452
Tehuacán
Cosamaloapan
Tuxtla
1879
Coatzacoalcos
TABASCO
Balancán
Uaxactún
San Ignacio
Benque
Viejo
Belmopan
BELIZE
Dangriga

Iguala
Chiautla
Huajuapan
de León
Chilac
Acatlán
Tres Valles
Minatitlán
Villahermosa
Cárdenas
Macuspana
LA VENTA
Teapa
Tenosique
TIKAL
Is. de
la Bahía

ERO
Chilapa
Asunción
Nochixtlán
Presa
Miguel
Alemán
San Juan Bautista
Valle Nacional
Istmo
de
Jesús Carranza
Presa
Malpaso
Netzahualcoyotl
Raudales de
Simojovel
Ocosingo
L. Petén Itzá
La Libertad
Flores
Maya Mts.
Monkey River
Roatán
Puerto
Castilla
Iriona

Chilpancingo
Tierra Colorada
Silacayoapan
Huautla
de Jiménez
Tehuantepec
Copainalá
Chiapa de
San Cristóbal de
las Casas
La Independencia
San Luis
San Antonio
Punta Gorda
Puerto
Barrios
Tela
Balfate
Sava

Acapulco
Ometepec
Ayutla
Tlaxiaco
Oaxaca
Tlacolula
Matías Romero
Gutiérrez
Tuxtla
Corzo
Comitán
Sebol
GUATEMALA
Livingston
San Pedro Sula
Olanchito
E

Pinotepa
Nacional
Tututepec
San Jeronimo
Ixtepec
Táviche
Ejutla
Arriaga
Tonalá
La Concordia
Uchumatanes
Cobán
Las Minas
Zacapa
Santa
Bárbara
L. de
Yojoa
Comayagua
Catacamas

Punta
Maldonado
Jamiltepec
San Pedro
Mixtepec
Miahuatlán
3139
Pochutla
Salina Cruz
Puerto
Arista
Pijijiapan
Mapastepec
Motozintla
Cuilco
3993
Huehuetenango
Guián
El Progreso
Santa Rosa de Copán
La Paz
HONDURAS
Juticalpa
Patuca

Puerto
Escondido
Puerto Ángel
Golfo de
Mar Muerto
Huixtla
Tapachula
San Marcos
Totonicapán
Sololá
Jalapa
Chiquimula
Comayagua
Danlí
Yuscarán

Tehuantepec
Retalhuleu
Mazate-
nango
Coatepeque
Amatitlán
Antigua
GUATEMALA
La Esperanza
Tegucigalpa

Golfo
de
Campeche

G U L F

O F

M E X I C O

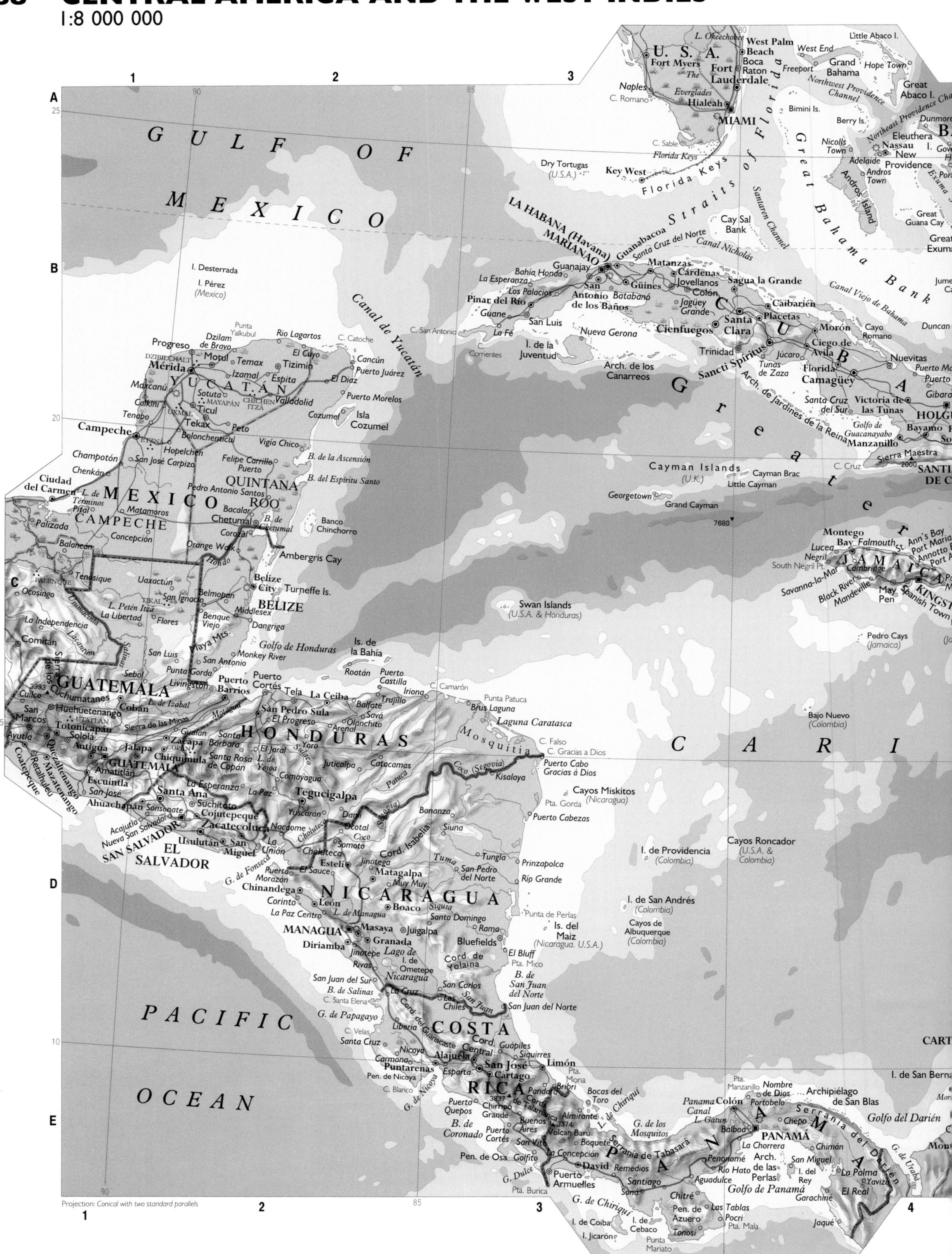

GULF OF MEXICO

PACIFIC OCEAN

U.S.A.

Projection: Conical with two standard parallels

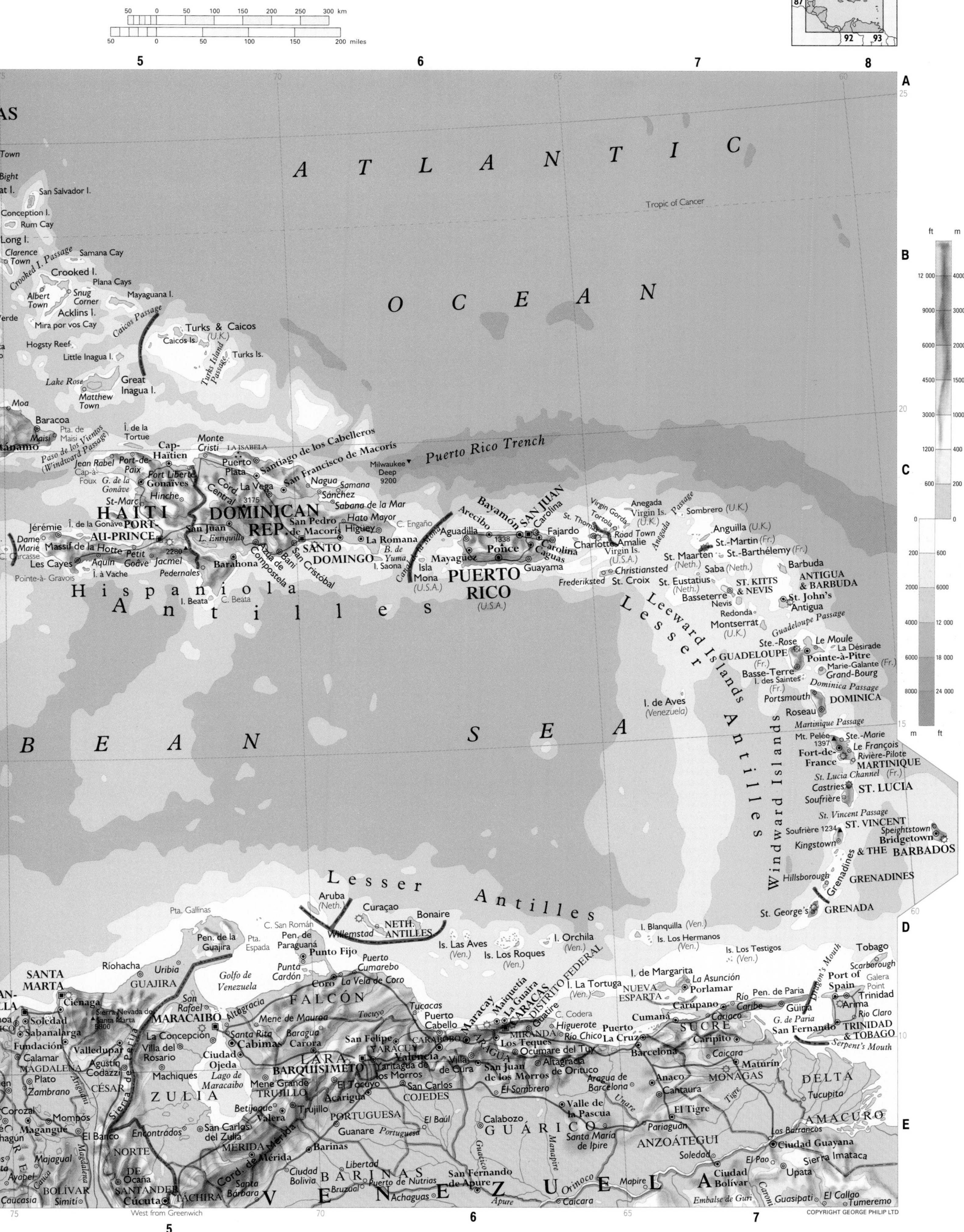
ATLANTIC OCEAN
Tropic of Cancer
Puerto Rico Trench
Milwaukee Deep 9200
CARIBBEAN SEA
Hispaniola
Antilles
HAITI
PORT-AU-PRINCE
DOMINICAN REP.
SANTO DOMINGO
PUERTO RICO (U.S.A.)
SAN JUAN
Turks & Caicos (U.K.)
Great Inagua I.
Acklins I.
Crooked I.
Mayaguana I.
Leeward Islands
Lesser Antilles
Windward Islands
Virgin Is. (U.K.)
Virgin Is. (U.S.A.)
Anguilla (U.K.)
St.-Martin (Fr.)
ANTIGUA & BARBUDA
St. John's
ST. KITTS & NEVIS
Basseterre
Montserrat (U.K.)
GUADELOUPE (Fr.)
Pointe-à-Pitre
Basse-Terre
DOMINICA
Roseau
MARTINIQUE (Fr.)
Fort-de-France
ST. LUCIA
Castries
ST. VINCENT & THE GRENADINES
Kingstown
BARBADOS
Bridgetown
GRENADA
St. George's
TRINIDAD & TOBAGO
Port of Spain
Aruba (Neth.)
Curaçao
Bonaire
NETH. ANTILLES
Willemstad
I. de Aves (Venezuela)
I. Orchila (Ven.)
I. de Margarita
VENEZUELA
CARACAS
MARACAIBO
Golfo de Venezuela
Lago de Maracaibo
BARQUISIMETO
Valencia
Barcelona
Cumaná
Maturín
Ciudad Guayana
Ciudad Bolívar
Orinoco
SANTA MARTA
Cúcuta
West from Greenwich
COPYRIGHT GEORGE PHILIP LTD

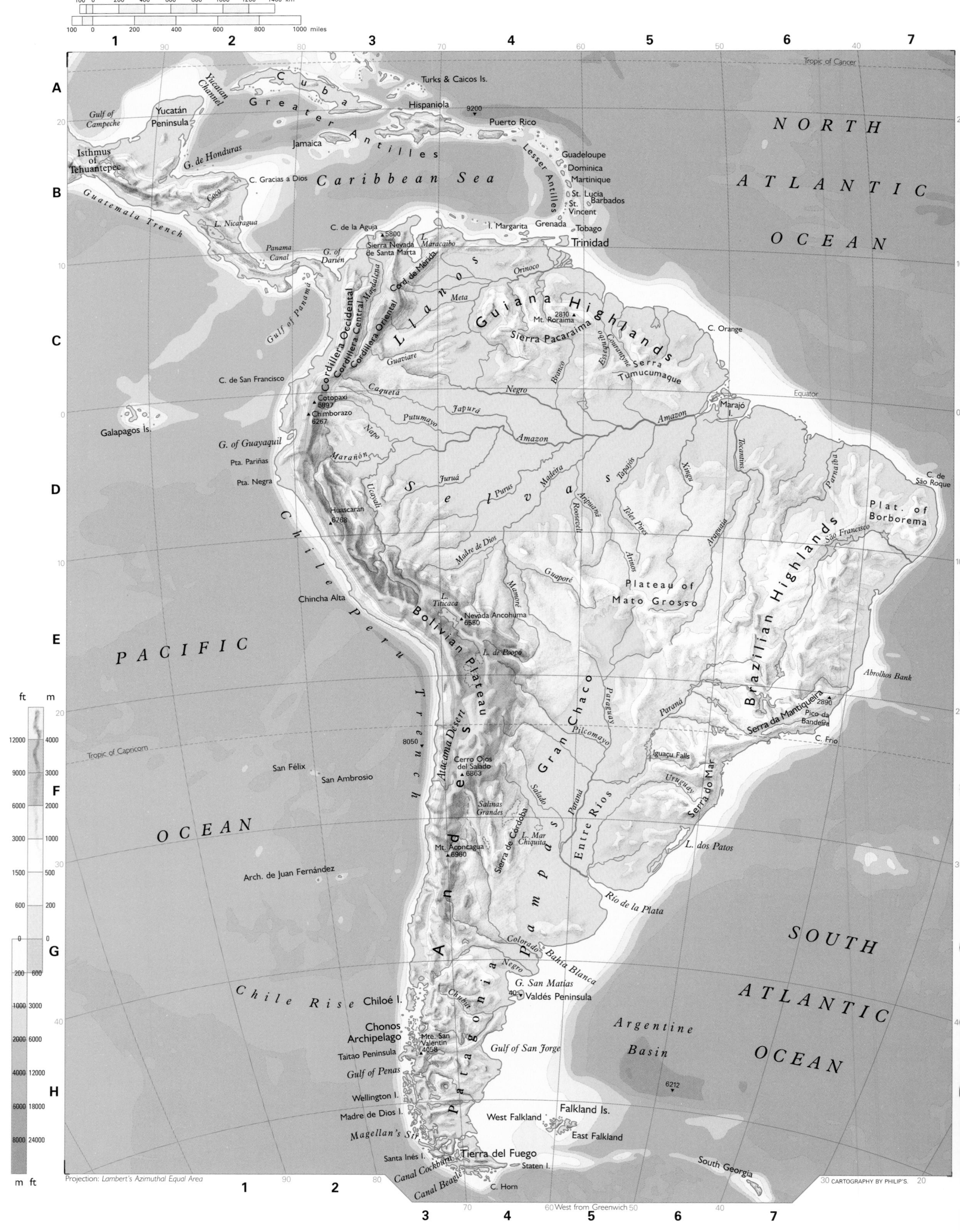

Projection: Lambert's Azimuthal Equal Area

CARTOGRAPHY BY PHILIP'S.

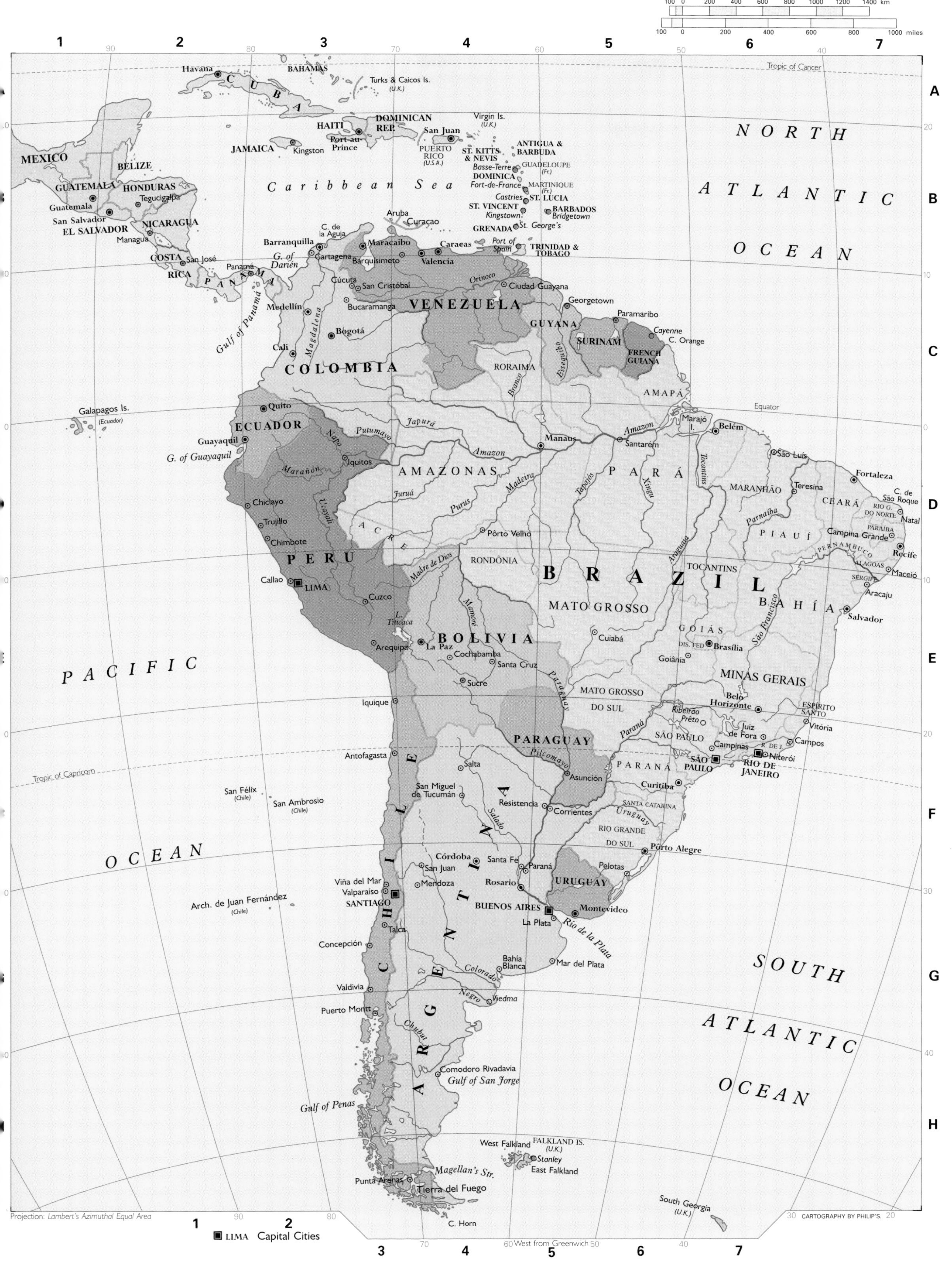
NORTH ATLANTIC OCEAN
SOUTH ATLANTIC OCEAN
PACIFIC OCEAN
Caribbean Sea
MEXICO
BELIZE
GUATEMALA
HONDURAS
EL SALVADOR
NICARAGUA
COSTA RICA
PANAMA
CUBA
BAHAMAS
JAMAICA
HAITI
DOMINICAN REP.
COLOMBIA
VENEZUELA
GUYANA
SURINAM
FRENCH GUIANA
ECUADOR
PERU
BOLIVIA
BRAZIL
PARAGUAY
CHILE
ARGENTINA
URUGUAY
TRINIDAD & TOBAGO
FALKLAND IS. (U.K.)
Galapagos Is. (Ecuador)
Tropic of Cancer
Tropic of Capricorn
Equator
Amazon
Orinoco
Río de la Plata
Magellan's Str.
Tierra del Fuego
C. Horn
LIMA
Capital Cities
Projection: Lambert's Azimuthal Equal Area
West from Greenwich
CARTOGRAPHY BY PHILIP'S.

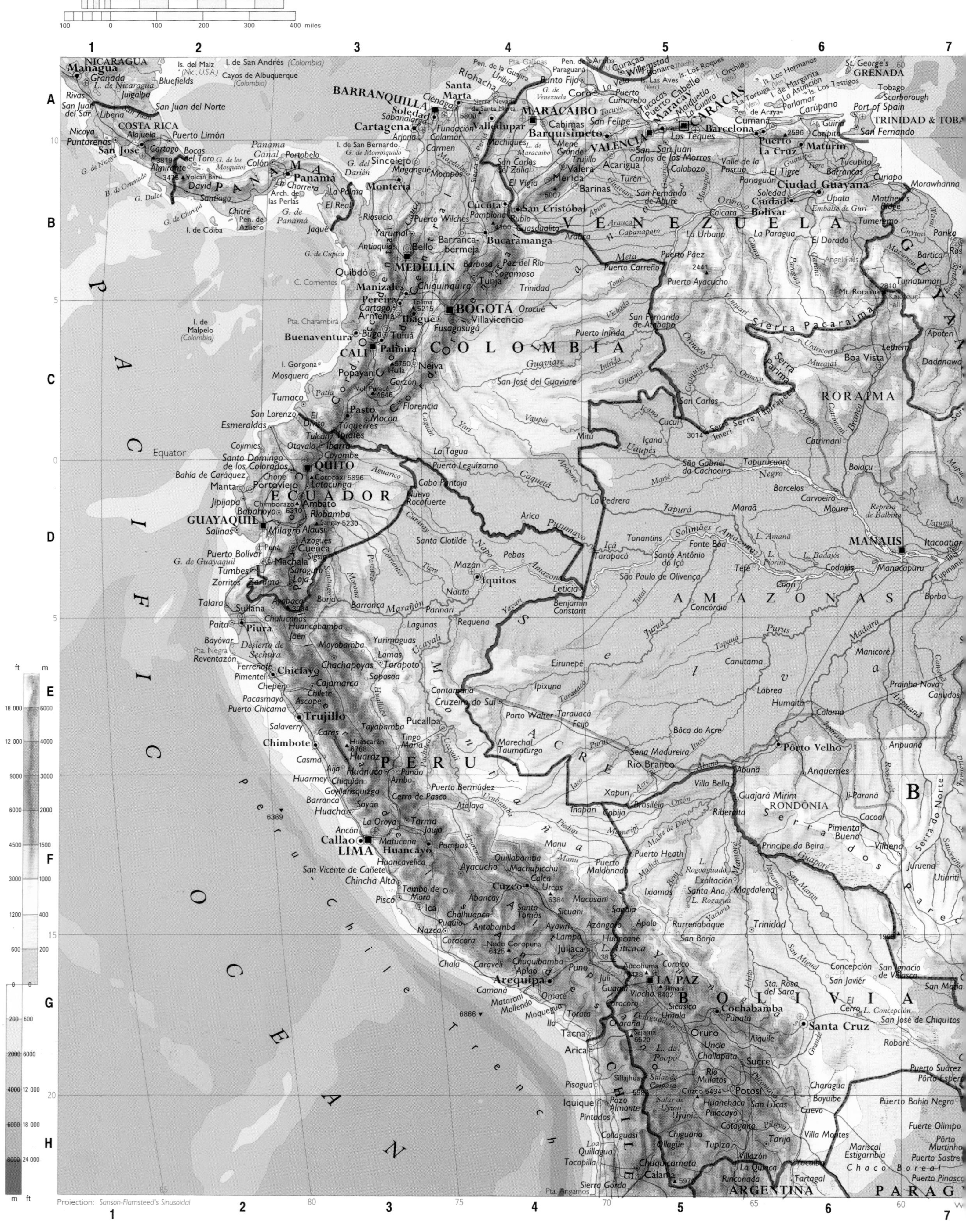

100 0 100 200 300 400 500 km
100 0 100 200 300 400 miles
1 2 3 4 5 6 7
A B C D E F G H
NICARAGUA
Managua
Granada
L. de Nicaragua
Is. del Maiz (Nic., U.S.A.)
Bluefields
I. de San Andrés (Colombia)
Cayos de Albuquerque (Colombia)
Rivas
San Juan del Sur
Juigalpa
San Juan del Norte
Liberia
COSTA RICA
Nicoya
Alajuela
Puerto Limón
Puntarenas
San José
Cartago
Bocas del Toro
Panama Canal
Colón
Portobelo
PANAMA
Panamá
David
Santiago
Chitré
Pen. de Azuero
I. de Coiba
G. de Panamá
Arch. de las Perlas
La Chorrera
La Palma
El Real
Jaqué
Volcán Barú
G. de Chiriquí
G. Dulce
BARRANQUILLA
Ciénaga
Santa Marta
Soledad
Sabanalarga
Cartagena
Arjona
Riohacha
Uribia
Pen. de la Guajira
Sierra Nevada de Santa Marta
5800
Valledupar
Fundación
Calamar
Carmen
I. de San Bernardo
G. de Morrosquillo
Sincelejo
G. del Darién
Magangué
Mompós
Montería
Riosucio
Puerto Wilches
Yarumal
Antioquia
Bello
MEDELLÍN
Barrancabermeja
Bucaramanga
Cúcuta
Pamplona
Quibdó
G. de Cupica
C. Corrientes
Manizales
Chiquinquirá
Tunja
Sogamoso
Paz del Rio
Barbosa
Pereira
Cartago
Armenia
Ibagué
Tolima 5215
BOGOTÁ
Villavicencio
Fusagasugá
Orocué
Trinidad
Buenaventura
Buga
Tuluá
CALI
Palmira
I. de Malpelo (Colombia)
Pta. Charambirá
I. Gorgona
Mosquera
Popayán
Huila 5750
Neiva
Garzón
Vol. Puracé 4646
Tumaco
Patía
Pasto
Mocoa
Florencia
San Lorenzo
Esmeraldas
Túquerres
Ipiales
Tulcán
Ibarra
Otavalo
Cojimies
Cayambe
Equator
Santo Domingo de los Colorados
QUITO
Cotopaxi 5896
Latacunga
Bahía de Caráquez
Chone
Manta
Portoviejo
ECUADOR
Jipijapa
Chimborazo 6310
Ambato
Babahoyo
Riobamba
Sangay 5230
GUAYAQUIL
Salinas
Milagro
Alausí
Puerto Bolívar
I. Puná
Azogues
Cuenca
Sígsig
G. de Guayaquil
Machala
Tumbes
Zorritos
Saraguro
Loja
Zaruma
Talara
Sullana
Ayabaca
Paita
Piura
Chulucanas
Huancabamba
Jaén
Bayóvar
Desierto de Sechura
Pta. Negra
Reventazón
Ferreñafe
Chiclayo
Pimentel
Chepén
Pacasmayo
Puerto Chicama
Cajamarca
Chilete
Ascope
Trujillo
Salaverry
Chimbote
Casma
Huascarán 6768
Caraz
Huaraz
Aija
Huarmey
Chiquián
Huánuco
Gollarisquizga
Barranca
Huacho
Sayán
6369
Ancón
Callao
LIMA
La Oroya
Tarma
Jauja
Matucana
Huancayo
Pampas
Huancavelica
San Vicente de Cañete
Chincha Alta
Pisco
Tambo de Mora
Ica
Nazca
Puquio
Chalhuanca
Coracora
Chala
Caravelí
Nudo Coropuna 6425
Chuquibamba
Aplao
Arequipa
Camaná
Matarani
Mollendo
Omate
Moquegua
Ilo
6866
Tacna
Arica
Pisagua
Iquique
Pozo Almonte
Pintados
Collaguasi
Ollagüe
Quillagua
Tocopilla
Chuquicamata
Calama
Sierra Gorda
Pta. Angamos
CHILE
PACIFIC OCEAN
Peru-Chile Trench
PERU
Moyobamba
Chachapoyas
Yurimaguas
Lamas
Tarapoto
Soposoa
Tayabamba
Pucallpa
Tingo María
Panao
Ambo
Cerro de Pasco
Puerto Bermúdez
Atalaya
Urubamba
Ayacucho
Quillabamba
Machupicchu
Calca
Cuzco
Urcos
Abancay
Santo Tomás
6384
Sicuani
Macusani
Ayaviri
Lampa
Juliaca
Puno
Azángaro
Huancané
L. Titicaca
3812
Juli
Ancohuma 6428
Illimani 6402
LA PAZ
Viacha
Guaqui
Corocoro
Sorata
Coroico
Sicasica
Umala
Oruro
Sajama 6520
Charaña
L. de Poopó
Uncía
Challapata
Cochabamba
Punata
Aiquile
Sucre
Potosí
Río Mulatos
Salar de Coipasa
Salar de Uyuni
Uyuni
Cuzco 5434
Huanchaca
Pulacayo
Cotagaita
San Lucas
Chiguana
Tupiza
Tarija
Villazón
La Quiaca
Yacuiba
Tartagal
Rinconada
5970
ARGENTINA
BOLIVIA
Santa Cruz
Trinidad
San Borja
Rurrenabaque
Apolo
Exaltación
Santa Ana
Magdalena
Puerto Heath
Puerto Maldonado
Ixiamas
Riberalta
Guajará Mirim
Villa Bella
RONDÔNIA
Principe da Beira
Concepción
San Ignacio de Velasco
San Javier
San José de Chiquitos
Roboré
Charagua
Boyuibe
Cuevo
Villa Montes
Mariscal Estigarribia
Puerto Suárez
Pôrto Esperança
Puerto Bahía Negra
Fuerte Olimpo
Pôrto Murtinho
Puerto Sastre
Puerto Pinasco
Chaco Boreal
PARAGUAY
Pta. Gallinas
Pen. de Paraguaná
Aruba
Curaçao
Willemstad
Bonaire (Neth.)
Is. Los Roques
Las Aves
La Orchila
Punto Fijo
Coro
La Vela
Puerto Cumarebo
Tucacas
Puerto Cabello
Maracay
Maiquetía
La Guaira
CARACAS
MARACAIBO
G. de Venezuela
Cabimas
San Felipe
Barquisimeto
VALENCIA
Los Teques
Barcelona
Cumaná
Carúpano
Güiria
Pen. de Araya
L. de Maracaibo
Machiques
Mene Grande
Trujillo
Valera
Acarigua
San Carlos
San Carlos del Zulia
El Vigía
Mérida
5007
Barinas
Turén
San Juan de los Morros
Calabozo
Valle de la Pascua
San Fernando de Apure
San Cristóbal
Rubio
Guasdualito
4100
Arauca
Capanaparo
Puerto Carreño
Puerto Páez
Puerto Ayacucho
La Urbana
Caicara
Ciudad Bolívar
Soledad
Pariaguán
Ciudad Guayana
Tucupita
Barrancas
El Tigre
Maturín
Puerto La Cruz
2596
La Asunción
I. de Margarita
La Tortuga
Is. Los Hermanos
Is. Los Testigos
Porlamar
St. George's
GRENADA
Tobago
Scarborough
Port of Spain
TRINIDAD & TOBAGO
San Fernando
Curiapo
Upata
El Dorado
Embalse de Guri
Tumeremo
La Paragua
VENEZUELA
Angel Falls
2441
Sierra Pacaraima
Mt. Roraima
2810
Serra Parima
San Carlos
Cucuí
Imeri
Serra Tapirapecó
3014
Santa Elena
Boa Vista
RORAIMA
Caracaraí
Catrimani
Morawhanna
Matthews Ridge
Bartica
Tumatumari
Apoteri
Lethem
Dadanawa
Mitú
San Fernando de Atabapo
Puerto Inírida
COLOMBIA
San José del Guaviare
La Tagua
Puerto Leguízamo
Cabo Pantoja
Nuevo Rocafuerte
Santa Clotilde
Mazán
Pebas
Iquitos
Nauta
Arica
La Pedrera
Tarapacá
Leticia
Benjamin Constant
Tonantins
Fonte Boa
Santo Antônio do Içá
São Paulo de Olivença
Tefé
Coari
Codajás
Manacapuru
MANAUS
Itacoatiara
Barcelos
Carvoeiro
Moura
Represa de Balbina
São Gabriel da Cachoeira
Tapurucuará
Içana
Uaupés
Barranca
Borja
Parinari
Lagunas
Requena
Contamana
Cruzeiro do Sul
Ipixuna
Eirunepé
Porto Walter
Tarauacá
Feijó
Marechal Taumaturgo
Sena Madureira
Rio Branco
Xapuri
Brasiléia
Cobija
Iñapari
Boca do Acre
Lábrea
Canutama
Humaitá
Pôrto Velho
Abunã
Ariquemes
Ji-Paraná
Pimenta Bueno
Cacoal
Vilhena
Aripuanã
Manicoré
Borba
Prainha Nova
Calama
Concórdia
AMAZONAS
ACRE
Projection: Sanson-Flamsteed's Sinusoidal

A T L A N T I C

O C E A N

Equator

São Paulo
(Braz.)

Fernando de Noronha
(Braz.)

**FRENCH
GUIANA**

AMAPÁ

PARÁ

MARANHÃO

PIAUÍ

CEARÁ

RIO GRANDE
DO NORTE

PARAÍBA

PERNAMBUCO

ALAGOAS

SERGIPE

BAHIA

TOCANTINS

GOIÁS

MINAS GERAIS

MATO GROSSO

Planalto do

Mato Grosso

GROSSO

DO SUL

BRASÍLIA

BELÉM

São Luís

FORTALEZA

Teresina

Natal

João Pessoa

RECIFE

Maceió

Aracaju

SALVADOR

BELO HORIZONTE

Vitória

RIO DE JANEIRO

Trindade
(Braz.)

COPYRIGHT GEORGE PHILIP LTD.

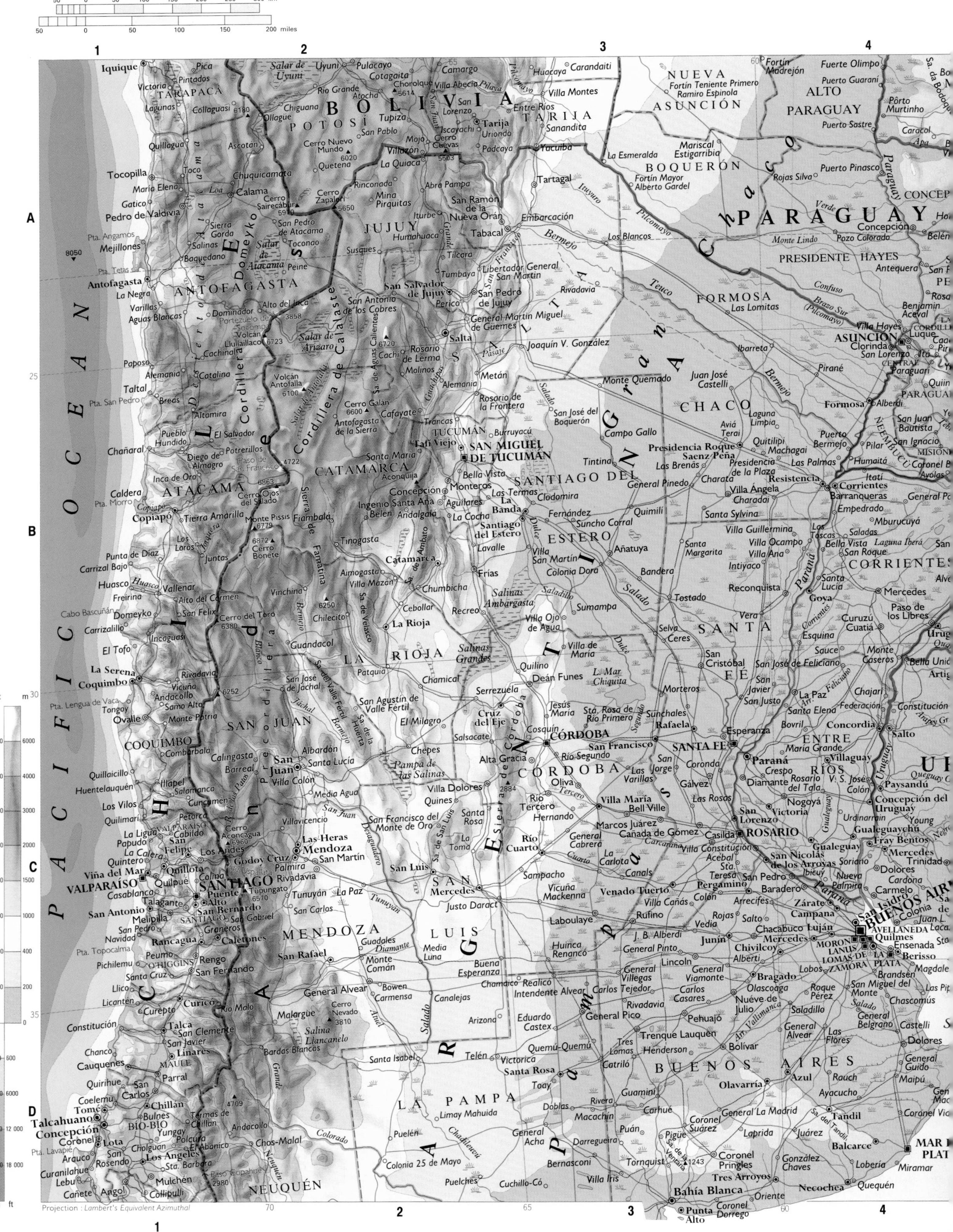

Projection : Lambert's Equivalent Azimuthal
PACIFIC OCEAN
BOLIVIA
PARAGUAY
ARGENTINA
CHILE
Gran Chaco
Pampas
Andes
Iquique
Antofagasta
Calama
Salta
SAN MIGUEL DE TUCUMÁN
CÓRDOBA
SANTA FE
ROSARIO
Mendoza
SANTIAGO
VALPARAÍSO
Concepción
Talcahuano
BUENOS AIRES
Bahía Blanca
ASUNCIÓN
Corrientes
San Juan
La Rioja
Catamarca
Santiago del Estero
San Luis
Santa Rosa
Paraná
Formosa
Resistencia

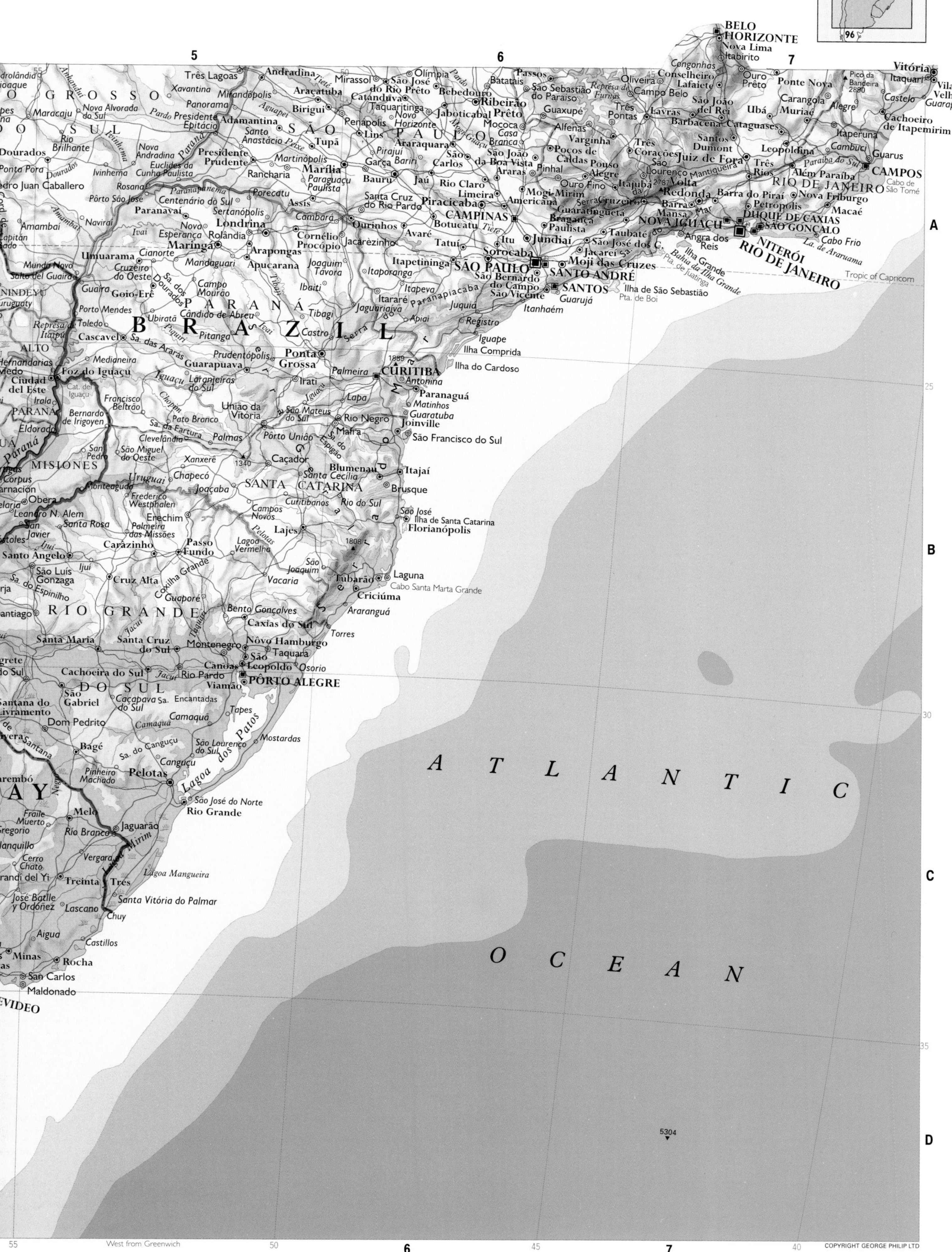

92
93
96
5
6
7
A
B
C
D
BELO HORIZONTE
Nova Lima
Itabirito
Vitória
Vila Velha
Guarapari
Cachoeiro de Itapemirim
Três Lagoas
Andradina
Araçatuba
Mirassol
São José do Rio Prêto
Olímpia
Bebedouro
Catanduva
Ribeirão Prêto
Passos
Batatais
São Sebastião do Paraíso
Conselheiro Lafaiete
Barbacena
Juiz de Fora
Campos
RIO DE JANEIRO
NITERÓI
DUQUE DE CAXIAS
NOVA IGUAÇU
SÃO GONÇALO
Petrópolis
Nova Friburgo
Macaé
Cabo Frio
Tropic of Capricorn
Volta Redonda
Taubaté
São José dos Campos
Jacareí
Moji das Cruzes
SÃO PAULO
SANTO ANDRÉ
SANTOS
Guarujá
São Bernardo do Campo
São Vicente
Ilha de São Sebastião
Itanhaém
CAMPINAS
Jundiaí
Sorocaba
Piracicaba
Limeira
Americana
Rio Claro
São Carlos
Araraquara
Bauru
Jaú
Marília
Presidente Prudente
Tupã
Assis
Ourinhos
Botucatu
Itapetininga
Londrina
Maringá
Apucarana
Arapongas
Cornélio Procópio
Umuarama
Cianorte
B R A Z I L
PARANÁ
SÃO PAULO
Ponta Grossa
Guarapuava
Cascavel
Foz do Iguaçu
Ciudad del Este
CURITIBA
Paranaguá
Antonina
Guaratuba
Joinville
São Francisco do Sul
Ilha do Cardoso
Iguape
Ilha Comprida
Registro
Blumenau
Itajaí
Brusque
Florianópolis
Ilha de Santa Catarina
SANTA CATARINA
Lajes
Tubarão
Laguna
Criciúma
Araranguá
Cabo Santa Marta Grande
Torres
Passo Fundo
Santo Ângelo
Cruz Alta
Caxias do Sul
Bento Gonçalves
Novo Hamburgo
São Leopoldo
Canoas
PÔRTO ALEGRE
Viamão
Osório
Santa Maria
Santa Cruz do Sul
Cachoeira do Sul
RIO GRANDE DO SUL
Bagé
Pelotas
Lagoa dos Patos
Rio Grande
São José do Norte
Mostardas
Jaguarão
Lagoa Mirim
Lagoa Mangueira
Santa Vitória do Palmar
Chuy
Melo
Treinta y Tres
Rocha
Maldonado
San Carlos
Castillos
Aiguá
Minas
Rivera
Santana do Livramento
Dom Pedrito
MISIONES
Posadas
Oberá
Eldorado
ATLANTIC OCEAN
5304
West from Greenwich
55
50
45
40
25
30
35

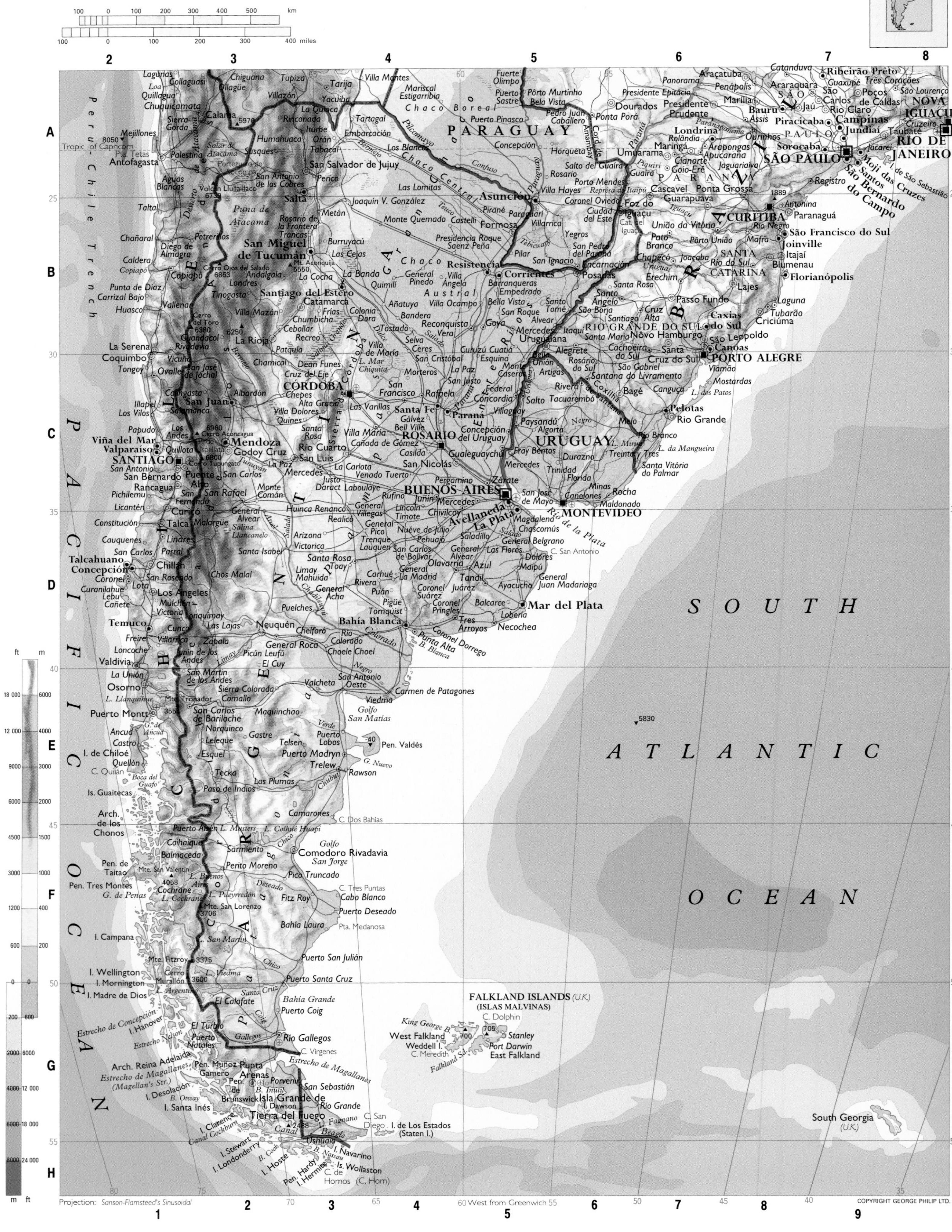
PARAGUAY
URUGUAY
SOUTH ATLANTIC OCEAN
PACIFIC OCEAN
FALKLAND ISLANDS (U.K.)
(ISLAS MALVINAS)
South Georgia
(U.K.)
BUENOS AIRES
MONTEVIDEO
SANTIAGO
Asunción
PORTO ALEGRE
SÃO PAULO
RIO DE JANEIRO
Projection: Sanson-Flamsteed's Sinusoidal
West from Greenwich
COPYRIGHT GEORGE PHILIP LTD.

INDEX

The index contains the names of all the principal places and features shown on the World Maps. Each name is followed by an additional entry in italics giving the country or region within which it is located. The alphabetical order of names composed of two or more words is governed primarily by the first word and then by the second. This is an example of the rule:

Mīr Kūh, *Iran*	**45 E8**	26 22N	58 55 E
Mīr Shahdād, *Iran*	**45 E8**	26 15N	58 29 E
Mira, *Italy*	**20 B5**	45 26N	12 8 E
Mira por vos Cay, *Bahamas* .	**89 B5**	22 9N	74 30W
Miraj, *India*	**40 L9**	16 50N	74 45 E

Physical features composed of a proper name (Erie) and a description (Lake) are positioned alphabetically by the proper name. The description is positioned after the proper name and is usually abbreviated:

Erie, L., *N. Amer.*	**78 D4**	42 15N	81 0W

Where a description forms part of a settlement or administrative name however, it is always written in full and put in its true alphabetic position:

Mount Morris, *U.S.A.*	**78 D7**	42 44N	77 52W

Names beginning with M' and Mc are indexed as if they were spelled Mac. Names beginning St. are alphabetised under Saint, but Sankt, Sint, Sant', Santa and San are all spelt in full and are alphabetised accordingly. If the same place name occurs two or more times in the index and all are in the same country, each is followed by the name of the administrative subdivision in which it is located. The names are placed in the alphabetical order of the subdivisions. For example:

Jackson, *Ky., U.S.A.*	**76 G4**	37 33N	83 23W
Jackson, *Mich., U.S.A.*	**76 D3**	42 15N	84 24W
Jackson, *Minn., U.S.A.*	**80 D7**	43 37N	95 1W

The number in bold type which follows each name in the index refers to the number of the map page where that feature or place will be found. This is usually the largest scale at which the place or feature appears.

The letter and figure which are in bold type immediately after the page number give the grid square on the map page, within which the feature is situated. The letter represents the latitude and the figure the longitude.

In some cases the feature itself may fall within the specified square, while the name is outside. This is usually the case only with features which are larger than a grid square.

For a more precise location the geographical coordinates which follow the letter/figure references give the latitude and the longitude of each place. The first set of figures represent the latitude which is the distance north or south of the Equator measured as an angle at the centre of the earth. The Equator is latitude 0°, the North Pole is 90°N, and the South Pole 90°S.

The second set of figures represent the longitude, which is the distance East or West of the prime meridian, which runs through Greenwich, England. Longitude is also measured as an angle at the centre of the earth and is given East or West of the prime meridian, from 0° to 180° in either direction.

The unit of measurement for latitude and longitude is the degree, which is subdivided into 60 minutes. Each index entry states the position of a place in degrees and minutes, a space being left between the degrees and the minutes.

The latitude is followed by N(orth) or S(outh) and the longitude by E(ast) or W(est).

Rivers are indexed to their mouths or confluences, and carry the symbol → after their names. A solid square ■ follows the name of a country, while an open square □ refers to a first order administrative area.

Abbreviations used in the index

A.C.T. – Australian Capital Territory
Afghan. – Afghanistan
Ala. – Alabama
Alta. – Alberta
Amer. – America(n)
Arch. – Archipelago
Ariz. – Arizona
Ark. – Arkansas
Atl. Oc. – Atlantic Ocean
B. – Baie, Bahía, Bay, Bucht, Bugt
B.C. – British Columbia
Bangla. – Bangladesh
Barr. – Barrage
Bos.-H. – Bosnia-Herzegovina
C. – Cabo, Cap, Cape, Coast
C.A.R. – Central African Republic
C. Prov. – Cape Province
Calif. – California
Cent. – Central
Chan. – Channel
Colo. – Colorado
Conn. – Connecticut
Cord. – Cordillera
Cr. – Creek
Czech. – Czech Republic
D.C. – District of Columbia
Del. – Delaware
Dep. – Dependency
Des. – Desert
Dist. – District
Dj. – Djebel
Domin. – Dominica
Dom. Rep. – Dominican Republic
E. – East

E. Salv. – El Salvador
Eq. Guin. – Equatorial Guinea
Fla. – Florida
Falk. Is. – Falkland Is.
G. – Golfe, Golfo, Gulf, Guba, Gebel
Ga. – Georgia
Gt. – Great, Greater
Guinea-Biss. – Guinea-Bissau
H.K. – Hong Kong
H.P. – Himachal Pradesh
Hants. – Hampshire
Harb. – Harbor, Harbour
Hd. – Head
Hts. – Heights
I.(s). – Île, Ilha, Insel, Isla, Island, Isle
Ill. – Illinois
Ind. – Indiana
Ind. Oc. – Indian Ocean
Ivory C. – Ivory Coast
J. – Jabal, Jebel, Jazira
Junc. – Junction
K. – Kap, Kapp
Kans. – Kansas
Kep. – Kepulauan
Ky. – Kentucky
L. – Lac, Lacul, Lago, Lagoa, Lake, Limni, Loch, Lough
La. – Louisiana
Liech. – Liechtenstein
Lux. – Luxembourg
Mad. P. – Madhya Pradesh
Madag. – Madagascar
Man. – Manitoba
Mass. – Massachusetts

Md. – Maryland
Me. – Maine
Medit. S. – Mediterranean Sea
Mich. – Michigan
Minn. – Minnesota
Miss. – Mississippi
Mo. – Missouri
Mont. – Montana
Mozam. – Mozambique
Mt.(e) – Mont, Monte, Monti, Montaña, Mountain
N. – Nord, Norte, North, Northern, Nouveau
N.B. – New Brunswick
N.C. – North Carolina
N. Cal. – New Caledonia
N. Dak. – North Dakota
N.H. – New Hampshire
N.I. – North Island
N.J. – New Jersey
N. Mex. – New Mexico
N.S. – Nova Scotia
N.S.W. – New South Wales
N.W.T. – North West Territory
N.Y. – New York
N.Z. – New Zealand
Nebr. – Nebraska
Neths. – Netherlands
Nev. – Nevada
Nfld. – Newfoundland
Nic. – Nicaragua
O. – Oued, Ouadi
Occ. – Occidentale
Okla. – Oklahoma
Ont. – Ontario
Or. – Orientale

Oreg. – Oregon
Os. – Ostrov
Oz. – Ozero
P. – Pass, Passo, Pasul, Pulau
P.E.I. – Prince Edward Island
Pa. – Pennsylvania
Pac. Oc. – Pacific Ocean
Papua N.G. – Papua New Guinea
Pass. – Passage
Pen. – Peninsula, Péninsule
Phil. – Philippines
Pk. – Park, Peak
Plat. – Plateau
Prov. – Province, Provincial
Pt. – Point
Pta. – Ponta, Punta
Pte. – Pointe
Qué. – Québec
Queens. – Queensland
R. – Rio, River
R.I. – Rhode Island
Ra.(s). – Range(s)
Raj. – Rajasthan
Reg. – Region
Rep. – Republic
Res. – Reserve, Reservoir
S. – San, South, Sea
Si. Arabia – Saudi Arabia
S.C. – South Carolina
S. Dak. – South Dakota
S.I. – South Island
S. Leone – Sierra Leone
Sa. – Serra, Sierra
Sask. – Saskatchewan
Scot. – Scotland
Sd. – Sound

Sev. – Severnaya
Sib. – Siberia
Sprs. – Springs
St. – Saint
Sta. – Santa, Station
Ste. – Sainte
Sto. – Santo
Str. – Strait, Stretto
Switz. – Switzerland
Tas. – Tasmania
Tenn. – Tennessee
Tex. – Texas
Tg. – Tanjung
Trin. & Tob. – Trinidad & Tobago
U.A.E. – United Arab Emirates
U.K. – United Kingdom
U.S.A. – United States of America
Ut. P. – Uttar Pradesh
Va. – Virginia
Vdkhr. – Vodokhranilishche
Vf. – Vírful
Vic. – Victoria
Vol. – Volcano
Vt. – Vermont
W. – Wadi, West
W. Va. – West Virginia
Wash. – Washington
Wis. – Wisconsin
Wlkp. – Wielkopolski
Wyo. – Wyoming
Yorks. – Yorkshire
Yug. – Yugoslavia

A Coruña

A

A Coruña, *Spain* **19 A1** 43 20N 8 25W
A Estrada, *Spain* **19 A1** 42 43N 8 27W
A Fonsagrada, *Spain* **19 A2** 43 8N 7 4W
Aachen, *Germany* **16 C4** 50 45N 6 6 E
Aalborg = Ålborg, *Denmark* **9 H13** 57 2N 9 54 E
Aalen, *Germany* **16 D6** 48 51N 10 6 E
Aalst, *Belgium* **15 D4** 50 56N 4 2 E
Aalten, *Neths.* **15 C6** 51 56N 6 35 E
Aalter, *Belgium* **15 C3** 51 5N 3 28 E
Äänekoski, *Finland* **9 E21** 62 36N 25 44 E
Aarau, *Switz.* **18 C8** 47 23N 8 4 E
Aare →, *Switz.* **18 C8** 47 33N 8 14 E
Aarhus = Århus, *Denmark* **9 H14** 56 8N 10 11 E
Aarschot, *Belgium* **15 D4** 50 59N 4 49 E
Aba, *Dem. Rep. of the Congo* **54 B3** 3 58N 30 17 E
Aba, *Nigeria* **50 G7** 5 10N 7 19 E
Ābādān, *Iran* **45 D6** 30 22N 48 20 E
Ābādeh, *Iran* **45 D7** 31 8N 52 40 E
Abadla, *Algeria* **50 B5** 31 2N 2 45W
Abaetetuba, *Brazil* **93 D9** 1 40S 48 50W
Abagnar Qi, *China* **34 C9** 43 52N 116 2 E
Abai, *Paraguay* **95 B4** 25 58S 55 54W
Abakan, *Russia* **27 D10** 53 40N 91 10 E
Abancay, *Peru* **92 F4** 13 35S 72 55W
Abariringa, *Kiribati* **64 H10** 2 50S 171 40W
Abarqū, *Iran* **45 D7** 31 10N 53 20 E
Abashiri, *Japan* **30 C12** 44 0N 144 15 E
Abashiri-Wan, *Japan* **30 C12** 44 0N 144 30 E
Abay, *Kazakstan* **26 E8** 49 38N 72 53 E
Abaya, L., *Ethiopia* **46 F2** 6 30N 37 50 E
Abaza, *Russia* **26 D10** 52 39N 90 6 E
'Abbāsābād, *Iran* **45 C8** 33 34N 58 23 E
Abbay = Nîl el Azraq →, *Sudan* **51 E12** 15 38N 32 31 E
Abbaye, Pt., *U.S.A.* **76 B1** 46 58N 88 8W
Abbé, L., *Ethiopia* **46 E3** 11 8N 41 47 E
Abbeville, *France* **18 A4** 50 6N 1 49 E
Abbeville, *Ala., U.S.A.* **77 K3** 31 34N 85 15W
Abbeville, *La., U.S.A.* **81 L8** 29 58N 92 8W
Abbeville, *S.C., U.S.A.* **77 H4** 34 11N 82 23W
Abbot Ice Shelf, *Antarctica* **5 D16** 73 0S 92 0W
Abbottabad, *Pakistan* **42 B5** 34 10N 73 15 E
Abd al Kūrī, *Ind. Oc.* **46 E5** 12 5N 52 20 E
Ābdar, *Iran* **45 D7** 30 16N 55 19 E
'Abdolābād, *Iran* **45 C8** 34 12N 56 30 E
Abdulpur, *Bangla.* **43 G13** 24 15N 88 59 E
Abéché, *Chad* **51 F10** 13 50N 20 35 E
Abengourou, *Ivory C.* **50 G5** 6 42N 3 27W
Åbenrå, *Denmark* **9 J13** 55 3N 9 25 E
Abeokuta, *Nigeria* **50 G6** 7 3N 3 19 E
Aber, *Uganda* **54 B3** 2 12N 32 25 E
Aberaeron, *U.K.* **11 E3** 52 15N 4 15W
Aberayron = Aberaeron, *U.K.* **11 E3** 52 15N 4 15W
Aberchirder, *U.K.* **12 D6** 57 34N 2 37W
Abercorn = Mbala, *Zambia* **55 D3** 8 46S 31 24 E
Abercorn, *Australia* **63 D5** 25 12S 151 5 E
Aberdare, *U.K.* **11 F4** 51 43N 3 27W
Aberdare Ra., *Kenya* **54 C4** 0 15S 36 50 E
Aberdeen, *Australia* **63 E5** 32 9S 150 56 E
Aberdeen, *Canada* **73 C7** 52 20N 106 8W
Aberdeen, *S. Africa* **56 E3** 32 28S 24 2 E
Aberdeen, *U.K.* **12 D6** 57 9N 2 5W
Aberdeen, *Ala., U.S.A.* **77 J1** 33 49N 88 33W
Aberdeen, *Idaho, U.S.A.* **82 E7** 42 57N 112 50W
Aberdeen, *Md., U.S.A.* **76 F7** 39 31N 76 10W
Aberdeen, *S. Dak., U.S.A.* **80 C5** 45 28N 98 29W
Aberdeen, *Wash., U.S.A.* **84 D3** 46 59N 123 50W
Aberdeen, City of □, *U.K.* **12 D6** 57 10N 2 10W
Aberdeenshire □, *U.K.* **12 D6** 57 17N 2 36W
Aberdovey = Aberdyfi, *U.K.* **11 E3** 52 33N 4 3W
Aberdyfi, *U.K.* **11 E3** 52 33N 4 3W
Aberfeldy, *U.K.* **12 E5** 56 37N 3 51W
Abergavenny, *U.K.* **11 F4** 51 49N 3 1W
Abergele, *U.K.* **10 D4** 53 17N 3 35W
Abernathy, *U.S.A.* **81 J4** 33 50N 101 51W
Abert, L., *U.S.A.* **82 E3** 42 38N 120 14W
Aberystwyth, *U.K.* **11 E3** 52 25N 4 5W
Abhā, *Si. Arabia* **46 D3** 18 0N 42 34 E
Abhar, *Iran* **45 B6** 36 9N 49 13 E
Abhayapuri, *India* **43 F14** 26 24N 90 38 E
Abidjan, *Ivory C.* **50 G5** 5 26N 3 58W
Abilene, *Kans., U.S.A.* **80 F6** 38 55N 97 13W
Abilene, *Tex., U.S.A.* **81 J5** 32 28N 99 43W
Abingdon, *U.K.* **11 F6** 51 40N 1 17W
Abingdon, *U.S.A.* **77 G5** 36 43N 81 59W
Abington Reef, *Australia* **62 B4** 18 0S 149 35 E
Abitau →, *Canada* **73 B7** 59 53N 109 3W
Abitibi →, *Canada* **70 B3** 51 3N 80 55W
Abitibi, L., *Canada* **70 C4** 48 40N 79 40W
Abkhaz Republic = Abkhazia □, *Georgia* **25 F7** 43 12N 41 5 E
Abkhazia □, *Georgia* **25 F7** 43 12N 41 5 E
Abminga, *Australia* **63 D1** 26 8S 134 51 E
Åbo = Turku, *Finland* **9 F20** 60 30N 22 19 E
Abohar, *India* **42 D6** 30 10N 74 10 E
Abolo, *Congo* **52 D2** 0 8N 14 16 E
Abomey, *Benin* **50 G6** 7 10N 2 5 E
Abong-Mbang, *Cameroon* **52 D2** 4 0N 13 8 E
Abou-Deïa, *Chad* **51 F9** 11 20N 19 20 E
Aboyne, *U.K.* **12 D6** 57 4N 2 47W
Abra Pampa, *Argentina* **94 A2** 22 43S 65 42W
Abraham L., *Canada* **72 C5** 52 15N 116 35W
Abreojos, Pta., *Mexico* **86 B2** 26 50N 113 40W
Abrud, *Romania* **17 E12** 46 19N 23 5 E
Absaroka Range, *U.S.A.* **82 D9** 44 45N 109 50W
Abu, *India* **42 G5** 24 41N 72 50 E
Abu al Abyad, *U.A.E.* **45 E7** 24 11N 53 50 E
Abū al Khaşīb, *Iraq* **45 D6** 30 25N 48 0 E
Abū 'Alī, *Si. Arabia* **45 E6** 27 20N 49 27 E
Abū 'Alī →, *Lebanon* **47 A4** 34 25N 35 50 E
Abu Dhabi = Abū Ẓāby, *U.A.E.* **45 E7** 24 28N 54 22 E
Abū Du'ān, *Syria* **44 B3** 36 25N 38 15 E
Abu el Gairi, W. →, *Egypt* **47 F2** 29 35N 33 30 E
Abu Ga'da, W. →, *Egypt* **47 F1** 29 15N 32 53 E
Abū Ḩadrīyah, *Si. Arabia* **45 E6** 27 20N 48 58 E
Abu Hamed, *Sudan* **51 E12** 19 32N 33 13 E
Abū Kamāl, *Syria* **44 C4** 34 30N 41 0 E
Abū Madd, Ra's, *Si. Arabia* **44 E3** 24 50N 37 7 E
Abū Mūsā, *U.A.E.* **45 E7** 25 52N 55 3 E
Abu Şafāt, W. →, *Jordan* **47 E5** 30 24N 36 7 E
Abu Simbel, *Egypt* **51 D12** 22 18N 31 40 E
Abū Şukhayr, *Iraq* **44 D5** 31 54N 44 30 E
Abû Zabad, *Sudan* **51 F11** 12 25N 29 10 E
Abū Ẓāby, *U.A.E.* **45 E7** 24 28N 54 22 E
Abū Zeydābād, *Iran* **45 C6** 33 54N 51 45 E
Abuja, *Nigeria* **50 G7** 9 16N 7 2 E
Abukuma-Gawa →, *Japan* **30 E10** 38 6N 140 52 E
Abukuma-Sammyaku, *Japan* **30 F10** 37 30N 140 45 E
Abunã, *Brazil* **92 E5** 9 40S 65 20W
Abunã →, *Brazil* **92 E5** 9 41S 65 20W
Aburo, *Dem. Rep. of the Congo* **54 B3** 2 4N 30 53 E
Abut Hd., *N.Z.* **59 K3** 43 7S 170 15 E
Acadia National Park, *U.S.A.* **77 C11** 44 20N 68 13W
Açailândia, *Brazil* **93 D9** 4 57S 47 0W
Acajutla, *El Salv.* **88 D2** 13 36N 89 50W
Acámbaro, *Mexico* **86 D4** 20 0N 100 40W
Acaponeta, *Mexico* **86 C3** 22 30N 105 20W
Acapulco, *Mexico* **87 D5** 16 51N 99 56W
Acarai, Serra, *Brazil* **92 C7** 1 50N 57 50W
Acarigua, *Venezuela* **92 B5** 9 33N 69 12W
Acatlán, *Mexico* **87 D5** 18 10N 98 3W
Acayucan, *Mexico* **87 D6** 17 59N 94 58W
Accomac, *U.S.A.* **76 G8** 37 43N 75 40W
Accra, *Ghana* **50 G5** 5 35N 0 6W
Accrington, *U.K.* **10 D5** 53 45N 2 22W
Acebal, *Argentina* **94 C3** 33 20S 60 50W
Aceh □, *Indonesia* **36 D1** 4 15N 97 30 E
Achalpur, *India* **40 J10** 21 22N 77 32 E
Acheng, *China* **35 B14** 45 30N 126 58 E
Acher, *India* **42 H5** 23 10N 72 32 E
Achill Hd., *Ireland* **13 C1** 53 58N 10 15W
Achill I., *Ireland* **13 C1** 53 58N 10 1W
Achinsk, *Russia* **27 D10** 56 20N 90 20 E
Acireale, *Italy* **20 F6** 37 37N 15 10 E
Ackerman, *U.S.A.* **81 J10** 33 19N 89 11W
Acklins I., *Bahamas* **89 B5** 22 30N 74 0W
Acme, *Canada* **72 C6** 51 33N 113 30W
Acme, *U.S.A.* **78 F5** 40 8N 79 26W
Aconcagua, Cerro, *Argentina* **94 C2** 32 39S 70 0W
Aconquija, Mt., *Argentina* **94 B2** 27 0S 66 0W
Açores, Is. dos = Azores, *Atl. Oc.* **50 A1** 38 44N 29 0W
Acraman, L., *Australia* **63 E2** 32 2S 135 23 E
Acre = 'Akko, *Israel* **47 C4** 32 55N 35 4 E
Acre □, *Brazil* **92 E4** 9 1S 71 0W
Acre →, *Brazil* **92 E5** 8 45S 67 22W
Acton, *Canada* **78 C4** 43 38N 80 3W
Acuña, *Mexico* **86 B4** 29 18N 100 55W
Ad Dammām, *Si. Arabia* **45 E6** 26 20N 50 5 E
Ad Dāmūr, *Lebanon* **47 B4** 33 44N 35 27 E
Ad Dawādimī, *Si. Arabia* **44 E5** 24 35N 44 15 E
Ad Dawḩah, *Qatar* **45 E6** 25 15N 51 35 E
Ad Dawr, *Iraq* **44 C4** 34 27N 43 47 E
Ad Dir'īyah, *Si. Arabia* **44 E5** 24 44N 46 35 E
Ad Dīwānīyah, *Iraq* **44 D5** 32 0N 45 0 E
Ad Dujayl, *Iraq* **44 C5** 33 51N 44 14 E
Ad Duwayd, *Si. Arabia* **44 D4** 30 15N 42 17 E
Ada, *Minn., U.S.A.* **80 B6** 47 18N 96 31W
Ada, *Okla., U.S.A.* **81 H6** 34 46N 96 41W
Adabiya, *Egypt* **47 F1** 29 53N 32 28 E
Adair, C., *Canada* **69 A12** 71 31N 71 24W
Adaja →, *Spain* **19 B3** 41 32N 4 52W
Adak I., *U.S.A.* **68 C2** 51 45N 176 45W
Adamaoua, Massif de l', *Cameroon* **52 C2** 7 20N 12 20 E
Adamawa Highlands = Adamaoua, Massif de l', *Cameroon* **52 C2** 7 20N 12 20 E
Adamello, Mte., *Italy* **18 C9** 46 9N 10 30 E
Adaminaby, *Australia* **63 F4** 36 0S 148 45 E
Adams, *Mass., U.S.A.* **79 D11** 42 38N 73 7W
Adams, *N.Y., U.S.A.* **79 C8** 43 49N 76 1W
Adams, *Wis., U.S.A.* **80 D10** 43 57N 89 49W
Adam's Bridge, *Sri Lanka* **40 Q11** 9 15N 79 40 E
Adams L., *Canada* **72 C5** 51 10N 119 40W
Adams Mt., *U.S.A.* **84 D5** 46 12N 121 30W
Adam's Peak, *Sri Lanka* **40 R12** 6 48N 80 30 E
Adana, *Turkey* **25 G6** 37 0N 35 16 E
Adapazarı = Sakarya, *Turkey* **25 F5** 40 48N 30 25 E
Adarama, *Sudan* **51 E12** 17 10N 34 52 E
Adare, C., *Antarctica* **5 D11** 71 0S 171 0 E
Adaut, *Indonesia* **37 F8** 8 8S 131 7 E
Adavale, *Australia* **63 D3** 25 52S 144 32 E
Adda →, *Italy* **18 D8** 45 8N 9 53 E
Addis Ababa = Addis Abeba, *Ethiopia* **46 F2** 9 2N 38 42 E
Addis Abeba, *Ethiopia* **46 F2** 9 2N 38 42 E
Addison, *U.S.A.* **78 D7** 42 1N 77 14W
Addo, *S. Africa* **56 E4** 33 32S 25 45 E
Ādeh, *Iran* **44 B5** 37 42N 45 11 E
Adel, *U.S.A.* **77 K4** 31 8N 83 25W
Adelaide, *Australia* **63 E2** 34 52S 138 30 E
Adelaide, *Bahamas* **88 A4** 25 4N 77 31W
Adelaide, *S. Africa* **56 E4** 32 42S 26 20 E
Adelaide I., *Antarctica* **5 C17** 67 15S 68 30W
Adelaide Pen., *Canada* **68 B10** 68 15N 97 30W
Adelaide River, *Australia* **60 B5** 13 15S 131 7 E
Adelanto, *U.S.A.* **85 L9** 34 35N 117 22W
Adele I., *Australia* **60 C3** 15 32S 123 9 E
Adélie, Terre, *Antarctica* **5 C10** 68 0S 140 0 E
Adélie Land = Adélie, Terre, *Antarctica* **5 C10** 68 0S 140 0 E
Aden = Al 'Adan, *Yemen* **46 E4** 12 45N 45 0 E
Aden, G. of, *Asia* **46 E4** 12 30N 47 30 E
Adendorp, *S. Africa* **56 E3** 32 15S 24 30 E
Adh Dhayd, *U.A.E.* **45 E7** 25 17N 55 53 E
Adhoi, *India* **42 H4** 23 26N 70 32 E
Adi, *Indonesia* **37 E8** 4 15S 133 30 E
Adieu, C., *Australia* **61 F5** 32 0S 132 10 E
Adieu Pt., *Australia* **60 C3** 15 14S 124 35 E
Adige →, *Italy* **20 B5** 45 9N 12 20 E
Adigrat, *Ethiopia* **46 E2** 14 20N 39 26 E
Adilabad, *India* **40 K11** 19 33N 78 20 E
Adin Khel, *Afghan.* **40 C6** 32 45N 68 5 E
Adirondack Mts., *U.S.A.* **79 C10** 44 0N 74 0W
Adjumani, *Uganda* **54 B3** 3 20N 31 50 E
Adlavik Is., *Canada* **71 A8** 55 2N 57 45W
Admiralty G., *Australia* **60 B4** 14 20S 125 55 E
Admiralty I., *U.S.A.* **72 B2** 57 30N 134 30W
Admiralty Is., *Papua N. G.* **64 H6** 2 0S 147 0 E
Adonara, *Indonesia* **37 F6** 8 15S 123 5 E
Adoni, *India* **40 M10** 15 33N 77 18 E
Adour →, *France* **18 E3** 43 32N 1 32W
Adra, *India* **43 H12** 23 30N 86 42 E
Adra, *Spain* **19 D4** 36 43N 3 3W
Adrano, *Italy* **20 F6** 37 40N 14 50 E
Adrar, *Algeria* **48 D4** 27 51N 0 11 E
Adrar, *Mauritania* **50 D3** 20 30N 7 30 E
Adrian, *Mich., U.S.A.* **76 E3** 41 54N 84 2W
Adrian, *Tex., U.S.A.* **81 H3** 35 16N 102 40W
Adriatic Sea, *Medit. S.* **20 C6** 43 0N 16 0 E
Adua, *Indonesia* **37 E7** 1 45S 129 50 E
Adwa, *Ethiopia* **46 E2** 14 15N 38 52 E
Adygea □, *Russia* **25 F7** 45 0N 40 0 E
Adzhar Republic = Ajaria □, *Georgia* **25 F7** 41 30N 42 0 E
Adzopé, *Ivory C.* **50 G5** 6 7N 3 49W
Ægean Sea, *Medit. S.* **21 E11** 38 30N 25 0 E
Aerhtai Shan, *Mongolia* **32 B4** 46 40N 92 45 E
'Afak, *Iraq* **44 C5** 32 4N 45 15 E
Afándou, *Greece* **23 C10** 36 18N 28 12 E
Afghanistan ■, *Asia* **40 C4** 33 0N 65 0 E
Aflou, *Algeria* **50 B6** 34 7N 2 3 E
Africa **48 E6** 10 0N 20 0 E
'Afrīn, *Syria* **44 B3** 36 32N 36 50 E
Afton, *N.Y., U.S.A.* **79 D9** 42 14N 75 32W
Afton, *Wyo., U.S.A.* **82 E8** 42 44N 110 56W
Afuá, *Brazil* **93 D8** 0 15S 50 20W
'Afula, *Israel* **47 C4** 32 37N 35 17 E
Afyon, *Turkey* **25 G5** 38 45N 30 33 E
Afyonkarahisar = Afyon, *Turkey* **25 G5** 38 45N 30 33 E
Agadès = Agadez, *Niger* **50 E7** 16 58N 7 59 E
Agadez, *Niger* **50 E7** 16 58N 7 59 E
Agadir, *Morocco* **50 B4** 30 28N 9 55W
Agaete, *Canary Is.* **22 F4** 28 6N 15 43W
Agar, *India* **42 H7** 23 40N 76 2 E
Agartala, *India* **41 H17** 23 50N 91 23 E
Agassiz, *Canada* **72 D4** 49 14N 121 46W
Agats, *Indonesia* **37 F9** 5 33S 138 0 E
Agawam, *U.S.A.* **79 D12** 42 5N 72 37W
Agboville, *Ivory C.* **50 G5** 5 55N 4 15W
Ağdam, *Azerbaijan* **44 B5** 40 0N 46 58 E
Agde, *France* **18 E5** 43 19N 3 28 E
Agen, *France* **18 D4** 44 12N 0 38 E
Āgh Kand, *Iran* **45 B6** 37 15N 48 4 E
Aginskoye, *Russia* **27 D12** 51 6N 114 32 E
Agnew, *Australia* **61 E3** 28 1S 120 31 E
Agori, *India* **43 G10** 24 33N 82 57 E
Agra, *India* **42 F7** 27 17N 77 58 E
Ağrı, *Turkey* **25 G7** 39 44N 43 3 E
Agri →, *Italy* **20 D7** 40 13N 16 44 E
Ağrı Dağı, *Turkey* **25 G7** 39 50N 44 15 E
Ağrı Karakose = Ağrı, *Turkey* **25 G7** 39 44N 43 3 E
Agrigento, *Italy* **20 F5** 37 19N 13 34 E
Agrínion, *Greece* **21 E9** 38 37N 21 27 E
Agua Caliente, *Baja Calif., Mexico* **85 N10** 32 29N 116 59W
Agua Caliente, *Sinaloa, Mexico* **86 B3** 26 30N 108 20W
Agua Caliente Springs, *U.S.A.* **85 N10** 32 56N 116 19W
Água Clara, *Brazil* **93 H8** 20 25S 52 45W
Agua Hechicero, *Mexico* **85 N10** 32 26N 116 14W
Agua Prieta, *Mexico* **86 A3** 31 20N 109 32W
Aguadilla, *Puerto Rico* **89 C6** 18 26N 67 10W
Aguadulce, *Panama* **88 E3** 8 15N 80 32W
Aguanga, *U.S.A.* **85 M10** 33 27N 116 51W
Aguanish, *Canada* **71 B7** 50 14N 62 2W
Aguanus →, *Canada* **71 B7** 50 13N 62 5W
Aguapey →, *Argentina* **94 B4** 29 7S 56 36W
Aguaray Guazú →, *Paraguay* **94 A4** 24 47S 57 19W
Aguarico →, *Ecuador* **92 D3** 0 59S 75 11W
Aguas Blancas, *Chile* **94 A2** 24 15S 69 55W
Aguas Calientes, Sierra de, *Argentina* **94 B2** 25 26S 66 40W
Aguascalientes, *Mexico* **86 C4** 21 53N 102 12W
Aguascalientes □, *Mexico* **86 C4** 22 0N 102 20W
Aguilares, *Argentina* **94 B2** 27 26S 65 35W
Aguilas, *Spain* **19 D5** 37 23N 1 35W
Agüimes, *Canary Is.* **22 G4** 27 58N 15 27W
Aguja, C. de la, *Colombia* **90 B3** 11 18N 74 12W
Agulhas, C., *S. Africa* **56 E3** 34 52S 20 0 E
Agulo, *Canary Is.* **22 F2** 28 11N 17 12W
Agung, *Indonesia* **36 F5** 8 20S 115 28 E
Agur, *Uganda* **54 B3** 2 28N 32 55 E
Agusan →, *Phil.* **37 C7** 9 0N 125 30 E
Aha Mts., *Botswana* **56 B3** 19 45S 21 0 E
Ahaggar, *Algeria* **50 D7** 23 0N 6 30 E
Ahar, *Iran* **44 B5** 38 35N 47 0 E
Ahipara B., *N.Z.* **59 F4** 35 5S 173 5 E
Ahiri, *India* **40 K12** 19 30N 80 0 E
Ahmad Wal, *Pakistan* **42 E1** 29 18N 65 58 E
Ahmadabad, *India* **42 H5** 23 0N 72 40 E
Aḩmadābād, *Khorāsān, Iran* **45 C9** 35 3N 60 50 E
Aḩmadābād, *Khorāsān, Iran* **45 C8** 35 49N 59 42 E
Aḩmadī, *Iran* **45 E8** 27 56N 56 42 E
Ahmadnagar, *India* **40 K9** 19 7N 74 46 E
Ahmadpur, *Pakistan* **42 E4** 29 12N 71 10 E
Ahmadpur Lamma, *Pakistan* **42 E4** 28 19N 70 3 E
Ahmedabad = Ahmadabad, *India* **42 H5** 23 0N 72 40 E
Ahmednagar = Ahmadnagar, *India* **40 K9** 19 7N 74 46 E
Ahome, *Mexico* **86 B3** 25 55N 109 11W
Ahoskie, *U.S.A.* **77 G7** 36 17N 76 59W
Ahram, *Iran* **45 D6** 28 52N 51 16 E
Ahrax Pt., *Malta* **23 D1** 35 59N 14 22 E
Āhū, *Iran* **45 C6** 34 33N 50 2 E
Ahuachapán, *El Salv.* **88 D2** 13 54N 89 52W
Ahvāz, *Iran* **45 D6** 31 20N 48 40 E
Ahvenanmaa = Åland, *Finland* **9 F19** 60 15N 20 0 E
Aḩwar, *Yemen* **46 E4** 13 30N 46 40 E
Ai →, *India* **43 F14** 26 26N 90 44 E
Aichi □, *Japan* **31 G8** 35 0N 137 15 E
Aigua, *Uruguay* **95 C5** 34 13S 54 46W
Aigues-Mortes, *France* **18 E6** 43 35N 4 12 E
Aihui, *China* **33 A7** 50 10N 127 30 E
Aija, *Peru* **92 E3** 9 50S 77 45W
Aikawa, *Japan* **30 E9** 38 2N 138 15 E
Aiken, *U.S.A.* **77 J5** 33 34N 81 43W
Aileron, *Australia* **62 C1** 22 39S 133 20 E
Aillik, *Canada* **71 A8** 55 11N 59 18W
Ailsa Craig, *U.K.* **12 F3** 55 15N 5 6W
'Ailūn, *Jordan* **47 C4** 32 18N 35 47 E
Aim, *Russia* **27 D14** 59 0N 133 55 E
Aimere, *Indonesia* **37 F6** 8 45S 121 3 E
Aimogasta, *Argentina* **94 B2** 28 33S 66 50W
Aïn Ben Tili, *Mauritania* **50 C4** 25 59N 9 27W
Aïn-Sefra, *Algeria* **50 B5** 32 47N 0 37W
'Ain Sudr, *Egypt* **47 F2** 29 50N 33 6 E
Ainaži, *Latvia* **9 H21** 57 50N 24 24 E
Ainsworth, *U.S.A.* **80 D5** 42 33N 99 52W
Aiquile, *Bolivia* **92 G5** 18 10S 65 10W
Aïr, *Niger* **50 E7** 18 30N 8 0 E
Air Force I., *Canada* **69 B12** 67 58N 74 5W
Air Hitam, *Malaysia* **39 M4** 1 55N 103 11 E
Airdrie, *Canada* **72 C6** 51 18N 114 2W
Airdrie, *U.K.* **12 F5** 55 52N 3 57W
Aire →, *U.K.* **10 D7** 53 43N 0 55W
Aire, I. de l', *Spain* **22 B11** 39 48N 4 16 E
Airlie Beach, *Australia* **62 C4** 20 16S 148 43 E
Aisne →, *France* **18 B5** 49 26N 2 50 E
Ait, *India* **43 G8** 25 54N 79 14 E
Aitkin, *U.S.A.* **80 B8** 46 32N 93 42W
Aiud, *Romania* **17 E12** 46 19N 23 44 E
Aix-en-Provence, *France* **18 E6** 43 32N 5 27 E
Aix-la-Chapelle = Aachen, *Germany* **16 C4** 50 45N 6 6 E
Aix-les-Bains, *France* **18 D6** 45 41N 5 53 E
Aíyion, *Greece* **21 E10** 38 15N 22 5 E
Aizawl, *India* **41 H18** 23 40N 92 44 E
Aizkraukle, *Latvia* **9 H21** 56 36N 25 11 E
Aizpute, *Latvia* **9 H19** 56 43N 21 40 E
Aizuwakamatsu, *Japan* **30 F9** 37 30N 139 56 E
Ajaccio, *France* **18 F8** 41 55N 8 40 E
Ajaigarh, *India* **43 G9** 24 52N 80 16 E
Ajalpan, *Mexico* **87 D5** 18 22N 97 15W
Ajanta Ra., *India* **40 J9** 20 28N 75 50 E
Ajari Rep. = Ajaria □, *Georgia* **25 F7** 41 30N 42 0 E
Ajaria □, *Georgia* **25 F7** 41 30N 42 0 E
Ajax, *Canada* **78 C5** 43 50N 79 1W
Ajdâbiyah, *Libya* **51 B10** 30 54N 20 4 E
Ajka, *Hungary* **17 E9** 47 4N 17 31 E
'Ajmān, *U.A.E.* **45 E7** 25 25N 55 30 E
Ajmer, *India* **42 F6** 26 28N 74 37 E
Ajnala, *India* **42 D6** 31 50N 74 48 E
Ajo, *U.S.A.* **83 K7** 32 22N 112 52W
Ajo, C. de, *Spain* **19 A4** 43 31N 3 35W
Akabira, *Japan* **30 C11** 43 33N 142 5 E
Akamas □, *Cyprus* **23 D11** 35 3N 32 18 E
Akanthou, *Cyprus* **23 D12** 35 22N 33 45 E
Akaroa, *N.Z.* **59 K4** 43 49S 172 59 E
Akashi, *Japan* **31 G7** 34 45N 134 58 E
Akbarpur, *Bihar, India* **43 G10** 24 39N 83 58 E
Akbarpur, *Ut. P., India* **43 F10** 26 25N 82 32 E
Akelamo, *Indonesia* **37 D7** 1 35N 129 40 E
Aketi, *Dem. Rep. of the Congo* **52 D4** 2 38N 23 47 E
Akharnaí, *Greece* **21 E10** 38 5N 23 44 E
Akhelóös →, *Greece* **21 E9** 38 19N 21 7 E
Akhisar, *Turkey* **21 E12** 38 56N 27 48 E
Akhnur, *India* **43 C6** 32 52N 74 45 E
Akhtyrka = Okhtyrka, *Ukraine* **25 D5** 50 25N 35 0 E
Aki, *Japan* **31 H6** 33 30N 133 54 E
Akimiski I., *Canada* **70 B3** 52 50N 81 30W
Akita, *Japan* **30 E10** 39 45N 140 7 E
Akita □, *Japan* **30 E10** 39 40N 140 30 E
Akjoujt, *Mauritania* **50 E3** 19 45N 14 15W
Akkeshi, *Japan* **30 C12** 43 2N 144 51 E
'Akko, *Israel* **47 C4** 32 55N 35 4 E
Aklavik, *Canada* **68 B6** 68 12N 135 0W
Aklera, *India* **42 G7** 24 26N 76 32 E
Akmolinsk = Astana, *Kazakstan* **26 D8** 51 10N 71 30 E
Akō, *Japan* **31 G7** 34 45N 134 24 E
Akola, *India* **40 J10** 20 42N 77 2 E
Akordat, *Eritrea* **46 D2** 15 30N 37 40 E
Akpatok I., *Canada* **69 B13** 60 25N 68 8W
Åkrahamn, *Norway* **9 G11** 59 15N 5 10 E
Akranes, *Iceland* **8 D2** 64 19N 22 5W
Akron, *Colo., U.S.A.* **80 E3** 40 10N 103 13W
Akron, *Ohio, U.S.A.* **78 E3** 41 5N 81 31W
Akrotiri, *Cyprus* **23 E11** 34 36N 32 57 E
Akrotiri Bay, *Cyprus* **23 E12** 34 35N 33 10 E
Aksai Chin, *India* **43 B8** 35 15N 79 55 E
Aksaray, *Turkey* **25 G5** 38 25N 34 2 E
Aksay, *Kazakstan* **25 D9** 51 11N 53 0 E
Akşehir, *Turkey* **44 B1** 38 18N 31 30 E
Akşehir Gölü, *Turkey* **25 G5** 38 30N 31 25 E
Aksu, *China* **32 B3** 41 5N 80 10 E
Aksum, *Ethiopia* **46 E2** 14 5N 38 40 E
Aktogay, *Kazakstan* **26 E8** 46 57N 79 40 E
Aktsyabrski, *Belarus* **17 B15** 52 38N 28 53 E
Aktyubinsk = Aqtöbe, *Kazakstan* **25 D10** 50 17N 57 10 E
Akure, *Nigeria* **50 G7** 7 15N 5 5 E
Akureyri, *Iceland* **8 D4** 65 40N 18 6W
Akuseki-Shima, *Japan* **31 K4** 29 27N 129 37 E
Akyab = Sittwe, *Burma* **41 J18** 20 18N 92 45 E
Al 'Adan, *Yemen* **46 E4** 12 45N 45 0 E
Al Aḩsā = Hasa □, *Si. Arabia* **45 E6** 25 50N 49 0 E
Al Ajfar, *Si. Arabia* **44 E4** 27 26N 43 0 E
Al Amādīyah, *Iraq* **44 B4** 37 5N 43 30 E
Al 'Amārah, *Iraq* **44 D5** 31 55N 47 15 E
Al 'Aqabah, *Jordan* **47 F4** 29 31N 35 0 E
Al Arak, *Syria* **44 C3** 34 38N 38 35 E
Al 'Aramah, *Si. Arabia* **44 E5** 25 30N 46 0 E
Al Arţāwīyah, *Si. Arabia* **44 E5** 26 31N 45 20 E
Al 'Āşimah = 'Ammān □, *Jordan* **47 D5** 31 40N 36 30 E
Al 'Assāfīyah, *Si. Arabia* **44 D3** 28 17N 38 59 E
Al 'Ayn, *Oman* **45 E7** 24 15N 55 45 E
Al 'Ayn, *Si. Arabia* **44 E3** 25 4N 38 6 E
Al 'Aẓamīyah, *Iraq* **44 C5** 33 22N 44 22 E
Al 'Azīzīyah, *Iraq* **44 C5** 32 54N 45 4 E
Al Bāb, *Syria* **44 B3** 36 23N 37 29 E
Al Bad', *Si. Arabia* **44 D2** 28 28N 35 1 E
Al Bādī, *Iraq* **44 C4** 35 56N 41 32 E
Al Baḩrah, *Kuwait* **44 D5** 29 40N 47 52 E
Al Baḩral Mayyit = Dead Sea, *Asia* **47 D4** 31 30N 35 30 E
Al Balqā' □, *Jordan* **47 C4** 32 5N 35 45 E
Al Bārūk, J., *Lebanon* **47 B4** 33 39N 35 40 E
Al Başrah, *Iraq* **44 D5** 30 30N 47 50 E
Al Baţḩā, *Iraq* **44 D5** 31 6N 45 53 E
Al Batrūn, *Lebanon* **47 A4** 34 15N 35 40 E
Al Bayḑā, *Libya* **51 B10** 32 50N 21 44 E
Al Biqā, *Lebanon* **47 A5** 34 10N 36 10 E
Al Bi'r, *Si. Arabia* **44 D3** 28 51N 36 16 E
Al Burayj, *Syria* **47 A5** 34 15N 36 46 E
Al Faḑilī, *Si. Arabia* **45 E6** 26 58N 49 10 E

Amadeus, L.

Al Fallūjah, *Iraq* **44 C4** 33 20N 43 55 E
Al Fāw, *Iraq* **45 D6** 30 0N 48 30 E
Al Fujayrah, *U.A.E.* **45 E8** 25 7N 56 18 E
Al Ghadaf, W. →, *Jordan* **47 D5** 31 26N 36 43 E
Al Ghammās, *Iraq* **44 D5** 31 45N 44 37 E
Al Ghazālah, *Si. Arabia* **44 E4** 26 48N 41 19 E
Al Hābah, *Si. Arabia* **44 E5** 27 10N 47 0 E
Al Ḩadīthah, *Iraq* **44 C4** 34 0N 41 13 E
Al Ḩadīthah, *Si. Arabia* **47 D6** 31 28N 37 8 E
Al Ḩaḑr, *Iraq* **44 C4** 35 35N 42 44 E
Al Hājānah, *Syria* **47 B5** 33 20N 36 33 E
Al Hajar al Gharbī, *Oman* **45 E8** 24 10N 56 15 E
Al Hāmad, *Si. Arabia* **44 D3** 31 30N 39 30 E
Al Hamdānīyah, *Syria* **44 C3** 35 25N 36 50 E
Al Ḩamīdīyah, *Syria* **47 A4** 34 42N 35 57 E
Al Ḩammār, *Iraq* **44 D5** 30 57N 46 51 E
Al Ḩamrā', *Si. Arabia* **44 E3** 24 2N 38 55 E
Al Ḩanākīyah, *Si. Arabia* **44 E4** 24 51N 40 31 E
Al Harīr, W. →, *Syria* **47 C4** 32 44N 35 59 E
Al Ḩasā, W. →, *Jordan* **47 D4** 31 4N 35 29 E
Al Ḩasakah, *Syria* **44 B4** 36 35N 40 45 E
Al Haydān, W. →, *Jordan* **47 D4** 31 29N 35 34 E
Al Ḩayy, *Iraq* **44 C5** 32 5N 46 5 E
Al Ḩijarah, *Asia* **44 D4** 30 0N 44 0 E
Al Ḩillah, *Iraq* **44 C5** 32 30N 44 25 E
Al Hindīyah, *Iraq* **44 C5** 32 30N 44 10 E
Al Hirmil, *Lebanon* **47 A5** 34 26N 36 24 E
Al Hoceïma, *Morocco* **50 A5** 35 8N 3 58W
Al Ḩudaydah, *Yemen* **46 E3** 14 50N 43 0 E
Al Hufūf, *Si. Arabia* **45 E6** 25 25N 49 45 E
Al Ḩumayḑah, *Si. Arabia* **44 D2** 29 14N 34 56 E
Al Ḩunayy, *Si. Arabia* **45 E6** 25 58N 48 45 E
Al Īsāwīyah, *Si. Arabia* **44 D3** 30 43N 37 59 E
Al Jafr, *Jordan* **47 E5** 30 18N 36 14 E
Al Jāfūrah, *Si. Arabia* **45 E7** 25 0N 50 15 E
Al Jaghbūb, *Libya* **51 C10** 29 42N 24 38 E
Al Jahrah, *Kuwait* **44 D5** 29 25N 47 40 E
Al Jalāmīd, *Si. Arabia* **44 D3** 31 20N 40 6 E
Al Jamalīyah, *Qatar* **45 E6** 25 37N 51 5 E
Al Janūb □, *Lebanon* **47 B4** 33 20N 35 20 E
Al Jawf, *Libya* **51 D10** 24 10N 23 24 E
Al Jawf, *Si. Arabia* **44 D3** 29 55N 39 40 E
Al Jazirah, *Iraq* **44 C5** 33 30N 44 0 E
Al Jithāmīyah, *Si. Arabia* **44 E4** 27 41N 41 43 E
Al Jubayl, *Si. Arabia* **45 E6** 27 0N 49 50 E
Al Jubaylah, *Si. Arabia* **44 E5** 24 55N 46 25 E
Al Jubb, *Si. Arabia* **44 E4** 27 11N 42 17 E
Al Junaynah, *Sudan* **51 F10** 13 27N 22 45 E
Al Kabā'ish, *Iraq* **44 D5** 30 58N 47 0 E
Al Karak, *Jordan* **47 D4** 31 11N 35 42 E
Al Karak □, *Jordan* **47 E5** 31 0N 36 0 E
Al Kāzim Tyah, *Iraq* **44 C5** 33 22N 44 12 E
Al Khābūra, *Oman* **45 F8** 23 57N 57 5 E
Al Khafji, *Si. Arabia* **45 E6** 28 24N 48 29 E
Al Khalīl, *West Bank* **47 D4** 31 32N 35 6 E
Al Khāliş, *Iraq* **44 C5** 33 49N 44 32 E
Al Kharsānīyah, *Si. Arabia* **45 E6** 27 13N 49 18 E
Al Khaşab, *Oman* **45 E8** 26 14N 56 15 E
Al Khawr, *Qatar* **45 E6** 25 41N 51 30 E
Al Khiḑr, *Iraq* **44 D5** 31 12N 45 33 E
Al Khiyām, *Lebanon* **47 B4** 33 20N 35 36 E
Al Khums, *Libya* **51 B8** 32 40N 14 17 E
Al Kiswah, *Syria* **47 B5** 33 23N 36 14 E
Al Kūfah, *Iraq* **44 C5** 32 2N 44 24 E
Al Kufrah, *Libya* **51 D10** 24 17N 23 15 E
Al Kuhayfiyah, *Si. Arabia* **44 E4** 27 12N 43 3 E
Al Kūt, *Iraq* **44 C5** 32 30N 46 0 E
Al Kuwayt, *Kuwait* **44 D5** 29 30N 48 0 E
Al Labwah, *Lebanon* **47 A5** 34 11N 36 20 E
Al Lādhiqīyah, *Syria* **44 C2** 35 30N 35 45 E
Al Līth, *Si. Arabia* **46 C3** 20 9N 40 15 E
Al Liwā', *Oman* **45 E8** 24 31N 56 36 E
Al Luḩayyah, *Yemen* **46 D3** 15 45N 42 40 E
Al Madīnah, *Iraq* **44 D5** 30 57N 47 16 E
Al Madīnah, *Si. Arabia* **46 C2** 24 35N 39 52 E
Al Mafraq, *Jordan* **47 C5** 32 17N 36 14 E
Al Maḩmūdīyah, *Iraq* **44 C5** 33 3N 44 21 E
Al Majma'ah, *Si. Arabia* **44 E5** 25 57N 45 22 E
Al Makhruq, W. →, *Jordan* **47 D6** 31 28N 37 0 E
Al Makḩūl, *Si. Arabia* **44 E4** 26 37N 42 39 E
Al Manāmah, *Bahrain* **45 E6** 26 10N 50 30 E
Al Maqwa', *Kuwait* **44 D5** 29 10N 47 59 E
Al Marj, *Libya* **51 B10** 32 25N 20 30 E
Al Maţlā, *Kuwait* **44 D5** 29 24N 47 40 E
Al Mawjib, W. →, *Jordan* **47 D4** 31 28N 35 36 E
Al Mawşil, *Iraq* **44 B4** 36 15N 43 5 E
Al Mayādin, *Syria* **44 C4** 35 1N 40 27 E
Al Mazār, *Jordan* **47 D4** 31 4N 35 41 E
Al Midhnab, *Si. Arabia* **44 E5** 25 50N 44 18 E
Al Minā', *Lebanon* **47 A4** 34 24N 35 49 E
Al Miqdādīyah, *Iraq* **44 C5** 34 0N 45 0 E
Al Mubarraz, *Si. Arabia* **45 E6** 25 30N 49 40 E
Al Mudawwarah, *Jordan* **47 F5** 29 19N 36 0 E
Al Mughayrā', *U.A.E.* **45 E7** 24 5N 53 32 E
Al Muḩarraq, *Bahrain* **45 E6** 26 15N 50 40 E
Al Mukallā, *Yemen* **46 E4** 14 33N 49 2 E
Al Mukhā, *Yemen* **46 E3** 13 18N 43 15 E
Al Musayjīd, *Si. Arabia* **44 E3** 24 5N 39 5 E
Al Musayyib, *Iraq* **44 C5** 32 49N 44 20 E
Al Muwayliḩ, *Si. Arabia* **44 E2** 27 40N 35 30 E
Al Qā'im, *Iraq* **44 C4** 34 21N 41 7 E
Al Qalībah, *Si. Arabia* **44 D3** 28 24N 37 42 E
Al Qāmishli, *Syria* **44 B4** 37 10N 41 10 E
Al Qaryatayn, *Syria* **47 A6** 34 12N 37 13 E
Al Qaşīm, *Si. Arabia* **44 E4** 26 0N 43 0 E
Al Qaţ'ā, *Syria* **44 C4** 34 40N 40 48 E
Al Qaţīf, *Si. Arabia* **45 E6** 26 35N 50 0 E
Al Qatrānah, *Jordan* **47 D5** 31 12N 36 6 E
Al Qaţrūn, *Libya* **51 D9** 24 56N 15 3 E
Al Qayşūmah, *Si. Arabia* **44 D5** 28 20N 46 7 E
Al Quds = Jerusalem, *Israel* **47 D4** 31 47N 35 10 E
Al Qunayţirah, *Syria* **47 C4** 32 55N 35 45 E
Al Qurnah, *Iraq* **44 D5** 31 1N 47 25 E
Al Quşayr, *Iraq* **44 D5** 30 39N 45 50 E
Al Quşayr, *Syria* **47 A5** 34 31N 36 34 E
Al Qutayfah, *Syria* **47 B5** 33 44N 36 36 E
Al 'Ubaylah, *Si. Arabia* **46 C5** 21 59N 50 57 E
Al 'Uḑaylīyah, *Si. Arabia* **45 E6** 25 8N 49 18 E
Al 'Ulā, *Si. Arabia* **44 E3** 26 35N 38 0 E
Al 'Uqayr, *Si. Arabia* **45 E6** 25 40N 50 15 E
Al 'Uthmānīyah, *Si. Arabia* **45 E6** 25 5N 49 22 E
Al 'Uwaynid, *Si. Arabia* **44 E5** 24 50N 46 0 E
Al 'Uwayqīlah, *Si. Arabia* **44 D4** 30 30N 42 10 E
Al 'Uyūn, Ḩijāz, *Si. Arabia* **44 E3** 24 33N 39 35 E
Al 'Uyūn, Najd, *Si. Arabia* **44 E4** 26 30N 43 50 E
Al 'Uzayr, *Iraq* **44 D5** 31 19N 47 25 E
Al Wajh, *Si. Arabia* **44 E3** 26 10N 36 30 E
Al Wakrah, *Qatar* **45 E6** 25 10N 51 40 E
Al Wannān, *Si. Arabia* **45 E6** 26 55N 48 24 E
Al Waqbah, *Si. Arabia* **44 D5** 28 48N 45 33 E
Al Wari'āh, *Si. Arabia* **44 E5** 27 51N 47 25 E
Al Wusayl, *Qatar* **45 E6** 25 29N 51 29 E
Ala Dağ, *Turkey* **44 B2** 37 44N 35 9 E
Ala Tau Shankou = Dzungarian Gates, *Kazakstan* **32 B3** 45 0N 82 0 E
Alabama □, *U.S.A.* **77 J2** 33 0N 87 0W
Alabama →, *U.S.A.* **77 K2** 31 8N 87 57W
Alabaster, *U.S.A.* **77 J2** 33 15N 86 49W
Alaçam Dağları, *Turkey* **21 E13** 39 18N 28 49 E
Alachua, *U.S.A.* **77 L4** 29 47N 82 30W
Alaérma, *Greece* **23 C9** 36 9N 27 57 E
Alagoa Grande, *Brazil* **93 E11** 7 3S 35 35W
Alagoas □, *Brazil* **93 E11** 9 0S 36 0W
Alagoinhas, *Brazil* **93 F11** 12 7S 38 20W
Alaior, *Spain* **22 B11** 39 57N 4 8 E
Alajero, *Canary Is.* **22 F2** 28 3N 17 13W
Alajuela, *Costa Rica* **88 D3** 10 2N 84 8W
Alakamisy, *Madag.* **57 C8** 21 19S 47 14 E
Alaknanda →, *India* **43 D8** 30 8N 78 36 E
Alakurtti, *Russia* **24 A5** 67 0N 30 30 E
Alamarvdasht, *Iran* **45 E7** 27 37N 52 59 E
Alameda, *Calif., U.S.A.* **84 H4** 37 46N 122 15W
Alameda, *N. Mex., U.S.A.* **83 J10** 35 11N 106 37W
Alamo, *U.S.A.* **85 J11** 37 22N 115 10W
Alamo Crossing, *U.S.A.* **85 L13** 34 16N 113 33W
Alamogordo, *U.S.A.* **83 K11** 32 54N 105 57W
Alamos, *Mexico* **86 B3** 27 0N 109 0W
Alamosa, *U.S.A.* **83 H11** 37 28N 105 52W
Åland, *Finland* **9 F19** 60 15N 20 0 E
Ålands hav, *Sweden* **9 F18** 60 0N 19 30 E
Alandur, *India* **40 N12** 13 0N 80 15 E
Alania = North Ossetia □, *Russia* **25 F7** 43 30N 44 30 E
Alanya, *Turkey* **25 G5** 36 38N 32 0 E
Alaotra, Farihin', *Madag.* **57 B8** 17 30S 48 30 E
Alapayevsk, *Russia* **26 D7** 57 52N 61 42 E
Alaşehir, *Turkey* **21 E13** 38 23N 28 30 E
Alaska □, *U.S.A.* **68 B5** 64 0N 154 0W
Alaska, G. of, *Pac. Oc.* **68 C5** 58 0N 145 0W
Alaska Peninsula, *U.S.A.* **68 C4** 56 0N 159 0W
Alaska Range, *U.S.A.* **68 B4** 62 50N 151 0W
Älät, *Azerbaijan* **25 G8** 39 58N 49 25 E
Alatyr, *Russia* **24 D8** 54 55N 46 35 E
Alausi, *Ecuador* **92 D3** 2 0S 78 50W
Alava, C., *U.S.A.* **82 B1** 48 10N 124 44W
Alavus, *Finland* **9 E20** 62 35N 23 36 E
Alawoona, *Australia* **63 E3** 34 45S 140 30 E
'Alayh, *Lebanon* **47 B4** 33 46N 35 33 E
Alba, *Italy* **18 D8** 44 42N 8 2 E
Alba-Iulia, *Romania* **17 E12** 46 8N 23 39 E
Albacete, *Spain* **19 C5** 39 0N 1 50W
Albacutya, L., *Australia* **63 F3** 35 45S 141 58 E
Albanel, L., *Canada* **70 B5** 50 55N 73 12W
Albania ■, *Europe* **21 D9** 41 0N 20 0 E
Albany, *Australia* **61 G2** 35 1S 117 58 E
Albany, *Ga., U.S.A.* **77 K3** 31 35N 84 10W
Albany, *N.Y., U.S.A.* **79 D11** 42 39N 73 45W
Albany, *Oreg., U.S.A.* **82 D2** 44 38N 123 6W
Albany, *Tex., U.S.A.* **81 J5** 32 44N 99 18W
Albany →, *Canada* **70 B3** 52 17N 81 31W
Albardón, *Argentina* **94 C2** 31 20S 68 30W
Albatross B., *Australia* **62 A3** 12 45S 141 30 E
Albemarle, *U.S.A.* **77 H5** 35 21N 80 11W
Albemarle Sd., *U.S.A.* **77 H7** 36 5N 76 0W
Alberche →, *Spain* **19 C3** 39 58N 4 46W
Alberdi, *Paraguay* **94 B4** 26 14S 58 20W
Albert, L., *Australia* **63 F2** 35 30S 139 10 E
Albert Edward Ra., *Australia* **60 C4** 18 17S 127 57 E
Albert L., *Africa* **54 B3** 1 30N 31 0 E
Albert Lea, *U.S.A.* **80 D8** 43 39N 93 22W
Albert Nile →, *Uganda* **54 B3** 3 36N 32 2 E
Albert Town, *Bahamas* **89 B5** 22 37N 74 33W
Alberta □, *Canada* **72 C6** 54 40N 115 0W
Alberti, *Argentina* **94 D3** 35 1S 60 16W
Albertinia, *S. Africa* **56 E3** 34 11S 21 34 E
Alberton, *Canada* **71 C7** 46 50N 64 0W
Albertville = Kalemie, *Dem. Rep. of the Congo* **54 D2** 5 55S 29 9 E
Albertville, *France* **18 D7** 45 40N 6 22 E
Albertville, *U.S.A.* **77 H2** 34 16N 86 13W
Albi, *France* **18 E5** 43 56N 2 9 E
Albia, *U.S.A.* **80 E8** 41 2N 92 48W
Albina, *Surinam* **93 B8** 5 37N 54 15W
Albina, Ponta, *Angola* **56 B1** 15 52S 11 44 E
Albion, *Mich., U.S.A.* **76 D3** 42 15N 84 45W
Albion, *Nebr., U.S.A.* **80 E6** 41 42N 98 0W
Albion, *Pa., U.S.A.* **78 E4** 41 53N 80 22W
Alborán, *Medit. S.* **19 E4** 35 57N 3 0W
Ålborg, *Denmark* **9 H13** 57 2N 9 54 E
Alborz, Reshteh-ye Kūhhā-ye, *Iran* **45 C7** 36 0N 52 0 E
Albuquerque, *U.S.A.* **83 J10** 35 5N 106 39W
Albuquerque, Cayos de, *Caribbean* **88 D3** 12 10N 81 50W
Alburg, *U.S.A.* **79 B11** 44 59N 73 18W
Albury-Wodonga, *Australia* **63 F4** 36 3S 146 56 E
Alcalá de Henares, *Spain* **19 B4** 40 28N 3 22W
Alcalá la Real, *Spain* **19 D4** 37 27N 3 57W
Álcamo, *Italy* **20 F5** 37 59N 12 55 E
Alcaniz, *Spain* **19 B5** 41 2N 0 8W
Alcântara, *Brazil* **93 D10** 2 20S 44 30W
Alcántara, Embalse de, *Spain* **19 C2** 39 44N 6 50W
Alcantarilla, *Spain* **19 D5** 37 59N 1 12W
Alcaraz, Sierra de, *Spain* **19 C4** 38 40N 2 20W
Alcaudete, *Spain* **19 D3** 37 35N 4 5W
Alcázar de San Juan, *Spain* **19 C4** 39 24N 3 12W
Alchevsk, *Ukraine* **25 E6** 48 30N 38 45 E
Alcira = Alzira, *Spain* **19 C5** 39 9N 0 30W
Alcova, *U.S.A.* **82 E10** 42 34N 106 43W
Alcoy, *Spain* **19 C5** 38 43N 0 30W
Alcúdia, *Spain* **22 B10** 39 51N 3 7 E
Alcúdia, B. d', *Spain* **22 B10** 39 47N 3 15 E
Aldabra Is., *Seychelles* **49 G8** 9 22S 46 28 E
Aldama, *Mexico* **87 C5** 23 0N 98 4W
Aldan, *Russia* **27 D13** 58 40N 125 30 E
Aldan →, *Russia* **27 C13** 63 28N 129 35 E
Aldea, Pta. de la, *Canary Is.* **22 G4** 28 0N 15 50W
Aldeburgh, *U.K.* **11 E9** 52 10N 1 37 E
Alder Pk., *U.S.A.* **84 K5** 35 53N 121 22W
Alderney, *U.K.* **11 H5** 49 42N 2 11W
Aldershot, *U.K.* **11 F7** 51 15N 0 44W
Aledo, *U.S.A.* **80 E9** 41 12N 90 45W
Aleg, *Mauritania* **50 E3** 17 3N 13 55W
Alegranza, *Canary Is.* **22 E6** 29 23N 13 32W
Alegranza, I., *Canary Is.* **22 E6** 29 23N 13 32W
Alegre, *Brazil* **95 A7** 20 50S 41 30W
Alegrete, *Brazil* **95 B4** 29 40S 56 0W
Aleisk, *Russia* **26 D9** 52 40N 83 0 E
Aleksandriya = Oleksandriya, *Ukraine* **17 C14** 50 37N 26 19 E
Aleksandrov Gay, *Russia* **25 D8** 50 9N 48 34 E
Aleksandrovsk-Sakhalinskiy, *Russia* **27 D15** 50 50N 142 20 E
Além Paraíba, *Brazil* **95 A7** 21 52S 42 41W
Alemania, *Argentina* **94 B2** 25 40S 65 30W
Alemania, *Chile* **94 B2** 25 10S 69 55W
Alençon, *France* **18 B4** 48 27N 0 4 E
Alenquer, *Brazil* **93 D8** 1 56S 54 46W
Alenuihaha Channel, *U.S.A.* **74 H17** 20 30N 156 0W
Aleppo = Ḩalab, *Syria* **44 B3** 36 10N 37 15 E
Alès, *France* **18 D6** 44 9N 4 5 E
Alessándria, *Italy* **18 D8** 44 54N 8 37 E
Ålesund, *Norway* **9 E12** 62 28N 6 12 E
Aleutian Is., *Pac. Oc.* **68 C2** 52 0N 175 0W
Aleutian Trench, *Pac. Oc.* **64 C10** 48 0N 180 0 E
Alexander, *U.S.A.* **80 B3** 47 51N 103 39W
Alexander, Mt., *Australia* **61 E3** 28 58S 120 16 E
Alexander Arch., *U.S.A.* **68 C6** 56 0N 136 0W
Alexander Bay, *S. Africa* **56 D2** 28 40S 16 30 E
Alexander City, *U.S.A.* **77 J3** 32 56N 85 58W
Alexander I., *Antarctica* **5 C17** 69 0S 70 0W
Alexandra, *Australia* **63 F4** 37 8S 145 40 E
Alexandra, *N.Z.* **59 L2** 45 14S 169 25 E
Alexandra Falls, *Canada* **72 A5** 60 29N 116 18W
Alexandria = El Iskandarîya, *Egypt* **51 B11** 31 13N 29 58 E
Alexandria, *B.C., Canada* **72 C4** 52 35N 122 27W
Alexandria, *Ont., Canada* **79 A10** 45 19N 74 38W
Alexandria, *Romania* **17 G13** 43 57N 25 24 E
Alexandria, *S. Africa* **56 E4** 33 38S 26 28 E
Alexandria, *U.K.* **12 F4** 55 59N 4 35W
Alexandria, *La., U.S.A.* **81 K8** 31 18N 92 27W
Alexandria, *Minn., U.S.A.* **80 C7** 45 53N 95 22W
Alexandria, *S. Dak., U.S.A.* **80 D6** 43 39N 97 47W
Alexandria, *Va., U.S.A.* **76 F7** 38 48N 77 3W
Alexandria Bay, *U.S.A.* **79 B9** 44 20N 75 55W
Alexandrina, L., *Australia* **63 F2** 35 25S 139 10 E
Alexandroúpolis, *Greece* **21 D11** 40 50N 25 54 E
Alexis →, *Canada* **71 B8** 52 33N 56 8W
Alexis Creek, *Canada* **72 C4** 52 10N 123 20W
Alfabia, *Spain* **22 B9** 39 44N 2 44 E
Alfenas, *Brazil* **95 A6** 21 20S 46 10W
Alford, *Aberds., U.K.* **12 D6** 57 14N 2 41W
Alford, *Lincs., U.K.* **10 D8** 53 15N 0 10 E
Alfred, *Maine, U.S.A.* **79 C14** 43 29N 70 43W
Alfred, *N.Y., U.S.A.* **78 D7** 42 16N 77 48W
Alfreton, *U.K.* **10 D6** 53 6N 1 24W
Alga, *Kazakstan* **25 E10** 49 53N 57 20 E
Algaida, *Spain* **22 B9** 39 33N 2 53 E
Ålgård, *Norway* **9 G11** 58 46N 5 53 E
Algarve, *Portugal* **19 D1** 36 58N 8 20W
Algeciras, *Spain* **19 D3** 36 9N 5 28W
Algemesí, *Spain* **19 C5** 39 11N 0 27W
Alger, *Algeria* **50 A6** 36 42N 3 8 E
Algeria ■, *Africa* **50 C6** 28 30N 2 0 E
Alghero, *Italy* **20 D3** 40 33N 8 19 E
Algiers = Alger, *Algeria* **50 A6** 36 42N 3 8 E
Algoa B., *S. Africa* **56 E4** 33 50S 25 45 E
Algoma, *U.S.A.* **76 C2** 44 36N 87 26W
Algona, *U.S.A.* **80 D7** 43 4N 94 14W
Algonac, *U.S.A.* **78 D2** 42 37N 82 32W
Algonquin Prov. Park, *Canada* **70 C4** 45 50N 78 30W
Algorta, *Uruguay* **96 C5** 32 25S 57 23W
Alhambra, *U.S.A.* **85 L8** 34 8N 118 6W
Alhucemas = Al Hoceïma, *Morocco* **50 A5** 35 8N 3 58W
'Alī al Gharbī, *Iraq* **44 C5** 32 30N 46 45 E
Alī ash Sharqī, *Iraq* **44 C5** 32 7N 46 44 E
'Alī Khēl, *Afghan.* **42 C3** 33 57N 69 43 E
Alī Shāh, *Iran* **44 B5** 38 9N 45 50 E
'Alīābād, *Khorāsān, Iran* **45 C8** 32 30N 57 30 E
'Alīābād, *Kordestān, Iran* **44 C5** 35 4N 46 58 E
'Alīābād, *Yazd, Iran* **45 D7** 31 41N 53 49 E
Aliağa, *Turkey* **21 E12** 38 47N 26 59 E
Aliákmon →, *Greece* **21 D10** 40 30N 22 36 E
Alicante, *Spain* **19 C5** 38 23N 0 30W
Alice, *S. Africa* **56 E4** 32 48S 26 55 E
Alice, *U.S.A.* **81 M5** 27 45N 98 5W
Alice →, *Queens., Australia* **62 C3** 24 2S 144 50 E
Alice →, *Queens., Australia* **62 B3** 15 35S 142 20 E
Alice Arm, *Canada* **72 B3** 55 29N 129 31W
Alice Springs, *Australia* **62 C1** 23 40S 133 50 E
Alicedale, *S. Africa* **56 E4** 33 15S 26 4 E
Aliceville, *U.S.A.* **77 J1** 33 8N 88 9W
Aliganj, *India* **43 F8** 27 30N 79 10 E
Aligarh, *Raj., India* **42 G7** 25 55N 76 15 E
Aligarh, *Ut. P., India* **42 F8** 27 55N 78 10 E
Alīgūdarz, *Iran* **45 C6** 33 25N 49 45 E
Alimnia, *Greece* **23 C9** 36 16N 27 43 E
Alingsås, *Sweden* **9 H15** 57 56N 12 31 E
Alipur, *Pakistan* **42 E4** 29 25N 70 55 E
Alipur Duar, *India* **41 F16** 26 30N 89 35 E
Aliquippa, *U.S.A.* **78 F4** 40 37N 80 15W
Alitus = Alytus, *Lithuania* **9 J21** 54 24N 24 3 E
Aliwal North, *S. Africa* **56 E4** 30 45S 26 45 E
Alix, *Canada* **72 C6** 52 24N 113 11W
Aljustrel, *Portugal* **19 D1** 37 55N 8 10W
Alkmaar, *Neths.* **15 B4** 52 37N 4 45 E
All American Canal, *U.S.A.* **83 K6** 32 45N 115 15W
Allagash →, *U.S.A.* **77 B11** 47 5N 69 3W
Allah Dad, *Pakistan* **42 G2** 25 38N 67 34 E
Allahabad, *India* **43 G9** 25 25N 81 58 E
Allan, *Canada* **73 C7** 51 53N 106 4W
Allanmyo, *Burma* **41 K19** 19 30N 95 17 E
Allanridge, *S. Africa* **56 D4** 27 45S 26 40 E
Allegany, *U.S.A.* **78 D6** 42 6N 78 30W
Allegheny →, *U.S.A.* **78 F5** 40 27N 80 1W
Allegheny Mts., *U.S.A.* **76 G6** 38 15N 80 10W
Allegheny Reservoir, *U.S.A.* **78 E6** 41 50N 79 0W
Allen, Bog of, *Ireland* **13 C5** 53 15N 7 0W
Allen, L., *Ireland* **13 B3** 54 8N 8 4W
Allendale, *U.S.A.* **77 J5** 33 1N 81 18W
Allende, *Mexico* **86 B4** 28 20N 100 50W
Allentown, *U.S.A.* **79 F9** 40 37N 75 29W
Alleppey, *India* **40 Q10** 9 30N 76 28 E
Aller →, *Germany* **16 B5** 52 56N 9 12 E
Alliance, *Nebr., U.S.A.* **80 D3** 42 6N 102 52W
Alliance, *Ohio, U.S.A.* **78 F3** 40 55N 81 6W
Allier →, *France* **18 C5** 46 57N 3 4 E
Alliford Bay, *Canada* **72 C2** 53 12N 131 58W
Alliston, *Canada* **78 B5** 44 9N 79 52W
Alloa, *U.K.* **12 E5** 56 7N 3 47W
Allora, *Australia* **63 D5** 28 2S 152 0 E
Alluitsup Paa = Sydprøven, *Greenland* **4 C5** 60 30N 45 35W
Alma, *Canada* **71 C5** 48 35N 71 40W
Alma, *Ga., U.S.A.* **77 K4** 31 33N 82 28W
Alma, *Kans., U.S.A.* **80 F6** 39 1N 96 17W
Alma, *Mich., U.S.A.* **76 D3** 43 23N 84 39W
Alma, *Nebr., U.S.A.* **80 E5** 40 6N 99 22W
Alma Ata = Almaty, *Kazakstan* **26 E8** 43 15N 76 57 E
Almada, *Portugal* **19 C1** 38 40N 9 9W
Almaden, *Australia* **62 B3** 17 22S 144 40 E
Almadén, *Spain* **19 C3** 38 49N 4 52W
Almanor, L., *U.S.A.* **82 F3** 40 14N 121 9W
Almansa, *Spain* **19 C5** 38 51N 1 5W
Almanzor, Pico, *Spain* **19 B3** 40 15N 5 18W
Almanzora →, *Spain* **19 D5** 37 14N 1 46W
Almaty, *Kazakstan* **26 E8** 43 15N 76 57 E
Almazán, *Spain* **19 B4** 41 30N 2 30W
Almeirim, *Brazil* **93 D8** 1 30S 52 34W
Almelo, *Neths.* **15 B6** 52 22N 6 42 E
Almendralejo, *Spain* **19 C2** 38 41N 6 26W
Almere-Stad, *Neths.* **15 B5** 52 20N 5 15 E
Almería, *Spain* **19 D4** 36 52N 2 27W
Almirante, *Panama* **88 E3** 9 10N 82 30W
Almiroú, Kólpos, *Greece* **23 D6** 35 23N 24 20 E
Almond, *U.S.A.* **78 D7** 42 19N 77 44W
Almont, *U.S.A.* **78 D1** 42 55N 83 3W
Almonte, *Canada* **79 A8** 45 14N 76 12W
Almora, *India* **43 E8** 29 38N 79 40 E
Alness, *U.K.* **12 D4** 57 41N 4 16W
Alnmouth, *U.K.* **10 B6** 55 24N 1 37W
Alnwick, *U.K.* **10 B6** 55 24N 1 42W
Aloi, *Uganda* **54 B3** 2 16N 33 10 E
Alon, *Burma* **41 H19** 22 12N 95 5 E
Alor, *Indonesia* **37 F6** 8 15S 124 30 E
Alor Setar, *Malaysia* **39 J3** 6 7N 100 22 E
Alot, *India* **42 H6** 23 56N 75 40 E
Aloysius, Mt., *Australia* **61 E4** 26 0S 128 38 E
Alpaugh, *U.S.A.* **84 K7** 35 53N 119 29W
Alpena, *U.S.A.* **76 C4** 45 4N 83 27W
Alpha, *Australia* **62 C4** 23 39S 146 37 E
Alphen aan den Rijn, *Neths.* **15 B4** 52 7N 4 40 E
Alpine, *Ariz., U.S.A.* **83 K9** 33 51N 109 9W
Alpine, *Calif., U.S.A.* **85 N10** 32 50N 116 46W
Alpine, *Tex., U.S.A.* **81 K3** 30 22N 103 40W
Alps, *Europe* **18 C8** 46 30N 9 30 E
Alsace, *France* **18 B7** 48 15N 7 25 E
Alsask, *Canada* **73 C7** 51 21N 109 59W
Alsasua, *Spain* **19 A4** 42 54N 2 10W
Alsek →, *U.S.A.* **72 B1** 59 10N 138 12W
Alsten, *Norway* **8 D15** 65 58N 12 40 E
Alston, *U.K.* **10 C5** 54 49N 2 25W
Alta, *Norway* **8 B20** 69 57N 23 10 E
Alta Gracia, *Argentina* **94 C3** 31 40S 64 30W
Alta Sierra, *U.S.A.* **85 K8** 35 42N 118 33W
Altaelva →, *Norway* **8 B20** 69 54N 23 17 E
Altafjorden, *Norway* **8 A20** 70 5N 23 5 E
Altai = Aerhtai Shan, *Mongolia* **32 B4** 46 40N 92 45 E
Altamaha →, *U.S.A.* **77 K5** 31 20N 81 20W
Altamira, *Brazil* **93 D8** 3 12S 52 10W
Altamira, *Chile* **94 B2** 25 47S 69 51W
Altamira, *Mexico* **87 C5** 22 24N 97 55W
Altamont, *U.S.A.* **79 D10** 42 43N 74 3W
Altamura, *Italy* **20 D7** 40 49N 16 33 E
Altanbulag, *Mongolia* **32 A5** 50 16N 106 30 E
Altar, *Mexico* **86 A2** 30 40N 111 50W
Altar, Desierto de, *Mexico* **86 B2** 30 10N 112 0W
Altata, *Mexico* **86 C3** 24 30N 108 0W
Altavista, *U.S.A.* **76 G6** 37 6N 79 17W
Altay, *China* **32 B3** 47 48N 88 10 E
Altea, *Spain* **19 C5** 38 38N 0 2W
Altiplano = Bolivian Plateau, *S. Amer.* **90 E4** 20 0S 67 30W
Alto Araguaia, *Brazil* **93 G8** 17 15S 53 20W
Alto Cuchumatanes = Cuchumatanes, Sierra de los, *Guatemala* **88 C1** 15 35N 91 25W
Alto del Carmen, *Chile* **94 B1** 28 46S 70 30W
Alto del Inca, *Chile* **94 A2** 24 10S 68 10W
Alto Ligonha, *Mozam.* **55 F4** 15 30S 38 11 E
Alto Molocue, *Mozam.* **55 F4** 15 50S 37 35 E
Alto Paraguay □, *Paraguay* **94 A4** 21 0S 58 30W
Alto Paraná □, *Paraguay* **95 B5** 25 30S 54 50W
Alton, *Canada* **78 C4** 43 54N 80 5W
Alton, *U.K.* **11 F7** 51 9N 0 59W
Alton, *Ill., U.S.A.* **80 F9** 38 53N 90 11W
Alton, *N.H., U.S.A.* **79 C13** 43 27N 71 13W
Altoona, *U.S.A.* **78 F6** 40 31N 78 24W
Altūn Kūprī, *Iraq* **44 C5** 35 45N 44 9 E
Altun Shan, *China* **32 C3** 38 30N 88 0 E
Alturas, *U.S.A.* **82 F3** 41 29N 120 32W
Altus, *U.S.A.* **81 H5** 34 38N 99 20W
Alucra, *Turkey* **25 F6** 40 22N 38 47 E
Alūksne, *Latvia* **9 H22** 57 24N 27 3 E
Alunite, *U.S.A.* **85 K12** 35 59N 114 55W
Alusi, *Indonesia* **37 F8** 7 35S 131 40 E
Alva, *U.S.A.* **81 G5** 36 48N 98 40W
Alvarado, *Mexico* **87 D5** 18 40N 95 50W
Alvarado, *U.S.A.* **81 J6** 32 24N 97 13W
Alvaro Obregón, Presa, *Mexico* **86 B3** 27 55N 109 52W
Alvear, *Argentina* **94 B4** 29 5S 56 30W
Alvesta, *Sweden* **9 H16** 56 54N 14 35 E
Alvin, *U.S.A.* **81 L7** 29 26N 95 15W
Alvinston, *Canada* **78 D3** 42 49N 81 52W
Älvkarleby, *Sweden* **9 F17** 60 34N 17 26 E
Alvord Desert, *U.S.A.* **82 E4** 42 30N 118 25W
Älvsbyn, *Sweden* **8 D19** 65 40N 21 0 E
Alwar, *India* **42 F7** 27 38N 76 34 E
Alxa Zuoqi, *China* **34 E3** 38 50N 105 40 E
Alyangula, *Australia* **62 A2** 13 55S 136 30 E
Alyata = Älät, *Azerbaijan* **25 G8** 39 58N 49 25 E
Alyth, *U.K.* **12 E5** 56 38N 3 13W
Alytus, *Lithuania* **9 J21** 54 24N 24 3 E
Alzada, *U.S.A.* **80 C2** 45 2N 104 25W
Alzira, *Spain* **19 C5** 39 9N 0 30W
Am-Timan, *Chad* **51 F10** 11 0N 20 10 E
Amadeus, L., *Australia* **61 D5** 24 54S 131 0 E

Amadi

Amadi, *Dem. Rep. of the Congo* **54 B2** 3 40N 26 40 E
Amâdi, *Sudan* **51 G12** 5 29N 30 25 E
Amadjuak L., *Canada* **69 B12** 65 0N 71 8W
Amagansett, *U.S.A.* **79 F12** 40 59N 72 9W
Amagasaki, *Japan* **31 G7** 34 42N 135 20 E
Amahai, *Indonesia* **37 E7** 3 20S 128 55 E
Amakusa-Shotō, *Japan* **31 H5** 32 15N 130 10 E
Åmål, *Sweden* **9 G15** 59 3N 12 42 E
Amaliás, *Greece* **21 F9** 37 47N 21 22 E
Amalner, *India* **40 J9** 21 5N 75 5 E
Amamapare, *Indonesia* **37 E9** 4 53S 136 38 E
Amambaí, *Brazil* **95 A4** 23 5S 55 13W
Amambaí →, *Brazil* **95 A5** 23 22S 53 56W
Amambay □, *Paraguay* **95 A4** 23 0S 56 0W
Amambay, Cordillera de, *S. Amer.* **95 A4** 23 0S 55 45W
Amami-Guntō, *Japan* **31 L4** 27 16N 129 21 E
Amami-Ō-Shima, *Japan* **31 L4** 28 0N 129 0 E
Amaná, L., *Brazil* **92 D6** 2 35S 64 40W
Amanat →, *India* **43 G11** 24 7N 84 4 E
Amanda Park, *U.S.A.* **84 C3** 47 28N 123 55W
Amangeldy, *Kazakstan* **26 D7** 50 10N 65 10 E
Amapá, *Brazil* **93 C8** 2 5N 50 50W
Amapá □, *Brazil* **93 C8** 1 40N 52 0W
Amarante, *Brazil* **93 E10** 6 14S 42 50W
Amaranth, *Canada* **73 C9** 50 36N 98 43W
Amargosa →, *U.S.A.* **85 J10** 36 14N 116 51W
Amargosa Range, *U.S.A.* **85 J10** 36 20N 116 45W
Amári, *Greece* **23 D6** 35 13N 24 40 E
Amarillo, *U.S.A.* **81 H4** 35 13N 101 50W
Amarkantak, *India* **43 H9** 22 40N 81 45 E
Amaro, Mte., *Italy* **20 C6** 42 5N 14 5 E
Amarpur, *India* **43 G12** 25 5N 87 0 E
Amarwara, *India* **43 H8** 22 18N 79 10 E
Amasya □, *Turkey* **25 F6** 40 40N 35 50 E
Amata, *Australia* **61 E5** 26 9S 131 9 E
Amatikulu, *S. Africa* **57 D5** 29 3S 31 33 E
Amatitlán, *Guatemala* **88 D1** 14 29N 90 38W
Amay, *Belgium* **15 D5** 50 33N 5 19 E
Amazon = Amazonas →, *S. Amer.* **93 D9** 0 5S 50 0W
Amazonas □, *Brazil* **92 E6** 5 0S 65 0W
Amazonas →, *S. Amer.* **93 D9** 0 5S 50 0W
Ambah, *India* **42 F8** 26 43N 78 13 E
Ambahakily, *Madag.* **57 C7** 21 36S 43 41 E
Ambala, *India* **42 D7** 30 23N 76 56 E
Ambalavao, *Madag.* **57 C8** 21 50S 46 56 E
Ambanja, *Madag.* **57 A8** 13 40S 48 27 E
Ambarchik, *Russia* **27 C17** 69 40N 162 20 E
Ambarijeby, *Madag.* **57 A8** 14 56S 47 41 E
Ambaro, Helodranon', *Madag.* **57 A8** 13 23S 48 38 E
Ambato, *Ecuador* **92 D3** 1 5S 78 42W
Ambato, Sierra de, *Argentina* **94 B2** 28 25S 66 10W
Ambato Boeny, *Madag.* **57 B8** 16 28S 46 43 E
Ambatofinandrahana, *Madag.* **57 C8** 20 33S 46 48 E
Ambatolampy, *Madag.* **57 B8** 19 20S 47 35 E
Ambatondrazaka, *Madag.* **57 B8** 17 55S 48 28 E
Ambatosoratra, *Madag.* **57 B8** 17 37S 48 31 E
Ambenja, *Madag.* **57 B8** 15 17S 46 58 E
Amberg, *Germany* **16 D6** 49 26N 11 52 E
Ambergris Cay, *Belize* **87 D7** 18 0N 88 0W
Amberley, *N.Z.* **59 K4** 43 9S 172 44 E
Ambikapur, *India* **43 H10** 23 15N 83 15 E
Ambilobé, *Madag.* **57 A8** 13 10S 49 3 E
Ambinanindrano, *Madag.* **57 C8** 20 5S 48 23 E
Amble, *U.K.* **10 B6** 55 20N 1 36W
Ambleside, *U.K.* **10 C5** 54 26N 2 58W
Ambo, *Peru* **92 F3** 10 5S 76 10W
Ambodifototra, *Madag.* **57 B8** 16 59S 49 52 E
Ambodilazana, *Madag.* **57 B8** 18 6S 49 10 E
Ambohimahasoa, *Madag.* **57 C8** 21 7S 47 13 E
Ambohimanga, *Madag.* **57 C8** 20 52S 47 36 E
Ambohitra, *Madag.* **57 A8** 12 30S 49 10 E
Amboise, *France* **18 C4** 47 24N 1 2 E
Ambon, *Indonesia* **37 E7** 3 35S 128 20 E
Amboseli, L., *Kenya* **54 C4** 2 40S 37 10 E
Ambositra, *Madag.* **57 C8** 20 31S 47 25 E
Ambovombe, *Madag.* **57 D8** 25 11S 46 5 E
Amboy, *U.S.A.* **85 L11** 34 33N 115 45W
Amboyna Cay, *S. China Sea* **36 C4** 7 50N 112 50 E
Ambridge, *U.S.A.* **78 F4** 40 36N 80 14W
Ambriz, *Angola* **52 F2** 7 48S 13 8 E
Amchitka I., *U.S.A.* **68 C1** 51 32N 179 0 E
Amderma, *Russia* **26 C7** 69 45N 61 30 E
Amdhi, *India* **43 H9** 23 51N 81 27 E
Ameca, *Mexico* **86 C4** 20 30N 104 0W
Ameca →, *Mexico* **86 C3** 20 40N 105 15W
Amecameca, *Mexico* **87 D5** 19 7N 98 46W
Ameland, *Neths.* **15 A5** 53 27N 5 45 E
Amenia, *U.S.A.* **79 E11** 41 51N 73 33W
American Falls, *U.S.A.* **82 E7** 42 47N 112 51W
American Falls Reservoir, *U.S.A.* **82 E7** 42 47N 112 52W
American Fork, *U.S.A.* **82 F8** 40 23N 111 48W
American Highland, *Antarctica* **5 D6** 73 0S 75 0 E
American Samoa ■, *Pac. Oc.* **59 B13** 14 20S 170 40W
Americana, *Brazil* **95 A6** 22 45S 47 20W
Americus, *U.S.A.* **77 K3** 32 4N 84 14W
Amersfoort, *Neths.* **15 B5** 52 9N 5 23 E
Amersfoort, *S. Africa* **57 D4** 26 59S 29 53 E
Amery Ice Shelf, *Antarctica* **5 C6** 69 30S 72 0 E
Ames, *U.S.A.* **80 E8** 42 2N 93 37W
Amesbury, *U.S.A.* **79 D14** 42 51N 70 56W
Amet, *India* **42 G5** 25 18N 73 56 E
Amga, *Russia* **27 C14** 60 50N 132 0 E
Amga →, *Russia* **27 C14** 62 38N 134 32 E
Amgu, *Russia* **27 E14** 45 45N 137 15 E
Amgun →, *Russia* **27 D14** 52 56N 139 38 E
Amherst, *Burma* **41 L20** 16 2N 97 20 E
Amherst, *Canada* **71 C7** 45 48N 64 8W
Amherst, *Mass., U.S.A.* **79 D12** 42 23N 72 31W
Amherst, *N.Y., U.S.A.* **78 D6** 42 59N 78 48W
Amherst, *Ohio, U.S.A.* **78 E2** 41 24N 82 14W
Amherst I., *Canada* **79 B8** 44 8N 76 43W
Amherstburg, *Canada* **70 D3** 42 6N 83 6W
Amiata, Mte., *Italy* **20 C4** 42 53N 11 37 E
Amidon, *U.S.A.* **80 B3** 46 29N 103 19W
Amiens, *France* **18 B5** 49 54N 2 16 E
Amīrābād, *Iran* **44 C5** 33 20N 46 16 E
Amirante Is., *Seychelles* **28 K9** 6 0S 53 0 E
Amisk L., *Canada* **73 C8** 54 35N 102 15W
Amistad, Presa de la, *Mexico* **86 B4** 29 24N 101 0W
Amite, *U.S.A.* **81 K9** 30 44N 90 30W
Amla, *India* **42 J8** 21 56N 78 7 E
Amlia I., *U.S.A.* **68 C2** 52 4N 173 30W
Amlwch, *U.K.* **10 D3** 53 24N 4 20W
'Ammān, *Jordan* **47 D4** 31 57N 35 52 E
'Ammān □, *Jordan* **47 D5** 31 40N 36 30 E
Ammanford, *U.K.* **11 F4** 51 48N 3 59W
Ammassalik = Angmagssalik, *Greenland* **4 C6** 65 40N 37 20W
Ammon, *U.S.A.* **82 E8** 43 28N 111 58W
Amnat Charoen, *Thailand* **38 E5** 15 51N 104 38 E
Amnura, *Bangla.* **43 G13** 24 37N 88 25 E
Āmol, *Iran* **45 B7** 36 23N 52 20 E
Amorgós, *Greece* **21 F11** 36 50N 25 57 E
Amory, *U.S.A.* **77 J1** 33 59N 88 29W
Amos, *Canada* **70 C4** 48 35N 78 5W
Åmot, *Norway* **9 G13** 59 57N 9 54 E
Amoy = Xiamen, *China* **33 D6** 24 25N 118 4 E
Ampang, *Malaysia* **39 L3** 3 8N 101 45 E
Ampanihy, *Madag.* **57 C7** 24 40S 44 45 E
Ampasindava, Helodranon', *Madag.* **57 A8** 13 40S 48 15 E
Ampasindava, Saikanosy, *Madag.* **57 A8** 13 42S 47 55 E
Ampenan, *Indonesia* **36 F5** 8 35S 116 13 E
Amper →, *Germany* **16 D6** 48 29N 11 55 E
Ampotaka, *Madag.* **57 D7** 25 3S 44 41 E
Ampoza, *Madag.* **57 C7** 22 20S 44 44 E
Amqui, *Canada* **71 C6** 48 28N 67 27W
Amravati, *India* **40 J10** 20 55N 77 45 E
Amreli, *India* **42 J4** 21 35N 71 17 E
Amritsar, *India* **42 D6** 31 35N 74 57 E
Amroha, *India* **43 E8** 28 53N 78 30 E
Amsterdam, *Neths.* **15 B4** 52 23N 4 54 E
Amsterdam, *U.S.A.* **79 D10** 42 56N 74 11W
Amsterdam, I., *Ind. Oc.* **3 F13** 38 30S 77 30 E
Amstetten, *Austria* **16 D8** 48 7N 14 51 E
Amudarya →, *Uzbekistan* **26 E6** 43 58N 59 34 E
Amundsen Gulf, *Canada* **68 A7** 71 0N 124 0W
Amundsen Sea, *Antarctica* **5 D15** 72 0S 115 0W
Amuntai, *Indonesia* **36 E5** 2 28S 115 25 E
Amur →, *Russia* **27 D15** 52 56N 141 10 E
Amurang, *Indonesia* **37 D6** 1 5N 124 40 E
Amuri Pass, *N.Z.* **59 K4** 42 31S 172 11 E
Amursk, *Russia* **27 D14** 50 14N 136 54 E
Amyderya = Amudarya →, *Uzbekistan* **26 E6** 43 58N 59 34 E
An Bien, *Vietnam* **39 H5** 9 45N 105 0 E
An Hoa, *Vietnam* **38 E7** 15 40N 108 5 E
An Nabatīyah at Tahta, *Lebanon* **47 B4** 33 23N 35 27 E
An Nabk, *Si. Arabia* **44 D3** 31 20N 37 20 E
An Nabk, *Syria* **47 A5** 34 2N 36 44 E
An Nabk Abū Qaṣr, *Si. Arabia* **44 D3** 30 21N 38 34 E
An Nafūd, *Si. Arabia* **44 D4** 28 15N 41 0 E
An Najaf, *Iraq* **44 C5** 32 3N 44 15 E
An Nāṣirīyah, *Iraq* **44 D5** 31 0N 46 15 E
An Nhon, *Vietnam* **38 F7** 13 55N 109 7 E
An Nu'ayrīyah, *Si. Arabia* **45 E6** 27 30N 48 30 E
An Nuwayb'ī, W. →, *Si. Arabia* **47 F3** 29 18N 34 57 E
An Thoi, Dao, *Vietnam* **39 H5** 9 58N 104 0 E
An Uaimh, *Ireland* **13 C5** 53 39N 6 41W
Anabar →, *Russia* **27 B12** 73 8N 113 36 E
'Anabtā, *West Bank* **47 C4** 32 19N 35 7 E
Anaconda, *U.S.A.* **82 C7** 46 8N 112 57W
Anacortes, *U.S.A.* **84 B4** 48 30N 122 37W
Anadarko, *U.S.A.* **81 H5** 35 4N 98 15W
Anadolu, *Turkey* **25 G5** 39 0N 30 0 E
Anadyr, *Russia* **27 C18** 64 35N 177 20 E
Anadyr →, *Russia* **27 C18** 64 55N 176 5 E
Anadyrskiy Zaliv, *Russia* **27 C19** 64 0N 180 0 E
Anaga, Pta. de, *Canary Is.* **22 F3** 28 34N 16 9W
'Ānah, *Iraq* **44 C4** 34 25N 42 0 E
Anaheim, *U.S.A.* **85 M9** 33 50N 117 55W
Anahim Lake, *Canada* **72 C3** 52 28N 125 18W
Anáhuac, *Mexico* **86 B4** 27 14N 100 9W
Anakapalle, *India* **41 L13** 17 42N 83 6 E
Anakie, *Australia* **62 C4** 23 32S 147 45 E
Analalava, *Madag.* **57 A8** 14 35S 48 0 E
Análipsis, *Greece* **23 A3** 39 36N 19 55 E
Anambar →, *Pakistan* **42 D3** 30 15N 68 50 E
Anambas, Kepulauan, *Indonesia* **39 L6** 3 20N 106 30 E
Anambas Is. = Anambas, Kepulauan, *Indonesia* **39 L6** 3 20N 106 30 E
Anamosa, *U.S.A.* **80 D9** 42 7N 91 17W
Anamur, *Turkey* **25 G5** 36 8N 32 58 E
Anan, *Japan* **31 H7** 33 54N 134 40 E
Anand, *India* **42 H5** 22 32N 72 59 E
Anantnag, *India* **43 C6** 33 45N 75 10 E
Ananyiv, *Ukraine* **17 E15** 47 44N 29 58 E
Anapodháris →, *Greece* **23 E7** 34 59N 25 20 E
Anápolis, *Brazil* **93 G9** 16 15S 48 50W
Anapu →, *Brazil* **93 D8** 1 53S 50 53W
Anār, *Iran* **45 D7** 30 55N 55 13 E
Anārak, *Iran* **45 C7** 33 25N 53 40 E
Anas →, *India* **42 H5** 23 26N 74 0 E
Anatolia = Anadolu, *Turkey* **25 G5** 39 0N 30 0 E
Anatsogno, *Madag.* **57 C7** 23 33S 43 46 E
Añatuya, *Argentina* **94 B3** 28 20S 62 50W
Anaunethad L., *Canada* **73 A8** 60 55N 104 25W
Anbyŏn, *N. Korea* **35 E14** 39 1N 127 35 E
Ancaster, *Canada* **78 C5** 43 13N 79 59W
Anchor Bay, *U.S.A.* **84 G3** 38 48N 123 34W
Anchorage, *U.S.A.* **68 B5** 61 13N 149 54W
Anci, *China* **34 E9** 39 20N 116 40 E
Ancohuma, Nevada, *Bolivia* **92 G5** 16 0S 68 50W
Ancón, *Peru* **92 F3** 11 50S 77 10W
Ancona, *Italy* **20 C5** 43 38N 13 30 E
Ancud, *Chile* **96 E2** 42 0S 73 50W
Ancud, G. de, *Chile* **96 E2** 42 0S 73 0W
Anda, *China* **33 B7** 46 24N 125 19 E
Andacollo, *Argentina* **94 D1** 37 10S 70 42W
Andacollo, *Chile* **94 C1** 30 14S 71 6W
Andalgalá, *Argentina* **94 B2** 27 40S 66 30W
Åndalsnes, *Norway* **9 E12** 62 35N 7 43 E
Andalucía □, *Spain* **19 D3** 37 35N 5 0W
Andalusia = Andalucía □, *Spain* **19 D3** 37 35N 5 0W
Andalusia, *U.S.A.* **77 K2** 31 18N 86 29W
Andaman Is., *Ind. Oc.* **28 H13** 12 30N 92 30 E
Andaman Sea, *Ind. Oc.* **36 B1** 13 0N 96 0 E
Andamooka Opal Fields, *Australia* **63 E2** 30 27S 137 9 E
Andapa, *Madag.* **53 G9** 14 30S 49 30 E
Andara, *Namibia* **56 B3** 18 2S 21 9 E
Andenes, *Norway* **8 B17** 69 19N 16 18 E
Andenne, *Belgium* **15 D5** 50 28N 5 5 E
Anderson, *Alaska, U.S.A.* **68 B5** 64 25N 149 15W
Anderson, *Calif., U.S.A.* **82 F2** 40 27N 122 18W
Anderson, *Ind., U.S.A.* **76 E3** 40 10N 85 41W
Anderson, *Mo., U.S.A.* **81 G7** 36 39N 94 27W
Anderson, *S.C., U.S.A.* **77 H4** 34 31N 82 39W
Anderson →, *Canada* **68 B7** 69 42N 129 0W
Andes, *U.S.A.* **79 D10** 42 12N 74 47W
Andes, Cord. de los, *S. Amer.* **92 H5** 20 0S 68 0W
Andfjorden, *Norway* **8 B17** 69 10N 16 20 E
Andhra Pradesh □, *India* **40 L11** 18 0N 79 0 E
Andijon, *Uzbekistan* **26 E8** 41 10N 72 15 E
Andikíthira, *Greece* **21 G10** 35 52N 23 15 E
Andīmeshk, *Iran* **45 C6** 32 27N 48 21 E
Andizhan = Andijon, *Uzbekistan* **26 E8** 41 10N 72 15 E
Andoany, *Madag.* **57 A8** 13 25S 48 16 E
Andong, *S. Korea* **35 F15** 36 40N 128 43 E
Andongwei, *China* **35 G10** 35 6N 119 20 E
Andoom, *Australia* **62 A3** 12 25S 141 53 E
Andorra ■, *Europe* **18 E4** 42 30N 1 30 E
Andorra La Vella, *Andorra* **18 E4** 42 31N 1 32 E
Andover, *U.K.* **11 F6** 51 12N 1 29W
Andover, *Maine, U.S.A.* **79 B14** 44 38N 70 45W
Andover, *Mass., U.S.A.* **79 D13** 42 40N 71 8W
Andover, *N.J., U.S.A.* **79 F10** 40 59N 74 45W
Andover, *N.Y., U.S.A.* **78 D7** 42 10N 77 48W
Andover, *Ohio, U.S.A.* **78 E4** 41 36N 80 34W
Andøya, *Norway* **8 B16** 69 10N 15 50 E
Andradina, *Brazil* **93 H8** 20 54S 51 23W
Andrahary, Mt., *Madag.* **57 A8** 13 37S 49 17 E
Andramasina, *Madag.* **57 B8** 19 11S 47 35 E
Andranopasy, *Madag.* **57 C7** 21 17S 43 44 E
Andratx, *Spain* **22 B9** 39 39N 2 25 E
Andreanof Is., *U.S.A.* **68 C2** 51 30N 176 0W
Andrews, *S.C., U.S.A.* **77 J6** 33 27N 79 34W
Andrews, *Tex., U.S.A.* **81 J3** 32 19N 102 33W
Ándria, *Italy* **20 D7** 41 13N 16 17 E
Andriba, *Madag.* **57 B8** 17 30S 46 58 E
Androka, *Madag.* **57 C7** 24 58S 44 2 E
Andropov = Rybinsk, *Russia* **24 C6** 58 5N 38 50 E
Ándros, *Greece* **21 F11** 37 50N 24 57 E
Andros I., *Bahamas* **88 B4** 24 30N 78 0W
Andros Town, *Bahamas* **88 B4** 24 43N 77 47W
Androscoggin →, *U.S.A.* **79 C14** 43 58N 70 0W
Andselv, *Norway* **8 B18** 69 4N 18 34 E
Andújar, *Spain* **19 C3** 38 3N 4 5W
Andulo, *Angola* **52 G3** 11 25S 16 45 E
Anegada I., *Virgin Is.* **89 C7** 18 45N 64 20W
Anegada Passage, *W. Indies* **89 C7** 18 15N 63 45W
Aneto, Pico de, *Spain* **19 A6** 42 37N 0 40 E
Ang Thong, *Thailand* **38 E3** 14 35N 100 31 E
Angamos, Punta, *Chile* **94 A1** 23 1S 70 32W
Angara →, *Russia* **27 D10** 58 5N 94 20 E
Angarsk, *Russia* **27 D11** 52 30N 104 0 E
Angas Hills, *Australia* **60 D4** 23 0S 127 50 E
Angaston, *Australia* **63 E2** 34 30S 139 8 E
Angaur I., *Pac. Oc.* **37 C8** 6 54N 134 9 E
Ånge, *Sweden* **9 E16** 62 31N 15 35 E
Ángel, Salto = Angel Falls, *Venezuela* **92 B6** 5 57N 62 30W
Ángel de la Guarda, I., *Mexico* **86 B2** 29 30N 113 30W
Angel Falls, *Venezuela* **92 B6** 5 57N 62 30W
Angeles, *Phil.* **37 A6** 15 9N 120 33 E
Ängelholm, *Sweden* **9 H15** 56 15N 12 58 E
Angels Camp, *U.S.A.* **84 G6** 38 4N 120 32W
Ångermanälven →, *Sweden* **8 E17** 62 40N 18 0 E
Ångermanland, *Sweden* **8 E18** 63 36N 17 45 E
Angers, *Canada* **79 A9** 45 31N 75 29W
Angers, *France* **18 C3** 47 30N 0 35W
Ängesån →, *Sweden* **8 C20** 66 16N 22 47 E
Angikuni L., *Canada* **73 A9** 62 0N 100 0W
Angkor, *Cambodia* **38 F4** 13 22N 103 50 E
Anglesey, *U.K.* **10 D3** 53 17N 4 20W
Anglesey, Isle of □, *U.K.* **10 D3** 53 16N 4 18W
Angleton, *U.S.A.* **81 L7** 29 10N 95 26W
Anglisidhes, *Cyprus* **23 E12** 34 51N 33 27 E
Angmagssalik, *Greenland* **4 C6** 65 40N 37 20W
Ango, *Dem. Rep. of the Congo* **54 B2** 4 10N 26 5 E
Angoche, *Mozam.* **55 F4** 16 8S 39 55 E
Angoche, I., *Mozam.* **55 F4** 16 20S 39 50 E
Angol, *Chile* **94 D1** 37 56S 72 45W
Angola, *Ind., U.S.A.* **76 E3** 41 38N 85 0W
Angola, *N.Y., U.S.A.* **78 D5** 42 38N 79 2W
Angola ■, *Africa* **53 G3** 12 0S 18 0 E
Angoulême, *France* **18 D4** 45 39N 0 10 E
Angoumois, *France* **18 D3** 45 50N 0 25 E
Angra dos Reis, *Brazil* **95 A7** 23 0S 44 10W
Angren, *Uzbekistan* **26 E8** 41 1N 70 12 E
Angtassom, *Cambodia* **39 G5** 11 1N 104 41 E
Angu, *Dem. Rep. of the Congo* **54 B1** 3 25N 24 28 E
Anguang, *China* **35 B12** 45 15N 123 45 E
Anguilla ■, *W. Indies* **89 C7** 18 14N 63 5W
Anguo, *China* **34 E8** 38 28N 115 15 E
Angurugu, *Australia* **62 A2** 14 0S 136 25 E
Angus □, *U.K.* **12 E6** 56 46N 2 56W
Anhanduí →, *Brazil* **95 A5** 21 46S 52 9W
Anholt, *Denmark* **9 H14** 56 42N 11 33 E
Anhui □, *China* **33 C6** 32 0N 117 0 E
Anhwei = Anhui □, *China* **33 C6** 32 0N 117 0 E
Anichab, *Namibia* **56 C1** 21 0S 14 46 E
Animas →, *U.S.A.* **83 H9** 36 43N 108 13W
Anivorano, *Madag.* **57 B8** 18 44S 48 58 E
Anjalankoski, *Finland* **9 F22** 60 45N 26 51 E
Anjar, *India* **42 H4** 23 6N 70 10 E
Anjidiv I., *India* **40 M9** 14 40N 74 10 E
Anjou, *France* **18 C3** 47 20N 0 15W
Anjozorobe, *Madag.* **57 B8** 18 22S 47 52 E
Anju, *N. Korea* **35 E13** 39 36N 125 40 E
Ankaboa, Tanjon, *Madag.* **57 C7** 21 58S 43 20 E
Ankang, *China* **34 H5** 32 40N 109 1 E
Ankara, *Turkey* **25 G5** 39 57N 32 54 E
Ankaramena, *Madag.* **57 C8** 21 57S 46 39 E
Ankaratra, *Madag.* **53 H9** 19 25S 47 12 E
Ankazoabo, *Madag.* **57 C7** 22 18S 44 31 E
Ankazobe, *Madag.* **57 B8** 18 20S 47 10 E
Ankeny, *U.S.A.* **80 E8** 41 44N 93 36W
Ankisabe, *Madag.* **57 B8** 19 17S 46 29 E
Ankoro, *Dem. Rep. of the Congo* **54 D2** 6 45S 26 55 E
Anmyŏn-do, *S. Korea* **35 F14** 36 25N 126 25 E
Ann, C., *U.S.A.* **79 D14** 42 38N 70 35W
Ann Arbor, *U.S.A.* **76 D4** 42 17N 83 45W
Anna, *U.S.A.* **81 G10** 37 28N 89 15W
Annaba, *Algeria* **50 A7** 36 50N 7 46 E
Annalee →, *Ireland* **13 B4** 54 2N 7 24W
Annam, *Vietnam* **38 E7** 16 0N 108 0 E
Annamitique, Chaîne, *Asia* **38 D6** 17 0N 106 0 E
Annan, *U.K.* **12 G5** 54 59N 3 16W
Annan →, *U.K.* **12 G5** 54 58N 3 16W
Annapolis, *U.S.A.* **76 F7** 38 59N 76 30W
Annapolis Royal, *Canada* **71 D6** 44 44N 65 32W
Annapurna, *Nepal* **43 E10** 28 34N 83 50 E
Annean, L., *Australia* **61 E2** 26 54S 118 14 E
Annecy, *France* **18 D7** 45 55N 6 8 E
Anning, *China* **32 D5** 24 55N 102 26 E
Anniston, *U.S.A.* **77 J3** 33 39N 85 50W
Annobón, *Atl. Oc.* **49 G4** 1 25S 5 36 E
Annotto Bay, *Jamaica* **88 C4** 18 17N 76 45W
Annville, *U.S.A.* **79 F8** 40 20N 76 31W
Áno Viánnos, *Greece* **23 D7** 35 2N 25 21 E
Anorotsangana, *Madag.* **57 A8** 13 56S 47 55 E
Anóyia, *Greece* **23 D6** 35 16N 24 52 E
Anping, *Hebei, China* **34 E8** 38 15N 115 30 E
Anping, *Liaoning, China* **35 D12** 41 5N 123 30 E
Anqing, *China* **33 C6** 30 30N 117 3 E
Anqiu, *China* **35 F10** 36 25N 119 10 E
Ansai, *China* **34 F5** 36 50N 109 20 E
Ansbach, *Germany* **16 D6** 49 28N 10 34 E
Anshan, *China* **35 D12** 41 5N 122 58 E
Anshun, *China* **32 D5** 26 18N 105 57 E
Ansley, *U.S.A.* **80 E5** 41 18N 99 23W
Anson, *U.S.A.* **81 J5** 32 45N 99 54W
Anson B., *Australia* **60 B5** 13 20S 130 6 E
Ansongo, *Mali* **50 E6** 15 25N 0 35 E
Ansonia, *U.S.A.* **79 E11** 41 21N 73 5W
Anstruther, *U.K.* **12 E6** 56 14N 2 41W
Ansudu, *Indonesia* **37 E9** 2 11S 139 22 E
Antabamba, *Peru* **92 F4** 14 40S 73 0W
Antakya, *Turkey* **25 G6** 36 14N 36 10 E
Antalaha, *Madag.* **57 A9** 14 57S 50 20 E
Antalya, *Turkey* **25 G5** 36 52N 30 45 E
Antalya Körfezi, *Turkey* **25 G5** 36 15N 31 30 E
Antananarivo, *Madag.* **57 B8** 18 55S 47 31 E
Antananarivo □, *Madag.* **57 B8** 19 0S 47 0 E
Antanimbaribe, *Madag.* **57 C7** 21 30S 44 48 E
Antarctic Pen., *Antarctica* **5 C18** 67 0S 60 0W
Antarctica **5 E3** 90 0S 0 0 E
Antelope, *Zimbabwe* **55 G2** 21 2S 28 31 E
Antequera, *Paraguay* **94 A4** 24 8S 57 7W
Antequera, *Spain* **19 D3** 37 5N 4 33W
Antero, Mt., *U.S.A.* **83 G10** 38 41N 106 15W
Anthony, *Kans., U.S.A.* **81 G5** 37 9N 98 2W
Anthony, *N. Mex., U.S.A.* **83 K10** 32 0N 106 36W
Anti Atlas, *Morocco* **50 C4** 30 0N 8 30W
Anti-Lebanon = Ash Sharqi, Al Jabal, *Lebanon* **47 B5** 33 40N 36 10 E
Antibes, *France* **18 E7** 43 34N 7 6 E
Anticosti, Î. d', *Canada* **71 C7** 49 30N 63 0W
Antigo, *U.S.A.* **80 C10** 45 9N 89 9W
Antigonish, *Canada* **71 C7** 45 38N 61 58W
Antigua, *Canary Is.* **22 F5** 28 24N 14 1W
Antigua, *W. Indies* **89 C7** 17 0N 61 50W
Antigua & Barbuda ■, *W. Indies* **89 C7** 17 20N 61 48W
Antigua Guatemala, *Guatemala* **88 D1** 14 34N 90 41W
Antilla, *Cuba* **88 B4** 20 40N 75 50W
Antilles = West Indies, *Cent. Amer.* **89 D7** 15 0N 65 0W
Antioch, *U.S.A.* **84 G5** 38 1N 121 48W
Antioquia, *Colombia* **92 B3** 6 40N 75 55W
Antipodes Is., *Pac. Oc.* **64 M9** 49 45S 178 40 E
Antlers, *U.S.A.* **81 H7** 34 14N 95 37W
Antofagasta, *Chile* **94 A1** 23 50S 70 30W
Antofagasta □, *Chile* **94 A2** 24 0S 69 0W
Antofagasta de la Sierra, *Argentina* **94 B2** 26 5S 67 20W
Antofalla, *Argentina* **94 B2** 25 30S 68 5W
Antofalla, Salar de, *Argentina* **94 B2** 25 40S 67 45W
Anton, *U.S.A.* **81 J3** 33 49N 102 10W
Antongila, Helodrano, *Madag.* **57 B8** 15 30S 49 50 E
Antonibé, *Madag.* **57 B8** 15 7S 47 24 E
Antonibé, Presqu'île d', *Madag.* **57 A8** 14 55S 47 20 E
Antonina, *Brazil* **95 B6** 25 26S 48 42W
Antrim, *U.K.* **13 B5** 54 43N 6 14W
Antrim, *U.S.A.* **78 F3** 40 7N 81 21W
Antrim □, *U.K.* **13 B5** 54 56N 6 25W
Antrim, Mts. of, *U.K.* **13 A5** 55 3N 6 14W
Antrim Plateau, *Australia* **60 C4** 18 8S 128 20 E
Antsalova, *Madag.* **57 B7** 18 40S 44 37 E
Antsirabe, *Madag.* **57 B8** 19 55S 47 2 E
Antsiranana, *Madag.* **57 A8** 12 25S 49 20 E
Antsohihy, *Madag.* **57 A8** 14 50S 47 59 E
Antsohimbondrona Seranana, *Madag.* **57 A8** 13 7S 48 48 E
Antu, *China* **35 C15** 42 30N 128 20 E
Antwerp = Antwerpen, *Belgium* **15 C4** 51 13N 4 25 E
Antwerp, *U.S.A.* **79 B9** 44 12N 75 37W
Antwerpen, *Belgium* **15 C4** 51 13N 4 25 E
Antwerpen □, *Belgium* **15 C4** 51 15N 4 40 E
Anupgarh, *India* **42 E5** 29 10N 73 10 E
Anuppur, *India* **43 H9** 23 6N 81 41 E
Anuradhapura, *Sri Lanka* **40 Q12** 8 22N 80 28 E
Anveh, *Iran* **45 E7** 27 23N 54 11 E
Anvers = Antwerpen, *Belgium* **15 C4** 51 13N 4 25 E
Anvers I., *Antarctica* **5 C17** 64 30S 63 40W
Anxi, *China* **32 B4** 40 30N 95 43 E
Anxious B., *Australia* **63 E1** 33 24S 134 45 E
Anyang, *China* **34 F8** 36 5N 114 21 E
Anyer-Kidul, *Indonesia* **37 G11** 6 4S 105 53 E
Anyi, *China* **34 G6** 35 2N 111 2 E
Anza, *U.S.A.* **85 M10** 33 35N 116 39W
Anze, *China* **34 F7** 36 10N 112 12 E
Anzhero-Sudzhensk, *Russia* **26 D9** 56 10N 86 0 E
Ánzio, *Italy* **20 D5** 41 27N 12 37 E
Aoga-Shima, *Japan* **31 H9** 32 28N 139 46 E
Aomen = Macau, *China* **33 D6** 22 16N 113 35 E
Aomori, *Japan* **30 D10** 40 45N 140 45 E

Asmera

Asmera, *Eritrea* **46 D2** 15 19N 38 55 E
Åsnen, *Sweden* **9 H16** 56 37N 14 45 E
Aspen, *U.S.A.* **83 G10** 39 11N 106 49W
Aspermont, *U.S.A.* **81 J4** 33 8N 100 14W
Aspiring, Mt., *N.Z.* **59 L2** 44 23S 168 46 E
Asprókavos, Ákra, *Greece* **23 B4** 39 21N 20 6 E
Aspur, *India* **42 H6** 23 58N 74 7 E
Asquith, *Canada* **73 C7** 52 8N 107 13W
Assam □, *India* **41 G18** 26 0N 93 0 E
Asse, *Belgium* **15 D4** 50 24N 4 10 E
Assen, *Neths.* **15 A6** 53 0N 6 35 E
Assiniboia, *Canada* **73 D7** 49 40N 105 59W
Assiniboine →, *Canada* **73 D9** 49 53N 97 8W
Assiniboine, Mt., *Canada* **72 C5** 50 52N 115 39W
Assis, *Brazil* **95 A5** 22 40S 50 20W
Assisi, *Italy* **20 C5** 43 4N 12 37 E
Assynt, L., *U.K.* **12 C3** 58 10N 5 3W
Astana, *Kazakstan* **26 D8** 51 10N 71 30 E
Āstāneh, *Iran* **45 B6** 37 17N 49 59 E
Astara, *Azerbaijan* **25 G8** 38 30N 48 50 E
Asteroúsia, *Greece* **23 E7** 34 59N 25 3 E
Asti, *Italy* **18 D8** 44 54N 8 12 E
Astipálaia, *Greece* **21 F12** 36 32N 26 22 E
Astorga, *Spain* **19 A2** 42 29N 6 8W
Astoria, *U.S.A.* **84 D3** 46 11N 123 50W
Astrakhan, *Russia* **25 E8** 46 25N 48 5 E
Asturias □, *Spain* **19 A3** 43 15N 6 0W
Asunción, *Paraguay* **94 B4** 25 10S 57 30W
Asunción Nochixtlán, *Mexico* **87 D5** 17 28N 97 14W
Aswa →, *Uganda* **54 B3** 3 43N 31 55 E
Aswân, *Egypt* **51 D12** 24 4N 32 57 E
Aswân High Dam = Sadd el Aali, *Egypt* **51 D12** 23 54N 32 54 E
Asyût, *Egypt* **51 C12** 27 11N 31 4 E
At Ţafīlah, *Jordan* **47 E4** 30 45N 35 30 E
Aţ Tā'if, *Si. Arabia* **46 C3** 21 5N 40 27 E
Aţ Ţirāq, *Si. Arabia* **44 E5** 27 19N 44 33 E
Aţ Tubayq, *Si. Arabia* **44 D3** 29 30N 37 0 E
Atacama □, *Chile* **94 B2** 27 30S 70 0W
Atacama, Desierto de, *Chile* **94 A2** 24 0S 69 20W
Atacama, Salar de, *Chile* **94 A2** 23 30S 68 20W
Atalaya, *Peru* **92 F4** 10 45S 73 50W
Atalaya de Femes, *Canary Is.* **22 F6** 28 56N 13 47W
Atami, *Japan* **31 G9** 35 5N 139 4 E
Atapupu, *Indonesia* **37 F6** 9 0S 124 51 E
Atâr, *Mauritania* **50 D3** 20 30N 13 5W
Atari, *Pakistan* **42 D6** 30 56N 74 2 E
Atascadero, *U.S.A.* **84 K6** 35 29N 120 40W
Atasu, *Kazakstan* **26 E8** 48 30N 71 0 E
Atatürk Barajı, *Turkey* **25 G6** 37 28N 38 30 E
Atauro, *Indonesia* **37 F7** 8 10S 125 30 E
Atbara, *Sudan* **51 E12** 17 42N 33 59 E
'Atbara →, *Sudan* **51 E12** 17 40N 33 56 E
Atbasar, *Kazakstan* **26 D7** 51 48N 68 20 E
Atchafalaya B., *U.S.A.* **81 L9** 29 25N 91 25W
Atchison, *U.S.A.* **80 F7** 39 34N 95 7W
Āteshān, *Iran* **45 C7** 35 35N 52 37 E
Ath, *Belgium* **15 D3** 50 38N 3 47 E
Athabasca, *Canada* **72 C6** 54 45N 113 20W
Athabasca →, *Canada* **73 B6** 58 40N 110 50W
Athabasca, L., *Canada* **73 B7** 59 15N 109 15W
Athboy, *Ireland* **13 C5** 53 37N 6 56W
Athenry, *Ireland* **13 C3** 53 18N 8 44W
Athens = Athínai, *Greece* **21 F10** 37 58N 23 46 E
Athens, *Ala., U.S.A.* **77 H2** 34 48N 86 58W
Athens, *Ga., U.S.A.* **77 J4** 33 57N 83 23W
Athens, *N.Y., U.S.A.* **79 D11** 42 16N 73 49W
Athens, *Ohio, U.S.A.* **76 F4** 39 20N 82 6W
Athens, *Pa., U.S.A.* **79 E8** 41 57N 76 31W
Athens, *Tenn., U.S.A.* **77 H3** 35 27N 84 36W
Athens, *Tex., U.S.A.* **81 J7** 32 12N 95 51W
Atherley, *Canada* **78 B5** 44 37N 79 20W
Atherton, *Australia* **62 B4** 17 17S 145 30 E
Athienou, *Cyprus* **23 D12** 35 3N 33 32 E
Athínai, *Greece* **21 F10** 37 58N 23 46 E
Athlone, *Ireland* **13 C4** 53 25N 7 56W
Athna, *Cyprus* **23 D12** 35 3N 33 47 E
Athol, *U.S.A.* **79 D12** 42 36N 72 14W
Atholl, Forest of, *U.K.* **12 E5** 56 51N 3 50W
Atholville, *Canada* **71 C6** 47 59N 66 43W
Áthos, *Greece* **21 D11** 40 9N 24 22 E
Athy, *Ireland* **13 C5** 53 0N 7 0W
Ati, *Chad* **51 F9** 13 13N 18 20 E
Atiak, *Uganda* **54 B3** 3 12N 32 2 E
Atik L., *Canada* **73 B9** 55 15N 96 0W
Atikameg →, *Canada* **70 B3** 52 30N 82 46W
Atikokan, *Canada* **70 C1** 48 45N 91 37W
Atikonak L., *Canada* **71 B7** 52 40N 64 32W
Atka, *Russia* **27 C16** 60 50N 151 48 E
Atka I., *U.S.A.* **68 C2** 52 7N 174 30W
Atkinson, *U.S.A.* **80 D5** 42 32N 98 59W
Atlanta, *Ga., U.S.A.* **77 J3** 33 45N 84 23W
Atlanta, *Tex., U.S.A.* **81 J7** 33 7N 94 10W
Atlantic, *U.S.A.* **80 E7** 41 24N 95 1W
Atlantic City, *U.S.A.* **76 F8** 39 21N 74 27W
Atlantic Ocean **2 E9** 0 0 20 0W
Atlas Mts. = Haut Atlas, *Morocco* **50 B4** 32 30N 5 0W
Atlin, *Canada* **72 B2** 59 31N 133 41W
Atlin, L., *Canada* **72 B2** 59 26N 133 45W
Atlin Prov. Park, *Canada* **72 B2** 59 10N 134 30W
Atmore, *U.S.A.* **77 K2** 31 2N 87 29W
Atoka, *U.S.A.* **81 H6** 34 23N 96 8W
Atolia, *U.S.A.* **85 K9** 35 19N 117 37W
Atrai →, *Bangla.* **43 G13** 24 7N 89 22 E
Atrak = Atrek →, *Turkmenistan* **45 B8** 37 35N 53 58 E
Atrauli, *India* **42 E8** 28 2N 78 20 E
Atrek →, *Turkmenistan* **45 B8** 37 35N 53 58 E
Atsuta, *Japan* **30 C10** 43 24N 141 26 E
Attalla, *U.S.A.* **77 H2** 34 1N 86 6W
Attapu, *Laos* **38 E6** 14 48N 106 50 E
Attáviros, *Greece* **23 C9** 36 12N 27 50 E
Attawapiskat, *Canada* **70 B3** 52 56N 82 24W
Attawapiskat →, *Canada* **70 B3** 52 57N 82 18W
Attawapiskat L., *Canada* **70 B2** 52 18N 87 54W
Attica, *Ind., U.S.A.* **76 E2** 40 18N 87 15W
Attica, *Ohio, U.S.A.* **78 E2** 41 4N 82 53W
Attikamagen L., *Canada* **71 B6** 55 0N 66 30W
Attleboro, *U.S.A.* **79 E13** 41 57N 71 17W
Attock, *Pakistan* **42 C5** 33 52N 72 20 E
Attopeu = Attapu, *Laos* **38 E6** 14 48N 106 50 E
Attu I., *U.S.A.* **68 C1** 52 55N 172 55 E
Attur, *India* **40 P11** 11 35N 78 30 E
Atuel →, *Argentina* **94 D2** 36 17S 66 50W
Åtvidaberg, *Sweden* **9 G17** 58 12N 16 0 E
Atwater, *U.S.A.* **84 H6** 37 21N 120 37W
Atwood, *Canada* **78 C3** 43 40N 81 1W
Atwood, *U.S.A.* **80 F4** 39 48N 101 3W
Atyraū, *Kazakstan* **25 E9** 47 5N 52 0 E
Au Sable, *U.S.A.* **78 B1** 44 25N 83 20W
Au Sable →, *U.S.A.* **76 C4** 44 25N 83 20W
Au Sable Forks, *U.S.A.* **79 B11** 44 27N 73 41W
Au Sable Pt., *U.S.A.* **78 B1** 44 20N 83 20W
Aubagne, *France* **18 E6** 43 17N 5 37 E
Aubarca, C. d', *Spain* **22 B7** 39 4N 1 22 E
Aube →, *France* **18 B5** 48 34N 3 43 E
Auberry, *U.S.A.* **84 H7** 37 7N 119 29W
Auburn, *Ala., U.S.A.* **77 J3** 32 36N 85 29W
Auburn, *Calif., U.S.A.* **84 G5** 38 54N 121 4W
Auburn, *Ind., U.S.A.* **76 E3** 41 22N 85 4W
Auburn, *Maine, U.S.A.* **77 C10** 44 6N 70 14W
Auburn, *N.Y., U.S.A.* **79 D8** 42 56N 76 34W
Auburn, *Nebr., U.S.A.* **80 E7** 40 23N 95 51W
Auburn, *Pa., U.S.A.* **79 F8** 40 36N 76 6W
Auburn, *Wash., U.S.A.* **84 C4** 47 18N 122 14W
Auburn Ra., *Australia* **63 D5** 25 15S 150 30 E
Aubusson, *France* **18 D5** 45 57N 2 11 E
Auch, *France* **18 E4** 43 39N 0 36 E
Auckland, *N.Z.* **59 G5** 36 52S 174 46 E
Auckland Is., *Pac. Oc.* **64 N8** 50 40S 166 5 E
Aude →, *France* **18 E5** 43 13N 3 14 E
Auden, *Canada* **70 B2** 50 14N 87 53W
Audubon, *U.S.A.* **80 E7** 41 43N 94 56W
Augathella, *Australia* **63 D4** 25 48S 146 35 E
Aughnacloy, *U.K.* **13 B5** 54 25N 6 59W
Augrabies Falls, *S. Africa* **56 D3** 28 35S 20 20 E
Augsburg, *Germany* **16 D6** 48 25N 10 52 E
Augusta, *Australia* **61 F2** 34 19S 115 9 E
Augusta, *Italy* **20 F6** 37 13N 15 13 E
Augusta, *Ark., U.S.A.* **81 H9** 35 17N 91 22W
Augusta, *Ga., U.S.A.* **77 J5** 33 28N 81 58W
Augusta, *Kans., U.S.A.* **81 G6** 37 41N 96 59W
Augusta, *Maine, U.S.A.* **69 D13** 44 19N 69 47W
Augusta, *Mont., U.S.A.* **82 C7** 47 30N 112 24W
Augustów, *Poland* **17 B12** 53 51N 23 0 E
Augustus, Mt., *Australia* **61 D2** 24 20S 116 50 E
Augustus I., *Australia* **60 C3** 15 20S 124 30 E
Aukum, *U.S.A.* **84 G6** 38 34N 120 43W
Auld, L., *Australia* **60 D3** 22 25S 123 50 E
Ault, *U.S.A.* **80 E2** 40 35N 104 44W
Aunis, *France* **18 C3** 46 5N 0 50W
Auponhia, *Indonesia* **37 E7** 1 58S 125 27 E
Aur, Pulau, *Malaysia* **39 L5** 2 35N 104 10 E
Auraiya, *India* **43 F8** 26 28N 79 33 E
Aurangabad, *Bihar, India* **43 G11** 24 45N 84 18 E
Aurangabad, *Maharashtra, India* **40 K9** 19 50N 75 23 E
Aurich, *Germany* **16 B4** 53 28N 7 28 E
Aurillac, *France* **18 D5** 44 55N 2 26 E
Aurora, *Canada* **78 C5** 44 0N 79 28W
Aurora, *S. Africa* **56 E2** 32 40S 18 29 E
Aurora, *Colo., U.S.A.* **80 F2** 39 44N 104 52W
Aurora, *Ill., U.S.A.* **76 E1** 41 45N 88 19W
Aurora, *Mo., U.S.A.* **81 G8** 36 58N 93 43W
Aurora, *N.Y., U.S.A.* **79 D8** 42 45N 76 42W
Aurora, *Nebr., U.S.A.* **80 E6** 40 52N 98 0W
Aurora, *Ohio, U.S.A.* **78 E3** 41 21N 81 20W
Aurukun, *Australia* **62 A3** 13 20S 141 45 E
Aus, *Namibia* **56 D2** 26 35S 16 12 E
Ausable →, *Canada* **78 C3** 43 19N 81 46W
Auschwitz = Oświęcim, *Poland* **17 C10** 50 2N 19 11 E
Austin, *Minn., U.S.A.* **80 D8** 43 40N 92 58W
Austin, *Nev., U.S.A.* **82 G5** 39 30N 117 4W
Austin, *Pa., U.S.A.* **78 E6** 41 38N 78 6W
Austin, *Tex., U.S.A.* **81 K6** 30 17N 97 45W
Austin, L., *Australia* **61 E2** 27 40S 118 0 E
Austin I., *Canada* **73 A10** 61 10N 94 0W
Austra, *Norway* **8 D14** 65 8N 11 55 E
Austral Is. = Tubuai Is., *Pac. Oc.* **65 K13** 25 0S 150 0W
Austral Seamount Chain, *Pac. Oc.* **65 K13** 24 0S 150 0W
Australia ■, *Oceania* **64 K5** 23 0S 135 0 E
Australian Capital Territory □, *Australia* **63 F4** 35 30S 149 0 E
Australind, *Australia* **61 F2** 33 17S 115 42 E
Austria ■, *Europe* **16 E8** 47 0N 14 0 E
Austvågøy, *Norway* **8 B16** 68 20N 14 40 E
Autlán, *Mexico* **86 D4** 19 40N 104 30W
Autun, *France* **18 C6** 46 58N 4 17 E
Auvergne, *France* **18 D5** 45 20N 3 15 E
Auvergne, Mts. d', *France* **18 D5** 45 20N 2 55 E
Auxerre, *France* **18 C5** 47 48N 3 32 E
Ava, *U.S.A.* **81 G8** 36 57N 92 40W
Avallon, *France* **18 C5** 47 30N 3 53 E
Avalon, *U.S.A.* **85 M8** 33 21N 118 20W
Avalon Pen., *Canada* **71 C9** 47 30N 53 20W
Avanos, *Turkey* **44 B2** 38 43N 34 51 E
Avaré, *Brazil* **95 A6** 23 4S 48 58W
Avawatz Mts., *U.S.A.* **85 K10** 35 40N 116 30W
Aveiro, *Brazil* **93 D7** 3 10S 55 5W
Aveiro, *Portugal* **19 B1** 40 37N 8 38W
Āvej, *Iran* **45 C6** 35 40N 49 15 E
Avellaneda, *Argentina* **94 C4** 34 50S 58 10W
Avellino, *Italy* **20 D6** 40 54N 14 47 E
Avenal, *U.S.A.* **84 K6** 36 0N 120 8W
Aversa, *Italy* **20 D6** 40 58N 14 12 E
Avery, *U.S.A.* **82 C6** 47 15N 115 49W
Aves, Is. las, *Venezuela* **89 D6** 12 0N 67 30W
Avesta, *Sweden* **9 F17** 60 9N 16 10 E
Avezzano, *Italy* **20 C5** 42 2N 13 25 E
Aviá Terai, *Argentina* **94 B3** 26 45S 60 50W
Aviemore, *U.K.* **12 D5** 57 12N 3 50W
Avignon, *France* **18 E6** 43 57N 4 50 E
Ávila, *Spain* **19 B3** 40 39N 4 43W
Avila Beach, *U.S.A.* **85 K6** 35 11N 120 44W
Avilés, *Spain* **19 A3** 43 35N 5 57W
Avis, *U.S.A.* **78 E7** 41 11N 77 19W
Avoca, *U.S.A.* **78 D7** 42 25N 77 25W
Avoca →, *Australia* **63 F3** 35 40S 143 43 E
Avoca →, *Ireland* **13 D5** 52 48N 6 10W
Avola, *Canada* **72 C5** 51 45N 119 19W
Avola, *Italy* **20 F6** 36 56N 15 7 E
Avon, *U.S.A.* **78 D7** 42 55N 77 45W
Avon →, *Australia* **61 F2** 31 40S 116 7 E
Avon →, *Bristol, U.K.* **11 F5** 51 29N 2 41W
Avon →, *Dorset, U.K.* **11 G6** 50 44N 1 46W
Avon →, *Warks., U.K.* **11 E5** 52 0N 2 8W
Avon Park, *U.S.A.* **77 M5** 27 36N 81 31W
Avondale, *Zimbabwe* **55 F3** 17 43S 30 58 E
Avonlea, *Canada* **73 D8** 50 0N 105 0W
Avonmore, *Canada* **79 A10** 45 10N 74 58W
Avranches, *France* **18 B3** 48 40N 1 20W
A'waj →, *Syria* **47 B5** 33 23N 36 20 E
Awaji-Shima, *Japan* **31 G7** 34 30N 134 50 E
'Awālī, *Bahrain* **45 E6** 26 0N 50 30 E
Awantipur, *India* **43 C6** 33 55N 75 3 E
Awasa, *Ethiopia* **46 F2** 7 3N 38 28 E
Awash, *Ethiopia* **46 F3** 9 1N 40 10 E
Awatere →, *N.Z.* **59 J5** 41 37S 174 10 E
Awbārī, *Libya* **51 C8** 26 46N 12 57 E
Awe, L., *U.K.* **12 E3** 56 17N 5 16W
Awjilah, *Libya* **51 C10** 29 8N 21 7 E
Axe →, *U.K.* **11 F5** 50 42N 3 4W
Axel Heiberg I., *Canada* **4 B3** 80 0N 90 0W
Axim, *Ghana* **50 H5** 4 51N 2 15W
Axiós →, *Greece* **21 D10** 40 57N 22 35 E
Axminster, *U.K.* **11 G4** 50 46N 3 0W
Ayabaca, *Peru* **92 D3** 4 40S 79 53W
Ayabe, *Japan* **31 G7** 35 20N 135 20 E
Ayacucho, *Argentina* **94 D4** 37 5S 58 20W
Ayacucho, *Peru* **92 F4** 13 0S 74 0W
Ayaguz, *Kazakstan* **26 E9** 48 10N 80 10 E
Ayamonte, *Spain* **19 D2** 37 12N 7 24W
Ayan, *Russia* **27 D14** 56 30N 138 16 E
Ayaviri, *Peru* **92 F4** 14 50S 70 35W
Aydın, *Turkey* **21 F12** 37 51N 27 51 E
Aydin □, *Turkey* **25 G4** 37 50N 28 0 E
Ayer, *U.S.A.* **79 D13** 42 34N 71 35W
Ayer's Cliff, *Canada* **79 A12** 45 10N 72 3W
Ayers Rock, *Australia* **61 E5** 25 23S 131 5 E
Ayia Aikateríni, Ákra, *Greece* **23 A3** 39 50N 19 50 E
Ayia Dhéka, *Greece* **23 D6** 35 3N 24 58 E
Ayia Gálini, *Greece* **23 D6** 35 6N 24 41 E
Ayia Napa, *Cyprus* **23 E13** 34 59N 34 0 E
Ayia Phyla, *Cyprus* **23 E12** 34 43N 33 1 E
Ayia Varvára, *Greece* **23 D7** 35 8N 25 1 E
Áyios Amvrósios, *Cyprus* **23 D12** 35 20N 33 35 E
Áyios Evstrátios, *Greece* **21 E11** 39 34N 24 58 E
Áyios Ioánnis, Ákra, *Greece* **23 D7** 35 20N 25 40 E
Áyios Isidhoros, *Greece* **23 C9** 36 9N 27 51 E
Áyios Matthaíos, *Greece* **23 B3** 39 30N 19 47 E
Áyios Nikólaos, *Greece* **23 D7** 35 11N 25 41 E
Áyios Seryios, *Cyprus* **23 D12** 35 12N 33 53 E
Ayios Theodhoros, *Cyprus* **23 D13** 35 22N 34 1 E
Aykino, *Russia* **24 B8** 62 15N 49 56 E
Aylesbury, *U.K.* **11 F7** 51 49N 0 49W
Aylmer, *Canada* **78 D4** 42 46N 80 59W
Aylmer, L., *Canada* **68 B8** 64 0N 110 8W
'Ayn, Wādī al, *Oman* **45 F7** 22 15N 55 28 E
Ayn Dār, *Si. Arabia* **45 E7** 25 55N 49 10 E
Ayn Zālah, *Iraq* **44 B4** 36 45N 42 35 E
Ayolas, *Paraguay* **94 B4** 27 10S 56 59W
Ayon, Ostrov, *Russia* **27 C17** 69 50N 169 0 E
'Ayoûn el 'Atroûs, *Mauritania* **50 E4** 16 40N 9 37W
Ayr, *Australia* **62 B4** 19 35S 147 25 E
Ayr, *Canada* **78 C4** 43 17N 80 27W
Ayr, *U.K.* **12 F4** 55 28N 4 38W
Ayr →, *U.K.* **12 F4** 55 28N 4 38W
Ayre, Pt. of, *U.K.* **10 C3** 54 25N 4 21W
Ayton, *Australia* **62 B4** 15 56S 145 22 E
Aytos, *Bulgaria* **21 C12** 42 42N 27 16 E
Ayu, Kepulauan, *Indonesia* **37 D8** 0 35N 131 5 E
Ayutla, *Guatemala* **88 D1** 14 40N 92 10W
Ayutla, *Mexico* **87 D5** 16 58N 99 17W
Ayvacık, *Turkey* **21 E12** 39 36N 26 24 E
Ayvalık, *Turkey* **21 E12** 39 20N 26 46 E
Az Zabadānī, *Syria* **47 B5** 33 43N 36 5 E
Aẓ Ẓāhirīyah, *West Bank* **47 D3** 31 25N 34 58 E
Aẓ Ẓahrān, *Si. Arabia* **45 E6** 26 10N 50 7 E
Az Zarqā, *Jordan* **47 C5** 32 5N 36 4 E
Az Zarqā', *U.A.E.* **45 E7** 24 53N 53 4 E
Az Zāwiyah, *Libya* **51 B8** 32 52N 12 56 E
Az Zībār, *Iraq* **44 B5** 36 52N 44 4 E
Az-Zilfī, *Si. Arabia* **44 E5** 26 12N 44 52 E
Az Zubayr, *Iraq* **44 D5** 30 26N 47 40 E
Azamgarh, *India* **43 F10** 26 5N 83 13 E
Azangaro, *Peru* **92 F4** 14 55S 70 13W
Āzār Shahr, *Iran* **44 B5** 37 45N 45 59 E
Azarān, *Iran* **44 B5** 37 25N 47 16 E
Azärbayjan = Azerbaijan ■, *Asia* **25 F8** 40 20N 48 0 E
Āzarbāyjān-e Gharbī □, *Iran* **44 B5** 37 0N 44 30 E
Āzarbāyjān-e Sharqī □, *Iran* **44 B5** 37 20N 47 0 E
Azare, *Nigeria* **50 F8** 11 55N 10 10 E
A'zāz, *Syria* **44 B3** 36 36N 37 4 E
Azbine = Aïr, *Niger* **50 E7** 18 30N 8 0 E
Azerbaijan ■, *Asia* **25 F8** 40 20N 48 0 E
Azerbaijchan = Azerbaijan ■, *Asia* **25 F8** 40 20N 48 0 E
Azimganj, *India* **43 G13** 24 14N 88 16 E
Azogues, *Ecuador* **92 D3** 2 35S 78 0W
Azores, *Atl. Oc.* **50 A1** 38 44N 29 0W
Azov, *Russia* **25 E6** 47 3N 39 25 E
Azov, Sea of, *Europe* **25 E6** 46 0N 36 30 E
Azovskoye More = Azov, Sea of, *Europe* **25 E6** 46 0N 36 30 E
Azraq ash Shīshān, *Jordan* **47 D5** 31 50N 36 49 E
Aztec, *U.S.A.* **83 H10** 36 49N 107 59W
Azúa de Compostela, *Dom. Rep.* **89 C5** 18 25N 70 44W
Azuaga, *Spain* **19 C3** 38 16N 5 39W
Azuero, Pen. de, *Panama* **88 E3** 7 30N 80 30W
Azul, *Argentina* **94 D4** 36 42S 59 43W
Azusa, *U.S.A.* **85 L9** 34 8N 117 52W

B

Ba Don, *Vietnam* **38 D6** 17 45N 106 26 E
Ba Dong, *Vietnam* **39 H6** 9 40N 106 33 E
Ba Ngoi = Cam Lam, *Vietnam* **39 G7** 11 54N 109 10 E
Ba Tri, *Vietnam* **39 G6** 10 2N 106 36 E
Ba Xian = Bazhou, *China* **34 E9** 39 8N 116 22 E
Baa, *Indonesia* **37 F6** 10 50S 123 0 E
Baarle-Nassau, *Belgium* **15 C4** 51 27N 4 56 E
Bab el Mandeb, *Red Sea* **46 E3** 12 35N 43 25 E
Baba Burnu, *Turkey* **21 E12** 39 29N 26 2 E
Bābā Kalū, *Iran* **45 D6** 30 7N 50 49 E
Babadag, *Romania* **17 F15** 44 53N 28 44 E
Babadayhan, *Turkmenistan* **26 F7** 37 42N 60 23 E
Babaeski, *Turkey* **21 D12** 41 26N 27 6 E
Babahoyo, *Ecuador* **92 D3** 1 40S 79 30W
Babai = Sarju →, *India* **43 F9** 27 21N 81 23 E
Babar, *Indonesia* **37 F7** 8 0S 129 30 E
Babar, *Pakistan* **42 D3** 31 7N 69 32 E
Babarkach, *Pakistan* **42 E3** 29 45N 68 0 E
Babb, *U.S.A.* **82 B7** 48 51N 113 27W
Babelthuap, *Pac. Oc.* **37 C8** 7 30N 134 30 E
Baberu, *India* **43 G9** 25 33N 80 43 E
Babi Besar, Pulau, *Malaysia* **39 L4** 2 25N 103 59 E
Babinda, *Australia* **62 B4** 17 20S 145 56 E
Babine, *Canada* **72 B3** 55 22N 126 37W
Babine →, *Canada* **72 B3** 55 45N 127 44W
Babine L., *Canada* **72 C3** 54 48N 126 0W
Babo, *Indonesia* **37 E8** 2 30S 133 30 E
Bābol, *Iran* **45 B7** 36 40N 52 50 E
Bābol Sar, *Iran* **45 B7** 36 45N 52 45 E
Babruysk, *Belarus* **17 B15** 53 10N 29 15 E
Babuhri, *India* **42 F3** 26 49N 69 43 E
Babusar Pass, *Pakistan* **43 B5** 35 12N 73 59 E
Babuyan Chan., *Phil.* **37 A6** 18 40N 121 30 E
Babylon, *Iraq* **44 C5** 32 34N 44 22 E
Bac Lieu, *Vietnam* **39 H5** 9 17N 105 43 E
Bac Phan, *Vietnam* **38 B5** 22 0N 105 0 E
Bacabal, *Brazil* **93 D10** 4 15S 44 45W
Bacalar, *Mexico* **87 D7** 18 50N 87 27W
Bacan, Kepulauan, *Indonesia* **37 E7** 0 35S 127 30 E
Bacarra, *Phil.* **37 A6** 18 15N 120 37 E
Bacău, *Romania* **17 E14** 46 35N 26 55 E
Bacerac, *Mexico* **86 A3** 30 18N 108 50W
Bach Long Vi, Dao, *Vietnam* **38 B6** 20 10N 107 40 E
Bachelina, *Russia* **26 D7** 57 45N 67 20 E
Bachhwara, *India* **43 G11** 25 35N 85 54 E
Back →, *Canada* **68 B9** 65 10N 104 0W
Bacolod, *Phil.* **37 B6** 10 40N 122 57 E
Bacuk, *Malaysia* **39 J4** 6 4N 102 25 E
Bād, *Iran* **45 C7** 33 41N 52 1 E
Bad →, *U.S.A.* **80 C4** 44 21N 100 22W
Bad Axe, *U.S.A.* **78 C2** 43 48N 83 0W
Bad Ischl, *Austria* **16 E7** 47 44N 13 38 E
Bad Kissingen, *Germany* **16 C6** 50 11N 10 4 E
Bad Lands, *U.S.A.* **80 D3** 43 40N 102 10W
Bada Barabil, *India* **43 H11** 22 7N 85 24 E
Badagara, *India* **40 P9** 11 35N 75 40 E
Badajós, L., *Brazil* **92 D6** 3 15S 62 50W
Badajoz, *Spain* **19 C2** 38 50N 6 59W
Badalona, *Spain* **19 B7** 41 26N 2 15 E
Badalzai, *Afghan.* **42 E1** 29 50N 65 35 E
Badampahar, *India* **41 H15** 22 10N 86 10 E
Badanah, *Si. Arabia* **44 D4** 30 58N 41 30 E
Badarinath, *India* **43 D8** 30 45N 79 30 E
Badas, Kepulauan, *Indonesia* **36 D3** 0 45N 107 5 E
Baddo →, *Pakistan* **40 F4** 28 0N 64 20 E
Bade, *Indonesia* **37 F9** 7 10S 139 35 E
Baden, *Austria* **16 D9** 48 1N 16 13 E
Baden, *U.S.A.* **78 F4** 40 38N 80 14W
Baden-Baden, *Germany* **16 D5** 48 44N 8 13 E
Baden-Württemberg □, *Germany* **16 D5** 48 20N 8 40 E
Badgastein, *Austria* **16 E7** 47 7N 13 9 E
Badger, *Canada* **71 C8** 49 0N 56 4W
Badger, *U.S.A.* **84 J7** 36 38N 119 1W
Bādghīsāt □, *Afghan.* **40 B3** 35 0N 63 0 E
Badgom, *India* **43 B6** 34 1N 74 45 E
Badin, *Pakistan* **42 G3** 24 38N 68 54 E
Badlands National Park, *U.S.A.* **80 D3** 43 38N 102 56W
Badrah, *Iraq* **44 C5** 33 6N 45 58 E
Badrinath, *India* **43 D8** 30 44N 79 29 E
Badulla, *Sri Lanka* **40 R12** 7 1N 81 7 E
Baena, *Spain* **19 D3** 37 37N 4 20W
Baeza, *Spain* **19 D4** 37 57N 3 25W
Baffin B., *Canada* **4 B4** 72 0N 64 0W
Baffin I., *Canada* **69 B12** 68 0N 75 0W
Bafing →, *Mali* **50 F3** 13 49N 10 50W
Bafliyūn, *Syria* **44 B3** 36 37N 36 59 E
Bafoulabé, *Mali* **50 F3** 13 50N 10 55W
Bafoussam, *Cameroon* **52 C2** 5 28N 10 25 E
Bāfq, *Iran* **45 D7** 31 40N 55 25 E
Bafra, *Turkey* **25 F6** 41 34N 35 54 E
Bāft, *Iran* **45 D8** 29 15N 56 38 E
Bafwasende, *Dem. Rep. of the Congo* **54 B2** 1 3N 27 5 E
Bagamoyo, *Tanzania* **54 D4** 6 28S 38 55 E
Bagan Datoh, *Malaysia* **39 L3** 3 59N 100 47 E
Bagan Serai, *Malaysia* **39 K3** 5 1N 100 32 E
Baganga, *Phil.* **37 C7** 7 34N 126 33 E
Bagani, *Namibia* **56 B3** 18 7S 21 41 E
Bagansiapiapi, *Indonesia* **36 D2** 2 12N 100 50 E
Bagasra, *India* **42 J4** 21 30N 71 0 E
Bagaud, *India* **42 H6** 22 19N 75 53 E
Bagdad, *U.S.A.* **85 L11** 34 35N 115 53W
Bagdarin, *Russia* **27 D12** 54 26N 113 36 E
Bagé, *Brazil* **95 C5** 31 20S 54 15W
Bagenalstown = Muine Bheag, *Ireland* **13 D5** 52 42N 6 58W
Baggs, *U.S.A.* **82 F10** 41 2N 107 39W
Bagh, *Pakistan* **43 C5** 33 59N 73 45 E
Baghain →, *India* **43 G9** 25 32N 81 1 E
Baghdād, *Iraq* **44 C5** 33 20N 44 30 E
Bagheria, *Italy* **20 E5** 38 5N 13 30 E
Baghlān, *Afghan.* **40 A6** 36 12N 69 0 E
Bagley, *U.S.A.* **80 B7** 47 32N 95 24W
Bagodar, *India* **43 G11** 24 5N 85 52 E
Bagrationovsk, *Russia* **9 J19** 54 23N 20 39 E
Baguio, *Phil.* **37 A6** 16 26N 120 34 E
Bah, *India* **43 F8** 26 53N 78 36 E
Bahadurganj, *India* **43 F12** 26 16N 87 49 E
Bahadurgarh, *India* **42 E7** 28 40N 76 57 E
Bahama, Canal Viejo de, *W. Indies* **88 B4** 22 10N 77 30W
Bahamas ■, *N. Amer.* **89 B5** 24 0N 75 0W
Baharampur, *India* **43 G13** 24 2N 88 27 E
Bahawalnagar, *Pakistan* **42 E5** 30 0N 73 15 E
Bahawalpur, *Pakistan* **42 E4** 29 24N 71 40 E
Baheri, *India* **43 E8** 28 45N 79 34 E
Bahgul →, *India* **43 F8** 27 45N 79 36 E
Bahi, *Tanzania* **54 D4** 5 58S 35 21 E
Bahi Swamp, *Tanzania* **54 D4** 6 10S 35 0 E
Bahía = Salvador, *Brazil* **93 F11** 13 0S 38 30W
Bahía □, *Brazil* **93 F10** 12 0S 42 0W
Bahía, Is. de la, *Honduras* **88 C2** 16 45N 86 15W
Bahía Blanca, *Argentina* **94 D3** 38 35S 62 13W
Bahía de Caráquez, *Ecuador* **92 D2** 0 40S 80 27W
Bahía Honda, *Cuba* **88 B3** 22 54N 83 10W
Bahía Laura, *Argentina* **96 F3** 48 10S 66 30W
Bahía Negra, *Paraguay* **92 H7** 20 5S 58 5W

Bardstown

ahir Dar, *Ethiopia* **46 E2** 11 37N 37 10 E
ahmanzād, *Iran* **45 D6** 31 15N 51 47 E
ahr el Ghazâl □, *Sudan* **51 G11** 7 0N 28 0 E
ahraich, *India* **43 F9** 27 38N 81 37 E
ahrain ■, *Asia* **45 E6** 26 0N 50 35 E
ahror, *India* **42 F7** 27 51N 76 20 E
āhū Kalāt, *Iran* **45 E9** 25 43N 61 25 E
ai Bung, Mui = Ca Mau, Mui, *Vietnam* **39 H5** 8 38N 104 44 E
ai Duc, *Vietnam* **38 C5** 18 3N 105 49 E
ai Thuong, *Vietnam* **38 C5** 19 54N 105 23 E
aia Mare, *Romania* **17 E12** 47 40N 23 35 E
aião, *Brazil* **93 D9** 2 40S 49 40W
aïbokoum, *Chad* **51 G9** 7 46N 15 43 E
aicheng, *China* **35 B12** 45 38N 122 42 E
aidoa, *Somali Rep.* **46 G3** 3 8N 43 30 E
aie Comeau, *Canada* **71 C6** 49 12N 68 10W
aie-St-Paul, *Canada* **71 C5** 47 28N 70 32W
aie Trinité, *Canada* **71 C6** 49 25N 67 20W
aie Verte, *Canada* **71 C8** 49 55N 56 12W
aihar, *India* **43 H9** 22 6N 80 33 E
aihe, *China* **34 H6** 32 50N 110 5 E
a'ījī, *Iraq* **44 C4** 35 0N 43 30 E
aijnath, *India* **43 E8** 29 55N 79 37 E
aikal, L. = Baykal, Oz., *Russia* **27 D11** 53 0N 108 0 E
aikunthpur, *India* **43 H10** 23 15N 82 33 E
aile Atha Cliath = Dublin, *Ireland* **13 C5** 53 21N 6 15W
ăilești, *Romania* **17 F12** 44 1N 23 20 E
ainbridge, *Ga., U.S.A.* **77 K3** 30 55N 84 35W
ainbridge, *N.Y., U.S.A.* **79 D9** 42 18N 75 29W
aing, *Indonesia* **37 F6** 10 14S 120 34 E
ainiu, *China* **34 H7** 32 50N 112 15 E
ā'ir, *Jordan* **47 E5** 30 45N 36 55 E
airin Youqi, *China* **35 C10** 43 30N 118 35 E
airin Zuoqi, *China* **35 C10** 43 58N 119 15 E
airnsdale, *Australia* **63 F4** 37 48S 147 36 E
aisha, *China* **34 G7** 34 20N 112 32 E
aitadi, *Nepal* **43 E9** 29 35N 80 25 E
aiyin, *China* **34 F3** 36 45N 104 14 E
aiyu Shan, *China* **34 F4** 37 15N 107 30 E
aj Baj, *India* **43 H13** 22 30N 88 5 E
aja, *Hungary* **17 E10** 46 12N 18 59 E
aja, Pta., *Mexico* **86 B1** 29 50N 116 0W
aja California, *Mexico* **86 A1** 31 10N 115 12W
aja California □, *Mexico* **86 B2** 30 0N 115 0W
aja California Sur □, *Mexico* **86 B2** 25 50N 111 50W
ajag, *India* **43 H9** 22 40N 81 21 E
ajamar, *Canary Is.* **22 F3** 28 33N 16 20W
ajana, *India* **42 H4** 23 7N 71 49 E
ājgīrān, *Iran* **45 B8** 37 36N 58 24 E
ajimba, Mt., *Australia* **63 D5** 29 17S 152 6 E
ajo Nuevo, *Caribbean* **88 C4** 15 40N 78 50W
ajoga, *Nigeria* **51 F8** 10 57N 11 20 E
ajool, *Australia* **62 C5** 23 40S 150 35 E
akel, *Senegal* **50 F3** 14 56N 12 20W
aker, *Calif., U.S.A.* **85 K10** 35 16N 116 4W
aker, *Mont., U.S.A.* **80 B2** 46 22N 104 17W
aker, L., *Canada* **68 B10** 64 0N 96 0W
aker City, *U.S.A.* **82 D5** 44 47N 117 50W
aker I., *Pac. Oc.* **64 G10** 0 10N 176 35W
aker I., *U.S.A.* **72 B2** 55 20N 133 40W
aker L., *Australia* **61 E4** 26 54S 126 5 E
aker Lake, *Canada* **68 B10** 64 20N 96 3W
aker Mt., *U.S.A.* **82 B3** 48 50N 121 49W
akers Creek, *Australia* **62 C4** 21 13S 149 7 E
aker's Dozen Is., *Canada* **70 A4** 56 45N 78 45W
akersfield, *Calif., U.S.A.* **85 K8** 35 23N 119 1W
akersfield, *Vt., U.S.A.* **79 B12** 44 45N 72 48W
ākhtarān, *Iran* **44 C5** 34 23N 47 0 E
ākhtarān □, *Iran* **44 C5** 34 0N 46 30 E
akı, *Azerbaijan* **25 F8** 40 29N 49 56 E
akkafjörður, *Iceland* **8 C6** 66 2N 14 48W
akony, *Hungary* **17 E9** 47 10N 17 30 E
akony Forest = Bakony, *Hungary* **17 E9** 47 10N 17 30 E
akouma, *C.A.R.* **52 C4** 5 40N 22 56 E
akswaho, *India* **43 G8** 24 15N 79 18 E
aku = Bakı, *Azerbaijan* **25 F8** 40 29N 49 56 E
akutis Coast, *Antarctica* **5 D15** 74 0S 120 0W
aky = Bakı, *Azerbaijan* **25 F8** 40 29N 49 56 E
ala, *Canada* **78 A5** 45 1N 79 37W
ala, *U.K.* **10 E4** 52 54N 3 36W
ala, L., *U.K.* **10 E4** 52 53N 3 37W
alabac I., *Phil.* **36 C5** 8 0N 117 0 E
alabac Str., *E. Indies* **36 C5** 7 53N 117 5 E
alabagh, *Afghan.* **42 B4** 34 25N 70 12 E
a'labakk, *Lebanon* **47 B5** 34 0N 36 10 E
alabalangan, Kepulauan, *Indonesia* **36 E5** 2 20S 117 30 E
alad, *Iraq* **44 C5** 34 1N 44 9 E
alad Rūz, *Iraq* **44 C5** 33 42N 45 5 E
ālādeh, *Fārs, Iran* **45 D6** 29 17N 51 56 E
ālādeh, *Māzandaran, Iran* **45 B6** 36 12N 51 48 E
alaghat, *India* **40 J12** 21 49N 80 12 E
alaghat Ra., *India* **40 K10** 18 50N 76 30 E
alaguer, *Spain* **19 B6** 41 50N 0 50 E
alaklava, *Ukraine* **25 F5** 44 30N 33 30 E
alakovo, *Russia* **24 D8** 52 4N 47 55 E
alamau, *India* **43 F9** 27 10N 80 21 E
alancán, *Mexico* **87 D6** 17 48N 91 32W
alashov, *Russia* **25 D7** 51 30N 43 10 E
alasinor, *India* **42 H5** 22 57N 73 23 E
alasore = Baleshwar, *India* **41 J15** 21 35N 87 3 E
alaton, *Hungary* **17 E9** 46 50N 17 40 E
albina, Reprêsa de, *Brazil* **92 D7** 2 0S 59 30W
alboa, *Panama* **88 E4** 8 57N 79 34W
albriggan, *Ireland* **13 C5** 53 37N 6 11W
alcarce, *Argentina* **94 D4** 38 0S 58 10W
alcarres, *Canada* **73 C8** 50 50N 103 35W
alchik, *Bulgaria* **21 C13** 43 28N 28 11 E
alclutha, *N.Z.* **59 M2** 46 15S 169 45 E
alcones Escarpment, *U.S.A.* **81 L5** 29 30N 99 15W
ald Hd., *Australia* **61 G2** 35 6S 118 1 E
ald I., *Australia* **61 F2** 34 57S 118 27 E
ald Knob, *U.S.A.* **81 H9** 35 19N 91 34W
aldock L., *Canada* **73 B9** 56 33N 97 57W
aldwin, *Mich., U.S.A.* **76 D3** 43 54N 85 51W
aldwin, *Pa., U.S.A.* **78 F5** 40 23N 79 59W
aldwinsville, *U.S.A.* **79 C8** 43 10N 76 20W
aldy Mt., *U.S.A.* **82 B9** 48 9N 109 39W
aldy Peak, *U.S.A.* **83 K9** 33 54N 109 34W
aleares, Is., *Spain* **22 B10** 39 30N 3 0 E
Balearic Is. = Baleares, Is., *Spain* **22 B10** 39 30N 3 0 E
Baleine = Whale →, *Canada* **71 A6** 58 15N 67 40W
Baler, *Phil.* **37 A6** 15 46N 121 34 E
Baleshare, *U.K.* **12 D1** 57 31N 7 22W
Baleshwar, *India* **41 J15** 21 35N 87 3 E
Balfate, *Honduras* **88 C2** 15 48N 86 25W
Balí, *Greece* **23 D6** 35 25N 24 47 E
Bali, *India* **42 G5** 25 11N 73 17 E
Bali □, *Indonesia* **36 F5** 8 20S 115 0 E
Bali, Selat, *Indonesia* **37 H16** 8 18S 114 25 E
Baliapal, *India* **43 J12** 21 40N 87 17 E
Balikeşir, *Turkey* **21 E12** 39 39N 27 53 E
Balikpapan, *Indonesia* **36 E5** 1 10S 116 55 E
Balimbing, *Phil.* **37 C5** 5 5N 119 58 E
Baling, *Malaysia* **39 K3** 5 41N 100 55 E
Balipara, *India* **41 F18** 26 50N 92 45 E
Balkan Mts. = Stara Planina, *Bulgaria* **21 C10** 43 15N 23 0 E
Balkhash = Balqash, *Kazakstan* **26 E8** 46 50N 74 50 E
Balkhash, Ozero = Balqash Köl, *Kazakstan* **26 E8** 46 0N 74 50 E
Balla, *Bangla.* **41 G17** 24 10N 91 35 E
Ballachulish, *U.K.* **12 E3** 56 41N 5 8W
Balladonia, *Australia* **61 F3** 32 27S 123 51 E
Ballaghaderreen, *Ireland* **13 C3** 53 55N 8 34W
Ballarat, *Australia* **63 F3** 37 33S 143 50 E
Ballard, L., *Australia* **61 E3** 29 20S 120 40 E
Ballater, *U.K.* **12 D5** 57 3N 3 3W
Ballenas, Canal de, *Mexico* **86 B2** 29 10N 113 45W
Balleny Is., *Antarctica* **5 C11** 66 30S 163 0 E
Ballia, *India* **43 G11** 25 46N 84 12 E
Ballina, *Australia* **63 D5** 28 50S 153 31 E
Ballina, *Ireland* **13 B2** 54 7N 9 9W
Ballinasloe, *Ireland* **13 C3** 53 20N 8 13W
Ballinger, *U.S.A.* **81 K5** 31 45N 99 57W
Ballinrobe, *Ireland* **13 C2** 53 38N 9 13W
Ballinskelligs B., *Ireland* **13 E1** 51 48N 10 13W
Ballston Spa, *U.S.A.* **79 D11** 43 0N 73 51W
Ballycastle, *U.K.* **13 A5** 55 12N 6 15W
Ballyclare, *U.K.* **13 B5** 54 46N 6 0W
Ballyhaunis, *Ireland* **13 C3** 53 46N 8 46W
Ballymena, *U.K.* **13 B5** 54 52N 6 17W
Ballymoney, *U.K.* **13 A5** 55 5N 6 31W
Ballymote, *Ireland* **13 B3** 54 5N 8 31W
Ballynahinch, *U.K.* **13 B6** 54 24N 5 54W
Ballyquintin Pt., *U.K.* **13 B6** 54 20N 5 30W
Ballyshannon, *Ireland* **13 B3** 54 30N 8 11W
Balmaceda, *Chile* **96 F2** 46 0S 71 50W
Balmertown, *Canada* **73 C10** 51 4N 93 41W
Balmoral, *Australia* **63 F3** 37 15S 141 48 E
Balmorhea, *U.S.A.* **81 K3** 30 59N 103 45W
Balonne →, *Australia* **63 D4** 28 47S 147 56 E
Balotra, *India* **42 G5** 25 50N 72 14 E
Balqash, *Kazakstan* **26 E8** 46 50N 74 50 E
Balqash Köl, *Kazakstan* **26 E8** 46 0N 74 50 E
Balrampur, *India* **43 F10** 27 30N 82 20 E
Balranald, *Australia* **63 E3** 34 38S 143 33 E
Balsas, *Mexico* **87 D5** 18 0N 99 40W
Balsas →, *Brazil* **93 E9** 7 15S 44 35W
Balsas →, *Mexico* **86 D4** 17 55N 102 10W
Balston Spa, *U.S.A.* **79 D11** 43 0N 73 52W
Balta, *Ukraine* **17 D15** 48 2N 29 45 E
Bălți, *Moldova* **17 E14** 47 48N 27 58 E
Baltic Sea, *Europe* **9 H18** 57 0N 19 0 E
Baltimore, *Ireland* **13 E2** 51 29N 9 22W
Baltimore, *Md., U.S.A.* **76 F7** 39 17N 76 37W
Baltimore, *Ohio, U.S.A.* **78 G2** 39 51N 82 36W
Baltit, *Pakistan* **43 A6** 36 15N 74 40 E
Baltiysk, *Russia* **9 J18** 54 41N 19 58 E
Baluchistan □, *Pakistan* **40 F4** 27 30N 65 0 E
Balurghat, *India* **43 G13** 25 15N 88 44 E
Balvi, *Latvia* **9 H22** 57 8N 27 15 E
Balya, *Turkey* **21 E12** 39 44N 27 35 E
Bam, *Iran* **45 D8** 29 7N 58 14 E
Bama, *Nigeria* **51 F8** 11 33N 13 41 E
Bamaga, *Australia* **62 A3** 10 50S 142 25 E
Bamaji L., *Canada* **70 B1** 51 9N 91 25W
Bamako, *Mali* **50 F4** 12 34N 7 55W
Bambari, *C.A.R.* **52 C4** 5 40N 20 35 E
Bambaroo, *Australia* **62 B4** 18 50S 146 10 E
Bamberg, *Germany* **16 D6** 49 54N 10 54 E
Bamberg, *U.S.A.* **77 J5** 33 18N 81 2W
Bambili, *Dem. Rep. of the Congo* **54 B2** 3 40N 26 0 E
Bamenda, *Cameroon* **52 C1** 5 57N 10 11 E
Bamfield, *Canada* **72 D3** 48 45N 125 10W
Bāmīān □, *Afghan.* **40 B5** 35 0N 67 0 E
Bamiancheng, *China* **35 C13** 43 15N 124 2 E
Bampūr, *Iran* **45 E9** 27 15N 60 21 E
Ban Ban, *Laos* **38 C4** 19 31N 103 30 E
Ban Bang Hin, *Thailand* **39 H2** 9 32N 98 35 E
Ban Chiang Klang, *Thailand* **38 C3** 19 25N 100 55 E
Ban Chik, *Laos* **38 D4** 17 15N 102 22 E
Ban Choho, *Thailand* **38 E4** 15 2N 102 9 E
Ban Dan Lan Hoi, *Thailand* **38 D2** 17 0N 99 35 E
Ban Don = Surat Thani, *Thailand* **39 H2** 9 6N 99 20 E
Ban Don, *Vietnam* **38 F6** 12 53N 107 48 E
Ban Don, Ao →, *Thailand* **39 H2** 9 20N 99 25 E
Ban Dong, *Thailand* **38 C3** 19 30N 100 59 E
Ban Hong, *Thailand* **38 C2** 18 18N 98 50 E
Ban Kaeng, *Thailand* **38 D3** 17 29N 100 7 E
Ban Kantang, *Thailand* **39 J2** 7 25N 99 31 E
Ban Keun, *Laos* **38 C4** 18 22N 102 35 E
Ban Khai, *Thailand* **38 F3** 12 46N 101 18 E
Ban Kheun, *Laos* **38 B3** 20 13N 101 7 E
Ban Khlong Kua, *Thailand* **39 J3** 6 57N 100 8 E
Ban Khuan Mao, *Thailand* **39 J2** 7 50N 99 37 E
Ban Ko Yai Chim, *Thailand* **39 G2** 11 17N 99 26 E
Ban Kok, *Thailand* **38 D4** 16 40N 103 40 E
Ban Laem, *Thailand* **38 F2** 13 13N 99 59 E
Ban Lao Ngam, *Laos* **38 E6** 15 28N 106 10 E
Ban Le Kathe, *Thailand* **38 E2** 15 49N 98 53 E
Ban Mae Chedi, *Thailand* **38 C2** 19 11N 99 31 E
Ban Mae Laeng, *Thailand* **38 B2** 20 1N 99 17 E
Ban Mae Sariang, *Thailand* **38 C1** 18 10N 97 56 E
Ban Mê Thuôt = Buon Ma Thuot, *Vietnam* **38 F7** 12 40N 108 3 E
Ban Mi, *Thailand* **38 E3** 15 3N 100 32 E
Ban Muong Mo, *Laos* **38 C4** 19 4N 103 58 E
Ban Na Mo, *Laos* **38 D5** 17 7N 105 40 E
Ban Na San, *Thailand* **39 H2** 8 53N 99 52 E
Ban Na Tong, *Laos* **38 B3** 20 56N 101 47 E
Ban Nam Bac, *Laos* **38 B4** 20 38N 102 20 E
Ban Nam Ma, *Laos* **38 A3** 22 2N 101 37 E
Ban Ngang, *Laos* **38 E6** 15 59N 106 11 E
Ban Nong Bok, *Laos* **38 D5** 17 5N 104 48 E
Ban Nong Boua, *Laos* **38 E6** 15 40N 106 33 E
Ban Nong Pling, *Thailand* **38 E3** 15 40N 100 10 E
Ban Pak Chan, *Thailand* **39 G2** 10 32N 98 51 E
Ban Phai, *Thailand* **38 D4** 16 4N 102 44 E
Ban Pong, *Thailand* **38 F2** 13 50N 99 55 E
Ban Ron Phibun, *Thailand* **39 H2** 8 9N 99 51 E
Ban Sanam Chai, *Thailand* **39 J3** 7 33N 100 25 E
Ban Sangkha, *Thailand* **38 E4** 14 37N 103 52 E
Ban Tak, *Thailand* **38 D2** 17 2N 99 4 E
Ban Tako, *Thailand* **38 E4** 14 5N 102 40 E
Ban Tha Dua, *Thailand* **38 D2** 17 59N 98 39 E
Ban Tha Li, *Thailand* **38 D3** 17 37N 101 25 E
Ban Tha Nun, *Thailand* **39 H2** 8 12N 98 18 E
Ban Thahine, *Laos* **38 E5** 14 12N 105 33 E
Ban Xien Kok, *Laos* **38 B3** 20 54N 100 39 E
Ban Yen Nhan, *Vietnam* **38 B6** 20 57N 106 2 E
Banaba, *Kiribati* **64 H8** 0 45S 169 50 E
Banalia, *Dem. Rep. of the Congo* **54 B2** 1 32N 25 5 E
Banam, *Cambodia* **39 G5** 11 20N 105 17 E
Bananal, I. do, *Brazil* **93 F8** 11 30S 50 30W
Banaras = Varanasi, *India* **43 G10** 25 22N 83 0 E
Banas →, *Gujarat, India* **42 H4** 23 45N 71 25 E
Banas →, *Mad. P., India* **43 G9** 24 15N 81 30 E
Bânâs, Ras, *Egypt* **51 D13** 23 57N 35 59 E
Banbān, *Si. Arabia* **44 E5** 25 1N 46 35 E
Banbridge, *U.K.* **13 B5** 54 22N 6 16W
Banbury, *U.K.* **11 E6** 52 4N 1 20W
Banchory, *U.K.* **12 D6** 57 3N 2 29W
Bancroft, *Canada* **78 A7** 45 3N 77 51W
Band Bonī, *Iran* **45 E8** 25 30N 59 33 E
Band Qīr, *Iran* **45 D6** 31 39N 48 53 E
Banda, *India* **43 G9** 25 30N 80 26 E
Banda, *Mad. P., India* **43 G8** 24 3N 78 57 E
Banda, Kepulauan, *Indonesia* **37 E7** 4 37S 129 50 E
Banda Aceh, *Indonesia* **36 C1** 5 35N 95 20 E
Banda Banda, Mt., *Australia* **63 E5** 31 10S 152 28 E
Banda Elat, *Indonesia* **37 F8** 5 40S 133 5 E
Banda Is. = Banda, Kepulauan, *Indonesia* **37 E7** 4 37S 129 50 E
Banda Sea, *Indonesia* **37 F8** 6 0S 130 0 E
Bandai-San, *Japan* **30 F10** 37 36N 140 4 E
Bandān, *Iran* **45 D9** 31 23N 60 44 E
Bandanaira, *Indonesia* **37 E7** 4 32S 129 54 E
Bandanwara, *India* **42 F6** 26 9N 74 38 E
Bandar = Machilipatnam, *India* **41 L12** 16 12N 81 8 E
Bandār 'Abbās, *Iran* **45 E8** 27 15N 56 15 E
Bandar-e Anzalī, *Iran* **45 B6** 37 30N 49 30 E
Bandar-e Bushehr = Būshehr, *Iran* **45 D6** 28 55N 50 55 E
Bandar-e Chārak, *Iran* **45 E7** 26 45N 54 20 E
Bandar-e Deylam, *Iran* **45 D6** 30 5N 50 10 E
Bandar-e Khomeynı, *Iran* **45 D6** 30 30N 49 5 E
Bandar-e Lengeh, *Iran* **45 E7** 26 35N 54 58 E
Bandar-e Maqām, *Iran* **45 E7** 26 56N 53 29 E
Bandar-e Ma'shur, *Iran* **45 D6** 30 35N 49 10 E
Bandar-e Nakhīlū, *Iran* **45 E7** 26 58N 53 30 E
Bandar-e Rīg, *Iran* **45 D6** 29 29N 50 38 E
Bandar-e Torkeman, *Iran* **45 B7** 37 0N 54 10 E
Bandar Maharani = Muar, *Malaysia* **39 L4** 2 3N 102 34 E
Bandar Penggaram = Batu Pahat, *Malaysia* **39 M4** 1 50N 102 56 E
Bandar Seri Begawan, *Brunei* **36 D5** 4 52N 115 0 E
Bandar Sri Aman, *Malaysia* **36 D4** 1 15N 111 32 E
Bandawe, *Malawi* **55 E3** 11 58S 34 5 E
Bandeira, Pico da, *Brazil* **95 A7** 20 26S 41 47W
Bandera, *Argentina* **94 B3** 28 55S 62 20W
Banderas, B. de, *Mexico* **86 C3** 20 40N 105 30W
Bandhogarh, *India* **43 H9** 23 40N 81 2 E
Bandi →, *India* **42 F6** 26 12N 75 47 E
Bandikui, *India* **42 F7** 27 3N 76 34 E
Bandırma, *Turkey* **21 D13** 40 20N 28 0 E
Bandon, *Ireland* **13 E3** 51 44N 8 44W
Bandon →, *Ireland* **13 E3** 51 43N 8 37W
Bandula, *Mozam.* **55 F3** 19 0S 33 7 E
Bandundu, *Dem. Rep. of the Congo* **52 E3** 3 15S 17 22 E
Bandung, *Indonesia* **37 G12** 6 54S 107 36 E
Bāneh, *Iran* **44 C5** 35 59N 45 53 E
Banes, *Cuba* **89 B4** 21 0N 75 42W
Banff, *Canada* **72 C5** 51 10N 115 34W
Banff, *U.K.* **12 D6** 57 40N 2 33W
Banff Nat. Park, *Canada* **72 C5** 51 30N 116 15W
Bang Fai →, *Laos* **38 D5** 16 57N 104 45 E
Bang Hieng →, *Laos* **38 D5** 16 10N 105 10 E
Bang Krathum, *Thailand* **38 D3** 16 34N 100 18 E
Bang Lamung, *Thailand* **38 F3** 13 3N 100 56 E
Bang Mun Nak, *Thailand* **38 D3** 16 2N 100 23 E
Bang Pa In, *Thailand* **38 E3** 14 14N 100 35 E
Bang Rakam, *Thailand* **38 D3** 16 45N 100 7 E
Bang Saphan, *Thailand* **39 G2** 11 14N 99 28 E
Bangaduni I., *India* **43 J13** 21 34N 88 52 E
Bangala Dam, *Zimbabwe* **55 G3** 21 7S 31 25 E
Bangalore, *India* **40 N10** 12 59N 77 40 E
Banganga →, *India* **42 F6** 27 6N 77 25 E
Bangaon, *India* **43 H13** 23 0N 88 47 E
Bangassou, *C.A.R.* **52 D4** 4 55N 23 7 E
Banggai, *Indonesia* **37 E6** 1 34S 123 30 E
Banggai, Kepulauan, *Indonesia* **37 E6** 1 40S 123 30 E
Banggai Arch. = Banggai, Kepulauan, *Indonesia* **37 E6** 1 40S 123 30 E
Banggi, *Malaysia* **36 C5** 7 17N 117 12 E
Banghāzī, *Libya* **51 B10** 32 11N 20 3 E
Bangka, *Sulawesi, Indonesia* **37 D7** 1 50N 125 5 E
Bangka, *Sumatera, Indonesia* **36 E3** 2 0S 105 50 E
Bangka, Selat, *Indonesia* **36 E3** 2 30S 105 30 E
Bangkalan, *Indonesia* **37 G15** 7 2S 112 46 E
Bangkinang, *Indonesia* **36 D2** 0 18N 101 5 E
Bangko, *Indonesia* **36 E2** 2 5S 102 9 E
Bangkok, *Thailand* **38 F3** 13 45N 100 35 E
Bangladesh ■, *Asia* **41 H17** 24 0N 90 0 E
Bangong Co, *India* **43 B8** 35 50N 79 20 E
Bangor, *Down, U.K.* **13 B6** 54 40N 5 40W
Bangor, *Gwynedd, U.K.* **10 D3** 53 14N 4 8W
Bangor, *Maine, U.S.A.* **69 D13** 44 48N 68 46W
Bangor, *Pa., U.S.A.* **79 F9** 40 52N 75 13W
Bangued, *Phil.* **37 A6** 17 40N 120 37 E
Bangui, *C.A.R.* **52 D3** 4 23N 18 35 E
Banguru, *Dem. Rep. of the Congo* **54 B2** 0 30N 27 10 E
Bangweulu, L., *Zambia* **55 E3** 11 0S 30 0 E
Bangweulu Swamp, *Zambia* **55 E3** 11 20S 30 15 E
Bani, *Dom. Rep.* **89 C5** 18 16N 70 22W
Banī Sa'd, *Iraq* **44 C5** 33 34N 44 32 E
Banihal Pass, *India* **43 C6** 33 30N 75 12 E
Bāniyās, *Syria* **44 C3** 35 10N 36 0 E
Banja Luka, *Bos.-H.* **20 B7** 44 49N 17 11 E
Banjar, *India* **42 D7** 31 38N 77 21 E
Banjar →, *India* **43 H9** 22 36N 80 22 E
Banjarmasin, *Indonesia* **36 E4** 3 20S 114 35 E
Banjul, *Gambia* **50 F2** 13 28N 16 40W
Banka, *India* **43 G12** 24 53N 86 55 E
Banket, *Zimbabwe* **55 F3** 17 27S 30 19 E
Bankipore, *India* **41 G14** 25 35N 85 10 E
Banks I., *B.C., Canada* **72 C3** 53 20N 130 0W
Banks I., *N.W.T., Canada* **68 A7** 73 15N 121 30W
Banks Pen., *N.Z.* **59 K4** 43 45S 173 15 E
Banks Str., *Australia* **62 G4** 40 40S 148 10 E
Bankura, *India* **43 H12** 23 11N 87 18 E
Banmankhi, *India* **43 G12** 25 53N 87 11 E
Bann →, *Arm., U.K.* **13 B5** 54 30N 6 31W
Bann →, *L'derry., U.K.* **13 A5** 55 8N 6 41W
Bannang Sata, *Thailand* **39 J3** 6 16N 101 16 E
Banning, *U.S.A.* **85 M10** 33 56N 116 53W
Banningville = Bandundu, *Dem. Rep. of the Congo* **52 E3** 3 15S 17 22 E
Bannockburn, *Canada* **78 B7** 44 39N 77 33W
Bannockburn, *U.K.* **12 E5** 56 5N 3 55W
Bannockburn, *Zimbabwe* **55 G2** 20 17S 29 48 E
Bannu, *Pakistan* **40 C7** 33 0N 70 18 E
Bano, *India* **43 H11** 22 40N 84 55 E
Bansgaon, *India* **43 F10** 26 33N 83 21 E
Banská Bystrica, *Slovak Rep.* **17 D10** 48 46N 19 14 E
Banswara, *India* **42 H6** 23 32N 74 24 E
Bantaeng, *Indonesia* **37 F5** 5 32S 119 56 E
Bantry, *Ireland* **13 E2** 51 41N 9 27W
Bantry B., *Ireland* **13 E2** 51 37N 9 44W
Bantul, *Indonesia* **37 G14** 7 55S 110 19 E
Bantva, *India* **42 J4** 21 29N 70 12 E
Banu, *Afghan.* **40 B6** 35 35N 69 5 E
Banyak, Kepulauan, *Indonesia* **36 D1** 2 10N 97 10 E
Banyalbufar, *Spain* **22 B9** 39 42N 2 31 E
Banyo, *Cameroon* **52 C2** 6 52N 11 45 E
Banyumas, *Indonesia* **37 G13** 7 32S 109 18 E
Banyuwangi, *Indonesia* **37 H16** 8 13S 114 21 E
Banzare Coast, *Antarctica* **5 C9** 68 0S 125 0 E
Banzyville = Mobayi, *Dem. Rep. of the Congo* **52 D4** 4 15N 21 8 E
Bao Lac, *Vietnam* **38 A5** 22 57N 105 40 E
Bao Loc, *Vietnam* **39 G6** 11 32N 107 48 E
Baocheng, *China* **34 H4** 33 12N 106 56 E
Baode, *China* **34 E6** 39 1N 111 5 E
Baodi, *China* **35 E9** 39 38N 117 20 E
Baoding, *China* **34 E8** 38 50N 115 28 E
Baoji, *China* **34 G4** 34 20N 107 5 E
Baoshan, *China* **32 D4** 25 10N 99 5 E
Baotou, *China* **34 D6** 40 32N 110 2 E
Baoying, *China* **35 H10** 33 17N 119 20 E
Bap, *India* **42 F5** 27 23N 72 18 E
Bapatla, *India* **41 M12** 15 55N 80 30 E
Bāqerābād, *Iran* **45 C6** 33 2N 51 58 E
Ba'qūbah, *Iraq* **44 C5** 33 45N 44 50 E
Baquedano, *Chile* **94 A2** 23 20S 69 52W
Bar, *Montenegro, Yug.* **21 C8** 42 8N 19 6 E
Bar, *Ukraine* **17 D14** 49 4N 27 40 E
Bar Bigha, *India* **43 G11** 25 21N 85 47 E
Bar Harbor, *U.S.A.* **77 C11** 44 23N 68 13W
Bar-le-Duc, *France* **18 B6** 48 47N 5 10 E
Bara, *India* **43 G9** 25 16N 81 43 E
Bara Banki, *India* **43 F9** 26 55N 81 12 E
Barabai, *Indonesia* **36 E5** 2 32S 115 34 E
Baraboo, *U.S.A.* **80 D10** 43 28N 89 45W
Baracoa, *Cuba* **89 B5** 20 20N 74 30W
Baradā →, *Syria* **47 B5** 33 33N 36 34 E
Baradero, *Argentina* **94 C4** 33 52S 59 29W
Baradine, *Australia* **63 E4** 30 56S 149 4 E
Baraga, *U.S.A.* **80 B10** 46 47N 88 30W
Barah →, *India* **42 F6** 27 42N 77 5 E
Barahona, *Dom. Rep.* **89 C5** 18 13N 71 7W
Barail Range, *India* **41 G18** 25 15N 93 20 E
Barakaldo, *Spain* **19 A4** 43 18N 2 59W
Barakar →, *India* **43 G12** 24 7N 86 14 E
Barakhola, *India* **41 G18** 25 0N 92 45 E
Barakot, *India* **43 J11** 21 33N 84 59 E
Barakpur, *India* **43 H13** 22 44N 88 30 E
Baralaba, *Australia* **62 C4** 24 13S 149 50 E
Baralzon L., *Canada* **73 B9** 60 0N 98 3W
Baramula, *India* **43 B6** 34 15N 74 20 E
Baran, *India* **42 G7** 25 9N 76 40 E
Baran →, *Pakistan* **42 G3** 25 13N 68 17 E
Baranavichy, *Belarus* **17 B14** 53 10N 26 0 E
Baranof, *U.S.A.* **72 B2** 57 5N 134 50W
Baranof I., *U.S.A.* **68 C6** 57 0N 135 0W
Barapasi, *Indonesia* **37 E9** 2 15S 137 5 E
Barasat, *India* **43 H13** 22 46N 88 31 E
Barat Daya, Kepulauan, *Indonesia* **37 F7** 7 30S 128 0 E
Barataria B., *U.S.A.* **81 L10** 29 20N 89 55W
Barauda, *India* **42 H6** 23 33N 75 15 E
Baraut, *India* **42 E7** 29 13N 77 7 E
Barbacena, *Brazil* **95 A7** 21 15S 43 56W
Barbados ■, *W. Indies* **89 D8** 13 10N 59 30W
Barbària, C. de, *Spain* **22 C7** 38 39N 1 24 E
Barbastro, *Spain* **19 A6** 42 2N 0 5 E
Barberton, *S. Africa* **57 D5** 25 42S 31 2 E
Barberton, *U.S.A.* **78 E3** 41 0N 81 39W
Barbosa, *Colombia* **92 B4** 5 57N 73 37W
Barbourville, *U.S.A.* **77 G4** 36 52N 83 53W
Barbuda, *W. Indies* **89 C7** 17 30N 61 40W
Barcaldine, *Australia* **62 C4** 23 43S 145 6 E
Barcellona Pozzo di Gotto, *Italy* **20 E6** 38 9N 15 13 E
Barcelona, *Spain* **19 B7** 41 21N 2 10 E
Barcelona, *Venezuela* **92 A6** 10 10N 64 40W
Barcelos, *Brazil* **92 D6** 1 0S 63 0W
Barcoo →, *Australia* **62 D3** 25 30S 142 50 E
Bardaï, *Chad* **51 D9** 21 25N 17 0 E
Bardas Blancas, *Argentina* **94 D2** 35 49S 69 45W
Barddhaman, *India* **43 H12** 23 14N 87 39 E
Bardejov, *Slovak Rep.* **17 D11** 49 18N 21 15 E
Bardera, *Somali Rep.* **46 G3** 2 20N 42 27 E
Bardīyah, *Libya* **51 B10** 31 45N 25 5 E
Bardsey I., *U.K.* **10 E3** 52 45N 4 47W
Bardstown, *U.S.A.* **76 G3** 37 49N 85 28W

Big Timber

fast, Maine, U.S.A. 77 C11 44 26N 69 1W
fast, N.Y., U.S.A. 78 D6 42 21N 78 7W
fast L., U.K. 13 B6 54 40N 5 50W
field, U.S.A. 80 B3 46 53N 103 12W
fort, France 18 C7 47 38N 6 50 E
fry, U.S.A. 82 D9 45 9N 109 1W
gaum, India 40 M9 15 55N 74 35 E
gium ■, Europe 15 D4 50 30N 5 0 E
gorod, Russia 25 D6 50 35N 36 35 E
gorod-Dnestrovskiy = Bilhorod-Dnistrovskyy, Ukraine 25 E5 46 11N 30 23 E
lgrade = Beograd, Serbia, Yug. 21 B9 44 50N 20 37 E
lgrade, U.S.A. 82 D8 45 47N 111 11W
lhaven, U.S.A. 77 H7 35 33N 76 37W
li Drim →, Europe 21 C9 42 6N 20 25 E
linyu, Indonesia 36 E3 1 35 S 105 50 E
liton Is. = Belitung, Indonesia 36 E3 3 10 S 107 50 E
litung, Indonesia 36 E3 3 10 S 107 50 E
lize ■, Cent. Amer. 87 D7 17 0N 88 30W
lize City, Belize 87 D7 17 25N 88 0W
lkovskiy, Ostrov, Russia 27 B14 75 32N 135 44 E
ll →, Canada 70 C4 49 48N 77 38W
ll I., Canada 71 B8 50 46N 55 35W
ll-Irving →, Canada 72 B3 56 12N 129 5W
ll Peninsula, Canada 69 B11 63 50N 82 0W
ll Ville, Argentina 94 C3 32 40 S 62 40W
lla Bella, Canada 72 C3 52 10N 128 10W
lla Coola, Canada 72 C3 52 25N 126 40W
lla Unión, Uruguay 94 C4 30 15 S 57 40W
lla Vista, Corrientes, Argentina 94 B4 28 33 S 59 0W
lla Vista, Tucuman, Argentina 94 B2 27 10 S 65 25W
llaire, U.S.A. 78 F4 40 1N 80 45W
llary, India 40 M10 15 10N 76 56 E
llata, Australia 63 D4 29 53 S 149 46 E
lle-Chasse, U.S.A. 81 L10 29 51N 89 59W
lle Fourche, U.S.A. 80 C3 44 40N 103 51W
lle Fourche →, U.S.A. 80 C3 44 26N 102 18W
lle Glade, U.S.A. 77 M5 26 41N 80 40W
lle-Île, France 18 C2 47 20N 3 10W
lle Isle, Canada 71 B8 51 57N 55 25W
lle Isle, Str. of, Canada 71 B8 51 30N 56 30W
lle Plaine, U.S.A. 80 E8 41 54N 92 17W
llefontaine, U.S.A. 76 E4 40 22N 83 46W
llefonte, U.S.A. 78 F7 40 55N 77 47W
lleoram, Canada 71 C8 47 31N 55 25W
lleville, Canada 78 B7 44 10N 77 23W
lleville, Ill., U.S.A. 80 F10 38 31N 89 59W
lleville, Kans., U.S.A. 80 F6 39 50N 97 38W
lleville, N.Y., U.S.A. 79 C8 43 46N 76 10W
llevue, Canada 72 D6 49 35N 114 22W
llevue, Idaho, U.S.A. 82 E6 43 28N 114 16W
llevue, Nebr., U.S.A. 80 E7 41 8N 95 53W
llevue, Ohio, U.S.A. 78 E2 41 17N 82 51W
llevue, Wash., U.S.A. 84 C4 47 37N 122 12W
llin = Kangirsuk, Canada 69 C13 60 0N 70 0W
llingen, Australia 63 E5 30 25 S 152 50 E
llingham, U.S.A. 68 D7 48 46N 122 29W
llingshausen Sea, Antarctica 5 C17 66 0 S 80 0W
llinzona, Switz. 18 C8 46 11N 9 1 E
llo, Colombia 92 B3 6 20N 75 33W
llows Falls, U.S.A. 79 C12 43 8N 72 27W
llpat, Pakistan 42 E3 29 0N 68 5 E
lluno, Italy 20 A5 46 9N 12 13 E
llwood, U.S.A. 78 F6 40 36N 78 20W
lmont, Canada 78 D3 42 53N 81 5W
lmont, S. Africa 56 D3 29 28 S 24 22 E
lmont, U.S.A. 78 D6 42 14N 78 2W
lmonte, Brazil 93 G11 16 0 S 39 0W
lmopan, Belize 87 D7 17 18N 88 30W
lmullet, Ireland 13 B2 54 14N 9 58W
lo Horizonte, Brazil 93 G10 19 55 S 43 56W
lo-sur-Mer, Madag. 57 C7 20 42 S 44 0 E
lo-Tsiribihina, Madag. 57 B7 19 40 S 44 30 E
logorsk, Russia 27 D13 51 0N 128 20 E
loha, Madag. 57 D8 25 10 S 45 3 E
loit, Kans., U.S.A. 80 F5 39 28N 98 6W
loit, Wis., U.S.A. 80 D10 42 31N 89 2W
lokorovichi, Ukraine 17 C15 51 7N 28 2 E
lomorsk, Russia 24 B5 64 35N 34 54 E
lonia, India 41 H17 23 15N 91 30 E
loretsk, Russia 24 D10 53 58N 58 24 E
lorussia = Belarus ■, Europe 17 B14 53 30N 27 0 E
lovo, Russia 26 D9 54 30N 86 0 E
loye, Ozero, Russia 24 B6 60 10N 37 35 E
loye More, Russia 24 A6 66 30N 38 0 E
lozersk, Russia 24 B6 60 1N 37 45 E
lpre, U.S.A. 76 F5 39 17N 81 34W
lrain, India 43 E9 28 23N 80 55 E
lt, U.S.A. 82 C8 47 23N 110 55W
ltana, Australia 63 E2 30 48 S 138 25 E
lterra, Brazil 93 D8 2 45 S 55 0W
lton, U.S.A. 81 K6 31 3N 97 28W
lton L., U.S.A. 81 K6 31 8N 97 32W
ltsy = Bălţi, Moldova 17 E14 47 48N 27 58 E
lturbet, Ireland 13 B4 54 6N 7 26W
lukha, Russia 26 E9 49 50N 86 50 E
luran, Malaysia 36 C5 5 48N 117 35 E
lvidere, Ill., U.S.A. 80 D10 42 15N 88 50W
lvidere, N.J., U.S.A. 79 F9 40 50N 75 5W
lyando →, Australia 62 C4 21 38 S 146 50 E
lyy, Ostrov, Russia 26 B8 73 30N 71 0 E
lyy Yar, Russia 26 D9 58 26N 84 39 E
lzoni, U.S.A. 81 J9 33 11N 90 29W
maraha, Lembalemban' i, Madag. 57 B7 18 40 S 44 45 E
marivo, Madag. 57 C7 21 45 S 44 45 E
marivo →, Madag. 57 B8 15 27 S 47 40 E
mavo, Madag. 57 C8 21 33 S 45 25 E
mbéréke, Benin 50 F6 10 11N 2 43 E
mbesi, Zimbabwe 55 G2 20 0 S 28 58 E
mbesi →, Zimbabwe 55 F2 18 57 S 27 47 E
metara, India 43 J9 21 42N 81 32 E
midji, U.S.A. 80 B7 47 28N 94 53W
en, Iran 45 C6 32 32N 50 45 E
en Cruachan, U.K. 12 E3 56 26N 5 8W
en Dearg, U.K. 12 D4 57 47N 4 56W
en Hope, U.K. 12 C4 58 25N 4 36W
en Lawers, U.K. 12 E4 56 32N 4 14W
en Lomond, N.S.W., Australia 63 E5 30 1 S 151 43 E
Ben Lomond, Tas., Australia 62 G4 41 38 S 147 42 E
Ben Lomond, U.K. 12 E4 56 11N 4 38W
Ben Luc, Vietnam 39 G6 10 39N 106 29 E
Ben Macdhui, U.K. 12 D5 57 4N 3 40W
Ben Mhor, U.K. 12 D1 57 15N 7 18W
Ben More, Arg. & Bute, U.K. 12 E2 56 26N 6 1W
Ben More, Stirl., U.K. 12 E4 56 23N 4 32W
Ben More Assynt, U.K. 12 C4 58 8N 4 52W
Ben Nevis, U.K. 12 E3 56 48N 5 1W
Ben Quang, Vietnam 38 D6 17 3N 106 55 E
Ben Vorlich, U.K. 12 E4 56 21N 4 14W
Ben Wyvis, U.K. 12 D4 57 40N 4 35W
Bena, Nigeria 50 F7 11 20N 5 50 E
Benalla, Australia 63 F4 36 30 S 146 0 E
Benares = Varanasi, India 43 G10 25 22N 83 0 E
Benavente, Spain 19 A3 42 2N 5 43W
Benavides, U.S.A. 81 M5 27 36N 98 25W
Benbecula, U.K. 12 D1 57 26N 7 21W
Benbonyathe, Australia 63 E2 30 25 S 139 11 E
Bend, U.S.A. 82 D3 44 4N 121 19W
Bendemeer, Australia 63 E5 30 53 S 151 8 E
Bender Beila, Somali Rep. 46 F5 9 30N 50 48 E
Bendery = Tighina, Moldova 17 E15 46 50N 29 30 E
Bendigo, Australia 63 F3 36 40 S 144 15 E
Benē Beraq, Israel 47 C3 32 6N 34 51 E
Benenitra, Madag. 57 C8 23 27 S 45 5 E
Benevento, Italy 20 D6 41 8N 14 45 E
Benga, Mozam. 55 F3 16 11 S 33 40 E
Bengal, Bay of, Ind. Oc. 41 M17 15 0N 90 0 E
Bengbu, China 35 H9 32 58N 117 20 E
Benghazi = Banghāzī, Libya 51 B10 32 11N 20 3 E
Bengkalis, Indonesia 36 D2 1 30N 102 10 E
Bengkulu, Indonesia 36 E2 3 50 S 102 12 E
Bengkulu □, Indonesia 36 E2 3 48 S 102 16 E
Bengough, Canada 73 D7 49 25N 105 10W
Benguela, Angola 53 G2 12 37 S 13 25 E
Benguérua, I., Mozam. 57 C6 21 58 S 35 28 E
Beni, Dem. Rep. of the Congo 54 B2 0 30N 29 27 E
Beni →, Bolivia 92 F5 10 23 S 65 24W
Beni Mellal, Morocco 50 B4 32 21N 6 21W
Beni Suef, Egypt 51 C12 29 5N 31 6 E
Beniah L., Canada 72 A6 63 23N 112 17W
Benicia, U.S.A. 84 G4 38 3N 122 9W
Benidorm, Spain 19 C5 38 33N 0 9W
Benin ■, Africa 50 G6 10 0N 2 0 E
Benin, Bight of, W. Afr. 50 H6 5 0N 3 0 E
Benin City, Nigeria 50 G7 6 20N 5 31 E
Benitses, Greece 23 A3 39 32N 19 55 E
Benjamin Aceval, Paraguay 94 A4 24 58 S 57 34W
Benjamin Constant, Brazil 92 D4 4 40 S 70 15W
Benjamin Hill, Mexico 86 A2 30 10N 111 10W
Benkelman, U.S.A. 80 E4 40 3N 101 32W
Bennett, Canada 72 B2 59 56N 134 53W
Bennett, L., Australia 60 D5 22 50 S 131 2 E
Bennetta, Ostrov, Russia 27 B15 76 21N 148 56 E
Bennettsville, U.S.A. 77 H6 34 37N 79 41W
Bennington, N.H., U.S.A. 79 D11 43 0N 71 55W
Bennington, Vt., U.S.A. 79 D11 42 53N 73 12W
Benoni, S. Africa 57 D4 26 11 S 28 18 E
Benque Viejo, Belize 87 D7 17 5N 89 8W
Benson, Ariz., U.S.A. 83 L8 31 58N 110 18W
Benson, Minn., U.S.A. 80 C7 45 19N 95 36W
Bent, Iran 45 E8 26 20N 59 31 E
Benteng, Indonesia 37 F6 6 10 S 120 30 E
Bentinck I., Australia 62 B2 17 3 S 139 35 E
Bento Gonçalves, Brazil 95 B5 29 10 S 51 31W
Benton, Ark., U.S.A. 81 H8 34 34N 92 35W
Benton, Calif., U.S.A. 84 H8 37 48N 118 32W
Benton, Ill., U.S.A. 80 G10 38 0N 88 55W
Benton, Pa., U.S.A. 79 E8 41 12N 76 23W
Benton Harbor, U.S.A. 76 D2 42 6N 86 27W
Bentonville, U.S.A. 81 G7 36 22N 94 13W
Bentung, Malaysia 39 L3 3 31N 101 55 E
Benue →, Nigeria 50 G7 7 48N 6 46 E
Benxi, China 35 D12 41 20N 123 48 E
Beo, Indonesia 37 D7 4 25N 126 50 E
Beograd, Serbia, Yug. 21 B9 44 50N 20 37 E
Beppu, Japan 31 H5 33 15N 131 30 E
Beqaa Valley = Al Biqā, Lebanon 47 A5 34 10N 36 10 E
Ber Mota, India 42 H3 23 27N 68 34 E
Berach →, India 42 G6 25 15N 75 2 E
Berati, Albania 21 D8 40 43N 19 59 E
Berau, Teluk, Indonesia 37 E8 2 30 S 132 30 E
Berber, Sudan 51 E12 18 0N 34 0 E
Berbera, Somali Rep. 46 E4 10 30N 45 2 E
Berbérati, C.A.R. 52 D3 4 15N 15 40 E
Berbice →, Guyana 92 B7 6 20N 57 32W
Berdichev = Berdychiv, Ukraine 17 D15 49 57N 28 30 E
Berdsk, Russia 26 D9 54 47N 83 2 E
Berdyansk, Ukraine 25 E6 46 45N 36 50 E
Berdychiv, Ukraine 17 D15 49 57N 28 30 E
Berea, U.S.A. 76 G3 37 34N 84 17W
Berebere, Indonesia 37 D7 2 25N 128 45 E
Bereda, Somali Rep. 46 E5 11 45N 51 0 E
Berehove, Ukraine 17 D12 48 15N 22 35 E
Berekum, Ghana 50 G5 7 29N 2 34W
Berens →, Canada 73 C9 52 25N 97 2W
Berens I., Canada 73 C9 52 18N 97 18W
Berens River, Canada 73 C9 52 25N 97 0W
Beresford, U.S.A. 80 D6 43 5N 96 47W
Berestechko, Ukraine 17 C13 50 22N 25 5 E
Berevo, Mahajanga, Madag. 57 B7 17 14 S 44 17 E
Berevo, Toliara, Madag. 57 B7 19 44 S 44 58 E
Bereza, Belarus 17 B13 52 31N 24 51 E
Berezhany, Ukraine 17 D13 49 26N 24 58 E
Berezina = Byarezina →, Belarus 17 B16 52 33N 30 14 E
Bereznik, Russia 24 B7 62 51N 42 40 E
Berezniki, Russia 24 C10 59 24N 56 46 E
Berezovo, Russia 26 C7 64 0N 65 0 E
Berga, Spain 19 A6 42 6N 1 48 E
Bergama, Turkey 21 E12 39 8N 27 11 E
Bérgamo, Italy 18 D8 45 41N 9 43 E
Bergen, Neths. 15 B4 52 40N 4 43 E
Bergen, Norway 9 F11 60 20N 5 20 E
Bergen, U.S.A. 78 C7 43 5N 77 57W
Bergen op Zoom, Neths. 15 C4 51 28N 4 18 E
Bergerac, France 18 D4 44 51N 0 30 E
Bergholz, U.S.A. 78 F4 40 31N 80 53W
Bergisch Gladbach, Germany 15 D7 50 59N 7 8 E
Bergville, S. Africa 57 D4 28 52 S 29 18 E
Berhala, Selat, Indonesia 36 E2 1 0 S 104 15 E
Berhampore = Baharampur, India 43 G13 24 2N 88 27 E
Berhampur = Brahmapur, India 41 K14 19 15N 84 54 E
Bering Sea, Pac. Oc. 68 C1 58 0N 171 0 E
Bering Strait, Pac. Oc. 68 B3 65 30N 169 0W
Beringovskiy, Russia 27 C18 63 3N 179 19 E
Berisso, Argentina 94 C4 34 56 S 57 50W
Berja, Spain 19 D4 36 50N 2 56W
Berkeley, U.S.A. 84 H4 37 52N 122 16W
Berkner I., Antarctica 5 D18 79 30 S 50 0W
Berkshire, U.S.A. 79 D8 42 19N 76 11W
Berkshire Downs, U.K. 11 F6 51 33N 1 29W
Berlin, Germany 16 B7 52 30N 13 25 E
Berlin, Md., U.S.A. 76 F8 38 20N 75 13W
Berlin, N.H., U.S.A. 79 B13 44 28N 71 11W
Berlin, N.Y., U.S.A. 79 D11 42 42N 73 23W
Berlin, Wis., U.S.A. 76 D1 43 58N 88 57W
Berlin L., U.S.A. 78 E4 41 3N 81 0W
Bermejo →, Formosa, Argentina 94 B4 26 51 S 58 23W
Bermejo →, San Juan, Argentina 94 C2 32 30 S 67 30W
Bermen, L., Canada 71 B6 53 35N 68 55W
Bermuda ■, Atl. Oc. 66 F13 32 45N 65 0W
Bern, Switz. 18 C7 46 57N 7 28 E
Bernalillo, U.S.A. 83 J10 35 18N 106 33W
Bernardo de Irigoyen, Argentina 95 B5 26 15 S 53 40W
Bernardo O'Higgins □, Chile 94 C1 34 15 S 70 45W
Bernardsville, U.S.A. 79 F10 40 43N 74 34W
Bernasconi, Argentina 94 D3 37 55 S 63 44W
Bernburg, Germany 16 C6 51 47N 11 44 E
Berne = Bern, Switz. 18 C7 46 57N 7 28 E
Berneray, U.K. 12 D1 57 43N 7 11W
Bernier I., Australia 61 D1 24 50 S 113 12 E
Bernina, Piz, Switz. 18 C8 46 20N 9 54 E
Beroroha, Madag. 57 C8 21 40 S 45 10 E
Beroun, Czech Rep. 16 D8 49 57N 14 5 E
Berri, Australia 63 E3 34 14 S 140 35 E
Berriane, Algeria 50 B6 32 50N 3 46 E
Berrigan, Australia 63 F4 35 38 S 145 49 E
Berry, Australia 63 E5 34 46 S 150 43 E
Berry, France 18 C5 46 50N 2 0 E
Berry Is., Bahamas 88 A4 25 40N 77 50W
Berryessa L., U.S.A. 84 G4 38 31N 122 6W
Berryville, U.S.A. 81 G8 36 22N 93 34W
Bershad, Ukraine 17 D15 48 22N 29 31 E
Berthold, U.S.A. 80 A4 48 19N 101 44W
Berthoud, U.S.A. 80 E2 40 19N 105 5W
Bertoua, Cameroon 52 D2 4 30N 13 45 E
Bertraghboy B., Ireland 13 C2 53 22N 9 54W
Berwick, U.S.A. 79 E8 41 3N 76 14W
Berwick-upon-Tweed, U.K. 10 B6 55 46N 2 0W
Berwyn Mts., U.K. 10 E4 52 54N 3 26W
Besal, Pakistan 43 B5 35 4N 73 56 E
Besalampy, Madag. 57 B7 16 43 S 44 29 E
Besançon, France 18 C7 47 15N 6 2 E
Besar, Indonesia 36 E5 2 40 S 116 0 E
Besnard L., Canada 73 B7 55 25N 106 0W
Besni, Turkey 44 B3 37 41N 37 52 E
Besor, N. →, Egypt 47 D3 31 28N 34 22 E
Bessarabiya, Moldova 17 E15 47 0N 28 10 E
Bessarabka = Basarabeasca, Moldova 17 E15 46 21N 28 58 E
Bessemer, Ala., U.S.A. 77 J2 33 24N 86 58W
Bessemer, Mich., U.S.A. 80 B9 46 29N 90 3W
Bessemer, Pa., U.S.A. 78 F4 40 59N 80 30W
Beswick, Australia 60 B5 14 34 S 132 53 E
Bet She'an, Israel 47 C4 32 30N 35 30 E
Bet Shemesh, Israel 47 D4 31 44N 35 0 E
Betafo, Madag. 57 B8 19 50 S 46 51 E
Betancuria, Canary Is. 22 F5 28 25N 14 3W
Betanzos, Spain 19 A1 43 15N 8 12W
Bétaré Oya, Cameroon 52 C2 5 40N 14 5 E
Bethal, S. Africa 57 D4 26 27 S 29 28 E
Bethanien, Namibia 56 D2 26 31 S 17 8 E
Bethany, Canada 78 B6 44 11N 78 34W
Bethany, U.S.A. 80 E7 40 16N 94 2W
Bethel, Alaska, U.S.A. 68 B3 60 48N 161 45W
Bethel, Conn., U.S.A. 79 E11 41 22N 73 25W
Bethel, Maine, U.S.A. 79 B14 44 25N 70 47W
Bethel, Vt., U.S.A. 79 C12 43 50N 72 38W
Bethel Park, U.S.A. 78 F4 40 20N 80 1W
Bethlehem = Bayt Lahm, West Bank 47 D4 31 43N 35 12 E
Bethlehem, S. Africa 57 D4 28 14 S 28 18 E
Bethlehem, U.S.A. 79 F9 40 37N 75 23W
Bethulie, S. Africa 56 E4 30 30 S 25 59 E
Béthune, France 18 A5 50 30N 2 38 E
Betioky, Madag. 57 C7 23 48 S 44 20 E
Betong, Thailand 39 K3 5 45N 101 5 E
Betoota, Australia 62 D3 25 45 S 140 42 E
Betroka, Madag. 57 C8 23 16 S 46 0 E
Betsiamites, Canada 71 C6 48 56N 68 40W
Betsiamites →, Canada 71 C6 48 56N 68 38W
Betsiboka →, Madag. 57 B8 16 3 S 46 36 E
Bettendorf, U.S.A. 80 E9 41 32N 90 30W
Bettiah, India 43 F11 26 48N 84 33 E
Betul, India 40 J10 21 58N 77 59 E
Betung, Malaysia 36 D4 1 24N 111 31 E
Betws-y-Coed, U.K. 10 D4 53 5N 3 48W
Beulah, Mich., U.S.A. 76 C2 44 38N 86 6W
Beulah, N. Dak., U.S.A. 80 B4 47 16N 101 47W
Beveren, Belgium 15 C4 51 12N 4 16 E
Beverley, Australia 61 F2 32 9 S 116 56 E
Beverley, U.K. 10 D7 53 51N 0 26W
Beverley Hills, U.S.A. 77 L4 28 56N 82 28W
Beverly, U.S.A. 79 D14 42 33N 70 53W
Beverly Hills, U.S.A. 85 L8 34 4N 118 25W
Bewas →, India 43 H8 23 59N 79 21 E
Bexhill, U.K. 11 G8 50 51N 0 29 E
Beyānlū, Iran 44 C5 36 0N 47 51 E
Beyneu, Kazakstan 25 E10 45 18N 55 9 E
Beypazarı, Turkey 25 F5 40 10N 31 56 E
Beyşehir Gölü, Turkey 25 G5 37 41N 31 33 E
Béziers, France 18 E5 43 20N 3 12 E
Bezwada = Vijayawada, India 41 L12 16 31N 80 39 E
Bhabua, India 43 G10 25 3N 83 37 E
Bhachau, India 40 H7 23 20N 70 16 E
Bhadar →, Gujarat, India 42 H5 22 17N 72 20 E
Bhadar →, Gujarat, India 42 J3 21 27N 69 47 E
Bhadarwah, India 43 C6 32 58N 75 46 E
Bhadohi, India 43 G10 25 25N 82 34 E
Bhadra, India 42 E6 29 8N 75 14 E
Bhadrakh, India 41 J15 21 10N 86 30 E
Bhadran, India 42 H5 22 19N 72 6 E
Bhadravati, India 40 N9 13 49N 75 40 E
Bhag, Pakistan 42 E2 29 2N 67 49 E
Bhagalpur, India 43 G12 25 10N 87 0 E
Bhagirathi →, Ut. P., India 43 D8 30 8N 78 35 E
Bhagirathi →, W. Bengal, India 43 H13 23 25N 88 23 E
Bhakkar, Pakistan 42 D4 31 40N 71 5 E
Bhakra Dam, India 42 D7 31 30N 76 45 E
Bhamo, Burma 41 G20 24 15N 97 15 E
Bhandara, India 40 J11 21 5N 79 42 E
Bhanpura, India 42 G6 24 31N 75 44 E
Bhanrer Ra., India 43 H8 23 40N 79 45 E
Bhaptiahi, India 43 F12 26 19N 86 44 E
Bharat = India ■, Asia 40 K11 20 0N 78 0 E
Bharatpur, Mad. P., India 43 H9 23 44N 81 46 E
Bharatpur, Raj., India 42 F7 27 15N 77 30 E
Bharno, India 43 H11 23 14N 84 53 E
Bhatinda, India 42 D6 30 15N 74 57 E
Bhatpara, India 43 H13 22 50N 88 25 E
Bhattu, India 42 E6 29 36N 75 19 E
Bhaun, Pakistan 42 C5 32 55N 72 40 E
Bhaunagar = Bhavnagar, India 40 J8 21 45N 72 10 E
Bhavnagar, India 40 J8 21 45N 72 10 E
Bhawanipatna, India 41 K12 19 55N 80 10 E
Bhawari, India 42 G5 25 42N 73 4 E
Bhayavadar, India 42 J4 21 51N 70 15 E
Bhera, Pakistan 42 C5 32 29N 72 57 E
Bhikangaon, India 42 J6 21 52N 75 57 E
Bhilsa = Vidisha, India 42 H7 23 28N 77 53 E
Bhilwara, India 42 G6 25 25N 74 38 E
Bhima →, India 40 L10 16 25N 77 17 E
Bhimavaram, India 41 L12 16 30N 81 30 E
Bhimbar, Pakistan 43 C6 32 59N 74 3 E
Bhind, India 43 F8 26 30N 78 46 E
Bhinga, India 43 F9 27 43N 81 56 E
Bhinmal, India 42 G5 25 0N 72 15 E
Bhiwandi, India 40 K8 19 20N 73 0 E
Bhiwani, India 42 E7 28 50N 76 9 E
Bhogava →, India 42 H5 22 26N 72 20 E
Bhola, Bangla. 41 H17 22 45N 90 35 E
Bholari, Pakistan 42 G3 25 19N 68 13 E
Bhopal, India 42 H7 23 20N 77 30 E
Bhubaneshwar, India 41 J14 20 15N 85 50 E
Bhuj, India 42 H3 23 15N 69 49 E
Bhusaval, India 40 J9 21 3N 75 46 E
Bhutan ■, Asia 41 F17 27 25N 90 30 E
Biafra, B. of = Bonny, Bight of, Africa 52 D1 3 30N 9 20 E
Biak, Indonesia 37 E9 1 10 S 136 6 E
Biała Podlaska, Poland 17 B12 52 4N 23 6 E
Białogard, Poland 16 A8 54 2N 15 58 E
Białystok, Poland 17 B12 53 10N 23 10 E
Biaora, India 42 H7 23 56N 76 56 E
Bīārjmand, Iran 45 B7 36 6N 55 53 E
Biaro, Indonesia 37 D7 2 5N 125 26 E
Biarritz, France 18 E3 43 29N 1 33W
Bibai, Japan 30 C10 43 19N 141 52 E
Bibby I., Canada 73 A10 61 55N 93 0W
Biberach, Germany 16 D5 48 5N 9 47 E
Bibungwa, Dem. Rep. of the Congo 54 C2 2 40 S 28 15 E
Bic, Canada 71 C6 48 20N 68 41W
Bicester, U.K. 11 F6 51 54N 1 9W
Bicheno, Australia 62 G4 41 52 S 148 18 E
Bichia, India 43 H9 22 27N 80 42 E
Bickerton I., Australia 62 A2 13 45 S 136 10 E
Bida, Nigeria 50 G7 9 3N 5 58 E
Bidar, India 40 L10 17 55N 77 35 E
Biddeford, U.S.A. 77 D10 43 30N 70 28W
Bideford, U.K. 11 F3 51 1N 4 13W
Bideford Bay, U.K. 11 F3 51 5N 4 20W
Bidhuna, India 43 F8 26 49N 79 31 E
Bidor, Malaysia 39 K3 4 6N 101 15 E
Bié, Planalto de, Angola 53 G3 12 0 S 16 0 E
Bieber, U.S.A. 82 F3 41 7N 121 8W
Biel, Switz. 18 C7 47 8N 7 14 E
Bielefeld, Germany 16 B5 52 1N 8 33 E
Biella, Italy 18 D8 45 34N 8 3 E
Bielsk Podlaski, Poland 17 B12 52 47N 23 12 E
Bielsko-Biała, Poland 17 D10 49 50N 19 2 E
Bien Hoa, Vietnam 39 G6 10 57N 106 49 E
Bienne = Biel, Switz. 18 C7 47 8N 7 14 E
Bienville, L., Canada 70 A5 55 5N 72 40W
Biesiesfontein, S. Africa 56 E2 30 57 S 17 58 E
Big →, Canada 71 B8 54 50N 58 55W
Big B., Canada 71 A7 55 43N 60 35W
Big Bear City, U.S.A. 85 L10 34 16N 116 51W
Big Bear Lake, U.S.A. 85 L10 34 15N 116 56W
Big Belt Mts., U.S.A. 82 C8 46 30N 111 25W
Big Bend, Swaziland 57 D5 26 50 S 31 58 E
Big Bend National Park, U.S.A. 81 L3 29 20N 103 5W
Big Black →, U.S.A. 81 K9 32 3N 91 4W
Big Blue →, U.S.A. 80 F6 39 35N 96 34W
Big Creek, U.S.A. 84 H7 37 11N 119 14W
Big Cypress National Preserve, U.S.A. 77 M5 26 0N 81 10W
Big Cypress Swamp, U.S.A. 77 M5 26 12N 81 10W
Big Falls, U.S.A. 80 A8 48 12N 93 48W
Big Fork →, U.S.A. 80 A8 48 31N 93 43W
Big Horn Mts. = Bighorn Mts., U.S.A. 82 D10 44 30N 107 30W
Big I., Canada 72 A5 61 7N 116 45W
Big Lake, U.S.A. 81 K4 31 12N 101 28W
Big Moose, U.S.A. 79 C10 43 49N 74 58W
Big Muddy Cr. →, U.S.A. 80 A2 48 8N 104 36W
Big Pine, U.S.A. 84 H8 37 10N 118 17W
Big Piney, U.S.A. 82 E8 42 32N 110 7W
Big Rapids, U.S.A. 76 D3 43 42N 85 29W
Big Rideau L., Canada 79 B8 44 40N 76 15W
Big River, Canada 73 C7 53 50N 107 0W
Big Run, U.S.A. 78 F6 40 57N 78 55W
Big Sable Pt., U.S.A. 76 C2 44 3N 86 1W
Big Salmon →, Canada 72 A2 61 52N 134 55W
Big Sand L., Canada 73 B9 57 45N 99 45W
Big Sandy, U.S.A. 82 B8 48 11N 110 7W
Big Sandy →, U.S.A. 76 F4 38 25N 82 36W
Big Sandy Cr. →, U.S.A. 80 F3 38 6N 102 29W
Big Sioux →, U.S.A. 80 D6 42 29N 96 27W
Big Spring, U.S.A. 81 J4 32 15N 101 28W
Big Stone City, U.S.A. 80 C6 45 18N 96 28W
Big Stone Gap, U.S.A. 77 G4 36 52N 82 47W
Big Stone L., U.S.A. 80 C6 45 30N 96 35W
Big Sur, U.S.A. 84 J5 36 15N 121 48W
Big Timber, U.S.A. 82 D9 45 50N 109 57W

Broad

Bolton, U.K. 10 D5 53 35N 2 26W
Bolton Landing, U.S.A. 79 C11 43 32N 73 35W
Bolu, Turkey 25 F5 40 45N 31 35 E
Bolungavík, Iceland 8 C2 66 9N 23 15W
Bolvadin, Turkey 25 G5 38 45N 31 4 E
Bolzano, Italy 20 A4 46 31N 11 22 E
Bom Jesus da Lapa, Brazil 93 F10 13 15S 43 25W
Boma, Dem. Rep. of the Congo 52 F2 5 50S 13 4 E
Bombala, Australia 63 F4 36 56S 149 15 E
Bombay = Mumbai, India 40 K8 18 55N 72 50 E
Bomboma, Dem. Rep. of the Congo 52 D3 2 25N 18 55 E
Bombombwa, Dem. Rep. of the Congo 54 B2 1 40N 25 40 E
Bomili, Dem. Rep. of the Congo 54 B2 1 45N 27 5 E
Bømlo, Norway 9 G11 59 37N 5 13 E
Bomokandi →, Dem. Rep. of the Congo 54 B2 3 39N 26 8 E
Bomu →, C.A.R. 52 D4 4 40N 22 30 E
Bon, C., Tunisia 48 C5 37 1N 11 2 E
Bon Sar Pa, Vietnam 38 F6 12 24N 107 35 E
Bonaigarh, India 43 J11 21 50N 84 57 E
Bonaire, Neth. Ant. 89 D6 12 10N 68 15W
Bonang, Australia 63 F4 37 11S 148 41 E
Bonanza, Nic. 88 D3 13 54N 84 35W
Bonaparte Arch., Australia 60 B3 14 0S 124 30 E
Bonaventure, Canada 71 C6 48 5N 65 32W
Bonavista, Canada 71 C9 48 40N 53 5W
Bonavista, C., Canada 71 C9 48 42N 53 5W
Bonavista B., Canada 71 C9 48 45N 53 25W
Bondo, Dem. Rep. of the Congo 54 B1 3 55N 23 53 E
Bondoukou, Ivory C. 50 G5 8 2N 2 47W
Bondowoso, Indonesia 37 G15 7 55S 113 49 E
Bone, Teluk, Indonesia 37 E6 4 10S 120 50 E
Bonerate, Indonesia 37 F6 7 25S 121 5 E
Bonerate, Kepulauan, Indonesia 37 F6 6 30S 121 10 E
Bo'ness, U.K. 12 E5 56 1N 3 37W
Bonete, Cerro, Argentina 94 B2 27 55S 68 40W
Bong Son = Hoai Nhon, Vietnam 38 E7 14 28N 109 1 E
Bongor, Chad 51 F9 10 35N 15 20 E
Bonham, U.S.A. 81 J6 33 35N 96 11W
Bonifacio, France 18 F8 41 24N 9 10 E
Bonifacio, Bouches de, Medit. S. 20 D3 41 12N 9 15 E
Bonin Is. = Ogasawara Gunto, Pac. Oc. 28 G18 27 0N 142 0 E
Bonn, Germany 16 C4 50 46N 7 6 E
Bonne Terre, U.S.A. 81 G9 37 55N 90 33W
Bonners Ferry, U.S.A. 82 B5 48 42N 116 19W
Bonney, L., Australia 63 F3 37 50S 140 20 E
Bonnie Rock, Australia 61 F2 30 29S 118 22 E
Bonny, Bight of, Africa 52 D1 3 30N 9 20 E
Bonnyrigg, U.K. 12 F5 55 53N 3 6W
Bonnyville, Canada 73 C6 54 20N 110 45W
Bonoi, Indonesia 37 E9 1 45S 137 41 E
Bonsall, U.S.A. 85 M9 33 16N 117 14W
Bontang, Indonesia 36 D5 0 10N 117 30 E
Bonthe, S. Leone 50 G3 7 30N 12 33W
Bontoc, Phil. 37 A6 17 7N 120 58 E
Bonython Ra., Australia 60 D4 23 40S 128 45 E
Bookabie, Australia 61 F5 31 50S 132 41 E
Booker, U.S.A. 81 G4 36 27N 100 32W
Booligal, Australia 63 E3 33 58S 144 53 E
Boonah, Australia 63 D5 27 58S 152 41 E
Boone, Iowa, U.S.A. 80 D8 42 4N 93 53W
Boone, N.C., U.S.A. 77 G5 36 13N 81 41W
Booneville, Ark., U.S.A. 81 H8 35 8N 93 55W
Booneville, Miss., U.S.A. 77 H1 34 39N 88 34W
Boonville, Calif., U.S.A. 84 F3 39 1N 123 22W
Boonville, Ind., U.S.A. 76 F2 38 3N 87 16W
Boonville, Mo., U.S.A. 80 F8 38 58N 92 44W
Boonville, N.Y., U.S.A. 79 C9 43 29N 75 20W
Boorindal, Australia 63 E4 30 22S 146 11 E
Boorowa, Australia 63 E4 34 28S 148 44 E
Boothia, Gulf of, Canada 69 A11 71 0N 90 0W
Boothia Pen., Canada 68 A10 71 0N 94 0W
Bootle, U.K. 10 D4 53 28N 3 1W
Booué, Gabon 52 E2 0 5S 11 55 E
Boquete, Panama 88 E3 8 46N 82 27W
Boquilla, Presa de la, Mexico 86 B3 27 40N 105 30W
Boquillas del Carmen, Mexico 86 B4 29 17N 102 53W
Bor, Serbia, Yug. 21 B10 44 5N 22 7 E
Bôr, Sudan 51 G12 6 10N 31 40 E
Bor Mashash, Israel 47 D3 31 7N 34 50 E
Borah Peak, U.S.A. 82 D7 44 8N 113 47W
Borås, Sweden 9 H15 57 43N 12 56 E
Borāzjān, Iran 45 D6 29 22N 51 10 E
Borba, Brazil 92 D7 4 12S 59 34W
Borborema, Planalto da, Brazil 90 D7 7 0S 37 0W
Bord Khūn-e Now, Iran 45 D6 28 3N 51 28 E
Borda, C., Australia 63 F2 35 45S 136 34 E
Bordeaux, France 18 D3 44 50N 0 36W
Borden, Australia 61 F2 34 3S 118 12 E
Borden, Canada 71 C7 46 18N 63 47W
Borden I., Canada 4 B2 78 30N 111 30W
Borden Pen., Canada 69 A11 73 0N 83 0W
Borders = Scottish Borders □, U.K. 12 F6 55 35N 2 50W
Bordertown, Australia 63 F3 36 19S 140 45 E
Borðeyri, Iceland 8 D3 65 12N 21 6W
Bordj Fly Ste. Marie, Algeria 50 C5 27 19N 2 32W
Bordj-in-Eker, Algeria 50 D7 24 9N 5 3 E
Bordj Omar Driss, Algeria 50 C7 28 10N 6 40 E
Borehamwood, U.K. 11 F7 51 40N 0 15W
Borgå = Porvoo, Finland 9 F21 60 24N 25 40 E
Borgarfjörður, Iceland 8 D7 65 31N 13 49W
Borgarnes, Iceland 8 D3 64 32N 21 55W
Børgefjellet, Norway 8 D15 65 20N 13 45 E
Borger, Neths. 15 B6 52 54N 6 44 E
Borger, U.S.A. 81 H4 35 39N 101 24W
Borgholm, Sweden 9 H17 56 52N 16 39 E
Borhoyn Tal, Mongolia 34 C6 43 50N 111 58 E
Borikhane, Laos 38 C4 18 33N 103 43 E
Borisoglebsk, Russia 25 D7 51 27N 42 5 E
Borisov = Barysaw, Belarus 17 A15 54 17N 28 28 E
Borja, Peru 92 D3 4 20S 77 40W
Borkou, Chad 51 E9 18 15N 18 50 E
Borkum, Germany 16 B4 53 34N 6 40 E
Borlänge, Sweden 9 F16 60 29N 15 26 E
Borley, C., Antarctica 5 C5 66 15S 52 30 E
Borneo, E. Indies 36 D5 1 0N 115 0 E
Bornholm, Denmark 9 J16 55 10N 15 0 E
Borogontsy, Russia 27 C14 62 42N 131 8 E
Boron, U.S.A. 85 L9 35 0N 117 39W
Borongan, Phil. 37 B7 11 37N 125 26 E
Borovichi, Russia 24 C5 58 25N 33 55 E
Borrego Springs, U.S.A. 85 M10 33 15N 116 23W
Borroloola, Australia 62 B2 16 4S 136 17 E
Borşa, Romania 17 E13 47 41N 24 50 E
Borsad, India 42 H5 22 25N 72 54 E
Borth, U.K. 11 E3 52 29N 4 2W
Borūjerd, Iran 45 C6 33 55N 48 50 E
Boryslav, Ukraine 17 D12 49 18N 23 28 E
Borzya, Russia 27 D12 50 24N 116 31 E
Bosa, Italy 20 D3 40 18N 8 30 E
Bosanska Gradiška, Bos.-H. 20 B7 45 10N 17 15 E
Bosaso, Somali Rep. 46 E4 11 12N 49 18 E
Boscastle, U.K. 11 G3 50 41N 4 42W
Boshan, China 35 F9 36 28N 117 49 E
Boshof, S. Africa 56 D4 28 31S 25 13 E
Boshrūyeh, Iran 45 C8 33 50N 57 30 E
Bosna →, Bos.-H. 21 B8 45 4N 18 29 E
Bosna i Hercegovina = Bosnia-Herzegovina ■, Europe 20 B7 44 0N 18 0 E
Bosnia-Herzegovina ■, Europe 20 B7 44 0N 18 0 E
Bosnik, Indonesia 37 E9 1 5S 136 10 E
Bosobolo, Dem. Rep. of the Congo 52 D3 4 15N 19 50 E
Bosporus = İstanbul Boğazı, Turkey 21 D13 41 10N 29 10 E
Bosque Farms, U.S.A. 83 J10 34 53N 106 40W
Bossangoa, C.A.R. 52 C3 6 35N 17 30 E
Bossier City, U.S.A. 81 J8 32 31N 93 44W
Bosso, Niger 51 F8 13 43N 13 19 E
Bostan, Pakistan 42 D2 30 26N 67 2 E
Bostānābād, Iran 44 B5 37 50N 46 50 E
Bosten Hu, China 32 B3 41 55N 87 40 E
Boston, U.K. 10 E7 52 59N 0 2W
Boston, U.S.A. 79 D13 42 22N 71 4W
Boston Bar, Canada 72 D4 49 52N 121 30W
Boston Mts., U.S.A. 81 H8 35 42N 93 15W
Boswell, Canada 72 D5 49 28N 116 45W
Boswell, U.S.A. 78 F5 40 10N 79 2W
Botad, India 42 H4 22 15N 71 40 E
Botene, Laos 38 D3 17 35N 101 12 E
Bothaville, S. Africa 56 D4 27 23S 26 34 E
Bothnia, G. of, Europe 8 E19 63 0N 20 15 E
Bothwell, Australia 62 G4 42 20S 147 1 E
Bothwell, Canada 78 D3 42 38N 81 52W
Botletle →, Botswana 56 C3 20 10S 23 15 E
Botoşani, Romania 17 E14 47 42N 26 41 E
Botou, Burkina Faso 50 F6 12 40N 2 3 E
Botswana ■, Africa 56 C3 22 0S 24 0 E
Bottineau, U.S.A. 80 A4 48 50N 100 27W
Bottrop, Germany 15 C6 51 31N 6 58 E
Botucatu, Brazil 95 A6 22 55S 48 30W
Botwood, Canada 71 C8 49 6N 55 23W
Bouaflé, Ivory C. 50 G4 7 1N 5 47W
Bouaké, Ivory C. 50 G4 7 40N 5 2W
Bouar, C.A.R. 52 C3 6 0N 15 40 E
Bouârfa, Morocco 50 B5 32 32N 1 58W
Boucaut B., Australia 62 A1 12 0S 134 25 E
Bougainville, C., Australia 60 B4 13 57S 126 4 E
Bougainville I., Papua N. G. 64 H7 6 0S 155 0 E
Bougainville Reef, Australia 62 B4 15 30S 147 5 E
Bougie = Bejaia, Algeria 50 A7 36 42N 5 2 E
Bougouni, Mali 50 F4 11 30N 7 20W
Bouillon, Belgium 15 E5 49 44N 5 3 E
Boulder, Colo., U.S.A. 80 E2 40 1N 105 17W
Boulder, Mont., U.S.A. 82 C7 46 14N 112 7W
Boulder City, U.S.A. 85 K12 35 59N 114 50W
Boulder Creek, U.S.A. 84 H4 37 7N 122 7W
Boulder Dam = Hoover Dam, U.S.A. 85 K12 36 1N 114 44W
Boulia, Australia 62 C2 22 52S 139 51 E
Boulogne-sur-Mer, France 18 A4 50 42N 1 36 E
Boultoum, Niger 51 F8 14 45N 10 25 E
Boun Neua, Laos 38 B3 21 38N 101 54 E
Boun Tai, Laos 38 B3 21 23N 101 58 E
Bouna, Ivory C. 50 G5 9 10N 3 0W
Boundary Peak, U.S.A. 84 H8 37 51N 118 21W
Boundiali, Ivory C. 50 G4 9 30N 6 20W
Bountiful, U.S.A. 82 F8 40 53N 111 53W
Bounty Is., Pac. Oc. 64 M9 48 0S 178 30 E
Bourbonnais, France 18 C5 46 28N 3 0 E
Bourdel L., Canada 70 A5 56 43N 74 10W
Bourem, Mali 50 E5 17 0N 0 24W
Bourg-en-Bresse, France 18 C6 46 13N 5 12 E
Bourg-St-Maurice, France 18 D7 45 35N 6 46 E
Bourges, France 18 C5 47 9N 2 25 E
Bourget, Canada 79 A9 45 26N 75 9W
Bourgogne, France 18 C6 47 0N 4 50 E
Bourke, Australia 63 E4 30 8S 145 55 E
Bourne, U.K. 10 E7 52 47N 0 22W
Bournemouth, U.K. 11 G6 50 43N 1 52W
Bournemouth □, U.K. 11 G6 50 43N 1 52W
Bouse, U.S.A. 85 M13 33 56N 114 0W
Bouvet I. = Bouvetøya, Antarctica 3 G10 54 26S 3 24 E
Bouvetøya, Antarctica 3 G10 54 26S 3 24 E
Bovill, U.S.A. 82 C5 46 51N 116 24W
Bovril, Argentina 94 C4 31 21S 59 26W
Bow →, Canada 72 C6 49 57N 111 41W
Bow Island, Canada 72 D6 49 50N 111 23W
Bowbells, U.S.A. 80 A3 48 48N 102 15W
Bowdle, U.S.A. 80 C5 45 27N 99 39W
Bowelling, Australia 61 F2 33 25S 116 30 E
Bowen, Argentina 94 D2 35 0S 67 31W
Bowen, Australia 62 C4 20 0S 148 16 E
Bowen Mts., Australia 63 F4 37 0S 147 50 E
Bowie, Ariz., U.S.A. 83 K9 32 19N 109 29W
Bowie, Tex., U.S.A. 81 J6 33 34N 97 51W
Bowkān, Iran 44 B5 36 31N 46 12 E
Bowland, Forest of, U.K. 10 D5 54 0N 2 30W
Bowling Green, Ky., U.S.A. 76 G2 36 59N 86 27W
Bowling Green, Ohio, U.S.A. 76 E4 41 23N 83 39W
Bowling Green, C., Australia 62 B4 19 19S 147 25 E
Bowman, U.S.A. 80 B3 46 11N 103 24W
Bowman I., Antarctica 5 C8 65 0S 104 0 E
Bowmanville, Canada 78 C6 43 55N 78 41W
Bowmore, U.K. 12 F2 55 45N 6 17W
Bowral, Australia 63 E5 34 26S 150 27 E
Bowraville, Australia 63 E5 30 37S 152 52 E
Bowron →, Canada 72 C4 54 3N 121 50W
Bowron Lake Prov. Park, Canada 72 C4 53 10N 121 5W
Bowser L., Canada 72 B3 56 30N 129 30W
Bowsman, Canada 73 C8 52 14N 101 12W
Bowwood, Zambia 55 F2 17 5S 26 20 E
Box Cr. →, Australia 63 E3 34 10S 143 50 E
Boxmeer, Neths. 15 C5 51 38N 5 56 E
Boxtel, Neths. 15 C5 51 36N 5 20 E
Boyce, U.S.A. 81 K8 31 23N 92 40W
Boyd L., Canada 70 B4 52 46N 76 42W
Boyle, Canada 72 C6 54 35N 112 49W
Boyle, Ireland 13 C3 53 59N 8 18W
Boyne →, Ireland 13 C5 53 43N 6 15W
Boyne City, U.S.A. 76 C3 45 13N 85 1W
Boynton Beach, U.S.A. 77 M5 26 32N 80 4W
Boyolali, Indonesia 37 G14 7 32S 110 35 E
Boyoma, Chutes, Dem. Rep. of the Congo 54 B2 0 35N 25 23 E
Boysen Reservoir, U.S.A. 82 E9 43 25N 108 11W
Boyuibe, Bolivia 92 G6 20 25S 63 17W
Boyup Brook, Australia 61 F2 33 50S 116 23 E
Boz Dağları, Turkey 21 E13 38 20N 28 0 E
Bozburun, Turkey 21 F13 36 43N 28 4 E
Bozcaada, Turkey 21 E12 39 49N 26 3 E
Bozdoğan, Turkey 21 F13 37 40N 28 17 E
Bozeman, U.S.A. 82 D8 45 41N 111 2W
Bozen = Bolzano, Italy 20 A4 46 31N 11 22 E
Bozhou, China 34 H8 33 55N 115 41 E
Bozoum, C.A.R. 52 C3 6 25N 16 35 E
Bra, Italy 18 D7 44 42N 7 51 E
Brabant □, Belgium 15 D4 50 46N 4 30 E
Brabant L., Canada 73 B8 55 58N 103 43W
Brač, Croatia 20 C7 43 20N 16 40 E
Bracadale, L., U.K. 12 D2 57 20N 6 30W
Bracciano, L. di, Italy 20 C5 42 7N 12 14 E
Bracebridge, Canada 78 A5 45 2N 79 19W
Brach, Libya 51 C8 27 31N 14 20 E
Bräcke, Sweden 9 E16 62 45N 15 26 E
Brackettville, U.S.A. 81 L4 29 19N 100 25W
Bracknell, U.K. 11 F7 51 25N 0 43W
Bracknell Forest □, U.K. 11 F7 51 25N 0 44W
Brad, Romania 17 E12 46 10N 22 50 E
Bradenton, U.S.A. 77 M4 27 30N 82 34W
Bradford, Canada 78 B5 44 7N 79 34W
Bradford, U.K. 10 D6 53 47N 1 45W
Bradford, Pa., U.S.A. 78 E6 41 58N 78 38W
Bradford, Vt., U.S.A. 79 C12 43 59N 72 9W
Bradley, Ark., U.S.A. 81 J8 33 6N 93 39W
Bradley, Calif., U.S.A. 84 K6 35 52N 120 48W
Bradley Institute, Zimbabwe 55 F3 17 7S 31 25 E
Brady, U.S.A. 81 K5 31 9N 99 20W
Braemar, U.K. 12 D5 57 0N 3 23W
Braeside, Canada 79 A8 45 28N 76 24W
Braga, Portugal 19 B1 41 35N 8 25W
Bragado, Argentina 94 D3 35 2S 60 27W
Bragança, Brazil 93 D9 1 0S 47 2W
Bragança, Portugal 19 B2 41 48N 6 50W
Bragança Paulista, Brazil 95 A6 22 55S 46 32W
Brahmanbaria, Bangla. 41 H17 23 58N 91 15 E
Brahmani →, India 41 J15 20 39N 86 46 E
Brahmapur, India 41 K14 19 15N 84 54 E
Brahmaputra →, India 43 H13 23 58N 89 50 E
Braich-y-pwll, U.K. 10 E3 52 47N 4 46W
Braidwood, Australia 63 F4 35 27S 149 49 E
Brăila, Romania 17 F14 45 19N 27 59 E
Brainerd, U.S.A. 80 B7 46 22N 94 12W
Braintree, U.K. 11 F8 51 53N 0 34 E
Braintree, U.S.A. 79 D14 42 13N 71 0W
Brak →, S. Africa 56 D3 29 35S 22 55 E
Brakwater, Namibia 56 C2 22 28S 17 3 E
Brampton, Canada 78 C5 43 45N 79 45W
Brampton, U.K. 10 C5 54 57N 2 44W
Branco →, Brazil 92 D6 1 20S 61 50W
Brandenburg = Neubrandenburg, Germany 16 B7 53 33N 13 15 E
Brandenburg, Germany 16 B7 52 25N 12 33 E
Brandenburg □, Germany 16 B6 52 50N 13 0 E
Brandfort, S. Africa 56 D4 28 40S 26 30 E
Brandon, Canada 73 D9 49 50N 99 57W
Brandon, U.S.A. 79 C11 43 48N 73 4W
Brandon B., Ireland 13 D1 52 17N 10 8W
Brandon Mt., Ireland 13 D1 52 15N 10 15W
Brandsen, Argentina 94 D4 35 10S 58 15W
Brandvlei, S. Africa 56 E3 30 25S 20 30 E
Branford, U.S.A. 79 E12 41 17N 72 49W
Braniewo, Poland 17 A10 54 25N 19 50 E
Bransfield Str., Antarctica 5 C18 63 0S 59 0W
Branson, U.S.A. 81 G8 36 39N 93 13W
Brantford, Canada 78 C4 43 10N 80 15W
Bras d'Or L., Canada 71 C7 45 50N 60 50W
Brasher Falls, U.S.A. 79 B10 44 49N 74 47W
Brasil, Planalto, Brazil 90 E6 18 0S 46 30W
Brasiléia, Brazil 92 F5 11 0S 68 45W
Brasília, Brazil 93 G9 15 47S 47 55W
Brasília Legal, Brazil 93 D7 3 49S 55 36W
Braslaw, Belarus 9 J22 55 38N 27 0 E
Braşov, Romania 17 F13 45 38N 25 35 E
Brasschaat, Belgium 15 C4 51 19N 4 27 E
Brassey, Banjaran, Malaysia 36 D5 5 0N 117 15 E
Brassey Ra., Australia 61 E3 25 8S 122 15 E
Brasstown Bald, U.S.A. 77 H4 34 53N 83 49W
Brastad, Sweden 9 G14 58 23N 11 30 E
Bratislava, Slovak Rep. 17 D9 48 10N 17 7 E
Bratsk, Russia 27 D11 56 10N 101 30 E
Brattleboro, U.S.A. 79 D12 42 51N 72 34W
Braunau, Austria 16 D7 48 15N 13 3 E
Braunschweig, Germany 16 B6 52 15N 10 31 E
Braunton, U.K. 11 F3 51 7N 4 10W
Bravo del Norte, Rio = Grande, Rio →, U.S.A. 81 N6 25 58N 97 9W
Brawley, U.S.A. 85 N11 32 59N 115 31W
Bray, Ireland 13 C5 53 13N 6 7W
Bray, Mt., Australia 62 A1 14 0S 134 30 E
Bray, Pays de, France 18 B4 49 46N 1 26 E
Brazeau →, Canada 72 C5 52 55N 115 14W
Brazil, U.S.A. 76 F2 39 32N 87 8W
Brazil ■, S. Amer. 93 F9 12 0S 50 0W
Brazilian Highlands = Brasil, Planalto, Brazil 90 E6 18 0S 46 30W
Brazo Sur →, S. Amer. 94 B4 25 21S 57 42W
Brazos →, U.S.A. 81 L7 28 53N 95 23W
Brazzaville, Congo 52 E3 4 9S 15 12 E
Brčko, Bos.-H. 21 B8 44 54N 18 46 E
Breaden, L., Australia 61 E4 25 51S 125 28 E
Breaksea Sd., N.Z. 59 L1 45 35S 166 35 E
Bream B., N.Z. 59 F5 35 56S 174 28 E
Bream Hd., N.Z. 59 F5 35 51S 174 36 E
Breas, Chile 94 B1 25 29S 70 24W
Brebes, Indonesia 37 G13 6 52S 109 3 E
Brechin, Canada 78 B5 44 32N 79 10W
Brechin, U.K. 12 E6 56 44N 2 39W
Brecht, Belgium 15 C4 51 21N 4 38 E
Breckenridge, Colo., U.S.A. 82 G10 39 29N 106 3W
Breckenridge, Minn., U.S.A. 80 B6 46 16N 96 35W
Breckenridge, Tex., U.S.A. 81 J5 32 45N 98 54W
Breckland, U.K. 11 E8 52 30N 0 40 E
Brecon, U.K. 11 F4 51 57N 3 23W
Brecon Beacons, U.K. 11 F4 51 53N 3 26W
Breda, Neths. 15 C4 51 35N 4 45 E
Bredasdorp, S. Africa 56 E3 34 33S 20 2 E
Bree, Belgium 15 C5 51 8N 5 35 E
Bregenz, Austria 16 E5 47 30N 9 45 E
Breiðafjörður, Iceland 8 D2 65 15N 23 15W
Brejo, Brazil 93 D10 3 41S 42 47W
Bremen, Germany 16 B5 53 4N 8 47 E
Bremer Bay, Australia 61 F2 34 21S 119 20 E
Bremer I., Australia 62 A2 12 5S 136 45 E
Bremerhaven, Germany 16 B5 53 33N 8 36 E
Bremerton, U.S.A. 84 C4 47 34N 122 38W
Brenham, U.S.A. 81 K6 30 10N 96 24W
Brennerpass, Austria 16 E6 47 2N 11 30 E
Brent, U.S.A. 77 J2 32 56N 87 10W
Brentwood, U.K. 11 F8 51 37N 0 19 E
Brentwood, Calif., U.S.A. 84 H5 37 56N 121 42W
Brentwood, N.Y., U.S.A. 79 F11 40 47N 73 15W
Bréscia, Italy 18 D9 45 33N 10 15 E
Breskens, Neths. 15 C3 51 23N 3 33 E
Breslau = Wrocław, Poland 17 C9 51 5N 17 5 E
Bressanone, Italy 20 A4 46 43N 11 39 E
Bressay, U.K. 12 A7 60 9N 1 6W
Brest, Belarus 17 B12 52 10N 23 40 E
Brest, France 18 B1 48 24N 4 31W
Brest-Litovsk = Brest, Belarus 17 B12 52 10N 23 40 E
Bretagne, France 18 B2 48 10N 3 0W
Breton, Canada 72 C6 53 7N 114 28W
Breton Sd., U.S.A. 81 L10 29 35N 89 15W
Brett, C., N.Z. 59 F5 35 10S 174 20 E
Brevard, U.S.A. 77 H4 35 14N 82 44W
Breves, Brazil 93 D8 1 40S 50 29W
Brewarrina, Australia 63 E4 30 0S 146 51 E
Brewer, U.S.A. 77 C11 44 48N 68 46W
Brewer, Mt., U.S.A. 84 J8 36 44N 118 28W
Brewster, N.Y., U.S.A. 79 E11 41 23N 73 37W
Brewster, Ohio, U.S.A. 78 F3 40 43N 81 36W
Brewster, Wash., U.S.A. 82 B4 48 6N 119 47W
Brewster, Kap, Greenland 4 B6 70 7N 22 0W
Brewton, U.S.A. 77 K2 31 7N 87 4W
Breyten, S. Africa 57 D5 26 16S 30 0 E
Brezhnev = Naberezhnyye Chelny, Russia 24 C9 55 42N 52 19 E
Briançon, France 18 D7 44 54N 6 39 E
Bribie I., Australia 63 D5 27 0S 153 10 E
Bribri, Costa Rica 88 E3 9 38N 82 50W
Bridgehampton, U.S.A. 79 F12 40 56N 72 19W
Bridgend, U.K. 11 F4 51 30N 3 34W
Bridgend □, U.K. 11 F4 51 36N 3 36W
Bridgeport, Calif., U.S.A. 84 G7 38 15N 119 14W
Bridgeport, Conn., U.S.A. 79 E11 41 11N 73 12W
Bridgeport, Nebr., U.S.A. 80 E3 41 40N 103 6W
Bridgeport, Tex., U.S.A. 81 J6 33 13N 97 45W
Bridger, U.S.A. 82 D9 45 18N 108 55W
Bridgeton, U.S.A. 76 F8 39 26N 75 14W
Bridgetown, Australia 61 F2 33 58S 116 7 E
Bridgetown, Barbados 89 D8 13 5N 59 30W
Bridgetown, Canada 71 D6 44 55N 65 18W
Bridgewater, Canada 71 D7 44 25N 64 31W
Bridgewater, Mass., U.S.A. 79 E14 41 59N 70 58W
Bridgewater, N.Y., U.S.A. 79 D9 42 53N 75 15W
Bridgewater, C., Australia 63 F3 38 23S 141 23 E
Bridgewater-Gagebrook, Australia 62 G4 42 44S 147 14 E
Bridgnorth, U.K. 11 E5 52 32N 2 25W
Bridgton, U.S.A. 79 B14 44 3N 70 42W
Bridgwater, U.K. 11 F5 51 8N 2 59W
Bridgwater B., U.K. 11 F4 51 15N 3 15W
Bridlington, U.K. 10 C7 54 5N 0 12W
Bridlington B., U.K. 10 C7 54 4N 0 10W
Bridport, Australia 62 G4 40 59S 147 23 E
Bridport, U.K. 11 G5 50 44N 2 45W
Brig, Switz. 18 C7 46 18N 7 59 E
Brigg, U.K. 10 D7 53 34N 0 28W
Brigham City, U.S.A. 82 F7 41 31N 112 1W
Bright, Australia 63 F4 36 42S 146 56 E
Brighton, Australia 63 F2 35 5S 138 30 E
Brighton, Canada 78 B7 44 2N 77 44W
Brighton, U.K. 11 G7 50 49N 0 7W
Brighton, Colo., U.S.A. 80 F2 39 59N 104 49W
Brighton, N.Y., U.S.A. 78 C7 43 8N 77 34W
Brilliant, U.S.A. 78 F4 40 15N 80 39W
Brindisi, Italy 21 D7 40 39N 17 55 E
Brinkley, U.S.A. 81 H9 34 53N 91 12W
Brinnon, U.S.A. 84 C4 47 41N 122 54W
Brion, I., Canada 71 C7 47 46N 61 26W
Brisbane, Australia 63 D5 27 25S 153 2 E
Brisbane →, Australia 63 D5 27 24S 153 9 E
Bristol, U.K. 11 F5 51 26N 2 35W
Bristol, Conn., U.S.A. 79 E12 41 40N 72 57W
Bristol, Pa., U.S.A. 79 F10 40 6N 74 51W
Bristol, R.I., U.S.A. 79 E13 41 40N 71 16W
Bristol, Tenn., U.S.A. 77 G4 36 36N 82 11W
Bristol, City of □, U.K. 11 F5 51 27N 2 36W
Bristol B., U.S.A. 68 C4 58 0N 160 0W
Bristol Channel, U.K. 11 F3 51 18N 4 30W
Bristol I., Antarctica 5 B1 58 45S 28 0W
Bristol L., U.S.A. 83 J5 34 23N 116 50W
Bristow, U.S.A. 81 H6 35 50N 96 23W
Britain = Great Britain, Europe 6 E5 54 0N 2 15W
British Columbia □, Canada 72 C3 55 0N 125 15W
British Indian Ocean Terr. = Chagos Arch., Ind. Oc. 29 K11 6 0S 72 0 E
British Isles, Europe 6 E5 54 0N 4 0W
Brits, S. Africa 57 D4 25 37S 27 48 E
Britstown, S. Africa 56 E3 30 37S 23 30 E
Britt, Canada 70 C3 45 46N 80 34W
Brittany = Bretagne, France 18 B2 48 10N 3 0W
Britton, U.S.A. 80 C6 45 48N 97 45W
Brive-la-Gaillarde, France 18 D4 45 10N 1 32 E
Brixen = Bressanone, Italy 20 A4 46 43N 11 39 E
Brixham, U.K. 11 G4 50 23N 3 31W
Brno, Czech Rep. 17 D9 49 10N 16 35 E
Broad →, U.S.A. 77 J5 34 1N 81 4W

Broad Arrow

Broad Arrow, Australia 61 F3 30 23S 121 15 E
Broad B., U.K. 12 C2 58 14N 6 18W
Broad Haven, Ireland 13 B2 54 20N 9 55W
Broad Law, U.K. 12 F5 55 30N 3 21W
Broad Sd., Australia 62 C4 22 0S 149 45 E
Broadalbin, U.S.A. 79 C10 43 4N 74 12W
Broadback →, Canada 70 B4 51 21N 78 52W
Broadford, Australia 63 F4 37 14S 145 4 E
Broadhurst Ra., Australia 60 D3 22 30S 122 30 E
Broads, The, U.K. 10 E9 52 45N 1 30 E
Broadus, U.S.A. 80 C2 45 27N 105 25W
Brochet, Canada 73 B8 57 53N 101 40W
Brochet, L., Canada 73 B8 58 36N 101 35W
Brocken, Germany 16 C6 51 47N 10 37 E
Brockport, U.S.A. 78 C7 43 13N 77 56W
Brockton, U.S.A. 79 D13 42 5N 71 1W
Brockville, Canada 79 B9 44 35N 75 41W
Brockway, Mont., U.S.A. 80 B2 47 18N 105 45W
Brockway, Pa., U.S.A. 78 E6 41 15N 78 47W
Brocton, U.S.A. 78 D5 42 23N 79 26W
Brodeur Pen., Canada 69 A11 72 30N 88 10W
Brodhead, Mt., U.S.A. 78 E7 41 39N 77 47W
Brodick, U.K. 12 F3 55 35N 5 9W
Brodnica, Poland 17 B10 53 15N 19 25 E
Brody, Ukraine 17 C13 50 5N 25 10 E
Brogan, U.S.A. 82 D5 44 15N 117 31W
Broken Arrow, U.S.A. 81 G7 36 3N 95 48W
Broken Bow, Nebr., U.S.A. 80 E5 41 24N 99 38W
Broken Bow, Okla., U.S.A. 81 H7 34 2N 94 44W
Broken Bow Lake, U.S.A. 81 H7 34 9N 94 40W
Broken Hill = Kabwe, Zambia 55 E2 14 30S 28 29 E
Broken Hill, Australia 63 E3 31 58S 141 29 E
Bromley, U.K. 11 F8 51 24N 0 2 E
Bromsgrove, U.K. 11 E5 52 21N 2 2W
Brønderslev, Denmark 9 H13 57 16N 9 57 E
Bronkhorstspruit, S. Africa 57 D4 25 46S 28 45 E
Brønnøysund, Norway 8 D15 65 28N 12 14 E
Brook Park, U.S.A. 78 E4 41 24N 81 51W
Brookhaven, U.S.A. 81 K9 31 35N 90 26W
Brookings, Oreg., U.S.A. 82 E1 42 3N 124 17W
Brookings, S. Dak., U.S.A. 80 C6 44 19N 96 48W
Brooklin, Canada 78 C6 43 55N 78 55W
Brooklyn Park, U.S.A. 80 C8 45 6N 93 23W
Brooks, Canada 72 C6 50 35N 111 55W
Brooks Range, U.S.A. 68 B5 68 0N 152 0W
Brooksville, U.S.A. 77 L4 28 33N 82 23W
Brookton, Australia 61 F2 32 22S 117 0 E
Brookville, U.S.A. 78 E5 41 10N 79 5W
Broom, L., U.K. 12 D3 57 55N 5 15W
Broome, Australia 60 C3 18 0S 122 15 E
Brora, U.K. 12 C5 58 0N 3 52W
Brora →, U.K. 12 C5 58 0N 3 51W
Brosna →, Ireland 13 C4 53 14N 7 58W
Brothers, U.S.A. 82 E3 43 49N 120 36W
Brough, U.K. 10 C5 54 32N 2 18W
Brough Hd., U.K. 12 B5 59 8N 3 20W
Broughton Island = Qikiqtarjuaq, Canada 69 B13 67 33N 63 0W
Brown, L., Australia 61 F2 31 5S 118 15 E
Brown, Pt., Australia 63 E1 32 32S 133 50 E
Brown City, U.S.A. 78 C2 43 13N 82 59W
Brown Willy, U.K. 11 G3 50 35N 4 37W
Brownfield, U.S.A. 81 J3 33 11N 102 17W
Browning, U.S.A. 82 B7 48 34N 113 1W
Brownsville, Oreg., U.S.A. 82 D2 44 24N 122 59W
Brownsville, Pa., U.S.A. 78 F5 40 1N 79 53W
Brownsville, Tenn., U.S.A. 81 H10 35 36N 89 16W
Brownsville, Tex., U.S.A. 81 N6 25 54N 97 30W
Brownville, U.S.A. 79 C9 44 0N 75 59W
Brownwood, U.S.A. 81 K5 31 43N 98 59W
Browse I., Australia 60 B3 14 7S 123 33 E
Bruas, Malaysia 39 K3 4 30N 100 47 E
Bruay-la-Buissière, France 18 A5 50 29N 2 33 E
Bruce, Mt., Australia 60 D2 22 37S 118 8 E
Bruce Pen., Canada 78 B3 45 0N 81 30W
Bruce Rock, Australia 61 F2 31 52S 118 8 E
Bruck an der Leitha, Austria 17 D9 48 1N 16 47 E
Bruck an der Mur, Austria 16 E8 47 24N 15 16 E
Brue →, U.K. 11 F5 51 13N 2 59W
Bruges = Brugge, Belgium 15 C3 51 13N 3 13 E
Brugge, Belgium 15 C3 51 13N 3 13 E
Bruin, U.S.A. 78 E5 41 3N 79 43W
Brûlé, Canada 72 C5 53 15N 117 58W
Brumado, Brazil 93 F10 14 14S 41 40W
Brumunddal, Norway 9 F14 60 53N 10 56 E
Bruneau, U.S.A. 82 E6 42 53N 115 48W
Bruneau →, U.S.A. 82 E6 42 56N 115 57W
Brunei = Bandar Seri Begawan, Brunei 36 D5 4 52N 115 0 E
Brunei ■, Asia 36 D5 4 50N 115 0 E
Brunner, L., N.Z. 59 K3 42 37S 171 27 E
Brunssum, Neths. 15 D5 50 57N 5 59 E
Brunswick = Braunschweig, Germany 16 B6 52 15N 10 31 E
Brunswick, Ga., U.S.A. 77 K5 31 10N 81 30W
Brunswick, Maine, U.S.A. 77 D11 43 55N 69 58W
Brunswick, Md., U.S.A. 76 F7 39 19N 77 38W
Brunswick, Mo., U.S.A. 80 F8 39 26N 93 8W
Brunswick, Ohio, U.S.A. 78 E3 41 14N 81 51W
Brunswick, Pen. de, Chile 96 G2 53 30S 71 30W
Brunswick B., Australia 60 C3 15 15S 124 50 E
Brunswick Junction, Australia 61 F2 33 15S 115 50 E
Bruny I., Australia 62 G4 43 20S 147 15 E
Brus Laguna, Honduras 88 C3 15 47N 84 35W
Brush, U.S.A. 80 E3 40 15N 103 37W
Brushton, U.S.A. 79 B10 44 50N 74 31W
Brusque, Brazil 95 B6 27 5S 49 0W
Brussel, Belgium 15 D4 50 51N 4 21 E
Brussels = Brussel, Belgium 15 D4 50 51N 4 21 E
Brussels, Canada 78 C3 43 44N 81 15W
Bruthen, Australia 63 F4 37 42S 147 50 E
Bruxelles = Brussel, Belgium 15 D4 50 51N 4 21 E
Bryan, Ohio, U.S.A. 76 E3 41 28N 84 33W
Bryan, Tex., U.S.A. 81 K6 30 40N 96 22W
Bryan, Mt., Australia 63 E2 33 30S 139 0 E
Bryansk, Russia 24 D5 53 13N 34 25 E
Bryce Canyon National Park, U.S.A. 83 H7 37 30N 112 10W
Bryne, Norway 9 G11 58 44N 5 38 E
Bryson City, U.S.A. 77 H4 35 26N 83 27W
Bsharri, Lebanon 47 A5 34 15N 36 0 E
Bū Baqarah, U.A.E. 45 E8 25 35N 56 25 E
Bu Craa, W. Sahara 50 C3 26 45N 12 50W
Bū Ḥasā, U.A.E. 45 F7 23 30N 53 20 E
Bua Yai, Thailand 38 E4 15 33N 102 26 E
Buapinang, Indonesia 37 E6 4 40S 121 30 E
Bubanza, Burundi 54 C2 3 6S 29 23 E
Būbiyān, Kuwait 45 D6 29 45N 48 15 E
Bucaramanga, Colombia 92 B4 7 0N 73 0W
Bucasia, Australia 62 C4 21 2S 149 10 E
Buccaneer Arch., Australia 60 C3 16 7S 123 20 E
Buchach, Ukraine 17 D13 49 5N 25 25 E
Buchan, U.K. 12 D6 57 32N 2 21W
Buchan Ness, U.K. 12 D7 57 29N 1 46W
Buchanan, Canada 73 C8 51 40N 102 45W
Buchanan, Liberia 50 G3 5 57N 10 2W
Buchanan, L., Queens., Australia 62 C4 21 35S 145 52 E
Buchanan, L., W. Austral., Australia 61 E3 25 33S 123 2 E
Buchanan, L., U.S.A. 81 K5 30 45N 98 25W
Buchanan Cr. →, Australia 62 B2 19 13S 136 33 E
Buchans, Canada 71 C8 48 50N 56 52W
Bucharest = Bucureşti, Romania 17 F14 44 27N 26 10 E
Buchon, Pt., U.S.A. 84 K6 35 15N 120 54W
Buck Hill Falls, U.S.A. 79 E9 41 11N 75 16W
Buckeye, U.S.A. 83 K7 33 22N 112 35W
Buckeye Lake, U.S.A. 78 G2 39 55N 82 29W
Buckhannon, U.S.A. 76 F5 39 0N 80 8W
Buckhaven, U.K. 12 E5 56 11N 3 3W
Buckhorn L., Canada 78 B6 44 29N 78 23W
Buckie, U.K. 12 D6 57 41N 2 58W
Buckingham, Canada 70 C4 45 37N 75 24W
Buckingham, U.K. 11 F7 51 59N 0 57W
Buckingham B., Australia 62 A2 12 10S 135 40 E
Buckinghamshire □, U.K. 11 F7 51 53N 0 55W
Buckle Hd., Australia 60 B4 14 26S 127 52 E
Buckleboo, Australia 63 E2 32 54S 136 12 E
Buckley, U.K. 10 D4 53 10N 3 5W
Buckley →, Australia 62 C2 20 10S 138 49 E
Bucklin, U.S.A. 81 G5 37 33N 99 38W
Bucks L., U.S.A. 84 F5 39 54N 121 12W
Buctouche, Canada 71 C7 46 30N 64 45W
Bucureşti, Romania 17 F14 44 27N 26 10 E
Bucyrus, U.S.A. 76 E4 40 48N 82 59W
Budalin, Burma 41 H19 22 20N 95 10 E
Budapest, Hungary 17 E10 47 29N 19 5 E
Budaun, India 43 E8 28 5N 79 10 E
Budd Coast, Antarctica 5 C8 68 0S 112 0 E
Bude, U.K. 11 G3 50 49N 4 34W
Budennovsk, Russia 25 F7 44 50N 44 10 E
Budge Budge = Baj Baj, India 43 H13 22 30N 88 5 E
Budgewoi, Australia 63 E5 33 13S 151 34 E
Budjala, Dem. Rep. of the Congo 52 D3 2 50N 19 40 E
Buellton, U.S.A. 85 L6 34 37N 120 12W
Buena Esperanza, Argentina 94 C2 34 45S 65 15W
Buena Park, U.S.A. 85 M9 33 52N 117 59W
Buena Vista, Colo., U.S.A. 83 G10 38 51N 106 8W
Buena Vista, Va., U.S.A. 76 G6 37 44N 79 21W
Buena Vista Lake Bed, U.S.A. 85 K7 35 12N 119 18W
Buenaventura, Colombia 92 C3 3 53N 77 4W
Buenaventura, Mexico 86 B3 29 50N 107 30W
Buenos Aires, Argentina 94 C4 34 30S 58 20W
Buenos Aires, Costa Rica 88 E3 9 10N 83 20W
Buenos Aires □, Argentina 94 D4 36 30S 60 0W
Buenos Aires, L., Chile 96 F2 46 35S 72 30W
Buffalo, Mo., U.S.A. 81 G8 37 39N 93 6W
Buffalo, N.Y., U.S.A. 78 D6 42 53N 78 53W
Buffalo, Okla., U.S.A. 81 G5 36 50N 99 38W
Buffalo, S. Dak., U.S.A. 80 C3 45 35N 103 33W
Buffalo, Wyo., U.S.A. 82 D10 44 21N 106 42W
Buffalo →, Canada 72 A5 60 5N 115 5W
Buffalo Head Hills, Canada 72 B5 57 25N 115 55W
Buffalo L., Canada 72 A5 60 12N 115 25W
Buffalo L., Alta., Canada 72 C6 52 27N 112 54W
Buffalo Narrows, Canada 73 B7 55 51N 108 29W
Buffels →, S. Africa 56 D2 29 36S 17 3 E
Buford, U.S.A. 77 H4 34 10N 84 0W
Bug = Buh →, Ukraine 25 E5 46 59N 31 58 E
Bug →, Poland 17 B11 52 31N 21 5 E
Buga, Colombia 92 C3 4 0N 76 15W
Buganda, Uganda 54 C3 0 0 31 30 E
Buganga, Uganda 54 C3 0 3S 32 0 E
Bugel, Tanjung, Indonesia 37 G14 6 26S 111 3 E
Bugibba, Malta 23 D1 35 57N 14 25 E
Bugsuk, Phil. 36 C5 8 15N 117 15 E
Bugulma, Russia 24 D9 54 33N 52 48 E
Bugun Shara, Mongolia 32 B5 49 0N 104 0 E
Buguruslan, Russia 24 D9 53 39N 52 26 E
Buh →, Ukraine 25 E5 46 59N 31 58 E
Buhl, U.S.A. 82 E6 42 36N 114 46W
Builth Wells, U.K. 11 E4 52 9N 3 25W
Buir Nur, Mongolia 33 B6 47 50N 117 42 E
Bujumbura, Burundi 54 C2 3 16S 29 18 E
Bukachacha, Russia 27 D12 52 55N 116 50 E
Bukama, Dem. Rep. of the Congo 55 D2 9 10S 25 50 E
Bukavu, Dem. Rep. of the Congo 54 C2 2 20S 28 52 E
Bukene, Tanzania 54 C3 4 15S 32 48 E
Bukhara = Bukhoro, Uzbekistan 26 F7 39 48N 64 25 E
Bukhoro, Uzbekistan 26 F7 39 48N 64 25 E
Bukima, Tanzania 54 C3 1 50S 33 25 E
Bukit Mertajam, Malaysia 39 K3 5 22N 100 28 E
Bukittinggi, Indonesia 36 E2 0 20S 100 20 E
Bukoba, Tanzania 54 C3 1 20S 31 49 E
Bukuya, Uganda 54 B3 0 40N 31 52 E
Būl, Kuh-e, Iran 45 D7 30 48N 52 45 E
Bula, Indonesia 37 E8 3 6S 130 30 E
Bulahdelah, Australia 63 E5 32 23S 152 13 E
Bulan, Phil. 37 B6 12 40N 123 52 E
Bulandshahr, India 42 E7 28 28N 77 51 E
Bulawayo, Zimbabwe 55 G2 20 7S 28 32 E
Buldan, Turkey 21 E13 38 2N 28 50 E
Bulgar, Russia 24 D8 54 57N 49 4 E
Bulgaria ■, Europe 21 C11 42 35N 25 30 E
Buli, Teluk, Indonesia 37 D7 1 5N 128 25 E
Buliluyan, C., Phil. 36 C5 8 20N 117 15 E
Bulkley →, Canada 72 B3 55 15N 127 40W
Bull Shoals L., U.S.A. 81 G8 36 22N 92 35W
Bullhead City, U.S.A. 85 K12 35 8N 114 32W
Büllingen, Belgium 15 D6 50 25N 6 16 E
Bullock Creek, Australia 62 B3 17 43S 144 31 E
Bulloo →, Australia 63 D3 28 43S 142 30 E
Bulloo L., Australia 63 D3 28 43S 142 25 E
Bulls, N.Z. 59 J5 40 10S 175 24 E
Bulnes, Chile 94 D1 36 42S 72 19W
Bulsar = Valsad, India 40 J8 20 40N 72 58 E
Bultfontein, S. Africa 56 D4 28 18S 26 10 E
Bulukumba, Indonesia 37 F6 5 33S 120 11 E
Bulun, Russia 27 B13 70 37N 127 30 E
Bumba, Dem. Rep. of the Congo 52 D4 2 13N 22 30 E
Bumbiri I., Tanzania 54 C3 1 40S 31 55 E
Bumhpa Bum, Burma 41 F20 26 51N 97 14 E
Bumi →, Zimbabwe 55 F2 17 0S 28 20 E
Buna, Kenya 54 B4 2 58N 39 30 E
Bunazi, Tanzania 54 C3 1 3S 31 23 E
Bunbury, Australia 61 F2 33 20S 115 35 E
Bunclody, Ireland 13 D5 52 39N 6 40W
Buncrana, Ireland 13 A4 55 8N 7 27W
Bundaberg, Australia 63 C5 24 54S 152 22 E
Bundey →, Australia 62 C2 21 46S 135 37 E
Bundi, India 42 G6 25 30N 75 35 E
Bundoran, Ireland 13 B3 54 28N 8 16W
Bung Kan, Thailand 38 C4 18 23N 103 37 E
Bungatakada, Japan 31 H5 33 35N 131 25 E
Bungay, U.K. 11 E9 52 27N 1 28 E
Bungil Cr. →, Australia 63 D4 27 5S 149 5 E
Bungo-Suidō, Japan 31 H6 33 0N 132 15 E
Bungoma, Kenya 54 B3 0 34N 34 34 E
Bungu, Tanzania 54 D4 7 35S 39 0 E
Bunia, Dem. Rep. of the Congo 54 B3 1 35N 30 20 E
Bunji, Pakistan 43 B6 35 45N 74 40 E
Bunkie, U.S.A. 81 K8 30 57N 92 11W
Buntok, Indonesia 36 E4 1 40S 114 58 E
Bunyu, Indonesia 36 D5 3 35N 117 50 E
Buol, Indonesia 37 D6 1 15N 121 32 E
Buon Brieng, Vietnam 38 F7 13 9N 108 12 E
Buon Ma Thuot, Vietnam 38 F7 12 40N 108 3 E
Buong Long, Cambodia 38 F6 13 44N 106 59 E
Buorkhaya, Mys, Russia 27 B14 71 50N 132 40 E
Buqayq, Si. Arabia 45 E6 26 0N 49 45 E
Bur Acaba, Somali Rep. 46 G3 3 12N 44 20 E
Bûr Safâga, Egypt 44 E2 26 43N 33 57 E
Bûr Sa'îd, Egypt 51 B12 31 16N 32 18 E
Bûr Sûdân, Sudan 51 E13 19 32N 37 9 E
Bura, Kenya 54 C4 1 4S 39 58 E
Burakin, Australia 61 F2 30 31S 117 10 E
Burao, Somali Rep. 46 F4 9 32N 45 32 E
Burāq, Syria 47 B5 33 11N 36 29 E
Buraydah, Si. Arabia 44 E5 26 20N 44 8 E
Burbank, U.S.A. 85 L8 34 11N 118 19W
Burda, India 42 G6 25 50N 77 35 E
Burdekin →, Australia 62 B4 19 38S 147 25 E
Burdur, Turkey 25 G5 37 45N 30 17 E
Burdwan = Barddhaman, India 43 H12 23 14N 87 39 E
Bure, Ethiopia 46 E2 10 40N 37 4 E
Bure →, U.K. 10 E9 52 38N 1 43 E
Bureya →, Russia 27 E13 49 27N 129 30 E
Burford, Canada 78 C4 43 7N 80 27W
Burgas, Bulgaria 21 C12 42 33N 27 29 E
Burgeo, Canada 71 C8 47 37N 57 38W
Burgersdorp, S. Africa 56 E4 31 0S 26 20 E
Burges, Mt., Australia 61 F3 30 50S 121 5 E
Burgos, Spain 19 A4 42 21N 3 41W
Burgsvik, Sweden 9 H18 57 3N 18 19 E
Burgundy = Bourgogne, France 18 C6 47 0N 4 50 E
Burhaniye, Turkey 21 E12 39 30N 26 58 E
Burhanpur, India 40 J10 21 18N 76 14 E
Burhi Gandak →, India 43 G12 25 20N 86 37 E
Burhner →, India 43 H9 22 43N 80 31 E
Burias, Phil. 37 B6 12 55N 123 5 E
Burica, Pta., Costa Rica 88 E3 8 3N 82 51W
Burien, U.S.A. 84 C4 47 28N 122 21W
Burigi, L., Tanzania 54 C3 2 2S 31 22 E
Burin, Canada 71 C8 47 1N 55 14W
Buriram, Thailand 38 E4 15 0N 103 0 E
Burj Sāfitā, Syria 44 C3 34 48N 36 7 E
Burkburnett, U.S.A. 81 H5 34 6N 98 34W
Burke →, Australia 62 C2 23 12S 139 33 E
Burke Chan., Canada 72 C3 52 10N 127 30W
Burketown, Australia 62 B2 17 45S 139 33 E
Burkina Faso ■, Africa 50 F5 12 0N 1 0W
Burk's Falls, Canada 70 C4 45 37N 79 24W
Burleigh Falls, Canada 78 B6 44 33N 78 12W
Burley, U.S.A. 82 E7 42 32N 113 48W
Burlingame, U.S.A. 84 H4 37 35N 122 21W
Burlington, Canada 78 C5 43 18N 79 45W
Burlington, Colo., U.S.A. 80 F3 39 18N 102 16W
Burlington, Iowa, U.S.A. 80 E9 40 49N 91 14W
Burlington, Kans., U.S.A. 80 F7 38 12N 95 45W
Burlington, N.C., U.S.A. 77 G6 36 6N 79 26W
Burlington, N.J., U.S.A. 79 F10 40 4N 74 51W
Burlington, Vt., U.S.A. 79 B11 44 29N 73 12W
Burlington, Wash., U.S.A. 84 B4 48 28N 122 20W
Burlington, Wis., U.S.A. 76 D1 42 41N 88 17W
Burlyu-Tyube, Kazakstan 26 E8 46 30N 79 10 E
Burma ■, Asia 41 J20 21 0N 96 30 E
Burnaby I., Canada 72 C2 52 25N 131 19W
Burnet, U.S.A. 81 K5 30 45N 98 14W
Burney, U.S.A. 82 F3 40 53N 121 40W
Burnham, U.S.A. 78 F7 40 38N 77 34W
Burnham-on-Sea, U.K. 11 F5 51 14N 3 0W
Burnie, Australia 62 G4 41 4S 145 56 E
Burnley, U.K. 10 D5 53 47N 2 14W
Burns, U.S.A. 82 E4 43 35N 119 3W
Burns Lake, Canada 72 C3 54 20N 125 45W
Burnside →, Canada 68 B9 66 51N 108 4W
Burnside, L., Australia 61 E3 25 22S 123 0 E
Burnsville, U.S.A. 80 C8 44 47N 93 17W
Burnt L., Canada 71 B7 53 35N 64 4W
Burnt River, Canada 78 B6 44 41N 78 42W
Burntwood →, Canada 73 B9 56 8N 96 34W
Burntwood L., Canada 73 B8 55 22N 100 26W
Burqān, Kuwait 44 D5 29 0N 47 57 E
Burra, Australia 63 E2 33 40S 138 55 E
Burray, U.K. 12 C6 58 51N 2 54W
Burren Junction, Australia 63 E4 30 7S 148 59 E
Burrinjuck Res., Australia 63 F4 35 0S 148 36 E
Burro, Serranías del, Mexico 86 B4 29 0N 102 0W
Burrow Hd., U.K. 12 G4 54 41N 4 24W
Burruyacú, Argentina 94 B3 26 30S 64 40W
Burry Port, U.K. 11 F3 51 41N 4 15W
Bursa, Turkey 21 D13 40 15N 29 5 E
Burstall, Canada 73 C7 50 39N 109 54W
Burton, Ohio, U.S.A. 78 E3 41 28N 81 8W
Burton, S.C., U.S.A. 77 J5 32 25N 80 45W
Burton, L., Canada 70 B4 54 45N 78 20W
Burton upon Trent, U.K. 10 E6 52 48N 1 38W
Buru, Indonesia 37 E7 3 30S 126 30 E
Burûn, Râs, Egypt 47 D2 31 14N 33 7 E
Burundi ■, Africa 54 C3 3 15S 30 0 E
Bururi, Burundi 54 C2 3 57S 29 37 E
Burutu, Nigeria 50 G7 5 20N 5 29 E
Burwell, U.S.A. 80 E5 41 47N 99 8W
Burwick, U.K. 12 C5 58 45N 2 58W
Bury, U.K. 10 D5 53 35N 2 17W
Bury St. Edmunds, U.K. 11 E8 52 15N 0 43 E
Buryatia □, Russia 27 D12 53 0N 110 0 E
Busango Swamp, Zambia 55 E2 14 15S 25 45 E
Buşayrah, Syria 44 C4 35 9N 40 26 E
Būshehr, Iran 45 D6 28 55N 50 55 E
Būshehr □, Iran 45 D6 28 20N 51 45 E
Bushell, Canada 73 B7 59 31N 108 45W
Bushenyi, Uganda 54 C3 0 35S 30 10 E
Bushire = Būshehr, Iran 45 D6 28 55N 50 55 E
Businga, Dem. Rep. of the Congo 52 D4 3 16N 20 59 E
Buşra ash Shām, Syria 47 C5 32 30N 36 25 E
Busselton, Australia 61 F2 33 42S 115 15 E
Bussum, Neths. 15 B5 52 16N 5 10 E
Busto Arsizio, Italy 18 D8 45 37N 8 51 E
Busu-Djanoa, Dem. Rep. of the Congo 52 D4 1 43N 21 23 E
Busuanga, Phil. 37 B6 12 10N 120 0 E
Buta, Dem. Rep. of the Congo 54 B1 2 50N 24 53 E
Butare, Rwanda 54 C2 2 31S 29 52 E
Butaritari, Kiribati 64 G9 3 30N 174 0 E
Bute, U.K. 12 F3 55 48N 5 2W
Bute Inlet, Canada 72 C4 50 40N 124 53W
Butemba, Uganda 54 B3 1 9N 31 37 E
Butembo, Dem. Rep. of the Congo 54 B2 0 9N 29 18 E
Butha Qi, China 33 B7 48 0N 122 32 E
Butiaba, Uganda 54 B3 1 50N 31 20 E
Butler, Mo., U.S.A. 80 F7 38 16N 94 20W
Butler, Pa., U.S.A. 78 F5 40 52N 79 54W
Buton, Indonesia 37 F6 5 0S 122 45 E
Butte, Mont., U.S.A. 82 C7 46 0N 112 32W
Butte, Nebr., U.S.A. 80 D5 42 58N 98 51W
Butte Creek →, U.S.A. 84 F5 39 12N 121 56W
Butterworth = Gcuwa, S. Africa 57 E4 32 20S 28 11 E
Butterworth, Malaysia 39 K3 5 24N 100 23 E
Buttevant, Ireland 13 D3 52 14N 8 40W
Buttfield, Mt., Australia 61 D4 24 45S 128 9 E
Button B., Canada 73 B10 58 45N 94 23W
Buttonwillow, U.S.A. 85 K7 35 24N 119 28W
Butty Hd., Australia 61 F3 33 54S 121 39 E
Butuan, Phil. 37 C7 8 57N 125 33 E
Butung = Buton, Indonesia 37 F6 5 0S 122 45 E
Buturlinovka, Russia 25 D7 50 50N 40 35 E
Buxa Duar, India 43 F13 27 45N 89 35 E
Buxar, India 43 G10 25 34N 83 58 E
Buxtehude, Germany 16 B5 53 28N 9 39 E
Buxton, U.K. 10 D6 53 16N 1 54W
Buy, Russia 24 C7 58 28N 41 28 E
Büyük Menderes →, Turkey 21 F12 37 28N 27 11 E
Büyükçekmece, Turkey 21 D13 41 2N 28 35 E
Buzău, Romania 17 F14 45 10N 26 50 E
Buzău →, Romania 17 F14 45 26N 27 44 E
Buzen, Japan 31 H5 33 35N 131 5 E
Buzi →, Mozam. 55 F3 19 50S 34 43 E
Buzuluk, Russia 24 D9 52 48N 52 12 E
Buzzards B., U.S.A. 79 E14 41 45N 70 37W
Buzzards Bay, U.S.A. 79 E14 41 44N 70 37W
Bwana Mkubwe, Dem. Rep. of the Congo 55 E2 13 8S 28 38 E
Byarezina →, Belarus 17 B16 52 33N 30 14 E
Bydgoszcz, Poland 17 B9 53 10N 18 0 E
Byelarus = Belarus ■, Europe 17 B14 53 30N 27 0 E
Byelorussia = Belarus ■, Europe 17 B14 53 30N 27 0 E
Byers, U.S.A. 80 F2 39 43N 104 14W
Byesville, U.S.A. 78 G3 39 58N 81 32W
Byford, Australia 61 F2 32 15S 116 0 E
Bykhaw, Belarus 17 B16 53 31N 30 14 E
Bykhov = Bykhaw, Belarus 17 B16 53 31N 30 14 E
Bylas, U.S.A. 83 K8 33 8N 110 7W
Bylot, Canada 73 B10 58 25N 94 8W
Bylot I., Canada 69 A12 73 13N 78 34W
Byrd, C., Antarctica 5 C17 69 38S 76 7W
Byrock, Australia 63 E4 30 40S 146 27 E
Byron Bay, Australia 63 D5 28 43S 153 37 E
Byrranga, Gory, Russia 27 B11 75 0N 100 0 E
Byrranga Mts. = Byrranga, Gory, Russia 27 B11 75 0N 100 0 E
Byske, Sweden 8 D19 64 57N 21 11 E
Byske älv →, Sweden 8 D19 64 57N 21 13 E
Bytom, Poland 17 C10 50 25N 18 54 E
Bytów, Poland 17 A9 54 10N 17 30 E
Byumba, Rwanda 54 C3 1 35S 30 4 E

C

Ca →, Vietnam 38 C5 18 45N 105 45 E
Ca Mau, Vietnam 39 H5 9 7N 105 8 E
Ca Mau, Mui, Vietnam 39 H5 8 38N 104 44 E
Ca Na, Vietnam 39 G7 11 20N 108 54 E
Caacupé, Paraguay 94 B4 25 23S 57 5W
Caála, Angola 53 G3 12 46S 15 30 E
Caamano Sd., Canada 72 C3 52 55N 129 25W
Caazapá, Paraguay 94 B4 26 8S 56 19W
Caazapá □, Paraguay 95 B4 26 10S 56 0W
Cabanatuan, Phil. 37 A6 15 30N 120 58 E
Cabano, Canada 71 C6 47 40N 68 56W
Cabazon, U.S.A. 85 M10 33 55N 116 47W
Cabedelo, Brazil 93 E12 7 0S 34 50W
Cabildo, Chile 94 C1 32 30S 71 5W
Cabimas, Venezuela 92 A4 10 23N 71 25W
Cabinda, Angola 52 F2 5 33S 12 11 E
Cabinda □, Angola 52 F2 5 0S 12 30 E
Cabinet Mts., U.S.A. 82 C6 48 0N 115 30W
Cabo Blanco, Argentina 96 F3 47 15S 65 47W
Cabo Frio, Brazil 95 A7 22 51S 42 3W
Cabo Pantoja, Peru 92 D3 1 0S 75 10W
Cabonga, Réservoir, Canada 70 C4 47 20N 76 40W
Cabool, U.S.A. 81 G8 37 7N 92 6W
Caboolture, Australia 63 D5 27 5S 152 58 E

Cárdenas

Cabora Bassa Dam = Cahora Bassa, Reprêsa de, Mozam. **55 F3** 15 20S 32 50 E
Caborca, Mexico **86 A2** 30 40N 112 10W
Cabot, Mt., U.S.A. **79 B13** 44 30N 71 25W
Cabot Hd., Canada **78 A3** 45 14N 81 17W
Cabot Str., Canada **71 C8** 47 15N 59 40W
Cabra, Spain **19 D3** 37 30N 4 28W
Cabrera, Spain **22 B9** 39 8N 2 57 E
Cabri, Canada **73 C7** 50 35N 108 25W
Cabriel →, Spain **19 C5** 39 14N 1 3W
Caçador, Brazil **95 B5** 26 47S 51 0W
Čačak, Serbia, Yug. **21 C9** 43 54N 20 20 E
Caçapava do Sul, Brazil **95 C5** 30 30S 53 30W
Cáceres, Brazil **92 G7** 16 5S 57 40W
Cáceres, Spain **19 C2** 39 26N 6 23W
Cache Bay, Canada **70 C4** 46 22N 80 0W
Cache Cr. →, U.S.A. **84 G5** 38 42N 121 42W
Cache Creek, Canada **72 C4** 50 48N 121 19W
Cachi, Argentina **94 B2** 25 5S 66 10W
Cachimbo, Serra do, Brazil **93 E7** 9 30S 55 30W
Cachinal de la Sierra, Chile **94 A2** 24 58S 69 32W
Cachoeira, Brazil **93 F11** 12 30S 39 0W
Cachoeira de Itapemirim, Brazil **95 A7** 20 51S 41 7W
Cachoeira do Sul, Brazil **95 C5** 30 3S 52 53W
Cacoal, Brazil **92 F6** 11 32S 61 18W
Cacólo, Angola **52 G3** 10 9S 19 21 E
Caconda, Angola **53 G3** 13 48S 15 8 E
Caddo, U.S.A. **81 H6** 34 7N 96 16W
Cader Idris, U.K. **11 E4** 52 42N 3 53W
Cadereyta, Mexico **86 B5** 25 36N 100 0W
Cadibarrawirracanna, L., Australia **63 D2** 28 52S 135 27 E
Cadillac, U.S.A. **76 C3** 44 15N 85 24W
Cadiz, Phil. **37 B6** 10 57N 123 15 E
Cádiz, Spain **19 D2** 36 30N 6 20W
Cadiz, Calif., U.S.A. **85 L11** 34 30N 115 28W
Cadiz, Ohio, U.S.A. **78 F4** 40 22N 81 0W
Cádiz, G. de, Spain **19 D2** 36 40N 7 0W
Cadiz L., U.S.A. **83 J6** 34 18N 115 24W
Cadney Park, Australia **63 D1** 27 55S 134 3 E
Cadomin, Canada **72 C5** 53 2N 117 20W
Cadotte Lake, Canada **72 B5** 56 26N 116 23W
Cadoux, Australia **61 F2** 30 46S 117 7 E
Caen, France **18 B3** 49 10N 0 22W
Caernarfon, U.K. **10 D3** 53 8N 4 16W
Caernarfon B., U.K. **10 D3** 53 4N 4 40W
Caernarvon = Caernarfon, U.K. **10 D3** 53 8N 4 16W
Caerphilly, U.K. **11 F4** 51 35N 3 13W
Caerphilly □, U.K. **11 F4** 51 37N 3 12W
Caesarea, Israel **47 C3** 32 30N 34 53 E
Caetité, Brazil **93 F10** 13 50S 42 32W
Cafayate, Argentina **94 B2** 26 2S 66 0W
Cafu, Angola **56 B2** 16 30S 15 8 E
Cagayan de Oro, Phil. **37 C6** 8 30N 124 40 E
Cagayan Is., Phil. **37 C5** 9 40N 121 16 E
Cágliari, Italy **20 E3** 39 13N 9 7 E
Cágliari, G. di, Italy **20 E3** 39 8N 9 11 E
Caguán →, Colombia **92 D4** 0 8S 74 18W
Caguas, Puerto Rico **89 C6** 18 14N 66 2W
Caha Mts., Ireland **13 E2** 51 45N 9 40W
Cahama, Angola **56 B1** 16 17S 14 19 E
Caher, Ireland **13 D4** 52 22N 7 56W
Cahersiveen, Ireland **13 E1** 51 56N 10 14W
Cahora Bassa, Reprêsa de, Mozam. **55 F3** 15 20S 32 50 E
Cahore Pt., Ireland **13 D5** 52 33N 6 12W
Cahors, France **18 D4** 44 27N 1 27 E
Cahul, Moldova **17 F15** 45 50N 28 15 E
Cai Nuoc, Vietnam **39 H5** 8 56N 105 1 E
Caia, Mozam. **55 F4** 17 51S 35 24 E
Caianda, Angola **55 E1** 11 2S 23 31 E
Caibarién, Cuba **88 B4** 22 30N 79 30W
Caicara, Venezuela **92 B5** 7 38N 66 10W
Caicó, Brazil **93 E11** 6 20S 37 0W
Caicos Is., W. Indies **89 B5** 21 40N 71 40W
Caicos Passage, W. Indies **89 B5** 22 45N 72 45W
Caird Coast, Antarctica **5 D1** 75 0S 25 0W
Cairn Gorm, U.K. **12 D5** 57 7N 3 39W
Cairngorm Mts., U.K. **12 D5** 57 6N 3 42W
Cairnryan, U.K. **12 G3** 54 59N 5 1W
Cairns, Australia **62 B4** 16 57S 145 45 E
Cairns L., Canada **73 C10** 51 42N 94 30W
Cairo = El Qâhira, Egypt **51 B12** 30 1N 31 14 E
Cairo, Ga., U.S.A. **77 K3** 30 52N 84 13W
Cairo, Ill., U.S.A. **81 G10** 37 0N 89 11W
Cairo, N.Y., U.S.A. **79 D11** 42 18N 74 0W
Caithness, Ord of, U.K. **12 C5** 58 8N 3 36W
Cajamarca, Peru **92 E3** 7 5S 78 28W
Cajàzeiras, Brazil **93 E11** 6 52S 38 30W
Cala d'Or, Spain **22 B10** 39 23N 3 14 E
Cala en Porter, Spain **22 B11** 39 52N 4 8 E
Cala Figuera, C. de, Spain **22 B9** 39 27N 2 31 E
Cala Forcat, Spain **22 B10** 40 0N 3 47 E
Cala Major, Spain **22 B9** 39 33N 2 37 E
Cala Mezquida = Sa Mesquida, Spain **22 B11** 39 55N 4 16 E
Cala Millor, Spain **22 B10** 39 35N 3 22 E
Cala Ratjada, Spain **22 B10** 39 43N 3 27 E
Cala Santa Galdana, Spain **22 B10** 39 56N 3 58 E
Calabar, Nigeria **50 H7** 4 57N 8 20 E
Calabogie, Canada **79 A8** 45 18N 76 43W
Calabozo, Venezuela **92 B5** 9 0N 67 28W
Calábria □, Italy **20 E7** 39 0N 16 30 E
Calafate, Argentina **96 G2** 50 19S 72 15W
Calahorra, Spain **19 A5** 42 18N 1 59W
Calais, France **18 A4** 50 57N 1 56 E
Calais, U.S.A. **77 C12** 45 11N 67 17W
Calalaste, Cord. de, Argentina **94 B2** 25 0S 67 0W
Calama, Brazil **92 E6** 8 0S 62 50W
Calama, Chile **94 A2** 22 30S 68 55W
Calamar, Colombia **92 A4** 10 15N 74 55W
Calamian Group, Phil. **37 B5** 11 50N 119 55 E
Calamocha, Spain **19 B5** 40 50N 1 17W
Calang, Indonesia **36 D1** 4 37N 95 37 E
Calapan, Phil. **37 B6** 13 25N 121 7 E
Călăraşi, Romania **17 F14** 44 12N 27 20 E
Calatayud, Spain **19 B5** 41 20N 1 40W
Calauag, Phil. **37 B6** 13 55N 122 15 E
Calavite, C., Phil. **37 B6** 13 26N 120 20 E
Calbayog, Phil. **37 B6** 12 4N 124 38 E
Calca, Peru **92 F4** 13 22S 72 0W
Calcasieu L., U.S.A. **81 L8** 29 55N 93 18W
Calcutta, India **43 H13** 22 36N 88 24 E
Calcutta, U.S.A. **78 F4** 40 40N 80 34W
Caldas da Rainha, Portugal **19 C1** 39 24N 9 8W
Calder →, U.K. **10 D6** 53 44N 1 22W
Caldera, Chile **94 B1** 27 5S 70 55W
Caldwell, Idaho, U.S.A. **82 E5** 43 40N 116 41W
Caldwell, Kans., U.S.A. **81 G6** 37 2N 97 37W
Caldwell, Tex., U.S.A. **81 K6** 30 32N 96 42W
Caledon, S. Africa **56 E2** 34 14S 19 26 E
Caledon →, S. Africa **56 E4** 30 31S 26 5 E
Caledon B., Australia **62 A2** 12 45S 137 0 E
Caledonia, Canada **78 C5** 43 7N 79 58W
Caledonia, U.S.A. **78 D7** 42 58N 77 51W
Calemba, Angola **56 B2** 16 0S 15 44 E
Calen, Australia **62 C4** 20 56S 148 48 E
Caletones, Chile **94 C1** 34 6S 70 27W
Calexico, U.S.A. **85 N11** 32 40N 115 30W
Calf of Man, U.K. **10 C3** 54 3N 4 48W
Calgary, Canada **72 C6** 51 0N 114 10W
Calheta, Madeira **22 D2** 32 44N 17 11W
Calhoun, U.S.A. **77 H3** 34 30N 84 57W
Cali, Colombia **92 C3** 3 25N 76 35W
Calicut, India **40 P9** 11 15N 75 43 E
Caliente, U.S.A. **83 H6** 37 37N 114 31W
California, Mo., U.S.A. **80 F8** 38 38N 92 34W
California, Pa., U.S.A. **78 F5** 40 4N 79 54W
California □, U.S.A. **84 H7** 37 30N 119 30W
California, Baja, Mexico **86 A1** 32 10N 115 12W
California, Baja, T.N. = Baja California □, Mexico **86 B2** 30 0N 115 0W
California, Baja, T.S. = Baja California Sur □, Mexico **86 B2** 25 50N 111 50W
California, G. de, Mexico **86 B2** 27 0N 111 0W
California City, U.S.A. **85 K9** 35 10N 117 55W
California Hot Springs, U.S.A. **85 K8** 35 51N 118 41W
Calingasta, Argentina **94 C2** 31 15S 69 30W
Calipatria, U.S.A. **85 M11** 33 8N 115 31W
Calistoga, U.S.A. **84 G4** 38 35N 122 35W
Calitzdorp, S. Africa **56 E3** 33 33S 21 42 E
Callabonna, L., Australia **63 D3** 29 40S 140 5 E
Callan, Ireland **13 D4** 52 32N 7 24W
Callander, U.K. **12 E4** 56 15N 4 13W
Callao, Peru **92 F3** 12 0S 77 0W
Calles, Mexico **87 C5** 23 2N 98 42W
Callicoon, U.S.A. **79 E9** 41 46N 75 3W
Calling Lake, Canada **72 B6** 55 15N 113 12W
Calliope, Australia **62 C5** 24 0S 151 16 E
Calne, U.K. **11 F6** 51 26N 2 0W
Calola, Angola **56 B2** 16 25S 17 48 E
Caloundra, Australia **63 D5** 26 45S 153 10 E
Calpella, U.S.A. **84 F3** 39 14N 123 12W
Calpine, U.S.A. **84 F6** 39 40N 120 27W
Calstock, Canada **70 C3** 49 47N 84 9W
Caltagirone, Italy **20 F6** 37 14N 14 31 E
Caltanissetta, Italy **20 F6** 37 29N 14 4 E
Calulo, Angola **52 G2** 10 1S 14 56 E
Caluquembe, Angola **53 G2** 13 47S 14 44 E
Calvert →, Australia **62 B2** 16 17S 137 44 E
Calvert I., Canada **72 C3** 51 30N 128 0W
Calvert Ra., Australia **60 D3** 24 0S 122 30 E
Calvi, France **18 E8** 42 34N 8 45 E
Calviá, Spain **19 C7** 39 34N 2 31 E
Calvillo, Mexico **86 C4** 21 51N 102 43W
Calvinia, S. Africa **56 E2** 31 28S 19 45 E
Calwa, U.S.A. **84 J7** 36 42N 119 46W
Cam →, U.K. **11 E8** 52 21N 0 16 E
Cam Lam, Vietnam **39 G7** 11 54N 109 10 E
Cam Ranh, Vietnam **39 G7** 11 54N 109 12 E
Cam Xuyen, Vietnam **38 C6** 18 15N 106 0 E
Camabatela, Angola **52 F3** 8 20S 15 26 E
Camacha, Madeira **22 D3** 32 41N 16 49W
Camacho, Mexico **86 C4** 24 25N 102 18W
Camacupa, Angola **53 G3** 11 58S 17 22 E
Camagüey, Cuba **88 B4** 21 20N 78 0W
Camaná, Peru **92 G4** 16 30S 72 50W
Camanche Reservoir, U.S.A. **84 G6** 38 14N 121 1W
Camaquã, Brazil **95 C5** 30 51S 51 49W
Camaquã →, Brazil **95 C5** 31 17S 51 47W
Câmara de Lobos, Madeira **22 D3** 32 39N 16 59W
Camargo, Mexico **87 B5** 26 19N 98 50W
Camargue, France **18 E6** 43 34N 4 34 E
Camarillo, U.S.A. **85 L7** 34 13N 119 2W
Camarón, C., Honduras **88 C2** 16 0N 85 5W
Camarones, Argentina **96 E3** 44 50S 65 40W
Camas, U.S.A. **84 E4** 45 35N 122 24W
Camas Valley, U.S.A. **82 E2** 43 2N 123 40W
Camballin, Australia **60 C3** 17 59S 124 12 E
Cambará, Brazil **95 A5** 23 2S 50 5W
Cambay = Khambhat, India **42 H5** 22 23N 72 33 E
Cambay, G. of = Khambhat, G. of, India **40 J8** 20 45N 72 30 E
Cambodia ■, Asia **38 F5** 12 15N 105 0 E
Camborne, U.K. **11 G2** 50 12N 5 19W
Cambrai, France **18 A5** 50 11N 3 14 E
Cambria, U.S.A. **84 K5** 35 34N 121 5W
Cambrian Mts., U.K. **11 E4** 52 3N 3 57W
Cambridge, Canada **78 C4** 43 23N 80 15W
Cambridge, Jamaica **88 C4** 18 18N 77 54W
Cambridge, N.Z. **59 G5** 37 54S 175 29 E
Cambridge, U.K. **11 E8** 52 12N 0 8 E
Cambridge, Mass., U.S.A. **79 D13** 42 22N 71 6W
Cambridge, Md., U.S.A. **75 C11** 38 34N 76 5W
Cambridge, Minn., U.S.A. **80 C8** 45 34N 93 13W
Cambridge, N.Y., U.S.A. **79 C11** 43 2N 73 22W
Cambridge, Nebr., U.S.A. **80 E4** 40 17N 100 10W
Cambridge, Ohio, U.S.A. **78 F3** 40 2N 81 35W
Cambridge Bay = Ikaluktutiak, Canada **68 B9** 69 10N 105 0W
Cambridge G., Australia **60 B4** 14 55S 128 15 E
Cambridge Springs, U.S.A. **78 E4** 41 48N 80 4W
Cambridgeshire □, U.K. **11 E7** 52 25N 0 7W
Cambuci, Brazil **95 A7** 21 35S 41 55W
Cambundi-Catembo, Angola **52 G3** 10 10S 17 35 E
Camden, Ala., U.S.A. **77 K2** 31 59N 87 17W
Camden, Ark., U.S.A. **81 J8** 33 35N 92 50W
Camden, Maine, U.S.A. **77 C11** 44 13N 69 4W
Camden, N.J., U.S.A. **79 G9** 39 56N 75 7W
Camden, N.Y., U.S.A. **79 C9** 43 20N 75 45W
Camden, S.C., U.S.A. **77 H5** 34 16N 80 36W
Camden Sd., Australia **60 C3** 15 27S 124 25 E
Camdenton, U.S.A. **81 F8** 38 1N 92 45W
Cameron, Ariz., U.S.A. **83 J8** 35 53N 111 25W
Cameron, La., U.S.A. **81 L8** 29 48N 93 20W
Cameron, Mo., U.S.A. **80 F7** 39 44N 94 14W
Cameron, Tex., U.S.A. **81 K6** 30 51N 96 59W
Cameron Highlands, Malaysia **39 K3** 4 27N 101 22 E
Cameron Hills, Canada **72 B5** 59 48N 118 0W
Cameroon ■, Africa **52 C2** 6 0N 12 30 E
Cameroun, Mt., Cameroon **52 D1** 4 13N 9 10 E
Cametá, Brazil **93 D9** 2 12S 49 30W
Camiguin I., Phil. **37 C6** 18 56N 121 55 E
Camilla, U.S.A. **77 K3** 31 14N 84 12W
Caminha, Portugal **19 B1** 41 50N 8 50W
Camino, U.S.A. **84 G6** 38 44N 120 41W
Camira Creek, Australia **63 D5** 29 15S 152 58 E
Cammal, U.S.A. **78 E7** 41 24N 77 28W
Camocim, Brazil **93 D10** 2 55S 40 50W
Camooweal, Australia **62 B2** 19 56S 138 7 E
Camopi, Fr. Guiana **93 C8** 3 12N 52 17W
Camp Borden, Canada **78 B5** 44 18N 79 56W
Camp Hill, U.S.A. **78 F8** 40 14N 76 55W
Camp Nelson, U.S.A. **85 J8** 36 8N 118 39W
Camp Pendleton, U.S.A. **85 M9** 33 16N 117 23W
Camp Verde, U.S.A. **83 J8** 34 34N 111 51W
Camp Wood, U.S.A. **81 L5** 29 40N 100 1W
Campana, Argentina **94 C4** 34 10S 58 55W
Campana, I., Chile **96 F1** 48 20S 75 20W
Campanário, Madeira **22 D2** 32 39N 17 2W
Campánia □, Italy **20 D6** 41 0N 14 30 E
Campbell, S. Africa **56 D3** 28 48S 23 44 E
Campbell, Calif., U.S.A. **84 H5** 37 17N 121 57W
Campbell, Ohio, U.S.A. **78 E4** 41 5N 80 37W
Campbell I., Pac. Oc. **64 N8** 52 30S 169 0 E
Campbell L., Canada **73 A7** 63 14N 106 55W
Campbell River, Canada **72 C3** 50 5N 125 20W
Campbell Town, Australia **62 G4** 41 52S 147 30 E
Campbellford, Canada **78 B7** 44 18N 77 48W
Campbellpur, Pakistan **42 C5** 33 46N 72 26 E
Campbellsville, U.S.A. **76 G3** 37 21N 85 20W
Campbellton, Canada **71 C6** 47 57N 66 43W
Campbelltown, Australia **63 E5** 34 4S 150 49 E
Campbeltown, U.K. **12 F3** 55 26N 5 36W
Campeche, Mexico **87 D6** 19 50N 90 32W
Campeche □, Mexico **87 D6** 19 50N 90 32W
Campeche, Golfo de, Mexico **87 D6** 19 30N 93 0W
Camperdown, Australia **63 F3** 38 14S 143 9 E
Camperville, Canada **73 C8** 51 59N 100 9W
Câmpina, Romania **17 F13** 45 10N 25 45 E
Campina Grande, Brazil **93 E11** 7 20S 35 47W
Campinas, Brazil **95 A6** 22 50S 47 0W
Campo Grande, Brazil **93 H8** 20 25S 54 40W
Campo Maíor, Brazil **93 D10** 4 50S 42 12W
Campo Mourão, Brazil **95 A5** 24 3S 52 22W
Campobasso, Italy **20 D6** 41 34N 14 39 E
Campos, Brazil **95 A7** 21 50S 41 20W
Campos Belos, Brazil **93 F9** 13 10S 47 3W
Campos del Puerto, Spain **22 B10** 39 26N 3 1 E
Campos Novos, Brazil **95 B5** 27 21S 51 50W
Camptonville, U.S.A. **84 F5** 39 27N 121 3W
Camptown, U.S.A. **79 E8** 41 44N 76 14W
Câmpulung, Romania **17 F13** 45 17N 25 3 E
Camrose, Canada **72 C6** 53 0N 112 50W
Camsell Portage, Canada **73 B7** 59 37N 109 15W
Çan, Turkey **21 D12** 40 2N 27 3 E
Can Clavo, Spain **22 C7** 38 57N 1 27 E
Can Creu, Spain **22 C7** 38 58N 1 28 E
Can Gio, Vietnam **39 G6** 10 25N 106 58 E
Can Tho, Vietnam **39 G5** 10 2N 105 46 E
Canaan, U.S.A. **79 D11** 42 2N 73 20W
Canada ■, N. Amer. **68 C10** 60 0N 100 0W
Cañada de Gómez, Argentina **94 C3** 32 40S 61 30W
Canadian, U.S.A. **81 H4** 35 55N 100 23W
Canadian →, U.S.A. **81 H7** 35 28N 95 3W
Canajoharie, U.S.A. **79 D10** 42 54N 74 35W
Çanakkale, Turkey **21 D12** 40 8N 26 24 E
Çanakkale Boğazı, Turkey **21 D12** 40 17N 26 32 E
Canal Flats, Canada **72 C5** 50 10N 115 48W
Canalejas, Argentina **94 D2** 35 15S 66 34W
Canals, Argentina **94 C3** 33 35S 62 53W
Canandaigua, U.S.A. **78 D7** 42 54N 77 17W
Canandaigua L., U.S.A. **78 D7** 42 47N 77 19W
Cananea, Mexico **86 A2** 31 0N 110 20W
Canarias, Is., Atl. Oc. **22 F4** 28 30N 16 0W
Canarreos, Arch. de los, Cuba **88 B3** 21 35N 81 40W
Canary Is. = Canarias, Is., Atl. Oc. **22 F4** 28 30N 16 0W
Canaseraga, U.S.A. **78 D7** 42 27N 77 45W
Canatlán, Mexico **86 C4** 24 31N 104 47W
Canaveral, C., U.S.A. **77 L5** 28 27N 80 32W
Canavieiras, Brazil **93 G11** 15 39S 39 0W
Canberra, Australia **63 F4** 35 15S 149 8 E
Canby, Calif., U.S.A. **82 F3** 41 27N 120 52W
Canby, Minn., U.S.A. **80 C6** 44 43N 96 16W
Canby, Oreg., U.S.A. **84 E4** 45 16N 122 42W
Cancún, Mexico **87 C7** 21 8N 86 44W
Candelaria, Argentina **95 B4** 27 29S 55 44W
Candelaria, Canary Is. **22 F3** 28 22N 16 22W
Candelo, Australia **63 F4** 36 47S 149 43 E
Candia = Iráklion, Greece **23 D7** 35 20N 25 12 E
Candle L., Canada **73 C7** 53 50N 105 18W
Candlemas I., Antarctica **5 B1** 57 3S 26 40W
Cando, U.S.A. **80 A5** 48 32N 99 12W
Canea = Khaniá, Greece **23 D6** 35 30N 24 4 E
Canelones, Uruguay **95 C4** 34 32S 56 17W
Cañete, Chile **94 D1** 37 50S 73 30W
Cañete, Peru **92 F3** 13 8S 76 30W
Cangas de Narcea, Spain **19 A2** 43 10N 6 32W
Canguaretama, Brazil **93 E11** 6 20S 35 5W
Canguçu, Brazil **95 C5** 31 22S 52 43W
Canguçu, Serra do, Brazil **95 C5** 31 20S 52 40W
Cangzhou, China **34 E9** 38 19N 116 52 E
Caniapiscau →, Canada **71 A6** 56 40N 69 30W
Caniapiscau Rés. de, Canada **71 B6** 54 10N 69 55W
Canicattì, Italy **20 F5** 37 21N 13 51 E
Canim Lake, Canada **72 C4** 51 47N 120 54W
Canindeyu □, Paraguay **95 A5** 24 10S 55 0W
Canisteo, U.S.A. **78 D7** 42 16N 77 36W
Canisteo →, U.S.A. **78 D7** 42 7N 77 8W
Cañitas, Mexico **86 C4** 23 36N 102 43W
Çankırı, Turkey **25 F5** 40 40N 33 37 E
Cankuzo, Burundi **54 C3** 3 10S 30 31 E
Canmore, Canada **72 C5** 51 7N 115 18W
Cann River, Australia **63 F4** 37 35S 149 7 E
Canna, U.K. **12 D2** 57 3N 6 33W
Cannanore, India **40 P9** 11 53N 75 27 E
Cannes, France **18 E7** 43 32N 7 1 E
Canning Town = Port Canning, India **43 H13** 22 23N 88 40 E
Cannington, Canada **78 B5** 44 20N 79 2W
Cannock, U.K. **11 E5** 52 41N 2 1W
Cannon Ball →, U.S.A. **80 B4** 46 20N 100 38W
Cannondale Mt., Australia **62 D4** 25 13S 148 57 E
Cannonsville Reservoir, U.S.A. **79 D9** 42 4N 75 22W
Cannonvale, Australia **62 C4** 20 17S 148 43 E
Canoas, Brazil **95 B5** 29 56S 51 11W
Canoe L., Canada **73 B7** 55 10N 108 15W
Canon City, U.S.A. **80 F2** 38 27N 105 14W
Canora, Canada **73 C8** 51 40N 102 30W
Canowindra, Australia **63 E4** 33 35S 148 38 E
Canso, Canada **71 C7** 45 20N 61 0W
Cantabria □, Spain **19 A4** 43 10N 4 0W
Cantabrian Mts. = Cantábrica, Cordillera, Spain **19 A3** 43 0N 5 10W
Cantábrica, Cordillera, Spain **19 A3** 43 0N 5 10W
Cantal, Plomb du, France **18 D5** 45 3N 2 45 E
Canterbury, Australia **62 D3** 25 23S 141 53 E
Canterbury, U.K. **11 F9** 51 16N 1 6 E
Canterbury □, N.Z. **59 K3** 43 45S 171 19 E
Canterbury Bight, N.Z. **59 L3** 44 16S 171 55 E
Canterbury Plains, N.Z. **59 K3** 43 55S 171 22 E
Cantil, U.S.A. **85 K9** 35 18N 117 58W
Canton = Guangzhou, China **33 D6** 23 5N 113 10 E
Canton, Ga., U.S.A. **77 H3** 34 14N 84 29W
Canton, Ill., U.S.A. **80 E9** 40 33N 90 2W
Canton, Miss., U.S.A. **81 J9** 32 37N 90 2W
Canton, Mo., U.S.A. **80 E9** 40 8N 91 32W
Canton, N.Y., U.S.A. **79 B9** 44 36N 75 10W
Canton, Ohio, U.S.A. **78 F3** 40 48N 81 23W
Canton, Pa., U.S.A. **78 E8** 41 39N 76 51W
Canton, S. Dak., U.S.A. **80 D6** 43 18N 96 35W
Canton L., U.S.A. **81 G5** 36 6N 98 35W
Canudos, Brazil **92 E7** 7 13S 58 5W
Canumã →, Brazil **92 D7** 3 55S 59 10W
Canutama, Brazil **92 E6** 6 30S 64 20W
Canutillo, U.S.A. **83 L10** 31 55N 106 36W
Canvey, U.K. **11 F8** 51 31N 0 37 E
Canyon, U.S.A. **81 H4** 34 59N 101 55W
Canyonlands National Park, U.S.A. **83 G9** 38 15N 110 0W
Canyonville, U.S.A. **82 E2** 42 56N 123 17W
Cao He →, China **35 D13** 40 10N 124 32 E
Cao Lanh, Vietnam **39 G5** 10 27N 105 38 E
Cao Xian, China **34 G8** 34 50N 115 35 E
Cap-aux-Meules, Canada **71 C7** 47 23N 61 52W
Cap-Chat, Canada **71 C6** 49 6N 66 40W
Cap-de-la-Madeleine, Canada **70 C5** 46 22N 72 31W
Cap-Haïtien, Haiti **89 C5** 19 40N 72 20W
Capac, U.S.A. **78 C2** 43 1N 82 56W
Capanaparo →, Venezuela **92 B5** 7 1N 67 7W
Cape →, Australia **62 C4** 20 59S 146 51 E
Cape Barren I., Australia **62 G4** 40 25S 148 15 E
Cape Breton Highlands Nat. Park, Canada **71 C7** 46 50N 60 40W
Cape Breton I., Canada **71 C7** 46 0N 60 30W
Cape Charles, U.S.A. **76 G8** 37 16N 76 1W
Cape Coast, Ghana **50 G5** 5 5N 1 15W
Cape Coral, U.S.A. **77 M5** 26 33N 81 57W
Cape Dorset, Canada **69 B12** 64 14N 76 32W
Cape Fear →, U.S.A. **77 H6** 33 53N 78 1W
Cape Girardeau, U.S.A. **81 G10** 37 19N 89 32W
Cape May, U.S.A. **76 F8** 38 56N 74 56W
Cape May Point, U.S.A. **75 C12** 38 56N 74 58W
Cape Province □, S. Africa **53 L3** 32 0S 23 0 E
Cape Tormentine, Canada **71 C7** 46 8N 63 47W
Cape Town, S. Africa **56 E2** 33 55S 18 22 E
Cape Verde Is. ■, Atl. Oc. **49 E1** 17 10N 25 20W
Cape Vincent, U.S.A. **79 B8** 44 8N 76 20W
Cape York Peninsula, Australia **62 A3** 12 0S 142 30 E
Capela, Brazil **93 F11** 10 30S 37 0W
Capella, Australia **62 C4** 23 2S 148 1 E
Capenda Camulemba, Angola **52 F3** 9 24S 18 27 E
Capim →, Brazil **93 D9** 1 40S 47 47W
Capitan, U.S.A. **83 K11** 33 35N 105 35W
Capitol Reef National Park, U.S.A. **83 G8** 38 15N 111 10W
Capitola, U.S.A. **84 J5** 36 59N 121 57W
Capoche →, Mozam. **55 F3** 15 35S 33 0 E
Capraia, Italy **18 E8** 43 2N 9 50 E
Capreol, Canada **70 C3** 46 43N 80 56W
Capri, Italy **20 D6** 40 33N 14 14 E
Capricorn Group, Australia **62 C5** 23 30S 151 55 E
Capricorn Ra., Australia **60 D2** 23 20S 116 50 E
Caprivi Strip, Namibia **56 B3** 18 0S 23 0 E
Captain's Flat, Australia **63 F4** 35 35S 149 27 E
Caquetá →, Colombia **92 D5** 1 15S 69 15W
Caracal, Romania **17 F13** 44 8N 24 22 E
Caracas, Venezuela **92 A5** 10 30N 66 55W
Caracol, Brazil **94 A4** 22 18S 57 1W
Caracol, Piauí, Brazil **93 E10** 9 15S 43 22W
Carajas, Brazil **93 E8** 6 5S 50 23W
Carajás, Serra dos, Brazil **93 E8** 6 0S 51 30W
Carangola, Brazil **95 A7** 20 44S 42 5W
Caransebeş, Romania **17 F12** 45 28N 22 18 E
Caraquet, Canada **71 C6** 47 48N 64 57W
Caras, Peru **92 E3** 9 3S 77 47W
Caratasca, L., Honduras **88 C3** 15 20N 83 40W
Caratinga, Brazil **93 G10** 19 50S 42 10W
Caraúbas, Brazil **93 E11** 5 43S 37 33W
Caravaca = Caravaca de la Cruz, Spain **19 C5** 38 8N 1 52W
Caravaca de la Cruz, Spain **19 C5** 38 8N 1 52W
Caravelas, Brazil **93 G11** 17 45S 39 15W
Caraveli, Peru **92 G4** 15 45S 73 25W
Caràzinho, Brazil **95 B5** 28 16S 52 46W
Carballo, Spain **19 A1** 43 13N 8 41W
Carberry, Canada **73 D9** 49 50N 99 25W
Carbó, Mexico **86 B2** 29 42N 110 58W
Carbonara, C., Italy **20 E3** 39 6N 9 31 E
Carbondale, Colo., U.S.A. **82 G10** 39 24N 107 13W
Carbondale, Ill., U.S.A. **81 G10** 37 44N 89 13W
Carbondale, Pa., U.S.A. **79 E9** 41 35N 75 30W
Carbonear, Canada **71 C9** 47 42N 53 13W
Carbónia, Italy **20 E3** 39 10N 8 30 E
Carcajou, Canada **72 B5** 57 47N 117 6W
Carcarana →, Argentina **94 C3** 32 27S 60 48W
Carcasse, C., Haiti **89 C5** 18 30N 74 28W
Carcassonne, France **18 E5** 43 13N 2 20 E
Carcross, Canada **72 A2** 60 13N 134 45W
Cardamon Hills, India **40 Q10** 9 30N 77 15 E
Cárdenas, Cuba **88 B3** 23 0N 81 30W
Cárdenas, San Luis Potosí, Mexico **87 C5** 22 0N 99 41W

Chamical, Argentina 94 C2 30 22S 66 27W
Chamkar Luong, Cambodia 39 G4 11 0N 103 45 E
Chamoli, India 43 D8 30 24N 79 21 E
Chamonix-Mont Blanc, France 18 D7 45 55N 6 51 E
Chamouchouane →, Canada 70 C5 48 37N 72 20W
Champa, India 43 H10 22 2N 82 43 E
Champagne, Canada 72 A1 60 49N 136 30W
Champagne, France 18 B6 48 40N 4 20 E
Champaign, U.S.A. 76 E1 40 7N 88 15W
Champassak, Laos 38 E5 14 53N 105 52 E
Champawat, India 43 E9 29 20N 80 6 E
Champdoré, L., Canada 71 A6 55 55N 65 49W
Champion, U.S.A. 78 E4 41 19N 80 51W
Champlain, U.S.A. 79 B11 44 59N 73 27W
Champlain, L., U.S.A. 79 B11 44 40N 73 20W
Champotón, Mexico 87 D6 19 20N 90 50W
Champua, India 43 H11 22 5N 85 40 E
Chana, Thailand 39 J3 6 55N 100 44 E
Chañaral, Chile 94 B1 26 23S 70 40W
Chanārān, Iran 45 B8 36 39N 59 6 E
Chanasma, India 42 H5 23 44N 72 5 E
Chanco, Chile 94 D1 35 44S 72 32W
Chand, India 43 J8 21 57N 79 7 E
Chandan, India 43 G12 24 38N 86 40 E
Chandan Chauki, India 43 E9 28 33N 80 47 E
Chandannagar, India 43 H13 22 52N 88 24 E
Chandausi, India 43 E8 28 27N 78 49 E
Chandeleur Is., U.S.A. 81 L10 29 55N 88 57W
Chandeleur Sd., U.S.A. 81 L10 29 55N 89 0W
Chandigarh, India 42 D7 30 43N 76 47 E
Chandil, India 43 H12 22 58N 86 3 E
Chandler, Australia 63 D1 27 0S 133 19 E
Chandler, Canada 71 C7 48 18N 64 46W
Chandler, Ariz., U.S.A. 83 K8 33 18N 111 50W
Chandler, Okla., U.S.A. 81 H6 35 42N 96 53W
Chandod, India 42 J5 21 59N 73 28 E
Chandpur, Bangla. 41 H17 23 8N 90 45 E
Chandrapur, India 40 K11 19 57N 79 25 E
Chānf, Iran 45 E9 26 38N 60 29 E
Chang, Pakistan 42 F3 26 59N 68 30 E
Chang, Ko, Thailand 39 G4 12 0N 102 23 E
Ch'ang Chiang = Chang Jiang →, China 33 C7 31 48N 121 10 E
Chang Jiang →, China 33 C7 31 48N 121 10 E
Changa, India 43 C7 33 53N 77 35 E
Changanacheri, India 40 Q10 9 25N 76 31 E
Changane →, Mozam. 57 C5 24 30S 33 30 E
Changbai, China 35 D15 41 25N 128 5 E
Changbai Shan, China 35 C15 42 20N 129 0 E
Changchiak'ou = Zhangjiakou, China 34 D8 40 48N 114 55 E
Ch'angchou = Changzhou, China 33 C6 31 47N 119 58 E
Changchun, China 35 C13 43 57N 125 17 E
Changchunling, China 35 B13 45 18N 125 27 E
Changde, China 33 D6 29 4N 111 35 E
Changdo-ri, N. Korea 35 E14 38 30N 127 40 E
Changhai = Shanghai, China 33 C7 31 15N 121 26 E
Changhua, Taiwan 33 D7 24 2N 120 30 E
Changhŭng, S. Korea 35 G14 34 41N 126 52 E
Changhŭngni, N. Korea 35 D15 40 24N 128 19 E
Changjiang, China 38 C7 19 20N 108 55 E
Changjin, N. Korea 35 D14 40 23N 127 15 E
Changjin-chŏsuji, N. Korea 35 D14 40 30N 127 15 E
Changli, China 35 E10 39 40N 119 13 E
Changling, China 35 B12 44 20N 123 58 E
Changlun, Malaysia 39 J3 6 25N 100 26 E
Changping, China 34 D9 40 14N 116 12 E
Changsha, China 33 D6 28 12N 113 0 E
Changwu, China 34 G4 35 10N 107 45 E
Changyi, China 35 F10 36 40N 119 30 E
Changyŏn, N. Korea 35 E13 38 15N 125 6 E
Changyuan, China 34 G8 35 15N 114 42 E
Changzhi, China 34 F7 36 10N 113 6 E
Changzhou, China 33 C6 31 47N 119 58 E
Chanhanga, Angola 56 B1 16 0S 14 8 E
Channapatna, India 40 N10 12 40N 77 15 E
Channel Is., U.K. 11 H5 49 19N 2 24W
Channel Is., U.S.A. 85 M7 33 40N 119 15W
Channel Islands National Park, U.S.A. 85 M8 33 30N 119 0W
Channel-Port aux Basques, Canada 71 C8 47 30N 59 9W
Channel Tunnel, Europe 11 F9 51 0N 1 30 E
Channing, U.S.A. 81 H3 35 41N 102 20W
Chantada, Spain 19 A2 42 36N 7 46W
Chanthaburi, Thailand 38 F4 12 38N 102 12 E
Chantrey Inlet, Canada 68 B10 67 48N 96 20W
Chanute, U.S.A. 81 G7 37 41N 95 27W
Chao Phraya →, Thailand 38 F3 13 32N 100 36 E
Chao Phraya Lowlands, Thailand 38 E3 15 30N 100 0 E
Chaocheng, China 34 F8 36 4N 115 37 E
Chaoyang, China 35 D11 41 35N 120 22 E
Chaozhou, China 33 D6 23 42N 116 32 E
Chapais, Canada 70 C5 49 47N 74 51W
Chapala, Mozam. 55 F4 15 50S 37 35 E
Chapala, L. de, Mexico 86 C4 20 10N 103 20W
Chapayev, Kazakstan 25 D9 50 25N 51 10 E
Chapayevsk, Russia 24 D8 53 0N 49 40 E
Chapecó, Brazil 95 B5 27 14S 52 41W
Chapel Hill, U.S.A. 77 H6 35 55N 79 4W
Chapleau, Canada 70 C3 47 50N 83 24W
Chaplin, Canada 73 C7 50 28N 106 40W
Chaplin L., Canada 73 C7 50 22N 106 36W
Chappell, U.S.A. 80 E3 41 6N 102 28W
Chapra = Chhapra, India 43 G11 25 48N 84 44 E
Chara, Russia 27 D12 56 54N 118 20 E
Charadai, Argentina 94 B4 27 35S 59 55W
Charagua, Bolivia 92 G6 19 45S 63 10W
Charambirá, Punta, Colombia 92 C3 4 16N 77 32W
Charaña, Bolivia 92 G5 17 30S 69 25W
Charanwala, India 42 F5 27 51N 72 10 E
Charata, Argentina 94 B3 27 13S 61 14W
Charcas, Mexico 86 C4 23 10N 101 20W
Chard, U.K. 11 G5 50 52N 2 58W
Chardon, U.S.A. 78 E3 41 35N 81 12W
Chardzhou = Chärjew, Turkmenistan 26 F7 39 6N 63 34 E
Charente →, France 18 D3 45 57N 1 5W
Chari →, Chad 51 F8 12 58N 14 31 E
Chārīkār, Afghan. 40 B6 35 0N 69 10 E
Chariton →, U.S.A. 80 F8 39 19N 92 58W
Chärjew, Turkmenistan 26 F7 39 6N 63 34 E
Charkhari, India 43 G8 25 24N 79 45 E
Charkhi Dadri, India 42 E7 28 37N 76 17 E
Charleroi, Belgium 15 D4 50 24N 4 27 E
Charleroi, U.S.A. 78 F5 40 9N 79 57W
Charles, C., U.S.A. 76 G8 37 7N 75 58W
Charles City, U.S.A. 80 D8 43 4N 92 41W
Charles L., Canada 73 B6 59 50N 110 33W
Charles Town, U.S.A. 76 F7 39 17N 77 52W
Charleston, Ill., U.S.A. 76 F1 39 30N 88 10W
Charleston, Miss., U.S.A. 81 H9 34 1N 90 4W
Charleston, Mo., U.S.A. 81 G10 36 55N 89 21W
Charleston, S.C., U.S.A. 77 J6 32 46N 79 56W
Charleston, W. Va., U.S.A. 76 F5 38 21N 81 38W
Charleston L., Canada 79 B9 44 32N 76 0W
Charleston Peak, U.S.A. 85 J11 36 16N 115 42W
Charlestown, Ireland 13 C3 53 58N 8 48W
Charlestown, S. Africa 57 D4 27 26S 29 53 E
Charlestown, Ind., U.S.A. 76 F3 38 27N 85 40W
Charlestown, N.H., U.S.A. 79 C12 43 14N 72 25W
Charleville = Rath Luirc, Ireland 13 D3 52 21N 8 40W
Charleville, Australia 63 D4 26 24S 146 15 E
Charleville-Mézières, France 18 B6 49 44N 4 40 E
Charlevoix, U.S.A. 76 C3 45 19N 85 16W
Charlotte, Mich., U.S.A. 76 D3 42 34N 84 50W
Charlotte, N.C., U.S.A. 77 H5 35 13N 80 51W
Charlotte, Vt., U.S.A. 79 B11 44 19N 73 14W
Charlotte Amalie, Virgin Is. 89 C7 18 21N 64 56W
Charlotte Harbor, U.S.A. 77 M4 26 50N 82 10W
Charlotte L., Canada 72 C3 52 12N 125 19W
Charlottesville, U.S.A. 76 F6 38 2N 78 30W
Charlottetown, Nfld., Canada 71 B8 52 46N 56 7W
Charlottetown, P.E.I., Canada 71 C7 46 14N 63 8W
Charlton, Australia 63 F3 36 16S 143 24 E
Charlton, U.S.A. 80 E8 40 59N 93 20W
Charlton I., Canada 70 B4 52 0N 79 20W
Charny, Canada 71 C5 46 43N 71 15W
Charolles, France 18 C6 46 27N 4 16 E
Charre, Mozam. 55 F4 17 13S 35 10 E
Charsadda, Pakistan 42 B4 34 7N 71 45 E
Charters Towers, Australia 62 C4 20 5S 146 13 E
Chartres, France 18 B4 48 29N 1 30 E
Chascomús, Argentina 94 D4 35 30S 58 0W
Chasefu, Zambia 55 E3 11 55S 33 8 E
Chashma Barrage, Pakistan 42 C4 32 27N 71 20 E
Chāt, Iran 45 B7 37 59N 55 16 E
Châteaubriant, France 18 C3 47 43N 1 23W
Chateaugay, U.S.A. 79 B10 44 56N 74 5W
Châteauguay, L., Canada 71 A5 56 26N 70 3W
Châteaulin, France 18 B1 48 11N 4 8W
Châteauroux, France 18 C4 46 50N 1 40 E
Châtellerault, France 18 C4 46 50N 0 30 E
Chatham = Miramichi, Canada 71 C6 47 2N 65 28W
Chatham, Canada 78 D2 42 24N 82 11W
Chatham, U.K. 11 F8 51 22N 0 32 E
Chatham, U.S.A. 79 D11 42 21N 73 36W
Chatham Is., Pac. Oc. 64 M10 44 0S 176 40W
Chatmohar, Bangla. 43 G13 24 15N 89 15 E
Chatra, India 43 G11 24 12N 84 56 E
Chatrapur, India 41 K14 19 22N 85 2 E
Chats, L. des, Canada 79 A8 45 30N 76 20W
Chatsu, India 42 F6 26 36N 75 57 E
Chatsworth, Canada 78 B4 44 27N 80 54W
Chatsworth, Zimbabwe 55 F3 19 38S 31 13 E
Chattahoochee, U.S.A. 77 K3 30 42N 84 51W
Chattahoochee →, U.S.A. 77 K3 30 54N 84 57W
Chattanooga, U.S.A. 77 H3 35 3N 85 19W
Chatteris, U.K. 11 E8 52 28N 0 2 E
Chaturat, Thailand 38 E3 15 40N 101 51 E
Chau Doc, Vietnam 39 G5 10 42N 105 7 E
Chauk, Burma 41 J19 20 53N 94 49 E
Chaukan La, Burma 41 F20 27 0N 97 15 E
Chaumont, France 18 B6 48 7N 5 8 E
Chaumont, U.S.A. 79 B8 44 4N 76 8W
Chautauqua L., U.S.A. 78 D5 42 10N 79 24W
Chauvin, Canada 73 C6 52 45N 110 10W
Chaves, Brazil 93 D9 0 15S 49 55W
Chaves, Portugal 19 B2 41 45N 7 32W
Chawang, Thailand 39 H2 8 25N 99 30 E
Chaykovskiy, Russia 24 C9 56 47N 54 9 E
Chazy, U.S.A. 79 B11 44 53N 73 26W
Cheb, Czech Rep. 16 C7 50 9N 12 28 E
Cheboksary, Russia 24 C8 56 8N 47 12 E
Cheboygan, U.S.A. 76 C3 45 39N 84 29W
Chech, Erg, Africa 50 D5 25 0N 2 15W
Chechenia □, Russia 25 F8 43 30N 45 29 E
Checheno-Ingush Republic = Chechenia □, Russia 25 F8 43 30N 45 29 E
Chechnya = Chechenia □, Russia 25 F8 43 30N 45 29 E
Chech'ŏn, S. Korea 35 F15 37 8N 128 12 E
Checotah, U.S.A. 81 H7 35 28N 95 31W
Chedabucto B., Canada 71 C7 45 25N 61 8W
Cheduba I., Burma 41 K18 18 45N 93 40 E
Cheepie, Australia 63 D4 26 33S 145 1 E
Chegdomyn, Russia 27 D14 51 7N 133 1 E
Chegga, Mauritania 50 C4 25 27N 5 40W
Chegutu, Zimbabwe 55 F3 18 10S 30 14 E
Chehalis, U.S.A. 84 D4 46 40N 122 58W
Chehalis →, U.S.A. 84 D3 46 57N 123 50W
Cheju do, S. Korea 35 H14 33 29N 126 34 E
Chekiang = Zhejiang □, China 33 D7 29 0N 120 0 E
Chela, Sa. da, Angola 56 B1 16 20S 13 20 E
Chelan, U.S.A. 82 C4 47 51N 120 1W
Chelan, L., U.S.A. 82 B3 48 11N 120 30W
Cheleken, Turkmenistan 25 G9 39 34N 53 16 E
Cheleken Yarymadasy, Turkmenistan 45 B7 39 30N 53 15 E
Chelforó, Argentina 96 D3 39 0S 66 33W
Chelkar = Shalqar, Kazakstan 26 E6 47 48N 59 39 E
Chelkar Tengiz, Solonchak, Kazakstan 26 E7 48 5N 63 7 E
Chełm, Poland 17 C12 51 8N 23 30 E
Chełmno, Poland 17 B10 53 20N 18 30 E
Chelmsford, U.K. 11 F8 51 44N 0 29 E
Chelsea, U.S.A. 79 C12 43 59N 72 27W
Cheltenham, U.K. 11 F5 51 54N 2 4W
Chelyabinsk, Russia 26 D7 55 10N 61 24 E
Chelyuskin, C., Russia 28 B14 77 30N 103 0 E
Chemainus, Canada 84 B3 48 55N 123 42W
Chemba, Mozam. 53 H6 17 9S 34 53 E
Chemnitz, Germany 16 C7 50 51N 12 54 E
Chemult, U.S.A. 82 E3 43 14N 121 47W
Chen, Gora, Russia 27 C15 65 16N 141 50 E
Chenab →, Pakistan 42 D4 30 23N 71 2 E
Chenango Forks, U.S.A. 79 D9 42 15N 75 51W
Cheney, U.S.A. 82 C5 47 30N 117 35W
Cheng Xian, China 34 H3 33 43N 105 42 E
Chengcheng, China 34 G5 35 8N 109 56 E
Chengchou = Zhengzhou, China 34 G7 34 45N 113 34 E
Chengde, China 35 D9 40 59N 117 58 E
Chengdu, China 32 C5 30 38N 104 2 E
Chenggu, China 34 H4 33 10N 107 21 E
Chengjiang, China 32 D5 24 39N 103 0 E
Ch'engmai, China 38 C7 19 50N 109 58 E
Ch'engtu = Chengdu, China 32 C5 30 38N 104 2 E
Chengwu, China 34 G8 34 58N 115 50 E
Chengyang, China 35 F11 36 18N 120 21 E
Chenjiagang, China 35 G10 34 23N 119 47 E
Chenkán, Mexico 87 D6 19 8N 90 58W
Chennai, India 40 N12 13 8N 80 19 E
Cheo Reo, Vietnam 36 B3 13 25N 108 28 E
Cheom Ksan, Cambodia 38 E5 14 13N 104 56 E
Chepén, Peru 92 E3 7 15S 79 23W
Chepes, Argentina 94 C2 31 20S 66 35W
Chepo, Panama 88 E4 9 10N 79 6W
Chepstow, U.K. 11 F5 51 38N 2 41W
Cheptulil, Mt., Kenya 54 B4 1 25N 35 35 E
Chequamegon B., U.S.A. 80 B9 46 40N 90 30W
Cher →, France 18 C4 47 21N 0 29 E
Cheraw, U.S.A. 77 H6 34 42N 79 53W
Cherbourg, France 18 B3 49 39N 1 40W
Cherdyn, Russia 24 B10 60 24N 56 29 E
Cheremkhovo, Russia 27 D11 53 8N 103 1 E
Cherepanovo, Russia 26 D9 54 15N 83 30 E
Cherepovets, Russia 24 C6 59 5N 37 55 E
Chergui, Chott ech, Algeria 50 B6 34 21N 0 25 E
Cherikov = Cherykaw, Belarus 17 B16 53 32N 31 20 E
Cherkasy, Ukraine 25 E5 49 27N 32 4 E
Cherkessk, Russia 25 F7 44 15N 42 5 E
Cherlak, Russia 26 D8 54 15N 74 55 E
Chernaya, Russia 27 B9 70 30N 89 10 E
Chernigov = Chernihiv, Ukraine 24 D5 51 28N 31 20 E
Chernihiv, Ukraine 24 D5 51 28N 31 20 E
Chernivtsi, Ukraine 17 D13 48 15N 25 52 E
Chernobyl = Chornobyl, Ukraine 17 C16 51 20N 30 15 E
Chernogorsk, Russia 27 D10 53 49N 91 18 E
Chernovtsy = Chernivtsi, Ukraine 17 D13 48 15N 25 52 E
Chernyakhovsk, Russia 9 J19 54 36N 21 48 E
Chernysheyskiy, Russia 27 C12 63 0N 112 30 E
Cherokee, Iowa, U.S.A. 80 D7 42 45N 95 33W
Cherokee, Okla., U.S.A. 81 G5 36 45N 98 21W
Cherokee Village, U.S.A. 81 G9 36 17N 91 30W
Cherokees, Grand Lake O' The, U.S.A. 81 G7 36 28N 95 2W
Cherrapunji, India 41 G17 25 17N 91 47 E
Cherry Valley, Calif., U.S.A. 85 M10 33 59N 116 57W
Cherry Valley, N.Y., U.S.A. 79 D10 42 48N 74 45W
Cherskiy, Russia 27 C17 68 45N 161 18 E
Cherskogo Khrebet, Russia 27 C15 65 0N 143 0 E
Cherven, Belarus 17 B15 53 45N 28 28 E
Chervonohrad, Ukraine 17 C13 50 25N 24 10 E
Cherwell →, U.K. 11 F6 51 44N 1 14W
Cherykaw, Belarus 17 B16 53 32N 31 20 E
Chesapeake, U.S.A. 76 G7 36 50N 76 17W
Chesapeake B., U.S.A. 76 G7 38 0N 76 10W
Cheshire □, U.K. 10 D5 53 14N 2 30W
Cheshskaya Guba, Russia 24 A8 67 20N 47 0 E
Cheshunt, U.K. 11 F7 51 43N 0 1W
Chesil Beach, U.K. 11 G5 50 37N 2 33W
Chesley, Canada 78 B3 44 17N 81 5W
Chester, U.K. 10 D5 53 12N 2 53W
Chester, Calif., U.S.A. 82 F3 40 19N 121 14W
Chester, Ill., U.S.A. 81 G10 37 55N 89 49W
Chester, Mont., U.S.A. 82 B8 48 31N 110 58W
Chester, Pa., U.S.A. 76 F8 39 51N 75 22W
Chester, S.C., U.S.A. 77 H5 34 43N 81 12W
Chester, Vt., U.S.A. 79 C12 43 16N 72 36W
Chester, W. Va., U.S.A. 78 F4 40 37N 80 34W
Chester-le-Street, U.K. 10 C6 54 51N 1 34W
Chesterfield, U.K. 10 D6 53 15N 1 25W
Chesterfield, Is., N. Cal. 64 J7 19 52S 158 15 E
Chesterfield Inlet, Canada 68 B10 63 30N 90 45W
Chesterton Ra., Australia 63 D4 25 30S 147 27 E
Chestertown, U.S.A. 79 C11 43 40N 73 48W
Chesterville, Canada 79 A9 45 6N 75 14W
Chestnut Ridge, U.S.A. 78 F5 40 20N 79 10W
Chesuncook L., U.S.A. 77 C11 46 0N 69 21W
Chéticamp, Canada 71 C7 46 37N 60 59W
Chetumal, Mexico 87 D7 18 30N 88 20W
Chetumal, B. de, Mexico 87 D7 18 40N 88 10W
Chetwynd, Canada 72 B4 55 45N 121 36W
Cheviot, The, U.K. 10 B5 55 29N 2 9W
Cheviot Hills, U.K. 10 B5 55 20N 2 30W
Cheviot Ra., Australia 62 D3 25 20S 143 45 E
Chew Bahir, Ethiopia 46 G2 4 40N 36 50 E
Chewelah, U.S.A. 82 B5 48 17N 117 43W
Cheyenne, Okla., U.S.A. 81 H5 35 37N 99 40W
Cheyenne, Wyo., U.S.A. 80 E2 41 8N 104 49W
Cheyenne →, U.S.A. 80 C4 44 41N 101 18W
Cheyenne Wells, U.S.A. 80 F3 38 49N 102 21W
Cheyne B., Australia 61 F2 34 35S 118 50 E
Chhabra, India 42 G7 24 40N 76 54 E
Chhaktala, India 42 H6 22 6N 74 11 E
Chhapra, India 43 G11 25 48N 84 44 E
Chhata, India 42 F7 27 42N 77 30 E
Chhatarpur, Bihar, India 43 G11 24 23N 84 11 E
Chhatarpur, Mad. P., India 43 G8 24 55N 79 35 E
Chhep, Cambodia 38 F5 13 45N 105 24 E
Chhindwara, Mad. P., India 43 H8 23 3N 79 29 E
Chhindwara, Mad. P., India 43 H8 22 2N 78 59 E
Chhlong, Cambodia 39 F5 12 15N 105 58 E
Chhota Tawa →, India 42 H7 22 14N 76 36 E
Chhoti Kali Sindh →, India 42 G6 24 2N 75 31 E
Chhuikhadan, India 43 J9 21 32N 80 59 E
Chhuk, Cambodia 39 G5 10 46N 104 28 E
Chi →, Thailand 38 E5 15 11N 104 43 E
Chiai, Taiwan 33 D7 23 29N 120 25 E
Chiamboni, Somali Rep. 52 E8 1 39S 41 35 E
Chiamussu = Jiamusi, China 33 B8 46 40N 130 26 E
Chiang Dao, Thailand 38 C2 19 22N 98 58 E
Chiang Kham, Thailand 38 C3 19 32N 100 18 E
Chiang Khan, Thailand 38 D3 17 52N 101 36 E
Chiang Mai, Thailand 38 C2 18 47N 98 59 E
Chiang Rai, Thailand 38 C2 19 52N 99 50 E
Chiapa →, Mexico 87 D6 16 42N 93 0W
Chiapa de Corzo, Mexico 87 D6 16 42N 93 0W
Chiapas □, Mexico 87 D6 17 0N 92 45W
Chiautla, Mexico 87 D5 18 18N 98 34W
Chiávari, Italy 18 D8 44 19N 9 19 E
Chiavenna, Italy 18 C8 46 19N 9 24 E
Chiba, Japan 31 G10 35 30N 140 7 E
Chiba □, Japan 31 G10 35 30N 140 20 E
Chibabava, Mozam. 57 C5 20 17S 33 35 E
Chibemba, Cunene, Angola 53 H2 15 48S 14 8 E
Chibemba, Huila, Angola 56 B2 16 20S 15 20 E
Chibia, Angola 53 H2 15 10S 13 42 E
Chibougamau, Canada 70 C5 49 56N 74 24W
Chibougamau, L., Canada 70 C5 49 50N 74 20W
Chic-Chocs, Mts., Canada 71 C6 48 55N 66 0W
Chicacole = Srikakulam, India 41 K13 18 14N 83 58 E
Chicago, U.S.A. 76 E2 41 53N 87 38W
Chicago Heights, U.S.A. 76 E2 41 30N 87 38W
Chichagof I., U.S.A. 68 C6 57 30N 135 30W
Chichén-Itzá, Mexico 87 C7 20 40N 88 36W
Chicheng, China 34 D8 40 55N 115 55 E
Chichester, U.K. 11 G7 50 50N 0 47W
Chichester Ra., Australia 60 D2 22 12S 119 15 E
Chichibu, Japan 31 F9 36 5N 139 10 E
Ch'ich'ihaerh = Qiqihar, China 27 E13 47 26N 124 0 E
Chicholi, India 42 H8 22 1N 77 40 E
Chickasha, U.S.A. 81 H6 35 3N 97 58W
Chiclana de la Frontera, Spain 19 D2 36 26N 6 9W
Chiclayo, Peru 92 E3 6 42S 79 50W
Chico, U.S.A. 84 F5 39 44N 121 50W
Chico →, Chubut, Argentina 96 E3 44 0S 67 0W
Chico →, Santa Cruz, Argentina 96 G3 50 0S 68 30W
Chicomo, Mozam. 57 C5 24 31S 34 6 E
Chicontepec, Mexico 87 C5 20 58N 98 10W
Chicopee, U.S.A. 79 D12 42 9N 72 37W
Chicoutimi, Canada 71 C5 48 28N 71 5W
Chicualacuala, Mozam. 57 C5 22 6S 31 42 E
Chidambaram, India 40 P11 11 20N 79 45 E
Chidenguele, Mozam. 57 C5 24 55S 34 11 E
Chidley, C., Canada 69 B13 60 23N 64 26W
Chiede, Angola 56 B2 17 15S 16 22 E
Chiefs Pt., Canada 78 B3 44 41N 81 18W
Chiem Hoa, Vietnam 38 A5 22 12N 105 17 E
Chiemsee, Germany 16 E7 47 53N 12 28 E
Chiengi, Zambia 55 D2 8 45S 29 10 E
Chiengmai = Chiang Mai, Thailand 38 C2 18 47N 98 59 E
Chiese →, Italy 18 D9 45 8N 10 25 E
Chieti, Italy 20 C6 42 21N 14 10 E
Chifeng, China 35 C10 42 18N 118 58 E
Chignecto B., Canada 71 C7 45 30N 64 40W
Chiguana, Bolivia 94 A2 21 0S 67 58W
Chigwell, U.K. 11 F8 51 37N 0 5 E
Chiha-ri, N. Korea 35 E14 38 40N 126 30 E
Chihli, G. of = Bo Hai, China 35 E10 39 0N 119 0 E
Chihuahua, Mexico 86 B3 28 40N 106 3W
Chihuahua □, Mexico 86 B3 28 40N 106 3W
Chiili, Kazakstan 26 E7 44 20N 66 15 E
Chik Bollapur, India 40 N10 13 25N 77 45 E
Chikmagalur, India 40 N9 13 15N 75 45 E
Chikwawa, Malawi 55 F3 16 2S 34 50 E
Chilac, Mexico 87 D5 18 20N 97 24W
Chilam Chavki, Pakistan 43 B6 35 5N 75 5 E
Chilanga, Zambia 55 F2 15 33S 28 16 E
Chilapa, Mexico 87 D5 17 40N 99 11W
Chilas, Pakistan 43 B6 35 25N 74 5 E
Chilaw, Sri Lanka 40 R11 7 30N 79 50 E
Chilcotin →, Canada 72 C4 51 44N 122 23W
Childers, Australia 63 D5 25 15S 152 17 E
Childress, U.S.A. 81 H4 34 25N 100 13W
Chile ■, S. Amer. 96 D2 35 0S 72 0W
Chile Rise, Pac. Oc. 65 L18 38 0S 92 0W
Chilecito, Argentina 94 B2 29 10S 67 30W
Chilete, Peru 92 E3 7 10S 78 50W
Chililabombwe, Zambia 55 E2 12 18S 27 43 E
Chilin = Jilin, China 35 C14 43 44N 126 30 E
Chilka L., India 41 K14 19 40N 85 25 E
Chilko →, Canada 72 C4 52 0N 123 40W
Chilko L., Canada 72 C4 51 20N 124 10W
Chillagoe, Australia 62 B3 17 7S 144 33 E
Chillán, Chile 94 D1 36 40S 72 10W
Chillicothe, Ill., U.S.A. 80 E10 40 55N 89 29W
Chillicothe, Mo., U.S.A. 80 F8 39 48N 93 33W
Chillicothe, Ohio, U.S.A. 76 F4 39 20N 82 59W
Chilliwack, Canada 72 D4 49 10N 121 54W
Chilo, India 42 F5 27 25N 73 32 E
Chiloane, I., Mozam. 57 C5 20 40S 34 55 E
Chiloé, I. de, Chile 96 E2 42 30S 73 50W
Chilpancingo, Mexico 87 D5 17 30N 99 30W
Chiltern Hills, U.K. 11 F7 51 40N 0 53W
Chilton, U.S.A. 76 C1 44 2N 88 10W
Chilubi, Zambia 55 E2 11 5S 29 58 E
Chilubula, Zambia 55 E3 10 14S 30 51 E
Chilumba, Malawi 55 E3 10 28S 34 12 E
Chilung, Taiwan 33 D7 25 3N 121 45 E
Chilwa, L., Malawi 55 F4 15 15S 35 40 E
Chimaltitán, Mexico 86 C4 21 46N 103 50W
Chimán, Panama 88 E4 8 45N 78 40W
Chimay, Belgium 15 D4 50 3N 4 20 E
Chimayo, U.S.A. 83 H11 36 0N 105 56W
Chimbay, Uzbekistan 26 E6 42 57N 59 47 E
Chimborazo, Ecuador 92 D3 1 29S 78 55W
Chimbote, Peru 92 E3 9 0S 78 35W
Chimkent = Shymkent, Kazakstan 26 E7 42 18N 69 36 E
Chimoio, Mozam. 55 F3 19 4S 33 30 E
Chimpembe, Zambia 55 D2 9 31S 29 33 E
Chin □, Burma 41 J18 22 0N 93 0 E
Chin Ling Shan = Qinling Shandi, China 34 H5 33 50N 108 10 E
China, Mexico 87 B5 25 40N 99 20W
China ■, Asia 33 D6 30 0N 110 0 E
China Lake, U.S.A. 85 K9 35 44N 117 37W
Chinan = Jinan, China 34 F9 36 38N 117 1 E
Chinandega, Nic. 88 D2 12 35N 87 12W
Chinati Peak, U.S.A. 81 L2 29 57N 104 29W
Chincha Alta, Peru 92 F3 13 25S 76 7W
Chinchaga →, Canada 72 B5 58 53N 118 20W
Chinchilla, Australia 63 D5 26 45S 150 38 E

Corrientes

Cobán, Guatemala 88 C1 15 30N 90 21W
Cobar, Australia 63 E4 31 27S 145 48 E
Cobargo, Australia 63 F4 36 20S 149 55 E
Cóbh, Ireland 13 E3 51 51N 8 17W
Cobija, Bolivia 92 F5 11 0S 68 50W
Cobleskill, U.S.A. 79 D10 42 41N 74 29W
Coboconk, Canada 78 B6 44 39N 78 48W
Cobourg, Canada 78 C6 43 58N 78 10W
Cobourg Pen., Australia 60 B5 11 20S 132 15 E
Cobram, Australia 63 F4 35 54S 145 40 E
Cóbué, Mozam. 55 E3 12 0S 34 58 E
Coburg, Germany 16 C6 50 15N 10 58 E
Cocanada = Kakinada, India 41 L13 16 57N 82 11 E
Cochabamba, Bolivia 92 G5 17 26S 66 10W
Cochemane, Mozam. 55 F3 17 0S 32 54 E
Cochin, India 40 Q10 9 59N 76 22 E
Cochin China, Vietnam 39 G6 10 30N 106 0 E
Cochran, U.S.A. 77 J4 32 23N 83 21W
Cochrane, Alta., Canada 72 C6 51 11N 114 30W
Cochrane, Ont., Canada 70 C3 49 0N 81 0W
Cochrane, Chile 96 F2 47 15S 72 33W
Cochrane →, Canada 73 B8 59 0N 103 40W
Cochrane, L., Chile 96 F2 47 10S 72 0W
Cochranton, U.S.A. 78 E4 41 31N 80 3W
Cockburn, Australia 63 E3 32 5S 141 0 E
Cockburn, Canal, Chile 96 G2 54 30S 72 0W
Cockburn I., Canada 70 C3 45 55N 83 22W
Cockburn Ra., Australia 60 C4 15 46S 128 0 E
Cockermouth, U.K. 10 C4 54 40N 3 22W
Cocklebiddy, Australia 61 F4 32 0S 126 3 E
Coco →, Cent. Amer. 88 D3 15 0N 83 8W
Coco, I. del, Pac. Oc. 65 G19 5 25N 87 55W
Cocoa, U.S.A. 77 L5 28 21N 80 44W
Cocobeach, Gabon 52 D1 0 59N 9 34 E
Cocos Is., Ind. Oc. 64 J1 12 10S 96 55 E
Cod, C., U.S.A. 76 D10 42 5N 70 10W
Codajás, Brazil 92 D6 3 55S 62 0W
Codó, Brazil 93 D10 4 30S 43 55W
Cody, U.S.A. 82 D9 44 32N 109 3W
Coe Hill, Canada 78 B7 44 52N 77 50W
Coelemu, Chile 94 D1 36 30S 72 48W
Coen, Australia 62 A3 13 52S 143 12 E
Cœur d'Alene, U.S.A. 82 C5 47 45N 116 51W
Cœur d'Alene L., U.S.A. 82 C5 47 32N 116 48W
Coevorden, Neths. 15 B6 52 40N 6 44 E
Cofete, Canary Is. 22 F5 28 6N 14 23W
Coffeyville, U.S.A. 81 G7 37 2N 95 37W
Coffin B., Australia 63 E2 34 38S 135 28 E
Coffin Bay, Australia 63 E2 34 37S 135 29 E
Coffin Bay Peninsula, Australia 63 E2 34 32S 135 15 E
Coffs Harbour, Australia 63 E5 30 16S 153 5 E
Cognac, France 18 D3 45 41N 0 20W
Cohocton, U.S.A. 78 D7 42 30N 77 30W
Cohocton →, U.S.A. 78 D7 42 9N 77 6W
Cohoes, U.S.A. 79 D11 42 46N 73 42W
Cohuna, Australia 63 F3 35 45S 144 15 E
Coiba, I., Panama 88 E3 7 30N 81 40W
Coig →, Argentina 96 G3 51 0S 69 10W
Coigeach, Rubha, U.K. 12 C3 58 6N 5 26W
Coihaique, Chile 96 F2 45 30S 71 45W
Coimbatore, India 40 P10 11 2N 76 59 E
Coimbra, Brazil 92 G7 19 55S 57 48W
Coimbra, Portugal 19 B1 40 15N 8 27W
Coín, Spain 19 D3 36 40N 4 48W
Coipasa, Salar de, Bolivia 92 G5 19 26S 68 9W
Cojimies, Ecuador 92 C3 0 20N 80 0W
Cojutepequé, El Salv. 88 D2 13 41N 88 54W
Cokeville, U.S.A. 82 E8 42 5N 110 57W
Colac, Australia 63 F3 38 21S 143 35 E
Colatina, Brazil 93 G10 19 32S 40 37W
Colbeck, C., Antarctica 5 D13 77 6S 157 48W
Colborne, Canada 78 C7 44 0N 77 53W
Colby, U.S.A. 80 F4 39 24N 101 3W
Colchester, U.K. 11 F8 51 54N 0 55 E
Cold L., Canada 73 C7 54 33N 110 5W
Coldstream, Canada 72 C5 50 13N 119 11W
Coldstream, U.K. 12 F6 55 39N 2 15W
Coldwater, Canada 78 B5 44 42N 79 40W
Coldwater, Kans., U.S.A. 81 G5 37 16N 99 20W
Coldwater, Mich., U.S.A. 76 E3 41 57N 85 0W
Coleambally, Australia 63 E4 34 49S 145 52 E
Colebrook, U.S.A. 79 B13 44 54N 71 30W
Coleman, U.S.A. 81 K5 31 50N 99 26W
Coleman →, Australia 62 B3 15 6S 141 38 E
Colenso, S. Africa 57 D4 28 44S 29 50 E
Coleraine, Australia 63 F3 37 36S 141 40 E
Coleraine, U.K. 13 A5 55 8N 6 41W
Coleridge, L., N.Z. 59 K3 43 17S 171 30 E
Colesberg, S. Africa 56 E4 30 45S 25 5 E
Coleville, U.S.A. 84 G7 38 34N 119 30W
Colfax, Calif., U.S.A. 84 F6 39 6N 120 57W
Colfax, La., U.S.A. 81 K8 31 31N 92 42W
Colfax, Wash., U.S.A. 82 C5 46 53N 117 22W
Colhué Huapi, L., Argentina 96 F3 45 30S 69 0W
Coligny, S. Africa 57 D4 26 17S 26 15 E
Colima, Mexico 86 D4 19 14N 103 43W
Colima □, Mexico 86 D4 19 10N 103 40W
Colima, Nevado de, Mexico 86 D4 19 35N 103 45W
Colina, Chile 94 C1 33 13S 70 45W
Colinas, Brazil 93 E10 6 0S 44 10W
Coll, U.K. 12 E2 56 39N 6 34W
Collaguasi, Chile 94 A2 21 5S 68 45W
Collarenebri, Australia 63 D4 29 33S 148 34 E
Colleen Bawn, Zimbabwe 55 G2 21 0S 29 12 E
College Park, U.S.A. 77 J3 33 40N 84 27W
College Station, U.S.A. 81 K6 30 37N 96 21W
Collie, Australia 61 F2 33 22S 116 8 E
Collier B., Australia 60 C3 16 10S 124 15 E
Collier Ra., Australia 61 D2 24 45S 119 10 E
Collina, Passo di, Italy 20 B4 44 2N 10 56 E
Collingwood, Canada 78 B4 44 29N 80 13W
Collingwood, N.Z. 59 J4 40 41S 172 40 E
Collins, Canada 70 B2 50 17N 89 27W
Collinsville, Australia 62 C4 20 30S 147 56 E
Collipulli, Chile 94 D1 37 55S 72 30W
Collooney, Ireland 13 B3 54 11N 8 29W
Colmar, France 18 B7 48 5N 7 20 E
Colo →, Australia 63 E5 33 25S 150 52 E
Cologne = Köln, Germany 16 C4 50 56N 6 57 E
Colom, I. d'en, Spain 22 B11 39 58N 4 16 E
Coloma, U.S.A. 84 G6 38 48N 120 53W
Colomb-Béchar = Béchar, Algeria 50 B5 31 38N 2 18W
Colombia ■, S. Amer. 92 C4 3 45N 73 0W
Colombian Basin, S. Amer. 66 H12 14 0N 76 0W
Colombo, Sri Lanka 40 R11 6 56N 79 58 E
Colón, Buenos Aires, Argentina 94 C3 33 53S 61 7W
Colón, Entre Ríos, Argentina 94 C4 32 12S 58 10W
Colón, Cuba 88 B3 22 42N 80 54W
Colón, Panama 88 E4 9 20N 79 54W
Colonia de Sant Jordi, Spain 22 B9 39 19N 2 59 E
Colonia del Sacramento, Uruguay 94 C4 34 25S 57 50W
Colonia Dora, Argentina 94 B3 28 34S 62 59W
Colonial Beach, U.S.A. 76 F7 38 15N 76 58W
Colonie, U.S.A. 79 D11 42 43N 73 50W
Colonsay, Canada 73 C7 51 59N 105 52W
Colonsay, U.K. 12 E2 56 5N 6 12W
Colorado □, U.S.A. 83 G10 39 30N 105 30W
Colorado →, Argentina 96 D4 39 50S 62 8W
Colorado →, N. Amer. 83 L6 31 45N 114 40W
Colorado →, U.S.A. 81 L7 28 36N 95 59W
Colorado City, U.S.A. 81 J4 32 24N 100 52W
Colorado Desert, U.S.A. 74 D3 34 20N 116 0W
Colorado Plateau, U.S.A. 83 H8 37 0N 111 0W
Colorado River Aqueduct, U.S.A. 85 L12 34 17N 114 10W
Colorado Springs, U.S.A. 80 F2 38 50N 104 49W
Colotlán, Mexico 86 C4 22 6N 103 16W
Colstrip, U.S.A. 82 D10 45 53N 106 38W
Colton, U.S.A. 79 B10 44 33N 74 56W
Columbia, Ky., U.S.A. 76 G3 37 6N 85 18W
Columbia, La., U.S.A. 81 J8 32 6N 92 5W
Columbia, Miss., U.S.A. 81 K10 31 15N 89 50W
Columbia, Mo., U.S.A. 80 F8 38 57N 92 20W
Columbia, Pa., U.S.A. 79 F8 40 2N 76 30W
Columbia, S.C., U.S.A. 77 J5 34 0N 81 2W
Columbia, Tenn., U.S.A. 77 H2 35 37N 87 2W
Columbia →, N. Amer. 84 D2 46 15N 124 5W
Columbia, C., Canada 4 A4 83 0N 70 0W
Columbia, District of □, U.S.A. 76 F7 38 55N 77 0W
Columbia, Mt., Canada 72 C5 52 8N 117 20W
Columbia Basin, U.S.A. 82 C4 46 45N 119 5W
Columbia Falls, U.S.A. 82 B6 48 23N 114 11W
Columbia Mts., Canada 72 C5 52 0N 119 0W
Columbia Plateau, U.S.A. 82 D5 44 0N 117 30W
Columbiana, U.S.A. 78 F4 40 53N 80 42W
Columbretes, Is., Spain 19 C6 39 50N 0 50 E
Columbus, Ga., U.S.A. 77 J3 32 28N 84 59W
Columbus, Ind., U.S.A. 76 F3 39 13N 85 55W
Columbus, Kans., U.S.A. 81 G7 37 10N 94 50W
Columbus, Miss., U.S.A. 77 J1 33 30N 88 25W
Columbus, Mont., U.S.A. 82 D9 45 38N 109 15W
Columbus, N. Mex., U.S.A. 83 L10 31 50N 107 38W
Columbus, Nebr., U.S.A. 80 E6 41 26N 97 22W
Columbus, Ohio, U.S.A. 76 F4 39 58N 83 0W
Columbus, Tex., U.S.A. 81 L6 29 42N 96 33W
Colusa, U.S.A. 84 F4 39 13N 122 1W
Colville, U.S.A. 82 B5 48 33N 117 54W
Colville →, U.S.A. 68 A4 70 25N 150 30W
Colville, C., N.Z. 59 G5 36 29S 175 21 E
Colwood, Canada 84 B3 48 26N 123 29W
Colwyn Bay, U.K. 10 D4 53 18N 3 44W
Comácchio, Italy 20 B5 44 42N 12 11 E
Comalcalco, Mexico 87 D6 18 16N 93 13W
Comallo, Argentina 96 E2 41 0S 70 5W
Comanche, U.S.A. 81 K5 31 54N 98 36W
Comayagua, Honduras 88 D2 14 25N 87 37W
Combahee →, U.S.A. 77 J5 32 30N 80 31W
Combarbalá, Chile 94 C1 31 11S 71 2W
Comber, Canada 78 D2 42 14N 82 33W
Comber, U.K. 13 B6 54 33N 5 45W
Combermere, Canada 78 A7 45 22N 77 37W
Comblain-au-Pont, Belgium 15 D5 50 29N 5 35 E
Comeragh Mts., Ireland 13 D4 52 18N 7 34W
Comet, Australia 62 C4 23 36S 148 38 E
Comilla, Bangla. 41 H17 23 28N 91 10 E
Comino, Malta 23 C1 36 2N 14 20 E
Comino, C., Italy 20 D3 40 32N 9 49 E
Comitán, Mexico 87 D6 16 18N 92 9W
Commerce, Ga., U.S.A. 77 H4 34 12N 83 28W
Commerce, Tex., U.S.A. 81 J7 33 15N 95 54W
Committee B., Canada 69 B11 68 30N 86 30W
Commonwealth B., Antarctica 5 C10 67 0S 144 0 E
Commoron Cr. →, Australia 63 D5 28 22S 150 8 E
Communism Pk. = Kommunizma, Pik, Tajikistan 26 F8 39 0N 72 2 E
Como, Italy 18 D8 45 47N 9 5 E
Como, Lago di, Italy 18 D8 46 0N 9 11 E
Comodoro Rivadavia, Argentina 96 F3 45 50S 67 40W
Comorin, C., India 40 Q10 8 3N 77 40 E
Comoro Is. = Comoros ■, Ind. Oc. 49 H8 12 10S 44 15 E
Comoros ■, Ind. Oc. 49 H8 12 10S 44 15 E
Comox, Canada 72 D4 49 42N 124 55W
Compiègne, France 18 B5 49 24N 2 50 E
Compostela, Mexico 86 C4 21 15N 104 53W
Comprida, I., Brazil 95 A6 24 50S 47 42W
Compton, Canada 79 A13 45 14N 71 49W
Compton, U.S.A. 85 M8 33 54N 118 13W
Comrat, Moldova 17 E15 46 18N 28 40 E
Con Cuong, Vietnam 38 C5 19 2N 104 54 E
Con Son, Vietnam 39 H6 8 41N 106 37 E
Conakry, Guinea 50 G3 9 29N 13 49W
Conara, Australia 62 G4 41 50S 147 26 E
Concarneau, France 18 C2 47 52N 3 56W
Conceição, Mozam. 55 F4 18 47S 36 7 E
Conceição da Barra, Brazil 93 G11 18 35S 39 45W
Conceição do Araguaia, Brazil 93 E9 8 0S 49 2W
Concepción, Argentina 94 B2 27 20S 65 35W
Concepción, Bolivia 92 G6 16 15S 62 8W
Concepción, Chile 94 D1 36 50S 73 0W
Concepción, Mexico 87 D6 18 15N 90 5W
Concepción, Paraguay 94 A4 23 22S 57 26W
Concepción □, Chile 94 D1 37 0S 72 30W
Concepción →, Mexico 86 A2 30 32N 113 2W
Concepción, Est. de, Chile 96 G2 50 30S 74 55W
Concepción, L., Bolivia 92 G6 17 20S 61 20W
Concepción, Punta, Mexico 86 B2 26 55N 111 59W
Concepción del Oro, Mexico 86 C4 24 40N 101 30W
Concepción del Uruguay, Argentina 94 C4 32 35S 58 20W
Conception, Pt., U.S.A. 85 L6 34 27N 120 28W
Conception B., Canada 71 C9 47 45N 53 0W
Conception B., Namibia 56 C1 23 55S 14 22 E
Conception I., Bahamas 89 B4 23 52N 75 9W
Concession, Zimbabwe 55 F3 17 27S 30 56 E
Conchas Dam, U.S.A. 81 H2 35 22N 104 11W
Concho, U.S.A. 83 J9 34 28N 109 36W
Concho →, U.S.A. 81 K5 31 34N 99 43W
Conchos →, Chihuahua, Mexico 86 B4 29 32N 105 0W
Conchos →, Tamaulipas, Mexico 87 B5 25 9N 98 35W
Concord, Calif., U.S.A. 84 H4 37 59N 122 2W
Concord, N.C., U.S.A. 77 H5 35 25N 80 35W
Concord, N.H., U.S.A. 79 C13 43 12N 71 32W
Concordia, Argentina 94 C4 31 20S 58 2W
Concórdia, Brazil 92 D5 4 36S 66 36W
Concordia, Mexico 86 C3 23 18N 106 2W
Concordia, U.S.A. 80 F6 39 34N 97 40W
Concrete, U.S.A. 82 B3 48 32N 121 45W
Condamine, Australia 63 D5 26 56S 150 9 E
Conde, U.S.A. 80 C5 45 9N 98 6W
Condeúba, Brazil 93 F10 14 52S 42 0W
Condobolin, Australia 63 E4 33 4S 147 6 E
Condon, U.S.A. 82 D3 45 14N 120 11W
Conegliano, Italy 20 B5 45 53N 12 18 E
Conejera, I. = Conills, I. des, Spain 22 B9 39 11N 2 58 E
Conejos, Mexico 86 B4 26 14N 103 53W
Confuso →, Paraguay 94 B4 25 9S 57 34W
Congleton, U.K. 10 D5 53 10N 2 13W
Congo (Kinshasa) = Congo, Dem. Rep. of the ■, Africa 52 E4 3 0S 23 0 E
Congo ■, Africa 52 E3 1 0S 16 0 E
Congo →, Africa 52 F2 6 4S 12 24 E
Congo, Dem. Rep. of the ■, Africa 52 E4 3 0S 23 0 E
Congo Basin, Africa 52 E4 0 10S 24 30 E
Congonhas, Brazil 95 A7 20 30S 43 52W
Congress, U.S.A. 83 J7 34 9N 112 51W
Conills, I. des, Spain 22 B9 39 11N 2 58 E
Coniston, Canada 70 C3 46 29N 80 51W
Conjeeveram = Kanchipuram, India 40 N11 12 52N 79 45 E
Conklin, Canada 73 B6 55 38N 111 5W
Conklin, U.S.A. 79 D9 42 2N 75 49W
Conn, L., Ireland 13 B2 54 3N 9 15W
Connacht □, Ireland 13 C2 53 43N 9 12W
Conneaut, U.S.A. 78 E4 41 57N 80 34W
Connecticut □, U.S.A. 79 E12 41 30N 72 45W
Connecticut →, U.S.A. 79 E12 41 16N 72 20W
Connell, U.S.A. 82 C4 46 40N 118 52W
Connellsville, U.S.A. 78 F5 40 1N 79 35W
Connemara, Ireland 13 C2 53 29N 9 45W
Connemaugh →, U.S.A. 78 F5 40 28N 79 19W
Connersville, U.S.A. 76 F3 39 39N 85 8W
Connors Ra., Australia 62 C4 21 40S 149 10 E
Conquest, Canada 73 C7 51 32N 107 14W
Conrad, U.S.A. 82 B8 48 10N 111 57W
Conran, C., Australia 63 F4 37 49S 148 44 E
Conroe, U.S.A. 81 K7 30 19N 95 27W
Consecon, Canada 78 C7 44 0N 77 31W
Conselheiro Lafaiete, Brazil 95 A7 20 40S 43 48W
Consett, U.K. 10 C6 54 51N 1 50W
Consort, Canada 73 C6 52 1N 110 46W
Constance = Konstanz, Germany 16 E5 47 40N 9 10 E
Constance, L. = Bodensee, Europe 18 C8 47 35N 9 25 E
Constanța, Romania 17 F15 44 14N 28 38 E
Constantia, U.S.A. 79 C8 43 15N 76 1W
Constantine, Algeria 50 A7 36 25N 6 42 E
Constitución, Chile 94 D1 35 20S 72 30W
Constitución, Uruguay 94 C4 31 0S 57 50W
Consul, Canada 73 D7 49 20N 109 30W
Contact, U.S.A. 82 F6 41 46N 114 45W
Contai, India 43 J12 21 54N 87 46 E
Contamana, Peru 92 E4 7 19S 74 55W
Contas →, Brazil 93 F11 14 17S 39 1W
Contoocook, U.S.A. 79 C13 43 13N 71 45W
Contra Costa, Mozam. 57 D5 25 9S 33 30 E
Contwoyto L., Canada 68 B8 65 42N 110 50W
Conway = Conwy, U.K. 10 D4 53 17N 3 50W
Conway = Conwy →, U.K. 10 D4 53 17N 3 50W
Conway, Ark., U.S.A. 81 H8 35 5N 92 26W
Conway, N.H., U.S.A. 79 C13 43 59N 71 7W
Conway, S.C., U.S.A. 77 J6 33 51N 79 3W
Conway, L., Australia 63 D2 28 17S 135 35 E
Conwy, U.K. 10 D4 53 17N 3 50W
Conwy □, U.K. 10 D4 53 10N 3 44W
Conwy →, U.K. 10 D4 53 17N 3 50W
Coober Pedy, Australia 63 D1 29 1S 134 43 E
Cooch Behar = Koch Bihar, India 41 F16 26 22N 89 29 E
Cooinda, Australia 60 B5 13 15S 130 5 E
Cook, Australia 61 F5 30 37S 130 25 E
Cook, U.S.A. 80 B8 47 49N 92 39W
Cook, B., Chile 96 H3 55 10S 70 0W
Cook, C., Canada 72 C3 50 8N 127 55W
Cook, Mt., N.Z. 59 K3 43 36S 170 9 E
Cook Inlet, U.S.A. 68 C4 60 0N 152 0W
Cook Is., Pac. Oc. 65 J12 17 0S 160 0W
Cook Strait, N.Z. 59 J5 41 15S 174 29 E
Cookeville, U.S.A. 77 G3 36 10N 85 30W
Cookhouse, S. Africa 56 E4 32 44S 25 47 E
Cookshire, Canada 79 A13 45 25N 71 38W
Cookstown, U.K. 13 B5 54 39N 6 45W
Cooksville, Canada 78 C5 43 36N 79 35W
Cooktown, Australia 62 B4 15 30S 145 16 E
Coolabah, Australia 63 E4 31 1S 146 43 E
Cooladdi, Australia 63 D4 26 37S 145 23 E
Coolah, Australia 63 E4 31 48S 149 41 E
Coolamon, Australia 63 E4 34 46S 147 8 E
Coolgardie, Australia 61 F3 30 55S 121 8 E
Coolidge, U.S.A. 83 K8 32 59N 111 31W
Coolidge Dam, U.S.A. 83 K8 33 0N 110 20W
Cooma, Australia 63 F4 36 12S 149 8 E
Coon Rapids, U.S.A. 80 C8 45 9N 93 19W
Coonabarabran, Australia 63 E4 31 14S 149 18 E
Coonalpyn, Australia 63 F2 35 43S 139 52 E
Coonamble, Australia 63 E4 30 56S 148 27 E
Coonana, Australia 61 F3 31 0S 123 0 E
Coondapoor, India 40 N9 13 42N 74 40 E
Cooninie, L., Australia 63 D2 26 4S 139 59 E
Cooper, U.S.A. 81 J7 33 23N 95 42W
Cooper Cr. →, Australia 63 D2 28 29S 137 46 E
Cooperstown, N. Dak., U.S.A. 80 B5 47 27N 98 8W
Cooperstown, N.Y., U.S.A. 79 D10 42 42N 74 56W
Coorabie, Australia 61 F5 31 54S 132 18 E
Coorow, Australia 61 E2 29 53S 116 2 E
Cooroy, Australia 63 D5 26 22S 152 54 E
Coos Bay, U.S.A. 82 E1 43 22N 124 13W
Coosa →, U.S.A. 77 J2 32 30N 86 16W
Cootamundra, Australia 63 E4 34 36S 148 1 E
Cootehill, Ireland 13 B4 54 4N 7 5W
Copahue Paso, Argentina 94 D1 37 49S 71 8W
Copainalá, Mexico 87 D6 17 8N 93 11W
Copake Falls, U.S.A. 79 D11 42 7N 73 31W
Copán, Honduras 88 D2 14 50N 89 9W
Cope, U.S.A. 80 F3 39 40N 102 51W
Copenhagen = København, Denmark 9 J15 55 41N 12 34 E
Copenhagen, U.S.A. 79 C9 43 54N 75 41W
Copiapó, Chile 94 B1 27 30S 70 20W
Copiapó →, Chile 94 B1 27 19S 70 56W
Coplay, U.S.A. 79 F9 40 44N 75 29W
Copp L., Canada 72 A6 60 14N 114 40W
Coppename →, Surinam 93 B7 5 48N 55 55W
Copper Harbor, U.S.A. 76 B2 47 28N 87 53W
Copper Queen, Zimbabwe 55 F2 17 29S 29 18 E
Copperas Cove, U.S.A. 81 K6 31 8N 97 54W
Copperbelt □, Zambia 55 E2 13 15S 27 30 E
Coppermine = Kugluktuk, Canada 68 B8 67 50N 115 5W
Coppermine →, Canada 68 B8 67 49N 116 4W
Copperopolis, U.S.A. 84 H6 37 58N 120 38W
Coquet →, U.K. 10 B6 55 20N 1 32W
Coquilhatville = Mbandaka, Dem. Rep. of the Congo 52 D3 0 1N 18 18 E
Coquille, U.S.A. 82 E1 43 11N 124 11W
Coquimbo, Chile 94 C1 30 0S 71 20W
Coquimbo □, Chile 94 C1 31 0S 71 0W
Corabia, Romania 17 G13 43 48N 24 30 E
Coracora, Peru 92 G4 15 5S 73 45W
Coraki, Australia 63 D5 28 59S 153 17 E
Coral, U.S.A. 78 F5 40 29N 79 10W
Coral Gables, U.S.A. 77 N5 25 45N 80 16W
Coral Harbour = Salliq, Canada 69 B11 64 8N 83 10W
Coral Sea, Pac. Oc. 64 J7 15 0S 150 0 E
Coral Springs, U.S.A. 77 M5 26 16N 80 13W
Coraopolis, U.S.A. 78 F4 40 31N 80 10W
Corato, Italy 20 D7 41 9N 16 25 E
Corbin, U.S.A. 76 G3 36 57N 84 6W
Corby, U.K. 11 E7 52 30N 0 41W
Corcaigh = Cork, Ireland 13 E3 51 54N 8 29W
Corcoran, U.S.A. 84 J7 36 6N 119 33W
Corcubión, Spain 19 A1 42 56N 9 12W
Cordele, U.S.A. 77 K4 31 58N 83 47W
Cordell, U.S.A. 81 H5 35 17N 98 59W
Córdoba, Argentina 94 C3 31 20S 64 10W
Córdoba, Mexico 87 D5 18 50N 97 0W
Córdoba, Spain 19 D3 37 50N 4 50W
Córdoba □, Argentina 94 C3 31 22S 64 15W
Córdoba, Sierra de, Argentina 94 C3 31 10S 64 25W
Cordova, U.S.A. 68 B5 60 33N 145 45W
Corella →, Australia 62 B3 19 34S 140 47 E
Corfield, Australia 62 C3 21 40S 143 21 E
Corfu = Kérkira, Greece 23 A3 39 38N 19 50 E
Corfu, Str. of, Greece 23 A4 39 34N 20 0 E
Coria, Spain 19 C2 39 58N 6 33W
Corigliano Cálabro, Italy 20 E7 39 36N 16 31 E
Coringa Is., Australia 62 B4 16 58S 149 58 E
Corinth = Kórinthos, Greece 21 F10 37 56N 22 55 E
Corinth, Miss., U.S.A. 77 H1 34 56N 88 31W
Corinth, N.Y., U.S.A. 79 C11 43 14N 73 49W
Corinth, N.Y., U.S.A. 79 C11 43 15N 73 49W
Corinth, G. of = Korinthiakós Kólpos, Greece 21 E10 38 16N 22 30 E
Corinto, Brazil 93 G10 18 20S 44 30W
Corinto, Nic. 88 D2 12 30N 87 10W
Cork, Ireland 13 E3 51 54N 8 29W
Cork □, Ireland 13 E3 51 57N 8 40W
Cork Harbour, Ireland 13 E3 51 47N 8 16W
Çorlu, Turkey 21 D12 41 11N 27 49 E
Cormack L., Canada 72 A4 60 56N 121 37W
Cormorant, Canada 73 C8 54 14N 100 35W
Cormorant L., Canada 73 C8 54 15N 100 50W
Corn Is. = Maiz, Is. del, Nic. 88 D3 12 15N 83 4W
Cornélio Procópio, Brazil 95 A5 23 7S 50 40W
Corner Brook, Canada 71 C8 48 57N 57 58W
Cornești, Moldova 17 E15 47 21N 28 1 E
Corning, Ark., U.S.A. 81 G9 36 25N 90 35W
Corning, Calif., U.S.A. 82 G2 39 56N 122 11W
Corning, Iowa, U.S.A. 80 E7 40 59N 94 44W
Corning, N.Y., U.S.A. 78 D7 42 9N 77 3W
Cornwall, Canada 79 A10 45 2N 74 44W
Cornwall, U.S.A. 79 F8 40 17N 76 25W
Cornwall □, U.K. 11 G3 50 26N 4 40W
Corny Pt., Australia 63 E2 34 55S 137 0 E
Coro, Venezuela 92 A5 11 25N 69 41W
Coroatá, Brazil 93 D10 4 8S 44 0W
Corocoro, Bolivia 92 G5 17 15S 68 28W
Coroico, Bolivia 92 G5 16 0S 67 50W
Coromandel, N.Z. 59 G5 36 45S 175 31 E
Coromandel Coast, India 40 N12 12 30N 81 0 E
Corona, Calif., U.S.A. 85 M9 33 53N 117 34W
Corona, N. Mex., U.S.A. 83 J11 34 15N 105 36W
Coronach, Canada 73 D7 49 7N 105 31W
Coronado, U.S.A. 85 N9 32 41N 117 11W
Coronado, B. de, Costa Rica 88 E3 9 0N 83 40W
Coronados, Is. los, U.S.A. 85 N9 32 25N 117 15W
Coronation, Canada 72 C6 52 5N 111 27W
Coronation Gulf, Canada 68 B9 68 25N 110 0W
Coronation I., Antarctica 5 C18 60 45S 46 0W
Coronation Is., Australia 60 B3 14 57S 124 55 E
Coronda, Argentina 94 C3 31 58S 60 56W
Coronel, Chile 94 D1 37 0S 73 10W
Coronel Bogado, Paraguay 94 B4 27 11S 56 18W
Coronel Dorrego, Argentina 94 D3 38 40S 61 10W
Coronel Oviedo, Paraguay 94 B4 25 24S 56 30W
Coronel Pringles, Argentina 94 D3 38 0S 61 30W
Coronel Suárez, Argentina 94 D3 37 30S 61 52W
Coronel Vidal, Argentina 94 D4 37 28S 57 45W
Coropuna, Nevado, Peru 92 G4 15 30S 72 41W
Corowa, Australia 63 F4 35 58S 146 21 E
Corozal, Belize 87 D7 18 23N 88 23W
Corpus, Argentina 95 B4 27 10S 55 30W
Corpus Christi, U.S.A. 81 M6 27 47N 97 24W
Corpus Christi, L., U.S.A. 81 L6 28 2N 97 52W
Corralejo, Canary Is. 22 F6 28 43N 13 53W
Corraun Pen., Ireland 13 C2 53 54N 9 54W
Correntes, C. das, Mozam. 57 C6 24 6S 35 34 E
Corrib, L., Ireland 13 C2 53 27N 9 16W
Corrientes, Argentina 94 B4 27 30S 58 45W

Corrientes

Corrientes □, Argentina ... 94 B4 28 0S 57 0W
Corrientes →, Argentina . 94 C4 30 42S 59 38W
Corrientes →, Peru 92 D4 3 43S 74 35W
Corrientes, C., Colombia .. 92 B3 5 30N 77 34W
Corrientes, C., Cuba 88 B3 21 43N 84 30W
Corrientes, C., Mexico 86 C3 20 25N 105 42W
Corrigan, U.S.A. 81 K7 31 0N 94 52W
Corrigin, Australia .... 61 F2 32 20S 117 53 E
Corry, U.S.A. 78 E5 41 55N 79 39W
Corryong, Australia .... 63 F4 36 12S 147 53 E
Corse, France .... 18 F8 42 0N 9 0 E
Corse, C., France .... 18 E8 43 1N 9 25 E
Corsica = Corse, France ... 18 F8 42 0N 9 0 E
Corsicana, U.S.A. 81 J6 32 6N 96 28W
Corte, France .... 18 E8 42 19N 9 11 E
Cortez, U.S.A. 83 H9 37 21N 108 35W
Cortland, N.Y., U.S.A. 79 D8 42 36N 76 11W
Cortland, Ohio, U.S.A. 78 E4 41 20N 80 44W
Çorum, Turkey .... 25 F5 40 30N 34 57 E
Corumbá, Brazil 92 G7 19 0S 57 30W
Corunna = A Coruña, Spain 19 A1 43 20N 8 25W
Corvallis, U.S.A. 82 D2 44 34N 123 16W
Corvette, L. de la, Canada . 70 B5 53 25N 74 3W
Corydon, U.S.A. 80 E8 40 46N 93 19W
Cosalá, Mexico 86 C3 24 28N 106 40W
Cosamaloapan, Mexico ... 87 D5 18 23N 95 50W
Cosenza, Italy .... 20 E7 39 18N 16 15 E
Coshocton, U.S.A. 78 F3 40 16N 81 51W
Cosmo Newberry, Australia 61 E3 28 0S 122 54 E
Coso Junction, U.S.A. 85 J9 36 3N 117 57W
Coso Pk., U.S.A. 85 J9 36 13N 117 44W
Cosquín, Argentina 94 C3 31 15S 64 30W
Costa Blanca, Spain 19 C5 38 25N 0 10W
Costa Brava, Spain ...... 19 B7 41 30N 3 0 E
Costa del Sol, Spain 19 D3 36 30N 4 30W
Costa Dorada, Spain ...... 19 B6 41 12N 1 15 E
Costa Mesa, U.S.A. 85 M9 33 38N 117 55W
Costa Rica ■, Cent. Amer. . 88 E3 10 0N 84 0W
Cosumnes →, U.S.A. 84 G5 38 16N 121 26W
Cotabato, Phil. .... 37 C6 7 14N 124 15 E
Cotagaita, Bolivia 94 A2 20 45S 65 40W
Côte d'Azur, France ...... 18 E7 43 25N 7 10 E
Côte-d'Ivoire = Ivory
Coast ■, Africa 50 G4 7 30N 5 0W
Coteau des Prairies, U.S.A. 80 C6 45 20N 97 50W
Coteau du Missouri, U.S.A. 80 B4 47 0N 100 0W
Coteau Landing, Canada .. 79 A10 45 15N 74 13W
Cotentin, France 18 B3 49 15N 1 30W
Cotillo, Canary Is. 22 F5 28 41N 14 1W
Cotonou, Benin .... 50 G6 6 20N 2 25 E
Cotopaxi, Ecuador 92 D3 0 40S 78 30W
Cotswold Hills, U.K. 11 F5 51 42N 2 10W
Cottage Grove, U.S.A. 82 E2 43 48N 123 3W
Cottbus, Germany .... 16 C8 51 45N 14 20 E
Cottonwood, U.S.A. 83 J7 34 45N 112 1W
Cotulla, U.S.A. 81 L5 28 26N 99 14W
Coudersport, U.S.A. 78 E6 41 46N 78 1W
Couedic, C. du, Australia .. 63 F2 36 5S 136 40 E
Coulee City, U.S.A. 82 C4 47 37N 119 17W
Coulman I., Antarctica .... 5 D11 73 35S 170 0 E
Coulonge →, Canada 70 C4 45 52N 76 46W
Coulterville, U.S.A. 84 H6 37 43N 120 12W
Council, U.S.A. 82 D5 44 44N 116 26W
Council Bluffs, U.S.A. 80 E7 41 16N 95 52W
Council Grove, U.S.A. 80 F6 38 40N 96 29W
Coupeville, U.S.A. 84 B4 48 13N 122 41W
Courantyne →, S. Amer. . 92 B7 5 55N 57 5W
Courcelles, Belgium ...... 15 D4 50 28N 4 22 E
Courtenay, Canada 72 D4 49 45N 125 0W
Courtland, U.S.A. 84 G5 38 20N 121 34W
Courtrai = Kortrijk, Belgium 15 D3 50 50N 3 17 E
Courtright, Canada 78 D2 42 49N 82 28W
Coushatta, U.S.A. 81 J8 32 1N 93 21W
Coutts Crossing, Australia . 63 D5 29 49S 152 55 E
Couvin, Belgium .... 15 D4 50 3N 4 29 E
Cove I., Canada 78 A3 45 17N 81 44W
Coventry, U.K. 11 E6 52 25N 1 28W
Covilhã, Portugal 19 B2 40 17N 7 31W
Covington, Ga., U.S.A. 77 J4 33 36N 83 51W
Covington, Ky., U.S.A. 76 F3 39 5N 84 31W
Covington, Okla., U.S.A. ... 81 G6 36 18N 97 35W
Covington, Tenn., U.S.A. ... 81 H10 35 34N 89 39W
Covington, Va., U.S.A. 76 G5 37 47N 79 59W
Cowal, L., Australia ...... 63 E4 33 40S 147 25 E
Cowan, L., Australia ...... 61 F3 31 45S 121 45 E
Cowan L., Canada 73 C7 54 0N 107 15W
Cowangie, Australia ...... 63 F3 35 12S 141 26 E
Cowansville, Canada 79 A12 45 14N 72 46W
Coward Springs, Australia . 63 D2 29 24S 136 49 E
Cowcowing Lakes, Australia 61 F2 30 55S 117 20 E
Cowdenbeath, U.K. 12 E5 56 7N 3 21W
Cowell, Australia .... 63 E2 33 39S 136 56 E
Cowes, U.K. 11 G6 50 45N 1 18W
Cowichan L., Canada 84 B2 48 53N 124 17W
Cowlitz →, U.S.A. 84 D4 46 6N 122 55W
Cowra, Australia .... 63 E4 33 49S 148 42 E
Coxilha Grande, Brazil 95 B5 28 18S 51 30W
Coxim, Brazil 93 G8 18 30S 54 55W
Cox's Bazar, Bangla. ...... 41 J17 21 26N 91 59 E
Coyote Wells, U.S.A. 85 N11 32 44N 115 58W
Coyuca de Benítez, Mexico 87 D4 17 1N 100 8W
Coyuca de Catalan, Mexico 86 D4 18 18N 100 41W
Cozad, U.S.A. 80 E5 40 52N 99 59W
Cozumel, Mexico 87 C7 20 31N 86 55W
Cozumel, Isla, Mexico 87 C7 20 30N 86 40W
Cracow = Kraków, Poland . 17 C10 50 4N 19 57 E
Cracow, Australia .... 63 D5 25 17S 150 17 E
Cradock, Australia .... 63 E2 32 6S 138 31 E
Cradock, S. Africa .... 56 E4 32 8S 25 36 E
Craig, U.S.A. 82 F10 40 31N 107 33W
Craigavon, U.K. 13 B5 54 27N 6 23W
Craigmore, Zimbabwe ..... 55 G3 20 28S 32 50 E
Craik, Canada 73 C7 51 3N 105 49W
Crailsheim, Germany ..... 16 D6 49 8N 10 5 E
Craiova, Romania .... 17 F12 44 21N 23 48 E
Cramsie, Australia .... 62 C3 23 20S 144 15 E
Cranberry L., U.S.A. 79 B10 44 11N 74 50W
Cranberry Portage, Canada 73 C8 54 35N 101 23W
Cranbrook, Australia ..... 61 F2 34 18S 117 33 E
Cranbrook, Canada 72 D5 49 30N 115 46W
Crandon, U.S.A. 80 C10 45 34N 88 54W
Crane, Oreg., U.S.A. 82 E4 43 25N 118 35W
Crane, Tex., U.S.A. 81 K3 31 24N 102 21W
Cranston, U.S.A. 79 E13 41 47N 71 26W
Crater L., U.S.A. 82 E2 42 56N 122 6W
Crater Lake National Park,
U.S.A. 82 E2 42 55N 122 10W
Crateús, Brazil 93 E10 5 10S 40 39W
Crato, Brazil 93 E11 7 10S 39 25W
Craven, L., Canada 70 B4 54 20N 76 56W
Crawford, U.S.A. 80 D3 42 41N 103 25W
Crawfordsville, U.S.A. 76 E2 40 2N 86 54W
Crawley, U.K. 11 F7 51 7N 0 11W
Crazy Mts., U.S.A. 82 C8 46 12N 110 20W
Crean L., Canada 73 C7 54 5N 106 9W
Crediton, Canada 78 C3 43 17N 81 33W
Cree →, Canada 73 B7 58 57N 105 47W
Cree →, U.K. 12 G4 54 55N 4 25W
Cree L., Canada 73 B7 57 30N 106 30W
Creede, U.S.A. 83 H10 37 51N 106 56W
Creekside, U.S.A. 78 F5 40 40N 79 11W
Creel, Mexico 86 B3 27 45N 107 38W
Creemore, Canada 78 B4 44 19N 80 6W
Creighton, Canada 73 C8 54 45N 101 54W
Creighton, U.S.A. 80 D6 42 28N 97 54W
Crema, Italy .... 18 D8 45 22N 9 41 E
Cremona, Italy .... 18 D9 45 7N 10 2 E
Cres, Croatia .... 16 F8 44 58N 14 25 E
Crescent City, U.S.A. 82 F1 41 45N 124 12W
Crespo, Argentina 94 C3 32 2S 60 19W
Cresson, U.S.A. 78 F6 40 28N 78 36W
Crestline, Calif., U.S.A. ... 85 L9 34 14N 117 18W
Crestline, Ohio, U.S.A. 78 F2 40 47N 82 44W
Creston, Canada 72 D5 49 10N 116 31W
Creston, Calif., U.S.A. 84 K6 35 32N 120 33W
Creston, Iowa, U.S.A. 80 E7 41 4N 94 22W
Crestview, Calif., U.S.A. ... 84 H8 37 46N 118 58W
Crestview, Fla., U.S.A. 77 K2 30 46N 86 34W
Crete = Kríti, Greece ..... 23 D7 35 15N 25 0 E
Crete, U.S.A. 80 E6 40 38N 96 58W
Créteil, France .... 18 B5 48 47N 2 28 E
Creus, C. de, Spain ...... 19 A7 42 20N 3 19 E
Creuse →, France .... 18 C4 47 0N 0 34 E
Crewe, U.K. 10 D5 53 6N 2 26W
Crewkerne, U.K. 11 G5 50 53N 2 48W
Criciúma, Brazil 95 B6 28 40S 49 23W
Crieff, U.K. 12 E5 56 22N 3 50W
Crimea □, Ukraine .... 25 E5 45 30N 33 10 E
Crimean Pen. = Krymskyy
Pivostriv, Ukraine ...... 25 F5 45 0N 34 0 E
Crişul Alb →, Romania ... 17 E11 46 42N 21 17 E
Crişul Negru →, Romania 17 E11 46 42N 21 16 E
Crna →, Macedonia ..... 21 D9 41 33N 21 59 E
Crna Gora = Montenegro □,
Yugoslavia .... 21 C8 42 40N 19 20 E
Crna Gora, Macedonia .... 21 C9 42 10N 21 30 E
Crna Reka = Crna →,
Macedonia .... 21 D9 41 33N 21 59 E
Croagh Patrick, Ireland ... 13 C2 53 46N 9 40W
Croatia ■, Europe .... 16 F9 45 20N 16 0 E
Crocker, Banjaran, Malaysia 36 C5 5 40N 116 30 E
Crockett, U.S.A. 81 K7 31 19N 95 27W
Crocodile = Krokodil →,
Mozam. .... 57 D5 25 14S 32 18 E
Crocodile Is., Australia ... 62 A1 12 3S 134 58 E
Crohy Hd., Ireland 13 B3 54 55N 8 26W
Croix, L. La, Canada 70 C1 48 20N 92 15W
Croker, C., Australia ..... 60 B5 10 58S 132 35 E
Croker, C., Canada 78 B4 44 58N 80 59W
Croker I., Australia ...... 60 B5 11 12S 132 32 E
Cromarty, U.K. 12 D4 57 40N 4 2W
Cromer, U.K. .... 10 E9 52 56N 1 17 E
Cromwell, N.Z. .... 59 L2 45 3S 169 14 E
Cromwell, U.S.A. 79 E12 41 36N 72 39W
Crook, U.K. 10 C6 54 43N 1 45W
Crooked →, Canada 72 C4 54 50N 122 54W
Crooked →, U.S.A. 82 D3 44 32N 121 16W
Crooked I., Bahamas 89 B5 22 50N 74 10W
Crooked Island Passage,
Bahamas 89 B5 23 0N 74 30W
Crookston, Minn., U.S.A. .. 80 B6 47 47N 96 37W
Crookston, Nebr., U.S.A. .. 80 D4 42 56N 100 45W
Crookwell, Australia ..... 63 E4 34 28S 149 24 E
Crosby, U.K. 10 D4 53 30N 3 3W
Crosby, U.S.A. 78 E6 41 45N 78 23W
Crosbyton, U.S.A. 81 J4 33 40N 101 14W
Cross City, U.S.A. 77 L4 29 38N 83 7W
Cross Fell, U.K. 10 C5 54 43N 2 28W
Cross L., Canada 73 C9 54 45N 97 30W
Cross Lake, Canada 73 C9 54 37N 97 47W
Cross Sound, U.S.A. 68 C6 58 0N 135 0W
Crossett, U.S.A. 81 J9 33 8N 91 58W
Crosshaven, Ireland 13 E3 51 47N 8 17W
Crossville, U.S.A. 77 G3 35 57N 85 2W
Croswell, U.S.A. 78 C2 43 16N 82 37W
Croton-on-Hudson, U.S.A. . 79 E11 41 12N 73 55W
Crotone, Italy .... 20 E7 39 5N 17 8 E
Crow →, Canada 72 B4 59 41N 124 20W
Crow Agency, U.S.A. 82 D10 45 36N 107 28W
Crow Hd., Ireland 13 E1 51 35N 10 9W
Crowell, U.S.A. 81 J5 33 59N 99 43W
Crowley, U.S.A. 81 K8 30 13N 92 22W
Crowley, L., U.S.A. 84 H8 37 35N 118 42W
Crown Point, Ind., U.S.A. . 76 E2 41 25N 87 22W
Crown Point, N.Y., U.S.A. . 79 C11 43 57N 73 26W
Crownpoint, U.S.A. 83 J9 35 41N 108 9W
Crows Landing, U.S.A. ... 84 H5 37 23N 121 6W
Crows Nest, Australia .... 63 D5 27 16S 152 4 E
Crowsnest Pass, Canada .. 72 D6 49 40N 114 40W
Croydon, Australia ...... 62 B3 18 13S 142 14 E
Croydon, U.K. 11 F7 51 22N 0 5W
Crozet Is., Ind. Oc. ...... 3 G12 46 27S 52 0 E
Cruz, C., Cuba 88 C4 19 50N 77 50W
Cruz Alta, Brazil 95 B5 28 45S 53 40W
Cruz del Eje, Argentina ... 94 C3 30 45S 64 50W
Cruzeiro, Brazil 95 A7 22 33S 45 0W
Cruzeiro do Oeste, Brazil . 95 A5 23 46S 53 4W
Cruzeiro do Sul, Brazil ... 92 E4 7 35S 72 35W
Cry L., Canada 72 B3 58 45N 129 0W
Crystal Bay, U.S.A. 84 F7 39 15N 120 0W
Crystal Brook, Australia .. 63 E2 33 21S 138 12 E
Crystal City, U.S.A. 81 L5 28 41N 99 50W
Crystal Falls, U.S.A. 76 B1 46 5N 88 20W
Crystal River, U.S.A. 77 L4 28 54N 82 35W
Crystal Springs, U.S.A. ... 81 K9 31 59N 90 21W
Csongrád, Hungary ...... 17 E11 46 43N 20 12 E
Cu Lao Hon, Vietnam .... 39 G7 10 54N 108 18 E
Cua Rao, Vietnam .... 38 C5 19 16N 104 27 E
Cuácua →, Mozam. ..... 55 F4 17 54S 37 0 E
Cuamato, Angola .... 56 B2 17 2S 15 7 E
Cuamba, Mozam. .... 55 E4 14 45S 36 22 E
Cuando →, Angola ..... 53 H4 17 30S 23 15 E
Cuando Cubango □, Angola 56 B3 16 25S 20 0 E
Cuangar, Angola .... 56 B2 17 36S 18 39 E
Cuanza →, Angola ...... 52 F2 9 2S 13 30 E
Cuarto →, Argentina 94 C3 33 25S 63 2W
Cuatrociénegas, Mexico ... 86 B4 26 59N 102 5W
Cuauhtémoc, Mexico 86 B3 28 25N 106 52W
Cuba, N. Mex., U.S.A. 83 J10 36 1N 107 4W
Cuba, N.Y., U.S.A. 78 D6 42 13N 78 17W
Cuba ■, W. Indies 88 B4 22 0N 79 0W
Cubal, Angola .... 53 G2 12 26S 14 3 E
Cubango →, Africa ..... 56 B3 18 50S 22 25 E
Cuchumatanes, Sierra de
los, Guatemala 88 C1 15 35N 91 25W
Cuckfield, U.K. 11 F7 51 1N 0 8W
Cucuí, Brazil 92 C5 1 12N 66 50W
Cucurpe, Mexico 86 A2 30 20N 110 43W
Cúcuta, Colombia 92 B4 7 54N 72 31W
Cuddalore, India .... 40 P11 11 46N 79 45 E
Cuddapah, India .... 40 M11 14 30N 78 47 E
Cuddapan, L., Australia ... 62 D3 25 45S 141 26 E
Cue, Australia .... 61 E2 27 25S 117 54 E
Cuenca, Ecuador 92 D3 2 50S 79 9W
Cuenca, Spain 19 B4 40 5N 2 10W
Cuenca, Serranía de, Spain 19 C5 39 55N 1 50W
Cuernavaca, Mexico 87 D5 18 55N 99 15W
Cuero, U.S.A. 81 L6 29 6N 97 17W
Cuevas del Almanzora,
Spain 19 D5 37 18N 1 58W
Cuevo, Bolivia 92 H6 20 15S 63 30W
Cuiabá, Brazil 93 G7 15 30S 56 0W
Cuiabá →, Brazil 93 G7 17 5S 56 36W
Cuijk, Neths. .... 15 C5 51 44N 5 50 E
Cuilco, Guatemala 88 C1 15 24N 91 58W
Cuillin Hills, U.K. 12 D2 57 13N 6 15W
Cuillin Sd., U.K. 12 D2 57 4N 6 20W
Cuito →, Angola .... 56 B3 18 1S 20 48 E
Cuitzeo, L. de, Mexico ... 86 D4 19 55N 101 5W
Cukai, Malaysia .... 39 K4 4 13N 103 25 E
Culbertson, U.S.A. 80 A2 48 9N 104 31W
Culcairn, Australia ...... 63 F4 35 41S 147 3 E
Culgoa →, Australia .... 63 D4 29 56S 146 20 E
Culiacán, Mexico 86 C3 24 50N 107 23W
Culiacán →, Mexico 86 C3 24 30N 107 42W
Culion, Phil. .... 37 B6 11 54N 119 58 E
Cullarin Ra., Australia ... 63 E4 34 30S 149 30 E
Cullen, U.K. 12 D6 57 42N 2 49W
Cullen Pt., Australia ..... 62 A3 11 57S 141 54 E
Cullera, Spain 19 C5 39 9N 0 17W
Cullman, U.S.A. 77 H2 34 11N 86 51W
Culpeper, U.S.A. 76 F7 38 30N 78 0W
Culuene →, Brazil 93 F8 12 56S 52 51W
Culver, Pt., Australia ..... 61 F3 32 54S 124 43 E
Culverden, N.Z. .... 59 K4 42 47S 172 49 E
Cumaná, Venezuela 92 A6 10 30N 64 5W
Cumberland, B.C., Canada . 72 D4 49 40N 125 0W
Cumberland, Ont., Canada . 79 A9 45 29N 75 24W
Cumberland, U.S.A. 76 F6 39 39N 78 46W
Cumberland →, U.S.A. .. 77 G2 36 15N 87 0W
Cumberland, L., U.S.A. ... 77 G3 36 57N 84 55W
Cumberland I., U.S.A. 77 K5 30 50N 81 25W
Cumberland Is., Australia .. 62 C4 20 35S 149 10 E
Cumberland L., Canada ... 73 C8 54 3N 102 18W
Cumberland Pen., Canada . 69 B13 67 0N 64 0W
Cumberland Plateau, U.S.A. 77 H3 36 0N 85 0W
Cumberland Sd., Canada .. 69 B13 65 30N 66 0W
Cumbernauld, U.K. 12 F5 55 57N 3 58W
Cumborah, Australia ..... 63 D4 29 40S 147 45 E
Cumbria □, U.K. 10 C5 54 42N 2 52W
Cumbrian Mts., U.K. 10 C5 54 30N 3 0W
Cumbum, India .... 40 M11 15 40N 79 10 E
Cuminá →, Brazil 93 D7 1 30S 56 0W
Cummings Mt., U.S.A. ... 85 K8 35 2N 118 34W
Cummins, Australia ...... 63 E2 34 16S 135 43 E
Cumnock, Australia ...... 63 E4 32 59S 148 46 E
Cumnock, U.K. 12 F4 55 28N 4 17W
Cumpas, Mexico 86 B3 30 0N 109 48W
Cumplida, Pta., Canary Is. . 22 F2 28 50N 17 48W
Cunco, Chile 96 D2 38 55S 72 2W
Cuncumén, Chile 94 C1 31 53S 70 38W
Cunderdin, Australia ..... 61 F2 31 37S 117 12 E
Cunene →, Angola ...... 56 B1 17 20S 11 50 E
Cúneo, Italy .... 18 D7 44 23N 7 32 E
Çüngüş, Turkey .... 44 B3 38 13N 39 17 E
Cunillera, I. = Sa Conillera,
Spain .... 22 C7 38 59N 1 13 E
Cunnamulla, Australia .... 63 D4 28 2S 145 38 E
Cupar, Canada 73 C8 50 57N 104 10W
Cupar, U.K. 12 E5 56 19N 3 1W
Cupica, G. de, Colombia .. 92 B3 6 25N 77 30W
Curaçao, Neth. Ant. 89 D6 12 10N 69 0W
Curanilahue, Chile 94 D1 37 29S 73 28W
Curaray →, Peru 92 D4 2 20S 74 5W
Curepto, Chile 94 D1 35 8S 72 1W
Curiapo, Venezuela 92 B6 8 33N 61 5W
Curicó, Chile 94 C1 34 55S 71 20W
Curitiba, Brazil 95 B6 25 20S 49 10W
Curitibanos, Brazil 95 B5 27 18S 50 36W
Currabubula, Australia ... 63 E5 31 16S 150 44 E
Currais Novos, Brazil 93 E11 6 13S 36 30W
Curralinho, Brazil 93 D9 1 45S 49 46W
Currant, U.S.A. 82 G6 38 51N 115 32W
Current →, U.S.A. 81 G9 36 15N 90 55W
Currie, Australia .... 62 F3 39 56S 143 53 E
Currie, U.S.A. 82 F6 40 16N 114 45W
Curtea de Argeş, Romania . 17 F13 45 12N 24 42 E
Curtis, U.S.A. 80 E4 40 38N 100 31W
Curtis Group, Australia ... 62 F4 39 30S 146 37 E
Curtis I., Australia ...... 62 C5 23 35S 151 10 E
Curuápanema →, Brazil .. 93 D7 2 25S 55 2W
Curuçá, Brazil 93 D9 0 43S 47 50W
Curuguaty, Paraguay 95 A4 24 31S 55 42W
Curup, Indonesia .... 36 E2 4 26S 102 13 E
Cururupu, Brazil 93 D10 1 50S 44 50W
Curuzú Cuatiá, Argentina . 94 B4 29 50S 58 5W
Curvelo, Brazil 93 G10 18 45S 44 27W
Cushing, U.S.A. 81 H6 35 59N 96 46W
Cushing, Mt., Canada 72 B3 57 35N 126 57W
Cusihuiriáchic, Mexico 86 B3 28 10N 106 50W
Custer, U.S.A. 80 D3 43 46N 103 36W
Cut Bank, U.S.A. 82 B7 48 38N 112 20W
Cutchogue, U.S.A. 79 E12 41 1N 72 30W
Cuthbert, U.S.A. 77 K3 31 46N 84 48W
Cutler, U.S.A. 84 J7 36 31N 119 17W
Cuttaburra →, Australia .. 63 D3 29 43S 144 22 E
Cuttack, India .... 41 J14 20 25N 85 57 E
Cuvier, C., Australia ..... 61 D1 23 14S 113 22 E
Cuvier I., N.Z. .... 59 G5 36 27S 175 50 E
Cuxhaven, Germany ..... 16 B5 53 51N 8 41 E
Cuyahoga Falls, U.S.A. 78 E3 41 8N 81 29W
Cuyo, Phil. .... 37 B6 10 50N 121 5 E
Cuyuni →, Guyana 92 B7 6 23N 58 41W
Cuzco, Bolivia 92 H5 20 0S 66 50W
Cuzco, Peru 92 F4 13 32S 72 0W
Cwmbran, U.K. 11 F4 51 39N 3 2W
Cyangugu, Rwanda .... 54 C2 2 29S 28 54 E
Cyclades = Kikládhes,
Greece .... 21 F11 37 0N 24 30 E
Cygnet, Australia .... 62 G4 43 8S 147 1 E
Cynthiana, U.S.A. 76 F3 38 23N 84 18W
Cypress Hills, Canada 73 D7 49 40N 109 30W
Cypress Hills Prov. Park,
Canada 73 D7 49 40N 109 30W
Cyprus ■, Asia .... 23 E12 35 0N 33 0 E
Cyrenaica, Libya .... 51 C10 27 0N 23 0 E
Czar, Canada 73 C6 52 27N 110 50W
Czech Rep. ■, Europe .... 16 D8 50 0N 15 0 E
Częstochowa, Poland .... 17 C10 50 49N 19 7 E

D

Da Hinggan Ling, China ... 33 B7 48 0N 121 0 E
Da Lat, Vietnam .... 39 G7 11 56N 108 25 E
Da Nang, Vietnam .... 38 D7 16 4N 108 13 E
Da Qaidam, China .... 32 C4 37 50N 95 15 E
Da Yunhe →, China ..... 35 G11 34 25N 120 5 E
Da'an, China .... 35 B13 45 30N 124 7 E
Daba Shan, China .... 33 C5 32 0N 109 0 E
Dabbagh, Jabal, Si. Arabia 44 E2 27 52N 35 45 E
Dabhoi, India .... 42 H5 22 10N 73 20 E
Dabo = Pasirkuning,
Indonesia .... 36 E2 0 30S 104 33 E
Dabola, Guinea 50 F3 10 50N 11 5W
Dabung, Malaysia .... 39 K4 5 23N 102 1 E
Dacca = Dhaka, Bangla. .. 43 H14 23 43N 90 26 E
Dacca = Dhaka □, Bangla. . 43 G14 24 25N 90 25 E
Dachau, Germany .... 16 D6 48 15N 11 26 E
Dadanawa, Guyana 92 C7 2 50N 59 30W
Dade City, U.S.A. 77 L4 28 22N 82 11W
Dadhar, Pakistan .... 42 E2 29 28N 67 39 E
Dadra & Nagar Haveli □,
India .... 40 J8 20 5N 73 0 E
Dadri = Charkhi Dadri, India 42 E7 28 37N 76 17 E
Dadu, Pakistan .... 42 F2 26 45N 67 45 E
Daet, Phil. .... 37 B6 14 2N 122 55 E
Dagana, Senegal 50 E2 16 30N 15 35W
Dagestan □, Russia ...... 25 F8 42 30N 47 0 E
Daggett, U.S.A. 85 L10 34 52N 116 52W
Daghestan Republic =
Dagestan □, Russia .... 25 F8 42 30N 47 0 E
Dağlıq Qarabağ = Nagorno-
Karabakh, Azerbaijan ... 25 F8 39 55N 46 45 E
Dagö = Hiiumaa, Estonia .. 9 G20 58 50N 22 45 E
Dagu, China .... 35 E9 38 59N 117 40 E
Dagupan, Phil. .... 37 A6 16 3N 120 20 E
Daguragu, Australia ..... 60 C5 17 33S 130 30 E
Dahlak Kebir, Eritrea .... 46 D3 15 50N 40 10 E
Dahlonega, U.S.A. 77 H4 34 32N 83 59W
Dahod, India .... 42 H6 22 50N 74 15 E
Dahomey = Benin ■, Africa 50 G6 10 0N 2 0 E
Dahūk, Iraq .... 44 B3 36 50N 43 1 E
Dai Hao, Vietnam .... 38 C6 18 1N 106 25 E
Dai-Sen, Japan .... 31 G6 35 22N 133 32 E
Dai Xian, China .... 34 E7 39 4N 112 58 E
Daicheng, China .... 34 E9 38 42N 116 38 E
Daingean, Ireland 13 C4 53 18N 7 17W
Daintree, Australia ...... 62 B4 16 20S 145 20 E
Daiō-Misaki, Japan ...... 31 G8 34 15N 136 45 E
Daisetsu-Zan, Japan ..... 30 C11 43 30N 142 57 E
Dajarra, Australia .... 62 C2 21 42S 139 30 E
Dak Dam, Cambodia ..... 38 F6 12 20N 107 21 E
Dak Nhe, Vietnam .... 38 E6 15 28N 107 48 E
Dak Pek, Vietnam .... 38 E6 15 4N 107 44 E
Dak Song, Vietnam ...... 39 F6 12 19N 107 35 E
Dak Sui, Vietnam .... 38 E6 14 55N 107 43 E
Dakar, Senegal 50 F2 14 34N 17 29W
Dakhla, W. Sahara 50 D2 23 50N 15 53W
Dakhla, El Wâhât el-, Egypt 51 C11 25 30N 28 50 E
Dakor, India .... 42 H5 22 45N 73 11 E
Dakota City, U.S.A. 80 D6 42 25N 96 25W
Đakovica, Yugoslavia .... 21 C9 42 22N 20 26 E
Dalachi, China .... 34 F3 36 48N 105 0 E
Dalai Nur, China .... 34 C9 43 20N 116 45 E
Dālakī, Iran .... 45 D6 29 26N 51 17 E
Dalälven, Sweden .... 9 F17 60 12N 16 43 E
Dalaman →, Turkey ..... 21 F13 36 41N 28 43 E
Dalandzadgad, Mongolia .. 34 C3 43 27N 104 30 E
Dalap-Uliga-Darrit,
Marshall Is. .... 64 G9 7 7N 171 24 E
Dalarna, Sweden .... 9 F16 61 0N 14 0 E
Dālbandīn, Pakistan ..... 40 E4 29 0N 64 23 E
Dalbeattie, U.K. 12 G5 54 56N 3 50W
Dalbeg, Australia .... 62 C4 20 16S 147 18 E
Dalby, Australia .... 63 D5 27 10S 151 17 E
Dale City, U.S.A. 76 F7 38 38N 77 18W
Dale Hollow L., U.S.A. ... 77 G3 36 32N 85 27W
Dalgān, Iran .... 45 E8 27 31N 59 19 E
Dalhart, U.S.A. 81 G3 36 4N 102 31W
Dalhousie, Canada 71 C6 48 5N 66 26W
Dalhousie, India .... 42 C6 32 38N 75 58 E
Dali, Shaanxi, China ..... 34 G5 34 48N 109 58 E
Dali, Yunnan, China ..... 32 D5 25 40N 100 10 E
Dalian, China .... 35 E11 38 50N 121 40 E
Daliang Shan, China ..... 32 D5 28 0N 102 45 E
Daling He →, China .... 35 D11 40 55N 121 40 E
Dāliyat el Karmel, Israel .. 47 C4 32 43N 35 2 E
Dalkeith, U.K. 12 F5 55 54N 3 4W
Dallas, Oreg., U.S.A. 82 D2 44 55N 123 19W
Dallas, Tex., U.S.A. 81 J6 32 47N 96 49W
Dalmā, U.A.E. .... 45 E7 24 30N 52 20 E
Dalmacija, Croatia .... 20 C7 43 20N 17 0 E
Dalmas, L., Canada 71 B5 53 30N 71 50W
Dalmatia = Dalmacija,
Croatia .... 20 C7 43 20N 17 0 E
Dalmau, India .... 43 F9 26 4N 81 2 E
Dalmellington, U.K. 12 F4 55 19N 4 23W
Dalnegorsk, Russia ...... 27 E14 44 32N 135 33 E
Dalnerechensk, Russia ... 27 E14 45 50N 133 40 E
Daloa, Ivory C. 50 G4 7 0N 6 30W
Dalry, U.K. 12 F4 55 42N 4 43W
Dalrymple, L., Australia .. 62 C4 20 40S 147 0 E
Dalsland, Sweden .... 9 G14 58 50N 12 15 E
Daltenganj, India .... 43 H11 24 0N 84 4 E
Dalton, Ga., U.S.A. 77 H3 34 46N 84 58W

Desolación, I.

Dalton, Mass., U.S.A. 79 D11 42 28N 73 11W
Dalton, Nebr., U.S.A. 80 E3 41 25N 102 58W
Dalton Iceberg Tongue, Antarctica 5 C9 66 15S 121 30 E
Dalton-in-Furness, U.K. 10 C4 54 10N 3 11W
Dalvík, Iceland 8 D4 65 58N 18 32W
Dalwallinu, Australia 61 F2 30 17S 116 40 E
Daly →, Australia 60 B5 13 35S 130 19 E
Daly City, U.S.A. 84 H4 37 42N 122 28W
Daly L., Canada 73 B7 56 32N 105 39W
Daly River, Australia 60 B5 13 46S 130 42 E
Daly Waters, Australia 62 B1 16 15S 133 24 E
Dam Doi, Vietnam 39 H5 8 50N 105 12 E
Dam Ha, Vietnam 38 B6 21 21N 107 36 E
Daman, India 40 J8 20 25N 72 57 E
Dāmaneh, Iran 45 C6 33 1N 50 29 E
Damanhûr, Egypt 51 B12 31 0N 30 30 E
Damant L., Canada 73 A7 61 45N 105 5W
Damanzhuang, China 34 E9 38 5N 116 35 E
Damar, Indonesia 37 F7 7 7S 128 40 E
Damaraland, Namibia 56 C2 20 0S 15 0 E
Damascus = Dimashq, Syria 47 B5 33 30N 36 18 E
Damāvand, Iran 45 C7 35 47N 52 0 E
Damāvand, Qolleh-ye, Iran 45 C7 35 56N 52 10 E
Damba, Angola 52 F3 6 44S 15 20 E
Dâmboviţa →, Romania 17 F14 44 12N 26 26 E
Dame Marie, Haiti 89 C5 18 36N 74 26W
Dāmghān, Iran 45 B7 36 10N 54 17 E
Damiel, Spain 19 C4 39 4N 3 37W
Damietta = Dumyât, Egypt 51 B12 31 24N 31 48 E
Daming, China 34 F8 36 15N 115 6 E
Damīr Qābū, Syria 44 B4 36 58N 41 51 E
Dammam = Ad Dammām, Si. Arabia 45 E6 26 20N 50 5 E
Damodar →, India 43 H12 23 17N 87 35 E
Damoh, India 43 H8 23 50N 79 28 E
Dampier, Australia 60 D2 20 41S 116 42 E
Dampier, Selat, Indonesia 37 E8 0 40S 131 0 E
Dampier Arch., Australia 60 D2 20 38S 116 32 E
Damrei, Chuor Phnum, Cambodia 39 G4 11 30N 103 0 E
Dan Xian, China 38 C7 19 31N 109 33 E
Dana, Indonesia 37 F6 11 0S 122 52 E
Dana, L., Canada 70 B4 50 53N 77 20W
Dana, Mt., U.S.A. 84 H7 37 54N 119 12W
Danakil Depression, Ethiopia 46 E3 12 45N 41 0 E
Danané, Ivory C. 50 G4 7 16N 8 9W
Danau Poso, Indonesia 37 E6 1 52S 120 35 E
Danbury, U.S.A. 79 E11 41 24N 73 28W
Danby L., U.S.A. 83 J6 34 13N 115 5W
Dand, Afghan. 42 D1 31 28N 65 32 E
Dandeldhura, Nepal 43 E9 29 20N 80 35 E
Dandeli, India 40 M9 15 5N 74 30 E
Dandenong, Australia 63 F4 38 0S 145 15 E
Dandong, China 35 D13 40 10N 124 20 E
Danfeng, China 34 H6 33 45N 110 25 E
Danger Is. = Pukapuka, Cook Is. 65 J11 10 53S 165 49W
Danger Pt., S. Africa 56 E2 34 40S 19 17 E
Dangla Shan = Tanggula Shan, China 32 C4 32 40N 92 10 E
Dangrek, Phnom, Thailand 38 E5 14 15N 105 0 E
Dangriga, Belize 87 D7 17 0N 88 13W
Dangshan, China 34 G9 34 27N 116 22 E
Daniel, U.S.A. 82 E8 42 52N 110 4W
Daniel's Harbour, Canada 71 B8 50 13N 57 35W
Danielskuil, S. Africa 56 D3 28 11S 23 33 E
Danielson, U.S.A. 79 E13 41 48N 71 53W
Danilov, Russia 24 C7 58 16N 40 13 E
Daning, China 34 F6 36 28N 110 45 E
Danissa, Kenya 54 B5 3 15N 40 58 E
Dank, Oman 45 F8 23 33N 56 16 E
Dankhar Gompa, India 40 C11 32 10N 78 10 E
Danlí, Honduras 88 D2 14 4N 86 35W
Dannemora, U.S.A. 79 B11 44 43N 73 44W
Dannevirke, N.Z. 59 J6 40 12S 176 8 E
Dannhauser, S. Africa 57 D5 28 0S 30 3 E
Dansville, U.S.A. 78 D7 42 34N 77 42W
Danta, India 42 G5 24 11N 72 46 E
Dantan, India 43 J12 21 57N 87 20 E
Dante, Somali Rep. 46 E5 10 25N 51 16 E
Danube = Dunărea →, Europe 17 F15 45 20N 29 40 E
Danvers, U.S.A. 79 D14 42 34N 70 56W
Danville, Ill., U.S.A. 76 E2 40 8N 87 37W
Danville, Ky., U.S.A. 76 G3 37 39N 84 46W
Danville, Pa., U.S.A. 79 F8 40 58N 76 37W
Danville, Va., U.S.A. 77 G6 36 36N 79 23W
Danville, Vt., U.S.A. 79 B12 44 25N 72 9W
Danzig = Gdańsk, Poland 17 A10 54 22N 18 40 E
Dapaong, Togo 50 F6 10 55N 0 16 E
Daqing Shan, China 34 D6 40 40N 111 0 E
Dar Banda, Africa 48 F6 8 0N 23 0 E
Dar el Beida = Casablanca, Morocco 50 B4 33 36N 7 36W
Dar es Salaam, Tanzania 54 D4 6 50S 39 12 E
Dar Mazār, Iran 45 D8 29 14N 57 20 E
Dar'ā, Syria 47 C5 32 36N 36 7 E
Dar'ā □, Syria 47 C5 32 55N 36 10 E
Dārāb, Iran 45 D7 28 50N 54 30 E
Daraban, Pakistan 42 D4 31 44N 70 20 E
Daraj, Libya 51 B8 30 10N 10 28 E
Dārān, Iran 45 C6 32 59N 50 24 E
Dārayyā, Syria 47 B5 33 28N 36 15 E
Darband, Pakistan 42 B5 34 20N 72 50 E
Darband, Kūh-e, Iran 45 D8 31 34N 57 8 E
Darbhanga, India 43 F11 26 15N 85 55 E
D'Arcy, Canada 72 C4 50 27N 122 35W
Dardanelle, Ark., U.S.A. 81 H8 35 13N 93 9W
Dardanelle, Calif., U.S.A. 84 G7 38 20N 119 50W
Dardanelles = Çanakkale Boğazı, Turkey 21 D12 40 17N 26 32 E
Dārestān, Iran 45 D8 29 9N 58 42 E
Dârfûr, Sudan 51 F10 13 40N 24 0 E
Dargai, Pakistan 42 B4 34 25N 71 55 E
Dargan Ata, Uzbekistan 26 E7 40 29N 62 10 E
Dargaville, N.Z. 59 F4 35 57S 173 52 E
Darhan, Mongolia 32 B5 49 37N 106 21 E
Darhan Muminggan Lianheqi, China 34 D6 41 40N 110 28 E
Darıca, Turkey 21 D13 40 45N 29 23 E
Darién, G. del, Colombia 92 B3 9 0N 77 0W
Dariganga = Ovoot, Mongolia 34 B7 45 21N 113 45 E
Darjeeling = Darjiling, India 43 F13 27 3N 88 18 E
Darjiling, India 43 F13 27 3N 88 18 E
Darkan, Australia 61 F2 33 20S 116 43 E
Darkhana, Pakistan 42 D5 30 39N 72 11 E
Darkhazīneh, Iran 45 D6 31 54N 48 39 E
Darkot Pass, Pakistan 43 A5 36 45N 73 26 E
Darling →, Australia 63 E3 34 4S 141 54 E
Darling Downs, Australia 63 D5 27 30S 150 30 E
Darling Ra., Australia 61 F2 32 30S 116 0 E
Darlington, U.K. 10 C6 54 32N 1 33W
Darlington, U.S.A. 77 H6 34 18N 79 52W
Darlington □, U.K. 10 C6 54 32N 1 33W
Darlington, L., S. Africa 56 E4 33 10S 25 9 E
Darlington Point, Australia 63 E4 34 37S 146 1 E
Darlot, L., Australia 61 E3 27 48S 121 35 E
Darłowo, Poland 16 A9 54 25N 16 25 E
Darmstadt, Germany 16 D5 49 51N 8 39 E
Darnah, Libya 51 B10 32 45N 22 45 E
Darnall, S. Africa 57 D5 29 23S 31 18 E
Darnley, C., Antarctica 5 C6 68 0S 69 0 E
Darnley B., Canada 68 B7 69 30N 123 30W
Darr →, Australia 62 C3 23 39S 143 50 E
Darra Pezu, Pakistan 42 C4 32 19N 70 44 E
Darrequeira, Argentina 94 D3 37 42S 63 10W
Darrington, U.S.A. 82 B3 48 15N 121 36W
Dart →, U.K. 11 G4 50 24N 3 39W
Dart, C., Antarctica 5 D14 73 6S 126 20W
Dartford, U.K. 11 F8 51 26N 0 13 E
Dartmoor, U.K. 11 G4 50 38N 3 57W
Dartmouth, Canada 71 D7 44 40N 63 30W
Dartmouth, U.K. 11 G4 50 21N 3 36W
Dartmouth, L., Australia 63 D4 26 4S 145 18 E
Dartuch, C. = Artrutx, C. de, Spain 22 B10 39 55N 3 49 E
Darvaza, Turkmenistan 26 E6 40 11N 58 24 E
Darvel, Teluk = Lahad Datu, Teluk, Malaysia 37 D5 4 50N 118 20 E
Darwen, U.K. 10 D5 53 42N 2 29W
Darwha, India 40 J10 20 15N 77 45 E
Darwin, Australia 60 B5 12 25S 130 51 E
Darwin, U.S.A. 85 J9 36 15N 117 35W
Darya Khan, Pakistan 42 D4 31 48N 71 6 E
Daryoi Amu = Amudarya →, Uzbekistan 26 E6 43 58N 59 34 E
Dās, U.A.E. 45 E7 25 20N 53 30 E
Dashetai, China 34 D5 41 0N 109 5 E
Dashhowuz, Turkmenistan 26 E6 41 49N 59 58 E
Dashköpri, Turkmenistan 45 B9 36 16N 62 8 E
Dasht, Iran 45 B8 37 17N 56 7 E
Dasht →, Pakistan 40 G2 25 10N 61 40 E
Dasht-e Mārgow, Afghan. 40 D3 30 40N 62 30 E
Dasht-i-Nawar, Afghan. 42 C3 33 52N 68 0 E
Daska, Pakistan 42 C6 32 20N 74 20 E
Dasuya, India 42 D6 31 49N 75 38 E
Datça, Turkey 21 F12 36 46N 27 40 E
Datia, India 43 G8 25 39N 78 27 E
Datong, China 34 D7 40 6N 113 18 E
Dattakhel, Pakistan 42 C3 32 54N 69 46 E
Datu, Tanjung, Indonesia 36 D3 2 5N 109 39 E
Datu Piang, Phil. 37 C6 7 2N 124 30 E
Daud Khel, Pakistan 42 C4 32 53N 71 34 E
Daudnagar, India 43 G11 25 2N 84 24 E
Daugava →, Latvia 9 H21 57 4N 24 3 E
Daugavpils, Latvia 9 J22 55 53N 26 32 E
Daulpur, India 42 F7 26 45N 77 59 E
Dauphin, Canada 73 C8 51 9N 100 5W
Dauphin, U.S.A. 78 F8 40 22N 76 56W
Dauphin L., Canada 73 C9 51 20N 99 45W
Dauphiné, France 18 D6 45 15N 5 25 E
Dausa, India 42 F7 26 52N 76 20 E
Davangere, India 40 M9 14 25N 75 55 E
Davao, Phil. 37 C7 7 0N 125 40 E
Davao, G. of, Phil. 37 C7 6 30N 125 48 E
Dāvar Panāh, Iran 45 E9 27 25N 62 15 E
Davenport, Calif., U.S.A. 84 H4 37 1N 122 12W
Davenport, Iowa, U.S.A. 80 E9 41 32N 90 35W
Davenport, Wash., U.S.A. 82 C4 47 39N 118 9W
Davenport Ra., Australia 62 C1 20 28S 134 0 E
Daventry, U.K. 11 E6 52 16N 1 10W
David, Panama 88 E3 8 30N 82 30W
David City, U.S.A. 80 E6 41 15N 97 8W
David Gorodok = Davyd Haradok, Belarus 17 B14 52 4N 27 8 E
Davidson, Canada 73 C7 51 16N 105 59W
Davis, U.S.A. 84 G5 38 33N 121 44W
Davis Dam, U.S.A. 85 K12 35 11N 114 34W
Davis Inlet, Canada 71 A7 55 50N 60 59W
Davis Mts., U.S.A. 81 K2 30 50N 103 55W
Davis Sea, Antarctica 5 C7 66 0S 92 0 E
Davis Str., N. Amer. 69 B14 65 0N 58 0W
Davos, Switz. 18 C8 46 48N 9 49 E
Davy L., Canada 73 B7 58 53N 108 18W
Davyd Haradok, Belarus 17 B14 52 4N 27 8 E
Dawei, Burma 38 E2 14 2N 98 12 E
Dawes Ra., Australia 62 C5 24 40S 150 40 E
Dawlish, U.K. 11 G4 50 35N 3 28W
Dawros Hd., Ireland 13 B3 54 50N 8 33W
Dawson, Canada 68 B6 64 10N 139 30W
Dawson, U.S.A. 77 K3 31 46N 84 27W
Dawson, I., Chile 96 G2 53 50S 70 50W
Dawson B., Canada 73 C8 52 53N 100 49W
Dawson Creek, Canada 72 B4 55 45N 120 15W
Dawson Inlet, Canada 73 A10 61 50N 93 25W
Dawson Ra., Australia 62 C4 24 30S 149 48 E
Dax, France 18 E3 43 44N 1 3W
Daxian, China 32 C5 31 15N 107 23 E
Daxindian, China 35 F11 37 30N 120 50 E
Daxinggou, China 35 C15 43 25N 129 40 E
Daxue Shan, China 32 C5 30 30N 101 30 E
Daylesford, Australia 63 F3 37 21S 144 9 E
Dayr az Zawr, Syria 44 C4 35 20N 40 5 E
Daysland, Canada 72 C6 52 50N 112 20W
Dayton, Nev., U.S.A. 84 F7 39 14N 119 36W
Dayton, Ohio, U.S.A. 76 F3 39 45N 84 12W
Dayton, Pa., U.S.A. 78 F5 40 53N 79 15W
Dayton, Tenn., U.S.A. 77 H3 35 30N 85 1W
Dayton, Wash., U.S.A. 82 C4 46 19N 117 59W
Dayton, Wyo., U.S.A. 82 D10 44 53N 107 16W
Daytona Beach, U.S.A. 77 L5 29 13N 81 1W
Dayville, U.S.A. 82 D4 44 28N 119 32W
De Aar, S. Africa 56 E3 30 39S 24 0 E
De Funiak Springs, U.S.A. 77 K2 30 43N 86 7W
De Grey →, Australia 60 D2 20 12S 119 13 E
De Haan, Belgium 15 C3 51 16N 3 2 E
De Kalb, U.S.A. 80 E10 41 56N 88 46W
De Land, U.S.A. 77 L5 29 2N 81 18W
De Leon, U.S.A. 81 J5 32 7N 98 32W
De Panne, Belgium 15 C2 51 6N 2 34 E
De Pere, U.S.A. 76 C1 44 27N 88 4W
De Queen, U.S.A. 81 H7 34 2N 94 21W
De Quincy, U.S.A. 81 K8 30 27N 93 26W
De Ridder, U.S.A. 81 K8 30 51N 93 17W
De Smet, U.S.A. 80 C6 44 23N 97 33W
De Soto, U.S.A. 80 F9 38 8N 90 34W
De Tour Village, U.S.A. 76 C4 46 0N 83 56W
De Witt, U.S.A. 81 H9 34 18N 91 20W
Dead Sea, Asia 47 D4 31 30N 35 30 E
Deadwood, U.S.A. 80 C3 44 23N 103 44W
Deadwood L., Canada 72 B3 59 10N 128 30W
Deal, U.K. 11 F9 51 13N 1 25 E
Deal I., Australia 62 F4 39 30S 147 20 E
Dealesville, S. Africa 56 D4 28 41S 25 44 E
Dean →, Canada 72 C3 52 49N 126 58W
Dean, Forest of, U.K. 11 F5 51 45N 2 33W
Dean Chan., Canada 72 C3 52 30N 127 15W
Deán Funes, Argentina 94 C3 30 20S 64 20W
Dease →, Canada 72 B3 59 56N 128 32W
Dease L., Canada 72 B2 58 40N 130 5W
Dease Lake, Canada 72 B2 58 25N 130 6W
Death Valley, U.S.A. 85 J10 36 15N 116 50W
Death Valley Junction, U.S.A. 85 J10 36 20N 116 25W
Death Valley National Park, U.S.A. 85 J10 36 45N 117 15W
Debar, Macedonia 21 D9 41 31N 20 30 E
Debden, Canada 73 C7 53 30N 106 50W
Dębica, Poland 17 C11 50 2N 21 25 E
Debolt, Canada 72 B5 55 12N 118 1W
Deborah East, L., Australia 61 F2 30 45S 119 0 E
Deborah West, L., Australia 61 F2 30 45S 118 50 E
Debre Markos, Ethiopia 46 E2 10 20N 37 40 E
Debre Tabor, Ethiopia 46 E2 11 50N 38 26 E
Debre Zeyit, Ethiopia 46 F2 11 48N 38 30 E
Debrecen, Hungary 17 E11 47 33N 21 42 E
Decatur, Ala., U.S.A. 77 H2 34 36N 86 59W
Decatur, Ga., U.S.A. 77 J3 33 47N 84 18W
Decatur, Ill., U.S.A. 80 F10 39 51N 88 57W
Decatur, Ind., U.S.A. 76 E3 40 50N 84 56W
Decatur, Tex., U.S.A. 81 J6 33 14N 97 35W
Deccan, India 40 L11 18 0N 79 0 E
Deception Bay, Australia 63 D5 27 10S 153 5 E
Deception L., Canada 73 B8 56 33N 104 13W
Dechhu, India 42 F5 26 46N 72 20 E
Děčín, Czech Rep. 16 C8 50 47N 14 12 E
Deckerville, U.S.A. 78 C2 43 32N 82 44W
Decorah, U.S.A. 80 D9 43 18N 91 48W
Dedéagach = Alexandroúpolis, Greece 21 D11 40 50N 25 54 E
Dedham, U.S.A. 79 D13 42 15N 71 10W
Dedza, Malawi 55 E3 14 20S 34 20 E
Dee →, Aberds., U.K. 12 D6 57 9N 2 5W
Dee →, Dumf. & Gall., U.K. 12 G4 54 51N 4 3W
Dee →, Wales, U.K. 10 D4 53 22N 3 17W
Deep B., Canada 72 A5 61 15N 116 35W
Deepwater, Australia 63 D5 29 25S 151 51 E
Deer →, Canada 73 B10 58 23N 94 13W
Deer L., Canada 73 C10 52 40N 94 20W
Deer Lake, Nfld., Canada 71 C8 49 11N 57 27W
Deer Lake, Ont., Canada 73 C10 52 36N 94 20W
Deer Lodge, U.S.A. 82 C7 46 24N 112 44W
Deer Park, U.S.A. 82 C5 47 57N 117 28W
Deer River, U.S.A. 80 B8 47 20N 93 48W
Deeragun, Australia 62 B4 19 16S 146 33 E
Deerdepoort, S. Africa 56 C4 24 37S 26 27 E
Deferiet, U.S.A. 79 B9 44 2N 75 41W
Defiance, U.S.A. 76 E3 41 17N 84 22W
Degana, India 42 F6 26 50N 74 20 E
Dégelis, Canada 71 C6 47 30N 68 35W
Deggendorf, Germany 16 D7 48 50N 12 57 E
Degh →, Pakistan 42 D5 31 3N 73 21 E
Deh Bīd, Iran 45 D7 30 39N 53 11 E
Deh-e Shīr, Iran 45 D7 31 29N 53 45 E
Dehaj, Iran 45 D7 30 42N 54 53 E
Dehak, Iran 45 E9 27 11N 62 37 E
Dehdez, Iran 45 D6 31 43N 50 17 E
Dehej, India 42 J5 21 44N 72 40 E
Dehestān, Iran 45 D7 28 30N 55 35 E
Dehgolān, Iran 44 C5 35 17N 47 25 E
Dehi Titan, Afghan. 40 C3 33 45N 63 50 E
Dehibat, Tunisia 51 B8 32 0N 10 47 E
Dehlorān, Iran 44 C5 32 41N 47 16 E
Dehnow-e Kūhestān, Iran 45 E8 27 58N 58 32 E
Dehra Dun, India 42 D8 30 20N 78 4 E
Dehri, India 43 G11 24 50N 84 15 E
Dehui, China 35 B13 44 30N 125 40 E
Deinze, Belgium 15 D3 50 59N 3 32 E
Dej, Romania 17 E12 47 10N 23 52 E
Dekese, Dem. Rep. of the Congo 52 E4 3 24S 21 24 E
Del Mar, U.S.A. 85 N9 32 58N 117 16W
Del Norte, U.S.A. 83 H10 37 41N 106 21W
Del Rio, U.S.A. 81 L4 29 22N 100 54W
Delambre I., Australia 60 D2 20 26S 117 5 E
Delano, U.S.A. 85 K7 35 46N 119 15W
Delano Peak, U.S.A. 83 G7 38 22N 112 22W
Delareyville, S. Africa 56 D4 26 41S 25 26 E
Delaronde L., Canada 73 C7 54 3N 107 3W
Delavan, U.S.A. 80 D10 42 38N 88 39W
Delaware, U.S.A. 76 E4 40 18N 83 4W
Delaware □, U.S.A. 76 F8 39 0N 75 20W
Delaware →, U.S.A. 79 G9 39 15N 75 20W
Delaware B., U.S.A. 76 F8 39 0N 75 10W
Delay →, Canada 71 A5 56 56N 71 28W
Delegate, Australia 63 F4 37 4S 148 56 E
Delevan, U.S.A. 78 D6 42 29N 78 29W
Delft, Neths. 15 B4 52 1N 4 22 E
Delfzijl, Neths. 15 A6 53 20N 6 55 E
Delgado, C., Mozam. 55 E5 10 45S 40 40 E
Delgerhet, Mongolia 34 B6 45 50N 110 30 E
Delgo, Sudan 51 D12 20 6N 30 40 E
Delhi, Canada 78 D4 42 51N 80 30W
Delhi, India 42 E7 28 38N 77 17 E
Delhi, La., U.S.A. 81 J9 32 28N 91 30W
Delhi, N.Y., U.S.A. 79 D10 42 17N 74 55W
Delia, Canada 72 C6 51 38N 112 23W
Delice, Turkey 25 G5 39 54N 34 2 E
Delicias, Mexico 86 B3 28 10N 105 30W
Delījān, Iran 45 C6 33 59N 50 40 E
Déline, Canada 68 B7 65 10N 123 30W
Delisle, Canada 73 C7 51 55N 107 8W
Dell City, U.S.A. 83 L11 31 56N 105 12W
Dell Rapids, U.S.A. 80 D6 43 50N 96 43W
Delmar, U.S.A. 79 D11 42 37N 73 47W
Delmenhorst, Germany 16 B5 53 3N 8 37 E
Delong, Ostrova, Russia 27 B15 76 40N 149 20 E
Deloraine, Australia 62 G4 41 30S 146 40 E
Deloraine, Canada 73 D8 49 15N 100 29W
Delphi, U.S.A. 76 E2 40 36N 86 41W
Delphos, U.S.A. 76 E3 40 51N 84 21W
Delportshoop, S. Africa 56 D3 28 22S 24 20 E
Delray Beach, U.S.A. 77 M5 26 28N 80 4W
Delta, Colo., U.S.A. 83 G9 38 44N 108 4W
Delta, Utah, U.S.A. 82 G7 39 21N 112 35W
Delta Junction, U.S.A. 68 B5 64 2N 145 44W
Deltona, U.S.A. 77 L5 28 54N 81 16W
Delungra, Australia 63 D5 29 39S 150 51 E
Delvada, India 42 J4 20 46N 71 2 E
Delvinë, Albania 21 E9 39 59N 20 6 E
Demak, Indonesia 37 G14 6 53S 110 38 E
Demanda, Sierra de la, Spain 19 A4 42 15N 3 0W
Demavand = Damāvand, Iran 45 C7 35 47N 52 0 E
Dembia, Dem. Rep. of the Congo 54 B2 3 33N 25 48 E
Dembidolo, Ethiopia 46 F1 8 34N 34 50 E
Demchok, India 43 C8 32 42N 79 29 E
Demer →, Belgium 15 D4 50 57N 4 42 E
Deming, N. Mex., U.S.A. 83 K10 32 16N 107 46W
Deming, Wash., U.S.A. 84 B4 48 50N 122 13W
Demini →, Brazil 92 D6 0 46S 62 56W
Demirci, Turkey 21 E13 39 2N 28 38 E
Demirköy, Turkey 21 D12 41 49N 27 45 E
Demopolis, U.S.A. 77 J2 32 31N 87 50W
Dempo, Indonesia 36 E2 4 2S 103 15 E
Den Burg, Neths. 15 A4 53 3N 4 47 E
Den Chai, Thailand 38 D3 17 59N 100 4 E
Den Haag = 's-Gravenhage, Neths. 15 B4 52 7N 4 17 E
Den Helder, Neths. 15 B4 52 57N 4 45 E
Den Oever, Neths. 15 B5 52 56N 5 2 E
Denair, U.S.A. 84 H6 37 32N 120 48W
Denau, Uzbekistan 26 F7 38 16N 67 54 E
Denbigh, Canada 78 A7 45 8N 77 15W
Denbigh, U.K. 10 D4 53 12N 3 25W
Denbighshire □, U.K. 10 D4 53 8N 3 22W
Dendang, Indonesia 36 E3 3 7S 107 56 E
Dendermonde, Belgium 15 C4 51 2N 4 5 E
Dengfeng, China 34 G7 34 25N 113 2 E
Dengkou, China 34 D4 40 18N 106 55 E
Denham, Australia 61 E1 25 56S 113 31 E
Denham Ra., Australia 62 C4 21 55S 147 46 E
Denham Sd., Australia 61 E1 25 45S 113 15 E
Denholm, Canada 73 C7 52 39N 108 1W
Denia, Spain 19 C6 38 49N 0 8 E
Denial B., Australia 63 E1 32 14S 133 32 E
Deniliquin, Australia 63 F3 35 30S 144 58 E
Denison, Iowa, U.S.A. 80 E7 42 1N 95 21W
Denison, Tex., U.S.A. 81 J6 33 45N 96 33W
Denison Plains, Australia 60 C4 18 35S 128 0 E
Denizli, Turkey 25 G4 37 42N 29 2 E
Denman Glacier, Antarctica 5 C7 66 45S 99 25 E
Denmark, Australia 61 F2 34 59S 117 25 E
Denmark ■, Europe 9 J13 55 45N 10 0 E
Denmark Str., Atl. Oc. 4 C6 66 0N 30 0W
Dennison, U.S.A. 78 F3 40 24N 81 19W
Denny, U.K. 12 E5 56 1N 3 55W
Denpasar, Indonesia 36 F5 8 45S 115 14 E
Denton, Mont., U.S.A. 82 C9 47 19N 109 57W
Denton, Tex., U.S.A. 81 J6 33 13N 97 8W
D'Entrecasteaux, Pt., Australia 61 F2 34 50S 115 57 E
Denver, Colo., U.S.A. 80 F2 39 44N 104 59W
Denver, Pa., U.S.A. 79 F8 40 14N 76 8W
Denver City, U.S.A. 81 J3 32 58N 102 50W
Deoband, India 42 E7 29 42N 77 43 E
Deogarh, India 42 G5 25 32N 73 54 E
Deoghar, India 43 G12 24 30N 86 42 E
Deolali, India 40 K8 19 58N 73 50 E
Deoli = Devli, India 42 G6 25 50N 75 20 E
Deora, India 42 F4 26 22N 70 55 E
Deori, India 43 H8 23 24N 79 1 E
Deoria, India 43 F10 26 31N 83 48 E
Deosai Mts., Pakistan 43 B6 35 40N 75 0 E
Deosri, India 43 F14 26 46N 90 29 E
Depalpur, India 42 H6 22 51N 75 33 E
Deping, China 35 F9 37 25N 116 58 E
Deposit, U.S.A. 79 D9 42 4N 75 25W
Depuch I., Australia 60 D2 20 37S 117 44 E
Deputatskiy, Russia 27 C14 69 18N 139 54 E
Dera Ghazi Khan, Pakistan 42 D4 30 5N 70 43 E
Dera Ismail Khan, Pakistan 42 D4 31 50N 70 50 E
Derabugti, Pakistan 42 E3 29 2N 69 9 E
Derawar Fort, Pakistan 42 E4 28 46N 71 20 E
Derbent, Russia 25 F8 42 5N 48 15 E
Derby, Australia 60 C3 17 18S 123 38 E
Derby, U.K. 10 E6 52 56N 1 28W
Derby, Conn., U.S.A. 79 E11 41 19N 73 5W
Derby, Kans., U.S.A. 81 G6 37 33N 97 16W
Derby, N.Y., U.S.A. 78 D6 42 41N 78 58W
Derby City □, U.K. 10 E6 52 56N 1 28W
Derby Line, U.S.A. 79 B12 45 0N 72 6W
Derbyshire □, U.K. 10 D6 53 11N 1 38W
Derg →, U.K. 13 B4 54 44N 7 26W
Derg, L., Ireland 13 D3 53 0N 8 20W
Dergaon, India 41 F19 26 45N 94 0 E
Dermott, U.S.A. 81 J9 33 32N 91 26W
Derry = Londonderry, U.K. 13 B4 55 0N 7 20W
Derry = Londonderry □, U.K. 13 B4 55 0N 7 20W
Derry, N.H., U.S.A. 79 D13 42 53N 71 19W
Derry, Pa., U.S.A. 78 F5 40 20N 79 18W
Derryveagh Mts., Ireland 13 B3 54 56N 8 11W
Derwent →, Cumb., U.K. 10 C4 54 39N 3 33W
Derwent →, Derby, U.K. 10 E6 52 57N 1 28W
Derwent →, N. Yorks., U.K. 10 D7 53 45N 0 58W
Derwent Water, U.K. 10 C4 54 35N 3 9W
Des Moines, Iowa, U.S.A. 80 E8 41 35N 93 37W
Des Moines, N. Mex., U.S.A. 81 G3 36 46N 103 50W
Des Moines →, U.S.A. 80 E9 40 23N 91 25W
Desaguadero →, Argentina 94 C2 34 30S 66 46W
Desaguadero →, Bolivia 92 G5 16 35S 69 5W
Descanso, Pta., Mexico 85 N9 32 21N 117 3W
Deschaillons, Canada 71 C5 46 32N 72 7W
Deschambault L., Canada 73 C8 54 50N 103 30W
Deschutes →, U.S.A. 82 D3 45 38N 120 55W
Dese, Ethiopia 46 E2 11 5N 39 40 E
Deseado →, Argentina 96 F3 47 45S 65 54W
Desert Center, U.S.A. 85 M11 33 43N 115 24W
Desert Hot Springs, U.S.A. 85 M10 33 58N 116 30W
Deshnok, India 42 F5 27 48N 73 21 E
Desna →, Ukraine 17 C16 50 33N 30 35 E
Desolación, I., Chile 96 G2 53 0S 74 0W

Despeñaperros, Paso

Despeñaperros, Paso, Spain 19 C4 38 24N 3 30W
Dessau, Germany 16 C7 51 51N 12 14 E
Dessye = Dese, Ethiopia 46 E2 11 5N 39 40 E
D'Estrees B., Australia 63 F2 35 55S 137 45 E
Desuri, India 42 G5 25 18N 73 35 E
Det Udom, Thailand 38 E5 14 54N 105 5 E
Dete, Zimbabwe 55 F2 18 38S 26 50 E
Detmold, Germany 16 C5 51 56N 8 52 E
Detour, Pt., U.S.A. 76 C2 45 40N 86 40W
Detroit, U.S.A. 78 D1 42 20N 83 3W
Detroit Lakes, U.S.A. 80 B7 46 49N 95 51W
Deurne, Neths. 15 C5 51 27N 5 49 E
Deutsche Bucht, Germany 16 A5 54 15N 8 0 E
Deva, Romania 17 F12 45 53N 22 55 E
Devakottai, India 40 Q11 9 55N 78 45 E
Devaprayag, India 43 D8 30 13N 78 35 E
Deventer, Neths. 15 B6 52 15N 6 10 E
Deveron →, U.K. 12 D6 57 41N 2 32W
Devgadh Bariya, India 42 H5 22 40N 73 55 E
Devikot, India 42 F4 26 42N 71 12 E
Devils Den, U.S.A. 84 K7 35 46N 119 58W
Devils Lake, U.S.A. 80 A5 48 7N 98 52W
Devils Paw, Canada 72 B2 58 47N 134 0W
Devils Tower Junction, U.S.A. 80 C2 44 31N 104 57W
Devine, U.S.A. 81 L5 29 8N 98 54W
Devizes, U.K. 11 F6 51 22N 1 58W
Devli, India 42 G6 25 50N 75 20 E
Devon, Canada 72 C6 53 24N 113 44W
Devon □, U.K. 11 G4 50 50N 3 40W
Devon I., Canada 4 B3 75 10N 85 0W
Devonport, Australia 62 G4 41 10S 146 22 E
Devonport, N.Z. 59 G5 36 49S 174 49 E
Dewas, India 42 H7 22 59N 76 3 E
Dewetsdorp, S. Africa 56 D4 29 33S 26 39 E
Dexter, Maine, U.S.A. 77 C11 45 1N 69 18W
Dexter, Mo., U.S.A. 81 G10 36 48N 89 57W
Dexter, N. Mex., U.S.A. 81 J2 33 12N 104 22W
Dey-Dey, L., Australia 61 E5 29 12S 131 4 E
Deyhük, Iran 45 C8 33 15N 57 30 E
Deyyer, Iran 45 E6 27 55N 51 55 E
Dezadeash L., Canada 72 A1 60 28N 136 58W
Dezfūl, Iran 45 C6 32 20N 48 30 E
Dezhneva, Mys, Russia 27 C19 66 5N 169 40W
Dezhou, China 34 F9 37 26N 116 18 E
Dhadhar →, India 43 G11 24 56N 85 24 E
Dháfni, Greece 23 D7 35 13N 25 3 E
Dhahiriya = Az Zāhirīyah, West Bank 47 D3 31 25N 34 58 E
Dhahran = Az Zahrān, Si. Arabia 45 E6 26 10N 50 7 E
Dhak, Pakistan 42 C5 32 25N 72 33 E
Dhaka, Bangla. 43 H14 23 43N 90 26 E
Dhaka □, Bangla. 43 G14 24 25N 90 25 E
Dhali, Cyprus 23 D12 35 1N 33 25 E
Dhampur, India 43 E8 29 19N 78 33 E
Dhamtari, India 41 J12 20 42N 81 35 E
Dhanbad, India 43 H12 23 50N 86 30 E
Dhangarhi, Nepal 41 E12 28 55N 80 40 E
Dhankuta, Nepal 43 F12 26 55N 87 40 E
Dhar, India 42 H6 22 35N 75 26 E
Dharampur, India 42 H6 22 13N 75 18 E
Dharamsala = Dharmsala, India 42 C7 32 16N 76 23 E
Dhariwal, India 42 D6 31 57N 75 19 E
Dharla →, Bangla. 43 G13 25 46N 89 42 E
Dharmapuri, India 40 N11 12 10N 78 10 E
Dharmjaygarh, India 43 H10 22 28N 83 13 E
Dharmsala, India 42 C7 32 16N 76 23 E
Dharni, India 42 J7 21 33N 76 53 E
Dhasan →, India 43 G8 25 48N 79 24 E
Dhaulagiri, Nepal 43 E10 28 39N 83 28 E
Dhebar, L., India 42 G6 24 10N 74 0 E
Dheftera, Cyprus 23 D12 35 5N 33 16 E
Dhenkanal, India 41 J14 20 45N 85 35 E
Dherinia, Cyprus 23 D12 35 3N 33 57 E
Dhiarrizos →, Cyprus 23 E11 34 41N 32 34 E
Dhībān, Jordan 47 D4 31 30N 35 46 E
Dhíkti Óros, Greece 23 D7 35 8N 25 30 E
Dhilwan, India 42 D6 31 31N 75 21 E
Dhimarkhera, India 43 H9 23 28N 80 22 E
Dhírfis = Dhírfis Óros, Greece 21 E10 38 40N 23 54 E
Dhírfis Óros, Greece 21 E10 38 40N 23 54 E
Dhodhekánisos, Greece 21 F12 36 35N 27 0 E
Dholka, India 42 H5 22 44N 72 29 E
Dhoraji, India 42 J4 21 45N 70 37 E
Dhráhstis, Ákra, Greece 23 A3 39 48N 19 40 E
Dhrangadhra, India 42 H4 22 59N 71 31 E
Dhrápanon, Ákra, Greece 23 D6 35 28N 24 14 E
Dhrol, India 42 H4 22 33N 70 25 E
Dhuburi, India 41 F16 26 2N 89 59 E
Dhule, India 40 J9 20 58N 74 50 E
Di Linh, Vietnam 39 G7 11 35N 108 4 E
Di Linh, Cao Nguyen, Vietnam 39 G7 11 30N 108 0 E
Día, Greece 23 D7 35 28N 25 14 E
Diablo, Mt., U.S.A. 84 H5 37 53N 121 56W
Diablo Range, U.S.A. 84 J5 37 20N 121 25W
Diafarabé, Mali 50 F5 14 9N 4 57W
Diamante, Argentina 94 C3 32 5S 60 40W
Diamante →, Argentina 94 C2 34 30S 66 46W
Diamantina, Brazil 93 G10 18 17S 43 40W
Diamantina →, Australia 63 D2 26 45S 139 10 E
Diamantino, Brazil 93 F7 14 30S 56 30W
Diamond Bar, U.S.A. 85 L9 34 1N 117 48W
Diamond Harbour, India 43 H13 22 11N 88 14 E
Diamond Is., Australia 62 B5 17 25S 151 5 E
Diamond Mts., U.S.A. 82 G6 39 50N 115 30W
Diamond Springs, U.S.A. 84 G6 38 42N 120 49W
Dībā, Oman 45 E8 25 45N 56 16 E
Dibai, India 42 E8 28 13N 78 15 E
Dibaya-Lubue, Dem. Rep. of the Congo 52 E3 4 12S 19 54 E
Dibete, Botswana 56 C4 23 45S 26 32 E
Dibrugarh, India 41 F19 27 29N 94 55 E
Dickens, U.S.A. 81 J4 33 37N 100 50W
Dickinson, U.S.A. 80 B3 46 53N 102 47W
Dickson = Dikson, Russia 26 B9 73 40N 80 5 E
Dickson, U.S.A. 77 G2 36 5N 87 23W
Dickson City, U.S.A. 79 E9 41 29N 75 40W
Didiéni, Mali 50 F4 13 53N 8 6W
Didsbury, Canada 72 C6 51 35N 114 10W
Didwana, India 42 F6 27 23N 74 36 E
Diefenbaker, L., Canada 73 C7 51 0N 106 55W
Diego de Almagro, Chile 94 B1 26 22S 70 3W
Diego Garcia, Ind. Oc. 3 E13 7 50S 72 50 E
Diekirch, Lux. 15 E6 49 52N 6 10 E
Dien Ban, Vietnam 38 E7 15 53N 108 16 E
Dien Khanh, Vietnam 39 F7 12 15N 109 6 E
Dieppe, France 18 B4 49 54N 1 4 E
Dierks, U.S.A. 81 H8 34 7N 94 1W
Diest, Belgium 15 D5 50 58N 5 4 E
Dif, Somali Rep. 46 G3 0 59N 0 56 E
Differdange, Lux. 15 E5 49 31N 5 54 E
Dig, India 42 F7 27 28N 77 20 E
Digba, Dem. Rep. of the Congo 54 B2 4 25N 25 48 E
Digby, Canada 71 D6 44 38N 65 50W
Diggi, India 42 F6 26 22N 75 26 E
Dighinala, Bangla. 41 H18 23 15N 92 5 E
Dighton, U.S.A. 80 F4 38 29N 100 28W
Digne-les-Bains, France 18 D7 44 5N 6 12 E
Digos, Phil. 37 C7 6 45N 125 20 E
Digranes, Iceland 8 C6 66 4N 14 44W
Digul →, Indonesia 37 F9 7 7S 138 42 E
Dihang →, India 41 F19 27 48N 95 30 E
Dijlah, Nahr →, Asia 44 D5 31 0N 47 25 E
Dijon, France 18 C6 47 20N 5 3 E
Dikkil, Djibouti 46 E3 11 8N 42 20 E
Dikomu di Kai, Botswana 56 C3 24 58S 24 36 E
Diksmuide, Belgium 15 C2 51 2N 2 52 E
Dikson, Russia 26 B9 73 40N 80 5 E
Dila, Ethiopia 46 F2 6 21N 38 22 E
Dili, Indonesia 37 F7 8 39S 125 34 E
Dilley, U.S.A. 81 L5 28 40N 99 10W
Dillingham, U.S.A. 68 C4 59 3N 158 28W
Dillon, Canada 73 B7 55 56N 108 35W
Dillon, Mont., U.S.A. 82 D7 45 13N 112 38W
Dillon, S.C., U.S.A. 77 H6 34 25N 79 22W
Dillon →, Canada 73 B7 55 56N 108 56W
Dillsburg, U.S.A. 78 F7 40 7N 77 2W
Dilolo, Dem. Rep. of the Congo 52 G4 10 28S 22 18 E
Dimas, Mexico 86 C3 23 43N 106 47W
Dimashq, Syria 47 B5 33 30N 36 18 E
Dimashq □, Syria 47 B5 33 30N 36 30 E
Dimbaza, S. Africa 57 E4 32 50S 27 14 E
Dimboola, Australia 63 F3 36 28S 142 7 E
Dîmbovița = Dâmbovița →, Romania 17 F14 44 12N 26 26 E
Dimbulah, Australia 62 B4 17 8S 145 4 E
Dimitrovgrad, Bulgaria 21 C11 42 5N 25 35 E
Dimitrovgrad, Russia 24 D8 54 14N 49 39 E
Dimitrovo = Pernik, Bulgaria 21 C10 42 35N 23 2 E
Dimmitt, U.S.A. 81 H3 34 33N 102 19W
Dimona, Israel 47 D4 31 2N 35 1 E
Dinagat, Phil. 37 B7 10 10N 125 40 E
Dinajpur, Bangla. 41 G16 25 33N 88 43 E
Dinan, France 18 B2 48 28N 2 2W
Dīnān Āb, Iran 45 C8 32 4N 56 49 E
Dinant, Belgium 15 D4 50 16N 4 55 E
Dinapur, India 43 G11 25 38N 85 5 E
Dīnār, Kūh-e, Iran 45 D6 30 42N 51 46 E
Dinara Planina, Croatia 20 C7 44 0N 16 30 E
Dinard, France 18 B2 48 38N 2 6W
Dinaric Alps = Dinara Planina, Croatia 20 C7 44 0N 16 30 E
Dindigul, India 40 P11 10 25N 78 0 E
Dindori, India 43 H9 22 57N 81 5 E
Ding Xian = Dingzhou, China 34 E8 38 30N 114 59 E
Dinga, Pakistan 42 G2 25 26N 67 10 E
Dingbian, China 34 F4 37 35N 107 32 E
Dingle, Ireland 13 D1 52 9N 10 17W
Dingle B., Ireland 13 D1 52 3N 10 20W
Dingmans Ferry, U.S.A. 79 E10 41 13N 74 55W
Dingo, Australia 62 C4 23 38S 149 19 E
Dingtao, China 34 G8 35 5N 115 35 E
Dingwall, U.K. 12 D4 57 36N 4 26W
Dingxi, China 34 G3 35 30N 104 33 E
Dingxiang, China 34 E7 38 30N 112 58 E
Dingzhou, China 34 E8 38 30N 114 59 E
Dinh, Mui, Vietnam 39 G7 11 22N 109 1 E
Dinokwe, Botswana 56 C4 23 29S 26 37 E
Dinorwic, Canada 73 D10 49 41N 92 30W
Dinosaur National Monument, U.S.A. 82 F9 40 30N 108 45W
Dinosaur Prov. Park, Canada 72 C6 50 47N 111 30W
Dinuba, U.S.A. 84 J7 36 32N 119 23W
Dipalpur, Pakistan 42 D5 30 40N 73 39 E
Diplo, Pakistan 42 G3 24 35N 69 35 E
Dipolog, Phil. 37 C6 8 36N 123 20 E
Dir, Pakistan 40 B7 35 8N 71 59 E
Dire Dawa, Ethiopia 46 F3 9 35N 41 45 E
Diriamba, Nic. 88 D2 11 51N 86 19W
Dirk Hartog I., Australia 61 E1 25 50S 113 5 E
Dirranbandi, Australia 63 D4 28 33S 148 17 E
Disa, India 42 G5 24 18N 72 10 E
Disappointment, C., U.S.A. 82 C2 46 18N 124 5W
Disappointment, L., Australia 60 D3 23 20S 122 40 E
Disaster B., Australia 63 F4 37 15S 149 58 E
Discovery B., Australia 63 F3 38 10S 140 40 E
Disko, Greenland 4 C5 69 45N 53 30W
Disko Bugt, Greenland 4 C5 69 10N 52 0W
Diss, U.K. 11 E9 52 23N 1 7 E
Disteghil Sar, Pakistan 43 A6 36 20N 75 12 E
Distrito Federal □, Brazil 93 G9 15 45S 47 45W
Distrito Federal □, Mexico 87 D5 19 15N 99 10W
Diu, India 42 J4 20 45N 70 58 E
Dīvāndarreh, Iran 44 C5 35 55N 47 2 E
Divide, U.S.A. 82 D7 45 45N 112 45W
Dividing Ra., Australia 61 E2 27 45S 116 0 E
Divinópolis, Brazil 93 H10 20 10S 44 54W
Divnoye, Russia 25 E7 45 55N 43 21 E
Divo, Ivory C. 50 G4 5 48N 5 15W
Dīwāl Kol, Afghan. 42 B2 34 23N 67 52 E
Dixie Mt., U.S.A. 84 F6 39 55N 120 16W
Dixon, Calif., U.S.A. 84 G5 38 27N 121 49W
Dixon, Ill., U.S.A. 80 E10 41 50N 89 29W
Dixon Entrance, U.S.A. 68 C6 54 30N 132 0W
Dixville, Canada 79 A13 45 4N 71 46W
Diyālā →, Iraq 44 C5 33 14N 44 31 E
Diyarbakır, Turkey 25 G7 37 55N 40 18 E
Diyodar, India 42 G4 24 8N 71 50 E
Djakarta = Jakarta, Indonesia 37 G12 6 9S 106 49 E
Djamba, Angola 56 B1 16 45S 13 58 E
Djambala, Congo 52 E2 2 32S 14 30 E
Djanet, Algeria 50 D7 24 35N 9 32 E
Djawa = Jawa, Indonesia 37 G14 7 0S 110 0 E
Djelfa, Algeria 50 B6 34 40N 3 15 E
Djema, C.A.R. 54 A2 6 3N 25 15 E
Djerba, I. de, Tunisia 51 B8 33 50N 10 48 E
Djerid, Chott, Tunisia 50 B7 33 42N 8 30 E
Djibouti, Djibouti 46 E3 11 30N 43 5 E
Djibouti ■, Africa 46 E3 12 0N 43 0 E
Djolu, Dem. Rep. of the Congo 52 D4 0 35N 22 5 E
Djoum, Cameroon 52 D2 2 41N 12 35 E
Djourab, Erg du, Chad 51 E9 16 40N 18 50 E
Djugu, Dem. Rep. of the Congo 54 B3 1 55N 30 35 E
Djúpivogur, Iceland 8 D6 64 39N 14 17W
Dmitriya Lapteva, Proliv, Russia 27 B15 73 0N 140 0 E
Dnepr → = Dnipro →, Ukraine 25 E5 46 30N 32 18 E
Dneprodzerzhinsk = Dniprodzerzhynsk, Ukraine 25 E5 48 32N 34 37 E
Dnepropetrovsk = Dnipropetrovsk, Ukraine 25 E6 48 30N 35 0 E
Dnestr → = Dnister →, Europe 17 E16 46 18N 30 17 E
Dnestrovski = Belgorod, Russia 25 D6 50 35N 36 35 E
Dnieper = Dnipro →, Ukraine 25 E5 46 30N 32 18 E
Dniester = Dnister →, Europe 17 E16 46 18N 30 17 E
Dnipro →, Ukraine 25 E5 46 30N 32 18 E
Dniprodzerzhynsk, Ukraine 25 E5 48 32N 34 37 E
Dnipropetrovsk, Ukraine 25 E6 48 30N 35 0 E
Dnister →, Europe 17 E16 46 18N 30 17 E
Dnistrovskyy Lyman, Ukraine 17 E16 46 15N 30 17 E
Dno, Russia 24 C4 57 50N 29 58 E
Dnyapro = Dnipro →, Ukraine 25 E5 46 30N 32 18 E
Doaktown, Canada 71 C6 46 33N 66 8W
Doba, Chad 51 G9 8 40N 16 50 E
Dobandi, Pakistan 42 D2 31 13N 66 50 E
Dobbyn, Australia 62 B3 19 44S 140 2 E
Dobele, Latvia 9 H20 56 37N 23 16 E
Doberai, Jazirah, Indonesia 37 E8 1 25S 133 0 E
Doblas, Argentina 94 D3 37 5S 64 0W
Dobo, Indonesia 37 F8 5 45S 134 15 E
Doboj, Bos.-H. 21 B8 44 46N 18 4 E
Dobreta-Turnu Severin, Romania 17 F12 44 39N 22 41 E
Dobrich, Bulgaria 21 C12 43 37N 27 49 E
Dobruja, Europe 17 F15 44 30N 28 15 E
Dobrush, Belarus 17 B16 52 25N 31 22 E
Doc, Mui, Vietnam 38 D6 17 58N 106 30 E
Docker River, Australia 61 D4 24 52S 129 5 E
Doctor Arroyo, Mexico 86 C4 23 40N 100 11W
Doda, India 43 C6 33 10N 75 34 E
Doda, L., Canada 70 C4 49 25N 75 13W
Dodecanese = Dhodhekánisos, Greece 21 F12 36 35N 27 0 E
Dodge City, U.S.A. 81 G5 37 45N 100 1W
Dodge L., Canada 73 B7 59 50N 105 36W
Dodgeville, U.S.A. 80 D9 42 58N 90 8W
Dodoma, Tanzania 54 D4 6 8S 35 45 E
Dodoma □, Tanzania 54 D4 6 0S 36 0 E
Dodsland, Canada 73 C7 51 50N 108 45W
Dodson, U.S.A. 82 B9 48 24N 108 15W
Doesburg, Neths. 15 B6 52 1N 6 9 E
Doetinchem, Neths. 15 C6 51 59N 6 18 E
Dog Creek, Canada 72 C4 51 35N 122 14W
Dog L., Man., Canada 73 C9 51 2N 98 31W
Dog L., Ont., Canada 70 C2 48 48N 89 30W
Dogi, Afghan. 40 C3 32 20N 62 50 E
Dogran, Pakistan 42 D5 31 48N 73 35 E
Doğubayazıt, Turkey 44 B5 39 31N 44 5 E
Doha = Ad Dawḩah, Qatar 46 B5 25 15N 51 35 E
Dohazari, Bangla. 41 H18 22 10N 92 5 E
Dohrighat, India 43 F10 26 16N 83 31 E
Doi, Indonesia 37 D7 2 14N 127 49 E
Doi Luang, Thailand 38 C3 18 30N 101 0 E
Doi Saket, Thailand 38 C2 18 52N 99 9 E
Dois Irmãos, Sa., Brazil 93 E10 9 0S 42 30W
Dokkum, Neths. 15 A5 53 20N 5 59 E
Dokri, Pakistan 42 F3 27 25N 68 7 E
Dolak, Pulau, Indonesia 37 F9 8 0S 138 30 E
Dolbeau, Canada 71 C5 48 53N 72 18W
Dole, France 18 C6 47 7N 5 31 E
Dolgellau, U.K. 10 E4 52 45N 3 53W
Dolgelley = Dolgellau, U.K. 10 E4 52 45N 3 53W
Dollard, Neths. 15 A7 53 20N 7 10 E
Dolo, Ethiopia 46 G3 4 11N 42 3 E
Dolomites = Dolomiti, Italy 20 A4 46 23N 11 51 E
Dolomiti, Italy 20 A4 46 23N 11 51 E
Dolores, Argentina 94 D4 36 20S 57 40W
Dolores, Uruguay 94 C4 33 34S 58 15W
Dolores, U.S.A. 83 H9 37 28N 108 30W
Dolores →, U.S.A. 83 G9 38 49N 109 17W
Dolphin, C., Falk. Is. 96 G5 51 10S 59 0W
Dolphin and Union Str., Canada 68 B8 69 5N 114 45W
Dom Pedrito, Brazil 95 C5 31 0S 54 40W
Domariaganj →, India 43 F10 26 17N 83 44 E
Domasi, Malawi 55 F4 15 15S 35 22 E
Dombarovskiy, Russia 26 D6 50 46N 59 32 E
Dombås, Norway 9 E13 62 4N 9 8 E
Domel I. = Letsôk-aw Kyun, Burma 39 G2 11 30N 98 25 E
Domeyko, Chile 94 B1 29 0S 71 0W
Domeyko, Cordillera, Chile 94 A2 24 30S 69 0W
Dominador, Chile 94 A2 24 21S 69 20W
Dominica ■, W. Indies 89 C7 15 20N 61 20W
Dominica Passage, W. Indies 89 C7 15 10N 61 20W
Dominican Rep. ■, W. Indies 89 C5 19 0N 70 30W
Domodóssola, Italy 18 C8 46 7N 8 17 E
Domville, Mt., Australia 63 D5 28 1S 151 15 E
Don →, Russia 25 E6 47 4N 39 18 E
Don →, Aberds., U.K. 12 D6 57 11N 2 5W
Don →, S. Yorks., U.K. 10 D7 53 41N 0 52W
Don, C., Australia 60 B5 11 18S 131 46 E
Don Benito, Spain 19 C3 38 53N 5 51W
Dona Ana = Nhamaabué, Mozam. 55 F4 17 25S 35 5 E
Donaghadee, U.K. 13 B6 54 39N 5 33W
Donald, Australia 63 F3 36 23S 143 0 E
Donaldsonville, U.S.A. 81 K9 30 6N 90 59W
Donalsonville, U.S.A. 77 K3 31 3N 84 53W
Donau = Dunărea →, Europe 17 F15 45 20N 29 40 E
Donau →, Austria 15 D3 48 10N 17 0 E
Donauwörth, Germany 16 D6 48 43N 10 47 E
Doncaster, U.K. 10 D6 53 32N 1 6W
Dondo, Mozam. 55 F3 19 33S 34 46 E
Dondo, Teluk, Indonesia 37 D6 0 50N 120 30 E
Dondra Head, Sri Lanka 40 S12 5 55N 80 40 E
Donegal, Ireland 13 B3 54 39N 8 5W
Donegal □, Ireland 13 B4 54 53N 8 0W
Donegal B., Ireland 13 B3 54 31N 8 49W
Donets →, Russia 25 E7 47 33N 40 55 E
Donetsk, Ukraine 25 E6 48 0N 37 45 E
Dong Ba Thin, Vietnam 39 F7 12 8N 109 13 E
Dong Giam, Vietnam 38 C5 19 25N 105 31 E
Dong Ha, Vietnam 38 D6 16 55N 107 8 E
Dong Hene, Laos 38 D5 16 40N 105 18 E
Dong Hoi, Vietnam 38 D6 17 29N 106 36 E
Dong Khe, Vietnam 38 A6 22 26N 106 27 E
Dong Ujimqin Qi, China 34 B9 45 32N 116 55 E
Dong Van, Vietnam 38 A5 23 16N 105 22 E
Dong Xoai, Vietnam 39 G6 11 32N 106 55 E
Dongara, Australia 61 E1 29 14S 114 57 E
Dongbei, China 35 D13 45 0N 125 0 E
Dongchuan, China 32 D5 26 8N 103 1 E
Dongfang, China 38 C7 18 50N 108 33 E
Dongfeng, China 35 C13 42 40N 125 34 E
Donggala, Indonesia 37 E5 0 30S 119 40 E
Donggou, China 35 E13 39 52N 124 10 E
Dongguang, China 34 F9 37 50N 116 30 E
Dongjingcheng, China 35 B15 44 5N 129 10 E
Dongning, China 35 B16 44 2N 131 5 E
Dongola, Sudan 51 E12 19 9N 30 22 E
Dongping, China 34 G9 35 55N 116 20 E
Dongsheng, China 34 E6 39 50N 110 0 E
Dongtai, China 35 H11 32 51N 120 21 E
Dongting Hu, China 33 D6 29 18N 112 45 E
Donington, C., Australia 63 E2 34 45S 136 0 E
Doniphan, U.S.A. 81 G9 36 37N 90 50W
Dønna, Norway 8 C15 66 6N 12 30 E
Donna, U.S.A. 81 M5 26 9N 98 4W
Donnaconna, Canada 71 C5 46 41N 71 41W
Donnelly's Crossing, N.Z. 59 F4 35 42S 173 38 E
Donnybrook, Australia 61 F2 33 34S 115 48 E
Donnybrook, S. Africa 57 D4 29 59S 29 48 E
Donora, U.S.A. 78 F5 40 11N 79 52W
Donostia = Donostia-San Sebastián, Spain 19 A5 43 17N 1 58W
Donostia-San Sebastián, Spain 19 A5 43 17N 1 58W
Doon →, U.K. 12 F4 55 27N 4 39W
Dora, L., Australia 60 D3 22 0S 123 0 E
Dora Báltea →, Italy 18 D8 45 11N 8 3 E
Doran L., Canada 73 A7 61 13N 108 6W
Dorchester, U.K. 11 G5 50 42N 2 27W
Dorchester, C., Canada 69 B12 65 27N 77 27W
Dordogne →, France 18 D3 45 2N 0 36W
Dordrecht, Neths. 15 C4 51 48N 4 39 E
Dordrecht, S. Africa 56 E4 31 20S 27 3 E
Doré L., Canada 73 C7 54 46N 107 17W
Doré Lake, Canada 73 C7 54 38N 107 36W
Dori, Burkina Faso 50 F5 14 3N 0 2W
Doring →, S. Africa 56 E2 31 54S 18 39 E
Doringbos, S. Africa 56 E2 31 59S 19 16 E
Dorion, Canada 79 A10 45 23N 74 3W
Dornbirn, Austria 16 E5 47 25N 9 45 E
Dornie, U.K. 12 D3 57 17N 5 31W
Dornoch, U.K. 12 D4 57 53N 4 2W
Dornoch Firth, U.K. 12 D4 57 51N 4 4W
Dornogovĭ □, Mongolia 34 C6 44 0N 110 0 E
Dorohoi, Romania 17 E14 47 56N 26 23 E
Döröö Nuur, Mongolia 32 B4 48 0N 93 0 E
Dorr, Iran 45 C6 33 17N 50 38 E
Dorre I., Australia 61 E1 25 13S 113 12 E
Dorrigo, Australia 63 E5 30 20S 152 44 E
Dorris, U.S.A. 82 F3 41 58N 121 55W
Dorset, Canada 78 A6 45 14N 78 54W
Dorset, U.S.A. 78 E4 41 40N 80 40W
Dorset □, U.K. 11 G5 50 45N 2 26W
Dortmund, Germany 16 C4 51 30N 7 28 E
Doruma, Dem. Rep. of the Congo 54 B2 4 42N 27 33 E
Dorūneh, Iran 45 C8 35 10N 57 18 E
Dos Bahías, C., Argentina 96 E3 44 58S 65 32W
Dos Hermanas, Spain 19 D3 37 16N 5 55W
Dos Palos, U.S.A. 84 J6 36 59N 120 37W
Dosso, Niger 50 F6 13 0N 3 13 E
Dothan, U.S.A. 77 K3 31 13N 85 24W
Doty, U.S.A. 84 D3 46 38N 123 17W
Douai, France 18 A5 50 21N 3 4 E
Douala, Cameroon 52 D1 4 0N 9 45 E
Douarnenez, France 18 B1 48 6N 4 21W
Double Island Pt., Australia 63 D5 25 56S 153 11 E
Double Mountain Fork →, U.S.A. 81 J4 33 16N 100 0W
Doubs →, France 18 C6 46 53N 5 1 E
Doubtful Sd., N.Z. 59 L1 45 20S 166 49 E
Doubtless B., N.Z. 59 F4 34 55S 173 26 E
Douglas, S. Africa 56 D3 29 4S 23 46 E
Douglas, U.K. 10 C3 54 10N 4 28W
Douglas, Ariz., U.S.A. 83 L9 31 21N 109 33W
Douglas, Ga., U.S.A. 77 K4 31 31N 82 51W
Douglas, Wyo., U.S.A. 80 D2 42 45N 105 24W
Douglas Chan., Canada 72 C3 53 40N 129 20W
Douglas Pt., Canada 78 B3 44 19N 81 37W
Douglasville, U.S.A. 77 J3 33 45N 84 45W
Dounreay, U.K. 12 C5 58 35N 3 44W
Dourada, Serra, Brazil 93 F9 13 10S 48 45W
Dourados, Brazil 95 A5 22 9S 54 50W
Dourados →, Brazil 95 A5 21 58S 54 18W
Dourados, Serra dos, Brazil 95 A5 23 30S 53 30W
Douro →, Europe 19 B1 41 8N 8 40W
Dove →, U.K. 10 E6 52 51N 1 36W
Dove Creek, U.S.A. 83 H9 37 46N 108 54W
Dover, Australia 62 G4 43 18S 147 2 E
Dover, U.K. 11 F9 51 7N 1 19 E
Dover, Del., U.S.A. 76 F8 39 10N 75 32W
Dover, N.H., U.S.A. 79 C14 43 12N 70 56W
Dover, N.J., U.S.A. 79 F10 40 53N 74 34W
Dover, Ohio, U.S.A. 78 F3 40 32N 81 29W
Dover, Pt., Australia 61 F4 32 32S 125 32 E
Dover, Str. of, Europe 11 G9 51 0N 1 30 E
Dover-Foxcroft, U.S.A. 77 C11 45 11N 69 13W
Dover Plains, U.S.A. 79 E11 41 43N 73 35W
Dovey = Dyfi →, U.K. 11 E3 52 32N 4 3W
Dovrefjell, Norway 9 E13 62 15N 9 33 E
Dow Rūd, Iran 45 C6 33 28N 49 4 E
Dowa, Malawi 55 E3 13 38S 33 58 E
Dowagiac, U.S.A. 76 E2 41 59N 86 6W

E

Ede, *Neths.* **15 B5** 52 4N 5 40 E
Edehon L., *Canada* **73 A9** 60 25N 97 15W
Eden, *Australia* **63 F4** 37 3S 149 55 E
Eden, *N.C., U.S.A.* **77 G6** 36 29N 79 53W
Eden, *N.Y., U.S.A.* **78 D6** 42 39N 78 55W
Eden, *Tex., U.S.A.* **81 K5** 31 13N 99 51W
Eden →, *U.K.* **10 C4** 54 57N 3 1W
Edenburg, *S. Africa* **56 D4** 29 43S 25 58 E
Edendale, *S. Africa* **57 D5** 29 39S 30 18 E
Edenderry, *Ireland* **13 C4** 53 21N 7 4W
Edenhope, *Australia* **63 F3** 37 4S 141 19 E
Edenton, *U.S.A.* **77 G7** 36 4N 76 39W
Edenville, *S. Africa* **57 D4** 27 37S 27 34 E
Eder →, *Germany* **16 C5** 51 12N 9 28 E
Edgar, *U.S.A.* **80 E6** 40 22N 97 58W
Edgartown, *U.S.A.* **79 E14** 41 23N 70 31W
Edge Hill, *U.K.* **11 E6** 52 8N 1 26W
Edgefield, *U.S.A.* **77 J5** 33 47N 81 56W
Edgeley, *U.S.A.* **80 B5** 46 22N 98 43W
Edgemont, *U.S.A.* **80 D3** 43 18N 103 50W
Edgeøya, *Svalbard* **4 B9** 77 45N 22 30 E
Édhessa, *Greece* **21 D10** 40 48N 22 5 E
Edievale, *N.Z.* **59 L2** 45 49S 169 22 E
Edina, *U.S.A.* **80 E8** 40 10N 92 11W
Edinboro, *U.S.A.* **78 E4** 41 52N 80 8W
Edinburg, *U.S.A.* **81 M5** 26 18N 98 10W
Edinburgh, *U.K.* **12 F5** 55 57N 3 13W
Edineţ, *Moldova* **17 D14** 48 9N 27 18 E
Edirne, *Turkey* **21 D12** 41 40N 26 34 E
Edison, *U.S.A.* **84 B4** 48 33N 122 27W
Edithburgh, *Australia* **63 F2** 35 5S 137 43 E
Edmeston, *U.S.A.* **79 D9** 42 42N 75 15W
Edmond, *U.S.A.* **81 H6** 35 39N 97 29W
Edmonds, *U.S.A.* **84 C4** 47 49N 122 23W
Edmonton, *Australia* **62 B4** 17 2S 145 46 E
Edmonton, *Canada* **72 C6** 53 30N 113 30W
Edmund L., *Canada* **70 B1** 54 45N 93 17W
Edmundston, *Canada* **71 C6** 47 23N 68 20W
Edna, *U.S.A.* **81 L6** 28 59N 96 39W
Edremit, *Turkey* **21 E12** 39 34N 27 0 E
Edremit Körfezi, *Turkey* **21 E12** 39 30N 26 45 E
Edson, *Canada* **72 C5** 53 35N 116 28W
Eduardo Castex, *Argentina* **94 D3** 35 50S 64 18W
Edward →, *Australia* **63 F3** 35 5S 143 30 E
Edward, L., *Africa* **54 C2** 0 25S 29 40 E
Edward River, *Australia* **62 A3** 14 59S 141 26 E
Edward VII Land, *Antarctica* **5 E13** 80 0S 150 0W
Edwards, *Calif., U.S.A.* **85 L9** 34 55N 117 51W
Edwards, *N.Y., U.S.A.* **79 B9** 44 20N 75 15W
Edwards Air Force Base, *U.S.A.* **85 L9** 34 50N 117 40W
Edwards Plateau, *U.S.A.* **81 K4** 30 45N 101 20W
Edwardsville, *U.S.A.* **79 E9** 41 15N 75 56W
Edzo, *Canada* **72 A5** 62 49N 116 4W
Eeklo, *Belgium* **15 C3** 51 11N 3 33 E
Effingham, *U.S.A.* **76 F1** 39 7N 88 33W
Égadi, Ísole, *Italy* **20 F5** 37 55N 12 16 E
Egan Range, *U.S.A.* **82 G6** 39 35N 114 55W
Eganville, *Canada* **78 A7** 45 32N 77 5W
Eger = Cheb, *Czech Rep.* **16 C7** 50 9N 12 28 E
Eger, *Hungary* **17 E11** 47 53N 20 27 E
Egersund, *Norway* **9 G12** 58 26N 6 1 E
Egg L., *Canada* **73 B7** 55 5N 105 30W
Éghezée, *Belgium* **15 D4** 50 35N 4 55 E
Egmont, *Canada* **72 D4** 49 45N 123 56W
Egmont, C., *N.Z.* **59 H4** 39 16S 173 45 E
Egmont, Mt., *N.Z.* **59 H5** 39 17S 174 5 E
Egra, *India* **43 J12** 21 54N 87 32 E
Eğridir, *Turkey* **25 G5** 37 52N 30 51 E
Eğridir Gölü, *Turkey* **25 G5** 37 53N 30 50 E
Egvekinot, *Russia* **27 C19** 66 19N 179 50W
Egypt ■, *Africa* **51 C12** 28 0N 31 0 E
Ehime □, *Japan* **31 H6** 33 30N 132 40 E
Ehrenberg, *U.S.A.* **85 M12** 33 36N 114 31W
Eibar, *Spain* **19 A4** 43 11N 2 28W
Eidsvold, *Australia* **63 D5** 25 25S 151 12 E
Eidsvoll, *Norway* **9 F14** 60 19N 11 14 E
Eifel, *Germany* **16 C4** 50 15N 6 50 E
Eiffel Flats, *Zimbabwe* **55 F3** 18 20S 30 0 E
Eigg, *U.K.* **12 E2** 56 54N 6 10W
Eighty Mile Beach, *Australia* **60 C3** 19 30S 120 40 E
Eil, *Somali Rep.* **46 F4** 8 0N 49 50 E
Eil, L., *U.K.* **12 E3** 56 51N 5 16W
Eildon, *Australia* **63 F4** 37 14S 145 55 E
Eildon, L., *Australia* **63 F4** 37 10S 146 0 E
Einasleigh, *Australia* **62 B3** 18 32S 144 5 E
Einasleigh →, *Australia* **62 B3** 17 30S 142 17 E
Eindhoven, *Neths.* **15 C5** 51 26N 5 28 E
Eire = Ireland ■, *Europe* **13 C4** 53 50N 7 52W
Eiríksjökull, *Iceland* **8 D3** 64 46N 20 24W
Eirunepé, *Brazil* **92 E5** 6 35S 69 53W
Eisenach, *Germany* **16 C6** 50 58N 10 19 E
Eisenerz, *Austria* **16 E8** 47 32N 14 54 E
Eivissa, *Spain* **22 C7** 38 54N 1 26 E
Ejutla, *Mexico* **87 D5** 16 34N 96 44W
Ekalaka, *U.S.A.* **80 C2** 45 53N 104 33W
Eketahuna, *N.Z.* **59 J5** 40 38S 175 43 E
Ekibastuz, *Kazakstan* **26 D8** 51 50N 75 10 E
Ekoli, *Dem. Rep. of the Congo* **54 C1** 0 23S 24 13 E
Eksjö, *Sweden* **9 H16** 57 40N 14 58 E
Ekwan →, *Canada* **70 B3** 53 12N 82 15W
Ekwan Pt., *Canada* **70 B3** 53 16N 82 7W
El Aaiún, *W. Sahara* **50 C3** 27 9N 13 12W
El Abanico, *Chile* **94 D1** 37 20S 71 31W
El 'Agrûd, *Egypt* **47 E3** 30 14N 34 24 E
El Alamein, *Egypt* **51 B11** 30 48N 28 58 E
El 'Aqaba, W. →, *Egypt* **47 E2** 30 7N 33 54 E
El Arīḥā, *West Bank* **47 D4** 31 52N 35 27 E
El 'Arîsh, *Egypt* **47 D2** 31 8N 33 50 E
El 'Arîsh, W. →, *Egypt* **47 D2** 31 8N 33 47 E
El Asnam = Ech Cheliff, *Algeria* **50 A6** 36 10N 1 20 E
El Bayadh, *Algeria* **50 B6** 33 40N 1 1 E
El Bluff, *Nic.* **88 D3** 11 59N 83 40W
El Brûk, W. →, *Egypt* **47 E2** 30 15N 33 50 E
El Cajon, *U.S.A.* **85 N10** 32 48N 116 58W
El Campo, *U.S.A.* **81 L6** 29 12N 96 16W
El Centro, *U.S.A.* **85 N11** 32 48N 115 34W
El Cerro, *Bolivia* **92 G6** 17 30S 61 40W
El Compadre, *Mexico* **85 N10** 32 20N 116 14W
El Cuy, *Argentina* **96 D3** 39 55S 68 25W
El Cuyo, *Mexico* **87 C7** 21 30N 87 40W
El Daheir, *Egypt* **47 D3** 31 13N 34 10 E
El Dátil, *Mexico* **86 B2** 30 7N 112 15W
El Dere, *Somali Rep.* **46 G4** 3 50N 47 8 E
El Descanso, *Mexico* **85 N10** 32 12N 116 58W
El Desemboque, *Mexico* **86 A2** 30 30N 112 57W
El Diviso, *Colombia* **92 C3** 1 22N 78 14W
El Djouf, *Mauritania* **50 D4** 20 0N 9 0W
El Dorado, *Ark., U.S.A.* **81 J8** 33 12N 92 40W
El Dorado, *Kans., U.S.A.* **81 G6** 37 49N 96 52W
El Dorado, *Venezuela* **92 B6** 6 55N 61 37W
El Escorial, *Spain* **19 B3** 40 35N 4 7W
El Faiyûm, *Egypt* **51 C12** 29 19N 30 50 E
El Fâsher, *Sudan* **51 F11** 13 33N 25 26 E
El Ferrol = Ferrol, *Spain* **19 A1** 43 29N 8 15W
El Fuerte, *Mexico* **86 B3** 26 30N 108 40W
El Gal, *Somali Rep.* **46 E5** 10 58N 50 20 E
El Geneina = Al Junaynah, *Sudan* **51 F10** 13 27N 22 45 E
El Gîza, *Egypt* **51 C12** 30 0N 31 10 E
El Goléa, *Algeria* **50 B6** 30 30N 2 50 E
El Iskandarîya, *Egypt* **51 B11** 31 13N 29 58 E
El Istiwa'iya, *Sudan* **51 G11** 5 0N 28 0 E
El Jadida, *Morocco* **50 B4** 33 11N 8 17W
El Jardal, *Honduras* **88 D2** 14 54N 88 50W
El Kabrît, G., *Egypt* **47 F2** 29 42N 33 16 E
El Khârga, *Egypt* **51 C12** 25 30N 30 33 E
El Khartûm, *Sudan* **51 E12** 15 31N 32 35 E
El Kuntilla, *Egypt* **47 E3** 30 1N 34 45 E
El Maestrazgo, *Spain* **19 B5** 40 30N 0 25W
El Mahalla el Kubra, *Egypt* **51 B12** 31 0N 31 0 E
El Mansûra, *Egypt* **51 B12** 31 0N 31 19 E
El Medano, *Canary Is.* **22 F3** 28 3N 16 32W
El Milagro, *Argentina* **94 C2** 30 59S 65 59W
El Minyâ, *Egypt* **51 C12** 28 7N 30 33 E
El Monte, *U.S.A.* **85 L8** 34 4N 118 1W
El Obeid, *Sudan* **51 F12** 13 8N 30 10 E
El Odaiya, *Sudan* **51 F11** 12 8N 28 12 E
El Oro, *Mexico* **87 D4** 19 48N 100 8W
El Oued, *Algeria* **50 B7** 33 20N 6 58 E
El Palmito, Presa, *Mexico* **86 B3** 25 40N 105 30W
El Paso, *U.S.A.* **83 L10** 31 45N 106 29W
El Paso Robles, *U.S.A.* **84 K6** 35 38N 120 41W
El Portal, *U.S.A.* **84 H7** 37 41N 119 47W
El Porvenir, *Mexico* **86 A3** 31 15N 105 51W
El Prat de Llobregat, *Spain* **19 B7** 41 18N 2 3 E
El Progreso, *Honduras* **88 C2** 15 26N 87 51W
El Pueblito, *Mexico* **86 B3** 29 3N 105 4W
El Pueblo, *Canary Is.* **22 F2** 28 36N 17 47W
El Puerto de Santa María, *Spain* **19 D2** 36 36N 6 13W
El Qâhira, *Egypt* **51 B12** 30 1N 31 14 E
El Qantara, *Egypt* **47 E1** 30 51N 32 20 E
El Quseima, *Egypt* **47 E3** 30 40N 34 15 E
El Real, *Panama* **92 B3** 8 0N 77 40W
El Reno, *U.S.A.* **81 H6** 35 32N 97 57W
El Rio, *U.S.A.* **85 L7** 34 14N 119 10W
El Roque, Pta., *Canary Is.* **22 F4** 28 10N 15 25W
El Rosarito, *Mexico* **86 B2** 28 38N 114 4W
El Saheira, W. →, *Egypt* **47 E2** 30 5N 33 25 E
El Salto, *Mexico* **86 C3** 23 47N 105 22W
El Salvador ■, *Cent. Amer.* **88 D2** 13 50N 89 0W
El Sauce, *Nic.* **88 D2** 13 0N 86 40W
El Sueco, *Mexico* **86 B3** 29 54N 106 24W
El Suweis, *Egypt* **51 C12** 29 58N 32 31 E
El Tamarâni, W. →, *Egypt* **47 E3** 30 7N 34 43 E
El Thamad, *Egypt* **47 F3** 29 40N 34 28 E
El Tigre, *Venezuela* **92 B6** 8 44N 64 15W
El Tîh, Gebal, *Egypt* **47 F2** 29 40N 33 50 E
El Tîna, Khalîg, *Egypt* **47 D1** 31 10N 32 40 E
El Tofo, *Chile* **94 B1** 29 22S 71 18W
El Tránsito, *Chile* **94 B1** 28 52S 70 17W
El Tûr, *Egypt* **44 D2** 28 14N 33 36 E
El Turbio, *Argentina* **96 G2** 51 45S 72 5W
El Uqsur, *Egypt* **51 C12** 25 41N 32 38 E
El Venado, *Mexico* **86 C4** 22 56N 101 10W
El Vergel, *Mexico* **86 B3** 26 28N 106 22W
El Vigía, *Venezuela* **92 B4** 8 38N 71 39W
El Wabeira, *Egypt* **47 F2** 29 34N 33 6 E
El Wak, *Kenya* **54 B5** 2 49N 40 56 E
El Wuz, *Sudan* **51 E12** 15 5N 30 7 E
Elat, *Israel* **47 F3** 29 30N 34 56 E
Elâzığ, *Turkey* **25 G6** 38 37N 39 14 E
Elba, *Italy* **20 C4** 42 46N 10 17 E
Elba, *U.S.A.* **77 K2** 31 25N 86 4W
Elbasani, *Albania* **21 D9** 41 9N 20 9 E
Elbe, *U.S.A.* **84 D4** 46 45N 122 10W
Elbe →, *Europe* **16 B5** 53 50N 9 0 E
Elbert, Mt., *U.S.A.* **83 G10** 39 7N 106 27W
Elberton, *U.S.A.* **77 H4** 34 7N 82 52W
Elbeuf, *France* **18 B4** 49 17N 1 2 E
Elbidtan, *Turkey* **44 B3** 38 13N 37 12 E
Elbing = Elbląg, *Poland* **17 A10** 54 10N 19 25 E
Elbląg, *Poland* **17 A10** 54 10N 19 25 E
Elbow, *Canada* **73 C7** 51 7N 106 35W
Elbrus, *Asia* **25 F7** 43 21N 42 30 E
Elburz Mts. = Alborz, Reshteh-ye Kūhhā-ye, *Iran* **45 C7** 36 0N 52 0 E
Elche, *Spain* **19 C5** 38 15N 0 42W
Elcho I., *Australia* **62 A2** 11 55S 135 45 E
Elda, *Spain* **19 C5** 38 29N 0 47W
Elde →, *Germany* **16 B6** 53 7N 11 15 E
Eldon, *Mo., U.S.A.* **80 F8** 38 21N 92 35W
Eldon, *Wash., U.S.A.* **84 C3** 47 33N 123 3W
Eldora, *U.S.A.* **80 D8** 42 22N 93 5W
Eldorado, *Argentina* **95 B5** 26 28S 54 43W
Eldorado, *Canada* **78 B7** 44 35N 77 31W
Eldorado, *Mexico* **86 C3** 24 20N 107 22W
Eldorado, *Ill., U.S.A.* **76 G1** 37 49N 88 26W
Eldorado, *Tex., U.S.A.* **81 K4** 30 52N 100 36W
Eldorado Springs, *U.S.A.* **81 G8** 37 52N 94 1W
Eldoret, *Kenya* **54 B4** 0 30N 35 17 E
Eldred, *U.S.A.* **78 E6** 41 58N 78 23W
Elea, C., *Cyprus* **23 D13** 35 19N 34 4 E
Eleanora, Pk., *Australia* **61 F3** 32 57S 121 9 E
Electra, *U.S.A.* **74 D7** 34 2N 98 55W
Elefantes →, *Mozam.* **57 C5** 24 10S 32 40 E
Elektrostal, *Russia* **24 C6** 55 41N 38 32 E
Elephant Butte Reservoir, *U.S.A.* **83 K10** 33 9N 107 11W
Elephant I., *Antarctica* **5 C18** 61 0S 55 0W
Eleuthera, *Bahamas* **88 B4** 25 0N 76 20W
Elgin, *Canada* **79 B8** 44 36N 76 13W
Elgin, *U.K.* **12 D5** 57 39N 3 19W
Elgin, *Ill., U.S.A.* **76 D1** 42 2N 88 17W
Elgin, *N. Dak., U.S.A.* **80 B4** 46 24N 101 51W
Elgin, *Oreg., U.S.A.* **82 D5** 45 34N 117 55W
Elgin, *Tex., U.S.A.* **81 K6** 30 21N 97 22W
Elgon, Mt., *Africa* **54 B3** 1 10N 34 30 E
Eliase, *Indonesia* **37 F8** 8 21S 130 48 E
Elim, *S. Africa* **56 E2** 34 35S 19 45 E
Elisabethville = Lubumbashi, *Dem. Rep. of the Congo* **55 E2** 11 40S 27 28 E
Elista, *Russia* **25 E7** 46 16N 44 14 E
Elizabeth, *Australia* **63 E2** 34 42S 138 41 E
Elizabeth, *N.J., U.S.A.* **79 F10** 40 39N 74 13W
Elizabeth, *N.J., U.S.A.* **79 F10** 40 40N 74 13W
Elizabeth City, *U.S.A.* **77 G7** 36 18N 76 14W
Elizabethton, *U.S.A.* **77 G4** 36 21N 82 13W
Elizabethtown, *Ky., U.S.A.* **76 G3** 37 42N 85 52W
Elizabethtown, *N.Y., U.S.A.* **79 B11** 44 13N 73 36W
Elizabethtown, *Pa., U.S.A.* **79 F8** 40 9N 76 36W
Ełk, *Poland* **17 B12** 53 50N 22 21 E
Elk →, *Canada* **72 C5** 49 11N 115 14W
Elk →, *U.S.A.* **77 H2** 34 46N 87 16W
Elk City, *U.S.A.* **81 H5** 35 25N 99 25W
Elk Creek, *U.S.A.* **84 F4** 39 36N 122 32W
Elk Grove, *U.S.A.* **84 G5** 38 25N 121 22W
Elk Island Nat. Park, *Canada* **72 C6** 53 35N 112 59W
Elk Lake, *Canada* **70 C3** 47 40N 80 25W
Elk Point, *Canada* **73 C6** 53 54N 110 55W
Elk River, *Idaho, U.S.A.* **82 C5** 46 47N 116 11W
Elk River, *Minn., U.S.A.* **80 C8** 45 18N 93 35W
Elkedra →, *Australia* **62 C2** 21 8S 136 22 E
Elkhart, *Ind., U.S.A.* **76 E3** 41 41N 85 58W
Elkhart, *Kans., U.S.A.* **81 G4** 37 0N 101 54W
Elkhorn, *Canada* **73 D8** 49 59N 101 14W
Elkhorn →, *U.S.A.* **80 E6** 41 8N 96 19W
Elkhovo, *Bulgaria* **21 C12** 42 10N 26 35 E
Elkin, *U.S.A.* **77 G5** 36 15N 80 51W
Elkins, *U.S.A.* **76 F6** 38 55N 79 51W
Elkland, *U.S.A.* **78 E7** 41 59N 77 19W
Elko, *Canada* **72 D5** 49 20N 115 10W
Elko, *U.S.A.* **82 F6** 40 50N 115 46W
Elkton, *U.S.A.* **78 C1** 43 49N 83 11W
Ell, L., *Australia* **61 E4** 29 13S 127 46 E
Ellef Ringnes I., *Canada* **4 B2** 78 30N 102 2W
Ellen, Mt., *U.S.A.* **79 B12** 44 9N 72 56W
Ellenburg, *U.S.A.* **79 B11** 44 54N 73 48W
Ellendale, *U.S.A.* **80 B5** 46 0N 98 32W
Ellensburg, *U.S.A.* **82 C3** 46 59N 120 34W
Ellenville, *U.S.A.* **79 E10** 41 43N 74 24W
Ellery, Mt., *Australia* **63 F4** 37 28S 148 47 E
Ellesmere, L., *N.Z.* **59 M4** 47 47S 172 28 E
Ellesmere I., *Canada* **4 B4** 79 30N 80 0W
Ellesmere Port, *U.K.* **10 D5** 53 17N 2 54W
Ellice Is. = Tuvalu ■, *Pac. Oc.* **64 H9** 8 0S 178 0 E
Ellicottville, *U.S.A.* **78 D6** 42 17N 78 40W
Elliot, *Australia* **62 B1** 17 33S 133 32 E
Elliot, *S. Africa* **57 E4** 31 22S 27 48 E
Elliot Lake, *Canada* **70 C3** 46 25N 82 35W
Elliotdale = Xhora, *S. Africa* **57 E4** 31 55S 28 38 E
Ellis, *U.S.A.* **80 F5** 38 56N 99 34W
Elliston, *Australia* **63 E1** 33 39S 134 53 E
Ellisville, *U.S.A.* **81 K10** 31 36N 89 12W
Ellon, *U.K.* **12 D6** 57 22N 2 4W
Ellore = Eluru, *India* **41 L12** 16 48N 81 8 E
Ellsworth, *Kans., U.S.A.* **80 F5** 38 44N 98 14W
Ellsworth, *Maine, U.S.A.* **77 C11** 44 33N 68 25W
Ellsworth Land, *Antarctica* **5 D16** 76 0S 89 0W
Ellsworth Mts., *Antarctica* **5 D16** 78 30S 85 0W
Ellwood City, *U.S.A.* **78 F4** 40 52N 80 17W
Elma, *Canada* **73 D9** 49 52N 95 55W
Elma, *U.S.A.* **84 D3** 47 0N 123 25W
Elmalı, *Turkey* **25 G4** 36 44N 29 56 E
Elmhurst, *U.S.A.* **76 E2** 41 53N 87 56W
Elmira, *Canada* **78 C4** 43 36N 80 33W
Elmira, *U.S.A.* **78 D8** 42 6N 76 48W
Elmira Heights, *U.S.A.* **78 D8** 42 8N 76 50W
Elmore, *Australia* **63 F3** 36 30S 144 37 E
Elmore, *U.S.A.* **85 M11** 33 7N 115 49W
Elmshorn, *Germany* **16 B5** 53 43N 9 40 E
Elmvale, *Canada* **78 B5** 44 35N 79 52W
Elora, *Canada* **78 C4** 43 41N 80 26W
Eloúnda, *Greece* **23 D7** 35 16N 25 42 E
Eloy, *U.S.A.* **83 K8** 32 45N 111 33W
Elrose, *Canada* **73 C7** 51 12N 108 0W
Elsie, *U.S.A.* **84 E3** 45 52N 123 36W
Elsinore = Helsingør, *Denmark* **9 H15** 56 2N 12 35 E
Eltham, *N.Z.* **59 H5** 39 26S 174 19 E
Eluru, *India* **41 L12** 16 48N 81 8 E
Elvas, *Portugal* **19 C2** 38 50N 7 10W
Elverum, *Norway* **9 F14** 60 53N 11 34 E
Elvire →, *Australia* **60 C4** 17 51S 128 11 E
Elvire, Mt., *Australia* **61 E2** 29 22S 119 36 E
Elwell, L., *U.S.A.* **82 B8** 48 22N 111 17W
Elwood, *Ind., U.S.A.* **76 E3** 40 17N 85 50W
Elwood, *Nebr., U.S.A.* **80 E5** 40 36N 99 52W
Elx = Elche, *Spain* **19 C5** 38 15N 0 42W
Ely, *U.K.* **11 E8** 52 24N 0 16 E
Ely, *Minn., U.S.A.* **80 B9** 47 55N 91 51W
Ely, *Nev., U.S.A.* **82 G6** 39 15N 114 54W
Elyria, *U.S.A.* **78 E2** 41 22N 82 7W
Emāmrūd, *Iran* **45 B7** 36 30N 55 0 E
Emba, *Kazakstan* **26 E6** 48 50N 58 8 E
Emba →, *Kazakstan* **25 E9** 46 55N 53 28 E
Embarcación, *Argentina* **94 A3** 23 10S 64 0W
Embarras Portage, *Canada* **73 B6** 58 27N 111 28W
Embetsu, *Japan* **30 B10** 44 44N 141 47 E
Embi = Emba, *Kazakstan* **26 E6** 48 50N 58 8 E
Embi = Emba →, *Kazakstan* **25 E9** 46 55N 53 28 E
Embóna, *Greece* **23 C9** 36 13N 27 51 E
Embrun, *France* **18 D7** 44 34N 6 30 E
Embu, *Kenya* **54 C4** 0 32S 37 38 E
Emden, *Germany* **16 B4** 53 21N 7 12 E
Emerald, *Australia* **62 C4** 23 32S 148 10 E
Emerson, *Canada* **73 D9** 49 0N 97 10W
Emet, *Turkey* **21 E13** 39 20N 29 15 E
Emi Koussi, *Chad* **51 E9** 19 45N 18 55 E
Eminabad, *Pakistan* **42 C6** 32 2N 74 8 E
Emine, Nos, *Bulgaria* **21 C12** 42 40N 27 56 E
Emlenton, *U.S.A.* **78 E5** 41 11N 79 43W
Emmaus, *U.S.A.* **79 F9** 40 32N 75 30W
Emmeloord, *Neths.* **15 B5** 52 44N 5 46 E
Emmen, *Neths.* **15 B6** 52 48N 6 57 E
Emmet, *Australia* **62 C3** 24 45S 144 30 E
Emmetsburg, *U.S.A.* **80 D7** 43 7N 94 41W
Emmett, *Idaho, U.S.A.* **82 E5** 43 52N 116 30W
Emmett, *Mich., U.S.A.* **78 D2** 42 59N 82 46W
Emmonak, *U.S.A.* **68 B3** 62 46N 164 30W
Emo, *Canada* **73 D10** 48 38N 93 50W
Empalme, *Mexico* **86 B2** 28 1N 110 49W
Empangeni, *S. Africa* **57 D5** 28 50S 31 52 E
Empedrado, *Argentina* **94 B4** 28 0S 58 46W
Emperor Seamount Chain, *Pac. Oc.* **64 D9** 40 0N 170 0 E
Emporia, *Kans., U.S.A.* **80 F6** 38 25N 96 11W
Emporia, *Va., U.S.A.* **77 G7** 36 42N 77 32W
Emporium, *U.S.A.* **78 E6** 41 31N 78 14W
Empress, *Canada* **73 C7** 50 57N 110 0W
Empty Quarter = Rub' al Khālī, *Si. Arabia* **46 D4** 18 0N 48 0 E
Ems →, *Germany* **16 B4** 53 20N 7 12 E
Emsdale, *Canada* **78 A5** 45 32N 79 19W
Emu, *China* **35 C15** 43 40N 128 6 E
Emu Park, *Australia* **62 C5** 23 13S 150 50 E
'En 'Avrona, *Israel* **47 F4** 29 43N 35 0 E
En Nahud, *Sudan* **51 F11** 12 45N 28 25 E
Ena, *Japan* **31 G8** 35 25N 137 25 E
Enana, *Namibia* **56 B2** 17 30S 16 23 E
Enaratoli, *Indonesia* **37 E9** 3 55S 136 21 E
Enard B., *U.K.* **12 C3** 58 5N 5 20W
Enare = Inarijärvi, *Finland* **8 B22** 69 0N 28 0 E
Encampment, *U.S.A.* **82 F10** 41 12N 106 47W
Encantadas, Serra, *Brazil* **95 C5** 30 40S 53 0W
Encarnación, *Paraguay* **95 B4** 27 15S 55 50W
Encarnación de Diaz, *Mexico* **86 C4** 21 30N 102 13W
Encinitas, *U.S.A.* **85 M9** 33 3N 117 17W
Encino, *U.S.A.* **83 J11** 34 39N 105 28W
Encounter B., *Australia* **63 F2** 35 45S 138 45 E
Endako, *Canada* **72 C3** 54 6N 125 2W
Ende, *Indonesia* **37 F6** 8 45S 121 40 E
Endeavour Str., *Australia* **62 A3** 10 45S 142 0 E
Enderbury I., *Kiribati* **64 H10** 3 8S 171 5W
Enderby, *Canada* **72 C5** 50 35N 119 10W
Enderby I., *Australia* **60 D2** 20 35S 116 30 E
Enderby Land, *Antarctica* **5 C5** 66 0S 53 0 E
Enderlin, *U.S.A.* **80 B6** 46 38N 97 36W
Endicott, *U.S.A.* **79 D8** 42 6N 76 4W
Endwell, *U.S.A.* **79 D8** 42 6N 76 2W
Endyalgout I., *Australia* **60 B5** 11 40S 132 35 E
Eneabba, *Australia* **61 E2** 29 49S 115 16 E
Enewetak Atoll, *Marshall Is.* **64 F8** 11 30N 162 15 E
Enez, *Turkey* **21 D12** 40 45N 26 5 E
Enfield, *Canada* **71 D7** 44 56N 63 32W
Enfield, *Conn., U.S.A.* **79 E12** 41 58N 72 36W
Enfield, *N.H., U.S.A.* **79 C12** 43 39N 72 9W
Engadin, *Switz.* **18 C9** 46 45N 10 10 E
Engaño, C., *Dom. Rep.* **89 C6** 18 30N 68 20W
Engaño, C., *Phil.* **37 A6** 18 35N 122 23 E
Engaru, *Japan* **30 B11** 44 3N 143 31 E
Engcobo, *S. Africa* **57 E4** 31 37S 28 0 E
Engels, *Russia* **25 D8** 51 28N 46 6 E
Engemann L., *Canada* **73 B7** 58 0N 106 55W
Enggano, *Indonesia* **36 F2** 5 20S 102 40 E
England, *U.S.A.* **81 H9** 34 33N 91 58W
England □, *U.K.* **10 D7** 53 0N 2 0W
Englee, *Canada* **71 B8** 50 45N 56 5W
Englehart, *Canada* **70 C4** 47 49N 79 52W
Englewood, *U.S.A.* **80 F2** 39 39N 104 59W
English →, *Canada* **73 C10** 50 35N 93 30W
English Bazar = Ingraj Bazar, *India* **43 G13** 24 58N 88 10 E
English Channel, *Europe* **11 G6** 50 0N 2 0W
English River, *Canada* **70 C1** 49 14N 91 0W
Enid, *U.S.A.* **81 G6** 36 24N 97 53W
Enkhuizen, *Neths.* **15 B5** 52 42N 5 17 E
Enna, *Italy* **20 F6** 37 34N 14 16 E
Ennadai, *Canada* **73 A8** 61 8N 100 53W
Ennadai L., *Canada* **73 A8** 61 0N 101 0W
Ennedi, *Chad* **51 E10** 17 15N 22 0 E
Enngonia, *Australia* **63 D4** 29 21S 145 50 E
Ennis, *Ireland* **13 D3** 52 51N 8 59W
Ennis, *Mont., U.S.A.* **82 D8** 45 21N 111 44W
Ennis, *Tex., U.S.A.* **81 J6** 32 20N 96 38W
Enniscorthy, *Ireland* **13 D5** 52 30N 6 34W
Enniskillen, *U.K.* **13 B4** 54 21N 7 39W
Ennistimon, *Ireland* **13 D2** 52 57N 9 17W
Enns →, *Austria* **16 D8** 48 14N 14 32 E
Enontekiö, *Finland* **8 B20** 68 23N 23 37 E
Enosburg Falls, *U.S.A.* **79 B12** 44 55N 72 48W
Enriquillo, L., *Dom. Rep.* **89 C5** 18 20N 72 5W
Enschede, *Neths.* **15 B6** 52 13N 6 53 E
Ensenada, *Argentina* **94 C4** 34 55S 57 55W
Ensenada, *Mexico* **86 A1** 31 50N 116 50W
Ensenada de los Muertos, *Mexico* **86 C2** 23 59N 109 50W
Ensiola, Pta. de n', *Spain* **22 B9** 39 7N 2 55 E
Entebbe, *Uganda* **54 B3** 0 4N 32 28 E
Enterprise, *Canada* **72 A5** 60 47N 115 45W
Enterprise, *Ala., U.S.A.* **77 K3** 31 19N 85 51W
Enterprise, *Oreg., U.S.A.* **82 D5** 45 25N 117 17W
Entre Ríos, *Bolivia* **94 A3** 21 30S 64 25W
Entre Ríos □, *Argentina* **94 C4** 30 30S 58 30W
Entroncamento, *Portugal* **19 C1** 39 28N 8 28W
Enugu, *Nigeria* **50 G7** 6 20N 7 30 E
Enumclaw, *U.S.A.* **84 C5** 47 12N 121 59W
Eólie, Ís., *Italy* **20 E6** 38 30N 14 57 E
Epe, *Neths.* **15 B5** 52 21N 5 59 E
Épernay, *France* **18 B5** 49 3N 3 56 E
Ephesus, *Turkey* **21 F12** 37 55N 27 22 E
Ephraim, *U.S.A.* **82 G8** 39 22N 111 35W
Ephrata, *Pa., U.S.A.* **79 F8** 40 11N 76 11W
Ephrata, *Wash., U.S.A.* **82 C4** 47 19N 119 33W
Épinal, *France* **18 B7** 48 10N 6 27 E
Episkopi, *Cyprus* **23 E11** 34 40N 32 54 E
Episkopí, *Greece* **23 D6** 35 20N 24 20 E
Episkopi Bay, *Cyprus* **23 E11** 34 35N 32 50 E
Epsom, *U.K.* **11 F7** 51 19N 0 16W
Epukiro, *Namibia* **56 C2** 21 40S 19 9 E
Equatorial Guinea ■, *Africa* **52 D1** 2 0N 8 0 E
Er Rahad, *Sudan* **51 F12** 12 45N 30 32 E
Er Rif, *Morocco* **50 A5** 35 1N 4 1W
Erāwadī Myit = Irrawaddy →, *Burma* **41 M19** 15 50N 95 6 E
Erbil = Arbīl, *Iraq* **44 B5** 36 15N 44 5 E
Erçek, *Turkey* **44 B4** 38 39N 43 36 E
Erciyaş Dağı, *Turkey* **25 G6** 38 30N 35 30 E
Érd, *Hungary* **17 E10** 47 22N 18 56 E
Erdao Jiang →, *China* **35 C14** 43 0N 127 0 E
Erdek, *Turkey* **21 D12** 40 23N 27 47 E
Erdene = Ulaan-Uul, *Mongolia* **34 B6** 44 13N 111 10 E
Erdenetsogt, *Mongolia* **34 C4** 42 55N 106 5 E
Erebus, Mt., *Antarctica* **5 D11** 77 35S 167 0 E
Erechim, *Brazil* **95 B5** 27 35S 52 15W
Ereğli, *Konya, Turkey* **25 G5** 37 31N 34 4 E
Ereğli, *Zonguldak, Turkey* **25 F5** 41 15N 31 24 E
Erenhot, *China* **34 C7** 43 48N 112 2 E
Eresma →, *Spain* **19 B3** 41 26N 4 45W
Erewadi Myitwanya, *Burma* **41 M19** 15 30N 95 0 E

Feldkirch

Erfenisdam, S. Africa 56 D4 28 30S 26 50 E
Erfurt, Germany 16 C6 50 58N 11 2 E
Erg Iguidi, Africa 50 C4 27 0N 7 0 E
Ergani, Turkey 44 B3 38 17N 39 49 E
Ergel, Mongolia 34 C5 43 8N 109 5 E
Ergeni Vozvyshennost, Russia 25 E7 47 0N 44 0 E
Ērgli, Latvia 9 H21 56 54N 25 38 E
Eriboll, L., U.K. 12 C4 58 30N 4 42W
Érice, Italy 20 E5 38 2N 12 35 E
Erie, U.S.A. 78 D4 42 8N 80 5W
Erie, L., N. Amer. 78 D4 42 15N 81 0W
Erie Canal, U.S.A. 78 C7 43 5N 78 43W
Erieau, Canada 78 D3 42 16N 81 57W
Erigavo, Somali Rep. 46 E4 10 35N 47 20 E
Erikoúsa, Greece 23 A3 39 53N 19 34 E
Eriksdale, Canada 73 C9 50 52N 98 7W
Erímanthos, Greece 21 F9 37 57N 21 50 E
Erimo-misaki, Japan 30 D11 41 50N 143 15 E
Erinpura, India 42 G5 25 9N 73 3 E
Eriskay, U.K. 12 D1 57 4N 7 18W
Eritrea ■, Africa 46 D2 14 0N 38 30 E
Erlangen, Germany 16 D6 49 36N 11 0 E
Erldunda, Australia 62 D1 25 14S 133 12 E
Ermelo, Neths. 15 B5 52 18N 5 35 E
Ermelo, S. Africa 57 D4 26 31S 29 59 E
Ermenek, Turkey 44 B2 36 38N 33 0 E
Ermones, Greece 23 A3 39 37N 19 46 E
Ermoúpolis = Síros, Greece 21 F11 37 28N 24 57 E
Ernakulam = Cochin, India 40 Q10 9 59N 76 22 E
Erne →, Ireland 13 B3 54 30N 8 16W
Erne, Lower L., U.K. 13 B4 54 28N 7 47W
Erne, Upper L., U.K. 13 B4 54 14N 7 32W
Ernest Giles Ra., Australia 61 E3 27 0S 123 45 E
Erode, India 40 P10 11 24N 77 45 E
Eromanga, Australia 63 D3 26 40S 143 11 E
Erongo, Namibia 56 C2 21 39S 15 58 E
Erramala Hills, India 40 M11 15 30N 78 15 E
Errigal, Ireland 13 A3 55 2N 8 6W
Erris Hd., Ireland 13 B1 54 19N 10 0W
Erskine, U.S.A. 80 B7 47 40N 96 0W
Ertis = Irtysh →, Russia 26 C7 61 4N 68 52 E
Erwin, U.S.A. 77 G4 36 9N 82 25W
Erzgebirge, Germany 16 C7 50 27N 12 55 E
Erzin, Russia 27 D10 50 15N 95 10 E
Erzincan, Turkey 25 G6 39 46N 39 30 E
Erzurum, Turkey 25 G7 39 57N 41 15 E
Es Caló, Spain 22 C8 38 40N 1 30 E
Es Canar, Spain 22 B8 39 2N 1 36 E
Es Mercadal, Spain 22 B11 39 59N 4 5 E
Es Migjorn Gran, Spain 22 B11 39 57N 4 3 E
Es Sahrâ' Esh Sharqîya, Egypt 51 C12 27 30N 32 30 E
Es Sînâ', Egypt 47 F3 29 0N 34 0 E
Es Vedrà, Spain 22 C7 38 52N 1 12 E
Esambo, Dem. Rep. of the Congo 54 C1 3 48S 23 30 E
Esan-Misaki, Japan 30 D10 41 40N 141 10 E
Esashi, Hokkaidō, Japan 30 B11 44 56N 142 35 E
Esashi, Hokkaidō, Japan 30 D10 41 52N 140 7 E
Esbjerg, Denmark 9 J13 55 29N 8 29 E
Escalante, U.S.A. 83 H8 37 47N 111 36W
Escalante →, U.S.A. 83 H8 37 24N 110 57W
Escalón, Mexico 86 B4 26 46N 104 20W
Escambia →, U.S.A. 77 K2 30 32N 87 11W
Escanaba, U.S.A. 76 C2 45 45N 87 4W
Esch-sur-Alzette, Lux. 18 B6 49 32N 6 0 E
Escondido, U.S.A. 85 M9 33 7N 117 5W
Escuinapa, Mexico 86 C3 22 50N 105 50W
Escuintla, Guatemala 88 D1 14 20N 90 48W
Esenguly, Turkmenistan 26 F6 37 37N 53 59 E
Eşfahān, Iran 45 C6 32 39N 51 43 E
Eşfahān □, Iran 45 C6 32 50N 51 50 E
Esfarāyen, Iran 45 B8 37 4N 57 30 E
Esfideh, Iran 45 C8 33 39N 59 46 E
Esh Sham = Dimashq, Syria 47 B5 33 30N 36 18 E
Esha Ness, U.K. 12 A7 60 29N 1 38W
Esher, U.K. 11 F7 51 21N 0 20W
Eshowe, S. Africa 57 D5 28 50S 31 30 E
Esil = Ishim →, Russia 26 D8 57 45N 71 10 E
Esk →, Cumb., U.K. 12 G5 54 58N 3 2W
Esk →, N. Yorks., U.K. 10 C7 54 30N 0 37W
Eskān, Iran 45 E9 26 48N 63 9 E
Esker, Canada 71 B6 53 53N 66 25W
Eskifjörður, Iceland 8 D7 65 3N 13 55W
Eskilstuna, Sweden 9 G17 59 22N 16 32 E
Eskimo Pt., Canada 68 B10 61 10N 94 15W
Eskişehir, Turkey 25 G5 39 50N 30 30 E
Esla →, Spain 19 B2 41 29N 6 3W
Eslāmābād-e Gharb, Iran 44 C5 34 10N 46 30 E
Eslāmshahr, Iran 45 C6 35 40N 51 10 E
Eşme, Turkey 21 E13 38 23N 28 58 E
Esmeraldas, Ecuador 92 C3 1 0N 79 40W
Esnagi L., Canada 70 C3 48 36N 84 33W
Espanola, Canada 70 C3 46 15N 81 46W
Espanola, U.S.A. 83 H10 35 59N 106 5W
Esparta, Costa Rica 88 E3 9 59N 84 40W
Esperance, Australia 61 F3 33 45S 121 55 E
Esperance B., Australia 61 F3 33 48S 121 55 E
Esperanza, Argentina 94 C3 31 29S 61 3W
Espichel, C., Portugal 19 C1 38 22N 9 16W
Espigão, Serra do, Brazil 95 B5 26 35S 50 30W
Espinazo, Sierra del = Espinhaço, Serra do, Brazil 93 G10 17 30S 43 30W
Espinhaço, Serra do, Brazil 93 G10 17 30S 43 30W
Espinilho, Serra do, Brazil 95 B5 28 30S 55 0W
Espírito Santo □, Brazil 93 H10 20 0S 40 45W
Espíritu Santo, Vanuatu 64 J8 15 15S 166 50 E
Espíritu Santo, B. del, Mexico 87 D7 19 15N 87 0W
Espíritu Santo, I., Mexico 86 C2 24 30N 110 23W
Espita, Mexico 87 C7 21 1N 88 19W
Espoo, Finland 9 F21 60 12N 24 40 E
Espungabera, Mozam. 57 C5 20 29S 32 45 E
Esquel, Argentina 96 E2 42 55S 71 20W
Esquimalt, Canada 72 D4 48 26N 123 25W
Esquina, Argentina 94 C4 30 0S 59 30W
Essaouira, Morocco 50 B4 31 32N 9 42W
Essebie, Dem. Rep. of the Congo 54 B3 2 58N 30 40 E
Essen, Belgium 15 C4 51 28N 4 28 E
Essen, Germany 16 C4 51 28N 7 2 E
Essendon, Mt., Australia 61 E3 25 0S 120 29 E
Essequibo →, Guyana 92 B7 6 50N 58 30W
Essex, Canada 78 D2 42 10N 82 49W
Essex, Calif., U.S.A. 85 L11 34 44N 115 15W
Essex, N.Y., U.S.A. 79 B11 44 19N 73 21W
Essex □, U.K. 11 F8 51 54N 0 27 E
Essex Junction, U.S.A. 79 B11 44 29N 73 7W
Esslingen, Germany 16 D5 48 44N 9 18 E
Estados, I. de Los, Argentina 96 G4 54 40S 64 30W
Eşţahbānāt, Iran 45 D7 29 8N 54 4 E
Estância, Brazil 93 F11 11 16S 37 26W
Estancia, U.S.A. 83 J10 34 46N 106 4W
Estārm, Iran 45 D8 28 21N 58 21 E
Estcourt, S. Africa 57 D4 29 0S 29 53 E
Estelí, Nic. 88 D2 13 9N 86 22W
Estellencs, Spain 22 B9 39 39N 2 29 E
Esterhazy, Canada 73 C8 50 37N 102 5W
Estevan, Canada 73 D8 49 10N 102 59W
Estevan Group, Canada 72 C3 53 3N 129 38W
Estherville, U.S.A. 80 D7 43 24N 94 50W
Eston, Canada 73 C7 51 8N 108 40W
Estonia ■, Europe 9 G21 58 30N 25 30 E
Estreito, Brazil 93 E9 6 32S 47 25W
Estrela, Serra da, Portugal 19 B2 40 10N 7 45W
Estremoz, Portugal 19 C2 38 51N 7 39W
Estrondo, Serra do, Brazil 93 E9 7 20S 48 0W
Esztergom, Hungary 17 E10 47 47N 18 44 E
Etah, India 43 F8 27 35N 78 40 E
Étampes, France 18 B5 48 26N 2 10 E
Etanga, Namibia 56 B1 17 55S 13 0 E
Etawah, India 43 F8 26 48N 79 6 E
Etawney L., Canada 73 B9 57 50N 96 50W
Ethel, U.S.A. 84 D4 46 32N 122 46W
Ethelbert, Canada 73 C8 51 32N 100 25W
Ethiopia ■, Africa 46 F3 8 0N 40 0 E
Ethiopian Highlands, Ethiopia 28 J7 10 0N 37 0 E
Etive, L., U.K. 12 E3 56 29N 5 10W
Etna, Italy 20 F6 37 50N 14 55 E
Etoile, Dem. Rep. of the Congo 55 E2 11 33S 27 30 E
Etosha Pan, Namibia 56 B2 18 40S 16 30 E
Etowah, U.S.A. 77 H3 35 20N 84 32W
Ettelbruck, Lux. 15 E6 49 51N 6 5 E
Ettrick Water →, U.K. 12 F6 55 31N 2 55W
Etuku, Dem. Rep. of the Congo 54 C2 3 42S 25 45 E
Etzatlán, Mexico 86 C4 20 48N 104 5W
Etzná, Mexico 87 D6 19 35N 90 15W
Euboea = Évvoia, Greece 21 E11 38 30N 24 0 E
Eucla, Australia 61 F4 31 41S 128 52 E
Euclid, U.S.A. 78 E3 41 34N 81 32W
Eucumbene, L., Australia 63 F4 36 2S 148 40 E
Eudora, U.S.A. 81 J9 33 7N 91 16W
Eufaula, Ala., U.S.A. 77 K3 31 54N 85 9W
Eufaula, Okla., U.S.A. 81 H7 35 17N 95 35W
Eufaula L., U.S.A. 81 H7 35 18N 95 21W
Eugene, U.S.A. 82 E2 44 5N 123 4W
Eugowra, Australia 63 E4 33 22S 148 24 E
Eulo, Australia 63 D4 28 10S 145 3 E
Eunice, La., U.S.A. 81 K8 30 30N 92 25W
Eunice, N. Mex., U.S.A. 81 J3 32 26N 103 10W
Eupen, Belgium 15 D6 50 37N 6 3 E
Euphrates = Furāt, Nahr al →, Asia 44 D5 31 0N 47 25 E
Eureka, Canada 4 B3 80 0N 85 56W
Eureka, Calif., U.S.A. 82 F1 40 47N 124 9W
Eureka, Kans., U.S.A. 81 G6 37 49N 96 17W
Eureka, Mont., U.S.A. 82 B6 48 53N 115 3W
Eureka, Nev., U.S.A. 82 G5 39 31N 115 58W
Eureka, S. Dak., U.S.A. 80 C5 45 46N 99 38W
Eureka, Mt., Australia 61 E3 26 35S 121 35 E
Euroa, Australia 63 F4 36 44S 145 35 E
Europa, Île, Ind. Oc. 53 J8 22 20S 40 22 E
Europa, Picos de, Spain 19 A3 43 10N 4 49W
Europa, Pta. de, Gib. 19 D3 36 3N 5 21W
Europe 6 E10 50 0N 20 0 E
Europoort, Neths. 15 C4 51 57N 4 10 E
Eustis, U.S.A. 77 L5 28 51N 81 41W
Euston, Australia 63 E3 34 30S 142 46 E
Eutsuk L., Canada 72 C3 53 20N 126 45W
Evale, Angola 56 B2 16 33S 15 44 E
Evans, U.S.A. 80 E2 40 23N 104 41W
Evans, L., Canada 70 B4 50 50N 77 0W
Evans City, U.S.A. 78 F4 40 46N 80 4W
Evans Head, Australia 63 D5 29 7S 153 27 E
Evans Mills, U.S.A. 79 B9 44 6N 75 48W
Evansburg, Canada 72 C5 53 36N 114 59W
Evanston, Ill., U.S.A. 76 E2 42 3N 87 41W
Evanston, Wyo., U.S.A. 82 F8 41 16N 110 58W
Evansville, U.S.A. 76 G2 37 58N 87 35W
Evaz, Iran 45 E7 27 46N 53 59 E
Eveleth, U.S.A. 80 B8 47 28N 92 32W
Evensk, Russia 27 C16 62 12N 159 30 E
Everard, L., Australia 63 E2 31 30S 135 0 E
Everard Ranges, Australia 61 E5 27 5S 132 28 E
Everest, Mt., Nepal 43 E12 28 5N 86 58 E
Everett, Pa., U.S.A. 78 F6 40 1N 78 23W
Everett, Wash., U.S.A. 84 C4 47 59N 122 12W
Everglades, The, U.S.A. 77 N5 25 50N 81 0W
Everglades National Park, U.S.A. 77 N5 25 30N 81 0W
Evergreen, Ala., U.S.A. 77 K2 31 26N 86 57W
Evergreen, Mont., U.S.A. 82 B6 48 9N 114 13W
Evesham, U.K. 11 E6 52 6N 1 56W
Evje, Norway 9 G12 58 36N 7 51 E
Évora, Portugal 19 C2 38 33N 7 57W
Evowghlī, Iran 44 B5 38 43N 45 13 E
Évreux, France 18 B4 49 3N 1 8 E
Évros →, Bulgaria 21 D12 41 40N 26 34 E
Évry, France 18 B5 48 38N 2 27 E
Évvoia, Greece 21 E11 38 30N 24 0 E
Ewe, L., U.K. 12 D3 57 49N 5 38W
Ewing, U.S.A. 80 D5 42 16N 98 21W
Ewo, Congo 52 E2 0 48S 14 45 E
Exaltación, Bolivia 92 F5 13 10S 65 20W
Excelsior Springs, U.S.A. 80 F7 39 20N 94 13W
Exe →, U.K. 11 G4 50 41N 3 29W
Exeter, Canada 78 C3 43 21N 81 29W
Exeter, U.K. 11 G4 50 43N 3 31W
Exeter, Calif., U.S.A. 84 J7 36 18N 119 9W
Exeter, N.H., U.S.A. 79 D14 42 59N 70 57W
Exmoor, U.K. 11 F4 51 12N 3 45W
Exmouth, Australia 60 D1 21 54S 114 10 E
Exmouth, U.K. 11 G4 50 37N 3 25W
Exmouth G., Australia 60 D1 22 15S 114 15 E
Expedition Ra., Australia 62 C4 24 30S 149 12 E
Extremadura □, Spain 19 C2 39 30N 6 5W
Exuma Sound, Bahamas 88 B4 24 30N 76 20W
Eyasi, L., Tanzania 54 C4 3 30S 35 0 E
Eye Pen., U.K. 12 C2 58 13N 6 10W
Eyemouth, U.K. 12 F6 55 52N 2 5W
Eyjafjörður, Iceland 8 C4 66 15N 18 30W
Eyre (North), L., Australia 63 D2 28 30S 137 20 E
Eyre (South), L., Australia 63 D2 29 18S 137 25 E
Eyre Mts., N.Z. 59 L2 45 25S 168 25 E
Eyre Pen., Australia 63 E2 33 30S 136 17 E
Eysturoy, Færoe Is. 8 E9 62 13N 6 54W
Eyvānkī, Iran 45 C6 35 24N 51 56 E
Ezine, Turkey 21 E12 39 48N 26 20 E
Ezouza →, Cyprus 23 E11 34 44N 32 27 E

F

F.Y.R.O.M. = Macedonia ■, Europe 21 D9 41 53N 21 40 E
Fabala, Guinea 50 G4 9 44N 9 5W
Fabens, U.S.A. 83 L10 31 30N 106 10W
Fabriano, Italy 20 C5 43 20N 12 54 E
Fachi, Niger 51 E8 18 6N 11 34 E
Fada, Chad 51 E10 17 13N 21 34 E
Fada-n-Gourma, Burkina Faso 50 F6 12 10N 0 30 E
Faddeyevskiy, Ostrov, Russia 27 B15 76 0N 144 0 E
Fadghāmī, Syria 44 C4 35 53N 40 52 E
Faenza, Italy 20 B4 44 17N 11 53 E
Færoe Is. = Føroyar, Atl. Oc. 8 F9 62 0N 7 0W
Făgăraş, Romania 17 F13 45 48N 24 58 E
Fagersta, Sweden 9 F16 60 1N 15 46 E
Fagnano, L., Argentina 96 G3 54 30S 68 0W
Fahlīān, Iran 45 D6 30 11N 51 28 E
Fahraj, Kermān, Iran 45 D8 29 0N 59 0 E
Fahraj, Yazd, Iran 45 D7 31 46N 54 36 E
Faial, Madeira 22 D3 32 47N 16 53W
Fair Haven, U.S.A. 76 D9 43 36N 73 16W
Fair Hd., U.K. 13 A5 55 14N 6 9W
Fair Oaks, U.S.A. 84 G5 38 39N 121 16W
Fairbanks, U.S.A. 68 B5 64 51N 147 43W
Fairbury, U.S.A. 80 E6 40 8N 97 11W
Fairfax, U.S.A. 79 B11 44 40N 73 1W
Fairfield, Ala., U.S.A. 77 J2 33 29N 86 55W
Fairfield, Calif., U.S.A. 84 G4 38 15N 122 3W
Fairfield, Conn., U.S.A. 79 E11 41 9N 73 16W
Fairfield, Idaho, U.S.A. 82 E6 43 21N 114 44W
Fairfield, Ill., U.S.A. 76 F1 38 23N 88 22W
Fairfield, Iowa, U.S.A. 80 E9 40 56N 91 57W
Fairfield, Tex., U.S.A. 81 K7 31 44N 96 10W
Fairford, Canada 73 C9 51 37N 98 38W
Fairhope, U.S.A. 77 K2 30 31N 87 54W
Fairlie, N.Z. 59 L3 44 5S 170 49 E
Fairmead, U.S.A. 84 H6 37 5N 120 10W
Fairmont, Minn., U.S.A. 80 D7 43 39N 94 28W
Fairmont, W. Va., U.S.A. 76 F5 39 29N 80 9W
Fairmount, Calif., U.S.A. 85 L8 34 45N 118 26W
Fairmount, N.Y., U.S.A. 79 C8 43 5N 76 12W
Fairplay, U.S.A. 83 G11 39 15N 106 2W
Fairport, U.S.A. 78 C7 43 6N 77 27W
Fairport Harbor, U.S.A. 78 E3 41 45N 81 17W
Fairview, Canada 72 B5 56 5N 118 25W
Fairview, Mont., U.S.A. 80 B2 47 51N 104 3W
Fairview, Okla., U.S.A. 81 G5 36 16N 98 29W
Fairweather, Mt., U.S.A. 72 B1 58 55N 137 32W
Faisalabad, Pakistan 42 D5 31 30N 73 5 E
Faith, U.S.A. 80 C3 45 2N 102 2W
Faizabad, India 43 F10 26 45N 82 10 E
Fajardo, Puerto Rico 89 C6 18 20N 65 39W
Fajr, Wādī, Si. Arabia 44 D3 29 10N 38 10 E
Fakenham, U.K. 10 E8 52 51N 0 51 E
Fakfak, Indonesia 37 E8 3 0S 132 15 E
Faku, China 35 C12 42 32N 123 21 E
Falaise, France 18 B3 48 54N 0 12W
Falaise, Mui, Vietnam 38 C5 19 6N 105 45 E
Falam, Burma 41 H18 23 0N 93 45 E
Falcó, C. des, Spain 22 C7 38 50N 1 23 E
Falcón, Presa, Mexico 87 B5 26 35N 99 10W
Falcon Lake, Canada 73 D9 49 42N 95 15W
Falcon Reservoir, U.S.A. 81 M5 26 34N 99 10W
Falconara Maríttima, Italy 20 C5 43 37N 13 24 E
Falcone, C. del, Italy 20 D3 40 58N 8 12 E
Falconer, U.S.A. 78 D5 42 7N 79 13W
Faleshty = Făleşti, Moldova 17 E14 47 32N 27 44 E
Făleşti, Moldova 17 E14 47 32N 27 44 E
Falfurrias, U.S.A. 81 M5 27 14N 98 9W
Falher, Canada 72 B5 55 44N 117 15W
Faliraki, Greece 23 C10 36 22N 28 12 E
Falkenberg, Sweden 9 H15 56 54N 12 30 E
Falkirk, U.K. 12 F5 56 0N 3 47W
Falkirk □, U.K. 12 F5 55 58N 3 49W
Falkland, U.K. 12 E5 56 16N 3 12W
Falkland Is. □, Atl. Oc. 96 G5 51 30S 59 0W
Falkland Sd., Falk. Is. 96 G5 52 0S 60 0W
Falköping, Sweden 9 G15 58 12N 13 33 E
Fall River, U.S.A. 79 E13 41 43N 71 10W
Fallbrook, U.S.A. 85 M9 33 23N 117 15W
Fallon, U.S.A. 82 G4 39 28N 118 47W
Falls City, U.S.A. 80 E7 40 3N 95 36W
Falls Creek, U.S.A. 78 E6 41 9N 78 48W
Falmouth, Jamaica 88 C4 18 30N 77 40W
Falmouth, U.K. 11 G2 50 9N 5 5W
Falmouth, U.S.A. 79 E14 41 33N 70 37W
Falsa, Pta., Mexico 86 B1 27 51N 115 3W
False B., S. Africa 56 E2 34 15S 18 40 E
Falso, C., Honduras 88 C3 15 12N 83 21W
Falster, Denmark 9 J14 54 45N 11 55 E
Falsterbo, Sweden 9 J15 55 23N 12 50 E
Fălticeni, Romania 17 E14 47 21N 26 20 E
Falun, Sweden 9 F16 60 37N 15 37 E
Famagusta, Cyprus 23 D12 35 8N 33 55 E
Famagusta Bay, Cyprus 23 D13 35 15N 34 0 E
Famalé, Niger 50 F6 14 33N 1 5 E
Famatina, Sierra de, Argentina 94 B2 27 30S 68 0W
Family L., Canada 73 C9 51 54N 95 27W
Famoso, U.S.A. 85 K7 35 37N 119 12W
Fan Xian, China 34 G8 35 55N 115 38 E
Fanad Hd., Ireland 13 A4 55 17N 7 38W
Fandriana, Madag. 57 C8 20 14S 47 21 E
Fangcheng, China 34 H7 33 18N 112 59 E
Fangshan, China 34 E6 38 3N 111 25 E
Fangzi, China 35 F10 36 33N 119 10 E
Fanjiatun, China 35 C13 43 40N 125 15 E
Fannich, L., U.K. 12 D4 57 38N 4 59W
Fannūj, Iran 45 E8 26 35N 59 38 E
Fanø, Denmark 9 J13 55 25N 8 25 E
Fano, Italy 20 C5 43 50N 13 1 E
Fanshi, China 34 E7 39 12N 113 20 E
Fao = Al Fāw, Iraq 45 D6 30 0N 48 30 E
Faqirwali, Pakistan 42 E5 29 27N 73 0 E
Faradje, Dem. Rep. of the Congo 54 B2 3 50N 29 45 E
Farafangana, Madag. 57 C8 22 49S 47 50 E
Farāh, Afghan. 40 C3 32 20N 62 7 E
Farāh □, Afghan. 40 C3 32 25N 62 10 E
Farahalana, Madag. 57 A9 14 26S 50 10 E
Faranah, Guinea 50 F3 10 3N 10 45W
Farasān, Jazā'ir, Si. Arabia 46 D3 16 45N 41 55 E
Farasan Is. = Farasān, Jazā'ir, Si. Arabia 46 D3 16 45N 41 55 E
Faratsiho, Madag. 57 B8 19 24S 46 57 E
Fareham, U.K. 11 G6 50 51N 1 11W
Farewell, C., N.Z. 59 J4 40 29S 172 43 E
Farewell C. = Farvel, Kap, Greenland 4 D5 59 48N 43 55W
Farghona, Uzbekistan 26 E8 40 23N 71 19 E
Fargo, U.S.A. 80 B6 46 53N 96 48W
Fār'iah, W. al →, West Bank 47 C4 32 12N 35 27 E
Faribault, U.S.A. 80 C8 44 18N 93 16W
Faridabad, India 42 E6 28 26N 77 19 E
Faridkot, India 42 D6 30 44N 74 45 E
Faridpur, Bangla. 43 H13 23 15N 89 55 E
Faridpur, India 43 E8 28 13N 79 33 E
Farīmān, Iran 45 C8 35 40N 59 49 E
Farina, Australia 63 E2 30 3S 138 15 E
Fariones, Pta., Canary Is. 22 E6 29 13N 13 28W
Farmerville, U.S.A. 81 J8 32 47N 92 24W
Farmingdale, U.S.A. 79 F10 40 12N 74 10W
Farmington, Canada 72 B4 55 54N 120 30W
Farmington, Calif., U.S.A. 84 H6 37 55N 120 59W
Farmington, Maine, U.S.A. 77 C10 44 40N 70 9W
Farmington, Mo., U.S.A. 81 G9 37 47N 90 25W
Farmington, N.H., U.S.A. 79 C13 43 24N 71 4W
Farmington, N. Mex., U.S.A. 83 H9 36 44N 108 12W
Farmington, Utah, U.S.A. 82 F8 41 0N 111 12W
Farmington →, U.S.A. 79 E12 41 51N 72 38W
Farmville, U.S.A. 76 G6 37 18N 78 24W
Farne Is., U.K. 10 B6 55 38N 1 37W
Farnham, Canada 79 A12 45 17N 72 59W
Farnham, Mt., Canada 72 C5 50 29N 116 30W
Faro, Brazil 93 D7 2 10S 56 39W
Faro, Canada 68 B6 62 11N 133 22W
Faro, Portugal 19 D2 37 2N 7 55W
Fårö, Sweden 9 H18 57 55N 19 5 E
Farquhar, C., Australia 61 D1 23 50S 113 36 E
Farrars Cr. →, Australia 62 D3 25 35S 140 43 E
Farrāshband, Iran 45 D7 28 57N 52 5 E
Farrell, U.S.A. 78 E4 41 13N 80 30W
Farrokhī, Iran 45 C8 33 50N 59 31 E
Farruch, C. = Ferrutx, C., Spain 22 B10 39 47N 3 21 E
Farrukhabad-cum-Fatehgarh, India 40 F11 27 30N 79 32 E
Fārs □, Iran 45 D7 29 30N 55 0 E
Fársala, Greece 21 E10 39 17N 22 23 E
Farson, U.S.A. 82 E9 42 6N 109 27W
Farsund, Norway 9 G12 58 5N 6 55 E
Fartak, Râs, Si. Arabia 44 D2 28 5N 34 34 E
Fartak, Ra's, Yemen 46 D5 15 38N 52 15 E
Fartura, Serra da, Brazil 95 B5 26 21S 52 52W
Fārūj, Iran 45 B8 37 14N 58 14 E
Farvel, Kap, Greenland 4 D5 59 48N 43 55W
Farwell, U.S.A. 81 H3 34 23N 103 2W
Fasā, Iran 45 D7 29 0N 53 39 E
Fasano, Italy 20 D7 40 50N 17 22 E
Fastiv, Ukraine 17 C15 50 7N 29 57 E
Fastov = Fastiv, Ukraine 17 C15 50 7N 29 57 E
Fatagar, Tanjung, Indonesia 37 E8 2 46S 131 57 E
Fatehabad, Haryana, India 42 E6 29 31N 75 27 E
Fatehabad, Ut. P., India 42 F8 27 1N 78 19 E
Fatehgarh, India 43 F8 27 25N 79 35 E
Fatehpur, Bihar, India 43 G11 24 38N 85 14 E
Fatehpur, Raj., India 42 F6 28 0N 74 40 E
Fatehpur, Ut. P., India 43 G9 25 56N 81 13 E
Fatehpur, Ut. P., India 43 F9 27 10N 81 13 E
Fatehpur Sikri, India 42 F6 27 6N 77 40 E
Fatima, Canada 71 C7 47 24N 61 53W
Faulkton, U.S.A. 80 C5 45 2N 99 8W
Faure I., Australia 61 E1 25 52S 113 50 E
Fauresmith, S. Africa 56 D4 29 44S 25 17 E
Fauske, Norway 8 C16 67 17N 15 25 E
Favara, Italy 20 F5 37 19N 13 39 E
Favàritx, C. de, Spain 22 B11 40 0N 4 15 E
Favignana, Italy 20 F5 37 56N 12 20 E
Fawcett, Pt., Australia 60 B5 11 46S 130 2 E
Fawn →, Canada 70 A2 55 20N 87 35W
Fawnskin, U.S.A. 85 L10 34 16N 116 56W
Faxaflói, Iceland 8 D2 64 29N 23 0W
Faya-Largeau, Chad 51 E9 17 58N 19 6 E
Fayd, Si. Arabia 44 E4 27 1N 42 52 E
Fayette, Ala., U.S.A. 77 J2 33 41N 87 50W
Fayette, Mo., U.S.A. 80 F8 39 9N 92 41W
Fayetteville, Ark., U.S.A. 81 G7 36 4N 94 10W
Fayetteville, N.C., U.S.A. 77 H6 35 3N 78 53W
Fayetteville, Tenn., U.S.A. 77 H2 35 9N 86 34W
Fazilka, India 42 D6 30 27N 74 2 E
Fazilpur, Pakistan 42 E4 29 18N 70 29 E
Fdérik, Mauritania 50 D3 22 40N 12 45W
Feale →, Ireland 13 D2 52 27N 9 37W
Fear, C., U.S.A. 77 J7 33 50N 77 58W
Feather →, U.S.A. 82 G3 38 47N 121 36W
Feather Falls, U.S.A. 84 F5 39 36N 121 16W
Featherston, N.Z. 59 J5 41 6S 175 20 E
Featherstone, Zimbabwe 55 F3 18 42S 30 55 E
Fécamp, France 18 B4 49 45N 0 22 E
Fedala = Mohammedia, Morocco 50 B4 33 44N 7 21W
Federación, Argentina 94 C4 31 0S 57 55W
Féderal, Argentina 96 C5 30 57S 58 48W
Federal Way, U.S.A. 84 C4 47 18N 122 19W
Fedeshkūh, Iran 45 D7 28 49N 53 50 E
Fehmarn, Germany 16 A6 54 27N 11 7 E
Fehmarn Bælt, Europe 9 J14 54 35N 11 20 E
Fehmarn Belt = Fehmarn Bælt, Europe 9 J14 54 35N 11 20 E
Fei Xian, China 35 G9 35 18N 117 59 E
Feijó, Brazil 92 E4 8 9S 70 21W
Feilding, N.Z. 59 J5 40 13S 175 35 E
Feira de Santana, Brazil 93 F11 12 15S 38 57W
Feixiang, China 34 F8 36 30N 114 45 E
Felanitx, Spain 22 B10 39 28N 3 9 E
Feldkirch, Austria 16 E5 47 15N 9 37 E

Felipe Carrillo Puerto

Felipe Carrillo Puerto, Mexico 87 D7 19 38N 88 3W
Felixstowe, U.K. 11 F9 51 58N 1 23 E
Felton, U.S.A. 84 H4 37 3N 122 4W
Femer Bælt = Fehmarn Bælt, Europe 9 J14 54 35N 11 20 E
Femunden, Norway 9 E14 62 10N 11 53 E
Fen He →, China 34 G6 35 36N 110 42 E
Fenelon Falls, Canada 78 B6 44 32N 78 45W
Feng Xian, Jiangsu, China 34 G9 34 43N 116 35 E
Feng Xian, Shaanxi, China 34 H4 33 54N 106 40 E
Fengcheng, China 35 D13 40 28N 124 5 E
Fengfeng, China 34 F8 36 28N 114 8 E
Fengjie, China 33 C5 31 5N 109 36 E
Fengning, China 34 D9 41 10N 116 33 E
Fengqiu, China 34 G8 35 2N 114 25 E
Fengrun, China 35 E10 39 48N 118 8 E
Fengtai, China 34 E9 39 50N 116 18 E
Fengxiang, China 34 G4 34 29N 107 25 E
Fengyang, China 35 H9 32 51N 117 29 E
Fengzhen, China 34 D7 40 25N 113 2 E
Fenoarivo Afovoany, Madag. 57 B8 18 26S 46 34 E
Fenoarivo Atsinanana, Madag. 57 B8 17 22S 49 25 E
Fens, The, U.K. 10 E7 52 38N 0 2W
Fenton, U.S.A. 76 D4 42 48N 83 42W
Fenxi, China 34 F6 36 40N 111 31 E
Fenyang, China 34 F6 37 18N 111 48 E
Feodosiya, Ukraine 25 E6 45 2N 35 16 E
Ferdows, Iran 45 C8 33 58N 58 2 E
Ferfer, Somali Rep. 46 F4 5 4N 45 9 E
Fergana = Farghona, Uzbekistan 26 E8 40 23N 71 19 E
Fergus, Canada 78 C4 43 43N 80 24W
Fergus Falls, U.S.A. 80 B6 46 17N 96 4W
Ferkéssédougou, Ivory C. 50 G4 9 35N 5 6W
Ferland, Canada 70 B2 50 19N 88 27W
Fermanagh □, U.K. 13 B4 54 21N 7 40W
Fermo, Italy 20 C5 43 9N 13 43 E
Fermont, Canada 71 B6 52 47N 67 5W
Fermont, Qué., Canada 69 C13 50 28N 67 29W
Fermoy, Ireland 13 D3 52 9N 8 16W
Fernández, Argentina 94 B3 27 55S 63 50W
Fernandina Beach, U.S.A. 77 K5 30 40N 81 27W
Fernando de Noronha, Brazil 93 D12 4 0S 33 10W
Fernando Póo = Bioko, Eq. Guin. 52 D1 3 30N 8 40 E
Ferndale, U.S.A. 84 B4 48 51N 122 36W
Fernie, Canada 72 D5 49 30N 115 5W
Fernlees, Australia 62 C4 23 51S 148 7 E
Fernley, U.S.A. 82 G4 39 36N 119 15W
Ferozepore = Firozpur, India 42 D6 30 55N 74 40 E
Ferrara, Italy 20 B4 44 50N 11 35 E
Ferreñafe, Peru 92 E3 6 42S 79 50W
Ferrerías, Spain 22 B11 39 59N 4 1 E
Ferret, C., France 18 D3 44 38N 1 15W
Ferriday, U.S.A. 81 K9 31 38N 91 33W
Ferrol, Spain 19 A1 43 29N 8 15W
Ferron, U.S.A. 83 G8 39 5N 111 8W
Ferrutx, C., Spain 22 B10 39 47N 3 21 E
Ferryland, Canada 71 C9 47 2N 52 53W
Fertile, U.S.A. 80 B6 47 32N 96 17W
Fès, Morocco 50 B5 34 0N 5 0W
Fessenden, U.S.A. 80 B5 47 39N 99 38W
Festus, U.S.A. 80 F9 38 13N 90 24W
Feteşti, Romania 17 F14 44 22N 27 51 E
Fethiye, Turkey 25 G4 36 36N 29 6 E
Fetlar, U.K. 12 A8 60 36N 0 52W
Feuilles →, Canada 69 C12 58 47N 70 4W
Fez = Fès, Morocco 50 B5 34 0N 5 0W
Fezzan, Libya 51 C8 27 0N 13 0 E
Fiambalá, Argentina 94 B2 27 45S 67 37W
Fianarantsoa, Madag. 57 C8 21 26S 47 5 E
Fianarantsoa □, Madag. 57 B8 19 30S 47 0 E
Ficksburg, S. Africa 57 D4 28 51S 27 53 E
Field →, Australia 62 C2 23 48S 138 0 E
Field I., Australia 60 B5 12 5S 132 23 E
Fieri, Albania 21 D8 40 43N 19 33 E
Fife □, U.K. 12 E5 56 16N 3 1W
Fife Ness, U.K. 12 E6 56 17N 2 35W
Fifth Cataract, Sudan 51 E12 18 23N 33 47 E
Figeac, France 18 D5 44 37N 2 2 E
Figtree, Zimbabwe 55 G2 20 22S 28 20 E
Figueira da Foz, Portugal 19 B1 40 7N 8 54W
Figueres, Spain 19 A7 42 18N 2 58 E
Figuig, Morocco 50 B5 32 5N 1 11W
Fihaonana, Madag. 57 B8 18 36S 47 12 E
Fiherenana, Madag. 57 B8 18 29S 48 24 E
Fiherenana →, Madag. 57 C7 23 19S 43 37 E
Fiji ■, Pac. Oc. 59 C8 17 20S 179 0 E
Filey, U.K. 10 C7 54 12N 0 18W
Filey B., U.K. 10 C7 54 12N 0 15W
Filfla, Malta 23 D1 35 47N 14 24 E
Filiatrá, Greece 21 F9 37 9N 21 35 E
Filingué, Niger 50 F6 14 21N 3 22 E
Filipstad, Sweden 9 G16 59 43N 14 9 E
Fillmore, Calif., U.S.A. 85 L8 34 24N 118 55W
Fillmore, Utah, U.S.A. 83 G7 38 58N 112 20W
Finch, Canada 79 A9 45 11N 75 7W
Findhorn →, U.K. 12 D5 57 38N 3 38W
Findlay, U.S.A. 76 E4 41 2N 83 39W
Finger L., Canada 70 B1 53 33N 93 30W
Finger Lakes, U.S.A. 79 D8 42 40N 76 30W
Fingoè, Mozam. 55 E3 14 55S 31 50 E
Finisterre, C. = Fisterra, C., Spain 19 A1 42 50N 9 19W
Finke, Australia 62 D1 25 34S 134 35 E
Finland ■, Europe 8 E22 63 0N 27 0 E
Finland, G. of, Europe 9 G21 60 0N 26 0 E
Finlay →, Canada 72 B3 57 0N 125 10W
Finley, Australia 63 F4 35 38S 145 35 E
Finley, U.S.A. 80 B6 47 31N 97 50W
Finn →, Ireland 13 B4 54 51N 7 28W
Finnigan, Mt., Australia 62 B4 15 49S 145 17 E
Finniss, C., Australia 63 E1 33 8S 134 51 E
Finnmark, Norway 8 B20 69 37N 23 57 E
Finnsnes, Norway 8 B18 69 14N 18 0 E
Finspång, Sweden 9 G16 58 43N 15 47 E
Fiora →, Italy 20 C4 42 20N 11 34 E
Fiq, Syria 47 C4 32 46N 35 41 E
Firat = Furāt, Nahr al →, Asia 44 D5 31 0N 47 25 E
Firebag →, Canada 73 B6 57 45N 111 21W
Firebaugh, U.S.A. 84 J6 36 52N 120 27W
Firedrake L., Canada 73 A8 61 25N 104 30W
Firenze, Italy 20 C4 43 46N 11 15 E
Firk →, Iraq 44 D5 30 59N 44 34 E
Firozabad, India 43 F8 27 10N 78 25 E
Firozpur, India 42 D6 30 55N 74 40 E
Firozpur-Jhirka, India 42 F7 27 48N 76 57 E
Fīrūzābād, Iran 45 D7 28 52N 52 35 E
Fīrūzkūh, Iran 45 C7 35 50N 52 50 E
Firvale, Canada 72 C3 52 27N 126 13W
Fish →, Namibia 56 D2 28 7S 17 10 E
Fish →, S. Africa 56 E3 31 30S 20 16 E
Fisher, Australia 61 F5 30 30S 131 0 E
Fisher B., Canada 73 C9 51 35N 97 13W
Fishers I., U.S.A. 79 E13 41 15N 72 0W
Fishguard, U.K. 11 E3 52 0N 4 58W
Fishing L., Canada 73 C9 52 10N 95 24W
Fishkill, U.S.A. 79 E11 41 32N 73 53W
Fisterra, C., Spain 19 A1 42 50N 9 19W
Fitchburg, U.S.A. 79 D13 42 35N 71 48W
Fitz Roy, Argentina 96 F3 47 0S 67 0W
Fitzgerald, Canada 72 B6 59 51N 111 36W
Fitzgerald, U.S.A. 77 K4 31 43N 83 15W
Fitzmaurice →, Australia 60 B5 14 45S 130 5 E
Fitzroy →, Queens., Australia 62 C5 23 32S 150 52 E
Fitzroy →, W. Austral., Australia 60 C3 17 31S 123 35 E
Fitzroy, Mte., Argentina 96 F2 49 17S 73 5W
Fitzroy Crossing, Australia 60 C4 18 9S 125 38 E
Fitzwilliam I., Canada 78 A3 45 30N 81 45W
Fiume = Rijeka, Croatia 16 F8 45 20N 14 21 E
Five Points, U.S.A. 84 J6 36 26N 120 6W
Fizi, Dem. Rep. of the Congo 54 C2 4 17S 28 55 E
Flagstaff, U.S.A. 83 J8 35 12N 111 39W
Flagstaff L., Maine, U.S.A. 77 C10 45 12N 70 19W
Flagstaff L., Maine, U.S.A. 79 A14 45 12N 70 18W
Flaherty I., Canada 70 A4 56 15N 79 15W
Flåm, Norway 9 F12 60 50N 7 7 E
Flambeau →, U.S.A. 80 C9 45 18N 91 14W
Flamborough Hd., U.K. 10 C7 54 7N 0 5W
Flaming Gorge Reservoir, U.S.A. 82 F9 41 10N 109 25W
Flamingo, Teluk, Indonesia 37 F9 5 30S 138 0 E
Flanders = Flandre, Europe 18 A5 50 50N 2 30 E
Flandre, Europe 18 A5 50 50N 2 30 E
Flandre Occidentale = West-Vlaanderen □, Belgium 15 D2 51 0N 3 0 E
Flandre Orientale = Oost-Vlaanderen □, Belgium 15 C3 51 5N 3 50 E
Flandreau, U.S.A. 80 C6 44 3N 96 36W
Flanigan, U.S.A. 84 E7 40 10N 119 53W
Flannan Is., U.K. 12 C1 58 9N 7 52W
Flåsjön, Sweden 8 D16 64 5N 15 40 E
Flat →, Canada 72 A3 61 33N 125 18W
Flathead L., U.S.A. 82 C7 47 51N 114 8W
Flattery, C., Australia 62 A4 14 58S 145 21 E
Flattery, C., U.S.A. 84 B2 48 23N 124 29W
Flatwoods, U.S.A. 76 F4 38 31N 82 43W
Fleetwood, U.K. 10 D4 53 55N 3 1W
Fleetwood, U.S.A. 79 F9 40 27N 75 49W
Flekkefjord, Norway 9 G12 58 18N 6 39 E
Flemington, U.S.A. 78 E7 41 7N 77 28W
Flensburg, Germany 16 A5 54 47N 9 27 E
Flers, France 18 B3 48 47N 0 33W
Flesherton, Canada 78 B4 44 16N 80 33W
Flesko, Tanjung, Indonesia 37 D6 0 29N 124 30 E
Fleurieu Pen., Australia 63 F2 35 40S 138 5 E
Flevoland □, Neths. 15 B5 52 30N 5 30 E
Flin Flon, Canada 73 C8 54 46N 101 53W
Flinders →, Australia 62 B3 17 36S 140 36 E
Flinders B., Australia 61 F2 34 19S 115 19 E
Flinders Group, Australia 62 A3 14 11S 144 15 E
Flinders I., S. Austral., Australia 63 E1 33 44S 134 41 E
Flinders I., Tas., Australia 62 G4 40 0S 148 0 E
Flinders Ranges, Australia 63 E2 31 30S 138 30 E
Flinders Reefs, Australia 62 B4 17 37S 148 31 E
Flint, U.K. 10 D4 53 15N 3 8W
Flint, U.S.A. 76 D4 43 1N 83 41W
Flint →, U.S.A. 77 K3 30 57N 84 34W
Flint I., Kiribati 65 J12 11 26S 151 48W
Flintshire □, U.K. 10 D4 53 17N 3 17W
Flodden, U.K. 10 B5 55 37N 2 8W
Floodwood, U.S.A. 80 B8 46 55N 92 55W
Flora, U.S.A. 76 F1 38 40N 88 29W
Florala, U.S.A. 77 K2 31 0N 86 20W
Florence = Firenze, Italy 20 C4 43 46N 11 15 E
Florence, Ala., U.S.A. 77 H2 34 48N 87 41W
Florence, Ariz., U.S.A. 83 K8 33 2N 111 23W
Florence, Colo., U.S.A. 80 F2 38 23N 105 8W
Florence, Oreg., U.S.A. 82 E1 43 58N 124 7W
Florence, S.C., U.S.A. 77 H6 34 12N 79 46W
Florence, L., Australia 63 D2 28 53S 138 9 E
Florencia, Colombia 92 1 36N 75 36W
Florennes, Belgium 15 D4 50 15N 4 35 E
Florenville, Belgium 15 E5 49 40N 5 19 E
Flores, Guatemala 88 C2 16 59N 89 50W
Flores, Indonesia 37 F6 8 35S 121 0 E
Flores I., Canada 72 D3 49 20N 126 10W
Flores Sea, Indonesia 37 F6 6 30S 120 0 E
Floreşti, Moldova 17 E15 47 53N 28 17 E
Floresville, U.S.A. 81 L5 29 8N 98 10W
Floriano, Brazil 93 E10 6 50S 43 0W
Florianópolis, Brazil 95 B6 27 30S 48 30W
Florida, Cuba 88 B4 21 32N 78 14W
Florida, Uruguay 95 C4 34 7S 56 10W
Florida □, U.S.A. 77 L5 28 0N 82 0W
Florida, Straits of, U.S.A. 88 B4 25 0N 80 0W
Florida B., U.S.A. 88 B3 25 0N 80 45W
Florida Keys, U.S.A. 77 N5 24 40N 81 0W
Flórina, Greece 21 D9 40 48N 21 26 E
Florø, Norway 9 F11 61 35N 5 1 E
Flower Station, Canada 79 A8 45 10N 76 41W
Flowerpot I., Canada 78 A3 45 18N 81 38W
Floydada, U.S.A. 81 J4 33 59N 101 20W
Fluk, Indonesia 37 E7 1 42S 127 44 E
Flushing = Vlissingen, Neths. 15 C3 51 26N 3 34 E
Flying Fish, C., Antarctica 5 D15 72 6S 102 29W
Foam Lake, Canada 73 C8 51 40N 103 32W
Foça, Turkey 21 E12 38 39N 26 46 E
Focşani, Romania 17 F14 45 41N 27 15 E
Fóggia, Italy 20 D6 41 27N 15 34 E
Fogo, Canada 71 C9 49 43N 54 17W
Fogo I., Canada 71 C9 49 40N 54 5W
Föhr, Germany 16 A5 54 43N 8 30 E
Foix, France 18 E4 42 58N 1 38 E
Folda, Nord-Trøndelag, Norway 8 D14 64 32N 10 30 E
Folda, Nordland, Norway 8 C16 67 38N 14 50 E
Foley, U.S.A. 77 K2 30 24N 87 41W
Foleyet, Canada 70 C3 48 15N 82 25W
Folgefonni, Norway 9 F12 60 3N 6 23 E
Foligno, Italy 20 C5 42 57N 12 42 E
Folkestone, U.K. 11 F9 51 5N 1 12 E
Folkston, U.S.A. 77 K5 30 50N 82 0W
Follansbee, U.S.A. 78 F4 40 19N 80 35W
Folsom L., U.S.A. 84 G5 38 42N 121 9W
Fond-du-Lac, Canada 73 B7 59 19N 107 12W
Fond du Lac, U.S.A. 80 D10 43 47N 88 27W
Fond-du-Lac →, Canada 73 B7 59 17N 106 0W
Fonda, U.S.A. 79 D10 42 57N 74 22W
Fondi, Italy 20 D5 41 21N 13 25 E
Fongafale, Tuvalu 64 H9 8 31S 179 13 E
Fonsagrada = A Fonsagrada, Spain 19 A2 43 8N 7 4W
Fonseca, G. de, Cent. Amer. 88 D2 13 10N 87 40W
Fontainebleau, France 18 B5 48 24N 2 40 E
Fontana, U.S.A. 85 L9 34 6N 117 26W
Fontas →, Canada 72 B4 58 14N 121 48W
Fonte Boa, Brazil 92 D5 2 33S 66 0W
Fontenay-le-Comte, France 18 C3 46 28N 0 48W
Fontenelle Reservoir, U.S.A. 82 E8 42 1N 110 3W
Fontur, Iceland 8 C6 66 23N 14 32W
Foochow = Fuzhou, China 33 D6 26 5N 119 16 E
Foping, China 34 H5 33 41N 108 0 E
Forbes, Australia 63 E4 33 22S 148 0 E
Forbesganj, India 43 F12 26 17N 87 18 E
Ford City, Calif., U.S.A. 85 K7 35 9N 119 27W
Ford City, Pa., U.S.A. 78 F5 40 46N 79 32W
Førde, Norway 9 F11 61 27N 5 53 E
Ford's Bridge, Australia 63 D4 29 41S 145 29 E
Fordyce, U.S.A. 81 J8 33 49N 92 25W
Forel, Mt., Greenland 4 C6 66 52N 36 55W
Foremost, Canada 72 D6 49 26N 111 34W
Forest, Canada 78 C3 43 6N 82 0W
Forest, U.S.A. 81 J10 32 22N 89 29W
Forest City, Iowa, U.S.A. 80 D8 43 16N 93 39W
Forest City, N.C., U.S.A. 77 H5 35 20N 81 52W
Forest City, Pa., U.S.A. 79 E9 41 39N 75 28W
Forest Grove, U.S.A. 84 E3 45 31N 123 7W
Forestburg, Canada 72 C6 52 35N 112 1W
Foresthill, U.S.A. 84 F6 39 1N 120 49W
Forestier Pen., Australia 62 G4 43 0S 148 0 E
Forestville, Canada 71 C6 48 48N 69 2W
Forestville, Calif., U.S.A. 84 G4 38 28N 122 54W
Forestville, N.Y., U.S.A. 78 D5 42 28N 79 10W
Forfar, U.K. 12 E6 56 39N 2 53W
Forks, U.S.A. 84 C2 47 57N 124 23W
Forksville, U.S.A. 79 E8 41 29N 76 35W
Forlì, Italy 20 B5 44 13N 12 3 E
Forman, U.S.A. 80 B6 46 7N 97 38W
Formby Pt., U.K. 10 D4 53 33N 3 6W
Formentera, Spain 22 C7 38 43N 1 27 E
Formentor, C. de, Spain 22 B10 39 58N 3 13 E
Former Yugoslav Republic of Macedonia = Macedonia ■, Europe 21 D9 41 53N 21 40 E
Fórmia, Italy 20 D5 41 15N 13 37 E
Formosa = Taiwan ■, Asia 33 D7 23 30N 121 0 E
Formosa, Argentina 94 B4 26 15S 58 10W
Formosa, Brazil 93 G9 15 32S 47 20W
Formosa □, Argentina 94 B4 25 0S 60 0W
Formosa, Serra, Brazil 93 F8 12 0S 55 0W
Formosa Bay, Kenya 54 C5 2 40S 40 20 E
Fornells, Spain 22 A11 40 3N 4 7 E
Føroyar, Atl. Oc. 8 F9 62 0N 7 0W
Forres, U.K. 12 D5 57 37N 3 37W
Forrest, Australia 61 F4 30 51S 128 6 E
Forrest, Mt., Australia 61 D4 24 48S 127 45 E
Forrest City, U.S.A. 81 H9 35 1N 90 47W
Forsayth, Australia 62 B3 18 33S 143 34 E
Forssa, Finland 9 F20 60 49N 23 38 E
Forst, Germany 16 C8 51 45N 14 37 E
Forsyth, U.S.A. 82 C10 46 16N 106 41W
Fort Abbas, Pakistan 42 E5 29 12N 72 52 E
Fort Albany, Canada 70 B3 52 15N 81 35W
Fort Ann, U.S.A. 79 C11 43 25N 73 30W
Fort Assiniboine, Canada 72 C6 54 20N 114 45W
Fort Augustus, U.K. 12 D4 57 9N 4 42W
Fort Beaufort, S. Africa 56 E4 32 46S 26 40 E
Fort Benton, U.S.A. 82 C8 47 49N 110 40W
Fort Bragg, U.S.A. 82 G2 39 26N 123 48W
Fort Bridger, U.S.A. 82 F8 41 19N 110 23W
Fort Chipewyan, Canada 73 B6 58 42N 111 8W
Fort Collins, U.S.A. 80 E2 40 35N 105 5W
Fort-Coulonge, Canada 70 C4 45 50N 76 45W
Fort Covington, U.S.A. 79 B10 44 59N 74 29W
Fort Davis, U.S.A. 81 K3 30 35N 103 54W
Fort-de-France, Martinique 89 D7 14 36N 61 2W
Fort Defiance, U.S.A. 83 J9 35 45N 109 5W
Fort Dodge, U.S.A. 80 D7 42 30N 94 11W
Fort Edward, U.S.A. 79 C11 43 16N 73 35W
Fort Erie, Canada 78 D6 42 54N 78 56W
Fort Fairfield, U.S.A. 77 B12 46 46N 67 50W
Fort Frances, Canada 73 D10 48 36N 93 24W
Fort Garland, U.S.A. 83 H11 37 26N 105 26W
Fort George = Chisasibi, Canada 70 B4 53 50N 79 0W
Fort Good-Hope, Canada 68 B7 66 14N 128 40W
Fort Hancock, U.S.A. 83 L11 31 18N 105 51W
Fort Hertz = Putao, Burma 41 F20 27 28N 97 30 E
Fort Hope, Canada 70 B2 51 30N 88 0W
Fort Irwin, U.S.A. 85 K10 35 16N 116 34W
Fort Jameson = Chipata, Zambia 55 E3 13 38S 32 28 E
Fort Kent, U.S.A. 77 B11 47 15N 68 36W
Fort Klamath, U.S.A. 82 E3 42 42N 122 0W
Fort-Lamy = Ndjamena, Chad 51 F8 12 10N 14 59 E
Fort Laramie, U.S.A. 80 D2 42 13N 104 31W
Fort Lauderdale, U.S.A. 77 M5 26 7N 80 8W
Fort Liard, Canada 72 A4 60 14N 123 30W
Fort Liberté, Haiti 89 C5 19 42N 71 51W
Fort Lupton, U.S.A. 80 E2 40 5N 104 49W
Fort Mackay, Canada 72 B6 57 12N 111 41W
Fort Macleod, Canada 72 D6 49 45N 113 30W
Fort McMurray, Canada 72 B6 56 44N 111 7W
Fort McPherson, Canada 68 B6 67 30N 134 55W
Fort Madison, U.S.A. 80 E9 40 38N 91 27W
Fort Meade, U.S.A. 77 M5 27 45N 81 48W
Fort Morgan, U.S.A. 80 E3 40 15N 103 48W
Fort Munro, Pakistan 42 E3 29 54N 69 58 E
Fort Myers, U.S.A. 77 M5 26 39N 81 52W
Fort Nelson, Canada 72 B4 58 50N 122 44W
Fort Nelson →, Canada 72 B4 59 32N 124 0W
Fort Norman = Tulita, Canada 68 B7 64 57N 125 30W
Fort Payne, U.S.A. 77 H3 34 26N 85 43W
Fort Peck, U.S.A. 82 B10 48 1N 106 27W
Fort Peck Dam, U.S.A. 82 C10 48 0N 106 26W
Fort Peck L., U.S.A. 82 C10 48 0N 106 26W
Fort Pierce, U.S.A. 77 M5 27 27N 80 20W
Fort Pierre, U.S.A. 80 C4 44 21N 100 22W
Fort Plain, U.S.A. 79 D10 42 56N 74 37W
Fort Portal, Uganda 54 B3 0 40N 30 20 E
Fort Providence, Canada 72 A5 61 3N 117 40W
Fort Qu'Appelle, Canada 73 C8 50 45N 103 50W
Fort Resolution, Canada 72 A6 61 10N 113 40W
Fort Rixon, Zimbabwe 55 G2 20 2S 29 17 E
Fort Rosebery = Mansa, Zambia 55 E2 11 13S 28 55 E
Fort Ross, U.S.A. 84 G3 38 32N 123 13W
Fort Rousset = Owando, Congo 52 E3 0 29S 15 55 E
Fort Rupert = Waskaganish, Canada 70 B4 51 30N 78 40W
Fort St. James, Canada 72 C4 54 30N 124 10W
Fort St. John, Canada 72 B4 56 15N 120 50W
Fort Sandeman = Zhob, Pakistan 42 D3 31 20N 69 31 E
Fort Saskatchewan, Canada 72 C6 53 40N 113 15W
Fort Scott, U.S.A. 81 G7 37 50N 94 42W
Fort Severn, Canada 70 A2 56 0N 87 40W
Fort Shevchenko, Kazakstan 25 F9 44 35N 50 23 E
Fort Simpson, Canada 72 A4 61 45N 121 15W
Fort Smith, Canada 72 B6 60 0N 111 51W
Fort Smith, U.S.A. 81 H7 35 23N 94 25W
Fort Stockton, U.S.A. 81 K3 30 53N 102 53W
Fort Sumner, U.S.A. 81 H2 34 28N 104 15W
Fort Thompson, U.S.A. 80 C5 44 3N 99 26W
Fort Trinquet = Bir Mogreïn, Mauritania 50 C3 25 10N 11 25W
Fort Valley, U.S.A. 77 J4 32 33N 83 53W
Fort Vermilion, Canada 72 B5 58 24N 116 0W
Fort Walton Beach, U.S.A. 77 K2 30 25N 86 36W
Fort Wayne, U.S.A. 76 E3 41 4N 85 9W
Fort William, U.K. 12 E3 56 49N 5 7W
Fort Worth, U.S.A. 81 J6 32 45N 97 18W
Fort Yates, U.S.A. 80 B4 46 5N 100 38W
Fort Yukon, U.S.A. 68 B5 66 34N 145 16W
Fortaleza, Brazil 93 D11 3 45S 38 35W
Forteau, Canada 71 B8 51 28N 56 58W
Fortescue →, Australia 60 D2 21 0S 116 4 E
Forth →, U.K. 12 E5 56 9N 3 50W
Forth, Firth of, U.K. 12 E6 56 5N 2 55W
Fortrose, U.K. 12 D4 57 35N 4 9W
Fortuna, Calif., U.S.A. 82 F1 40 36N 124 9W
Fortuna, N. Dak., U.S.A. 80 A3 48 55N 103 47W
Fortune, Canada 71 C8 47 4N 55 50W
Fortune B., Canada 71 C8 47 30N 55 22W
Forūr, Iran 45 E7 26 17N 54 32 E
Foshan, China 33 D6 23 4N 113 5 E
Fosna, Norway 8 E14 63 50N 10 20 E
Fosnavåg, Norway 9 E11 62 22N 5 38 E
Fossano, Italy 18 D7 44 33N 7 43 E
Fossil, U.S.A. 82 D3 45 0N 120 9W
Foster, Australia 63 F4 38 40S 146 15 E
Foster, Canada 79 A12 45 17N 72 30W
Foster →, Canada 73 B7 55 47N 105 49W
Fosters Ra., Australia 62 C1 21 35S 133 48 E
Fostoria, U.S.A. 76 E4 41 10N 83 25W
Fougères, France 18 B3 48 21N 1 14W
Foul Pt., Sri Lanka 40 Q12 8 35N 81 18 E
Foula, U.K. 12 A6 60 10N 2 5W
Foulness I., U.K. 11 F8 51 36N 0 55 E
Foulpointe, Madag. 57 B8 17 41S 49 31 E
Foulweather, C., U.S.A. 74 B2 44 50N 124 5W
Foumban, Cameroon 52 C2 5 45N 10 50 E
Fountain, U.S.A. 80 F2 38 41N 104 42W
Fountain Springs, U.S.A. 85 K8 35 54N 118 51W
Fouriesburg, S. Africa 56 D4 28 38S 28 14 E
Foúrnoi, Greece 21 F12 37 36N 26 32 E
Fourth Cataract, Sudan 51 E12 18 47N 32 3 E
Fouta Djalon, Guinea 50 F3 11 20N 12 10W
Foux, Cap-à-, Haiti 89 C5 19 43N 73 27W
Foveaux Str., N.Z. 59 M2 46 42S 168 10 E
Fowey, U.K. 11 G3 50 20N 4 39W
Fowler, Calif., U.S.A. 84 J7 36 38N 119 41W
Fowler, Colo., U.S.A. 80 F3 38 8N 104 2W
Fowlers B., Australia 61 F5 31 59S 132 34 E
Fowman, Iran 45 B6 37 13N 49 19 E
Fox →, Canada 73 B10 56 3N 93 18W
Fox Creek, Canada 72 C5 54 24N 116 48W
Fox Lake, Canada 72 B6 58 28N 114 31W
Fox Valley, Canada 73 C7 50 30N 109 25W
Foxboro, U.S.A. 79 D13 42 4N 71 16W
Foxe Basin, Canada 69 B12 66 0N 77 0W
Foxe Chan., Canada 69 B12 65 0N 80 0W
Foxe Pen., Canada 69 B12 65 0N 76 0W
Foxton, N.Z. 59 J5 40 29S 175 18 E
Foyle, Lough, U.K. 13 A4 55 7N 7 4W
Foynes, Ireland 13 D2 52 37N 9 7W
Fóz do Cunene, Angola 56 B1 17 15S 11 48 E
Foz do Iguaçu, Brazil 95 B5 25 30S 54 30W
Frackville, U.S.A. 79 F8 40 47N 76 14W
Fraile Muerto, Uruguay 95 C5 32 31S 54 32W
Framingham, U.S.A. 79 D13 42 17N 71 25W
Franca, Brazil 93 H9 20 33S 47 30W
Francavilla Fontana, Italy 21 D7 40 32N 17 35 E
France ■, Europe 18 C5 47 0N 3 0 E
Frances, Australia 63 F3 36 41S 140 55 E
Frances →, Canada 72 A3 60 16N 129 10W
Frances L., Canada 72 A3 61 23N 129 30W
Franceville, Gabon 52 E2 1 40S 13 32 E
Franche-Comté, France 18 C6 46 50N 5 55 E
Francis Case, L., U.S.A. 80 D5 43 4N 98 34W
Francisco Beltrão, Brazil 95 B5 26 5S 53 4W
Francisco I. Madero, Coahuila, Mexico 86 B4 25 48N 103 18W
Francisco I. Madero, Durango, Mexico 86 C4 24 32N 104 22W
Francistown, Botswana 57 C4 21 7S 27 33 E
François, Canada 71 C8 47 35N 56 45W
François L., Canada 72 C3 54 0N 125 30W
Franeker, Neths. 15 A5 53 12N 5 33 E
Frankford, Canada 78 B7 44 12N 77 36W
Frankfort, S. Africa 57 D4 27 17S 28 30 E
Frankfort, Ind., U.S.A. 76 E2 40 17N 86 31W
Frankfort, Kans., U.S.A. 80 F6 39 42N 96 25W
Frankfort, Ky., U.S.A. 76 F3 38 12N 84 52W
Frankfort, N.Y., U.S.A. 79 C9 43 2N 75 4W

Gatton

Frankfurt, Brandenburg, Germany 16 B8 52 20N 14 32 E
Frankfurt, Hessen, Germany 16 C5 50 7N 8 41 E
Fränkische Alb, Germany 16 D6 49 10N 11 23 E
Frankland →, Australia 61 G2 35 0S 116 48 E
Franklin, Ky., U.S.A. 77 G2 36 43N 86 35W
Franklin, La., U.S.A. 81 L9 29 48N 91 30W
Franklin, Mass., U.S.A. 79 D13 42 5N 71 24W
Franklin, N.H., U.S.A. 79 C13 43 27N 71 39W
Franklin, Nebr., U.S.A. 80 E5 40 6N 98 57W
Franklin, Pa., U.S.A. 78 E5 41 24N 79 50W
Franklin, Va., U.S.A. 77 G7 36 41N 76 56W
Franklin, W. Va., U.S.A. 76 F6 38 39N 79 20W
Franklin B., Canada 68 B7 69 45N 126 0W
Franklin D. Roosevelt L., U.S.A. 82 B4 48 18N 118 9W
Franklin I., Antarctica 5 D11 76 10S 168 30 E
Franklin L., U.S.A. 82 F6 40 25N 115 22W
Franklin Mts., Canada 68 B7 65 0N 125 0W
Franklin Str., Canada 68 A10 72 0N 96 0W
Franklinton, U.S.A. 81 K9 30 51N 90 9W
Franklinville, U.S.A. 78 D6 42 20N 78 27W
Franks Pk., U.S.A. 82 E9 43 58N 109 18W
Frankston, Australia 63 F4 38 8S 145 8 E
Frantsa Iosifa, Zemlya, Russia 26 A6 82 0N 55 0 E
Franz, Canada 70 C3 48 25N 84 30W
Franz Josef Land = Frantsa Iosifa, Zemlya, Russia 26 A6 82 0N 55 0 E
Fraser, U.S.A. 78 D2 42 32N 82 57W
Fraser →, B.C., Canada 72 D4 49 7N 123 11W
Fraser →, Nfld., Canada 71 A7 56 39N 62 10W
Fraser, Mt., Australia 61 E2 25 35S 118 20 E
Fraser I., Australia 63 D5 25 15S 153 10 E
Fraser Lake, Canada 72 C4 54 0N 124 50W
Fraserburg, S. Africa 56 E3 31 55S 21 30 E
Fraserburgh, U.K. 12 D6 57 42N 2 1W
Fraserdale, Canada 70 C3 49 55N 81 37W
Fray Bentos, Uruguay 94 C4 33 10S 58 15W
Fredericia, Denmark 9 J13 55 34N 9 45 E
Frederick, Md., U.S.A. 76 F7 39 25N 77 25W
Frederick, Okla., U.S.A. 81 H5 34 23N 99 1W
Frederick, S. Dak., U.S.A. 80 C5 45 50N 98 31W
Fredericksburg, Pa., U.S.A. 79 F8 40 27N 76 26W
Fredericksburg, Tex., U.S.A. 81 K5 30 16N 98 52W
Fredericksburg, Va., U.S.A. 76 F7 38 18N 77 28W
Fredericktown, Mo., U.S.A. 81 G9 37 34N 90 18W
Fredericktown, Ohio, U.S.A. 78 F2 40 29N 82 33W
Frederico I. Madero, Presa, Mexico 86 B3 28 7N 105 40W
Frederico Westphalen, Brazil 95 B5 27 22S 53 24W
Fredericton, Canada 71 C6 45 57N 66 40W
Fredericton Junction, Canada 71 C6 45 41N 66 40W
Frederikshåb, Greenland 4 C5 62 0N 49 43W
Frederikshavn, Denmark 9 H14 57 28N 10 31 E
Frederiksted, Virgin Is. 89 C7 17 43N 64 53W
Fredonia, Ariz., U.S.A. 83 H7 36 57N 112 32W
Fredonia, Kans., U.S.A. 81 G7 37 32N 95 49W
Fredonia, N.Y., U.S.A. 78 D5 42 26N 79 20W
Fredrikstad, Norway 9 G14 59 13N 10 57 E
Free State □, S. Africa 56 D4 28 30S 27 0 E
Freehold, U.S.A. 79 F10 40 16N 74 17W
Freel Peak, U.S.A. 84 G7 38 52N 119 54W
Freeland, U.S.A. 79 E9 41 1N 75 54W
Freels, C., Canada 71 C9 49 15N 53 30W
Freeman, Calif., U.S.A. 85 K9 35 35N 117 53W
Freeman, S. Dak., U.S.A. 80 D6 43 21N 97 26W
Freeport, Bahamas 88 A4 26 30N 78 47W
Freeport, Ill., U.S.A. 80 D10 42 17N 89 36W
Freeport, N.Y., U.S.A. 79 F11 40 39N 73 35W
Freeport, Ohio, U.S.A. 78 F3 40 12N 81 15W
Freeport, Pa., U.S.A. 78 F5 40 41N 79 41W
Freeport, Tex., U.S.A. 81 L7 28 57N 95 21W
Freetown, S. Leone 50 G3 8 30N 13 17W
Frégate, L., Canada 70 B5 53 15N 74 45W
Fregenal de la Sierra, Spain 19 C2 38 10N 6 39W
Freibourg = Fribourg, Switz. 18 C7 46 49N 7 9 E
Freiburg, Germany 16 E4 47 59N 7 51 E
Freire, Chile 96 D2 38 54S 72 38W
Freirina, Chile 94 B1 28 30S 71 10W
Freising, Germany 16 D6 48 24N 11 45 E
Freistadt, Austria 16 D8 48 30N 14 30 E
Fréjus, France 18 E7 43 25N 6 44 E
Fremantle, Australia 61 F2 32 7S 115 47 E
Fremont, Calif., U.S.A. 84 H4 37 32N 121 57W
Fremont, Mich., U.S.A. 76 D3 43 28N 85 57W
Fremont, Nebr., U.S.A. 80 E6 41 26N 96 30W
Fremont, Ohio, U.S.A. 76 E4 41 21N 83 7W
Fremont →, U.S.A. 83 G8 38 24N 110 42W
French Camp, U.S.A. 84 H5 37 53N 121 16W
French Creek →, U.S.A. 78 E5 41 24N 79 50W
French Guiana ■, S. Amer. 93 C8 4 0N 53 0W
French Pass, N.Z. 59 J4 40 55S 173 55 E
French Polynesia ■, Pac. Oc. 65 K13 20 0S 145 0W
Frenchman Cr. →, N. Amer. 82 B10 48 31N 107 10W
Frenchman Cr. →, U.S.A. 80 E4 40 14N 100 50W
Fresco →, Brazil 93 E8 7 15S 51 30W
Freshfield, C., Antarctica 5 C10 68 25S 151 10 E
Fresnillo, Mexico 86 C4 23 10N 103 0W
Fresno, U.S.A. 84 J7 36 44N 119 47W
Fresno Reservoir, U.S.A. 82 B9 48 36N 109 57W
Frew →, Australia 62 C2 20 0S 135 38 E
Frewsburg, U.S.A. 78 D5 42 3N 79 10W
Freycinet Pen., Australia 62 G4 42 10S 148 25 E
Fria, C., Namibia 56 B1 18 0S 12 0 E
Friant, U.S.A. 84 J7 36 59N 119 43W
Frías, Argentina 94 B2 28 40S 65 5W
Fribourg, Switz. 18 C7 46 49N 7 9 E
Friday Harbor, U.S.A. 84 B3 48 32N 123 1W
Friedens, U.S.A. 78 F6 40 3N 78 59W
Friedrichshafen, Germany 16 E5 47 39N 9 30 E
Friendly Is. = Tonga ■, Pac. Oc. 59 D11 19 50S 174 30W
Friendship, U.S.A. 78 D6 42 12N 78 8W
Friesland □, Neths. 15 A5 53 5N 5 50 E
Frio →, U.S.A. 81 L5 28 26N 98 11W
Frio, C., Brazil 90 F6 22 50S 41 50W
Friona, U.S.A. 81 H3 34 38N 102 43W
Fritch, U.S.A. 81 H4 35 38N 101 36W
Frobisher B., Canada 69 B13 62 30N 66 0W
Frobisher Bay = Iqaluit, Canada 69 B13 63 44N 68 31W
Frobisher L., Canada 73 B7 56 20N 108 15W
Frohavet, Norway 8 E13 64 0N 9 30 E
Frome, U.K. 11 F5 51 14N 2 19W
Frome →, U.K. 11 G5 50 41N 2 6W
Frome, L., Australia 63 E2 30 45S 139 45 E
Front Range, U.S.A. 74 C5 40 25N 105 45W
Front Royal, U.S.A. 76 F6 38 55N 78 12W
Frontera, Canary Is. 22 G2 27 47N 17 59W
Frontera, Mexico 87 D6 18 30N 92 40W
Fronteras, Mexico 86 A3 30 56N 109 31W
Frosinone, Italy 20 D5 41 38N 13 19 E
Frostburg, U.S.A. 76 F6 39 39N 78 56W
Frostisen, Norway 8 B17 68 14N 17 10 E
Frøya, Norway 8 E13 63 43N 8 40 E
Frunze = Bishkek, Kyrgyzstan 26 E8 42 54N 74 46 E
Frutal, Brazil 93 H9 20 0S 49 0W
Frýdek-Místek, Czech Rep. 17 D10 49 40N 18 20 E
Fryeburg, U.S.A. 79 B14 44 1N 70 59W
Fu Xian = Wafangdian, China 35 E11 39 38N 121 58 E
Fu Xian, China 34 G5 36 0N 109 20 E
Fucheng, China 34 F9 37 50N 116 10 E
Fuchou = Fuzhou, China 33 D6 26 5N 119 16 E
Fuchū, Japan 31 G6 34 34N 133 14 E
Fuencaliente, Canary Is. 22 F2 28 28N 17 50W
Fuencaliente, Pta., Canary Is. 22 F2 28 27N 17 51W
Fuengirola, Spain 19 D3 36 32N 4 41W
Fuentes de Oñoro, Spain 19 B2 40 33N 6 52W
Fuerte →, Mexico 86 B3 25 50N 109 25W
Fuerte Olimpo, Paraguay 94 A4 21 0S 57 51W
Fuerteventura, Canary Is. 22 F6 28 30N 14 0W
Fufeng, China 34 G5 34 22N 108 0 E
Fugou, China 34 G8 34 3N 114 25 E
Fugu, China 34 E6 39 2N 111 3 E
Fuhai, China 32 B3 47 2N 87 25 E
Fuhaymī, Iraq 44 C4 34 16N 42 10 E
Fuji, Japan 31 G9 35 9N 138 39 E
Fuji-San, Japan 31 G9 35 22N 138 44 E
Fuji-yoshida, Japan 31 G9 35 30N 138 46 E
Fujian □, China 33 D6 26 0N 118 0 E
Fujinomiya, Japan 31 G9 35 10N 138 40 E
Fujisawa, Japan 31 G9 35 22N 139 29 E
Fujiyama, Mt. = Fuji-San, Japan 31 G9 35 22N 138 44 E
Fukien = Fujian □, China 33 D6 26 0N 118 0 E
Fukuchiyama, Japan 31 G7 35 19N 135 9 E
Fukue-Shima, Japan 31 H4 32 40N 128 45 E
Fukui, Japan 31 F8 36 5N 136 10 E
Fukui □, Japan 31 G8 36 0N 136 12 E
Fukuoka, Japan 31 H5 33 39N 130 21 E
Fukuoka □, Japan 31 H5 33 30N 131 0 E
Fukushima, Japan 30 F10 37 44N 140 28 E
Fukushima □, Japan 30 F10 37 30N 140 15 E
Fukuyama, Japan 31 G6 34 35N 133 20 E
Fulda, Germany 16 C5 50 32N 9 40 E
Fulda →, Germany 16 C5 51 25N 9 39 E
Fulford Harbour, Canada 84 B3 48 47N 123 27W
Fullerton, Calif., U.S.A. 85 M9 33 53N 117 56W
Fullerton, Nebr., U.S.A. 80 E6 41 22N 97 58W
Fulongquan, China 35 B13 44 20N 124 42 E
Fulton, Mo., U.S.A. 80 F9 38 52N 91 57W
Fulton, N.Y., U.S.A. 79 C8 43 19N 76 25W
Funabashi, Japan 31 G10 35 45N 140 0 E
Funchal, Madeira 22 D3 32 38N 16 54W
Fundación, Colombia 92 A4 10 31N 74 11W
Fundão, Portugal 19 B2 40 8N 7 30W
Fundy, B. of, Canada 71 D6 45 0N 66 0W
Funing, Hebei, China 35 E10 39 53N 119 12 E
Funing, Jiangsu, China 35 H10 33 45N 119 50 E
Funiu Shan, China 34 H7 33 30N 112 20 E
Funtua, Nigeria 50 F7 11 30N 7 18 E
Fuping, Hebei, China 34 E8 38 48N 114 12 E
Fuping, Shaanxi, China 34 G5 34 42N 109 10 E
Furano, Japan 30 C11 43 21N 142 23 E
Furāt, Nahr al →, Asia 44 D5 31 0N 47 25 E
Fūrg, Iran 45 D7 28 18N 55 13 E
Furnás, Spain 22 B8 39 3N 1 32 E
Furnas, Reprêsa de, Brazil 95 A6 20 50S 45 30W
Furneaux Group, Australia 62 G4 40 10S 147 50 E
Furqlus, Syria 47 A6 34 36N 37 8 E
Fürstenwalde, Germany 16 B8 52 22N 14 3 E
Fürth, Germany 16 D6 49 28N 10 59 E
Furukawa, Japan 30 E10 38 34N 140 58 E
Fury and Hecla Str., Canada 69 B11 69 56N 84 0W
Fusagasuga, Colombia 92 C4 4 21N 74 22W
Fushan, Shandong, China 35 F11 37 30N 121 15 E
Fushan, Shanxi, China 34 G6 35 58N 111 51 E
Fushun, China 35 D12 41 50N 123 56 E
Fusong, China 35 C14 42 20N 127 15 E
Futuna, Wall. & F. Is. 59 B8 14 25S 178 20 E
Fuxin, China 35 C11 42 5N 121 48 E
Fuyang, China 34 H8 33 0N 115 48 E
Fuyang He →, China 34 E9 38 12N 117 0 E
Fuyu, China 35 B13 45 12N 124 43 E
Fuzhou, China 33 D6 26 5N 119 16 E
Fylde, U.K. 10 D5 53 50N 2 58W
Fyn, Denmark 9 J14 55 20N 10 30 E
Fyne, L., U.K. 12 F3 55 59N 5 23W

G

Gabela, Angola 52 G2 11 0S 14 24 E
Gabès, Tunisia 51 B8 33 53N 10 2 E
Gabès, G. de, Tunisia 51 B8 34 0N 10 30 E
Gabon ■, Africa 52 E2 0 10S 10 0 E
Gaborone, Botswana 56 C4 24 45S 25 57 E
Gabriels, U.S.A. 79 B10 44 26N 74 12W
Gābrīk, Iran 45 E8 25 44N 58 28 E
Gabrovo, Bulgaria 21 C11 42 52N 25 19 E
Gāch Sār, Iran 45 B6 36 7N 51 19 E
Gachsārān, Iran 45 D6 30 15N 50 45 E
Gadag, India 40 M9 15 30N 75 45 E
Gadap, Pakistan 42 G2 25 5N 67 28 E
Gadarwara, India 43 H8 22 50N 78 50 E
Gadhada, India 42 J4 22 0N 71 35 E
Gadra, Pakistan 42 G4 25 40N 70 38 E
Gadsden, U.S.A. 77 H3 34 1N 86 1W
Gadwal, India 40 L10 16 10N 77 50 E
Gaffney, U.S.A. 77 H5 35 5N 81 39W
Gafsa, Tunisia 50 B7 34 24N 8 43 E
Gagaria, India 42 G4 25 43N 70 46 E
Gagnoa, Ivory C. 50 G4 6 56N 5 16W
Gagnon, Canada 71 B6 51 50N 68 5W
Gagnon, L., Canada 73 A6 62 3N 110 27W
Gahini, Rwanda 54 C3 1 50S 30 30 E
Gahmar, India 43 G10 25 27N 83 49 E
Gai Xian = Gaizhou, China 35 D12 40 22N 122 20 E
Gaïdhouronísi, Greece 23 E7 34 53N 25 41 E
Gail, U.S.A. 81 J4 32 46N 101 27W
Gaillimh = Galway, Ireland 13 C2 53 17N 9 3W
Gaines, U.S.A. 78 E7 41 46N 77 35W
Gainesville, Fla., U.S.A. 77 L4 29 40N 82 20W
Gainesville, Ga., U.S.A. 77 H4 34 18N 83 50W
Gainesville, Mo., U.S.A. 81 G8 36 36N 92 26W
Gainesville, Tex., U.S.A. 81 J6 33 38N 97 8W
Gainsborough, U.K. 10 D7 53 24N 0 46W
Gairdner, L., Australia 63 E2 31 30S 136 0 E
Gairloch, L., U.K. 12 D3 57 43N 5 45W
Gaizhou, China 35 D12 40 22N 122 20 E
Gaj →, Pakistan 42 F2 26 26N 67 21 E
Gakuch, Pakistan 43 A5 36 7N 73 45 E
Galán, Cerro, Argentina 94 B2 25 55S 66 52W
Galana →, Kenya 54 C5 3 9S 40 8 E
Galápagos, Pac. Oc. 90 D1 0 0 91 0W
Galashiels, U.K. 12 F6 55 37N 2 49W
Galaţi, Romania 17 F15 45 27N 28 2 E
Galatina, Italy 21 D8 40 10N 18 10 E
Galax, U.S.A. 77 G5 36 40N 80 56W
Galcaio, Somali Rep. 46 F4 6 30N 47 30 E
Galdhøpiggen, Norway 9 F12 61 38N 8 18 E
Galeana, Mexico 86 C4 24 50N 100 4W
Galeana, Nuevo León, Mexico 86 A3 24 50N 100 4W
Galela, Indonesia 37 D7 1 50N 127 49 E
Galena, U.S.A. 68 B4 64 44N 156 56W
Galera Point, Trin. & Tob. 89 D7 10 8N 61 0W
Galesburg, U.S.A. 80 E9 40 57N 90 22W
Galeton, U.S.A. 78 E7 41 44N 77 39W
Galich, Russia 24 C7 58 22N 42 24 E
Galicia □, Spain 19 A2 42 43N 7 45W
Galilee = Hagalil, Israel 47 C4 32 53N 35 18 E
Galilee, L., Australia 62 C4 22 20S 145 50 E
Galilee, Sea of = Yam Kinneret, Israel 47 C4 32 45N 35 35 E
Galinoporni, Cyprus 23 D13 35 31N 34 18 E
Galion, U.S.A. 78 F2 40 44N 82 47W
Galiuro Mts., U.S.A. 83 K8 32 30N 110 20W
Galiwinku, Australia 62 A2 12 2S 135 34 E
Gallan Hd., U.K. 12 C1 58 15N 7 2W
Gallatin, U.S.A. 77 G2 36 24N 86 27W
Galle, Sri Lanka 40 R12 6 5N 80 10 E
Gállego →, Spain 19 B5 41 39N 0 51W
Gallegos →, Argentina 96 G3 51 35S 69 0W
Galley Hd., Ireland 13 E3 51 32N 8 55W
Gallinas, Pta., Colombia 92 A4 12 28N 71 40W
Gallipoli = Gelibolu, Turkey 21 D12 40 28N 26 43 E
Gallipoli, Italy 21 D8 40 3N 17 58 E
Gallipolis, U.S.A. 76 F4 38 49N 82 12W
Gällivare, Sweden 8 C19 67 9N 20 40 E
Galloo I., U.S.A. 79 C8 43 55N 76 25W
Galloway, U.K. 12 F4 55 1N 4 29W
Galloway, Mull of, U.K. 12 G4 54 39N 4 52W
Gallup, U.S.A. 83 J9 35 32N 108 45W
Galoya, Sri Lanka 40 Q12 8 10N 80 55 E
Galt, U.S.A. 84 G5 38 15N 121 18W
Galty Mts., Ireland 13 D3 52 22N 8 10W
Galtymore, Ireland 13 D3 52 21N 8 11W
Galva, U.S.A. 80 E9 41 10N 90 3W
Galveston, U.S.A. 81 L7 29 18N 94 48W
Galveston B., U.S.A. 81 L7 29 36N 94 50W
Gálvez, Argentina 94 C3 32 0S 61 14W
Galway, Ireland 13 C2 53 17N 9 3W
Galway □, Ireland 13 C2 53 22N 9 1W
Galway B., Ireland 13 C2 53 13N 9 10W
Gam →, Vietnam 38 B5 21 55N 105 12 E
Gamagori, Japan 31 G8 34 50N 137 14 E
Gambat, Pakistan 42 F3 27 17N 68 26 E
Gambhir →, India 42 F6 26 58N 77 27 E
Gambia ■, W. Afr. 50 F2 13 25N 16 0W
Gambia →, W. Afr. 50 F2 13 28N 16 34W
Gambier, U.S.A. 78 F2 40 22N 82 23W
Gambier, C., Australia 60 B5 11 56S 130 57 E
Gambier Is., Australia 63 F2 35 3S 136 30 E
Gambo, Canada 71 C9 48 47N 54 13W
Gamboli, Pakistan 42 E3 29 53N 68 24 E
Gamboma, Congo 52 E3 1 55S 15 52 E
Gamlakarleby = Kokkola, Finland 8 E20 63 50N 23 8 E
Gammon →, Canada 73 C9 51 24N 95 44W
Gan Jiang →, China 33 D6 29 15N 116 0 E
Ganado, U.S.A. 83 J9 35 43N 109 33W
Gananoque, Canada 79 B8 44 20N 76 10W
Ganāveh, Iran 45 D6 29 35N 50 35 E
Gäncä, Azerbaijan 25 F8 40 45N 46 20 E
Gancheng, China 38 C7 18 51N 108 37 E
Gand = Gent, Belgium 15 C3 51 2N 3 42 E
Ganda, Angola 53 G2 13 3S 14 35 E
Gandajika, Dem. Rep. of the Congo 52 F4 6 45S 23 57 E
Gandak →, India 43 G11 25 39N 85 13 E
Gandava, Pakistan 42 E2 28 32N 67 32 E
Gander, Canada 71 C9 48 58N 54 35W
Gander L., Canada 71 C9 48 58N 54 35W
Ganderowe Falls, Zimbabwe 55 F2 17 20S 29 10 E
Gandhi Sagar, India 42 G6 24 40N 75 40 E
Gandhinagar, India 42 H5 23 15N 72 45 E
Gandía, Spain 19 C5 38 58N 0 9W
Gando, Pta., Canary Is. 22 G4 27 55N 15 22W
Ganedidalem = Gani, Indonesia 37 E7 0 48S 128 14 E
Ganga →, India 43 H14 23 20N 90 30 E
Ganga Sagar, India 43 J13 21 38N 88 5 E
Gangan →, India 43 E8 28 38N 78 58 E
Ganganagar, India 42 E5 29 56N 73 56 E
Gangapur, India 42 F7 26 32N 76 49 E
Gangaw, Burma 41 H19 22 5N 94 5 E
Gangdisê Shan, China 41 D12 31 20N 81 0 E
Ganges = Ganga →, India 43 H14 23 20N 90 30 E
Ganges, Canada 72 D4 48 51N 123 31W
Ganges, Mouths of the, India 43 J14 21 30N 90 0 E
Gangoh, India 42 E7 29 46N 77 18 E
Gangroti, India 43 D8 30 50N 79 10 E
Gangtok, India 41 F16 27 20N 88 37 E
Gangu, China 34 G3 34 40N 105 15 E
Gangyao, China 35 B14 44 12N 126 37 E
Gani, Indonesia 37 E7 0 48S 128 14 E
Ganj, India 43 F8 27 45N 78 57 E
Gannett Peak, U.S.A. 82 E9 43 11N 109 39W
Ganquan, China 34 F5 36 20N 109 20 E
Gansu □, China 34 G3 36 0N 104 0 E
Ganta, Liberia 50 G4 7 15N 8 59W
Gantheaume, C., Australia 63 F2 36 4S 137 32 E
Gantheaume B., Australia 61 E1 27 40S 114 10 E
Gantsevichi = Hantsavichy, Belarus 17 B14 52 49N 26 30 E
Ganyem = Genyem, Indonesia 37 E10 2 46S 140 12 E
Ganyu, China 35 G10 34 50N 119 8 E
Ganzhou, China 33 D6 25 51N 114 56 E
Gao, Mali 50 E5 16 15N 0 5W
Gaomi, China 35 F10 36 20N 119 42 E
Gaoping, China 34 G7 35 45N 112 55 E
Gaotang, China 34 F9 36 50N 116 15 E
Gaoua, Burkina Faso 50 F5 10 20N 3 8W
Gaoual, Guinea 50 F3 11 45N 13 25W
Gaoxiong = Kaohsiung, Taiwan 33 D7 22 35N 120 16 E
Gaoyang, China 34 E8 38 40N 115 45 E
Gaoyou Hu, China 35 H10 32 45N 119 20 E
Gaoyuan, China 35 F9 37 8N 117 58 E
Gap, France 18 D7 44 33N 6 5 E
Gapat →, India 43 G10 24 30N 82 28 E
Gapuwiyak, Australia 62 A2 12 25S 135 43 E
Gar, China 32 C2 32 10N 79 58 E
Garabogazköl Aylagy, Turkmenistan 25 F9 41 0N 53 30 E
Garachico, Canary Is. 22 F3 28 22N 16 46W
Garachiné, Panama 88 E4 8 0N 78 12W
Garafia, Canary Is. 22 F2 28 48N 17 57W
Garah, Australia 63 D4 29 5S 149 38 E
Garajonay, Canary Is. 22 F2 28 7N 17 14W
Garanhuns, Brazil 93 E11 8 50S 36 30W
Garautha, India 43 G8 25 34N 79 18 E
Garba Tula, Kenya 54 B4 0 30N 38 32 E
Garberville, U.S.A. 82 F2 40 6N 123 48W
Garbiyang, India 43 D9 30 8N 80 54 E
Garda, L. di, Italy 20 B4 45 40N 10 41 E
Garde L., Canada 73 A7 62 50N 106 13W
Garden City, Ga., U.S.A. 77 J5 32 6N 81 9W
Garden City, Kans., U.S.A. 81 G4 37 58N 100 53W
Garden City, Tex., U.S.A. 81 K4 31 52N 101 29W
Garden Grove, U.S.A. 85 M9 33 47N 117 55W
Gardēz, Afghan. 42 C3 33 37N 69 9 E
Gardiner, Maine, U.S.A. 77 C11 44 14N 69 47W
Gardiner, Mont., U.S.A. 82 D8 45 2N 110 22W
Gardiners I., U.S.A. 79 E12 41 6N 72 6W
Gardner, U.S.A. 79 D13 42 34N 71 59W
Gardner Canal, Canada 72 C3 53 27N 128 8W
Gardnerville, U.S.A. 84 G7 38 56N 119 45W
Gardo, Somali Rep. 46 F4 9 30N 49 6 E
Garey, U.S.A. 85 L6 34 53N 120 19W
Garfield, U.S.A. 82 C5 47 1N 117 9W
Garforth, U.K. 10 D6 53 47N 1 24W
Gargano, Mte., Italy 20 D6 41 43N 15 43 E
Garibaldi Prov. Park, Canada 72 D4 49 50N 122 40W
Garies, S. Africa 56 E2 30 32S 17 59 E
Garigliano →, Italy 20 D5 41 13N 13 45 E
Garissa, Kenya 54 C4 0 25S 39 40 E
Garland, Tex., U.S.A. 81 J6 32 55N 96 38W
Garland, Utah, U.S.A. 82 F7 41 47N 112 10W
Garm, Tajikistan 26 F8 39 0N 70 20 E
Garmāb, Iran 45 C8 35 25N 56 45 E
Garmisch-Partenkirchen, Germany 16 E6 47 30N 11 6 E
Garmsār, Iran 45 C7 35 20N 52 25 E
Garner, U.S.A. 80 D8 43 6N 93 36W
Garnett, U.S.A. 80 F7 38 17N 95 14W
Garo Hills, India 43 G14 25 30N 90 30 E
Garoe, Somali Rep. 46 F4 8 25N 48 33 E
Garonne →, France 18 D3 45 2N 0 36W
Garot, India 42 G6 24 19N 75 41 E
Garoua, Cameroon 51 G8 9 19N 13 21 E
Garrauli, India 43 G8 25 5N 79 22 E
Garrison, Mont., U.S.A. 82 C7 46 31N 112 49W
Garrison, N. Dak., U.S.A. 80 B4 47 40N 101 25W
Garrison Res. = Sakakawea, L., U.S.A. 80 B4 47 30N 101 25W
Garron Pt., U.K. 13 A6 55 3N 5 59W
Garry →, U.K. 12 E5 56 44N 3 47W
Garry, L., Canada 68 B9 65 58N 100 18W
Garsen, Kenya 54 C5 2 20S 40 5 E
Garson L., Canada 73 B6 56 19N 110 2W
Garu, India 43 H11 23 40N 84 14 E
Garub, Namibia 56 D2 26 37S 16 0 E
Garut, Indonesia 37 G12 7 14S 107 53 E
Garvie Mts., N.Z. 59 L2 45 30S 168 50 E
Garwa = Garoua, Cameroon 51 G8 9 19N 13 21 E
Garwa, India 43 G10 24 11N 83 47 E
Gary, U.S.A. 76 E2 41 36N 87 20W
Garzê, China 32 C5 31 38N 100 1 E
Garzón, Colombia 92 C3 2 10N 75 40W
Gas-San, Japan 30 E10 38 32N 140 1 E
Gasan Kuli = Esenguly, Turkmenistan 26 F6 37 37N 53 59 E
Gascogne, France 18 E4 43 45N 0 20 E
Gascogne, G. de, Europe 18 D2 44 0N 2 0W
Gascony = Gascogne, France 18 E4 43 45N 0 20 E
Gascoyne →, Australia 61 D1 24 52S 113 37 E
Gascoyne Junction, Australia 61 E2 25 2S 115 17 E
Gashaka, Nigeria 51 G8 7 20N 11 29 E
Gasherbrum, Pakistan 43 B7 35 40N 76 40 E
Gashua, Nigeria 51 F8 12 54N 11 0 E
Gaspé, Canada 71 C7 48 52N 64 30W
Gaspé, C. de, Canada 71 C7 48 48N 64 7W
Gaspé, Pén. de, Canada 71 C6 48 45N 65 40W
Gaspésie, Parc de Conservation de la, Canada 71 C6 48 55N 65 50W
Gasteiz = Vitoria-Gasteiz, Spain 19 A4 42 50N 2 41W
Gastonia, U.S.A. 77 H5 35 16N 81 11W
Gastre, Argentina 96 E3 42 20S 69 15W
Gata, C., Cyprus 23 E12 34 34N 33 2 E
Gata, C. de, Spain 19 D4 36 41N 2 13W
Gata, Sierra de, Spain 19 B2 40 20N 6 45W
Gataga →, Canada 72 B3 58 35N 126 59W
Gatehouse of Fleet, U.K. 12 G4 54 53N 4 12W
Gates, U.S.A. 78 C7 43 9N 77 42W
Gateshead, U.K. 10 C6 54 57N 1 35W
Gatesville, U.S.A. 81 K6 31 26N 97 45W
Gaths, Zimbabwe 55 G3 20 2S 30 32 E
Gatico, Chile 94 A1 22 29S 70 20W
Gatineau, Canada 79 A9 45 29N 75 38W
Gatineau →, Canada 70 C4 45 27N 75 42W
Gatineau, Parc Nat. de la, Canada 70 C4 45 40N 76 0W
Gatton, Australia 63 D5 27 32S 152 17 E

Grenen

Grenen, *Denmark* . . . . **9 H14** 57 44N 10 40 E
Grenfell, *Australia* . . . . . . **63 E4** 33 52S 148 8 E
Grenfell, *Canada* **73 C8** 50 30N 102 56W
Grenoble, *France* . . . . **18 D6** 45 12N 5 42 E
Grenville, C., *Australia* . . . . **62 A3** 12 0S 143 13 E
Grenville Chan., *Canada* . . . **72 C3** 53 40N 129 46W
Gresham, *U.S.A.* **84 E4** 45 30N 122 26W
Gresik, *Indonesia* . . . . **37 G15** 7 13S 112 38 E
Gretna, *U.K.* **12 F5** 55 0N 3 3W
Grevenmacher, *Lux.* . . . . **15 E6** 49 41N 6 26 E
Grey →, *Canada* **71 C8** 47 34N 57 6W
Grey →, *N.Z.* . . . . **59 K3** 42 27S 171 12 E
Grey, C., *Australia* . . . . **62 A2** 13 0S 136 35 E
Grey Ra., *Australia* . . . . **63 D3** 27 0S 143 30 E
Greybull, *U.S.A.* **82 D9** 44 30N 108 3W
Greymouth, *N.Z.* . . . . **59 K3** 42 29S 171 13 E
Greystones, *Ireland* **13 C5** 53 9N 6 5W
Greytown, *N.Z.* . . . . **59 J5** 41 5S 175 29 E
Greytown, *S. Africa* . . . . . . **57 D5** 29 1S 30 36 E
Gribbell I., *Canada* **72 C3** 53 23N 129 0W
Gridley, *U.S.A.* **84 F5** 39 22N 121 42W
Griekwastad, *S. Africa* . . . . . **56 D3** 28 49S 23 15 E
Griffin, *U.S.A.* **77 J3** 33 15N 84 16W
Griffith, *Australia* . . . . **63 E4** 34 18S 146 2 E
Griffith, *Canada* **78 A7** 45 15N 77 10W
Griffith I., *Canada* **78 B4** 44 50N 80 55W
Grimaylov = Hrymayliv, *Ukraine* . . . . **17 D14** 49 20N 26 5 E
Grimes, *U.S.A.* **84 F5** 39 4N 121 54W
Grimsay, *U.K.* **12 D1** 57 29N 7 14W
Grimsby, *Canada* **78 C5** 43 12N 79 34W
Grimsby, *U.K.* **10 D7** 53 34N 0 5W
Grímsey, *Iceland* **8 C5** 66 33N 17 58W
Grimshaw, *Canada* **72 B5** 56 10N 117 40W
Grimstad, *Norway* . . . . **9 G13** 58 20N 8 35 E
Grindstone I., *Canada* **79 B8** 44 43N 76 14W
Grinnell, *U.S.A.* **80 E8** 41 45N 92 43W
Gris-Nez, C., *France* . . . . . . **18 A4** 50 52N 1 35 E
Groais I., *Canada* **71 B8** 50 55N 55 35W
Groblersdal, *S. Africa* . . . . . **57 D4** 25 15S 29 25 E
Grodno = Hrodna, *Belarus* . **17 B12** 53 42N 23 52 E
Grodzyanka = Hrodzyanka, *Belarus* . . . . **17 B15** 53 31N 28 42 E
Groesbeck, *U.S.A.* **81 K6** 30 48N 96 31W
Grójec, *Poland* . . . . **17 C11** 51 50N 20 58 E
Grong, *Norway* . . . . **8 D15** 64 25N 12 8 E
Groningen, *Neths.* . . . . **15 A6** 53 15N 6 35 E
Groningen □, *Neths.* . . . . . **15 A6** 53 16N 6 40 E
Groom, *U.S.A.* **81 H4** 35 12N 101 6W
Groot →, *S. Africa* . . . . . . **56 E3** 33 45S 24 36 E
Groot Berg →, *S. Africa* . . **56 E2** 32 47S 18 8 E
Groot-Brakrivier, *S. Africa* . **56 E3** 34 2S 22 18 E
Groot-Kei →, *S. Africa* . . . **57 E4** 32 41S 28 22 E
Groot Vis →, *S. Africa* . . . **56 E4** 33 28S 27 5 E
Groote Eylandt, *Australia* . . **62 A2** 14 0S 136 40 E
Grootfontein, *Namibia* . . . . . **56 B2** 19 31S 18 6 E
Grootlaagte →, *Africa* . . . **56 C3** 20 55S 21 27 E
Grootvloer, *S. Africa* . . . . . **56 E3** 30 0S 20 40 E
Gros C., *Canada* **72 A6** 61 59N 113 32W
Gros Morne Nat. Park, *Canada* **71 C8** 49 40N 57 50W
Grossa, Pta., *Spain* . . . . **22 B8** 39 6N 1 36 E
Grosser Arber, *Germany* . . . **16 D7** 49 6N 13 8 E
Grosseto, *Italy* . . . . **20 C4** 42 46N 11 8 E
Grossglockner, *Austria* . . . . **16 E7** 47 5N 12 40 E
Groswater B., *Canada* **71 B8** 54 20N 57 40W
Groton, *Conn., U.S.A.* **79 E12** 41 21N 72 5W
Groton, *N.Y., U.S.A.* **79 D8** 42 36N 76 22W
Groton, *S. Dak., U.S.A.* **80 C5** 45 27N 98 6W
Grouard Mission, *Canada* . . **72 B5** 55 33N 116 9W
Groundhog →, *Canada* . . . **70 C3** 48 45N 82 58W
Grouw, *Neths.* . . . . **15 A5** 53 5N 5 51 E
Grove City, *U.S.A.* **78 E4** 41 10N 80 5W
Grove Hill, *U.S.A.* **77 K2** 31 42N 87 47W
Groveland, *U.S.A.* **84 H6** 37 50N 120 14W
Grover City, *U.S.A.* **85 K6** 35 7N 120 37W
Groves, *U.S.A.* **81 L8** 29 57N 93 54W
Groveton, *U.S.A.* **79 B13** 44 36N 71 31W
Groznyy, *Russia* . . . . **25 F8** 43 20N 45 45 E
Grudziądz, *Poland* . . . . **17 B10** 53 30N 18 47 E
Gruinard B., *U.K.* **12 D3** 57 56N 5 35W
Grundy Center, *U.S.A.* **80 D8** 42 22N 92 47W
Gruver, *U.S.A.* **81 G4** 36 16N 101 24W
Gryazi, *Russia* . . . . **24 D6** 52 30N 39 58 E
Gryazovets, *Russia* . . . . **24 C7** 58 50N 40 10 E
Gua, *India* . . . . **41 H14** 22 18N 85 20 E
Gua Musang, *Malaysia* . . . . . **39 K3** 4 53N 101 58 E
Guacanayabo, G. de, *Cuba* . . **88 B4** 20 40N 77 20W
Guachípas →, *Argentina* . . **94 B2** 25 40S 65 30W
Guadalajara, *Mexico* **86 C4** 20 40N 103 20W
Guadalajara, *Spain* **19 B4** 40 37N 3 12W
Guadalcanal, *Solomon Is.* . . **64 H8** 9 32S 160 12 E
Guadales, *Argentina* **94 C2** 34 30S 67 55W
Guadalete →, *Spain* **19 D2** 36 35N 6 13W
Guadalquivir →, *Spain* . . . **19 D2** 36 47N 6 22W
Guadalupe = Guadeloupe ■, *W. Indies* . . **89 C7** 16 20N 61 40W
Guadalupe, *Mexico* **85 N10** 32 4N 116 32W
Guadalupe, *U.S.A.* **85 L6** 34 59N 120 33W
Guadalupe →, *Mexico* **85 N10** 32 6N 116 51W
Guadalupe →, *U.S.A.* **81 L6** 28 27N 96 47W
Guadalupe, Sierra de, *Spain* **19 C3** 39 28N 5 30W
Guadalupe Bravos, *Mexico* . **86 A3** 31 20N 106 10W
Guadalupe I., *Pac. Oc.* **66 G8** 29 0N 118 50W
Guadalupe Mts. Nat. Park, *U.S.A.* **81 K2** 32 0N 104 30W
Guadalupe Peak, *U.S.A.* **81 K2** 31 50N 104 52W
Guadalupe y Calvo, *Mexico* **86 B3** 26 6N 106 58W
Guadarrama, Sierra de, *Spain* **19 B4** 41 0N 4 0W
Guadeloupe ■, *W. Indies* . . **89 C7** 16 20N 61 40W
Guadeloupe Passage, *W. Indies* **89 C7** 16 50N 62 15W
Guadiana →, *Portugal* . . . **19 D2** 37 14N 7 22W
Guadix, *Spain* **19 D4** 37 18N 3 11W
Guafo, Boca del, *Chile* **96 E2** 43 35S 74 0W
Guainía →, *Colombia* **92 C5** 2 1N 67 7W
Guaíra, *Brazil* **95 A5** 24 5S 54 10W
Guaíra □, *Paraguay* **94 B4** 25 45S 56 30W
Guaitecas, Is., *Chile* **96 E2** 44 0S 74 30W
Guajará-Mirim, *Brazil* **92 F5** 10 50S 65 20W
Guajira, Pen. de la, *Colombia* **92 A4** 12 0N 72 0W
Gualán, *Guatemala* **88 C2** 15 8N 89 22W
Gualeguay, *Argentina* **94 C4** 33 10S 59 14W
Gualeguaychú, *Argentina* . **94 C4** 33 3S 59 31W
Gualequay →, *Argentina* . **94 C4** 33 19S 59 39W
Guam ■, *Pac. Oc.* . . . . **64 F6** 13 27N 144 45 E
Guaminí, *Argentina* **94 D3** 37 1S 62 28W
Guamúchil, *Mexico* **86 B3** 25 25N 108 3W
Guanabacoa, *Cuba* **88 B3** 23 8N 82 18W
Guanacaste, Cordillera del, *Costa Rica* **88 D2** 10 40N 85 4W
Guanaceví, *Mexico* **86 B3** 25 40N 106 0W
Guanahani = San Salvador I., *Bahamas* **89 B5** 24 0N 74 40W
Guanajay, *Cuba* **88 B3** 22 56N 82 42W
Guanajuato, *Mexico* **86 C4** 21 0N 101 20W
Guanajuato □, *Mexico* **86 C4** 20 40N 101 20W
Guandacol, *Argentina* **94 B2** 29 30S 68 40W
Guane, *Cuba* **88 B3** 22 10N 84 7W
Guangdong □, *China* . . . . . **33 D6** 23 0N 113 0 E
Guangling, *China* . . . . **34 E8** 39 47N 114 22 E
Guangrao, *China* . . . . **35 F10** 37 5N 118 25 E
Guangwu, *China* . . . . **34 F3** 37 48N 105 57 E
Guangxi Zhuangzu Zizhiqu □, *China* . . . . **33 D5** 24 0N 109 0 E
Guangzhou, *China* . . . . **33 D6** 23 5N 113 10 E
Guanipa →, *Venezuela* . . . **92 B6** 9 56N 62 26W
Guannan, *China* . . . . **35 G10** 34 8N 119 21 E
Guantánamo, *Cuba* **89 B4** 20 10N 75 14W
Guantao, *China* . . . . **34 F8** 36 42N 115 25 E
Guanyun, *China* . . . . **35 G10** 34 20N 119 18 E
Guápiles, *Costa Rica* **88 D3** 10 10N 83 46W
Guaporé, *Brazil* **95 B5** 28 51S 51 54W
Guaporé →, *Brazil* **92 F5** 11 55S 65 4W
Guaqui, *Bolivia* **92 G5** 16 41S 68 54W
Guarapari, *Brazil* **95 A7** 20 40S 40 30W
Guarapuava, *Brazil* **95 B5** 25 20S 51 30W
Guaratinguetá, *Brazil* **95 A6** 22 49S 45 9W
Guaratuba, *Brazil* **95 B6** 25 53S 48 38W
Guarda, *Portugal* **19 B2** 40 32N 7 20W
Guardafui, C. = Asir, Ras, *Somali Rep.* . . . . **46 E5** 11 55N 51 10 E
Guárico □, *Venezuela* **92 B5** 8 40N 66 35W
Guarujá, *Brazil* **95 A6** 24 2S 46 25W
Guarus, *Brazil* **95 A7** 21 44S 41 20W
Guasave, *Mexico* **86 B3** 25 34N 108 27W
Guasdualito, *Venezuela* **92 B4** 7 15N 70 44W
Guatemala, *Guatemala* **88 D1** 14 40N 90 22W
Guatemala ■, *Cent. Amer.* . . **88 C1** 15 40N 90 30W
Guaviare →, *Colombia* . . . **92 C5** 4 3N 67 44W
Guaxupé, *Brazil* **95 A6** 21 10S 47 5W
Guayama, *Puerto Rico* **89 C6** 17 59N 66 7W
Guayaquil, *Ecuador* **92 D3** 2 15S 79 52W
Guayaquil, G. de, *Ecuador* . **92 D2** 3 10S 81 0W
Guaymas, *Mexico* **86 B2** 27 59N 110 54W
Guba, *Dem. Rep. of the Congo* . **55 E2** 10 38S 26 27 E
Gubkin, *Russia* . . . . **25 D6** 51 17N 37 32 E
Gudbrandsdalen, *Norway* . . **9 F14** 61 33N 10 10 E
Guddu Barrage, *Pakistan* . . . **40 E6** 28 30N 69 50 E
Gudivada, *India* . . . . **41 L12** 16 30N 81 3 E
Gudur, *India* . . . . **40 M11** 14 12N 79 55 E
Guecho = Getxo, *Spain* **19 A4** 43 21N 2 59W
Guelph, *Canada* **78 C4** 43 35N 80 20W
Guéret, *France* . . . . **18 C4** 46 11N 1 51 E
Guerneville, *U.S.A.* **84 G4** 38 30N 123 0W
Guernica = Gernika-Lumo, *Spain* **19 A4** 43 19N 2 40W
Guernsey, *U.K.* **11 H5** 49 26N 2 35W
Guernsey, *U.S.A.* **80 D2** 42 19N 104 45W
Guerrero □, *Mexico* **87 D5** 17 30N 100 0W
Gügher, *Iran* . . . . **45 D8** 29 28N 56 27 E
Guhakolak, Tanjung, *Indonesia* . . . . **37 G11** 6 50S 105 14 E
Guia, *Canary Is.* **22 F4** 28 8N 15 38W
Guia de Isora, *Canary Is.* . . . **22 F3** 28 12N 16 46W
Guia Lopes da Laguna, *Brazil* **95 A4** 21 26S 56 7W
Guiana, *S. Amer.* **90 C4** 5 10N 60 40W
Guider, *Cameroon* . . . . **51 G8** 9 56N 13 57 E
Guidónia-Montecélio, *Italy* . **20 C5** 42 1N 12 45 E
Guijá, *Mozam.* . . . . **57 C5** 24 27S 33 0 E
Guildford, *U.K.* **11 F7** 51 14N 0 34W
Guilford, *U.S.A.* **79 E12** 41 17N 72 41W
Guilin, *China* . . . . **33 D6** 25 18N 110 15 E
Guillaume-Delisle L., *Canada* **70 A4** 56 15N 76 17W
Güimar, *Canary Is.* **22 F3** 28 18N 16 24W
Guimarães, *Portugal* **19 B1** 41 28N 8 24W
Guimaras, *Phil.* . . . . **37 B6** 10 35N 122 37 E
Guinda, *U.S.A.* **84 G4** 38 50N 122 12W
Guinea, *Africa* . . . . **48 F4** 8 0N 8 0 E
Guinea ■, *W. Afr.* **50 F3** 10 20N 11 30W
Guinea, Gulf of, *Atl. Oc.* . . . . **48 F4** 3 0N 2 30 E
Guinea-Bissau ■, *Africa* . . . **50 F3** 12 0N 15 0W
Güines, *Cuba* **88 B3** 22 50N 82 0W
Guingamp, *France* **18 B2** 48 34N 3 10W
Güiria, *Venezuela* **92 A6** 10 32N 62 18W
Guiuan, *Phil.* . . . . **37 B7** 11 5N 125 55 E
Guiyang, *China* . . . . **32 D5** 26 32N 106 40 E
Guizhou □, *China* . . . . **32 D5** 27 0N 107 0 E
Gujar Khan, *Pakistan* . . . . . . **42 C5** 33 16N 73 19 E
Gujarat □, *India* . . . . **42 H4** 23 20N 71 0 E
Gujranwala, *Pakistan* . . . . . . **42 C6** 32 10N 74 12 E
Gujrat, *Pakistan* . . . . **42 C6** 32 40N 74 2 E
Gulargambone, *Australia* . . . **63 E4** 31 20S 148 30 E
Gulbarga, *India* . . . . **40 L10** 17 20N 76 50 E
Gulbene, *Latvia* . . . . **9 H22** 57 8N 26 52 E
Gulf, The, *Asia* . . . . **45 E6** 27 0N 50 0 E
Gulfport, *U.S.A.* **81 K10** 30 22N 89 6W
Gulgong, *Australia* . . . . **63 E4** 32 20S 149 49 E
Gulistan, *Pakistan* . . . . **42 D2** 30 30N 66 35 E
Gull Lake, *Canada* **73 C7** 50 10N 108 29W
Güllük, *Turkey* . . . . **21 F12** 37 14N 27 35 E
Gulmarg, *India* . . . . **43 B6** 34 3N 74 25 E
Gulshad, *Kazakstan* . . . . **26 E8** 46 45N 74 25 E
Gulu, *Uganda* . . . . **54 B3** 2 48N 32 17 E
Gulwe, *Tanzania* . . . . **54 D4** 6 30S 36 25 E
Gumal →, *Pakistan* . . . . . . **42 D4** 31 40N 71 50 E
Gumbaz, *Pakistan* . . . . **42 D3** 30 2N 69 0 E
Gumel, *Nigeria* . . . . **50 F7** 12 39N 9 22 E
Gumla, *India* . . . . **43 H11** 23 3N 84 33 E
Gumlu, *Australia* . . . . **62 B4** 19 53S 147 41 E
Gumma □, *Japan* . . . . **31 F9** 36 30N 138 20 E
Gumzai, *Indonesia* . . . . **37 F8** 5 28S 134 42 E
Guna, *India* . . . . **42 G7** 24 40N 77 19 E
Gunisao →, *Canada* **73 C9** 53 56N 97 53W
Gunisao L., *Canada* **73 C9** 53 33N 96 15W
Gunjyal, *Pakistan* . . . . **42 C4** 32 20N 71 55 E
Gunnbjørn Fjeld, *Greenland* . **4 C6** 68 55N 29 47W
Gunnedah, *Australia* . . . . . . **63 E5** 30 59S 150 15 E
Gunnewin, *Australia* . . . . . . **63 D4** 25 59S 148 33 E
Gunningbar Cr. →, *Australia* . . . . **63 E4** 31 14S 147 6 E
Gunnison, *Colo., U.S.A.* **83 G10** 38 33N 106 56W
Gunnison, *Utah, U.S.A.* **82 G8** 39 9N 111 49W
Gunnison →, *U.S.A.* **83 G9** 39 4N 108 35W
Gunpowder, *Australia* . . . . . **62 B2** 19 42S 139 22 E
Guntakal, *India* . . . . **40 M10** 15 11N 77 27 E
Guntersville, *U.S.A.* **77 H2** 34 21N 86 18W
Guntong, *Malaysia* . . . . **39 K3** 4 36N 101 3 E
Guntur, *India* . . . . **41 L12** 16 23N 80 30 E
Gunungapi, *Indonesia* . . . . . **37 F7** 6 45S 126 30 E
Gunungsitoli, *Indonesia* . . . **36 D1** 1 15N 97 30 E
Gunza, *Angola* . . . . **52 G2** 10 50S 13 50 E
Guo He →, *China* . . . . **35 H9** 32 59N 117 10 E
Guoyang, *China* . . . . **34 H9** 33 32N 116 12 E
Gupis, *Pakistan* . . . . **43 A5** 36 15N 73 20 E
Gurdaspur, *India* . . . . **42 C6** 32 5N 75 31 E
Gurdon, *U.S.A.* **81 J8** 33 55N 93 9W
Gurgaon, *India* . . . . **42 E7** 28 27N 77 1 E
Gurgueia →, *Brazil* **93 E10** 6 50S 43 24W
Gurha, *India* . . . . **42 G4** 25 12N 71 39 E
Guri, Embalse de, *Venezuela* **92 B6** 7 50N 62 52W
Gurkha, *Nepal* . . . . **43 E11** 28 5N 84 40 E
Gurley, *Australia* . . . . **63 D4** 29 45S 149 48 E
Gurnet Point, *U.S.A.* **79 D14** 42 1N 70 34W
Gurué, *Mozam.* . . . . **55 F4** 15 25S 36 58 E
Gurun, *Malaysia* . . . . **39 K3** 5 49N 100 27 E
Gürün, *Turkey* . . . . **25 G6** 38 43N 37 15 E
Gurupá, *Brazil* **93 D8** 1 25S 51 35W
Gurupá, I. Grande de, *Brazil* **93 D8** 1 25S 51 45W
Gurupi, *Brazil* **93 F9** 11 43S 49 4W
Gurupi →, *Brazil* **93 D9** 1 13S 46 6W
Guryev = Atyraū, *Kazakstan* **25 E9** 47 5N 52 0 E
Gusau, *Nigeria* . . . . **50 F7** 12 12N 6 40 E
Gusev, *Russia* . . . . **9 J20** 54 35N 22 10 E
Gushan, *China* . . . . **35 E12** 39 50N 123 35 E
Gushgy, *Turkmenistan* . . . . . **26 F7** 35 20N 62 18 E
Gusinoozersk, *Russia* . . . . . **27 D11** 51 16N 106 27 E
Gustavus, *U.S.A.* **72 B1** 58 25N 135 44W
Gustine, *U.S.A.* **84 H6** 37 16N 121 0W
Güstrow, *Germany* . . . . **16 B7** 53 47N 12 10 E
Gütersloh, *Germany* . . . . **16 C5** 51 54N 8 24 E
Gutha, *Australia* . . . . **61 E2** 28 58S 115 55 E
Guthalungra, *Australia* . . . . **62 B4** 19 52S 147 50 E
Guthrie, *Okla., U.S.A.* **81 H6** 35 53N 97 25W
Guthrie, *Tex., U.S.A.* **81 J4** 33 37N 100 19W
Guttenberg, *U.S.A.* **80 D9** 42 47N 91 6W
Guyana ■, *S. Amer.* **92 C7** 5 0N 59 0W
Guyane française = French Guiana ■, *S. Amer.* **93 C8** 4 0N 53 0W
Guyang, *China* . . . . **34 D6** 41 0N 110 5 E
Guyenne, *France* . . . . **18 D4** 44 30N 0 40 E
Guymon, *U.S.A.* **81 G4** 36 41N 101 29W
Guyra, *Australia* . . . . **63 E5** 30 15S 151 40 E
Guyuan, *Hebei, China* . . . . . **34 D8** 41 37N 115 40 E
Guyuan, *Ningxia Huizu, China* . . . . **34 G4** 36 0N 106 20 E
Guzhen, *China* . . . . **35 H9** 33 22N 117 18 E
Guzmán, L. de, *Mexico* **86 A3** 31 25N 107 25W
Gvardeysk, *Russia* . . . . **9 J19** 54 39N 21 5 E
Gwa, *Burma* . . . . **41 L19** 17 36N 94 34 E
Gwaai, *Zimbabwe* . . . . **55 F2** 19 15S 27 45 E
Gwabegar, *Australia* . . . . . . **63 E4** 30 31S 149 0 E
Gwādar, *Pakistan* . . . . **40 G3** 25 10N 62 18 E
Gwalior, *India* . . . . **42 F8** 26 12N 78 10 E
Gwanda, *Zimbabwe* . . . . **55 G2** 20 55S 29 0 E
Gwane, *Dem. Rep. of the Congo* . **54 B2** 4 45N 25 48 E
Gweebarra B., *Ireland* **13 B3** 54 51N 8 23W
Gweedore, *Ireland* **13 A3** 55 3N 8 13W
Gweru, *Zimbabwe* . . . . **55 F2** 19 28S 29 45 E
Gwinn, *U.S.A.* **76 B2** 46 19N 87 27W
Gwydir →, *Australia* . . . . . . **63 D4** 29 27S 149 48 E
Gwynedd □, *U.K.* **10 E3** 52 52N 4 10W
Gyandzha = Gäncä, *Azerbaijan* . . . . **25 F8** 40 45N 46 20 E
Gyaring Hu, *China* . . . . **32 C4** 34 50N 97 40 E
Gydanskiy Poluostrov, *Russia* . . . . **26 C8** 70 0N 78 0 E
Gympie, *Australia* . . . . **63 D5** 26 11S 152 38 E
Gyöngyös, *Hungary* . . . . **17 E10** 47 48N 19 56 E
Győr, *Hungary* . . . . **17 E9** 47 41N 17 40 E
Gypsum Pt., *Canada* **72 A6** 61 53N 114 35W
Gypsumville, *Canada* **73 C9** 51 45N 98 40W
Gyula, *Hungary* . . . . **17 E11** 46 38N 21 17 E
Gyumri, *Armenia* . . . . **25 F7** 40 47N 43 50 E
Gyzylarbat, *Turkmenistan* . . **26 F6** 39 4N 56 23 E
Gyzyletrek, *Turkmenistan* . . **45 B7** 37 36N 54 46 E

H

Ha 'Arava →, *Israel* . . . . . . **47 E4** 30 50N 35 20 E
Ha Tien, *Vietnam* . . . . **39 G5** 10 23N 104 29 E
Ha Tinh, *Vietnam* . . . . **38 C5** 18 20N 105 54 E
Ha Trung, *Vietnam* . . . . **38 C5** 19 58N 105 50 E
Haaksbergen, *Neths.* . . . . . . **15 B6** 52 9N 6 45 E
Haapsalu, *Estonia* . . . . **9 G20** 58 56N 23 30 E
Haarlem, *Neths.* . . . . **15 B4** 52 23N 4 39 E
Haast →, *N.Z.* . . . . **59 K2** 43 50S 169 2 E
Haast Bluff, *Australia* . . . . . **60 D5** 23 22S 132 0 E
Hab →, *Pakistan* . . . . **42 G3** 24 53N 66 41 E
Hab Nadi Chauki, *Pakistan* . **42 G2** 25 0N 66 50 E
Habaswein, *Kenya* . . . . **54 B4** 1 2N 39 30 E
Habay, *Canada* **72 B5** 58 50N 118 44W
Ḩabbānīyah, *Iraq* . . . . **44 C4** 33 17N 43 29 E
Haboro, *Japan* . . . . **30 B10** 44 22N 141 42 E
Ḩabshān, *U.A.E.* . . . . **45 F7** 23 50N 53 37 E
Hachijō-Jima, *Japan* . . . . **31 H9** 33 5N 139 45 E
Hachinohe, *Japan* . . . . **30 D10** 40 30N 141 29 E
Hachiōji, *Japan* . . . . **31 G9** 35 40N 139 20 E
Hachŏn, *N. Korea* . . . . **35 D15** 41 29N 129 2 E
Hackensack, *U.S.A.* **79 F10** 40 53N 74 3W
Hackettstown, *U.S.A.* **79 F10** 40 51N 74 50W
Hadali, *Pakistan* . . . . **42 C5** 32 16N 72 11 E
Hadarba, Ras, *Sudan* . . . . . . **51 D13** 22 4N 36 51 E
Hadarom □, *Israel* . . . . **47 E4** 31 0N 35 0 E
Hadd, Ra's al, *Oman* . . . . **46 C6** 22 35N 59 50 E
Hadejia, *Nigeria* . . . . **50 F7** 12 30N 10 5 E
Hadera, *Israel* . . . . **47 C3** 32 27N 34 55 E
Hadera, N. →, *Israel* . . . . . . **47 C3** 32 28N 34 52 E
Haderslev, *Denmark* . . . . **9 J13** 55 15N 9 30 E
Hadhramaut = Ḩaḑramawt, *Yemen* . . . . **46 D4** 15 30N 49 30 E
Hadibu, *Yemen* . . . . **46 E5** 12 39N 54 2 E
Hadong, *S. Korea* **35 G14** 35 5N 127 44
Ḩaḑramawt, *Yemen* **46 D4** 15 30N 49 30
Ḩadrānīyah, *Iraq* **44 C4** 35 38N 43 14
Hadrian's Wall, *U.K.* **10 B5** 55 0N 2 30
Haeju, *N. Korea* **35 E13** 38 3N 125 45
Haenam, *S. Korea* **35 G14** 34 34N 126 35
Haerhpin = Harbin, *China* . . **35 B14** 45 48N 126 40
Hafar al Bāṭin, *Si. Arabia* . . **44 D5** 28 32N 45 52
Ḩafirat al 'Aydā, *Si. Arabia* . **44 E3** 26 26N 39 12
Ḩafit, *Oman* **45 F7** 23 59N 55 49
Ḩafit, Jabal, *Oman* **45 E7** 24 3N 55 46
Hafizabad, *Pakistan* **42 C5** 32 5N 73 40
Haflong, *India* **41 G18** 25 10N 93 5
Hafnarfjörður, *Iceland* **8 D3** 64 4N 21 57
Haft Gel, *Iran* **45 D6** 31 30N 49 32
Hafun, Ras, *Somali Rep.* . . . **46 E5** 10 29N 51 30
Hagalil, *Israel* **47 C4** 32 53N 35 18
Hagen, *Germany* **16 C4** 51 21N 7 27
Hagerman, *U.S.A.* **81 J2** 33 7N 104 20
Hagerstown, *U.S.A.* **76 F7** 39 39N 77 43
Hagersville, *Canada* **78 D4** 42 58N 80 3
Hagfors, *Sweden* **9 F15** 60 3N 13 45
Hagi, *Japan* **31 G5** 34 30N 131 22
Hagolan, *Syria* **47 C4** 33 0N 35 45
Hagondange, *France* **18 B7** 49 16N 6 11
Hags Hd., *Ireland* **13 D2** 52 57N 9 28
Hague, C. de la, *France* **18 B3** 49 44N 1 56
Hague, The = 's-Gravenhage, *Neths.* **15 B4** 52 7N 4 17
Haguenau, *France* **18 B7** 48 49N 7 47
Haicheng, *China* **35 D12** 40 50N 122 45
Haidar Khel, *Afghan.* **42 C3** 33 58N 68 38
Haidargarh, *India* **43 F9** 26 37N 81 22
Haifa = Ḩefa, *Israel* **47 C4** 32 46N 35 0
Haikou, *China* **33 D6** 20 1N 110 16
Ḩā'il, *Si. Arabia* **44 E4** 27 28N 41 45
Hailar, *China* **33 B6** 49 10N 119 38
Hailey, *U.S.A.* **82 E6** 43 31N 114 19
Haileybury, *Canada* **70 C4** 47 30N 79 38
Hailin, *China* **35 B15** 44 37N 129 30
Hailong, *China* **35 C13** 42 32N 125 40
Hailuoto, *Finland* **8 D21** 65 3N 24 45
Hainan □, *China* **33 E5** 19 0N 109 30
Hainaut □, *Belgium* **15 D4** 50 30N 4 0
Haines, *Alaska, U.S.A.* **72 B1** 59 14N 135 26
Haines, *Oreg., U.S.A.* **82 D5** 44 55N 117 56
Haines City, *U.S.A.* **77 L5** 28 7N 81 38
Haines Junction, *Canada* . . **72 A1** 60 45N 137 30
Haiphong, *Vietnam* **32 D5** 20 47N 106 41
Haiti ■, *W. Indies* **89 C5** 19 0N 72 30
Haiya, *Sudan* **51 E13** 18 20N 36 21
Haiyang, *China* **35 F11** 36 47N 121 9
Haiyuan, *China* **34 F3** 36 35N 105 52
Haizhou, *China* **35 G10** 34 37N 119 7
Haizhou Wan, *China* **35 G10** 34 50N 119 20
Hajdúböszörmény, *Hungary* **17 E11** 47 40N 21 30
Hajipur, *India* **43 G11** 25 45N 85 13
Ḩājjī Muḩsin, *Iraq* **44 C5** 32 35N 45 29
Ḩājjīābād, *Iran* **45 D7** 28 19N 55 55
Ḩājjīābād-e Zarrīn, *Iran* . . . **45 C7** 33 9N 54 51
Hajnówka, *Poland* **17 B12** 52 47N 23 35
Hakansson, Mts., *Dem. Rep. of the Congo* . **55 D2** 8 40S 25 45
Hakkâri, *Turkey* **44 B4** 37 34N 43 44
Hakken-Zan, *Japan* **31 G7** 34 10N 135 54
Hakodate, *Japan* **30 D10** 41 45N 140 44
Haku-San, *Japan* **31 F8** 36 9N 136 46
Hakui, *Japan* **31 F8** 36 53N 136 47
Hala, *Pakistan* **40 G6** 25 43N 68 20
Ḩalab, *Syria* **44 B3** 36 10N 37 15
Ḩalabjah, *Iraq* **44 C5** 35 10N 45 58
Halaib, *Sudan* **51 D13** 22 12N 36 30
Hālat 'Ammār, *Si. Arabia* . . **44 D3** 29 10N 36 4
Halbā, *Lebanon* **47 A5** 34 34N 36 6
Halberstadt, *Germany* **16 C6** 51 54N 11 3
Halcombe, *N.Z.* **59 J5** 40 8S 175 30
Halcon, *Phil.* **37 B6** 13 0N 121 30
Halden, *Norway* **9 G14** 59 9N 11 23
Haldia, *India* **41 H16** 22 5N 88 3
Haldwani, *India* **43 E8** 29 31N 79 30
Hale →, *Australia* **62 C2** 24 56S 135 53
Haleakala Crater, *U.S.A.* **74 H16** 20 43N 156 16
Halesowen, *U.K.* **11 E5** 52 27N 2 3
Haleyville, *U.S.A.* **77 H2** 34 14N 87 37
Halfway →, *Canada* **72 B4** 56 12N 121 32
Halia, *India* **43 G10** 24 50N 82 19
Haliburton, *Canada* **78 A6** 45 3N 78 30
Halifax, *Australia* **62 B4** 18 32S 146 22
Halifax, *Canada* **71 D7** 44 38N 63 35
Halifax, *U.K.* **10 D6** 53 43N 1 52
Halifax, *U.S.A.* **78 F8** 40 25N 76 55
Halifax B., *Australia* **62 B4** 18 50S 147 0
Halifax I., *Namibia* **56 D2** 26 38S 15 4
Halīl →, *Iran* **45 E8** 27 40N 58 30
Halkirk, *U.K.* **12 C5** 58 30N 3 29
Hall Beach = Sanirajak, *Canada* **69 B11** 68 46N 81 12
Hall Pen., *Canada* **69 B13** 63 30N 66 0
Hall Pt., *Australia* **60 C3** 15 40S 124 23
Halland, *Sweden* **9 H15** 57 8N 12 47
Halle, *Belgium* **15 D4** 50 44N 4 13
Halle, *Germany* **16 C6** 51 30N 11 56
Hällefors, *Sweden* **9 G16** 59 47N 14 31
Hallett, *Australia* **63 E2** 33 25S 138 55
Hallettsville, *U.S.A.* **81 L6** 29 27N 96 57
Hallim, *S. Korea* **35 H14** 33 24N 126 15
Hallingdalselvi →, *Norway* **9 F13** 60 23N 9 35
Halls Creek, *Australia* **60 C4** 18 16S 127 38
Hallsberg, *Sweden* **9 G16** 59 5N 15 7
Hallstead, *U.S.A.* **79 E9** 41 58N 75 45
Halmahera, *Indonesia* **37 D7** 0 40N 128 0
Halmstad, *Sweden* **9 H15** 56 41N 12 52
Hälsingborg = Helsingborg, *Sweden* **9 H15** 56 3N 12 42
Hälsingland, *Sweden* **9 F16** 61 40N 16 5
Halstead, *U.K.* **11 F8** 51 57N 0 40
Halti, *Finland* **8 B19** 69 17N 21 18
Halton □, *U.K.* **10 D5** 53 22N 2 45
Haltwhistle, *U.K.* **10 C5** 54 58N 2 26
Halul, *Qatar* **45 E7** 25 40N 52 40
Halvad, *India* **42 H4** 23 1N 71 11
Ḩalvān, *Iran* **45 C8** 33 57N 56 15
Ham Tan, *Vietnam* **39 G6** 10 40N 107 45
Ham Yen, *Vietnam* **38 A5** 22 4N 105 3
Hamab, *Namibia* **56 D2** 28 7S 19 16
Hamada, *Japan* **31 G6** 34 56N 132 4
Hamadān, *Iran* **45 C6** 34 52N 48 32

Indonesia

oyerswerda, *Germany* **16 C8** 51 26N 14 14 E
oylake, *U.K.* **10 D4** 53 24N 3 10W
pungan Pass, *Burma* **41 F20** 27 30N 96 55 E
radec Králové, *Czech Rep.* **16 C8** 50 15N 15 50 E
rodna, *Belarus* **17 B12** 53 42N 23 52 E
rodzyanka, *Belarus* **17 B15** 53 31N 28 42 E
on →, *Slovak Rep.* **17 E10** 47 49N 18 45 E
vatska = Croatia ■, *Europe* **16 F9** 45 20N 16 0 E
ymayliv, *Ukraine* **17 D14** 49 20N 26 5 E
senwi, *Burma* **41 H20** 23 22N 97 55 E
siamen = Xiamen, *China* **33 D6** 24 25N 118 4 E
sian = Xi'an, *China* **34 G5** 34 15N 109 0 E
sinchu, *Taiwan* **33 D7** 24 48N 120 58 E
sinhailien = Lianyungang, *China* **35 G10** 34 40N 119 11 E
süchou = Xuzhou, *China* **35 G9** 34 18N 117 10 E
u Xian, *China* **34 G5** 34 8N 108 42 E
ua Hin, *Thailand* **38 F2** 12 34N 99 58 E
ua Xian, *Henan, China* **34 G8** 35 30N 114 30 E
ua Xian, *Shaanxi, China* **34 G5** 34 30N 109 48 E
uachinera, *Mexico* **86 A3** 30 9N 108 55W
uacho, *Peru* **92 F3** 11 10S 77 35W
uade, *China* **34 D7** 41 55N 113 59 E
uadian, *China* **35 C14** 43 0N 126 40 E
uai He →, *China* **33 C6** 33 0N 118 30 E
uai Yot, *Thailand* **39 J2** 7 45N 99 37 E
uai'an, *Hebei, China* **34 D8** 40 30N 114 20 E
uai'an, *Jiangsu, China* **35 H10** 33 30N 119 10 E
uaibei, *China* **34 G9** 34 0N 116 48 E
uaide = Gongzhuling, *China* **35 C13** 43 30N 124 40 E
uaidezhen, *China* **35 C13** 43 48N 124 50 E
uainan, *China* **33 C6** 32 38N 116 58 E
uairen, *China* **34 E7** 39 48N 113 20 E
uairou, *China* **34 D9** 40 20N 116 35 E
uaiyang, *China* **34 H8** 33 40N 114 52 E
uaiyin, *China* **35 H10** 33 30N 119 2 E
uaiyuan, *China* **35 H9** 32 55N 117 10 E
uajianzi, *China* **35 D13** 41 23N 125 20 E
uajuapan de Leon, *Mexico* **87 D5** 17 50N 97 48W
ualapai Peak, *U.S.A.* **83 J7** 35 5N 113 54W
uallaga →, *Peru* **92 E3** 5 15S 75 30W
uambo, *Angola* **53 G3** 12 42S 15 54 E
uan Jiang →, *China* **34 G5** 34 28N 109 0 E
uan Xian, *China* **34 F4** 36 33N 107 7 E
uancabamba, *Peru* **92 E3** 5 10S 79 15W
uancane, *Peru* **92 G5** 15 10S 69 44W
uancavelica, *Peru* **92 F3** 12 50S 75 5W
uancayo, *Peru* **92 F3** 12 5S 75 12W
uanchaca, *Bolivia* **92 H5** 20 15S 66 40W
uang Hai = Yellow Sea, *China* **35 G12** 35 0N 123 0 E
uang He →, *China* **35 F10** 37 55N 118 50 E
uang Xian, *China* **35 F11** 37 38N 120 30 E
uangling, *China* **34 G5** 35 34N 109 15 E
uanglong, *China* **34 G5** 35 30N 109 59 E
uangshan, *China* **33 D6** 29 42N 118 25 E
uangshi, *China* **33 C6** 30 10N 115 3 E
uangsongdian, *China* **35 C14** 43 45N 127 25 E
uantai, *China* **35 F9** 36 58N 117 56 E
uánuco, *Peru* **92 E3** 9 55S 76 15W
uaraz, *Peru* **92 E3** 9 30S 77 32W
uarmey, *Peru* **92 F3** 10 5S 78 5W
uascarán, *Peru* **92 E3** 9 8S 77 36W
uasco, *Chile* **94 B1** 28 30S 71 15W
uasco →, *Chile* **94 B1** 28 27S 71 13W
uasna, *U.S.A.* **85 K6** 35 6N 120 24W
uatabampo, *Mexico* **86 B3** 26 50N 109 50W
uauchinango, *Mexico* **87 C5** 20 11N 98 3W
uautla de Jiménez, *Mexico* **87 D5** 18 8N 96 51W
uay Namota, *Mexico* **86 C4** 21 56N 104 30W
uayin, *China* **34 G6** 34 35N 110 5 E
ubbard, *Ohio, U.S.A.* **78 E4** 41 9N 80 34W
ubbard, *Tex., U.S.A.* **81 K6** 31 51N 96 48W
ubbart Pt., *Canada* **73 B10** 59 21N 94 41W
ubei □, *China* **33 C6** 31 0N 112 0 E
ubli, *India* **40 M9** 15 22N 75 15 E
uch'ang, *N. Korea* **35 D14** 41 25N 127 2 E
ucknall, *U.K.* **10 D6** 53 3N 1 13W
uddersfield, *U.K.* **10 D6** 53 39N 1 47W
udiksvall, *Sweden* **9 F17** 61 43N 17 10 E
udson, *Canada* **70 B1** 50 6N 92 9W
udson, *Mass., U.S.A.* **79 D13** 42 23N 71 34W
udson, *N.Y., U.S.A.* **79 D11** 42 15N 73 46W
udson, *Wis., U.S.A.* **80 C8** 44 58N 92 45W
udson, *Wyo., U.S.A.* **82 E9** 42 54N 108 35W
udson →, *U.S.A.* **79 F10** 40 42N 74 2W
udson Bay, *N.W.T., Canada* **69 C11** 60 0N 86 0W
udson Bay, *Sask., Canada* **73 C8** 52 51N 102 23W
udson Falls, *U.S.A.* **79 C11** 43 18N 73 35W
udson Mts., *Antarctica* **5 D16** 74 32S 99 20W
udson Str., *Canada* **69 B13** 62 0N 70 0W
udson's Hope, *Canada* **72 B4** 56 0N 121 54W
ue, *Vietnam* **38 D6** 16 30N 107 35 E
uehuetenango, *Guatemala* **88 C1** 15 20N 91 28W
uejúcar, *Mexico* **86 C4** 22 21N 103 13W
uelva, *Spain* **19 D2** 37 18N 6 57W
uentelauquén, *Chile* **94 C1** 31 38S 71 33W
uerta, Sa. de la, *Argentina* **94 C2** 31 10S 67 30W
uesca, *Spain* **19 A5** 42 8N 0 25W
uetamo, *Mexico* **86 D4** 18 36N 100 54W
ugh →, *Australia* **62 D1** 25 1S 134 1 E
ughenden, *Australia* **62 C3** 20 52S 144 10 E
ughes, *Australia* **61 F4** 30 42S 129 31 E
ughesville, *U.S.A.* **79 E8** 41 14N 76 44W
ugli →, *India* **43 J13** 21 56N 88 4 E
ugo, *Colo., U.S.A.* **80 F3** 39 8N 103 28W
ugo, *Okla., U.S.A.* **81 H7** 34 1N 95 31W
ugoton, *U.S.A.* **81 G4** 37 11N 101 21W
ui Xian = Huixian, *China* **34 G7** 35 27N 113 12 E
ui Xian, *China* **34 H4** 33 50N 106 4 E
ui'anbu, *China* **34 F4** 37 28N 106 38 E
uichapán, *Mexico* **87 C5** 20 24N 99 40W
uifa He →, *China* **35 C14** 43 0N 127 50 E
uila, Nevado del, *Colombia* **92 C3** 3 0N 76 0W
uimin, *China* **35 F9** 37 27N 117 28 E
uinan, *China* **35 C14** 42 40N 126 2 E
uinca Renancó, *Argentina* **94 C3** 34 51S 64 22W
uining, *China* **34 G3** 35 38N 105 0 E
uinong, *China* **34 E4** 39 5N 106 35 E
uisache, *Mexico* **86 C4** 22 55N 100 25W
iiting, *China* **34 G9** 34 5N 116 5 E
ixian, *China* **34 G7** 35 27N 113 12 E
uixtla, *Mexico* **87 D6** 15 9N 92 28W
Huize, *China* **32 D5** 26 24N 103 15 E
Hukawng Valley, *Burma* **41 F20** 26 30N 96 30 E
Hukuntsi, *Botswana* **56 C3** 23 58S 21 45 E
Ḥulayfā', *Si. Arabia* **44 E4** 25 58N 40 45 E
Huld = Ulaanjirem, *Mongolia* **34 B3** 45 5N 105 30 E
Hulin He →, *China* **35 B12** 45 0N 122 10 E
Hull = Kingston upon Hull, *U.K.* **10 D7** 53 45N 0 21W
Hull, *Canada* **79 A9** 45 25N 75 44W
Hull →, *U.K.* **10 D7** 53 44N 0 20W
Hulst, *Neths.* **15 C4** 51 17N 4 2 E
Hulun Nur, *China* **33 B6** 49 0N 117 30 E
Humahuaca, *Argentina* **94 A2** 23 10S 65 25W
Humaitá, *Brazil* **92 E6** 7 35S 63 1W
Humaitá, *Paraguay* **94 B4** 27 2S 58 31W
Humansdorp, *S. Africa* **56 E3** 34 2S 24 46 E
Humbe, *Angola* **56 B1** 16 40S 14 55 E
Humber →, *U.K.* **10 D7** 53 42N 0 27W
Humboldt, *Canada* **73 C7** 52 15N 105 9W
Humboldt, *Iowa, U.S.A.* **80 D7** 42 44N 94 13W
Humboldt, *Tenn., U.S.A.* **81 H10** 35 50N 88 55W
Humboldt →, *U.S.A.* **82 F4** 39 59N 118 36W
Humboldt Gletscher, *Greenland* **4 B4** 79 30N 62 0W
Hume, *U.S.A.* **84 J8** 36 48N 118 54W
Hume, L., *Australia* **63 F4** 36 0S 147 5 E
Humenné, *Slovak Rep.* **17 D11** 48 55N 21 50 E
Humphreys, Mt., *U.S.A.* **84 H8** 37 17N 118 40W
Humphreys Peak, *U.S.A.* **83 J8** 35 21N 111 41W
Humptulips, *U.S.A.* **84 C3** 47 14N 123 57W
Hūn, *Libya* **51 C9** 29 2N 16 0 E
Hun Jiang →, *China* **35 D13** 40 50N 125 38 E
Húnaflói, *Iceland* **8 D3** 65 50N 20 50W
Hunan □, *China* **33 D6** 27 30N 112 0 E
Hunchun, *China* **35 C16** 42 52N 130 28 E
Hundewali, *Pakistan* **42 D5** 31 55N 72 38 E
Hundred Mile House, *Canada* **72 C4** 51 38N 121 18W
Hunedoara, *Romania* **17 F12** 45 40N 22 50 E
Hungary ■, *Europe* **17 E10** 47 20N 19 20 E
Hungary, Plain of, *Europe* **6 F10** 47 0N 20 0 E
Hungerford, *Australia* **63 D3** 28 58S 144 24 E
Hŭngnam, *N. Korea* **35 E14** 39 49N 127 45 E
Hunsberge, *Namibia* **56 D2** 27 45S 17 12 E
Hunsrück, *Germany* **16 D4** 49 56N 7 27 E
Hunstanton, *U.K.* **10 E8** 52 56N 0 29 E
Hunter, *U.S.A.* **79 D10** 42 13N 74 13W
Hunter I., *Australia* **62 G3** 40 30S 144 45 E
Hunter I., *Canada* **72 C3** 51 55N 128 0W
Hunter Ra., *Australia* **63 E5** 32 45S 150 15 E
Hunters Road, *Zimbabwe* **55 F2** 19 9S 29 49 E
Hunterville, *N.Z.* **59 H5** 39 56S 175 35 E
Huntingburg, *U.S.A.* **76 F2** 38 18N 86 57W
Huntingdon, *Canada* **70 C5** 45 6N 74 10W
Huntingdon, *U.K.* **11 E7** 52 20N 0 11W
Huntingdon, *U.S.A.* **78 F6** 40 30N 78 1W
Huntington, *Ind., U.S.A.* **76 E3** 40 53N 85 30W
Huntington, *Oreg., U.S.A.* **82 D5** 44 21N 117 16W
Huntington, *Utah, U.S.A.* **82 G8** 39 20N 110 58W
Huntington, *W. Va., U.S.A.* **76 F4** 38 25N 82 27W
Huntington Beach, *U.S.A.* **85 M9** 33 40N 118 5W
Huntington Station, *U.S.A.* **79 F11** 40 52N 73 26W
Huntly, *N.Z.* **59 G5** 37 34S 175 11 E
Huntly, *U.K.* **12 D6** 57 27N 2 47W
Huntsville, *Canada* **78 A5** 45 20N 79 14W
Huntsville, *Ala., U.S.A.* **77 H2** 34 44N 86 35W
Huntsville, *Tex., U.S.A.* **81 K7** 30 43N 95 33W
Hunyani →, *Zimbabwe* **55 F3** 15 57S 30 39 E
Hunyuan, *China* **34 E7** 39 42N 113 42 E
Hunza →, *India* **43 B6** 35 54N 74 20 E
Huo Xian = Huozhou, *China* **34 F6** 36 36N 111 42 E
Huong Hoa, *Vietnam* **38 D6** 16 37N 106 45 E
Huong Khe, *Vietnam* **38 C5** 18 13N 105 41 E
Huonville, *Australia* **62 G4** 43 0S 147 5 E
Huozhou, *China* **34 F6** 36 36N 111 42 E
Hupeh = Hubei □, *China* **33 C6** 31 0N 112 0 E
Ḥūr, *Iran* **45 D8** 30 50N 57 7 E
Hurd, C., *Canada* **78 A3** 45 13N 81 44W
Hure Qi, *China* **35 C11** 42 45N 121 45 E
Hurghada, *Egypt* **51 C12** 27 15N 33 50 E
Hurley, *N. Mex., U.S.A.* **83 K9** 32 42N 108 8W
Hurley, *Wis., U.S.A.* **80 B9** 46 27N 90 11W
Huron, *Calif., U.S.A.* **84 J6** 36 12N 120 6W
Huron, *Ohio, U.S.A.* **78 E2** 41 24N 82 33W
Huron, *S. Dak., U.S.A.* **80 C5** 44 22N 98 13W
Huron, L., *U.S.A.* **78 B2** 44 30N 82 40W
Hurricane, *U.S.A.* **83 H7** 37 11N 113 17W
Hurunui →, *N.Z.* **59 K4** 42 54S 173 18 E
Húsavík, *Iceland* **8 C5** 66 3N 17 21W
Huşi, *Romania* **17 E15** 46 41N 28 7 E
Huskvarna, *Sweden* **9 H16** 57 47N 14 15 E
Hustadvika, *Norway* **8 E12** 63 0N 7 0 E
Hustontown, *U.S.A.* **78 F6** 40 3N 78 2W
Hutchinson, *Kans., U.S.A.* **81 F6** 38 5N 97 56W
Hutchinson, *Minn., U.S.A.* **80 C7** 44 54N 94 22W
Hutte Sauvage, L. de la, *Canada* **71 A7** 56 15N 64 45W
Hutton, Mt., *Australia* **63 D4** 25 51S 148 20 E
Huy, *Belgium* **15 D5** 50 31N 5 15 E
Huzhou, *China* **33 C7** 30 51N 120 8 E
Hvammstangi, *Iceland* **8 D3** 65 24N 20 57W
Hvar, *Croatia* **20 C7** 43 11N 16 28 E
Hvítá →, *Iceland* **8 D3** 64 30N 21 58W
Hwachŏn-chŏsuji, *S. Korea* **35 E14** 38 5N 127 50 E
Hwang Ho = Huang He →, *China* **35 F10** 37 55N 118 50 E
Hwange, *Zimbabwe* **55 F2** 18 18S 26 30 E
Hwange Nat. Park, *Zimbabwe* **56 B4** 19 0S 26 30 E
Hyannis, *Mass., U.S.A.* **76 E10** 41 39N 70 17W
Hyannis, *Nebr., U.S.A.* **80 E4** 42 0N 101 46W
Hyargas Nuur, *Mongolia* **32 B4** 49 0N 93 0 E
Hydaburg, *U.S.A.* **72 B2** 55 15N 132 50W
Hyde Park, *U.S.A.* **79 E11** 41 47N 73 56W
Hyden, *Australia* **61 F2** 32 24S 118 53 E
Hyder, *U.S.A.* **72 B2** 55 55N 130 5W
Hyderabad, *India* **40 L11** 17 22N 78 29 E
Hyderabad, *Pakistan* **42 G3** 25 23N 68 24 E
Hyères, *France* **18 E7** 43 8N 6 9 E
Hyères, Îs. d', *France* **18 E7** 43 0N 6 20 E
Hyesan, *N. Korea* **35 D15** 41 20N 128 10 E
Hyland →, *Canada* **72 B3** 59 52N 128 12W
Hymia, *India* **43 C8** 33 40N 78 2 E
Hyndman Peak, *U.S.A.* **82 E6** 43 45N 114 8W
Hyōgo □, *Japan* **31 G7** 35 15N 134 50 E
Hyrum, *U.S.A.* **82 F8** 41 38N 111 51W
Hysham, *U.S.A.* **82 C10** 46 18N 107 14W
Hythe, *U.K.* **11 F9** 51 4N 1 5 E
Hyūga, *Japan* **31 H5** 32 25N 131 35 E
Hyvinge = Hyvinkää, *Finland* **9 F21** 60 38N 24 50 E
Hyvinkää, *Finland* **9 F21** 60 38N 24 50 E

I

I-n-Gall, *Niger* **50 E7** 16 51N 7 1 E
Iaco →, *Brazil* **92 E5** 9 3S 68 34W
Iakora, *Madag.* **57 C8** 23 6S 46 40 E
Ialomiţa →, *Romania* **17 F14** 44 42N 27 51 E
Iaşi, *Romania* **17 E14** 47 10N 27 40 E
Ib →, *India* **43 J10** 21 34N 83 48 E
Iba, *Phil.* **37 A6** 15 22N 120 0 E
Ibadan, *Nigeria* **50 G6** 7 22N 3 58 E
Ibagué, *Colombia* **92 C3** 4 20N 75 20W
Ibar →, *Serbia, Yug.* **21 C9** 43 43N 20 45 E
Ibaraki □, *Japan* **31 F10** 36 10N 140 10 E
Ibarra, *Ecuador* **92 C3** 0 21N 78 7W
Ibembo, *Dem. Rep. of the Congo* **54 B1** 2 35N 23 35 E
Ibera, L., *Argentina* **94 B4** 28 30S 57 9W
Iberian Peninsula, *Europe* **6 H5** 40 0N 5 0W
Iberville, *Canada* **79 A11** 45 19N 73 17W
Iberville, Lac d', *Canada* **70 A5** 55 55N 73 15W
Ibiá, *Brazil* **93 G9** 19 30S 46 30W
Ibicuí →, *Brazil* **95 B4** 29 25S 56 47W
Ibicuy, *Argentina* **94 C4** 33 55S 59 10W
Ibioapaba, Sa. da, *Brazil* **93 D10** 4 0S 41 30W
Ibiza = Eivissa, *Spain* **22 C7** 38 54N 1 26 E
Ibo, *Mozam.* **55 E5** 12 22S 40 40 E
Ibonma, *Indonesia* **37 E8** 3 29S 133 31 E
Ibotirama, *Brazil* **93 F10** 12 13S 43 12W
Ibrāhīm →, *Lebanon* **47 A4** 34 4N 35 38 E
'Ibrī, *Oman* **45 F8** 23 14N 56 30 E
Ibu, *Indonesia* **37 D7** 1 35N 127 33 E
Ibusuki, *Japan* **31 J5** 31 12N 130 40 E
Ica, *Peru* **92 F3** 14 0S 75 48W
Içá →, *Brazil* **92 D5** 2 55S 67 58W
Içana, *Brazil* **92 C5** 0 21N 67 19W
Içana →, *Brazil* **92 C5** 0 26N 67 19W
Içel = Mersin, *Turkey* **25 G5** 36 51N 34 36 E
Iceland ■, *Europe* **8 D4** 64 45N 19 0W
Ich'ang = Yichang, *China* **33 C6** 30 40N 111 20 E
Ichchapuram, *India* **41 K14** 19 10N 84 40 E
Ichhawar, *India* **42 H7** 23 1N 77 1 E
Ichihara, *Japan* **31 G10** 35 28N 140 5 E
Ichikawa, *Japan* **31 G9** 35 44N 139 55 E
Ichilo →, *Bolivia* **92 G6** 15 57S 64 50W
Ichinohe, *Japan* **30 D10** 40 13N 141 17 E
Ichinomiya, *Japan* **31 G8** 35 18N 136 48 E
Ichinoseki, *Japan* **30 E10** 38 55N 141 8 E
Ichŏn, *S. Korea* **35 F14** 37 17N 127 27 E
Icod, *Canary Is.* **22 F3** 28 22N 16 43W
Ida Grove, *U.S.A.* **80 D7** 42 21N 95 28W
Idabel, *U.S.A.* **81 J7** 33 54N 94 50W
Idaho □, *U.S.A.* **82 D7** 45 0N 115 0W
Idaho City, *U.S.A.* **82 E6** 43 50N 115 50W
Idaho Falls, *U.S.A.* **82 E7** 43 30N 112 2W
Idar-Oberstein, *Germany* **16 D4** 49 43N 7 16 E
Idfû, *Egypt* **51 D12** 24 55N 32 49 E
Ídhi Óros, *Greece* **23 D6** 35 15N 24 45 E
Ídhra, *Greece* **21 F10** 37 20N 23 28 E
Idi, *Indonesia* **36 C1** 5 2N 97 37 E
Idiofa, *Dem. Rep. of the Congo* **52 E3** 4 55S 19 42 E
Idlib, *Syria* **44 C3** 35 55N 36 36 E
Idria, *U.S.A.* **84 J6** 36 25N 120 41W
Idutywa, *S. Africa* **57 E4** 32 8S 28 18 E
Ieper, *Belgium* **15 D2** 50 51N 2 53 E
Ierápetra, *Greece* **23 E7** 35 1N 25 44 E
Iesi, *Italy* **20 C5** 43 31N 13 14 E
Ifakara, *Tanzania* **52 F7** 8 8S 36 41 E
'Ifāl, W. al →, *Si. Arabia* **44 D2** 28 7N 35 3 E
Ifanadiana, *Madag.* **57 C8** 21 19S 47 39 E
Ife, *Nigeria* **50 G6** 7 30N 4 31 E
Iférouâne, *Niger* **50 E7** 19 5N 8 24 E
Iffley, *Australia* **62 B3** 18 53S 141 12 E
Ifni, *Morocco* **50 C3** 29 29N 10 12W
Iforas, Adrar des, *Mali* **50 E6** 19 40N 1 40 E
Ifould, L., *Australia* **61 F5** 30 52S 132 6 E
Iganga, *Uganda* **54 B3** 0 37N 33 28 E
Igarapava, *Brazil* **93 H9** 20 3S 47 47W
Igarka, *Russia* **26 C9** 67 30N 86 33 E
Igatimi, *Paraguay* **95 A4** 24 5S 55 40W
Iggesund, *Sweden* **9 F17** 61 39N 17 10 E
Iglésias, *Italy* **20 E3** 39 19N 8 32 E
Igloolik, *Canada* **69 B11** 69 20N 81 49W
Igluligaarjuk, *Canada* **69 B10** 63 21N 90 42W
Ignace, *Canada* **70 C1** 49 30N 91 40W
İğneada Burnu, *Turkey* **21 D13** 41 53N 28 2 E
Igoumenítsa, *Greece* **21 E9** 39 32N 20 18 E
Iguaçu →, *Brazil* **95 B5** 25 36S 54 36W
Iguaçu, Cat. del, *Brazil* **95 B5** 25 41S 54 26W
Iguaçu Falls = Iguaçu, Cat. del, *Brazil* **95 B5** 25 41S 54 26W
Iguala, *Mexico* **87 D5** 18 20N 99 40W
Igualada, *Spain* **19 B6** 41 37N 1 37 E
Iguassu = Iguaçu →, *Brazil* **95 B5** 25 36S 54 36W
Iguatu, *Brazil* **93 E11** 6 20S 39 18W
Iharana, *Madag.* **57 A9** 13 25S 50 0 E
Ihbulag, *Mongolia* **34 C4** 43 11N 107 10 E
Iheya-Shima, *Japan* **31 L3** 27 4N 127 58 E
Ihosy, *Madag.* **57 C8** 22 24S 46 8 E
Ihotry, L., *Madag.* **57 C7** 21 56S 43 41 E
Ii, *Finland* **8 D21** 65 19N 25 22 E
Ii-Shima, *Japan* **31 L3** 26 43N 127 47 E
Iida, *Japan* **31 G8** 35 35N 137 50 E
Iijoki →, *Finland* **8 D21** 65 20N 25 20 E
Iisalmi, *Finland* **8 E22** 63 32N 27 10 E
Iiyama, *Japan* **31 F9** 36 51N 138 22 E
Iizuka, *Japan* **31 H5** 33 38N 130 42 E
Ijebu-Ode, *Nigeria* **50 G6** 6 47N 3 58 E
IJmuiden, *Neths.* **15 B4** 52 28N 4 35 E
IJssel →, *Neths.* **15 B5** 52 35N 5 50 E
IJsselmeer, *Neths.* **15 B5** 52 45N 5 20 E
Ijuí, *Brazil* **95 B5** 28 23S 53 55W
Ijuí →, *Brazil* **95 B4** 27 58S 55 20W
Ikaluktutiak, *Canada* **68 B9** 69 10N 105 0W
Ikare, *Nigeria* **50 G7** 7 32N 5 40 E
Ikaría, *Greece* **21 F12** 37 35N 26 10 E
Ikeda, *Japan* **31 G6** 34 1N 133 48 E
Ikela, *Dem. Rep. of the Congo* **52 E4** 1 6S 23 6 E
Iki, *Japan* **31 H4** 33 45N 129 42 E
Ikimba L., *Tanzania* **54 C3** 1 30S 31 20 E
Ikopa →, *Madag.* **57 B8** 16 45S 46 40 E
Ikungu, *Tanzania* **54 C3** 1 33S 33 42 E
Ilagan, *Phil.* **37 A6** 17 7N 121 53 E
Īlām, *Iran* **44 C5** 33 36N 46 36 E
Ilam, *Nepal* **43 F12** 26 58N 87 58 E
Ilam □, *Iran* **44 C5** 33 0N 47 0 E
Ilanskiy, *Russia* **27 D10** 56 14N 96 3 E
Iława, *Poland* **17 B10** 53 36N 19 34 E
Ile-à-la-Crosse, *Canada* **73 B7** 55 27N 107 53W
Ile-à-la-Crosse, Lac, *Canada* **73 B7** 55 40N 107 45W
Île-de-France □, *France* **18 B5** 49 0N 2 20 E
Ilebo, *Dem. Rep. of the Congo* **52 E4** 4 17S 20 55 E
Ilek, *Russia* **26 D6** 51 32N 53 21 E
Ilek →, *Russia* **24 D9** 51 30N 53 22 E
Ilesha, *Nigeria* **50 G6** 7 37N 4 40 E
Ilford, *Canada* **73 B9** 56 4N 95 35W
Ilfracombe, *Australia* **62 C3** 23 30S 144 30 E
Ilfracombe, *U.K.* **11 F3** 51 12N 4 8W
Ilhéus, *Brazil* **93 F11** 14 49S 39 2W
Ili →, *Kazakstan* **26 E8** 45 53N 77 10 E
Iliamna L., *U.S.A.* **68 C4** 59 30N 155 0W
Iligan, *Phil.* **37 C6** 8 12N 124 13 E
Ilion, *U.S.A.* **79 D9** 43 1N 75 2W
Ilkeston, *U.K.* **10 E6** 52 58N 1 19W
Ilkley, *U.K.* **10 D6** 53 56N 1 48W
Illampu = Ancohuma, Nevada, *Bolivia* **92 G5** 16 0S 68 50W
Illana B., *Phil.* **37 C6** 7 35N 123 45 E
Illapel, *Chile* **94 C1** 32 0S 71 10W
Iller →, *Germany* **16 D6** 48 23N 9 58 E
Illetas, *Spain* **22 B9** 39 32N 2 35 E
Illimani, Nevado, *Bolivia* **92 G5** 16 30S 67 50W
Illinois □, *U.S.A.* **80 E10** 40 15N 89 30W
Illinois →, *U.S.A.* **75 C8** 38 58N 90 28W
Illium = Troy, *Turkey* **21 E12** 39 57N 26 12 E
Illizi, *Algeria* **50 C7** 26 31N 8 32 E
Ilmajoki, *Finland* **9 E20** 62 44N 22 34 E
Ilmen, Ozero, *Russia* **24 C5** 58 15N 31 10 E
Ilo, *Peru* **92 G4** 17 40S 71 20W
Iloilo, *Phil.* **37 B6** 10 45N 122 33 E
Ilorin, *Nigeria* **50 G6** 8 30N 4 35 E
Ilwaco, *U.S.A.* **84 D2** 46 19N 124 3W
Ilwaki, *Indonesia* **37 F7** 7 55S 126 30 E
Imabari, *Japan* **31 G6** 34 4N 133 0 E
Imaloto →, *Madag.* **57 C8** 23 27S 45 13 E
Imandra, Ozero, *Russia* **24 A5** 67 30N 33 0 E
Imari, *Japan* **31 H4** 33 15N 129 52 E
Imatra, *Finland* **24 B4** 61 12N 28 48 E
Imbil, *Australia* **63 D5** 26 22S 152 32 E
imeni 26 Bakinskikh Komissarov = Neftçala, *Azerbaijan* **25 G8** 39 19N 49 12 E
Imeri, Serra, *Brazil* **92 C5** 0 50N 65 25W
Imerimandroso, *Madag.* **57 B8** 17 26S 48 35 E
Imi, *Ethiopia* **46 F3** 6 28N 42 10 E
Imlay, *U.S.A.* **82 F4** 40 40N 118 9W
Imlay City, *U.S.A.* **78 D1** 43 2N 83 5W
Immingham, *U.K.* **10 D7** 53 37N 0 13W
Immokalee, *U.S.A.* **77 M5** 26 25N 81 25W
Ímola, *Italy* **20 B4** 44 20N 11 42 E
Imperatriz, *Brazil* **93 E9** 5 30S 47 29W
Impéria, *Italy* **18 E8** 43 53N 8 3 E
Imperial, *Canada* **73 C7** 51 21N 105 28W
Imperial, *Calif., U.S.A.* **85 N11** 32 51N 115 34W
Imperial, *Nebr., U.S.A.* **80 E4** 40 31N 101 39W
Imperial Beach, *U.S.A.* **85 N9** 32 35N 117 8W
Imperial Dam, *U.S.A.* **85 N12** 32 55N 114 25W
Imperial Reservoir, *U.S.A.* **85 N12** 32 53N 114 28W
Imperial Valley, *U.S.A.* **85 N11** 33 0N 115 30W
Imperieuse Reef, *Australia* **60 C2** 17 36S 118 50 E
Impfondo, *Congo* **52 D3** 1 40N 18 0 E
Imphal, *India* **41 G18** 24 48N 93 56 E
İmroz = Gökçeada, *Turkey* **21 D11** 40 10N 25 50 E
Imuris, *Mexico* **86 A2** 30 47N 110 52W
Imuruan B., *Phil.* **37 B5** 10 40N 119 10 E
In Salah, *Algeria* **50 C6** 27 10N 2 32 E
Ina, *Japan* **31 G8** 35 50N 137 55 E
Inangahua Junction, *N.Z.* **59 J3** 41 52S 171 59 E
Inanwatan, *Indonesia* **37 E8** 2 10S 132 14 E
Iñapari, *Peru* **92 F5** 11 0S 69 40W
Inari, *Finland* **8 B22** 68 54N 27 5 E
Inarijärvi, *Finland* **8 B22** 69 0N 28 0 E
Inawashiro-Ko, *Japan* **30 F10** 37 29N 140 6 E
Inca, *Spain* **22 B9** 39 43N 2 54 E
Inca de Oro, *Chile* **94 B2** 26 45S 69 54W
Incaguasi, *Chile* **94 B1** 29 12S 71 5W
İnce Burun, *Turkey* **25 F5** 42 7N 34 56 E
İncesu, *Turkey* **44 B2** 38 38N 35 11 E
Inch'ŏn, *S. Korea* **35 F14** 37 27N 126 40 E
İncirliova, *Turkey* **21 F12** 37 50N 27 41 E
Incline Village, *U.S.A.* **82 G4** 39 10N 119 58W
Incomáti →, *Mozam.* **57 D5** 25 46S 32 43 E
Indalsälven →, *Sweden* **9 E17** 62 36N 17 30 E
Indaw, *Burma* **41 G20** 24 15N 96 5 E
Independence, *Calif., U.S.A.* **84 J8** 36 48N 118 12W
Independence, *Iowa, U.S.A.* **80 D9** 42 28N 91 54W
Independence, *Kans., U.S.A.* **81 G7** 37 14N 95 42W
Independence, *Ky., U.S.A.* **76 F3** 38 57N 84 33W
Independence, *Mo., U.S.A.* **80 F7** 39 6N 94 25W
Independence Fjord, *Greenland* **4 A6** 82 10N 29 0W
Independence Mts., *U.S.A.* **82 F5** 41 20N 116 0W
Index, *U.S.A.* **84 C5** 47 50N 121 33W
India ■, *Asia* **40 K11** 20 0N 78 0 E
Indian →, *U.S.A.* **77 M5** 27 59N 80 34W
Indian Cabins, *Canada* **72 B5** 59 52N 117 40W
Indian Harbour, *Canada* **71 B8** 54 27N 57 13W
Indian Head, *Canada* **73 C8** 50 30N 103 41W
Indian Lake, *U.S.A.* **79 C10** 43 47N 74 16W
Indian Ocean **28 K11** 5 0S 75 0 E
Indian Springs, *U.S.A.* **85 J11** 36 35N 115 40W
Indiana, *U.S.A.* **78 F5** 40 37N 79 9W
Indiana □, *U.S.A.* **76 F3** 40 0N 86 0W
Indianapolis, *U.S.A.* **76 F2** 39 46N 86 9W
Indianola, *Iowa, U.S.A.* **80 E8** 41 22N 93 34W
Indianola, *Miss., U.S.A.* **81 J9** 33 27N 90 39W
Indiga, *Russia* **24 A8** 67 38N 49 9 E
Indigirka →, *Russia* **27 B15** 70 48N 148 54 E
Indio, *U.S.A.* **85 M10** 33 43N 116 13W
Indo-China, *Asia* **28 H14** 15 0N 102 0 E
Indonesia ■, *Asia* **36 F5** 5 0S 115 0 E

Indore

Indore, *India* **42 H6** 22 42N 75 53 E
Indramayu, *Indonesia* **37 G13** 6 20S 108 19 E
Indravati →, *India* **41 K12** 19 20N 80 20 E
Indre →, *France* **18 C4** 47 16N 0 11 E
Indulkana, *Australia* **63 D1** 26 58S 133 5 E
Indus →, *Pakistan* **42 G2** 24 20N 67 47 E
Indus, Mouth of the, *Pakistan* **42 H3** 24 0N 68 0 E
İnebolu, *Turkey* **25 F5** 41 55N 33 40 E
Infiernillo, Presa del, *Mexico* **86 D4** 18 9N 102 0W
Ingenio, *Canary Is.* **22 G4** 27 55N 15 26W
Ingenio Santa Ana, *Argentina* **94 B2** 27 25S 65 40W
Ingersoll, *Canada* **78 C4** 43 4N 80 55W
Ingham, *Australia* **62 B4** 18 43S 146 10 E
Ingleborough, *U.K.* **10 C5** 54 10N 2 22W
Inglewood, *Queens., Australia* **63 D5** 28 25S 151 2 E
Inglewood, *Vic., Australia* **63 F3** 36 29S 143 53 E
Inglewood, *N.Z.* **59 H5** 39 9S 174 14 E
Inglewood, *U.S.A.* **85 M8** 33 58N 118 21W
Ingólfshöfði, *Iceland* **8 E5** 63 48N 16 39W
Ingolstadt, *Germany* **16 D6** 48 46N 11 26 E
Ingomar, *U.S.A.* **82 C10** 46 35N 107 23W
Ingonish, *Canada* **71 C7** 46 42N 60 18W
Ingraj Bazar, *India* **43 G13** 24 58N 88 10 E
Ingrid Christensen Coast, *Antarctica* **5 C6** 69 30S 76 0 E
Ingulec = Inhulec, *Ukraine* **25 E5** 47 42N 33 14 E
Ingushetia □, *Russia* **25 E8** 43 20N 44 50 E
Ingwavuma, *S. Africa* **57 D5** 27 9S 31 59 E
Inhaca, I., *Mozam.* **57 D5** 26 1S 32 57 E
Inhafenga, *Mozam.* **57 C5** 20 36S 33 53 E
Inhambane, *Mozam.* **57 C6** 23 54S 35 30 E
Inhambane □, *Mozam.* **57 C5** 22 30S 34 20 E
Inhaminga, *Mozam.* **55 F4** 18 26S 35 0 E
Inharrime, *Mozam.* **57 C6** 24 30S 35 0 E
Inharrime →, *Mozam.* **57 C6** 24 30S 35 0 E
Inhulec, *Ukraine* **25 E5** 47 42N 33 14 E
Ining = Yining, *China* **26 E9** 43 58N 81 10 E
Inírida →, *Colombia* **92 C5** 3 55N 67 52W
Inishbofin, *Ireland* **13 C1** 53 37N 10 13W
Inisheer, *Ireland* **13 C2** 53 3N 9 32W
Inishfree B., *Ireland* **13 A3** 55 4N 8 23W
Inishkea North, *Ireland* **13 B1** 54 9N 10 11W
Inishkea South, *Ireland* **13 B1** 54 7N 10 12W
Inishmaan, *Ireland* **13 C2** 53 5N 9 35W
Inishmore, *Ireland* **13 C2** 53 8N 9 45W
Inishowen Pen., *Ireland* **13 A4** 55 14N 7 15W
Inishshark, *Ireland* **13 C1** 53 37N 10 16W
Inishturk, *Ireland* **13 C1** 53 42N 10 7W
Inishvickillane, *Ireland* **13 D1** 52 3N 10 37W
Injune, *Australia* **63 D4** 25 53S 148 32 E
Inklin →, *Canada* **72 B2** 58 50N 133 10W
Inle L., *Burma* **41 J20** 20 30N 96 58 E
Inlet, *U.S.A.* **79 C10** 43 45N 74 48W
Inn →, *Austria* **16 D7** 48 35N 13 28 E
Innamincka, *Australia* **63 D3** 27 44S 140 46 E
Inner Hebrides, *U.K.* **12 E2** 57 0N 6 30W
Inner Mongolia = Nei Monggol Zizhiqu □, *China* **34 D7** 42 0N 112 0 E
Inner Sound, *U.K.* **12 D3** 57 30N 5 55W
Innerkip, *Canada* **78 C4** 43 13N 80 42W
Innetalling I., *Canada* **70 A4** 56 0N 79 0W
Innisfail, *Australia* **62 B4** 17 33S 146 5 E
Innisfail, *Canada* **72 C6** 52 0N 113 57W
In'no-shima, *Japan* **31 G6** 34 19N 133 10 E
Innsbruck, *Austria* **16 E6** 47 16N 11 23 E
Inny →, *Ireland* **13 C4** 53 30N 7 50W
Inongo, *Dem. Rep. of the Congo* **52 E3** 1 55S 18 30 E
Inoucdjouac = Inukjuak, *Canada* **69 C12** 58 25N 78 15W
Inowrocław, *Poland* **17 B10** 52 50N 18 12 E
Inpundong, *N. Korea* **35 D14** 41 25N 126 34 E
Inscription, C., *Australia* **61 E1** 25 29S 112 59 E
Insein, *Burma* **41 L20** 16 50N 96 5 E
Inta, *Russia* **24 A11** 66 5N 60 8 E
Intendente Alvear, *Argentina* **94 D3** 35 12S 63 32W
Interlaken, *Switz.* **18 C7** 46 41N 7 50 E
Interlaken, *U.S.A.* **79 D8** 42 37N 76 44W
International Falls, *U.S.A.* **80 A8** 48 36N 93 25W
Intiyaco, *Argentina* **94 B3** 28 43S 60 5W
Inukjuak, *Canada* **69 C12** 58 25N 78 15W
Inútil, B., *Chile* **96 G2** 53 30S 70 15W
Inuvik, *Canada* **68 B6** 68 16N 133 40W
Inveraray, *U.K.* **12 E3** 56 14N 5 5W
Inverbervie, *U.K.* **12 E6** 56 51N 2 17W
Invercargill, *N.Z.* **59 M2** 46 24S 168 24 E
Inverclyde □, *U.K.* **12 F4** 55 55N 4 49W
Inverell, *Australia* **63 D5** 29 45S 151 8 E
Invergordon, *U.K.* **12 D4** 57 41N 4 10W
Inverloch, *Australia* **63 F4** 38 38S 145 45 E
Invermere, *Canada* **72 C5** 50 30N 116 2W
Inverness, *Canada* **71 C7** 46 15N 61 19W
Inverness, *U.K.* **12 D4** 57 29N 4 13W
Inverness, *U.S.A.* **77 L4** 28 50N 82 20W
Inverurie, *U.K.* **12 D6** 57 17N 2 23W
Investigator Group, *Australia* **63 E1** 34 45S 134 20 E
Investigator Str., *Australia* **63 F2** 35 30S 137 0 E
Inya, *Russia* **26 D9** 50 28N 86 37 E
Inyanga, *Zimbabwe* **55 F3** 18 12S 32 40 E
Inyangani, *Zimbabwe* **55 F3** 18 5S 32 50 E
Inyantue, *Zimbabwe* **55 F2** 18 30S 26 40 E
Inyo Mts., *U.S.A.* **84 J9** 36 40N 118 0W
Inyokern, *U.S.A.* **85 K9** 35 39N 117 49W
Inza, *Russia* **24 D8** 53 55N 46 25 E
Iō-Jima, *Japan* **31 J5** 30 48N 130 18 E
Ioánnina, *Greece* **21 E9** 39 42N 20 47 E
Iola, *U.S.A.* **81 G7** 37 55N 95 24W
Iona, *U.K.* **12 E2** 56 20N 6 25W
Ione, *U.S.A.* **84 G6** 38 21N 120 56W
Ionia, *U.S.A.* **76 D3** 42 59N 85 4W
Ionian Is. = Iónioi Nísoi, *Greece* **21 E9** 38 40N 20 0 E
Ionian Sea, *Medit. S.* **21 E7** 37 30N 17 30 E
Iónioi Nísoi, *Greece* **21 E9** 38 40N 20 0 E
Íos, *Greece* **21 F11** 36 41N 25 20 E
Iowa □, *U.S.A.* **80 D8** 42 18N 93 30W
Iowa →, *U.S.A.* **80 E9** 41 10N 91 1W
Iowa City, *U.S.A.* **80 E9** 41 40N 91 32W
Iowa Falls, *U.S.A.* **80 D8** 42 31N 93 16W
Iowa Park, *U.S.A.* **81 J5** 33 57N 98 40W
Ipala, *Tanzania* **54 C3** 4 30S 32 52 E
Ipameri, *Brazil* **93 G9** 17 44S 48 9W
Ipatinga, *Brazil* **93 G10** 19 32S 42 30W
Ipiales, *Colombia* **92 C3** 0 50N 77 37W
Ipin = Yibin, *China* **32 D5** 28 45N 104 32 E
Ipixuna, *Brazil* **92 E4** 7 0S 71 40W
Ipoh, *Malaysia* **39 K3** 4 35N 101 5 E
Ippy, *C.A.R.* **52 C4** 6 5N 21 7 E
İpsala, *Turkey* **21 D12** 40 55N 26 23 E
Ipswich, *Australia* **63 D5** 27 35S 152 40 E
Ipswich, *U.K.* **11 E9** 52 4N 1 10 E
Ipswich, *Mass., U.S.A.* **79 D14** 42 41N 70 50W
Ipswich, *S. Dak., U.S.A.* **80 C5** 45 27N 99 2W
Ipu, *Brazil* **93 D10** 4 23S 40 44W
Iqaluit, *Canada* **69 B13** 63 44N 68 31W
Iquique, *Chile* **92 H4** 20 19S 70 5W
Iquitos, *Peru* **92 D4** 3 45S 73 10W
Irabu-Jima, *Japan* **31 M2** 24 50N 125 10 E
Iracoubo, *Fr. Guiana* **93 B8** 5 30N 53 10W
Īrafshān, *Iran* **45 E9** 26 42N 61 56 E
Iráklion, *Greece* **23 D7** 35 20N 25 12 E
Iráklion □, *Greece* **23 D7** 35 10N 25 10 E
Irala, *Paraguay* **95 B5** 25 55S 54 35W
Iran ■, *Asia* **45 C7** 33 0N 53 0 E
Iran, Gunung-Gunung, *Malaysia* **36 D4** 2 20N 114 50 E
Iran, Plateau of, *Asia* **28 F9** 32 0N 55 0 E
Iran Ra. = Iran, Gunung-Gunung, *Malaysia* **36 D4** 2 20N 114 50 E
Īrānshahr, *Iran* **45 E9** 27 15N 60 40 E
Irapuato, *Mexico* **86 C4** 20 40N 101 30W
Iraq ■, *Asia* **44 C5** 33 0N 44 0 E
Irati, *Brazil* **95 B5** 25 25S 50 38W
Irbid, *Jordan* **47 C4** 32 35N 35 48 E
Irbid □, *Jordan* **47 C5** 32 15N 36 35 E
Ireland ■, *Europe* **13 C4** 53 50N 7 52W
Irhyangdong, *N. Korea* **35 D15** 41 15N 129 30 E
Iri, *S. Korea* **35 G14** 35 59N 127 0 E
Irian Jaya □, *Indonesia* **37 E9** 4 0S 137 0 E
Iringa, *Tanzania* **54 D4** 7 48S 35 43 E
Iringa □, *Tanzania* **54 D4** 7 48S 35 43 E
Iriomote-Jima, *Japan* **31 M1** 24 19N 123 48 E
Iriona, *Honduras* **88 C2** 15 57N 85 11W
Iriri →, *Brazil* **93 D8** 3 52S 52 37W
Irish Republic ■, *Europe* **13 C3** 53 0N 8 0W
Irish Sea, *U.K.* **10 D3** 53 38N 4 48W
Irkutsk, *Russia* **27 D11** 52 18N 104 20 E
Irma, *Canada* **73 C6** 52 55N 111 14W
Irō-Zaki, *Japan* **31 G9** 34 36N 138 51 E
Iron Baron, *Australia* **63 E2** 32 58S 137 11 E
Iron Gate = Portile de Fier, *Europe* **17 F12** 44 44N 22 30 E
Iron Knob, *Australia* **63 E2** 32 46S 137 8 E
Iron Mountain, *U.S.A.* **76 C1** 45 49N 88 4W
Iron River, *U.S.A.* **80 B10** 46 6N 88 39W
Irondequoit, *U.S.A.* **78 C7** 43 13N 77 35W
Ironstone Kopje, *Botswana* **56 D3** 25 17S 24 5 E
Ironton, *Mo., U.S.A.* **81 G9** 37 36N 90 38W
Ironton, *Ohio, U.S.A.* **76 F4** 38 32N 82 41W
Ironwood, *U.S.A.* **80 B9** 46 27N 90 9W
Iroquois, *Canada* **79 B9** 44 51N 75 19W
Iroquois Falls, *Canada* **70 C3** 48 46N 80 41W
Irpin, *Ukraine* **17 C16** 50 30N 30 15 E
Irrara Cr. →, *Australia* **63 D4** 29 35S 145 31 E
Irrawaddy □, *Burma* **41 L19** 17 0N 95 0 E
Irrawaddy →, *Burma* **41 M19** 15 50N 95 6 E
Irricana, *Canada* **72 C6** 51 19N 113 37W
Irtysh →, *Russia* **26 C7** 61 4N 68 52 E
Irumu, *Dem. Rep. of the Congo* **54 B2** 1 32N 29 53 E
Irún, *Spain* **19 A5** 43 20N 1 52W
Irunea = Pamplona, *Spain* **19 A5** 42 48N 1 38W
Irvine, *Canada* **73 D6** 49 57N 110 16W
Irvine, *U.K.* **12 F4** 55 37N 4 41W
Irvine, *Calif., U.S.A.* **85 M9** 33 41N 117 46W
Irvine, *Ky., U.S.A.* **76 G4** 37 42N 83 58W
Irvinestown, *U.K.* **13 B4** 54 28N 7 39W
Irving, *U.S.A.* **81 J6** 32 49N 96 56W
Irvona, *U.S.A.* **78 F6** 40 46N 78 33W
Irwin →, *Australia* **61 E1** 29 15S 114 54 E
Irymple, *Australia* **63 E3** 34 14S 142 8 E
Isa Khel, *Pakistan* **42 C4** 32 41N 71 17 E
Isaac →, *Australia* **62 C4** 22 55S 149 20 E
Isabel, *U.S.A.* **80 C4** 45 24N 101 26W
Isabela, I., *Mexico* **86 C3** 21 51N 105 55W
Isabelia, Cord., *Nic.* **88 D2** 13 30N 85 25W
Isabella, *Phil.* **37 C6** 6 40N 122 10 E
Isabella Ra., *Australia* **60 D3** 21 0S 121 4 E
Ísafjarðardjúp, *Iceland* **8 C2** 66 10N 23 0W
Ísafjörður, *Iceland* **8 C2** 66 5N 23 9W
Isagarh, *India* **42 G7** 24 48N 77 51 E
Isahaya, *Japan* **31 H5** 32 52N 130 2 E
Isaka, *Tanzania* **54 C3** 3 56S 32 59 E
Isan →, *India* **43 F9** 26 51N 80 7 E
Isana = Içana →, *Brazil* **92 C5** 0 26N 67 19W
Isar →, *Germany* **16 D7** 48 48N 12 57 E
Íschia, *Italy* **20 D5** 40 44N 13 57 E
Isdell →, *Australia* **60 C3** 16 27S 124 51 E
Ise, *Japan* **31 G8** 34 25N 136 45 E
Ise-Wan, *Japan* **31 G8** 34 43N 136 43 E
Iseramagazi, *Tanzania* **54 C3** 4 37S 32 10 E
Isère →, *France* **18 D6** 44 59N 4 51 E
Isérnia, *Italy* **20 D6** 41 36N 14 14 E
Isfahan = Eşfahān, *Iran* **45 C6** 32 39N 51 43 E
Ishigaki-Shima, *Japan* **31 M2** 24 20N 124 10 E
Ishikari-Gawa →, *Japan* **30 C10** 43 15N 141 23 E
Ishikari-Sammyaku, *Japan* **30 C11** 43 30N 143 0 E
Ishikari-Wan, *Japan* **30 C10** 43 25N 141 1 E
Ishikawa □, *Japan* **31 F8** 36 30N 136 30 E
Ishim, *Russia* **26 D7** 56 10N 69 30 E
Ishim →, *Russia* **26 D8** 57 45N 71 10 E
Ishinomaki, *Japan* **30 E10** 38 32N 141 20 E
Ishioka, *Japan* **31 F10** 36 11N 140 16 E
Ishkuman, *Pakistan* **43 A5** 36 30N 73 50 E
Ishpeming, *U.S.A.* **76 B2** 46 29N 87 40W
Isil Kul, *Russia* **26 D8** 54 55N 71 16 E
Isiolo, *Kenya* **54 B4** 0 24N 37 33 E
Isiro, *Dem. Rep. of the Congo* **54 B2** 2 53N 27 40 E
Isisford, *Australia* **62 C3** 24 15S 144 21 E
İskenderun, *Turkey* **25 G6** 36 32N 36 10 E
İskenderun Körfezi, *Turkey* **25 G6** 36 40N 35 50 E
İskŭr →, *Bulgaria* **21 C11** 43 45N 24 25 E
Iskut →, *Canada* **72 B2** 56 45N 131 49W
Isla →, *U.K.* **12 E5** 56 32N 3 20W
Isla Vista, *U.S.A.* **85 L7** 34 25N 119 53W
Islam Headworks, *Pakistan* **42 E5** 29 49N 72 33 E
Islamabad, *Pakistan* **42 C5** 33 40N 73 10 E
Islamgarh, *Pakistan* **42 F4** 27 51N 70 48 E
Islamkot, *Pakistan* **42 G4** 24 42N 70 13 E
Islampur, *India* **43 G11** 25 9N 85 12 E
Island L., *Canada* **73 C10** 53 47N 94 25W
Island Lagoon, *Australia* **63 E2** 31 30S 136 40 E
Island Pond, *U.S.A.* **79 B13** 44 49N 71 53W
Islands, B. of, *Canada* **71 C8** 49 11N 58 15W
Islay, *U.K.* **12 F2** 55 46N 6 10W
Isle →, *France* **18 D3** 44 55N 0 15W
Isle aux Morts, *Canada* **71 C8** 47 35N 59 0W
Isle of Wight □, *U.K.* **11 G6** 50 41N 1 17W
Isle Royale, *U.S.A.* **80 B10** 48 0N 88 54W
Isle Royale National Park, *U.S.A.* **80 B10** 48 0N 88 55W
Isleton, *U.S.A.* **84 G5** 38 10N 121 37W
Ismail = Izmayil, *Ukraine* **17 F15** 45 22N 28 46 E
Ismâ'ilîya, *Egypt* **51 B12** 30 37N 32 18 E
Isogstalo, *India* **43 B8** 34 15N 78 46 E
Isparta, *Turkey* **25 G5** 37 47N 30 30 E
Ispica, *Italy* **20 F6** 36 47N 14 55 E
Israel ■, *Asia* **47 D3** 32 0N 34 50 E
Issoire, *France* **18 D5** 45 32N 3 15 E
Issyk-Kul = Ysyk-Köl, *Kyrgyzstan* **28 E11** 42 26N 76 12 E
Issyk-Kul, Ozero = Ysyk-Köl, Ozero, *Kyrgyzstan* **26 E8** 42 25N 77 15 E
İstanbul, *Turkey* **21 D13** 41 0N 29 0 E
İstanbul Boğazı, *Turkey* **21 D13** 41 10N 29 10 E
Istiaía, *Greece* **21 E10** 38 57N 23 9 E
Istokpoga, L., *U.S.A.* **77 M5** 27 23N 81 17W
Istra, *Croatia* **16 F7** 45 10N 14 0 E
Istres, *France* **18 E6** 43 31N 4 59 E
Istria = Istra, *Croatia* **16 F7** 45 10N 14 0 E
Itá, *Paraguay* **94 B4** 25 29S 57 21W
Itaberaba, *Brazil* **93 F10** 12 32S 40 18W
Itabira, *Brazil* **93 G10** 19 37S 43 13W
Itabirito, *Brazil* **95 A7** 20 15S 43 48W
Itabuna, *Brazil* **93 F11** 14 48S 39 16W
Itacaunas →, *Brazil* **93 E9** 5 21S 49 8W
Itacoatiara, *Brazil* **92 D7** 3 8S 58 25W
Itaipú, Représa de, *Brazil* **95 B5** 25 30S 54 30W
Itaituba, *Brazil* **93 D7** 4 10S 55 50W
Itajaí, *Brazil* **95 B6** 27 50S 48 39W
Itajubá, *Brazil* **95 A6** 22 24S 45 30W
Itaka, *Tanzania* **55 D3** 8 50S 32 49 E
Italy ■, *Europe* **20 C5** 42 0N 13 0 E
Itamaraju, *Brazil* **93 G11** 17 5S 39 31W
Itampolo, *Madag.* **57 C7** 24 41S 43 57 E
Itapecuru-Mirim, *Brazil* **93 D10** 3 24S 44 20W
Itaperuna, *Brazil* **95 A7** 21 10S 41 54W
Itapetininga, *Brazil* **95 A6** 23 36S 48 7W
Itapeva, *Brazil* **95 A6** 23 59S 48 59W
Itapicuru →, *Bahia, Brazil* **93 F11** 11 47S 37 32W
Itapicuru →, *Maranhão, Brazil* **93 D10** 2 52S 44 12W
Itapipoca, *Brazil* **93 D11** 3 30S 39 35W
Itapuá □, *Paraguay* **95 B4** 26 40S 55 40W
Itaquari, *Brazil* **95 A7** 20 20S 40 25W
Itaquí, *Brazil* **94 B4** 29 8S 56 30W
Itararé, *Brazil* **95 A6** 24 6S 49 23W
Itarsi, *India* **42 H7** 22 36N 77 51 E
Itatí, *Argentina* **94 B4** 27 16S 58 15W
Itchen →, *U.K.* **11 G6** 50 55N 1 22W
Itezhi Tezhi, L., *Zambia* **55 F2** 15 30S 25 30 E
Ithaca = Itháki, *Greece* **21 E9** 38 25N 20 40 E
Ithaca, *U.S.A.* **79 D8** 42 27N 76 30W
Itháki, *Greece* **21 E9** 38 25N 20 40 E
Itiquira →, *Brazil* **93 G7** 17 18S 56 44W
Ito, *Japan* **31 G9** 34 58N 139 5 E
Ito Aba I., *S. China Sea* **36 B4** 10 23N 114 21 E
Itoigawa, *Japan* **31 F8** 37 2N 137 51 E
Itonamas →, *Bolivia* **92 F6** 12 28S 64 24W
Ittoqqortoormiit = Scoresbysund, *Greenland* **4 B6** 70 20N 23 0W
Itu, *Brazil* **95 A6** 23 17S 47 15W
Ituiutaba, *Brazil* **93 G9** 19 0S 49 25W
Itumbiara, *Brazil* **93 G9** 18 20S 49 10W
Ituna, *Canada* **73 C8** 51 10N 103 24W
Itunge Port, *Tanzania* **55 D3** 9 40S 33 55 E
Iturbe, *Argentina* **94 A2** 23 0S 65 25W
Ituri →, *Dem. Rep. of the Congo* **54 B2** 1 40N 27 1 E
Iturup, Ostrov, *Russia* **27 E15** 45 0N 148 0 E
Ituxi →, *Brazil* **92 E6** 7 18S 64 51W
Ituyuro →, *Argentina* **94 A3** 22 40S 63 50W
Itzehoe, *Germany* **16 B5** 53 55N 9 31 E
Ivaí →, *Brazil* **95 A5** 23 18S 53 42W
Ivalo, *Finland* **8 B22** 68 38N 27 35 E
Ivalojoki →, *Finland* **8 B22** 68 40N 27 40 E
Ivanava, *Belarus* **17 B13** 52 7N 25 29 E
Ivanhoe, *Australia* **63 E3** 32 56S 144 20 E
Ivanhoe, *Calif., U.S.A.* **84 J7** 36 23N 119 13W
Ivanhoe, *Minn., U.S.A.* **80 C6** 44 28N 96 15W
Ivano-Frankivsk, *Ukraine* **17 D13** 48 40N 24 40 E
Ivano-Frankovsk = Ivano-Frankivsk, *Ukraine* **17 D13** 48 40N 24 40 E
Ivanovo = Ivanava, *Belarus* **17 B13** 52 7N 25 29 E
Ivanovo, *Russia* **24 C7** 57 5N 41 0 E
Ivato, *Madag.* **57 C8** 20 37S 47 10 E
Ivatsevichy, *Belarus* **17 B13** 52 43N 25 21 E
Ivdel, *Russia* **24 B11** 60 42N 60 24 E
Ivindo →, *Gabon* **52 D2** 0 9S 12 9 E
Ivinheima →, *Brazil* **95 A5** 23 14S 53 42W
Ivinhema, *Brazil* **95 A5** 22 10S 53 37W
Ivohibe, *Madag.* **57 C8** 22 31S 46 57 E
Ivory Coast, *Africa* **50 H4** 5 0N 5 0W
Ivory Coast ■, *Africa* **50 G4** 7 30N 5 0W
Ivrea, *Italy* **18 D7** 45 28N 7 52 E
Ivujivik, *Canada* **69 B12** 62 24N 77 55W
Ivybridge, *U.K.* **11 G4** 50 23N 3 56W
Iwaizumi, *Japan* **30 E10** 39 50N 141 45 E
Iwaki, *Japan* **31 F10** 37 3N 140 55 E
Iwakuni, *Japan* **31 G6** 34 15N 132 8 E
Iwamizawa, *Japan* **30 C10** 43 12N 141 46 E
Iwanai, *Japan* **30 C10** 42 58N 140 30 E
Iwata, *Japan* **31 G8** 34 42N 137 51 E
Iwate □, *Japan* **30 E10** 39 30N 141 30 E
Iwate-San, *Japan* **30 E10** 39 51N 141 0 E
Iwo, *Nigeria* **50 G6** 7 39N 4 9 E
Ixiamas, *Bolivia* **92 F5** 13 50S 68 5W
Ixopo, *S. Africa* **57 E5** 30 11S 30 5 E
Ixtepec, *Mexico* **87 D5** 16 32N 95 10W
Ixtlán del Río, *Mexico* **86 C4** 21 5N 104 21W
Iyo, *Japan* **31 H6** 33 45N 132 45 E
Izabal, L. de, *Guatemala* **88 C2** 15 30N 89 10W
Izamal, *Mexico* **87 C7** 20 56N 89 1W
Izena-Shima, *Japan* **31 L3** 26 56N 127 56 E
Izhevsk, *Russia* **24 C9** 56 51N 53 14 E
Izhma →, *Russia* **24 A9** 65 19N 52 54 E
Izmayil, *Ukraine* **17 F15** 45 22N 28 46
İzmir, *Turkey* **21 E12** 38 25N 27 8
İzmit = Kocaeli, *Turkey* **25 F4** 40 45N 29 50
İznik Gölü, *Turkey* **21 D13** 40 27N 29 30
Izra, *Syria* **47 C5** 32 51N 36 15
Izu-Shotō, *Japan* **31 G10** 34 30N 140 0
Izúcar de Matamoros, *Mexico* **87 D5** 18 36N 98 28
Izumi-sano, *Japan* **31 G7** 34 23N 135 18
Izumo, *Japan* **31 G6** 35 20N 132 46
Izyaslav, *Ukraine* **17 C14** 50 5N 26 50

J

Jabalpur, *India* **43 H8** 23 9N 79 58
Jabbūl, *Syria* **44 B3** 36 4N 37 30
Jabiru, *Australia* **60 B5** 12 40S 132 53
Jablah, *Syria* **44 C3** 35 20N 36 0
Jablonec nad Nisou, *Czech Rep.* **16 C8** 50 43N 15 10
Jaboatão, *Brazil* **93 E11** 8 7S 35 1
Jaboticabal, *Brazil* **95 A6** 21 15S 48 17
Jaca, *Spain* **19 A5** 42 35N 0 33
Jacareí, *Brazil* **95 A6** 23 20S 46 0
Jacarèzinho, *Brazil* **95 A6** 23 5S 49 58
Jackman, *U.S.A.* **77 C10** 45 35N 70 17
Jacksboro, *U.S.A.* **81 J5** 33 14N 98 15
Jackson, *Ala., U.S.A.* **77 K2** 31 31N 87 53
Jackson, *Calif., U.S.A.* **84 G6** 38 21N 120 46
Jackson, *Ky., U.S.A.* **76 G4** 37 33N 83 23
Jackson, *Mich., U.S.A.* **76 D3** 42 15N 84 24
Jackson, *Minn., U.S.A.* **80 D7** 43 37N 95 1
Jackson, *Miss., U.S.A.* **81 J9** 32 18N 90 12
Jackson, *Mo., U.S.A.* **81 G10** 37 23N 89 40
Jackson, *N.H., U.S.A.* **79 B13** 44 10N 71 11
Jackson, *Ohio, U.S.A.* **76 F4** 39 3N 82 39
Jackson, *Tenn., U.S.A.* **77 H1** 35 37N 88 49
Jackson, *Wyo., U.S.A.* **82 E8** 43 29N 110 46
Jackson B., *N.Z.* **59 K2** 43 58S 168 42
Jackson L., *U.S.A.* **82 E8** 43 52N 110 36
Jacksons, *N.Z.* **59 K3** 42 46S 171 32
Jackson's Arm, *Canada* **71 C8** 49 52N 56 47
Jacksonville, *Ala., U.S.A.* **77 J3** 33 49N 85 46
Jacksonville, *Ark., U.S.A.* **81 H8** 34 52N 92 7
Jacksonville, *Calif., U.S.A.* **84 H6** 37 52N 120 24
Jacksonville, *Fla., U.S.A.* **77 K5** 30 20N 81 39
Jacksonville, *Ill., U.S.A.* **80 F9** 39 44N 90 14
Jacksonville, *N.C., U.S.A.* **77 H7** 34 45N 77 26
Jacksonville, *Tex., U.S.A.* **81 K7** 31 58N 95 17
Jacksonville Beach, *U.S.A.* **77 K5** 30 17N 81 24
Jacmel, *Haiti* **89 C5** 18 14N 72 32
Jacob Lake, *U.S.A.* **83 H7** 36 43N 112 13
Jacobabad, *Pakistan* **42 E3** 28 20N 68 29
Jacobina, *Brazil* **93 F10** 11 11S 40 30
Jacques Cartier, Dét. de, *Canada* **71 C7** 50 0N 63 30
Jacques-Cartier, Mt., *Canada* **71 C6** 48 57N 66 0
Jacques Cartier, Parc Prov., *Canada* **71 C5** 47 15N 71 33
Jacuí →, *Brazil* **95 C5** 30 2S 51 15
Jacumba, *U.S.A.* **85 N10** 32 37N 116 11
Jacundá →, *Brazil* **93 D8** 1 57S 50 26
Jadotville = Likasi, *Dem. Rep. of the Congo* **55 E2** 10 55S 26 48
Jaén, *Peru* **92 E3** 5 25S 78 40
Jaén, *Spain* **19 D4** 37 44N 3 43
Jafarabad, *India* **42 J4** 20 52N 71 22
Jaffa = Tel Aviv-Yafo, *Israel* **47 C3** 32 4N 34 48
Jaffa, C., *Australia* **63 F2** 36 58S 139 40
Jaffna, *Sri Lanka* **40 Q12** 9 45N 80 2
Jaffrey, *U.S.A.* **79 D12** 42 49N 72 2
Jagadhri, *India* **42 D7** 30 10N 77 20
Jagadishpur, *India* **43 G11** 25 30N 84 21
Jagdalpur, *India* **41 K13** 19 3N 82 0
Jagersfontein, *S. Africa* **56 D4** 29 44S 25 27
Jaghīn →, *Iran* **45 E8** 27 17N 57 13
Jagodina, *Serbia, Yug.* **21 C9** 44 5N 21 15
Jagraon, *India* **40 D9** 30 50N 75 25
Jagtial, *India* **40 K11** 18 50N 79 0
Jaguariaíva, *Brazil* **95 A6** 24 10S 49 50
Jaguaribe →, *Brazil* **93 D11** 4 25S 37 45
Jagüey Grande, *Cuba* **88 B3** 22 35N 81 7
Jahanabad, *India* **43 G11** 25 13N 84 59
Jahazpur, *India* **42 G6** 25 37N 75 17
Jahrom, *Iran* **45 D7** 28 30N 53 31
Jaijon, *India* **42 D7** 31 21N 76 9
Jailolo, *Indonesia* **37 D7** 1 5N 127 30
Jailolo, Selat, *Indonesia* **37 D7** 0 5N 129 5
Jaipur, *India* **42 F6** 27 0N 75 50
Jais, *India* **43 F9** 26 15N 81 32
Jaisalmer, *India* **42 F4** 26 55N 70 54
Jaisinghnagar, *India* **43 H8** 23 38N 78 34
Jaitaran, *India* **42 F5** 26 12N 73 56
Jaithari, *India* **43 H8** 23 14N 78 37
Jājarm, *Iran* **45 B8** 36 58N 56 27
Jakam →, *India* **42 H6** 23 54N 74 13
Jakarta, *Indonesia* **37 G12** 6 9S 106 49
Jakhal, *India* **42 E6** 29 48N 75 50
Jakhau, *India* **42 H3** 23 13N 68 43
Jakobstad = Pietarsaari, *Finland* **8 E20** 63 40N 22 43
Jal, *U.S.A.* **81 J3** 32 7N 103 12
Jalalabad, *Afghan.* **42 B4** 34 30N 70 29
Jalalabad, *India* **43 F8** 27 41N 79 42
Jalalpur Jattan, *Pakistan* **42 C6** 32 38N 74 11
Jalama, *U.S.A.* **85 L6** 34 29N 120 29
Jalapa, *Guatemala* **88 D2** 14 39N 89 59
Jalapa Enríquez, *Mexico* **87 D5** 19 32N 96 55
Jalasjärvi, *Finland* **9 E20** 62 29N 22 47
Jalaun, *India* **43 F8** 26 8N 79 25
Jaldhaka →, *Bangla.* **43 F13** 26 16N 89 16
Jalesar, *India* **42 F8** 27 29N 78 19
Jaleswar, *Nepal* **43 F11** 26 38N 85 48
Jalgaon, *Maharashtra, India* **40 J10** 21 2N 76 31
Jalgaon, *Maharashtra, India* **40 J9** 21 0N 75 42
Jalībah, *Iraq* **44 D5** 30 35N 46 32
Jalisco □, *Mexico* **86 D4** 20 0N 104 0
Jalkot, *Pakistan* **43 B5** 35 14N 73 24
Jalna, *India* **40 K9** 19 48N 75 38
Jalón →, *Spain* **19 B5** 41 47N 1 4
Jalor, *India* **42 G5** 25 21N 72 37
Jalpa, *Mexico* **86 C4** 21 38N 102 58
Jalpaiguri, *India* **41 F16** 26 32N 88 46
Jaluit I., *Marshall Is.* **64 G8** 6 0N 169 30

Juruena

Juruena →, Brazil 92 E7 7 20S 58 3W
Juruti, Brazil 93 D7 2 9S 56 4W
Justo Daract, Argentina 94 C2 33 52S 65 12W
Jutaí →, Brazil 92 D5 2 43S 66 57W
Juticalpa, Honduras 88 D2 14 40N 86 12W
Jutland = Jylland, Denmark 9 H13 56 25N 9 30 E
Juventud, I. de la, Cuba 88 B3 21 40N 82 40W
Juwain, Afghan. 40 D2 31 45N 61 30 E
Jūy Zar, Iran 44 C5 33 50N 46 18 E
Juye, China 34 G9 35 22N 116 5 E
Jwaneng, Botswana 53 J4 24 45S 24 50 E
Jylland, Denmark 9 H13 56 25N 9 30 E
Jyväskylä, Finland 9 E21 62 14N 25 50 E

K

K2, Pakistan 43 B7 35 58N 76 32 E
Kaap Plateau, S. Africa 56 D3 28 30S 24 0 E
Kaapkruis, Namibia 56 C1 21 55S 13 57 E
Kaapstad = Cape Town, S. Africa 56 E2 33 55S 18 22 E
Kabaena, Indonesia 37 F6 5 15S 122 0 E
Kabala, S. Leone 50 G3 9 38N 11 37W
Kabale, Uganda 54 C3 1 15S 30 0 E
Kabalo, Dem. Rep. of the Congo 54 D2 6 0S 27 0 E
Kabambare, Dem. Rep. of the Congo 54 C2 4 41S 27 39 E
Kabango, Dem. Rep. of the Congo 55 D2 8 35S 28 30 E
Kabanjahe, Indonesia 36 D1 3 6N 98 30 E
Kabardino-Balkar Republic = Kabardino-Balkaria □, Russia 25 F7 43 30N 43 30 E
Kabardino-Balkaria □, Russia 25 F7 43 30N 43 30 E
Kabarega Falls = Murchison Falls, Uganda 54 B3 2 15N 31 30 E
Kabasalan, Phil. 37 C6 7 47N 122 44 E
Kabetogama, U.S.A. 80 A8 48 28N 92 59W
Kabin Buri, Thailand 38 F3 13 57N 101 43 E
Kabinakagami L., Canada 70 C3 48 54N 84 25W
Kabinda, Dem. Rep. of the Congo 52 F4 6 19S 24 20 E
Kabompo, Zambia 55 E1 13 36S 24 14 E
Kabompo →, Zambia 53 G4 14 10S 23 11 E
Kabondo, Dem. Rep. of the Congo 55 D2 8 58S 25 40 E
Kabongo, Dem. Rep. of the Congo 54 D2 7 22S 25 33 E
Kabūd Gonbad, Iran 45 B8 37 5N 59 45 E
Kābul, Afghan. 42 B3 34 28N 69 11 E
Kābul □, Afghan. 40 B6 34 30N 69 0 E
Kabul →, Pakistan 42 C5 33 55N 72 14 E
Kabunga, Dem. Rep. of the Congo 54 C2 1 38S 28 3 E
Kaburuang, Indonesia 37 D7 3 50N 126 30 E
Kabwe, Zambia 55 E2 14 30S 28 29 E
Kachchh, Gulf of, India 42 H3 22 50N 69 15 E
Kachchh, Rann of, India 42 H4 24 0N 70 0 E
Kachchhidhana, India 43 J8 21 44N 78 46 E
Kachebera, Zambia 55 E3 13 50S 32 50 E
Kachin □, Burma 41 G20 26 0N 97 30 E
Kachira, L., Uganda 54 C3 0 40S 31 7 E
Kachiry, Kazakstan 26 D8 53 10N 75 50 E
Kachnara, India 42 H6 23 50N 75 6 E
Kachot, Cambodia 39 G4 11 30N 103 3 E
Kaçkar, Turkey 25 F7 40 45N 41 10 E
Kadan Kyun, Burma 38 F2 12 30N 98 20 E
Kadanai →, Afghan. 42 D1 31 22N 65 45 E
Kadi, India 42 H5 23 18N 72 23 E
Kadina, Australia 63 E2 33 55S 137 43 E
Kadipur, India 43 F10 26 10N 82 23 E
Kadirli, Turkey 44 B3 37 23N 36 5 E
Kadiyevka = Stakhanov, Ukraine 25 E6 48 35N 38 40 E
Kadoka, U.S.A. 80 D4 43 50N 101 31W
Kadoma, Zimbabwe 55 F2 18 20S 29 52 E
Kâdugli, Sudan 51 F11 11 0N 29 45 E
Kaduna, Nigeria 50 F7 10 30N 7 21 E
Kaédi, Mauritania 50 E3 16 9N 13 28W
Kaeng Khoï, Thailand 38 E3 14 35N 101 0 E
Kaesŏng, N. Korea 35 F14 37 58N 126 35 E
Kāf, Si. Arabia 44 D3 31 25N 37 29 E
Kafan = Kapan, Armenia 25 G8 39 18N 46 27 E
Kafanchan, Nigeria 50 G7 9 40N 8 20 E
Kafinda, Zambia 55 E3 12 32S 30 20 E
Kafirévs, Ákra, Greece 21 E11 38 9N 24 38 E
Kafue, Zambia 55 F2 15 46S 28 9 E
Kafue →, Zambia 53 H5 15 30S 29 0 E
Kafue Flats, Zambia 55 F2 15 40S 27 25 E
Kafue Nat. Park, Zambia 55 F2 15 0S 25 30 E
Kafulwe, Zambia 55 D2 9 0S 29 1 E
Kaga, Afghan. 42 B4 34 14N 70 10 E
Kaga Bandoro, C.A.R. 52 C3 7 0N 19 10 E
Kagan, Uzbekistan 26 F7 39 43N 64 33 E
Kagawa □, Japan 31 G7 34 15N 134 0 E
Kagera □, Tanzania 54 C3 2 0S 31 30 E
Kagera →, Uganda 54 C3 0 57S 31 47 E
Kağızman, Turkey 44 A4 40 5N 43 10 E
Kagoshima, Japan 31 J5 31 35N 130 33 E
Kagoshima □, Japan 31 J5 31 30N 130 30 E
Kagul = Cahul, Moldova 17 F15 45 50N 28 15 E
Kahak, Iran 45 B6 36 6N 49 46 E
Kahama, Tanzania 54 C3 4 8S 32 30 E
Kahan, Pakistan 42 E3 29 18N 68 54 E
Kahang, Malaysia 39 L4 2 12N 103 32 E
Kahayan →, Indonesia 36 E4 3 40S 114 0 E
Kahe, Tanzania 54 C4 3 30S 37 25 E
Kahnūj, Iran 45 E8 27 55N 57 40 E
Kahoka, U.S.A. 80 E9 40 25N 91 44W
Kahoolawe, U.S.A. 74 H16 20 33N 156 37W
Kahramanmaraş, Turkey 25 G6 37 37N 36 53 E
Kahuta, Pakistan 42 C5 33 35N 73 24 E
Kai, Kepulauan, Indonesia 37 F8 5 55S 132 45 E
Kai Besar, Indonesia 37 F8 5 35S 133 0 E
Kai Is. = Kai, Kepulauan, Indonesia 37 F8 5 55S 132 45 E
Kai Kecil, Indonesia 37 F8 5 45S 132 40 E
Kaiapoi, N.Z. 59 K4 43 24S 172 40 E
Kaieteur Falls, Guyana 92 B7 5 1N 59 10W
Kaifeng, China 34 G8 34 48N 114 21 E
Kaikohe, N.Z. 59 F4 35 25S 173 49 E
Kaikoura, N.Z. 59 K4 42 25S 173 43 E
Kaikoura Ra., N.Z. 59 J4 41 59S 173 41 E
Kailu, China 35 C11 43 38N 121 18 E
Kailua Kona, U.S.A. 74 J17 19 39N 155 59W
Kaimana, Indonesia 37 E8 3 39S 133 45 E
Kaimanawa Mts., N.Z. 59 H5 39 15S 175 56 E
Kaimganj, India 43 F8 27 33N 79 24 E
Kaimur Hills, India 43 G10 24 30N 82 0 E
Kaingaroa Forest, N.Z. 59 H6 38 24S 176 30 E
Kainji Res., Nigeria 50 F6 10 1N 4 40 E
Kainuu, Finland 8 D23 64 30N 29 7 E
Kaipara Harbour, N.Z. 59 G5 36 25S 174 14 E
Kaipokok B., Canada 71 B8 54 54N 59 47W
Kaira, India 42 H5 22 45N 72 50 E
Kairana, India 42 E7 29 24N 77 15 E
Kaironi, Indonesia 37 E8 0 47S 133 40 E
Kairouan, Tunisia 51 A8 35 45N 10 5 E
Kaiserslautern, Germany 16 D4 49 26N 7 45 E
Kaitaia, N.Z. 59 F4 35 8S 173 17 E
Kaitangata, N.Z. 59 M2 46 17S 169 51 E
Kaithal, India 42 E7 29 48N 76 26 E
Kaitu →, Pakistan 42 C4 33 10N 70 30 E
Kaiwi Channel, U.S.A. 74 H16 21 15N 157 30W
Kaiyuan, China 35 C13 42 28N 124 1 E
Kajaani, Finland 8 D22 64 17N 27 46 E
Kajabbi, Australia 62 C3 20 0S 140 1 E
Kajana = Kajaani, Finland 8 D22 64 17N 27 46 E
Kajang, Malaysia 39 L3 2 59N 101 48 E
Kajiado, Kenya 54 C4 1 53S 36 48 E
Kajo Kaji, Sudan 51 H12 3 58N 31 40 E
Kakabeka Falls, Canada 70 C2 48 24N 89 37W
Kakadu Nat. Park, Australia 60 B5 12 30S 132 5 E
Kakamas, S. Africa 56 D3 28 45S 20 33 E
Kakamega, Kenya 54 B3 0 20N 34 46 E
Kakanui Mts., N.Z. 59 L3 45 10S 170 30 E
Kakdwip, India 43 J13 21 53N 88 11 E
Kake, Japan 31 G6 34 36N 132 19 E
Kake, U.S.A. 72 B2 56 59N 133 57W
Kakegawa, Japan 31 G9 34 45N 138 1 E
Kakeroma-Jima, Japan 31 K4 28 8N 129 14 E
Kakhovka, Ukraine 25 E5 46 45N 33 30 E
Kakhovske Vdskh., Ukraine 25 E5 47 5N 34 0 E
Kakinada, India 41 L13 16 57N 82 11 E
Kakisa →, Canada 72 A5 61 3N 118 10W
Kakisa L., Canada 72 A5 60 56N 117 43W
Kakogawa, Japan 31 G7 34 46N 134 51 E
Kakwa →, Canada 72 C5 54 37N 118 28W
Kāl Gūsheh, Iran 45 D8 30 59N 58 12 E
Kal Safīd, Iran 44 C5 34 52N 47 23 E
Kalabagh, Pakistan 42 C4 33 0N 71 28 E
Kalabahi, Indonesia 37 F6 8 13S 124 31 E
Kalach, Russia 25 D7 50 22N 41 0 E
Kaladan →, Burma 41 J18 20 20N 93 5 E
Kaladar, Canada 78 B7 44 37N 77 5W
Kalahari, Africa 56 C3 24 0S 21 30 E
Kalahari Gemsbok Nat. Park, S. Africa 56 D3 25 30S 20 30 E
Kalajoki, Finland 8 D20 64 12N 24 10 E
Kālak, Iran 45 E8 25 29N 59 22 E
Kalakamati, Botswana 57 C4 20 40S 27 25 E
Kalakan, Russia 27 D12 55 15N 116 45 E
K'alak'unlun Shank'ou, Pakistan 43 B7 35 33N 77 46 E
Kalam, Pakistan 43 B5 35 34N 72 30 E
Kalama, Dem. Rep. of the Congo 54 C2 2 52S 28 35 E
Kalama, U.S.A. 84 E4 46 1N 122 51W
Kalámai, Greece 21 F10 37 3N 22 10 E
Kalamata = Kalámai, Greece 21 F10 37 3N 22 10 E
Kalamazoo, U.S.A. 76 D3 42 17N 85 35W
Kalamazoo →, U.S.A. 76 D2 42 40N 86 10W
Kalambo Falls, Tanzania 55 D3 8 37S 31 35 E
Kalan, Turkey 44 B3 39 7N 39 32 E
Kalannie, Australia 61 F2 30 22S 117 5 E
Kalāntarī, Iran 45 C7 32 10N 54 8 E
Kalao, Indonesia 37 F6 7 21S 121 0 E
Kalaotoa, Indonesia 37 F6 7 20S 121 50 E
Kalasin, Thailand 38 D4 16 26N 103 30 E
Kalat, Pakistan 40 E5 29 8N 66 31 E
Kalāteh, Iran 45 B7 36 33N 55 41 E
Kalāteh-ye Ganj, Iran 45 E8 27 31N 57 55 E
Kalbarri, Australia 61 E1 27 40S 114 10 E
Kalce, Slovenia 16 F8 45 54N 14 13 E
Kale, Turkey 21 F13 37 27N 28 49 E
Kalegauk Kyun, Burma 41 M20 15 33N 97 35 E
Kalehe, Dem. Rep. of the Congo 54 C2 2 6S 28 50 E
Kalema, Tanzania 54 C3 1 12S 31 55 E
Kalemie, Dem. Rep. of the Congo 54 D2 5 55S 29 9 E
Kalewa, Burma 41 H19 23 10N 94 15 E
Kaleybar, Iran 44 B5 38 47N 47 2 E
Kalgan = Zhangjiakou, China 34 D8 40 48N 114 55 E
Kalgoorlie-Boulder, Australia 61 F3 30 40S 121 22 E
Kali →, India 43 F8 27 6N 79 55 E
Kali Sindh →, India 42 G6 25 32N 76 17 E
Kaliakra, Nos, Bulgaria 21 C13 43 21N 28 30 E
Kalianda, Indonesia 36 F3 5 50S 105 45 E
Kalibo, Phil. 37 B6 11 43N 122 22 E
Kalima, Dem. Rep. of the Congo 54 C2 2 33S 26 32 E
Kalimantan □, Indonesia 36 E4 0 0 114 0 E
Kalimantan Barat □, Indonesia 36 E4 0 0 110 30 E
Kalimantan Selatan □, Indonesia 36 E5 2 30S 115 30 E
Kalimantan Tengah □, Indonesia 36 E4 2 0S 113 30 E
Kalimantan Timur □, Indonesia 36 D5 1 30N 116 30 E
Kálimnos, Greece 21 F12 37 0N 27 0 E
Kalimpong, India 43 F13 27 4N 88 35 E
Kalinin = Tver, Russia 24 C6 56 55N 35 55 E
Kaliningrad, Russia 9 J19 54 42N 20 32 E
Kalinkavichy, Belarus 17 B15 52 12N 29 20 E
Kalinkovichi = Kalinkavichy, Belarus 17 B15 52 12N 29 20 E
Kaliro, Uganda 54 B3 0 56N 33 30 E
Kalispell, U.S.A. 82 B6 48 12N 114 19W
Kalisz, Poland 17 C10 51 45N 18 8 E
Kaliua, Tanzania 54 D3 5 5S 31 48 E
Kalix, Sweden 8 D20 65 53N 23 12 E
Kalix →, Sweden 8 D20 65 50N 23 11 E
Kalka, India 42 D7 30 46N 76 57 E
Kalkarindji, Australia 60 C5 17 30S 130 47 E
Kalkaska, U.S.A. 76 C3 44 44N 85 11W
Kalkfeld, Namibia 56 C2 20 57S 16 14 E
Kalkfontein, Botswana 56 C3 22 4S 20 57 E
Kalkrand, Namibia 56 C2 24 1S 17 35 E
Kallavesi, Finland 8 E22 62 58N 27 30 E
Kallsjön, Sweden 8 E15 63 38N 13 0 E
Kalmar, Sweden 9 H17 56 40N 16 20 E
Kalmyk Republic = Kalmykia □, Russia 25 E8 46 5N 46 1 E
Kalmykia □, Russia 25 E8 46 5N 46 1 E
Kalmykovo, Kazakstan 25 E9 49 0N 51 47 E
Kalna, India 43 H13 23 13N 88 25 E
Kalnai, India 43 H10 22 46N 83 30 E
Kalocsa, Hungary 17 E10 46 32N 19 0 E
Kalokhorio, Cyprus 23 E12 34 51N 33 2 E
Kaloko, Dem. Rep. of the Congo 54 D2 6 47S 25 48 E
Kalol, Gujarat, India 42 H5 22 37N 73 31 E
Kalol, Gujarat, India 42 H5 23 15N 72 33 E
Kalomo, Zambia 55 F2 17 0S 26 30 E
Kalpi, India 43 F8 26 8N 79 47 E
Kalu, Pakistan 42 G2 25 5N 67 39 E
Kaluga, Russia 24 D6 54 35N 36 10 E
Kalulushi, Zambia 55 E2 12 50S 28 3 E
Kalundborg, Denmark 9 J14 55 41N 11 5 E
Kalush, Ukraine 17 D13 49 3N 24 23 E
Kalutara, Sri Lanka 40 R12 6 35N 80 0 E
Kalya, Russia 24 B10 60 15N 59 59 E
Kama, Dem. Rep. of the Congo 54 C2 3 30S 27 5 E
Kama →, Russia 24 C9 55 45N 52 0 E
Kamachumu, Tanzania 54 C3 1 37S 31 37 E
Kamaishi, Japan 30 E10 39 16N 141 53 E
Kamalia, Pakistan 42 D5 30 44N 72 42 E
Kaman, India 42 F6 27 39N 77 16 E
Kamapanda, Zambia 55 E1 12 5S 24 0 E
Kamaran, Yemen 46 D3 15 21N 42 35 E
Kamativi, Zimbabwe 55 F2 18 15S 27 27 E
Kambalda, Australia 61 F3 31 10S 121 37 E
Kambar, Pakistan 42 F3 27 37N 68 1 E
Kambarka, Russia 24 C9 56 15N 54 11 E
Kambolé, Zambia 55 D3 8 47S 30 48 E
Kambos, Cyprus 23 D11 35 2N 32 44 E
Kambove, Dem. Rep. of the Congo 55 E2 10 51S 26 33 E
Kamchatka, Poluostrov, Russia 27 D17 57 0N 160 0 E
Kamchatka Pen. = Kamchatka, Poluostrov, Russia 27 D17 57 0N 160 0 E
Kamchiya →, Bulgaria 21 C12 43 4N 27 44 E
Kamen, Russia 26 D9 53 50N 81 30 E
Kamen-Rybolov, Russia 30 B6 44 46N 132 2 E
Kamenjak, Rt., Croatia 16 F7 44 47N 13 55 E
Kamenka, Russia 24 A7 65 58N 44 0 E
Kamenka Bugskaya = Kamyanka-Buzka, Ukraine 17 C13 50 8N 24 16 E
Kamensk Uralskiy, Russia 26 D7 56 25N 62 2 E
Kamenskoye, Russia 27 C17 62 45N 165 30 E
Kameoka, Japan 31 G7 35 0N 135 35 E
Kamiah, U.S.A. 82 C5 46 14N 116 2W
Kamieskroon, S. Africa 56 E2 30 9S 17 56 E
Kamilukuak, L., Canada 73 A8 62 22N 101 40W
Kamin-Kashyrskyy, Ukraine 17 C13 51 39N 24 56 E
Kamina, Dem. Rep. of the Congo 55 D2 8 45S 25 0 E
Kaminak L., Canada 73 A10 62 10N 95 0W
Kaministiquia, Canada 70 C1 48 32N 89 35W
Kaminoyama, Japan 30 E10 38 9N 140 17 E
Kamiros, Greece 23 C9 36 20N 27 56 E
Kamituga, Dem. Rep. of the Congo 54 C2 3 2S 28 10 E
Kamla →, India 43 G12 25 35N 86 36 E
Kamloops, Canada 72 C4 50 40N 120 20W
Kamo, Japan 30 F9 37 39N 139 3 E
Kamoke, Pakistan 42 C6 32 4N 74 4 E
Kampala, Uganda 54 B3 0 20N 32 30 E
Kampang Chhnang, Cambodia 39 F5 12 20N 104 35 E
Kampar, Malaysia 39 K3 4 18N 101 9 E
Kampar →, Indonesia 36 D2 0 30N 103 8 E
Kampen, Neths. 15 B5 52 33N 5 53 E
Kampene, Dem. Rep. of the Congo 52 E5 3 36S 26 40 E
Kamphaeng Phet, Thailand 38 D2 16 28N 99 30 E
Kampolombo, L., Zambia 55 E2 11 37S 29 42 E
Kampong Saom, Cambodia 39 G4 10 38N 103 30 E
Kampong Saom, Chaak, Cambodia 36 B2 10 45N 103 30 E
Kampong Saom, Chaak, Cambodia 39 G4 10 50N 103 32 E
Kampong To, Thailand 39 J3 6 3N 101 13 E
Kampot, Cambodia 39 G5 10 36N 104 10 E
Kampuchea = Cambodia ■, Asia 38 F5 12 15N 105 0 E
Kampung Air Putih, Malaysia 39 K4 4 15N 103 10 E
Kampung Jerangau, Malaysia 39 K4 4 50N 103 10 E
Kampung Raja, Malaysia 39 K4 5 45N 102 35 E
Kampungbaru = Tolitoli, Indonesia 37 D6 1 5N 120 50 E
Kamrau, Teluk, Indonesia 37 E8 3 30S 133 36 E
Kamsack, Canada 73 C8 51 34N 101 54W
Kamskoye Vdkhr., Russia 24 C10 58 41N 56 7 E
Kamuchawie L., Canada 73 B8 56 18N 101 59W
Kamuela, U.S.A. 74 H17 20 1N 155 41W
Kamui-Misaki, Japan 30 C10 43 20N 140 21 E
Kamyanets-Podilskyy, Ukraine 17 D14 48 45N 26 40 E
Kamyanka-Buzka, Ukraine 17 C13 50 8N 24 16 E
Kāmyārān, Iran 44 C5 34 47N 46 56 E
Kamyshin, Russia 25 D8 50 10N 45 24 E
Kanaaupscow, Canada 70 B4 54 2N 76 30W
Kanaaupscow →, Canada 69 C12 53 39N 77 9W
Kanab, U.S.A. 83 H7 37 3N 112 32W
Kanab →, U.S.A. 83 H7 36 24N 112 38W
Kanagi, Japan 30 D10 40 54N 140 27 E
Kanairiktok →, Canada 71 A7 55 2N 60 18W
Kananga, Dem. Rep. of the Congo 52 F4 5 55S 22 18 E
Kanash, Russia 24 C8 55 30N 47 32 E
Kanaskat, U.S.A. 84 C5 47 19N 121 54W
Kanastraíon, Ákra = Palioúrion, Ákra, Greece 21 E10 39 57N 23 45 E
Kanawha →, U.S.A. 76 F4 38 50N 82 9W
Kanazawa, Japan 31 F8 36 30N 136 38 E
Kanchanaburi, Thailand 38 E2 14 2N 99 31 E
Kanchenjunga, Nepal 43 F13 27 50N 88 10 E
Kanchipuram, India 40 N11 12 52N 79 45 E
Kandaghat, India 42 D7 30 59N 77 7 E
Kandahar = Qandahār, Afghan. 40 D4 31 32N 65 30 E
Kandalaksha, Russia 24 A5 67 9N 32 30 E
Kandalakshkiy Zaliv, Russia 24 A6 66 0N 35 0 E
Kandalu, Afghan. 40 E3 29 55N 63 20 E
Kandangan, Indonesia 36 E5 2 50S 115 20 E
Kandanghaur, Indonesia 37 G13 6 21S 108 6 E
Kandanos, Greece 23 D5 35 19N 23 44 E
Kandhkot, Pakistan 42 E3 28 16N 69 8 E
Kandhla, India 42 E7 29 18N 77 19 E
Kandi, Benin 50 F6 11 7N 2 55 E
Kandi, India 43 H13 23 58N 88 5 E
Kandiaro, Pakistan 42 F3 27 4N 68 13 E
Kandla, India 42 H4 23 0N 70 10 E
Kandos, Australia 63 E4 32 45S 149 58 E
Kandy, Sri Lanka 40 R12 7 18N 80 43 E
Kane, U.S.A. 78 E6 41 40N 78 49W
Kane Basin, Greenland 4 B4 79 1N 70 0W
Kaneohe, U.S.A. 74 H16 21 25N 157 48W
Kangān, Fārs, Iran 45 E7 27 50N 52 3 E
Kangān, Hormozgān, Iran 45 E8 25 48N 57 28 E
Kangar, Malaysia 39 J3 6 27N 100 12 E
Kangaroo I., Australia 63 F2 35 45S 137 0 E
Kangaroo Mts., Australia 62 C3 23 29S 141 51 E
Kangasala, Finland 9 F21 61 28N 24 4 E
Kangāvar, Iran 45 C6 34 40N 48 0 E
Kangdong, N. Korea 35 E14 39 9N 126 5 E
Kangean, Kepulauan, Indonesia 36 F5 6 55S 115 23 E
Kangean Is. = Kangean, Kepulauan, Indonesia 36 F5 6 55S 115 23 E
Kanggye, N. Korea 35 D14 41 0N 126 35 E
Kanggyŏng, S. Korea 35 F14 36 10N 127 0 E
Kanghwa, S. Korea 35 F14 37 45N 126 30 E
Kangiqsualujjuaq, Canada 69 C13 58 30N 65 59W
Kangiqsujuaq, Canada 69 B12 61 30N 72 0W
Kangirsuk, Canada 69 C13 60 0N 70 0W
Kangnŭng, S. Korea 35 F15 37 45N 128 54 E
Kangping, China 35 C12 42 43N 123 18 E
Kangra, India 42 C7 32 6N 76 16 E
Kangto, India 41 F18 27 50N 92 35 E
Kanhar →, India 43 G10 24 28N 83 8 E
Kaniama, Dem. Rep. of the Congo 54 D1 7 30S 24 12 E
Kaniapiskau = Caniapiscau →, Canada 71 A6 56 40N 69 30W
Kaniapiskau, Res. = Caniapiscau Rés. de, Canada 71 B6 54 10N 69 55W
Kanin, Poluostrov, Russia 24 A8 68 0N 45 0 E
Kanin Nos, Mys, Russia 24 A7 68 39N 43 32 E
Kanin Pen. = Kanin, Poluostrov, Russia 24 A8 68 0N 45 0 E
Kaniva, Australia 63 F3 36 22S 141 18 E
Kanjut Sar, Pakistan 43 A6 36 7N 75 25 E
Kankaanpää, Finland 9 F20 61 44N 22 50 E
Kankakee, U.S.A. 76 E2 41 7N 87 52W
Kankakee →, U.S.A. 76 E1 41 23N 88 15W
Kankan, Guinea 50 F4 10 23N 9 15W
Kankendy = Xankändi, Azerbaijan 25 G8 39 52N 46 49 E
Kanker, India 41 J12 20 10N 81 40 E
Kankroli, India 42 G5 25 4N 73 53 E
Kannapolis, U.S.A. 77 H5 35 30N 80 37W
Kannauj, India 43 F8 27 3N 79 56 E
Kannod, India 40 H10 22 45N 76 40 E
Kano, Nigeria 50 F7 12 2N 8 30 E
Kan'onji, Japan 31 G6 34 7N 133 39 E
Kanowit, Malaysia 36 D4 2 14N 112 20 E
Kanoya, Japan 31 J5 31 25N 130 50 E
Kanpetlet, Burma 41 J18 21 10N 93 59 E
Kanpur, India 43 F9 26 28N 80 20 E
Kansas □, U.S.A. 80 F6 38 30N 99 0W
Kansas →, U.S.A. 80 F7 39 7N 94 37W
Kansas City, Kans., U.S.A. 80 F7 39 7N 94 38W
Kansas City, Mo., U.S.A. 80 F7 39 6N 94 35W
Kansenia, Dem. Rep. of the Congo 55 E2 10 20S 26 0 E
Kansk, Russia 27 D10 56 20N 95 37 E
Kansŏng, S. Korea 35 E15 38 24N 128 30 E
Kansu = Gansu □, China 34 G3 36 0N 104 0 E
Kantaphor, India 42 H7 22 35N 76 34 E
Kantharalak, Thailand 38 E5 14 39N 104 39 E
Kantli →, India 42 E6 28 20N 75 30 E
Kantō □, Japan 31 F9 36 15N 139 30 E
Kantō-Sanchi, Japan 31 G9 35 59N 138 50 E
Kanturk, Ireland 13 D3 52 11N 8 54W
Kanuma, Japan 31 F9 36 34N 139 42 E
Kanus, Namibia 56 D2 27 50S 18 39 E
Kanye, Botswana 56 C4 24 55S 25 28 E
Kanzenze, Dem. Rep. of the Congo 55 E2 10 30S 25 12 E
Kanzi, Ras, Tanzania 54 D4 7 1S 39 33 E
Kaohsiung, Taiwan 33 D7 22 35N 120 16 E
Kaokoveld, Namibia 56 B1 19 15S 14 30 E
Kaolack, Senegal 50 F2 14 5N 16 8W
Kaoshan, China 35 B13 44 38N 124 50 E
Kapaa, U.S.A. 74 G15 22 5N 159 19W
Kapadvanj, India 42 H5 23 5N 73 0 E
Kapan, Armenia 25 G8 39 18N 46 27 E
Kapanga, Dem. Rep. of the Congo 52 F4 8 30S 22 40 E
Kapchagai = Qapshaghay, Kazakstan 26 E8 43 51N 77 14 E
Kapela = Velika Kapela, Croatia 16 F8 45 10N 15 5 E
Kapema, Dem. Rep. of the Congo 55 E2 10 45S 28 22 E
Kapfenberg, Austria 16 E8 47 26N 15 18 E
Kapiri Mposhi, Zambia 55 E2 13 59S 28 43 E
Kapiskau →, Canada 70 B3 52 47N 81 55W
Kapit, Malaysia 36 D4 2 0N 112 55 E
Kapiti I., N.Z. 59 J5 40 50S 174 56 E
Kaplan, U.S.A. 81 K8 30 0N 92 17W
Kapoe, Thailand 39 H2 9 34N 98 32 E
Kapoeta, Sudan 51 H12 4 50N 33 35 E
Kaposvár, Hungary 17 E9 46 25N 17 47 E
Kapowsin, U.S.A. 84 D4 46 59N 122 13W
Kapps, Namibia 56 C2 22 32S 17 18 E
Kapsan, N. Korea 35 D15 41 4N 128 19 E
Kapsukas = Marijampole, Lithuania 9 J20 54 33N 23 19 E
Kapuas →, Indonesia 36 E3 0 25S 109 20 E
Kapuas Hulu, Pegunungan, Malaysia 36 D4 1 30N 113 30 E

Kościan

Kinsale, Old Hd. of, Ireland 13 E3 51 37N 8 33W
Kinsha = Chang Jiang →, China 33 C7 31 48N 121 10 E
Kinshasa, Dem. Rep. of the Congo 52 E3 4 20S 15 15 E
Kinsley, U.S.A. 81 G5 37 55N 99 25W
Kinsman, U.S.A. 78 E4 41 26N 80 35W
Kinston, U.S.A. 77 H7 35 16N 77 35W
Kintore Ra., Australia 60 D4 23 15S 128 47 E
Kintyre, U.K. 12 F3 55 30N 5 35W
Kintyre, Mull of, U.K. 12 F3 55 17N 5 47W
Kinushseo →, Canada 70 A3 55 15N 83 45W
Kinuso, Canada 72 B5 55 20N 115 25W
Kinyangiri, Tanzania 54 C3 4 25S 34 37 E
Kinzua, U.S.A. 78 E6 41 52N 78 58W
Kinzua Dam, U.S.A. 78 E6 41 53N 79 0W
Kiosk, Canada 70 C4 46 6N 78 53W
Kiowa, Kans., U.S.A. 81 G5 37 1N 98 29W
Kiowa, Okla., U.S.A. 81 H7 34 43N 95 54W
Kipahigan L., Canada 73 B8 55 20N 101 55W
Kipanga, Tanzania 54 D4 6 15S 35 20 E
Kiparissía, Greece 21 F9 37 15N 21 40 E
Kiparissiakós Kólpos, Greece 21 F9 37 25N 21 25 E
Kipawa, L., Canada 70 C4 46 50N 79 0W
Kipembawe, Tanzania 54 D3 7 38S 33 27 E
Kipengere Ra., Tanzania 55 D3 9 12S 34 15 E
Kipili, Tanzania 54 D3 7 28S 30 32 E
Kipini, Kenya 54 C5 2 30S 40 32 E
Kipling, Canada 73 C8 50 6N 102 38W
Kippure, Ireland 13 C5 53 11N 6 21W
Kipushi, Dem. Rep. of the Congo 55 E2 11 48S 27 12 E
Kirensk, Russia 27 D11 57 50N 107 55 E
Kirghizia = Kyrgyzstan ■, Asia 26 E8 42 0N 75 0 E
Kirghizstan = Kyrgyzstan ■, Asia 26 E8 42 0N 75 0 E
Kirgiziya Steppe, Eurasia 25 E10 50 0N 55 0 E
Kiribati ■, Pac. Oc. 64 H10 5 0S 180 0 E
Kırıkkale, Turkey 25 G5 39 51N 33 32 E
Kirillov, Russia 24 C6 59 49N 38 24 E
Kirin = Jilin, China 35 C14 43 44N 126 30 E
Kiritimati, Kiribati 65 G12 1 58N 157 27W
Kirkby, U.K. 10 D5 53 30N 2 54W
Kirkby Lonsdale, U.K. 10 C5 54 12N 2 36W
Kirkcaldy, U.K. 12 E5 56 7N 3 9W
Kirkcudbright, U.K. 12 G4 54 50N 4 2W
Kirkee, India 40 K8 18 34N 73 56 E
Kirkenes, Norway 8 B23 69 40N 30 5 E
Kirkfield, Canada 78 B6 44 34N 78 59W
Kirkjubæjarklaustur, Iceland 8 E4 63 47N 18 4W
Kirkkonummi, Finland 9 F21 60 8N 24 26 E
Kirkland Lake, Canada 70 C3 48 9N 80 2W
Kırklareli, Turkey 21 D12 41 44N 27 15 E
Kirksville, U.S.A. 80 E8 40 12N 92 35W
Kirkūk, Iraq 44 C5 35 30N 44 21 E
Kirkwall, U.K. 12 C6 58 59N 2 58W
Kirkwood, S. Africa 56 E4 33 22S 25 15 E
Kirov, Russia 24 C8 58 35N 49 40 E
Kirovabad = Gäncä, Azerbaijan 25 F8 40 45N 46 20 E
Kirovakan = Vanadzor, Armenia 25 F7 40 48N 44 30 E
Kirovograd = Kirovohrad, Ukraine 25 E5 48 35N 32 20 E
Kirovohrad, Ukraine 25 E5 48 35N 32 20 E
Kirovsk = Babadayhan, Turkmenistan 26 F7 37 42N 60 23 E
Kirovsk, Russia 24 A5 67 32N 33 41 E
Kirovskiy, Kamchatka, Russia 27 D16 54 27N 155 42 E
Kirovskiy, Primorsk, Russia 30 B6 45 7N 133 30 E
Kirriemuir, U.K. 12 E5 56 41N 3 1W
Kirsanov, Russia 24 D7 52 35N 42 40 E
Kırşehir, Turkey 25 G5 39 14N 34 5 E
Kirthar Range, Pakistan 42 F2 27 0N 67 0 E
Kirtland, U.S.A. 83 H9 36 44N 108 21W
Kiruna, Sweden 8 C19 67 52N 20 15 E
Kirundu, Dem. Rep. of the Congo 54 C2 0 50S 25 35 E
Kiryū, Japan 31 F9 36 24N 139 20 E
Kisaga, Tanzania 54 C3 4 30S 34 23 E
Kisalaya, Nic. 88 D3 14 40N 84 3W
Kisámou, Kólpos, Greece 23 D5 35 30N 23 38 E
Kisanga, Dem. Rep. of the Congo 54 B2 2 30N 26 35 E
Kisangani, Dem. Rep. of the Congo 54 B2 0 35N 25 15 E
Kisar, Indonesia 37 F7 8 5S 127 10 E
Kisarawe, Tanzania 54 D4 6 53S 39 0 E
Kisarazu, Japan 31 G9 35 23N 139 55 E
Kishanganga →, Pakistan 43 B5 34 18N 73 28 E
Kishanganj, India 43 F13 26 3N 88 14 E
Kishangarh, Raj., India 42 F6 26 34N 74 52 E
Kishangarh, Raj., India 42 F4 27 50N 70 30 E
Kishinev = Chişinău, Moldova 17 E15 47 2N 28 50 E
Kishiwada, Japan 31 G7 34 28N 135 22 E
Kishtwar, India 43 C6 33 20N 75 48 E
Kisii, Kenya 54 C3 0 40S 34 45 E
Kisiju, Tanzania 54 D4 7 23S 39 19 E
Kisizi, Uganda 54 C2 1 0S 29 58 E
Kiskőrös, Hungary 17 E10 46 37N 19 20 E
Kiskunfélegyháza, Hungary 17 E10 46 42N 19 53 E
Kiskunhalas, Hungary 17 E10 46 28N 19 37 E
Kislovodsk, Russia 25 F7 43 50N 42 45 E
Kismayu = Chisimaio, Somali Rep. 49 G8 0 22S 42 32 E
Kiso-Gawa →, Japan 31 G8 35 20N 136 45 E
Kiso-Sammyaku, Japan 31 G8 35 45N 137 45 E
Kisofukushima, Japan 31 G8 35 52N 137 43 E
Kisoro, Uganda 54 C2 1 17S 29 48 E
Kissidougou, Guinea 50 G3 9 5N 10 5W
Kissimmee, U.S.A. 77 L5 28 18N 81 24W
Kissimmee →, U.S.A. 77 M5 27 9N 80 52W
Kississing L., Canada 73 B8 55 10N 101 20W
Kissónerga, Cyprus 23 E11 34 49N 32 24 E
Kisumu, Kenya 54 C3 0 3S 34 45 E
Kiswani, Tanzania 54 C4 4 5S 37 57 E
Kiswere, Tanzania 55 D4 9 27S 39 30 E
Kit Carson, U.S.A. 80 F3 38 46N 102 48W
Kita, Mali 50 F4 13 5N 9 25W
Kitaibaraki, Japan 31 F10 36 50N 140 45 E
Kitakami, Japan 30 E10 39 20N 141 10 E
Kitakami-Gawa →, Japan 30 E10 38 25N 141 19 E
Kitakami-Sammyaku, Japan 30 E10 39 30N 141 30 E
Kitakata, Japan 30 F9 37 39N 139 52 E
Kitakyūshū, Japan 31 H5 33 50N 130 50 E
Kitale, Kenya 54 B4 1 0N 35 0 E
Kitami, Japan 30 C11 43 48N 143 54 E
Kitami-Sammyaku, Japan 30 B11 44 22N 142 43 E
Kitangiri, L., Tanzania 54 C3 4 5S 34 20 E
Kitaya, Tanzania 55 E5 10 38S 40 8 E
Kitchener, Canada 78 C4 43 27N 80 29W
Kitega = Gitega, Burundi 54 C2 3 26S 29 56 E
Kitengo, Dem. Rep. of the Congo 54 D1 7 26S 24 8 E
Kitgum, Uganda 54 B3 3 17N 32 52 E
Kíthira, Greece 21 F10 36 8N 23 0 E
Kíthnos, Greece 21 F11 37 26N 24 27 E
Kiti, Cyprus 23 E12 34 50N 33 34 E
Kiti, C., Cyprus 23 E12 34 48N 33 36 E
Kitimat, Canada 72 C3 54 3N 128 38W
Kitinen →, Finland 8 C22 67 14N 27 27 E
Kitsuki, Japan 31 H5 33 25N 131 37 E
Kittakittaooloo, L., Australia 63 D2 28 3S 138 14 E
Kittanning, U.S.A. 78 F5 40 49N 79 31W
Kittatinny Mts., U.S.A. 79 F10 41 0N 75 0W
Kittery, U.S.A. 77 D10 43 5N 70 45W
Kittilä, Finland 8 C21 67 40N 24 51 E
Kitui, Kenya 54 C4 1 17S 38 0 E
Kitwanga, Canada 72 B3 55 6N 128 4W
Kitwe, Zambia 55 E2 12 54S 28 13 E
Kivarli, India 42 G5 24 33N 72 46 E
Kivertsi, Ukraine 17 C13 50 50N 25 28 E
Kividhes, Cyprus 23 E11 34 46N 32 51 E
Kivu, L., Dem. Rep. of the Congo 54 C2 1 48S 29 0 E
Kiyev = Kyyiv, Ukraine 17 C16 50 30N 30 28 E
Kiyevskoye Vdkhr. = Kyyivske Vdskh., Ukraine 17 C16 51 0N 30 25 E
Kizel, Russia 24 C10 59 3N 57 40 E
Kiziguru, Rwanda 54 C3 1 46S 30 23 E
Kızıl Irmak →, Turkey 25 F6 41 44N 35 58 E
Kizil Jilga, India 43 B8 35 26N 78 50 E
Kızıltepe, Turkey 44 B4 37 12N 40 35 E
Kizimkazi, Tanzania 54 D4 6 28S 39 30 E
Kizlyar, Russia 25 F8 43 51N 46 40 E
Kizyl-Arvat = Gyzylarbat, Turkmenistan 26 F6 39 4N 56 23 E
Kjölur, Iceland 8 D4 64 50N 19 25W
Kladno, Czech Rep. 16 C8 50 10N 14 7 E
Klaeng, Thailand 38 F3 12 47N 101 39 E
Klagenfurt, Austria 16 E8 46 38N 14 20 E
Klaipeda, Lithuania 9 J19 55 43N 21 10 E
Klaksvík, Færoe Is. 8 E9 62 14N 6 35W
Klamath →, U.S.A. 82 F1 41 33N 124 5W
Klamath Falls, U.S.A. 82 E3 42 13N 121 46W
Klamath Mts., U.S.A. 82 F2 41 20N 123 0W
Klamono, Indonesia 37 E8 1 8S 131 30 E
Klappan →, Canada 72 B3 58 0N 129 43W
Klarälven →, Sweden 9 G15 59 23N 13 32 E
Klatovy, Czech Rep. 16 D7 49 23N 13 18 E
Klawer, S. Africa 56 E2 31 44S 18 36 E
Klazienaveen, Neths. 15 B6 52 44N 7 0 E
Kleena Kleene, Canada 72 C4 52 0N 124 59W
Klein-Karas, Namibia 56 D2 27 33S 18 7 E
Klerksdorp, S. Africa 56 D4 26 53S 26 38 E
Kletsk = Klyetsk, Belarus 17 B14 53 5N 26 45 E
Kletskiy, Russia 25 E7 49 16N 43 11 E
Klickitat, U.S.A. 82 D3 45 49N 121 9W
Klickitat →, U.S.A. 84 E5 45 42N 121 17W
Klidhes, Cyprus 23 D13 35 42N 34 36 E
Klinaklini →, Canada 72 C3 51 21N 125 40W
Klipdale, S. Africa 56 E2 34 19S 19 57 E
Klipplaat, S. Africa 56 E3 33 1S 24 22 E
Kłodzko, Poland 17 C9 50 28N 16 38 E
Klouto, Togo 50 G6 6 57N 0 44 E
Kluane L., Canada 68 B6 61 15N 138 40W
Kluane Nat. Park, Canada 72 A1 60 45N 139 30W
Kluczbork, Poland 17 C10 50 58N 18 12 E
Klukwan, U.S.A. 72 B1 59 24N 135 54W
Klyetsk, Belarus 17 B14 53 5N 26 45 E
Klyuchevskaya, Gora, Russia 27 D17 55 50N 160 30 E
Knaresborough, U.K. 10 C6 54 1N 1 28W
Knee L., Man., Canada 70 A1 55 3N 94 45W
Knee L., Sask., Canada 73 B7 55 51N 107 0W
Knight Inlet, Canada 72 C3 50 45N 125 40W
Knighton, U.K. 11 E4 52 21N 3 3W
Knights Ferry, U.S.A. 84 H6 37 50N 120 40W
Knights Landing, U.S.A. 84 G5 38 48N 121 43W
Knob, C., Australia 61 F2 34 32S 119 16 E
Knock, Ireland 13 C3 53 48N 8 55W
Knockmealdown Mts., Ireland 13 D4 52 14N 7 56W
Knokke-Heist, Belgium 15 C3 51 21N 3 17 E
Knossós, Greece 23 D7 35 16N 25 10 E
Knowlton, Canada 79 A12 45 13N 72 31W
Knox, U.S.A. 76 E2 41 18N 86 37W
Knox Coast, Antarctica 5 C8 66 30S 108 0 E
Knoxville, Iowa, U.S.A. 80 E8 41 19N 93 6W
Knoxville, Pa., U.S.A. 78 E7 41 57N 77 27W
Knoxville, Tenn., U.S.A. 77 H4 35 58N 83 55W
Knysna, S. Africa 56 E3 34 2S 23 2 E
Ko Kha, Thailand 38 C2 18 11N 99 24 E
Koartac = Quaqtaq, Canada 69 B13 60 55N 69 40W
Koba, Indonesia 37 F8 6 37S 134 37 E
Kobarid, Slovenia 16 E7 46 15N 13 30 E
Kobayashi, Japan 31 J5 31 56N 130 59 E
Kobdo = Hovd, Mongolia 32 B4 48 2N 91 37 E
Kōbe, Japan 31 G7 34 45N 135 10 E
København, Denmark 9 J15 55 41N 12 34 E
Kōbi-Sho, Japan 31 M1 25 56N 123 41 E
Koblenz, Germany 16 C4 50 21N 7 36 E
Kobryn, Belarus 17 B13 52 15N 24 22 E
Kocaeli, Turkey 25 F4 40 45N 29 50 E
Kočani, Macedonia 21 D10 41 55N 22 25 E
Koch Bihar, India 41 F16 26 22N 89 29 E
Kochang, S. Korea 35 G14 35 41N 127 55 E
Kochas, India 43 G10 25 15N 83 56 E
Kōchi, Japan 31 H6 33 30N 133 35 E
Kōchi □, Japan 31 H6 33 40N 133 30 E
Kochiu = Gejiu, China 32 D5 23 20N 103 10 E
Kodarma, India 43 G11 24 28N 85 36 E
Kodiak, U.S.A. 68 C4 57 47N 152 24W
Kodiak I., U.S.A. 68 C4 57 30N 152 45W
Kodinar, India 42 J4 20 46N 70 46 E
Koes, Namibia 56 D2 26 0S 19 15 E
Koffiefontein, S. Africa 56 D4 29 30S 25 0 E
Kofiau, Indonesia 37 E7 1 11S 129 50 E
Koforidua, Ghana 50 G5 6 3N 0 17W
Kōfu, Japan 31 G9 35 40N 138 30 E
Koga, Japan 31 F9 36 11N 139 43 E
Kogaluk →, Canada 71 A7 56 12N 61 44W
Køge, Denmark 9 J15 55 27N 12 11 E
Koh-i-Bābā, Afghan. 40 B5 34 30N 67 0 E
Koh-i-Khurd, Afghan. 42 C1 33 30N 65 59 E
Koh-i-Maran, Pakistan 42 E2 29 18N 66 50 E
Kohat, Pakistan 42 C4 33 40N 71 29 E
Kohima, India 41 G19 25 35N 94 10 E
Kohkīlūyeh va Būyer Aḥmadi □, Iran 45 D6 31 30N 50 30 E
Kohler Ra., Antarctica 5 D15 77 0S 110 0W
Kohlu, Pakistan 42 E3 29 54N 69 15 E
Kohtla-Järve, Estonia 9 G22 59 20N 27 20 E
Koillismaa, Finland 8 D23 65 44N 28 36 E
Koin-dong, N. Korea 35 D14 40 28N 126 18 E
Kojō, N. Korea 35 E14 38 58N 127 58 E
Kojonup, Australia 61 F2 33 48S 117 10 E
Kojūr, Iran 45 B6 36 23N 51 43 E
Kokand = Qūqon, Uzbekistan 26 E8 40 30N 70 57 E
Kokas, Indonesia 37 E8 2 42S 132 26 E
Kokchetav = Kökshetaū, Kazakstan 26 D7 53 20N 69 25 E
Kokemäenjoki →, Finland 9 F19 61 32N 21 44 E
Kokkola, Finland 8 E20 63 50N 23 8 E
Koko Kyunzu, Burma 41 M18 14 10N 93 25 E
Kokomo, U.S.A. 76 E2 40 29N 86 8W
Koksan, N. Korea 35 E14 38 46N 126 40 E
Kökshetaū, Kazakstan 26 D7 53 20N 69 25 E
Koksoak →, Canada 69 C13 58 30N 68 10W
Kokstad, S. Africa 57 E4 30 32S 29 29 E
Kokubu, Japan 31 J5 31 44N 130 46 E
Kola, Indonesia 37 F8 5 35S 134 30 E
Kola, Russia 24 A5 68 45N 33 8 E
Kola Pen. = Kolskiy Poluostrov, Russia 24 A6 67 30N 38 0 E
Kolachi →, Pakistan 42 F2 27 8N 67 2 E
Kolahoi, India 43 B6 34 12N 75 22 E
Kolaka, Indonesia 37 E6 4 3S 121 46 E
Kolar, India 40 N11 13 12N 78 15 E
Kolar Gold Fields, India 40 N11 12 58N 78 16 E
Kolaras, India 42 G6 25 14N 77 36 E
Kolari, Finland 8 C20 67 20N 23 48 E
Kolayat, India 40 F8 27 50N 72 50 E
Kolchugino = Leninsk-Kuznetskiy, Russia 26 D9 54 44N 86 10 E
Kolding, Denmark 9 J13 55 30N 9 29 E
Kolepom = Dolak, Pulau, Indonesia 37 F9 8 0S 138 30 E
Kolguyev, Ostrov, Russia 24 A8 69 20N 48 30 E
Kolhapur, India 40 L9 16 43N 74 15 E
Kolín, Czech Rep. 16 C8 50 2N 15 9 E
Kolkas rags, Latvia 9 H20 57 46N 22 37 E
Kollum, Neths. 15 A6 53 17N 6 10 E
Kolmanskop, Namibia 56 D2 26 45S 15 14 E
Köln, Germany 16 C4 50 56N 6 57 E
Koło, Poland 17 B10 52 14N 18 40 E
Kołobrzeg, Poland 16 A8 54 10N 15 35 E
Kolomna, Russia 24 C6 55 8N 38 45 E
Kolomyya, Ukraine 17 D13 48 31N 25 2 E
Kolonodale, Indonesia 37 E6 2 3S 121 25 E
Kolosib, India 41 G18 24 15N 92 45 E
Kolpashevo, Russia 26 D9 58 20N 83 5 E
Kolpino, Russia 24 C5 59 44N 30 39 E
Kolskiy Poluostrov, Russia 24 A6 67 30N 38 0 E
Kolskiy Zaliv, Russia 24 A5 69 23N 34 0 E
Kolwezi, Dem. Rep. of the Congo 55 E2 10 40S 25 25 E
Kolyma →, Russia 27 C17 69 30N 161 0 E
Kolymskoye Nagorye, Russia 27 C16 63 0N 157 0 E
Kôm Ombo, Egypt 51 D12 24 25N 32 52 E
Komandorskiye Is. = Komandorskiye Ostrova, Russia 27 D17 55 0N 167 0 E
Komandorskiye Ostrova, Russia 27 D17 55 0N 167 0 E
Komárno, Slovak Rep. 17 E10 47 49N 18 5 E
Komatipoort, S. Africa 57 D5 25 25S 31 55 E
Komatou Yialou, Cyprus 23 D13 35 25N 34 8 E
Komatsu, Japan 31 F8 36 25N 136 30 E
Komatsujima, Japan 31 H7 34 0N 134 35 E
Komi □, Russia 24 B10 64 0N 55 0 E
Kommunarsk = Alchevsk, Ukraine 25 E6 48 30N 38 45 E
Kommunizma, Pik, Tajikistan 26 F8 39 0N 72 2 E
Komodo, Indonesia 37 F5 8 37S 119 20 E
Komoran, Pulau, Indonesia 37 F9 8 18S 138 45 E
Komoro, Japan 31 F9 36 19N 138 26 E
Komotini, Greece 21 D11 41 9N 25 26 E
Kompasberg, S. Africa 56 E3 31 45S 24 32 E
Kompong Bang, Cambodia 39 F5 12 24N 104 40 E
Kompong Cham, Cambodia 39 G5 12 0N 105 30 E
Kompong Chhnang = Kampang Chhnang, Cambodia 39 F5 12 20N 104 35 E
Kompong Chikreng, Cambodia 38 F5 13 5N 104 18 E
Kompong Kleang, Cambodia 38 F5 13 6N 104 8 E
Kompong Luong, Cambodia 39 G5 11 49N 104 48 E
Kompong Pranak, Cambodia 38 F5 13 35N 104 55 E
Kompong Som = Kampong Saom, Cambodia 39 G4 10 38N 103 30 E
Kompong Som, Chhung = Kampong Saom, Chaak, Cambodia 39 G4 10 50N 103 32 E
Kompong Speu, Cambodia 39 G5 11 26N 104 32 E
Kompong Sralao, Cambodia 38 E5 14 5N 105 46 E
Kompong Thom, Cambodia 38 F5 12 35N 104 51 E
Kompong Trabeck, Cambodia 38 F5 13 6N 105 14 E
Kompong Trabeck, Cambodia 39 G5 11 9N 105 28 E
Kompong Trach, Cambodia 39 G5 11 25N 105 48 E
Kompong Tralach, Cambodia 39 G5 11 54N 104 47 E
Komrat = Comrat, Moldova 17 E15 46 18N 28 40 E
Komsberg, S. Africa 56 E3 32 40S 20 45 E
Komsomolets, Ostrov, Russia 27 A10 80 30N 95 0 E
Komsomolsk, Russia 27 D14 50 30N 137 0 E
Kon Tum, Vietnam 38 E7 14 24N 108 0 E
Kon Tum, Plateau du, Vietnam 38 E7 14 30N 108 30 E
Konarhā □, Afghan. 40 B7 35 30N 71 3 E
Konārī, Iran 45 D6 28 13N 51 36 E
Konch, India 43 G8 26 0N 79 10 E
Konde, Tanzania 54 C4 4 57S 39 45 E
Kondinin, Australia 61 F2 32 34S 118 8 E
Kondoa, Tanzania 54 C4 4 55S 35 50 E
Kondókali, Greece 23 A3 39 38N 19 51 E
Kondopaga, Russia 24 B5 62 12N 34 17 E
Kondratyevo, Russia 27 D10 57 22N 98 15 E
Köneürgench, Turkmenistan 26 E6 42 19N 59 10 E
Konevo, Russia 24 B6 62 8N 39 20 E
Kong = Khong →, Cambodia 38 F5 13 32N 105 58 E
Kong, Ivory C. 50 G5 8 54N 4 36W
Kong, Koh, Cambodia 39 G4 11 20N 103 0 E
Kong Christian IX.s Land, Greenland 4 C6 68 0N 36 0W
Kong Christian X.s Land, Greenland 4 B6 74 0N 29 0W
Kong Franz Joseph Fd., Greenland 4 B6 73 30N 24 30W
Kong Frederik IX.s Land, Greenland 4 C5 67 0N 52 0W
Kong Frederik VI.s Kyst, Greenland 4 C5 63 0N 43 0W
Kong Frederik VIII.s Land, Greenland 4 B6 78 30N 26 0W
Kong Oscar Fjord, Greenland 4 B6 72 20N 24 0W
Kongju, S. Korea 35 F14 36 30N 127 0 E
Konglu, Burma 41 F20 27 13N 97 57 E
Kongolo, Kasai-Or., Dem. Rep. of the Congo 54 D1 5 26S 24 49 E
Kongolo, Katanga, Dem. Rep. of the Congo 54 D2 5 22S 27 0 E
Kongsberg, Norway 9 G13 59 39N 9 39 E
Kongsvinger, Norway 9 F15 60 12N 12 2 E
Kongwa, Tanzania 54 D4 6 11S 36 26 E
Koni, Dem. Rep. of the Congo 55 E2 10 40S 27 11 E
Koni, Mts., Dem. Rep. of the Congo 55 E2 10 36S 27 10 E
Königsberg = Kaliningrad, Russia 9 J19 54 42N 20 32 E
Konin, Poland 17 B10 52 12N 18 15 E
Konjic, Bos.-H. 21 C7 43 42N 17 58 E
Konkiep, Namibia 56 D2 26 49S 17 15 E
Konosha, Russia 24 B7 61 0N 40 5 E
Kōnosu, Japan 31 F9 36 3N 139 31 E
Konotop, Ukraine 25 D5 51 12N 33 7 E
Końskie, Poland 17 C11 51 15N 20 23 E
Konstanz, Germany 16 E5 47 40N 9 10 E
Kont, Iran 45 E9 26 55N 61 50 E
Kontagora, Nigeria 50 F7 10 23N 5 27 E
Konya, Turkey 25 G5 37 52N 32 35 E
Konza, Kenya 54 C4 1 45S 37 7 E
Koocanusa, L., Canada 82 B6 49 20N 115 15W
Kookynie, Australia 61 E3 29 17S 121 22 E
Koolyanobbing, Australia 61 F2 30 48S 119 36 E
Koonibba, Australia 63 E1 31 54S 133 25 E
Koorawatha, Australia 63 E4 34 2S 148 33 E
Koorda, Australia 61 F2 30 48S 117 35 E
Kooskia, U.S.A. 82 C6 46 9N 115 59W
Kootenay →, U.S.A. 72 D5 49 19N 117 39W
Kootenay L., Canada 72 D5 49 45N 116 50W
Kootenay Nat. Park, Canada 72 C5 51 0N 116 0W
Kootjieskolk, S. Africa 56 E3 31 15S 20 21 E
Kopaonik, Serbia, Yug. 21 C9 43 10N 20 50 E
Kópavogur, Iceland 8 D3 64 6N 21 55W
Koper, Slovenia 16 F7 45 31N 13 44 E
Kopervik, Norway 9 G11 59 17N 5 17 E
Kopet Dagh, Asia 45 B8 38 0N 58 0 E
Kopi, Australia 63 E2 33 24S 135 40 E
Köping, Sweden 9 G17 59 31N 16 3 E
Koppeh Dāgh = Kopet Dagh, Asia 45 B8 38 0N 58 0 E
Koppies, S. Africa 57 D4 27 20S 27 30 E
Koprivnica, Croatia 20 A7 46 12N 16 45 E
Kopychyntsi, Ukraine 17 D13 49 7N 25 58 E
Korab, Macedonia 21 D9 41 44N 20 40 E
Korakiána, Greece 23 A3 39 42N 19 45 E
Koral, India 42 J5 21 50N 73 12 E
Korba, India 43 H10 22 20N 82 45 E
Korbu, G., Malaysia 39 K3 4 41N 101 18 E
Korça, Albania 21 D9 40 37N 20 50 E
Korce = Korça, Albania 21 D9 40 37N 20 50 E
Korčula, Croatia 20 C7 42 56N 16 57 E
Kord Kūy, Iran 45 B7 36 48N 54 7 E
Kord Sheykh, Iran 45 D7 28 31N 52 53 E
Kordestān □, Iran 44 C5 36 0N 47 0 E
Kordofân, Sudan 51 F11 13 0N 29 0 E
Korea, North ■, Asia 35 E14 40 0N 127 0 E
Korea, South ■, Asia 35 G15 36 0N 128 0 E
Korea Bay, Korea 35 E13 39 0N 124 0 E
Korea Strait, Asia 35 H15 34 0N 129 30 E
Korets, Ukraine 17 C14 50 40N 27 5 E
Korhogo, Ivory C. 50 G4 9 29N 5 28W
Korinthiakós Kólpos, Greece 21 E10 38 16N 22 30 E
Kórinthos, Greece 21 F10 37 56N 22 55 E
Koríssa, Límni, Greece 23 B3 39 27N 19 53 E
Kōriyama, Japan 30 F10 37 24N 140 23 E
Korla, China 32 B3 41 45N 86 4 E
Kormakiti, C., Cyprus 23 D11 35 23N 32 56 E
Korneshty = Corneşti, Moldova 17 E15 47 21N 28 1 E
Koro, Fiji 59 C8 17 19S 179 23 E
Koro, Ivory C. 50 G4 8 32N 7 30W
Koro Sea, Fiji 59 C9 17 30S 179 45W
Korogwe, Tanzania 54 D4 5 5S 38 25 E
Koronadal, Phil. 37 C6 6 12N 125 1 E
Koror, Palau 37 C8 7 20N 134 28 E
Körös →, Hungary 17 E11 46 43N 20 12 E
Korosten, Ukraine 17 C15 50 54N 28 36 E
Korostyshev, Ukraine 17 C15 50 19N 29 4 E
Korraraika, Helodranon' i, Madag. 57 B7 17 45S 43 57 E
Korsakov, Russia 27 E15 46 36N 142 42 E
Korshunovo, Russia 27 D12 58 37N 110 10 E
Korsør, Denmark 9 J14 55 20N 11 9 E
Kortrijk, Belgium 15 D3 50 50N 3 17 E
Korwai, India 42 G8 24 7N 78 5 E
Koryakskoye Nagorye, Russia 27 C18 61 0N 171 0 E
Koryŏng, S. Korea 35 G15 35 44N 128 15 E
Kos, Greece 21 F12 36 50N 27 15 E
Koschagyl, Kazakstan 25 E9 46 40N 54 0 E
Kościan, Poland 17 B9 52 5N 16 40 E

Kosciusko

Kosciusko, *U.S.A.* **81 J10** 33 4N 89 35W
Kosciuszko, Mt., *Australia* . **63 F4** 36 27S 148 16 E
Kosha, *Sudan* .... **51 D12** 20 50N 30 30 E
K'oshih = Kashi, *China* ... **32 C2** 39 30N 76 2 E
Koshiki-Rettō, *Japan* ...... **31 J4** 31 45N 129 49 E
Kosi, *India* .... **42 F7** 27 48N 77 29 E
Kosi →, *India* .... **43 E8** 28 41N 78 57 E
Košice, *Slovak Rep.* ...... **17 D11** 48 42N 21 15 E
Koskhinoú, *Greece* .... **23 C10** 36 23N 28 13 E
Koslan, *Russia* .... **24 B8** 63 34N 49 14 E
Kosŏng, *N. Korea* .... **35 E15** 38 40N 128 22 E
Kosovo □, *Yugoslavia* .... **21 C9** 42 30N 21 0 E
Kosovska Mitrovica,
Yugoslavia .... **21 C9** 42 54N 20 52 E
Kossou, L. de, *Ivory C.* **50 G4** 6 59N 5 31W
Koster, *S. Africa* .... **56 D4** 25 52S 26 54 E
Kôstî, *Sudan* .... **51 F12** 13 8N 32 43 E
Kostopil, *Ukraine* .... **17 C14** 50 51N 26 22 E
Kostroma, *Russia* .... **24 C7** 57 50N 40 58 E
Kostrzyn, *Poland* .... **16 B8** 52 35N 14 39 E
Koszalin, *Poland* .... **16 A9** 54 11N 16 8 E
Kot Addu, *Pakistan* .... **42 D4** 30 30N 71 0 E
Kot Kapura, *India* .... **42 D6** 30 35N 74 50 E
Kot Moman, *Pakistan* ...... **42 C5** 32 13N 73 0 E
Kot Sultan, *Pakistan* ...... **42 D4** 30 46N 70 56 E
Kota, *India* .... **42 G6** 25 14N 75 49 E
Kota Baharu, *Malaysia* .... **39 J4** 6 7N 102 14 E
Kota Barrage, *India* .... **42 G6** 25 6N 75 51 E
Kota Belud, *Malaysia* ..... **36 C5** 6 21N 116 26 E
Kota Kinabalu, *Malaysia* ... **36 C5** 6 0N 116 4 E
Kota Kubu Baharu, *Malaysia* **39 L3** 3 34N 101 39 E
Kota Tinggi, *Malaysia* ..... **39 M4** 1 44N 103 53 E
Kotaagung, *Indonesia* ..... **36 F2** 5 38S 104 29 E
Kotabaru, *Indonesia* ...... **36 E5** 3 20S 116 20 E
Kotabumi, *Indonesia* ...... **36 E2** 4 49S 104 54 E
Kotamobagu, *Indonesia* .... **37 D6** 0 57N 124 31 E
Kotcho L., *Canada* **72 B4** 59 7N 121 12W
Kotdwara, *India* .... **43 E8** 29 45N 78 32 E
Kotelnich, *Russia* .... **24 C8** 58 22N 48 24 E
Kotelnikovo, *Russia* ...... **25 E7** 47 38N 43 8 E
Kotelnyy, Ostrov, *Russia* .. **27 B14** 75 10N 139 0 E
Kothari →, *India* .... **42 G6** 25 20N 75 4 E
Kothi, *Mad. P., India* ...... **43 H10** 23 21N 82 3 E
Kothi, *Mad. P., India* ...... **43 G9** 24 45N 80 40 E
Kotiro, *Pakistan* .... **42 F2** 26 17N 67 13 E
Kotka, *Finland* .... **9 F22** 60 28N 26 58 E
Kotlas, *Russia* .... **24 B8** 61 17N 46 43 E
Kotli, *Pakistan* .... **42 C5** 33 30N 73 55 E
Kotma, *India* .... **43 H9** 23 12N 81 58 E
Kotmul, *Pakistan* .... **43 B6** 35 32N 75 10 E
Kotor, *Montenegro, Yug.* .. **21 C8** 42 25N 18 47 E
Kotovsk, *Ukraine* .... **17 E15** 47 45N 29 35 E
Kotputli, *India* .... **42 F7** 27 43N 76 12 E
Kotri, *Pakistan* .... **42 G3** 25 22N 68 22 E
Kottayam, *India* .... **40 Q10** 9 35N 76 33 E
Kotturu, *India* .... **40 M10** 14 45N 76 10 E
Kotuy →, *Russia* .... **27 B11** 71 54N 102 6 E
Kotzebue, *U.S.A.* **68 B3** 66 53N 162 39W
Koudougou, *Burkina Faso* . **50 F5** 12 10N 2 20W
Koufonísi, *Greece* .... **23 E8** 34 56N 26 8 E
Kougaberge, *S. Africa* .... **56 E3** 33 48S 23 50 E
Kouilou →, *Congo* ...... **52 E2** 4 10S 12 5 E
Koula Moutou, *Gabon* ..... **52 E2** 1 15S 12 25 E
Koulen = Kulen, *Cambodia* **38 F5** 13 50N 104 40 E
Kouloúra, *Greece* .... **23 A3** 39 42N 19 54 E
Koúm-bournoú, Ákra,
Greece .... **23 C10** 36 15N 28 11 E
Koumala, *Australia* .... **62 C4** 21 38S 149 15 E
Koumra, *Chad* .... **51 G9** 8 50N 17 35 E
Kounradskiy, *Kazakstan* ... **26 E8** 46 59N 75 0 E
Kountze, *U.S.A.* **81 K7** 30 22N 94 19W
Kouris →, *Cyprus* .... **23 E11** 34 38N 32 54 E
Kourou, *Fr. Guiana* **93 B8** 5 9N 52 39W
Kousseri, *Cameroon* ...... **51 F8** 12 0N 14 55 E
Kouvola, *Finland* .... **9 F22** 60 52N 26 43 E
Kovdor, *Russia* .... **24 A5** 67 34N 30 24 E
Kovel, *Ukraine* .... **17 C13** 51 11N 24 38 E
Kovrov, *Russia* .... **24 C7** 56 25N 41 25 E
Kowanyama, *Australia* .... **62 B3** 15 29S 141 44 E
Kowŏn, *N. Korea* .... **35 E14** 39 26N 127 14 E
Köyceğiz, *Turkey* .... **21 F13** 36 57N 28 40 E
Koza, *Japan* .... **31 L3** 26 19N 127 46 E
Kozan, *Turkey* .... **44 B2** 37 26N 35 50 E
Kozáni, *Greece* .... **21 D9** 40 19N 21 47 E
Kozhikode = Calicut, *India* . **40 P9** 11 15N 75 43 E
Kozhva, *Russia* .... **24 A10** 65 10N 57 0 E
Kozyatyn, *Ukraine* .... **17 D15** 49 45N 28 50 E
Kra, Isthmus of = Kra, Kho
Khot, *Thailand* .... **39 G2** 10 15N 99 30 E
Kra, Kho Khot, *Thailand* ... **39 G2** 10 15N 99 30 E
Kra Buri, *Thailand* .... **39 G2** 10 22N 98 46 E
Krabi, *Thailand* .... **39 H2** 8 4N 98 55 E
Kracheh, *Cambodia* .... **38 F6** 12 32N 106 10 E
Kragan, *Indonesia* .... **37 G14** 6 43S 111 38 E
Kragerø, *Norway* .... **9 G13** 58 52N 9 25 E
Kragujevac, *Serbia, Yug.* .. **21 B9** 44 2N 20 56 E
Krajina, *Bos.-H.* .... **20 B7** 44 45N 16 35 E
Krakatau = Rakata, Pulau,
Indonesia .... **36 F3** 6 10S 105 20 E
Krakatoa = Rakata, Pulau,
Indonesia .... **36 F3** 6 10S 105 20 E
Krakor, *Cambodia* .... **38 F5** 12 32N 104 12 E
Kraków, *Poland* .... **17 C10** 50 4N 19 57 E
Kralanh, *Cambodia* .... **38 F4** 13 35N 103 25 E
Kraljevo, *Serbia, Yug.* ..... **21 C9** 43 44N 20 41 E
Kramatorsk, *Ukraine* ...... **25 E6** 48 50N 37 30 E
Kramfors, *Sweden* .... **9 E17** 62 55N 17 48 E
Kranj, *Slovenia* .... **16 E8** 46 16N 14 22 E
Krankskop, *S. Africa* ...... **57 D5** 28 0S 30 47 E
Krasavino, *Russia* .... **24 B8** 60 58N 46 29 E
Kraskino, *Russia* .... **27 E14** 42 44N 130 48 E
Kraśnik, *Poland* .... **17 C12** 50 55N 22 15 E
Krasnoarmeysk, *Russia* ... **26 D5** 51 0N 45 42 E
Krasnodar, *Russia* .... **25 E6** 45 5N 39 0 E
Krasnokamsk, *Russia* ..... **24 C10** 58 4N 55 48 E
Krasnoperekopsk, *Ukraine* . **25 E5** 46 0N 33 54 E
Krasnorechenskiy, *Russia* . **30 B7** 44 41N 135 14 E
Krasnoselkup, *Russia* ..... **26 C9** 65 20N 82 10 E
Krasnoturinsk, *Russia* ..... **24 C11** 59 46N 60 12 E
Krasnoufimsk, *Russia* ..... **24 C10** 56 36N 57 38 E
Krasnouralsk, *Russia* ..... **24 C11** 58 21N 60 3 E
Krasnovishersk, *Russia* .... **24 B10** 60 23N 57 3 E
Krasnovodsk =
Türkmenbashi,
Turkmenistan .... **25 G9** 40 5N 53 5 E
Krasnoyarsk, *Russia* ...... **27 D10** 56 8N 93 0 E
Krasnyy Kut, *Russia* ...... **25 D8** 50 50N 47 0 E
Krasnyy Luch, *Ukraine* .... **25 E6** 48 13N 39 0 E
Krasnyy Yar, *Russia* ...... **25 E8** 46 43N 48 23 E
Kratie = Kracheh, *Cambodia* **38 F6** 12 32N 106 10 E
Krau, *Indonesia* .... **37 E10** 3 19S 140 5 E
Kravanh, Chuor Phnum,
Cambodia .... **39 G4** 12 0N 103 32 E
Krefeld, *Germany* .... **16 C4** 51 20N 6 33 E
Kremen, *Croatia* .... **16 F8** 44 28N 15 53 E
Kremenchug =
Kremenchuk, *Ukraine* ... **25 E5** 49 5N 33 25 E
Kremenchuk, *Ukraine* ..... **25 E5** 49 5N 33 25 E
Kremenchuksk Vdskh.,
Ukraine .... **25 E5** 49 20N 32 30 E
Kremenets, *Ukraine* ...... **17 C13** 50 8N 25 43 E
Kremmling, *U.S.A.* **82 F10** 40 4N 106 24W
Krems, *Austria* .... **16 D8** 48 25N 15 36 E
Kretinga, *Lithuania* .... **9 J19** 55 53N 21 15 E
Kribi, *Cameroon* .... **52 D1** 2 57N 9 56 E
Krichev = Krychaw, *Belarus* **17 B16** 53 40N 31 41 E
Kriós, Ákra, *Greece* .... **23 D5** 35 13N 23 34 E
Krishna →, *India* .... **41 M12** 15 57N 80 59 E
Krishnanagar, *India* ...... **43 H13** 23 24N 88 33 E
Kristiansand, *Norway* ..... **9 G13** 58 8N 8 1 E
Kristianstad, *Sweden* ..... **9 H16** 56 2N 14 9 E
Kristiansund, *Norway* ..... **8 E12** 63 7N 7 45 E
Kristiinankaupunki, *Finland* **9 E19** 62 16N 21 21 E
Kristinehamn, *Sweden* .... **9 G16** 59 18N 14 7 E
Kristinestad =
Kristiinankaupunki,
Finland .... **9 E19** 62 16N 21 21 E
Kríti, *Greece* .... **23 D7** 35 15N 25 0 E
Kritsá, *Greece* .... **23 D7** 35 10N 25 41 E
Krivoy Rog = Kryvyy Rih,
Ukraine .... **25 E5** 47 51N 33 20 E
Krk, *Croatia* .... **16 F8** 45 8N 14 40 E
Krokodil →, *Mozam.* .... **57 D5** 25 14S 32 18 E
Krong Kaoh Kong,
Cambodia .... **36 B2** 11 35N 103 0 E
Kronprins Olav Kyst,
Antarctica .... **5 C5** 69 0S 42 0 E
Kronshtadt, *Russia* .... **24 B4** 59 57N 29 51 E
Kroonstad, *S. Africa* ...... **56 D4** 27 43S 27 19 E
Kropotkin, *Russia* .... **25 E7** 45 28N 40 28 E
Krosno, *Poland* .... **17 D11** 49 42N 21 46 E
Krotoszyn, *Poland* .... **17 C9** 51 42N 17 23 E
Kroussón, *Greece* .... **23 D6** 35 13N 24 59 E
Kruger Nat. Park, *S. Africa* . **57 C5** 23 30S 31 40 E
Krugersdorp, *S. Africa* .... **57 D4** 26 5S 27 46 E
Kruisfontein, *S. Africa* .... **56 E3** 33 59S 24 43 E
Krung Thep = Bangkok,
Thailand .... **38 F3** 13 45N 100 35 E
Krupki, *Belarus* .... **17 A15** 54 19N 29 8 E
Kruševac, *Serbia, Yug.* .... **21 C9** 43 35N 21 28 E
Krychaw, *Belarus* .... **17 B16** 53 40N 31 41 E
Krymskiy Poluostrov =
Krymskyy Pivostriv,
Ukraine .... **25 F5** 45 0N 34 0 E
Krymskyy Pivostriv, *Ukraine* **25 F5** 45 0N 34 0 E
Kryvyy Rih, *Ukraine* ...... **25 E5** 47 51N 33 20 E
Ksar el Kebir, *Morocco* **50 B4** 35 0N 6 0W
Ksar es Souk = Ar
Rachidiya, *Morocco* **50 B5** 31 58N 4 20W
Kuala Belait, *Malaysia* .... **36 D4** 4 35N 114 11 E
Kuala Berang, *Malaysia* ... **39 K4** 5 5N 103 1 E
Kuala Dungun = Dungun,
Malaysia .... **39 K4** 4 45N 103 25 E
Kuala Kangsar, *Malaysia* .. **39 K3** 4 46N 100 56 E
Kuala Kelawang, *Malaysia* . **39 L4** 2 56N 102 5 E
Kuala Kerai, *Malaysia* ..... **39 K4** 5 30N 102 12 E
Kuala Lipis, *Malaysia* ..... **39 K4** 4 10N 102 3 E
Kuala Lumpur, *Malaysia* .. **39 L3** 3 9N 101 41 E
Kuala Nerang, *Malaysia* ... **39 J3** 6 16N 100 37 E
Kuala Pilah, *Malaysia* ..... **39 L4** 2 45N 102 15 E
Kuala Rompin, *Malaysia* ... **39 L4** 2 49N 103 29 E
Kuala Selangor, *Malaysia* . **39 L3** 3 20N 101 15 E
Kuala Sepetang, *Malaysia* . **39 K3** 4 49N 100 28 E
Kuala Terengganu, *Malaysia* **39 K4** 5 20N 103 8 E
Kualajelai, *Indonesia* ..... **36 E4** 2 58S 110 46 E
Kualakapuas, *Indonesia* ... **36 E4** 2 55S 114 20 E
Kualakurun, *Indonesia* .... **36 E4** 1 10S 113 50 E
Kualapembuang, *Indonesia* **36 E4** 3 14S 112 38 E
Kualasimpang, *Indonesia* .. **36 D1** 4 17N 98 3 E
Kuancheng, *China* .... **35 D10** 40 37N 118 30 E
Kuandang, *Indonesia* ..... **37 D6** 0 56N 123 1 E
Kuandian, *China* .... **35 D13** 40 45N 124 45 E
Kuangchou = Guangzhou,
China .... **33 D6** 23 5N 113 10 E
Kuantan, *Malaysia* .... **39 L4** 3 49N 103 20 E
Kuba = Quba, *Azerbaijan* . **25 F8** 41 21N 48 32 E
Kuban →, *Russia* .... **25 E6** 45 20N 37 30 E
Kubokawa, *Japan* .... **31 H6** 33 12N 133 8 E
Kucha Gompa, *India* ...... **43 B7** 34 25N 76 56 E
Kuchaman, *India* .... **42 F6** 27 13N 74 47 E
Kuchinda, *India* .... **43 J11** 21 44N 84 21 E
Kuching, *Malaysia* .... **36 D4** 1 33N 110 25 E
Kuchino-eruba-Jima, *Japan* **31 J5** 30 28N 130 12 E
Kuchino-Shima, *Japan* .... **31 K4** 29 57N 129 55 E
Kuchinotsu, *Japan* .... **31 H5** 32 36N 130 11 E
Kucing = Kuching, *Malaysia* **36 D4** 1 33N 110 25 E
Kud →, *Pakistan* .... **42 F2** 26 5N 66 20 E
Kuda, *India* .... **40 H7** 23 10N 71 15 E
Kudat, *Malaysia* .... **36 C5** 6 55N 116 55 E
Kudus, *Indonesia* .... **37 G14** 6 48S 110 51 E
Kudymkar, *Russia* .... **24 C9** 59 1N 54 39 E
Kueiyang = Guiyang, *China* **32 D5** 26 32N 106 40 E
Kufra Oasis = Al Kufrah,
Libya .... **51 D10** 24 17N 23 15 E
Kufstein, *Austria* .... **16 E7** 47 35N 12 11 E
Kugluktuk, *Canada* **68 B8** 67 50N 115 5W
Kugong I., *Canada* **70 A4** 56 18N 79 50W
Kūhak, *Iran* .... **40 F3** 27 12N 63 10 E
Kuhan, *Pakistan* .... **42 E2** 28 19N 67 14 E
Kūhbonān, *Iran* .... **45 D8** 31 23N 56 19 E
Kūhestak, *Iran* .... **45 E8** 26 47N 57 2 E
Kuhin, *Iran* .... **45 B6** 36 22N 49 40 E
Kūhīrī, *Iran* .... **45 E9** 26 55N 61 2 E
Kūhpāyeh, *Eşfahan, Iran* .. **45 C7** 32 44N 52 20 E
Kūhpāyeh, *Kermān, Iran* ... **45 D8** 30 35N 57 15 E
Kūhrān, Kūh-e, *Iran* ...... **45 E8** 26 46N 58 12 E
Kui Buri, *Thailand* .... **39 F2** 12 3N 99 52 E
Kuito, *Angola* .... **53 G3** 12 22S 16 55 E
Kuiu I., *U.S.A.* **72 B2** 57 45N 134 10W
Kujang, *N. Korea* .... **35 E14** 39 57N 126 1 E
Kuji, *Japan* .... **30 D10** 40 11N 141 46 E
Kujū-San, *Japan* .... **31 H5** 33 5N 131 15 E
Kukësi, *Albania* .... **21 C9** 42 5N 20 27 E
Kukup, *Malaysia* .... **39 M4** 1 20N 103 27 E
Kula, *Turkey* .... **21 E13** 38 32N 28 40 E
Kulachi, *Pakistan* .... **42 D4** 31 56N 70 27 E
Kulai, *Malaysia* .... **39 M4** 1 44N 103 35 E
Kulal, Mt., *Kenya* .... **54 B4** 2 42N 36 57 E
Kulasekarappattinam, *India* **40 Q11** 8 20N 78 5 E
Kuldīga, *Latvia* .... **9 H19** 56 58N 21 59 E
Kuldja = Yining, *China* .... **26 E9** 43 58N 81 10 E
Kulen, *Cambodia* .... **38 F5** 13 50N 104 40 E
Kulgam, *India* .... **43 C6** 33 36N 75 2 E
Kulgera, *Australia* .... **62 D1** 25 50S 133 18 E
Kulim, *Malaysia* .... **39 K3** 5 22N 100 34 E
Kulin, *Australia* .... **61 F2** 32 40S 118 2 E
Kŭlob, *Tajikistan* .... **26 F7** 37 55N 69 50 E
Kulsary, *Kazakstan* .... **25 E9** 46 59N 54 1 E
Kulti, *India* .... **43 H12** 23 43N 86 50 E
Kulu, *India* .... **42 D7** 31 58N 77 6 E
Kulumbura, *Australia* ..... **60 B4** 13 55S 126 35 E
Kulunda, *Russia* .... **26 D8** 52 35N 78 57 E
Kulungar, *Afghan.* .... **42 C3** 34 0N 69 2 E
Kūlvand, *Iran* .... **45 D7** 31 21N 54 35 E
Kulwin, *Australia* .... **63 F3** 35 0S 142 42 E
Kulyab = Kŭlob, *Tajikistan* **26 F7** 37 55N 69 50 E
Kuma →, *Russia* .... **25 F8** 44 55N 47 0 E
Kumagaya, *Japan* .... **31 F9** 36 9N 139 22 E
Kumai, *Indonesia* .... **36 E4** 2 44S 111 43 E
Kumamba, Kepulauan,
Indonesia .... **37 E9** 1 36S 138 45 E
Kumamoto, *Japan* .... **31 H5** 32 45N 130 45 E
Kumamoto □, *Japan* ...... **31 H5** 32 55N 130 55 E
Kumanovo, *Macedonia* .... **21 C9** 42 9N 21 42 E
Kumara, *N.Z.* .... **59 K3** 42 37S 171 12 E
Kumarina, *Australia* ...... **61 D2** 24 41S 119 32 E
Kumasi, *Ghana* **50 G5** 6 41N 1 38W
Kumayri = Gyumri, *Armenia* **25 F7** 40 47N 43 50 E
Kumba, *Cameroon* .... **52 D1** 4 36N 9 24 E
Kumbakonam, *India* ...... **40 P11** 10 58N 79 25 E
Kumbarilla, *Australia* ..... **63 D5** 27 15S 150 55 E
Kumbhraj, *India* .... **42 G7** 24 22N 77 3 E
Kumbia, *Australia* .... **63 D5** 26 41S 151 39 E
Kŭmch'ŏn, *N. Korea* ...... **35 E14** 38 10N 126 29 E
Kumdok, *India* .... **43 C8** 33 32N 78 10 E
Kume-Shima, *Japan* ...... **31 L3** 26 20N 126 47 E
Kumertau, *Russia* .... **24 D10** 52 45N 55 57 E
Kumharsain, *India* .... **42 D7** 31 19N 77 27 E
Kŭmhwa, *S. Korea* .... **35 E14** 38 17N 127 28 E
Kumi, *Uganda* .... **54 B3** 1 30N 33 58 E
Kumla, *Sweden* .... **9 G16** 59 8N 15 10 E
Kumo, *Nigeria* .... **51 F8** 10 1N 11 12 E
Kumon Bum, *Burma* ...... **41 F20** 26 30N 97 15 E
Kunashir, Ostrov, *Russia* .. **27 E15** 44 0N 146 0 E
Kunda, *Estonia* .... **9 G22** 59 30N 26 34 E
Kunda, *India* .... **43 G9** 25 43N 81 31 E
Kundar →, *Pakistan* ..... **42 D3** 31 56N 69 19 E
Kundian, *Pakistan* .... **42 C4** 32 27N 71 28 E
Kundla, *India* .... **42 J4** 21 21N 71 25 E
Kunga →, *Bangla.* .... **43 J13** 21 46N 89 30 E
Kunghit I., *Canada* **72 C2** 52 6N 131 3W
Kungrad = Qŭnghirot,
Uzbekistan .... **26 E6** 43 6N 58 54 E
Kungsbacka, *Sweden* ..... **9 H15** 57 30N 12 5 E
Kungur, *Russia* .... **24 C10** 57 25N 56 57 E
Kunhar →, *Pakistan* ..... **43 B5** 34 20N 73 30 E
Kuningan, *Indonesia* ..... **37 G13** 6 59S 108 29 E
Kunlong, *Burma* .... **41 H21** 23 20N 98 50 E
Kunlun Shan, *Asia* .... **32 C3** 36 0N 86 30 E
Kunming, *China* .... **32 D5** 25 1N 102 41 E
Kunsan, *S. Korea* .... **35 G14** 35 59N 126 45 E
Kunununrra, *Australia* ..... **60 C4** 15 40S 128 50 E
Kunwari →, *India* .... **43 F8** 26 26N 79 11 E
Kunya-Urgench =
Köneürgench,
Turkmenistan .... **26 E6** 42 19N 59 10 E
Kuopio, *Finland* .... **8 E22** 62 53N 27 35 E
Kupa →, *Croatia* .... **16 F9** 45 28N 16 24 E
Kupang, *Indonesia* .... **37 F6** 10 19S 123 39 E
Kupreanof I., *U.S.A.* **72 B2** 56 50N 133 30W
Kupyansk-Uzlovoi, *Ukraine* **25 E6** 49 40N 37 43 E
Kuqa, *China* .... **32 B3** 41 35N 82 30 E
Kür →, *Azerbaijan* ...... **25 G8** 39 29N 49 15 E
Kür Dili, *Azerbaijan* .... **45 B6** 39 3N 49 13 E
Kura = Kür →, *Azerbaijan* **25 G8** 39 29N 49 15 E
Kuranda, *Australia* .... **62 B4** 16 48S 145 35 E
Kuranga, *India* .... **42 H3** 22 4N 69 10 E
Kurashiki, *Japan* .... **31 G6** 34 40N 133 50 E
Kurayoshi, *Japan* .... **31 G6** 35 26N 133 50 E
Kŭrdzhali, *Bulgaria* .... **21 D11** 41 38N 25 21 E
Kure, *Japan* .... **31 G6** 34 14N 132 32 E
Kuressaare, *Estonia* ...... **9 G20** 58 15N 22 30 E
Kurgan, *Russia* .... **26 D7** 55 26N 65 18 E
Kuri, *India* .... **42 F4** 26 37N 70 43 E
Kuria Maria Is. = Khurīyā
Murīyā, Jazā 'ir, *Oman* .. **46 D6** 17 30N 55 58 E
Kuridala, *Australia* .... **62 C3** 21 16S 140 29 E
Kurigram, *Bangla.* .... **41 G16** 25 49N 89 39 E
Kurikka, *Finland* .... **9 E20** 62 36N 22 24 E
Kuril Is. = Kurilskiye
Ostrova, *Russia* .... **27 E16** 45 0N 150 0 E
Kuril Trench, *Pac. Oc.* ..... **28 E19** 44 0N 153 0 E
Kurilsk, *Russia* .... **27 E15** 45 14N 147 53 E
Kurilskiye Ostrova, *Russia* . **27 E16** 45 0N 150 0 E
Kurino, *Japan* .... **31 J5** 31 57N 130 43 E
Kurinskaya Kosa = Kür Dili,
Azerbaijan .... **45 B6** 39 3N 49 13 E
Kurnool, *India* .... **40 M11** 15 45N 78 0 E
Kuro-Shima, *Kagoshima,*
Japan .... **31 J4** 30 50N 129 57 E
Kuro-Shima, *Okinawa,*
Japan .... **31 M2** 24 14N 124 1 E
Kurow, *N.Z.* .... **59 L3** 44 44S 170 29 E
Kurram →, *Pakistan* ..... **42 C4** 32 36N 71 20 E
Kurri Kurri, *Australia* ..... **63 E5** 32 50S 151 28 E
Kurrimine, *Australia* ...... **62 B4** 17 47S 146 6 E
Kurshskiy Zaliv, *Russia* ... **9 J19** 55 9N 21 6 E
Kursk, *Russia* .... **24 D6** 51 42N 36 11 E
Kuruçay, *Turkey* .... **44 B3** 39 39N 38 29 E
Kuruktag, *China* .... **32 B3** 41 0N 89 0 E
Kuruman, *S. Africa* .... **56 D3** 27 28S 23 28 E
Kuruman →, *S. Africa* ... **56 D3** 26 56S 20 39 E
Kurume, *Japan* .... **31 H5** 33 15N 130 30 E
Kurunegala, *Sri Lanka* .... **40 R12** 7 30N 80 23 E
Kurya, *Russia* .... **24 B10** 61 42N 57 9 E
Kus Gölü, *Turkey* .... **21 D12** 40 10N 27 55 E
Kuşadası, *Turkey* .... **21 F12** 37 52N 27 15 E
Kusatsu, *Japan* .... **31 F9** 36 37N 138 36 E
Kusawa L., *Canada* **72 A1** 60 20N 136 13W
Kushalgarh, *India* .... **42 H6** 23 10N 74 27 E
Kushikino, *Japan* .... **31 J5** 31 44N 130 16 E
Kushima, *Japan* .... **31 J5** 31 29N 131 14 E
Kushimoto, *Japan* .... **31 H7** 33 28N 135 47 E
Kushiro, *Japan* .... **30 C12** 43 0N 144 25 E
Kushiro-Gawa →, *Japan* . **30 C12** 42 59N 144 23 E
Kūshk, *Iran* .... **45 D8** 28 46N 56 51 E
Kushka = Gushgy,
Turkmenistan .... **26 F7** 35 20N 62 18 E
Kūshkī, *Iran* .... **44 C5** 33 31N 47 13 E
Kushol, *India* .... **43 C7** 33 40N 76 36 E
Kushtia, *Bangla.* .... **41 H16** 23 55N 89 5 E
Kushva, *Russia* .... **24 C10** 58 18N 59 45 E
Kuskokwim B., *U.S.A.* **68 C3** 59 45N 162 25W
Kusmi, *India* .... **43 H10** 23 17N 83 55 E
Kussharo-Ko, *Japan* ...... **30 C12** 43 38N 144 21 E
Kustanay = Qostanay,
Kazakstan .... **26 D7** 53 10N 63 35 E
Kut, Ko, *Thailand* .... **39 G4** 11 40N 102 35 E
Kütahya, *Turkey* .... **25 G5** 39 30N 30 2 E
Kutaisi, *Georgia* .... **25 F7** 42 19N 42 40 E
Kutaraja = Banda Aceh,
Indonesia .... **36 C1** 5 35N 95 20 E
Kutch, Gulf of = Kachchh,
Gulf of, *India* .... **42 H3** 22 50N 69 15 E
Kutch, Rann of = Kachchh,
Rann of, *India* .... **42 H4** 24 0N 70 0 E
Kutiyana, *India* .... **42 J4** 21 36N 70 2 E
Kutno, *Poland* .... **17 B10** 52 15N 19 23 E
Kutu,
Dem. Rep. of the Congo . **52 E3** 2 40S 18 11 E
Kutum, *Sudan* .... **51 F10** 14 10N 24 40 E
Kuujjuaq, *Canada* **69 C13** 58 6N 68 15W
Kuujjuarapik, *Canada* **70 A4** 55 20N 77 35W
Kuŭp-tong, *N. Korea* ...... **35 D14** 40 45N 126 1 E
Kuusamo, *Finland* .... **8 D23** 65 57N 29 8 E
Kuusankoski, *Finland* ..... **9 F22** 60 55N 26 38 E
Kuvango, *Angola* .... **53 G3** 14 28S 16 20 E
Kuwait = Al Kuwayt, *Kuwait* **44 D5** 29 30N 48 0 E
Kuwait ■, *Asia* .... **44 D5** 29 30N 47 30 E
Kuwana, *Japan* .... **31 G8** 35 5N 136 43 E
Kuwana →, *India* .... **43 F10** 26 25N 83 15 E
Kuybyshev = Samara,
Russia .... **24 D9** 53 8N 50 6 E
Kuybyshev, *Russia* .... **26 D8** 55 27N 78 19 E
Kuybyshevskoye Vdkhr.,
Russia .... **24 C8** 55 2N 49 30 E
Kuye He →, *China* ...... **34 E6** 38 23N 110 46 E
Kūyeh, *Iran* .... **44 B5** 38 45N 47 57 E
Kūysanjaq, *Iraq* .... **44 B5** 36 5N 44 38 E
Kuyto, Ozero, *Russia* ..... **24 B5** 65 6N 31 20 E
Kuyumba, *Russia* .... **27 C10** 60 58N 96 59 E
Kuzey Anadolu Dağları,
Turkey .... **25 F6** 41 30N 35 0 E
Kuznetsk, *Russia* .... **24 D8** 53 12N 46 40 E
Kuzomen, *Russia* .... **24 A6** 66 22N 36 50 E
Kvænangen, *Norway* ..... **8 A19** 70 5N 21 15 E
Kvaløy, *Norway* .... **8 B18** 69 40N 18 30 E
Kvarner, *Croatia* .... **16 F8** 44 50N 14 10 E
Kvarnerič, *Croatia* .... **16 F8** 44 43N 14 37 E
Kwa-Nobuhle, *S. Africa* ... **53 L5** 33 50S 25 22 E
Kwabhaca, *S. Africa* ..... **57 E4** 30 51S 29 0 E
Kwakhanai, *Botswana* .... **56 C3** 21 39S 21 16 E
Kwakoegron, *Surinam* **93 B7** 5 12N 55 25W
Kwale, *Kenya* .... **54 C4** 4 15S 39 31 E
KwaMashu, *S. Africa* ..... **57 D5** 29 45S 30 58 E
Kwando →, *Africa* ...... **56 B3** 18 27S 23 32 E
Kwangdaeri, *N. Korea* .... **35 D14** 40 31N 127 32 E
Kwangju, *S. Korea* .... **35 G14** 35 9N 126 54 E
Kwango →,
Dem. Rep. of the Congo . **52 E3** 3 14S 17 22 E
Kwangsi-Chuang = Guangxi
Zhuangzu Zizhiqu □,
China .... **33 D5** 24 0N 109 0 E
Kwangtung =
Guangdong □, *China* ... **33 D6** 23 0N 113 0 E
Kwataboahegan →,
Canada **70 B3** 51 9N 80 50W
Kwatisore, *Indonesia* ..... **37 E8** 3 18S 134 50 E
KwaZulu Natal □, *S. Africa* **57 D5** 29 0S 30 0 E
Kweichow = Guizhou □,
China .... **32 D5** 27 0N 107 0 E
Kwekwe, *Zimbabwe* ...... **55 F2** 18 58S 29 48 E
Kwidzyn, *Poland* .... **17 B10** 53 44N 18 55 E
Kwinana New Town,
Australia .... **61 F2** 32 15S 115 47 E
Kwoka, *Indonesia* .... **37 E8** 0 31S 132 27 E
Kyabra Cr. →, *Australia* .. **63 D3** 25 36S 142 55 E
Kyabram, *Australia* .... **63 F4** 36 19S 145 4 E
Kyaikto, *Burma* .... **38 D1** 17 20N 97 3 E
Kyakhta, *Russia* .... **27 D11** 50 30N 106 25 E
Kyancutta, *Australia* ...... **63 E2** 33 8S 135 33 E
Kyangin, *Burma* .... **41 K19** 18 20N 95 20 E
Kyaukpadaung, *Burma* .... **41 J19** 20 52N 95 8 E
Kyaukpyu, *Burma* .... **41 K18** 19 28N 93 30 E
Kyaukse, *Burma* .... **41 J20** 21 36N 96 10 E
Kyburz, *U.S.A.* **84 G6** 38 47N 120 18W
Kyelang, *India* .... **42 C7** 32 35N 77 2 E
Kyenjojo, *Uganda* .... **54 B3** 0 40N 30 37 E
Kyle, *Canada* **73 C7** 50 50N 108 2W
Kyle Dam, *Zimbabwe* ..... **55 G3** 20 15S 31 0 E
Kyle of Lochalsh, *U.K.* **12 D3** 57 17N 5 44W
Kymijoki →, *Finland* ..... **9 F22** 60 30N 26 55 E
Kyneton, *Australia* .... **63 F3** 37 10S 144 29 E
Kynuna, *Australia* .... **62 C3** 21 37S 141 55 E
Kyō-ga-Saki, *Japan* ...... **31 G7** 35 45N 135 15 E
Kyoga, L., *Uganda* .... **54 B3** 1 35N 33 0 E
Kyogle, *Australia* .... **63 D5** 28 40S 153 0 E
Kyongju, *S. Korea* .... **35 G15** 35 51N 129 14 E
Kyongpyaw, *Burma* ...... **41 L19** 17 12N 95 10 E
Kyŏngsŏng, *N. Korea* ..... **35 D15** 41 35N 129 36 E
Kyōto, *Japan* .... **31 G7** 35 0N 135 45 E
Kyōto □, *Japan* .... **31 G7** 35 15N 135 45 E
Kyparissovouno, *Cyprus* .. **23 D12** 35 19N 33 10 E
Kyperounda, *Cyprus* ...... **23 E11** 34 56N 32 58 E
Kyrenia, *Cyprus* .... **23 D12** 35 20N 33 20 E
Kyrgyzstan ■, *Asia* ...... **26 E8** 42 0N 75 0 E
Kyrönjoki →, *Finland* .... **8 E19** 63 14N 21 45 E
Kystatyam, *Russia* .... **27 C13** 67 20N 123 10 E
Kythréa, *Cyprus* .... **23 D12** 35 15N 33 29 E
Kyunhla, *Burma* .... **41 H19** 23 25N 95 15 E
Kyuquot Sound, *Canada* .. **72 D3** 50 2N 127 22W
Kyūshū, *Japan* .... **31 H5** 33 0N 131 0 E
Kyūshū □, *Japan* .... **31 H5** 33 0N 131 0 E
Kyūshū-Sanchi, *Japan* .... **31 H5** 32 35N 131 17 E

Mallaig

:Conaughy, L., *U.S.A.* **80 E4** 41 14N 101 40W
:Cook, *U.S.A.* **80 E4** 40 12N 100 38W
:Creary, *Canada* **73 C9** 50 47N 99 29W
:Cullough Mt., *U.S.A.* **85 K11** 35 35N 115 13W
:Cusker →, *Canada* **73 B7** 55 32N 108 39W
:Dame, *Canada* **72 B3** 59 44N 128 59W
:Dermitt, *U.S.A.* **82 F5** 41 59N 117 43W
:Donald, *U.S.A.* **78 F4** 40 22N 80 14W
acdonald, L., *Australia* **60 D4** 23 30S 129 0 E
:Donald Is., *Ind. Oc.* **3 G13** 53 0S 73 0 E
acDonnell Ranges, *Australia* **60 D5** 23 40S 133 0 E
acDowell L., *Canada* **70 B1** 52 15N 92 45W
acduff, *U.K.* **12 D6** 57 40N 2 31W
acedonia = Makedhonia □, *Greece* **21 D10** 40 39N 22 0 E
acedonia, *U.S.A.* **78 E3** 41 19N 81 31W
acedonia ■, *Europe* **21 D9** 41 53N 21 40 E
aceió, *Brazil* **93 E11** 9 40S 35 41W
acerata, *Italy* **20 C5** 43 18N 13 27 E
:Farland, *U.S.A.* **85 K7** 35 41N 119 14W
:Farlane →, *Canada* **73 B7** 59 12N 107 58W
acfarlane, L., *Australia* **63 E2** 32 0S 136 40 E
:Gehee, *U.S.A.* **81 J9** 33 38N 91 24W
:Gill, *U.S.A.* **82 G6** 39 23N 114 47W
acgillycuddy's Reeks, *Ireland* **13 E2** 51 58N 9 45W
:Graw, *U.S.A.* **79 D8** 42 36N 76 8W
:Gregor, *U.S.A.* **80 D9** 43 1N 91 11W
:Gregor Ra., *Australia* **63 D3** 27 0S 142 45 E
ach, *Pakistan* **40 E5** 29 50N 67 20 E
ach Kowr, *Iran* **45 E9** 25 48N 61 28 E
achado = Jiparaná →, *Brazil* **92 E6** 8 3S 62 52W
achagai, *Argentina* **94 B3** 26 56S 60 2W
achakos, *Kenya* **54 C4** 1 30S 37 15 E
achala, *Ecuador* **92 D3** 3 20S 79 57W
achanga, *Mozam.* **57 C6** 20 59S 35 0 E
achattie, L., *Australia* **62 C2** 24 50S 139 48 E
achava, *Mozam.* **57 D5** 25 54S 32 28 E
achece, *Mozam.* **55 F4** 19 15S 35 32 E
achhu →, *India* **42 H4** 23 6N 70 46 E
achias, *Maine, U.S.A.* **77 C12** 44 43N 67 28W
achias, *N.Y., U.S.A.* **78 D6** 42 25N 78 30W
achichi →, *Canada* **73 B10** 57 3N 92 6W
achico, *Madeira* **22 D3** 32 43N 16 44W
achilipatnam, *India* **41 L12** 16 12N 81 8 E
achiques, *Venezuela* **92 A4** 10 4N 72 34W
achupicchu, *Peru* **92 F4** 13 8S 72 30W
achynlleth, *U.K.* **11 E4** 52 35N 3 50W
:llwraith Ra., *Australia* **62 A3** 13 50S 143 20 E
:Innes L., *Canada* **73 C10** 52 13N 93 45W
:Intosh, *U.S.A.* **80 C4** 45 55N 101 21W
:Intosh L., *Canada* **73 B8** 55 45N 105 0W
acintosh Ra., *Australia* **61 E4** 27 39S 125 32 E
acintyre →, *Australia* **63 D5** 28 37S 150 47 E
ackay, *Australia* **62 C4** 21 8S 149 11 E
ackay, *U.S.A.* **82 E7** 43 55N 113 37W
acKay →, *Canada* **72 B6** 57 10N 111 38W
ackay, L., *Australia* **60 D4** 22 30S 129 0 E
:Kay Ra., *Australia* **60 D3** 23 0S 122 30 E
:Keesport, *U.S.A.* **78 F5** 40 21N 79 52W
:Kellar, *Canada* **78 A5** 45 30N 79 55W
:Kenna, *U.S.A.* **84 D4** 46 56N 122 33W
ackenzie, *Canada* **72 B4** 55 20N 123 5W
:Kenzie, *U.S.A.* **77 G1** 36 8N 88 31W
ackenzie →, *Australia* **62 C4** 23 38S 149 46 E
ackenzie →, *Canada* **68 B6** 69 10N 134 20W
:Kenzie →, *U.S.A.* **82 D2** 44 7N 123 6W
ackenzie Bay, *Canada* **4 B1** 69 0N 137 30W
ackenzie City = Linden, *Guyana* **92 B7** 6 0N 58 10W
ackenzie Mts., *Canada* **68 B7** 64 0N 130 0W
ackinaw City, *U.S.A.* **76 C3** 45 47N 84 44W
:Kinlay, *Australia* **62 C3** 21 16S 141 18 E
:Kinlay →, *Australia* **62 C3** 20 50S 141 28 E
:Kinley, Mt., *U.S.A.* **68 B4** 63 4N 151 0W
:Kinley Sea, *Arctic* **4 A7** 82 0N 0 0 E
:Kinney, *U.S.A.* **81 J6** 33 12N 96 37W
ackinnon Road, *Kenya* **54 C4** 3 40S 39 1 E
:Kittrick, *U.S.A.* **85 K7** 35 18N 119 37W
acklin, *Canada* **73 C7** 52 20N 109 56W
acksville, *Australia* **63 E5** 30 40S 152 56 E
:Laughlin, *U.S.A.* **80 C4** 45 49N 100 49W
aclean, *Australia* **63 D5** 29 26S 153 16 E
:Lean, *U.S.A.* **81 H4** 35 14N 100 36W
:Leansboro, *U.S.A.* **80 F10** 38 6N 88 32W
aclear, *S. Africa* **57 E4** 31 2S 28 23 E
acleay →, *Australia* **63 E5** 30 56S 153 0 E
:Lennan, *Canada* **72 B5** 55 42N 116 50W
:Leod →, *Canada* **72 C5** 54 9N 115 44W
acLeod, B., *Canada* **73 A7** 62 53N 110 0W
acLeod, L., *Australia* **61 D1** 24 9S 113 47 E
acLeod Lake, *Canada* **72 C4** 54 58N 123 0W
:Loughlin, Mt., *U.S.A.* **82 E2** 42 27N 122 19W
:Mechen, *U.S.A.* **78 G4** 39 57N 80 44W
:Minnville, *Oreg., U.S.A.* **82 D2** 45 13N 123 12W
:Minnville, *Tenn., U.S.A.* **77 H3** 35 41N 85 46W
:Murdo Sd., *Antarctica* **5 D11** 77 0S 170 0 E
:Murray = Fort McMurray, *Canada* **72 B6** 56 44N 111 7W
:Murray, *U.S.A.* **84 B4** 48 19N 122 14W
acodoene, *Mozam.* **57 C6** 23 32S 35 5 E
acomb, *U.S.A.* **80 E9** 40 27N 90 40W
acon, *France* **18 C6** 46 19N 4 50 E
acon, *Ga., U.S.A.* **77 J4** 32 51N 83 38W
acon, *Miss., U.S.A.* **77 J1** 33 7N 88 34W
acon, *Mo., U.S.A.* **80 F8** 39 44N 92 28W
acossa, *Mozam.* **55 F3** 17 55S 33 56 E
acoun L., *Canada* **73 B8** 56 32N 103 40W
acovane, *Mozam.* **57 C6** 21 30S 35 2 E
:Pherson, *U.S.A.* **80 F6** 38 22N 97 40W
:Pherson Pk., *U.S.A.* **85 L7** 34 53N 119 53W
:Pherson Ra., *Australia* **63 D5** 28 15S 153 15 E
acquarie →, *Australia* **63 E4** 30 5S 147 30 E
acquarie Harbour, *Australia* **62 G4** 42 15S 145 23 E
acquarie Is., *Pac. Oc.* **64 N7** 54 36S 158 55 E
acRobertson Land, *Antarctica* **5 D6** 71 0S 64 0 E
acroom, *Ireland* **13 E3** 51 54N 8 57W
acTier, *Canada* **78 A5** 45 9N 79 46W
acubela, *Mozam.* **55 F4** 16 53S 37 49 E
acuiza, *Mozam.* **55 F3** 18 7S 34 29 E
acusani, *Peru* **92 F4** 14 4S 70 29W
acuse, *Mozam.* **55 F4** 17 45S 37 10 E
Macuspana, *Mexico* **87 D6** 17 46N 92 36W
Macusse, *Angola* **56 B3** 17 48S 20 23 E
Madadeni, *S. Africa* **57 D5** 27 43S 30 3 E
Madagascar ■, *Africa* **57 C8** 20 0S 47 0 E
Madā'in Sālih, *Si. Arabia* **44 E3** 26 46N 37 57 E
Madama, *Niger* **51 D8** 22 0N 13 40 E
Madame I., *Canada* **71 C7** 45 30N 60 58W
Madaripur, *Bangla.* **41 H17** 23 19N 90 15 E
Madauk, *Burma* **41 L20** 17 56N 96 52 E
Madawaska, *Canada* **78 A7** 45 30N 78 0W
Madawaska →, *Canada* **78 A8** 45 27N 76 21W
Madaya, *Burma* **41 H20** 22 12N 96 10 E
Maddalena, *Italy* **20 D3** 41 16N 9 23 E
Madeira, *Atl. Oc.* **22 D3** 32 50N 17 0W
Madeira →, *Brazil* **92 D7** 3 22S 58 45W
Madeleine, Îs. de la, *Canada* **71 C7** 47 30N 61 40W
Madera, *Mexico* **86 B3** 29 12N 108 7W
Madera, *Calif., U.S.A.* **84 J6** 36 57N 120 3W
Madera, *Pa., U.S.A.* **78 F6** 40 49N 78 26W
Madha, *India* **40 L9** 18 0N 75 30 E
Madhavpur, *India* **42 J3** 21 15N 69 58 E
Madhepura, *India* **43 F12** 26 11N 86 23 E
Madhubani, *India* **43 F12** 26 21N 86 7 E
Madhupur, *India* **43 G12** 24 16N 86 39 E
Madhya Pradesh □, *India* **42 J8** 22 50N 78 0 E
Madidi →, *Bolivia* **92 F5** 12 32S 66 52W
Madikeri, *India* **40 N9** 12 30N 75 45 E
Madill, *U.S.A.* **81 H6** 34 6N 96 46W
Madimba, *Dem. Rep. of the Congo* **52 E3** 4 58S 15 5 E
Ma'din, *Syria* **44 C3** 35 45N 39 36 E
Madingou, *Congo* **52 E2** 4 10S 13 33 E
Madirovalo, *Madag.* **57 B8** 16 26S 46 32 E
Madison, *Calif., U.S.A.* **84 G5** 38 41N 121 59W
Madison, *Fla., U.S.A.* **77 K4** 30 28N 83 25W
Madison, *Ind., U.S.A.* **76 F3** 38 44N 85 23W
Madison, *Nebr., U.S.A.* **80 E6** 41 50N 97 27W
Madison, *Ohio, U.S.A.* **78 E3** 41 46N 81 3W
Madison, *S. Dak., U.S.A.* **80 D6** 44 0N 97 7W
Madison, *Wis., U.S.A.* **80 D10** 43 4N 89 24W
Madison →, *U.S.A.* **82 D8** 45 56N 111 31W
Madison Heights, *U.S.A.* **76 G6** 37 25N 79 8W
Madisonville, *Ky., U.S.A.* **76 G2** 37 20N 87 30W
Madisonville, *Tex., U.S.A.* **81 K7** 30 57N 95 55W
Madista, *Botswana* **56 C4** 21 15S 25 6 E
Madiun, *Indonesia* **37 G14** 7 38S 111 32 E
Madoc, *Canada* **78 B7** 44 30N 77 28W
Madona, *Latvia* **9 H22** 56 53N 26 5 E
Madrakah, Ra's al, *Oman* **46 D6** 19 0N 57 50 E
Madras = Chennai, *India* **40 N12** 13 8N 80 19 E
Madras = Tamil Nadu □, *India* **40 P10** 11 0N 77 0 E
Madras, *U.S.A.* **82 D3** 44 38N 121 8W
Madre, L., *Mexico* **87 C5** 25 0N 97 30W
Madre, Laguna, *U.S.A.* **81 M6** 27 0N 97 30W
Madre, Sierra, *Phil.* **37 A6** 17 0N 122 0 E
Madre de Dios →, *Bolivia* **92 F5** 10 59S 66 8W
Madre de Dios, I., *Chile* **96 G1** 50 20S 75 10W
Madre del Sur, Sierra, *Mexico* **87 D5** 17 30N 100 0W
Madre Occidental, Sierra, *Mexico* **86 B3** 27 0N 107 0W
Madre Oriental, Sierra, *Mexico* **86 C5** 25 0N 100 0W
Madri, *India* **42 G5** 24 16N 73 32 E
Madrid, *Spain* **19 B4** 40 25N 3 45W
Madrid, *U.S.A.* **79 B9** 44 45N 75 8W
Madura, *Australia* **61 F4** 31 55S 127 0 E
Madura, *Indonesia* **37 G15** 7 30S 114 0 E
Madura, Selat, *Indonesia* **37 G15** 7 30S 113 20 E
Madurai, *India* **40 Q11** 9 55N 78 10 E
Madurantakam, *India* **40 N11** 12 30N 79 50 E
Mae Chan, *Thailand* **38 B2** 20 9N 99 52 E
Mae Hong Son, *Thailand* **38 C2** 19 16N 97 56 E
Mae Khlong →, *Thailand* **38 F3** 13 24N 100 0 E
Mae Phrik, *Thailand* **38 D2** 17 27N 99 7 E
Mae Ramat, *Thailand* **38 D2** 16 58N 98 31 E
Mae Rim, *Thailand* **38 C2** 18 54N 98 57 E
Mae Sot, *Thailand* **38 D2** 16 43N 98 34 E
Mae Suai, *Thailand* **38 C2** 19 39N 99 33 E
Mae Tha, *Thailand* **38 C2** 18 28N 99 8 E
Maebashi, *Japan* **31 F9** 36 24N 139 4 E
Maesteg, *U.K.* **11 F4** 51 36N 3 40W
Maestra, Sierra, *Cuba* **88 B4** 20 15N 77 0W
Maevatanana, *Madag.* **57 B8** 16 56S 46 49 E
Mafeking = Mafikeng, *S. Africa* **56 D4** 25 50S 25 38 E
Mafeking, *Canada* **73 C8** 52 40N 101 10W
Mafeteng, *Lesotho* **56 D4** 29 51S 27 15 E
Maffra, *Australia* **63 F4** 37 53S 146 58 E
Mafia I., *Tanzania* **54 D4** 7 45S 39 50 E
Mafikeng, *S. Africa* **56 D4** 25 50S 25 38 E
Mafra, *Brazil* **95 B6** 26 10S 49 55W
Mafra, *Portugal* **19 C1** 38 55N 9 20W
Mafungabusi Plateau, *Zimbabwe* **55 F2** 18 30S 29 8 E
Magadan, *Russia* **27 D16** 59 38N 150 50 E
Magadi, *Kenya* **54 C4** 1 54S 36 19 E
Magadi, L., *Kenya* **54 C4** 1 54S 36 19 E
Magaliesburg, *S. Africa* **57 D4** 26 0S 27 32 E
Magallanes, Estrecho de, *Chile* **96 G2** 52 30S 75 0W
Magangué, *Colombia* **92 B4** 9 14N 74 45W
Magdalen Is. = Madeleine, Îs. de la, *Canada* **71 C7** 47 30N 61 40W
Magdalena, *Argentina* **94 D4** 35 5S 57 30W
Magdalena, *Bolivia* **92 F6** 13 13S 63 57W
Magdalena, *Mexico* **86 A2** 30 50N 112 0W
Magdalena, *U.S.A.* **83 J10** 34 7N 107 15W
Magdalena →, *Colombia* **92 A4** 11 6N 74 51W
Magdalena →, *Mexico* **86 A2** 30 40N 112 25W
Magdalena, B., *Mexico* **86 C2** 24 30N 112 10W
Magdalena, Llano de la, *Mexico* **86 C2** 25 0N 111 30W
Magdeburg, *Germany* **16 B6** 52 7N 11 38 E
Magdelaine Cays, *Australia* **62 B5** 16 33S 150 18 E
Magee, *U.S.A.* **81 K10** 31 52N 89 44W
Magelang, *Indonesia* **37 G14** 7 29S 110 13 E
Magellan's Str. = Magallanes, Estrecho de, *Chile* **96 G2** 52 30S 75 0W
Magenta, L., *Australia* **61 F2** 33 30S 119 2 E
Magerøya, *Norway* **8 A21** 71 3N 25 40 E
Maggiore, Lago, *Italy* **18 D8** 45 57N 8 39 E
Maghâgha, *Egypt* **51 C12** 28 38N 30 50 E
Magherafelt, *U.K.* **13 B5** 54 45N 6 37W
Maghreb, *N. Afr.* **50 B5** 32 0N 4 0W
Magistralnyy, *Russia* **27 D11** 56 16N 107 36 E
Magnetic Pole (North) = North Magnetic Pole, *Canada* **4 B2** 77 58N 102 8W
Magnetic Pole (South) = South Magnetic Pole, *Antarctica* **5 C9** 64 8S 138 8 E
Magnitogorsk, *Russia* **24 D10** 53 27N 59 4 E
Magnolia, *Ark., U.S.A.* **81 J8** 33 16N 93 14W
Magnolia, *Miss., U.S.A.* **81 K9** 31 9N 90 28W
Magog, *Canada* **79 A12** 45 18N 72 9W
Magoro, *Uganda* **54 B3** 1 45N 34 12 E
Magosa = Famagusta, *Cyprus* **23 D12** 35 8N 33 55 E
Magouládhes, *Greece* **23 A3** 39 45N 19 42 E
Magoye, *Zambia* **55 F2** 16 1S 27 30 E
Magozal, *Mexico* **87 C5** 21 34N 97 59W
Magpie, L., *Canada* **71 B7** 51 0N 64 41W
Magrath, *Canada* **72 D6** 49 25N 112 50W
Maguarinho, C., *Brazil* **93 D9** 0 15S 48 30W
Mağusa = Famagusta, *Cyprus* **23 D12** 35 8N 33 55 E
Maguse L., *Canada* **73 A9** 61 40N 95 10W
Maguse Pt., *Canada* **73 A10** 61 20N 93 50W
Magvana, *India* **42 H3** 23 13N 69 22 E
Magwe, *Burma* **41 J19** 20 10N 95 0 E
Maha Sarakham, *Thailand* **38 D4** 16 12N 103 16 E
Mahābād, *Iran* **44 B5** 36 50N 45 45 E
Mahabharat Lekh, *Nepal* **43 E10** 28 30N 82 0 E
Mahabo, *Madag.* **57 C7** 20 23S 44 40 E
Mahadeo Hills, *India* **43 H8** 22 20N 78 30 E
Mahaffey, *U.S.A.* **78 F6** 40 53N 78 44W
Mahagi, *Dem. Rep. of the Congo* **54 B3** 2 20N 31 0 E
Mahajamba →, *Madag.* **57 B8** 15 33S 47 8 E
Mahajamba, Helodranon' i, *Madag.* **57 B8** 15 24S 47 5 E
Mahajan, *India* **42 E5** 28 48N 73 56 E
Mahajanga, *Madag.* **57 B8** 15 40S 46 25 E
Mahajanga □, *Madag.* **57 B8** 17 0S 47 0 E
Mahajilo →, *Madag.* **57 B8** 19 42S 45 22 E
Mahakam →, *Indonesia* **36 E5** 0 35S 117 17 E
Mahalapye, *Botswana* **56 C4** 23 1S 26 51 E
Maḩallāt, *Iran* **45 C6** 33 55N 50 30 E
Māhān, *Iran* **45 D8** 30 5N 57 18 E
Mahan →, *India* **43 H10** 23 30N 82 50 E
Mahanadi →, *India* **41 J15** 20 20N 86 25 E
Mahananda →, *India* **43 G12** 25 12N 87 52 E
Mahanoro, *Madag.* **57 B8** 19 54S 48 48 E
Mahanoy City, *U.S.A.* **79 F8** 40 49N 76 9W
Maharashtra □, *India* **40 J9** 20 30N 75 30 E
Mahari Mts., *Tanzania* **54 D3** 6 20S 30 0 E
Mahasham, W. →, *Egypt* **47 E3** 30 15N 34 10 E
Mahasolo, *Madag.* **57 B8** 19 7S 46 22 E
Mahattat ash Shīdīyah, *Jordan* **47 F4** 29 55N 35 55 E
Mahattat 'Unayzah, *Jordan* **47 E4** 30 30N 35 47 E
Mahaxay, *Laos* **38 D5** 17 22N 105 12 E
Mahbubnagar, *India* **40 L10** 16 45N 77 59 E
Maḩḑah, *Oman* **45 E7** 24 24N 55 59 E
Mahdia, *Tunisia* **51 A8** 35 28N 11 0 E
Mahe, *India* **43 C8** 33 10N 78 32 E
Mahendragarh, *India* **42 E7** 28 17N 76 14 E
Mahenge, *Tanzania* **55 D4** 8 45S 36 41 E
Maheno, *N.Z.* **59 L3** 45 10S 170 50 E
Mahesana, *India* **42 H5** 23 39N 72 26 E
Maheshwar, *India* **42 H6** 22 11N 75 35 E
Mahgawan, *India* **43 F8** 26 29N 78 37 E
Mahi →, *India* **42 H5** 22 15N 72 55 E
Mahia Pen., *N.Z.* **59 H6** 39 9S 177 55 E
Mahilyow, *Belarus* **17 B16** 53 55N 30 18 E
Mahmud Kot, *Pakistan* **42 D4** 30 16N 71 0 E
Mahnomen, *U.S.A.* **80 B7** 47 19N 95 58W
Mahoba, *India* **43 G8** 25 15N 79 55 E
Mahón = Maó, *Spain* **22 B11** 39 53N 4 16 E
Mahone Bay, *Canada* **71 D7** 44 30N 64 20W
Mahopac, *U.S.A.* **79 E11** 41 22N 73 45W
Mahuva, *India* **42 J4** 21 5N 71 48 E
Mai-Ndombe, L., *Dem. Rep. of the Congo* **52 E3** 2 0S 18 20 E
Mai-Sai, *Thailand* **38 B2** 20 20N 99 55 E
Maicurú →, *Brazil* **93 D8** 2 14S 54 17W
Maidan Khula, *Afghan.* **42 C3** 33 36N 69 50 E
Maidenhead, *U.K.* **11 F7** 51 31N 0 42W
Maidstone, *Canada* **73 C7** 53 5N 109 20W
Maidstone, *U.K.* **11 F8** 51 16N 0 32 E
Maiduguri, *Nigeria* **51 F8** 12 0N 13 20 E
Maihar, *India* **43 G9** 24 16N 80 45 E
Maijdi, *Bangla.* **41 H17** 22 48N 91 10 E
Maikala Ra., *India* **41 J12** 22 0N 81 0 E
Mailani, *India* **43 E9** 28 17N 80 21 E
Mailsi, *Pakistan* **42 E5** 29 48N 72 15 E
Main →, *Germany* **16 C5** 50 0N 8 18 E
Main →, *U.K.* **13 B5** 54 48N 6 18W
Maine, *France* **18 C3** 48 20N 0 15W
Maine □, *U.S.A.* **77 C11** 45 20N 69 0W
Maine →, *Ireland* **13 D2** 52 9N 9 45W
Maingkwan, *Burma* **41 F20** 26 15N 96 37 E
Mainit, L., *Phil.* **37 C7** 9 31N 125 30 E
Mainland, *Orkney, U.K.* **12 C5** 58 59N 3 8W
Mainland, *Shet., U.K.* **12 A7** 60 15N 1 22W
Mainoru, *Australia* **62 A1** 14 0S 134 6 E
Mainpuri, *India* **43 F8** 27 18N 79 4 E
Maintirano, *Madag.* **57 B7** 18 3S 44 1 E
Mainz, *Germany* **16 C5** 50 1N 8 14 E
Maipú, *Argentina* **94 D4** 36 52S 57 50W
Maiquetía, *Venezuela* **92 A5** 10 36N 66 57W
Mairabari, *India* **41 F18** 26 30N 92 22 E
Maisí, *Cuba* **89 B5** 20 17N 74 9W
Maisí, Pta. de, *Cuba* **89 B5** 20 10N 74 10W
Maitland, *N.S.W., Australia* **63 E5** 32 33S 151 36 E
Maitland, *S. Austral., Australia* **63 E2** 34 23S 137 40 E
Maitland →, *Canada* **78 C3** 43 45N 81 43W
Maiz, Is. del, *Nic.* **88 D3** 12 15N 83 4W
Maizuru, *Japan* **31 G7** 35 25N 135 22 E
Majalengka, *Indonesia* **37 G13** 6 50S 108 13 E
Majene, *Indonesia* **37 E5** 3 38S 118 57 E
Majorca = Mallorca, *Spain* **22 B10** 39 30N 3 0 E
Makale, *Indonesia* **37 E5** 3 6S 119 51 E
Makamba, *Burundi* **54 C2** 4 8S 29 49 E
Makarikari = Makgadikgadi Salt Pans, *Botswana* **56 C4** 20 40S 25 45 E
Makarovo, *Russia* **27 D11** 57 40N 107 45 E
Makasar = Ujung Pandang, *Indonesia* **37 F5** 5 10S 119 20 E
Makasar, Selat, *Indonesia* **37 E5** 1 0S 118 20 E
Makasar, Str. of = Makasar, Selat, *Indonesia* **37 E5** 1 0S 118 20 E
Makat, *Kazakstan* **25 E9** 47 39N 53 19 E
Makedhonía □, *Greece* **21 D10** 40 39N 22 0 E
Makedonija = Macedonia ■, *Europe* **21 D9** 41 53N 21 40 E
Makena, *U.S.A.* **74 H16** 20 39N 156 27W
Makeyevka = Makiyivka, *Ukraine* **25 E6** 48 0N 38 0 E
Makgadikgadi Salt Pans, *Botswana* **56 C4** 20 40S 25 45 E
Makhachkala, *Russia* **25 F8** 43 0N 47 30 E
Makhmūr, *Iraq* **44 C4** 35 46N 43 35 E
Makian, *Indonesia* **37 D7** 0 20N 127 20 E
Makindu, *Kenya* **54 C4** 2 18S 37 50 E
Makinsk, *Kazakstan* **26 D8** 52 37N 70 26 E
Makiyivka, *Ukraine* **25 E6** 48 0N 38 0 E
Makkah, *Si. Arabia* **46 C2** 21 30N 39 54 E
Makkovik, *Canada* **71 A8** 55 10N 59 10W
Makó, *Hungary* **17 E11** 46 14N 20 33 E
Makokou, *Gabon* **52 D2** 0 40N 12 50 E
Makongo, *Dem. Rep. of the Congo* **54 B2** 3 25N 26 17 E
Makoro, *Dem. Rep. of the Congo* **54 B2** 3 10N 29 59 E
Makrai, *India* **40 H10** 22 2N 77 0 E
Makran Coast Range, *Pakistan* **40 G4** 25 40N 64 0 E
Makrana, *India* **42 F6** 27 2N 74 46 E
Makríyialos, *Greece* **23 D7** 35 2N 25 59 E
Mākū, *Iran* **44 B5** 39 15N 44 31 E
Makunda, *Botswana* **56 C3** 22 30S 20 7 E
Makurazaki, *Japan* **31 J5** 31 15N 130 20 E
Makurdi, *Nigeria* **50 G7** 7 43N 8 35 E
Makūyeh, *Iran* **45 D7** 28 7N 53 9 E
Makwassie, *S. Africa* **56 D4** 27 17S 26 0 E
Mal B., *Ireland* **13 D2** 52 50N 9 30W
Mala, Pta., *Panama* **88 E3** 7 28N 80 2W
Malabar Coast, *India* **40 P9** 11 0N 75 0 E
Malabo = Rey Malabo, *Eq. Guin.* **52 D1** 3 45N 8 50 E
Malacca, Str. of, *Indonesia* **39 L3** 3 0N 101 0 E
Malad City, *U.S.A.* **82 E7** 42 12N 112 15W
Maladzyechna, *Belarus* **17 A14** 54 20N 26 50 E
Málaga, *Spain* **19 D3** 36 43N 4 23W
Malagarasi, *Tanzania* **54 D3** 5 5S 30 50 E
Malagarasi →, *Tanzania* **54 D2** 5 12S 29 47 E
Malagasy Rep. = Madagascar ■, *Africa* **57 C8** 20 0S 47 0 E
Malahide, *Ireland* **13 C5** 53 26N 6 9W
Malaimbandy, *Madag.* **57 C8** 20 20S 45 36 E
Malakâl, *Sudan* **51 G12** 9 33N 31 40 E
Malakand, *Pakistan* **42 B4** 34 40N 71 55 E
Malakwal, *Pakistan* **42 C5** 32 34N 73 13 E
Malamala, *Indonesia* **37 E6** 3 21S 120 55 E
Malanda, *Australia* **62 B4** 17 22S 145 35 E
Malang, *Indonesia* **37 G15** 7 59S 112 45 E
Malangen, *Norway* **8 B18** 69 24N 18 37 E
Malanje, *Angola* **52 F3** 9 36S 16 17 E
Mälaren, *Sweden* **9 G17** 59 30N 17 10 E
Malargüe, *Argentina* **94 D2** 35 32S 69 30W
Malartic, *Canada* **70 C4** 48 9N 78 9W
Malaryta, *Belarus* **17 C13** 51 50N 24 3 E
Malatya, *Turkey* **25 G6** 38 25N 38 20 E
Malawi ■, *Africa* **55 E3** 11 55S 34 0 E
Malawi, L. = Nyasa, L., *Africa* **55 E3** 12 30S 34 30 E
Malay Pen., *Asia* **39 J3** 7 25N 100 0 E
Malaya Vishera, *Russia* **24 C5** 58 55N 32 25 E
Malaybalay, *Phil.* **37 C7** 8 5N 125 7 E
Malāyer, *Iran* **45 C6** 34 19N 48 51 E
Malaysia ■, *Asia* **39 K4** 5 0N 110 0 E
Malazgirt, *Turkey* **25 G7** 39 10N 42 33 E
Malbon, *Australia* **62 C3** 21 5S 140 17 E
Malbooma, *Australia* **63 E1** 30 41S 134 11 E
Malbork, *Poland* **17 B10** 54 3N 19 1 E
Malcolm, *Australia* **61 E3** 28 51S 121 25 E
Malcolm, Pt., *Australia* **61 F3** 33 48S 123 45 E
Maldah, *India* **43 G13** 25 2N 88 9 E
Maldegem, *Belgium* **15 C3** 51 14N 3 26 E
Malden, *Mass., U.S.A.* **79 D13** 42 26N 71 4W
Malden, *Mo., U.S.A.* **81 G10** 36 34N 89 57W
Malden I., *Kiribati* **65 H12** 4 3S 155 1W
Maldives ■, *Ind. Oc.* **29 J11** 5 0N 73 0 E
Maldonado, *Uruguay* **95 C5** 34 59S 55 0W
Maldonado, Punta, *Mexico* **87 D5** 16 19N 98 35W
Malé, *Maldives* **29 J11** 4 0N 73 28 E
Malé Karpaty, *Slovak Rep.* **17 D9** 48 30N 17 20 E
Maléa, Ákra, *Greece* **21 F10** 36 28N 23 7 E
Malegaon, *India* **40 J9** 20 30N 74 38 E
Malei, *Mozam.* **55 F4** 17 12S 36 58 E
Malek Kandī, *Iran* **44 B5** 37 9N 46 6 E
Malela, *Dem. Rep. of the Congo* **54 C2** 4 22S 26 8 E
Malema, *Mozam.* **55 E4** 14 57S 37 20 E
Máleme, *Greece* **23 D5** 35 31N 23 49 E
Maleny, *Australia* **63 D5** 26 45S 152 52 E
Malerkotla, *India* **42 D6** 30 32N 75 58 E
Máles, *Greece* **23 D7** 35 6N 25 35 E
Malgomaj, *Sweden* **8 D17** 64 40N 16 30 E
Malha, *Sudan* **51 E11** 15 8N 25 10 E
Malhargarh, *India* **42 G6** 24 17N 74 59 E
Malheur →, *U.S.A.* **82 D5** 44 4N 116 59W
Malheur L., *U.S.A.* **82 E4** 43 20N 118 48W
Mali ■, *Africa* **50 E5** 17 0N 3 0W
Mali →, *Burma* **41 G20** 25 40N 97 40 E
Mali Kyun, *Burma* **38 F2** 13 0N 98 20 E
Malibu, *U.S.A.* **85 L8** 34 2N 118 41W
Maliku, *Indonesia* **37 E6** 0 39S 123 16 E
Malili, *Indonesia* **37 E6** 2 42S 121 6 E
Malimba, Mts., *Dem. Rep. of the Congo* **54 D2** 7 30S 29 30 E
Malin Hd., *Ireland* **13 A4** 55 23N 7 23W
Malin Pen., *Ireland* **13 A4** 55 20N 7 17W
Malindi, *Kenya* **54 C5** 3 12S 40 5 E
Malines = Mechelen, *Belgium* **15 C4** 51 2N 4 29 E
Malino, *Indonesia* **37 D6** 1 0N 121 0 E
Malinyi, *Tanzania* **55 D4** 8 56S 36 0 E
Malita, *Phil.* **37 C7** 6 19N 125 39 E
Maliwun, *Burma* **36 B1** 10 17N 98 40 E
Maliya, *India* **42 H4** 23 5N 70 46 E
Malkara, *Turkey* **21 D12** 40 53N 26 53 E
Mallacoota Inlet, *Australia* **63 F4** 37 34S 149 40 E
Mallaig, *U.K.* **12 D3** 57 0N 5 50W

Mallawan, *India* **43 F9** 27 4N 80 12 E
Mallawi, *Egypt* **51 C12** 27 44N 30 44 E
Mállia, *Greece* **23 D7** 35 17N 25 32 E
Mallión, Kólpos, *Greece* **23 D7** 35 19N 25 27 E
Mallorca, *Spain* **22 B10** 39 30N 3 0 E
Mallorytown, *Canada* **79 B9** 44 29N 75 53W
Mallow, *Ireland* **13 D3** 52 8N 8 39W
Malmberget, *Sweden* **8 C19** 67 11N 20 40 E
Malmédy, *Belgium* **15 D6** 50 25N 6 2 E
Malmesbury, *S. Africa* **56 E2** 33 28S 18 41 E
Malmö, *Sweden* **9 J15** 55 36N 12 59 E
Malolos, *Phil.* **37 B6** 14 50N 120 49 E
Malombe L., *Malawi* **55 E4** 14 40S 35 15 E
Malone, *U.S.A.* **79 B10** 44 51N 74 18W
Måløy, *Norway* **9 F11** 61 57N 5 6 E
Malpaso, *Canary Is.* **22 G1** 27 43N 18 3W
Malpelo, I. de, *Colombia* **92 C2** 4 3N 81 35W
Malpur, *India* **42 H5** 23 21N 73 27 E
Malpura, *India* **42 F6** 26 17N 75 23 E
Malta, *Idaho, U.S.A.* **82 E7** 42 18N 113 22W
Malta, *Mont., U.S.A.* **82 B10** 48 21N 107 52W
Malta ■, *Europe* **23 D2** 35 50N 14 30 E
Maltahöhe, *Namibia* **56 C2** 24 55S 17 0 E
Malton, *Canada* **78 C5** 43 42N 79 38W
Malton, *U.K.* **10 C7** 54 8N 0 49W
Maluku, *Indonesia* **37 E7** 1 0S 127 0 E
Maluku □, *Indonesia* **37 E7** 3 0S 128 0 E
Maluku Sea = Molucca Sea, *Indonesia* **37 E6** 2 0S 124 0 E
Malvan, *India* **40 L8** 16 2N 73 30 E
Malvern, *U.S.A.* **81 H8** 34 22N 92 49W
Malvern Hills, *U.K.* **11 E5** 52 0N 2 19W
Malvinas, Is. = Falkland Is. □, *Atl. Oc.* **96 G5** 51 30S 59 0W
Malya, *Tanzania* **54 C3** 3 5S 33 38 E
Malyn, *Ukraine* **17 C15** 50 46N 29 3 E
Malyy Lyakhovskiy, Ostrov, *Russia* **27 B15** 74 7N 140 36 E
Mama, *Russia* **27 D12** 58 18N 112 54 E
Mamanguape, *Brazil* **93 E11** 6 50S 35 4W
Mamarr Mitlā, *Egypt* **47 E1** 30 2N 32 54 E
Mamasa, *Indonesia* **37 E5** 2 55S 119 20 E
Mambasa, *Dem. Rep. of the Congo* **54 B2** 1 22N 29 3 E
Mamberamo →, *Indonesia* **37 E9** 2 0S 137 50 E
Mambilima Falls, *Zambia* **55 E2** 10 31S 28 45 E
Mambirima, *Dem. Rep. of the Congo* **55 E2** 11 25S 27 33 E
Mambo, *Tanzania* **54 C4** 4 52S 38 22 E
Mambrui, *Kenya* **54 C5** 3 5S 40 5 E
Mamburao, *Phil.* **37 B6** 13 13N 120 39 E
Mameigwess L., *Canada* **70 B2** 52 35N 87 50W
Mammoth, *U.S.A.* **83 K8** 32 43N 110 39W
Mammoth Cave National Park, *U.S.A.* **76 G3** 37 8N 86 13W
Mamoré →, *Bolivia* **92 F5** 10 23S 65 53W
Mamou, *Guinea* **50 F3** 10 15N 12 0W
Mamuju, *Indonesia* **37 E5** 2 41S 118 50 E
Man, *Ivory C.* **50 G4** 7 30N 7 40W
Man, I. of, *U.K.* **10 C3** 54 15N 4 30W
Man-Bazar, *India* **43 H12** 23 4N 86 39 E
Man Na, *Burma* **41 H20** 23 27N 97 19 E
Mana →, *Fr. Guiana* **93 B8** 5 45N 53 55W
Manaar, G. of = Mannar, G. of, *Asia* **40 Q11** 8 30N 79 0 E
Manacapuru, *Brazil* **92 D6** 3 16S 60 37W
Manacor, *Spain* **22 B10** 39 34N 3 13 E
Manado, *Indonesia* **37 D6** 1 29N 124 51 E
Managua, *Nic.* **88 D2** 12 6N 86 20W
Managua, L. de, *Nic.* **88 D2** 12 20N 86 30W
Manakara, *Madag.* **57 C8** 22 8S 48 1 E
Manali, *India* **42 C7** 32 16N 77 10 E
Manama = Al Manāmah, *Bahrain* **45 E6** 26 10N 50 30 E
Manambao →, *Madag.* **57 B7** 17 35S 44 0 E
Manambato, *Madag.* **57 A8** 13 43S 49 7 E
Manambolo →, *Madag.* **57 B7** 19 18S 44 22 E
Manambolosy, *Madag.* **57 B8** 16 2S 49 40 E
Mananara, *Madag.* **57 B8** 16 10S 49 46 E
Mananara →, *Madag.* **57 C8** 23 21S 47 42 E
Mananjary, *Madag.* **57 C8** 21 13S 48 20 E
Manantenina, *Madag.* **57 C8** 24 17S 47 19 E
Manaos = Manaus, *Brazil* **92 D7** 3 0S 60 0W
Manapire →, *Venezuela* **92 B5** 7 42N 66 7W
Manapouri, *N.Z.* **59 L1** 45 34S 167 39 E
Manapouri, L., *N.Z.* **59 L1** 45 32S 167 32 E
Manār, Jabal, *Yemen* **46 E3** 14 2N 44 17 E
Manas, *China* **32 B3** 44 17N 85 56 E
Manas →, *India* **41 F17** 26 12N 90 40 E
Manaslu, *Nepal* **43 E11** 28 33N 84 33 E
Manasquan, *U.S.A.* **79 F10** 40 8N 74 3W
Manassa, *U.S.A.* **83 H11** 37 11N 105 56W
Manaung, *Burma* **41 K18** 18 45N 93 40 E
Manaus, *Brazil* **92 D7** 3 0S 60 0W
Manawan L., *Canada* **73 B8** 55 24N 103 14W
Manbij, *Syria* **44 B3** 36 31N 37 57 E
Manchegorsk, *Russia* **26 C4** 67 54N 32 58 E
Manchester, *U.K.* **10 D5** 53 29N 2 12W
Manchester, *Calif., U.S.A.* **84 G3** 38 58N 123 41W
Manchester, *Conn., U.S.A.* **79 E12** 41 47N 72 31W
Manchester, *Ga., U.S.A.* **77 J3** 32 51N 84 37W
Manchester, *Iowa, U.S.A.* **80 D9** 42 29N 91 27W
Manchester, *Ky., U.S.A.* **76 G4** 37 9N 83 46W
Manchester, *N.H., U.S.A.* **79 D13** 42 59N 71 28W
Manchester, *N.Y., U.S.A.* **78 D7** 42 56N 77 16W
Manchester, *Pa., U.S.A.* **79 F8** 40 4N 76 43W
Manchester, *Tenn., U.S.A.* **77 H2** 35 29N 86 5W
Manchester, *Vt., U.S.A.* **79 C11** 43 10N 73 5W
Manchester L., *Canada* **73 A7** 61 28N 107 29W
Manchhar L., *Pakistan* **42 F2** 26 25N 67 39 E
Manchuria = Dongbei, *China* **35 D13** 45 0N 125 0 E
Manchurian Plain, *China* **28 E16** 47 0N 124 0 E
Mand →, *India* **43 J10** 21 42N 83 15 E
Mand →, *Iran* **45 D7** 28 20N 52 30 E
Manda, *Chunya, Tanzania* **54 D3** 6 51S 32 29 E
Manda, *Ludewe, Tanzania* **55 E3** 10 30S 34 40 E
Mandabé, *Madag.* **57 C7** 21 0S 44 55 E
Mandaguari, *Brazil* **95 A5** 23 32S 51 42W
Mandah = Töhöm, *Mongolia* **34 B5** 44 27N 108 2 E
Mandal, *Norway* **9 G12** 58 2N 7 25 E
Mandala, Puncak, *Indonesia* **37 E10** 4 44S 140 20 E
Mandalay, *Burma* **41 J20** 22 0N 96 4 E
Mandale = Mandalay, *Burma* **41 J20** 22 0N 96 4 E
Mandalgarh, *India* **42 G6** 25 12N 75 6 E
Mandalgovi, *Mongolia* **34 B4** 45 45N 106 10 E
Mandalī, *Iraq* **44 C5** 33 43N 45 28 E
Mandan, *U.S.A.* **80 B4** 46 50N 100 54W
Mandar, Teluk, *Indonesia* **37 E5** 3 35S 119 15 E
Mandaue, *Phil.* **37 B6** 10 20N 123 56 E
Mandera, *Kenya* **54 B5** 3 55N 41 53 E
Mandi, *India* **42 D7** 31 39N 76 58 E
Mandi Dabwali, *India* **42 E6** 29 58N 74 42 E
Mandimba, *Mozam.* **55 E4** 14 20S 35 40 E
Mandioli, *Indonesia* **37 E7** 0 40S 127 20 E
Mandla, *India* **43 H9** 22 39N 80 30 E
Mandorah, *Australia* **60 B5** 12 32S 130 42 E
Mandoto, *Madag.* **57 B8** 19 34S 46 17 E
Mandra, *Pakistan* **42 C5** 33 23N 73 12 E
Mandrare →, *Madag.* **57 D8** 25 10S 46 30 E
Mandritsara, *Madag.* **57 B8** 15 50S 48 49 E
Mandsaur, *India* **42 G6** 24 3N 75 8 E
Mandurah, *Australia* **61 F2** 32 36S 115 48 E
Mandvi, *India* **42 H3** 22 51N 69 22 E
Mandya, *India* **40 N10** 12 30N 77 0 E
Mandzai, *Pakistan* **42 D2** 30 55N 67 6 E
Maneh, *Iran* **45 B8** 37 39N 57 7 E
Maneroo Cr. →, *Australia* **62 C3** 23 21S 143 53 E
Manfalût, *Egypt* **51 C12** 27 20N 30 52 E
Manfredónia, *Italy* **20 D6** 41 38N 15 55 E
Mangabeiras, Chapada das, *Brazil* **93 F9** 10 0S 46 30W
Mangalia, *Romania* **17 G15** 43 50N 28 35 E
Mangalore, *India* **40 N9** 12 55N 74 47 E
Mangan, *India* **43 F13** 27 31N 88 32 E
Mangaung, *S. Africa* **53 K5** 29 10S 26 25 E
Mangawan, *India* **43 G9** 24 41N 81 33 E
Mangaweka, *N.Z.* **59 H5** 39 48S 175 47 E
Manggar, *Indonesia* **36 E3** 2 50S 108 10 E
Manggawitu, *Indonesia* **37 E8** 4 8S 133 32 E
Mangkalihat, Tanjung, *Indonesia* **37 D5** 1 2N 118 59 E
Mangla, *Pakistan* **42 C5** 33 7N 73 39 E
Mangla Dam, *Pakistan* **43 C5** 33 9N 73 44 E
Manglaur, *India* **42 E7** 29 44N 77 49 E
Mangnai, *China* **32 C4** 37 52N 91 43 E
Mango, *Togo* **50 F6** 10 20N 0 30 E
Mangoche, *Malawi* **55 E4** 14 25S 35 16 E
Mangoky →, *Madag.* **57 C7** 21 29S 43 41 E
Mangole, *Indonesia* **37 E6** 1 50S 125 55 E
Mangombe, *Dem. Rep. of the Congo* **54 C2** 1 20S 26 48 E
Mangonui, *N.Z.* **59 F4** 35 1S 173 32 E
Mangrol, *Mad. P., India* **42 J4** 21 7N 70 7 E
Mangrol, *Raj., India* **42 G6** 25 20N 76 31 E
Mangueira, L. da, *Brazil* **95 C5** 33 0S 52 50W
Mangum, *U.S.A.* **81 H5** 34 53N 99 30W
Mangyshlak Poluostrov, *Kazakstan* **26 E6** 44 30N 52 30 E
Manhattan, *U.S.A.* **80 F6** 39 11N 96 35W
Manhiça, *Mozam.* **57 D5** 25 23S 32 49 E
Mania →, *Madag.* **57 B8** 19 42S 45 22 E
Manica, *Mozam.* **57 B5** 18 58S 32 59 E
Manica e Sofala □, *Mozam.* **57 B5** 19 10S 33 45 E
Manicaland □, *Zimbabwe* **55 F3** 19 0S 32 30 E
Manicoré, *Brazil* **92 E6** 5 48S 61 16W
Manicouagan →, *Canada* **71 C6** 49 30N 68 30W
Manicouagan, Rés., *Canada* **71 B6** 51 5N 68 40W
Maniema □, *Dem. Rep. of the Congo* **54 C2** 3 0S 26 0 E
Manīfah, *Si. Arabia* **45 E6** 27 44N 49 0 E
Manifold, C., *Australia* **62 C5** 22 41S 150 50 E
Manigotagan, *Canada* **73 C9** 51 6N 96 18W
Manigotagan →, *Canada* **73 C9** 51 7N 96 20W
Manihari, *India* **43 G12** 25 21N 87 38 E
Manihiki, *Cook Is.* **65 J11** 10 24S 161 1W
Manika, Plateau de la, *Dem. Rep. of the Congo* **55 E2** 10 0S 25 5 E
Manikpur, *India* **43 G9** 25 4N 81 7 E
Manila, *Phil.* **37 B6** 14 40N 121 3 E
Manila, *U.S.A.* **82 F9** 40 59N 109 43W
Manila B., *Phil.* **37 B6** 14 40N 120 35 E
Manilla, *Australia* **63 E5** 30 45S 150 43 E
Maningrida, *Australia* **62 A1** 12 3S 134 13 E
Manipur □, *India* **41 G19** 25 0N 94 0 E
Manipur →, *Burma* **41 H19** 23 45N 94 20 E
Manisa, *Turkey* **21 E12** 38 38N 27 30 E
Manistee, *U.S.A.* **76 C2** 44 15N 86 19W
Manistee →, *U.S.A.* **76 C2** 44 15N 86 21W
Manistique, *U.S.A.* **76 C2** 45 57N 86 15W
Manito L., *Canada* **73 C7** 52 43N 109 43W
Manitoba □, *Canada* **73 B9** 55 30N 97 0W
Manitoba, L., *Canada* **73 C9** 51 0N 98 45W
Manitou, *Canada* **73 D9** 49 15N 98 32W
Manitou, L., *Canada* **71 B6** 50 55N 65 17W
Manitou Is., *U.S.A.* **76 C3** 45 8N 86 0W
Manitou Springs, *U.S.A.* **80 F2** 38 52N 104 55W
Manitoulin I., *Canada* **70 C3** 45 40N 82 30W
Manitouwadge, *Canada* **70 C2** 49 8N 85 48W
Manitowoc, *U.S.A.* **76 C2** 44 5N 87 40W
Manizales, *Colombia* **92 B3** 5 5N 75 32W
Manja, *Madag.* **57 C7** 21 26S 44 20 E
Manjacaze, *Mozam.* **57 C5** 24 45S 34 0 E
Manjakandriana, *Madag.* **57 B8** 18 55S 47 47 E
Manjhand, *Pakistan* **42 G3** 25 50N 68 10 E
Manjil, *Iran* **45 B6** 36 46N 49 30 E
Manjimup, *Australia* **61 F2** 34 15S 116 6 E
Manjra →, *India* **40 K10** 18 49N 77 52 E
Mankato, *Kans., U.S.A.* **80 F5** 39 47N 98 13W
Mankato, *Minn., U.S.A.* **80 C8** 44 10N 94 0W
Mankayane, *Swaziland* **57 D5** 26 40S 31 4 E
Mankera, *Pakistan* **42 D4** 31 23N 71 26 E
Mankota, *Canada* **73 D7** 49 25N 107 5W
Manlay = Üydzin, *Mongolia* **34 B4** 44 9N 107 0 E
Manmad, *India* **40 J9** 20 18N 74 28 E
Mann Ranges, *Australia* **61 E5** 26 6S 130 5 E
Manna, *Indonesia* **36 E2** 4 25S 102 55 E
Mannahill, *Australia* **63 E3** 32 25S 140 0 E
Mannar, *Sri Lanka* **40 Q11** 9 1N 79 54 E
Mannar, G. of, *Asia* **40 Q11** 8 30N 79 0 E
Mannar I., *Sri Lanka* **40 Q11** 9 5N 79 45 E
Mannheim, *Germany* **16 D5** 49 29N 8 29 E
Manning, *Canada* **72 B5** 56 53N 117 39W
Manning, *Oreg., U.S.A.* **84 E3** 45 45N 123 13W
Manning, *S.C., U.S.A.* **77 J5** 33 42N 80 13W
Manning Prov. Park, *Canada* **72 D4** 49 5N 120 45W
Mannum, *Australia* **63 E2** 34 50S 139 20 E
Manoharpur, *India* **43 H11** 22 23N 85 12 E
Manokwari, *Indonesia* **37 E8** 0 54S 134 0 E
Manombo, *Madag.* **57 C7** 22 57S 43 28 E
Manono, *Dem. Rep. of the Congo* **54 D2** 7 15S 27 25 E
Manosque, *France* **18 E6** 43 49N 5 47 E
Manotick, *Canada* **79 A9** 45 13N 75 41W
Manouane →, *Canada* **71 C5** 49 30N 71 10W
Manouane, L., *Canada* **71 B5** 50 45N 70 45W
Manp'o, *N. Korea* **35 D14** 41 6N 126 24 E
Manpojin = Manp'o, *N. Korea* **35 D14** 41 6N 126 24 E
Manpur, *Mad. P., India* **42 H6** 22 26N 75 37 E
Manpur, *Mad. P., India* **43 H10** 23 17N 83 35 E
Manresa, *Spain* **19 B6** 41 48N 1 50 E
Mansa, *Gujarat, India* **42 H5** 23 27N 72 45 E
Mansa, *Punjab, India* **42 E6** 30 0N 75 27 E
Mansa, *Zambia* **55 E2** 11 13S 28 55 E
Mansehra, *Pakistan* **42 B5** 34 20N 73 15 E
Mansel I., *Canada* **69 B12** 62 0N 80 0W
Mansfield, *Australia* **63 F4** 37 4S 146 6 E
Mansfield, *U.K.* **10 D6** 53 9N 1 11W
Mansfield, *La., U.S.A.* **81 J8** 32 2N 93 43W
Mansfield, *Mass., U.S.A.* **79 D13** 42 2N 71 13W
Mansfield, *Ohio, U.S.A.* **78 F2** 40 45N 82 31W
Mansfield, *Pa., U.S.A.* **78 E7** 41 48N 77 5W
Mansfield, Mt., *U.S.A.* **79 B12** 44 33N 72 49W
Manson Creek, *Canada* **72 B4** 55 37N 124 32W
Manta, *Ecuador* **92 D2** 1 0S 80 40W
Mantalingajan, Mt., *Phil.* **36 C5** 8 55N 117 45 E
Mantare, *Tanzania* **54 C3** 2 42S 33 13 E
Manteca, *U.S.A.* **84 H5** 37 48N 121 13W
Manteo, *U.S.A.* **77 H8** 35 55N 75 40W
Mantes-la-Jolie, *France* **18 B4** 48 58N 1 41 E
Manthani, *India* **40 K11** 18 40N 79 35 E
Manti, *U.S.A.* **82 G8** 39 16N 111 38W
Mantiqueira, Serra da, *Brazil* **95 A7** 22 0S 44 0W
Manton, *U.S.A.* **76 C3** 44 25N 85 24W
Mántova, *Italy* **20 B4** 45 9N 10 48 E
Mänttä, *Finland* **9 E21** 62 0N 24 40 E
Mantua = Mántova, *Italy* **20 B4** 45 9N 10 48 E
Manu, *Peru* **92 F4** 12 10S 70 51W
Manu →, *Peru* **92 F4** 12 16S 70 55W
Manua Is., *Amer. Samoa* **59 B14** 14 13S 169 35W
Manuel Alves →, *Brazil* **93 F9** 11 19S 48 28W
Manui, *Indonesia* **37 E6** 3 35S 123 5 E
Manuripi →, *Bolivia* **92 F5** 11 6S 67 36W
Many, *U.S.A.* **81 K8** 31 34N 93 29W
Manyara, L., *Tanzania* **54 C4** 3 40S 35 50 E
Manych-Gudilo, Ozero, *Russia* **25 E7** 46 24N 42 38 E
Manyonga →, *Tanzania* **54 C3** 4 10S 34 15 E
Manyoni, *Tanzania* **54 D3** 5 45S 34 55 E
Manzai, *Pakistan* **42 C4** 32 12N 70 15 E
Manzanares, *Spain* **19 C4** 39 2N 3 22W
Manzanillo, *Cuba* **88 B4** 20 20N 77 31W
Manzanillo, *Mexico* **86 D4** 19 0N 104 20W
Manzanillo, Pta., *Panama* **88 E4** 9 30N 79 40W
Manzano Mts., *U.S.A.* **83 J10** 34 40N 106 20W
Manzarīyeh, *Iran* **45 C6** 34 53N 50 50 E
Manzhouli, *China* **33 B6** 49 35N 117 25 E
Manzini, *Swaziland* **57 D5** 26 30S 31 25 E
Mao, *Chad* **51 F9** 14 4N 15 19 E
Maó, *Spain* **22 B11** 39 53N 4 16 E
Maoke, Pegunungan, *Indonesia* **37 E9** 3 40S 137 30 E
Maolin, *China* **35 C12** 43 58N 123 30 E
Maoming, *China* **33 D6** 21 50N 110 54 E
Maoxing, *China* **35 B13** 45 28N 124 40 E
Mapam Yumco, *China* **32 C3** 30 45N 81 28 E
Mapastepec, *Mexico* **87 D6** 15 26N 92 54W
Mapia, Kepulauan, *Indonesia* **37 D8** 0 50N 134 20 E
Mapimí, *Mexico* **86 B4** 25 50N 103 50W
Mapimí, Bolsón de, *Mexico* **86 B4** 27 30N 104 15W
Mapinga, *Tanzania* **54 D4** 6 40S 39 12 E
Mapinhane, *Mozam.* **57 C6** 22 20S 35 0 E
Maple Creek, *Canada* **73 D7** 49 55N 109 29W
Maple Valley, *U.S.A.* **84 C4** 47 25N 122 3W
Mapleton, *U.S.A.* **82 D2** 44 2N 123 52W
Mapuera →, *Brazil* **92 D7** 1 5S 57 2W
Maputo, *Mozam.* **57 D5** 25 58S 32 32 E
Maputo, B. de, *Mozam.* **57 D5** 25 50S 32 45 E
Maqiaohe, *China* **35 B16** 44 40N 130 30 E
Maqnā, *Si. Arabia* **44 D2** 28 25N 34 50 E
Maquela do Zombo, *Angola* **52 F3** 6 0S 15 15 E
Maquinchao, *Argentina* **96 E3** 41 15S 68 50W
Maquoketa, *U.S.A.* **80 D9** 42 4N 90 40W
Mar, Serra do, *Brazil* **95 B6** 25 30S 49 0W
Mar Chiquita, L., *Argentina* **94 C3** 30 40S 62 50W
Mar del Plata, *Argentina* **94 D4** 38 0S 57 30W
Mar Menor, *Spain* **19 D5** 37 40N 0 45W
Mara, *Tanzania* **54 C3** 1 30S 34 32 E
Mara □, *Tanzania* **54 C3** 1 45S 34 20 E
Maraã, *Brazil* **92 D5** 1 52S 65 25W
Marabá, *Brazil* **93 E9** 5 20S 49 5W
Maracá, I. de, *Brazil* **93 C8** 2 10N 50 30W
Maracaibo, *Venezuela* **92 A4** 10 40N 71 37W
Maracaibo, L. de, *Venezuela* **92 B4** 9 40N 71 30W
Maracaju, *Brazil* **95 A4** 21 38S 55 9W
Maracay, *Venezuela* **92 A5** 10 15N 67 28W
Maradi, *Niger* **50 F7** 13 29N 7 20 E
Marāgheh, *Iran* **44 B5** 37 30N 46 12 E
Marāh, *Si. Arabia* **44 E5** 25 0N 45 35 E
Marajó, I. de, *Brazil* **93 D9** 1 0S 49 30W
Marākand, *Iran* **44 B5** 38 51N 45 16 E
Maralal, *Kenya* **54 B4** 1 0N 36 38 E
Maralinga, *Australia* **61 F5** 30 13S 131 32 E
Maran, *Malaysia* **39 L4** 3 35N 102 45 E
Marana, *U.S.A.* **83 K8** 32 27N 111 13W
Maranboy, *Australia* **60 B5** 14 40S 132 39 E
Marand, *Iran* **44 B5** 38 30N 45 45 E
Marang, *Malaysia* **39 K4** 5 12N 103 13 E
Maranguape, *Brazil* **93 D11** 3 55S 38 50W
Maranhão = São Luís, *Brazil* **93 D10** 2 39S 44 15W
Maranhão □, *Brazil* **93 E9** 5 0S 46 0W
Maranoa →, *Australia* **63 D4** 27 50S 148 37 E
Marañón →, *Peru* **92 D4** 4 30S 73 35W
Marão, *Mozam.* **57 C5** 24 18S 34 2 E
Maraş = Kahramanmaraş, *Turkey* **25 G6** 37 37N 36 53 E
Marathasa □, *Cyprus* **23 E11** 34 59N 32 51 E
Marathon, *Australia* **62 C3** 20 51S 143 32 E
Marathon, *Canada* **70 C2** 48 44N 86 23W
Marathon, *N.Y., U.S.A.* **79 D8** 42 26N 76 2W
Marathon, *N.Y., U.S.A.* **79 D8** 42 27N 76 2W
Marathon, *Tex., U.S.A.* **81 K3** 30 12N 103 15W
Marathóvouno, *Cyprus* **23 D12** 35 13N 33 37 E
Maratua, *Indonesia* **37 D5** 2 10N 118 35 E
Maravatío, *Mexico* **86 D4** 19 51N 100 25
Marāwih, *U.A.E.* **45 E7** 24 18N 53 18
Marbella, *Spain* **19 D3** 36 30N 4 57
Marble Bar, *Australia* **60 D2** 21 9S 119 44
Marble Falls, *U.S.A.* **81 K5** 30 35N 98 16
Marblehead, *U.S.A.* **79 D14** 42 30N 70 51
Marburg, *Germany* **16 C5** 50 47N 8 46
March, *U.K.* **11 E8** 52 33N 0 5
Marche, *France* **18 C4** 46 5N 1 20
Marche-en-Famenne, *Belgium* **15 D5** 50 14N 5 19
Marchena, *Spain* **19 D3** 37 18N 5 23
Marco, *U.S.A.* **77 N5** 25 58N 81 44
Marcos Juárez, *Argentina* **94 C3** 32 42S 62 5
Marcus I. = Minami-Tori-Shima, *Pac. Oc.* **64 E7** 24 20N 153 58
Marcus Necker Ridge, *Pac. Oc.* **64 F9** 20 0N 175 0
Marcy, Mt., *U.S.A.* **79 B11** 44 7N 73 56
Mardan, *Pakistan* **42 B5** 34 20N 72 0
Mardin, *Turkey* **25 G7** 37 20N 40 43
Maree, L., *U.K.* **12 D3** 57 40N 5 26
Mareeba, *Australia* **62 B4** 16 59S 145 28
Marek = Stanke Dimitrov, *Bulgaria* **21 C10** 42 17N 23 9
Marengo, *U.S.A.* **80 E8** 41 48N 92 4
Marenyi, *Kenya* **54 C4** 4 22S 39 8
Marerano, *Madag.* **57 C7** 21 23S 44 52
Marfa, *U.S.A.* **81 K2** 30 19N 104 1
Marfa Pt., *Malta* **23 D1** 35 59N 14 19
Margaret →, *Australia* **60 C4** 18 9S 125 41
Margaret Bay, *Canada* **72 C3** 51 20N 127 35
Margaret L., *Canada* **72 B5** 58 56N 115 25
Margaret River, *Australia* **61 F2** 33 57S 115 4
Margarita, I. de, *Venezuela* **92 A6** 11 0N 64 0
Margaritovo, *Russia* **30 C7** 43 25N 134 45
Margate, *S. Africa* **57 E5** 30 50S 30 20
Margate, *U.K.* **11 F9** 51 23N 1 23
Marguerite, *Canada* **72 C4** 52 30N 122 25
Mari El □, *Russia* **24 C8** 56 30N 48 0
Mari Indus, *Pakistan* **42 C4** 32 57N 71 34
Mari Republic = Mari El □, *Russia* **24 C8** 56 30N 48 0
María Elena, *Chile* **94 A2** 22 18S 69 40
María Grande, *Argentina* **94 C4** 31 45S 59 55
Maria I., *N. Terr., Australia* **62 A2** 14 52S 135 45
Maria I., *Tas., Australia* **62 G4** 42 35S 148 0
Maria van Diemen, C., *N.Z.* **59 F4** 34 29S 172 40
Mariakani, *Kenya* **54 C4** 3 50S 39 27
Marian, *Australia* **62 C4** 21 9S 148 57
Marian L., *Canada* **72 A5** 63 0N 116 15
Mariana Trench, *Pac. Oc.* **28 H18** 13 0N 145 0
Marianao, *Cuba* **88 B3** 23 8N 82 24
Marianna, *Ark., U.S.A.* **81 H9** 34 46N 90 46
Marianna, *Fla., U.S.A.* **77 K3** 30 46N 85 14
Marias →, *U.S.A.* **82 C8** 47 56N 110 30
Mariato, Punta, *Panama* **88 E3** 7 12N 80 52
Maribor, *Slovenia* **16 E8** 46 36N 15 40
Marico →, *Africa* **56 C4** 23 35S 26 57
Maricopa, *Ariz., U.S.A.* **83 K7** 33 4N 112 3
Maricopa, *Calif., U.S.A.* **85 K7** 35 4N 119 24
Marié →, *Brazil* **92 D5** 0 27S 66 26
Marie Byrd Land, *Antarctica* **5 D14** 79 30S 125 0
Marie-Galante, *Guadeloupe* **89 C7** 15 56N 61 16
Mariecourt = Kangiqsujuaq, *Canada* **69 B12** 61 30N 72 0
Mariembourg, *Belgium* **15 D4** 50 6N 4 31
Mariental, *Namibia* **56 C2** 24 36S 18 0
Marienville, *U.S.A.* **78 E5** 41 28N 79 8
Mariestad, *Sweden* **9 G15** 58 43N 13 50
Marietta, *Ga., U.S.A.* **77 J3** 33 57N 84 33
Marietta, *Ohio, U.S.A.* **76 F5** 39 25N 81 27
Marieville, *Canada* **79 A11** 45 26N 73 10
Mariinsk, *Russia* **26 D9** 56 10N 87 20
Marijampole, *Lithuania* **9 J20** 54 33N 23 19
Marília, *Brazil* **95 A6** 22 13S 50 0
Marín, *Spain* **19 A1** 42 23N 8 42
Marina, *U.S.A.* **84 J5** 36 41N 121 48
Marinduque, *Phil.* **37 B6** 13 25N 122 0
Marinette, *U.S.A.* **76 C2** 45 6N 87 38
Maringá, *Brazil* **95 A5** 23 26S 52 2
Marion, *Ala., U.S.A.* **77 J2** 32 38N 87 19
Marion, *Ill., U.S.A.* **81 G10** 37 44N 88 56
Marion, *Ind., U.S.A.* **76 E3** 40 32N 85 40
Marion, *Iowa, U.S.A.* **80 D9** 42 2N 91 36
Marion, *Kans., U.S.A.* **80 F6** 38 21N 97 1
Marion, *N.C., U.S.A.* **77 H5** 35 41N 82 1
Marion, *Ohio, U.S.A.* **76 E4** 40 35N 83 8
Marion, *S.C., U.S.A.* **77 H6** 34 11N 79 24
Marion, *Va., U.S.A.* **77 G5** 36 50N 81 31
Marion, L., *U.S.A.* **77 J5** 33 28N 80 10
Mariposa, *U.S.A.* **84 H7** 37 29N 119 58
Mariscal Estigarribia, *Paraguay* **94 A3** 22 3S 60 40
Maritime Alps = Maritimes, Alpes, *Europe* **18 D7** 44 10N 7 10
Maritimes, Alpes, *Europe* **18 D7** 44 10N 7 10
Maritsa = Évros →, *Bulgaria* **21 D12** 41 40N 26 34
Maritsá, *Greece* **23 C10** 36 22N 28 8
Mariupol, *Ukraine* **25 E6** 47 5N 37 31
Marīvān, *Iran* **44 C5** 35 30N 46 25
Marj 'Uyūn, *Lebanon* **47 B4** 33 20N 35 35
Markazī □, *Iran* **45 C6** 35 0N 49 30
Markdale, *Canada* **78 B4** 44 19N 80 39
Marked Tree, *U.S.A.* **81 H9** 35 32N 90 25
Market Drayton, *U.K.* **10 E5** 52 54N 2 29
Market Harborough, *U.K.* **11 E7** 52 29N 0 55
Market Rasen, *U.K.* **10 D7** 53 24N 0 20
Markham, *Canada* **78 C5** 43 52N 79 16
Markham, Mt., *Antarctica* **5 E11** 83 0S 164 0
Markleeville, *U.S.A.* **84 G7** 38 42N 119 47
Markovo, *Russia* **27 C17** 64 40N 170 24
Marks, *Russia* **24 D8** 51 45N 46 50
Marksville, *U.S.A.* **81 K8** 31 8N 92 4
Marla, *Australia* **63 D1** 27 19S 133 33
Marlbank, *Canada* **78 B7** 44 26N 77 6
Marlboro, *Mass., U.S.A.* **79 D13** 42 19N 71 33
Marlboro, *N.Y., U.S.A.* **79 E11** 41 36N 73 59
Marlborough, *Australia* **62 C4** 22 46S 149 52
Marlborough, *U.K.* **11 F6** 51 25N 1 43
Marlborough Downs, *U.K.* **11 F6** 51 27N 1 53
Marlin, *U.S.A.* **81 K6** 31 18N 96 54
Marlow, *U.S.A.* **81 H6** 34 39N 97 58
Marmagao, *India* **40 M8** 15 25N 73 56
Marmara, *Turkey* **21 D12** 40 35N 27 38

Mehndawal

armara, Sea of = Marmara Denizi, *Turkey* **21 D13** 40 45N 28 15 E
armara Denizi, *Turkey* **21 D13** 40 45N 28 15 E
armaris, *Turkey* **21 F13** 36 50N 28 14 E
armion, Mt., *Australia* **61 E2** 29 16S 119 50 E
armion L., *Canada* **70 C1** 48 55N 91 20W
armolada, Mte., *Italy* **20 A4** 46 26N 11 51 E
armora, *Canada* **78 B7** 44 28N 77 41W
arne →, *France* **18 B5** 48 48N 2 24 E
aroala, *Madag.* **57 B8** 15 23S 47 59 E
aroantsetra, *Madag.* **57 B8** 15 26S 49 44 E
aromandia, *Madag.* **57 A8** 14 13S 48 5 E
arondera, *Zimbabwe* **55 F3** 18 5S 31 42 E
aroni →, *Fr. Guiana* **93 B8** 5 30N 54 0W
aroochydore, *Australia* **63 D5** 26 29S 153 5 E
aroona, *Australia* **63 F3** 37 27S 142 54 E
arosakoa, *Madag.* **57 B8** 15 26S 46 38 E
aroua, *Cameroon* **51 F8** 10 40N 14 20 E
arovoay, *Madag.* **57 B8** 16 6S 46 39 E
arquard, *S. Africa* **56 D4** 28 40S 27 28 E
arquesas Is. = Marquises, Is., *Pac. Oc.* **65 H14** 9 30S 140 0W
arquette, *U.S.A.* **76 B2** 46 33N 87 24W
arquises, Is., *Pac. Oc.* **65 H14** 9 30S 140 0W
arra, Djebel, *Sudan* **51 F10** 13 10N 24 22 E
arracuene, *Mozam.* **57 D5** 25 45S 32 35 E
arrakech, *Morocco* **50 B4** 31 9N 8 0W
arrawah, *Australia* **62 G3** 40 55S 144 42 E
arree, *Australia* **63 D2** 29 39S 138 1 E
arrero, *U.S.A.* **81 L9** 29 54N 90 6W
arrimane, *Mozam.* **57 C5** 22 58S 33 34 E
arromeu, *Mozam.* **57 B6** 18 15S 36 25 E
arrowie Cr. →, *Australia* **63 E4** 33 23S 145 40 E
arrubane, *Mozam.* **55 F4** 18 0S 37 0 E
arrupa, *Mozam.* **55 E4** 13 8S 37 30 E
ars Hill, *U.S.A.* **77 B12** 46 31N 67 52W
arsá Matrûh, *Egypt* **51 B11** 31 19N 27 9 E
arsabit, *Kenya* **54 B4** 2 18N 38 0 E
arsala, *Italy* **20 F5** 37 48N 12 26 E
arsalforn, *Malta* **23 C1** 36 4N 14 15 E
arsden, *Australia* **63 E4** 33 47S 147 32 E
arseille, *France* **18 E6** 43 18N 5 23 E
arseilles = Marseille, *France* **18 E6** 43 18N 5 23 E
arsh I., *U.S.A.* **81 L9** 29 34N 91 53W
arshall, *Ark., U.S.A.* **81 H8** 35 55N 92 38W
arshall, *Mich., U.S.A.* **76 D3** 42 16N 84 58W
arshall, *Minn., U.S.A.* **80 C7** 44 25N 95 45W
arshall, *Mo., U.S.A.* **80 F8** 39 7N 93 12W
arshall, *Tex., U.S.A.* **81 J7** 32 33N 94 23W
arshall →, *Australia* **62 C2** 22 59S 136 59 E
arshall Is. ■, *Pac. Oc.* **64 G9** 9 0N 171 0 E
arshalltown, *U.S.A.* **80 D8** 42 3N 92 55W
arshfield, *Mo., U.S.A.* **81 G8** 37 15N 92 54W
arshfield, *Vt., U.S.A.* **79 B12** 44 20N 72 20W
arshfield, *Wis., U.S.A.* **80 C9** 44 40N 90 10W
arshūn, *Iran* **45 B6** 36 19N 49 23 E
ärsta, *Sweden* **9 G17** 59 37N 17 52 E
art, *U.S.A.* **81 K6** 31 33N 96 50W
artaban, *Burma* **41 L20** 16 30N 97 35 E
artaban, G. of, *Burma* **41 L20** 16 5N 96 30 E
artapura, *Kalimantan, Indonesia* **36 E4** 3 22S 114 47 E
artapura, *Sumatera, Indonesia* **36 E2** 4 19S 104 22 E
artelange, *Belgium* **15 E5** 49 49N 5 43 E
artha's Vineyard, *U.S.A.* **79 E14** 41 25N 70 38W
artigny, *Switz.* **18 C7** 46 6N 7 3 E
artigues, *France* **18 E6** 43 24N 5 4 E
artin, *Slovak Rep.* **17 D10** 49 6N 18 58 E
artin, *S. Dak., U.S.A.* **80 D4** 43 11N 101 44W
artin, *Tenn., U.S.A.* **81 G10** 36 21N 88 51W
artin L., *U.S.A.* **77 J3** 32 41N 85 55W
artina Franca, *Italy* **20 D7** 40 42N 17 20 E
artinborough, *N.Z.* **59 J5** 41 14S 175 29 E
artinez, *Calif., U.S.A.* **84 G4** 38 1N 122 8W
artinez, *Ga., U.S.A.* **77 J4** 33 31N 82 4W
artinique ■, *W. Indies* **89 D7** 14 40N 61 0W
artinique Passage, *W. Indies* **89 C7** 15 15N 61 0W
artinópolis, *Brazil* **95 A5** 22 11S 51 12W
artins Ferry, *U.S.A.* **78 F4** 40 6N 80 44W
artinsburg, *Pa., U.S.A.* **78 F6** 40 19N 78 20W
artinsburg, *W. Va., U.S.A.* **76 F7** 39 27N 77 58W
artinsville, *Ind., U.S.A.* **76 F2** 39 26N 86 25W
artinsville, *Va., U.S.A.* **77 G6** 36 41N 79 52W
arton, *N.Z.* **59 J5** 40 4S 175 23 E
artos, *Spain* **19 D4** 37 44N 3 58W
arudi, *Malaysia* **36 D4** 4 11N 114 19 E
a'ruf, *Afghan.* **40 D5** 31 30N 67 6 E
arugame, *Japan* **31 G6** 34 15N 133 40 E
arunga, *Angola* **56 B3** 17 28S 20 2 E
arungu, Mts., *Dem. Rep. of the Congo* **54 D3** 7 30S 30 0 E
arv Dasht, *Iran* **45 D7** 29 50N 52 40 E
arvast, *Iran* **45 D7** 30 30N 54 15 E
arvel Loch, *Australia* **61 F2** 31 28S 119 29 E
arwar, *India* **42 G5** 25 43N 73 45 E
ary, *Turkmenistan* **26 F7** 37 40N 61 50 E
aryborough = Port Laoise, *Ireland* **13 C4** 53 2N 7 18W
aryborough, *Queens., Australia* **63 D5** 25 31S 152 37 E
aryborough, *Vic., Australia* **63 F3** 37 0S 143 44 E
aryfield, *Canada* **73 D8** 49 50N 101 35W
aryland □, *U.S.A.* **76 F7** 39 0N 76 30W
aryland Junction, *Zimbabwe* **55 F3** 17 45S 30 31 E
aryport, *U.K.* **10 C4** 54 44N 3 28W
ary's Harbour, *Canada* **71 B8** 52 18N 55 51W
arystown, *Canada* **71 C8** 47 10N 55 10W
arysville, *Canada* **72 D5** 49 35N 116 0W
arysville, *Calif., U.S.A.* **84 F5** 39 9N 121 35W
arysville, *Kans., U.S.A.* **80 F6** 39 51N 96 39W
arysville, *Mich., U.S.A.* **78 D2** 42 54N 82 29W
arysville, *Ohio, U.S.A.* **76 E4** 40 14N 83 22W
arysville, *Wash., U.S.A.* **84 B4** 48 3N 122 11W
ryville, *Mo., U.S.A.* **80 E7** 40 21N 94 52W
ryville, *Tenn., U.S.A.* **77 H4** 35 46N 83 58W
arzūq, *Libya* **51 C8** 25 53N 13 57 E
asahunga, *Tanzania* **54 C3** 2 6S 33 18 E
asai Steppe, *Tanzania* **54 C4** 4 30S 36 30 E
asaka, *Uganda* **54 C3** 0 21S 31 45 E
asalembo, Kepulauan, *Indonesia* **36 F4** 5 35S 114 30 E
asalima, Kepulauan, *Indonesia* **36 F5** 5 4S 117 5 E
Masamba, *Indonesia* **37 E6** 2 30S 120 15 E
Masan, *S. Korea* **35 G15** 35 11N 128 32 E
Masandam, Ra's, *Oman* **45 E8** 26 30N 56 30 E
Masasi, *Tanzania* **55 E4** 10 45S 38 52 E
Masaya, *Nic.* **88 D2** 12 0N 86 7W
Masbate, *Phil.* **37 B6** 12 21N 123 36 E
Mascara, *Algeria* **50 A6** 35 26N 0 6 E
Mascota, *Mexico* **86 C4** 20 30N 104 50W
Masela, *Indonesia* **37 F7** 8 9S 129 51 E
Maseru, *Lesotho* **56 D4** 29 18S 27 30 E
Mashaba, *Zimbabwe* **55 G3** 20 2S 30 29 E
Mashābih, *Si. Arabia* **44 E3** 25 35N 36 30 E
Masherbrum, *Pakistan* **43 B7** 35 38N 76 18 E
Mashhad, *Iran* **45 B8** 36 20N 59 35 E
Mashīz, *Iran* **45 D8** 29 56N 56 37 E
Mashkel, Hamun-i, *Pakistan* **40 E3** 28 20N 62 56 E
Mashki Chāh, *Pakistan* **40 E3** 29 5N 62 30 E
Mashonaland, *Zimbabwe* **53 H6** 16 30S 31 0 E
Mashonaland Central □, *Zimbabwe* **57 B5** 17 30S 31 0 E
Mashonaland East □, *Zimbabwe* **57 B5** 18 0S 32 0 E
Mashonaland West □, *Zimbabwe* **57 B4** 17 30S 29 30 E
Mashrakh, *India* **43 F11** 26 7N 84 48 E
Masindi, *Uganda* **54 B3** 1 40N 31 43 E
Masindi Port, *Uganda* **54 B3** 1 43N 32 2 E
Maşīrah, *Oman* **46 C6** 21 0N 58 50 E
Maşīrah, Khalīj, *Oman* **46 C6** 20 10N 58 10 E
Masisi, *Dem. Rep. of the Congo* **54 C2** 1 23S 28 49 E
Masjed Soleyman, *Iran* **45 D6** 31 55N 49 18 E
Mask, L., *Ireland* **13 C2** 53 36N 9 22W
Maskin, *Oman* **45 F8** 23 30N 56 50 E
Masoala, Tanjon' i, *Madag.* **57 B9** 15 59S 50 13 E
Masoarivo, *Madag.* **57 B7** 19 3S 44 19 E
Masohi = Amahai, *Indonesia* **37 E7** 3 20S 128 55 E
Masomeloka, *Madag.* **57 C8** 20 17S 48 37 E
Mason, *Nev., U.S.A.* **84 G7** 38 56N 119 8W
Mason, *Tex., U.S.A.* **81 K5** 30 45N 99 14W
Mason City, *U.S.A.* **80 D8** 43 9N 93 12W
Maspalomas, *Canary Is.* **22 G4** 27 46N 15 35W
Maspalomas, Pta., *Canary Is.* **22 G4** 27 43N 15 36W
Masqat, *Oman* **46 C6** 23 37N 58 36 E
Massa, *Italy* **18 D9** 44 1N 10 9 E
Massachusetts □, *U.S.A.* **79 D13** 42 30N 72 0W
Massachusetts B., *U.S.A.* **79 D14** 42 20N 70 50W
Massakory, *Chad* **51 F9** 13 0N 15 49 E
Massanella, *Spain* **22 B9** 39 48N 2 51 E
Massangena, *Mozam.* **57 C5** 21 34S 33 0 E
Massango, *Angola* **52 F3** 8 2S 16 21 E
Massawa = Mitsiwa, *Eritrea* **46 D2** 15 35N 39 25 E
Massena, *U.S.A.* **79 B10** 44 56N 74 54W
Massénya, *Chad* **51 F9** 11 21N 16 9 E
Masset, *Canada* **72 C2** 54 2N 132 10W
Massif Central, *France* **18 D5** 44 55N 3 0 E
Massillon, *U.S.A.* **78 F3** 40 48N 81 32W
Massinga, *Mozam.* **57 C6** 23 15S 35 22 E
Masson, *Canada* **79 A9** 45 32N 75 25W
Masson I., *Antarctica* **5 C7** 66 10S 93 20 E
Mastanli = Momchilgrad, *Bulgaria* **21 D11** 41 33N 25 23 E
Masterton, *N.Z.* **59 J5** 40 56S 175 39 E
Mastic, *U.S.A.* **79 F12** 40 47N 72 54W
Mastuj, *Pakistan* **43 A5** 36 20N 72 36 E
Mastung, *Pakistan* **40 E5** 29 50N 66 56 E
Masty, *Belarus* **17 B13** 53 27N 24 38 E
Masuda, *Japan* **31 G5** 34 40N 131 51 E
Masvingo, *Zimbabwe* **55 G3** 20 8S 30 49 E
Masvingo □, *Zimbabwe* **55 G3** 21 0S 31 30 E
Maşyāf, *Syria* **44 C3** 35 4N 36 20 E
Matabeleland, *Zimbabwe* **53 H5** 18 0S 27 0 E
Matabeleland North □, *Zimbabwe* **55 F2** 19 0S 28 0 E
Matabeleland South □, *Zimbabwe* **55 G2** 21 0S 29 0 E
Matachewan, *Canada* **70 C3** 47 56N 80 39W
Matadi, *Dem. Rep. of the Congo* **52 F2** 5 52S 13 31 E
Matagalpa, *Nic.* **88 D2** 13 0N 85 58W
Matagami, *Canada* **70 C4** 49 45N 77 34W
Matagami, L., *Canada* **70 C4** 49 50N 77 40W
Matagorda B., *U.S.A.* **81 L6** 28 40N 96 0W
Matagorda I., *U.S.A.* **81 L6** 28 15N 96 30W
Matak, *Indonesia* **39 L6** 3 18N 106 16 E
Mátala, *Greece* **23 E6** 34 59N 24 45 E
Matam, *Senegal* **50 E3** 15 34N 13 17W
Matamoros, *Campeche, Mexico* **87 D6** 18 50N 90 50W
Matamoros, *Coahuila, Mexico* **86 B4** 25 33N 103 15W
Matamoros, *Tamaulipas, Mexico* **87 B5** 25 50N 97 30W
Ma'ţan as Sarra, *Libya* **51 D10** 21 45N 22 0 E
Matandu →, *Tanzania* **55 D3** 8 45S 34 19 E
Matane, *Canada* **71 C6** 48 50N 67 33W
Matanomadh, *India* **42 H3** 23 33N 68 57 E
Matanzas, *Cuba* **88 B3** 23 0N 81 40W
Matapan, C. = Taínaron, Ákra, *Greece* **21 F10** 36 22N 22 27 E
Matapédia, *Canada* **71 C6** 48 0N 66 59W
Matara, *Sri Lanka* **40 S12** 5 58N 80 30 E
Mataram, *Indonesia* **36 F5** 8 41S 116 10 E
Matarani, *Peru* **92 G4** 17 0S 72 10W
Mataranka, *Australia* **60 B5** 14 55S 133 4 E
Matarma, Râs, *Egypt* **47 E1** 30 27N 32 44 E
Mataró, *Spain* **19 B7** 41 32N 2 29 E
Matatiele, *S. Africa* **57 E4** 30 20S 28 49 E
Mataura, *N.Z.* **59 M2** 46 11S 168 51 E
Matehuala, *Mexico* **86 C4** 23 40N 100 40W
Mateke Hills, *Zimbabwe* **55 G3** 21 48S 31 0 E
Matera, *Italy* **20 D7** 40 40N 16 36 E
Matetsi, *Zimbabwe* **55 F2** 18 12S 26 0 E
Mathis, *U.S.A.* **81 L6** 28 6N 97 50W
Mathráki, *Greece* **23 A3** 39 48N 19 31 E
Mathura, *India* **42 F7** 27 30N 77 40 E
Mati, *Phil.* **37 C7** 6 55N 126 15 E
Matiali, *India* **43 F13** 26 56N 88 49 E
Matías Romero, *Mexico* **87 D5** 16 53N 95 2W
Matibane, *Mozam.* **55 E5** 14 49S 40 45 E
Matima, *Botswana* **56 C3** 20 15S 24 26 E
Matiri Ra., *N.Z.* **59 J4** 41 38S 172 20 E
Matla →, *India* **43 J13** 21 40N 88 40 E
Matli, *Pakistan* **42 G3** 25 2N 68 39 E
Matlock, *U.K.* **10 D6** 53 9N 1 33W
Mato Grosso □, *Brazil* **93 F8** 14 0S 55 0W
Mato Grosso, Planalto do, *Brazil* **93 G8** 15 0S 55 0W
Mato Grosso do Sul □, *Brazil* **93 G8** 18 0S 55 0W
Matochkin Shar, *Russia* **26 B6** 73 10N 56 40 E
Matopo Hills, *Zimbabwe* **55 G2** 20 36S 28 20 E
Matopos, *Zimbabwe* **55 G2** 20 20S 28 29 E
Matosinhos, *Portugal* **19 B1** 41 11N 8 42W
Maţraḩ, *Oman* **46 C6** 23 37N 58 30 E
Matsue, *Japan* **31 G6** 35 25N 133 10 E
Matsumae, *Japan* **30 D10** 41 26N 140 7 E
Matsumoto, *Japan* **31 F9** 36 15N 138 0 E
Matsusaka, *Japan* **31 G8** 34 34N 136 32 E
Matsutō, *Japan* **31 F8** 36 31N 136 34 E
Matsuura, *Japan* **31 H4** 33 20N 129 49 E
Matsuyama, *Japan* **31 H6** 33 45N 132 45 E
Mattagami →, *Canada* **70 B3** 50 43N 81 29W
Mattancheri, *India* **40 Q10** 9 50N 76 15 E
Mattawa, *Canada* **70 C4** 46 20N 78 45W
Matterhorn, *Switz.* **18 D7** 45 58N 7 39 E
Matthew Town, *Bahamas* **89 B5** 20 57N 73 40W
Matthew's Ridge, *Guyana* **92 B6** 7 37N 60 10W
Mattice, *Canada* **70 C3** 49 40N 83 20W
Mattituck, *U.S.A.* **79 F12** 40 59N 72 32W
Mattoon, *U.S.A.* **76 F1** 39 29N 88 23W
Matuba, *Mozam.* **57 C5** 24 28S 32 49 E
Matucana, *Peru* **92 F3** 11 55S 76 25W
Matūn = Khowst, *Afghan.* **42 C3** 33 22N 69 58 E
Maturín, *Venezuela* **92 B6** 9 45N 63 11W
Mau, *India* **43 G10** 25 56N 83 33 E
Mau, *Mad. P., India* **43 F8** 26 17N 78 41 E
Mau, *Ut. P., India* **43 G9** 25 17N 81 23 E
Mau Escarpment, *Kenya* **54 C4** 0 40S 36 0 E
Mau Ranipur, *India* **43 G8** 25 16N 79 8 E
Maubeuge, *France* **18 A6** 50 17N 3 57 E
Maud, Pt., *Australia* **60 D1** 23 6S 113 45 E
Maude, *Australia* **63 E3** 34 29S 144 18 E
Maudin Sun, *Burma* **41 M19** 16 0N 94 30 E
Maués, *Brazil* **92 D7** 3 20S 57 45W
Mauganj, *India* **41 G12** 24 50N 81 55 E
Maughold Hd., *U.K.* **10 C3** 54 18N 4 18W
Maui, *U.S.A.* **74 H16** 20 48N 156 20W
Maulamyaing = Moulmein, *Burma* **41 L20** 16 30N 97 40 E
Maule □, *Chile* **94 D1** 36 5S 72 30W
Maumee, *U.S.A.* **76 E4** 41 34N 83 39W
Maumee →, *U.S.A.* **76 E4** 41 42N 83 28W
Maumere, *Indonesia* **37 F6** 8 38S 122 13 E
Maun, *Botswana* **56 C3** 20 0S 23 26 E
Mauna Kea, *U.S.A.* **74 J17** 19 50N 155 28W
Mauna Loa, *U.S.A.* **74 J17** 19 30N 155 35W
Maungmagan Is., *Burma* **38 F1** 14 0N 97 30 E
Maungmagan Kyunzu, *Burma* **41 N20** 14 0N 97 48 E
Maupin, *U.S.A.* **82 D3** 45 11N 121 5W
Maurepas, L., *U.S.A.* **81 K9** 30 15N 90 30W
Maurice, L., *Australia* **61 E5** 29 30S 131 0 E
Mauricie, Parc Nat. de la, *Canada* **70 C5** 46 45N 73 0W
Mauritania ■, *Africa* **50 E3** 20 50N 10 0W
Mauritius ■, *Ind. Oc.* **49 J9** 20 0S 57 0 E
Mauston, *U.S.A.* **80 D9** 43 48N 90 5W
Mavli, *India* **42 G5** 24 45N 73 55 E
Mavuradonha Mts., *Zimbabwe* **55 F3** 16 30S 31 30 E
Mawa, *Dem. Rep. of the Congo* **54 B2** 2 45N 26 40 E
Mawai, *India* **43 H9** 22 30N 81 4 E
Mawana, *India* **42 E7** 29 6N 77 58 E
Mawand, *Pakistan* **42 E3** 29 33N 68 38 E
Mawk Mai, *Burma* **41 J20** 20 14N 97 37 E
Mawlaik, *Burma* **41 H19** 23 40N 94 26 E
Mawqaq, *Si. Arabia* **44 E4** 27 25N 41 8 E
Mawson Coast, *Antarctica* **5 C6** 68 30S 63 0 E
Max, *U.S.A.* **80 B4** 47 49N 101 18W
Maxcanú, *Mexico* **87 C6** 20 40N 92 0W
Maxesibeni, *S. Africa* **57 E4** 30 49S 29 23 E
Maxhamish L., *Canada* **72 B4** 59 50N 123 17W
Maxixe, *Mozam.* **57 C6** 23 54S 35 17 E
Maxville, *Canada* **79 A10** 45 17N 74 51W
Maxwell, *U.S.A.* **84 F4** 39 17N 122 11W
Maxwelton, *Australia* **62 C3** 20 43S 142 41 E
May, C., *U.S.A.* **76 F8** 38 56N 74 58W
May Pen, *Jamaica* **88 C4** 17 58N 77 15W
Maya →, *Russia* **27 D14** 60 28N 134 28 E
Maya Mts., *Belize* **87 D7** 16 30N 89 0W
Mayaguana, *Bahamas* **89 B5** 22 30N 72 44W
Mayagüez, *Puerto Rico* **89 C6** 18 12N 67 9W
Mayāmey, *Iran* **45 B7** 36 24N 55 42 E
Mayanup, *Australia* **61 F2** 33 57S 116 27 E
Mayapan, *Mexico* **87 C7** 20 30N 89 25W
Mayarí, *Cuba* **89 B4** 20 40N 75 41W
Maybell, *U.S.A.* **82 F9** 40 31N 108 5W
Maybole, *U.K.* **12 F4** 55 21N 4 42W
Maydān, *Iraq* **44 C5** 34 55N 45 37 E
Maydena, *Australia* **62 G4** 42 45S 146 30 E
Mayenne →, *France* **18 C3** 47 30N 0 32W
Mayer, *U.S.A.* **83 J7** 34 24N 112 14W
Mayerthorpe, *Canada* **72 C5** 53 57N 115 8W
Mayfield, *Ky., U.S.A.* **77 G1** 36 44N 88 38W
Mayfield, *N.Y., U.S.A.* **79 C10** 43 6N 74 16W
Mayhill, *U.S.A.* **83 K11** 32 53N 105 29W
Maykop, *Russia* **25 F7** 44 35N 40 10 E
Maymyo, *Burma* **38 A1** 22 2N 96 28 E
Maynard, *Mass., U.S.A.* **79 D13** 42 26N 71 27W
Maynard, *Wash., U.S.A.* **84 C4** 47 59N 122 55W
Maynard Hills, *Australia* **61 E2** 28 28S 119 49 E
Mayne →, *Australia* **62 C3** 23 40S 141 55 E
Maynooth, *Ireland* **13 C5** 53 23N 6 34W
Mayo, *Canada* **68 B6** 63 38N 135 57W
Mayo □, *Ireland* **13 C2** 53 53N 9 3W
Mayon Volcano, *Phil.* **37 B6** 13 15N 123 41 E
Mayor I., *N.Z.* **59 G6** 37 16S 176 17 E
Mayotte, I., *Mayotte* **53 G9** 12 50S 45 10 E
Maysville, *U.S.A.* **76 F4** 38 39N 83 46W
Mayu, *Indonesia* **37 D7** 1 30N 126 30 E
Mayumba, *Gabon* **52 E2** 3 25S 10 39 E
Mayville, *N. Dak., U.S.A.* **80 B6** 47 30N 97 20W
Mayville, *N.Y., U.S.A.* **78 D5** 42 15N 79 30W
Mayya, *Russia* **27 C14** 61 44N 130 18 E
Mazabuka, *Zambia* **55 F2** 15 52S 27 44 E
Mazagán = El Jadida, *Morocco* **50 B4** 33 11N 8 17W
Mazagão, *Brazil* **93 D8** 0 7S 51 16W
Mazán, *Peru* **92 D4** 3 30S 73 0W
Māzandarān □, *Iran* **45 B7** 36 30N 52 0 E
Mazapil, *Mexico* **86 C4** 24 38N 101 34W
Mazara del Vallo, *Italy* **20 F5** 37 39N 12 35 E
Mazarrón, *Spain* **19 D5** 37 38N 1 19W
Mazaruni →, *Guyana* **92 B7** 6 25N 58 35W
Mazatán, *Mexico* **86 B2** 29 0N 110 8W
Mazatenango, *Guatemala* **88 D1** 14 35N 91 30W
Mazatlán, *Mexico* **86 C3** 23 13N 106 25W
Mažeikiai, *Lithuania* **9 H20** 56 20N 22 20 E
Māzhān, *Iran* **45 C8** 32 30N 59 0 E
Mazīnān, *Iran* **45 B8** 36 19N 56 56 E
Mazoe, *Mozam.* **55 F3** 16 42S 33 7 E
Mazoe →, *Mozam.* **55 F3** 16 20S 33 30 E
Mazowe, *Zimbabwe* **55 F3** 17 28S 30 58 E
Mazurian Lakes = Mazurski, Pojezierze, *Poland* **17 B11** 53 50N 21 0 E
Mazurski, Pojezierze, *Poland* **17 B11** 53 50N 21 0 E
Mazyr, *Belarus* **17 B15** 51 59N 29 15 E
Mbabane, *Swaziland* **57 D5** 26 18S 31 6 E
Mbaïki, *C.A.R.* **52 D3** 3 53N 18 1 E
Mbala, *Zambia* **55 D3** 8 46S 31 24 E
Mbale, *Uganda* **54 B3** 1 8N 34 12 E
Mbalmayo, *Cameroon* **52 D2** 3 33N 11 33 E
Mbamba Bay, *Tanzania* **55 E3** 11 13S 34 49 E
Mbandaka, *Dem. Rep. of the Congo* **52 D3** 0 1N 18 18 E
Mbanza Congo, *Angola* **52 F2** 6 18S 14 16 E
Mbanza Ngungu, *Dem. Rep. of the Congo* **52 F2** 5 12S 14 53 E
Mbarara, *Uganda* **54 C3** 0 35S 30 40 E
Mbashe →, *S. Africa* **57 E4** 32 15S 28 54 E
Mbenkuru →, *Tanzania* **55 D4** 9 25S 39 50 E
Mberengwa, *Zimbabwe* **55 G2** 20 29S 29 57 E
Mberengwa, Mt., *Zimbabwe* **55 G2** 20 37S 29 55 E
Mbesuma, *Zambia* **55 E3** 10 0S 32 2 E
Mbeya, *Tanzania* **55 D3** 8 54S 33 29 E
Mbeya □, *Tanzania* **54 D3** 8 15S 33 30 E
Mbinga, *Tanzania* **55 E4** 10 50S 35 0 E
Mbini □, *Eq. Guin.* **52 D2** 1 30N 10 0 E
Mbour, *Senegal* **50 F2** 14 22N 16 54W
Mbuji-Mayi, *Dem. Rep. of the Congo* **54 D1** 6 9S 23 40 E
Mbulu, *Tanzania* **54 C4** 3 45S 35 30 E
Mburucuyá, *Argentina* **94 B4** 28 1S 58 14W
Mchinja, *Tanzania* **55 D4** 9 44S 39 45 E
Mchinji, *Malawi* **55 E3** 13 47S 32 58 E
Mdantsane, *S. Africa* **53 L5** 32 56S 27 46 E
Mead, L., *U.S.A.* **85 J12** 36 1N 114 44W
Meade, *U.S.A.* **81 G4** 37 17N 100 20W
Meadow Lake, *Canada* **73 C7** 54 10N 108 26W
Meadow Lake Prov. Park, *Canada* **73 C7** 54 27N 109 0W
Meadow Valley Wash →, *U.S.A.* **85 J12** 36 40N 114 34W
Meadville, *U.S.A.* **78 E4** 41 39N 80 9W
Meaford, *Canada* **78 B4** 44 36N 80 35W
Mealy Mts., *Canada* **71 B8** 53 10N 58 0W
Meander River, *Canada* **72 B5** 59 2N 117 42W
Meares, C., *U.S.A.* **82 D2** 45 37N 124 0W
Mearim →, *Brazil* **93 D10** 3 4S 44 35W
Meath □, *Ireland* **13 C5** 53 40N 6 57W
Meath Park, *Canada* **73 C7** 53 27N 105 22W
Meaux, *France* **18 B5** 48 58N 2 50 E
Mebechi-Gawa →, *Japan* **30 D10** 40 31N 141 31 E
Mecanhelas, *Mozam.* **55 F4** 15 12S 35 54 E
Mecca = Makkah, *Si. Arabia* **46 C2** 21 30N 39 54 E
Mecca, *U.S.A.* **85 M10** 33 34N 116 5W
Mechanicsburg, *U.S.A.* **78 F8** 40 13N 77 1W
Mechanicville, *U.S.A.* **79 D11** 42 54N 73 41W
Mechelen, *Belgium* **15 C4** 51 2N 4 29 E
Mecheria, *Algeria* **50 B5** 33 35N 0 18W
Mecklenburg, *Germany* **16 B6** 53 33N 11 40 E
Mecklenburger Bucht, *Germany* **16 A6** 54 20N 11 40 E
Meconta, *Mozam.* **55 E4** 14 59S 39 50 E
Medan, *Indonesia* **36 D1** 3 40N 98 38 E
Medanosa, Pta., *Argentina* **96 F3** 48 8S 66 0W
Médéa, *Algeria* **50 A6** 36 12N 2 50 E
Medellín, *Colombia* **92 B3** 6 15N 75 35W
Medelpad, *Sweden* **9 E17** 62 33N 16 30 E
Medemblik, *Neths.* **15 B5** 52 46N 5 8 E
Medford, *Mass., U.S.A.* **79 D13** 42 25N 71 7W
Medford, *Oreg., U.S.A.* **82 E2** 42 19N 122 52W
Medford, *Wis., U.S.A.* **80 C9** 45 9N 90 20W
Medgidia, *Romania* **17 F15** 44 15N 28 19 E
Media Agua, *Argentina* **94 C2** 31 58S 68 25W
Media Luna, *Argentina* **94 C2** 34 45S 66 44W
Medianeira, *Brazil* **95 B5** 25 17S 54 5W
Mediaş, *Romania* **17 E13** 46 9N 24 22 E
Medicine Bow, *U.S.A.* **82 F10** 41 54N 106 12W
Medicine Bow Pk., *U.S.A.* **82 F10** 41 21N 106 19W
Medicine Bow Ra., *U.S.A.* **82 F10** 41 10N 106 25W
Medicine Hat, *Canada* **73 D6** 50 0N 110 45W
Medicine Lake, *U.S.A.* **80 A2** 48 30N 104 30W
Medicine Lodge, *U.S.A.* **81 G5** 37 17N 98 35W
Medina = Al Madīnah, *Si. Arabia* **46 C2** 24 35N 39 52 E
Medina, *N. Dak., U.S.A.* **80 B5** 46 54N 99 18W
Medina, *N.Y., U.S.A.* **78 C6** 43 13N 78 23W
Medina, *Ohio, U.S.A.* **78 E3** 41 8N 81 52W
Medina →, *U.S.A.* **81 L5** 29 16N 98 29W
Medina del Campo, *Spain* **19 B3** 41 18N 4 55W
Medina L., *U.S.A.* **81 L5** 29 32N 98 56W
Medina Sidonia, *Spain* **19 D3** 36 28N 5 57W
Medinipur, *India* **43 H12** 22 25N 87 21 E
Mediterranean Sea, *Europe* **6 H7** 35 0N 15 0 E
Médoc, *France* **18 D3** 45 10N 0 50W
Medveditsa →, *Russia* **25 E7** 49 35N 42 41 E
Medvezhi, Ostrava, *Russia* **27 B17** 71 0N 161 0 E
Medvezhyegorsk, *Russia* **24 B5** 63 0N 34 25 E
Medway →, *U.K.* **11 F8** 51 27N 0 46 E
Medway Towns □, *U.K.* **11 F8** 51 25N 0 32 E
Meekatharra, *Australia* **61 E2** 26 32S 118 29 E
Meeker, *U.S.A.* **82 F10** 40 2N 107 55W
Meelpaeg Res., *Canada* **71 C8** 48 15N 56 33W
Meerut, *India* **42 E7** 29 1N 77 42 E
Meeteetse, *U.S.A.* **82 D9** 44 9N 108 52W
Mega, *Ethiopia* **46 G2** 3 57N 38 19 E
Mégara, *Greece* **21 F10** 37 58N 23 22 E
Megasini, *India* **43 J12** 21 38N 86 21 E
Meghalaya □, *India* **41 G17** 25 50N 91 0 E
Mégiscane, L., *Canada* **70 C4** 48 35N 75 55W
Meharry, Mt., *Australia* **60 D2** 22 59S 118 35 E
Mehlville, *U.S.A.* **80 F9** 38 30N 90 19W
Mehndawal, *India* **43 F10** 26 58N 83 5 E

Mehr Jān

Mehr Jān, *Iran* 45 C7 33 50N 55 6 E
Mehrābād, *Iran* 44 B5 36 53N 47 55 E
Mehrān, *Iran* 44 C5 33 7N 46 10 E
Mehrīz, *Iran* 45 D7 31 35N 54 28 E
Mei Xian, *China* 34 G4 34 18N 107 55 E
Meiktila, *Burma* 41 J19 20 53N 95 54 E
Meissen, *Germany* 16 C7 51 9N 13 29 E
Meizhou, *China* 33 D6 24 16N 116 6 E
Meja, *India* 43 G10 25 9N 82 7 E
Mejillones, *Chile* 94 A1 23 10S 70 30W
Mekele, *Ethiopia* 46 E2 13 33N 39 30 E
Mekhtar, *Pakistan* 40 D6 30 30N 69 15 E
Meknès, *Morocco* 50 B4 33 57N 5 33W
Mekong →, *Asia* 39 H6 9 30N 106 15 E
Mekongga, *Indonesia* 37 E6 3 39S 121 15 E
Mekvari = Kür →, *Azerbaijan* 25 G8 39 29N 49 15 E
Melagiri Hills, *India* 40 N10 12 20N 77 30 E
Melaka, *Malaysia* 39 L4 2 15N 102 15 E
Melalap, *Malaysia* 36 C5 5 10N 116 5 E
Mélambes, *Greece* 23 D6 35 8N 24 40 E
Melanesia, *Pac. Oc.* 64 H7 4 0S 155 0 E
Melbourne, *Australia* 63 F4 37 50S 145 0 E
Melbourne, *U.S.A.* 77 L5 28 5N 80 37W
Melchor Múzquiz, *Mexico* 86 B4 27 50N 101 30W
Melchor Ocampo, *Mexico* 86 C4 24 52N 101 40W
Mélèzes →, *Canada* 69 C12 57 30N 71 0W
Mélèzes →, *Qué., Canada* 70 A5 57 40N 69 29W
Melfort, *Canada* 73 C8 52 50N 104 37W
Melfort, *Zimbabwe* 55 F3 18 0S 31 25 E
Melhus, *Norway* 8 E14 63 17N 10 18 E
Melilla, *N. Afr.* 19 E4 35 21N 2 57W
Melipilla, *Chile* 94 C1 33 42S 71 15W
Mélissa, Ákra, *Greece* 23 D6 35 6N 24 33 E
Melita, *Canada* 73 D8 49 15N 101 0W
Melitopol, *Ukraine* 25 E6 46 50N 35 22 E
Melk, *Austria* 16 D8 48 13N 15 20 E
Mellansel, *Sweden* 8 E18 63 25N 18 17 E
Mellen, *U.S.A.* 80 B9 46 20N 90 40W
Mellerud, *Sweden* 9 G15 58 41N 12 28 E
Mellette, *U.S.A.* 80 C5 45 9N 98 30W
Mellieha, *Malta* 23 D1 35 57N 14 21 E
Melo, *Uruguay* 95 C5 32 20S 54 10W
Melolo, *Indonesia* 37 F6 9 53S 120 40 E
Melouprey, *Cambodia* 38 F5 13 48N 105 16 E
Melrose, *Australia* 63 E4 32 42S 146 57 E
Melrose, *U.K.* 12 F6 55 36N 2 43W
Melrose, *Minn., U.S.A.* 80 C7 45 40N 94 49W
Melrose, *N. Mex., U.S.A.* 81 H3 34 26N 103 38W
Melstone, *U.S.A.* 82 C10 46 36N 107 52W
Melton Mowbray, *U.K.* 10 E7 52 47N 0 54W
Melun, *France* 18 B5 48 32N 2 39 E
Melville, *Canada* 73 C8 50 55N 102 50W
Melville, C., *Australia* 62 A3 14 11S 144 30 E
Melville, L., *Canada* 71 B8 53 30N 60 0W
Melville B., *Australia* 62 A2 12 0S 136 45 E
Melville I., *Australia* 60 B5 11 30S 131 0 E
Melville I., *Canada* 4 B2 75 30N 112 0W
Melville Pen., *Canada* 69 B11 68 0N 84 0W
Memba, *Mozam.* 55 E5 14 11S 40 30 E
Memboro, *Indonesia* 37 F5 9 30S 119 30 E
Memel = Klaipėda, *Lithuania* 9 J19 55 43N 21 10 E
Memel, *S. Africa* 57 D4 27 38S 29 36 E
Memmingen, *Germany* 16 E6 47 58N 10 10 E
Mempawah, *Indonesia* 36 D3 0 30N 109 5 E
Memphis, *Mich., U.S.A.* 78 D2 42 54N 82 46W
Memphis, *Tenn., U.S.A.* 81 H10 35 8N 90 3W
Memphis, *Tex., U.S.A.* 81 H4 34 44N 100 33W
Memphremagog, L., *U.S.A.* 79 B12 45 0N 72 12W
Mena, *U.S.A.* 81 H7 34 35N 94 15W
Menai Strait, *U.K.* 10 D3 53 11N 4 13W
Ménaka, *Mali* 50 E6 15 59N 2 18 E
Menan = Chao Phraya →, *Thailand* 38 F3 13 32N 100 36 E
Menarandra →, *Madag.* 57 D7 25 17S 44 30 E
Menard, *U.S.A.* 81 K5 30 55N 99 47W
Mendawai →, *Indonesia* 36 E4 3 30S 113 0 E
Mende, *France* 18 D5 44 31N 3 30 E
Mendez, *Mexico* 87 B5 25 7N 98 34W
Mendhar, *India* 43 C6 33 35N 74 10 E
Mendip Hills, *U.K.* 11 F5 51 17N 2 40W
Mendocino, *U.S.A.* 82 G2 39 19N 123 48W
Mendocino, C., *U.S.A.* 82 F1 40 26N 124 25W
Mendooran, *Australia* 63 E4 31 50S 149 6 E
Mendota, *Calif., U.S.A.* 84 J6 36 45N 120 23W
Mendota, *Ill., U.S.A.* 80 E10 41 33N 89 7W
Mendoza, *Argentina* 94 C2 32 50S 68 52W
Mendoza □, *Argentina* 94 C2 33 0S 69 0W
Mene Grande, *Venezuela* 92 B4 9 49N 70 56W
Menemen, *Turkey* 21 E12 38 34N 27 3 E
Menen, *Belgium* 15 D3 50 47N 3 7 E
Menggala, *Indonesia* 36 E3 4 30S 105 15 E
Mengjin, *China* 34 G7 34 55N 112 45 E
Mengyin, *China* 35 G9 35 40N 117 58 E
Mengzi, *China* 32 D5 23 20N 103 22 E
Menihek, *Canada* 71 B6 54 28N 56 36W
Menihek L., *Canada* 71 B6 54 0N 67 0W
Menin = Menen, *Belgium* 15 D3 50 47N 3 7 E
Menindee, *Australia* 63 E3 32 20S 142 25 E
Menindee L., *Australia* 63 E3 32 20S 142 25 E
Meningie, *Australia* 63 F2 35 50S 139 18 E
Menlo Park, *U.S.A.* 84 H4 37 27N 122 12W
Menominee, *U.S.A.* 76 C2 45 6N 87 37W
Menominee →, *U.S.A.* 76 C2 45 6N 87 36W
Menomonie, *U.S.A.* 80 C9 44 53N 91 55W
Menongue, *Angola* 53 G3 14 48S 17 52 E
Menorca, *Spain* 22 B11 40 0N 4 0 E
Mentakab, *Malaysia* 39 L4 3 29N 102 21 E
Mentawai, Kepulauan, *Indonesia* 36 E1 2 0S 99 0 E
Menton, *France* 18 E7 43 50N 7 29 E
Mentor, *U.S.A.* 78 E3 41 40N 81 21W
Menzelinsk, *Russia* 24 C9 55 47N 53 11 E
Menzies, *Australia* 61 E3 29 40S 121 2 E
Me'ona, *Israel* 47 B4 33 1N 35 15 E
Meoqui, *Mexico* 86 B3 28 17N 105 29W
Mepaco, *Mozam.* 55 F3 15 57S 30 48 E
Meppel, *Neths.* 15 B6 52 42N 6 12 E
Merabéllou, Kólpos, *Greece* 23 D7 35 10N 25 50 E
Merak, *Indonesia* 37 F12 6 10N 106 26 E
Meramangye, L., *Australia* 61 E5 28 25S 132 13 E
Meran = Merano, *Italy* 20 A4 46 40N 11 9 E
Merano, *Italy* 20 A4 46 40N 11 9 E
Merauke, *Indonesia* 37 F10 8 29S 140 24 E
Merbein, *Australia* 63 E3 34 10S 142 2 E
Merca, *Somali Rep.* 46 G3 1 48N 44 50 E
Merced, *U.S.A.* 84 H6 37 18N 120 29W
Merced →, *U.S.A.* 84 H6 37 21N 120 59W
Merced Pk., *U.S.A.* 84 H7 37 36N 119 24W
Mercedes, *Buenos Aires, Argentina* 94 C4 34 40S 59 30W
Mercedes, *Corrientes, Argentina* 94 B4 29 10S 58 5W
Mercedes, *San Luis, Argentina* 94 C2 33 40S 65 21W
Mercedes, *Uruguay* 94 C4 33 12S 58 0W
Mercedes, *U.S.A.* 81 M6 26 9N 97 55W
Merceditas, *Chile* 94 B1 28 20S 70 35W
Mercer, *N.Z.* 59 G5 37 16S 175 5 E
Mercer, *U.S.A.* 78 E4 41 14N 80 15W
Mercer Island, *U.S.A.* 84 C4 47 35N 122 15W
Mercury, *U.S.A.* 85 J11 36 40N 115 58W
Mercy C., *Canada* 69 B13 65 0N 63 30W
Mere, *U.K.* 11 F5 51 6N 2 16W
Meredith, C., *Falk. Is.* 96 G4 52 15S 60 40W
Meredith, L., *U.S.A.* 81 H4 35 43N 101 33W
Mergui, *Burma* 38 F2 12 26N 98 34 E
Mergui Arch. = Myeik Kyunzu, *Burma* 39 G1 11 30N 97 30 E
Mérida, *Mexico* 87 C7 20 58N 89 37W
Mérida, *Spain* 19 C2 38 55N 6 25W
Mérida, *Venezuela* 92 B4 8 24N 71 8W
Mérida, Cord. de, *Venezuela* 90 C3 9 0N 71 0W
Meriden, *U.K.* 11 E6 52 26N 1 38W
Meriden, *U.S.A.* 79 E12 41 32N 72 48W
Meridian, *Calif., U.S.A.* 84 F5 39 9N 121 55W
Meridian, *Idaho, U.S.A.* 82 E5 43 37N 116 24W
Meridian, *Miss., U.S.A.* 77 J1 32 22N 88 42W
Merimbula, *Australia* 63 F4 36 53S 149 54 E
Merinda, *Australia* 62 C4 20 2S 148 11 E
Meringur, *Australia* 63 E3 34 20S 141 19 E
Merir, *Pac. Oc.* 37 D8 4 10N 132 30 E
Merirumã, *Brazil* 93 C8 1 15N 54 50W
Merkel, *U.S.A.* 81 J5 32 28N 100 1W
Mermaid Reef, *Australia* 60 C2 17 6S 119 36 E
Merredin, *Australia* 61 F2 31 28S 118 18 E
Merrick, *U.K.* 12 F4 55 8N 4 28W
Merrickville, *Canada* 79 B9 44 55N 75 50W
Merrill, *Oreg., U.S.A.* 82 E3 42 1N 121 36W
Merrill, *Wis., U.S.A.* 80 C10 45 11N 89 41W
Merrimack →, *U.S.A.* 79 D14 42 49N 70 49W
Merriman, *U.S.A.* 80 D4 42 55N 101 42W
Merritt, *Canada* 72 C4 50 10N 120 45W
Merritt Island, *U.S.A.* 77 L5 28 21N 80 42W
Merriwa, *Australia* 63 E5 32 6S 150 22 E
Merry I., *Canada* 70 A4 55 29N 77 31W
Merryville, *U.S.A.* 81 K8 30 45N 93 33W
Mersch, *Lux.* 15 E6 49 44N 6 7 E
Mersea I., *U.K.* 11 F8 51 47N 0 58 E
Merseburg, *Germany* 16 C6 51 22N 11 59 E
Mersey →, *U.K.* 10 D4 53 25N 3 1W
Merseyside □, *U.K.* 10 D4 53 31N 3 2W
Mersin, *Turkey* 25 G5 36 51N 34 36 E
Mersing, *Malaysia* 39 L4 2 25N 103 50 E
Merta, *India* 42 F6 26 39N 74 4 E
Merta Road, *India* 42 F5 26 43N 73 55 E
Merthyr Tydfil, *U.K.* 11 F4 51 45N 3 22W
Merthyr Tydfil □, *U.K.* 11 F4 51 46N 3 21W
Mértola, *Portugal* 19 D2 37 40N 7 40W
Mertzon, *U.S.A.* 81 K4 31 16N 100 49W
Meru, *Kenya* 54 B4 0 3N 37 40 E
Meru, *Tanzania* 54 C4 3 15S 36 46 E
Mesa, *U.S.A.* 83 K8 33 25N 111 50W
Mesa Verde National Park, *U.S.A.* 83 H9 37 11N 108 29W
Mesanagrós, *Greece* 23 C9 36 1N 27 49 E
Mesaoría □, *Cyprus* 23 D12 35 12N 33 14 E
Mesarás, Kólpos, *Greece* 23 D6 35 6N 24 47 E
Mesgouez, L., *Canada* 70 B5 51 20N 75 0W
Meshed = Mashhad, *Iran* 45 B8 36 20N 59 35 E
Meshoppen, *U.S.A.* 79 E8 41 36N 76 3W
Mesilinka →, *Canada* 72 B4 56 6N 124 30W
Mesilla, *U.S.A.* 83 K10 32 16N 106 48W
Mesolóngion, *Greece* 21 E9 38 21N 21 28 E
Mesopotamia = Al Jazirah, *Iraq* 44 C5 33 30N 44 0 E
Mesopotamia, *U.S.A.* 78 E4 41 27N 80 57W
Mesquite, *U.S.A.* 83 H6 36 47N 114 6W
Messaad, *Algeria* 50 B6 34 8N 3 30 E
Messalo →, *Mozam.* 55 E4 12 25S 39 15 E
Messina, *Italy* 20 E6 38 11N 15 34 E
Messina, *S. Africa* 57 C5 22 20S 30 5 E
Messina, Str. di, *Italy* 20 F6 38 15N 15 35 E
Messíni, *Greece* 21 F10 37 4N 22 1 E
Messiniakós Kólpos, *Greece* 21 F10 36 45N 22 5 E
Messonghi, *Greece* 23 B3 39 29N 19 56 E
Mesta →, *Bulgaria* 21 D11 40 54N 24 49 E
Meta →, *S. Amer.* 92 B5 6 12N 67 28W
Meta Incognita Peninsula, *Canada* 69 B13 62 40N 68 0W
Metabetchouan, *Canada* 71 C5 48 26N 71 52W
Metairie, *U.S.A.* 81 L9 29 58N 90 10W
Metaline Falls, *U.S.A.* 82 B5 48 52N 117 22W
Metán, *Argentina* 94 B3 25 30S 65 0W
Metangula, *Mozam.* 55 E3 12 40S 34 50 E
Metengobalame, *Mozam.* 55 E3 14 49S 34 30 E
Methven, *N.Z.* 59 K3 43 38S 171 40 E
Metil, *Mozam.* 55 F4 16 24S 39 0 E
Metlakatla, *U.S.A.* 68 C6 55 8N 131 35W
Metropolis, *U.S.A.* 81 G10 37 9N 88 44W
Mettur Dam, *India* 40 P10 11 45N 77 45 E
Metu, *Ethiopia* 46 F2 8 18N 35 35 E
Metz, *France* 18 B7 49 8N 6 10 E
Meulaboh, *Indonesia* 36 D1 4 11N 96 3 E
Meureudu, *Indonesia* 36 C1 5 19N 96 10 E
Meuse →, *Europe* 18 A6 50 45N 5 41 E
Mexia, *U.S.A.* 81 K6 31 41N 96 29W
Mexiana, I., *Brazil* 93 D9 0 0 49 30W
Mexicali, *Mexico* 85 N11 32 40N 115 30W
Mexican Plateau, *Mexico* 66 G9 25 0N 104 0W
Mexican Water, *U.S.A.* 83 H9 36 57N 109 32W
México, *Mexico* 87 D5 19 20N 99 10W
Mexico, *Maine, U.S.A.* 79 B14 44 34N 70 33W
Mexico, *Mo., U.S.A.* 80 F9 39 10N 91 53W
Mexico, *N.Y., U.S.A.* 79 C8 43 28N 76 18W
México □, *Mexico* 87 D5 19 20N 99 10W
Mexico ■, *Cent. Amer.* 86 C4 25 0N 105 0W
Mexico, G. of, *Cent. Amer.* 87 C7 25 0N 90 0W
Mexico B., *U.S.A.* 79 C8 43 35N 76 20W
Meydān-e Naftūn, *Iran* 45 D6 31 56N 49 18 E
Meydani, Ra's-e, *Iran* 45 E8 25 24N 59 6 E
Meymaneh, *Afghan.* 40 B4 35 53N 64 38 E
Mezen, *Russia* 24 A7 65 50N 44 20 E
Mezen →, *Russia* 24 A7 65 44N 44 22 E
Mézenc, Mt., *France* 18 D6 44 54N 4 11 E
Mezhdurechenskiy, *Russia* 26 D7 59 36N 65 56 E
Mezőkövesd, *Hungary* 17 E11 47 49N 20 35 E
Mezőtúr, *Hungary* 17 E11 47 1N 20 41 E
Mezquital, *Mexico* 86 C4 23 29N 104 23W
Mgeta, *Tanzania* 55 D4 8 22S 36 6 E
Mhlaba Hills, *Zimbabwe* 55 F3 18 30S 30 30 E
Mhow, *India* 42 H6 22 33N 75 50 E
Miahuatlán, *Mexico* 87 D5 16 21N 96 36W
Miami, *Fla., U.S.A.* 77 N5 25 47N 80 11W
Miami, *Okla., U.S.A.* 81 G7 36 53N 94 53W
Miami, *Tex., U.S.A.* 81 H4 35 42N 100 38W
Miami Beach, *U.S.A.* 77 N5 25 47N 80 8W
Mian Xian, *China* 34 H4 33 10N 106 32 E
Mianchi, *China* 34 G6 34 48N 111 48 E
Mīāndarreh, *Iran* 45 C7 35 37N 53 39 E
Mīāndowāb, *Iran* 44 B5 37 0N 46 5 E
Miandrivazo, *Madag.* 57 B8 19 31S 45 29 E
Mīāneh, *Iran* 44 B5 37 30N 47 40 E
Mianwali, *Pakistan* 42 C4 32 38N 71 28 E
Miarinarivo, *Madag.* 57 B8 18 57S 46 55 E
Miass, *Russia* 24 D11 54 59N 60 6 E
Michalovce, *Slovak Rep.* 17 D11 48 47N 21 58 E
Michigan □, *U.S.A.* 76 C3 44 0N 85 0W
Michigan, L., *U.S.A.* 76 D2 44 0N 87 0W
Michigan City, *U.S.A.* 76 E2 41 43N 86 54W
Michipicoten I., *Canada* 70 C2 47 40N 85 40W
Michoacan □, *Mexico* 86 D4 19 0N 102 0W
Michurin, *Bulgaria* 21 C12 42 9N 27 51 E
Michurinsk, *Russia* 24 D7 52 58N 40 27 E
Mico, Pta., *Nic.* 88 D3 12 0N 83 30W
Micronesia, *Pac. Oc.* 64 G7 11 0N 160 0 E
Micronesia, Federated States of ■, *Pac. Oc.* 64 G7 9 0N 150 0 E
Midai, *Indonesia* 39 L6 3 0N 107 47 E
Midale, *Canada* 73 D8 49 25N 103 20W
Middelburg, *Neths.* 15 C3 51 30N 3 36 E
Middelburg, *Eastern Cape, S. Africa* 56 E4 31 30S 25 0 E
Middelburg, *Mpumalanga, S. Africa* 57 D4 25 49S 29 28 E
Middelwit, *S. Africa* 56 C4 24 51S 27 3 E
Middle Alkali L., *U.S.A.* 82 F3 41 27N 120 5W
Middle Bass I., *U.S.A.* 78 E2 41 41N 82 49W
Middle East, *Asia* 28 F7 38 0N 40 0 E
Middle Fork Feather →, *U.S.A.* 84 F5 38 33N 121 30W
Middle I., *Australia* 61 F3 34 6S 123 11 E
Middle Loup →, *U.S.A.* 80 E5 41 17N 98 24W
Middle Sackville, *Canada* 71 D7 44 47N 63 42W
Middleboro, *U.S.A.* 79 E14 41 54N 70 55W
Middleburg, *Fla., U.S.A.* 77 K5 30 4N 81 52W
Middleburg, *N.Y., U.S.A.* 79 D10 42 36N 74 20W
Middleburg, *Pa., U.S.A.* 78 F7 40 47N 77 3W
Middlebury, *U.S.A.* 79 B11 44 1N 73 10W
Middlemount, *Australia* 62 C4 22 50S 148 40 E
Middleport, *N.Y., U.S.A.* 78 C6 43 13N 78 29W
Middleport, *Ohio, U.S.A.* 76 F4 39 0N 82 3W
Middlesboro, *U.S.A.* 77 G4 36 36N 83 43W
Middlesbrough, *U.K.* 10 C6 54 35N 1 13W
Middlesbrough □, *U.K.* 10 C6 54 28N 1 13W
Middlesex, *Belize* 88 C2 17 2N 88 31W
Middlesex, *N.J., U.S.A.* 79 F10 40 36N 74 30W
Middlesex, *N.Y., U.S.A.* 78 D7 42 42N 77 16W
Middleton, *Australia* 62 C3 22 22S 141 32 E
Middleton, *Canada* 71 D6 44 57N 65 4W
Middleton Cr. →, *Australia* 62 C3 22 35S 141 51 E
Middletown, *U.K.* 13 B5 54 17N 6 51W
Middletown, *Calif., U.S.A.* 84 G4 38 45N 122 37W
Middletown, *Conn., U.S.A.* 79 E12 41 34N 72 39W
Middletown, *N.Y., U.S.A.* 79 E10 41 27N 74 25W
Middletown, *Ohio, U.S.A.* 76 F3 39 31N 84 24W
Middletown, *Pa., U.S.A.* 79 F8 40 12N 76 44W
Midhurst, *U.K.* 11 G7 50 59N 0 44W
Midi, Canal du →, *France* 18 E4 43 45N 1 21 E
Midland, *Canada* 78 B5 44 45N 79 50W
Midland, *Calif., U.S.A.* 85 M12 33 52N 114 48W
Midland, *Mich., U.S.A.* 76 D3 43 37N 84 14W
Midland, *Pa., U.S.A.* 78 F4 40 39N 80 27W
Midland, *Tex., U.S.A.* 81 K3 32 0N 102 3W
Midlands □, *Zimbabwe* 55 F2 19 40S 29 0 E
Midleton, *Ireland* 13 E3 51 55N 8 10W
Midlothian, *U.S.A.* 81 J6 32 30N 97 0W
Midlothian □, *U.K.* 12 F5 55 51N 3 5W
Midongy, Tangorombohitr' i, *Madag.* 57 C8 23 30S 47 0 E
Midongy Atsimo, *Madag.* 57 C8 23 35S 47 1 E
Midway Is., *Pac. Oc.* 64 E10 28 13N 177 22W
Midway Wells, *U.S.A.* 85 N11 32 41N 115 7W
Midwest, *U.S.A.* 75 B9 42 0N 90 0W
Midwest, *Wyo., U.S.A.* 82 E10 43 25N 106 16W
Midwest City, *U.S.A.* 81 H6 35 27N 97 24W
Midyat, *Turkey* 44 B4 37 25N 41 23 E
Midzŏr, *Bulgaria* 21 C10 43 24N 22 40 E
Mie □, *Japan* 31 G8 34 30N 136 10 E
Międzychód, *Poland* 16 B8 52 35N 15 53 E
Międzyrzec Podlaski, *Poland* 17 C12 51 58N 22 45 E
Mielec, *Poland* 17 C11 50 15N 21 25 E
Mienga, *Angola* 56 B2 17 12S 19 48 E
Miercurea-Ciuc, *Romania* 17 E13 46 21N 25 48 E
Mieres, *Spain* 19 A3 43 18N 5 48W
Mifflintown, *U.S.A.* 78 F7 40 34N 77 24W
Mifraz Hefa, *Israel* 47 C4 32 52N 35 0 E
Miguel Alemán, Presa, *Mexico* 87 D5 18 15N 96 40W
Mihara, *Japan* 31 G6 34 24N 133 5 E
Mikese, *Tanzania* 54 D4 6 48S 37 55 E
Mikhaylovgrad = Montana, *Bulgaria* 21 C10 43 27N 23 16 E
Mikhaylovka, *Russia* 25 D7 50 3N 43 5 E
Mikkeli, *Finland* 9 F22 61 43N 27 15 E
Mikkwa →, *Canada* 72 B6 58 25N 114 46W
Mikonos, *Greece* 21 F11 37 30N 25 25 E
Mikumi, *Tanzania* 54 D4 7 26S 37 0 E
Mikun, *Russia* 24 B9 62 20N 50 0 E
Milaca, *U.S.A.* 80 C8 45 45N 93 39W
Milagro, *Ecuador* 92 D3 2 11S 79 36W
Milan = Milano, *Italy* 18 D8 45 28N 9 12 E
Milan, *Mo., U.S.A.* 80 E8 40 12N 93 7W
Milan, *Tenn., U.S.A.* 77 H1 35 55N 88 46W
Milang, *Australia* 63 F2 35 24S 138 58 E
Milange, *Mozam.* 55 F4 16 3S 35 45 E
Milano, *Italy* 18 D8 45 28N 9 12 E
Milâs, *Turkey* 21 F12 37 20N 27 50
Mílatos, *Greece* 23 D7 35 18N 25 34
Milazzo, *Italy* 20 E6 38 13N 15 15
Milbank, *U.S.A.* 80 C6 45 13N 96 38
Milbanke Sd., *Canada* 72 C3 52 15N 128 35
Milden, *Canada* 73 C7 51 29N 107 32
Mildenhall, *U.K.* 11 E8 52 21N 0 32
Mildmay, *Canada* 78 B3 44 3N 81 7
Mildura, *Australia* 63 E3 34 13S 142 9
Miles, *Australia* 63 D5 26 40S 150 9
Miles City, *U.S.A.* 80 B2 46 25N 105 51
Milestone, *Canada* 73 D8 49 59N 104 31
Miletus, *Turkey* 21 F12 37 30N 27 18
Milford, *Calif., U.S.A.* 84 E6 40 10N 120 22
Milford, *Conn., U.S.A.* 79 E11 41 14N 73 3
Milford, *Del., U.S.A.* 76 F8 38 55N 75 26
Milford, *Mass., U.S.A.* 79 D13 42 8N 71 31
Milford, *N.H., U.S.A.* 79 D13 42 50N 71 39
Milford, *Pa., U.S.A.* 79 E10 41 19N 74 48
Milford, *Utah, U.S.A.* 83 G7 38 24N 113 1
Milford Haven, *U.K.* 11 F2 51 42N 5 7
Milford Sd., *N.Z.* 59 L1 44 41S 167 47
Milḥ, Baḥr al, *Iraq* 44 C4 32 40N 43 35
Milikapiti, *Australia* 60 B5 11 26S 130 40
Miling, *Australia* 61 F2 30 30S 116 17
Milk →, *U.S.A.* 82 B10 48 4N 106 19
Milk River, *Canada* 72 D6 49 10N 112 5
Mill I., *Antarctica* 5 C8 66 0S 101 30
Mill Valley, *U.S.A.* 84 H4 37 54N 122 32
Millau, *France* 18 D5 44 8N 3 4
Millbridge, *Canada* 78 B7 44 41N 77 36
Millbrook, *Canada* 78 B6 44 10N 78 29
Millbrook, *U.S.A.* 79 E11 41 47N 73 42
Mille Lacs, L. des, *Canada* 70 C1 48 45N 90 35
Mille Lacs L., *U.S.A.* 80 B8 46 15N 93 39
Milledgeville, *U.S.A.* 77 J4 33 5N 83 14
Millen, *U.S.A.* 77 J5 32 48N 81 57
Miller, *U.S.A.* 80 C5 44 31N 98 59
Millersburg, *Ohio, U.S.A.* 78 F3 40 33N 81 55
Millersburg, *Pa., U.S.A.* 78 F8 40 32N 76 58
Millerton, *U.S.A.* 79 E11 41 57N 73 31
Millerton L., *U.S.A.* 84 J7 37 1N 119 41
Millheim, *U.S.A.* 78 F7 40 54N 77 29
Millicent, *Australia* 63 F3 37 34S 140 21
Millington, *U.S.A.* 81 H10 35 20N 89 53
Millinocket, *U.S.A.* 77 C11 45 39N 68 43
Millmerran, *Australia* 63 D5 27 53S 151 16
Millom, *U.K.* 10 C4 54 13N 3 16
Mills L., *Canada* 72 A5 61 30N 118 20
Millsboro, *U.S.A.* 78 G5 40 0N 80 0
Milltown Malbay, *Ireland* 13 D2 52 52N 9 24
Millville, *N.J., U.S.A.* 76 F8 39 24N 75 2
Millville, *Pa., U.S.A.* 79 E8 41 7N 76 32
Millwood L., *U.S.A.* 81 J8 33 42N 93 58
Milne →, *Australia* 62 C2 21 10S 137 33
Milo, *U.S.A.* 77 C11 45 15N 68 59
Mílos, *Greece* 21 F11 36 44N 24 25
Milparinka, *Australia* 63 D3 29 46S 141 57
Milton, *N.S., Canada* 71 D7 44 4N 64 45
Milton, *Ont., Canada* 78 C5 43 31N 79 53
Milton, *N.Z.* 59 M2 46 7S 169 59
Milton, *Calif., U.S.A.* 84 G6 38 3N 120 51
Milton, *Fla., U.S.A.* 77 K2 30 38N 87 3
Milton, *Pa., U.S.A.* 78 F8 41 1N 76 51
Milton, *Vt., U.S.A.* 79 B11 44 38N 73 7
Milton-Freewater, *U.S.A.* 82 D4 45 56N 118 23
Milton Keynes, *U.K.* 11 E7 52 1N 0 44
Milton Keynes □, *U.K.* 11 E7 52 1N 0 44
Milverton, *Canada* 78 C4 43 34N 80 55
Milwaukee, *U.S.A.* 76 D2 43 2N 87 55
Milwaukee Deep, *Atl. Oc.* 89 C6 19 50N 68 0
Milwaukie, *U.S.A.* 84 E4 45 27N 122 38
Min Jiang →, *Fujian, China* 33 D6 26 0N 119 35
Min Jiang →, *Sichuan, China* 32 D5 28 45N 104 40
Min Xian, *China* 34 G3 34 25N 104 5
Mina Pirquitas, *Argentina* 94 A2 22 40S 66 30
Mīnā Su'ud, *Si. Arabia* 45 D6 28 45N 48 28
Mīnā'al Aḥmadī, *Kuwait* 45 D6 29 5N 48 10
Minago →, *Canada* 73 C9 54 33N 98 59
Minaki, *Canada* 73 D10 49 59N 94 40
Minamata, *Japan* 31 H5 32 10N 130 30
Minami-Tori-Shima, *Pac. Oc.* 64 E7 24 20N 153 58
Minas, *Uruguay* 95 C4 34 20S 55 10
Minas, Sierra de las, *Guatemala* 88 C2 15 9N 89 31
Minas Basin, *Canada* 71 C7 45 20N 64 12
Minas Gerais □, *Brazil* 93 G9 18 50S 46 0
Minatitlán, *Mexico* 87 D6 17 59N 94 31
Minbu, *Burma* 41 J19 20 10N 94 52
Minchinabad, *Pakistan* 42 D5 30 10N 73 34
Mindanao, *Phil.* 37 C7 8 0N 125 0
Mindanao Sea = Bohol Sea, *Phil.* 37 C6 9 0N 124 0
Mindanao Trench, *Pac. Oc.* 37 B7 12 0N 126 6
Minden, *Canada* 78 B6 44 55N 78 43
Minden, *Germany* 16 B5 52 17N 8 55
Minden, *La., U.S.A.* 81 J8 32 37N 93 17
Minden, *Nev., U.S.A.* 84 G7 38 57N 119 46
Mindiptana, *Indonesia* 37 F10 5 55S 140 22
Mindoro, *Phil.* 37 B6 13 0N 121 0
Mindoro Str., *Phil.* 37 B6 12 30N 120 30
Mine, *Japan* 31 G5 34 12N 131 7
Minehead, *U.K.* 11 F4 51 12N 3 29
Mineola, *N.Y., U.S.A.* 79 F11 40 45N 73 39
Mineola, *Tex., U.S.A.* 81 J7 32 40N 95 29
Mineral King, *U.S.A.* 84 J8 36 27N 118 36
Mineral Wells, *U.S.A.* 81 J5 32 48N 98 7
Minersville, *U.S.A.* 79 F8 40 41N 76 16
Minerva, *U.S.A.* 78 F3 40 44N 81 6
Minetto, *U.S.A.* 79 C8 43 24N 76 28
Mingäçevir Su Anbarı, *Azerbaijan* 25 F8 40 57N 46 50
Mingan, *Canada* 71 B7 50 20N 64 0
Mingechaurskoye Vdkhr. = Mingäçevir Su Anbarı, *Azerbaijan* 25 F8 40 57N 46 50
Mingela, *Australia* 62 B4 19 52S 146 38
Mingenew, *Australia* 61 E2 29 12S 115 21
Mingera Cr. →, *Australia* 62 C2 20 38S 137 45
Mingin, *Burma* 41 H19 22 50N 94 30
Mingo Junction, *U.S.A.* 78 F4 40 19N 80 37
Mingyuegue, *China* 35 C15 43 2N 128 50
Minho = Miño →, *Spain* 19 A2 41 52N 8 40
Minho, *Portugal* 19 B1 41 25N 8 20
Minidoka, *U.S.A.* 82 E7 42 45N 113 29

Montour Falls

Minigwal, L., *Australia* .... **61 E3** 29 31S 123 14 E
Minilya →, *Australia* .... **61 D1** 23 45S 114 0 E
Minilya Roadhouse, *Australia* .... **61 D1** 23 55S 114 0 E
Minipi L., *Canada* **71 B7** 52 25N 60 45W
Mink L., *Canada* **72 A5** 61 54N 117 40W
Minna, *Nigeria* .... **50 G7** 9 37N 6 30 E
Minneapolis, *Kans., U.S.A.* **80 F6** 39 8N 97 42W
Minneapolis, *Minn., U.S.A.* **80 C8** 44 59N 93 16W
Minnedosa, *Canada* **73 C9** 50 14N 99 50W
Minnesota □, *U.S.A.* **80 B8** 46 0N 94 15W
Minnesota →, *U.S.A.* **80 C8** 44 54N 93 9W
Minnewaukan, *U.S.A.* **80 A5** 48 4N 99 15W
Minnipa, *Australia* .... **63 E2** 32 51S 135 9 E
Minnitaki L., *Canada* **70 C1** 49 57N 92 10W
Mino, *Japan* .... **31 G8** 35 32N 136 55 E
Miño →, *Spain* **19 A2** 41 52N 8 40W
Minorca = Menorca, *Spain* **22 B11** 40 0N 4 0 E
Minot, *U.S.A.* **80 A4** 48 14N 101 18W
Minqin, *China* .... **34 E2** 38 38N 103 20 E
Minsk, *Belarus* .... **17 B14** 53 52N 27 30 E
Mińsk Mazowiecki, *Poland* . **17 B11** 52 10N 21 33 E
Mintabie, *Australia* .... **63 D1** 27 15S 133 7 E
Mintaka Pass, *Pakistan* .... **43 A6** 37 0N 74 58 E
Minteke Daban = Mintaka Pass, *Pakistan* .... **43 A6** 37 0N 74 58 E
Minto, *Canada* **71 C6** 46 5N 66 5W
Minto, L., *Canada* **70 A5** 57 13N 75 0W
Minton, *Canada* **73 D8** 49 10N 104 35W
Minturn, *U.S.A.* **82 G10** 39 35N 106 26W
Minusinsk, *Russia* .... **27 D10** 53 43N 91 20 E
Minutang, *India* .... **41 E20** 28 15N 96 30 E
Miquelon, *Canada* **70 C4** 49 25N 76 27W
Miquelon, *St- P. & M.* **71 C8** 47 8N 56 22W
Mīr Kūh, *Iran* .... **45 E8** 26 22N 58 55 E
Mīr Shahdād, *Iran* .... **45 E8** 26 15N 58 29 E
Mira, *Italy* .... **20 B5** 45 26N 12 8 E
Mira por vos Cay, *Bahamas* **89 B5** 22 9N 74 30W
Miraj, *India* .... **40 L9** 16 50N 74 45 E
Miram Shah, *Pakistan* .... **42 C4** 33 0N 70 2 E
Miramar, *Argentina* **94 D4** 38 15S 57 50W
Miramar, *Mozam.* .... **57 C6** 23 50S 35 35 E
Miramichi, *Canada* **71 C6** 47 2N 65 28W
Miramichi B., *Canada* **71 C7** 47 15N 65 0W
Miranda, *Brazil* **93 H7** 20 10S 56 15W
Miranda →, *Brazil* **92 G7** 19 25S 57 20W
Miranda de Ebro, *Spain* **19 A4** 42 41N 2 57W
Miranda do Douro, *Portugal* **19 B2** 41 30N 6 16W
Mirandópolis, *Brazil* **95 A5** 21 9S 51 6W
Mirango, *Malawi* .... **55 E3** 13 32S 34 58 E
Mirassol, *Brazil* **95 A6** 20 46S 49 28W
Mirbāţ, *Oman* .... **46 D5** 17 0N 54 45 E
Miri, *Malaysia* .... **36 D4** 4 23N 113 59 E
Miriam Vale, *Australia* .... **62 C5** 24 20S 151 33 E
Mirim, L., *S. Amer.* **95 C5** 32 45S 52 50W
Mirnyy, *Russia* .... **27 C12** 62 33N 113 53 E
Mirokhan, *Pakistan* .... **42 F3** 27 46N 68 6 E
Mirond L., *Canada* **73 B8** 55 6N 102 47W
Mirpur, *Pakistan* .... **43 C5** 33 32N 73 56 E
Mirpur Batoro, *Pakistan* .... **42 G3** 24 44N 68 16 E
Mirpur Bibiwari, *Pakistan* .. **42 E2** 28 33N 67 44 E
Mirpur Khas, *Pakistan* .... **42 G3** 25 30N 69 0 E
Mirpur Sakro, *Pakistan* .... **42 G2** 24 33N 67 41 E
Mirtağ, *Turkey* .... **44 B4** 38 23N 41 56 E
Miryang, *S. Korea* .... **35 G15** 35 31N 128 44 E
Mirzapur, *India* .... **43 G10** 25 10N 82 34 E
Mirzapur-cum-Vindhyachal = Mirzapur, *India* .... **43 G10** 25 10N 82 34 E
Misantla, *Mexico* **87 D5** 19 56N 96 50W
Misawa, *Japan* .... **30 D10** 40 41N 141 24 E
Miscou I., *Canada* **71 C7** 47 57N 64 31W
Mish'āb, Ra's al, *Si. Arabia* **45 D6** 28 15N 48 43 E
Mishan, *China* .... **33 B8** 45 37N 131 48 E
Mishawaka, *U.S.A.* **76 E2** 41 40N 86 11W
Mishima, *Japan* .... **31 G9** 35 10N 138 52 E
Misión, *Mexico* **85 N10** 32 6N 116 53W
Misiones □, *Argentina* **95 B5** 27 0S 55 0W
Misiones □, *Paraguay* **94 B4** 27 0S 56 0W
Miskah, *Si. Arabia* .... **44 E4** 24 49N 42 56 E
Miskitos, Cayos, *Nic.* **88 D3** 14 26N 82 50W
Miskolc, *Hungary* .... **17 D11** 48 7N 20 50 E
Misoke, *Dem. Rep. of the Congo* . **54 C2** 0 42S 28 2 E
Misool, *Indonesia* .... **37 E8** 1 52S 130 10 E
Misrātah, *Libya* .... **51 B9** 32 24N 15 3 E
Missanabie, *Canada* **70 C3** 48 20N 84 6W
Missinaibi →, *Canada* **70 B3** 50 43N 81 29W
Missinaibi L., *Canada* **70 C3** 48 23N 83 40W
Mission, *Canada* **72 D4** 49 10N 122 15W
Mission, *S. Dak., U.S.A.* **80 D4** 43 18N 100 39W
Mission, *Tex., U.S.A.* **81 M5** 26 13N 98 20W
Mission Beach, *Australia* .. **62 B4** 17 53S 146 6 E
Mission Viejo, *U.S.A.* **85 M9** 33 36N 117 40W
Missisa L., *Canada* **70 B2** 52 20N 85 7W
Missisicabi →, *Canada* **70 B4** 51 14N 79 31W
Mississagi →, *Canada* **70 C3** 46 15N 83 9W
Mississauga, *Canada* **78 C5** 43 32N 79 35W
Mississippi □, *U.S.A.* **81 J10** 33 0N 90 0W
Mississippi →, *U.S.A.* **81 L10** 29 9N 89 15W
Mississippi L., *Canada* **79 A8** 45 5N 76 10W
Mississippi River Delta, *U.S.A.* **81 L9** 29 10N 89 15W
Mississippi Sd., *U.S.A.* **81 K10** 30 20N 89 0W
Missoula, *U.S.A.* **82 C7** 46 52N 114 1W
Missouri □, *U.S.A.* **80 F8** 38 25N 92 30W
Missouri →, *U.S.A.* **80 F9** 38 49N 90 7W
Missouri City, *U.S.A.* **81 L7** 29 37N 95 32W
Missouri Valley, *U.S.A.* **80 E7** 41 34N 95 53W
Mist, *U.S.A.* **84 E3** 45 59N 123 15W
Mistassibi →, *Canada* **71 B5** 48 53N 72 13W
Mistassini, *Canada* **71 C5** 48 53N 72 12W
Mistassini →, *Canada* **71 C5** 48 42N 72 20W
Mistassini, L., *Canada* **70 B5** 51 0N 73 30W
Mistastin L., *Canada* **71 A7** 55 57N 63 20W
Mistinibi, L., *Canada* **71 A7** 55 56N 64 17W
Misty L., *Canada* **73 B8** 58 53N 101 40W
Misurata = Misrātah, *Libya* **51 B9** 32 24N 15 3 E
Mitchell, *Australia* .... **63 D4** 26 29S 147 58 E
Mitchell, *Canada* **78 C3** 43 28N 81 12W
Mitchell, *Nebr., U.S.A.* **80 E3** 41 57N 103 49W
Mitchell, *Oreg., U.S.A.* **82 D3** 44 34N 120 9W
Mitchell, *S. Dak., U.S.A.* **80 D6** 43 43N 98 2W
Mitchell →, *Australia* .... **62 B3** 15 12S 141 35 E
Mitchell, Mt., *U.S.A.* **77 H4** 35 46N 82 16W
Mitchell Ranges, *Australia* . **62 A2** 12 49S 135 36 E
Mitchelstown, *Ireland* **13 D3** 52 15N 8 16W
Mitha Tiwana, *Pakistan* .... **42 C5** 32 13N 72 6 E
Mithi, *Pakistan* .... **42 G3** 24 44N 69 48 E
Mithrao, *Pakistan* .... **42 F3** 27 28N 69 40 E
Mitilíni, *Greece* .... **21 E12** 39 6N 26 35 E
Mito, *Japan* .... **31 F10** 36 20N 140 30 E
Mitrovica = Kosovska Mitrovica, *Serbia, Yug.* .. **21 C9** 42 54N 20 52 E
Mitsinjo, *Madag.* .... **57 B8** 16 1S 45 52 E
Mitsiwa, *Eritrea* .... **46 D2** 15 35N 39 25 E
Mitsukaidō, *Japan* .... **31 F9** 36 1N 139 59 E
Mittagong, *Australia* .... **63 E5** 34 28S 150 29 E
Mitú, *Colombia* **92 C4** 1 15N 70 13W
Mitumba, *Tanzania* .... **54 D3** 7 8S 31 2 E
Mitumba, Mts., *Dem. Rep. of the Congo* . **54 D2** 7 0S 27 30 E
Mitwaba, *Dem. Rep. of the Congo* . **55 D2** 8 2S 27 17 E
Mityana, *Uganda* .... **54 B3** 0 23N 32 2 E
Mixteco →, *Mexico* **87 D5** 18 11N 98 30W
Miyagi □, *Japan* .... **30 E10** 38 15N 140 45 E
Miyah, W. el →, *Syria* .... **44 C3** 34 44N 39 57 E
Miyake-Jima, *Japan* .... **31 G9** 34 5N 139 30 E
Miyako, *Japan* .... **30 E10** 39 40N 141 59 E
Miyako-Jima, *Japan* .... **31 M2** 24 45N 125 20 E
Miyako-Rettō, *Japan* .... **31 M2** 24 24N 125 0 E
Miyakonojō, *Japan* .... **31 J5** 31 40N 131 5 E
Miyani, *India* .... **42 J3** 21 50N 69 26 E
Miyanoura-Dake, *Japan* .... **31 J5** 30 20N 130 31 E
Miyazaki, *Japan* .... **31 J5** 31 56N 131 30 E
Miyazaki □, *Japan* .... **31 H5** 32 30N 131 30 E
Miyazu, *Japan* .... **31 G7** 35 35N 135 10 E
Miyet, Bahr el = Dead Sea, *Asia* .... **47 D4** 31 30N 35 30 E
Miyoshi, *Japan* .... **31 G6** 34 48N 132 51 E
Miyun, *China* .... **34 D9** 40 28N 116 50 E
Miyun Shuiku, *China* .... **35 D9** 40 30N 117 0 E
Mizdah, *Libya* .... **51 B8** 31 30N 13 0 E
Mizen Hd., *Cork, Ireland* **13 E2** 51 27N 9 50W
Mizen Hd., *Wick., Ireland* .. **13 D5** 52 51N 6 4W
Mizhi, *China* .... **34 F6** 37 47N 110 12 E
Mizoram □, *India* .... **41 H18** 23 30N 92 40 E
Mizpe Ramon, *Israel* .... **47 E3** 30 34N 34 49 E
Mizusawa, *Japan* .... **30 E10** 39 8N 141 8 E
Mjölby, *Sweden* .... **9 G16** 58 20N 15 10 E
Mjøsa, *Norway* .... **9 F14** 60 40N 11 0 E
Mkata, *Tanzania* .... **54 D4** 5 45S 38 20 E
Mkokotoni, *Tanzania* .... **54 D4** 5 55S 39 15 E
Mkomazi, *Tanzania* .... **54 C4** 4 40S 38 7 E
Mkomazi →, *S. Africa* .... **57 E5** 30 12S 30 50 E
Mkulwe, *Tanzania* .... **55 D3** 8 37S 32 20 E
Mkumbi, Ras, *Tanzania* .... **54 D4** 7 38S 39 55 E
Mkushi, *Zambia* .... **55 E2** 14 25S 29 15 E
Mkushi River, *Zambia* .... **55 E2** 13 32S 29 45 E
Mkuze, *S. Africa* .... **57 D5** 27 10S 32 0 E
Mladá Boleslav, *Czech Rep.* **16 C8** 50 27N 14 53 E
Mlala Hills, *Tanzania* .... **54 D3** 6 50S 31 40 E
Mlange = Mulanje, *Malawi* **55 F4** 16 2S 35 33 E
Mlanje, Pic, *Malawi* .... **53 H7** 15 57S 35 38 E
Mława, *Poland* .... **17 B11** 53 9N 20 25 E
Mljet, *Croatia* .... **20 C7** 42 43N 17 30 E
Mmabatho, *S. Africa* .... **56 D4** 25 49S 25 30 E
Mo i Rana, *Norway* .... **8 C16** 66 20N 14 7 E
Moa, *Cuba* **89 B4** 20 40N 74 56W
Moa, *Indonesia* .... **37 F7** 8 0S 128 0 E
Moab, *U.S.A.* **83 G9** 38 35N 109 33W
Moala, *Fiji* .... **59 D8** 18 36S 179 53 E
Moama, *Australia* .... **63 F3** 36 7S 144 46 E
Moapa, *U.S.A.* **85 J12** 36 40N 114 37W
Moate, *Ireland* **13 C4** 53 24N 7 44W
Moba, *Dem. Rep. of the Congo* . **54 D2** 7 0S 29 48 E
Mobārakābād, *Iran* .... **45 D7** 28 24N 53 20 E
Mobaye, *C.A.R.* .... **52 D4** 4 25N 21 5 E
Mobayi, *Dem. Rep. of the Congo* . **52 D4** 4 15N 21 8 E
Moberley Lake, *Canada* **72 B4** 55 50N 121 44W
Moberly, *U.S.A.* **80 F8** 39 25N 92 26W
Mobile, *U.S.A.* **77 K1** 30 41N 88 3W
Mobile B., *U.S.A.* **77 K2** 30 30N 88 0W
Mobridge, *U.S.A.* **80 C4** 45 32N 100 26W
Mobutu Sese Seko, L. = Albert L., *Africa* .... **54 B3** 1 30N 31 0 E
Moc Chau, *Vietnam* .... **38 B5** 20 50N 104 38 E
Moc Hoa, *Vietnam* .... **39 G5** 10 46N 105 56 E
Mocabe Kasari, *Dem. Rep. of the Congo* . **55 D2** 9 58S 26 12 E
Moçambique, *Mozam.* .... **55 F5** 15 3S 40 42 E
Moçâmedes = Namibe, *Angola* .... **53 H2** 15 7S 12 11 E
Mocanaqua, *U.S.A.* **79 E8** 41 9N 76 8W
Mochudi, *Botswana* .... **56 C4** 24 27S 26 7 E
Mocimboa da Praia, *Mozam.* **55 E5** 11 25S 40 20 E
Moclips, *U.S.A.* **84 C2** 47 14N 124 13W
Mocoa, *Colombia* **92 C3** 1 7N 76 35W
Mococa, *Brazil* **95 A6** 21 28S 47 0W
Mocorito, *Mexico* **86 B3** 25 30N 107 53W
Moctezuma, *Mexico* **86 B3** 29 50N 109 0W
Moctezuma →, *Mexico* .. **87 C5** 21 59N 98 34W
Mocuba, *Mozam.* .... **55 F4** 16 54S 36 57 E
Mocúzari, Presa, *Mexico* .. **86 B3** 27 10N 109 10W
Modane, *France* .... **18 D7** 45 12N 6 40 E
Modasa, *India* .... **42 H5** 23 30N 73 21 E
Modder →, *S. Africa* .... **56 D3** 29 2S 24 37 E
Modderrivier, *S. Africa* .... **56 D3** 29 2S 24 38 E
Módena, *Italy* .... **20 B4** 44 40N 10 55 E
Modena, *U.S.A.* **83 H7** 37 48N 113 56W
Modesto, *U.S.A.* **84 H6** 37 39N 121 0W
Módica, *Italy* .... **20 F6** 36 52N 14 46 E
Moe, *Australia* .... **63 F4** 38 12S 146 19 E
Moebase, *Mozam.* .... **55 F4** 17 3S 38 41 E
Moengo, *Surinam* **93 B8** 5 45N 54 20W
Moffat, *U.K.* **12 F5** 55 21N 3 27W
Moga, *India* .... **42 D6** 30 48N 75 8 E
Mogadishu = Muqdisho, *Somali Rep.* .... **46 G4** 2 2N 45 25 E
Mogador = Essaouira, *Morocco* **50 B4** 31 32N 9 42W
Mogalakwena →, *S. Africa* **57 C4** 22 38S 28 40 E
Mogami-Gawa →, *Japan* . **30 E10** 38 45N 140 0 E
Mogán, *Canary Is.* **22 G4** 27 53N 15 43W
Mogaung, *Burma* .... **41 G20** 25 20N 97 0 E
Mogi das Cruzes, *Brazil* **95 A6** 23 31S 46 11W
Mogi-Guaçu →, *Brazil* **95 A6** 20 53S 48 10W
Mogi-Mirim, *Brazil* **95 A6** 22 29S 47 0W
Mogilev = Mahilyow, *Belarus* .... **17 B16** 53 55N 30 18 E
Mogilev-Podolskiy = Mohyliv-Podilskyy, *Ukraine* .... **17 D14** 48 26N 27 48 E
Mogincual, *Mozam.* .... **55 F5** 15 35S 40 25 E
Mogocha, *Russia* .... **27 D12** 53 40N 119 50 E
Mogok, *Burma* .... **41 H20** 23 0N 96 40 E
Mogollon Rim, *U.S.A.* **83 J8** 34 10N 110 50W
Mogumber, *Australia* .... **61 F2** 31 2S 116 3 E
Mohács, *Hungary* .... **17 F10** 45 58N 18 41 E
Mohales Hoek, *Lesotho* .... **56 E4** 30 7S 27 26 E
Mohall, *U.S.A.* **80 A4** 48 46N 101 31W
Moḩammadābād, *Iran* .... **45 B8** 37 52N 59 5 E
Mohammedia, *Morocco* **50 B4** 33 44N 7 21W
Mohana →, *India* .... **43 G11** 24 43N 85 0 E
Mohanlalganj, *India* .... **43 F9** 26 41N 80 58 E
Mohave, L., *U.S.A.* **85 K12** 35 12N 114 34W
Mohawk →, *U.S.A.* **79 D11** 42 47N 73 41W
Mohenjodaro, *Pakistan* .... **42 F3** 27 19N 68 7 E
Mohicanville Reservoir, *U.S.A.* **78 F3** 40 45N 82 0W
Mohoro, *Tanzania* .... **54 D4** 8 6S 39 8 E
Mohyliv-Podilskyy, *Ukraine* **17 D14** 48 26N 27 48 E
Moidart, L., *U.K.* **12 E3** 56 47N 5 52W
Moira →, *Canada* **78 B7** 44 21N 77 24W
Moíres, *Greece* .... **23 D6** 35 4N 24 56 E
Moisaküla, *Estonia* .... **9 G21** 58 3N 25 12 E
Moisie, *Canada* **71 B6** 50 12N 66 1W
Moisie →, *Canada* **71 B6** 50 14N 66 5W
Mojave, *U.S.A.* **85 K8** 35 3N 118 10W
Mojave Desert, *U.S.A.* **85 L10** 35 0N 116 30W
Mojo, *Bolivia* **94 A2** 21 48S 65 33W
Mojokerto, *Indonesia* .... **37 G15** 7 28S 112 26 E
Mokai, *N.Z.* .... **59 H5** 38 32S 175 56 E
Mokambo, *Dem. Rep. of the Congo* . **55 E2** 12 25S 28 20 E
Mokameh, *India* .... **43 G11** 25 24N 85 55 E
Mokelumne →, *U.S.A.* **84 G5** 38 13N 121 28W
Mokelumne Hill, *U.S.A.* **84 G6** 38 18N 120 43W
Mokhós, *Greece* .... **23 D7** 35 16N 25 27 E
Mokhotlong, *Lesotho* .... **57 D4** 29 22S 29 2 E
Mokokchung, *India* .... **41 F19** 26 15N 94 30 E
Mokp'o, *S. Korea* .... **35 G14** 34 50N 126 25 E
Mokra Gora, *Serbia, Yug.* . **21 C9** 42 50N 20 30 E
Mol, *Belgium* .... **15 C5** 51 11N 5 5 E
Molchanovo, *Russia* .... **26 D9** 57 40N 83 50 E
Mold, *U.K.* **10 D4** 53 9N 3 8W
Moldavia = Moldova ■, *Europe* .... **17 E15** 47 0N 28 0 E
Molde, *Norway* .... **8 E12** 62 45N 7 9 E
Moldova ■, *Europe* .... **17 E15** 47 0N 28 0 E
Moldoveana, Vf., *Romania* . **17 F13** 45 36N 24 45 E
Mole →, *U.K.* **11 F7** 51 24N 0 21W
Mole Creek, *Australia* .... **62 G4** 41 34S 146 24 E
Molepolole, *Botswana* .... **56 C4** 24 28S 25 28 E
Molfetta, *Italy* .... **20 D7** 41 12N 16 36 E
Moline, *U.S.A.* **80 E9** 41 30N 90 31W
Molinos, *Argentina* **94 B2** 25 28S 66 15W
Moliro, *Dem. Rep. of the Congo* . **54 D3** 8 12S 30 30 E
Mollendo, *Peru* **92 G4** 17 0S 72 0W
Mollerin, L., *Australia* .... **61 F2** 30 30S 117 35 E
Molodechno = Maladzyechna, *Belarus* .. **17 A14** 54 20N 26 50 E
Molokai, *U.S.A.* **74 H16** 21 8N 157 0W
Molong, *Australia* .... **63 E4** 33 5S 148 54 E
Molopo →, *Africa* .... **56 D3** 27 30S 20 13 E
Molotov = Perm, *Russia* .. **24 C10** 58 0N 56 10 E
Molson L., *Canada* **73 C9** 54 22N 96 40W
Molteno, *S. Africa* .... **56 E4** 31 22S 26 22 E
Molu, *Indonesia* .... **37 F8** 6 45S 131 40 E
Molucca Sea, *Indonesia* .... **37 E6** 2 0S 124 0 E
Moluccas = Maluku, *Indonesia* .... **37 E7** 1 0S 127 0 E
Moma, *Dem. Rep. of the Congo* . **54 C1** 1 35S 23 52 E
Moma, *Mozam.* .... **55 F4** 16 47S 39 4 E
Mombasa, *Kenya* .... **54 C4** 4 2S 39 43 E
Mombetsu, *Japan* .... **30 B11** 44 21N 143 22 E
Momchilgrad, *Bulgaria* .... **21 D11** 41 33N 25 23 E
Momi, *Dem. Rep. of the Congo* . **54 C2** 1 42S 27 0 E
Mompós, *Colombia* **92 B4** 9 14N 74 26W
Møn, *Denmark* .... **9 J15** 54 57N 12 20 E
Mon →, *Burma* .... **41 J19** 20 25N 94 30 E
Mona, Canal de la, *W. Indies* **89 C6** 18 30N 67 45W
Mona, Isla, *Puerto Rico* **89 C6** 18 5N 67 54W
Mona, Pta., *Costa Rica* **88 E3** 9 37N 82 36W
Monaca, *U.S.A.* **78 F4** 40 41N 80 17W
Monaco ■, *Europe* .... **18 E7** 43 46N 7 23 E
Monadhliath Mts., *U.K.* **12 D4** 57 10N 4 4W
Monadnock, Mt., *U.S.A.* **79 D12** 42 52N 72 7W
Monaghan, *Ireland* **13 B5** 54 15N 6 57W
Monaghan □, *Ireland* **13 B5** 54 11N 6 56W
Monahans, *U.S.A.* **81 K3** 31 36N 102 54W
Monapo, *Mozam.* .... **55 E5** 14 56S 40 19 E
Monar, L., *U.K.* **12 D3** 57 26N 5 8W
Monarch Mt., *Canada* **72 C3** 51 55N 125 57W
Monashee Mts., *Canada* **72 C5** 51 0N 118 43W
Monasterevin, *Ireland* **13 C4** 53 8N 7 4W
Monastir = Bitola, *Macedonia* .... **21 D9** 41 1N 21 20 E
Moncayo, Sierra del, *Spain* **19 B5** 41 48N 1 50W
Monchegorsk, *Russia* .... **24 A5** 67 54N 32 58 E
Mönchengladbach, *Germany* .... **16 C4** 51 11N 6 27 E
Monchique, *Portugal* **19 D1** 37 19N 8 38W
Moncks Corner, *U.S.A.* **77 J5** 33 12N 80 1W
Monclova, *Mexico* **86 B4** 26 50N 101 30W
Moncton, *Canada* **71 C7** 46 7N 64 51W
Mondego →, *Portugal* **19 B1** 40 9N 8 52W
Mondeodo, *Indonesia* .... **37 E6** 3 34S 122 9 E
Mondovì, *Italy* .... **18 D7** 44 23N 7 49 E
Mondrain I., *Australia* .... **61 F3** 34 9S 122 14 E
Monessen, *U.S.A.* **78 F5** 40 9N 79 54W
Monett, *U.S.A.* **81 G8** 36 55N 93 55W
Moneymore, *U.K.* **13 B5** 54 41N 6 40W
Monforte de Lemos, *Spain* **19 A2** 42 31N 7 33W
Mong Hsu, *Burma* .... **41 J21** 21 54N 98 30 E
Mong Kung, *Burma* .... **41 J20** 21 35N 97 35 E
Mong Nai, *Burma* .... **41 J20** 20 32N 97 46 E
Mong Pawk, *Burma* .... **41 H21** 22 4N 99 16 E
Mong Ton, *Burma* .... **41 J21** 20 17N 98 45 E
Mong Wa, *Burma* .... **41 J22** 21 26N 100 27 E
Mong Yai, *Burma* .... **41 H21** 22 21N 98 3 E
Mongalla, *Sudan* .... **51 G12** 5 8N 31 42 E
Mongers, L., *Australia* .... **61 E2** 29 25S 117 5 E
Monghyr = Munger, *India* . **43 G12** 25 23N 86 30 E
Mongibello = Etna, *Italy* .. **20 F6** 37 50N 14 55 E
Mongo, *Chad* .... **51 F9** 12 14N 18 43 E
Mongolia ■, *Asia* .... **27 E10** 47 0N 103 0 E
Mongu, *Zambia* .... **53 H4** 15 16S 23 12 E
Môngua, *Angola* .... **56 B2** 16 43S 15 20 E
Monifieth, *U.K.* **12 E6** 56 30N 2 48W
Monkey Bay, *Malawi* .... **55 E4** 14 7S 35 1 E
Monkey Mia, *Australia* .... **61 E1** 25 48S 113 43 E
Monkey River, *Belize* **87 D7** 16 22N 88 29W
Monkoto, *Dem. Rep. of the Congo* . **52 E4** 1 38S 20 35 E
Monkton, *Canada* **78 C3** 43 35N 81 5W
Monmouth, *U.K.* **11 F5** 51 48N 2 42W
Monmouth, *Ill., U.S.A.* **80 E9** 40 55N 90 39W
Monmouth, *Oreg., U.S.A.* . **82 D2** 44 51N 123 14W
Monmouthshire □, *U.K.* **11 F5** 51 48N 2 54W
Mono L., *U.S.A.* **84 H7** 38 1N 119 1W
Monolith, *U.S.A.* **85 K8** 35 7N 118 22W
Monólithos, *Greece* .... **23 C9** 36 7N 27 45 E
Monongahela, *U.S.A.* **78 F5** 40 12N 79 56W
Monópoli, *Italy* .... **20 D7** 40 57N 17 18 E
Monroe, *Ga., U.S.A.* **77 J4** 33 47N 83 43W
Monroe, *La., U.S.A.* **81 J8** 32 30N 92 7W
Monroe, *Mich., U.S.A.* **76 E4** 41 55N 83 24W
Monroe, *N.C., U.S.A.* **77 H5** 34 59N 80 33W
Monroe, *N.Y., U.S.A.* **79 E10** 41 20N 74 11W
Monroe, *Utah, U.S.A.* **83 G7** 38 38N 112 7W
Monroe, *Wash., U.S.A.* **84 C5** 47 51N 121 58W
Monroe, *Wis., U.S.A.* **80 D10** 42 36N 89 38W
Monroe City, *U.S.A.* **80 F9** 39 39N 91 44W
Monroeton, *U.S.A.* **79 E8** 41 43N 76 29W
Monroeville, *Ala., U.S.A.* .. **77 K2** 31 31N 87 20W
Monroeville, *Pa., U.S.A.* **78 F5** 40 26N 79 45W
Monrovia, *Liberia* **50 G3** 6 18N 10 47W
Mons, *Belgium* .... **15 D3** 50 27N 3 58 E
Monse, *Indonesia* .... **37 E6** 4 0S 123 10 E
Mont-de-Marsan, *France* .. **18 E3** 43 54N 0 31W
Mont-Joli, *Canada* **71 C6** 48 37N 68 10W
Mont-Laurier, *Canada* **70 C4** 46 35N 75 30W
Mont-Louis, *Canada* **71 C6** 49 15N 65 44W
Mont-St-Michel, Le = Le Mont-St-Michel, *France* . **18 B3** 48 40N 1 30W
Mont Tremblant, Parc Recr. du, *Canada* **70 C5** 46 30N 74 30W
Montagu, *S. Africa* .... **56 E3** 33 45S 20 8 E
Montagu I., *Antarctica* **5 B1** 58 25S 26 20W
Montague, *Canada* **71 C7** 46 10N 62 39W
Montague, I., *Mexico* **86 A2** 31 40N 114 56W
Montague Ra., *Australia* .... **61 E2** 27 15S 119 30 E
Montague Sd., *Australia* .. **60 B4** 14 28S 125 20 E
Montalbán, *Spain* **19 B5** 40 50N 0 45W
Montalvo, *U.S.A.* **85 L7** 34 15N 119 12W
Montana, *Bulgaria* .... **21 C10** 43 27N 23 16 E
Montaña, *Peru* **92 E4** 6 0S 73 0W
Montana □, *U.S.A.* **82 C9** 47 0N 110 0W
Montaña Clara, I., *Canary Is.* **22 E6** 29 17N 13 33W
Montargis, *France* .... **18 C5** 47 59N 2 43 E
Montauban, *France* .... **18 D4** 44 2N 1 21 E
Montauk, *U.S.A.* **79 E13** 41 3N 71 57W
Montauk Pt., *U.S.A.* **79 E13** 41 4N 71 52W
Montbéliard, *France* .... **18 C7** 47 31N 6 48 E
Montceau-les-Mines, *France* **18 C6** 46 40N 4 23 E
Montclair, *U.S.A.* **79 F10** 40 49N 74 13W
Monte Albán, *Mexico* **87 D5** 17 2N 96 45W
Monte Alegre, *Brazil* **93 D8** 2 0S 54 0W
Monte Azul, *Brazil* **93 G10** 15 9S 42 53W
Monte Bello Is., *Australia* .. **60 D2** 20 30S 115 45 E
Monte-Carlo, *Monaco* .... **18 E7** 43 46N 7 23 E
Monte Caseros, *Argentina* . **94 C4** 30 10S 57 50W
Monte Comán, *Argentina* .. **94 C2** 34 40S 67 53W
Monte Cristi, *Dom. Rep.* **89 C5** 19 52N 71 39W
Monte Lindo →, *Paraguay* **94 A4** 23 56S 57 12W
Monte Patria, *Chile* **94 C1** 30 42S 70 58W
Monte Quemado, *Argentina* **94 B3** 25 53S 62 41W
Monte Rio, *U.S.A.* **84 G4** 38 28N 123 0W
Monte Santu, C. di, *Italy* .. **20 D3** 40 5N 9 44 E
Monte Vista, *U.S.A.* **83 H10** 37 35N 106 9W
Monteagudo, *Argentina* **95 B5** 27 14S 54 8W
Montebello, *Canada* **70 C5** 45 40N 74 55W
Montecito, *U.S.A.* **85 L7** 34 26N 119 40W
Montecristo, *Italy* .... **20 C4** 42 20N 10 19 E
Montego Bay, *Jamaica* **88 C4** 18 30N 78 0W
Montélimar, *France* .... **18 D6** 44 33N 4 45 E
Montello, *U.S.A.* **80 D10** 43 48N 89 20W
Montemorelos, *Mexico* **87 B5** 25 11N 99 42W
Montenegro, *Brazil* **95 B5** 29 39S 51 29W
Montenegro □, *Yugoslavia* **21 C8** 42 40N 19 20 E
Montepuez, *Mozam.* .... **55 E4** 13 8S 38 59 E
Montepuez →, *Mozam.* .. **55 E5** 12 32S 40 27 E
Monterey, *U.S.A.* **84 J5** 36 37N 121 55W
Monterey B., *U.S.A.* **84 J5** 36 45N 122 0W
Montería, *Colombia* **92 B3** 8 46N 75 53W
Monteros, *Argentina* **94 B2** 27 11S 65 30W
Monterrey, *Mexico* **86 B4** 25 40N 100 30W
Montes Claros, *Brazil* **93 G10** 16 30S 43 50W
Montesano, *U.S.A.* **84 D3** 46 59N 123 36W
Montesilvano, *Italy* .... **20 C6** 42 29N 14 8 E
Montevideo, *Uruguay* **95 C4** 34 50S 56 11W
Montevideo, *U.S.A.* **80 C7** 44 57N 95 43W
Montezuma, *U.S.A.* **80 E8** 41 35N 92 32W
Montgomery = Sahiwal, *Pakistan* .... **42 D5** 30 45N 73 8 E
Montgomery, *U.K.* **11 E4** 52 34N 3 8W
Montgomery, *Ala., U.S.A.* . **77 J2** 32 23N 86 19W
Montgomery, *Pa., U.S.A.* .. **78 E8** 41 10N 76 53W
Montgomery, *W. Va., U.S.A.* **76 F5** 38 11N 81 19W
Montgomery City, *U.S.A.* .. **80 F9** 38 59N 91 30W
Monticello, *Ark., U.S.A.* **81 J9** 33 38N 91 47W
Monticello, *Fla., U.S.A.* **77 K4** 30 33N 83 52W
Monticello, *Ind., U.S.A.* **76 E2** 40 45N 86 46W
Monticello, *Iowa, U.S.A.* **80 D9** 42 15N 91 12W
Monticello, *Ky., U.S.A.* **77 G3** 36 50N 84 51W
Monticello, *Minn., U.S.A.* .. **80 C8** 45 18N 93 48W
Monticello, *Miss., U.S.A.* .. **81 K9** 31 33N 90 7W
Monticello, *N.Y., U.S.A.* **79 E10** 41 39N 74 42W
Monticello, *Utah, U.S.A.* **83 H9** 37 52N 109 21W
Montijo, *Portugal* **19 C1** 38 41N 8 54W
Montilla, *Spain* **19 D3** 37 36N 4 40W
Montluçon, *France* .... **18 C5** 46 22N 2 36 E
Montmagny, *Canada* **71 C5** 46 58N 70 34W
Montmartre, *Canada* **73 C8** 50 14N 103 27W
Montmorillon, *France* .... **18 C4** 46 26N 0 50 E
Monto, *Australia* .... **62 C5** 24 52S 151 6 E
Montoro, *Spain* **19 C3** 38 1N 4 27W
Montour Falls, *U.S.A.* **78 D8** 42 21N 76 51W

Nanching

Mulhouse, *France* **18 C7** 47 40N 7 20 E
Muling, *China* **35 B16** 44 35N 130 10 E
Mull, *U.K.* **12 E3** 56 25N 5 56W
Mull, Sound of, *U.K.* **12 E3** 56 30N 5 50W
Mullaittivu, *Sri Lanka* **40 Q12** 9 15N 80 49 E
Mullen, *U.S.A.* **80 D4** 42 3N 101 1W
Mullens, *U.S.A.* **76 G5** 37 35N 81 23W
Muller, Pegunungan, *Indonesia* **36 D4** 0 30N 113 30 E
Mullet Pen., *Ireland* **13 B1** 54 13N 10 2W
Mullewa, *Australia* **61 E2** 28 29S 115 30 E
Mulligan →, *Australia* **62 D2** 25 0S 139 0 E
Mullingar, *Ireland* **13 C4** 53 31N 7 21W
Mullins, *U.S.A.* **77 H6** 34 12N 79 15W
Mullumbimby, *Australia* **63 D5** 28 30S 153 30 E
Mulobezi, *Zambia* **55 F2** 16 45S 25 7 E
Mulroy B., *Ireland* **13 A4** 55 15N 7 46W
Multan, *Pakistan* **42 D4** 30 15N 71 36 E
Mulumbe, Mts., *Dem. Rep. of the Congo* **55 D2** 8 40S 27 30 E
Mulungushi Dam, *Zambia* **55 E2** 14 48S 28 48 E
Mulvane, *U.S.A.* **81 G6** 37 29N 97 15W
Mumbai, *India* **40 K8** 18 55N 72 50 E
Mumbwa, *Zambia* **55 F2** 15 0S 27 0 E
Mun →, *Thailand* **38 E5** 15 19N 105 30 E
Muna, *Indonesia* **37 F6** 5 0S 122 30 E
Munabao, *India* **42 G4** 25 45N 70 17 E
Munamagi, *Estonia* **9 H22** 57 43N 27 4 E
München, *Germany* **16 D6** 48 8N 11 34 E
Munchen-Gladbach = Mönchengladbach, *Germany* **16 C4** 51 11N 6 27 E
Muncho Lake, *Canada* **72 B3** 59 0N 125 50W
Munch'ŏn, *N. Korea* **35 E14** 39 14N 127 19 E
Muncie, *U.S.A.* **76 E3** 40 12N 85 23W
Muncoonie, L., *Australia* **62 D2** 25 12S 138 40 E
Mundabbera, *Australia* **63 D5** 25 36S 151 18 E
Munday, *U.S.A.* **81 J5** 33 27N 99 38W
Münden, *Germany* **16 C5** 51 25N 9 38 E
Mundiwindi, *Australia* **60 D3** 23 47S 120 9 E
Mundo Novo, *Brazil* **93 F10** 11 50S 40 29W
Mundra, *India* **42 H3** 22 54N 69 48 E
Mundrabilla, *Australia* **61 F4** 31 52S 127 51 E
Mungallala, *Australia* **63 D4** 26 28S 147 34 E
Mungallala Cr. →, *Australia* **63 D4** 28 53S 147 5 E
Mungana, *Australia* **62 B3** 17 8S 144 27 E
Mungaoli, *India* **42 G8** 24 24N 78 7 E
Mungari, *Mozam.* **55 F3** 17 12S 33 30 E
Mungbere, *Dem. Rep. of the Congo* **54 B2** 2 36N 28 28 E
Mungeli, *India* **43 H9** 22 4N 81 41 E
Munger, *India* **43 G12** 25 23N 86 30 E
Munich = München, *Germany* **16 D6** 48 8N 11 34 E
Munising, *U.S.A.* **76 B2** 46 25N 86 40W
Munku-Sardyk, *Russia* **27 D11** 51 45N 100 20 E
Muñoz Gamero, Pen., *Chile* **96 G2** 52 30S 73 5W
Munroe L., *Canada* **73 B9** 59 13N 98 35W
Munsan, *S. Korea* **35 F14** 37 51N 126 48 E
Münster, *Germany* **16 C4** 51 58N 7 37 E
Munster □, *Ireland* **13 D3** 52 18N 8 44W
Muntadgin, *Australia* **61 F2** 31 45S 118 33 E
Muntok, *Indonesia* **36 E3** 2 5S 105 10 E
Munyama, *Zambia* **55 F2** 16 5S 28 31 E
Muong Et, *Laos* **38 B5** 20 49N 104 1 E
Muong Hiem, *Laos* **38 B4** 20 5N 103 22 E
Muong Kau, *Laos* **38 E5** 15 6N 105 47 E
Muong Khao, *Laos* **38 C4** 19 38N 103 32 E
Muong Liep, *Laos* **38 C3** 18 29N 101 40 E
Muong May, *Laos* **38 E6** 14 49N 106 56 E
Muong Nong, *Laos* **38 D6** 16 22N 106 30 E
Muong Oua, *Laos* **38 C3** 18 18N 101 20 E
Muong Phalane, *Laos* **38 D5** 16 39N 105 34 E
Muong Phieng, *Laos* **38 C3** 19 6N 101 32 E
Muong Phine, *Laos* **38 D6** 16 32N 106 2 E
Muong Saiapoun, *Laos* **38 C3** 18 24N 101 31 E
Muong Sen, *Vietnam* **38 C5** 19 24N 104 8 E
Muong Soui, *Laos* **38 C4** 19 33N 102 52 E
Muong Xia, *Vietnam* **38 B5** 20 19N 104 50 E
Muonio, *Finland* **8 C20** 67 57N 23 40 E
Muonionjoki →, *Finland* **8 C20** 67 11N 23 34 E
Muping, *China* **35 F11** 37 22N 121 36 E
Muqdisho, *Somali Rep.* **46 G4** 2 2N 45 25 E
Mur →, *Austria* **17 E9** 46 18N 16 52 E
Murakami, *Japan* **30 E9** 38 14N 139 29 E
Murallón, Cerro, *Chile* **96 F2** 49 48S 73 30W
Muranda, *Rwanda* **54 C2** 1 52S 29 20 E
Murang'a, *Kenya* **54 C4** 0 45S 37 9 E
Murashi, *Russia* **24 C8** 59 30N 49 0 E
Murat →, *Turkey* **25 G7** 38 46N 40 0 E
Muratlı, *Turkey* **21 D12** 41 10N 27 29 E
Murayama, *Japan* **30 E10** 38 30N 140 25 E
Murban, *U.A.E.* **45 F7** 23 50N 53 45 E
Murchison →, *Australia* **61 E1** 27 45S 114 0 E
Murchison, Mt., *Antarctica* **5 D11** 73 0S 168 0 E
Murchison Falls, *Uganda* **54 B3** 2 15N 31 30 E
Murchison Ra., *Australia* **62 C1** 20 0S 134 10 E
Murchison Rapids, *Malawi* **55 F3** 15 55S 34 35 E
Murcia, *Spain* **19 D5** 38 5N 1 10W
Murcia □, *Spain* **19 D5** 37 50N 1 30W
Murdo, *U.S.A.* **80 D4** 43 53N 100 43W
Murdoch Pt., *Australia* **62 A3** 14 37S 144 55 E
Mureş →, *Romania* **17 E11** 46 15N 20 13 E
Mureşul = Mureş →, *Romania* **17 E11** 46 15N 20 13 E
Murfreesboro, *N.C., U.S.A.* **77 G7** 36 27N 77 6W
Murfreesboro, *Tenn., U.S.A.* **77 H2** 35 51N 86 24W
Murgab = Murghob, *Tajikistan* **26 F8** 38 10N 74 2 E
Murgab →, *Turkmenistan* **45 B9** 38 18N 61 12 E
Murgenella, *Australia* **60 B5** 11 34S 132 56 E
Murgha Kibzai, *Pakistan* **42 D3** 30 44N 69 25 E
Murghob, *Tajikistan* **26 F8** 38 10N 74 2 E
Murgon, *Australia* **63 D5** 26 15S 151 54 E
Muri, *India* **43 H11** 23 22N 85 52 E
Muria, *Indonesia* **37 G14** 6 36S 110 53 E
Muriaé, *Brazil* **95 A7** 21 8S 42 23W
Muriel Mine, *Zimbabwe* **55 F3** 17 14S 30 40 E
Müritz, *Germany* **16 B7** 53 25N 12 42 E
Murka, *Kenya* **54 C4** 3 27S 38 0 E
Murliganj, *India* **43 G12** 25 54N 86 59 E
Murmansk, *Russia* **24 A5** 68 57N 33 10 E
Muro, *Spain* **22 B10** 39 44N 3 3 E
Murom, *Russia* **24 C7** 55 35N 42 3 E
Muroran, *Japan* **30 C10** 42 25N 141 0 E
Muroto, *Japan* **31 H7** 33 18N 134 9 E
Muroto-Misaki, *Japan* **31 H7** 33 15N 134 10 E
Murphy, *U.S.A.* **82 E5** 43 13N 116 33W
Murphys, *U.S.A.* **84 G6** 38 8N 120 28W
Murray, *Ky., U.S.A.* **77 G1** 36 37N 88 19W
Murray, *Utah, U.S.A.* **82 F8** 40 40N 111 53W
Murray →, *Australia* **63 F2** 35 20S 139 22 E
Murray, L., *U.S.A.* **77 H5** 34 3N 81 13W
Murray Bridge, *Australia* **63 F2** 35 6S 139 14 E
Murray Harbour, *Canada* **71 C7** 46 0N 62 28W
Murraysburg, *S. Africa* **56 E3** 31 58S 23 47 E
Murree, *Pakistan* **42 C5** 33 56N 73 28 E
Murrieta, *U.S.A.* **85 M9** 33 33N 117 13W
Murrumbidgee →, *Australia* **63 E3** 34 43S 143 12 E
Murrumburrah, *Australia* **63 E4** 34 32S 148 22 E
Murrurundi, *Australia* **63 E5** 31 42S 150 51 E
Murshidabad, *India* **43 G13** 24 11N 88 19 E
Murtle L., *Canada* **72 C5** 52 8N 119 38W
Murtoa, *Australia* **63 F3** 36 35S 142 28 E
Murungu, *Tanzania* **54 C3** 4 12S 31 10 E
Mururoa, *Pac. Oc.* **65 K14** 21 52S 138 55W
Murwara, *India* **43 H9** 23 46N 80 28 E
Murwillumbah, *Australia* **63 D5** 28 18S 153 27 E
Mürzzuschlag, *Austria* **16 E8** 47 36N 15 41 E
Muş, *Turkey* **25 G7** 38 45N 41 30 E
Mûsa, Gebel, *Egypt* **44 D2** 28 33N 33 59 E
Musa Khel, *Pakistan* **42 D3** 30 59N 69 52 E
Mūsá Qal'eh, *Afghan.* **40 C4** 32 20N 64 50 E
Musaffargarh, *Pakistan* **40 D7** 30 10N 71 10 E
Musafirkhana, *India* **43 F9** 26 22N 81 48 E
Musala, *Bulgaria* **21 C10** 42 13N 23 37 E
Musala, *Indonesia* **36 D1** 1 41N 98 28 E
Musan, *N. Korea* **35 C15** 42 12N 129 12 E
Musangu, *Dem. Rep. of the Congo* **55 E1** 10 28S 23 55 E
Musasa, *Tanzania* **54 C3** 3 25S 31 30 E
Musay'īd, *Qatar* **45 E6** 25 0N 51 33 E
Muscat = Masqat, *Oman* **46 C6** 23 37N 58 36 E
Muscat & Oman = Oman ■, *Asia* **46 C6** 23 0N 58 0 E
Muscatine, *U.S.A.* **80 E9** 41 25N 91 3W
Musgrave Harbour, *Canada* **71 C9** 49 27N 53 58W
Musgrave Ranges, *Australia* **61 E5** 26 0S 132 0 E
Mushie, *Dem. Rep. of the Congo* **52 E3** 2 56S 16 55 E
Musi →, *Indonesia* **36 E2** 2 20S 104 56 E
Muskeg →, *Canada* **72 A4** 60 20N 123 20W
Muskegon, *U.S.A.* **76 D2** 43 14N 86 16W
Muskegon →, *U.S.A.* **76 D2** 43 14N 86 21W
Muskegon Heights, *U.S.A.* **76 D2** 43 12N 86 16W
Muskogee, *U.S.A.* **81 H7** 35 45N 95 22W
Muskoka, L., *Canada* **78 B5** 45 0N 79 25W
Muskwa →, *Canada* **72 B4** 58 47N 122 48W
Muslīmiyah, *Syria* **44 B3** 36 19N 37 12 E
Musofu, *Zambia* **55 E2** 13 30S 29 0 E
Musoma, *Tanzania* **54 C3** 1 30S 33 48 E
Musquaro, L., *Canada* **71 B7** 50 38N 61 5W
Musquodoboit Harbour, *Canada* **71 D7** 44 50N 63 9W
Musselburgh, *U.K.* **12 F5** 55 57N 3 2W
Musselshell →, *U.S.A.* **82 C10** 47 21N 107 57W
Mussoorie, *India* **42 D8** 30 27N 78 6 E
Mussuco, *Angola* **56 B2** 17 2S 19 3 E
Mustafakemalpaşa, *Turkey* **21 D13** 40 2N 28 24 E
Mustang, *Nepal* **43 E10** 29 10N 83 55 E
Musters, L., *Argentina* **96 F3** 45 20S 69 25W
Musudan, *N. Korea* **35 D15** 40 50N 129 43 E
Muswellbrook, *Australia* **63 E5** 32 16S 150 56 E
Mût, *Egypt* **51 C11** 25 28N 28 58 E
Mut, *Turkey* **44 B2** 36 40N 33 28 E
Mutanda, *Mozam.* **57 C5** 21 0S 33 34 E
Mutanda, *Zambia* **55 E2** 12 24S 26 13 E
Mutare, *Zimbabwe* **55 F3** 18 58S 32 38 E
Muting, *Indonesia* **37 F10** 7 23S 140 20 E
Mutoray, *Russia* **27 C11** 60 56N 101 0 E
Mutshatsha, *Dem. Rep. of the Congo* **55 E1** 10 35S 24 20 E
Mutsu, *Japan* **30 D10** 41 5N 140 55 E
Mutsu-Wan, *Japan* **30 D10** 41 5N 140 55 E
Muttaburra, *Australia* **62 C3** 22 38S 144 29 E
Mutton I., *Ireland* **13 D2** 52 49N 9 32W
Mutuáli, *Mozam.* **55 E4** 14 55S 37 0 E
Muweilih, *Egypt* **47 E3** 30 42N 34 19 E
Muy Muy, *Nic.* **88 D2** 12 39N 85 36W
Muyinga, *Burundi* **54 C3** 3 14S 30 33 E
Muynak, *Uzbekistan* **26 E6** 43 44N 59 10 E
Muzaffarabad, *Pakistan* **43 B5** 34 25N 73 30 E
Muzaffargarh, *Pakistan* **42 D4** 30 5N 71 14 E
Muzaffarnagar, *India* **42 E7** 29 26N 77 40 E
Muzaffarpur, *India* **43 F11** 26 7N 85 23 E
Muzafirpur, *Pakistan* **42 D3** 30 58N 69 9 E
Muzhi, *Russia* **24 A11** 65 25N 64 40 E
Mvuma, *Zimbabwe* **55 F3** 19 16S 30 30 E
Mvurwi, *Zimbabwe* **55 F3** 17 0S 30 57 E
Mwadui, *Tanzania* **54 C3** 3 26S 33 32 E
Mwambo, *Tanzania* **55 E5** 10 30S 40 22 E
Mwandi, *Zambia* **55 F1** 17 30S 24 51 E
Mwanza, *Dem. Rep. of the Congo* **54 D2** 7 55S 26 43 E
Mwanza, *Tanzania* **54 C3** 2 30S 32 58 E
Mwanza, *Zambia* **55 F1** 16 58S 24 28 E
Mwanza □, *Tanzania* **54 C3** 2 0S 33 0 E
Mwaya, *Tanzania* **55 D3** 9 32S 33 55 E
Mweelrea, *Ireland* **13 C2** 53 39N 9 49W
Mweka, *Dem. Rep. of the Congo* **52 E4** 4 50S 21 34 E
Mwene-Ditu, *Dem. Rep. of the Congo* **52 F4** 6 35S 22 27 E
Mwenezi, *Zimbabwe* **55 G3** 21 15S 30 48 E
Mwenezi →, *Mozam.* **55 G3** 22 40S 31 50 E
Mwenga, *Dem. Rep. of the Congo* **54 C2** 3 1S 28 28 E
Mweru, L., *Zambia* **55 D2** 9 0S 28 40 E
Mweza Range, *Zimbabwe* **55 G3** 21 0S 30 0 E
Mwilambwe, *Dem. Rep. of the Congo* **54 D2** 8 7S 25 5 E
Mwimbi, *Tanzania* **55 D3** 8 38S 31 39 E
Mwinilunga, *Zambia* **55 E1** 11 43S 24 25 E
My Tho, *Vietnam* **39 G6** 10 29N 106 23 E
Myajlar, *India* **42 F4** 26 15N 70 20 E
Myanaung, *Burma* **41 K19** 18 18N 95 22 E
Myanmar = Burma ■, *Asia* **41 J20** 21 0N 96 30 E
Myaungmya, *Burma* **41 L19** 16 30N 94 40 E
Mycenæ, *Greece* **21 F10** 37 39N 22 52 E
Myeik Kyunzu, *Burma* **39 G1** 11 30N 97 30 E
Myers Chuck, *U.S.A.* **72 B2** 55 44N 132 11W
Myerstown, *U.S.A.* **79 F8** 40 22N 76 19W
Myingyan, *Burma* **41 J19** 21 30N 95 20 E
Myitkyina, *Burma* **41 G20** 25 24N 97 26 E
Mykines, *Færoe Is.* **8 E9** 62 7N 7 35W
Mykolayiv, *Ukraine* **25 E5** 46 58N 32 0 E
Mymensingh, *Bangla.* **41 G17** 24 45N 90 24 E
Mynydd Du, *U.K.* **11 F4** 51 52N 3 50W
Mýrdalsjökull, *Iceland* **8 E4** 63 40N 19 6W
Myrtle Beach, *U.S.A.* **77 J6** 33 42N 78 53W
Myrtle Creek, *U.S.A.* **82 E2** 43 1N 123 17W
Myrtle Point, *U.S.A.* **82 E1** 43 4N 124 8W
Myrtou, *Cyprus* **23 D12** 35 18N 33 4 E
Mysia, *Turkey* **21 E12** 39 50N 27 0 E
Mysore = Karnataka □, *India* **40 N10** 13 15N 77 0 E
Mysore, *India* **40 N10** 12 17N 76 41 E
Mystic, *U.S.A.* **79 E13** 41 21N 71 58W
Myszków, *Poland* **17 C10** 50 45N 19 22 E
Mytishchi, *Russia* **24 C6** 55 50N 37 50 E
Mývatn, *Iceland* **8 D5** 65 36N 17 0W
Mzimba, *Malawi* **55 E3** 11 55S 33 39 E
Mzimkulu →, *S. Africa* **57 E5** 30 44S 30 28 E
Mzimvubu →, *S. Africa* **57 E4** 31 38S 29 33 E
Mzuzu, *Malawi* **55 E3** 11 30S 33 55 E

N

Na Hearadh = Harris, *U.K.* **12 D2** 57 50N 6 55W
Na Noi, *Thailand* **38 C3** 18 19N 100 43 E
Na Phao, *Laos* **38 D5** 17 35N 105 44 E
Na San, *Vietnam* **38 B5** 21 12N 104 2 E
Naab →, *Germany* **16 D6** 49 1N 12 2 E
Naantali, *Finland* **9 F19** 60 29N 22 2 E
Naas, *Ireland* **13 C5** 53 12N 6 40W
Nababiep, *S. Africa* **56 D2** 29 36S 17 46 E
Nabadwip = Navadwip, *India* **43 H13** 23 34N 88 20 E
Nabari, *Japan* **31 G8** 34 37N 136 5 E
Nabawa, *Australia* **61 E1** 28 30S 114 48 E
Nabberu, L., *Australia* **61 E3** 25 50S 120 30 E
Naberezhnyye Chelny, *Russia* **24 C9** 55 42N 52 19 E
Nabeul, *Tunisia* **51 A8** 36 30N 10 44 E
Nabha, *India* **42 D7** 30 26N 76 14 E
Nabīd, *Iran* **45 D8** 29 40N 57 38 E
Nabire, *Indonesia* **37 E9** 3 15S 135 26 E
Nabisar, *Pakistan* **42 G3** 25 8N 69 40 E
Nabisipi →, *Canada* **71 B7** 50 14N 62 13W
Nabiswera, *Uganda* **54 B3** 1 27N 32 15 E
Nablus = Nābulus, *West Bank* **47 C4** 32 14N 35 15 E
Naboomspruit, *S. Africa* **57 C4** 24 32S 28 40 E
Nābulus, *West Bank* **47 C4** 32 14N 35 15 E
Nacala, *Mozam.* **55 E5** 14 31S 40 34 E
Nacala-Velha, *Mozam.* **55 E5** 14 32S 40 34 E
Nacaome, *Honduras* **88 D2** 13 31N 87 30W
Nacaroa, *Mozam.* **55 E4** 14 22S 39 56 E
Naches, *U.S.A.* **82 C3** 46 44N 120 42W
Naches →, *U.S.A.* **84 D6** 46 38N 120 31W
Nachicapau, L., *Canada* **71 A6** 56 40N 68 5W
Nachingwea, *Tanzania* **55 E4** 10 23S 38 49 E
Nachna, *India* **42 F4** 27 34N 71 41 E
Nacimiento L., *U.S.A.* **84 K6** 35 46N 120 53W
Naco, *Mexico* **86 A3** 31 20N 109 56W
Nacogdoches, *U.S.A.* **81 K7** 31 36N 94 39W
Nácori Chico, *Mexico* **86 B3** 29 39N 109 1W
Nacozari, *Mexico* **86 A3** 30 24N 109 39W
Nadiad, *India* **42 H5** 22 41N 72 56 E
Nador, *Morocco* **50 B5** 35 14N 2 58W
Nadur, *Malta* **23 C1** 36 2N 14 17 E
Nadūshan, *Iran* **45 C7** 32 2N 53 35 E
Nadvirna, *Ukraine* **17 D13** 48 37N 24 30 E
Nadvoitsy, *Russia* **24 B5** 63 52N 34 14 E
Nadvornaya = Nadvirna, *Ukraine* **17 D13** 48 37N 24 30 E
Nadym, *Russia* **26 C8** 65 35N 72 42 E
Nadym →, *Russia* **26 C8** 66 12N 72 0 E
Nærbø, *Norway* **9 G11** 58 40N 5 39 E
Næstved, *Denmark* **9 J14** 55 13N 11 44 E
Naft-e Safīd, *Iran* **45 D6** 31 40N 49 17 E
Naftshahr, *Iran* **44 C5** 34 0N 45 30 E
Nafud Desert = An Nafūd, *Si. Arabia* **44 D4** 28 15N 41 0 E
Naga, *Phil.* **37 B6** 13 38N 123 15 E
Nagahama, *Japan* **31 G8** 35 23N 136 16 E
Nagai, *Japan* **30 E10** 38 6N 140 2 E
Nagaland □, *India* **41 G19** 26 0N 94 30 E
Nagano, *Japan* **31 F9** 36 40N 138 10 E
Nagano □, *Japan* **31 F9** 36 15N 138 0 E
Nagaoka, *Japan* **31 F9** 37 27N 138 51 E
Nagappattinam, *India* **40 P11** 10 46N 79 51 E
Nagar →, *Bangla.* **43 G13** 24 27N 89 12 E
Nagar Parkar, *Pakistan* **42 G4** 24 28N 70 46 E
Nagasaki, *Japan* **31 H4** 32 47N 129 50 E
Nagasaki □, *Japan* **31 H4** 32 50N 129 40 E
Nagato, *Japan* **31 G5** 34 19N 131 5 E
Nagaur, *India* **42 F5** 27 15N 73 45 E
Nagda, *India* **42 H6** 23 27N 75 25 E
Nagercoil, *India* **40 Q10** 8 12N 77 26 E
Nagina, *India* **43 E8** 29 30N 78 30 E
Nagīneh, *Iran* **45 C8** 34 20N 57 15 E
Nagir, *Pakistan* **43 A6** 36 12N 74 42 E
Nagod, *India* **43 G9** 24 34N 80 36 E
Nagoorin, *Australia* **62 C5** 24 17S 151 15 E
Nagorno-Karabakh, *Azerbaijan* **25 F8** 39 55N 46 45 E
Nagornyy, *Russia* **27 D13** 55 58N 124 57 E
Nagoya, *Japan* **31 G8** 35 10N 136 50 E
Nagpur, *India* **40 J11** 21 8N 79 10 E
Nagua, *Dom. Rep.* **89 C6** 19 23N 69 50W
Nagykanizsa, *Hungary* **17 E9** 46 28N 17 0 E
Nagykőrös, *Hungary* **17 E10** 47 5N 19 48 E
Naha, *Japan* **31 L3** 26 13N 127 42 E
Nahan, *India* **42 D7** 30 33N 77 18 E
Nahanni Butte, *Canada* **72 A4** 61 2N 123 31W
Nahanni Nat. Park, *Canada* **72 A4** 61 15N 125 0W
Nahargarh, *Mad. P., India* **42 G6** 24 10N 75 14 E
Nahargarh, *Raj., India* **42 G7** 24 55N 76 50 E
Nahariyya, *Israel* **44 C2** 33 1N 35 5 E
Nahāvand, *Iran* **45 C6** 34 10N 48 22 E
Naicá, *Mexico* **86 B3** 27 53N 105 31W
Naicam, *Canada* **73 C8** 52 30N 104 30W
Naikoon Prov. Park, *Canada* **72 C2** 53 55N 131 55W
Naimisharanya, *India* **43 F9** 27 21N 80 30 E
Nain, *Canada* **71 A7** 56 34N 61 40W
Nā'īn, *Iran* **45 C7** 32 54N 53 0 E
Naini Tal, *India* **43 E8** 29 30N 79 30 E
Nainpur, *India* **40 H12** 22 30N 80 10 E
Nainwa, *India* **42 G6** 25 46N 75 51 E
Nairn, *U.K.* **12 D5** 57 35N 3 53W
Nairobi, *Kenya* **54 C4** 1 17S 36 48 E
Naissaar, *Estonia* **9 G21** 59 34N 24 29 E
Naivasha, *Kenya* **54 C4** 0 40S 36 30 E
Naivasha, L., *Kenya* **54 C4** 0 48S 36 20 E
Najafābād, *Iran* **45 C6** 32 40N 51 15 E
Najd, *Si. Arabia* **46 B3** 26 30N 42 0 E
Najibabad, *India* **42 E8** 29 40N 78 20 E
Najin, *N. Korea* **35 C16** 42 12N 130 15 E
Najmah, *Si. Arabia* **45 E6** 26 42N 50 6 E
Naju, *S. Korea* **35 G14** 35 3N 126 43 E
Nakadōri-Shima, *Japan* **31 H4** 32 57N 129 4 E
Nakalagba, *Dem. Rep. of the Congo* **54 B2** 2 50N 27 58 E
Nakaminato, *Japan* **31 F10** 36 21N 140 36 E
Nakamura, *Japan* **31 H6** 32 59N 132 56 E
Nakano, *Japan* **31 F9** 36 45N 138 22 E
Nakano-Shima, *Japan* **31 K4** 29 51N 129 52 E
Nakashibetsu, *Japan* **30 C12** 43 33N 144 59 E
Nakfa, *Eritrea* **46 D2** 16 40N 38 32 E
Nakhfar al Buşayyah, *Iraq* **44 D5** 30 0N 46 10 E
Nakhichevan = Naxçıvan, *Azerbaijan* **25 G8** 39 12N 45 15 E
Nakhichevan Republic = Naxçıvan □, *Azerbaijan* **25 G8** 39 25N 45 26 E
Nakhl, *Egypt* **47 F2** 29 55N 33 43 E
Nakhl-e Taqī, *Iran* **45 E7** 27 28N 52 36 E
Nakhodka, *Russia* **27 E14** 42 53N 132 54 E
Nakhon Nayok, *Thailand* **38 E3** 14 12N 101 13 E
Nakhon Pathom, *Thailand* **38 F3** 13 49N 100 3 E
Nakhon Phanom, *Thailand* **38 D5** 17 23N 104 43 E
Nakhon Ratchasima, *Thailand* **38 E4** 14 59N 102 12 E
Nakhon Sawan, *Thailand* **38 E3** 15 35N 100 10 E
Nakhon Si Thammarat, *Thailand* **39 H3** 8 29N 100 0 E
Nakhon Thai, *Thailand* **38 D3** 17 5N 100 44 E
Nakhtarana, *India* **42 H3** 23 20N 69 15 E
Nakina, *Canada* **70 B2** 50 10N 86 40W
Nakodar, *India* **42 D6** 31 8N 75 31 E
Nakskov, *Denmark* **9 J14** 54 50N 11 8 E
Naktong →, *S. Korea* **35 G15** 35 7N 128 57 E
Nakuru, *Kenya* **54 C4** 0 15S 36 4 E
Nakuru, L., *Kenya* **54 C4** 0 23S 36 5 E
Nakusp, *Canada* **72 C5** 50 20N 117 45W
Nal, *Pakistan* **42 F2** 27 40N 66 12 E
Nal →, *Pakistan* **42 G1** 25 20N 65 30 E
Nalchik, *Russia* **25 F7** 43 30N 43 33 E
Nalgonda, *India* **40 L11** 17 6N 79 15 E
Nalhati, *India* **43 G12** 24 17N 87 52 E
Naliya, *India* **42 H3** 23 16N 68 50 E
Nallamalai Hills, *India* **40 M11** 15 30N 78 50 E
Nam Can, *Vietnam* **39 H5** 8 46N 104 59 E
Nam-ch'on, *N. Korea* **35 E14** 38 15N 126 26 E
Nam Co, *China* **32 C4** 30 30N 90 45 E
Nam Du, Hon, *Vietnam* **39 H5** 9 41N 104 21 E
Nam Ngum Dam, *Laos* **38 C4** 18 35N 102 34 E
Nam-Phan = Cochin China, *Vietnam* **39 G6** 10 30N 106 0 E
Nam Phong, *Thailand* **38 D4** 16 42N 102 52 E
Nam Tok, *Thailand* **38 E2** 14 21N 99 4 E
Namacunde, *Angola* **56 B2** 17 18S 15 50 E
Namacurra, *Mozam.* **57 B6** 17 30S 36 50 E
Namak, Daryācheh-ye, *Iran* **45 C7** 34 30N 52 0 E
Namak, Kavir-e, *Iran* **45 C8** 34 30N 57 30 E
Namakzār, Daryācheh-ye, *Iran* **45 C9** 34 0N 60 30 E
Namaland, *Namibia* **56 C2** 26 0S 17 0 E
Namangan, *Uzbekistan* **26 E8** 41 0N 71 40 E
Namapa, *Mozam.* **55 E4** 13 43S 39 50 E
Namaqualand, *S. Africa* **56 E2** 30 0S 17 25 E
Namasagali, *Uganda* **54 B3** 1 2N 33 0 E
Namber, *Indonesia* **37 E8** 1 2S 134 49 E
Nambour, *Australia* **63 D5** 26 32S 152 58 E
Nambucca Heads, *Australia* **63 E5** 30 37S 153 0 E
Namcha Barwa, *China* **32 D4** 29 40N 95 10 E
Namche Bazar, *Nepal* **43 F12** 27 51N 86 47 E
Namchonjŏm = Nam-ch'on, *N. Korea* **35 E14** 38 15N 126 26 E
Namecunda, *Mozam.* **55 E4** 14 54S 37 37 E
Nameponda, *Mozam.* **55 F4** 15 50S 39 50 E
Nametil, *Mozam.* **55 F4** 15 40S 39 21 E
Namew L., *Canada* **73 C8** 54 14N 101 56W
Namgia, *India* **43 D8** 31 48N 78 40 E
Namib Desert = Namibwoestyn, *Namibia* **56 C2** 22 30S 15 0 E
Namibe, *Angola* **53 H2** 15 7S 12 11 E
Namibe □, *Angola* **56 B1** 16 35S 12 30 E
Namibia ■, *Africa* **56 C2** 22 0S 18 9 E
Namibwoestyn, *Namibia* **56 C2** 22 30S 15 0 E
Namlea, *Indonesia* **37 E7** 3 18S 127 5 E
Namoi →, *Australia* **63 E4** 30 12S 149 30 E
Nampa, *U.S.A.* **82 E5** 43 34N 116 34W
Namp'o, *N. Korea* **35 E13** 38 52N 125 10 E
Nampō-Shotō, *Japan* **31 J10** 32 0N 140 0 E
Nampula, *Mozam.* **55 F4** 15 6S 39 15 E
Namrole, *Indonesia* **37 E7** 3 46S 126 46 E
Namse Shankou, *China* **41 E13** 30 0N 82 25 E
Namsen →, *Norway* **8 D14** 64 28N 11 37 E
Namsos, *Norway* **8 D14** 64 29N 11 30 E
Namtsy, *Russia* **27 C13** 62 43N 129 37 E
Namtu, *Burma* **41 H20** 23 5N 97 28 E
Namtumbo, *Tanzania* **55 E4** 10 30S 36 4 E
Namu, *Canada* **72 C3** 51 52N 127 50W
Namur, *Belgium* **15 D4** 50 27N 4 52 E
Namur □, *Belgium* **15 D4** 50 17N 5 0 E
Namutoni, *Namibia* **56 B2** 18 49S 16 55 E
Namwala, *Zambia* **55 F2** 15 44S 26 30 E
Namwŏn, *S. Korea* **35 G14** 35 23N 127 23 E
Nan, *Thailand* **38 C3** 18 48N 100 46 E
Nan →, *Thailand* **38 E3** 15 42N 100 9 E
Nan-ch'ang = Nanchang, *China* **33 D6** 28 42N 115 55 E
Nanaimo, *Canada* **72 D4** 49 10N 124 0W
Nanam, *N. Korea* **35 D15** 41 44N 129 40 E
Nanango, *Australia* **63 D5** 26 40S 152 0 E
Nanao, *Japan* **31 F8** 37 0N 137 0 E
Nanchang, *China* **33 D6** 28 42N 115 55 E
Nanching = Nanjing, *China* **33 C6** 32 2N 118 47 E

North Knife

lew Smyrna Beach, U.S.A. 77 L5 29 1N 80 56W
lew South Wales □, Australia 63 E4 33 0S 146 0 E
lew Town, U.S.A. 80 B3 47 59N 102 30W
lew Tredegar, U.K. 11 F4 51 44N 3 16W
lew Ulm, U.S.A. 80 C7 44 19N 94 28W
lew Waterford, Canada 71 C7 46 13N 60 4W
lew Westminster, Canada 84 A4 49 13N 122 55W
lew York, U.S.A. 79 F11 40 45N 74 0W
lew York □, U.S.A. 79 D9 43 0N 75 0W
lew York Mts., U.S.A. 83 J6 35 0N 115 20W
lew Zealand ■, Oceania 59 J6 40 0S 176 0 E
lewaj →, India 42 G7 24 24N 76 49 E
lewala, Tanzania 55 E4 10 58S 39 18 E
lewark, Del., U.S.A. 76 F8 39 41N 75 46W
lewark, N.J., U.S.A. 79 F10 40 44N 74 10W
lewark, N.Y., U.S.A. 78 C7 43 3N 77 6W
lewark, Ohio, U.S.A. 78 F2 40 3N 82 24W
lewark-on-Trent, U.K. 10 D7 53 5N 0 48W
lewark Valley, U.S.A. 79 D8 42 14N 76 11W
lewberg, U.S.A. 82 D2 45 18N 122 58W
lewberry, Mich., U.S.A. 76 B3 46 21N 85 30W
lewberry, S.C., U.S.A. 77 H5 34 17N 81 37W
lewberry Springs, U.S.A. 85 L10 34 50N 116 41W
lewboro L., Canada 79 B8 44 38N 76 20W
lewbridge = Droichead Nua, Ireland 13 C5 53 11N 6 48W
ewburgh, Canada 78 B8 44 19N 76 52W
ewburgh, U.S.A. 79 E10 41 30N 74 1W
ewbury, U.K. 11 F6 51 24N 1 20W
ewbury, N.H., U.S.A. 79 B12 43 19N 72 3W
ewbury, Vt., U.S.A. 79 B12 44 5N 72 4W
lewburyport, U.S.A. 77 D10 42 49N 70 53W
lewcastle, Australia 63 E5 33 0S 151 46 E
lewcastle, N.B., Canada 71 C6 47 1N 65 38W
lewcastle, Ont., Canada 70 D4 43 55N 78 35W
lewcastle, S. Africa 57 D4 27 45S 29 58 E
lewcastle, U.K. 13 B6 54 13N 5 54W
lewcastle, Calif., U.S.A. 84 G5 38 53N 121 8W
lewcastle, Wyo., U.S.A. 80 D2 43 50N 104 11W
lewcastle Emlyn, U.K. 11 E3 52 2N 4 28W
lewcastle Ra., Australia 60 C5 15 45S 130 15 E
lewcastle-under-Lyme, U.K. 10 D5 53 1N 2 14W
lewcastle-upon-Tyne, U.K. 10 C6 54 58N 1 36W
lewcastle Waters, Australia 62 B1 17 30S 133 28 E
lewcastle West, Ireland 13 D2 52 27N 9 3W
lewcomb, U.S.A. 79 C10 43 58N 74 10W
lewcomerstown, U.S.A. 78 F3 40 16N 81 36W
lewdegate, Australia 61 F2 33 6S 119 0 E
lewell, Australia 62 B4 16 20S 145 16 E
lewell, U.S.A. 80 C3 44 43N 103 25W
lewfane, U.S.A. 78 C6 43 17N 78 43W
lewfield, U.S.A. 79 D8 42 18N 76 33W
lewfound L., U.S.A. 79 C13 43 40N 71 47W
lewfoundland, N. Amer. 66 E14 49 0N 55 0W
lewfoundland, U.S.A. 79 E9 41 18N 75 19W
lewfoundland □, Canada 71 B8 53 0N 58 0W
lewhall, U.S.A. 85 L8 34 23N 118 32W
lewhaven, U.K. 11 G8 50 47N 0 3 E
lewkirk, U.S.A. 81 G6 36 53N 97 3W
lewlyn, U.K. 11 G2 50 6N 5 34W
lewman, Australia 60 D2 23 18S 119 45 E
lewman, U.S.A. 84 H5 37 19N 121 1W
lewmarket, Canada 78 B5 44 3N 79 28W
lewmarket, Ireland 13 D2 52 13N 9 0W
lewmarket, U.K. 11 E8 52 15N 0 25 E
lewmarket, N.H., U.S.A. 79 C14 43 4N 70 56W
lewmarket, N.H., U.S.A. 79 C14 43 5N 70 56W
lewnan, U.S.A. 77 J3 33 23N 84 48W
lewport, Ireland 13 C2 53 53N 9 33W
lewport, I. of W., U.K. 11 G6 50 42N 1 17W
lewport, Newp., U.K. 11 F5 51 35N 3 0W
lewport, Ark., U.S.A. 81 H9 35 37N 91 16W
lewport, Ky., U.S.A. 76 F3 39 5N 84 30W
lewport, N.H., U.S.A. 79 C12 43 22N 72 10W
lewport, N.Y., U.S.A. 79 C9 43 11N 75 1W
ewport, Oreg., U.S.A. 82 D1 44 39N 124 3W
ewport, Pa., U.S.A. 78 F7 40 29N 77 8W
ewport, R.I., U.S.A. 79 E13 41 29N 71 19W
ewport, Tenn., U.S.A. 77 H4 35 58N 83 11W
ewport, Vt., U.S.A. 79 B12 44 56N 72 13W
ewport, Wash., U.S.A. 82 B5 48 11N 117 3W
ewport □, U.K. 11 F4 51 33N 3 1W
ewport Beach, U.S.A. 85 M9 33 37N 117 56W
ewport News, U.S.A. 76 G7 36 59N 76 25W
ewport Pagnell, U.K. 11 E7 52 5N 0 43W
ewquay, U.K. 11 G2 50 25N 5 6W
ewry, U.K. 13 B5 54 11N 6 21W
ewton, Ill., U.S.A. 80 F10 38 59N 88 10W
ewton, Iowa, U.S.A. 80 E8 41 42N 93 3W
ewton, Kans., U.S.A. 81 F6 38 3N 97 21W
ewton, Mass., U.S.A. 79 D13 42 21N 71 12W
ewton, Miss., U.S.A. 81 J10 32 19N 89 10W
ewton, N.C., U.S.A. 77 H5 35 40N 81 13W
ewton, N.J., U.S.A. 79 E10 41 3N 74 45W
ewton, Tex., U.S.A. 81 K8 30 51N 93 46W
ewton Abbot, U.K. 11 G4 50 32N 3 37W
ewton Aycliffe, U.K. 10 C6 54 37N 1 34W
ewton Falls, U.S.A. 78 E4 41 11N 80 59W
ewton Stewart, U.K. 12 G4 54 57N 4 30W
ewtonmore, U.K. 12 D4 57 4N 4 8W
ewtown, U.K. 11 E4 52 31N 3 19W
ewtownabbey, U.K. 13 B6 54 40N 5 56W
ewtownards, U.K. 13 B6 54 36N 5 42W
ewtownbarry = Bunclody, Ireland 13 D5 52 39N 6 40W
ewtownstewart, U.K. 13 B4 54 43N 7 23W
ewville, U.S.A. 78 F7 40 10N 77 24W
eya, Russia 24 C7 58 21N 43 49 E
eyrīz, Iran 45 D7 29 15N 54 19 E
eyshābūr, Iran 45 B8 36 10N 58 50 E
ezhin = Nizhyn, Ukraine 25 D5 51 5N 31 55 E
ezperce, U.S.A. 82 C5 46 14N 116 14W
gabang, Indonesia 36 D3 0 23N 109 55 E
gabordamlu, Tanjung, Indonesia 37 F8 6 56S 134 11 E
'Gage, Angola 52 F3 7 46S 15 16 E
gami Depression, Botswana 56 C3 20 30S 22 46 E
gamo, Zimbabwe 55 F2 19 3S 27 32 E
ganglong Kangri, China 41 C12 33 0N 81 0 E
gao, Thailand 38 C2 18 46N 99 59 E
gaoundéré, Cameroon 52 C2 7 15N 13 35 E
gapara, N.Z. 59 L3 44 57S 170 46 E
gara, Tanzania 54 C3 2 29S 30 40 E
gawi, Indonesia 37 G14 7 24S 111 26 E
Ngoma, Malawi 55 E3 13 8S 33 45 E
Ngomahura, Zimbabwe 55 G3 20 26S 30 43 E
Ngomba, Tanzania 55 D3 8 20S 32 53 E
Ngoring Hu, China 32 C4 34 55N 97 5 E
Ngorongoro, Tanzania 54 C4 3 11S 35 32 E
Ngozi, Burundi 54 C2 2 54S 29 50 E
Ngudu, Tanzania 54 C3 2 58S 33 25 E
Nguigmi, Niger 51 F8 14 20N 13 20 E
Nguiu, Australia 60 B5 11 46S 130 38 E
Ngukurr, Australia 62 A1 14 44S 134 44 E
Ngulu Atoll, Pac. Oc. 37 C9 8 0N 137 30 E
Ngunga, Tanzania 54 C3 3 37S 33 37 E
Nguru, Nigeria 51 F8 12 56N 10 29 E
Nguru Mts., Tanzania 54 D4 6 0S 37 30 E
Nha Trang, Vietnam 39 F7 12 16N 109 10 E
Nhacoongo, Mozam. 57 C6 24 18S 35 14 E
Nhamaabué, Mozam. 55 F4 17 25S 35 5 E
Nhamundá →, Brazil 93 D7 2 12S 56 41W
Nhangutazi, L., Mozam. 57 C5 24 0S 34 30 E
Nhill, Australia 63 F3 36 18S 141 40 E
Nhulunbuy, Australia 62 A2 12 10S 137 20 E
Nia-nia, Dem. Rep. of the Congo 54 B2 1 30N 27 40 E
Niagara Falls, Canada 78 C5 43 7N 79 5W
Niagara Falls, U.S.A. 78 C6 43 5N 79 4W
Niagara-on-the-Lake, Canada 78 C5 43 15N 79 4W
Niah, Malaysia 36 D4 3 58N 113 46 E
Niamey, Niger 50 F6 13 27N 2 6 E
Niangara, Dem. Rep. of the Congo 54 B2 3 42N 27 50 E
Niantic, U.S.A. 79 E12 41 20N 72 11W
Nias, Indonesia 36 D1 1 0N 97 30 E
Niassa □, Mozam. 55 E4 13 30S 36 0 E
Nibāk, Si. Arabia 45 E7 24 25N 50 50 E
Nicaragua ■, Cent. Amer. 88 D2 11 40N 85 30W
Nicaragua, L. de, Nic. 88 D2 12 0N 85 30W
Nicastro, Italy 20 E7 38 59N 16 19 E
Nice, France 18 E7 43 42N 7 14 E
Niceville, U.S.A. 77 K2 30 31N 86 30W
Nichicun, L., Canada 71 B5 53 5N 71 0W
Nichinan, Japan 31 J5 31 38N 131 23 E
Nicholás, Canal, W. Indies 88 B3 23 30N 80 5W
Nicholasville, U.S.A. 76 G3 37 53N 84 34W
Nichols, U.S.A. 79 D8 42 1N 76 22W
Nicholson, Australia 60 C4 18 2S 128 54 E
Nicholson, U.S.A. 79 E9 41 37N 75 47W
Nicholson →, Australia 62 B2 17 31S 139 36 E
Nicholson L., Canada 73 A8 62 40N 102 40W
Nicholson Ra., Australia 61 E2 27 15S 116 45 E
Nicholville, U.S.A. 79 B10 44 41N 74 39W
Nicobar Is., Ind. Oc. 28 J13 9 0N 93 0 E
Nicola, Canada 72 C4 50 12N 120 40W
Nicolls Town, Bahamas 88 A4 25 8N 78 0W
Nicosia, Cyprus 23 D12 35 10N 33 25 E
Nicoya, Costa Rica 88 D2 10 9N 85 27W
Nicoya, G. de, Costa Rica 88 E3 10 0N 85 0W
Nicoya, Pen. de, Costa Rica 88 E2 9 45N 85 40W
Nidd →, U.K. 10 D6 53 59N 1 23W
Niedersachsen □, Germany 16 B5 52 50N 9 0 E
Niekerkshoop, S. Africa 56 D3 29 19S 22 51 E
Niemba, Dem. Rep. of the Congo 54 D2 5 58S 28 24 E
Niemen = Neman →, Lithuania 9 J20 55 25N 21 10 E
Nienburg, Germany 16 B5 52 39N 9 13 E
Nieu Bethesda, S. Africa 56 E3 31 51S 24 34 E
Nieuw Amsterdam, Surinam 93 B7 5 53N 55 5W
Nieuw Nickerie, Surinam 93 B7 6 0N 56 59W
Nieuwoudtville, S. Africa 56 E2 31 23S 19 7 E
Nieuwpoort, Belgium 15 C2 51 8N 2 45 E
Nieves, Pico de las, Canary Is. 22 G4 27 57N 15 35W
Niğde, Turkey 25 G5 37 58N 34 40 E
Nigel, S. Africa 57 D4 26 27S 28 25 E
Niger ■, W. Afr. 50 E7 17 30N 10 0 E
Niger →, W. Afr. 50 G7 5 33N 6 33 E
Nigeria ■, W. Afr. 50 G7 8 30N 8 0 E
Nighasin, India 43 E9 28 14N 80 52 E
Nightcaps, N.Z. 59 L2 45 57S 168 2 E
Nii-Jima, Japan 31 G9 34 20N 139 15 E
Niigata, Japan 30 F9 37 58N 139 0 E
Niigata □, Japan 31 F9 37 15N 138 45 E
Niihama, Japan 31 H6 33 55N 133 16 E
Niihau, U.S.A. 74 H14 21 54N 160 9W
Niimi, Japan 31 G6 34 59N 133 28 E
Niitsu, Japan 30 F9 37 48N 139 7 E
Nijil, Jordan 47 E4 30 32N 35 33 E
Nijkerk, Neths. 15 B5 52 13N 5 30 E
Nijmegen, Neths. 15 C5 51 50N 5 52 E
Nijverdal, Neths. 15 B6 52 22N 6 28 E
Nīk Pey, Iran 45 B6 36 50N 48 10 E
Nikiniki, Indonesia 37 F6 9 49S 124 30 E
Nikkō, Japan 31 F9 36 45N 139 35 E
Nikolayev = Mykolayiv, Ukraine 25 E5 46 58N 32 0 E
Nikolayevsk, Russia 25 E8 50 0N 45 35 E
Nikolayevsk-na-Amur, Russia 27 D15 53 8N 140 44 E
Nikolskoye, Russia 27 D17 55 12N 166 0 E
Nikopol, Ukraine 25 E5 47 35N 34 25 E
Nīkshahr, Iran 45 E9 26 15N 60 10 E
Nikšić, Montenegro, Yug. 21 C8 42 50N 18 57 E
Nîl, Nahr en →, Africa 51 B12 30 10N 31 6 E
Nîl el Abyad →, Sudan 51 E12 15 38N 32 31 E
Nîl el Azraq →, Sudan 51 E12 15 38N 32 31 E
Nila, Indonesia 37 F7 6 44S 129 31 E
Niland, U.S.A. 85 M11 33 14N 115 31W
Nile = Nîl, Nahr en →, Africa 51 B12 30 10N 31 6 E
Niles, Mich., U.S.A. 76 E2 41 50N 86 15W
Niles, Ohio, U.S.A. 78 E4 41 11N 80 46W
Nim Ka Thana, India 42 F6 27 44N 75 48 E
Nimach, India 42 G6 24 30N 74 56 E
Nimbahera, India 42 G6 24 37N 74 45 E
Nîmes, France 18 E6 43 50N 4 23 E
Nimfaíon, Ákra = Pínnes, Ákra, Greece 21 D11 40 5N 24 20 E
Nimmitabel, Australia 63 F4 36 29S 149 15 E
Nīnawá, Iraq 44 B4 36 25N 43 10 E
Nindigully, Australia 63 D4 28 21S 148 50 E
Nineveh = Nīnawá, Iraq 44 B4 36 25N 43 10 E
Ning Xian, China 34 G4 35 30N 107 58 E
Ning'an, China 35 B15 44 22N 129 20 E
Ningbo, China 33 D7 29 51N 121 28 E
Ningcheng, China 35 D10 41 32N 119 53 E
Ningjin, China 34 F8 37 35N 114 57 E
Ningjing Shan, China 32 D4 30 0N 98 20 E
Ningling, China 34 G8 34 25N 115 22 E
Ningpo = Ningbo, China 33 D7 29 51N 121 28 E
Ningqiang, China 34 H4 32 47N 106 15 E
Ningshan, China 34 H5 33 21N 108 21 E
Ningsia Hui A.R. = Ningxia Huizu Zizhiqu □, China 34 F4 38 0N 106 0 E
Ningwu, China 34 E7 39 0N 112 18 E
Ningxia Huizu Zizhiqu □, China 34 F4 38 0N 106 0 E
Ningyang, China 34 G9 35 47N 116 45 E
Ninh Giang, Vietnam 38 B6 20 44N 106 24 E
Ninh Hoa, Vietnam 38 F7 12 30N 109 7 E
Ninh Ma, Vietnam 38 F7 12 48N 109 21 E
Ninove, Belgium 15 D4 50 51N 4 2 E
Nioaque, Brazil 95 A4 21 5S 55 50W
Niobrara, U.S.A. 80 D6 42 45N 98 2W
Niobrara →, U.S.A. 80 D6 42 46N 98 3W
Nioro du Sahel, Mali 50 E4 15 15N 9 30W
Niort, France 18 C3 46 19N 0 29W
Nipawin, Canada 73 C8 53 20N 104 0W
Nipigon, Canada 70 C2 49 0N 88 17W
Nipigon, L., Canada 70 C2 49 50N 88 30W
Nipishish L., Canada 71 B7 54 12N 60 45W
Nipissing, L., Canada 70 C4 46 20N 80 0W
Nipomo, U.S.A. 85 K6 35 3N 120 29W
Nipton, U.S.A. 85 K11 35 28N 115 16W
Niquelândia, Brazil 93 F9 14 33S 48 23W
Nīr, Iran 44 B5 38 2N 47 59 E
Nirasaki, Japan 31 G9 35 42N 138 27 E
Nirmal, India 40 K11 19 3N 78 20 E
Nirmali, India 43 F12 26 20N 86 35 E
Niš, Serbia, Yug. 21 C9 43 19N 21 58 E
Nişāb, Si. Arabia 44 D5 29 11N 44 43 E
Nişāb, Yemen 46 E4 14 25N 46 29 E
Nishinomiya, Japan 31 G7 34 45N 135 20 E
Nishino'omote, Japan 31 J5 30 43N 130 59 E
Nishiwaki, Japan 31 G7 34 59N 134 58 E
Niskibi →, Canada 70 A2 56 29N 88 9W
Nisqually →, U.S.A. 84 C4 47 6N 122 42W
Nissáki, Greece 23 A3 39 43N 19 52 E
Nissum Bredning, Denmark 9 H13 56 40N 8 20 E
Nistru = Dnister →, Europe 17 E16 46 18N 30 17 E
Nisutlin →, Canada 72 A2 60 14N 132 34W
Nitchequon, Canada 71 B5 53 10N 70 58W
Niterói, Brazil 95 A7 22 52S 43 0W
Nith →, Canada 78 C4 43 12N 80 23W
Nith →, U.K. 12 F5 55 14N 3 33W
Nitra, Slovak Rep. 17 D10 48 19N 18 4 E
Nitra →, Slovak Rep. 17 E10 47 46N 18 10 E
Niuafo'ou, Tonga 59 B11 15 30S 175 58W
Niue, Cook Is. 65 J11 19 2S 169 54W
Niut, Indonesia 36 D4 0 55N 110 6 E
Niuzhuang, China 35 D12 40 58N 122 28 E
Nivala, Finland 8 E21 63 56N 24 57 E
Nivelles, Belgium 15 D4 50 35N 4 20 E
Nivernais, France 18 C5 47 15N 3 30 E
Niwas, India 43 H9 23 3N 80 26 E
Nixon, U.S.A. 81 L6 29 16N 97 46W
Nizamabad, India 40 K11 18 45N 78 7 E
Nizamghat, India 41 E19 28 20N 95 45 E
Nizhne Kolymsk, Russia 27 C17 68 34N 160 55 E
Nizhnekamsk, Russia 24 C9 55 38N 51 49 E
Nizhneudinsk, Russia 27 D10 54 54N 99 3 E
Nizhnevartovsk, Russia 26 C8 60 56N 76 38 E
Nizhniy Novgorod, Russia 24 C7 56 20N 44 0 E
Nizhniy Tagil, Russia 24 C10 57 55N 59 57 E
Nizhyn, Ukraine 25 D5 51 5N 31 55 E
Nizip, Turkey 44 B3 37 5N 37 50 E
Nízké Tatry, Slovak Rep. 17 D10 48 55N 19 30 E
Njakwa, Malawi 55 E3 11 1S 33 56 E
Njanji, Zambia 55 E3 14 25S 31 46 E
Njinjo, Tanzania 55 D4 8 48S 38 54 E
Njombe, Tanzania 55 D3 9 20S 34 50 E
Njombe →, Tanzania 54 D4 6 56S 35 6 E
Nkana, Zambia 55 E2 12 50S 28 8 E
Nkayi, Zimbabwe 55 F2 19 41S 29 20 E
Nkhotakota, Malawi 55 E3 12 56S 34 15 E
Nkongsamba, Cameroon 52 D1 4 55N 9 55 E
Nkurenkuru, Namibia 56 B2 17 42S 18 32 E
Nmai →, Burma 41 G20 25 30N 97 25 E
Noakhali = Maijdi, Bangla. 41 H17 22 48N 91 10 E
Nobel, Canada 78 A4 45 25N 80 6W
Nobeoka, Japan 31 H5 32 36N 131 41 E
Noblesville, U.S.A. 76 E3 40 3N 86 1W
Nocera Inferiore, Italy 20 D6 40 44N 14 38 E
Nocona, U.S.A. 81 J6 33 47N 97 44W
Noda, Japan 31 G9 35 56N 139 52 E
Nogales, Mexico 86 A2 31 20N 110 56W
Nogales, U.S.A. 83 L8 31 20N 110 56W
Nōgata, Japan 31 H5 33 48N 130 44 E
Noggerup, Australia 61 F2 33 32S 116 5 E
Noginsk, Russia 27 C10 64 30N 90 50 E
Nogoa →, Australia 62 C4 23 40S 147 55 E
Nogoyá, Argentina 94 C4 32 24S 59 48W
Nohar, India 42 E6 29 11N 74 49 E
Nohta, India 43 H8 23 40N 79 34 E
Noire, Mts., France 18 B2 48 7N 3 28W
Noirmoutier, Î. de, France 18 C2 46 58N 2 10W
Nojane, Botswana 56 C3 23 15S 20 14 E
Nojima-Zaki, Japan 31 G9 34 54N 139 53 E
Nok Kundi, Pakistan 40 E3 28 50N 62 45 E
Nokaneng, Botswana 56 B3 19 40S 22 17 E
Nokia, Finland 9 F20 61 30N 23 30 E
Nokomis, Canada 73 C8 51 35N 105 0W
Nokomis L., Canada 73 B8 57 0N 103 0W
Nola, C.A.R. 52 D3 3 35N 16 4 E
Noma Omuramba →, Namibia 56 B3 18 52S 20 53 E
Nombre de Dios, Panama 88 E4 9 34N 79 28W
Nome, U.S.A. 68 B3 64 30N 165 25W
Nomo-Zaki, Japan 31 H4 32 35N 129 44 E
Nonacho L., Canada 73 A7 61 42N 109 40W
Nonda, Australia 62 C3 20 40S 142 28 E
Nong Chang, Thailand 38 E2 15 23N 99 51 E
Nong Het, Laos 38 C4 19 29N 103 59 E
Nong Khai, Thailand 38 D4 17 50N 102 46 E
Nong'an, China 35 B13 44 25N 125 5 E
Nongoma, S. Africa 57 D5 27 58S 31 35 E
Nonoava, Mexico 86 B3 27 28N 106 44W
Nonoava →, Mexico 86 B3 27 29N 106 45W
Nonthaburi, Thailand 38 F3 13 51N 100 34 E
Noonamah, Australia 60 B5 12 40S 131 4 E
Noord Brabant □, Neths. 15 C5 51 40N 5 0 E
Noord Holland □, Neths. 15 B4 52 30N 4 45 E
Noordbeveland, Neths. 15 C3 51 35N 3 50 E
Noordoostpolder, Neths. 15 B5 52 45N 5 45 E
Noordwijk, Neths. 15 B4 52 14N 4 26 E
Nootka I., Canada 72 D3 49 32N 126 42W
Nopiming Prov. Park, Canada 73 C9 50 30N 95 37W
Noralee, Canada 72 C3 53 59N 126 26W
Noranda = Rouyn-Noranda, Canada 70 C4 48 20N 79 0W
Norco, U.S.A. 85 M9 33 56N 117 33W
Nord-Kivu □, Dem. Rep. of the Congo 54 C2 1 0S 29 0 E
Nord-Ostsee-Kanal, Germany 16 A5 54 12N 9 32 E
Nordaustlandet, Svalbard 4 B9 79 14N 23 0 E
Nordegg, Canada 72 C5 52 29N 116 5W
Norderney, Germany 16 B4 53 42N 7 9 E
Norderstedt, Germany 16 B5 53 42N 10 1 E
Nordfjord, Norway 9 F11 61 55N 5 30 E
Nordfriesische Inseln, Germany 16 A5 54 40N 8 20 E
Nordhausen, Germany 16 C6 51 30N 10 47 E
Norðoyar, Færoe Is. 8 E9 62 17N 6 35W
Nordkapp, Norway 8 A21 71 10N 25 50 E
Nordkapp, Svalbard 4 A9 80 31N 20 0 E
Nordkinn = Kinnarodden, Norway 6 A11 71 8N 27 40 E
Nordkinn-halvøya, Norway 8 A22 70 55N 27 40 E
Nordrhein-Westfalen □, Germany 16 C4 51 45N 7 30 E
Nordvik, Russia 27 B12 74 2N 111 32 E
Nore →, Ireland 13 D4 52 25N 6 58W
Norfolk, Nebr., U.S.A. 80 D6 42 2N 97 25W
Norfolk, Va., U.S.A. 76 G7 36 51N 76 17W
Norfolk □, U.K. 11 E8 52 39N 0 54 E
Norfolk I., Pac. Oc. 64 K8 28 58S 168 3 E
Norfork L., U.S.A. 81 G8 36 15N 92 14W
Norilsk, Russia 27 C9 69 20N 88 6 E
Norma, Mt., Australia 62 C3 20 55S 140 42 E
Normal, U.S.A. 80 E10 40 31N 88 59W
Norman, U.S.A. 81 H6 35 13N 97 26W
Norman →, Australia 62 B3 19 18S 141 51 E
Norman Wells, Canada 68 B7 65 17N 126 51W
Normanby →, Australia 62 A3 14 23S 144 10 E
Normandie, France 18 B4 48 45N 0 10 E
Normandin, Canada 70 C5 48 49N 72 31W
Normandy = Normandie, France 18 B4 48 45N 0 10 E
Normanhurst, Mt., Australia 61 E3 25 4S 122 30 E
Normanton, Australia 62 B3 17 40S 141 10 E
Normétal, Canada 70 C4 49 0N 79 22W
Norquay, Canada 73 C8 51 53N 102 5W
Norquinco, Argentina 96 E2 41 51S 70 55W
Norrbotten □, Sweden 8 C19 66 30N 22 30 E
Norris Point, Canada 71 C8 49 31N 57 53W
Norristown, U.S.A. 79 F9 40 7N 75 21W
Norrköping, Sweden 9 G17 58 37N 16 11 E
Norrland, Sweden 9 E16 62 15N 15 45 E
Norrtälje, Sweden 9 G18 59 46N 18 42 E
Norseman, Australia 61 F3 32 8S 121 43 E
Norsk, Russia 27 D14 52 30N 130 5 E
Norte, Pta. del, Canary Is. 22 G2 27 51N 17 57W
Norte, Serra do, Brazil 92 11 20S 59 0W
North, C., Canada 71 C7 47 2N 60 20W
North Adams, U.S.A. 79 D11 42 42N 73 7W
North Arm, Canada 72 A5 62 0N 114 30W
North Augusta, U.S.A. 77 J5 33 30N 81 59W
North Ayrshire □, U.K. 12 F4 55 45N 4 44W
North Bass I., U.S.A. 78 E2 41 43N 82 49W
North Battleford, Canada 73 C7 52 50N 108 17W
North Bay, Canada 70 C4 46 20N 79 30W
North Belcher Is., Canada 70 A4 56 50N 79 50W
North Bend, Oreg., U.S.A. 82 E1 43 24N 124 14W
North Bend, Pa., U.S.A. 78 E7 41 20N 77 42W
North Bend, Wash., U.S.A. 84 C5 47 30N 121 47W
North Bennington, U.S.A. 79 D11 42 56N 73 15W
North Berwick, U.K. 12 E6 56 4N 2 42W
North Berwick, U.S.A. 79 C14 43 18N 70 44W
North C., Canada 71 C7 47 5N 64 0W
North C., N.Z. 59 F4 34 23S 173 4 E
North Canadian →, U.S.A. 81 H7 35 16N 95 31W
North Canton, U.S.A. 78 F3 40 53N 81 24W
North Cape = Nordkapp, Norway 8 A21 71 10N 25 50 E
North Cape = Nordkapp, Svalbard 4 A9 80 31N 20 0 E
North Caribou L., Canada 70 B1 52 50N 90 40W
North Carolina □, U.S.A. 77 H6 35 30N 80 0W
North Cascades National Park, U.S.A. 82 B3 48 45N 121 10W
North Channel, Canada 70 C3 46 0N 83 0W
North Channel, U.K. 12 F3 55 13N 5 52W
North Charleston, U.S.A. 77 J6 32 53N 79 58W
North Chicago, U.S.A. 76 D2 42 19N 87 51W
North Creek, U.S.A. 79 C11 43 41N 73 59W
North Dakota □, U.S.A. 80 B5 47 30N 100 15W
North Downs, U.K. 11 F8 51 19N 0 21 E
North East, U.S.A. 78 D5 42 13N 79 50W
North East Frontier Agency = Arunachal Pradesh □, India 41 F19 28 0N 95 0 E
North East Lincolnshire □, U.K. 10 D7 53 34N 0 2W
North Eastern □, Kenya 54 B5 1 30N 40 0 E
North Esk →, U.K. 12 E6 56 46N 2 24W
North European Plain, Europe 6 E10 55 0N 25 0 E
North Foreland, U.K. 11 F9 51 22N 1 28 E
North Fork, U.S.A. 84 H7 37 14N 119 21W
North Fork American →, U.S.A. 84 G5 38 57N 120 59W
North Fork Feather →, U.S.A. 84 F5 38 33N 121 30W
North Fork Grand →, U.S.A. 80 C3 45 47N 102 16W
North Fork Red →, U.S.A. 81 H5 34 24N 99 14W
North Frisian Is. = Nordfriesische Inseln, Germany 16 A5 54 40N 8 20 E
North Gower, Canada 79 A9 45 8N 75 43W
North Hd., Australia 61 F1 30 14S 114 59 E
North Henik L., Canada 73 A9 61 45N 97 40W
North Highlands, U.S.A. 84 G5 38 40N 121 23W
North Horr, Kenya 54 B4 3 20N 37 8 E
North I., Kenya 54 B4 4 5N 36 5 E
North I., N.Z. 59 H5 38 0S 175 0 E
North Kingsville, U.S.A. 78 E4 41 50N 80 42W
North Knife →, Canada 73 B10 58 53N 94 45W

North Koel

North Koel →, India 43 G10 24 45N 83 50 E
North Korea ■, Asia 35 E14 40 0N 127 0 E
North Lakhimpur, India 41 F19 27 14N 94 7 E
North Lanarkshire □, U.K. 12 F5 55 52N 3 56W
North Las Vegas, U.S.A. 85 J11 36 12N 115 7W
North Lincolnshire □, U.K. 10 D7 53 36N 0 30W
North Little Rock, U.S.A. 81 H8 34 45N 92 16W
North Loup →, U.S.A. 80 E5 41 17N 98 24W
North Magnetic Pole, Canada 4 B2 77 58N 102 8W
North Minch, U.K. 12 C3 58 5N 5 55W
North Moose L., Canada 73 C8 54 11N 100 6W
North Myrtle Beach, U.S.A. 77 J6 33 48N 78 42W
North Nahanni →, Canada 72 A4 62 15N 123 20W
North Olmsted, U.S.A. 78 E3 41 25N 81 56W
North Ossetia □, Russia 25 F7 43 30N 44 30 E
North Pagai, I. = Pagai Utara, Pulau, Indonesia 36 E2 2 35S 100 0 E
North Palisade, U.S.A. 84 H8 37 6N 118 31W
North Platte, U.S.A. 80 E4 41 8N 100 46W
North Platte →, U.S.A. 80 E4 41 7N 100 42W
North Pole, Arctic 4 A 90 0N 0 0 E
North Portal, Canada 73 D8 49 0N 102 33W
North Powder, U.S.A. 82 D5 45 2N 117 55W
North Pt., U.S.A. 78 A1 45 2N 83 16W
North Rhine Westphalia = Nordrhein-Westfalen □, Germany 16 C4 51 45N 7 30 E
North River, Canada 71 B8 53 49N 57 6W
North Ronaldsay, U.K. 12 B6 59 22N 2 26W
North Saskatchewan →, Canada 73 C7 53 15N 105 5W
North Sea, Europe 6 D6 56 0N 4 0 E
North Seal →, Canada 73 B9 58 50N 98 7W
North Somerset □, U.K. 11 F5 51 24N 2 45W
North Sporades = Vóriai Sporádhes, Greece 21 E10 39 15N 23 30 E
North Sydney, Canada 71 C7 46 12N 60 15W
North Syracuse, U.S.A. 79 C8 43 8N 76 7W
North Taranaki Bight, N.Z. 59 H5 38 50S 174 15 E
North Thompson →, Canada 72 C4 50 40N 120 20W
North Tonawanda, U.S.A. 78 C6 43 2N 78 53W
North Troy, U.S.A. 79 B12 45 0N 72 24W
North Truchas Pk., U.S.A. 83 J11 36 0N 105 30W
North Twin I., Canada 70 B4 53 20N 80 0W
North Tyne →, U.K. 10 B5 55 0N 2 8W
North Uist, U.K. 12 D1 57 40N 7 15W
North Vancouver, Canada 72 D4 49 19N 123 4W
North Vernon, U.S.A. 76 F3 39 0N 85 38W
North Wabasca L., Canada 72 B6 56 0N 113 55W
North Walsham, U.K. 10 E9 52 50N 1 22 E
North-West □, S. Africa 56 D4 27 0S 25 0 E
North West C., Australia 60 D1 21 45S 114 9 E
North West Christmas I. Ridge, Pac. Oc. 65 G11 6 30N 165 0W
North West Frontier □, Pakistan 42 C4 34 0N 72 0 E
North West Highlands, U.K. 12 D4 57 33N 4 58W
North West River, Canada 71 B7 53 30N 60 10W
North Western □, Zambia 55 E2 13 30S 25 30 E
North Wildwood, U.S.A. 76 F8 39 0N 74 48W
North York Moors, U.K. 10 C7 54 23N 0 53W
North Yorkshire □, U.K. 10 C6 54 15N 1 25W
Northallerton, U.K. 10 C6 54 20N 1 26W
Northam, Australia 61 F2 31 35S 116 42 E
Northam, S. Africa 56 C4 24 56S 27 18 E
Northampton, Australia 61 E1 28 27S 114 33 E
Northampton, U.K. 11 E7 52 15N 0 53W
Northampton, Mass., U.S.A. 79 D12 42 19N 72 38W
Northampton, Pa., U.S.A. 79 F9 40 41N 75 30W
Northamptonshire □, U.K. 11 E7 52 16N 0 55W
Northbridge, U.S.A. 79 D13 42 9N 71 39W
Northcliffe, Australia 61 F2 34 39S 116 7 E
Northeast Providence Chan., W. Indies 88 A4 26 0N 76 0W
Northern □, Malawi 55 E3 11 0S 34 0 E
Northern □, Uganda 54 B3 3 5N 32 30 E
Northern □, Zambia 55 E3 10 30S 31 0 E
Northern Cape □, S. Africa 56 D3 30 0S 20 0 E
Northern Circars, India 41 L13 17 30N 82 30 E
Northern Indian L., Canada 73 B9 57 20N 97 20W
Northern Ireland □, U.K. 13 B5 54 45N 7 0W
Northern Light L., Canada 70 C1 48 15N 90 39W
Northern Marianas ■, Pac. Oc. 64 F6 17 0N 145 0 E
Northern Territory □, Australia 60 D5 20 0S 133 0 E
Northern Transvaal □, S. Africa 57 C4 24 0S 29 0 E
Northfield, Minn., U.S.A. 80 C8 44 27N 93 9W
Northfield, Vt., U.S.A. 79 B12 44 9N 72 40W
Northland □, N.Z. 59 F4 35 30S 173 30 E
Northome, U.S.A. 80 B7 47 52N 94 17W
Northport, Ala., U.S.A. 77 J2 33 14N 87 35W
Northport, Wash., U.S.A. 82 B5 48 55N 117 48W
Northumberland □, U.K. 10 B6 55 12N 2 0W
Northumberland, C., Australia 63 F3 38 5S 140 40 E
Northumberland Is., Australia 62 C4 21 30S 149 50 E
Northumberland Str., Canada 71 C7 46 20N 64 0W
Northville, U.S.A. 79 C10 43 13N 74 11W
Northwest Providence Channel, W. Indies 88 A4 26 0N 78 0W
Northwest Territories □, Canada 68 B9 67 0N 110 0W
Northwood, Iowa, U.S.A. 80 D8 43 27N 93 13W
Northwood, N. Dak., U.S.A. 80 B6 47 44N 97 34W
Norton, U.S.A. 80 F5 39 50N 99 53W
Norton, Zimbabwe 55 F3 17 52S 30 40 E
Norton Sd., U.S.A. 68 B3 63 50N 164 0W
Norwalk, Calif., U.S.A. 85 M8 33 54N 118 5W
Norwalk, Conn., U.S.A. 79 E11 41 7N 73 22W
Norwalk, Iowa, U.S.A. 80 E8 41 29N 93 41W
Norwalk, Ohio, U.S.A. 78 E2 41 15N 82 37W
Norway, Maine, U.S.A. 77 C10 44 13N 70 32W
Norway, Mich., U.S.A. 76 C2 45 47N 87 55W
Norway ■, Europe 8 E14 63 0N 11 0 E
Norway House, Canada 73 C9 53 59N 97 50W
Norwegian Sea, Atl. Oc. 4 C8 66 0N 1 0 E
Norwich, Canada 78 D4 42 59N 80 36W
Norwich, U.K. 11 E9 52 38N 1 18 E
Norwich, Conn., U.S.A. 79 E12 41 31N 72 5W
Norwich, N.Y., U.S.A. 79 D9 42 32N 75 32W
Norwood, Canada 78 B7 44 23N 77 59W
Norwood, U.S.A. 79 B10 44 45N 75 0W
Noshiro, Japan 30 D10 40 12N 140 0 E
Noşratābād, Iran 45 D8 29 55N 60 0 E
Noss Hd., U.K. 12 C5 58 28N 3 3W
Nossob →, S. Africa 56 D3 26 55S 20 45 E
Nosy Barren, Madag. 53 H8 18 25S 43 40 E
Nosy Be, Madag. 53 G9 13 25S 48 15 E
Nosy Boraha, Madag. 57 B8 16 50S 49 55 E
Nosy Varika, Madag. 57 C8 20 35S 48 32 E
Noteć →, Poland 16 B8 52 44N 15 26 E
Notikewin →, Canada 72 B5 57 2N 117 38W
Notodden, Norway 9 G13 59 35N 9 17 E
Notre Dame B., Canada 71 C8 49 45N 55 30W
Notre Dame de Koartac = Quaqtaq, Canada 69 B13 60 55N 69 40W
Notre-Dame-des-Bois, Canada 79 A13 45 24N 71 4W
Notre Dame d'Ivugivic = Ivujivik, Canada 69 B12 62 24N 77 55W
Notre-Dame-du-Nord, Canada 70 C4 47 36N 79 30W
Nottawasaga B., Canada 78 B4 44 35N 80 15W
Nottaway →, Canada 70 B4 51 22N 78 55W
Nottingham, U.K. 10 E6 52 58N 1 10W
Nottingham, City of □, U.K. 10 E6 52 58N 1 10W
Nottingham I., Canada 69 B12 63 20N 77 55W
Nottinghamshire □, U.K. 10 D6 53 10N 1 3W
Nottoway →, U.S.A. 76 G7 36 33N 76 55W
Notwane →, Botswana 56 C4 23 35S 26 58 E
Nouâdhibou, Mauritania 50 D2 20 54N 17 0W
Nouâdhibou, Ras, Mauritania 50 D2 20 50N 17 0W
Nouakchott, Mauritania 50 E2 18 9N 15 58W
Nouméa, N. Cal. 64 K8 22 17S 166 30 E
Noupoort, S. Africa 56 E3 31 10S 24 57 E
Nouveau Comptoir = Wemindji, Canada 70 B4 53 0N 78 49W
Nouvelle-Calédonie = New Caledonia ■, Pac. Oc. 64 K8 21 0S 165 0 E
Nova Casa Nova, Brazil 93 E10 9 25S 41 5W
Nova Esperança, Brazil 95 A5 23 8S 52 24W
Nova Friburgo, Brazil 95 A7 22 16S 42 30W
Nova Gaia = Cambundi-Catembo, Angola 52 G3 10 10S 17 35 E
Nova Iguaçu, Brazil 95 A7 22 45S 43 28W
Nova Iorque, Brazil 93 E10 7 0S 44 5W
Nova Lima, Brazil 95 A7 19 59S 43 51W
Nova Lisboa = Huambo, Angola 53 G3 12 42S 15 54 E
Nova Lusitânia, Mozam. 55 F3 19 50S 34 34 E
Nova Mambone, Mozam. 57 C6 21 0S 35 3 E
Nova Scotia □, Canada 71 C7 45 10N 63 0W
Nova Sofala, Mozam. 57 C5 20 7S 34 42 E
Nova Venécia, Brazil 93 G10 18 45S 40 24W
Nova Zagora, Bulgaria 21 C11 42 32N 26 1 E
Novar, Canada 78 A5 45 27N 79 15W
Novara, Italy 18 D8 45 28N 8 38 E
Novato, U.S.A. 84 G4 38 6N 122 35W
Novaya Ladoga, Russia 24 B5 60 7N 32 16 E
Novaya Lyalya, Russia 24 C11 59 4N 60 45 E
Novaya Sibir, Ostrov, Russia 27 B16 75 10N 150 0 E
Novaya Zemlya, Russia 26 B6 75 0N 56 0 E
Nové Zámky, Slovak Rep. 17 D10 48 2N 18 8 E
Novgorod, Russia 24 C5 58 30N 31 25 E
Novgorod-Severskiy = Novhorod-Siverskyy, Ukraine 24 D5 52 2N 33 10 E
Novhorod-Siverskyy, Ukraine 24 D5 52 2N 33 10 E
Novi Lígure, Italy 18 D8 44 46N 8 47 E
Novi Pazar, Serbia, Yug. 21 C9 43 12N 20 28 E
Novi Sad, Serbia, Yug. 21 B8 45 18N 19 52 E
Nôvo Hamburgo, Brazil 95 B5 29 37S 51 7W
Novo Mesto, Slovenia 20 B6 45 47N 15 12 E
Novo Remanso, Brazil 93 E10 9 41S 42 4W
Novoataysk, Russia 26 D9 53 30N 84 0 E
Novocherkassk, Russia 25 E7 47 27N 40 15 E
Novogrudok = Navahrudak, Belarus 17 B13 53 40N 25 50 E
Novohrad-Volynskyy, Ukraine 17 C14 50 34N 27 35 E
Novokachalinsk, Russia 30 B6 45 5N 132 0 E
Novokazalinsk = Zhangaqazaly, Kazakstan 26 E7 45 48N 62 6 E
Novokuybyshevsk, Russia 24 D8 53 7N 49 58 E
Novokuznetsk, Russia 26 D9 53 45N 87 10 E
Novomoskovsk, Russia 24 D6 54 5N 38 15 E
Novorossiysk, Russia 25 F6 44 43N 37 46 E
Novorybnoye, Russia 27 B11 72 50N 105 50 E
Novoselytsya, Ukraine 17 D14 48 14N 26 15 E
Novoshakhtinsk, Russia 25 E6 47 46N 39 58 E
Novosibirsk, Russia 26 D9 55 0N 83 5 E
Novosibirskiye Ostrova, Russia 27 B15 75 0N 142 0 E
Novotroitsk, Russia 24 D10 51 10N 58 15 E
Novouzensk, Russia 25 D8 50 32N 48 17 E
Novovolynsk, Ukraine 17 C13 50 45N 24 4 E
Novska, Croatia 20 B7 45 19N 17 0 E
Novvy Urengoy, Russia 26 C8 65 48N 76 52 E
Novyy Bor, Russia 24 A9 66 43N 52 19 E
Novyy Port, Russia 26 C8 67 40N 72 30 E
Now Shahr, Iran 45 B6 36 40N 51 30 E
Nowa Sól, Poland 16 C8 51 48N 15 44 E
Nowata, U.S.A. 81 G7 36 42N 95 38W
Nowbarān, Iran 45 C6 35 8N 49 42 E
Nowghāb, Iran 45 C8 33 53N 59 4 E
Nowgong, Assam, India 41 F18 26 20N 92 50 E
Nowgong, Mad. P., India 43 G8 25 4N 79 27 E
Nowra-Bomaderry, Australia 63 E5 34 53S 150 35 E
Nowshera, Pakistan 40 C8 34 0N 72 0 E
Nowy Sącz, Poland 17 D11 49 40N 20 41 E
Nowy Targ, Poland 17 D11 49 29N 20 2 E
Nowy Tomyśl, Poland 16 B9 52 19N 16 10 E
Noxen, U.S.A. 79 E8 41 25N 76 4W
Noxon, U.S.A. 82 C6 48 0N 115 43W
Noyabr'sk, Russia 26 C8 64 34N 76 21 E
Noyon, France 18 B5 49 34N 2 59 E
Noyon, Mongolia 34 C2 43 2N 102 4 E
Nsanje, Malawi 55 F4 16 55S 35 12 E
Nsomba, Zambia 55 E2 10 45S 29 51 E
Nu Jiang →, China 32 D4 29 58N 97 25 E
Nu Shan, China 32 D4 26 0N 99 20 E
Nubia, Africa 48 D7 21 0N 32 0 E
Nubian Desert = Nûbîya, Es Sahrâ en, Sudan 51 D12 21 30N 33 30 E
Nûbîya, Es Sahrâ en, Sudan 51 D12 21 30N 33 30 E
Nuboai, Indonesia 37 E9 2 10S 136 30 E
Nubra →, India 43 B7 34 35N 77 35 E
Nueces →, U.S.A. 81 M6 27 51N 97 30W
Nueltin L., Canada 73 A9 60 30N 99 30W
Nueva Asunción □, Paraguay 94 A3 21 0S 61 0W
Nueva Gerona, Cuba 88 B3 21 53N 82 49W
Nueva Palmira, Uruguay 94 C4 33 52S 58 20W
Nueva Rosita, Mexico 86 B4 28 0N 101 11W
Nueva San Salvador, El Salv. 88 D2 13 40N 89 18W
Nuéve de Julio, Argentina 94 D3 35 30S 61 0W
Nuevitas, Cuba 88 B4 21 30N 77 20W
Nuevo, G., Argentina 96 E4 43 0S 64 30W
Nuevo Casas Grandes, Mexico 86 A3 30 22N 108 0W
Nuevo Guerrero, Mexico 87 B5 26 34N 99 15W
Nuevo Laredo, Mexico 87 B5 27 30N 99 30W
Nuevo León □, Mexico 86 C5 25 0N 100 0W
Nuevo Rocafuerte, Ecuador 92 D3 0 55S 75 27W
Nugget Pt., N.Z. 59 M2 46 27S 169 50 E
Nuhaka, N.Z. 59 H6 39 3S 177 45 E
Nukey Bluff, Australia 63 E2 32 26S 135 29 E
Nukhuyb, Iraq 44 C4 32 4N 42 3 E
Nuku'alofa, Tonga 59 E12 21 10S 174 0W
Nukus, Uzbekistan 26 E6 42 27N 59 41 E
Nullagine, Australia 60 D3 21 53S 120 7 E
Nullagine →, Australia 60 D3 21 20S 120 20 E
Nullarbor, Australia 61 F5 31 28S 130 55 E
Nullarbor Plain, Australia 61 F4 31 10S 129 0 E
Numalla, L., Australia 63 D3 28 43S 144 20 E
Numan, Nigeria 51 G8 9 29N 12 3 E
Numata, Japan 31 F9 36 45N 139 4 E
Numazu, Japan 31 G9 35 7N 138 51 E
Numbulwar, Australia 62 A2 14 15S 135 45 E
Numfoor, Indonesia 37 E8 1 0S 134 50 E
Numurkah, Australia 63 F4 36 5S 145 26 E
Nunaksaluk I., Canada 71 A7 55 49N 60 20W
Nunavut □, Canada 69 B11 66 0N 85 0W
Nunda, U.S.A. 78 D7 42 35N 77 56W
Nungarin, Australia 61 F2 31 12S 118 6 E
Nungo, Mozam. 55 E4 13 23S 37 43 E
Nungwe, Tanzania 54 C3 2 48S 32 2 E
Nunivak I., U.S.A. 68 C3 60 10N 166 30W
Nunkun, India 43 C7 33 57N 76 2 E
Núoro, Italy 20 D3 40 20N 9 20 E
Nūrābād, Iran 45 E8 27 47N 57 12 E
Nuremberg = Nürnberg, Germany 16 D6 49 27N 11 3 E
Nuri, Mexico 86 B3 28 2N 109 22W
Nuriootpa, Australia 63 E2 34 27S 139 0 E
Nurmes, Finland 8 E23 63 33N 29 10 E
Nürnberg, Germany 16 D6 49 27N 11 3 E
Nurpur, Pakistan 42 D4 31 53N 71 54 E
Nurran, L. = Terewah, L., Australia 63 D4 29 52S 147 35 E
Nurrari Lakes, Australia 61 E5 29 1S 130 5 E
Nusa Barung, Indonesia 37 H15 8 30S 113 30 E
Nusa Kambangan, Indonesia 37 G13 7 40S 108 10 E
Nusa Tenggara Barat □, Indonesia 36 F5 8 50S 117 30 E
Nusa Tenggara Timur □, Indonesia 37 F6 9 30S 122 0 E
Nusaybin, Turkey 25 G7 37 3N 41 10 E
Nushki, Pakistan 42 E2 29 35N 66 0 E
Nuuk, Greenland 69 B14 64 10N 51 35W
Nuwakot, Nepal 43 E10 28 10N 83 55 E
Nuweiba', Egypt 44 D2 28 59N 34 39 E
Nuweveldberge, S. Africa 56 E3 32 10S 21 45 E
Nuyts, C., Australia 61 F5 32 2S 132 21 E
Nuyts, Pt., Australia 61 G2 35 4S 116 38 E
Nuyts Arch., Australia 63 E1 32 35S 133 20 E
Nxau-Nxau, Botswana 56 B3 18 57S 21 4 E
Nyabing, Australia 61 F2 33 33S 118 9 E
Nyack, U.S.A. 79 E11 41 5N 73 55W
Nyagan, Russia 26 C7 62 30N 65 38 E
Nyahanga, Tanzania 54 C3 2 20S 33 37 E
Nyahua, Tanzania 54 D3 5 25S 33 23 E
Nyahururu, Kenya 54 B4 0 2N 36 27 E
Nyainqentanglha Shan, China 32 D4 30 0N 90 0 E
Nyakanazi, Tanzania 54 C3 3 2S 31 10 E
Nyâlâ, Sudan 51 F10 12 2N 24 58 E
Nyamandhlovu, Zimbabwe 55 F2 19 55S 28 16 E
Nyambiti, Tanzania 54 C3 2 48S 33 27 E
Nyamwaga, Tanzania 54 C3 1 27S 34 33 E
Nyandekwa, Tanzania 54 C3 3 57S 32 32 E
Nyandoma, Russia 24 B7 61 40N 40 12 E
Nyangana, Namibia 56 B3 18 0S 20 40 E
Nyanguge, Tanzania 54 C3 2 30S 33 12 E
Nyanza, Rwanda 54 C2 2 20S 29 42 E
Nyanza □, Kenya 54 C3 0 10S 34 15 E
Nyanza-Lac, Burundi 54 C2 4 21S 29 36 E
Nyasa, L., Africa 55 E3 12 30S 34 30 E
Nyasvizh, Belarus 17 B14 53 14N 26 38 E
Nyazepetrovsk, Russia 24 C10 56 3N 59 36 E
Nyazura, Zimbabwe 55 F3 18 40S 32 16 E
Nyazwidzi →, Zimbabwe 55 G3 20 0S 31 17 E
Nybro, Sweden 9 H16 56 44N 15 55 E
Nyda, Russia 26 C8 66 40N 72 58 E
Nyeri, Kenya 54 C4 0 23S 36 56 E
Nyíregyháza, Hungary 17 E11 47 58N 21 47 E
Nykøbing, Storstrøm, Denmark 9 J14 54 56N 11 52 E
Nykøbing, Vestsjælland, Denmark 9 J14 55 55N 11 40 E
Nykøbing, Viborg, Denmark 9 H13 56 48N 8 51 E
Nyköping, Sweden 9 G17 58 45N 17 1 E
Nylstroom, S. Africa 57 C4 24 42S 28 22 E
Nymagee, Australia 63 E4 32 7S 146 20 E
Nynäshamn, Sweden 9 G17 58 54N 17 57 E
Nyngan, Australia 63 E4 31 30S 147 8 E
Nyoma Rap, India 43 C8 33 10N 78 40 E
Nyoman = Neman →, Lithuania 9 J20 55 25N 21 10 E
Nysa, Poland 17 C9 50 30N 17 22 E
Nysa →, Europe 16 B8 52 4N 14 46 E
Nyssa, U.S.A. 82 E5 43 53N 117 0W
Nyunzu, Dem. Rep. of the Congo 54 D2 5 57S 27 58 E
Nyurba, Russia 27 C12 63 17N 118 28 E
Nzega, Tanzania 54 C3 4 10S 33 12 E
N'zérékoré, Guinea 50 G4 7 49N 8 48W
Nzeto, Angola 52 F2 7 10S 12 52 E
Nzilo, Chutes de, Dem. Rep. of the Congo 55 E2 10 18S 25 27 E
Nzubuka, Tanzania 54 C3 4 45S 32 50 E

O

Ō-Shima, Japan 31 G9 34 44N 139 24 E
Oa, Mull of, U.K. 12 F2 55 35N 6 20W
Oacoma, U.S.A. 80 D5 43 48N 99 24W
Oahe, L., U.S.A. 80 C4 44 27N 100 24W
Oahe Dam, U.S.A. 80 C4 44 27N 100 24W
Oahu, U.S.A. 74 H16 21 28N 157 58W
Oak Harbor, U.S.A. 84 B4 48 18N 122 39W
Oak Hill, U.S.A. 76 G5 37 59N 81 9W
Oak Ridge, U.S.A. 77 G3 36 1N 84 16W
Oak View, U.S.A. 85 L7 34 24N 119 18W
Oakan-Dake, Japan 30 C12 43 27N 144 10 E
Oakdale, Calif., U.S.A. 84 H6 37 46N 120 51W
Oakdale, La., U.S.A. 81 K8 30 49N 92 40W
Oakes, U.S.A. 80 B5 46 8N 98 6W
Oakesdale, U.S.A. 82 C5 47 8N 117 15W
Oakey, Australia 63 D5 27 25S 151 43 E
Oakfield, U.S.A. 78 C6 43 4N 78 16W
Oakham, U.K. 11 E7 52 40N 0 43W
Oakhurst, U.S.A. 84 H7 37 19N 119 40W
Oakland, U.S.A. 84 H4 37 49N 122 16W
Oakley, Idaho, U.S.A. 82 E7 42 15N 113 53W
Oakley, Kans., U.S.A. 80 F4 39 8N 100 51W
Oakover →, Australia 60 D3 21 0S 120 40 E
Oakridge, U.S.A. 82 E2 43 45N 122 28W
Oakville, Canada 78 C5 43 27N 79 41W
Oakville, U.S.A. 84 D3 46 51N 123 14W
Oamaru, N.Z. 59 L3 45 5S 170 59 E
Oasis, Calif., U.S.A. 85 M10 33 28N 116 6W
Oasis, Nev., U.S.A. 84 H9 37 29N 117 55W
Oates Land, Antarctica 5 C11 69 0S 160 0 E
Oatlands, Australia 62 G4 42 17S 147 21 E
Oatman, U.S.A. 85 K12 35 1N 114 19W
Oaxaca, Mexico 87 D5 17 2N 96 40W
Oaxaca □, Mexico 87 D5 17 0N 97 0W
Ob →, Russia 26 C7 66 45N 69 30 E
Oba, Canada 70 C3 49 4N 84 7W
Obama, Japan 31 G7 35 30N 135 45 E
Oban, U.K. 12 E3 56 25N 5 29W
Obbia, Somali Rep. 46 F4 5 25N 48 30 E
Obera, Argentina 95 B4 27 21S 55 2W
Oberhausen, Germany 16 C4 51 28N 6 51 E
Oberlin, Kans., U.S.A. 80 F4 39 49N 100 32W
Oberlin, La., U.S.A. 81 K8 30 37N 92 46W
Oberlin, Ohio, U.S.A. 78 E2 41 18N 82 13W
Oberon, Australia 63 E4 33 45S 149 52 E
Obi, Kepulauan, Indonesia 37 E7 1 23S 127 45 E
Obi Is. = Obi, Kepulauan, Indonesia 37 E7 1 23S 127 45 E
Óbidos, Brazil 93 D7 1 50S 55 30W
Obihiro, Japan 30 C11 42 56N 143 12 E
Obilatu, Indonesia 37 E7 1 25S 127 20 E
Obluchye, Russia 27 E14 49 1N 131 4 E
Obo, C.A.R. 54 A2 5 20N 26 32 E
Oboa, Mt., Uganda 54 B3 1 45N 34 45 E
Oboyan, Russia 26 D4 51 15N 36 21 E
Obozerskaya = Obozerskiy, Russia 24 B7 63 34N 40 21 E
Obozerskiy, Russia 24 B7 63 34N 40 21 E
Observatory Inlet, Canada 72 B3 55 10N 129 54W
Obshchi Syrt, Russia 6 E16 52 0N 53 0 E
Obskaya Guba, Russia 26 C8 69 0N 73 0 E
Obuasi, Ghana 50 G5 6 17N 1 40W
Ocala, U.S.A. 77 L4 29 11N 82 8W
Ocampo, Mexico 86 B3 28 9N 108 24W
Ocampo, Tamaulipas, Mexico 87 C5 22 50N 99 20W
Ocaña, Spain 19 C4 39 55N 3 30W
Ocanomowoc, U.S.A. 80 D10 43 7N 88 30W
Occidental, Cordillera, Colombia 92 C3 5 0N 76 0W
Ocean City, Md., U.S.A. 76 F8 38 20N 75 5W
Ocean City, N.J., U.S.A. 76 F8 39 17N 74 35W
Ocean City, Wash., U.S.A. 84 C2 47 4N 124 10W
Ocean Falls, Canada 72 C3 52 18N 127 48W
Ocean I. = Banaba, Kiribati 64 H8 0 45S 169 50 E
Ocean Park, U.S.A. 84 D2 46 30N 124 3W
Oceano, U.S.A. 85 K6 35 6N 120 37W
Oceanport, U.S.A. 79 F10 40 19N 74 3W
Oceanside, U.S.A. 85 M9 33 12N 117 23W
Ochil Hills, U.K. 12 E5 56 14N 3 40W
Ocilla, U.S.A. 77 K4 31 36N 83 15W
Ocmulgee →, U.S.A. 77 K4 31 58N 82 33W
Ocniţa, Moldova 17 D14 48 25N 27 30 E
Oconee →, U.S.A. 77 K4 31 58N 82 33W
Oconto, U.S.A. 76 C2 44 53N 87 52W
Oconto Falls, U.S.A. 76 C1 44 52N 88 9W
Ocosingo, Mexico 87 D6 17 10N 92 15W
Ocotal, Nic. 88 D2 13 41N 86 31W
Ocotlán, Mexico 86 C4 20 21N 102 42W
Ocotlán de Morelos, Mexico 87 D5 16 48N 96 40W
Ōda, Japan 31 G6 35 11N 132 30 E
Ódáðahraun, Iceland 8 D5 65 5N 17 0W
Odate, Japan 30 D10 40 16N 140 34 E
Odawara, Japan 31 G9 35 20N 139 6 E
Odda, Norway 9 F12 60 3N 6 35 E
Odei →, Canada 73 B9 56 6N 96 54W
Ödemiş, Turkey 21 E13 38 15N 28 0 E
Odendaalsrus, S. Africa 56 D4 27 48S 26 45 E
Odense, Denmark 9 J14 55 22N 10 23 E
Oder →, Europe 16 B8 53 33N 14 38 E
Odesa, Ukraine 25 E5 46 30N 30 45 E
Odessa = Odesa, Ukraine 25 E5 46 30N 30 45 E
Odessa, Canada 79 B8 44 17N 76 43W
Odessa, Tex., U.S.A. 81 K3 31 52N 102 23W
Odessa, Wash., U.S.A. 82 C4 47 20N 118 41W
Odiakwe, Botswana 56 C4 20 12S 25 17 E
Odienné, Ivory C. 50 G4 9 30N 7 34W
Odintsovo, Russia 24 C6 55 39N 37 15 E
O'Donnell, U.S.A. 81 J4 32 58N 101 50W
Odorheiu Secuiesc, Romania 17 E13 46 21N 25 21 E
Odra = Oder →, Europe 16 B8 53 33N 14 38 E
Odzi, Zimbabwe 57 B5 19 0S 32 20 E
Oeiras, Brazil 93 E10 7 0S 42 8W
Oelrichs, U.S.A. 80 D3 43 11N 103 14W
Oelwein, U.S.A. 80 D9 42 41N 91 55W
Oenpelli, Australia 60 B5 12 20S 133 4 E
Ofanto →, Italy 20 D7 41 22N 16 13 E
Offa, Nigeria 50 G6 8 13N 4 42 E
Offaly □, Ireland 13 C4 53 15N 7 30W
Offenbach, Germany 16 C5 50 6N 8 44 E
Offenburg, Germany 16 D4 48 28N 7 56 E

Oshmyany

Oshmyany = Ashmyany, Belarus 9 J21 54 26N 25 52 E
Oshnoviyeh, Iran 44 B5 37 2N 45 6 E
Oshogbo, Nigeria 50 G6 7 48N 4 37 E
Oshtorīnān, Iran 45 C6 34 1N 48 38 E
Oshwe, Dem. Rep. of the Congo 52 E3 3 25S 19 28 E
Osijek, Croatia 21 B8 45 34N 18 41 E
Osipenko = Berdyansk, Ukraine 25 E6 46 45N 36 50 E
Osipovichi = Asipovichy, Belarus 17 B15 53 19N 28 33 E
Osiyan, India 42 F5 26 43N 72 55 E
Osizweni, S. Africa 57 D5 27 49S 30 7 E
Oskaloosa, U.S.A. 80 E8 41 18N 92 39W
Oskarshamn, Sweden 9 H17 57 15N 16 27 E
Oskélanéo, Canada 70 C4 48 5N 75 15W
Öskemen, Kazakstan 26 E9 50 0N 82 36 E
Oslo, Norway 9 G14 59 55N 10 45 E
Oslofjorden, Norway 9 G14 59 20N 10 35 E
Osmanabad, India 40 K10 18 5N 76 10 E
Osmaniye, Turkey 25 G6 37 5N 36 10 E
Osnabrück, Germany 16 B5 52 17N 8 3 E
Osorio, Brazil 95 B5 29 53S 50 17W
Osorno, Chile 96 E2 40 25S 73 0W
Osoyoos, Canada 72 D5 49 0N 119 30W
Osøyro, Norway 9 F11 60 9N 5 30 E
Ospika →, Canada 72 B4 56 20N 124 0W
Osprey Reef, Australia 62 A4 13 52S 146 36 E
Oss, Neths. 15 C5 51 46N 5 32 E
Ossa, Mt., Australia 62 G4 41 52S 146 3 E
Óssa, Óros, Greece 21 E10 39 47N 22 42 E
Ossabaw I., U.S.A. 77 K5 31 50N 81 5W
Ossining, U.S.A. 79 E11 41 10N 73 55W
Ossipee, U.S.A. 79 C13 43 41N 71 7W
Ossokmanuan L., Canada 71 B7 53 25N 65 0W
Ossora, Russia 27 D17 59 20N 163 13 E
Ostend = Oostende, Belgium 15 C2 51 15N 2 54 E
Oster, Ukraine 17 C16 50 57N 30 53 E
Osterburg, U.S.A. 78 F6 40 16N 78 31W
Österdalälven, Sweden 9 F16 61 30N 13 45 E
Østerdalen, Norway 9 F14 61 40N 10 50 E
Östersund, Sweden 8 E16 63 10N 14 38 E
Ostfriesische Inseln, Germany 16 B4 53 42N 7 0 E
Ostrava, Czech Rep. 17 D10 49 51N 18 18 E
Ostróda, Poland 17 B10 53 42N 19 58 E
Ostroh, Ukraine 17 C14 50 20N 26 30 E
Ostrołęka, Poland 17 B11 53 4N 21 32 E
Ostrów Mazowiecka, Poland 17 B11 52 50N 21 51 E
Ostrów Wielkopolski, Poland 17 C9 51 36N 17 44 E
Ostrowiec-Świętokrzyski, Poland 17 C11 50 55N 21 22 E
Ostuni, Italy 21 D7 40 44N 17 35 E
Ōsumi-Kaikyō, Japan 31 J5 30 55N 131 0 E
Ōsumi-Shotō, Japan 31 J5 30 30N 130 0 E
Osuna, Spain 19 D3 37 14N 5 8W
Oswegatchie →, U.S.A. 79 B9 44 42N 75 30W
Oswego, U.S.A. 79 C8 43 27N 76 31W
Oswego →, U.S.A. 79 C8 43 27N 76 30W
Oswestry, U.K. 10 E4 52 52N 3 3W
Oświęcim, Poland 17 C10 50 2N 19 11 E
Otago □, N.Z. 59 L2 45 15S 170 0 E
Otago Harbour, N.Z. 59 L3 45 47S 170 42 E
Ōtake, Japan 31 G6 34 12N 132 13 E
Otaki, N.Z. 59 J5 40 45S 175 10 E
Otaru, Japan 30 C10 43 10N 141 0 E
Otaru-Wan = Ishikari-Wan, Japan 30 C10 43 25N 141 1 E
Otavalo, Ecuador 92 C3 0 13N 78 20W
Otavi, Namibia 56 B2 19 40S 17 24 E
Otchinjau, Angola 56 B1 16 30S 13 56 E
Otelnuk L., Canada 71 A6 56 9N 68 12W
Othello, U.S.A. 82 C4 46 50N 119 10W
Otira Gorge, N.Z. 59 K3 42 53S 171 33 E
Otjiwarongo, Namibia 56 C2 20 30S 16 33 E
Otoineppu, Japan 30 B11 44 44N 142 16 E
Otorohanga, N.Z. 59 H5 38 12S 175 14 E
Otoskwin →, Canada 70 B2 52 13N 88 6W
Otra →, Norway 9 G13 58 9N 8 1 E
Otranto, Italy 21 D8 40 9N 18 28 E
Otranto, C. d', Italy 21 D8 40 7N 18 30 E
Otranto, Str. of, Italy 21 D8 40 15N 18 40 E
Otse, S. Africa 56 D4 25 2S 25 45 E
Ōtsu, Japan 31 G7 35 0N 135 50 E
Ōtsuki, Japan 31 G9 35 36N 138 57 E
Ottawa = Outaouais →, Canada 70 C5 45 27N 74 8W
Ottawa, Canada 79 A9 45 27N 75 42W
Ottawa, Ill., U.S.A. 80 E10 41 21N 88 51W
Ottawa, Kans., U.S.A. 80 F7 38 37N 95 16W
Ottawa Is., Canada 69 C11 59 35N 80 10W
Otter Cr. →, U.S.A. 79 B11 44 13N 73 17W
Otter L., Canada 73 B8 55 35N 104 39W
Otterville, Canada 78 D4 42 55N 80 36W
Ottery St. Mary, U.K. 11 G4 50 44N 3 17W
Otto Beit Bridge, Zimbabwe 55 F2 15 59S 28 56 E
Ottosdal, S. Africa 56 D4 26 46S 25 59 E
Ottumwa, U.S.A. 80 E8 41 1N 92 25W
Oturkpo, Nigeria 50 G7 7 16N 8 8 E
Otway, B., Chile 96 G2 53 30S 74 0W
Otway, C., Australia 63 F3 38 52S 143 30 E
Otwock, Poland 17 B11 52 5N 21 20 E
Ou →, Laos 38 B4 20 4N 102 13 E
Ou-Sammyaku, Japan 30 E10 39 20N 140 35 E
Ouachita →, U.S.A. 81 K9 31 38N 91 49W
Ouachita, L., U.S.A. 81 H8 34 34N 93 12W
Ouachita Mts., U.S.A. 81 H7 34 40N 94 25W
Ouagadougou, Burkina Faso 50 F5 12 25N 1 30W
Ouahran = Oran, Algeria 50 A5 35 45N 0 39W
Ouallene, Algeria 50 D6 24 41N 1 11 E
Ouargla, Algeria 50 B7 31 59N 5 16 E
Ouarzazate, Morocco 50 B4 30 55N 6 50W
Oubangi →, Dem. Rep. of the Congo 52 E3 0 30S 17 50 E
Ouddorp, Neths. 15 C3 51 50N 3 57 E
Oude Rijn →, Neths. 15 B4 52 12N 4 24 E
Oudenaarde, Belgium 15 D3 50 50N 3 37 E
Oudtshoorn, S. Africa 56 E3 33 35S 22 14 E
Ouessant, Î. d', France 18 B1 48 28N 5 6W
Ouesso, Congo 52 D3 1 37N 16 5 E
Ouest, Pte. de l', Canada 71 C7 49 52N 64 40W
Ouezzane, Morocco 50 B4 34 51N 5 35W
Oughterard, Ireland 13 C2 53 26N 9 18W
Oujda, Morocco 50 B5 34 41N 1 55W
Oulainen, Finland 8 D21 64 17N 24 47 E
Oulu, Finland 8 D21 65 1N 25 29 E
Oulujärvi, Finland 8 D22 64 25N 27 15 E
Oulujoki →, Finland 8 D21 65 1N 25 30 E
Oum Chalouba, Chad 51 E10 15 48N 20 46 E
Oum Hadjer, Chad 51 F9 13 18N 19 41 E
Ounasjoki →, Finland 8 C21 66 31N 25 40 E
Ounguati, Namibia 56 C2 22 0S 15 46 E
Ounianga Sérir, Chad 51 E10 18 54N 20 51 E
Our →, Lux. 15 E6 49 55N 6 5 E
Ouray, U.S.A. 83 G10 38 1N 107 40W
Ourense, Spain 19 A2 42 19N 7 55W
Ouricuri, Brazil 93 E10 7 53S 40 5W
Ourinhos, Brazil 95 A6 23 0S 49 54W
Ouro Fino, Brazil 95 A6 22 16S 46 25W
Ouro Prêto, Brazil 95 A7 20 20S 43 30W
Ourthe →, Belgium 15 D5 50 29N 5 35 E
Ouse →, E. Susx., U.K. 11 G8 50 47N 0 4 E
Ouse →, N. Yorks., U.K. 10 D7 53 44N 0 55W
Outaouais →, Canada 70 C5 45 27N 74 8W
Outardes →, Canada 71 C6 49 24N 69 30W
Outer Hebrides, U.K. 12 D1 57 30N 7 40W
Outjo, Namibia 56 C2 20 5S 16 7 E
Outlook, Canada 73 C7 51 30N 107 0W
Outokumpu, Finland 8 E23 62 43N 29 1 E
Ouyen, Australia 63 F3 35 1S 142 22 E
Ovalau, Fiji 59 C8 17 40S 178 48 E
Ovalle, Chile 94 C1 30 33S 71 18W
Ovamboland, Namibia 56 B2 18 30S 16 0 E
Overflakkee, Neths. 15 C4 51 44N 4 10 E
Overijssel □, Neths. 15 B6 52 25N 6 35 E
Overland Park, U.S.A. 80 F7 38 55N 94 50W
Overton, U.S.A. 85 J12 36 33N 114 27W
Övertorneå, Sweden 8 C20 66 23N 23 38 E
Ovid, U.S.A. 79 D8 42 41N 76 49W
Oviedo, Spain 19 A3 43 25N 5 50W
Oviši, Latvia 9 H19 57 33N 21 44 E
Ovoot, Mongolia 34 B7 45 21N 113 45 E
Övör Hangay □, Mongolia 34 B2 45 0N 102 30 E
Øvre Årdal, Norway 9 F12 61 19N 7 48 E
Ovruch, Ukraine 17 C15 51 25N 28 45 E
Owaka, N.Z. 59 M2 46 27S 169 40 E
Owambo = Ovamboland, Namibia 56 B2 18 30S 16 0 E
Owando, Congo 52 E3 0 29S 15 55 E
Owasco L., U.S.A. 79 D8 42 50N 76 31W
Owase, Japan 31 G8 34 7N 136 12 E
Owatonna, U.S.A. 80 C8 44 5N 93 14W
Owbeh, Afghan. 40 B3 34 28N 63 10 E
Owego, U.S.A. 79 D8 42 6N 76 16W
Owen Falls Dam, Uganda 54 B3 0 30N 33 5 E
Owen Sound, Canada 78 B4 44 35N 80 55W
Owens →, U.S.A. 84 J9 36 32N 117 59W
Owens L., U.S.A. 85 J9 36 26N 117 57W
Owensboro, U.S.A. 76 G2 37 46N 87 7W
Owl →, Canada 73 B10 57 51N 92 44W
Owo, Nigeria 50 G7 7 10N 5 39 E
Owosso, U.S.A. 76 D3 43 0N 84 10W
Owyhee, U.S.A. 82 F5 41 57N 116 6W
Owyhee →, U.S.A. 82 E5 43 49N 117 2W
Owyhee, L., U.S.A. 82 E5 43 38N 117 14W
Ox Mts. = Slieve Gamph, Ireland 13 B3 54 6N 9 0W
Öxarfjörður, Iceland 8 C5 66 15N 16 45W
Oxbow, Canada 73 D8 49 14N 102 10W
Oxelösund, Sweden 9 G17 58 43N 17 5 E
Oxford, N.Z. 59 K4 43 18S 172 11 E
Oxford, U.K. 11 F6 51 46N 1 15W
Oxford, Mass., U.S.A. 79 D13 42 7N 71 52W
Oxford, Miss., U.S.A. 81 H10 34 22N 89 31W
Oxford, N.C., U.S.A. 77 G6 36 19N 78 35W
Oxford, N.Y., U.S.A. 79 D9 42 27N 75 36W
Oxford, Ohio, U.S.A. 76 F3 39 31N 84 45W
Oxford L., Canada 73 C9 54 51N 95 37W
Oxfordshire □, U.K. 11 F6 51 48N 1 16W
Oxnard, U.S.A. 85 L7 34 12N 119 11W
Oxus = Amudarya →, Uzbekistan 26 E6 43 58N 59 34 E
Oya, Malaysia 36 D4 2 55N 111 55 E
Oyama, Japan 31 F9 36 18N 139 48 E
Oyem, Gabon 52 D2 1 34N 11 31 E
Oyen, Canada 73 C6 51 22N 110 28W
Oykel →, U.K. 12 D4 57 56N 4 26W
Oymyakon, Russia 27 C15 63 25N 142 44 E
Oyo, Nigeria 50 G6 7 46N 3 56 E
Oyster Bay, U.S.A. 79 F11 40 52N 73 32W
Öyübari, Japan 30 C11 43 1N 142 5 E
Ozamiz, Phil. 37 C6 8 15N 123 50 E
Ozark, Ala., U.S.A. 77 K3 31 28N 85 39W
Ozark, Ark., U.S.A. 81 H8 35 29N 93 50W
Ozark, Mo., U.S.A. 81 G8 37 1N 93 12W
Ozark Plateau, U.S.A. 81 G9 37 20N 91 40W
Ozarks, L. of the, U.S.A. 80 F8 38 12N 92 38W
Ózd, Hungary 17 D11 48 14N 20 15 E
Ozette L., U.S.A. 84 B2 48 6N 124 38W
Ozona, U.S.A. 81 K4 30 43N 101 12W
Ozuluama, Mexico 87 C5 21 40N 97 50W

P

Pa-an, Burma 41 L20 16 51N 97 40 E
Pa Mong Dam, Thailand 38 D4 18 0N 102 22 E
Pa Sak →, Thailand 36 B2 15 30N 101 0 E
Paamiut = Frederikshåb, Greenland 4 C5 62 0N 49 43W
Paarl, S. Africa 56 E2 33 45S 18 56 E
Paauilo, U.S.A. 74 H17 20 2N 155 22W
Pab Hills, Pakistan 42 F2 26 30N 66 45 E
Pabbay, U.K. 12 D1 57 46N 7 14W
Pabianice, Poland 17 C10 51 40N 19 20 E
Pabna, Bangla. 41 G16 24 1N 89 18 E
Pabo, Uganda 54 B3 3 1N 32 10 E
Pacaja →, Brazil 93 D8 1 56S 50 50W
Pacaraima, Sa., S. Amer. 92 C6 4 0N 62 30W
Pacasmayo, Peru 92 E3 7 20S 79 35W
Pachhar, India 42 G7 24 40N 77 42 E
Pachitea →, Peru 92 E4 8 46S 74 33W
Pachmarhi, India 43 H8 22 28N 78 26 E
Pachpadra, India 40 G8 25 58N 72 10 E
Pachuca, Mexico 87 C5 20 10N 98 40W
Pacific, Canada 72 C3 54 48N 128 28W
Pacific-Antarctic Ridge, Pac. Oc. 65 M16 43 0S 115 0W
Pacific Grove, U.S.A. 84 J5 36 38N 121 56W
Pacific Ocean, Pac. Oc. 65 G14 10 0N 140 0W
Pacific Rim Nat. Park, Canada 84 B2 48 40N 124 45W
Pacifica, U.S.A. 84 H4 37 36N 122 30W
Pacitan, Indonesia 37 H14 8 12S 111 7 E
Packwood, U.S.A. 84 D5 46 36N 121 40W
Padaido, Kepulauan, Indonesia 37 E9 1 5S 138 0 E
Padang, Indonesia 36 E2 1 0S 100 20 E
Padang Endau, Malaysia 39 L4 2 40N 103 38 E
Padangpanjang, Indonesia 36 E2 0 40S 100 20 E
Padangsidempuan, Indonesia 36 D1 1 30N 99 15 E
Paddle Prairie, Canada 72 B5 57 57N 117 29W
Paddockwood, Canada 73 C7 53 30N 105 30W
Paderborn, Germany 16 C5 51 42N 8 45 E
Padma, India 43 G11 24 12N 85 22 E
Pádova, Italy 20 B4 45 25N 11 53 E
Padra, India 42 H5 22 15N 73 7 E
Padrauna, India 43 F10 26 54N 83 59 E
Padre I., U.S.A. 81 M6 27 10N 97 25W
Padstow, U.K. 11 G3 50 33N 4 58W
Padua = Pádova, Italy 20 B4 45 25N 11 53 E
Paducah, Ky., U.S.A. 76 G1 37 5N 88 37W
Paducah, Tex., U.S.A. 81 H4 34 1N 100 18W
Paengnyŏng-do, S. Korea 35 F13 37 57N 124 40 E
Paeroa, N.Z. 59 G5 37 23S 175 41 E
Pafúri, Mozam. 57 C5 22 28S 31 17 E
Pag, Croatia 16 F8 44 25N 15 3 E
Pagadian, Phil. 37 C6 7 55N 123 30 E
Pagai Selatan, Pulau, Indonesia 36 E2 3 0S 100 15 E
Pagai Utara, Pulau, Indonesia 36 E2 2 35S 100 0 E
Pagalu = Annobón, Atl. Oc. 49 G4 1 25S 5 36 E
Pagara, India 43 G9 24 22N 80 1 E
Pagastikós Kólpos, Greece 21 E10 39 15N 23 0 E
Pagatan, Indonesia 36 E5 3 33S 115 59 E
Page, U.S.A. 83 H8 36 57N 111 27W
Pago Pago, Amer. Samoa 59 B13 14 16S 170 43W
Pagosa Springs, U.S.A. 83 H10 37 16N 107 1W
Pagwa River, Canada 70 B2 50 2N 85 14W
Pahala, U.S.A. 74 J17 19 12N 155 29W
Pahang →, Malaysia 39 L4 3 30N 103 9 E
Pahiatua, N.Z. 59 J5 40 27S 175 50 E
Pahokee, U.S.A. 77 M5 26 50N 80 40W
Pahrump, U.S.A. 85 J11 36 12N 115 59W
Pahute Mesa, U.S.A. 84 H10 37 20N 116 45W
Pai, Thailand 38 C2 19 19N 98 27 E
Paia, U.S.A. 74 H16 20 54N 156 22W
Paicines, U.S.A. 84 J5 36 44N 121 17W
Paide, Estonia 9 G21 58 57N 25 31 E
Paignton, U.K. 11 G4 50 26N 3 35W
Päijänne, Finland 9 F21 61 30N 25 30 E
Pailani, India 43 G9 25 45N 80 26 E
Pailin, Cambodia 38 F4 12 46N 102 36 E
Painan, Indonesia 36 E2 1 21S 100 34 E
Painesville, U.S.A. 78 E3 41 43N 81 15W
Paint Hills = Wemindji, Canada 70 B4 53 0N 78 49W
Paint L., Canada 73 B9 55 28N 97 57W
Painted Desert, U.S.A. 83 J8 36 0N 111 0W
Paintsville, U.S.A. 76 G4 37 49N 82 48W
País Vasco □, Spain 19 A4 42 50N 2 45W
Paisley, Canada 78 B3 44 18N 81 16W
Paisley, U.K. 12 F4 55 50N 4 25W
Paisley, U.S.A. 82 E3 42 42N 120 32W
Paita, Peru 92 E2 5 11S 81 9W
Pajares, Puerto de, Spain 19 A3 42 58N 5 46W
Pak Lay, Laos 38 C3 18 15N 101 27 E
Pak Phanang, Thailand 39 H3 8 21N 100 12 E
Pak Sane, Laos 38 C4 18 22N 103 39 E
Pak Song, Laos 38 E6 15 11N 106 14 E
Pakaur, India 43 G12 24 38N 87 51 E
Pakenham, Canada 79 A8 45 18N 76 18W
Pákhnes, Greece 23 D6 35 16N 24 4 E
Pakistan ■, Asia 42 E4 30 0N 70 0 E
Pakkading, Laos 38 C4 18 19N 103 59 E
Pakokku, Burma 41 J19 21 20N 95 0 E
Pakowki L., Canada 73 D6 49 20N 111 0W
Pakpattan, Pakistan 42 D5 30 25N 73 27 E
Paktīā □, Afghan. 40 C6 33 0N 69 15 E
Pakwach, Uganda 54 B3 2 28N 31 27 E
Pakxe, Laos 38 E5 15 5N 105 52 E
Pal Lahara, India 43 J11 21 27N 85 11 E
Pala, Chad 51 G9 9 25N 15 5 E
Pala, Dem. Rep. of the Congo 54 D2 6 45S 29 30 E
Pala, U.S.A. 85 M9 33 22N 117 5W
Palabek, Uganda 54 B3 3 22N 32 33 E
Palacios, U.S.A. 81 L6 28 42N 96 13W
Palagruža, Croatia 20 C7 42 24N 16 15 E
Palaiókastron, Greece 23 D8 35 12N 26 15 E
Palaiokhóra, Greece 23 D5 35 16N 23 39 E
Palam, India 40 K10 19 0N 77 0 E
Palampur, India 42 C7 32 10N 76 30 E
Palana, Australia 62 F4 39 45S 147 55 E
Palana, Russia 27 D16 59 10N 159 59 E
Palanan, Phil. 37 A6 17 8N 122 29 E
Palanan Pt., Phil. 37 A6 17 17N 122 30 E
Palandri, Pakistan 43 C5 33 42N 73 40 E
Palanga, Lithuania 9 J19 55 58N 21 3 E
Palangkaraya, Indonesia 36 E4 2 16S 113 56 E
Palani Hills, India 40 P10 10 14N 77 33 E
Palanpur, India 42 G5 24 10N 72 25 E
Palapye, Botswana 56 C4 22 30S 27 7 E
Palas, Pakistan 43 B5 35 4N 73 14 E
Palashi, India 43 H13 23 47N 88 15 E
Palasponga, India 43 J11 21 47N 85 34 E
Palatka, Russia 27 C16 60 6N 150 54 E
Palatka, U.S.A. 77 L5 29 39N 81 38W
Palau ■, Pac. Oc. 28 J17 7 30N 134 30 E
Palauk, Burma 38 F2 13 10N 98 40 E
Palawan, Phil. 36 C5 9 30N 118 30 E
Palayankottai, India 40 Q10 8 45N 77 45 E
Paldiski, Estonia 9 G21 59 23N 24 9 E
Paleleh, Indonesia 37 D6 1 10N 121 50 E
Palembang, Indonesia 36 E2 3 0S 104 50 E
Palencia, Spain 19 A3 42 1N 4 34W
Palenque, Mexico 87 D6 17 31N 91 58W
Paleokastrítsa, Greece 23 A3 39 40N 19 41 E
Paleometokho, Cyprus 23 D12 35 7N 33 11 E
Palermo, Italy 20 E5 38 7N 13 22 E
Palermo, U.S.A. 82 G3 39 26N 121 33W
Palestina, Chile 96 A3 23 50S 69 47W
Palestine, Asia 47 D4 32 0N 35 0 E
Palestine, U.S.A. 81 K7 31 46N 95 38W
Paletwa, Burma 41 J18 21 10N 92 50 E
Palghat, India 40 P10 10 46N 76 42 E
Palgrave, Mt., Australia 60 D2 23 22S 115 58 E
Pali, India 42 G5 25 50N 73 20 E
Palikir, Micronesia 64 G7 6 55N 158 9 E
Palioúrion, Ákra, Greece 21 E10 39 57N 23 45 E
Palisades Reservoir, U.S.A. 82 E8 43 20N 111 12W
Paliseul, Belgium 15 E5 49 54N 5 8 E
Palitana, India 42 J4 21 32N 71 49 E
Palizada, Mexico 87 D6 18 18N 92 8W
Palk Bay, Asia 40 Q11 9 30N 79 15 E
Palk Strait, Asia 40 Q11 10 0N 79 45 E
Palkānah, Iraq 44 C5 35 49N 44 26 E
Palkot, India 43 H11 22 53N 84 39 E
Palla Road = Dinokwe, Botswana 56 C4 23 29S 26 37 E
Pallanza = Verbània, Italy 18 D8 45 56N 8 33 E
Pallarenda, Australia 62 B4 19 12S 146 46 E
Pallinup →, Australia 61 F2 34 27S 118 50 E
Pallisa, Uganda 54 B3 1 12N 33 43 E
Pallu, India 42 E6 28 59N 74 14 E
Palm Bay, U.S.A. 77 L5 28 2N 80 35W
Palm Beach, U.S.A. 77 M6 26 43N 80 2W
Palm Coast, U.S.A. 77 L5 29 32N 81 10W
Palm Desert, U.S.A. 85 M10 33 43N 116 22W
Palm Is., Australia 62 B4 18 40S 146 35 E
Palm Springs, U.S.A. 85 M10 33 50N 116 33W
Palma, Mozam. 55 E5 10 46S 40 29 E
Palma, B. de, Spain 22 B9 39 30N 2 39 E
Palma de Mallorca, Spain 22 B9 39 35N 2 39 E
Palma Soriano, Cuba 88 B4 20 15N 76 0W
Palmares, Brazil 93 E11 8 41S 35 28W
Palmas, Brazil 95 B5 26 29S 52 0W
Palmas, C., Liberia 50 H4 4 27N 7 46W
Pálmas, G. di, Italy 20 E3 39 0N 8 30 E
Palmdale, U.S.A. 85 L8 34 35N 118 7W
Palmeira das Missões, Brazil 95 B5 27 55S 53 17W
Palmeira dos Índios, Brazil 93 E11 9 25S 36 37W
Palmer, U.S.A. 68 B5 61 36N 149 7W
Palmer →, Australia 62 B3 16 0S 142 26 E
Palmer Arch., Antarctica 5 C17 64 15S 65 0W
Palmer Lake, U.S.A. 80 F2 39 7N 104 55W
Palmer Land, Antarctica 5 D18 73 0S 63 0W
Palmerston, Canada 78 C4 43 50N 80 51W
Palmerston, N.Z. 59 L3 45 29S 170 43 E
Palmerston North, N.Z. 59 J5 40 21S 175 39 E
Palmerton, U.S.A. 79 F9 40 48N 75 37W
Palmetto, U.S.A. 77 M4 27 31N 82 34W
Palmi, Italy 20 E6 38 21N 15 51 E
Palmira, Argentina 94 C2 32 59S 68 34W
Palmira, Colombia 92 C3 3 32N 76 16W
Palmyra = Tudmur, Syria 44 C3 34 36N 38 15 E
Palmyra, Mo., U.S.A. 80 F9 39 48N 91 32W
Palmyra, N.J., U.S.A. 79 F9 40 1N 75 1W
Palmyra, N.Y., U.S.A. 78 C7 43 5N 77 18W
Palmyra, Pa., U.S.A. 79 F8 40 18N 76 36W
Palmyra Is., Pac. Oc. 65 G11 5 52N 162 5W
Palo Alto, U.S.A. 84 H4 37 27N 122 10W
Palo Verde, U.S.A. 85 M12 33 26N 114 44W
Palopo, Indonesia 37 E6 3 0S 120 16 E
Palos, C. de, Spain 19 D5 37 38N 0 40W
Palos Verdes, U.S.A. 85 M8 33 48N 118 23W
Palos Verdes, Pt., U.S.A. 85 M8 33 43N 118 26W
Palu, Indonesia 37 E5 1 0S 119 52 E
Palu, Turkey 25 G7 38 45N 40 0 E
Palwal, India 42 E7 28 8N 77 19 E
Pamanukan, Indonesia 37 G12 6 16S 107 49 E
Pamiers, France 18 E4 43 7N 1 39 E
Pamir, Tajikistan 26 F8 37 40N 73 0 E
Pamlico →, U.S.A. 77 H7 35 20N 76 28W
Pamlico Sd., U.S.A. 77 H8 35 20N 76 0W
Pampa, U.S.A. 81 H4 35 32N 100 58W
Pampa de las Salinas, Argentina 94 C2 32 1S 66 58W
Pampanua, Indonesia 37 E6 4 16S 120 8 E
Pampas, Argentina 94 D3 35 0S 63 0W
Pampas, Peru 92 F4 12 20S 74 50W
Pamplona, Colombia 92 B4 7 23N 72 39W
Pamplona, Spain 19 A5 42 48N 1 38W
Pampoenpoort, S. Africa 56 E3 31 3S 22 40 E
Pana, U.S.A. 80 F10 39 23N 89 5W
Panaca, U.S.A. 83 H6 37 47N 114 23W
Panaitan, Indonesia 37 G11 6 36S 105 12 E
Panaji, India 40 M8 15 25N 73 50 E
Panamá, Panama 88 E4 9 0N 79 25W
Panama ■, Cent. Amer. 88 E4 8 48N 79 55W
Panamá, G. de, Panama 88 E4 8 4N 79 20W
Panama Canal, Panama 88 E4 9 10N 79 37W
Panama City, U.S.A. 77 K3 30 10N 85 40W
Panamint Range, U.S.A. 85 J9 36 20N 117 20W
Panamint Springs, U.S.A. 85 J9 36 20N 117 28W
Panão, Peru 92 E3 9 55S 75 55W
Panare, Thailand 39 J3 6 51N 101 30 E
Panay, Phil. 37 B6 11 10N 122 30 E
Panay, G., Phil. 37 B6 11 0N 122 30 E
Pančevo, Serbia, Yug. 21 B9 44 52N 20 41 E
Pandan, Phil. 37 B6 11 45N 122 10 E
Pandegelang, Indonesia 37 G12 6 25S 106 5 E
Pandhana, India 42 J7 21 42N 76 13 E
Pandharpur, India 40 L9 17 41N 75 20 E
Pando, Uruguay 95 C4 34 44S 56 0W
Pando, L. = Hope, L., Australia 63 D2 28 24S 139 18 E
Pandokrátor, Greece 23 A3 39 45N 19 50 E
Pandora, Costa Rica 88 E3 9 43N 83 3W
Panevėžys, Lithuania 9 J21 55 42N 24 25 E
Panfilov, Kazakstan 26 E9 44 10N 80 0 E
Pang-Long, Burma 41 H21 23 11N 98 45 E
Pang-Yang, Burma 41 H21 22 7N 98 48 E
Panga, Dem. Rep. of the Congo 54 B2 1 52N 26 18 E
Pangalanes, Canal des, Madag. 57 C8 22 48S 47 50 E
Pangani, Tanzania 54 D4 5 25S 38 58 E
Pangani →, Tanzania 54 D4 5 26S 38 58 E
Pangfou = Bengbu, China 35 H9 32 58N 117 20 E
Pangil, Dem. Rep. of the Congo 54 C2 3 10S 26 35 E
Pangkah, Tanjung, Indonesia 37 G15 6 51S 112 33 E
Pangkajene, Indonesia 37 E5 4 46S 119 34 E
Pangkalanbrandan, Indonesia 36 D1 4 1N 98 20 E
Pangkalanbuun, Indonesia 36 E4 2 41S 111 37 E

Penn Hills

Pangkalpinang, Indonesia . 36 E3 2 0S 106 0 E
Pangnirtung, Canada 69 B13 66 8N 65 54W
Pangong Tso, India 42 B8 34 40N 78 40 E
Panguitch, U.S.A. 83 H7 37 50N 112 26W
Pangutaran Group, Phil. 37 C6 6 18N 120 34 E
Panhandle, U.S.A. 81 H4 35 21N 101 23W
Pani Mines, India 42 H5 22 29N 73 50 E
Pania-Mutombo, Dem. Rep. of the Congo 54 D1 5 11S 23 51 E
Panikota I., India 42 J4 20 46N 71 21 E
Panipat, India 42 E7 29 25N 77 2 E
Panjal Range, India 42 C7 32 30N 76 50 E
Panjang, Hon, Vietnam 39 H4 9 20N 103 28 E
Panjgur, Pakistan 40 F4 27 0N 64 5 E
Panjim = Panaji, India 40 M8 15 25N 73 50 E
Panjin, China 35 D12 41 3N 122 2 E
Panjinad Barrage, Pakistan 40 E7 29 22N 71 15 E
Panjnad →, Pakistan 42 E4 28 57N 70 30 E
Panjwai, Afghan. 42 D1 31 26N 65 27 E
Panmunjŏm, N. Korea 35 F14 37 59N 126 38 E
Panna, India 43 G9 24 40N 80 15 E
Panna Hills, India 43 G9 24 40N 81 15 E
Pannawonica, Australia 60 D2 21 39S 116 19 E
Pano Akil, Pakistan 42 F3 27 51N 69 7 E
Pano Lefkara, Cyprus 23 E12 34 53N 33 20 E
Pano Panayia, Cyprus 23 E11 34 55N 32 38 E
Panorama, Brazil 95 A5 21 21S 51 51W
Pánormon, Greece 23 D6 35 25N 24 41 E
Pansemal, India 42 J6 21 39N 74 42 E
Panshan = Panjin, China 35 D12 41 3N 122 2 E
Panshi, China 35 C14 42 58N 126 5 E
Pantanal, Brazil 92 H7 17 30S 57 40W
Pantar, Indonesia 37 F6 8 28S 124 10 E
Pante Macassar, Indonesia 37 F6 9 30S 123 58 E
Pantelleria, Italy 20 F4 36 50N 11 57 E
Pánuco, Mexico 87 C5 22 0N 98 15W
Paola, Malta 23 D2 35 52N 14 30 E
Paola, U.S.A. 80 F7 38 35N 94 53W
Paonia, U.S.A. 83 G10 38 52N 107 36W
Paoting = Baoding, China 34 E8 38 50N 115 28 E
Paot'ou = Baotou, China 34 D6 40 32N 110 2 E
Paoua, C.A.R. 52 C3 7 9N 16 20 E
Pápa, Hungary 17 E9 47 22N 17 30 E
Papa Stour, U.K. 12 A7 60 20N 1 42W
Papa Westray, U.K. 12 B6 59 20N 2 55W
Papagayo →, Mexico 87 D5 16 36N 99 43W
Papagayo, G. de, Costa Rica 88 D2 10 30N 85 50W
Papakura, N.Z. 59 G5 37 4S 174 59 E
Papantla, Mexico 87 C5 20 30N 97 30W
Papar, Malaysia 36 C5 5 45N 116 0 E
Papeete, Tahiti 65 J13 17 32S 149 34W
Paphos, Cyprus 23 E11 34 46N 32 25 E
Papigochic →, Mexico 86 B3 29 9N 109 40W
Paposo, Chile 94 B1 25 0S 70 30W
Papoutsa, Cyprus 23 E12 34 54N 33 4 E
Papua New Guinea ■, Oceania 64 H6 8 0S 145 0 E
Papudo, Chile 94 C1 32 29S 71 27W
Papun, Burma 41 K20 18 2N 97 30 E
Papunya, Australia 60 D5 23 15S 131 54 E
Pará = Belém, Brazil 93 D9 1 20S 48 30W
Pará □, Brazil 93 D8 3 20S 52 0W
Paraburdoo, Australia 60 D2 23 14S 117 32 E
Paracatu, Brazil 93 G9 17 10S 46 50W
Paracel Is., S. China Sea 36 A4 15 50N 112 0 E
Parachilna, Australia 63 E2 31 10S 138 21 E
Parachinar, Pakistan 42 C4 33 55N 70 5 E
Paradhísi, Greece 23 C10 36 18N 28 7 E
Paradip, India 41 J15 20 15N 86 35 E
Paradise, Calif., U.S.A. 84 F5 39 46N 121 37W
Paradise, Nev., U.S.A. 85 J11 36 9N 115 10W
Paradise →, Canada 71 B8 53 27N 57 19W
Paradise Hill, Canada 73 C7 53 32N 109 28W
Paradise River, Canada 71 B8 53 27N 57 17W
Paradise Valley, U.S.A. 82 F5 41 30N 117 32W
Parado, Indonesia 37 F5 8 42S 118 30 E
Paragould, U.S.A. 81 G9 36 3N 90 29W
Paragua →, Venezuela 92 B6 6 55N 62 55W
Paraguaçu →, Brazil 93 F11 12 45S 38 54W
Paraguaçu Paulista, Brazil 95 A5 22 22S 50 35W
Paraguaná, Pen. de, Venezuela 92 A5 12 0N 70 0W
Paraguarí, Paraguay 94 B4 25 36S 57 0W
Paraguarí □, Paraguay 94 B4 26 0S 57 10W
Paraguay ■, S. Amer. 94 A4 23 0S 57 0W
Paraguay →, Paraguay 94 B4 27 18S 58 38W
Paraíba = João Pessoa, Brazil 93 E12 7 10S 34 52W
Paraíba □, Brazil 93 E11 7 0S 36 0W
Paraíba do Sul →, Brazil 95 A7 21 37S 41 3W
Parainen, Finland 9 F20 60 18N 22 18 E
Paraiso, Mexico 87 D6 18 24N 93 14W
Parak, Iran 45 E7 27 38N 52 25 E
Parakou, Benin 50 G6 9 25N 2 40 E
Paralimni, Cyprus 23 D12 35 2N 33 58 E
Paramaribo, Surinam 93 B7 5 50N 55 10W
Paramushir, Ostrov, Russia 27 D16 50 24N 156 0 E
Paran →, Israel 47 E4 30 20N 35 10 E
Paraná, Argentina 94 C3 31 45S 60 30W
Paranã, Brazil 93 F9 12 30S 47 48W
Paraná □, Brazil 95 A5 24 30S 51 0W
Paraná →, Argentina 94 C4 33 43S 59 15W
Paranaguá, Brazil 95 B6 25 30S 48 30W
Paranaíba, Brazil 93 G8 19 40S 51 11W
Paranaíba →, Brazil 93 H8 20 6S 51 4W
Paranapanema →, Brazil 95 A5 22 40S 53 9W
Paranapiacaba, Serra do, Brazil 95 A6 24 31S 48 35W
Paranavaí, Brazil 95 A5 23 4S 52 56W
Parang, Jolo, Phil. 37 C6 5 55N 120 54 E
Parang, Mindanao, Phil. 37 C6 7 23N 124 16 E
Parângul Mare, Vf., Romania 17 F12 45 20N 23 37 E
Parbati →, India 42 F6 26 54N 77 53 E
Parbati →, India 42 G7 25 50N 76 30 E
Parbhani, India 40 K10 19 8N 76 52 E
Parchim, Germany 16 B6 53 26N 11 52 E
Pardes Hanna-Karkur, Israel 47 C3 32 28N 34 57 E
Pardo →, Bahia, Brazil 93 G11 15 40S 39 0W
Pardo →, Mato Grosso, Brazil 95 A5 21 46S 52 9W
Pardubice, Czech Rep. 16 C8 50 3N 15 45 E
Pare, Indonesia 37 G15 7 43S 112 12 E
Pare Mts., Tanzania 54 C4 4 0S 37 45 E
Parecis, Serra dos, Brazil 92 F7 13 0S 60 0W
Paren, Russia 27 C17 62 30N 163 15 E
Parent, Canada 70 C5 47 55N 74 35W
Parent, L., Canada 70 C4 48 31N 77 1W
Parepare, Indonesia 37 E5 4 0S 119 40 E
Párga, Greece 21 E9 39 15N 20 29 E
Pargo, Pta. do, Madeira 22 D2 32 49N 17 17W
Pariaguán, Venezuela 92 B6 8 51N 64 34W
Paricutín, Cerro, Mexico 86 D4 19 28N 102 15W
Parigi, Indonesia 37 E6 0 50S 120 5 E
Parika, Guyana 92 B7 6 50N 58 20W
Parima, Serra, Brazil 92 C6 2 30N 64 0W
Parinari, Peru 92 D4 4 35S 74 25W
Pariñas, Pta., S. Amer. 90 D2 4 30S 82 0W
Parintins, Brazil 93 D7 2 40S 56 50W
Pariparit Kyun, Burma 41 M18 14 55N 93 45 E
Paris, Canada 78 C4 43 12N 80 25W
Paris, France 18 B5 48 50N 2 20 E
Paris, Idaho, U.S.A. 82 E8 42 14N 111 24W
Paris, Ky., U.S.A. 76 F3 38 13N 84 15W
Paris, Tenn., U.S.A. 77 G1 36 18N 88 19W
Paris, Tex., U.S.A. 81 J7 33 40N 95 33W
Parish, U.S.A. 79 C8 43 25N 76 8W
Parishville, U.S.A. 79 B10 44 38N 74 49W
Park, U.S.A. 84 B4 48 45N 122 18W
Park City, U.S.A. 81 G6 37 48N 97 20W
Park Falls, U.S.A. 80 C9 45 56N 90 27W
Park Head, Canada 78 B3 44 36N 81 9W
Park Hills, U.S.A. 81 G9 37 53N 90 28W
Park Range, U.S.A. 82 G10 40 0N 106 30W
Park Rapids, U.S.A. 80 B7 46 55N 95 4W
Park River, U.S.A. 80 A6 48 24N 97 45W
Park Rynie, S. Africa 57 E5 30 25S 30 45 E
Parkā Bandar, Iran 45 E8 25 55N 59 35 E
Parkano, Finland 9 E20 62 1N 23 0 E
Parker, Ariz., U.S.A. 85 L12 34 9N 114 17W
Parker, Pa., U.S.A. 78 E5 41 5N 79 41W
Parker Dam, U.S.A. 85 L12 34 18N 114 8W
Parkersburg, U.S.A. 76 F5 39 16N 81 34W
Parkes, Australia 63 E4 33 9S 148 11 E
Parkfield, U.S.A. 84 K6 35 54N 120 26W
Parkhill, Canada 78 C3 43 15N 81 38W
Parkland, U.S.A. 84 C4 47 9N 122 26W
Parkston, U.S.A. 80 D6 43 24N 97 59W
Parksville, Canada 72 D4 49 20N 124 21W
Parla, Spain 19 B4 40 14N 3 46W
Parma, Italy 18 D9 44 48N 10 20 E
Parma, Idaho, U.S.A. 82 E5 43 47N 116 57W
Parma, Ohio, U.S.A. 78 E3 41 23N 81 43W
Parnaguá, Brazil 93 F10 10 10S 44 38W
Parnaíba, Brazil 93 D10 2 54S 41 47W
Parnaíba →, Brazil 93 D10 3 0S 41 50W
Parnassós, Greece 21 E10 38 35N 22 30 E
Pärnu, Estonia 9 G21 58 28N 24 33 E
Paroo →, Australia 63 E3 31 28S 143 32 E
Páros, Greece 21 F11 37 5N 25 12 E
Parowan, U.S.A. 83 H7 37 51N 112 50W
Parral, Chile 94 D1 36 10S 71 52W
Parras, Mexico 86 B4 25 30N 102 20W
Parrett →, U.K. 11 F4 51 12N 3 1W
Parris I., U.S.A. 77 J5 32 20N 80 41W
Parrsboro, Canada 71 C7 45 30N 64 25W
Parry I., Canada 78 A4 45 18N 80 10W
Parry Is., Canada 4 B2 77 0N 110 0W
Parry Sound, Canada 78 A5 45 20N 80 0W
Parsnip →, Canada 72 B4 55 10N 123 2W
Parsons, U.S.A. 81 G7 37 20N 95 16W
Parsons Ra., Australia 62 A2 13 30S 135 15 E
Partinico, Italy 20 E5 38 3N 13 7 E
Partridge I., Canada 70 A2 55 59N 87 37W
Paru →, Brazil 93 D8 1 33S 52 38W
Parvān □, Afghan. 40 B6 35 0N 69 0 E
Parvatipuram, India 41 K13 18 50N 83 25 E
Parvatsar, India 42 F6 26 52N 74 49 E
Parys, S. Africa 56 D4 26 52S 27 29 E
Pas, Pta. des, Spain 22 C7 38 46N 1 26 E
Pasadena, Canada 71 C8 49 1N 57 36W
Pasadena, Calif., U.S.A. 85 L8 34 9N 118 9W
Pasadena, Tex., U.S.A. 81 L7 29 43N 95 13W
Pasaje →, Argentina 94 B3 25 39S 63 56W
Pascagoula, U.S.A. 81 K10 30 21N 88 33W
Pascagoula →, U.S.A. 81 K10 30 23N 88 37W
Paşcani, Romania 17 E14 47 14N 26 45 E
Pasco, U.S.A. 82 C4 46 14N 119 6W
Pasco, Cerro de, Peru 92 F3 10 45S 76 10W
Pasco I., Australia 60 D2 20 57S 115 20 E
Pascoag, U.S.A. 79 E13 41 57N 71 42W
Pascua, I. de, Pac. Oc. 65 K17 27 0S 109 0W
Pasfield L., Canada 73 B7 58 24N 105 20W
Pashiwari, Pakistan 43 B6 34 40N 75 10 E
Pashmakli = Smolyan, Bulgaria 21 D11 41 36N 24 38 E
Pasir Mas, Malaysia 39 J4 6 2N 102 8 E
Pasir Putih, Malaysia 39 K4 5 50N 102 24 E
Pasirian, Indonesia 37 H15 8 13S 113 8 E
Pasirkuning, Indonesia 36 E2 0 30S 104 33 E
Pasküh, Iran 45 E9 27 34N 61 39 E
Pasley, C., Australia 61 F3 33 52S 123 35 E
Pašman, Croatia 16 G8 43 58N 15 20 E
Pasni, Pakistan 40 G3 25 15N 63 27 E
Paso Cantinela, Mexico 85 N11 32 33N 115 47W
Paso de Indios, Argentina 96 E3 43 55S 69 0W
Paso de los Libres, Argentina 94 B4 29 44S 57 10W
Paso de los Toros, Uruguay 94 C4 32 45S 56 30W
Paso Robles, U.S.A. 83 J3 35 38N 120 41W
Paspébiac, Canada 71 C6 48 3N 65 17W
Pasrur, Pakistan 42 C6 32 16N 74 43 E
Passage West, Ireland 13 E3 51 52N 8 21W
Passaic, U.S.A. 79 F10 40 51N 74 7W
Passau, Germany 16 D7 48 34N 13 28 E
Passero, C., Italy 20 F6 36 41N 15 10 E
Passo Fundo, Brazil 95 B5 28 10S 52 20W
Passos, Brazil 93 H9 20 45S 46 37W
Pastavy, Belarus 9 J22 55 4N 26 50 E
Pastaza →, Peru 92 D3 4 50S 76 52W
Pasto, Colombia 92 C3 1 13N 77 17W
Pasuruan, Indonesia 37 G15 7 40S 112 44 E
Patagonia, Argentina 96 F3 45 0S 69 0W
Patagonia, U.S.A. 83 L8 31 33N 110 45W
Patambar, Iran 45 D9 29 45N 60 17 E
Patan, India 40 H8 23 54N 72 14 E
Patan, Maharashtra, India 42 H5 23 54N 72 14 E
Patan, Nepal 41 F14 27 40N 85 20 E
Patani, Indonesia 37 D7 0 20N 128 50 E
Pataudi, India 42 E7 28 18N 76 48 E
Patchewollock, Australia 63 F3 35 22S 142 12 E
Patchogue, U.S.A. 79 F11 40 46N 73 1W
Patea, N.Z. 59 H5 39 45S 174 30 E
Patensie, S. Africa 56 E3 33 46S 24 49 E
Paternò, Italy 20 F6 37 34N 14 54 E
Pateros, U.S.A. 82 B4 48 3N 119 54W
Paterson, U.S.A. 79 F10 40 55N 74 11W
Paterson Ra., Australia 60 D3 21 45S 122 10 E
Pathankot, India 42 C6 32 18N 75 45 E
Pathfinder Reservoir, U.S.A. 82 E10 42 28N 106 51W
Pathiu, Thailand 39 G2 10 42N 99 19 E
Pathum Thani, Thailand 38 E3 14 1N 100 32 E
Pati, Indonesia 37 G14 6 45S 111 1 E
Patía →, Colombia 92 C3 2 13N 78 40W
Patiala, India 42 D7 30 23N 76 26 E
Patiala, India 43 F8 27 43N 79 1 E
Patkai Bum, India 41 F19 27 0N 95 30 E
Pátmos, Greece 21 F12 37 21N 26 36 E
Patna, India 43 G11 25 35N 85 12 E
Pato Branco, Brazil 95 B5 26 13S 52 40W
Patonga, Uganda 54 B3 2 45N 33 15 E
Patos, Brazil 93 E11 6 55S 37 16W
Patos, L. dos, Brazil 95 C5 31 20S 51 0W
Patos, Río de los →, Argentina 94 C2 31 18S 69 25W
Patos de Minas, Brazil 93 G9 18 35S 46 32W
Patquía, Argentina 94 C2 30 2S 66 55W
Pátrai, Greece 21 E9 38 14N 21 47 E
Pátraikós Kólpos, Greece 21 E9 38 17N 21 30 E
Patras = Pátrai, Greece 21 E9 38 14N 21 47 E
Patrocínio, Brazil 93 G9 18 57S 47 0W
Patta, Kenya 54 C5 2 10S 41 0 E
Pattani, Thailand 39 J3 6 48N 101 15 E
Pattaya, Thailand 36 B2 12 52N 100 55 E
Patten, U.S.A. 77 C11 46 0N 68 38W
Patterson, Calif., U.S.A. 84 H5 37 28N 121 8W
Patterson, La., U.S.A. 81 L9 29 42N 91 18W
Patterson, Mt., U.S.A. 84 G7 38 29N 119 20W
Patti, Punjab, India 42 D6 31 17N 74 54 E
Patti, Ut. P., India 43 G10 25 55N 82 12 E
Pattoki, Pakistan 42 D5 31 5N 73 52 E
Patton, U.S.A. 78 F6 40 38N 78 39W
Patuakhali, Bangla. 41 H17 22 20N 90 25 E
Patuanak, Canada 73 B7 55 55N 107 43W
Patuca →, Honduras 88 C3 15 50N 84 18W
Patuca, Punta, Honduras 88 C3 15 49N 84 14W
Pátzcuaro, Mexico 86 D4 19 30N 101 40W
Pau, France 18 E3 43 19N 0 25W
Pauk, Burma 41 J19 21 27N 94 30 E
Paul I., Canada 71 A7 56 30N 61 20W
Paul Smiths, U.S.A. 79 B10 44 26N 74 15W
Paulatuk, Canada 68 B7 69 25N 124 0W
Paulis = Isiro, Dem. Rep. of the Congo 54 B2 2 53N 27 40 E
Paulistana, Brazil 93 E10 8 9S 41 9W
Paulo Afonso, Brazil 93 E11 9 21S 38 15W
Paulpietersburg, S. Africa 57 D5 27 23S 30 50 E
Pauls Valley, U.S.A. 81 H6 34 44N 97 13W
Pauma Valley, U.S.A. 85 M10 33 16N 116 58W
Pauri, India 43 D8 30 9N 78 47 E
Pāveh, Iran 44 C5 35 3N 46 22 E
Pavia, Italy 18 D8 45 7N 9 8 E
Pavilion, U.S.A. 78 D6 42 52N 78 1W
Pāvilosta, Latvia 9 H19 56 53N 21 14 E
Pavlodar, Kazakstan 26 D8 52 33N 77 0 E
Pavlograd = Pavlohrad, Ukraine 25 E6 48 30N 35 52 E
Pavlohrad, Ukraine 25 E6 48 30N 35 52 E
Pavlovo, Russia 24 C7 55 58N 43 5 E
Pavlovsk, Russia 25 D7 50 26N 40 5 E
Pavlovskaya, Russia 25 E6 46 17N 39 47 E
Pawayan, India 43 E9 28 4N 80 6 E
Pawhuska, U.S.A. 81 G6 36 40N 96 20W
Pawling, U.S.A. 79 E11 41 34N 73 36W
Pawnee, U.S.A. 81 G6 36 20N 96 48W
Pawnee City, U.S.A. 80 E6 40 7N 96 9W
Pawtucket, U.S.A. 79 E13 41 53N 71 23W
Paximádhia, Greece 23 E6 35 0N 24 35 E
Paxoí, Greece 21 E9 39 14N 20 12 E
Paxton, Ill., U.S.A. 76 E1 40 27N 88 6W
Paxton, Nebr., U.S.A. 80 E4 41 7N 101 21W
Payakumbuh, Indonesia 36 E2 0 20S 100 35 E
Payette, U.S.A. 82 D5 44 5N 116 56W
Payne Bay = Kangirsuk, Canada 69 C13 60 0N 70 0W
Payne L., Canada 69 C12 59 30N 74 30W
Paynes Find, Australia 61 E2 29 15S 117 42 E
Paynesville, U.S.A. 80 C7 45 23N 94 43W
Paysandú, Uruguay 94 C4 32 19S 58 8W
Payson, Ariz., U.S.A. 83 J8 34 14N 111 20W
Payson, Utah, U.S.A. 74 B4 40 3N 111 44W
Paz →, Guatemala 88 D1 13 44N 90 10W
Paz, B. la, Mexico 86 C2 24 15N 110 25W
Pāzanān, Iran 45 D6 30 35N 49 59 E
Pazardzhik, Bulgaria 21 C11 42 12N 24 20 E
Pe Ell, U.S.A. 84 D3 46 34N 123 18W
Peabody, U.S.A. 79 D14 42 31N 70 56W
Peace →, Canada 72 B6 59 0N 111 25W
Peace Point, Canada 72 B6 59 7N 112 27W
Peace River, Canada 72 B5 56 15N 117 18W
Peach Springs, U.S.A. 83 J7 35 32N 113 25W
Peachland, Canada 72 D5 49 47N 119 45W
Peachtree City, U.S.A. 77 J3 33 25N 84 35W
Peak, The = Kinder Scout, U.K. 10 D6 53 24N 1 52W
Peak District, U.K. 10 D6 53 10N 1 50W
Peak Hill, N.S.W., Australia 63 E4 32 47S 148 11 E
Peak Hill, W. Austral., Australia 61 E2 25 35S 118 43 E
Peak Ra., Australia 62 C4 22 50S 148 20 E
Peake Cr. →, Australia 63 D2 28 2S 136 7 E
Peale, Mt., U.S.A. 83 G9 38 26N 109 14W
Pearblossom, U.S.A. 85 L9 34 30N 117 55W
Pearl →, U.S.A. 81 K10 30 11N 89 32W
Pearl City, U.S.A. 74 H16 21 24N 157 59W
Pearl Harbor, U.S.A. 74 H16 21 21N 157 57W
Pearl River, U.S.A. 79 E10 41 4N 74 2W
Pearsall, U.S.A. 81 L5 28 54N 99 6W
Peary Land, Greenland 4 A6 82 40N 33 0W
Pease →, U.S.A. 81 H5 34 12N 99 2W
Peawanuck, Canada 69 C11 55 15N 85 12W
Pebane, Mozam. 55 F4 17 10S 38 8 E
Pebas, Peru 92 D4 3 10S 71 46W
Pebble Beach, U.S.A. 84 J5 36 34N 121 57W
Peć, Yugoslavia 21 C9 42 40N 20 17 E
Pechenga, Russia 24 A5 69 29N 31 4 E
Pechenizhyn, Ukraine 17 D13 48 30N 24 48 E
Pechiguera, Pta., Canary Is. 22 F6 28 51N 13 53W
Pechora, Russia 24 A10 65 10N 57 11 E
Pechora →, Russia 24 A9 68 13N 54 15 E
Pechorskaya Guba, Russia 24 A9 68 40N 54 0 E
Pečory, Russia 9 H22 57 48N 27 40 E
Pecos, U.S.A. 81 K3 31 26N 103 30W
Pecos →, U.S.A. 81 L3 29 42N 101 22W
Pécs, Hungary 17 E10 46 5N 18 15 E
Pedder, L., Australia 62 G4 42 55S 146 10 E
Peddie, S. Africa 57 E4 33 14S 27 7 E
Pédernales, Dom. Rep. 89 C5 18 2N 71 44W
Pedieos →, Cyprus 23 D12 35 10N 33 54 E
Pedirka, Australia 63 D2 26 40S 135 14 E
Pedra Azul, Brazil 93 G10 16 2S 41 17W
Pedreiras, Brazil 93 D10 4 32S 44 40W
Pedro Afonso, Brazil 93 E9 9 0S 48 10W
Pedro Cays, Jamaica 88 C4 17 5N 77 48W
Pedro de Valdivia, Chile 94 A2 22 55S 69 38W
Pedro Juan Caballero, Paraguay 95 A4 22 30S 55 40W
Pee Dee →, U.S.A. 77 J6 33 22N 79 16W
Peebinga, Australia 63 E3 34 52S 140 57 E
Peebles, U.K. 12 F5 55 40N 3 11W
Peekskill, U.S.A. 79 E11 41 17N 73 55W
Peel, U.K. 10 C3 54 13N 4 40W
Peel →, Australia 63 E5 30 50S 150 29 E
Peel →, Canada 68 B6 67 0N 135 0W
Peel Sound, Canada 68 A10 73 0N 96 0W
Peera Peera Poolanna L., Australia 63 D2 26 30S 138 0 E
Peerless Lake, Canada 72 B6 56 37N 114 40W
Peers, Canada 72 C5 53 40N 116 0W
Pegasus Bay, N.Z. 59 K4 43 20S 173 10 E
Pegu, Burma 41 L20 17 20N 96 29 E
Pegu Yoma, Burma 41 K20 19 0N 96 0 E
Pehuajó, Argentina 94 D3 35 45S 62 0W
Pei Xian = Pizhou, China 34 G9 34 44N 116 55 E
Peine, Chile 94 A2 23 45S 68 8W
Peine, Germany 16 B6 52 19N 10 14 E
Peip'ing = Beijing, China 34 E9 39 55N 116 20 E
Peipus, L. = Chudskoye, Ozero, Russia 9 G22 58 13N 27 30 E
Peixe, Brazil 93 F9 12 0S 48 40W
Peixe →, Brazil 93 H8 21 31S 51 58W
Pekalongan, Indonesia 37 G13 6 53S 109 40 E
Pekan, Malaysia 39 L4 3 30N 103 25 E
Pekanbaru, Indonesia 36 D2 0 30N 101 15 E
Pekin, U.S.A. 80 E10 40 35N 89 40W
Peking = Beijing, China 34 E9 39 55N 116 20 E
Pelabuhan Kelang, Malaysia 39 L3 3 0N 101 23 E
Pelabuhan Ratu, Teluk, Indonesia 37 G12 7 5S 106 30 E
Pelabuhanratu, Indonesia 37 G12 7 0S 106 32 E
Pelagie, Is., Italy 20 G5 35 39N 12 33 E
Pelaihari, Indonesia 36 E4 3 55S 114 45 E
Peleaga, Vf., Romania 17 F12 45 22N 22 55 E
Pelée, Mt., Martinique 89 D7 14 48N 61 10W
Pelee, Pt., Canada 70 D3 41 54N 82 31W
Pelee I., Canada 78 E2 41 47N 82 40W
Pelekech, Kenya 54 B4 3 52N 35 8 E
Peleng, Indonesia 37 E6 1 20S 123 30 E
Pelican, U.S.A. 72 B1 57 58N 136 14W
Pelican L., Canada 73 C8 52 28N 100 20W
Pelican Narrows, Canada 73 B8 55 10N 102 56W
Pelješac, Croatia 20 C7 42 55N 17 25 E
Pelkosenniemi, Finland 8 C22 67 6N 27 28 E
Pella, S. Africa 56 D2 29 1S 19 6 E
Pella, U.S.A. 80 E8 41 25N 92 55W
Pello, Finland 8 C21 66 47N 23 59 E
Pelly →, Canada 68 B6 62 47N 137 19W
Pelly Bay, Canada 69 B11 68 38N 89 50W
Peloponnese = Pelopónnisos □, Greece 21 F10 37 10N 22 0 E
Pelopónnisos □, Greece 21 F10 37 10N 22 0 E
Pelorus Sd., N.Z. 59 J4 40 59S 173 59 E
Pelotas, Brazil 95 C5 31 42S 52 23W
Pelotas →, Brazil 95 B5 27 28S 51 55W
Pelvoux, Massif du, France 18 D7 44 52N 6 20 E
Pemalang, Indonesia 37 G13 6 53S 109 23 E
Pemanggil, Pulau, Malaysia 39 L5 2 37N 104 21 E
Pematangsiantar, Indonesia 36 D1 2 57N 99 5 E
Pemba, Mozam. 55 E5 12 58S 40 30 E
Pemba, Zambia 55 F2 16 30S 27 28 E
Pemba Channel, Tanzania 54 D4 5 0S 39 37 E
Pemba I., Tanzania 54 D4 5 0S 39 45 E
Pemberton, Australia 61 F2 34 30S 116 0 E
Pemberton, Canada 72 C4 50 25N 122 50W
Pembina, U.S.A. 80 A6 48 58N 97 15W
Pembroke, Canada 70 C4 45 50N 77 7W
Pembroke, U.K. 11 F3 51 41N 4 55W
Pembrokeshire □, U.K. 11 F3 51 52N 4 56W
Pen-y-Ghent, U.K. 10 C5 54 10N 2 14W
Penang = Pinang, Malaysia 39 K3 5 25N 100 15 E
Penápolis, Brazil 95 A6 21 30S 50 0W
Peñarroya-Pueblonuevo, Spain 19 C3 38 19N 5 16W
Penarth, U.K. 11 F4 51 26N 3 11W
Peñas, C. de, Spain 19 A3 43 42N 5 52W
Penas, G. de, Chile 96 F2 47 0S 75 0W
Peñas del Chache, Canary Is. 22 E6 29 6N 13 33W
Pench'i = Benxi, China 35 D12 41 20N 123 48 E
Pend Oreille →, U.S.A. 82 B5 49 4N 117 37W
Pend Oreille, L., U.S.A. 82 C5 48 10N 116 21W
Pendembu, S. Leone 50 G3 9 7N 11 14W
Pender B., Australia 60 C3 16 45S 122 42 E
Pendleton, U.S.A. 82 D4 45 40N 118 47W
Pendra, India 43 H9 22 46N 81 57 E
Penedo, Brazil 93 F11 10 15S 36 36W
Penetanguishene, Canada 78 B5 44 50N 79 55W
Penfield, U.S.A. 78 E6 41 13N 78 35W
Pengalengan, Indonesia 37 G12 7 9S 107 30 E
Penge, Kasai-Or., Dem. Rep. of the Congo 54 D1 5 30S 24 33 E
Penge, Sud-Kivu, Dem. Rep. of the Congo 54 C2 4 27S 28 25 E
Penglai, China 35 F11 37 48N 120 42 E
Penguin, Australia 62 G4 41 8S 146 6 E
Penhalonga, Zimbabwe 55 F3 18 52S 32 40 E
Peniche, Portugal 19 C1 39 19N 9 22W
Penicuik, U.K. 12 F5 55 50N 3 13W
Penida, Indonesia 36 F5 8 45S 115 30 E
Peninsular Malaysia □, Malaysia 39 L4 4 0N 102 0 E
Penitente, Serra do, Brazil 93 E9 8 45S 46 20W
Penkridge, U.K. 10 E5 52 44N 2 6W
Penmarch, Pte. de, France 18 C1 47 48N 4 22W
Penn Hills, U.S.A. 78 F5 40 28N 79 52W

Posong

itsilia □, *Cyprus* **23 E12** 34 55N 33 0 E
itt I., *Canada* **72 C3** 53 30N 129 50W
ittsburg, *Calif., U.S.A.* **84 G5** 38 2N 121 53W
ittsburg, *Kans., U.S.A.* **81 G7** 37 25N 94 42W
ittsburg, *Tex., U.S.A.* **81 J7** 33 0N 94 59W
ittsburgh, *U.S.A.* **78 F5** 40 26N 80 1W
ittsfield, *Ill., U.S.A.* **80 F9** 39 36N 90 49W
ittsfield, *Maine, U.S.A.* **77 C11** 44 47N 69 23W
ittsfield, *Mass., U.S.A.* **79 D11** 42 27N 73 15W
ittsfield, *N.H., U.S.A.* **79 C13** 43 18N 71 20W
ittston, *U.S.A.* **79 E9** 41 19N 75 47W
ittsworth, *Australia* **63 D5** 27 41S 151 37 E
ituri →, *Australia* **62 C2** 22 35S 138 30 E
iura, *Peru* **92 E2** 5 15S 80 38W
ixley, *U.S.A.* **84 K7** 35 58N 119 18W
izhou, *China* **34 G9** 34 44N 116 55 E
lacentia, *Canada* **71 C9** 47 20N 54 0W
lacentia B., *Canada* **71 C9** 47 0N 54 40W
lacerville, *U.S.A.* **84 G6** 38 44N 120 48W
lacetas, *Cuba* **88 B4** 22 15N 79 44W
lainfield, *N.J., U.S.A.* **79 F10** 40 37N 74 25W
lainfield, *Ohio, U.S.A.* **78 F3** 40 13N 81 43W
lainfield, *Vt., U.S.A.* **79 B12** 44 17N 72 26W
lains, *Mont., U.S.A.* **82 C6** 47 28N 114 53W
lains, *Tex., U.S.A.* **81 J3** 33 11N 102 50W
lainview, *Nebr., U.S.A.* **80 D6** 42 21N 97 47W
lainview, *Tex., U.S.A.* **81 H4** 34 11N 101 43W
lainwell, *U.S.A.* **76 D3** 42 27N 85 38W
laistow, *U.S.A.* **79 D13** 42 50N 71 6W
láka, Ákra, *Greece* **23 D8** 35 11N 26 19 E
lana Cays, *Bahamas* **89 B5** 22 38N 73 30W
lanada, *U.S.A.* **84 H6** 37 16N 120 19W
lano, *U.S.A.* **81 J6** 33 1N 96 42W
lant City, *U.S.A.* **77 M4** 28 1N 82 7W
laquemine, *U.S.A.* **81 K9** 30 17N 91 14W
lasencia, *Spain* **19 B2** 40 3N 6 8W
laster City, *U.S.A.* **85 N11** 32 47N 115 51W
laster Rock, *Canada* **71 C6** 46 53N 67 22W
lastun, *Russia* **30 B8** 44 45N 136 19 E
lata, Río de la, *S. Amer.* **94 C4** 34 45S 57 30W
látani →, *Italy* **20 F5** 37 23N 13 16 E
látanos, *Greece* **23 D5** 35 28N 23 33 E
latte, *U.S.A.* **80 D5** 43 23N 98 51W
latte →, *Mo., U.S.A.* **75 C8** 39 16N 94 50W
latte →, *Nebr., U.S.A.* **80 E7** 41 4N 95 53W
latteville, *U.S.A.* **80 D9** 42 44N 90 29W
lattsburgh, *U.S.A.* **79 B11** 44 42N 73 28W
lattsmouth, *U.S.A.* **80 E7** 41 1N 95 53W
lauen, *Germany* **16 C7** 50 30N 12 8 E
lavinas, *Latvia* **9 H21** 56 35N 25 46 E
laya Blanca, *Canary Is.* **22 F6** 28 55N 13 37W
laya Blanca Sur, *Canary Is.* **22 F6** 28 51N 13 50W
laya de las Americas, *Canary Is.* **22 F3** 28 5N 16 43W
laya de Mogán, *Canary Is.* **22 G4** 27 48N 15 47W
laya del Inglés, *Canary Is.* **22 G4** 27 45N 15 33W
laya Esmerelda, *Canary Is.* **22 F5** 28 8N 14 16W
laygreen L., *Canada* **73 C9** 54 0N 98 15W
leasant Bay, *Canada* **71 C7** 46 51N 60 48W
leasant Hill, *U.S.A.* **84 H4** 37 57N 122 4W
leasant Mount, *U.S.A.* **79 E9** 41 44N 75 26W
leasanton, *Calif., U.S.A.* **84 H5** 37 39N 121 52W
leasanton, *Tex., U.S.A.* **81 L5** 28 58N 98 29W
leasantville, *N.J., U.S.A.* **76 F8** 39 24N 74 32W
leasantville, *Pa., U.S.A.* **78 E5** 41 35N 79 34W
lei Ku, *Vietnam* **38 F7** 13 57N 108 0 E
lenty →, *Australia* **62 C2** 23 25S 136 31 E
lenty, B. of, *N.Z.* **59 G6** 37 45S 177 0 E
lentywood, *U.S.A.* **80 A2** 48 47N 104 34W
lesetsk, *Russia* **24 B7** 62 43N 40 20 E
lessisville, *Canada* **71 C5** 46 14N 71 47W
létipi, L., *Canada* **71 B5** 51 44N 70 6W
leven, *Bulgaria* **21 C11** 43 26N 24 37 E
levlja, *Montenegro, Yug.* **21 C8** 43 21N 19 21 E
levna, *Canada* **78 B8** 44 58N 76 59W
lock, *Poland* **17 B10** 52 32N 19 40 E
löckenstein, *Germany* **16 D7** 48 46N 13 51 E
loiești, *Romania* **17 F14** 44 57N 26 5 E
longe, Lac la, *Canada* **73 B7** 55 8N 107 20W
lovdiv, *Bulgaria* **21 C11** 42 8N 24 44 E
lum, *U.S.A.* **78 F5** 40 29N 79 47W
lum I., *U.S.A.* **79 E12** 41 11N 72 12W
lumas, *U.S.A.* **84 F7** 39 45N 120 4W
lummer, *U.S.A.* **82 C5** 47 20N 116 53W
umtree, *Zimbabwe* **55 G2** 20 27S 27 55 E
unge, *Lithuania* **9 J19** 55 53N 21 59 E
ymouth, *U.K.* **11 G3** 50 22N 4 10W
ymouth, *Calif., U.S.A.* **84 G6** 38 29N 120 51W
ymouth, *Ind., U.S.A.* **76 E2** 41 21N 86 19W
ymouth, *Mass., U.S.A.* **79 E14** 41 57N 70 40W
ymouth, *N.C., U.S.A.* **77 H7** 35 52N 76 43W
ymouth, *N.H., U.S.A.* **79 C13** 43 46N 71 41W
ymouth, *Pa., U.S.A.* **79 E9** 41 14N 75 57W
ymouth, *Wis., U.S.A.* **76 D2** 43 45N 87 59W
ynlimon = Pumlumon Fawr, *U.K.* **11 E4** 52 28N 3 46W
zeň, *Czech Rep.* **16 D7** 49 45N 13 22 E
o →, *Italy* **20 B5** 44 57N 12 4 E
o Hai = Bo Hai, *China* **35 E10** 39 0N 119 0 E
obeda, *Russia* **27 C15** 65 12N 146 12 E
obedy, Pik, *Kyrgyzstan* **26 E8** 42 0N 79 58 E
ocahontas, *Ark., U.S.A.* **81 G9** 36 16N 90 58W
ocahontas, *Iowa, U.S.A.* **80 D7** 42 44N 94 40W
ocatello, *U.S.A.* **82 E7** 42 52N 112 27W
ochutla, *Mexico* **87 D5** 15 50N 96 31W
ocito Casas, *Mexico* **86 B2** 28 32N 111 6W
ocomoke City, *U.S.A.* **76 F8** 38 5N 75 34W
oços de Caldas, *Brazil* **95 A6** 21 50S 46 33W
odgorica, *Montenegro, Yug.* **21 C8** 42 30N 19 19 E
odilska Vysochyna, *Ukraine* **17 D14** 49 0N 28 0 E
odolsk, *Russia* **24 C6** 55 25N 37 30 E
odporozhye, *Russia* **24 B5** 60 55N 34 2 E
ofadder, *S. Africa* **56 D2** 29 10S 19 22 E
ogranitšnyi, *Russia* **30 B5** 44 25N 131 24 E
oh, *Indonesia* **37 E6** 0 46S 122 51 E
ohang, *S. Korea* **35 F15** 36 1N 129 23 E
ohjanmaa, *Finland* **8 E20** 62 58N 22 50 E
ohnpei, *Micronesia* **64 G7** 6 55N 158 10 E
ohri, *India* **42 G6** 25 32N 77 22 E
oinsett, C., *Antarctica* **5 C8** 65 42S 113 18 E
oint Arena, *U.S.A.* **84 G3** 38 55N 123 41W
oint Baker, *U.S.A.* **72 B2** 56 21N 133 37W
oint Edward, *Canada* **70 D3** 43 0N 82 30W
oint Hope, *U.S.A.* **68 B3** 68 21N 166 47W
oint L., *Canada* **68 B8** 65 15N 113 4W
Point Pedro, *Sri Lanka* **40 Q12** 9 50N 80 15 E
Point Pleasant, *N.J., U.S.A.* **79 F10** 40 5N 74 4W
Point Pleasant, *W. Va., U.S.A.* **76 F4** 38 51N 82 8W
Pointe-à-Pitre, *Guadeloupe* **89 C7** 16 10N 61 30W
Pointe-Claire, *Canada* **79 A11** 45 26N 73 50W
Pointe-Gatineau, *Canada* **79 A9** 45 28N 75 42W
Pointe-Noire, *Congo* **52 E2** 4 48S 11 53 E
Poisonbush Ra., *Australia* **60 D3** 22 30S 121 30 E
Poissonnier Pt., *Australia* **60 C2** 19 57S 119 10 E
Poitiers, *France* **18 C4** 46 35N 0 20 E
Poitou, *France* **18 C3** 46 40N 0 10W
Pojoaque, *U.S.A.* **83 J11** 35 54N 106 1W
Pokaran, *India* **40 F7** 27 0N 71 50 E
Pokataroo, *Australia* **63 D4** 29 30S 148 36 E
Pokhara, *Nepal* **43 E10** 28 14N 83 58 E
Poko, *Dem. Rep. of the Congo* **54 B2** 3 7N 26 52 E
Pokrovsk = Engels, *Russia* **25 D8** 51 28N 46 6 E
Pokrovsk, *Russia* **27 C13** 61 29N 129 0 E
Pola = Pula, *Croatia* **16 F7** 44 54N 13 57 E
Polacca, *U.S.A.* **83 J8** 35 50N 110 23W
Polan, *Iran* **45 E9** 25 30N 61 10 E
Poland ■, *Europe* **17 C10** 52 0N 20 0 E
Polar Bear Prov. Park, *Canada* **70 A2** 55 0N 83 45W
Polatsk, *Belarus* **24 C4** 55 30N 28 50 E
Polcura, *Chile* **94 D1** 37 17S 71 43W
Polessk, *Russia* **9 J19** 54 50N 21 8 E
Polesye = Pripet Marshes, *Europe* **17 B15** 52 10N 28 10 E
Polevskoy, *Russia* **24 C11** 56 26N 60 11 E
Pŏlgyo-ri, *S. Korea* **35 G14** 34 51N 127 21 E
Police, *Poland* **16 B8** 53 33N 14 33 E
Polillo Is., *Phil.* **37 B6** 14 56N 122 0 E
Polis, *Cyprus* **23 D11** 35 2N 32 26 E
Políyiros, *Greece* **21 D10** 40 23N 23 25 E
Polk, *U.S.A.* **78 E5** 41 22N 79 56W
Pollachi, *India* **40 P10** 10 35N 77 0 E
Pollença, *Spain* **22 B10** 39 54N 3 1 E
Pollença, B. de, *Spain* **22 B10** 39 53N 3 8 E
Polnovat, *Russia* **26 C7** 63 50N 65 54 E
Polonne, *Ukraine* **17 C14** 50 6N 27 30 E
Polonnoye = Polonne, *Ukraine* **17 C14** 50 6N 27 30 E
Polson, *U.S.A.* **82 C6** 47 41N 114 9W
Poltava, *Ukraine* **25 E5** 49 35N 34 35 E
Põltsamaa, *Estonia* **9 G21** 58 41N 25 58 E
Polunochnoye, *Russia* **26 C7** 60 52N 60 25 E
Põlva, *Estonia* **9 G22** 58 3N 27 3 E
Polyarny, *Russia* **24 A5** 69 8N 33 20 E
Polynesia, *Pac. Oc.* **65 J11** 10 0S 162 0W
Polynésie française = French Polynesia ■, *Pac. Oc.* **65 K13** 20 0S 145 0W
Pomaro, *Mexico* **86 D4** 18 20N 103 18W
Pombal, *Portugal* **19 C1** 39 55N 8 40W
Pómbia, *Greece* **23 E6** 35 0N 24 51 E
Pomeroy, *Ohio, U.S.A.* **76 F4** 39 2N 82 2W
Pomeroy, *Wash., U.S.A.* **82 C5** 46 28N 117 36W
Pomézia, *Italy* **20 D5** 41 40N 12 30 E
Pomona, *Australia* **63 D5** 26 22S 152 52 E
Pomona, *U.S.A.* **85 L9** 34 4N 117 45W
Pomorskie, Pojezierze, *Poland* **17 B9** 53 40N 16 37 E
Pomos, *Cyprus* **23 D11** 35 9N 32 33 E
Pomos, C., *Cyprus* **23 D11** 35 10N 32 33 E
Pompano Beach, *U.S.A.* **77 M5** 26 14N 80 8W
Pompeys Pillar, *U.S.A.* **82 D10** 45 59N 107 57W
Pompton Lakes, *U.S.A.* **79 F10** 41 0N 74 17W
Ponape = Pohnpei, *Micronesia* **64 G7** 6 55N 158 10 E
Ponask L., *Canada* **70 B1** 54 0N 92 41W
Ponca, *U.S.A.* **80 D6** 42 34N 96 43W
Ponca City, *U.S.A.* **81 G6** 36 42N 97 5W
Ponce, *Puerto Rico* **89 C6** 18 1N 66 37W
Ponchatoula, *U.S.A.* **81 K9** 30 26N 90 26W
Poncheville, L., *Canada* **70 B4** 50 10N 76 55W
Pond, *U.S.A.* **85 K7** 35 43N 119 20W
Pond Inlet, *Canada* **69 A12** 72 40N 77 0W
Pondicherry, *India* **40 P11** 11 59N 79 50 E
Ponds, I. of, *Canada* **71 B8** 53 27N 55 52W
Ponferrada, *Spain* **19 A2** 42 32N 6 35W
Ponnani, *India* **40 P9** 10 45N 75 59 E
Ponnyadaung, *Burma* **41 J19** 22 0N 94 10 E
Ponoka, *Canada* **72 C6** 52 42N 113 40W
Ponorogo, *Indonesia* **37 G14** 7 52S 111 27 E
Ponoy, *Russia* **24 A7** 67 0N 41 13 E
Ponoy →, *Russia* **24 A7** 66 59N 41 17 E
Ponta do Sol, *Madeira* **22 D2** 32 42N 17 7W
Ponta Grossa, *Brazil* **95 B5** 25 7S 50 10W
Ponta Pora, *Brazil* **95 A4** 22 20S 55 35W
Pontarlier, *France* **18 C7** 46 54N 6 20 E
Pontchartrain L., *U.S.A.* **81 K10** 30 5N 90 5W
Ponte do Pungué, *Mozam.* **55 F3** 19 30S 34 33 E
Ponte Nova, *Brazil* **95 A7** 20 25S 42 54W
Ponteix, *Canada* **73 D7** 49 46N 107 29W
Pontevedra, *Spain* **19 A1** 42 26N 8 40W
Pontiac, *Ill., U.S.A.* **80 E10** 40 53N 88 38W
Pontiac, *Mich., U.S.A.* **76 D4** 42 38N 83 18W
Pontian Kecil, *Malaysia* **39 M4** 1 29N 103 23 E
Pontianak, *Indonesia* **36 E3** 0 3S 109 15 E
Pontine Is. = Ponziane, Ísole, *Italy* **20 D5** 40 55N 12 57 E
Pontine Mts. = Kuzey Anadolu Dağları, *Turkey* **25 F6** 41 30N 35 0 E
Pontivy, *France* **18 B2** 48 5N 2 58W
Pontoise, *France* **18 B5** 49 3N 2 5 E
Ponton →, *Canada* **72 B5** 58 27N 116 11W
Pontypool, *Canada* **78 B6** 44 6N 78 38W
Pontypool, *U.K.* **11 F4** 51 42N 3 2W
Ponziane, Ísole, *Italy* **20 D5** 40 55N 12 57 E
Poochera, *Australia* **63 E1** 32 43S 134 51 E
Poole, *U.K.* **11 G6** 50 43N 1 59W
Poole □, *U.K.* **11 G6** 50 43N 1 59W
Poona = Pune, *India* **40 K8** 18 29N 73 57 E
Pooncarie, *Australia* **63 E3** 33 22S 142 31 E
Poopelloe L., *Australia* **63 E3** 31 40S 144 0 E
Poopó, L. de, *Bolivia* **92 G5** 18 30S 67 35W
Popayán, *Colombia* **92 C3** 2 27N 76 36W
Poperinge, *Belgium* **15 D2** 50 51N 2 42 E
Popilta L., *Australia* **63 E3** 33 10S 141 42 E
Popio L., *Australia* **63 E3** 33 10S 141 52 E
Poplar, *U.S.A.* **80 A2** 48 7N 105 12W
Poplar →, *Canada* **73 C9** 53 0N 97 19W
Poplar Bluff, *U.S.A.* **81 G9** 36 46N 90 24W
Poplarville, *U.S.A.* **81 K10** 30 51N 89 32W
Popocatépetl, Volcán, *Mexico* **87 D5** 19 2N 98 38W
Popokabaka, *Dem. Rep. of the Congo* **52 F3** 5 41S 16 40 E
Poprad, *Slovak Rep.* **17 D11** 49 3N 20 18 E
Porali →, *Pakistan* **42 G2** 25 58N 66 26 E
Porbandar, *India* **40 J6** 21 44N 69 43 E
Porcher I., *Canada* **72 C2** 53 50N 130 30W
Porcupine →, *Canada* **73 B8** 59 11N 104 46W
Porcupine →, *U.S.A.* **68 B5** 66 34N 145 19W
Pordenone, *Italy* **20 B5** 45 57N 12 39 E
Pori, *Finland* **9 F19** 61 29N 21 48 E
Porlamar, *Venezuela* **92 A6** 10 57N 63 51W
Poronaysk, *Russia* **27 E15** 49 13N 143 0 E
Poroshiri-Dake, *Japan* **30 C11** 42 41N 142 52 E
Poroto Mts., *Tanzania* **55 D3** 9 0S 33 30 E
Porpoise B., *Antarctica* **5 C9** 66 0S 127 0 E
Porreres, *Spain* **22 B10** 39 31N 3 2 E
Porsangen, *Norway* **8 A21** 70 40N 25 40 E
Porsgrunn, *Norway* **9 G13** 59 10N 9 40 E
Port Alberni, *Canada* **72 D4** 49 14N 124 50W
Port Alfred, *S. Africa* **56 E4** 33 36S 26 55 E
Port Alice, *Canada* **72 C3** 50 20N 127 25W
Port Allegany, *U.S.A.* **78 E6** 41 48N 78 17W
Port Allen, *U.S.A.* **81 K9** 30 27N 91 12W
Port Alma, *Australia* **62 C5** 23 38S 150 53 E
Port Angeles, *U.S.A.* **84 B3** 48 7N 123 27W
Port Antonio, *Jamaica* **88 C4** 18 10N 76 30W
Port Aransas, *U.S.A.* **81 M6** 27 50N 97 4W
Port Arthur = Lüshun, *China* **35 E11** 38 45N 121 15 E
Port Arthur, *Australia* **62 G4** 43 7S 147 50 E
Port Arthur, *U.S.A.* **81 L8** 29 54N 93 56W
Port au Choix, *Canada* **71 B8** 50 43N 57 22W
Port au Port B., *Canada* **71 C8** 48 40N 58 50W
Port-au-Prince, *Haiti* **89 C5** 18 40N 72 20W
Port Augusta, *Australia* **63 E2** 32 30S 137 50 E
Port Austin, *U.S.A.* **78 B2** 44 3N 83 1W
Port Bell, *Uganda* **54 B3** 0 18N 32 35 E
Port Bergé Vaovao, *Madag.* **57 B8** 15 33S 47 40 E
Port Blandford, *Canada* **71 C9** 48 20N 54 10W
Port Bradshaw, *Australia* **62 A2** 12 30S 137 20 E
Port Broughton, *Australia* **63 E2** 33 37S 137 56 E
Port Burwell, *Canada* **78 D4** 42 40N 80 48W
Port Campbell, *Australia* **63 F3** 38 37S 143 1 E
Port Canning, *India* **43 H13** 22 23N 88 40 E
Port-Cartier, *Canada* **71 B6** 50 2N 66 50W
Port Chalmers, *N.Z.* **59 L3** 45 49S 170 30 E
Port Charlotte, *U.S.A.* **77 M4** 26 59N 82 6W
Port Chester, *U.S.A.* **79 F11** 41 0N 73 40W
Port Clements, *Canada* **72 C2** 53 40N 132 10W
Port Clinton, *U.S.A.* **76 E4** 41 31N 82 56W
Port Colborne, *Canada* **78 D5** 42 50N 79 10W
Port Coquitlam, *Canada* **72 D4** 49 15N 122 45W
Port Credit, *Canada* **78 C5** 43 33N 79 35W
Port Curtis, *Australia* **62 C5** 23 57S 151 20 E
Port d'Alcúdia, *Spain* **22 B10** 39 50N 3 7 E
Port Dalhousie, *Canada* **78 C5** 43 13N 79 16W
Port Darwin, *Australia* **60 B5** 12 24S 130 45 E
Port Darwin, *Falk. Is.* **96 G5** 51 50S 59 0W
Port Davey, *Australia* **62 G4** 43 16S 145 55 E
Port-de-Paix, *Haiti* **89 C5** 19 50N 72 50W
Port de Pollença, *Spain* **22 B10** 39 54N 3 4 E
Port de Sóller, *Spain* **22 B9** 39 48N 2 42 E
Port Dickson, *Malaysia* **39 L3** 2 30N 101 49 E
Port Douglas, *Australia* **62 B4** 16 30S 145 30 E
Port Dover, *Canada* **78 D4** 42 47N 80 12W
Port Edward, *Canada* **72 C2** 54 12N 130 10W
Port Elgin, *Canada* **78 B3** 44 25N 81 25W
Port Elizabeth, *S. Africa* **56 E4** 33 58S 25 40 E
Port Ellen, *U.K.* **12 F2** 55 38N 6 11W
Port Erin, *U.K.* **10 C3** 54 5N 4 45W
Port Essington, *Australia* **60 B5** 11 15S 132 10 E
Port Etienne = Nouâdhibou, *Mauritania* **50 D2** 20 54N 17 0W
Port Ewen, *U.S.A.* **79 E11** 41 54N 73 59W
Port Fairy, *Australia* **63 F3** 38 22S 142 12 E
Port Gamble, *U.S.A.* **84 C4** 47 51N 122 35W
Port-Gentil, *Gabon* **52 E1** 0 40S 8 50 E
Port Germein, *Australia* **63 E2** 33 1S 138 1 E
Port Gibson, *U.S.A.* **81 K9** 31 58N 90 59W
Port Glasgow, *U.K.* **12 F4** 55 56N 4 41W
Port Harcourt, *Nigeria* **50 H7** 4 40N 7 10 E
Port Hardy, *Canada* **72 C3** 50 41N 127 30W
Port Harrison = Inukjuak, *Canada* **69 C12** 58 25N 78 15W
Port Hawkesbury, *Canada* **71 C7** 45 36N 61 22W
Port Hedland, *Australia* **60 D2** 20 25S 118 35 E
Port Henry, *U.S.A.* **79 B11** 44 3N 73 28W
Port Hood, *Canada* **71 C7** 46 0N 61 32W
Port Hope, *Canada* **78 C6** 43 56N 78 20W
Port Hope, *U.S.A.* **78 C2** 43 57N 82 43W
Port Hope Simpson, *Canada* **71 B8** 52 33N 56 18W
Port Hueneme, *U.S.A.* **85 L7** 34 7N 119 12W
Port Huron, *U.S.A.* **78 D2** 42 58N 82 26W
Port Jefferson, *U.S.A.* **79 F11** 40 57N 73 3W
Port Jervis, *U.S.A.* **79 E10** 41 22N 74 41W
Port Kelang = Pelabuhan Kelang, *Malaysia* **39 L3** 3 0N 101 23 E
Port Kenny, *Australia* **63 E1** 33 10S 134 41 E
Port Lairge = Waterford, *Ireland* **13 D4** 52 15N 7 8W
Port Laoise, *Ireland* **13 C4** 53 2N 7 18W
Port Lavaca, *U.S.A.* **81 L6** 28 37N 96 38W
Port Leyden, *U.S.A.* **79 C9** 43 35N 75 21W
Port Lincoln, *Australia* **63 E2** 34 42S 135 52 E
Port Loko, *S. Leone* **50 G3** 8 48N 12 46W
Port Louis, *Mauritius* **49 H9** 20 10S 57 30 E
Port Lyautey = Kenitra, *Morocco* **50 B4** 34 15N 6 40W
Port MacDonnell, *Australia* **63 F3** 38 5S 140 48 E
Port McNeill, *Canada* **72 C3** 50 35N 127 6W
Port Macquarie, *Australia* **63 E5** 31 25S 152 25 E
Port Maria, *Jamaica* **88 C4** 18 25N 76 55W
Port Matilda, *U.S.A.* **78 F6** 40 48N 78 3W
Port Mellon, *Canada* **72 D4** 49 32N 123 31W
Port-Menier, *Canada* **71 C7** 49 51N 64 15W
Port Moody, *Canada* **84 A4** 49 17N 122 51W
Port Morant, *Jamaica* **88 C4** 17 54N 76 19W
Port Moresby, *Papua N. G.* **64 H6** 9 24S 147 8 E
Port Musgrave, *Australia* **62 A3** 11 55S 141 50 E
Port Neches, *U.S.A.* **81 L8** 30 0N 93 59W
Port Nolloth, *S. Africa* **56 D2** 29 17S 16 52 E
Port Nouveau-Québec = Kangiqsualujjuaq, *Canada* **69 C13** 58 30N 65 59W
Port of Spain, *Trin. & Tob.* **89 D7** 10 40N 61 31W
Port Orange, *U.S.A.* **77 L5** 29 9N 80 59W
Port Orchard, *U.S.A.* **84 C4** 47 32N 122 38W
Port Orford, *U.S.A.* **82 E1** 42 45N 124 30W
Port Pegasus, *N.Z.* **59 M1** 47 12S 167 41 E
Port Perry, *Canada* **78 B6** 44 6N 78 56W
Port Phillip B., *Australia* **63 F3** 38 10S 144 50 E
Port Pirie, *Australia* **63 E2** 33 10S 138 1 E
Port Radium = Echo Bay, *Canada* **68 B8** 66 5N 117 55W
Port Renfrew, *Canada* **72 D4** 48 30N 124 20W
Port Roper, *Australia* **62 A2** 14 45S 135 25 E
Port Rowan, *Canada* **78 D4** 42 40N 80 30W
Port Safaga = Bûr Safâga, *Egypt* **44 E2** 26 43N 33 57 E
Port Said = Bûr Sa'îd, *Egypt* **51 B12** 31 16N 32 18 E
Port St. Joe, *U.S.A.* **77 L3** 29 49N 85 18W
Port St. Johns, *S. Africa* **57 E4** 31 38S 29 33 E
Port St. Lucie, *U.S.A.* **77 M5** 27 20N 80 20W
Port Sanilac, *U.S.A.* **78 C2** 43 26N 82 33W
Port Severn, *Canada* **78 B5** 44 48N 79 43W
Port Shepstone, *S. Africa* **57 E5** 30 44S 30 28 E
Port Simpson, *Canada* **72 C2** 54 30N 130 20W
Port Stanley = Stanley, *Falk. Is.* **96 G5** 51 40S 59 51W
Port Stanley, *Canada* **78 D3** 42 40N 81 10W
Port Sudan = Bûr Sûdân, *Sudan* **51 E13** 19 32N 37 9 E
Port Sulphur, *U.S.A.* **81 L10** 29 29N 89 42W
Port Talbot, *U.K.* **11 F4** 51 35N 3 47W
Port Townsend, *U.S.A.* **84 B4** 48 7N 122 45W
Port-Vendres, *France* **18 E5** 42 32N 3 8 E
Port Vila, *Vanuatu* **64 J8** 17 45S 168 18 E
Port Vladimir, *Russia* **24 A5** 69 25N 33 6 E
Port Wakefield, *Australia* **63 E2** 34 12S 138 10 E
Port Washington, *U.S.A.* **76 D2** 43 23N 87 53W
Port Weld = Kuala Sepetang, *Malaysia* **39 K3** 4 49N 100 28 E
Porta Orientalis, *Romania* **17 F12** 45 6N 22 18 E
Portadown, *U.K.* **13 B5** 54 25N 6 27W
Portaferry, *U.K.* **13 B6** 54 23N 5 33W
Portage, *Pa., U.S.A.* **78 F6** 40 23N 78 41W
Portage, *Wis., U.S.A.* **80 D10** 43 33N 89 28W
Portage La Prairie, *Canada* **73 D9** 49 58N 98 18W
Portageville, *U.S.A.* **81 G10** 36 26N 89 42W
Portalegre, *Portugal* **19 C2** 39 19N 7 25W
Portales, *U.S.A.* **81 H3** 34 11N 103 20W
Portarlington, *Ireland* **13 C4** 53 9N 7 14W
Portbou, *Spain* **19 A7** 42 25N 3 9 E
Porter L., *N.W.T., Canada* **73 A7** 61 41N 108 5W
Porter L., *Sask., Canada* **73 B7** 56 20N 107 20W
Porterville, *S. Africa* **56 E2** 33 0S 19 0 E
Porterville, *U.S.A.* **84 J8** 36 4N 119 1W
Porthcawl, *U.K.* **11 F4** 51 29N 3 42W
Porthill, *U.S.A.* **82 B5** 48 59N 116 30W
Porthmadog, *U.K.* **10 E3** 52 55N 4 8W
Portile de Fier, *Europe* **17 F12** 44 44N 22 30 E
Portimão, *Portugal* **19 D1** 37 8N 8 32W
Portishead, *U.K.* **11 F5** 51 29N 2 46W
Portknockie, *U.K.* **12 D6** 57 42N 2 51W
Portland, *N.S.W., Australia* **63 E5** 33 20S 150 0 E
Portland, *Vic., Australia* **63 F3** 38 20S 141 35 E
Portland, *Canada* **79 B8** 44 42N 76 12W
Portland, *Conn., U.S.A.* **79 E12** 41 34N 72 38W
Portland, *Maine, U.S.A.* **69 D12** 43 39N 70 16W
Portland, *Mich., U.S.A.* **76 D3** 42 52N 84 54W
Portland, *Oreg., U.S.A.* **84 E4** 45 32N 122 37W
Portland, *Pa., U.S.A.* **79 F9** 40 55N 75 6W
Portland, *Tex., U.S.A.* **81 M6** 27 53N 97 20W
Portland, I. of, *U.K.* **11 G5** 50 33N 2 26W
Portland B., *Australia* **63 F3** 38 15S 141 45 E
Portland Bill, *U.K.* **11 G5** 50 31N 2 28W
Portland Canal, *U.S.A.* **72 B2** 55 56N 130 0W
Portmadoc = Porthmadog, *U.K.* **10 E3** 52 55N 4 8W
Porto, *Portugal* **19 B1** 41 8N 8 40W
Pôrto Alegre, *Brazil* **95 C5** 30 5S 51 10W
Porto Amboim = Gunza, *Angola* **52 G2** 10 50S 13 50 E
Porto Cristo, *Spain* **22 B10** 39 33N 3 20 E
Pôrto de Móz, *Brazil* **93 D8** 1 41S 52 13W
Porto Empédocle, *Italy* **20 F5** 37 17N 13 32 E
Pôrto Esperança, *Brazil* **92 G7** 19 37S 57 29W
Pôrto Franco, *Brazil* **93 E9** 6 20S 47 24W
Porto Mendes, *Brazil* **95 A5** 24 30S 54 15W
Porto Moniz, *Madeira* **22 D2** 32 52N 17 11W
Pôrto Murtinho, *Brazil* **92 H7** 21 45S 57 55W
Pôrto Nacional, *Brazil* **93 F9** 10 40S 48 30W
Porto-Novo, *Benin* **50 G6** 6 23N 2 42 E
Porto Petro, *Spain* **22 B10** 39 22N 3 13 E
Porto Santo, *Madeira* **50 B2** 33 45N 16 25W
Pôrto São José, *Brazil* **95 A5** 22 43S 53 10W
Pôrto Seguro, *Brazil* **93 G11** 16 26S 39 5W
Porto Tórres, *Italy* **20 D3** 40 50N 8 24 E
Pôrto Uniâo, *Brazil* **95 B5** 26 10S 51 10W
Pôrto Válter, *Brazil* **92 E4** 8 15S 72 40W
Porto-Vecchio, *France* **18 F8** 41 35N 9 16 E
Pôrto Velho, *Brazil* **92 E6** 8 46S 63 54W
Portobelo, *Panama* **88 E4** 9 35N 79 42W
Portoferráio, *Italy* **20 C4** 42 48N 10 20 E
Portola, *U.S.A.* **84 F6** 39 49N 120 28W
Portoscuso, *Italy* **20 E3** 39 12N 8 24 E
Portoviejo, *Ecuador* **92 D2** 1 7S 80 28W
Portpatrick, *U.K.* **12 G3** 54 51N 5 7W
Portree, *U.K.* **12 D2** 57 25N 6 12W
Portrush, *U.K.* **13 A5** 55 12N 6 40W
Portsmouth, *Domin.* **89 C7** 15 34N 61 27W
Portsmouth, *U.K.* **11 G6** 50 48N 1 6W
Portsmouth, *N.H., U.S.A.* **77 D10** 43 5N 70 45W
Portsmouth, *Ohio, U.S.A.* **76 F4** 38 44N 82 57W
Portsmouth, *R.I., U.S.A.* **79 E13** 41 36N 71 15W
Portsmouth, *Va., U.S.A.* **76 G7** 36 50N 76 18W
Portsmouth □, *U.K.* **11 G6** 50 48N 1 6W
Portsoy, *U.K.* **12 D6** 57 41N 2 41W
Portstewart, *U.K.* **13 A5** 55 11N 6 43W
Porttipahtan tekojärvi, *Finland* **8 B22** 68 5N 26 40 E
Portugal ■, *Europe* **19 C1** 40 0N 8 0W
Portumna, *Ireland* **13 C3** 53 6N 8 14W
Portville, *U.S.A.* **78 D6** 42 3N 78 20W
Porvenir, *Chile* **96 G2** 53 10S 70 16W
Porvoo, *Finland* **9 F21** 60 24N 25 40 E
Posadas, *Argentina* **95 B4** 27 30S 55 50W
Poshan = Boshan, *China* **35 F9** 36 28N 117 49 E
Posht-e-Badam, *Iran* **45 C7** 33 2N 55 23 E
Poso, *Indonesia* **37 E6** 1 20S 120 55 E
Posong, *S. Korea* **35 G14** 34 46N 127 5 E

Posse

Posse, *Brazil* **93 F9** 14 4S 46 18W
Possession I., *Antarctica* **5 D11** 72 4S 172 0 E
Possum Kingdom L., *U.S.A.* **81 J5** 32 52N 98 26W
Post, *U.S.A.* **81 J4** 33 12N 101 23W
Post Falls, *U.S.A.* **82 C5** 47 43N 116 57W
Postavy = Pastavy, *Belarus* **9 J22** 55 4N 26 50 E
Poste-de-la-Baleine = Kuujjuarapik, *Canada* **70 A4** 55 20N 77 35W
Postmasburg, *S. Africa* **56 D3** 28 18S 23 5 E
Postojna, *Slovenia* **16 F8** 45 46N 14 12 E
Poston, *U.S.A.* **85 M12** 34 0N 114 24W
Postville, *Canada* **71 B8** 54 54N 59 47W
Potchefstroom, *S. Africa* **56 D4** 26 41S 27 7 E
Poteau, *U.S.A.* **81 H7** 35 3N 94 37W
Poteet, *U.S.A.* **81 L5** 29 2N 98 35W
Potenza, *Italy* **20 D6** 40 38N 15 48 E
Poteriteri, L., *N.Z.* **59 M1** 46 5S 167 10 E
Potgietersrus, *S. Africa* **57 C4** 24 10S 28 55 E
Poti, *Georgia* **25 F7** 42 10N 41 38 E
Potiskum, *Nigeria* **51 F8** 11 39N 11 2 E
Potomac →, *U.S.A.* **76 G7** 38 0N 76 23W
Potosí, *Bolivia* **92 G5** 19 38S 65 50W
Potosi Mt., *U.S.A.* **85 K11** 35 57N 115 29W
Pototan, *Phil.* **37 B6** 10 54N 122 38 E
Potrerillos, *Chile* **94 B2** 26 30S 69 30W
Potsdam, *Germany* **16 B7** 52 25N 13 4 E
Potsdam, *U.S.A.* **79 B10** 44 40N 74 59W
Pottersville, *U.S.A.* **79 C11** 43 43N 73 50W
Pottstown, *U.S.A.* **79 F9** 40 15N 75 39W
Pottsville, *U.S.A.* **79 F8** 40 41N 76 12W
Pottuvil, *Sri Lanka* **40 R12** 6 55N 81 50 E
Pouce Coupé, *Canada* **72 B4** 55 40N 120 10W
Poughkeepsie, *U.S.A.* **79 E11** 41 42N 73 56W
Poulaphouca Res., *Ireland* **13 C5** 53 8N 6 30W
Poulsbo, *U.S.A.* **84 C4** 47 44N 122 39W
Poultney, *U.S.A.* **79 C11** 43 31N 73 14W
Poulton-le-Fylde, *U.K.* **10 D5** 53 51N 2 58W
Pouso Alegre, *Brazil* **95 A6** 22 14S 45 57W
Pouthisat, *Cambodia* **38 F4** 12 34N 103 50 E
Považská Bystrica, *Slovak Rep.* **17 D10** 49 8N 18 27 E
Povenets, *Russia* **24 B5** 62 50N 34 50 E
Poverty B., *N.Z.* **59 H7** 38 43S 178 2 E
Póvoa de Varzim, *Portugal* **19 B1** 41 25N 8 46W
Povungnituk = Puvirnituq, *Canada* **69 B12** 60 2N 77 10W
Powassan, *Canada* **70 C4** 46 5N 79 25W
Poway, *U.S.A.* **85 N9** 32 58N 117 2W
Powder →, *U.S.A.* **80 B2** 46 45N 105 26W
Powder River, *U.S.A.* **82 E10** 43 2N 106 59W
Powell, *U.S.A.* **82 D9** 44 45N 108 46W
Powell, L., *U.S.A.* **83 H8** 36 57N 111 29W
Powell River, *Canada* **72 D4** 49 50N 124 35W
Powers, *U.S.A.* **76 C2** 45 41N 87 32W
Powys □, *U.K.* **11 E4** 52 20N 3 20W
Poyang Hu, *China* **33 D6** 29 5N 116 20 E
Poyarkovo, *Russia* **27 E13** 49 36N 128 41 E
Poza Rica, *Mexico* **87 C5** 20 33N 97 27W
Požarevac, *Serbia, Yug.* **21 B9** 44 35N 21 18 E
Poznań, *Poland* **17 B9** 52 25N 16 55 E
Pozo, *U.S.A.* **85 K6** 35 20N 120 24W
Pozo Almonte, *Chile* **92 H5** 20 10S 69 50W
Pozo Colorado, *Paraguay* **94 A4** 23 30S 58 45W
Pozoblanco, *Spain* **19 C3** 38 23N 4 51W
Pozzuoli, *Italy* **20 D6** 40 49N 14 7 E
Prachin Buri, *Thailand* **38 F3** 14 0N 101 25 E
Prachuap Khiri Khan, *Thailand* **39 G2** 11 49N 99 48 E
Prado, *Brazil* **93 G11** 17 20S 39 13W
Prague = Praha, *Czech Rep.* **16 C8** 50 5N 14 22 E
Praha, *Czech Rep.* **16 C8** 50 5N 14 22 E
Praia, *C. Verde Is.* **49 E1** 14 55N 23 30W
Prainha, *Amazonas, Brazil* **92 E6** 7 10S 60 30W
Prainha, *Pará, Brazil* **93 D8** 1 45S 53 30W
Prairie, *Australia* **62 C3** 20 50S 144 35 E
Prairie City, *U.S.A.* **82 D4** 44 28N 118 43W
Prairie Dog Town Fork →, *U.S.A.* **81 H5** 34 30N 99 23W
Prairie du Chien, *U.S.A.* **80 D9** 43 3N 91 9W
Prairies, L. of the, *Canada* **73 C8** 51 16N 101 32W
Pran Buri, *Thailand* **38 F2** 12 23N 99 55 E
Prapat, *Indonesia* **36 D1** 2 41N 98 58 E
Prasonísi, Ákra, *Greece* **23 D9** 35 42N 27 46 E
Prata, *Brazil* **93 G9** 19 25S 48 54W
Pratabpur, *India* **43 H10** 23 28N 83 15 E
Pratapgarh, *Raj., India* **42 G6** 24 2N 74 40 E
Pratapgarh, *Ut. P., India* **43 G9** 25 56N 81 59 E
Prato, *Italy* **20 C4** 43 53N 11 6 E
Pratt, *U.S.A.* **81 G5** 37 39N 98 44W
Prattville, *U.S.A.* **77 J2** 32 28N 86 29W
Pravia, *Spain* **19 A2** 43 30N 6 12W
Praya, *Indonesia* **36 F5** 8 39S 116 17 E
Precordillera, *Argentina* **94 C2** 30 0S 69 1W
Preeceville, *Canada* **73 C8** 51 57N 102 40W
Preiļi, *Latvia* **9 H22** 56 18N 26 43 E
Premont, *U.S.A.* **81 M5** 27 22N 98 7W
Prentice, *U.S.A.* **80 C9** 45 33N 90 17W
Preobrazheniye, *Russia* **30 C6** 42 54N 133 54 E
Preparis North Channel, *Ind. Oc.* **41 M18** 15 12N 93 40 E
Preparis South Channel, *Ind. Oc.* **41 M18** 14 36N 93 40 E
Přerov, *Czech Rep.* **17 D9** 49 28N 17 27 E
Prescott, *Canada* **79 B9** 44 45N 75 30W
Prescott, *Ariz., U.S.A.* **83 J7** 34 33N 112 28W
Prescott, *Ark., U.S.A.* **81 J8** 33 48N 93 23W
Prescott Valley, *U.S.A.* **83 J7** 34 40N 112 18W
Preservation Inlet, *N.Z.* **59 M1** 46 8S 166 35 E
Presho, *U.S.A.* **80 D4** 43 54N 100 3W
Presidencia de la Plaza, *Argentina* **94 B4** 27 0S 59 50W
Presidencia Roque Saenz Peña, *Argentina* **94 B3** 26 45S 60 30W
Presidente Epitácio, *Brazil* **93 H8** 21 56S 52 6W
Presidente Hayes □, *Paraguay* **94 A4** 24 0S 59 0W
Presidente Prudente, *Brazil* **95 A5** 22 5S 51 25W
Presidio, *Mexico* **86 B4** 29 29N 104 23W
Presidio, *U.S.A.* **81 L2** 29 34N 104 22W
Prešov, *Slovak Rep.* **17 D11** 49 0N 21 15 E
Prespa, L. = Prespansko Jezero, *Macedonia* **21 D9** 40 55N 21 0 E
Prespansko Jezero, *Macedonia* **21 D9** 40 55N 21 0 E
Presque I., *U.S.A.* **78 D4** 42 9N 80 6W
Presque Isle, *U.S.A.* **77 B12** 46 41N 68 1W
Prestatyn, *U.K.* **10 D4** 53 20N 3 24W
Presteigne, *U.K.* **11 E5** 52 17N 3 0W
Preston, *Canada* **78 C4** 43 23N 80 21W
Preston, *U.K.* **10 D5** 53 46N 2 42W
Preston, *Idaho, U.S.A.* **82 E8** 42 6N 111 53W
Preston, *Minn., U.S.A.* **80 D8** 43 40N 92 5W
Preston, C., *Australia* **60 D2** 20 51S 116 12 E
Prestonburg, *U.S.A.* **76 G4** 37 39N 82 46W
Prestwick, *U.K.* **12 F4** 55 29N 4 37W
Pretoria, *S. Africa* **57 D4** 25 44S 28 12 E
Préveza, *Greece* **21 E9** 38 57N 20 47 E
Prey Veng, *Cambodia* **39 G5** 11 35N 105 29 E
Pribilof Is., *U.S.A.* **68 C2** 57 0N 170 0W
Příbram, *Czech Rep.* **16 D8** 49 41N 14 2 E
Price, *U.S.A.* **82 G8** 39 36N 110 49W
Price I., *Canada* **72 C3** 52 23N 128 41W
Prichard, *U.S.A.* **77 K1** 30 44N 88 5W
Priekule, *Latvia* **9 H19** 56 26N 21 35 E
Prienai, *Lithuania* **9 J20** 54 38N 23 57 E
Prieska, *S. Africa* **56 D3** 29 40S 22 42 E
Priest L., *U.S.A.* **82 B5** 48 35N 116 52W
Priest River, *U.S.A.* **82 B5** 48 10N 116 54W
Priest Valley, *U.S.A.* **84 J6** 36 10N 120 39W
Prievidza, *Slovak Rep.* **17 D10** 48 46N 18 36 E
Prikaspiyskaya Nizmennost = Caspian Depression, *Eurasia* **25 E8** 47 0N 48 0 E
Prilep, *Macedonia* **21 D9** 41 21N 21 32 E
Priluki = Pryluky, *Ukraine* **25 D5** 50 30N 32 24 E
Prime Seal I., *Australia* **62 G4** 40 3S 147 43 E
Primrose L., *Canada* **73 C7** 54 55N 109 45W
Prince Albert, *Canada* **73 C7** 53 15N 105 50W
Prince Albert, *S. Africa* **56 E3** 33 12S 22 2 E
Prince Albert Mts., *Antarctica* **5 D11** 76 0S 161 30 E
Prince Albert Nat. Park, *Canada* **73 C7** 54 0N 106 25W
Prince Albert Pen., *Canada* **68 A8** 72 30N 116 0W
Prince Albert Sd., *Canada* **68 A8** 70 25N 115 0W
Prince Alfred, C., *Canada* **4 B1** 74 20N 124 40W
Prince Charles I., *Canada* **69 B12** 67 47N 76 12W
Prince Charles Mts., *Antarctica* **5 D6** 72 0S 67 0 E
Prince Edward I. □, *Canada* **71 C7** 46 20N 63 20W
Prince Edward Is., *Ind. Oc.* **3 G11** 46 35S 38 0 E
Prince Edward Pt., *Canada* **78 C8** 43 56N 76 52W
Prince George, *Canada* **72 C4** 53 55N 122 50W
Prince of Wales, C., *U.S.A.* **66 C3** 65 36N 168 5W
Prince of Wales I., *Australia* **62 A3** 10 40S 142 10 E
Prince of Wales I., *Canada* **68 A10** 73 0N 99 0W
Prince of Wales I., *U.S.A.* **68 C6** 55 47N 132 50W
Prince Patrick I., *Canada* **4 B2** 77 0N 120 0W
Prince Regent Inlet, *Canada* **4 B3** 73 0N 90 0W
Prince Rupert, *Canada* **72 C2** 54 20N 130 20W
Princess Charlotte B., *Australia* **62 A3** 14 25S 144 0 E
Princess May Ranges, *Australia* **60 C4** 15 30S 125 30 E
Princess Royal I., *Canada* **72 C3** 53 0N 128 40W
Princeton, *Canada* **72 D4** 49 27N 120 30W
Princeton, *Calif., U.S.A.* **84 F4** 39 24N 122 1W
Princeton, *Ill., U.S.A.* **80 E10** 41 23N 89 28W
Princeton, *Ind., U.S.A.* **76 F2** 38 21N 87 34W
Princeton, *Ky., U.S.A.* **76 G2** 37 7N 87 53W
Princeton, *Mo., U.S.A.* **80 E8** 40 24N 93 35W
Princeton, *N.J., U.S.A.* **79 F10** 40 21N 74 39W
Princeton, *W. Va., U.S.A.* **76 G5** 37 22N 81 6W
Principe, I. de, *Atl. Oc.* **48 F4** 1 37N 7 27 E
Principe da Beira, *Brazil* **92 F6** 12 20S 64 30W
Prineville, *U.S.A.* **82 D3** 44 18N 120 51W
Prins Harald Kyst, *Antarctica* **5 D4** 70 0S 35 1 E
Prinsesse Astrid Kyst, *Antarctica* **5 D3** 70 45S 12 30 E
Prinsesse Ragnhild Kyst, *Antarctica* **5 D4** 70 15S 27 30 E
Prinzapolca, *Nic.* **88 D3** 13 20N 83 35W
Priozersk, *Russia* **24 B5** 61 2N 30 7 E
Pripet = Prypyat →, *Europe* **17 C16** 51 20N 30 15 E
Pripet Marshes, *Europe* **17 B15** 52 10N 28 10 E
Pripyat Marshes = Pripet Marshes, *Europe* **17 B15** 52 10N 28 10 E
Pripyats = Prypyat →, *Europe* **17 C16** 51 20N 30 15 E
Priština, *Yugoslavia* **21 C9** 42 40N 21 13 E
Privas, *France* **18 D6** 44 45N 4 37 E
Privolzhskaya Vozvyshennost, *Russia* **25 D8** 51 0N 46 0 E
Prizren, *Yugoslavia* **21 C9** 42 13N 20 45 E
Probolinggo, *Indonesia* **37 G15** 7 46S 113 13 E
Proctor, *U.S.A.* **79 C11** 43 40N 73 2W
Proddatur, *India* **40 M11** 14 45N 78 30 E
Prodhromos, *Cyprus* **23 E11** 34 57N 32 50 E
Profitis Ilias, *Greece* **23 C9** 36 17N 27 56 E
Profondeville, *Belgium* **15 D4** 50 23N 4 52 E
Progreso, *Mexico* **87 C7** 21 20N 89 40W
Progreso, *Yucatán, Mexico* **86 B4** 21 17N 89 40W
Prokopyevsk, *Russia* **26 D9** 54 0N 86 45 E
Prokuplje, *Serbia, Yug.* **21 C9** 43 16N 21 36 E
Prome = Pyè, *Burma* **41 K19** 18 49N 95 13 E
Prophet →, *Canada* **72 B4** 58 48N 122 40W
Prophet River, *Canada* **72 B4** 58 6N 122 43W
Propriá, *Brazil* **93 F11** 10 13S 36 51W
Proserpine, *Australia* **62 C4** 20 21S 148 36 E
Prosna →, *Poland* **17 B9** 52 6N 17 44 E
Prospect, *U.S.A.* **79 C9** 43 18N 75 9W
Prosser, *U.S.A.* **82 C4** 46 12N 119 46W
Prostějov, *Czech Rep.* **17 D9** 49 30N 17 9 E
Proston, *Australia* **63 D5** 26 8S 151 32 E
Provence, *France* **18 E6** 43 40N 5 46 E
Providence, *Ky., U.S.A.* **76 G2** 37 24N 87 46W
Providence, *R.I., U.S.A.* **79 E13** 41 49N 71 24W
Providence Bay, *Canada* **70 C3** 45 41N 82 15W
Providence Mts., *U.S.A.* **85 K11** 35 10N 115 15W
Providencia, I. de, *Colombia* **88 D3** 13 25N 81 26W
Provideniya, *Russia* **27 C19** 64 23N 173 18W
Provins, *France* **18 B5** 48 33N 3 15 E
Provo, *U.S.A.* **82 F8** 40 14N 111 39W
Provost, *Canada* **73 C6** 52 25N 110 20W
Prudhoe Bay, *U.S.A.* **68 A5** 70 18N 148 22W
Prudhoe I., *Australia* **62 C4** 21 19S 149 41 E
Prud'homme, *Canada* **73 C7** 52 20N 105 54W
Pruszków, *Poland* **17 B11** 52 9N 20 49 E
Prut →, *Romania* **17 F15** 45 28N 28 10 E
Pruzhany, *Belarus* **17 B13** 52 33N 24 28 E
Prydz B., *Antarctica* **5 C6** 69 0S 74 0 E
Pryluky, *Ukraine* **25 D5** 50 30N 32 24 E
Pryor, *U.S.A.* **81 G7** 36 19N 95 19W
Prypyat →, *Europe* **17 C16** 51 20N 30 15 E
Przemyśl, *Poland* **17 D12** 49 50N 22 45 E
Przhevalsk, *Kyrgyzstan* **26 E8** 42 30N 78 20 E
Psará, *Greece* **21 E11** 38 37N 25 38 E
Psíra, *Greece* **23 D7** 35 12N 25 52 E
Pskov, *Russia* **24 C4** 57 50N 28 25 E
Pskovskoye, Ozero, *Russia* **9 H22** 58 0N 27 58 E
Ptich = Ptsich →, *Belarus* **17 B15** 52 9N 28 52 E
Ptolemaís, *Greece* **21 D9** 40 30N 21 43 E
Ptsich →, *Belarus* **17 B15** 52 9N 28 52 E
Pu Xian, *China* **34 F6** 36 24N 111 6 E
Pua, *Thailand* **38 C3** 19 11N 100 55 E
Puán, *Argentina* **94 D3** 37 30S 62 45W
Puan, *S. Korea* **35 G14** 35 44N 126 44 E
Pucallpa, *Peru* **92 E4** 8 25S 74 30W
Pudasjärvi, *Finland* **8 D22** 65 23N 26 53 E
Pudozh, *Russia* **24 B6** 61 48N 36 32 E
Pudukkottai, *India* **40 P11** 10 28N 78 47 E
Puebla, *Mexico* **87 D5** 19 3N 98 12W
Puebla □, *Mexico* **87 D5** 18 30N 98 0W
Pueblo, *U.S.A.* **80 F2** 38 16N 104 37W
Pueblo Hundido, *Chile* **94 B1** 26 20S 70 5W
Puelches, *Argentina* **94 D2** 38 5S 65 51W
Puelén, *Argentina* **94 D2** 37 32S 67 38W
Puente Alto, *Chile* **94 C1** 33 32S 70 35W
Puente-Genil, *Spain* **19 D3** 37 22N 4 47W
Puerco →, *U.S.A.* **83 J10** 34 22N 107 50W
Puerto, *Canary Is.* **22 F2** 28 5N 17 20W
Puerto Aisén, *Chile* **96 F2** 45 27S 73 0W
Puerto Ángel, *Mexico* **87 D5** 15 40N 96 29W
Puerto Arista, *Mexico* **87 D6** 15 56N 93 48W
Puerto Armuelles, *Panama* **88 E3** 8 20N 82 51W
Puerto Ayacucho, *Venezuela* **92 B5** 5 40N 67 35W
Puerto Barrios, *Guatemala* **88 C2** 15 40N 88 32W
Puerto Bermejo, *Argentina* **94 B4** 26 55S 58 34W
Puerto Bermúdez, *Peru* **92 F4** 10 20S 74 58W
Puerto Bolívar, *Ecuador* **92 D3** 3 19S 79 55W
Puerto Cabello, *Venezuela* **92 A5** 10 28N 68 1W
Puerto Cabezas, *Nic.* **88 D3** 14 0N 83 30W
Puerto Cabo Gracias á Dios, *Nic.* **88 D3** 15 0N 83 10W
Puerto Carreño, *Colombia* **92 B5** 6 12N 67 22W
Puerto Castilla, *Honduras* **88 C2** 16 0N 86 0W
Puerto Chicama, *Peru* **92 E3** 7 45S 79 20W
Puerto Coig, *Argentina* **96 G3** 50 54S 69 15W
Puerto Cortés, *Costa Rica* **88 E3** 8 55N 84 0W
Puerto Cortés, *Honduras* **88 C2** 15 51N 88 0W
Puerto Cumarebo, *Venezuela* **92 A5** 11 29N 69 30W
Puerto de Alcudia = Port d'Alcúdia, *Spain* **22 B10** 39 50N 3 7 E
Puerto de Andraitx, *Spain* **22 B9** 39 32N 2 23 E
Puerto de Cabrera, *Spain* **22 B9** 39 8N 2 56 E
Puerto de Gran Tarajal, *Canary Is.* **22 F5** 28 13N 14 1W
Puerto de la Cruz, *Canary Is.* **22 F3** 28 24N 16 32W
Puerto de Pozo Negro, *Canary Is.* **22 F6** 28 19N 13 55W
Puerto de Sóller = Port de Sóller, *Spain* **22 B9** 39 48N 2 42 E
Puerto del Carmen, *Canary Is.* **22 F6** 28 55N 13 38W
Puerto del Rosario, *Canary Is.* **22 F6** 28 30N 13 52W
Puerto Deseado, *Argentina* **96 F3** 47 55S 66 0W
Puerto Escondido, *Mexico* **87 D5** 15 50N 97 3W
Puerto Heath, *Bolivia* **92 F5** 12 34S 68 39W
Puerto Inírida, *Colombia* **92 C5** 3 53N 67 52W
Puerto Juárez, *Mexico* **87 C7** 21 11N 86 49W
Puerto La Cruz, *Venezuela* **92 A6** 10 13N 64 38W
Puerto Leguízamo, *Colombia* **92 D4** 0 12S 74 46W
Puerto Limón, *Colombia* **92 C4** 3 23N 73 30W
Puerto Lobos, *Argentina* **96 E3** 42 0S 65 3W
Puerto Madryn, *Argentina* **96 E3** 42 48S 65 4W
Puerto Maldonado, *Peru* **92 F5** 12 30S 69 10W
Puerto Manotí, *Cuba* **88 B4** 21 22N 76 50W
Puerto Montt, *Chile* **96 E2** 41 28S 73 0W
Puerto Morazán, *Nic.* **88 D2** 12 51N 87 11W
Puerto Morelos, *Mexico* **87 C7** 20 49N 86 52W
Puerto Natales, *Chile* **96 G2** 51 45S 72 15W
Puerto Padre, *Cuba* **88 B4** 21 13N 76 35W
Puerto Páez, *Venezuela* **92 B5** 6 13N 67 28W
Puerto Peñasco, *Mexico* **86 A2** 31 20N 113 33W
Puerto Pinasco, *Paraguay* **94 A4** 22 36S 57 50W
Puerto Plata, *Dom. Rep.* **89 C5** 19 48N 70 45W
Puerto Pollensa = Port de Pollença, *Spain* **22 B10** 39 54N 3 4 E
Puerto Princesa, *Phil.* **37 C5** 9 46N 118 45 E
Puerto Quepos, *Costa Rica* **88 E3** 9 29N 84 6W
Puerto Rico, *Canary Is.* **22 G4** 27 47N 15 42W
Puerto Rico ■, *W. Indies* **89 C6** 18 15N 66 45W
Puerto Rico Trench, *Atl. Oc.* **89 C6** 19 50N 66 0W
Puerto San Julián, *Argentina* **96 F3** 49 18S 67 43W
Puerto Sastre, *Paraguay* **94 A4** 22 2S 57 55W
Puerto Suárez, *Bolivia* **92 G7** 18 58S 57 52W
Puerto Vallarta, *Mexico* **86 C3** 20 36N 105 15W
Puerto Wilches, *Colombia* **92 B4** 7 21N 73 54W
Puertollano, *Spain* **19 C3** 38 43N 4 7W
Pueyrredón, L., *Argentina* **96 F2** 47 20S 72 0W
Puffin I., *Ireland* **13 E1** 51 50N 10 24W
Pugachev, *Russia* **24 D8** 52 0N 48 49 E
Pugal, *India* **42 E5** 28 30N 72 48 E
Puge, *Tanzania* **54 C3** 4 45S 33 11 E
Puget Sound, *U.S.A.* **82 C2** 47 50N 122 30W
Pugŏdong, *N. Korea* **35 C16** 42 5N 130 0 E
Pugu, *Tanzania* **54 D4** 6 55S 39 4 E
Pūgūnzī, *Iran* **45 E8** 25 49N 59 10 E
Puig Major, *Spain* **22 B9** 39 48N 2 47 E
Puigcerdà, *Spain* **19 A6** 42 24N 1 50 E
Puigpunyent, *Spain* **22 B9** 39 38N 2 32 E
Pujon-chŏsuji, *N. Korea* **35 D14** 40 35N 127 35 E
Pukaki L., *N.Z.* **59 L3** 44 4S 170 1 E
Pukapuka, *Cook Is.* **65 J11** 10 53S 165 49W
Pukaskwa Nat. Park, *Canada* **70 C2** 48 20N 86 0W
Pukatawagan, *Canada* **73 B8** 55 45N 101 20W
Pukchin, *N. Korea* **35 D13** 40 12N 125 45 E
Pukch'ŏng, *N. Korea* **35 D15** 40 14N 128 10 E
Pukekohe, *N.Z.* **59 G5** 37 12S 174 55 E
Pukhrayan, *India* **43 F8** 26 14N 79 51 E
Pula, *Croatia* **16 F7** 44 54N 13 57 E
Pulacayo, *Bolivia* **92 H5** 20 25S 66 41W
Pulandian, *China* **35 E11** 39 25N 121 58 E
Pularumpi, *Australia* **60 B5** 11 24S 130 26 E
Pulaski, *N.Y., U.S.A.* **79 C8** 43 34N 76 8W
Pulaski, *Tenn., U.S.A.* **77 H2** 35 12N 87 2W
Pulaski, *Va., U.S.A.* **76 G5** 37 3N 80 47W
Pulau →, *Indonesia* **37 F9** 5 50S 138 15 E
Puławy, *Poland* **17 C11** 51 23N 21 59 E
Pulga, *U.S.A.* **84 F5** 39 48N 121 29W
Pulicat L., *India* **40 N12** 13 40N 80 15 E
Pullman, *U.S.A.* **82 C5** 46 44N 117 10W
Pulo-Anna, *Pac. Oc.* **37 D8** 4 30N 132 5 E
Pulog, *Phil.* **37 A6** 16 40N 120 50 E
Pułtusk, *Poland* **17 B11** 52 43N 21 6 E
Pumlumon Fawr, *U.K.* **11 E4** 52 28N 3 46W
Puná, I., *Ecuador* **92 D2** 2 55S 80 5W
Punakha, *Bhutan* **41 F16** 27 42N 89 52 E
Punasar, *India* **42 F5** 27 6N 73 6 E
Punata, *Bolivia* **92 G5** 17 32S 65 50W
Punch, *India* **43 C6** 33 48N 74 4 E
Punch →, *Pakistan* **42 C5** 33 12N 73 40 E
Pune, *India* **40 K8** 18 29N 73 57 E
P'ungsan, *N. Korea* **35 D15** 40 50N 128 9 E
Pungue, Ponte de, *Mozam.* **55 F3** 19 0S 34 0 E
Punjab □, *India* **42 D7** 31 0N 76 0 E
Punjab □, *Pakistan* **42 E6** 32 0N 74 30 E
Puno, *Peru* **92 G4** 15 55S 70 3W
Punpun →, *India* **43 G11** 25 31N 85 18 E
Punta Alta, *Argentina* **96 D4** 38 53S 62 4W
Punta Arenas, *Chile* **96 G2** 53 10S 71 0W
Punta de Díaz, *Chile* **94 B1** 28 0S 70 45W
Punta Gorda, *Belize* **87 D7** 16 10N 88 45W
Punta Gorda, *U.S.A.* **77 M5** 26 56N 82 3W
Punta Prieta, *Mexico* **86 B2** 28 58N 114 17W
Punta Prima, *Spain* **22 B11** 39 48N 4 16 E
Puntarenas, *Costa Rica* **88 E3** 10 0N 84 50W
Punto Fijo, *Venezuela* **92 A4** 11 50N 70 13W
Punxsatawney, *U.S.A.* **78 F6** 40 57N 78 59W
Puquio, *Peru* **92 F4** 14 45S 74 10W
Pur →, *Russia* **26 C8** 67 31N 77 55 E
Purace, Vol., *Colombia* **92 C3** 2 21N 76 23W
Puralia = Puruliya, *India* **43 H12** 23 17N 86 24 E
Puranpur, *India* **43 E9** 28 31N 80 9 E
Purbeck, Isle of, *U.K.* **11 G6** 50 39N 1 59W
Purcell, *U.S.A.* **81 H6** 35 1N 97 22W
Purcell Mts., *Canada* **72 D5** 49 55N 116 15W
Puri, *India* **41 K14** 19 50N 85 58 E
Purmerend, *Neths.* **15 B4** 52 32N 4 58 E
Purnia, *India* **43 G12** 25 45N 87 31 E
Pursat = Pouthisat, *Cambodia* **38 F4** 12 34N 103 50 E
Purukcahu, *Indonesia* **36 E4** 0 35S 114 35 E
Puruliya, *India* **43 H12** 23 17N 86 24 E
Purus →, *Brazil* **92 D6** 3 42S 61 28W
Purvis, *U.S.A.* **81 K10** 31 9N 89 25W
Purwa, *India* **43 F9** 26 28N 80 47 E
Purwakarta, *Indonesia* **37 G12** 6 35S 107 29 E
Purwodadi, *Indonesia* **37 G14** 7 7S 110 55 E
Purwokerto, *Indonesia* **37 G13** 7 25S 109 14 E
Puryŏng, *N. Korea* **35 C15** 42 5N 129 43 E
Pusa, *India* **43 G11** 25 59N 85 41 E
Pusan, *S. Korea* **35 G15** 35 5N 129 0 E
Pushkino, *Russia* **25 D8** 51 16N 47 0 E
Putahow L., *Canada* **73 B8** 59 54N 100 40W
Putao, *Burma* **41 F20** 27 28N 97 30 E
Putaruru, *N.Z.* **59 H5** 38 2S 175 50 E
Puthein Myit →, *Burma* **41 M19** 15 56N 94 18 E
Putignano, *Italy* **20 D7** 40 51N 17 7 E
Puting, Tanjung, *Indonesia* **36 E4** 3 31S 111 46 E
Putnam, *U.S.A.* **79 E13** 41 55N 71 55W
Putorana, Gory, *Russia* **27 C10** 69 0N 95 0 E
Puttalam, *Sri Lanka* **40 Q11** 8 1N 79 55 E
Puttgarden, *Germany* **16 A6** 54 30N 11 10 E
Putumayo →, *S. Amer.* **92 D5** 3 7S 67 58W
Putussibau, *Indonesia* **36 D4** 0 50N 112 56 E
Puvirnituq, *Canada* **69 B12** 60 2N 77 10W
Puy-de-Dôme, *France* **18 D5** 45 46N 2 57 E
Puyallup, *U.S.A.* **84 C4** 47 12N 122 18W
Puyang, *China* **34 G8** 35 40N 115 1 E
Pūzeh Rīg, *Iran* **45 E8** 27 20N 58 40 E
Pwani □, *Tanzania* **54 D4** 7 0S 39 0 E
Pweto, *Dem. Rep. of the Congo* **55 D2** 8 25S 28 51 E
Pwllheli, *U.K.* **10 E3** 52 53N 4 25W
Pya-ozero, *Russia* **24 A5** 66 5N 30 58 E
Pyapon, *Burma* **41 L19** 16 20N 95 40 E
Pyasina →, *Russia* **27 B9** 73 30N 87 0 E
Pyatigorsk, *Russia* **25 F7** 44 2N 43 6 E
Pyè, *Burma* **41 K19** 18 49N 95 13 E
Pyetrikaw, *Belarus* **17 B15** 52 11N 28 29 E
Pyhäjoki, *Finland* **8 D21** 64 28N 24 14 E
Pyinmana, *Burma* **41 K20** 19 45N 96 12 E
Pyla, C., *Cyprus* **23 E12** 34 56N 33 51 E
Pymatuning Reservoir, *U.S.A.* **78 E4** 41 30N 80 28W
Pyŏktong, *N. Korea* **35 D13** 40 50N 125 50 E
Pyŏnggang, *N. Korea* **35 E14** 38 24N 127 17 E
P'yŏngt'aek, *S. Korea* **35 F14** 37 1N 127 4 E
P'yŏngyang, *N. Korea* **35 E13** 39 0N 125 30 E
Pyote, *U.S.A.* **81 K3** 31 32N 103 8W
Pyramid L., *U.S.A.* **82 G4** 40 1N 119 35W
Pyramid Pk., *U.S.A.* **85 J10** 36 25N 116 37W
Pyrénées, *Europe* **18 E4** 42 45N 0 18 E
Pyu, *Burma* **41 K20** 18 30N 96 28 E

Q

Qaanaaq = Thule, *Greenland* **4 B4** 77 40N 69 0W
Qachasnek, *S. Africa* **57 E4** 30 6S 28 42 E
Qa'el Jafr, *Jordan* **47 E5** 30 20N 36 25 E
Qa'emābād, *Iran* **45 D9** 31 44N 60 2 E
Qā'emshahr, *Iran* **45 B7** 36 30N 52 53 E
Qagan Nur, *China* **34 C8** 43 30N 114 55 E
Qahar Youyi Zhongqi, *China* **34 D7** 41 12N 112 40 E
Qahremānshahr = Bākhtarān, *Iran* **44 C5** 34 23N 47 0 E
Qaidam Pendi, *China* **32 C4** 37 0N 95 0 E
Qajarīyeh, *Iran* **45 D6** 31 1N 48 22 E
Qala, Ras il, *Malta* **23 C1** 36 1N 14 20 E
Qala-i-Jadid = Spīn Búldak, *Afghan.* **42 D2** 31 1N 66 25 E
Qala Viala, *Pakistan* **42 D2** 30 49N 67 17 E
Qala Yangi, *Afghan.* **42 B2** 34 20N 66 30 E

R

155

S

Sa, *Thailand* **38 C3** 18 34N 100 45 E
Sa Canal, *Spain* **22 C7** 38 51N 1 23 E
Sa Conillera, *Spain* **22 C7** 38 59N 1 13 E
Sa Dec, *Vietnam* **39 G5** 10 20N 105 46 E
Sa Dragonera, *Spain* **22 B9** 39 35N 2 19 E
Sa Mesquida, *Spain* **22 B11** 39 55N 4 16 E
Sa Savina, *Spain* **22 C7** 38 44N 1 25 E
Sa'ādatābād, *Fārs, Iran* **45 D7** 30 10N 53 5 E
Sa'ādatābād, *Hormozgān, Iran* **45 D7** 28 3N 55 53 E
Sa'ādatābād, *Kermān, Iran* **45 D7** 29 40N 55 51 E
Saale →, *Germany* **16 C6** 51 56N 11 54 E
Saalfeld, *Germany* **16 C6** 50 38N 11 21 E
Saar →, *Europe* **18 B7** 49 41N 6 32 E
Saarbrücken, *Germany* **16 D4** 49 14N 6 59 E
Saaremaa, *Estonia* **9 G20** 58 30N 22 30 E
Saarijärvi, *Finland* **9 E21** 62 43N 25 16 E
Saariselkä, *Finland* **8 B23** 68 16N 28 15 E
Sab 'Ābar, *Syria* **44 C3** 33 46N 37 41 E
Saba, *W. Indies* **89 C7** 17 42N 63 26W
Šabac, *Serbia, Yug.* **21 B8** 44 48N 19 42 E
Sabadell, *Spain* **19 B7** 41 28N 2 7 E
Sabah □, *Malaysia* **36 C5** 6 0N 117 0 E
Sabak Bernam, *Malaysia* **39 L3** 3 46N 100 58 E
Sabalān, Kūhhā-ye, *Iran* **44 B5** 38 15N 47 45 E
Sabalana, Kepulauan, *Indonesia* **37 F5** 6 45S 118 50 E
Sábana de la Mar, *Dom. Rep.* **89 C6** 19 7N 69 24W
Sábanalarga, *Colombia* **92 A4** 10 38N 74 55W
Sabang, *Indonesia* **36 C1** 5 50N 95 15 E
Sabará, *Brazil* **93 G10** 19 55S 43 46W
Sabarmati →, *India* **42 H5** 22 18N 72 22 E
Sabattis, *U.S.A.* **79 B10** 44 6N 74 40W
Saberania, *Indonesia* **37 E9** 2 5S 138 18 E
Sabhah, *Libya* **51 C8** 27 9N 14 29 E
Sabi →, *India* **42 E7** 28 29N 76 44 E
Sabie, *S. Africa* **57 D5** 25 10S 30 48 E
Sabinal, *Mexico* **86 A3** 30 58N 107 25W
Sabinal, *U.S.A.* **81 L5** 29 19N 99 28W
Sabinas, *Mexico* **86 B4** 27 50N 101 10W
Sabinas →, *Mexico* **86 B4** 27 37N 100 42W
Sabinas Hidalgo, *Mexico* **86 B4** 26 33N 100 10W
Sabine →, *U.S.A.* **81 L8** 29 59N 93 47W
Sabine L., *U.S.A.* **81 L8** 29 53N 93 51W
Sabine Pass, *U.S.A.* **81 L8** 29 44N 93 54W
Sabinsville, *U.S.A.* **78 E7** 41 52N 77 31W
Sabkhet el Bardawîl, *Egypt* **47 D2** 31 10N 33 15 E
Sablayan, *Phil.* **37 B6** 12 50N 120 50 E
Sable, *Canada* **71 A6** 55 30N 68 21W
Sable, C., *Canada* **71 D6** 43 29N 65 38W
Sable, C., *U.S.A.* **75 E10** 25 9N 81 8W
Sable I., *Canada* **71 D8** 44 0N 60 0W
Sabrina Coast, *Antarctica* **5 C9** 68 0S 120 0 E
Sabulubbek, *Indonesia* **36 E1** 1 36S 98 40 E
Sabzevār, *Iran* **45 B8** 36 15N 57 40 E
Sabzvārān, *Iran* **45 D8** 28 45N 57 50 E
Sac City, *U.S.A.* **80 D7** 42 25N 95 0W
Săcele, *Romania* **17 F13** 45 37N 25 41 E
Sachigo →, *Canada* **70 A2** 55 6N 88 58W
Sachigo, L., *Canada* **70 B1** 53 50N 92 12W
Sachsen □, *Germany* **16 C7** 50 55N 13 10 E
Sachsen-Anhalt □, *Germany* **16 C7** 52 0N 12 0 E
Sackets Harbor, *U.S.A.* **79 C8** 43 57N 76 7W
Sackville, *Canada* **71 C7** 45 54N 64 22W
Saco, *Maine, U.S.A.* **77 D10** 43 30N 70 27W
Saco, *Mont., U.S.A.* **82 B10** 48 28N 107 21W
Sacramento, *U.S.A.* **84 G5** 38 35N 121 29W
Sacramento →, *U.S.A.* **84 G5** 38 3N 121 56W
Sacramento Mts., *U.S.A.* **83 K11** 32 30N 105 30W
Sacramento Valley, *U.S.A.* **84 G5** 39 30N 122 0W
Sada-Misaki, *Japan* **31 H6** 33 20N 132 1 E
Sadabad, *India* **42 F8** 27 27N 78 3 E
Sadani, *Tanzania* **54 D4** 5 58S 38 35 E
Sadao, *Thailand* **39 J3** 6 38N 100 26 E
Sadd el Aali, *Egypt* **51 D12** 23 54N 32 54 E
Saddle Mt., *U.S.A.* **84 E3** 45 58N 123 41W
Sadimi, *Dem. Rep. of the Congo* **55 D1** 9 25S 23 32 E
Sado, *Japan* **30 F9** 38 0N 138 25 E
Sadon, *Burma* **41 G20** 25 28N 97 55 E
Sadra, *India* **42 H5** 23 21N 72 43 E
Sadri, *India* **42 G5** 25 11N 73 26 E
Sæby, *Denmark* **9 H14** 57 21N 10 30 E
Saegertown, *U.S.A.* **78 E4** 41 43N 80 9W
Şafājah, *Si. Arabia* **44 E3** 26 25N 39 0 E
Säffle, *Sweden* **9 G15** 59 8N 12 55 E
Safford, *U.S.A.* **83 K9** 32 50N 109 43W
Saffron Walden, *U.K.* **11 E8** 52 1N 0 16 E
Safi, *Morocco* **50 B4** 32 18N 9 20W
Şafīābād, *Iran* **45 B8** 36 45N 57 58 E
Safīd Dasht, *Iran* **45 C6** 33 27N 48 11 E
Safīd Kūh, *Afghan.* **40 B3** 34 45N 63 0 E
Safīd Rūd →, *Iran* **45 B6** 37 23N 50 11 E
Safipur, *India* **43 F9** 26 44N 80 21 E
Safwān, *Iraq* **44 D5** 30 7N 47 43 E
Sag Harbor, *U.S.A.* **79 F12** 41 0N 72 18W
Saga, *Japan* **31 H5** 33 15N 130 16 E
Saga □, *Japan* **31 H5** 33 15N 130 20 E
Sagae, *Japan* **30 E10** 38 22N 140 17 E
Sagamore, *U.S.A.* **78 F5** 40 46N 79 14W
Sagar, *India* **40 M9** 14 14N 75 6 E
Sagar, *Mad. P., India* **43 H8** 23 50N 78 44 E
Sagara, L., *Tanzania* **54 D3** 5 20S 31 0 E
Saginaw, *U.S.A.* **76 D4** 43 26N 83 56W
Saginaw →, *U.S.A.* **76 D4** 43 39N 83 51W
Saginaw B., *U.S.A.* **76 D4** 43 50N 83 40W
Saglouc = Salluit, *Canada* **69 B12** 62 14N 75 38W
Sagŏ-ri, *S. Korea* **35 G14** 35 25N 126 49 E
Sagua la Grande, *Cuba* **88 B3** 22 50N 80 10W
Saguache, *U.S.A.* **83 G10** 38 5N 106 8W
Saguaro Nat. Park, *U.S.A.* **83 K8** 32 12N 110 38W
Saguenay →, *Canada* **71 C5** 48 22N 71 0W
Sagunt, *Spain* **19 C5** 39 42N 0 18W
Sagunto = Sagunt, *Spain* **19 C5** 39 42N 0 18W
Sagwara, *India* **42 H6** 23 41N 74 1 E
Sahagún, *Spain* **19 A3** 42 18N 5 2W
Saḩam al Jawlān, *Syria* **47 C4** 32 45N 35 55 E
Sahand, Kūh-e, *Iran* **44 B5** 37 44N 46 27 E
Sahara, *Africa* **50 D6** 23 0N 5 0 E
Saharan Atlas = Saharien, Atlas, *Algeria* **50 B6** 33 30N 1 0 E
Saharanpur, *India* **42 E7** 29 58N 77 33 E
Saharien, Atlas, *Algeria* **50 B6** 33 30N 1 0 E
Saharsa, *India* **43 G12** 25 53N 86 36 E
Sahasinaka, *Madag.* **57 C8** 21 49S 47 49 E
Sahaswan, *India* **43 E8** 28 5N 78 45 E
Sahel, *Africa* **50 E5** 16 0N 5 0 E
Sahibganj, *India* **43 G12** 25 12N 87 40 E
Sāḩilīyah, *Iraq* **44 C4** 33 43N 42 42 E
Sahiwal, *Pakistan* **42 D5** 30 45N 73 8 E
Şaḩneh, *Iran* **44 C5** 34 29N 47 41 E
Sahuaripa, *Mexico* **86 B3** 29 0N 109 13W
Sahuarita, *U.S.A.* **83 L8** 31 57N 110 58W
Sahuayo, *Mexico* **86 C4** 20 4N 102 43W
Sai →, *India* **43 G10** 25 39N 82 47 E
Sai Buri, *Thailand* **39 J3** 6 43N 101 45 E
Sa'id Bundas, *Sudan* **51 G10** 8 24N 24 48 E
Sa'īdābād, *Kermān, Iran* **45 D7** 29 30N 55 45 E
Sa'īdābād, *Semnān, Iran* **45 B7** 36 8N 54 11 E
Sa'īdīyeh, *Iran* **45 B6** 36 20N 48 55 E
Saidpur, *Bangla.* **41 G16** 25 48N 89 0 E
Saidpur, *India* **43 G10** 25 33N 83 11 E
Saidu, *Pakistan* **43 B5** 34 43N 72 24 E
Saigon = Phanh Bho Ho Chi Minh, *Vietnam* **39 G6** 10 58N 106 40 E
Saijō, *Japan* **31 H6** 33 55N 133 11 E
Saikhoa Ghat, *India* **41 F19** 27 50N 95 40 E
Saiki, *Japan* **31 H5** 32 58N 131 51 E
Sailana, *India* **42 H6** 23 28N 74 55 E
Sailolof, *Indonesia* **37 E8** 1 7S 130 46 E
Saimaa, *Finland* **9 F23** 61 15N 28 15 E
Şa'in Dezh, *Iran* **44 B5** 36 40N 46 25 E
St. Abb's Head, *U.K.* **12 F6** 55 55N 2 8W
St. Alban's, *Canada* **71 C8** 47 51N 55 50W
St. Albans, *U.K.* **11 F7** 51 45N 0 19W
St. Albans, *Vt., U.S.A.* **79 B11** 44 49N 73 5W
St. Albans, *W. Va., U.S.A.* **76 F5** 38 23N 81 50W
St. Alban's Head, *U.K.* **11 G5** 50 34N 2 4W
St. Albert, *Canada* **72 C6** 53 37N 113 32W
St. Andrew's, *Canada* **71 C8** 47 45N 59 15W
St. Andrews, *U.K.* **12 E6** 56 20N 2 47W
St-Anicet, *Canada* **79 A10** 45 8N 74 22W
St. Ann B., *Canada* **71 C7** 46 22N 60 25W
St. Ann's Bay, *Jamaica* **88 C4** 18 26N 77 15W
St. Anthony, *Canada* **71 B8** 51 22N 55 35W
St. Anthony, *U.S.A.* **82 E8** 43 58N 111 41W
St. Antoine, *Canada* **71 C7** 46 22N 64 45W
St. Arnaud, *Australia* **63 F3** 36 40S 143 16 E
St-Augustin →, *Canada* **71 B8** 51 16N 58 40W
St-Augustin-Saguenay, *Canada* **71 B8** 51 13N 58 38W
St. Augustine, *U.S.A.* **77 L5** 29 54N 81 19W
St. Austell, *U.K.* **11 G3** 50 20N 4 47W
St. Barbe, *Canada* **71 B8** 51 12N 56 46W
St-Barthélemy, *W. Indies* **89 C7** 17 50N 62 50W
St. Bees Hd., *U.K.* **10 C4** 54 31N 3 38W
St. Bride's, *Canada* **71 C9** 46 56N 54 10W
St. Brides B., *U.K.* **11 F2** 51 49N 5 9W
St-Brieuc, *France* **18 B2** 48 30N 2 46W
St. Catharines, *Canada* **78 C5** 43 10N 79 15W
St. Catherines I., *U.S.A.* **77 K5** 31 40N 81 10W
St. Catherine's Pt., *U.K.* **11 G6** 50 34N 1 18W
St-Chamond, *France* **18 D6** 45 28N 4 31 E
St. Charles, *Ill., U.S.A.* **76 E1** 41 54N 88 19W
St. Charles, *Mo., U.S.A.* **80 F9** 38 47N 90 29W
St. Charles, *Va., U.S.A.* **76 F7** 36 48N 83 4W
St. Christopher-Nevis = St. Kitts & Nevis ■, *W. Indies* **89 C7** 17 20N 62 40W
St. Clair, *Mich., U.S.A.* **78 D2** 42 50N 82 30W
St. Clair, *Pa., U.S.A.* **79 F8** 40 43N 76 12W
St. Clair →, *U.S.A.* **78 D2** 42 38N 82 31W
St. Clair, L., *Canada* **70 D3** 42 30N 82 45W
St. Clair, L., *U.S.A.* **78 D2** 42 27N 82 39W
St. Clairsville, *U.S.A.* **78 F4** 40 5N 80 54W
St. Claude, *Canada* **73 D9** 49 40N 98 20W
St-Clet, *Canada* **79 A10** 45 21N 74 13W
St. Cloud, *Fla., U.S.A.* **77 L5** 28 15N 81 17W
St. Cloud, *Minn., U.S.A.* **80 C7** 45 34N 94 10W
St. Cricq, C., *Australia* **61 E1** 25 17S 113 6 E
St. Croix, *Virgin Is.* **89 C7** 17 45N 64 45W
St. Croix →, *U.S.A.* **80 C8** 44 45N 92 48W
St. Croix Falls, *U.S.A.* **80 C8** 45 24N 92 38W
St. David's, *Canada* **71 C8** 48 12N 58 52W
St. David's, *U.K.* **11 F2** 51 53N 5 16W
St. David's Head, *U.K.* **11 F2** 51 54N 5 19W
St-Denis, *France* **18 B5** 48 56N 2 22 E
St-Dizier, *France* **18 B6** 48 38N 4 56 E
St. Elias, Mt., *U.S.A.* **68 B5** 60 18N 140 56W
St. Elias Mts., *Canada* **72 A1** 60 33N 139 28W
St. Elias Mts., *U.S.A.* **68 C6** 60 0N 138 0W
St-Étienne, *France* **18 D6** 45 27N 4 22 E
St. Eugène, *Canada* **79 A10** 45 30N 74 28W
St. Eustatius, *W. Indies* **89 C7** 17 20N 63 0W
St-Félicien, *Canada* **70 C5** 48 40N 72 25W
St-Flour, *France* **18 D5** 45 2N 3 6 E
St. Francis, *U.S.A.* **80 F4** 39 47N 101 48W
St. Francis →, *U.S.A.* **81 H9** 34 38N 90 36W
St. Francis, C., *S. Africa* **56 E3** 34 14S 24 49 E
St. Francisville, *U.S.A.* **81 K9** 30 47N 91 23W
St-François, L., *Canada* **79 A10** 45 10N 74 22W
St-Gabriel, *Canada* **70 C5** 46 17N 73 24W
St. Gallen = Sankt Gallen, *Switz.* **18 C8** 47 26N 9 22 E
St-Gaudens, *France* **18 E4** 43 6N 0 44 E
St. George, *Australia* **63 D4** 28 1S 148 30 E
St. George, *Canada* **71 C6** 45 11N 66 50W
St. George, *S.C., U.S.A.* **77 J5** 33 11N 80 35W
St. George, *Utah, U.S.A.* **83 H7** 37 6N 113 35W
St. George, C., *Canada* **71 C8** 48 30N 59 16W
St. George, C., *U.S.A.* **77 L3** 29 40N 85 5W
St. George Ra., *Australia* **60 C4** 18 40S 125 0 E
St. George's, *Canada* **71 C8** 48 26N 58 31W
St-Georges, *Canada* **71 C5** 46 8N 70 40W
St. George's, *Grenada* **89 D7** 12 5N 61 43W
St. George's B., *Canada* **71 C8** 48 24N 58 53W
St. Georges Basin, *N.S.W., Australia* **63 F5** 35 7S 150 36 E
St. Georges Basin, *W. Austral., Australia* **60 C4** 15 23S 125 2 E
St. George's Channel, *Europe* **13 E6** 52 0N 6 0W
St. Georges Hd., *Australia* **63 F5** 35 12S 150 42 E
St. Gotthard P. = San Gottardo, P. del, *Switz.* **18 C8** 46 33N 8 33 E
St. Helena, *U.S.A.* **82 G2** 38 30N 122 28W
St. Helena ■, *Atl. Oc.* **49 H3** 15 55S 5 44W
St. Helena, Mt., *U.S.A.* **84 G4** 38 40N 122 36W
St. Helena B., *S. Africa* **56 E2** 32 40S 18 10 E
St. Helens, *Australia* **62 G4** 41 20S 148 15 E
St. Helens, *U.K.* **10 D5** 53 27N 2 44W
St. Helens, *U.S.A.* **84 E4** 45 52N 122 48W
St. Helens, Mt., *U.S.A.* **84 D4** 46 12N 122 12W
St. Helier, *U.K.* **11 H5** 49 10N 2 7W
St-Hubert, *Belgium* **15 D5** 50 2N 5 23 E
St-Hyacinthe, *Canada* **70 C5** 45 40N 72 58W
St. Ignace, *U.S.A.* **76 C3** 45 52N 84 44W
St. Ignace I., *Canada* **70 C2** 48 45N 88 0W
St. Ignatius, *U.S.A.* **82 C6** 47 19N 114 6W
St. Ives, *U.K.* **11 G2** 50 12N 5 30W
St. James, *U.S.A.* **80 D7** 43 59N 94 38W
St-Jean →, *Canada* **71 B7** 50 17N 64 20W
St-Jean, L., *Canada* **71 C5** 48 40N 72 0W
St-Jean-Port-Joli, *Canada* **71 C5** 47 15N 70 13W
St-Jean-sur-Richelieu, *Canada* **79 A11** 45 20N 73 20W
St-Jérôme, *Canada* **70 C5** 45 47N 74 0W
St. John, *Canada* **71 C6** 45 20N 66 8W
St. John, *U.S.A.* **81 G5** 38 0N 98 46W
St. John →, *U.S.A.* **77 C12** 45 12N 66 5W
St. John, C., *Canada* **71 C8** 50 0N 55 32W
St. John's, *Antigua* **89 C7** 17 6N 61 51W
St. John's, *Canada* **71 C9** 47 35N 52 40W
St. Johns, *Ariz., U.S.A.* **83 J9** 34 30N 109 22W
St. Johns, *Mich., U.S.A.* **76 D3** 43 0N 84 33W
St. Johns →, *U.S.A.* **77 K5** 30 24N 81 24W
St. John's Pt., *Ireland* **13 B3** 54 34N 8 27W
St. Johnsbury, *U.S.A.* **79 B12** 44 25N 72 1W
St. Johnsville, *U.S.A.* **79 D10** 43 0N 74 43W
St. Joseph, *La., U.S.A.* **81 K9** 31 55N 91 14W
St. Joseph, *Mich., U.S.A.* **75 B9** 42 6N 86 29W
St. Joseph, *Mo., U.S.A.* **80 F7** 39 46N 94 50W
St. Joseph →, *U.S.A.* **76 D2** 42 7N 86 29W
St. Joseph, I., *Canada* **70 C3** 46 12N 83 58W
St. Joseph, L., *Canada* **70 B1** 51 10N 90 35W
St-Jovite, *Canada* **70 C5** 46 8N 74 38W
St. Kilda, *N.Z.* **59 L3** 45 53S 170 31 E
St. Kitts & Nevis ■, *W. Indies* **89 C7** 17 20N 62 40W
St. Laurent, *Canada* **73 C9** 50 25N 97 58W
St. Lawrence, *Australia* **62 C4** 22 16S 149 31 E
St. Lawrence, *Canada* **71 C8** 46 54N 55 23W
St. Lawrence →, *Canada* **71 C6** 49 30N 66 0W
St. Lawrence, Gulf of, *Canada* **71 C7** 48 25N 62 0W
St. Lawrence I., *U.S.A.* **68 B3** 63 30N 170 30W
St. Leonard, *Canada* **71 C6** 47 12N 67 58W
St. Lewis →, *Canada* **71 B8** 52 26N 56 11W
St-Lô, *France* **18 B3** 49 7N 1 5W
St. Louis, *Senegal* **50 E2** 16 8N 16 27W
St. Louis, *U.S.A.* **80 F9** 38 37N 90 12W
St. Louis →, *U.S.A.* **80 B8** 47 15N 92 45W
St. Lucia ■, *W. Indies* **89 D7** 14 0N 60 50W
St. Lucia, L., *S. Africa* **57 D5** 28 5S 32 30 E
St. Lucia Channel, *W. Indies* **89 D7** 14 15N 61 0W
St. Maarten, *W. Indies* **89 C7** 18 0N 63 5W
St. Magnus B., *U.K.* **12 A7** 60 25N 1 35W
St-Malo, *France* **18 B2** 48 39N 2 1W
St-Marc, *Haiti* **89 C5** 19 10N 72 41W
St. Maries, *U.S.A.* **82 C5** 47 19N 116 35W
St-Martin, *W. Indies* **89 C7** 18 0N 63 0W
St. Martin, L., *Canada* **73 C9** 51 40N 98 30W
St. Mary Pk., *Australia* **63 E2** 31 32S 138 34 E
St. Marys, *Australia* **62 G4** 41 35S 148 11 E
St. Marys, *Canada* **78 C3** 43 20N 81 10W
St. Mary's, *Corn., U.K.* **11 H1** 49 55N 6 18W
St. Mary's, *Orkney, U.K.* **12 C6** 58 54N 2 54W
St. Marys, *Ga., U.S.A.* **77 K5** 30 44N 81 33W
St. Marys, *Pa., U.S.A.* **78 E6** 41 26N 78 34W
St. Mary's, C., *Canada* **71 C9** 46 50N 54 12W
St. Mary's B., *Canada* **71 C9** 46 50N 53 50W
St. Marys Bay, *Canada* **71 D6** 44 25N 66 10W
St-Mathieu, Pte., *France* **18 B1** 48 20N 4 45W
St. Matthew I., *U.S.A.* **68 B2** 60 24N 172 42W
St. Matthews, I. = Zadetkyi Kyun, *Burma* **39 H2** 10 0N 98 25 E
St-Maurice →, *Canada* **70 C5** 46 21N 72 31W
St-Nazaire, *France* **18 C2** 47 17N 2 12W
St. Neots, *U.K.* **11 E7** 52 14N 0 15W
St-Niklaas, *Belgium* **15 C4** 51 10N 4 8 E
St-Omer, *France* **18 A5** 50 45N 2 15 E
St-Pamphile, *Canada* **71 C6** 46 58N 69 48W
St. Pascal, *Canada* **71 C6** 47 32N 69 48W
St. Paul, *Canada* **72 C6** 54 0N 111 17W
St. Paul, *Minn., U.S.A.* **80 C8** 44 57N 93 6W
St. Paul, *Nebr., U.S.A.* **80 E5** 41 13N 98 27W
St-Paul →, *Canada* **71 B8** 51 27N 57 42W
St. Paul, I., *Ind. Oc.* **3 F13** 38 55S 77 34 E
St. Paul I., *Canada* **71 C7** 47 12N 60 9W
St. Peter, *U.S.A.* **80 C8** 44 20N 93 57W
St. Peter Port, *U.K.* **11 H5** 49 26N 2 33W
St. Peters, *N.S., Canada* **71 C7** 45 40N 60 53W
St. Peters, *P.E.I., Canada* **71 C7** 46 25N 62 35W
St. Petersburg = Sankt-Peterburg, *Russia* **24 C5** 59 55N 30 20 E
St. Petersburg, *U.S.A.* **77 M4** 27 46N 82 39W
St-Pie, *Canada* **79 A12** 45 30N 72 54W
St-Pierre, *St- P. & M.* **71 C8** 46 46N 56 12W
St-Pierre, L., *Canada* **70 C5** 46 12N 72 52W
St-Pierre et Miquelon □, *St- P. & M.* **71 C8** 46 55N 56 10W
St. Quentin, *Canada* **71 C6** 47 30N 67 23W
St-Quentin, *France* **18 B5** 49 50N 3 16 E
St. Regis, *U.S.A.* **82 C6** 47 18N 115 6W
St. Sebastien, Tanjon' i, *Madag.* **57 A8** 12 26S 48 44 E
St-Siméon, *Canada* **71 C6** 47 51N 69 54W
St. Simons I., *U.S.A.* **77 K5** 31 12N 81 15W
St. Simons Island, *U.S.A.* **77 K5** 31 9N 81 22W
St. Stephen, *Canada* **71 C6** 45 16N 67 17W
St. Thomas, *Canada* **78 D3** 42 45N 81 10W
St. Thomas I., *Virgin Is.* **89 C7** 18 20N 64 55W
St-Tite, *Canada* **70 C5** 46 45N 72 34W
St-Tropez, *France* **18 E7** 43 17N 6 38 E
St. Troud = St. Truiden, *Belgium* **15 D5** 50 48N 5 10 E
St. Truiden, *Belgium* **15 D5** 50 48N 5 10 E
St. Vincent, G., *Australia* **63 F2** 35 0S 138 0 E
St. Vincent & the Grenadines ■, *W. Indies* **89 D7** 13 0N 61 10W
St. Vincent Passage, *W. Indies* **89 D7** 13 30N 61 0W
St-Vith, *Belgium* **15 D6** 50 17N 6 9 E
St. Walburg, *Canada* **73 C7** 53 39N 109 12W
Ste-Agathe-des-Monts, *Canada* **70 C5** 46 3N 74 17W
Ste-Anne, L., *Canada* **71 B6** 50 0N 67 42W
Ste-Anne-des-Monts, *Canada* **71 C6** 49 8N 66 30W
Ste. Genevieve, *U.S.A.* **80 G9** 37 59N 90 2W
Ste-Marguerite →, *Canada* **71 B6** 50 9N 66 36W
Ste-Marie, *Martinique* **89 D7** 14 48N 61 1W
Ste-Marie de la Madeleine, *Canada* **71 C5** 46 26N 71 0W
Ste-Rose, *Guadeloupe* **89 C7** 16 20N 61 45W
Ste. Rose du Lac, *Canada* **73 C9** 51 4N 99 30W
Saintes, *France* **18 D3** 45 45N 0 37W
Saintes, I. des, *Guadeloupe* **89 C7** 15 50N 61 35W
Saintfield, *U.K.* **13 B6** 54 28N 5 49W
Sainthiya, *India* **43 H12** 23 57N 87 40 E
Saintonge, *France* **18 D3** 45 40N 0 50W
Saipan, *Pac. Oc.* **64 F6** 15 12N 145 45 E
Sairang, *India* **41 H18** 23 50N 92 45 E
Sairecábur, Cerro, *Bolivia* **94 A2** 22 43S 67 54W
Saitama □, *Japan* **31 F9** 36 25N 139 30 E
Saiyid, *Pakistan* **42 C5** 33 7N 73 2 E
Sajama, *Bolivia* **92 G5** 18 7S 69 0W
Sajószentpéter, *Hungary* **17 D11** 48 12N 20 44 E
Sajum, *India* **43 C8** 33 20N 79 0 E
Sak →, *S. Africa* **56 E3** 30 52S 20 25 E
Sakai, *Japan* **31 G7** 34 30N 135 30 E
Sakaide, *Japan* **31 G6** 34 15N 133 50 E
Sakaiminato, *Japan* **31 G6** 35 38N 133 11 E
Sakākah, *Si. Arabia* **44 D4** 30 0N 40 8 E
Sakakawea, L., *U.S.A.* **80 B4** 47 30N 101 25W
Sakami →, *Canada* **70 B4** 53 40N 76 40W
Sakami, L., *Canada* **70 B4** 53 15N 77 0W
Sakania, *Dem. Rep. of the Congo* **55 E2** 12 43S 28 30 E
Sakarya, *Turkey* **25 F5** 40 48N 30 25 E
Sakashima-Guntō, *Japan* **31 M2** 24 46N 124 0 E
Sakata, *Japan* **30 E9** 38 55N 139 50 E
Sakchu, *N. Korea* **35 D13** 40 23N 125 2 E
Sakeny →, *Madag.* **57 C8** 20 0S 45 25 E
Sakha □, *Russia* **27 C14** 66 0N 130 0 E
Sakhalin, *Russia* **27 D15** 51 0N 143 0 E
Sakhalinskiy Zaliv, *Russia* **27 D15** 54 0N 141 0 E
Šakiai, *Lithuania* **9 J20** 54 59N 23 2 E
Sakon Nakhon, *Thailand* **38 D5** 17 10N 104 9 E
Sakrand, *Pakistan* **42 F3** 26 10N 68 15 E
Sakri, *India* **43 F12** 26 13N 86 5 E
Sakrivier, *S. Africa* **56 E3** 30 54S 20 28 E
Sakti, *India* **43 H10** 22 2N 82 58 E
Sakuma, *Japan* **31 G8** 35 3N 137 49 E
Sakurai, *Japan* **31 G7** 34 30N 135 51 E
Sala, *Sweden* **9 G17** 59 58N 16 35 E
Sala Consilina, *Italy* **20 D6** 40 23N 15 36 E
Sala-y-Gómez, *Pac. Oc.* **65 K17** 26 28S 105 28W
Salaberry-de-Valleyfield, *Canada* **79 A10** 45 15N 74 8W
Saladas, *Argentina* **94 B4** 28 15S 58 40W
Saladillo, *Argentina* **94 D4** 35 40S 59 55W
Salado →, *Buenos Aires, Argentina* **94 D4** 35 44S 57 22W
Salado →, *La Pampa, Argentina* **96 D3** 37 30S 67 0W
Salado →, *Santa Fe, Argentina* **94 C3** 31 40S 60 41W
Salado →, *Mexico* **81 M5** 26 52N 99 19W
Salaga, *Ghana* **50 G5** 8 31N 0 31W
Sālah, *Syria* **47 C5** 32 40N 36 45 E
Sálakhos, *Greece* **23 C9** 36 17N 27 57 E
Salālah, *Oman* **46 D5** 16 56N 53 59 E
Salamanca, *Chile* **94 C1** 31 46S 70 59W
Salamanca, *Spain* **19 B3** 40 58N 5 39W
Salamanca, *U.S.A.* **78 D6** 42 10N 78 43W
Salāmatābād, *Iran* **44 C5** 35 39N 47 50 E
Salamis, *Cyprus* **23 D12** 35 11N 33 54 E
Salamís, *Greece* **21 F10** 37 56N 23 30 E
Salar de Atacama, *Chile* **94 A2** 23 30S 68 25W
Salar de Uyuni, *Bolivia* **92 H5** 20 30S 67 45W
Salatiga, *Indonesia* **37 G14** 7 19S 110 30 E
Salavat, *Russia* **24 D10** 53 21N 55 55 E
Salaverry, *Peru* **92 E3** 8 15S 79 0W
Salawati, *Indonesia* **37 E8** 1 7S 130 52 E
Salaya, *India* **42 H3** 22 19N 69 35 E
Salayar, *Indonesia* **37 F6** 6 7S 120 30 E
Salcombe, *U.K.* **11 G4** 50 14N 3 47W
Saldanha, *S. Africa* **56 E2** 33 0S 17 58 E
Saldanha B., *S. Africa* **56 E2** 33 6S 18 0 E
Saldus, *Latvia* **9 H20** 56 38N 22 30 E
Sale, *Australia* **63 F4** 38 6S 147 6 E
Salé, *Morocco* **50 B4** 34 3N 6 48W
Sale, *U.K.* **10 D5** 53 26N 2 19W
Salekhard, *Russia* **26 C7** 66 30N 66 35 E
Salem, *India* **40 P11** 11 40N 78 11 E
Salem, *Ill., U.S.A.* **76 F1** 38 38N 88 57W
Salem, *Ind., U.S.A.* **76 F2** 38 36N 86 6W
Salem, *Mass., U.S.A.* **79 D14** 42 31N 70 53W
Salem, *Mo., U.S.A.* **81 G9** 37 39N 91 32W
Salem, *N.H., U.S.A.* **79 D13** 42 45N 71 12W
Salem, *N.J., U.S.A.* **76 F8** 39 34N 75 28W
Salem, *N.Y., U.S.A.* **79 C11** 43 10N 73 20W
Salem, *Ohio, U.S.A.* **78 F4** 40 54N 80 52W
Salem, *Oreg., U.S.A.* **82 D2** 44 56N 123 2W
Salem, *S. Dak., U.S.A.* **80 D6** 43 44N 97 23W
Salem, *Va., U.S.A.* **76 G5** 37 18N 80 3W
Salerno, *Italy* **20 D6** 40 41N 14 47 E
Salford, *U.K.* **10 D5** 53 30N 2 18W
Salgótarján, *Hungary* **17 D10** 48 5N 19 47 E
Salgueiro, *Brazil* **93 E11** 8 4S 39 6W
Salibabu, *Indonesia* **37 D7** 3 51N 126 40 E
Salida, *U.S.A.* **74 C5** 38 32N 106 0W
Salihli, *Turkey* **21 E13** 38 28N 28 8 E
Salihorsk, *Belarus* **17 B14** 52 51N 27 27 E
Salima, *Malawi* **53 G6** 13 47S 34 28 E
Salina, *Italy* **20 E6** 38 34N 14 50 E
Salina, *Kans., U.S.A.* **80 F6** 38 50N 97 37W
Salina, *Utah, U.S.A.* **83 G8** 38 58N 111 51W
Salina Cruz, *Mexico* **87 D5** 16 10N 95 10W
Salinas, *Brazil* **93 G10** 16 10S 42 10W
Salinas, *Chile* **94 A2** 23 31S 69 29W
Salinas, *Ecuador* **92 D2** 2 10S 80 58W
Salinas, *U.S.A.* **84 J5** 36 40N 121 39W
Salinas →, *Guatemala* **87 D6** 16 28N 90 31W
Salinas →, *U.S.A.* **84 J5** 36 45N 121 48W
Salinas, B. de, *Nic.* **88 D2** 11 4N 85 45W
Salinas, Pampa de las, *Argentina* **94 C2** 31 58S 66 42W
Salinas Ambargasta, *Argentina* **94 B3** 29 0S 65 0W

Sanchahe

alinas de Hidalgo, Mexico 86 C4 22 30N 101 40W
alinas Grandes, Argentina 94 C3 30 0S 65 0W
aline →, Ark., U.S.A. 81 J8 33 10N 92 8W
aline →, Kans., U.S.A. 80 F6 38 52N 97 30W
alines, Spain 22 B10 39 21N 3 3 E
alines, C. de ses, Spain 22 B10 39 16N 3 4 E
alinópolis, Brazil 93 D9 0 40S 47 20W
alisbury = Harare, Zimbabwe 55 F3 17 43S 31 2 E
alisbury, U.K. 11 F6 51 4N 1 47W
alisbury, Md., U.S.A. 76 F8 38 22N 75 36W
alisbury, N.C., U.S.A. 77 H5 35 40N 80 29W
alisbury I., Canada 69 B12 63 30N 77 0W
alisbury Plain, U.K. 11 F6 51 14N 1 55W
alkhad, Syria 47 C5 32 29N 36 43 E
alla, Finland 8 C23 66 50N 28 49 E
alliq, Canada 69 B11 64 8N 83 10W
allisaw, U.S.A. 81 H7 35 28N 94 47W
alluit, Canada 69 B12 62 14N 75 38W
almās, Iran 44 B5 38 11N 44 47 E
almo, Canada 72 D5 49 10N 117 20W
almon, U.S.A. 82 D7 45 11N 113 54W
almon →, Canada 72 C4 54 3N 122 40W
almon →, U.S.A. 82 D5 45 51N 116 47W
almon Arm, Canada 72 C5 50 40N 119 15W
almon Gums, Australia 61 F3 32 59S 121 38 E
almon River Mts., U.S.A. 82 D6 45 0N 114 30W
alo, Finland 9 F20 60 22N 23 10 E
alome, U.S.A. 85 M13 33 47N 113 37W
alon, India 43 F9 26 2N 81 27 E
alon-de-Provence, France 18 E6 43 39N 5 6 E
alonica = Thessaloníki, Greece 21 D10 40 38N 22 58 E
alonta, Romania 17 E11 46 49N 21 42 E
alpausselkä, Finland 9 F22 61 0N 27 0 E
alsacate, Argentina 94 C2 31 20S 65 5W
alsk, Russia 25 E7 46 28N 41 30 E
also →, Italy 20 F5 37 6N 13 57 E
alt →, Canada 72 B6 60 0N 112 25W
alt →, U.S.A. 83 K7 33 23N 112 19W
alt Fork Arkansas →, U.S.A. 75 C7 36 36N 97 3W
alt Lake City, U.S.A. 82 F8 40 45N 111 53W
alt Range, Pakistan 42 C5 32 30N 72 25 E
alta, Argentina 94 A2 24 57S 65 25W
alta ☐, Argentina 94 A2 24 48S 65 30W
altash, U.K. 11 G3 50 24N 4 14W
altburn by the Sea, U.K. 10 C7 54 35N 0 58W
altcoats, U.K. 12 F4 55 38N 4 47W
altee Is., Ireland 13 D5 52 7N 6 37W
altfjellet, Norway 8 C16 66 40N 15 15 E
altfjorden, Norway 8 C16 67 15N 14 10 E
altillo, Mexico 86 B4 25 25N 101 0W
alto, Argentina 94 C3 34 20S 60 15W
alto, Uruguay 94 C4 31 27S 57 50W
alto →, Italy 20 C5 42 26N 12 25 E
alto del Guaíra, Paraguay 95 A5 24 3S 54 17W
alton City, U.S.A. 85 M11 33 29N 115 51W
alton Sea, U.S.A. 85 M11 33 15N 115 45W
altsburg, U.S.A. 78 F5 40 29N 79 27W
aluda →, U.S.A. 77 J5 34 1N 81 4W
alûm, Egypt 51 B11 31 31N 25 7 E
alur, India 41 K13 18 27N 83 18 E
alvador, Brazil 93 F11 13 0S 38 30W
alvador, Canada 73 C7 52 10N 109 32W
alvador, L., U.S.A. 81 L9 29 43N 90 15W
alween →, Burma 41 L20 16 31N 97 37 E
alyan, Azerbaijan 25 G8 39 33N 48 59 E
alzach →, Austria 16 D7 48 12N 12 56 E
alzburg, Austria 16 E7 47 48N 13 2 E
alzgitter, Germany 16 B6 52 9N 10 19 E
alzwedel, Germany 16 B6 52 52N 11 10 E
am, India 42 F4 26 50N 70 31 E
am Ngao, Thailand 38 D2 17 18N 99 0 E
am Rayburn Reservoir, U.S.A. 81 K7 31 4N 94 5W
am Son, Vietnam 38 C5 19 44N 105 54 E
am Teu, Laos 38 C5 19 59N 104 38 E
ama de Langreo = Langreo, Spain 19 A3 43 18N 5 40W
amagaltay, Russia 27 D10 50 36N 95 3 E
amales Group, Phil. 37 C6 6 0N 122 0 E
amana, India 42 D7 30 10N 76 13 E
amaná ☐, Dom. Rep. 89 C6 19 15N 69 27W
amana Cay, Bahamas 89 B5 23 3N 73 45W
amanga, Tanzania 55 D4 8 20S 39 13 E
amangwa, Dem. Rep. of the Congo 54 C1 4 23S 24 10 E
amani, Japan 30 C11 42 7N 142 56 E
amar, Phil. 37 B7 12 0N 125 0 E
amara, Russia 24 D9 53 8N 50 6 E
amaria = Shōmrōn, West Bank 47 C4 32 15N 35 13 E
amariá, Greece 23 D5 35 17N 23 58 E
amarinda, Indonesia 36 E5 0 30S 117 9 E
amarkand = Samarqand, Uzbekistan 26 F7 39 40N 66 55 E
amarqand, Uzbekistan 26 F7 39 40N 66 55 E
amarrā, Iraq 44 C4 34 12N 43 52 E
amastipur, India 43 G11 25 50N 85 50 E
amba, Dem. Rep. of the Congo 54 C2 4 38S 26 22 E
amba, India 43 C6 32 32N 75 10 E
ambalpur, India 41 J14 21 28N 84 4 E
ambar, Tanjung, Indonesia 36 E4 2 59S 110 19 E
ambas, Indonesia 36 D3 1 20N 109 20 E
ambava, Madag. 57 A9 14 16S 50 10 E
ambawizi, Zimbabwe 55 F2 18 24S 26 13 E
ambhal, India 43 E8 28 35N 78 37 E
ambhar, India 42 F6 26 52N 75 6 E
ambhar L., India 42 F6 26 55N 75 12 E
ambiase, Italy 20 E7 38 58N 16 17 E
ambir, Ukraine 17 D12 49 30N 23 10 E
ambor, Cambodia 38 F6 12 46N 106 0 E
amborombón, B., Argentina 94 D4 36 5S 57 20W
amch'ŏk, S. Korea 35 F15 37 30N 129 10 E
amch'onp'o, S. Korea 35 G15 35 0N 128 6 E
ame, Tanzania 54 C4 4 2S 37 38 E
amfya, Zambia 55 E2 11 22S 29 31 E
amnah, Si. Arabia 44 E3 25 10N 37 15 E
amo Alto, Chile 94 C1 30 22S 71 0W
amokov, Bulgaria 21 C10 42 18N 23 35 E
amos, Greece 21 F12 37 45N 26 50 E
amothráki = Mathráki, Greece 23 A3 39 48N 19 31 E
Samothráki, Greece 21 D11 40 28N 25 28 E
Sampacho, Argentina 94 C3 33 20S 64 50W
Sampang, Indonesia 37 G15 7 11S 113 13 E
Sampit, Indonesia 36 E4 2 34S 113 0 E
Sampit, Teluk, Indonesia 36 E4 3 5S 113 3 E
Samrong, Cambodia 38 E4 14 15N 103 30 E
Samrong, Thailand 38 E3 15 10N 100 40 E
Samsø, Denmark 9 J14 55 50N 10 35 E
Samsun, Turkey 25 F6 41 15N 36 22 E
Samui, Ko, Thailand 39 H3 9 30N 100 0 E
Samusole, Dem. Rep. of the Congo 55 E1 10 2S 24 0 E
Samut Prakan, Thailand 38 F3 13 32N 100 40 E
Samut Songkhram →, Thailand 36 B1 13 24N 100 1 E
Samwari, Pakistan 42 E2 28 30N 66 46 E
San, Mali 50 F5 13 15N 4 57W
San →, Cambodia 38 F5 13 32N 105 57 E
San →, Poland 17 C11 50 45N 21 51 E
San Agustin, C., Phil. 37 C7 6 20N 126 13 E
San Agustín de Valle Fértil, Argentina 94 C2 30 35S 67 30W
San Ambrosio, Pac. Oc. 90 F3 26 28S 79 53W
San Andreas, U.S.A. 84 G6 38 12N 120 41W
San Andrés, I. de, Caribbean 88 D3 12 42N 81 46W
San Andres Mts., U.S.A. 83 K10 33 0N 106 30W
San Andrés Tuxtla, Mexico 87 D5 18 30N 95 20W
San Angelo, U.S.A. 81 K4 31 28N 100 26W
San Anselmo, U.S.A. 84 H4 37 59N 122 34W
San Antonio, Belize 87 D7 16 15N 89 2W
San Antonio, Chile 94 C1 33 40S 71 40W
San Antonio, N. Mex., U.S.A. 83 K10 33 55N 106 52W
San Antonio, Tex., U.S.A. 81 L5 29 25N 98 30W
San Antonio →, U.S.A. 81 L6 28 30N 96 54W
San Antonio, C., Argentina 94 D4 36 15S 56 40W
San Antonio, C., Cuba 88 B3 21 50N 84 57W
San Antonio, Mt., U.S.A. 85 L9 34 17N 117 38W
San Antonio de los Baños, Cuba 88 B3 22 54N 82 31W
San Antonio de los Cobres, Argentina 94 A2 24 10S 66 17W
San Antonio Oeste, Argentina 96 E4 40 40S 65 0W
San Ardo, U.S.A. 84 J6 36 1N 120 54W
San Augustín, Canary Is. 22 G4 27 47N 15 32W
San Augustine, U.S.A. 81 K7 31 30N 94 7W
San Bartolomé, Canary Is. 22 F6 28 59N 13 37W
San Bartolomé de Tirajana, Canary Is. 22 G4 27 54N 15 34W
San Benedetto del Tronto, Italy 20 C5 42 57N 13 53 E
San Benedicto, I., Mexico 86 D2 19 18N 110 49W
San Benito, U.S.A. 81 M6 26 8N 97 38W
San Benito →, U.S.A. 84 J5 36 53N 121 34W
San Benito Mt., U.S.A. 84 J6 36 22N 120 37W
San Bernardino, U.S.A. 85 L9 34 7N 117 19W
San Bernardino Mts., U.S.A. 85 L10 34 10N 116 45W
San Bernardino Str., Phil. 37 B7 13 0N 125 0 E
San Bernardo, Chile 94 C1 33 40S 70 50W
San Bernardo, I. de, Colombia 92 B3 9 45N 75 50W
San Blas, Mexico 86 B3 26 4N 108 46W
San Blas, Arch. de, Panama 88 E4 9 50N 78 31W
San Blas, C., U.S.A. 77 L3 29 40N 85 21W
San Borja, Bolivia 92 F5 14 50S 66 52W
San Buenaventura, Mexico 86 B4 27 5N 101 32W
San Carlos = Sant Carles, Spain 22 B8 39 3N 1 34 E
San Carlos, Argentina 94 C2 33 50S 69 0W
San Carlos, Chile 94 D1 36 10S 72 0W
San Carlos, Mexico 86 B4 29 0N 100 54W
San Carlos, Mexico 86 C2 24 47N 112 6W
San Carlos, Nic. 88 D3 11 12N 84 50W
San Carlos, Phil. 37 B6 10 29N 123 25 E
San Carlos, Uruguay 95 C5 34 46S 54 58W
San Carlos, U.S.A. 83 K8 33 21N 110 27W
San Carlos, Venezuela 92 B5 9 40N 68 36W
San Carlos de Bariloche, Argentina 96 E2 41 10S 71 25W
San Carlos de Bolívar, Argentina 96 D4 36 15S 61 6W
San Carlos del Zulia, Venezuela 92 B4 9 1N 71 55W
San Carlos L., U.S.A. 83 K8 33 11N 110 32W
San Clemente, Chile 94 D1 35 30S 71 29W
San Clemente, U.S.A. 85 M9 33 26N 117 37W
San Clemente I., U.S.A. 85 N8 32 53N 118 29W
San Cristóbal = Es Migjorn Gran, Spain 22 B11 39 57N 4 3 E
San Cristóbal, Argentina 94 C3 30 20S 61 10W
San Cristóbal, Dom. Rep. 89 C5 18 25N 70 6W
San Cristóbal, Venezuela 92 B4 7 46N 72 14W
San Cristóbal de la Casas, Mexico 87 D6 16 50N 92 33W
San Diego, Calif., U.S.A. 85 N9 32 43N 117 9W
San Diego, Tex., U.S.A. 81 M5 27 46N 98 14W
San Diego, C., Argentina 96 G3 54 40S 65 10W
San Diego de la Unión, Mexico 86 C4 21 28N 100 52W
San Dimitri, Ras, Malta 23 C1 36 4N 14 11 E
San Estanislao, Paraguay 94 A4 24 39S 56 26W
San Felipe, Chile 94 C1 32 43S 70 42W
San Felipe, Mexico 86 A2 31 0N 114 52W
San Felipe, Venezuela 92 A5 10 20N 68 44W
San Felipe →, U.S.A. 85 M11 33 12N 115 49W
San Felix, Chile 94 B1 28 56S 70 28W
San Félix, Pac. Oc. 90 F2 26 23S 80 0W
San Fernando = Sant Ferran, Spain 22 C7 38 42N 1 28 E
San Fernando, Chile 94 C1 34 30S 71 0W
San Fernando, Mexico 86 B1 29 55N 115 10W
San Fernando, Tamaulipas, Mexico 87 C5 24 51N 98 10W
San Fernando, La Union, Phil. 37 A6 16 40N 120 23 E
San Fernando, Pampanga, Phil. 37 A6 15 5N 120 37 E
San Fernando, Spain 19 D2 36 28N 6 17W
San Fernando, Trin. & Tob. 89 D7 10 20N 61 30W
San Fernando, U.S.A. 85 L8 34 17N 118 26W
San Fernando de Apure, Venezuela 92 B5 7 54N 67 15W
San Fernando de Atabapo, Venezuela 92 C5 4 3N 67 42W
San Francisco, Argentina 94 C3 31 30S 62 5W
San Francisco, U.S.A. 84 H4 37 47N 122 25W
San Francisco →, U.S.A. 83 K9 32 59N 109 22W
San Francisco, Paso de, S. Amer. 94 B2 27 0S 68 0W
San Francisco de Macorís, Dom. Rep. 89 C5 19 19N 70 15W
San Francisco del Monte de Oro, Argentina 94 C2 32 36S 66 8W
San Francisco del Oro, Mexico 86 B3 26 52N 105 50W
San Francisco Javier = Sant Francesc de Formentera, Spain 22 C7 38 42N 1 26 E
San Francisco Solano, Pta., Colombia 90 C3 6 18N 77 29W
San Gabriel, Chile 94 C1 33 47S 70 15W
San Gabriel Mts., U.S.A. 85 L9 34 20N 118 0W
San Gorgonio Mt., U.S.A. 85 L10 34 7N 116 51W
San Gottardo, P. del, Switz. 18 C8 46 33N 8 33 E
San Gregorio, Uruguay 95 C4 32 37S 55 40W
San Gregorio, U.S.A. 84 H4 37 20N 122 23W
San Ignacio, Belize 87 D7 17 10N 89 0W
San Ignacio, Bolivia 92 G6 16 20S 60 55W
San Ignacio, Mexico 86 B2 27 27N 113 0W
San Ignacio, Paraguay 88 C2 26 52S 57 3W
San Ignacio, L., Mexico 86 B2 26 50N 113 11W
San Ildefonso, C., Phil. 37 A6 16 0N 122 1 E
San Isidro, Argentina 94 C4 34 29S 58 31W
San Jacinto, U.S.A. 85 M10 33 47N 116 57W
San Jaime = Sant Jaume, Spain 22 B11 39 54N 4 4 E
San Javier, Misiones, Argentina 95 B4 27 55S 55 5W
San Javier, Santa Fe, Argentina 94 C4 30 40S 59 55W
San Javier, Bolivia 92 G6 16 18S 62 30W
San Javier, Chile 94 D1 35 40S 71 45W
San Jeronimo Taviche, Mexico 87 D5 16 38N 96 32W
San Joaquin, U.S.A. 84 J6 36 36N 120 11W
San Joaquin →, U.S.A. 84 G5 38 4N 121 51W
San Joaquin Valley, U.S.A. 84 J6 37 20N 121 0W
San Jon, U.S.A. 81 H3 35 6N 103 20W
San Jordi = Sant Jordi, Spain 22 B9 39 33N 2 46 E
San Jorge, Argentina 94 C3 31 54S 61 50W
San Jorge, Spain 22 C7 38 54N 1 24 E
San Jorge, B. de, Mexico 86 A2 31 20N 113 20W
San Jorge, G., Argentina 96 F3 46 0S 66 0W
San Jorge, G. of, Argentina 90 H4 46 0S 66 0W
San José = San Josep, Spain 22 C7 38 55N 1 18 E
San José, Costa Rica 88 E3 9 55N 84 2W
San José, Guatemala 88 D1 14 0N 90 50W
San José, Mexico 86 C2 25 0N 110 50W
San Jose, Luzon, Phil. 37 A6 15 45N 120 55 E
San Jose, Mind. Or., Phil. 37 B6 12 27N 121 4 E
San Jose, U.S.A. 84 H5 37 20N 121 53W
San Jose →, U.S.A. 83 J10 34 25N 106 45W
San Jose Buenavista, Phil. 37 B6 10 45N 121 56 E
San José de Chiquitos, Bolivia 92 G6 17 53S 60 50W
San José de Feliciano, Argentina 94 C4 30 26S 58 46W
San José de Jáchal, Argentina 94 C2 30 15S 68 46W
San José de Mayo, Uruguay 94 C4 34 27S 56 40W
San José del Cabo, Mexico 86 C3 23 0N 109 40W
San José del Guaviare, Colombia 92 C4 2 35N 72 38W
San Josep, Spain 22 C7 38 55N 1 18 E
San Juan, Argentina 94 C2 31 30S 68 30W
San Juan, Mexico 86 C4 21 20N 102 50W
San Juan, Puerto Rico 89 C6 18 28N 66 7W
San Juan ☐, Argentina 94 C2 31 9S 69 0W
San Juan ☐, Dom. Rep. 89 C5 18 45N 71 25W
San Juan →, Argentina 94 C2 32 20S 67 25W
San Juan →, Nic. 88 D3 10 56N 83 42W
San Juan →, U.S.A. 83 H8 37 16N 110 26W
San Juan Bautista = Sant Joan Baptista, Spain 22 B8 39 5N 1 31 E
San Juan Bautista, Paraguay 94 B4 26 37S 57 6W
San Juan Bautista, U.S.A. 84 J5 36 51N 121 32W
San Juan Bautista Valle Nacional, Mexico 87 D5 17 47N 96 19W
San Juan Capistrano, U.S.A. 85 M9 33 30N 117 40W
San Juan Cr. →, U.S.A. 84 J5 35 40N 120 22W
San Juan de Guadalupe, Mexico 86 C4 24 38N 102 44W
San Juan de la Costa, Mexico 86 C2 24 23N 110 45W
San Juan de los Morros, Venezuela 92 B5 9 55N 67 21W
San Juan del Norte, Nic. 88 D3 10 58N 83 40W
San Juan del Norte, B. de, Nic. 88 D3 11 0N 83 40W
San Juan del Río, Mexico 87 C5 20 25N 100 0W
San Juan del Sur, Nic. 88 D2 11 20N 85 51W
San Juan I., U.S.A. 84 B3 48 32N 123 5W
San Juan Mts., U.S.A. 83 H10 37 30N 107 0W
San Justo, Argentina 94 C3 30 47S 60 30W
San Kamphaeng, Thailand 38 C2 18 45N 99 8 E
San Lázaro, C., Mexico 86 C2 24 50N 112 18W
San Lázaro, Sa., Mexico 86 C3 23 25N 110 0W
San Leandro, U.S.A. 84 H4 37 44N 122 9W
San Lorenzo = Sant Llorenç des Cardassar, Spain 22 B10 39 37N 3 17 E
San Lorenzo, Argentina 94 C3 32 45S 60 45W
San Lorenzo, Ecuador 92 C3 1 15N 78 50W
San Lorenzo, Paraguay 94 B4 25 20S 57 32W
San Lorenzo →, Mexico 86 C3 24 15N 107 24W
San Lorenzo, I., Mexico 86 B2 28 35N 112 50W
San Lorenzo, Mte., Argentina 96 F2 47 40S 72 20W
San Lucas, Bolivia 92 H5 20 5S 65 7W
San Lucas, Baja Calif. S., Mexico 86 C3 22 53N 109 54W
San Lucas, Baja Calif. S., Mexico 86 B2 27 10N 112 14W
San Lucas, U.S.A. 84 J5 36 8N 121 1W
San Lucas, C., Mexico 86 C3 22 50N 110 0W
San Luis, Argentina 94 C2 33 20S 66 20W
San Luis, Cuba 88 B3 22 17N 83 46W
San Luis, Guatemala 88 C2 16 14N 89 27W
San Luis, Ariz., U.S.A. 83 K6 32 29N 114 47W
San Luis, Colo., U.S.A. 83 H11 37 12N 105 25W
San Luis ☐, Argentina 94 C2 34 0S 66 0W
San Luis, I., Mexico 86 B2 29 58N 114 26W
San Luis, Sierra de, Argentina 94 C2 32 30S 66 10W
San Luis de la Paz, Mexico 86 C4 21 19N 100 32W
San Luis Obispo, U.S.A. 85 K6 35 17N 120 40W
San Luis Potosí, Mexico 86 C4 22 9N 100 59W
San Luis Potosí ☐, Mexico 86 C4 22 10N 101 0W
San Luis Reservoir, U.S.A. 84 H5 37 4N 121 5W
San Luis Río Colorado, Mexico 86 A2 32 29N 114 58W
San Manuel, U.S.A. 83 K8 32 36N 110 38W
San Marcos, Guatemala 88 D1 14 59N 91 52W
San Marcos, Mexico 86 B2 27 13N 112 6W
San Marcos, Calif., U.S.A. 85 M9 33 9N 117 10W
San Marcos, Tex., U.S.A. 81 L6 29 53N 97 56W
San Marino, San Marino 16 G7 43 55N 12 30 E
San Marino ■, Europe 20 C5 43 56N 12 25 E
San Martín, Argentina 94 C2 33 5S 68 28W
San Martin →, Bolivia 92 F6 13 8S 63 43W
San Martín, L., Argentina 96 F2 48 50S 72 50W
San Martin de los Andes, Argentina 96 E2 40 10S 71 20W
San Mateo = Sant Mateu, Spain 22 B7 39 3N 1 23 E
San Mateo, U.S.A. 84 H4 37 34N 122 19W
San Matías, Bolivia 92 G7 16 25S 58 20W
San Matías, G., Argentina 96 E4 41 30S 64 0W
San Miguel = Sant Miquel, Spain 22 B7 39 3N 1 26 E
San Miguel, El Salv. 88 D2 13 30N 88 12W
San Miguel, Panama 88 E4 8 27N 78 55W
San Miguel, U.S.A. 84 K6 35 45N 120 42W
San Miguel →, Bolivia 92 F6 13 52S 63 56W
San Miguel de Tucumán, Argentina 94 B2 26 50S 65 20W
San Miguel del Monte, Argentina 94 D4 35 23S 58 50W
San Miguel I., U.S.A. 85 L6 34 2N 120 23W
San Nicolás, Canary Is. 22 G4 27 58N 15 47W
San Nicolás de los Arroyas, Argentina 94 C3 33 25S 60 10W
San Nicolas I., U.S.A. 85 M7 33 15N 119 30W
San Onofre, U.S.A. 85 M9 33 22N 117 34W
San Pablo, Bolivia 94 A2 21 43S 66 38W
San Pablo, U.S.A. 84 H4 37 58N 122 21W
San Pedro, Argentina 94 C4 33 40S 59 40W
San Pedro, Buenos Aires, Argentina 95 B5 26 30S 54 10W
San Pedro, Chile 94 C1 33 54S 71 28W
San Pedro, Ivory C. 50 H4 4 50N 6 33W
San Pedro, Mexico 86 C2 23 55N 110 17W
San Pedro ☐, Paraguay 94 A4 24 0S 57 0W
San Pedro →, Chihuahua, Mexico 86 B3 28 20N 106 10W
San Pedro →, Nayarit, Mexico 86 C3 21 45N 105 30W
San Pedro →, U.S.A. 83 K8 32 59N 110 47W
San Pedro, Pta., Chile 94 B1 25 30S 70 38W
San Pedro Channel, U.S.A. 85 M8 33 30N 118 25W
San Pedro de Atacama, Chile 94 A2 22 55S 68 15W
San Pedro de Jujuy, Argentina 94 A3 24 12S 64 55W
San Pedro de las Colonias, Mexico 86 B4 25 50N 102 59W
San Pedro de Macorís, Dom. Rep. 89 C6 18 30N 69 18W
San Pedro del Norte, Nic. 88 D3 13 4N 84 33W
San Pedro del Paraná, Paraguay 94 B4 26 43S 56 13W
San Pedro Mártir, Sierra, Mexico 86 A1 31 0N 115 30W
San Pedro Mixtepec, Mexico 87 D5 16 2N 97 7W
San Pedro Ocampo = Melchor Ocampo, Mexico 86 C4 24 52N 101 40W
San Pedro Sula, Honduras 88 C2 15 30N 88 0W
San Pietro, Italy 20 E3 39 8N 8 17 E
San Quintín, Mexico 86 A1 30 29N 115 57W
San Rafael, Argentina 94 C2 34 40S 68 21W
San Rafael, Calif., U.S.A. 84 H4 37 58N 122 32W
San Rafael, N. Mex., U.S.A. 83 J10 35 7N 107 53W
San Rafael Mt., U.S.A. 85 L7 34 41N 119 52W
San Rafael Mts., U.S.A. 85 L7 34 40N 119 50W
San Ramón de la Nueva Orán, Argentina 94 A3 23 10S 64 20W
San Remo, Italy 18 E7 43 49N 7 46 E
San Roque, Argentina 94 B4 28 25S 58 45W
San Roque, Spain 19 D3 36 17N 5 21W
San Rosendo, Chile 94 D1 37 16S 72 43W
San Saba, U.S.A. 81 K5 31 12N 98 43W
San Salvador, El Salv. 88 D2 13 40N 89 10W
San Salvador, Spain 22 B10 39 27N 3 11 E
San Salvador de Jujuy, Argentina 94 A3 24 10S 64 48W
San Salvador I., Bahamas 89 B5 24 0N 74 40W
San Sebastián = Donostia-San Sebastián, Spain 19 A5 43 17N 1 58W
San Sebastián, Argentina 96 G3 53 10S 68 30W
San Sebastian de la Gomera, Canary Is. 22 F2 28 5N 17 7W
San Serra = Son Serra, Spain 22 B10 39 43N 3 13 E
San Severo, Italy 20 D6 41 41N 15 23 E
San Simeon, U.S.A. 84 K5 35 39N 121 11W
San Simon, U.S.A. 83 K9 32 16N 109 14W
San Telmo = Sant Telm, Spain 22 B9 39 35N 2 21 E
San Telmo, Mexico 86 A1 30 58N 116 6W
San Tiburcio, Mexico 86 C4 24 8N 101 32W
San Valentin, Mte., Chile 96 F2 46 30S 73 30W
San Vicente de la Barquera, Spain 19 A3 43 23N 4 29W
San Vito, Costa Rica 88 E3 8 50N 82 58W
Sana', Yemen 46 D3 15 27N 44 12 E
Sana →, Bos.-H. 16 F9 45 3N 16 23 E
Sanaga →, Cameroon 52 D1 3 35N 9 38 E
Sanaloa, Presa, Mexico 86 C3 24 50N 107 20W
Sanana, Indonesia 37 E7 2 4S 125 58 E
Sanand, India 42 H5 22 59N 72 25 E
Sanandaj, Iran 44 C5 35 18N 47 1 E
Sanandita, Bolivia 94 A3 21 40S 63 45W
Sanawad, India 42 H7 22 11N 76 5 E
Sancellas = Sencelles, Spain 22 B9 39 39N 2 54 E
Sanchahe, China 35 B14 44 50N 126 2 E

165

Tha Song Yang

Tha Song Yang, *Thailand* **38 D1** 17 34N 97 55 E
Thaba Putsoa, *Lesotho* **57 D4** 29 45S 28 0 E
Thabana Ntlenyana, *Lesotho* **57 D4** 29 30S 29 16 E
Thabazimbi, *S. Africa* **57 C4** 24 40S 27 21 E
Thādiq, *Si. Arabia* **44 E5** 25 18N 45 52 E
Thai Muang, *Thailand* **39 H2** 8 24N 98 16 E
Thailand ■, *Asia* **38 E4** 16 0N 102 0 E
Thailand, G. of, *Asia* **39 G3** 11 30N 101 0 E
Thakhek, *Laos* **38 D5** 17 25N 104 45 E
Thal, *Pakistan* **42 C4** 33 28N 70 33 E
Thal Desert, *Pakistan* **42 D4** 31 10N 71 30 E
Thala La, *Burma* **41 E20** 28 25N 97 23 E
Thalabarivat, *Cambodia* **38 F5** 13 33N 105 57 E
Thallon, *Australia* **63 D4** 28 39S 148 49 E
Thames, *N.Z.* **59 G5** 37 7S 175 34 E
Thames →, *Canada* **78 D2** 42 20N 82 25W
Thames →, *U.K.* **11 F8** 51 29N 0 34 E
Thames →, *U.S.A.* **79 E12** 41 18N 72 5W
Thames Estuary, *U.K.* **11 F8** 51 29N 0 52 E
Thamesford, *Canada* **78 C4** 43 4N 81 0W
Thamesville, *Canada* **78 D3** 42 33N 81 59W
Than, *India* **42 H4** 22 34N 71 11 E
Than Uyen, *Vietnam* **38 B4** 22 0N 103 54 E
Thana Gazi, *India* **42 F7** 27 25N 76 19 E
Thandla, *India* **42 H6** 23 0N 74 34 E
Thane, *India* **40 K8** 19 12N 72 59 E
Thanesar, *India* **42 D7** 30 1N 76 52 E
Thanet, I. of, *U.K.* **11 F9** 51 21N 1 20 E
Thangool, *Australia* **62 C5** 24 38S 150 42 E
Thanh Hoa, *Vietnam* **38 C5** 19 48N 105 46 E
Thanh Hung, *Vietnam* **39 H5** 9 55N 105 43 E
Thanh Pho Ho Chi Minh = Phanh Bho Ho Chi Minh, *Vietnam* **39 G6** 10 58N 106 40 E
Thanh Thuy, *Vietnam* **38 A5** 22 55N 104 51 E
Thanjavur, *India* **40 P11** 10 48N 79 12 E
Thano Bula Khan, *Pakistan* **42 G2** 25 22N 67 50 E
Thaolinta L., *Canada* **73 A9** 61 30N 96 25W
Thap Sakae, *Thailand* **39 G2** 11 30N 99 37 E
Thap Than, *Thailand* **38 E2** 15 27N 99 54 E
Thar Desert, *India* **42 F5** 28 0N 72 0 E
Tharad, *India* **42 G4** 24 30N 71 44 E
Thargomindah, *Australia* **63 D3** 27 58S 143 46 E
Tharrawaddy, *Burma* **41 L19** 17 38N 95 48 E
Tharthār, Mileh, *Iraq* **44 C4** 34 0N 43 15 E
Tharthār, W. ath →, *Iraq* **44 C4** 33 59N 43 12 E
Thásos, *Greece* **21 D11** 40 40N 24 40 E
Thatcher, *Ariz., U.S.A.* **83 K9** 32 51N 109 46W
Thatcher, *Colo., U.S.A.* **81 G2** 37 33N 104 7W
Thaton, *Burma* **41 L20** 16 55N 97 22 E
Thaungdut, *Burma* **41 G19** 24 30N 94 40 E
Thayer, *U.S.A.* **81 G9** 36 31N 91 33W
Thayetmyo, *Burma* **41 K19** 19 20N 95 10 E
Thazi, *Burma* **41 J20** 21 0N 96 5 E
The Alberga →, *Australia* **63 D2** 27 6S 135 33 E
The Bight, *Bahamas* **89 B4** 24 19N 75 24W
The Coorong, *Australia* **63 F2** 35 50S 139 20 E
The Dalles, *U.S.A.* **82 D3** 45 36N 121 10W
The English Company's Is., *Australia* **62 A2** 11 50S 136 32 E
The Frome →, *Australia* **63 D2** 29 8S 137 54 E
The Great Divide = Great Dividing Ra., *Australia* **62 C4** 23 0S 146 0 E
The Hague = 's-Gravenhage, *Neths.* **15 B4** 52 7N 4 17 E
The Hamilton →, *Australia* **63 D2** 26 40S 135 19 E
The Macumba →, *Australia* **63 D2** 27 52S 137 12 E
The Neales →, *Australia* **63 D2** 28 8S 136 47 E
The Officer →, *Australia* **61 E5** 27 46S 132 30 E
The Pas, *Canada* **73 C8** 53 45N 101 15W
The Range, *Zimbabwe* **55 F3** 19 2S 31 2 E
The Rock, *Australia* **63 F4** 35 15S 147 2 E
The Salt L., *Australia* **63 E3** 30 6S 142 8 E
The Sandheads, *India* **43 J13** 21 10N 88 20 E
The Stevenson →, *Australia* **63 D2** 27 6S 135 33 E
The Warburton →, *Australia* **63 D2** 28 4S 137 28 E
The Woodlands, *U.S.A.* **81 K7** 30 9N 95 27W
Thebes = Thívai, *Greece* **21 E10** 38 19N 23 19 E
Thebes, *Egypt* **51 C12** 25 40N 32 35 E
Thedford, *Canada* **78 C3** 43 9N 81 51W
Thedford, *U.S.A.* **80 E4** 41 59N 100 35W
Theebine, *Australia* **63 D5** 25 57S 152 34 E
Thekulthili L., *Canada* **73 A7** 61 3N 110 0W
Thelon →, *Canada* **73 A8** 62 35N 104 3W
Theodore, *Australia* **62 C5** 24 55S 150 3 E
Theodore, *Canada* **73 C8** 51 26N 102 55W
Theodore, *U.S.A.* **77 K1** 30 33N 88 10W
Theodore Roosevelt National Memorial Park, *U.S.A.* **80 B3** 47 0N 103 25W
Theodore Roosevelt Res., *U.S.A.* **83 K8** 33 46N 111 0W
Thepha, *Thailand* **39 J3** 6 52N 100 58 E
Theresa, *U.S.A.* **79 B9** 44 13N 75 48W
Thermaïkós Kólpos, *Greece* **21 D10** 40 15N 22 45 E
Thermopolis, *U.S.A.* **82 E9** 43 39N 108 13W
Thermopylae P., *Greece* **21 E10** 38 48N 22 35 E
Thessalon, *Canada* **70 C3** 46 20N 83 30W
Thessaloníki, *Greece* **21 D10** 40 38N 22 58 E
Thessaloniki, Gulf of = Thermaïkós Kólpos, *Greece* **21 D10** 40 15N 22 45 E
Thetford, *U.K.* **11 E8** 52 25N 0 45 E
Thetford Mines, *Canada* **71 C5** 46 8N 71 18W
Theun →, *Laos* **38 C5** 18 19N 104 0 E
Theunissen, *S. Africa* **56 D4** 28 26S 26 43 E
Thevenard, *Australia* **63 E1** 32 9S 133 38 E
Thibodaux, *U.S.A.* **81 L9** 29 48N 90 49W
Thicket Portage, *Canada* **73 B9** 55 19N 97 42W
Thief River Falls, *U.S.A.* **80 A6** 48 7N 96 10W
Thiel Mts., *Antarctica* **5 E16** 85 15S 91 0W
Thiers, *France* **18 D5** 45 52N 3 33 E
Thiès, *Senegal* **50 F2** 14 50N 16 51W
Thika, *Kenya* **54 C4** 1 1S 37 5 E
Thikombia, *Fiji* **59 B9** 15 44S 179 55W
Thimphu, *Bhutan* **41 F16** 27 31N 89 45 E
þingvallavatn, *Iceland* **8 D3** 64 11N 21 9W
Thionville, *France* **18 B7** 49 20N 6 10 E
Thíra, *Greece* **21 F11** 36 23N 25 27 E
Third Cataract, *Sudan* **51 E12** 19 49N 30 19 E
Thirsk, *U.K.* **10 C6** 54 14N 1 19W
Thisted, *Denmark* **9 H13** 56 58N 8 40 E
Thistle I., *Australia* **63 F2** 35 0S 136 8 E
Thívai, *Greece* **21 E10** 38 19N 23 19 E
þjórsá →, *Iceland* **8 E3** 63 47N 20 48W
Thlewiaza →, *Man., Canada* **73 B8** 59 43N 100 5W
Thlewiaza →, *N.W.T., Canada* **73 A10** 60 29N 94 40W
Thmar Puok, *Cambodia* **38 F4** 13 57N 103 4 E
Tho Vinh, *Vietnam* **38 C5** 19 16N 105 42 E
Thoa →, *Canada* **73 A7** 60 31N 109 47W
Thoen, *Thailand* **38 D2** 17 43N 99 12 E
Thoeng, *Thailand* **38 C3** 19 41N 100 12 E
Thohoyandou, *S. Africa* **53 J6** 22 58S 30 29 E
Tholdi, *Pakistan* **43 B7** 35 5N 76 6 E
Thomas, *U.S.A.* **81 H5** 35 45N 98 45W
Thomas, L., *Australia* **63 D2** 26 4S 137 58 E
Thomaston, *U.S.A.* **77 J3** 32 53N 84 20W
Thomasville, *Ala., U.S.A.* **77 K2** 31 55N 87 44W
Thomasville, *Ga., U.S.A.* **77 K4** 30 50N 83 59W
Thomasville, *N.C., U.S.A.* **77 H5** 35 53N 80 5W
Thompson, *Canada* **73 B9** 55 45N 97 52W
Thompson, *U.S.A.* **79 E9** 41 52N 75 31W
Thompson →, *Canada* **72 C4** 50 15N 121 24W
Thompson →, *U.S.A.* **80 F8** 39 46N 93 37W
Thompson Falls, *U.S.A.* **82 C6** 47 36N 115 21W
Thompson Pk., *U.S.A.* **82 F2** 41 0N 123 0W
Thompson Springs, *U.S.A.* **83 G9** 38 58N 109 43W
Thompsontown, *U.S.A.* **78 F7** 40 33N 77 14W
Thomson, *U.S.A.* **77 J4** 33 28N 82 30W
Thomson →, *Australia* **62 C3** 25 11S 142 53 E
Thomson's Falls = Nyahururu, *Kenya* **54 B4** 0 2N 36 27 E
þórisvatn, *Iceland* **8 D4** 64 20N 18 55W
Thornaby on Tees, *U.K.* **10 C6** 54 33N 1 18W
Thornbury, *Canada* **78 B4** 44 34N 80 26W
Thorne, *U.K.* **10 D7** 53 37N 0 57W
Thornhill, *Canada* **72 C3** 54 31N 128 32W
Thorold, *Canada* **78 C5** 43 7N 79 12W
þórshöfn, *Iceland* **8 C6** 66 12N 15 20W
Thouin, C., *Australia* **60 D2** 20 20S 118 10 E
Thousand Oaks, *U.S.A.* **85 L8** 34 10N 118 50W
Thrace, *Turkey* **21 D12** 41 0N 27 0 E
Three Forks, *U.S.A.* **82 D8** 45 54N 111 33W
Three Hills, *Canada* **72 C6** 51 43N 113 15W
Three Hummock I., *Australia* **62 G3** 40 25S 144 55 E
Three Points, C., *Ghana* **50 H5** 4 42N 2 6W
Three Rivers, *Calif., U.S.A.* **84 J8** 36 26N 118 54W
Three Rivers, *Tex., U.S.A.* **81 L5** 28 28N 98 11W
Three Sisters, *U.S.A.* **82 D3** 44 4N 121 51W
Three Springs, *Australia* **61 E2** 29 32S 115 45 E
Throssell, L., *Australia* **61 E3** 27 33S 124 10 E
Throssell Ra., *Australia* **60 D3** 22 3S 121 43 E
Thuan Hoa, *Vietnam* **39 H5** 8 58N 105 30 E
Thubun Lakes, *Canada* **73 A6** 61 30N 112 0W
Thuin, *Belgium* **15 D4** 50 20N 4 17 E
Thule, *Greenland* **4 B4** 77 40N 69 0W
Thun, *Switz.* **18 C7** 46 45N 7 38 E
Thunder B., *U.S.A.* **78 B1** 45 0N 83 20W
Thunder Bay, *Canada* **70 C2** 48 20N 89 15W
Thung Song, *Thailand* **39 H2** 8 10N 99 40 E
Thunkar, *Bhutan* **41 F17** 27 55N 91 0 E
Thuong Tra, *Vietnam* **38 D6** 16 2N 107 42 E
Thüringer Wald, *Germany* **16 C6** 50 35N 11 0 E
Thurles, *Ireland* **13 D4** 52 41N 7 49W
Thurrock □, *U.K.* **11 F8** 51 31N 0 23 E
Thursday I., *Australia* **62 A3** 10 30S 142 3 E
Thurso, *Canada* **70 C4** 45 36N 75 15W
Thurso, *U.K.* **12 C5** 58 36N 3 32W
Thurso →, *U.K.* **12 C5** 58 36N 3 32W
Thurston I., *Antarctica* **5 D16** 72 0S 100 0W
Thutade L., *Canada* **72 B3** 57 0N 126 55W
Thyolo, *Malawi* **55 F4** 16 7S 35 5 E
Thysville = Mbanza Ngungu, *Dem. Rep. of the Congo* **52 F2** 5 12S 14 53 E
Ti Tree, *Australia* **62 C1** 22 5S 133 22 E
Tian Shan, *Asia* **32 B3** 42 0N 76 0 E
Tianjin, *China* **35 E9** 39 8N 117 10 E
Tianshui, *China* **34 G3** 34 32N 105 40 E
Tianzhen, *China* **34 D8** 40 24N 114 5 E
Tianzhuangtai, *China* **35 D12** 40 43N 122 5 E
Tiaret, *Algeria* **50 A6** 35 20N 1 21 E
Tibagi, *Brazil* **95 A5** 24 30S 50 24W
Tibagi →, *Brazil* **95 A5** 22 47S 51 1W
Tiber = Tevere →, *Italy* **20 D5** 41 44N 12 14 E
Tiberias = Teverya, *Israel* **47 C4** 32 47N 35 32 E
Tiberias, L. = Yam Kinneret, *Israel* **47 C4** 32 45N 35 35 E
Tibesti, *Chad* **51 D9** 21 0N 17 30 E
Tibet = Xizang Zizhiqu □, *China* **32 C3** 32 0N 88 0 E
Tibet, Plateau of, *Asia* **28 F12** 32 0N 86 0 E
Tibnī, *Syria* **44 C3** 35 36N 39 50 E
Tibooburra, *Australia* **63 D3** 29 26S 142 1 E
Tiburón, I., *Mexico* **86 B2** 29 0N 112 30W
Ticino →, *Italy* **18 D8** 45 9N 9 14 E
Ticonderoga, *U.S.A.* **79 C11** 43 51N 73 26W
Ticul, *Mexico* **87 C7** 20 20N 89 31W
Tidaholm, *Sweden* **9 G15** 58 12N 13 58 E
Tiddim, *Burma* **41 H18** 23 28N 93 45 E
Tidioute, *U.S.A.* **78 E5** 41 41N 79 24W
Tidjikja, *Mauritania* **50 E3** 18 29N 11 35W
Tidore, *Indonesia* **37 D7** 0 40N 127 25 E
Tiel, *Neths.* **15 C5** 51 53N 5 26 E
Tieling, *China* **35 C12** 42 20N 123 55 E
Tielt, *Belgium* **15 C3** 51 0N 3 20 E
Tien Shan = Tian Shan, *Asia* **32 B3** 42 0N 76 0 E
Tien-tsin = Tianjin, *China* **35 E9** 39 8N 117 10 E
Tien Yen, *Vietnam* **38 B6** 21 20N 107 24 E
T'ienching = Tianjin, *China* **35 E9** 39 8N 117 10 E
Tienen, *Belgium* **15 D4** 50 48N 4 57 E
Tientsin = Tianjin, *China* **35 E9** 39 8N 117 10 E
Tieri, *Australia* **62 C4** 23 2S 148 21 E
Tierra Amarilla, *Chile* **94 B1** 27 28S 70 18W
Tierra Amarilla, *U.S.A.* **83 H10** 36 42N 106 33W
Tierra Colorada, *Mexico* **87 D5** 17 10N 99 35W
Tierra de Campos, *Spain* **19 A3** 42 10N 4 50W
Tierra del Fuego, I. Gr. de, *Argentina* **96 G3** 54 0S 69 0W
Tiétar →, *Spain* **19 C3** 39 50N 6 1W
Tieté →, *Brazil* **95 A5** 20 40S 51 35W
Tiffin, *U.S.A.* **76 E4** 41 7N 83 11W
Tiflis = Tbilisi, *Georgia* **25 F7** 41 43N 44 50 E
Tifton, *U.S.A.* **77 K4** 31 27N 83 31W
Tifu, *Indonesia* **37 E7** 3 39S 126 24 E
Tighina, *Moldova* **17 E15** 46 50N 29 30 E
Tigil, *Russia* **27 D16** 57 49N 158 40 E
Tignish, *Canada* **71 C7** 46 58N 64 2W
Tigre →, *Peru* **92 D4** 4 30S 74 10W
Tigre →, *Venezuela* **92 B6** 9 20N 62 30W
Tigris = Dijlah, Nahr →, *Asia* **44 D5** 31 0N 47 25 E
Tigyaing, *Burma* **41 H20** 23 45N 96 10 E
Tijara, *India* **42 F7** 27 56N 76 31 E
Tijuana, *Mexico* **85 N9** 32 30N 117 10W
Tikal, *Guatemala* **88 C2** 17 13N 89 24W
Tikamgarh, *India* **43 G8** 24 44N 78 50 E
Tikhoretsk, *Russia* **25 E7** 45 56N 40 5 E
Tikhvin, *Russia* **24 C5** 59 35N 33 30 E
Tikrīt, *Iraq* **44 C4** 34 35N 43 37 E
Tiksi, *Russia* **27 B13** 71 40N 128 45 E
Tilamuta, *Indonesia* **37 D6** 0 32N 122 23 E
Tilburg, *Neths.* **15 C5** 51 31N 5 6 E
Tilbury, *Canada* **78 D2** 42 17N 82 23W
Tilbury, *U.K.* **11 F8** 51 27N 0 22 E
Tilcara, *Argentina* **94 A2** 23 36S 65 23W
Tilden, *U.S.A.* **80 D6** 42 3N 97 50W
Tilhar, *India* **43 F8** 28 0N 79 45 E
Tilichiki, *Russia* **27 C17** 60 27N 166 5 E
Tílissos, *Greece* **23 D7** 35 20N 25 1 E
Till →, *U.K.* **10 B5** 55 41N 2 13W
Tillamook, *U.S.A.* **82 D2** 45 27N 123 51W
Tillsonburg, *Canada* **78 D4** 42 53N 80 44W
Tillyeria □, *Cyprus* **23 D11** 35 6N 32 40 E
Tílos, *Greece* **21 F12** 36 27N 27 27 E
Tilpa, *Australia* **63 E3** 30 57S 144 24 E
Tilsit = Sovetsk, *Russia* **9 J19** 55 6N 21 50 E
Tilt →, *U.K.* **12 E5** 56 46N 3 51W
Tilton, *U.S.A.* **79 C13** 43 27N 71 36W
Tiltonsville, *U.S.A.* **78 F4** 40 10N 80 41W
Timagami, L., *Canada* **70 C3** 47 0N 80 10W
Timanskiy Kryazh, *Russia* **24 A9** 65 58N 50 5 E
Timaru, *N.Z.* **59 L3** 44 23S 171 14 E
Timau, *Kenya* **54 B4** 0 4N 37 15 E
Timbákion, *Greece* **23 D6** 35 4N 24 45 E
Timber Creek, *Australia* **60 C5** 15 40S 130 29 E
Timber Lake, *U.S.A.* **80 C4** 45 26N 101 5W
Timber Mt., *U.S.A.* **84 H10** 37 6N 116 28W
Timbuktu = Tombouctou, *Mali* **50 E5** 16 50N 3 0W
Timi, *Cyprus* **23 E11** 34 44N 32 31 E
Timimoun, *Algeria* **50 C6** 29 14N 0 16 E
Timişoara, *Romania* **17 F11** 45 43N 21 15 E
Timmins, *Canada* **70 C3** 48 28N 81 25W
Timok →, *Serbia, Yug.* **21 B10** 44 10N 22 40 E
Timor, *Indonesia* **37 F7** 9 0S 125 0 E
Timor Sea, *Ind. Oc.* **60 B4** 12 0S 127 0 E
Timor Timur □, *Indonesia* **37 F7** 9 0S 125 0 E
Tin Can Bay, *Australia* **63 D5** 25 56S 153 0 E
Tin Mt., *U.S.A.* **84 J9** 36 50N 117 10W
Tinaca Pt., *Phil.* **37 C7** 5 30N 125 25 E
Tinajo, *Canary Is.* **22 E6** 29 4N 13 42W
Tindal, *Australia* **60 B5** 14 31S 132 22 E
Tindouf, *Algeria* **50 C4** 27 42N 8 10W
Tinggi, Pulau, *Malaysia* **39 L5** 2 18N 104 7 E
Tingo Maria, *Peru* **92 E3** 9 10S 75 54W
Tingrela, *Ivory C.* **50 F4** 10 27N 6 25W
Tinh Bien, *Vietnam* **39 G5** 10 36N 104 57 E
Tinnevelly = Tirunelveli, *India* **40 Q10** 8 45N 77 45 E
Tinogasta, *Argentina* **94 B2** 28 5S 67 32W
Tínos, *Greece* **21 F11** 37 33N 25 8 E
Tinpahar, *India* **43 G12** 24 59N 87 44 E
Tintina, *Argentina* **94 B3** 27 2S 62 45W
Tintinara, *Australia* **63 F3** 35 48S 140 2 E
Tioga, *N. Dak., U.S.A.* **80 A3** 48 23N 102 56W
Tioga, *Pa., U.S.A.* **78 E7** 41 55N 77 8W
Tioman, Pulau, *Malaysia* **39 L5** 2 50N 104 10 E
Tionesta, *U.S.A.* **78 E5** 41 30N 79 28W
Tipongpani, *India* **41 F19** 27 20N 95 55 E
Tipperary, *Ireland* **13 D3** 52 28N 8 10W
Tipperary □, *Ireland* **13 D4** 52 37N 7 55W
Tipton, *Calif., U.S.A.* **84 J7** 36 4N 119 19W
Tipton, *Iowa, U.S.A.* **80 E9** 41 46N 91 8W
Tipton Mt., *U.S.A.* **85 K12** 35 32N 114 12W
Tiptonville, *U.S.A.* **81 G10** 36 23N 89 29W
Tīrān, *Iran* **45 C6** 32 45N 51 8 E
Tirana, *Albania* **21 D8** 41 18N 19 49 E
Tiranë = Tirana, *Albania* **21 D8** 41 18N 19 49 E
Tiraspol, *Moldova* **17 E15** 46 55N 29 35 E
Tire, *Turkey* **21 E12** 38 5N 27 45 E
Tirebolu, *Turkey* **25 F6** 40 58N 38 45 E
Tiree, *U.K.* **12 E2** 56 31N 6 55W
Tiree, Passage of, *U.K.* **12 E2** 56 30N 6 30W
Tîrgovişte = Târgovişte, *Romania* **17 F13** 44 55N 25 27 E
Tîrgu-Jiu = Târgu-Jiu, *Romania* **17 F12** 45 5N 23 19 E
Tîrgu Mureş = Târgu Mureş, *Romania* **17 E13** 46 31N 24 38 E
Tirich Mir, *Pakistan* **40 A7** 36 15N 71 55 E
Tírnavos, *Greece* **21 E10** 39 45N 22 18 E
Tirodi, *India* **40 J11** 21 40N 79 44 E
Tirol □, *Austria* **16 E6** 47 3N 10 43 E
Tirso →, *Italy* **20 E3** 39 53N 8 32 E
Tiruchchirappalli, *India* **40 P11** 10 45N 78 45 E
Tirunelveli, *India* **40 Q10** 8 45N 77 45 E
Tirupati, *India* **40 N11** 13 39N 79 25 E
Tiruppur, *India* **40 P10** 11 5N 77 22 E
Tiruvannamalai, *India* **40 N11** 12 15N 79 5 E
Tisa, *India* **42 C7** 32 50N 76 9 E
Tisa →, *Serbia, Yug.* **21 B9** 45 15N 20 17 E
Tisdale, *Canada* **73 C8** 52 50N 104 0W
Tishomingo, *U.S.A.* **81 H6** 34 14N 96 41W
Tisza = Tisa →, *Serbia, Yug.* **21 B9** 45 15N 20 17 E
Tit-Ary, *Russia* **27 B13** 71 55N 127 2 E
Tithwal, *Pakistan* **43 B5** 34 21N 73 50 E
Titicaca, L., *S. Amer.* **92 G5** 15 30S 69 30W
Titograd = Podgorica, *Montenegro, Yug.* **21 C8** 42 30N 19 19 E
Titule, *Dem. Rep. of the Congo* **54 B2** 3 15N 25 31 E
Titusville, *Fla., U.S.A.* **77 L5** 28 37N 80 49W
Titusville, *Pa., U.S.A.* **78 E5** 41 38N 79 41W
Tivaouane, *Senegal* **50 F2** 14 56N 16 45W
Tiverton, *U.K.* **11 G4** 50 54N 3 29W
Tívoli, *Italy* **20 D5** 41 58N 12 45 E
Tizi-Ouzou, *Algeria* **50 A6** 36 42N 4 3 E
Tizimín, *Mexico* **87 C7** 21 0N 88 1W
Tjeggelvas, *Sweden* **8 C17** 66 37N 17 45 E
Tjirebon = Cirebon, *Indonesia* **37 G13** 6 45S 108 32 E
Tjörn, *Sweden* **9 G14** 58 0N 11 35 E
Tlacotalpan, *Mexico* **87 D5** 18 37N 95 40W
Tlahualilo, *Mexico* **86 B4** 26 20N 103 30W
Tlaquepaque, *Mexico* **86 C4** 20 39N 103 19W
Tlaxcala, *Mexico* **87 D5** 19 20N 98 14W
Tlaxcala □, *Mexico* **87 D5** 19 30N 98 20W
Tlaxiaco, *Mexico* **87 D5** 17 18N 97 40W
Tlemcen, *Algeria* **50 B5** 34 52N 1 21W
To Bong, *Vietnam* **38 F7** 12 45N 109 16 E
Toad →, *Canada* **72 B4** 59 25N 124 57W
Toad River, *Canada* **72 B3** 58 51N 125 14W
Toamasina, *Madag.* **57 B8** 18 10S 49 25 E
Toamasina □, *Madag.* **57 B8** 18 0S 49 0 E
Toay, *Argentina* **94 D3** 36 43S 64 38W
Toba, *Japan* **31 G8** 34 30N 136 51 E
Toba, Danau, *Indonesia* **36 D1** 2 30N 97 30 E
Toba Kakar, *Pakistan* **42 D3** 31 30N 69 0 E
Toba Tek Singh, *Pakistan* **42 D5** 30 55N 72 25 E
Tobago, *W. Indies* **89 D7** 11 10N 60 30W
Tobelo, *Indonesia* **37 D7** 1 45N 127 56 E
Tobermory, *Canada* **78 A3** 45 12N 81 40W
Tobermory, *U.K.* **12 E2** 56 38N 6 5W
Tobi, *Pac. Oc.* **37 D8** 2 40N 131 10 E
Tobin, *U.S.A.* **84 F5** 39 55N 121 19W
Tobin, L., *Australia* **60 D4** 21 45S 125 49 E
Tobin L., *Canada* **73 C8** 53 35N 103 30W
Toboali, *Indonesia* **36 E3** 3 0S 106 25 E
Tobol →, *Russia* **26 D7** 58 10N 68 12 E
Toboli, *Indonesia* **37 E6** 0 38S 120 5 E
Tobolsk, *Russia* **26 D7** 58 15N 68 10 E
Tobruk = Tubruq, *Libya* **51 B10** 32 7N 23 55 E
Tobyhanna, *U.S.A.* **79 E9** 41 11N 75 25W
Tobyl = Tobol →, *Russia* **26 D7** 58 10N 68 12 E
Tocantinópolis, *Brazil* **93 E9** 6 20S 47 25W
Tocantins □, *Brazil* **93 F9** 10 0S 48 0W
Tocantins →, *Brazil* **93 D9** 1 45S 49 10W
Toccoa, *U.S.A.* **77 H4** 34 35N 83 19W
Tochi →, *Pakistan* **42 C4** 32 49N 70 41 E
Tochigi, *Japan* **31 F9** 36 25N 139 45 E
Tochigi □, *Japan* **31 F9** 36 45N 139 45 E
Toconao, *Chile* **94 A2** 23 11S 68 1W
Tocopilla, *Chile* **94 A1** 22 5S 70 10W
Tocumwal, *Australia* **63 F4** 35 51S 145 31 E
Tocuyo →, *Venezuela* **92 A5** 11 3N 68 23W
Todd →, *Australia* **62 C2** 24 52S 135 48 E
Todeli, *Indonesia* **37 E6** 1 38S 124 34
Todenyang, *Kenya* **54 B4** 4 35N 35 56 E
Todgarh, *India* **42 G5** 25 42N 73 58
Todos os Santos, B. de, *Brazil* **93 F11** 12 48S 38 38W
Todos Santos, *Mexico* **86 C2** 23 27N 110 13W
Toe Hd., *U.K.* **12 D1** 57 50N 7 8W
Tofield, *Canada* **72 C6** 53 25N 112 40W
Tofino, *Canada* **72 D3** 49 11N 125 55W
Tofua, *Tonga* **59 D11** 19 45S 175 5W
Tōgane, *Japan* **31 G10** 35 33N 140 22
Togian, Kepulauan, *Indonesia* **37 E6** 0 20S 121 50 E
Togliatti, *Russia* **24 D8** 53 32N 49 24 E
Togo ■, *W. Afr.* **50 G6** 8 30N 1 35 E
Togtoh, *China* **34 D6** 40 15N 111 10 E
Tōhoku □, *Japan* **30 E10** 39 50N 141 45 E
Töhöm, *Mongolia* **34 B5** 44 27N 108 2 E
Toinya, *Sudan* **51 G11** 6 17N 29 46 E
Toiyabe Range, *U.S.A.* **82 G5** 39 30N 117 0W
Tojikiston = Tajikistan ■, *Asia* **26 F8** 38 30N 70 0 E
Tojo, *Indonesia* **37 E6** 1 20S 121 15
Tōjō, *Japan* **31 G6** 34 53N 133 16
Tok, *U.S.A.* **68 B5** 63 20N 142 59W
Tok-do, *Japan* **31 F5** 37 15N 131 52
Tokachi-Dake, *Japan* **30 C11** 43 17N 142 5
Tokachi-Gawa →, *Japan* **30 C11** 42 44N 143 42
Tokala, *Indonesia* **37 E6** 1 30S 121 40
Tōkamachi, *Japan* **31 F9** 37 8N 138 43
Tokanui, *N.Z.* **59 M2** 46 34S 168 56
Tokara-Rettō, *Japan* **31 K4** 29 37N 129 43
Tokarahi, *N.Z.* **59 L3** 44 56S 170 39
Tokashiki-Shima, *Japan* **31 L3** 26 11N 127 21
Tokat □, *Turkey* **25 F6** 40 15N 36 30
Tŏkch'ŏn, *N. Korea* **35 E14** 39 45N 126 18
Tokeland, *U.S.A.* **84 D3** 46 42N 123 59W
Tokelau Is., *Pac. Oc.* **64 H10** 9 0S 171 45W
Tokmak, *Kyrgyzstan* **26 E8** 42 49N 75 15
Toko Ra., *Australia* **62 C2** 23 5S 138 20
Tokoro-Gawa →, *Japan* **30 B12** 44 7N 144 5
Tokuno-Shima, *Japan* **31 L4** 27 56N 128 55
Tokushima, *Japan* **31 G7** 34 4N 134 34
Tokushima □, *Japan* **31 H7** 33 55N 134 0
Tokuyama, *Japan* **31 G5** 34 3N 131 50
Tōkyō, *Japan* **31 G9** 35 45N 139 45
Tolaga Bay, *N.Z.* **59 H7** 38 21S 178 20
Tolbukhin = Dobrich, *Bulgaria* **21 C12** 43 37N 27 49
Toledo, *Brazil* **95 A5** 24 44S 53 45W
Toledo, *Spain* **19 C3** 39 50N 4 2W
Toledo, *Ohio, U.S.A.* **76 E4** 41 39N 83 33W
Toledo, *Oreg., U.S.A.* **82 D2** 44 37N 123 56W
Toledo, *Wash., U.S.A.* **82 C2** 46 26N 122 51W
Toledo, Montes de, *Spain* **19 C3** 39 33N 4 20W
Toledo Bend Reservoir, *U.S.A.* **81 K8** 31 11N 93 34W
Tolga, *Australia* **62 B4** 17 15S 145 29
Toliara, *Madag.* **57 C7** 23 21S 43 40
Toliara □, *Madag.* **57 C8** 21 0S 45 0
Tolima, *Colombia* **92 C3** 4 40N 75 19W
Tolitoli, *Indonesia* **37 D6** 1 5N 120 50
Tollhouse, *U.S.A.* **84 H7** 37 1N 119 24W
Tolo, Teluk, *Indonesia* **37 E6** 2 20S 122 10
Toluca, *Mexico* **87 D5** 19 20N 99 40W
Tom Burke, *S. Africa* **57 C4** 23 5S 28 0
Tom Price, *Australia* **60 D2** 22 40S 117 48
Tomah, *U.S.A.* **80 D9** 43 59N 90 30W
Tomahawk, *U.S.A.* **80 C10** 45 28N 89 44W
Tomakomai, *Japan* **30 C10** 42 38N 141 36
Tomales, *U.S.A.* **84 G4** 38 15N 122 53W
Tomales B., *U.S.A.* **84 G3** 38 15N 123 58W
Tomar, *Portugal* **19 C1** 39 36N 8 25W
Tomaszów Mazowiecki, *Poland* **17 C10** 51 30N 20 2
Tomatlán, *Mexico* **86 D3** 19 56N 105 15W
Tombador, Serra do, *Brazil* **92 F7** 12 0S 58 0W
Tombigbee →, *U.S.A.* **77 K2** 31 8N 87 57W
Tombouctou, *Mali* **50 E5** 16 50N 3 0W
Tombstone, *U.S.A.* **83 L8** 31 43N 110 4W
Tombua, *Angola* **56 B1** 15 55S 11 55

Tukums

Tomé, *Chile* **94 D1** 36 36S 72 57W
Tomelloso, *Spain* **19 C4** 39 10N 3 2W
Tomini, *Indonesia* **37 D6** 0 30N 120 30 E
Tomini, Teluk, *Indonesia* **37 E6** 0 10S 122 0 E
Tomintoul, *U.K.* **12 D5** 57 15N 3 23W
Tomkinson Ranges, *Australia* **61 E4** 26 11S 129 5 E
Tommot, *Russia* **27 D13** 59 4N 126 20 E
Tomnop Ta Suos, *Cambodia* **39 G5** 11 20N 104 15 E
Tomo →, *Colombia* **92 B5** 5 20N 67 48W
Toms Place, *U.S.A.* **84 H8** 37 34N 118 41W
Toms River, *U.S.A.* **79 G10** 39 58N 74 12W
Tomsk, *Russia* **26 D9** 56 30N 85 5 E
Tonalá, *Mexico* **87 D6** 16 8N 93 41W
Tonantins, *Brazil* **92 D5** 2 45S 67 45W
Tonasket, *U.S.A.* **82 B4** 48 42N 119 26W
Tonawanda, *U.S.A.* **78 D6** 43 1N 78 53W
Tonbridge, *U.K.* **11 F8** 51 11N 0 17 E
Tondano, *Indonesia* **37 D6** 1 35N 124 54 E
Tone →, *Australia* **61 F2** 34 25S 116 25 E
Tone-Gawa →, *Japan* **31 F9** 35 44N 140 51 E
Tonekābon, *Iran* **45 B6** 36 45N 51 12 E
Tong Xian, *China* **34 E9** 39 55N 116 35 E
Tonga ■, *Pac. Oc.* **59 D11** 19 50S 174 30W
Tonga Trench, *Pac. Oc.* **64 J10** 18 0S 173 0W
Tongaat, *S. Africa* **57 D5** 29 33S 31 9 E
Tongareva, *Cook Is.* **65 H12** 9 0S 158 0W
Tongatapu, *Tonga* **59 E12** 21 10S 174 0W
Tongchŏn-ni, *N. Korea* **35 E14** 39 50N 127 25 E
Tongchuan, *China* **34 G5** 35 6N 109 3 E
Tongeren, *Belgium* **15 D5** 50 47N 5 28 E
Tongguan, *China* **34 G6** 34 40N 110 25 E
Tonghua, *China* **35 D13** 41 42N 125 58 E
Tongjosŏn Man, *N. Korea* **35 E15** 39 30N 128 0 E
Tongking, G. of, *Asia* **32 E5** 20 0N 108 0 E
Tongliao, *China* **35 C12** 43 38N 122 18 E
Tongling, *China* **33 C6** 30 55N 117 48 E
Tongnae, *S. Korea* **35 G15** 35 12N 129 5 E
Tongobory, *Madag.* **57 C7** 23 32S 44 20 E
Tongoy, *Chile* **94 C1** 30 16S 71 31W
Tongres = Tongeren, *Belgium* **15 D5** 50 47N 5 28 E
Tongsa Dzong, *Bhutan* **41 F17** 27 31N 90 31 E
Tongue, *U.K.* **12 C4** 58 29N 4 25W
Tongue →, *U.S.A.* **80 B2** 46 25N 105 52W
Tongwei, *China* **34 G3** 35 0N 105 5 E
Tongxin, *China* **34 F3** 36 59N 105 58 E
Tongyang, *N. Korea* **35 E14** 39 9N 126 53 E
Tongyu, *China* **35 B12** 44 45N 123 4 E
Tonj, *Sudan* **51 G11** 7 20N 28 44 E
Tonk, *India* **42 F6** 26 6N 75 54 E
Tonkawa, *U.S.A.* **81 G6** 36 41N 97 18W
Tonkin = Bac Phan, *Vietnam* **38 B5** 22 0N 105 0 E
Tonle Sap, *Cambodia* **38 F5** 13 0N 104 0 E
Tono, *Japan* **30 E10** 39 19N 141 32 E
Tonopah, *U.S.A.* **83 G5** 38 4N 117 14W
Tonosí, *Panama* **88 E3** 7 20N 80 20W
Tons →, *Haryana, India* **42 D7** 30 30N 77 39 E
Tons →, *Ut. P., India* **43 F10** 26 1N 83 33 E
Tønsberg, *Norway* **9 G14** 59 19N 10 25 E
Toobanna, *Australia* **62 B4** 18 42S 146 9 E
Toodyay, *Australia* **61 F2** 31 34S 116 28 E
Tooele, *U.S.A.* **82 F7** 40 32N 112 18W
Toompine, *Australia* **63 D3** 27 15S 144 19 E
Toora, *Australia* **63 F4** 38 39S 146 23 E
Toora-Khem, *Russia* **27 D10** 52 28N 96 17 E
Toowoomba, *Australia* **63 D5** 27 32S 151 56 E
Top-ozero, *Russia* **24 A5** 65 35N 32 0 E
Top Springs, *Australia* **60 C5** 16 37S 131 51 E
Topaz, *U.S.A.* **84 G7** 38 41N 119 30W
Topeka, *U.S.A.* **80 F7** 39 3N 95 40W
Topley, *Canada* **72 C3** 54 49N 126 18W
Topocalma, Pta., *Chile* **94 C1** 34 10S 72 2W
Topock, *U.S.A.* **85 L12** 34 46N 114 29W
Topol'čany, *Slovak Rep.* **17 D10** 48 35N 18 12 E
Topolobampo, *Mexico* **86 B3** 25 40N 109 4W
Toppenish, *U.S.A.* **82 C3** 46 23N 120 19W
Toraka Vestale, *Madag.* **57 B7** 16 20S 43 58 E
Torata, *Peru* **92 G4** 17 23S 70 1W
Torbalı, *Turkey* **21 E12** 38 10N 27 21 E
Torbat-e Heydārīyeh, *Iran* **45 C8** 35 15N 59 12 E
Torbat-e Jām, *Iran* **45 C9** 35 16N 60 35 E
Torbay, *Canada* **71 C9** 47 40N 52 42W
Torbay □, *U.K.* **11 G4** 50 26N 3 31W
Tordesillas, *Spain* **19 B3** 41 30N 5 0W
Torfaen □, *U.K.* **11 F4** 51 43N 3 3W
Torgau, *Germany* **16 C7** 51 34N 13 0 E
Torhout, *Belgium* **15 C3** 51 5N 3 7 E
Tori-Shima, *Japan* **31 J10** 30 29N 140 19 E
Torin, *Mexico* **86 B2** 27 33N 110 15W
Torino, *Italy* **18 D7** 45 3N 7 40 E
Torit, *Sudan* **51 H12** 4 27N 32 31 E
Torkamān, *Iran* **44 B5** 37 35N 47 23 E
Tormes →, *Spain* **19 B2** 41 18N 6 29W
Tornado Mt., *Canada* **72 D6** 49 55N 114 40W
Torne älv →, *Sweden* **8 D21** 65 50N 24 12 E
Torneå = Tornio, *Finland* **8 D21** 65 50N 24 12 E
Torneträsk, *Sweden* **8 B18** 68 24N 19 15 E
Tornio, *Finland* **8 D21** 65 50N 24 12 E
Tornionjoki →, *Finland* **8 D21** 65 50N 24 12 E
Tornquist, *Argentina* **94 D3** 38 8S 62 15W
Toro, *Spain* **22 B11** 39 59N 4 8 E
Toro, Cerro del, *Chile* **94 B2** 29 10S 69 50W
Toro Pk., *U.S.A.* **85 M10** 33 34N 116 24W
Toroníios Kólpos, *Greece* **21 D10** 40 5N 23 30 E
Toronto, *Canada* **78 C5** 43 39N 79 20W
Toronto, *U.S.A.* **78 F4** 40 28N 80 36W
Toropets, *Russia* **24 C5** 56 30N 31 40 E
Tororo, *Uganda* **54 B3** 0 45N 34 12 E
Toros Dağları, *Turkey* **25 G5** 37 0N 32 30 E
Torpa, *India* **43 H11** 22 57N 85 6 E
Torquay, *Australia* **63 F3** 38 20S 144 19 E
Torquay, *U.K.* **11 G4** 50 27N 3 32W
Torrance, *U.S.A.* **85 M8** 33 50N 118 19W
Torre de Moncorvo, *Portugal* **19 B2** 41 12N 7 8W
Torre del Greco, *Italy* **20 D6** 40 47N 14 22 E
Torrejón de Ardoz, *Spain* **19 B4** 40 27N 3 29W
Torrelavega, *Spain* **19 A3** 43 20N 4 5W
Torremolinos, *Spain* **19 D3** 36 38N 4 30W
Torrens, L., *Australia* **63 E2** 31 0S 137 50 E
Torrens Cr. →, *Australia* **62 C4** 22 23S 145 9 E
Torrens Creek, *Australia* **62 C4** 20 48S 145 3 E
Torrent, *Spain* **19 C5** 39 27N 0 28W
Torreón, *Mexico* **86 B4** 25 33N 103 26W
Torres, *Brazil* **95 B5** 29 21S 49 44W
Torres, *Mexico* **86 B2** 28 46N 110 47W
Torres Strait, *Australia* **64 H6** 9 50S 142 20 E
Torres Vedras, *Portugal* **19 C1** 39 5N 9 15W
Torrevieja, *Spain* **19 D5** 37 59N 0 42W
Torrey, *U.S.A.* **83 G8** 38 18N 111 25W
Torridge →, *U.K.* **11 G3** 51 0N 4 13W
Torridon, L., *U.K.* **12 D3** 57 35N 5 50W
Torrington, *Conn., U.S.A.* **79 E11** 41 48N 73 7W
Torrington, *Wyo., U.S.A.* **80 D2** 42 4N 104 11W
Tórshavn, *Færoe Is.* **8 E9** 62 5N 6 56W
Tortola, *Virgin Is.* **89 C7** 18 19N 64 45W
Tortosa, *Spain* **19 B6** 40 49N 0 31 E
Tortosa, C., *Spain* **19 B6** 40 41N 0 52 E
Tortue, I. de la, *Haiti* **89 B5** 20 5N 72 57W
Ţorūd, *Iran* **45 C7** 35 25N 55 5 E
Toruń, *Poland* **17 B10** 53 2N 18 39 E
Tory I., *Ireland* **13 A3** 55 16N 8 14W
Tosa, *Japan* **31 H6** 33 24N 133 23 E
Tosa-Shimizu, *Japan* **31 H6** 32 52N 132 58 E
Tosa-Wan, *Japan* **31 H6** 33 15N 133 30 E
Toscana □, *Italy* **20 C4** 43 25N 11 0 E
Toshkent, *Uzbekistan* **26 E7** 41 20N 69 10 E
Tostado, *Argentina* **94 B3** 29 15S 61 50W
Tostón, Pta. de, *Canary Is.* **22 F5** 28 42N 14 2W
Tosu, *Japan* **31 H5** 33 22N 130 31 E
Toteng, *Botswana* **56 C3** 20 22S 22 58 E
Totma, *Russia* **24 C7** 60 0N 42 40 E
Totnes, *U.K.* **11 G4** 50 26N 3 42W
Totness, *Surinam* **93 B7** 5 53N 56 19W
Totonicapán, *Guatemala* **88 D1** 14 58N 91 12W
Totten Glacier, *Antarctica* **5 C8** 66 45S 116 10 E
Tottenham, *Australia* **63 E4** 32 14S 147 21 E
Tottenham, *Canada* **78 B5** 44 1N 79 49W
Tottori, *Japan* **31 G7** 35 30N 134 15 E
Tottori □, *Japan* **31 G7** 35 30N 134 12 E
Toubkal, Djebel, *Morocco* **50 B4** 31 0N 8 0W
Tougan, *Burkina Faso* **50 F5** 13 11N 2 58W
Touggourt, *Algeria* **50 B7** 33 6N 6 4 E
Toul, *France* **18 B6** 48 40N 5 53 E
Toulon, *France* **18 E6** 43 10N 5 55 E
Toulouse, *France* **18 E4** 43 37N 1 27 E
Toummo, *Niger* **51 D8** 22 45N 14 8 E
Toungoo, *Burma* **41 K20** 19 0N 96 30 E
Touraine, *France* **18 C4** 47 20N 0 30 E
Tourane = Da Nang, *Vietnam* **38 D7** 16 4N 108 13 E
Tourcoing, *France* **18 A5** 50 42N 3 10 E
Touriñán, C., *Spain* **19 A1** 43 3N 9 18W
Tournai, *Belgium* **15 D3** 50 35N 3 25 E
Tournon-sur-Rhône, *France* **18 D6** 45 4N 4 50 E
Tours, *France* **18 C4** 47 22N 0 40 E
Tousidé, Pic, *Chad* **51 D9** 21 1N 16 29 E
Toussora, Mt., *C.A.R.* **52 C4** 9 7N 23 14 E
Touwsrivier, *S. Africa* **56 E3** 33 20S 20 2 E
Towada, *Japan* **30 D10** 40 37N 141 13 E
Towada-Ko, *Japan* **30 D10** 40 28N 140 55 E
Towanda, *U.S.A.* **79 E8** 41 46N 76 27W
Towang, *India* **41 F17** 27 37N 91 50 E
Tower, *U.S.A.* **80 B8** 47 48N 92 17W
Towerhill Cr. →, *Australia* **62 C3** 22 28S 144 35 E
Towner, *U.S.A.* **80 A4** 48 21N 100 25W
Townsend, *U.S.A.* **82 C8** 46 19N 111 31W
Townshend I., *Australia* **62 C5** 22 10S 150 31 E
Townsville, *Australia* **62 B4** 19 15S 146 45 E
Towson, *U.S.A.* **76 F7** 39 24N 76 36W
Towuti, Danau, *Indonesia* **37 E6** 2 45S 121 32 E
Toya-Ko, *Japan* **30 C10** 42 35N 140 51 E
Toyama, *Japan* **31 F8** 36 40N 137 15 E
Toyama □, *Japan* **31 F8** 36 45N 137 30 E
Toyama-Wan, *Japan* **31 F8** 37 0N 137 30 E
Toyohashi, *Japan* **31 G8** 34 45N 137 25 E
Toyokawa, *Japan* **31 G8** 34 48N 137 27 E
Toyonaka, *Japan* **31 G7** 34 50N 135 28 E
Toyooka, *Japan* **31 G7** 35 35N 134 48 E
Toyota, *Japan* **31 G8** 35 3N 137 7 E
Tozeur, *Tunisia* **50 B7** 33 56N 8 8 E
Trá Li = Tralee, *Ireland* **13 D2** 52 16N 9 42W
Tra On, *Vietnam* **39 H5** 9 58N 105 55 E
Trabzon, *Turkey* **25 F6** 41 0N 39 45 E
Tracadie, *Canada* **71 C7** 47 30N 64 55W
Tracy, *Calif., U.S.A.* **84 H5** 37 44N 121 26W
Tracy, *Minn., U.S.A.* **80 C7** 44 14N 95 37W
Trafalgar, C., *Spain* **19 D2** 36 10N 6 2W
Trail, *Canada* **72 D5** 49 5N 117 40W
Trainor L., *Canada* **72 A4** 60 24N 120 17W
Trákhonas, *Cyprus* **23 D12** 35 12N 33 21 E
Tralee, *Ireland* **13 D2** 52 16N 9 42W
Tralee B., *Ireland* **13 D2** 52 17N 9 55W
Tramore, *Ireland* **13 D4** 52 10N 7 10W
Tramore B., *Ireland* **13 D4** 52 9N 7 10W
Tran Ninh, Cao Nguyen, *Laos* **38 C4** 19 30N 103 10 E
Tranås, *Sweden* **9 G16** 58 3N 14 59 E
Trancas, *Argentina* **94 B2** 26 11S 65 20W
Trang, *Thailand* **39 J2** 7 33N 99 38 E
Trangahy, *Madag.* **57 B7** 19 7S 44 31 E
Trangan, *Indonesia* **37 F8** 6 40S 134 20 E
Trangie, *Australia* **63 E4** 32 4S 148 0 E
Trani, *Italy* **20 D7** 41 17N 16 25 E
Tranoroa, *Madag.* **57 C8** 24 42S 45 4 E
Tranqueras, *Uruguay* **95 C4** 31 13S 55 45W
Transantarctic Mts., *Antarctica* **5 E12** 85 0S 170 0W
Transilvania, *Romania* **17 E12** 46 30N 24 0 E
Transilvanian Alps = Carpaţii Meridionali, *Romania* **17 F13** 45 30N 25 0 E
Transvaal □, *S. Africa* **53 K5** 25 0S 29 0 E
Transylvania = Transilvania, *Romania* **17 E12** 46 30N 24 0 E
Trápani, *Italy* **20 E5** 38 1N 12 29 E
Trapper Pk., *U.S.A.* **82 D6** 45 54N 114 18W
Traralgon, *Australia* **63 F4** 38 12S 146 34 E
Trasimeno, L., *Italy* **20 C5** 43 8N 12 6 E
Trat, *Thailand* **39 F4** 12 14N 102 33 E
Tratani →, *Pakistan* **42 E3** 29 19N 68 20 E
Traun, *Austria* **16 D8** 48 14N 14 15 E
Travellers L., *Australia* **63 E3** 33 20S 142 0 E
Travemünde, *Germany* **16 B6** 53 57N 10 52 E
Travers, Mt., *N.Z.* **59 K4** 42 1S 172 45 E
Traverse City, *U.S.A.* **76 C3** 44 46N 85 38W
Travis, L., *U.S.A.* **81 K5** 30 24N 97 55W
Travnik, *Bos.-H.* **21 B7** 44 17N 17 39 E
Trébbia →, *Italy* **18 D8** 45 4N 9 41 E
Třebíč, *Czech Rep.* **16 D8** 49 14N 15 55 E
Trebinje, *Bos.-H.* **21 C8** 42 44N 18 22 E
Trebonne, *Australia* **62 B4** 18 37S 146 5 E
Tregaron, *U.K.* **11 E4** 52 14N 3 56W
Tregrosse Is., *Australia* **62 B5** 17 41S 150 43 E
Treherne, *Canada* **73 D9** 49 38N 98 42W
Treinta y Tres, *Uruguay* **95 C5** 33 16S 54 17W
Trelew, *Argentina* **96 E3** 43 10S 65 20W
Trelleborg, *Sweden* **9 J15** 55 20N 13 10 E
Tremadog Bay, *U.K.* **10 E3** 52 51N 4 18W
Tremonton, *U.S.A.* **82 F7** 41 43N 112 10W
Tremp, *Spain* **19 A6** 42 10N 0 52 E
Trenche →, *Canada* **70 C5** 47 46N 72 53W
Trenčín, *Slovak Rep.* **17 D10** 48 52N 18 4 E
Trenggalek, *Indonesia* **37 H14** 8 3S 111 43 E
Trenque Lauquen, *Argentina* **94 D3** 36 5S 62 45W
Trent →, *Canada* **78 B7** 44 6N 77 34W
Trent →, *U.K.* **10 D7** 53 41N 0 42W
Trento, *Italy* **20 A4** 46 4N 11 8 E
Trenton, *Canada* **78 B7** 44 10N 77 34W
Trenton, *Mo., U.S.A.* **80 E8** 40 5N 93 37W
Trenton, *N.J., U.S.A.* **79 F10** 40 14N 74 46W
Trenton, *Nebr., U.S.A.* **80 E4** 40 11N 101 1W
Trepassey, *Canada* **71 C9** 46 43N 53 25W
Tres Arroyos, *Argentina* **94 D3** 38 26S 60 20W
Três Corações, *Brazil* **95 A6** 21 44S 45 15W
Três Lagoas, *Brazil* **93 H8** 20 50S 51 43W
Tres Lomas, *Argentina* **94 D3** 36 27S 62 51W
Tres Marías, Islas, *Mexico* **86 C3** 21 25N 106 28W
Tres Montes, C., *Chile* **96 F1** 46 50S 75 30W
Tres Pinos, *U.S.A.* **84 J5** 36 48N 121 19W
Três Pontas, *Brazil* **95 A6** 21 23S 45 29W
Tres Puentes, *Chile* **94 B1** 27 50S 70 15W
Tres Puntas, C., *Argentina* **96 F3** 47 0S 66 0W
Três Rios, *Brazil* **95 A7** 22 6S 43 15W
Tres Valles, *Mexico* **87 D5** 18 15N 96 8W
Tresco, *U.K.* **11 H1** 49 57N 6 20W
Treviso, *Italy* **20 B5** 45 40N 12 15 E
Triabunna, *Australia* **62 G4** 42 30S 147 55 E
Triánda, *Greece* **23 C10** 36 25N 28 10 E
Tribulation, C., *Australia* **62 B4** 16 5S 145 29 E
Tribune, *U.S.A.* **80 F4** 38 28N 101 45W
Trichinopoly = Tiruchchirappalli, *India* **40 P11** 10 45N 78 45 E
Trichur, *India* **40 P10** 10 30N 76 18 E
Trida, *Australia* **63 E4** 33 1S 145 1 E
Trier, *Germany* **16 D4** 49 45N 6 38 E
Trieste, *Italy* **20 B5** 45 40N 13 46 E
Triglav, *Slovenia* **16 E7** 46 21N 13 50 E
Tríkkala, *Greece* **21 E9** 39 34N 21 47 E
Trikomo, *Cyprus* **23 D12** 35 17N 33 52 E
Trikora, Puncak, *Indonesia* **37 E9** 4 15S 138 45 E
Trim, *Ireland* **13 C5** 53 33N 6 48W
Trincomalee, *Sri Lanka* **40 Q12** 8 38N 81 15 E
Trindade, *Brazil* **93 G9** 16 40S 49 30W
Trindade, I., *Atl. Oc.* **2 F8** 20 20S 29 50W
Trinidad, *Bolivia* **92 F6** 14 46S 64 50W
Trinidad, *Cuba* **88 B4** 21 48N 80 0W
Trinidad, *Uruguay* **94 C4** 33 30S 56 50W
Trinidad, *U.S.A.* **81 G2** 37 10N 104 31W
Trinidad, *W. Indies* **89 D7** 10 30N 61 15W
Trinidad →, *Mexico* **87 D5** 17 49N 95 9W
Trinidad & Tobago ■, *W. Indies* **89 D7** 10 30N 61 20W
Trinity, *Canada* **71 C9** 48 59N 53 55W
Trinity, *U.S.A.* **81 K7** 30 57N 95 22W
Trinity →, *Calif., U.S.A.* **82 F2** 41 11N 123 42W
Trinity →, *Tex., U.S.A.* **81 L7** 29 45N 94 43W
Trinity B., *Canada* **71 C9** 48 20N 53 10W
Trinity Is., *U.S.A.* **68 C4** 56 33N 154 25W
Trinity Range, *U.S.A.* **82 F4** 40 15N 118 45W
Trinkitat, *Sudan* **51 E13** 18 45N 37 51 E
Trinway, *U.S.A.* **78 F2** 40 9N 82 1W
Tripoli = Tarābulus, *Lebanon* **47 A4** 34 31N 35 50 E
Tripoli = Tarābulus, *Libya* **51 B8** 32 49N 13 7 E
Trípolis, *Greece* **21 F10** 37 31N 22 25 E
Tripolitania, *Libya* **48 C5** 31 0N 12 0 E
Tripolitania, *N. Afr.* **51 B8** 31 0N 13 0 E
Tripura □, *India* **41 H18** 24 0N 92 0 E
Tripylos, *Cyprus* **23 E11** 34 59N 32 41 E
Tristan da Cunha, *Atl. Oc.* **49 K2** 37 6S 12 20W
Trisul, *India* **43 D8** 30 19N 79 47 E
Trivandrum, *India* **40 Q10** 8 41N 77 0 E
Trnava, *Slovak Rep.* **17 D9** 48 23N 17 35 E
Trochu, *Canada* **72 C6** 51 50N 113 13W
Trodely I., *Canada* **70 B4** 52 15N 79 26W
Troglav, *Croatia* **20 C7** 43 56N 16 36 E
Troilus, L., *Canada* **70 B5** 50 50N 74 35W
Trois-Pistoles, *Canada* **71 C6** 48 5N 69 10W
Trois-Rivières, *Canada* **70 C5** 46 25N 72 34W
Troitsk, *Russia* **26 D7** 54 10N 61 35 E
Troitsko Pechorsk, *Russia* **24 B10** 62 40N 56 10 E
Trölladyngja, *Iceland* **8 D5** 64 54N 17 16W
Trollhättan, *Sweden* **9 G15** 58 17N 12 20 E
Trollheimen, *Norway* **8 E13** 62 46N 9 1 E
Trombetas →, *Brazil* **93 D7** 1 55S 55 35W
Tromsø, *Norway* **8 B18** 69 40N 18 56 E
Trona, *U.S.A.* **85 K9** 35 46N 117 23W
Tronador, Mte., *Argentina* **96 E2** 41 10S 71 50W
Trøndelag, *Norway* **8 D14** 64 17N 11 50 E
Trondheim, *Norway* **8 E14** 63 36N 10 25 E
Trondheimsfjorden, *Norway* **8 E14** 63 35N 10 30 E
Troodos, *Cyprus* **23 E11** 34 55N 32 52 E
Troon, *U.K.* **12 F4** 55 33N 4 39W
Tropic, *U.S.A.* **83 H7** 37 37N 112 5W
Trostan, *U.K.* **13 A5** 55 3N 6 10W
Trout →, *Canada* **72 A5** 61 19N 119 51W
Trout L., *N.W.T., Canada* **72 A4** 60 40N 121 14W
Trout L., *Ont., Canada* **73 C10** 51 20N 93 15W
Trout Lake, *Canada* **72 B6** 56 30N 114 32W
Trout Lake, *U.S.A.* **84 E5** 46 0N 121 32W
Trout River, *Canada* **71 C8** 49 29N 58 8W
Trout Run, *U.S.A.* **78 E7** 41 23N 77 3W
Trouville-sur-Mer, *France* **18 B4** 49 21N 0 5 E
Trowbridge, *U.K.* **11 F5** 51 18N 2 12W
Troy, *Turkey* **21 E12** 39 57N 26 12 E
Troy, *Ala., U.S.A.* **77 K3** 31 48N 85 58W
Troy, *Kans., U.S.A.* **80 F7** 39 47N 95 5W
Troy, *Mo., U.S.A.* **80 F9** 38 59N 90 59W
Troy, *Mont., U.S.A.* **82 B6** 48 28N 115 53W
Troy, *N.Y., U.S.A.* **79 D11** 42 44N 73 41W
Troy, *Ohio, U.S.A.* **76 E3** 40 2N 84 12W
Troy, *Pa., U.S.A.* **79 E8** 41 47N 76 47W
Troyes, *France* **18 B6** 48 19N 4 3 E
Truchas Peak, *U.S.A.* **81 H2** 35 58N 105 39W
Trucial States = United Arab Emirates ■, *Asia* **45 F7** 23 50N 54 0 E
Truckee, *U.S.A.* **84 F6** 39 20N 120 11W
Trudovoye, *Russia* **30 C6** 43 17N 132 5 E
Trujillo, *Honduras* **88 C2** 16 0N 86 0W
Trujillo, *Peru* **92 E3** 8 6S 79 0W
Trujillo, *Spain* **19 C3** 39 28N 5 55W
Trujillo, *U.S.A.* **81 H2** 35 32N 104 42W
Trujillo, *Venezuela* **92 B4** 9 22N 70 38W
Truk, *Micronesia* **64 G7** 7 25N 151 46 E
Trumann, *U.S.A.* **81 H9** 35 41N 90 31W
Trumansburg, *U.S.A.* **79 D8** 42 33N 76 40W
Trumbull, Mt., *U.S.A.* **83 H7** 36 25N 113 8W
Trundle, *Australia* **63 E4** 32 53S 147 35 E
Trung-Phan = Annam, *Vietnam* **38 E7** 16 0N 108 0 E
Truro, *Canada* **71 C7** 45 21N 63 14W
Truro, *U.K.* **11 G2** 50 16N 5 4W
Truskavets, *Ukraine* **17 D12** 49 17N 23 30 E
Trutch, *Canada* **72 B4** 57 44N 122 57W
Truth or Consequences, *U.S.A.* **83 K10** 33 8N 107 15W
Trutnov, *Czech Rep.* **16 C8** 50 37N 15 54 E
Truxton, *U.S.A.* **79 D8** 42 45N 76 2W
Tryonville, *U.S.A.* **78 E5** 41 42N 79 48W
Tsaratanana, *Madag.* **57 B8** 16 47S 47 39 E
Tsaratanana, Mt. de, *Madag.* **57 A8** 14 0S 49 0 E
Tsarevo = Michurin, *Bulgaria* **21 C12** 42 9N 27 51 E
Tsau, *Botswana* **56 C3** 20 8S 22 22 E
Tselinograd = Astana, *Kazakstan* **26 D8** 51 10N 71 30 E
Tsetserleg, *Mongolia* **32 B5** 47 36N 101 32 E
Tshabong, *Botswana* **56 D3** 26 2S 22 29 E
Tshane, *Botswana* **56 C3** 24 5S 21 54 E
Tshela, *Dem. Rep. of the Congo* **52 E2** 4 57S 13 4 E
Tshesebe, *Botswana* **57 C4** 21 51S 27 32 E
Tshibeke, *Dem. Rep. of the Congo* **54 C2** 2 40S 28 35 E
Tshibinda, *Dem. Rep. of the Congo* **54 C2** 2 23S 28 43 E
Tshikapa, *Dem. Rep. of the Congo* **52 F4** 6 28S 20 48 E
Tshilenge, *Dem. Rep. of the Congo* **54 D1** 6 17S 23 48 E
Tshinsenda, *Dem. Rep. of the Congo* **55 E2** 12 20S 28 0 E
Tshofa, *Dem. Rep. of the Congo* **54 D2** 5 13S 25 16 E
Tshwane, *Botswana* **56 C3** 22 24S 22 1 E
Tsigara, *Botswana* **56 C4** 20 22S 25 54 E
Tsihombe, *Madag.* **57 D8** 25 10S 45 41 E
Tsiigehtchic, *Canada* **68 B6** 67 15N 134 0W
Tsimlyansk Res. = Tsimlyanskoye Vdkhr., *Russia* **25 E7** 48 0N 43 0 E
Tsimlyanskoye Vdkhr., *Russia* **25 E7** 48 0N 43 0 E
Tsinan = Jinan, *China* **34 F9** 36 38N 117 1 E
Tsineng, *S. Africa* **56 D3** 27 5S 23 5 E
Tsinghai = Qinghai □, *China* **32 C4** 36 0N 98 0 E
Tsingtao = Qingdao, *China* **35 F11** 36 5N 120 20 E
Tsinjomitondraka, *Madag.* **57 B8** 15 40S 47 8 E
Tsiroanomandidy, *Madag.* **57 B8** 18 46S 46 2 E
Tsivory, *Madag.* **57 C8** 24 4S 46 5 E
Tskhinvali, *Georgia* **25 F7** 42 14N 44 1 E
Tsna →, *Russia* **24 D7** 54 55N 41 58 E
Tso Moriri, L., *India* **43 C8** 32 50N 78 20 E
Tsodilo Hill, *Botswana* **56 B3** 18 49S 21 43 E
Tsogttsetsiy = Baruunsuu, *Mongolia* **34 C3** 43 43N 105 35 E
Tsolo, *S. Africa* **57 E4** 31 18S 28 37 E
Tsomo, *S. Africa* **57 E4** 32 0S 27 42 E
Tsu, *Japan* **31 G8** 34 45N 136 25 E
Tsu L., *Canada* **72 A6** 60 40N 111 52W
Tsuchiura, *Japan* **31 F10** 36 5N 140 15 E
Tsugaru-Kaikyō, *Japan* **30 D10** 41 35N 141 0 E
Tsumeb, *Namibia* **56 B2** 19 9S 17 44 E
Tsumis, *Namibia* **56 C2** 23 39S 17 29 E
Tsuruga, *Japan* **31 G8** 35 45N 136 2 E
Tsurugi-San, *Japan* **31 H7** 33 51N 134 6 E
Tsuruoka, *Japan* **30 E9** 38 44N 139 50 E
Tsushima, *Gifu, Japan* **31 G8** 35 10N 136 43 E
Tsushima, *Nagasaki, Japan* **31 G4** 34 20N 129 20 E
Tsuyama, *Japan* **31 G7** 35 3N 134 0 E
Tsyelyakhany, *Belarus* **17 B13** 52 30N 25 46 E
Tual, *Indonesia* **37 F8** 5 38S 132 44 E
Tuam, *Ireland* **13 C3** 53 31N 8 51W
Tuamotu Arch. = Tuamotu Is., *Pac. Oc.* **65 J13** 17 0S 144 0W
Tuamotu Is., *Pac. Oc.* **65 J13** 17 0S 144 0W
Tuamotu Ridge, *Pac. Oc.* **65 K14** 20 0S 138 0W
Tuao, *Phil.* **37 A6** 17 55N 121 22 E
Tuapse, *Russia* **25 F6** 44 5N 39 10 E
Tuatapere, *N.Z.* **59 M1** 46 8S 167 41 E
Tuba City, *U.S.A.* **83 H8** 36 8N 111 14W
Tuban, *Indonesia* **37 G15** 6 54S 112 3 E
Tubarão, *Brazil* **95 B6** 28 30S 49 0W
Tūbās, *West Bank* **47 C4** 32 20N 35 22 E
Tübingen, *Germany* **16 D5** 48 31N 9 4 E
Tubruq, *Libya* **51 B10** 32 7N 23 55 E
Tubuai Is., *Pac. Oc.* **65 K13** 25 0S 150 0W
Tuc Trung, *Vietnam* **39 G6** 11 1N 107 12 E
Tucacas, *Venezuela* **92 A5** 10 48N 68 19W
Tuchodi →, *Canada* **72 B4** 58 17N 123 42W
Tuckanarra, *Australia* **61 E2** 27 7S 118 5 E
Tucson, *U.S.A.* **83 K8** 32 13N 110 58W
Tucumán □, *Argentina* **94 B2** 26 48S 66 2W
Tucumcari, *U.S.A.* **81 H3** 35 10N 103 44W
Tucupita, *Venezuela* **92 B6** 9 2N 62 3W
Tucuruí, *Brazil* **93 D9** 3 42S 49 44W
Tucuruí, Represa de, *Brazil* **93 D9** 4 0S 49 30W
Tudela, *Spain* **19 A5** 42 4N 1 39W
Tudmur, *Syria* **44 C3** 34 36N 38 15 E
Tudor, L., *Canada* **71 A6** 55 50N 65 25W
Tugela →, *S. Africa* **57 D5** 29 14S 31 30 E
Tuguegarao, *Phil.* **37 A6** 17 35N 121 42 E
Tugur, *Russia* **27 D14** 53 44N 136 45 E
Tui, *Spain* **19 A1** 42 3N 8 39W
Tuineje, *Canary Is.* **22 F5** 28 19N 14 3W
Tukangbesi, Kepulauan, *Indonesia* **37 F6** 6 0S 124 0 E
Tukarak I., *Canada* **70 A4** 56 15N 78 45W
Tukayyid, *Iraq* **44 D5** 29 47N 45 36 E
Tuktoyaktuk, *Canada* **68 B6** 69 27N 133 2W
Tukums, *Latvia* **9 H20** 56 58N 23 10 E

173

West Indies

Yeysk

oodend, *Australia* **63 F3** 37 20S 144 33 E
oodford, *Australia* **63 D5** 26 58S 152 47 E
oodfords, *U.S.A.* **84 G7** 38 47N 119 50W
oodlake, *U.S.A.* **84 J7** 36 25N 119 6W
oodland, *Calif., U.S.A.* **84 G5** 38 41N 121 46W
oodland, *Maine, U.S.A.* **77 C12** 45 9N 67 25W
oodland, *Pa., U.S.A.* **78 F6** 40 59N 78 21W
oodland, *Wash., U.S.A.* **84 E4** 45 54N 122 45W
oodland Caribou Prov. Park, *Canada* **73 C10** 51 0N 94 45W
oodridge, *Canada* **73 D9** 49 20N 96 9W
oodroffe, Mt., *Australia* **61 E5** 26 20S 131 45 E
oods, L., *Australia* **62 B1** 17 50S 133 30 E
oods, L. of the, *Canada* **73 D10** 49 15N 94 45W
oodside, *Australia* **63 F4** 38 31S 146 52 E
oodstock, *Australia* **62 B4** 19 35S 146 50 E
oodstock, *N.B., Canada* **71 C6** 46 11N 67 37W
oodstock, *Ont., Canada* **78 C4** 43 10N 80 45W
oodstock, *U.K.* **11 F6** 51 51N 1 20W
oodstock, *Ill., U.S.A.* **80 D10** 42 19N 88 27W
oodstock, *Vt., U.S.A.* **79 C12** 43 37N 72 31W
oodsville, *U.S.A.* **79 B13** 44 9N 72 2W
oodville, *N.Z.* **59 J5** 40 20S 175 53 E
oodville, *Miss., U.S.A.* **81 K9** 31 6N 91 18W
oodville, *Tex., U.S.A.* **81 K7** 30 47N 94 25W
oodward, *U.S.A.* **81 G5** 36 26N 99 24W
oody, *U.S.A.* **85 K8** 35 42N 118 50W
oody →, *Canada* **73 C8** 52 31N 100 51W
oolamai, C., *Australia* **63 F4** 38 30S 145 23 E
ooler, *U.K.* **10 B5** 55 33N 2 1W
oolgoolga, *Australia* **63 E5** 30 6S 153 11 E
oomera, *Australia* **63 E2** 31 5S 136 50 E
oonsocket, *R.I., U.S.A.* **79 E13** 42 0N 71 31W
oonsocket, *S. Dak., U.S.A.* **80 C5** 44 3N 98 17W
ooramel →, *Australia* **61 E1** 25 47S 114 10 E
ooramel Roadhouse, *Australia* **61 E1** 25 45S 114 17 E
ooster, *U.S.A.* **78 F3** 40 48N 81 56W
orcester, *S. Africa* **56 E2** 33 39S 19 27 E
orcester, *U.K.* **11 E5** 52 11N 2 12W
orcester, *Mass., U.S.A.* **79 D13** 42 16N 71 48W
orcester, *N.Y., U.S.A.* **79 D10** 42 36N 74 45W
orcestershire □, *U.K.* **11 E5** 52 13N 2 10W
orkington, *U.K.* **10 C4** 54 39N 3 33W
orksop, *U.K.* **10 D6** 53 18N 1 7W
orkum, *Neths.* **15 B5** 52 59N 5 26 E
orland, *U.S.A.* **82 D10** 44 1N 107 57W
orms, *Germany* **16 D5** 49 37N 8 21 E
orsley, *Canada* **72 B5** 56 31N 119 8W
ortham, *U.S.A.* **81 K6** 31 47N 96 28W
orthing, *U.K.* **11 G7** 50 49N 0 21W
orthington, *Minn., U.S.A.* **80 D7** 43 37N 95 36W
orthington, *Pa., U.S.A.* **78 F5** 40 50N 79 38W
osi, *Indonesia* **37 E7** 0 15S 128 0 E
ou-han = Wuhan, *China* **33 C6** 30 31N 114 18 E
ousi = Wuxi, *China* **33 C7** 31 33N 120 18 E
owoni, *Indonesia* **37 E6** 4 5S 123 5 E
rangel I. = Vrangelya, Ostrov, *Russia* **27 B19** 71 0N 180 0 E
rangell, *U.S.A.* **72 B2** 56 28N 132 23W
rangell Mts., *U.S.A.* **68 B5** 61 30N 142 0W
rath, C., *U.K.* **12 C3** 58 38N 5 1W
ray, *U.S.A.* **80 E3** 40 5N 102 13W
rekin, The, *U.K.* **11 E5** 52 41N 2 32W
rens, *U.S.A.* **77 J4** 33 12N 82 23W
rexham, *U.K.* **10 D4** 53 3N 3 0W
rexham □, *U.K.* **10 D5** 53 1N 2 58W
right, *U.S.A.* **80 D2** 43 47N 105 30W
right Pt., *Canada* **78 C3** 43 48N 81 44W
rightson Mt., *U.S.A.* **83 L8** 31 42N 110 51W
rightwood, *U.S.A.* **85 L9** 34 21N 117 38W
rigley, *Canada* **68 B7** 63 16N 123 37W
rocław, *Poland* **17 C9** 51 5N 17 5 E
rześnia, *Poland* **17 B9** 52 21N 17 36 E
u Jiang →, *China* **32 D5** 29 40N 107 20 E
u'an, *China* **34 F8** 36 40N 114 15 E
ubin, *Australia* **61 F2** 30 6S 116 37 E
ubu, *China* **34 F6** 37 28N 110 42 E
uchang, *China* **35 B14** 44 55N 127 5 E
ucheng, *China* **34 F9** 37 12N 116 20 E
uchuan, *China* **34 D6** 41 5N 111 28 E
udi, *China* **35 F9** 37 40N 117 35 E
uding He →, *China* **34 F6** 37 2N 110 23 E
udinna, *Australia* **63 E2** 33 0S 135 22 E
udu, *China* **34 H3** 33 22N 104 54 E
uhan, *China* **33 C6** 30 31N 114 18 E
uhe, *China* **35 H9** 33 10N 117 50 E
uhsi = Wuxi, *China* **33 C7** 31 33N 120 18 E
uhu, *China* **33 C6** 31 22N 118 21 E
ukari, *Nigeria* **50 G7** 7 51N 9 42 E
ulajie, *China* **35 B14** 44 6N 126 33 E
ulanbulang, *China* **34 D6** 41 5N 110 55 E
ular L., *India* **43 B6** 34 20N 74 30 E
ulian, *China* **35 G10** 35 40N 119 12 E
uliaru, *Indonesia* **37 F8** 7 27S 131 0 E
uluk'omushih Ling, *China* **32 C3** 36 25N 87 25 E
ulumuchi = Ürümqi, *China* **26 E9** 43 45N 87 45 E
undowie, *Australia* **61 F2** 31 47S 116 23 E
unnummin L., *Canada* **70 B2** 52 55N 89 10W
untho, *Burma* **41 H19** 23 55N 95 45 E
uppertal, *Germany* **16 C4** 51 16N 7 12 E
uppertal, *S. Africa* **56 E2** 32 13S 19 12 E
uqing, *China* **35 E9** 39 23N 117 4 E
urtsboro, *U.S.A.* **79 E10** 41 35N 74 29W
ürzburg, *Germany* **16 D5** 49 46N 9 55 E
ushan, *China* **34 G3** 34 43N 104 53 E
usuli Jiang = Ussuri →, *Asia* **30 A7** 48 27N 135 0 E
utai, *China* **34 E7** 38 40N 113 12 E
uting = Huimin, *China* **35 F9** 37 27N 117 28 E
utonghaolai, *China* **35 C11** 42 50N 120 5 E
utongqiao, *China* **32 D5** 29 22N 103 50 E
uwei, *China* **32 C5** 37 57N 102 34 E
uxi, *China* **33 C7** 31 33N 120 18 E
uxiang, *China* **34 F7** 36 49N 112 50 E
uyang, *China* **34 H7** 33 25N 113 35 E
uyi, *China* **34 F8** 37 46N 115 56 E
uyi Shan, *China* **33 D6** 27 0N 117 0 E
uyuan, *China* **34 D5** 41 2N 108 20 E
uzhai, *China* **34 E6** 38 54N 111 48 E
uzhi Shan, *China* **38 C7** 18 45N 109 45 E
uzhong, *China* **34 E4** 38 2N 106 12 E
uzhou, *China* **33 D6** 23 30N 111 18 E
yaaba Cr. →, *Australia* **62 B3** 16 27S 141 35 E
yalkatchem, *Australia* **61 F2** 31 8S 117 22 E
Wyalusing, *U.S.A.* **79 E8** 41 40N 76 16W
Wyandotte, *U.S.A.* **76 D4** 42 12N 83 9W
Wyandra, *Australia* **63 D4** 27 12S 145 56 E
Wyangala Res., *Australia* **63 E4** 33 54S 149 0 E
Wyara, L., *Australia* **63 D3** 28 42S 144 14 E
Wycheproof, *Australia* **63 F3** 36 5S 143 17 E
Wye →, *U.K.* **11 F5** 51 38N 2 40W
Wyemandoo, *Australia* **61 E2** 28 28S 118 29 E
Wymondham, *U.K.* **11 E9** 52 35N 1 7 E
Wymore, *U.S.A.* **80 E6** 40 7N 96 40W
Wyndham, *Australia* **60 C4** 15 33S 128 3 E
Wyndham, *N.Z.* **59 M2** 46 20S 168 51 E
Wynne, *U.S.A.* **81 H9** 35 14N 90 47W
Wynyard, *Australia* **62 G4** 41 5S 145 44 E
Wynyard, *Canada* **73 C8** 51 45N 104 10W
Wyola L., *Australia* **61 E5** 29 8S 130 17 E
Wyoming, *Canada* **78 D2** 42 57N 82 7W
Wyoming □, *U.S.A.* **82 E10** 43 0N 107 30W
Wyomissing, *U.S.A.* **79 F9** 40 20N 75 59W
Wyong, *Australia* **63 E5** 33 14S 151 24 E
Wytheville, *U.S.A.* **76 G5** 36 57N 81 5W

X

Xaçmaz, *Azerbaijan* **25 F8** 41 31N 48 42 E
Xai-Xai, *Mozam.* **57 D5** 25 6S 33 31 E
Xainza, *China* **32 C3** 30 58N 88 35 E
Xangongo, *Angola* **56 B2** 16 45S 15 5 E
Xankändi, *Azerbaijan* **25 G8** 39 52N 46 49 E
Xánthi, *Greece* **21 D11** 41 10N 24 58 E
Xanxerê, *Brazil* **95 B5** 26 53S 52 23W
Xapuri, *Brazil* **92 F5** 10 35S 68 35W
Xar Moron He →, *China* **35 C11** 43 25N 120 35 E
Xátiva, *Spain* **19 C5** 38 59N 0 32W
Xau, L., *Botswana* **56 C3** 21 15S 24 44 E
Xavantina, *Brazil* **95 A5** 21 15S 52 48W
Xenia, *U.S.A.* **76 F4** 39 41N 83 56W
Xeropotamos →, *Cyprus* **23 E11** 34 42N 32 33 E
Xhora, *S. Africa* **57 E4** 31 55S 28 38 E
Xhumo, *Botswana* **56 C3** 21 7S 24 35 E
Xi Jiang →, *China* **33 D6** 22 5N 113 20 E
Xi Xian, *China* **34 F6** 36 41N 110 58 E
Xia Xian, *China* **34 G6** 35 8N 111 12 E
Xiachengzi, *China* **35 B16** 44 40N 130 18 E
Xiaguan, *China* **32 D5** 25 32N 100 16 E
Xiajin, *China* **34 F9** 36 56N 116 0 E
Xiamen, *China* **33 D6** 24 25N 118 4 E
Xi'an, *China* **34 G5** 34 15N 109 0 E
Xian Xian, *China* **34 E9** 38 12N 116 6 E
Xiang Jiang →, *China* **33 D6** 28 55N 112 50 E
Xiangcheng, *Henan, China* **34 H8** 33 29N 114 52 E
Xiangcheng, *Henan, China* **34 H7** 33 50N 113 27 E
Xiangfan, *China* **33 C6** 32 2N 112 8 E
Xianggang = Hong Kong □, *China* **33 D6** 22 11N 114 14 E
Xianghuang Qi, *China* **34 C7** 42 2N 113 50 E
Xiangning, *China* **34 G6** 35 58N 110 50 E
Xiangquan, *China* **34 F7** 36 30N 113 1 E
Xiangquan He = Sutlej →, *Pakistan* **42 E4** 29 23N 71 3 E
Xiangshui, *China* **35 G10** 34 12N 119 33 E
Xiangtan, *China* **33 D6** 27 51N 112 54 E
Xianyang, *China* **34 G5** 34 20N 108 40 E
Xiao Hinggan Ling, *China* **33 B7** 49 0N 127 0 E
Xiao Xian, *China* **34 G9** 34 15N 116 55 E
Xiaoyi, *China* **34 F6** 37 8N 111 48 E
Xiawa, *China* **35 C11** 42 35N 120 38 E
Xiayi, *China* **34 G9** 34 15N 116 10 E
Xichang, *China* **32 D5** 27 51N 102 19 E
Xichuan, *China* **34 H6** 33 0N 111 30 E
Xieng Khouang, *Laos* **38 C4** 19 17N 103 25 E
Xifei He →, *China* **34 H9** 32 45N 116 40 E
Xifeng, *Gansu, China* **34 G4** 35 40N 107 40 E
Xifeng, *Liaoning, China* **35 C13** 42 42N 124 45 E
Xifengzhen = Xifeng, *China* **34 G4** 35 40N 107 40 E
Xigazê, *China* **32 D3** 29 5N 88 45 E
Xihe, *China* **34 G3** 34 2N 105 20 E
Xihua, *China* **34 H8** 33 45N 114 30 E
Xiliao He →, *China* **35 C12** 43 32N 123 35 E
Xin Xian = Xinzhou, *China* **34 E7** 38 22N 112 46 E
Xinavane, *Mozam.* **57 D5** 25 2S 32 47 E
Xinbin, *China* **35 D13** 41 40N 125 2 E
Xing Xian, *China* **34 E6** 38 27N 111 7 E
Xing'an, *China* **33 D6** 25 38N 110 40 E
Xingcheng, *China* **35 D11** 40 40N 120 45 E
Xinghe, *China* **34 D7** 40 55N 113 55 E
Xinghua, *China* **35 H10** 32 58N 119 48 E
Xinglong, *China* **35 D9** 40 25N 117 30 E
Xingping, *China* **34 G5** 34 20N 108 28 E
Xingtai, *China* **34 F8** 37 3N 114 32 E
Xingu →, *Brazil* **93 D8** 1 30S 51 53W
Xingyang, *China* **34 G7** 34 45N 112 52 E
Xinhe, *China* **34 F8** 37 30N 115 15 E
Xining, *China* **32 C5** 36 34N 101 40 E
Xinjiang, *China* **34 G6** 35 34N 111 11 E
Xinjiang Uygur Zizhiqu □, *China* **32 C3** 42 0N 86 0 E
Xinjin = Pulandian, *China* **35 E11** 39 25N 121 58 E
Xinkai He →, *China* **35 C12** 43 32N 123 35 E
Xinle, *China* **34 E8** 38 25N 114 40 E
Xinlitun, *China* **35 D12** 42 0N 122 8 E
Xinmin, *China* **35 D12** 41 59N 122 50 E
Xintai, *China* **35 G9** 35 55N 117 45 E
Xinxiang, *China* **34 G7** 35 18N 113 50 E
Xinzhan, *China* **35 C14** 43 50N 127 18 E
Xinzheng, *China* **34 G7** 34 20N 113 45 E
Xinzhou, *China* **34 E7** 38 22N 112 46 E
Xiong Xian, *China* **34 E9** 38 59N 116 8 E
Xiongyuecheng, *China* **35 D12** 40 12N 122 5 E
Xiping, *Henan, China* **34 H8** 33 22N 114 5 E
Xiping, *Henan, China* **34 H6** 33 25N 111 8 E
Xique-Xique, *Brazil* **93 F10** 10 50S 42 40W
Xisha Qundao = Paracel Is., *S. China Sea* **36 A4** 15 50N 112 0 E
Xiuyan, *China* **35 D12** 40 18N 123 11 E
Xixabangma Feng, *China* **41 E14** 28 20N 85 40 E
Xixia, *China* **34 H6** 33 25N 111 29 E
Xixiang, *China* **34 H4** 33 0N 107 44 E
Xiyang, *China* **34 F7** 37 38N 113 38 E
Xizang Zizhiqu □, *China* **32 C3** 32 0N 88 0 E
Xlendi, *Malta* **23 C1** 36 1N 14 12 E
Xuan Loc, *Vietnam* **39 G6** 10 56N 107 14 E
Xuanhua, *China* **34 D8** 40 40N 115 2 E
Xuchang, *China* **34 G7** 34 2N 113 48 E
Xun Xian, *China* **34 G8** 35 42N 114 33 E
Xunyang, *China* **34 H5** 32 48N 109 22 E
Xunyi, *China* **34 G5** 35 8N 108 20 E
Xúquer →, *Spain* **19 C5** 39 5N 0 10W
Xushui, *China* **34 E8** 39 2N 115 40 E
Xuyen Moc, *Vietnam* **39 G6** 10 34N 107 25 E
Xuzhou, *China* **35 G9** 34 18N 117 10 E
Xylophagou, *Cyprus* **23 E12** 34 54N 33 51 E

Y

Ya Xian, *China* **38 C7** 18 14N 109 29 E
Yaamba, *Australia* **62 C5** 23 8S 150 22 E
Yaapeet, *Australia* **63 F3** 35 45S 142 3 E
Yablonovy Ra. = Yablonovyy Khrebet, *Russia* **27 D12** 53 0N 114 0 E
Yablonovyy Khrebet, *Russia* **27 D12** 53 0N 114 0 E
Yabrai Shan, *China* **34 E2** 39 40N 103 0 E
Yabrūd, *Syria* **47 B5** 33 58N 36 39 E
Yacheng, *China* **33 E5** 18 22N 109 6 E
Yacuiba, *Bolivia* **94 A3** 22 0S 63 43W
Yacuma →, *Bolivia* **92 F5** 13 38S 65 23W
Yadgir, *India* **40 L10** 16 45N 77 5 E
Yadkin →, *U.S.A.* **77 H5** 35 29N 80 9W
Yaeyama-Rettō, *Japan* **31 M1** 24 30N 123 40 E
Yagodnoye, *Russia* **27 C15** 62 33N 149 40 E
Yahila, *Dem. Rep. of the Congo* **54 B1** 0 13N 24 28 E
Yahk, *Canada* **72 D5** 49 6N 116 10W
Yahuma, *Dem. Rep. of the Congo* **52 D4** 1 0N 23 10 E
Yaita, *Japan* **31 F9** 36 48N 139 56 E
Yaiza, *Canary Is.* **22 F6** 28 57N 13 46W
Yakima, *U.S.A.* **82 C3** 46 36N 120 31W
Yakima →, *U.S.A.* **82 C3** 47 0N 120 30W
Yakobi I., *U.S.A.* **72 B1** 58 0N 136 30W
Yakovlevka, *Russia* **30 B6** 44 26N 133 28 E
Yaku-Shima, *Japan* **31 J5** 30 20N 130 30 E
Yakumo, *Japan* **30 C10** 42 15N 140 16 E
Yakutat, *U.S.A.* **68 C6** 59 33N 139 44W
Yakutia = Sakha □, *Russia* **27 C14** 66 0N 130 0 E
Yakutsk, *Russia* **27 C13** 62 5N 129 50 E
Yala, *Thailand* **39 J3** 6 33N 101 18 E
Yale, *U.S.A.* **78 C2** 43 8N 82 48W
Yalgoo, *Australia* **61 E2** 28 16S 116 39 E
Yalinga, *C.A.R.* **52 C4** 6 33N 23 10 E
Yalkubul, Punta, *Mexico* **87 C7** 21 32N 88 37W
Yalleroi, *Australia* **62 C4** 24 3S 145 42 E
Yalobusha →, *U.S.A.* **81 J9** 33 33N 90 10W
Yalong Jiang →, *China* **32 D5** 26 40N 101 55 E
Yalova, *Turkey* **21 D13** 40 41N 29 15 E
Yalta, *Ukraine* **25 F5** 44 30N 34 10 E
Yalu Jiang →, *China* **35 E13** 40 0N 124 22 E
Yam Ha Melaḥ = Dead Sea, *Asia* **47 D4** 31 30N 35 30 E
Yam Kinneret, *Israel* **47 C4** 32 45N 35 35 E
Yamada, *Japan* **31 H5** 33 33N 130 49 E
Yamagata, *Japan* **30 E10** 38 15N 140 15 E
Yamagata □, *Japan* **30 E10** 38 30N 140 0 E
Yamaguchi, *Japan* **31 G5** 34 10N 131 32 E
Yamaguchi □, *Japan* **31 G5** 34 20N 131 40 E
Yamal, Poluostrov, *Russia* **26 B8** 71 0N 70 0 E
Yamal Pen. = Yamal, Poluostrov, *Russia* **26 B8** 71 0N 70 0 E
Yamanashi □, *Japan* **31 G9** 35 40N 138 40 E
Yamantau, Gora, *Russia* **24 D10** 54 15N 58 6 E
Yamba, *Australia* **63 D5** 29 26S 153 23 E
Yambarran Ra., *Australia* **60 C5** 15 10S 130 25 E
Yâmbiô, *Sudan* **51 H11** 4 35N 28 16 E
Yambol, *Bulgaria* **21 C12** 42 30N 26 30 E
Yamdena, *Indonesia* **37 F8** 7 45S 131 20 E
Yame, *Japan* **31 H5** 33 13N 130 35 E
Yamethin, *Burma* **41 J20** 20 29N 96 18 E
Yamma-Yamma, L., *Australia* **63 D3** 26 16S 141 20 E
Yamoussoukro, *Ivory C.* **50 G4** 6 49N 5 17W
Yampa →, *U.S.A.* **82 F9** 40 32N 108 59W
Yampi Sd., *Australia* **60 C3** 16 8S 123 38 E
Yampil, *Moldova* **17 D15** 48 15N 28 15 E
Yampol = Yampil, *Moldova* **17 D15** 48 15N 28 15 E
Yamuna →, *India* **43 G9** 25 30N 81 53 E
Yamunanagar, *India* **42 D7** 30 7N 77 17 E
Yamzho Yumco, *China* **32 D4** 28 48N 90 35 E
Yana →, *Russia* **27 B14** 71 30N 136 0 E
Yanagawa, *Japan* **31 H5** 33 10N 130 24 E
Yanai, *Japan* **31 H6** 33 58N 132 7 E
Yan'an, *China* **34 F5** 36 35N 109 26 E
Yanaul, *Russia* **24 C10** 56 25N 55 0 E
Yanbu 'al Baḩr, *Si. Arabia* **46 C2** 24 0N 38 5 E
Yanchang, *China* **34 F6** 36 43N 110 1 E
Yancheng, *Henan, China* **34 H8** 33 35N 114 0 E
Yancheng, *Jiangsu, China* **35 H11** 33 23N 120 8 E
Yanchep Beach, *Australia* **61 F2** 31 33S 115 37 E
Yanchi, *China* **34 F4** 37 48N 107 20 E
Yanchuan, *China* **34 F6** 36 51N 110 10 E
Yanco, *Australia* **63 E4** 34 38S 146 27 E
Yanco Cr. →, *Australia* **63 F4** 35 14S 145 35 E
Yandoon, *Burma* **41 L19** 17 0N 95 40 E
Yang Xian, *China* **34 H4** 33 15N 107 30 E
Yangambi, *Dem. Rep. of the Congo* **54 B1** 0 47N 24 20 E
Yangcheng, *China* **34 G7** 35 28N 112 22 E
Yangch'ü = Taiyuan, *China* **34 F7** 37 52N 112 33 E
Yanggao, *China* **34 D7** 40 21N 113 55 E
Yanggu, *China* **34 F8** 36 8N 115 43 E
Yangliuqing, *China* **35 E9** 39 2N 117 5 E
Yangon = Rangoon, *Burma* **41 L20** 16 45N 96 20 E
Yangpingguan, *China* **34 H4** 32 58N 106 5 E
Yangquan, *China* **34 F7** 37 58N 113 31 E
Yangtse = Chang Jiang →, *China* **33 C7** 31 48N 121 10 E
Yangtze Kiang = Chang Jiang →, *China* **33 C7** 31 48N 121 10 E
Yangyang, *S. Korea* **35 E15** 38 4N 128 38 E
Yangyuan, *China* **34 D8** 40 1N 114 10 E
Yangzhou, *China* **33 C6** 32 21N 119 26 E
Yanji, *China* **35 C15** 42 59N 129 30 E
Yankton, *U.S.A.* **80 D6** 42 53N 97 23W
Yanonge, *Dem. Rep. of the Congo* **54 B1** 0 35N 24 38 E
Yanqi, *China* **32 B3** 42 5N 86 35 E
Yanqing, *China* **34 D8** 40 30N 115 58 E
Yanshan, *China* **35 E9** 38 4N 117 22 E
Yanshou, *China* **35 B15** 45 28N 128 22 E
Yantabulla, *Australia* **63 D4** 29 21S 145 0 E
Yantai, *China* **35 F11** 37 34N 121 22 E
Yanzhou, *China* **34 G9** 35 35N 116 49 E
Yao Xian, *China* **34 G5** 34 55N 108 59 E
Yao Yai, Ko, *Thailand* **39 J2** 8 0N 98 35 E
Yaoundé, *Cameroon* **52 D2** 3 50N 11 35 E
Yaowan, *China* **35 G10** 34 15N 118 3 E
Yap I., *Pac. Oc.* **64 G5** 9 30N 138 10 E
Yapen, *Indonesia* **37 E9** 1 50S 136 0 E
Yapen, Selat, *Indonesia* **37 E9** 1 20S 136 10 E
Yapero, *Indonesia* **37 E9** 4 59S 137 11 E
Yappar →, *Australia* **62 B3** 18 22S 141 16 E
Yaqui →, *Mexico* **86 B2** 27 37N 110 39W
Yar-Sale, *Russia* **26 C8** 66 50N 70 50 E
Yaraka, *Australia* **62 C3** 24 53S 144 3 E
Yaransk, *Russia* **24 C8** 57 22N 47 49 E
Yare →, *U.K.* **11 E9** 52 35N 1 38 E
Yaremcha, *Ukraine* **17 D13** 48 27N 24 33 E
Yarensk, *Russia* **24 B8** 62 11N 49 15 E
Yarí →, *Colombia* **92 D4** 0 20S 72 20W
Yarkand = Shache, *China* **32 C2** 38 20N 77 10 E
Yarker, *Canada* **79 B8** 44 23N 76 46W
Yarkhun →, *Pakistan* **43 A5** 36 17N 72 30 E
Yarmouth, *Canada* **71 D6** 43 50N 66 7W
Yarmūk →, *Syria* **47 C4** 32 42N 35 40 E
Yaroslavl, *Russia* **24 C6** 57 35N 39 55 E
Yarqa, W. →, *Egypt* **47 F2** 30 0N 33 49 E
Yarra Yarra Lakes, *Australia* **61 E2** 29 40S 115 45 E
Yarram, *Australia* **63 F4** 38 29S 146 39 E
Yarraman, *Australia* **63 D5** 26 50S 152 0 E
Yarras, *Australia* **63 E5** 31 25S 152 20 E
Yartsevo, *Russia* **27 C10** 60 20N 90 0 E
Yarumal, *Colombia* **92 B3** 6 58N 75 24W
Yasawa Group, *Fiji* **59 C7** 17 0S 177 23 E
Yaselda, *Belarus* **17 B14** 52 7N 26 28 E
Yasin, *Pakistan* **43 A5** 36 24N 73 23 E
Yasinski, L., *Canada* **70 B4** 53 16N 77 35W
Yasinya, *Ukraine* **17 D13** 48 16N 24 21 E
Yasothon, *Thailand* **38 E5** 15 50N 104 10 E
Yass, *Australia* **63 E4** 34 49S 148 54 E
Yatağan, *Turkey* **21 F13** 37 20N 28 10 E
Yates Center, *U.S.A.* **81 G7** 37 53N 95 44W
Yathkyed L., *Canada* **73 A9** 62 40N 98 0W
Yatsushiro, *Japan* **31 H5** 32 30N 130 40 E
Yatta Plateau, *Kenya* **54 C4** 2 0S 38 0 E
Yavari →, *Peru* **92 D4** 4 21S 70 2W
Yávaros, *Mexico* **86 B3** 26 42N 109 31W
Yavatmal, *India* **40 J11** 20 20N 78 15 E
Yavne, *Israel* **47 D3** 31 52N 34 45 E
Yavoriv, *Ukraine* **17 D12** 49 55N 23 20 E
Yavorov = Yavoriv, *Ukraine* **17 D12** 49 55N 23 20 E
Yawatahama, *Japan* **31 H6** 33 27N 132 24 E
Yazd, *Iran* **45 D7** 31 55N 54 27 E
Yazd □, *Iran* **45 D7** 32 0N 55 0 E
Yazd-e Khvāst, *Iran* **45 D7** 31 31N 52 7 E
Yazman, *Pakistan* **42 E4** 29 8N 71 45 E
Yazoo →, *U.S.A.* **81 J9** 32 22N 90 54W
Yazoo City, *U.S.A.* **81 J9** 32 51N 90 25W
Yding Skovhøj, *Denmark* **9 J13** 55 59N 9 46 E
Ye Xian = Laizhou, *China* **35 F10** 37 8N 119 57 E
Ye Xian, *China* **34 H7** 33 35N 113 25 E
Yebyu, *Burma* **38 E2** 14 15N 98 13 E
Yechŏn, *S. Korea* **35 F15** 36 39N 128 27 E
Yecla, *Spain* **19 C5** 38 35N 1 5W
Yécora, *Mexico* **86 B3** 28 20N 108 58W
Yedintsy = Edineţ, *Moldova* **17 D14** 48 9N 27 18 E
Yegros, *Paraguay* **94 B4** 26 20S 56 25W
Yehuda, Midbar, *Israel* **47 D4** 31 35N 35 15 E
Yei, *Sudan* **51 H12** 4 9N 30 40 E
Yekaterinburg, *Russia* **26 D7** 56 50N 60 30 E
Yekaterinodar = Krasnodar, *Russia* **25 E6** 45 5N 39 0 E
Yelarbon, *Australia* **63 D5** 28 33S 150 38 E
Yelets, *Russia* **24 D6** 52 40N 38 30 E
Yelizavetgrad = Kirovohrad, *Ukraine* **25 E5** 48 35N 32 20 E
Yell, *U.K.* **12 A7** 60 35N 1 5W
Yell Sd., *U.K.* **12 A7** 60 33N 1 15W
Yellow Sea, *China* **35 G12** 35 0N 123 0 E
Yellowhead Pass, *Canada* **72 C5** 52 53N 118 25W
Yellowknife, *Canada* **72 A6** 62 27N 114 29W
Yellowknife →, *Canada* **72 A6** 62 31N 114 19W
Yellowstone →, *U.S.A.* **80 B3** 47 59N 103 59W
Yellowstone L., *U.S.A.* **82 D8** 44 27N 110 22W
Yellowstone National Park, *U.S.A.* **82 D9** 44 40N 110 30W
Yelsk, *Belarus* **17 C15** 51 50N 29 10 E
Yemen ■, *Asia* **46 E3** 15 0N 44 0 E
Yenangyaung, *Burma* **41 J19** 20 30N 95 0 E
Yenbo = Yanbu 'al Baḩr, *Si. Arabia* **46 C2** 24 0N 38 5 E
Yenda, *Australia* **63 E4** 34 13S 146 14 E
Yenice, *Turkey* **21 E12** 39 55N 27 17 E
Yenisey →, *Russia* **26 B9** 71 50N 82 40 E
Yeniseysk, *Russia* **27 D10** 58 27N 92 13 E
Yeniseyskiy Zaliv, *Russia* **26 B9** 72 20N 81 0 E
Yennádhi, *Greece* **23 C9** 36 2N 27 56 E
Yenyuka, *Russia* **27 D13** 57 57N 121 15 E
Yeo →, *U.K.* **11 G5** 51 2N 2 49W
Yeo, L., *Australia* **61 E3** 28 0S 124 30 E
Yeo I., *Canada* **78 A3** 45 24N 81 48W
Yeola, *India* **40 J9** 20 2N 74 30 E
Yeoryioúpolis, *Greece* **23 D6** 35 20N 24 15 E
Yeovil, *U.K.* **11 G5** 50 57N 2 38W
Yeppoon, *Australia* **62 C5** 23 5S 150 47 E
Yerbent, *Turkmenistan* **26 F6** 39 30N 58 50 E
Yerbogachen, *Russia* **27 C11** 61 16N 108 0 E
Yerevan, *Armenia* **25 F7** 40 10N 44 31 E
Yerington, *U.S.A.* **82 G4** 38 59N 119 10W
Yermak, *Kazakstan* **26 D8** 52 2N 76 55 E
Yermo, *U.S.A.* **85 L10** 34 54N 116 50W
Yerólakkos, *Cyprus* **23 D12** 35 11N 33 15 E
Yeropol, *Russia* **27 C17** 65 15N 168 40 E
Yeropótamos →, *Greece* **23 D6** 35 3N 24 50 E
Yeroskipos, *Cyprus* **23 E11** 34 46N 32 28 E
Yershov, *Russia* **25 D8** 51 23N 48 27 E
Yerushalayim = Jerusalem, *Israel* **47 D4** 31 47N 35 10 E
Yes Tor, *U.K.* **11 G4** 50 41N 4 0W
Yesan, *S. Korea* **35 F14** 36 41N 126 51 E
Yeso, *U.S.A.* **81 H2** 34 26N 104 37W
Yessey, *Russia* **27 C11** 68 29N 102 10 E
Yetman, *Australia* **63 D5** 28 56S 150 48 E
Yeu, Î. d', *France* **18 C2** 46 42N 2 20W
Yevpatoriya, *Ukraine* **25 E5** 45 15N 33 20 E
Yeysk, *Russia* **25 E6** 46 40N 38 12 E

Yezd = Yazd, *Iran* **45 D7** 31 55N 54 27 E
Yhati, *Paraguay* **94 B4** 25 45S 56 35W
Yhú, *Paraguay* **95 B4** 25 0S 56 0W
Yi →, *Uruguay* **94 C4** 33 7S 57 8W
Yi 'Allaq, G., *Egypt* **47 E2** 30 22N 33 32 E
Yi He →, *China* **35 G10** 34 10N 118 8 E
Yi Xian, *Hebei, China* **34 E8** 39 20N 115 30 E
Yi Xian, *Liaoning, China* **35 D11** 41 30N 121 22 E
Yialiás →, *Cyprus* **23 D12** 35 9N 33 44 E
Yialousa, *Cyprus* **23 D13** 35 32N 34 10 E
Yianisádhes, *Greece* **23 D8** 35 20N 26 10 E
Yiannitsa, *Greece* **21 D10** 40 46N 22 24 E
Yibin, *China* **32 D5** 28 45N 104 32 E
Yichang, *China* **33 C6** 30 40N 111 20 E
Yicheng, *China* **34 G6** 35 42N 111 40 E
Yichuan, *China* **34 F6** 36 2N 110 10 E
Yichun, *China* **33 B7** 47 44N 128 52 E
Yidu, *China* **35 F10** 36 43N 118 28 E
Yijun, *China* **34 G5** 35 28N 109 8 E
Yıldız Dağları, *Turkey* **21 D12** 41 48N 27 36 E
Yilehuli Shan, *China* **33 A7** 51 20N 124 20 E
Yimianpo, *China* **35 B15** 45 7N 128 2 E
Yinchuan, *China* **34 E4** 38 30N 106 15 E
Yindarlgooda, L., *Australia* **61 F3** 30 40S 121 52 E
Ying He →, *China* **34 H9** 32 30N 116 30 E
Ying Xian, *China* **34 E7** 39 32N 113 10 E
Yingkou, *China* **35 D12** 40 37N 122 18 E
Yining, *China* **26 E9** 43 58N 81 10 E
Yinmabin, *Burma* **41 H19** 22 10N 94 55 E
Yiofiros →, *Greece* **23 D7** 35 20N 25 6 E
Yirga Alem, *Ethiopia* **46 F2** 6 48N 38 22 E
Yirrkala, *Australia* **62 A2** 12 14S 136 56 E
Yishan, *China* **32 D5** 24 28N 108 38 E
Yishui, *China* **35 G10** 35 47N 118 30 E
Yíthion, *Greece* **21 F10** 36 46N 22 34 E
Yitiaoshan, *China* **34 F3** 37 5N 104 2 E
Yitong, *China* **35 C13** 43 13N 125 20 E
Yiyang, *Henan, China* **34 G7** 34 27N 112 10 E
Yiyang, *Hunan, China* **33 D6** 28 35N 112 18 E
Yli-Kitka, *Finland* **8 C23** 66 8N 28 30 E
Ylitornio, *Finland* **8 C20** 66 19N 23 39 E
Ylivieska, *Finland* **8 D21** 64 4N 24 28 E
Yoakum, *U.S.A.* **81 L6** 29 17N 97 9W
Yog Pt., *Phil.* **37 B6** 14 6N 124 12 E
Yogyakarta, *Indonesia* **37 G14** 7 49S 110 22 E
Yoho Nat. Park, *Canada* **72 C5** 51 25N 116 30W
Yojoa, L. de, *Honduras* **88 D2** 14 53N 88 0W
Yŏju, *S. Korea* **35 F14** 37 20N 127 35 E
Yokadouma, *Cameroon* **52 D2** 3 26N 14 55 E
Yokkaichi, *Japan* **31 G8** 34 55N 136 38 E
Yoko, *Cameroon* **52 C2** 5 32N 12 20 E
Yokohama, *Japan* **31 G9** 35 27N 139 28 E
Yokosuka, *Japan* **31 G9** 35 20N 139 40 E
Yokote, *Japan* **30 E10** 39 20N 140 30 E
Yola, *Nigeria* **51 G8** 9 10N 12 29 E
Yolaina, Cordillera de, *Nic.* **88 D3** 11 30N 84 0W
Yoloten, *Turkmenistan* **45 B9** 37 18N 62 21 E
Yom →, *Thailand* **36 A2** 15 35N 100 1 E
Yonago, *Japan* **31 G6** 35 25N 133 19 E
Yonaguni-Jima, *Japan* **31 M1** 24 27N 123 0 E
Yŏnan, *N. Korea* **35 F14** 37 55N 126 11 E
Yonezawa, *Japan* **30 F10** 37 57N 140 4 E
Yong Peng, *Malaysia* **39 M4** 2 0N 103 3 E
Yong Sata, *Thailand* **39 J2** 7 8N 99 41 E
Yongamp'o, *N. Korea* **35 E13** 39 56N 124 23 E
Yongcheng, *China* **34 H9** 33 55N 116 20 E
Yŏngch'ŏn, *S. Korea* **35 G15** 35 58N 128 56 E
Yongdeng, *China* **34 F2** 36 38N 103 25 E
Yŏngdŏk, *S. Korea* **35 F15** 36 24N 129 22 E
Yŏngdŭngpo, *S. Korea* **35 F14** 37 31N 126 54 E
Yonghe, *China* **34 F6** 36 46N 110 38 E
Yŏnghŭng, *N. Korea* **35 E14** 39 31N 127 18 E
Yongji, *China* **34 G6** 34 52N 110 28 E
Yŏngju, *S. Korea* **35 F15** 36 50N 128 40 E
Yongnian, *China* **34 F8** 36 47N 114 29 E
Yongning, *China* **34 E4** 38 15N 106 14 E
Yongqing, *China* **34 E9** 39 25N 116 28 E
Yŏngwŏl, *S. Korea* **35 F15** 37 11N 128 28 E
Yonibana, *S. Leone* **50 G3** 8 30N 12 19W
Yonkers, *U.S.A.* **79 F11** 40 56N 73 54W
Yonne →, *France* **18 B5** 48 23N 2 58 E
York, *Australia* **61 F2** 31 52S 116 47 E
York, *U.K.* **10 D6** 53 58N 1 6W
York, *Nebr., U.S.A.* **80 E6** 40 52N 97 36W
York, *Pa., U.S.A.* **76 F7** 39 58N 76 44W
York, C., *Australia* **62 A3** 10 42S 142 31 E
York, City of □, *U.K.* **10 D6** 53 58N 1 6W
York, Kap, *Greenland* **4 B4** 75 55N 66 25W
York, Vale of, *U.K.* **10 C6** 54 15N 1 25W
York Haven, *U.S.A.* **78 F8** 40 7N 76 46W
York Sd., *Australia* **60 C4** 15 0S 125 5 E
Yorke Pen., *Australia* **63 E2** 34 50S 137 40 E
Yorketown, *Australia* **63 F2** 35 0S 137 33 E
Yorkshire Wolds, *U.K.* **10 C7** 54 8N 0 31W
Yorkton, *Canada* **73 C8** 51 11N 102 28W
Yorkville, *U.S.A.* **84 G3** 38 52N 123 13W
Yoro, *Honduras* **88 C2** 15 9N 87 7W
Yoron-Jima, *Japan* **31 L4** 27 2N 128 26 E
Yos Sudarso, Pulau = Dolak, Pulau, *Indonesia* **37 F9** 8 0S 138 30 E
Yosemite National Park, *U.S.A.* **84 H7** 37 45N 119 40W
Yosemite Village, *U.S.A.* **84 H7** 37 45N 119 35W
Yoshkar Ola, *Russia* **24 C8** 56 38N 47 55 E
Yŏsu, *S. Korea* **35 G14** 34 47N 127 45 E
Yotvata, *Israel* **47 F4** 29 55N 35 2 E
Youbou, *Canada* **84 B2** 48 53N 124 13W
Youghal, *Ireland* **13 E4** 51 56N 7 52W
Youghal B., *Ireland* **13 E4** 51 55N 7 49W
Young, *Australia* **63 E4** 34 19S 148 18 E
Young, *Canada* **73 C7** 51 47N 105 45W
Young, *Uruguay* **94 C4** 32 44S 57 36W
Younghusband, L., *Australia* **63 E2** 30 50S 136 5 E
Younghusband Pen., *Australia* **63 F2** 36 0S 139 25 E
Youngstown, *Canada* **73 C6** 51 35N 111 10W
Youngstown, *N.Y., U.S.A.* **78 C5** 43 15N 79 3W
Youngstown, *Ohio, U.S.A.* **78 E4** 41 6N 80 39W
Youngsville, *U.S.A.* **78 E5** 41 51N 79 19W
Youngwood, *U.S.A.* **78 F5** 40 14N 79 34W
Youyu, *China* **34 D7** 40 10N 112 20 E
Yozgat, *Turkey* **25 G5** 39 51N 34 47 E
Ypané →, *Paraguay* **94 A4** 23 29S 57 19W
Ypres = Ieper, *Belgium* **15 D2** 50 51N 2 53 E
Yreka, *U.S.A.* **82 F2** 41 44N 122 38W
Ystad, *Sweden* **9 J15** 55 26N 13 50 E
Ysyk-Köl, *Kyrgyzstan* **28 E11** 42 26N 76 12 E
Ysyk-Köl, Ozero, *Kyrgyzstan* **26 E8** 42 25N 77 15 E
Ythan →, *U.K.* **12 D7** 57 19N 1 59W
Ytyk Kyuyel, *Russia* **27 C14** 62 30N 133 45 E
Yu Jiang →, *China* **33 D6** 23 22N 110 3 E
Yu Xian = Yuzhou, *China* **34 G7** 34 10N 113 28 E
Yu Xian, *Hebei, China* **34 E8** 39 50N 114 35 E
Yu Xian, *Shanxi, China* **34 E7** 38 5N 113 20 E
Yuan Jiang →, *China* **33 D6** 28 55N 111 50 E
Yuanqu, *China* **34 G6** 35 18N 111 40 E
Yuanyang, *China* **34 G7** 35 3N 113 58 E
Yuba →, *U.S.A.* **84 F5** 39 8N 121 36W
Yuba City, *U.S.A.* **84 F5** 39 8N 121 37W
Yūbari, *Japan* **30 C10** 43 4N 141 59 E
Yūbetsu, *Japan* **30 B11** 44 13N 143 50 E
Yucatán □, *Mexico* **87 C7** 21 30N 86 30W
Yucatán, Canal de, *Caribbean* **88 B2** 22 0N 86 30W
Yucatán, Península de, *Mexico* **66 H11** 19 30N 89 0W
Yucatán Basin, *Cent. Amer.* **66 H11** 19 0N 86 0W
Yucatan Str. = Yucatán, Canal de, *Caribbean* **88 B2** 22 0N 86 30W
Yucca, *U.S.A.* **85 L12** 34 52N 114 9W
Yucca Valley, *U.S.A.* **85 L10** 34 8N 116 27W
Yucheng, *China* **34 F9** 36 55N 116 32 E
Yuci, *China* **34 F7** 37 42N 112 46 E
Yuendumu, *Australia* **60 D5** 22 16S 131 49 E
Yugoslavia ■, *Europe* **21 B9** 43 20N 20 0 E
Yukon →, *U.S.A.* **68 B3** 62 32N 163 54W
Yukon Territory □, *Canada* **68 B6** 63 0N 135 0W
Yukta, *Russia* **27 C11** 63 26N 105 42 E
Yukuhashi, *Japan* **31 H5** 33 44N 130 59 E
Yulara, *Australia* **61 E5** 25 10S 130 55 E
Yule →, *Australia* **60 D2** 20 41S 118 17 E
Yuleba, *Australia* **63 D4** 26 37S 149 24 E
Yulin, *Shaanxi, China* **34 E5** 38 20N 109 30 E
Yulin, *Shensi, China* **38 C7** 38 15N 109 30 E
Yuma, *Ariz., U.S.A.* **85 N12** 32 43N 114 37W
Yuma, *Colo., U.S.A.* **80 E3** 40 8N 102 43W
Yuma, B. de, *Dom. Rep.* **89 C6** 18 20N 68 35W
Yumbe, *Uganda* **54 B3** 3 28N 31 15 E
Yumbi, *Dem. Rep. of the Congo* **54 C2** 1 12S 26 15 E
Yumen, *China* **32 C4** 39 50N 97 30 E
Yun Ho →, *China* **35 E9** 39 10N 117 10 E
Yuna, *Australia* **61 E2** 28 20S 115 0 E
Yuncheng, *Henan, China* **34 G8** 35 36N 115 57 E
Yuncheng, *Shanxi, China* **34 G6** 35 2N 111 0 E
Yungas, *Bolivia* **92 G5** 17 0S 66 0W
Yungay, *Chile* **94 D1** 37 10S 72 5W
Yunnan □, *China* **32 D5** 25 0N 102 0 E
Yunta, *Australia* **63 E2** 32 34S 139 36 E
Yunxi, *China* **34 H6** 33 0N 110 22 E
Yupyongdong, *N. Korea* **35 D15** 41 49N 128 53 E
Yurga, *Russia* **26 D9** 55 42N 84 51 E
Yurimaguas, *Peru* **92 E3** 5 55S 76 7W
Yuryung Kaya, *Russia* **27 B12** 72 48N 113 23 E
Yuscarán, *Honduras* **88 D2** 13 58N 86 45W
Yushe, *China* **34 F7** 37 4N 112 58 E
Yushu, *Jilin, China* **35 B14** 44 43N 126 38 E
Yushu, *Qinghai, China* **32 C4** 33 5N 96 55 E
Yutai, *China* **34 G9** 35 0N 116 45 E
Yutian, *China* **35 E9** 39 53N 117 45 E
Yuxarı Qarabağ = Nagorno-Karabakh, *Azerbaijan* **25 F8** 39 55N 46 45 E
Yuxi, *China* **32 D5** 24 30N 102 35 E
Yuzawa, *Japan* **30 E10** 39 10N 140 30 E
Yuzhno-Sakhalinsk, *Russia* **27 E15** 46 58N 142 45 E
Yuzhou, *China* **34 G7** 34 10N 113 28 E
Yvetot, *France* **18 B4** 49 37N 0 44 E

Z

Zaanstad, *Neths.* **15 B4** 52 27N 4 50 E
Zāb al Kabīr →, *Iraq* **44 C4** 36 1N 43 24 E
Zāb aş Şagīr →, *Iraq* **44 C4** 35 17N 43 29 E
Zabaykalsk, *Russia* **27 E12** 49 40N 117 25 E
Zābol, *Iran* **45 D9** 31 0N 61 32 E
Zābolī, *Iran* **45 E9** 27 10N 61 35 E
Zabrze, *Poland* **17 C10** 50 18N 18 50 E
Zacapa, *Guatemala* **88 D2** 14 59N 89 31W
Zacapu, *Mexico* **86 D4** 19 50N 101 43W
Zacatecas, *Mexico* **86 C4** 22 49N 102 34W
Zacatecas □, *Mexico* **86 C4** 23 30N 103 0W
Zacatecoluca, *El Salv.* **88 D2** 13 29N 88 51W
Zachary, *U.S.A.* **81 K9** 30 39N 91 9W
Zacoalco, *Mexico* **86 C4** 20 14N 103 33W
Zacualtipán, *Mexico* **87 C5** 20 39N 98 36W
Zadar, *Croatia* **16 F8** 44 8N 15 14 E
Zadetkyi Kyun, *Burma* **39 H2** 10 0N 98 25 E
Zafarqand, *Iran* **45 C7** 33 11N 52 29 E
Zafra, *Spain* **19 C2** 38 26N 6 30W
Żagań, *Poland* **16 C8** 51 39N 15 22 E
Zagaoua, *Chad* **51 E10** 15 30N 22 24 E
Zagazig, *Egypt* **51 B12** 30 40N 31 30 E
Zāgheh, *Iran* **45 C6** 33 30N 48 42 E
Zagorsk = Sergiyev Posad, *Russia* **24 C6** 56 20N 38 10 E
Zagreb, *Croatia* **16 F9** 45 50N 15 58 E
Zāgros, Kūhhā-ye, *Iran* **45 C6** 33 45N 48 5 E
Zagros Mts. = Zāgros, Kūhhā-ye, *Iran* **45 C6** 33 45N 48 5 E
Zāhedān, *Fārs, Iran* **45 D7** 28 46N 53 52 E
Zāhedān, *Sīstān va Balūchestān, Iran* **45 D9** 29 30N 60 50 E
Zahlah, *Lebanon* **47 B4** 33 52N 35 50 E
Zaïre = Congo →, *Africa* **52 F2** 6 4S 12 24 E
Zaječar, *Serbia, Yug.* **21 C10** 43 53N 22 18 E
Zakamensk, *Russia* **27 D11** 50 23N 103 17 E
Zakhodnaya Dzvina = Daugava →, *Latvia* **9 H21** 57 4N 24 3 E
Zākhū, *Iraq* **44 B4** 37 10N 42 50 E
Zákinthos, *Greece* **21 F9** 37 47N 20 57 E
Zakopane, *Poland* **17 D10** 49 18N 19 57 E
Zákros, *Greece* **23 D8** 35 6N 26 10 E
Zalaegerszeg, *Hungary* **17 E9** 46 53N 16 47 E
Zalău, *Romania* **17 E12** 47 12N 23 3 E
Zaleshchiki = Zalishchyky, *Ukraine* **17 D13** 48 45N 25 45 E
Zalew Wiślany, *Poland* **17 A10** 54 20N 19 50 E
Zalingei, *Sudan* **51 F10** 12 51N 23 29 E
Zalishchyky, *Ukraine* **17 D13** 48 45N 25 45 E
Zama L., *Canada* **72 B5** 58 45N 119 5W
Zambeke, *Dem. Rep. of the Congo* **54 B2** 2 8N 25 17 E
Zambeze →, *Africa* **55 F4** 18 35S 36 20 E
Zambezi = Zambeze →, *Africa* **55 F4** 18 35S 36 20 E
Zambezi, *Zambia* **53 G4** 13 30S 23 15 E
Zambezia □, *Mozam.* **55 F4** 16 15S 37 30 E
Zambia ■, *Africa* **55 F2** 15 0S 28 0 E
Zamboanga, *Phil.* **37 C6** 6 59N 122 3 E
Zamora, *Mexico* **86 D4** 20 0N 102 21W
Zamora, *Spain* **19 B3** 41 30N 5 45W
Zamość, *Poland* **17 C12** 50 43N 23 15 E
Zandvoort, *Neths.* **15 B4** 52 22N 4 32 E
Zanesville, *U.S.A.* **78 G2** 39 56N 82 1W
Zangābād, *Iran* **44 B5** 38 26N 46 44 E
Zangue →, *Mozam.* **55 F4** 17 50S 35 21 E
Zanjān, *Iran* **45 B6** 36 40N 48 35 E
Zanjān □, *Iran* **45 B6** 37 20N 49 30 E
Zanjān →, *Iran* **45 B6** 37 8N 47 47 E
Zante = Zákinthos, *Greece* **21 F9** 37 47N 20 57 E
Zanthus, *Australia* **61 F3** 31 2S 123 34 E
Zanzibar, *Tanzania* **54 D4** 6 12S 39 12 E
Zaouiet El-Kala = Bordj Omar Driss, *Algeria* **50 C7** 28 10N 6 40 E
Zaouiet Reggane, *Algeria* **50 C6** 26 32N 0 3 E
Zaozhuang, *China* **35 G9** 34 50N 117 35 E
Zap Suyu = Zāb al Kabīr →, *Iraq* **44 C4** 36 1N 43 24 E
Zapadnaya Dvina = Daugava →, *Latvia* **9 H21** 57 4N 24 3 E
Západné Beskydy, *Europe* **17 D10** 49 30N 19 0 E
Zapala, *Argentina* **96 D2** 39 0S 70 5W
Zapaleri, Cerro, *Bolivia* **94 A2** 22 49S 67 11W
Zapata, *U.S.A.* **81 M5** 26 55N 99 16W
Zapolyarnyy, *Russia* **24 A5** 69 26N 30 51 E
Zaporizhzhya, *Ukraine* **25 E6** 47 50N 35 10 E
Zaporozhye = Zaporizhzhya, *Ukraine* **25 E6** 47 50N 35 10 E
Zara, *Turkey* **44 B3** 39 58N 37 43 E
Zaragoza, *Coahuila, Mexico* **86 B4** 28 30N 101 0W
Zaragoza, *Nuevo León, Mexico* **87 C5** 24 0N 99 46W
Zaragoza, *Spain* **19 B5** 41 39N 0 53W
Zarand, *Kermān, Iran* **45 D8** 30 46N 56 34 E
Zarand, *Markazī, Iran* **45 C6** 35 18N 50 25 E
Zaranj, *Afghan.* **40 D2** 30 55N 61 55 E
Zarasai, *Lithuania* **9 J22** 55 40N 26 20 E
Zarate, *Argentina* **94 C4** 34 7S 59 0W
Zard, Kūh-e, *Iran* **45 C6** 32 22N 50 4 E
Zāreh, *Iran* **45 C6** 35 7N 49 9 E
Zaria, *Nigeria* **50 F7** 11 0N 7 40 E
Zarneh, *Iran* **44 C5** 33 55N 46 10 E
Zarós, *Greece* **23 D6** 35 8N 24 54 E
Zarqā', Nahr az →, *Jordan* **47 C4** 32 10N 35 37 E
Zarrīn, *Iran* **45 C7** 32 46N 54 37 E
Zaruma, *Ecuador* **92 D3** 3 40S 79 38W
Żary, *Poland* **16 C8** 51 37N 15 10 E
Zarzis, *Tunisia* **51 B8** 33 31N 11 2 E
Zaskar →, *India* **43 B7** 34 13N 77 20 E
Zaskar Mts., *India* **43 C7** 33 15N 77 30 E
Zastron, *S. Africa* **56 E4** 30 18S 27 7 E
Zavāreh, *Iran* **45 C7** 33 29N 52 28 E
Zavitinsk, *Russia* **27 D13** 50 10N 129 20 E
Zavodovski, I., *Antarctica* **5 B1** 56 0S 27 45W
Zawiercie, *Poland* **17 C10** 50 30N 19 24 E
Zāwiyat al Bayḑā, *Libya* **51 B10** 32 50N 21 44 E
Zāyā, *Iraq* **44 C5** 33 33N 44 13 E
Zāyandeh →, *Iran* **45 C7** 32 35N 52 0 E
Zaysan, *Kazakstan* **26 E9** 47 28N 84 52 E
Zaysan, Oz., *Kazakstan* **26 E9** 48 0N 83 0 E
Zayü, *China* **32 D4** 28 48N 97 27 E
Zbarazh, *Ukraine* **17 D13** 49 43N 25 44 E
Zdolbuniv, *Ukraine* **17 C14** 50 30N 26 15 E
Zduńska Wola, *Poland* **17 C10** 51 37N 18 59 E
Zeballos, *Canada* **72 D3** 49 59N 126 50W
Zebediela, *S. Africa* **57 C4** 24 20S 29 17 E
Zeebrugge, *Belgium* **15 C3** 51 19N 3 12 E
Zeehan, *Australia* **62 G4** 41 52S 145 25 E
Zeeland □, *Neths.* **15 C3** 51 30N 3 50 E
Zeerust, *S. Africa* **56 D4** 25 31S 26 4 E
Zefat, *Israel* **47 C4** 32 58N 35 29 E
Zeil, Mt., *Australia* **60 D5** 23 30S 132 23 E
Zeila, *Somali Rep.* **46 E3** 11 21N 43 30 E
Zeist, *Neths.* **15 B5** 52 5N 5 15 E
Zeitz, *Germany* **16 C7** 51 2N 12 7 E
Zelenograd, *Russia* **24 C6** 56 1N 37 12 E
Zelenogradsk, *Russia* **9 J19** 54 53N 20 29 E
Zelienople, *U.S.A.* **78 F4** 40 48N 80 8W
Zémio, *C.A.R.* **54 A2** 5 2N 25 5 E
Zemun, *Serbia, Yug.* **21 B9** 44 51N 20 25 E
Zenica, *Bos.-H.* **21 B7** 44 10N 17 57 E
Žepče, *Bos.-H.* **21 B8** 44 28N 18 2 E
Zevenaar, *Neths.* **15 C6** 51 56N 6 5 E
Zeya, *Russia* **27 D13** 53 48N 127 14 E
Zeya →, *Russia* **27 D13** 51 42N 128 53 E
Zêzere →, *Portugal* **19 C1** 39 28N 8 20W
Zghartā, *Lebanon* **47 A4** 34 21N 35 53 E
Zgorzelec, *Poland* **16 C8** 51 10N 15 0 E
Zhabinka, *Belarus* **17 B13** 52 13N 24 2 E
Zhailma, *Kazakstan* **26 D7** 51 37N 61 33 E
Zhambyl, *Kazakstan* **26 E8** 42 54N 71 22 E
Zhangaqazaly, *Kazakstan* **26 E7** 45 48N 62 6 E
Zhangbei, *China* **34 D8** 41 10N 114 45 E
Zhangguangcai Ling, *China* **35 B15** 45 0N 129 0 E
Zhangjiakou, *China* **34 D8** 40 48N 114 55 E
Zhangwu, *China* **35 C12** 42 43N 123 52 E
Zhangye, *China* **32 C5** 38 50N 100 23 E
Zhangzhou, *China* **33 D6** 24 30N 117 35 E
Zhanhua, *China* **35 F10** 37 40N 118 8 E
Zhanjiang, *China* **33 D6** 21 15N 110 20 E
Zhannetty, Ostrov, *Russia* **27 B16** 76 43N 158 0 E
Zhanyi, *China* **32 D5** 25 38N 103 48 E
Zhanyu, *China* **35 B12** 44 30N 122 30 E
Zhao Xian, *China* **34 F8** 37 43N 114 45 E
Zhaocheng, *China* **34 F6** 36 22N 111 38 E
Zhaotong, *China* **32 D5** 27 20N 103 44 E
Zhaoyuan, *Heilongjiang, China* **35 B13** 45 27N 125 0 E
Zhaoyuan, *Shandong, China* **35 F11** 37 20N 120 23 E
Zhashkiv, *Ukraine* **17 D16** 49 15N 30 5 E
Zhashui, *China* **34 H5** 33 40N 109 8 E
Zhayyq →, *Kazakstan* **25 E9** 47 0N 51 48 E
Zhdanov = Mariupol, *Ukraine* **25 E6** 47 5N 37 31 E
Zhecheng, *China* **34 G8** 34 7N 115 20 E
Zhejiang □, *China* **33 D7** 29 0N 120 0 E
Zheleznodorozhnyy, *Russia* **24 B9** 62 35N 50 55 E
Zheleznogorsk-Ilimskiy, *Russia* **27 D11** 56 34N 104 8 E
Zhen'an, *China* **34 H5** 33 27N 109 9 E
Zhengding, *China* **34 E8** 38 8N 114 32 E
Zhengzhou, *China* **34 G7** 34 45N 113 34 E
Zhenlai, *China* **35 B12** 45 50N 123 5 E
Zhenping, *China* **34 H7** 33 10N 112 16 E
Zhenyuan, *China* **34 G4** 35 35N 107 30 E
Zhetiqara, *Kazakstan* **26 D7** 52 11N 61 12 E
Zhezqazghan, *Kazakstan* **26 E7** 47 44N 67 40 E
Zhidan, *China* **34 F5** 36 48N 108 48 E
Zhigansk, *Russia* **27 C13** 66 48N 123 27 E
Zhilinda, *Russia* **27 C12** 70 0N 114 20 E
Zhitomir = Zhytomyr, *Ukraine* **17 C15** 50 20N 28 40 E
Zhlobin, *Belarus* **17 B16** 52 55N 30 0 E
Zhmerinka = Zhmerynka, *Ukraine* **17 D15** 49 2N 28 2 E
Zhmerynka, *Ukraine* **17 D15** 49 2N 28 2 E
Zhob, *Pakistan* **42 D3** 31 20N 69 31 E
Zhob →, *Pakistan* **42 C3** 32 4N 69 50 E
Zhodino = Zhodzina, *Belarus* **17 A15** 54 5N 28 17 E
Zhodzina, *Belarus* **17 A15** 54 5N 28 17 E
Zhokhova, Ostrov, *Russia* **27 B16** 76 4N 152 40 E
Zhongdian, *China* **32 D4** 27 48N 99 42 E
Zhongning, *China* **34 F3** 37 29N 105 40 E
Zhongtiao Shan, *China* **34 G6** 35 0N 111 10 E
Zhongwei, *China* **34 F3** 37 30N 105 12 E
Zhongyang, *China* **34 F6** 37 20N 111 11 E
Zhoucun, *China* **35 F9** 36 47N 117 48 E
Zhouzhi, *China* **34 G5** 34 10N 108 12 E
Zhuanghe, *China* **35 E12** 39 40N 123 0 E
Zhucheng, *China* **35 G10** 36 0N 119 27 E
Zhugqu, *China* **34 H3** 33 40N 104 30 E
Zhumadian, *China* **34 H8** 32 59N 114 2 E
Zhuo Xian = Zhuozhou, *China* **34 E8** 39 28N 115 58 E
Zhuolu, *China* **34 D8** 40 20N 115 12 E
Zhuozhou, *China* **34 E8** 39 28N 115 58 E
Zhuozi, *China* **34 D7** 41 0N 112 25 E
Zhytomyr, *Ukraine* **17 C15** 50 20N 28 40 E
Zīārān, *Iran* **45 B6** 36 7N 50 32 E
Ziarat, *Pakistan* **42 D2** 30 25N 67 49 E
Zibo, *China* **35 F10** 36 47N 118 3 E
Zichang, *China* **34 F5** 37 18N 109 40 E
Zielona Góra, *Poland* **16 C8** 51 57N 15 31 E
Zierikzee, *Neths.* **15 C3** 51 40N 3 55 E
Zigey, *Chad* **51 F9** 14 43N 15 50 E
Zigong, *China* **32 D5** 29 15N 104 48 E
Ziguinchor, *Senegal* **50 F2** 12 35N 16 20W
Zihuatanejo, *Mexico* **86 D4** 17 38N 101 33W
Žilina, *Slovak Rep.* **17 D10** 49 12N 18 42 E
Zillah, *Libya* **51 C9** 28 30N 17 33 E
Zima, *Russia* **27 D11** 54 0N 102 5 E
Zimapán, *Mexico* **87 C5** 20 54N 99 20W
Zimba, *Zambia* **55 F2** 17 20S 26 11 E
Zimbabwe, *Zimbabwe* **55 G3** 20 16S 30 54 E
Zimbabwe ■, *Africa* **55 F3** 19 0S 30 0 E
Zimnicea, *Romania* **17 G13** 43 40N 25 22 E
Zinder, *Niger* **50 F7** 13 48N 9 0 E
Zinga, *Tanzania* **55 D4** 9 16S 38 49 E
Zion National Park, *U.S.A.* **83 H7** 37 15N 113 5W
Ziros, *Greece* **23 D8** 35 5N 26 8 E
Zitácuaro, *Mexico* **86 D4** 19 28N 100 21W
Zitundo, *Mozam.* **57 D5** 26 48S 32 47 E
Ziway, L., *Ethiopia* **46 F2** 8 0N 38 50 E
Ziyang, *China* **34 H5** 32 32N 108 31 E
Zlatograd, *Bulgaria* **21 D11** 41 22N 25 7 E
Zlatoust, *Russia* **24 C10** 55 10N 59 40 E
Zlín, *Czech Rep.* **17 D9** 49 14N 17 40 E
Zmeinogorsk, *Kazakstan* **26 D9** 51 10N 82 13 E
Znojmo, *Czech Rep.* **16 D9** 48 50N 16 2 E
Zobeyrī, *Iran* **44 C5** 34 10N 46 40 E
Zobia, *Dem. Rep. of the Congo* **54 B2** 3 0N 25 59 E
Zoetermeer, *Neths.* **15 B4** 52 3N 4 30 E
Zolochev = Zolochiv, *Ukraine* **17 D13** 49 45N 24 51 E
Zolochiv, *Ukraine* **17 D13** 49 45N 24 51 E
Zomba, *Malawi* **55 F4** 15 22S 35 19 E
Zongo, *Dem. Rep. of the Congo* **52 D3** 4 20N 18 35 E
Zonguldak, *Turkey* **25 F5** 41 28N 31 50 E
Zonqor Pt., *Malta* **23 D2** 35 51N 14 34 E
Zorritos, *Peru* **92 D2** 3 43S 80 40W
Zou Xiang, *China* **34 G9** 35 30N 116 58 E
Zouar, *Chad* **51 D9** 20 30N 16 32 E
Zouérate = Zouîrât, *Mauritania* **50 D3** 22 44N 12 21W
Zouîrât, *Mauritania* **50 D3** 22 44N 12 21W
Zoutkamp, *Neths.* **15 A6** 53 20N 6 18 E
Zrenjanin, *Serbia, Yug.* **21 B9** 45 22N 20 23 E
Zufār, *Oman* **46 D5** 17 40N 54 0 E
Zug, *Switz.* **18 C8** 47 10N 8 31 E
Zugspitze, *Germany* **16 E6** 47 25N 10 59 E
Zuid-Holland □, *Neths.* **15 C4** 52 0N 4 35 E
Zuidbeveland, *Neths.* **15 C3** 51 30N 3 50 E
Zuidhorn, *Neths.* **15 A6** 53 15N 6 23 E
Zula, *Eritrea* **46 D2** 15 17N 39 40 E
Zumbo, *Mozam.* **55 F3** 15 35S 30 26 E
Zumpango, *Mexico* **87 D5** 19 48N 99 6W
Zunhua, *China* **35 D9** 40 18N 117 58 E
Zuni, *U.S.A.* **83 J9** 35 4N 108 51W
Zunyi, *China* **32 D5** 27 42N 106 53 E
Zuoquan, *China* **34 F7** 37 5N 113 22 E
Zurbātīyah, *Iraq* **44 C5** 33 9N 46 3 E
Zürich, *Switz.* **18 C8** 47 22N 8 32 E
Zutphen, *Neths.* **15 B6** 52 9N 6 12 E
Zuwārah, *Libya* **51 B8** 32 58N 12 1 E
Zūzan, *Iran* **45 C8** 34 22N 59 53 E
Zverinogolovskoye, *Russia* **26 D7** 54 26N 64 50 E
Zvishavane, *Zimbabwe* **55 G3** 20 17S 30 2 E
Zvolen, *Slovak Rep.* **17 D10** 48 33N 19 10 E
Zwelitsha, *S. Africa* **53 L5** 32 55S 27 22 E
Zwettl, *Austria* **16 D8** 48 35N 15 9 E
Zwickau, *Germany* **16 C7** 50 44N 12 30 E
Zwolle, *Neths.* **15 B6** 52 31N 6 6 E
Zwolle, *U.S.A.* **81 K8** 31 38N 93 39W
Żyrardów, *Poland* **17 B11** 52 3N 20 28 E
Zyryan, *Kazakstan* **26 E9** 49 43N 84 20 E
Zyryanka, *Russia* **27 C16** 65 45N 150 51 E
Zyryanovsk = Zyryan, *Kazakstan* **26 E9** 49 43N 84 20 E
Żywiec, *Poland* **17 D10** 49 42N 19 10 E
Zyyi, *Cyprus* **23 E12** 34 43N 33 20 E